Lecture Notes in Computer Science 3806

Commenced Publication in 1973
Founding and Former Series Editors:
Gerhard Goos, Juris Hartmanis, and Jan van Leeuwen

T0189070

Anne H.H. Ngu   Masaru Kitsuregawa
Erich J. Neuhold   Jen-Yao Chung
Quan Z. Sheng (Eds.)

Web Information Systems Engineering – WISE 2005

6th International Conference on
Web Information Systems Engineering
New York, NY, USA, November 20-22, 2005
Proceedings

 Springer

Volume Editors

Anne H.H. Ngu
Texas State University, Department of Computer Science
601 University Drive, San Marcos, TX 78666-4616, USA
E-mail: angu@txstate.edu

Masaru Kitsuregawa
The University of Tokyo, Institute of Industrial Science
Komaba 4-6-1, Meguro Ku, Tokyo, 135-8505, Japan
E-mail: kitsure@tkl.iis.u-tokyo.ac.jp

Erich J. Neuhold
Fraunhofer IPSI
Dolivostraße 15, 64293 Darmstadt, Germany
E-mail: neuhold@ipsi.fhg.de

Jen-Yao Chung
IBM Research Division, Thomas J. Watson Research Center
P.O. Box 218, Yorktown Heights, NY 10598, USA
E-mail: jychung@us.ibm.com

Quan Z. Sheng
The University of New South Wales
School of Computer Science and Engineering
Sydney, NSW 2052, Australia
E-mail: qsheng@cse.unsw.edu.au

Library of Congress Control Number: 2005934894

CR Subject Classification (1998): H.4, H.2, H.3, H.5, K.4.4, C.2.4, I.2

ISSN   0302-9743
ISBN-10   3-540-30017-1 Springer Berlin Heidelberg New York
ISBN-13   978-3-540-30017-5 Springer Berlin Heidelberg New York

Springer is a part of Springer Science+Business Media

springeronline.com

© Springer-Verlag Berlin Heidelberg 2005
Printed in Germany

Typesetting: Camera-ready by author, data conversion by Scientific Publishing Services, Chennai, India
Printed on acid-free paper   SPIN: 11581062   06/3142   5 4 3 2 1 0

Message from the General Chairs

It is a pleasure and honor to welcome you to the proceedings of the 6th International Conference on Web Information Systems Engineering (WISE), November 2005, New York, NY. We had an excellent program comprising of the research track with regular, short and poster paper sessions, industry track sessions, three workshops and three tutorials that covered a variety of interests and disciplines in the area of Web information systems engineering.

Many individuals contributed to the success of this conference. First, we would like to thank Masaru Kitsuregawa, Erich Neuhold, and Anne Ngu, the research track program chairs, and the members of the Program Committee for selecting the papers in the research track. Second, we would like to thank the industry program chair, Jen-Yao Chung and the members of the Industry Program Committee for putting together a fantastic industry program.

We would like to extend our appreciation to Alexandros Biliris, the workshops chair, for leading the workshop program. We thank all the workshop program chairs/organizers who worked with Alex to put together the three WISE workshops, specifically: Roland Kascheck and Shonali Krishnaswamy for the "Web Information Systems Quality (WISQ 2005)" workshop; Woochun Jun for the "International Workshop on Web-Based Learning"; Mike Dean, Yuanbo Guo, and Zhengxiang Pan for the "Scalable Semantic Web Knowledge Base Systems (SSWS 2005)" workshop. Next, we would like to express our thanks to Boualem Benatallah for soliciting and selecting several excellent tutorials for this year's program, and James Geller for putting together a very interesting panel.

Thimios Panagos and Soon Ae Chun worked tirelessly to provide the local arrangements. We thank Michael Sheng for his dedicated effort in the preparation of the proceedings, and Helen Paik for maintaining the website and for taking care of the publicity. We wish to express our appreciation to the WISE Steering Committee members Yanchun Zhang and Marek Rusinkiewicz, for their continued support. We would also like to acknowledge Priscilla Rasmussen for helping with the registrations and helping with the selection of the hotel.

We wish to thank Adam Drobot and Telcordia for their generous financial support and backing that made a New York-based WISE organization possible.

We are grateful to the WISE keynote address speakers. Last but not least, our thanks go to all the authors who submitted papers and all the attendees. We hope they found the program stimulating and beneficial for their research.

September 2005   Dimitrios Georgakopoulos
                                                              Vijay Atluri

Message from the Program Chairs

The relentless growth in Internet functionality and bandwidth have enabled a new wave of innovations that are transforming the way all types of organizations (businesses, governments, ordinary citizens) collaborate and interact with partners, both within and across organizational boundaries. WISE 2005 aims at presenting novel topics and approaches to Web engineering in the dynamic, diverse, distributed and ever increasing volume of WWW data and applications. WISE 2005 was the first WISE conference to be held in the USA. Previous WISE conferences were held in China (2000), Japan (2001), Singapore (2002), Italy (2003), and Australia (2004).

The call for papers created a large interest. There were over 300 abstracts proposed and eventually 259 valid paper submissions arrived; an increase of over 30% compared to WISE 2004. The paper submissions came from 33 different countries. There are 43 papers from the USA; 40 papers received from China; 34 papers received from Korea; 20 papers received from Australia; 10–19 papers received from Italy, Japan, Spain, Germany and France; 5–9 papers received from India, UK, The Netherlands and Brazil; 1–4 papers received from Switzerland, Canada, Austria, Portugal, Turkey, Taiwan, Lebanon, Iran, Greece, Thailand, Romania, Poland, Mexico, Denmark, Columbia, Finland, Ireland, Chile, Bangladesh and Belgium.

The international Program Committee selected 30 full papers (acceptance rate of 12%), 20 short papers (acceptance rate of 8%) and 19 poster papers (acceptance rate of 9%). As a result, the technical track of the WISE 2005 program offered 10 sessions of full papers presentation, 4 sessions of short papers presentation and 2 sessions of poster papers presentation and demonstrations. The selected papers cover a wide and important variety of issues in Web information systems engineering such as Web mining, Semantic Web and Ontology, XML and semi-structured data, Web collaboration, P2P systems, and Web information extraction. A few selected papers from WISE 2005 will be published in a special issue of the "Internet and Web Information Systems", by Springer. In addition, $1000 will be awarded to the authors of the paper selected for the "Yahiko Kambayashi Best Paper".

We thank all authors who submitted their papers and the Program Committee members and external reviewers for their excellent work. We hope that the present proceedings will contain enough food for thought to push the Internet utilization to new heights.

September, 2005

Masaru Kitsuregawa
Erich Neuhold
Anne Ngu

Message from the Industrial Chair

The goals of the WISE 2005 Industry Program were to foster exchanges between practitioners and academics, to promote novel solutions to today's business challenges, to provide practitioners in the field an early opportunity to evaluate leading-edge research, and to identify new issues and directions for future research and development work. The focus of the WISE 2005 industrial program was related to innovative Web engineering including technologies, methodologies, and applications.

The international Program Committee went through a rigorous review process with at least four reviews for each paper in order to ensure the quality and fairness. The review processes gave favor to papers with industry related works. The accepted papers are grouped into four major categories: Semantic Web, Service Oriented Architecture (SOA), Business Performance Management (BPM), and Web Infrastructure.

We are very grateful to all Industrial Program Committee members for helping us review the papers. We had many productive discussions during the Industry program at WISE 2005. We hope the attendees had enjoyable experiences and fruitful meetings in New York City!

September, 2005   Jen-Yao Chung

Conference Organization

General Chairs

Dimitrios Georgakopoulos, *Telcordia, USA*
Vijay Atluri, *Rutgers University, USA*

Program Committee Chairs

Masaru Kitsuregawa, *University of Tokyo, Japan*
Erich Neuhold, *Fraunhofer-IPSI, Germany*
Anne H.H. Ngu, *Texas State University, USA*

Industrial Program Chair

Jen-Yao Chung, *IBM T.J. Watson Research Center, USA*

Tutorial Chair

Boualem Benatallah
University of New South Wales, Australia

Panel Chair

James Geller
New Jersey Institute of Technology, USA

Workshop Chair

Alexandros Biliris
Columbia University, USA

Publicity Chair

Helen Paik
University of New South Wales, Australia

Local Arrangements Chairs

Thimios Panagos
Telcordia, USA
Soon Ae Chun
City University of New York, USA

WISE Steering Committee Liaisons

Yanchun Zhang
Victoria University, Australia
Marek Rusinkiewicz
Telcordia, USA

Publication Chair

Quan Z. Sheng, *University of New South Wales, Australia*

Program Committee Members

Marco Aiello	Italy	Pat Martin	Canada
Rafael Alonso	USA	Carlo Meghini	Italy
Toshiyuki Amagasa	Japan	Rubens Melo	Brazil
Elisa Bertino	USA	Michele Missikoff	Italy
Athman Bouguettaya	USA	Miyuki Nakano	Japan
Shawn Bowers	USA	Mourad Ouzzani	USA
Dave Buttler	USA	Tamer Ozsu	Canada
Wojciech Cellary	Poland	Barbara Pernici	Italy
Sang Kyun Cha	Korea	Dewayne Perry	USA
Sharma Chakravarthy	USA	Rodion Podorozhny	USA
Edward Chang	USA	Dimitris Plexousakis	Greece
Arbee L.P. Chen	Taiwan	Dan Rocco	USA
Guihai Chen	China	Colette Rolland	France
Soon Ae Chun	USA	Louiqa Raschid	USA
Andrzej Cichocki	USA	Thomas Risse	Germany
Alex Delis	USA	Michael Rys	USA
Gill Dobbie	New Zealand	Keun Ho Ryu	Korea
Schahram Dustdar	Austria	Shazia Sadiq	Australia
Johann Eder	Austria	Yasushi Sakurai	Japan
Tina Eliassi-Rad	USA	Mark Segal	USA
Peter Fankhauser	Germany	John Shepherd	Australia
Paul Grefen	The Netherlands	Klaus-Dieter Schewe	New Zealand
Claude Godart	France	Ming-Chien Shan	USA
Wook-Shin Han	Korea	Monica Scannapieco	Italy
Manfred Hauswirth	Switzerland	Quan Z. Sheng	Australia
Carol Hazlewood	USA	Amit Sheth	USA
Christian Hueme	Austria	Jianwen Su	USA
George Karabatis	USA	Stanely Su	USA
Kamal Karlapalem	India	Katsumi Tanaka	Japan
Martin Kersten	The Netherlands	Frank Tompa	Canada
Ross King	Austria	Peter Trianatfillou	Greece
Hiroyuki Kitagawa	Japan	Aphrodite Tsalgatidou	Greece
Manolis Koubarakis	Greece	Andreas Wombacher	The Netherlands
Herman Lam	USA	Leah Wong	USA
Chen Li	USA	Limsoon Wong	Singapore
Jianzhong Li	China	Jian Yang	Australia
Qing Li	China	Ge Yu	China
Xuemin Lin	Australia	Jeffrey Yu	China
Tok Wang Ling	Singapore	Asano Yasuhito	Japan
Chengfei Liu	Australia	Masatoshi Yoshikawa	Japan
Peng Liu	USA	Carlo Zaniolo	USA
Jianguo Lu	Canada	Liangzhao Zeng	USA
Wei-Ying Ma	China	Xiaofang Zhou	Australia

Industrial Program Vice Chairs

Stephane Gagnon, New Jersey Institute of Technology, USA
Shu-Ping Chang, IBM T.J. Watson Research Center, USA
Shiwa S. Fu, IBM T.J. Watson Research Center, USA

Industrial Program Committee Members

Naga Ayachitula	USA	Althea Q. Liang	Singapore
Xiaoying Bai	China	James Lipscomb	USA
Ying Chen	China	William Song	UK
Paul Dantzig	USA	Yan Wang	Australia
Xiang Gao	The Netherlands	Yinsheng Li	China
Sang-Goo Lee	Korea	Dalu Zhang	China
Haifei Li	USA		

External Reviewers

Yannis Aekaterinidis	Karthik Gomadam	Kazuo Mogi
Vasiliki Alevizou	Qijun Gu	Anirban Mondal
Anastasia Analyti	Qi He	Shinsuke Nakajima
Samuli Angelov	Van Hai Ho	Zaiqing Nie
Yosuke Aragane	Du Huynh	Nikos Ntarmos
Danilo Ardagna	Noriko Imafuji	Masato Oguchi
George Athanasopoulos	Nobuto Inoguchi	Nunzia Osimi
Kun Bai	Yoshiharu Ishikawa	Hye-Young Paik
Luciano Baresi	Chen Jiang	Chichun Pan
Cassia Baruque	George-Dimitrios Kapos	Michael Pantazoglou
Lucia Baruque	Roland Kaschek	Matthew Perry
Fiore Basile	Kaikhah Khosrow	Willy Picard
A. Binemann-Zdanowicz	Natalia Kokash	Thomi Pilioura
Panagiotis Bouros	Woralak Kongdenfha	Theoni Pitoura
Xiao Chen	Eleni Koutrouli	Pierluigi Plebani
Amir H. Chinaei	Alexander Lazovik	Raymond Pon
Fulvio D'Antonio	Fengjun Li	Wendy Powley
Takeharu Eda	Lunquan Li	Iko Pramudiono
Reza Eslami	Yinhua Li	Arun Qamra
Flavio Ferrarotti	Xumin Liu	Hajo Reijers
Vangelis Floros	Jiaheng Lu	Jarogniew Rykowski
George Flouris	Jeroen van Luin	Derong Shen
Ganna Frankova	Massimo Mecella	Jialie Shen
Kei Fujimoto	Diego Milano	Shuming Shi
G.R. Gangadharan	Stefano Modafferi	Sean Siqueira

Yu Suzuki

Hiroyuki Toda

Nikos Tsatsakis

Daling Wang

Hai Wang

Ji-Rong Wen

Gan Wu

Yi Wu

Gu Xu

Guirong Xue

Jingling Xue

Chun Yuan

Hua-Jun Zeng

Bailing Zhang

Table of Contents

Ontology and Semantic Web

XML

Web Service Method

Web Service Structure

Collaborative Methodology

P2P, Ubiquitous and Mobile

Document Retrieval Applications

Short Paper Session 1: Web Services and E-Commerce

Short Paper Session 2: Recommendation and Web Information Extraction

Short Paper Session 3: P2P, Grid and Distributed Management

Short Paper Session 4: Advanced Issues

Poster Flash Session 1

Poster Flash Session 2

Industry-1: Semantic Web

Industry-2: SOA

Industry-3: BPM

Industry-4: Web Infrastructure

Tutorials and Panels

Poster

Mining Communities on the Web Using a Max-Flow and a Site-Oriented Framework

Yasuhito Asano[1], Takao Nishizeki[1], and Masashi Toyoda[2]

[1] Graduate School of Information Sciences, Tohoku University,
Aza-Aoba 6-6-05, Aramaki, Aoba-ku, Sendai, 980-8579, Japan
asano@nishizeki.ecei.tohoku.ac.jp, nishi@ecei.tohoku.ac.jp
[2] Institute of Industrial Science, the Univeristy of Tokyo,
Komaba 4-6-1, Meguro-ku, Tokyo, 153-8505, Japan
toyoda@tkl.iis.u-tokyo.ac.jp

Abstract. There are several methods for mining communities on the Web using hyperlinks. One of the well-known ones is a max-flow based method proposed by Flake *et al.* The method adopts a page-oriented framework, that is, it uses a page on the Web as a unit of information, like other methods including HITS and trawling. Recently, Asano *et al.* built a site-oriented framework which uses a site as a unit of information, and they experimentally showed that trawling on the site-oriented framework often outputs significantly better communities than trawling on the page-oriented framework. However, it has not been known whether the site-oriented framework is effective in mining communities through the max-flow based method. In this paper, we first point out several problems of the max-flow based method, mainly owing to the page-oriented framework, and then propose solutions to the problems by utilizing several advantages of the site-oriented framework. Computational experiments reveal that our max-flow based method on the site-oriented framework is significantly effective in mining communities, related to the topics of given pages, in comparison with the original max-flow based method on the page-oriented framework.

1 Introduction

A Web community is a set of sites or pages related to a topic. Several methods of mining communities have been recently developed by utilizing a graph structure of hyperlinks on the Web. The idea behind the methods is the following observation: if there is a link (u, v) from pages u to v, then v is considered to contain valuable information for the author of u. For example, HITS proposed by Kleinberg [10] regards a Web page as an *authority* of communities if it is linked from many pages, and as a *hub* if it has many links to authorities. Two of the other well-known methods are trawling proposed by Kumar *et al.* [11] and a max-flow based method proposed by Flake *et al.* [8]. The latter, in particular, is known as a useful method of mining communities related to the topics of given pages.

M. Kitsuregawa et al. (Eds.): WISE 2005, LNCS 3806, pp. 1–14, 2005.

Most of the methods of mining communities using hyperlinks [9], [14] adopt the following *page-oriented framework*:

(1) Collect data of URLs and links in Web pages. For example, the max-flow based method collects URLs and links of pages which are within two links from given pages.
(2) Construct from the data a Web graph $G = (V, E)$, where V is a set of Web pages and E is a set of links between pages in V.
(3) Find some characteristic subgraphs of the Web graph G as approximate communities. For example, the max-flow based method finds a dense subgraph as an approximate community.

It is often appropriate to regard a site, in place of a page, as a unit of information in the real Web. In fact, a *link* (u, v) *between sites*, i.e. a link (u, v) such that pages u and v are in the different sites, is created mostly as a reference to valuable information, while a *link* (u, v) *inside a site*, i.e. a link (u, v) such that both pages u and v are in the same site, may be created merely for convenience of Web browsing. However, the page-oriented framework deals with both kinds of links equally, and has some disadvantages for properly mining communities. Thus, Asano *et al.* [3], [4] proposed another framework for mining communities, named a *site-oriented framework*, as follows.

(1) Collect data of URLs and links in Web pages.
(2) Find "directory-based sites" by using the data.
(3) Construct an *inter-site graph*, whose vertices are directory-based sites, and whose edges are links between directory-based sites.
(4) Find some characteristic subgraphs in the inter-site graph as approximate communities.

This framework regards a site, instead of a page, as a unit of information, and is expected to be more useful for properly mining communities than the page-oriented framework. They implemented this framework by proposing a new model of a site, called a *directory-based site*, and by giving a method for finding directory-based sites from data of URLs and links. Asano *et al.* used data sets of .jp domain URLs crawled in 2000 and 2002 by Toyoda and Kitsuregawa [13], and verified that the method can correctly find directory-based sites in most cases. For the data sets above, they also showed [3], [4] that trawling on the site-oriented framework can find a number of communities which can never be found by trawling on the page-oriented framework. Thus, the site-oriented framework is effective in mining communities through trawling. However, it has not been known that whether the site-oriented framework is effective in mining communities through the max-flow based method.

In this paper, we show that the site-oriented framework is significantly effective in mining communities through the max-flow based method in regard to both quality and quantity. The *quantity* of a found approximate community is measured by the number of sites that are truly related to the topics of given pages. The *quality* is measured by the ratio of the number of related sites to the total number of sites in the community.

The rest of this paper is organized as follows. In Section 2, we overview the results obtained by computational experiments. In Section 3, we introduce the site-oriented framework proposed in [3], [4] In Section 4, we outline the max-flow based method proposed by Flake *et al.* In Section 5, we point out several problems of the max-flow based method on the page-oriented framework, and propose solutions to them by utilizing the site-oriented framework. We also analyze how the problems and the solutions affect the performance of the method. In Section 6, we present our concluding remarks.

2 Overview of Experimental Results

We implement our improved max-flow based method, and evaluate by computational experiments the performance of two methods: our method based on the site-oriented framework, and the original max-flow based method based on the page-oriented framework.

Table 1. Quality and quantity of found communities

Topic	1	2	3	4	5	6	7	8
Page, original	0/2	0/12	0/5	3/126	7/29	2/4	8/12	1/5
Site, improved	17/26	16/28	6/11	4/9	15/23	36/42	7/7	11/21

Topic	9	10	11	12	13	14	15	16
Page, original	7/11	7/10	1/3	10/17	11/15	37/52	8/8	3/3
Site, improved	18/21	8/9	13/25	15/20	24/28	4/5	7/7	16/23

Table 1 depicts the results of the experiments using the data set collected in 2003. The topics indexed 1 to 16 are "Studio Ziburi (Japanese famous animation studio)," "Tactics Ouga (computer game)," "dagashi-ya (Japanese traditional papa-mama shops)," "The Lord of the Rings (movie and novel)," "swords," "cats," "Chinese history," "Spitz (Japanese singer)," "guns," "dogs," "army," "Hirohiko Araki (Japanese comic artist)," "train photos," "Monopoly (board game) clubs," "beetles," and "mountain photos," respectively. For each topic, we select three or four seed pages from the search results of the topic by Google. As seed pages, we pick up pages in personal sites on servers of ISPs (Internet Service Providers), servers of universities or rental Web servers as much as possible so that, for every topic, at most one seed page is not a page in such sites. In Table 1, "Page, original", abbreviated to PO, denotes the original max-flow based method on the page-oriented framework, while "Site, improved", abbreviated to SI, denotes our improved method on the site-oriented framework. "Page, original" and "Site, improved" rows show the results of applying PO and SI to the seed pages for the sixteen topics, respectively. These two rows consist of sixteen cells, each corresponding to a topic. Each cell contains a fraction; the denominator is the number of the sites in the found approximate community other than the seeds; and the numerator is the number of the sites in the community that are truly related to the topic of the seeds. In other words, the numerator represents the quantity of the found community, and the fraction does the quality.

For example, we use three seed pages for topic 5, "swords." PO finds 29 sites other than the seeds, but only seven of them are truly related to the topics of the seeds. On the other hand, SI finds 23 sites, and 15 of them are truly related. Thus, the original method PO finds a community of quantity 7 and quality 7/29, while our method SI finds a community of quantity 15 and quality 15/23. It should be noted that the community found by SI contains nine personal sites in servers of ISPs, servers of universities or rental Web servers; these nine sites cannot be found by PO, although all the nine sites contain valuable information about the topic "swords."

The average number 13.6 of related sites found by SI is about 2.07 times as many as the average number 6.56 of related pages found by PO. The average quality 72.6% of the communities found by SI is significantly greater than the average quality 45.8% of those found by PO. In fact, SI achieves strictly better quality than PO for fourteen topics among all the sixteen topics. It still has relatively good quality for the remaining two topics 15 and 16; 100% and 69.6%, respectively. For topic 16, SI finds sixteen related sites, five times more than PO. As we will explain in Section 5, SI adopts several solutions utilizing some advantages of the site-oriented framework. Thus the site-oriented framework is fairly effective for improving the max-flow method both in quality and in quantity. Further analyses will be described in Section 5.

Table 2. The sizes of used graphs

Topic	1	2	3	4	5	6
Page	345, 1422	687, 2518	160, 610	1472, 9020	2216, 7550	385, 1484
Site	2109, 5050	2605, 6216	1969, 4678	489, 1154	2143, 5208	4854, 11580

Topic	7	8	9	10	11	12
Page	1055, 4822	484, 1826	416, 1768	325, 1210	1987, 7584	1745, 7394
Site	1957, 4510	7602, 18436	1595, 3750	3196, 7642	5969, 14614	6497, 15942

Topic	13	14	15	16
Page	466, 2110	745, 3404	877, 4074	744, 3086
Site	590, 1472	2187, 5670	3116, 7302	2164, 5048

Table 2 shows the sizes of the Web graphs and the inter-site graphs used for the topics in the experiments. In each cell, the left number denotes the number of vertices, while the right number denotes the number of edges. For example, for topic 5, the number of vertices and edges in the Web graph used by PO is 2,216 and 7,550, respectively; the number of vertices and edges in the inter-site graph used by SI is 2,143 and 5,208, respectively.

3   Implementation of Site-Oriented Framework

It is easy to propose a site-oriented framework, but is very difficult to implement it, because a site is a vague concept. Asano *et al.* [4], [5] have implemented it by using a directory-based site model and a method of identifying directory-based sites from data of URLs and links. In this section, we outline the implementation, and compare the sizes of a Web graph and an inter-site graph obtained from a data set of 2003, a new one different from the data sets used in [4], [5].

3.1   Directory-Based Sites

The phrase "Web site" is usually used ambiguously, and it is difficult to present a proper definition of a Web site.

Several methods including the max-flow based method, HITS, and trawling, have adopted an idea to use a Web server, instead of a site, as a unit of information. This idea works relatively well for a *single-site server*, which is a Web server containing a single site as in the case of official sites made by companies, governments or other organizations. On the other hand, the idea works poorly for a *multi-site server*, which is a Web server containing multiple sites. For example, a Web server of an ISP, a university's server or a rental Web server may contain a number of personal Web sites. Thus, adopting this idea would lose valuable information, since information about relatively minor or specialized topics is frequently held in such personal sites.

Li *et al.* proposed a *logical domain* as a unit of information smaller than a site [12]. However, the logical domain is used for clustering documents but not for mining communities.

Several researches [2], [6] and [7] defined a Web site as a set of Web pages that are written by a single person, company, or cohesive group, although they did not actually propose a method of finding sites on the Web according to their definitions. If every Web page contained information about its author, then one could identify a Web site according to this definition. Unfortunately, most pages contain no information about their authors, and hence it is difficult to identify Web sites according to this definition. Thus, we need a method of finding Web sites approximately according to some proper model.

Asano *et al.* [3], [4] proposed a new model of a site, called a *directory-based site*, and obtained a method to examine whether a given server is a single-site server or a multi-site server and to find a set of directories corresponding to the top directories of users' sites. Using their method, we have found 6,063,674 directory-based sites in 2,940,591 servers for the data set of 2003. The error rate for the results is only 1.9%, which has been estimated by random sampling.

3.2   Inter-site Graph

Once the directory-based sites have been found for a given data set, we can construct an inter-site graph G, as follows:

(1) If there is a link from a page v in a directory-based site A to a page w in another directory-based site B, we add to G a link from A to B, called a *global-link*.

(2) An *inter-site graph* G is a directed graph, whose vertices correspond to directory-based sites and whose edges correspond to global-links. A pair of oppositely directed global-links is called a *mutual-link*.

For the data sets of 2003, the numbers of vertices and edges of the Web (page) graph are 312,536,723 and 1,032,820,388, and the numbers of those of the inter-site graph are 6,063,674 and 43,197,249. The number of the edges of the inter-site graph is less than 5% of the number of the edges of the Web graph. One can thus deal with the inter-site graph more easily than the Web graph for mining communities especially in memory space.

4   Summary of Max-Flow Based Method

The max-flow based method proposed by Flake *et al.* [8] finds an approximate community from a Web graph composed of seed pages and their neighbor pages. The method finds a dense subgraph containing the seed pages, and regards it as a community, as outlined as follows.

1. Construct a Web graph $G = (V, E)$. The vertex set V is a union of three sets S, P and Q of pages; S is the set of seed pages given by a searcher, P is the set of all pages that either link to or are linked from pages in S, and Q is the set of all pages that are linked from pages in P. The edge set E consists of all the links from pages in S to pages in $S \cup P$ and all the links from pages in P to pages in $S \cup P \cup Q$. In Figure 1 all edges in E are drawn by solid lines.

2. Add to $G = (V, E)$ a virtual source s and a virtual sink t, and add to G a virtual edge (s, x) for each vertex $x \in S$ and a virtual edge (x, t) for each vertex $x \in V$. Let $G'_1 = (V', E')$ be the resulting network. Thus $V' = V \cup \{s\} \cup \{t\}$ and $E' = E \cup \{(s, x) \mid x \in S\} \cup \{(x, t) \mid x \in V\}$. In Figure 1 some of the virtual edges are drawn by dotted lines. The capacity $c(e)$ for each edge $e \in E'$ is given as follows:
   - $c(e) = k$ for each edge $e \in E$, where $k(> 1)$ is a given integer parameter, and is equal to the number of the seed pages in [8]. (Usually k is fairly small, say $2 \le k \le 4$.)
   - $c(e) = \infty$ for each edge $e = (s, x)$.
   - $c(e) = 1$ for each edge $e = (x, t)$.

3. For $i = 1$ to ℓ, do the following procedures (a)-(c), where ℓ is a given integer parameter. (Flake *et al.* usually set $\ell = 4$.)
   (a) Compute the min-cut of network G'_i, that separates s and t and is nearest to s, by finding a max-flow for G'_i. Let $E(X, V' \setminus X)$ be the set of edges in the min-cut, where $X \subseteq V'$ is a vertex set containing s.
   (b) If $i < \ell$, then find a vertex u of maximum degree in $X \setminus (S \cup \{s\})$, i.e. a vertex u such that $d(u) \ge d(u')$ for every vertex $u' \in X \setminus (S \cup \{s\})$, where $d(x)$ denotes the degree of vertex $x \in V'$ in G'_i, that is, $d(x)$ is the sum of in-degree and out-degree of x. Regard u as a new seed, set

$S := S \cup \{u\}$, and construct a new network G'_{i+1} for the new set S as in Steps 1 and 2. Increment i by one.

(c) Otherwise, i.e. $i = \ell$, output $X \setminus \{s\}$ as an approximate community.

Note that Flake *et al.* have adopted the following three policies in Step 1 [8].

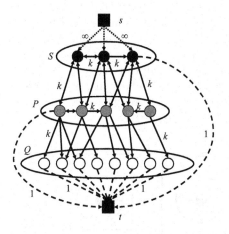

Fig. 1. A Web graph G and network G'_1

1. Regard every page with relatively large degree, say 50 or more, as a portal, and ignore it.
2. Every edge joining a vertex in S and a vertex in P is regarded as a bi-directed edge in G even if there is only a uni-directional link between the two pages corresponding to the vertices. Without this policy, some pages that link to but are not linked from pages in S cannot be reached from the virtual source and consequently cannot be members of the found community although they are sometimes related to the seed pages on the real Web.
3. Ignore all the links between pages in the same server. This policy will be further discussed in the next section.

5 Problems of Max-Flow Based Method and Solutions to Them

In this section, we first point out four problems of the max-flow based method, which mainly owe to the page-oriented framework, and then propose solutions to them by utilizing the site-oriented framework. We also analyze how the problems and the solutions affect the performance of the max-flow method. In subsections 5.1-5.4, we describe these four problems, which we call the *ignored link problem*, the *mutual-link problem*, the *missing link problem*, and the *capacity problem*, respectively.

5.1 Ignored Link Problem

The original max-flow based method adopts the policy of ignoring links in the same server. Consider a seed page belonging to an official site of companies, governments or other organizations. Such an official site usually consists of the whole pages in a Web server, and many links in the site are created merely for convenience of the reader of the site. Thus, a Web graph G would contain a dense subgraph consisting of pages in the official site if the max-flow based method on the page-oriented framework did not adopt the policy of ignoring links in the same server. Thus the quantity of the found community, corresponding to the dense subgraph, is only one. Hence, the policy is necessary for finding a community with large quantity by the max-flow based method on the page-oriented framework. However, the policy suffers from the following two problems.

Ignored Link Problem (1). Figure 2 illustrates two sites A and B; although there is a global-link going from A to B in an inter-site graph, the seed page $a \in A$ is isolated in a Web graph G since a link (a, b) is ignored and hence a link (b, c) cannot be found. Such a situation often occurs when a seed page is the top page of a site and all links to other sites are placed on other pages in this site. In such a case, the information of links from this site to the other sites is lost although it may be valuable for mining communities related to this site. There are a number of such cases in the real Web, particularly in personal sites in multi-site servers, and hence the lack of such information would be a serious problem. We call this problem the *ignored link problem (1)*.

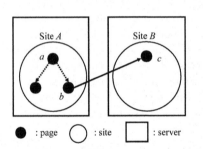

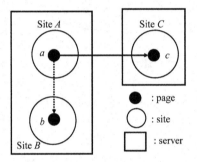

Fig. 2. Illustration for the ignored link problem (1)

Fig. 3. Illustration for the ignored link problem (2)

Ignored Link Problem (2). If we adopt the policy of ignoring links in the same server, then we cannot utilize information of links between sites in the same server. Figure 3 illustrates three sites A, B and C, among which there are two global-links (A, B) and (A, C). The global-link (A, C) can be found but (A, B) cannot be found, because A and B are contained in the same server. In the real Web there are a number of multi-site servers such as rental Web servers, ISPs' servers and universities' servers, and hence the lack of such information would be a serious problem in mining communities. We call this problem the *ignored link problem (2)*.

Table 3 shows the number of ignored links, the number of edges in Web graphs, and their ratio for each of the sixteen topics used in the experiments described in Section 2. The average ratio 60.6% is fairly large, and ignored links are frequently found around personal sites in multi-site servers. Thus, within the page-oriented framework, the loss of information due to ignored links would cause the poor quality of communities especially when given pages belong to personal sites in multi-site servers.

Table 3. The number of ignored links

Topic	1	2	3	4	5	6	7	8
Ignored Links	706	793	1081	8265	5182	1361	1690	1271
Edges	1422	2518	610	9020	7550	1484	4822	1826
Ratio (%)	49.6	31.5	177.2	91.6	68.6	91.7	35.0	69.6

Topic	9	10	11	12	13	14	15	16
Ignored Links	75	855	2333	3933	2826	807	1577	1196
Edges	1768	1210	3086	7584	7394	2110	3404	4074
Ratio (%)	4.2	70.7	75.6	51.9	38.2	38.2	46.3	29.4

The site-oriented framework gives a natural solution to the ignored link problems. The site-oriented framework does not need the policy of ignoring links in the same server, since there is no links in the same site in an inter-site graph. The ignored link problem (2) is also solved by using an inter-site graph instead of a Web graph, because a link between sites in the same server appears as a global-link in an inter-site graph.

5.2   Mutual-Link Problem

A mutual-link between two sites is frequently created when these sites are related and the authors of the sites know each other site, and hence a mutual-link is more useful for mining communities than a single-sided link. Asano *et al.* have indeed proposed a method of mining communities by enumerating maximal cliques composed of mutual-links, and have verified that the method is more suitable for mining communities of personal sites than trawling [4], [5]. However, the original max-flow based method cannot correctly find mutual-links due to the following two reasons (1) and (2), illustrated for the example in Figure 4.

(1) Since the max-flow based method adopts the policy of ignoring links in the same server, all the links drawn by dotted lines in Figure 4 are ignored. Thus, even if both the top pages $a \in A$ and $c \in B$ are given, the link from $b \in A$

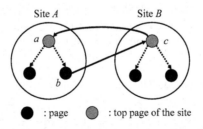

Fig. 4. Illustration for the mutual-link problem

to c cannot be found, and hence the mutual-link between A and B cannot be found.
(2) In Figure 4, there are links from b to c and from c to a, but there is no pair of pages mutually linked. Thus, there is no mutual-link between two pages in a Web graph composed of all the pages and links in Figure 4.

In the real Web there are a number of situations similar to the example above, and thus it would be a serious problem that such mutual-links cannot be found.

Moreover, the max-flow based method cannot fully utilize the found mutual-links, as follows.

(I) The method regards all the links emanating from seeds as bi-directed edges even if they are single-sided links. Hence, the mutual-links and the single-sided links emanating from seeds are equally treated in the max-flow based method.
(II) Most of the "path flows" [1] of the max flow in a network G' pass through vertices in the following order: vertices in S, vertices in P, and vertices in Q. That is, most of the path flows go along an edge from S to P and along an edge from P to Q, while very few of the path flows go along an edge from Q to P and along an edge from P to S. Thus, even we use a bi-directed edge to represent a mutual-link and use a uni-directed edge to represent a single-sided link in order to make a difference between a mutual-link and a single-sided link, the mutual-link would not contribute to finding good approximate communities.

Thus, the original max-flow based method on the page-oriented framework can neither find all mutual-links nor fully utilize the found mutual-links. We call this problem the *mutual-link problem*.

We now propose a solution to the mutual-link problem using the site-oriented framework. First, we construct an inter-site graph as G from a given set of seed sites and use a site, instead of a page, in the max-flow based method described in Section 4. Second, when we construct the last network G'_ℓ, let R be the set of vertices connected to one or more seed sites by mutual-links, and we add all the sites in R to the given set of seed sites, where ℓ is the parameter in Step 3 of the method. Some preliminary experiments reveal that adding the sites in R to the set of seed sites when constructing intermediate networks G_i, $1 \le i \le \ell - 1$, does not contribute to finding good approximate communities in quality. The solution above is based on the observation in [4], [5] that a mutual-link between two sites represents a strong relation between them.

Table 4. The numbers of mutual-links

Topic	1	2	3	4	5	6	7	8	9	10	11	12	13	14	15	16
Page	0	0	1	9	0	9	7	5	4	0	7	8	5	3	8	10
Site	12	19	10	0	8	14	7	17	5	19	10	28	15	3	18	11

Table 4 shows the numbers of mutual-links in the graphs used for the experiments in Section 2. For each topic, "Page" row shows the number of mutual-links in the Web graph, while "Site" row shows the number of mutual-links in the inter-site graphs. The average number 12.3 of mutual-links in an inter-site graph is about 2.58 times as many as the average number 4.75 of mutual-links in a Web graph, and hence the site-oriented framework is suitable for mining communities using mutual-links. Only for topic 4 "The Lord of the Rings," the Web graph has more mutual-links than the inter-site graph, although the quality of the community found by PO is worse than that by SI, as described in Table 1. In the Web graph, some of the seed pages for topic 4 have links to pages concerning a well-known HTML grammer checker *htmllint*, and all the mutual-links in the Web graph join two of the pages on *htmllint*. Hence, even if a page becomes a member of the community owing to the mutual-links, the page is related to *htmllint* but not to topic 4, and hence these mutual-links do not contribute to the quality of the community for topic 4.

For the topics other than topic 4, although the number of mutual-links is fairly small compared with the number of edges, their effect for mining communities is not small on the site-oriented framework. For example, for topic 6 "cats", the following five sites in the community found by SI would not be found without the solution above: `homepage2.nifty.com/yazu/`, `www10.ocn.ne.jp/~ne-help/`, `www5e.biglobe.ne.jp/~moyochu-/`, `www.kuma-kuma.net/~kylie/`, and `www.kuma-kuma.net/~nekoneko/`. Each of these five sites is a personal site in a multi-site server, and contains attractive contents about cats, and thus our solution based on the site-oriented framework is effective for mining communities containing personal sites in multi-site servers.

5.3 Missing Link Problem

In this paper, a link from pages a to b is called a *missing link* if a corresponds to a vertex in set Q and b corresponds to a vertex in set $P \cup Q$. The original max-flow based method ignores all these missing links in the construction step of a Web graph $G = (V, E)$. However, ignoring the missing links would lose valuable information and consequently be a serious problem for mining communities. We call this problem the *missing link problem*.

Using experiments with the same inputs described in Section 2, we have verified the fact that the average number of missing links for the site-oriented framework is larger than the average number of those for the page-oriented framework.

Table 5. The numbers of missing links

Topic	1	2	3	4	5	6	7	8	9	10	11	12	13	14	15	16
Page	18	24	2	80	34	56	88	34	46	6	80	88	132	30	210	138
Site	26	42	142	6	34	134	40	200	34	86	20	190	170	12	284	80

Table 5 shows the numbers of missing links in the experiments. For each topic, "Page" row shows the number of missing links for the page-oriented framework, while "Site" row shows the number of missing links for the site-oriented framework. The average number 93.8 of missing links for the site-oriented framework is about 1.41 times as many as the average number 66.6 of missing links for the page-oriented framework.

The fact implies that using missing links on the page-oriented framework would not much affect finding good approximate communities, but utilizing missing links on the site-oriented framework would be useful for mining communities. Thus, in order to solve the missing link problem, we include the missing links in a graph G on the site-oriented framework.

For example, for topic 6 "cats", the following two sites in the community found by SI could not be found without the solution above: `www.kt.rim.or.jp/~taya/`, and `www.iris.dti.ne.jp/~mya-/`. Each of these two sites is a personal site in a multi-site server, and contains attractive contents about cats, and thus our solution based on the site-oriented framework is effective for mining communities containing personal sites in multi-site servers.

5.4   Capacity Problem

Let $G' = (V', E')$ be a network used to find an approximate community. Let C be the set of vertices corresponding to the approximate community. Let $(X, V' \setminus X)$ be the min-cut of G' corresponding to C, where $s \in X \subseteq V'$. Thus $C = X \setminus \{s\}$. For a vertex v, we denote by $d^+(v)$ and $d^-(v)$ the out-degree and in-degree of v in G', respectively. We consider a situation in which the following condition (1) hold:

(1) G' has no edge (u, v) for any pair of vertices u and v such that $u, v \in P$ or $u, v \in Q$.

We then claim that the following (A) and (B) hold for the approximate community found by the original max-flow based method.

(A) A vertex $v \in P$ is contained in C if $d^-(v) > 1/k + d^+(v) - 1$, where k is the given parameter in Step 2 of the method.
(B) A vertex $v \in Q$ is contained in C if there is an edge $(u, v) \in E'$ for some vertex $u \in P \cap C$.

Proof of (A): Suppose that $d^-(v) > 1/k + d^+(v) - 1$ for a vertex $v \in P$. Then the sum $k \cdot d^-(v)$ of capacities of the edges entering v is larger than the sum $1 + k(d^+(v) - 1)$ of capacities of the edges emanating from v. The capacity of every edge connecting the virtual source s and a vertex in S is infinite. Therefore, v can be reached from the virtual source s via a vertex in S in the "residual network" [1] of G' for the max-flow, and hence v is contained in C.   □

Proof of (B): Suppose that there is an edge $(u, v) \in E'$ for some vertex $u \in P \cap C$. Let $P'(v) = \{u' \in P \cap C \mid (u', v) \in E'\}$, then $P'(v) \neq \emptyset$. Since G'

satisfies the condition (1), vertex $v \in Q$ has excatly one outgoing edge (v,t), and $c(v,t) = 1$. On the other hand, the total amount of capacities of all edges going from vertices in $P'(v)$ to v is more than 1 since $c(u,v) = k > 1$. Thus, edge (u,v) for $u \in P'(v)$ cannot be saturated by any max-flow in G', and hence the vertex v can be reached from the virtual source s through u in the residual network. Thus $v \in C$. □

(A) and (B) above immediately imply the following two facts (I) and (II).

(I) Even if a vertex v in Q has only one incoming edge (u,v), the max-flow based method regards v as a member of the community when $u \in P \cap C$.
(II) Even if a vertex v' in P has incoming edges from all the vertices in S, corresponding to the seed pages, the max-flow based method does not regard v' as a member of the community when $d^+(v') > |S|$.

In the real Web, a page corresponding to a vertex v in Q with only one incoming edge is usually not related to the topic of seed pages, while a page corresponding to a vertex v' in P linked from all the seeds is usually related to the topic. However, (I) and (II) imply that v often becomes a member of a community but v' often becomes a non-member of a community. Thus, (A) and (B) cause a problem for mining communities. This problem is serious, because many graphs used in the max-flow based method satisfy the condition (1); even if they do not satisfy the condition (1), the graphs obtained from them by removing few edges often satisfy the condition (1). We call this problem the *capacity problem*.

To solve the capacity problem, we propose to increase the capacity of every edge joining a vertex in S and a vertex in P. That is, we modify the original capacity function as follows:

- $c(e) = k'$ for every edge $e = (u,v)$, $u \in S$ and $v \in S \cup P$, where $k'(> 1)$ is a new parameter.
- $c(e) = 1$ for every edge $e = (u,v)$, $u \in P$ and $v \in P \cup Q$.
- $c(e) = \infty$ for each edge $e = (s,x)$.
- $c(e) = 1$ for each edge $e = (x,t)$.

We have made some preliminary experiments varying the parameter $k' \in \{3, 5, 10, 15, 20, 25\}$ for the sixteen topics described in Section 2, and confirmed that the method on the site-oriented framework finds approximate communities with good quality when $k' = 10$ or $k' = 15$ for these topics.

6   Concluding Remarks

We have pointed out several problems of the max-flow based method on the page-oriented framework, and proposed solutions to them utilizing the site-oriented framework. Our improved max-flow based method using the solutions on the site-oriented framework has achieved much better results, both in quality and in quantity, than the original max-flow based method on the page-oriented framework. Our solutions are relatively simple, but are particularly effective for mining communities containing personal sites in multi-site servers. Other methods for mining communities using hyperlinks suffer from the problems described in this paper, and hence the site-oriented framework and the proposed solutions in the paper would be useful for improving such methods.

References

1. R. K. Ahuja, T. L. Magnanti, and J. B. Orlin, "Network Flows – Theory, Algorithms, and Applications," Prentice Hall, New Jersey, 1993.
2. B. Amento, L. G. Terveen, and W. C. Hill, "Does "authority" mean quality? predicting expert quality ratings of web documents," *Proc. 23rd Annual International ACM SIGIR Conference*, pp. 296–303, 2000.
3. Y. Asano, H. Imai, M. Toyoda, and M. Kitsuregawa, "Applying the site information to the information retrieval from the Web," *Proc. 3rd International Conference on Web Information Systems Engineering*, IEEE CS, pp. 83–92, 2002.
4. Y. Asano, "A New Framework for Link-Based Information Retrieval from the Web," Ph.D. Thesis, the University of Tokyo, March 2003.
5. Y. Asano, H. Imai, M. Toyoda, and M. Kitsuregawa, "Finding neighbor communities in the Web using an inter-site graph," *Proc. 14th International Conference on Database and Expert Systems Applications*, LNCS 2736, pp. 558-568, 2003.
6. K. Bharat, B. W. Chang, M. Henzinger, and M. Ruhl, "Who links to whom: mining linkage between Web Sites," *Proc. 1st IEEE International Conference on Data Mining*, pp. 51–58, 2001.
7. N. Craswell, D. Hawking, and S. Robertson, "Effective site finding using link anchor information," *Proc. 24th Annual International ACM SIGIR Conference*, pp. 250–257, 2001.
8. G. W. Flake, S. Lawrence, and C. L. Giles, "Efficient identification of Web communities," *Proc. 6th ACM SIGKDD KDD2000*, pp. 150–160, 2000.
9. N. Imafuji and M. Kitsuregawa, "Finding Web communities by maximum flow algorithm using well-assigned edge capacity," *IEICE Trans. Special Section on Information Processing Technology for Web Utilization*, Vol. E87-D, No. 2, pp. 407-415, 2004.
10. J. Kleinberg, "Authoritative sources in a hyperlinked environment," *Proc. 9th Annual ACM-SIAM SODA*, pp. 668–677, 1998.
11. R. Kumar, P. Raghavan, S. Rajagopalan, and A. Tomkins, "Trawling the Web for emerging cyber-communities," *Computer Networks*, 31(11-16), pp. 1481–1493, 1999.
12. W. S. Li, N. F. Ayan, O. Kolak, and Q. Vuy, "Constructing multi-granular and topic-focused Web site maps," *Proc. 10th International World Wide Web Conference*, pp. 343–354, 2001.
13. M. Toyoda and M. Kitsuregawa, "Extracting evolution of Web communities from a series of Web archives," *Proc. 14th Conference on Hypertext and Hypermedia (Hypertext 03)*, ACM, pp. 28–37, 2003.
14. X. Wang, Z. Lu and A. Zhou, "Topic exploration and distillation for Web search by a similarity-based analysis," *Proc. 3rd International Conference of Advances in Web-Age Information Management (WAIM 2002)*, LNCS 2419, pp. 316–327, 2002.

A Web Recommendation Technique Based on Probabilistic Latent Semantic Analysis

Guandong Xu[1], Yanchun Zhang[1], and Xiaofang Zhou[2]

[1]School of Computer Science and Mathematics,
Victoria University, PO Box 14428, VIC 8001, Australia
{xu, yzhang}@csm.vu.edu.au
[2] School of Information Technology & Electrical Engineering,
University of Queensland, Brisbane QLD 4072, Australia
zxf@itee.uq.edu.au

Abstract. Web transaction data between Web visitors and Web functionalities usually convey user task-oriented behavior pattern. Mining such type of click-stream data will lead to capture usage pattern information. Nowadays Web usage mining technique has become one of most widely used methods for Web recommendation, which customizes Web content to user-preferred style. Traditional techniques of Web usage mining, such as Web user session or Web page clustering, association rule and frequent navigational path mining can only discover usage pattern explicitly. They, however, cannot reveal the underlying navigational activities and identify the latent relationships that are associated with the patterns among Web users as well as Web pages. In this work, we propose a Web recommendation framework incorporating Web usage mining technique based on *Probabilistic Latent Semantic Analysis* (PLSA) model. The main advantages of this method are, not only to discover usage-based access pattern, but also to reveal the underlying latent factor as well. With the discovered user access pattern, we then present user more interested content via collaborative recommendation. To validate the effectiveness of proposed approach, we conduct experiments on real world datasets and make comparisons with some existing traditional techniques. The preliminary experimental results demonstrate the usability of the proposed approach.

1 Introduction

With the popularizing and spreading of Internet applications, Web has recently become a powerful data repository for, not only retrieving information, but also discovering knowledge. Generally, Web users may exhibit various types of behaviors associated with their information needs and intended tasks when they are traversing the Web. These task-oriented behaviors are explicitly characterized by sequences of clicks on different Web objects (i.e. Web pages) performed by users. As a result, extracting the underlying usage pattern among the clickstream data is able to capture these interest-oriented tasks implicitly. For example, image a Web site designed for information about automobiles; there will be a variety of customer groups with various access interests during their visiting such an E-commerce Website. One type of

M. Kitsuregawa et al. (Eds.): WISE 2005, LNCS 3806, pp. 15–28, 2005.

customers intends to make comparison prior to shopping, a visitor planning to purchase one particular type car of wagon, for example, would have to browse the Web pages of each manufacturer, compare their offering, whereas another one will just be more interested in one specific brand car, such as "Ford", rather than one specific car category. In such scenario, these two visitors who exhibit different interests may follow distinct access tracks to accomplish their goals, and thus, corresponding clickstream data are recorded in Web sever log file accordingly. Mining Web log information, thus, will lead to reveal user access pattern. Moreover, the discovered informative knowledge (or patterns) will be utilized for providing better Web application, such as Web recommendation or personalization. Generally, Web recommendation can be viewed as a process that recommends customized Web presentation or predicts tailored Web content to users according to their specific tastes or preferences.

Related Work: With the significant development in data mining domain, many advanced techniques, such as k-Nearest Neighbor (*kNN*) algorithm [1-3], Web clustering [4-6], association rule mining [7, 8] and sequential pattern mining [9] are widely utilized to address Web usage mining recently. The successful progress shows that it will, not only, benefit Web structure and presentation design, e.g. Adaptive Web Design, but also, improve the quality of Web applications, such as practical Web personalization and recommendation systems [10-13].

To-date, there are two kinds of approaches commonly used in Web recommendation, namely content-based filtering and collaborative filtering systems [14, 15]. Content-based filtering systems such as WebWatcher [16] and client-side agent Letizia [11] generally generate recommendation based on the pre-constructed user profiles by measuring the similarity of Web content to these profiles, while collaborative filtering systems make recommendation by utilizing the rating of current user for objects via referring other users' preference that is closely similar to current one. Today collaborative filtering systems have been widely adopted in Web recommendation applications and have achieved great success as well [1-3]. In addition, Web usage mining has been proposed as an alternative method for Web recommendation recently [5]. The discovered usage pattern is utilized to determine user access interest, in turn, make collaborative recommendation efficiently.

On the other hand, *Latent Semantic Analysis* (LSA) is an approach to capture the latent or hidden semantic relationships among co-occurrence activities [17]. In practical applications, Single Value Decomposition (SVD) or Primary Component Analysis (PCA) algorithm is employed to generate a reduced latent space, which is the best approximation of original vector space and reserves the main latent information among the co-occurrence activities. [17-19]. LSA has been widely used in information indexing and retrieval applications [18, 20], Web linkage analysis [21, 22] and Web page clustering [23]. Although LSA has achieved great success in some applications, it still has some shortcomings [24]. *Probabilistic Latent Semantic Analysis* (PLSA) is a probabilistic variant of LSA based on maximum likelihood principle. Recently, approaches based on PLSA has been successfully applied in collaborative filtering [25] Web usage mining [26], text learning and mining [27, 28], co-citation analysis [28, 29] and related topics.

Our Approach: In this paper, we propose a Web recommendation framework based on PLSA model. The Web recommendation process exploits the usage pattern derived from Web usage mining to predict user preferred content and customize the presentation. By employing PLSA model on usage data, which is expressed as a page weight matrix, we can not only characterize the underlying relationships among Web access observation but also identify the latent semantic factors that are considered to represent the navigational tasks of users during their browsing period. Such relationships are determined by probability inference, and then are utilized to discover the usage-based access pattern. Furthermore, we make use of these discovered access pattern knowledge for Web recommendation by finding the most similar user access pattern to active user and predicting the preferred content based on the matched pattern.

The main contributions in this work are as follows: firstly, we present a Web recommendation unified framework incorporating Web usage mining technique based on PLSA model. Secondly, we investigate the discovery of user access patterns and latent factors related to these patterns via employing probability inference process, in turn, make use of the discovered usage knowledge for Web recommendation. Particularly, we develop a modified *k-means* clustering algorithm on the transformed session vectors and build up user access patterns in terms of centroids of generated session clusters, which reflect common navigational interests in same user category. Finally, we demonstrate the usability and effectiveness of the proposed model by conducting experiments on two real world datasets. The evaluation results show that usage-based approach is capable of predicting user preferred content more accurately and efficiently in comparison with some traditional techniques.

The rest of the paper is organized as follows. In section 2, we introduce the PLSA model. We present the algorithms for discovering latent factors, Web page categories in section 3. In section 4, we concentrate on how to construct usage-based user access pattern and Web recommendation model upon the discovered usage knowledge as well. To validate the proposed approach, we demonstrate experiment and comparison results conducted on two real world datasets in section 5, and conclude the paper in section 6.

2 Probabilistic Latent Semantic Analysis (PLSA) Model

2.1 Data Sessionization Process

Prior to introduce the principle of PLSA model, we discuss briefly the issue with respect to sessionization process of usage data. In general, the user access interests exhibited may be reflected by the varying degrees of visits in different Web pages during one session. Thus, we can represent a user session as a weighted page vector visited by user during a period. After data preprocessing, we can built up a page set of size n as $P = \{p_1, p_2, \cdots p_n\}$ and user session set of size m as $S = \{s_1, s_2, \cdots, s_m\}$. The whole procedures are called page identification and user sessionization respectively. By simplifying user session in the form of page vector, each session can be considered as an n-dimensional page vector $s_i = \{a_{i1}, a_{i2}, \cdots a_{in}\}$, where a_{ij} denotes the weight for page p_j in s_i session.

1) *Main* Movies: 20sec *Movies* News: 15sec *News*Box: 43sec *Box-Office* Evita: 52sec *News* Argentina:31 sec *Evita: 44sec*
2) *Music* Box: llsec *Box-Office* Crucible: 12sec *Crucible* Book: 13sec *Books: 19sec*
3) *Main* Movies: 33sec *Movies* Box: 21sec *Boxoffice* Evita: 44sec *News* Box: 53sec *Box-office* Evita: 61 sec *Evita : 31sec*
4) *Main* Movies: 19sec *Movies* News: 21sec *News box*: 38sec *Box-Office* Evita:61 sec *News* Evita:24sec *Evita* News: 31 sec *News* Argentina: 19sec *Evita: 39sec*
5) *Movies* Box: 32sec *Box-Office* News: 17sec *News* Jordan: 64sec *Box-Office* Evita: 19sec *Evita: 50sec*
6) *Main* Box: 17sec *Box-Office* Evita: 33sec *News* Box: 41 sec *Box-Office* Evita: 54sec *Evita* News: 56sec *News: 47sec*

$$SP_{ex} = \begin{bmatrix} 9.76 & 7.32 & 36.1 & 25.4 & 21.5 & 0.00 & 0.00 & 0.00 \\ 0.00 & 0.00 & 0.00 & 21.8 & 0.00 & 20.0 & 23.6 & 34.6 \\ 13.6 & 8.64 & 21.8 & 43.2 & 12.8 & 0.00 & 0.00 & 0.00 \\ 7.54 & 8.33 & 32.1 & 34.2 & 27.8 & 0.00 & 0.00 & 0.00 \\ 0.00 & 17.6 & 35.2 & 19.8 & 27.5 & 0.00 & 0.00 & 0.00 \\ 6.85 & 0.00 & 35.5 & 35.1 & 22.6 & 0.00 & 0.00 & 0.00 \end{bmatrix}$$

Fig. 1. A usage snapshot and its normalized session-page matrix expression

As a result, the user session data can be formed as Web usage data represented by a session-page matrix $SP = \{a_{ij}\}$. The entry in the session-page matrix, a_{ij}, is the weight associated with the page p_j in the user session s_i, which is usually determined by the number of hit or the amount time spent on the specific page. Generally, the weight a_{ij} associated with page p_j in the session s_i should be normalized across pages in same user session in order to eliminate the influence caused by the amount difference of visiting time durations or hit numbers. For example, Figure 1 depicts an usage data snapshot and its corresponding session-page matrix in the form of normalized weight matrix from [30, 31]. The element in the matrix is determined by the ratio of the visiting time on corresponding page to total visiting time, e.g. $a_{11} = 15/(15+43+52+31+44)*100 = 9.7\ldots$ and so on.

2.2 PLSA Model

The PLSA model is based on a statistic model called aspect model, which can be utilized to identify the hidden semantic relationships among general co-occurrence activities. Similarly, we can conceptually view the user sessions over Web page space as co-occurrence activities in the context of Web usage mining to discover the latent usage pattern. For the given aspect model, suppose that there is a latent factor space $Z = \{z_1, z_2, \cdots z_k\}$ and each co-occurrence observation data (s_i, p_j) is associated with the factor $z_k \in Z$ by varying degree to z_k.

According to the viewpoint of aspect model, thus, it can be inferred that there are existing different relationships among Web users or pages related to different factors, and the factors can be considered to represent the user access patterns. In this manner, each observation data (s_i, p_j) can convey the user navigational interests over the k-dimensional latent factor space. The degrees to which such relationships are "explained" by each factor derived from the factor-conditional probabilities. Our goal is to discover the underlying factors and characterize associated factor-conditional probabilities accordingly.

By combining probability definition and Bayesian rule, we can model the probability of an observation data (s_i, p_j) by adopting the latent factor variable z_k as:

$$P(s_i, p_j) = \sum_{z_k \in Z} P(z_k) \bullet P(s_i \mid z_k) \bullet P(p_j \mid z_k) \qquad (1)$$

Furthermore, the total likelihood of the observation is determined as

$$L_i = \sum_{s_i \in S, p_j \in P} m(s_i, p_j) \bullet \log P(s_i, p_j) \qquad (2)$$

where $m(s_i, p_j)$ is the element of the session-page matrix corresponding to session s_i and page p_j.

In order to estimate the desired probabilities, we utilize Expectation Maximization (EM) algorithm to perform maximum likelihood estimation in latent variable model [32]. Generally, two steps are needed to implement in this algorithm alternately: (1) Expectation (E) step where posterior probabilities are calculated for the latent factors based on the current estimates of conditional probability; and (2) Maximization (M) step, where the estimated conditional probabilities are updated and used to maximize the likelihood based on the posterior probabilities computed in the previous E-step. Iterating of E-step and M-step will result in the monotonically increasing of total likelihood L_i until a local optimal limit is reaching, which means the estimated results can represent the final probabilities of observation data. More details regarding EM algorithm is referred in [33]

It is easily found that the computational complexity of this algorithm is $O(mnk)$, where m is the number of user session, n is the number of page, and k is the number of factors.

3   Discovery of Latent Factors, Usage-Based Web Page Categories

Those probabilities generated in section 2 quantitatively measure the underlying relationships among Web users, pages as well as latent factors. We, thus, utilize the class-conditional probability estimates and clustering algorithm to identify user access interests, partition Web pages and user sessions into various usage-based categories.

3.1   Characterizing Latent Factor

First, we discuss how to capture the latent factor associated with user navigational behavior by characterizing the "dominant" pages. Note that $P(p_j \mid z_k)$ represents the conditional occurrence probability over the page space corresponding to a specific factor, whereas $P(z_k \mid p_j)$ represents the conditional probability distribution over the factor space corresponding to a specific page. In such case, we may consider that the pages whose conditional probabilities $P(z_k \mid p_j)$ and $P(p_j \mid z_k)$ are both greater than a predefined threshold μ can be viewed to contribute to one particular functionality related to the latent factor. By exploring and interpreting the content of these pages satisfying aforementioned condition, we may characterize the semantic meaning of each factor. The algorithm to characterize the task-oriented semantic latent factor is described as follows:

Algorithm 1. Characterizing Latent Factor

Input: $P(z_k \mid p_j)$ and $P(p_j \mid z_k)$, predefined threshold μ

Output: A set of characteristic page base sets $LF = (LF_1, LF_2, \cdots, LF_k)$

1. $LF_1 = LF_2 = \cdots = LF_k = \Phi$

2. For each z_k, choose all pages $p_j \in P$

   If $P(p_j \mid z_k) \geq \mu$ and $P(z_k \mid p_j) \geq \mu$ then

   $\quad LF_k = LF_k \cup p_j$

   Else go back to step 2

3. If there are still pages to be classified, go back to step 2

4. Output: $LF = \{LF_k\}$

3.2 Identifying Web Page Categories

Note that the set of $P(z_k \mid p_j)$ is conceptually representing the probability distribution over the latent factor space for a specific Web page p_j, we, thus, construct the page-factor matrix based on the calculated probability estimates, to reflect the relationship between Web pages and latent factors, which is expressed as follows:

$$pr_j = (c_{j,1}, c_{j,2}, ..., c_{j,k}) \tag{3}$$

Where $c_{j,s}$ is the occurrence probability of page p_j on factor z_s. In this manner, the distance between two page vectors may reflect the functionality similarity exhibited by them. We, therefore, define their similarity by applying well-known cosine similarity as:

$$sim(p_i, p_j) = \left(pr_i, pr_j \right) / \left(\|pr_i\|_2 \bullet \|pr_j\|_2 \right) \tag{4}$$

where $\left(pr_i, pr_j \right) = \sum_{m=1}^{k} c_{i,m} c_{j,m}$, $\|pr_i\|_2 = \sqrt{\sum_{l=1}^{k} c_{i,l}^2}$

With the page similarity measurement (4), we propose a modified k-means clustering algorithm to partition Web pages into corresponding categories. The detail of the clustering algorithm is described in [34]. The discovered Web page categories reflect, either user "sole" access interest or cross-interest navigational intention.

4   Clustering User Session and Making Web Recommendation

Similarly, we employ clustering algorithm on the probabilistic variable set of $P(z_k \mid s_i)$, which represents the probability of a latent class factor z_k exhibited by a given user session s_i to capture user access pattern. The clustering user session via modified k-means clustering algorithm is described as follows:

Algorithm 2. Clustering User Session
  Input: the set of $P(z_k \mid s_i)$, predefined threshold μ
  Output: A set of user session clusters $SCL = \{SCL_1, SCL_2, \cdots, SCL_p\}$ and corresponding centroids $Cid = \{Cid_1, Cid_2, \cdots, Cid_p\}$

1. Select the first session s_1 as the initial cluster SCL_1 and the centroid of this cluster: $SCL_1 = \{s_1\}$ and $Cid_1 = s_1$.

2. For each session s_i, measure the similarity between s_i and the centroid of each existing cluster $sim(s_i, Cid_j)$

3. If $sim(s_i, Cid_t) = \max_j(sim(s_i, Cid_j)) > \mu$, then insert s_i into the cluster SCL_t and update the centroid of SCL_t as

$$Cid_t = 1/|SCL_t| \bullet \sum_{j \in SCL_t} sr_j \tag{5}$$

where sr_j is the transformed user session over factor space, $|SCL_t|$ is the number of sessions in the cluster;
  Otherwise, s_i will create a new cluster and is the centroid of the new cluster.

4. If there are still sessions to be classified into one of existing clusters or a session that itself is a cluster, go back to step 2 iteratively until it converges (i.e. all clusters' centroid are no longer changed)
5. Output $SCL = \{SCL_p\}, Cid = \{Cid_p\}$

As we mentioned above, each user session is represented as a weighted page vector. In this manner, it is reasonable to derive the centroid of cluster obtained by aforementioned algorithm as the user access pattern (i.e. user profile).

Generally, Web recommendation process is usually carried out in two ways. On the one hand, we can take the current active user's historic behavior or pattern into consideration, and predict the preferable information to the specific user. On the other hand, by finding the most similar access pattern to the current active user from the learned models of other users, we can recommend the tailored Web content. The former one is sometime called memory-based approach, whereas the latter one is called model-based approach respectively. In this work, we adopt the model-based technique in our Web recommendation framework. We consider the usage-based access patterns generated in section 3 as the aggregated representations of common navigational behaviors, and utilize them as a basis for recommending potentially visited Web pages to current user.

Similar to the method proposed in [5], we utilize the commonly used *cosine* function to measure the similarity between the current active user session and discovered usage pattern. We, then, choose the best suitable pattern, which shares the highest similarity with the current session, as the matched pattern for current user. Finally, we generate the top-N recommendation pages based on the historically visited probabilities of pages visited by other users in the selected profile. The procedure is as follows:

Algorithm 3. Web Recommendation
  Input: An active user session and a set of user profiles
  Output: The top-N recommendation pages
  1. The active session and the patterns are to be treated as n-dimensional vectors over the page space within a site, i.e. $s_p = Cid_p = [w_1^p, w_2^p, \cdots, w_n^p]$, where w_i^p is the significance contributed by page p_i in this pattern, and $s_a = [w_1^a, w_2^a, \cdots w_n^a]$, where $w_i^a = 1$, if page p_i is already accessed, and otherwise $w_i^a = 0$.
  2. Measure the similarities between the active session and all derived usage patterns, and choose the maximum one out of the calculated similarities as the most matched pattern:

$$sim(s_a, s_p) = (s_a \Box s_p) / \|s_a\|_2 \|s_p\|_2, \ sim(s_a, s_p^{mat}) = \max_j (sim(s_a, s_p^j)) \qquad (6)$$

  3. Incorporate the selected pattern s_p^{mat} with the active session s_a, then calculate the recommendation score $rs(p_i)$ for each page p_i:

$$rs(p_i) = \sqrt{w_i^{mat} \times sim(s_a, s_p^{mat})} \qquad (7)$$

Thus, each page in the profile will be assigned a recommendation score between 0 and 1. Note that the recommendation score will be 0 if the page is already visited in the current session.

  4. Sort the calculated recommendation scores in step 3 in a descending order, i.e. $rs = (w_1^{mat}, w_2^{mat}, \cdots, w_n^{mat})$, and select the N pages with the highest recommendation score to construct the top-N recommendation set:

$$REC(S) = \{ p_j^{mat} \mid rs(p_j^{mat}) > rs(p_{j+1}^{mat}), j = 1, 2, \cdots N-1 \} \qquad (8)$$

5 Experiments and Evaluations

In order to evaluate the effectiveness of the proposed method based on PLSA model and efficiency of Web recommendation, we have conducted preliminary experiments on two real world data sets.

5.1 Data Sets

The first data set we used is downloaded from KDDCUP website. After data preparation, we have setup an evaluation data set including 9308 user sessions and 69 pages, where every session consists of 11.88 pages in average. We refer this data set to "KDDCUP data". In this data set, the numbers of Web page hits by the given user determines the elements in session-page matrix associated with the specific page in the given session.

The second data set is from a academic Website log files [35]. The data is based on a 2-week Web log file during April of 2002. After data preprocessing stage, the filtered data contains 13745 sessions and 683 pages. The entries in the table correspond to the amount of time (in seconds) spent on pages during a given session. For convenience, we refer this data as "CTI data".

5.2 Latent Factors Based on PLSA Model

We conduct the experiments on the two data sets to characterize the latent factors and group usage-based Web pages. Firstly, we present the experimental results of the derived latent factors from two real data sets based on PLSA model respectively. Table 1 illustrates the results extracted from the KDDCUP data set, whereas Table 2 presents the results of CTI data set. From these tables, it is shown that the descriptive labels of latent factors are characterized by some "prominent" pages whose probabilistic weights are exceeding one predefined threshold. This work is done by interpreting the contents of corresponding pages since these "dominant" pages contribute greatly to the latent factors. With the derived characteristic factor, we may semantically discover usage-based access pattern.

Table 1. Labels of factors from KDDCUP

Factor	Label	Dominant Page
1	Department search	6, 7
2	Product information of Legwear	4
3	Vendor service info	10,36,37,39
4	Freegift, especially legcare	1,9,33
5	Product information of Legcare	5
6	Online shopping process	27,29,32,42,44,45,60
7	Assortment of various lifestyle	3,26
8	Vendor2's Assortment	11,34
9	Boutique	2
10	Replenishment info of Department	6,25,26,30
11	Article regarding Department	12,13,22,23
12	Home page	8,35

5.3 Examples of Web Page Categories

At this stage, we utilize aforementioned clustering algorithm to partition Web pages into various clusters. By analyzing the discovered clusters, we may conclude that many of groups do really reflect the single user access task; whereas others may cover two or more tasks, which may be relevant in nature. As indicated above, the former can be considered to correspond to the primary latent factor, and the latter may reveal the "overlapping" of functionality in content.

In Table 3, we list two Web page categories out of total generated categories from KDDCUP data set, which is expressed by top ranked page information such as page numbers and their relative URLs as well. It is seen that each of these two page groups reflects sole usage task, which is consistent with the corresponding factor depicted in Table 1. Table 4 illustrates two Web page groups from CTI dataset accordingly. In this table, the upper row lists the top ranked pages and their corresponding contents from one of the generated page clusters, which reflect the task regarding searching postgraduate program information, and it is easily to conclude that these pages are all contributed to factor #13 displayed in Table 2. On the other hand, the listed significative pages in lower row in the table involve in the "overlapping" of two dominant tasks, which are corresponding to factor #3 and #15 depicted in Table 2.

Note that with these generated Web page categories, we may make use of these intrinsic relationships among Web pages to reinforce the improvement of Web organization or functionality design, e.g. *Adaptive Web Site Design*.

Table 2. Lables of factors from CTI

Factor	Label	Factor	Label
1	specific syllabi	11	international_study
2	grad_app_process	12	Faculty-search
3	grad_assist_app	13	postgrad_program
4	admission	14	UG_scholarship
5	advising	15	tutoring_gradassist
6	program_bacholer	16	Mycti_stud_profile
7	syllabi list	17	schedule
8	course info	18	CS_PhD_research
9	jobs	19	specific news
10	calendar	20	Home page

Table 3. Examples of Web page categories from KDDCUP dataset

Page	Content	Page	Content
10	main/vendor	38	articles/dpt_payment
28	articles/dpt_privacy	39	articles/dpt_shipping
37	articles/dpt_contact	40	articles/dpt_returns
27	main/login2	50	account/past_orders
32	main/registration	52	account/credit_info
42	account/your_account	60	checkout/thankyou
44	checkout/expresCheckout	64	account/create_credit
45	checkout/confirm_order	65	main/welcome
47	Account/address	66	account/edit_credit

Table 4. Examples of Web page categories from CTI dataset

Page	Content	Page	Content
386	/News	588	/Prog/2002/Gradect2002
575	/Programs	590	/Prog/2002/Gradis2002
586	/Prog/2002/Gradcs2002	591	/Prog/2002/Gradmis2002
587	/Prog/2002/Gradds2002	592	/Prog/2002/Gradse2002
65	/course/internship	406	/pdf/forms/assistantship
70	/course/studyabroad	666	/program/master
352	/cti/.../applicant_login	678	/resource/default
353	/cti/.../assistantship_form	679	/resource/tutoring
355	/cti/.../assistsubmit		

5.4 Evaluation Metric of Web Recommendation

From the view of the user, the efficiency of Web recommendation is evaluated by the precision of recommendation. Here, we exploit a metric called *hit precision* [5] to measure the effectiveness in the context of top-N recommendation. Given a user session in the test set, we extract the first j pages as an active session to generate a top-N recommendation set via the procedure described in section 4. Since the recommendation set is in descending order, we then obtain the rank of $j+1$ page in the sorted recommendation list. Furthermore, for each rank $r > 0$, we sum the number of test data that exactly rank the rth as $Nb(r)$. Let $S(r) = \sum_{i=1}^{r} Nb(i)$, and $hitp = S(N)/|T|$, where $|T|$ represents the number of testing data in the whole test set. Thus, *hitp* stands for the hit precision of Web recommendation process.

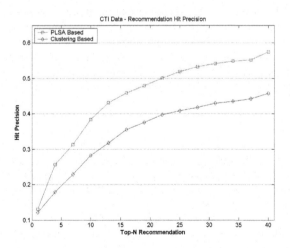

Fig. 2. Web recommendation evaluation upon hitp comparison for CTI dataset

In order to compare our approach with other existing methods, we implement a baseline method that is based on the clustering technique [5]. This method is to generate usage-based session clusters by performing k-means clustering process on usage data explicitly. Then the cluster centroids are derived as the aggregated access patterns.

Figure 2 depicts the comparison results of *hitp* coefficient using the two methods discussed above respectively performed on CTI dataset. The results demonstrate that the proposed PLSA-based technique consistently overweighs standard clustering-based algorithm in terms of hit precision parameter. In this scenario, it can be concluded that our approach is capable of making Web recommendation more accurately and effectively against conventional method. In addition to recommendation, this approach is able to identify the hidden factors why such user sessions or Web pages are grouped together in same category.

6   Conclusion and Future Work

Web usage mining is an emerging technique that can be utilized to, not only reveal Web user access interest, but also improve Web recommendation. This will provide benefits for improvement of Web applications, such as increasing the click-rate of Web site and providing more customized or preferred presentation to users.

In this paper, we have developed a Web recommendation technique by exploiting the pattern knowledge from Web usage mining process based on PLSA. With the proposed probabilistic method, we modeled the co-occurrence activities (i.e. user session) in terms of probability estimations to capture the underlying relationships among users and pages. Analysis of the estimated probabilities could result in building up usage-based Web page categories, discovering usage pattern, and identifying the hidden factors associated with corresponding interests. The discovered usage pattern has been utilized to improve the accuracy of Web recommendation. We demonstrated the effectiveness and efficiency of our technique through experiments performed on the real world datasets and comparison with previous work.

Our future work will focus on the following issues: we intend to conduct more experiments to validate the scalability of our approach. Meanwhile we plan to develop other methods by combining various types of Web data, such as content information into recommendation process to improve the accuracy.

References

1. Herlocker, J., et al. An Algorithmic Framework for Performing Collaborative Filtering. in Proceedings of the 22nd ACM Conference on Researchand Development in Information Retrieval (SIGIR'99). 1999. Berkeley, CA.
2. Konstan, J., et al., Grouplens: Applying Collaborative Filtering to Usenet News. Communications of the ACM, 1997. **40**: p. 77-87.
3. Shardanand, U. and P. Maes. Social Information Filtering: Algorithms for Automating 'Word of Mouth'. in Proceedings of the Computer-Human Interaction Conference (CHI95). 1995. Denver, CO.
4. Han, E., et al., Hypergraph Based Clustering in High-Dimensional Data Sets: A Summary of Results. IEEE Data Engineering Bulletin, 1998. **21**(1): p. 15-22.

5. Mobasher, B., et al., Discovery and Evaluation of Aggregate Usage Profiles for Web Personalization. Data Mining and Knowledge Discovery, 2002. **6**(1): p. 61-82.
6. Perkowitz, M. and O. Etzioni. Adaptive Web Sites: Automatically Synthesizing Web Pages. in Proceedings of the 15th National Conference on Artificial Intelligence. 1998. Madison, WI: AAAI.
7. Agarwal, R., C. Aggarwal, and V. Prasad, A Tree Projection Algorithm for Generation of Frequent Itemsets. Journal of Parallel and Distributed Computing, 1999. **61**(3): p. 350-371.
8. Agrawal, R. and R. Srikant. Jorge B. Bocca and Matthias Jarke and Carlo Zaniolo. in Proceedings of the 20th International Conference on Very Large Data Bases (VLDB). 1994. Santiago, Chile: Morgan Kaufmann.
9. Agrawal, R. and R. Srikant. Mining Sequential Patterns. in Proceedings of the International Conference on Data Engineering (ICDE). 1995. Taipei, Taiwan: IEEE Computer Society Press.
10. Joachims, T., D. Freitag, and T. Mitchell. Webwatcher: A tour guide for the world wide web. in The 15th International Joint Conference on Artificial Intelligence (ICJAI'97). 1997. Nagoya, Japan.
11. Lieberman, H. Letizia: An agent that assists web browsing. in Proc. of the 1995 International Joint Conference on Artificial Intelligence. 1995. Montreal, Canada: Morgan Kaufmann.
12. Mobasher, B., R. Cooley, and J. Srivastava. Creating adaptive web sites through usage-based clustering of URLs. in Proceedings of the 1999 Workshop on Knowledge and Data Engineering Exchange. 1999: IEEE Computer Society.
13. Ngu, D.S.W. and X. Wu. Sitehelper: A localized agent that helps incremental exploration of the world wide web. in Proceedings of 6th International World Wide Web Conference. 1997. Santa Clara, CA: ACM Press.
14. Herlocker, J.L., et al., Evaluating collaborative filtering recommender systems. ACM Transactions on Information Systems (TOIS), 2004. **22**(1): p. 5 - 53.
15. Dunja, M., Personal Web Watcher: design and implementation. 1996, Department of Intelligent Systems, J. Stefan Institute, Slovenia.
16. Joachims, T., D. Freitag, and T. Mitchell. WebWatcher: A Tour Guide for the World Wide Web. in Proceedings of the International Joint Conference in AI (IJCAI97). 1997. Los Angeles.
17. Baeza-Yates, R. and B. Ribeiro-Neto, Modern information retrieval. 1999, Sydney: Addison Wesley.
18. Deerwester, S., et al., Indexing by latent semantic analysis. Journal American Society for information retrieval, 1990. **41**(6): p. 391-407.
19. Dumais, S.T. Latent semantic indexing (LSI): Trec-3 report. in Proceeding of the Text REtrieval Conference (TREC-3). 1995.
20. Berry, M.W., S.T. Dumais, and G.W. O' Brie0146-4833n, Using linear algebra for intelligent information retrieval. SIAM Review, 1995. **37**(4): p. 573-595.
21. Hou, J. and Y. Zhang. Constructing Good Quality Web Page Communities. in Proc. of the 13th Australasian Database Conferences (ADC2002). 2002. Melbourne, Australia: ACS Inc.
22. Hou, J. and Y. Zhang, Effectively Finding Relevant Web Pages from Linkage Information. IEEE Trans. Knowl. Data Eng., 2003. **15**(4): p. 940-951.
23. Xu, G., Y. Zhang, and X. Zhou. A Latent Usage Approach for Clustering Web Transaction and Building User Profile. in The First International Conference on Advanced Data Mining and Applications (ADMA 2005). 2005. Wuhan, china: Springer.

24. Hofmann, T. Probabilistic Latent Semantic Analysis. in Proc. of the 22nd Annual ACM Conference on Research and Development in Information Retrieval. 1999. Berkeley, California: ACM Press.
25. Hofmann, T., Latent Semantic Models for Collaborative Filtering. ACM Transactions on Information Systems, 2004. **22**(1): p. 89-115.
26. Jin, X., Y. Zhou, and B. Mobasher. A Unified Approach to Personalization Based on Probabilistic Latent Semantic Models of Web Usage and Content. in Proceedings of the AAAI 2004 Workshop on Semantic Web Personalization (SWP'04). 2004. San Jose.
27. Cohn, D. and H. Chang. Learning to probabilistically identify authoritative documents. in Proc. of the 17th International Conference on Machine Learning. 2000. San Francisco, CA: Morgan Kaufmann.
28. Hofmann, T., Unsupervised Learning by Probabilistic Latent Semantic Analysis. Machine Learning Journal, 2001. **42**(1): p. 177-196.
29. Cohn, D. and T. Hofmann, The missing link: A probabilistic model of document content and hypertext connectivity, in Advances in Neural Information Processing Systems, T.G.D. Todd K. Leen, and Tresp, V., Editor. 2001, MIT Press.
30. Shahabi, C., et al. Knowledge discovery from user web-page navigational. in Proceedings of the 7th International Workshop on Research Issues in Data Engineering (RIDE '97). 1997: IEEE Computer Society.
31. Xiao, J., et al. Measuring similarity of interests for clustering web-users. in Proceedings of the 12th Australasian Database conference (ADC2001). 2001. Queensland, Australia: ACS Inc.
32. Dempster, A.P., N.M. Laird, and D.B. Rubin, Maximum likelihood from incomplete data via the EM algorithm. Journal Royal Statist. Soc. B, 1977. **39**(2): p. 1-38.
33. Xu, G., et al. Discovering User Access Pattern Based on Probabilistic Latent Factor Model. in Proceeding of 16th Australasian Database Conference. 2004. Newcastle, Australia: ACS Inc.
34. Xu, G., Y. Zhang, and X. Zhou. Using Probabilistic Semantic Latent Analysis for Web Page Grouping. in 15th International Workshop on Research Issues on Data Engineering: Stream Data Mining and Applications (RIDE-SDMA'2005). 2005. Tyoko, Japan.
35. Mobasher, B., Web Usage Mining and Personalization, in Practical Handbook of Internet Computing, M.P. Singh, Editor. 2004, CRC Press.

Constructing Interface Schemas for Search Interfaces of Web Databases

Hai He[1], Weiyi Meng[1], Clement Yu[2], and Zonghuan Wu[3]

[1] Dept. of Computer Science, SUNY at Binghamton, Binghamton, NY 13902
{haihe, meng}@cs.binghamton.edu
[2] Dept. of Computer Science, Univ. of Illinois at Chicago, Chicago, IL 60607
yu@cs.uic.edu
[3] Center for Adv. Compu. Studies, Univ. of Louisiana at Lafayette, Lafayette, LA 70504
zwu@cacs.louisiana.edu

Abstract. Many databases have become Web-accessible through form-based search interfaces (i.e., search forms) that allow users to specify complex and precise queries to access the underlying databases. In general, such a Web search interface can be considered as containing an *interface schema* with multiple *attributes* and rich *semantic/meta information*; however, the schema is not formally defined on the search interface. Many Web applications, such as Web database integration and deep Web crawling, require the construction of the schemas. In this paper, we introduce a schema model for complex search interfaces, and present a tool (WISE-*i*Extractor) for automatically extracting and deriving all the needed information to construct the schemas. Our experimental results on real search interfaces indicate that this tool is highly effective.

1 Introduction

With the explosive growth of the Internet, more and more databases supported by relational databases systems have become Web accessible through form-based search interfaces. For example, amazon.com uses the search interface as shown in Figure 1 to search its book database. The search interfaces of Web databases typically contain some form control *elements*, such as *textbox*, *radio button*, *checkbox* and *selection list*, which allow users to enter search information. A *label* (a descriptive text) is usually associated with an element to describe the semantic meaning of the element. Logically, elements and their associated labels together form different *attributes* (or query conditions) of the underlying database. Using such a schema-based interface, users can specify complex and precise queries to Web databases.

In order to understand Web databases and obtain the information from them, the first essential step is to understand search interfaces [2]. As Web search interfaces are designed in HTML for human users to use, their schemas are not formally defined. First of all, semantically related labels and elements are scattered in HTML text and the formal associations of these labels and elements do not exist. Moreover, search interfaces are heterogeneous in their contents, presentation styles and query capabilities. Therefore, it is difficult to automatically identify the attributes of each interface and to fully understand the semantics of the information related to the attributes. Although

M. Kitsuregawa et al. (Eds.): WISE 2005, LNCS 3806, pp. 29–42, 2005.
© Springer-Verlag Berlin Heidelberg 2005

some work on extracting search interfaces has been reported [4, 9, 10, 13, 16], they are highly inadequate as they focus on only labels and elements.

In fact, beyond labels and elements, a substantial amount of semantic/meta information about a search interface is "*hidden*" (i.e., not machine understandable) and needs to be revealed in order to better utilize the underlying Web database. For example, in Figure 1 "Publication date" implies that the attribute semantically has a *date* value type, and its two elements play different roles in specifying a query condition. As another example, in Figure 2 the values in the selection list (Title, Author, Keyword and Publisher) are in fact attribute names, and only one of them can be used to submit a query at a time (thus they are called *exclusive attributes* in this paper).

Fig. 1. The book search interface of amazon.com

Fig. 2. Example search interfaces containing exclusive attributes

Many Web applications are related to Web databases and require the contents of search interfaces of the Web databases to be understood and properly organized for computer processing. These applications include schema matching across multiple interfaces [1, 5, 7, 14], unified interface generation [7], deep Web crawling [13], programmatically interfacing with Web databases [3, 11], clustering/classifying Web databases [6, 12], and annotating the returned results of Web databases [15].

In this paper, we present a general framework for making the search interfaces of Web databases machine understandable. First, an *interface schema model* for capturing the semantic/meta information available on complex search interfaces is reported. Second, we present our method for automatically constructing the schema to make the "*hidden*" information on the search interfaces *explicit* and *machine understandable*. For this purpose, we introduce WISE-*i*Extractor whose main goals are: 1) *Attribute Extraction*, i.e., to associate semantically related labels and elements to form logical attributes and identify an appropriate label for each attribute; 2) *Attribute Analysis*, i.e., to reveal the "*hidden*" information to help understand the search interface.

This paper has the following contributions:

1) An interface schema model is proposed to describe the contents and capabilities of Web search interfaces for *deeper* understanding of them. This model contains not only attributes but also a substantial amount of semantic/meta information about the attributes, such as domain type, value type, and relationships among elements. This model is an extension of the model described in [8].

2) A practical solution is provided to automatically identify logical attributes on search interfaces. This solution consists of two novel components: (1) LEX, a *l*ayout-*ex*pression-based form extraction approach is designed to automatically extract attributes from search interfaces; (2) the knowledge from multiple interfaces in the same domain is leveraged to help extract *exclusive attributes*.

3) Extensive experimental results are reported, and they indicate that our solution for automatic search interface schema extraction is highly accurate and robust.

The rest of this paper is organized as follows. In Section 2, we present our schema model for search interfaces. In Sections 3 and 4, we discuss how to practically construct the schema, including attribute extraction and attribute analysis. The experimental results are reported in Section 5. In Section 6, we review related work. Finally, Section 7 contains the conclusions.

2   Schema Model for Representing Search Interfaces

In this section, we present a schema model for Web search interfaces that captures rich semantic information. For completeness of interface representation, the model also includes syntactic information of a search interface, such as element name and element type. In our model, an interface is represented as $F = (S, \{A_1, A_2, ..., A_n\}, C_f)$, where S is the site information associated with the form, such as the site URL, the server name and the HTTP communication method, $\{A_1, A_2, ..., A_n\}$ is an ordered list of attributes on the interface, and C_f is the form constraint (the logic relationship of the attributes for query submission). Each A_i is represented as $(L, P, DT, DF, VT, U, R_e, \{E_j, E_{j+1}, ..., E_k\}, C_a)$, where L is the attribute label of A_i (if applicable), P is the layout order position of A_i, DT is the domain type of A_i, DF is the default value of A_i, VT is the value type, U is the unit of A_i, $\{E_j, E_{j+1}, ..., E_k\}$ is an ordered list of domain elements of A_i, R_e is the relationship type of the domain elements, and C_a is the constraints of the attribute. Each domain element E_i is itself represented as (L_e, N, F_e, V, DV), where L_e is the element label (possibly empty), N is the name of E_i, F_e is the format (e.g., textbox, selection list, checkbox and radio button), V is the set of values of E_i, and DV is the default value of E_i (possibly null).

In the following, we will explain some of the concepts in the proposed interface schema model while some other concepts will be explained in subsequent sections.

Relationships of elements:
In a search form, an attribute may have multiple elements and they may be related differently. Generally, there exist four types of element relationships: *range type, part type, group type* and *constraint type*. For example, in Figure 3, the relationship between the elements of "Publication Year" is of *range type* (for specifying range query conditions); that of "Author" is of *part type* (i.e., last name and first name are parts of

a name); that of "Platform" is of *group type*; and finally "Exact phrase" is a *constraint type* of "Title keywords".

When an attribute has multiple associated elements, they shall be classified into two types: *domain elements* and *constraint elements* because they usually play different roles in specifying a query. Domain elements are used to specify domain values for the attribute while constraint elements specify some constraints on domain elements. For example, in Figure 3, element "Exact phrase" is a constraint element while the textbox following "Title keywords" is a domain element.

Identifying the relationship between the elements of each attribute helps interface schema integration [7, 14] and query mapping [3, 11]. As an example for query mapping, consider a local search interface containing an attribute "Title keywords" as shown in Figure 3. When a user specifies a query on the global attribute "Title" on a *mediated interface*, the query translation should map the query value to the domain element of "Title keywords" instead of the constraint element "Exact phrase".

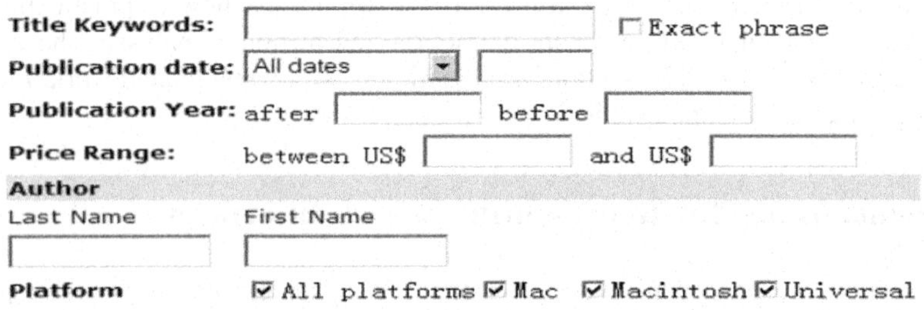

Title Keywords: [   ] □ Exact phrase
Publication date: [All dates ▼] [   ]
Publication Year: after [   ] before [   ]
Price Range: between US$ [   ] and US$ [   ]
Author
Last Name   First Name
[   ]   [   ]
Platform   ☑ All platforms ☑ Mac ☑ Macintosh ☑ Universal

Fig. 3. Examples of element relationship type

Element label:
In Figure 3, attribute "Publication Year" has two elements whose labels are "after" and "before" respectively. In this case, "Publication Year" is treated as the label of the attribute. Element labels are considered as the *child* labels of their attribute, which usually represent the semantics of the elements.

Logic relationship of attributes:
Attributes on a search interface can be logically combined in different ways to form a query to access the underlying database. Correctly identifying the logic relationship is important for successful query mapping and submission. Generally, there are four possibilities:

1) *Conjunctive*. All the attributes are combined through the "*and*" Boolean logic operator, meaning that all specified conditions must be satisfied at the same time.
2) *Disjunctive*. All the attributes are combined through the "*or*" Boolean logic operator, meaning that at least one specified condition must be satisfied.
3) *Exclusive*. In this case, only one attribute can be chosen to form a query at any given time. In Figure 2 the attribute names appear in a selection list (or a group of radio buttons) and only one attribute can be used at a time to form a query.
4) *Hybrid*. This is a combination of the above three cases. In this case, some conditions may be conjunctive, some may be disjunctive, and some may be exclusive.

3   Attribute Extraction

Labels and elements are the basic components of a search interface, but it is insufficient to just extract individual labels and elements because many applications (e.g., [1, 7, 11, 12, 13, 15]) rely on the *logical attributes* formed by related labels and elements. In order to extract logical attributes, it is essential to determine the semantic associations of labels and elements.

3.1   Interface Expression

On a search interface, labels and elements are *visually* arranged in one or more rows. To approximately capture the *visual layout* of these labels and elements, we introduce the concept of *interface expression* (IEXP). For a given search interface, its IEXP is a *string* consisting of three types of basic items 't', 'e' and 'l', where 't' denotes a label/text, 'e' for an element, and 'l' for a row delimiter that starts a new physical row.

For example, the search interface in Figure 1 can be represented as "te|eee|te|eee|te|eee|te|t|t|te|t|te|te|te|tee|t|te", where the first 't' denotes the label "Author", the first 'e' for the textbox following the label "Author", the first 'l' for the start of a new row on the interface, the following three 'e's for the three radio buttons below the textbox. The remaining items can be understood in a similar manner.

The IEXP is obtained when extracting individual labels and elements from a search interface (see Section 3.2 below). It provides a *high-level* description of the *visual layout* of different labels and elements on the interface while ignoring the details like the values of elements and the actual implementations of laying out labels and elements. Our method for automatic extraction of attributes will rely on this expression.

3.2   Extracting Individual Labels and Elements

This is the first step of our automatic attribute extraction method. Given a search interface, the extraction starts with its "<FORM>" tag. When a label or an element is encountered, a 't' or an 'e' will be appended to the IEXP (initially it is empty) accordingly. Each element contains its values (if available). Four types of input elements are considered: *textbox, selection list, checkbox* and *radio button*. When a row delimiter like "<BR>", "<P>" or "</TR>" is encountered, a 'l' is appended to the IEXP. This process continues until the "</FORM>" tag is encountered. In this process, some texts that are too long will be discarded. After this process, all labels and elements in the search interface are extracted, and the corresponding IEXP is also constructed.

3.3   Identifying the Names of Exclusive Attributes

Exclusive attributes are those whose names may appear as *values* in some elements, such as a group of *radio buttons* or a *selection list* (e.g., attribute names in Figures 2).

By our observation, exclusive attributes appear frequently on real Web search interfaces. Among the 184 real search interfaces we collected, more than 34% of the interfaces in the books, movies and music domains have exclusive attributes. A significant flaw of existing approaches [4, 9, 10, 13, 16] is that they do not extract them.

B. He et al [5] reported their discovery that the vocabulary of schemas in a domain stabilizes at a reasonably small size even though the number of search interfaces in the domain can be very large. We also observed that the names of exclusive attributes are often the *most commonly used attribute names* of a domain. Based on these, we propose a novel and simple statistical approach to tackle the problem of identifying exclusive attributes. The basic idea of our approach is the construction of a vocabulary for a domain by considering multiple interfaces in the same domain at the same time (Web interfaces can be clustered first such that each cluster contains the interfaces from the same domain [6, 12]).

To construct the vocabulary, we compute the **Label Interface Frequency** (*LIF*) of each extracted label of all considered search interfaces of a domain, which is the number of search interfaces of the domain that contain the label. Then only labels whose *LIF* $\geq$ *ft* are selected to construct the *common schema vocabulary* of the domain, where *ft* is computed by $ft = p*n$, with n being the total number of considered search interfaces of the domain, and p being the threshold known as the minimal percentage of search interfaces that contain the label.

Using this schema vocabulary, we find the search interfaces that contain some elements whose values are words in the vocabulary, and then extract the attribute names from these elements. Two patterns widely used in search interfaces as shown in Figure 2 are applied to identify such search interfaces: one pattern consists of a group of *radio buttons* and a *textbox*; the other consists of a *selection list* and a *textbox*. If enough values in the element(s) (selection list or radio buttons) are found to be contained in the vocabulary and the *textbox* is nearby, the values are extracted as attribute names, and the textbox is treated as the domain element of each attribute. After exclusive attributes are identified from the interface, the IEXP of the interface needs to be adjusted accordingly such that other attributes (if any) would not be affected for grouping in the next step (Section 3.4).

3.4 Grouping Labels and Elements

This step is to group the labels and elements that semantically correspond to the same attribute, and to find the appropriate attribute label/name for each group. For example, in Figure 1, label "Author", the textbox, the three radio buttons and their values below the textbox all belong to the same attribute, and this step aims to group them together and identify label "Author" as the name of the attribute.

To achieve this objective, a *layout-expression-based extraction* technique (LEX) is developed. The basic idea of LEX is as follows. The IEXP of an interface organizes texts/labels and elements into multiple rows. For each element e in a row, LEX finds the text either in the same row or within the two rows above the current row that is most likely to be the attribute label for e based on an *association weight* of the text with e computed using five measures (see below), and then groups e with this text. The process continues until all the elements in the IEXP are processed. The reason for considering two rows above the current row of an element is that related labels and elements are generally never laid out sparsely on a search interface.

During the above process, if the text closest to e is not recognized as the attribute label of e, it is assumed to be the element label of e. For example, in Figure 3 if text "after" is not recognized as the attribute label for the textbox, it will be considered as the element label of the textbox.

We identified five heuristic measures that are useful for predicting the association of labels and elements. The five heuristic measures are described below:

1) *Ending colon.* An attribute label often ends with a colon, while other texts do not.

2) *Textual similarity of element name and text.* An attribute label and its elements may have some words/characters in common.

3) *Distance of the element and text.* An attribute label and its elements usually are close to each other on a search interface. Such relationships are also expressed in the IEXP. If there exist multiple texts, then the closest text to an element is most likely to be the attribute label for the element. We define the distance of a text and an element as $dist = 1\ /\ |Ie - It|$, where Ie and It are the position indexes of the element and the text in the IEXP, respectively.

4) *Vertical alignment.* An element and its associated attribute label may be placed into different rows with one row having label and the row below it having the element. In this case, they are frequently aligned vertically. Thus, when we consider two rows above the current row of the element, we check if the element and the text are aligned vertically.

5) *Priority of the current row.* Although we consider two extra rows above the current row of an element, the current row is given higher priority because in most cases an attribute label appears in the same row as its elements.

4 Attribute Analysis

Once attribute extraction is finished, all labels and elements have been organized into logical attributes, and each attribute has an *element list* that maintains its elements. In this section, we discuss how to derive semantic information about attributes beyond labels and elements themselves as described in Section 2.

4.1 Differentiating Elements

As mentioned earlier, differentiating domain elements and constraint elements is important for precisely understanding the composition of attributes. Our observation indicates that domain elements often precede constraint elements either horizontally or vertically, and that constraint elements often appear in the form of a group of radio buttons (as shown in Figure 1) or a group of checkboxes. Based on the observation, a simple two-step method can be used to differentiate domain elements and constraint elements. First, identify the attributes whose elements are all radio buttons or checkboxes. Such attributes are considered to have only domain elements. Next, other attributes that may contain both domain elements and constraint elements can be easily recognized by following the regulations of the observation.

4.2 Identifying the Relationships and Semantics of Domain Elements

If an attribute has multiple *domain elements*, we identify their relationship and semantics. In our model, three types of relationships for multiple domain elements are defined and they are *group*, *range* and *part*.

We identify the group type by checking whether all the elements of the attribute are checkboxes or radio buttons and whether there are at least *two* (group implies at least two) checkboxes/radio buttons. If both are true, group type is recognized.

Range type is recognized by checking labels against certain domain-independent keywords and patterns that are widely used to represent range semantics. If some keywords and a pattern are found in the labels, the elements are considered to be of range type. For example, "between-and" and "from-to" are widely used range value patterns. At the same time, we also identify the semantic meaning of each element. For the "between-and" example, the element with "between" represents the lower bound of the range and the other with "and" represents the upper bound. Such semantics are useful for query mapping and schema matching.

The elements that are not of range type or group type will be treated as part type by default. The semantic meaning of each element involved in a part type relationship should also be identified whenever possible. Our approach is that we build a thesaurus of some commonly used concepts, such as date, time, name, address, etc. For example, if an attribute has three selection lists, each of them has its own set of values for "month", "day" and "year", respectively; by matching the patterns of values with the existing concepts, the system can derive what each element represents semantically.

4.3   Deriving Meta-information of Attributes

In our interface schema model four types of meta-information for each attribute are defined: *domain type*, *value type*, *default value* and *unit*. Note that these meta-data are for *domain elements* of each attribute only. Deriving meta-information is relatively straightforward as described below.

Domain type: Domain type indicates how many values can be specified on an attribute for each query. Four domain types are defined in our model: *range*, *finite* (with finite values but no range semantics), *infinite* (with possibly unlimited number of values, e.g., textbox, but no range semantics) and *Boolean*. The range domain type is addressed first. Given an attribute, if the relationship of its domain elements is of range type, then the domain type of the attribute is *range*. Otherwise, if a certain number of range keywords or a *range* pattern exists in the attribute label and the values of each element, the domain type of the attribute is recognized to be *range*. For example, keywords "less than" indicates a range; "from $10 to $30" satisfies a range pattern. If the domain type of the attribute is not a range type, it is then *infinite* if it involves a textbox. For the *Boolean* type, the attribute has just a single checkbox, and this checkbox is usually used to mark a yes-or-no selection. An example of such an attribute is "Used only" in Figure 1. *Boolean* type may be considered as a special case of the finite type because an attribute of Boolean type takes two (finite) possible values conceptually. In our model, *Boolean* type is separated from the regular *finite* type as this separation makes the Boolean property of the attribute more obvious and precise. If the attribute is not *Boolean* type, then *finite* type is set by default.

Value type: Value types currently defined in our model include *date*, *time*, *datetime*, *currency*, *id*, *number* and *char*, but more types could be added. To identify *date*, *time*, *datetime*, *currency* and *id*, commonly used keywords and patterns can be employed. For example, keyword "date" and value "12/01/2005" imply a date value type; keyword "morning" and value "10:30 AM" imply a time value type; "$" implies a currency value type. Value patterns can be expressed as regular expressions. If an attribute is not one of these five value types, the value type is declared to be *number* if the values of each element are numeric; otherwise the value type is *char*.

Default value: Default values in many cases indicate some semantics of the attributes. For example, in Figure 1 the attribute "Reader age" has a default value "all ages". Identifying default value is easy because it is always marked as "checked" or "selected" in an element.

Unit: A unit defines the meaning of an attribute value (e.g., *kilogram* is a unit for *weight*). Different sites may use different units for values of the same attributes. For example, a search interface may use "USD" as the unit of its "Price" attribute, while another may use "CAD" for its "Price" attribute. Identifying the correct units associated with attribute values can help understand attributes. Not all attributes have units. The unit information may be contained in labels or values for some attributes, which is easy to identify. Some resources available on the Web (e.g., the dictionary of units of measurement at www.unc.edu/~rowlett/units/) can also be utilized for helping identify the unit of an attribute.

4.4   Identifying the Logic Relationships

As the *exclusive* relationship of attributes is already addressed in Section 3.3, we focus on the other three relationships in the section.

Clearly, if two attributes are in a conjunctive relationship, the number of results returned from the search engine for a query using both attributes to specify conditions cannot be greater than that using only one of these two attributes in another query; and if two attributes are in a disjunctive relationship, then the number of results using both attributes cannot be less than that using only one of them. Thus, in principle, logic relationships between attributes could be identified by submitting appropriate queries to a search engine and comparing the numbers of hits for different queries.

In reality, however, it is rather difficult to automatically find appropriate queries to submit and to extract the numbers of results correctly. Therefore, in our current implementation, we take a simple and practical approach to tackle the problem. We observe that some search engines contain logic operators (i.e., *and, or*) on their interfaces. In this case, it is easy to identify the logic relationships among the involved attributes. Most interfaces have no explicit logic operators or exclusive attributes (e.g., Figure 1), so conjunctive relationships are assumed for attributes. If different types of logic relationships exist among the attributes on an interface, then a hybrid relationship is recognized for the interface. This simple approach, though heuristic, is really effective for identifying the logic relationships of attributes (by our experiments, 180 out of 184 forms used in our dataset are correctly identified).

5   Experiments

We have implemented an operational prototype of WISE-*i*Extractor using Java. WISE-*i*Extractor takes as input raw HTML pages containing search interfaces (search forms containing scripts such as Javascript or Vbscript are not considered) in the same domain, and outputs the schemas of these interfaces in XML format for use by other applications (say schema matching). The entire extraction process is fully automated.

5.1 Datasets

To evaluate the interface extraction technique proposed in this paper, we selected various numbers of search interfaces from 7 application domains: books (60 interfaces), electronics (21), games (12), movies (30), music (32), toys (13) and watches (16). The total number of search interfaces used is 184 from 146 different sites (some site has multiple search forms). We also use two independently collected datasets from the works [15, 16] for performance comparison.

5.2 Form Extraction Results

Grouping extracted labels and elements into separate attributes is the most complex problem in search interface extraction. To evaluate our LEX method for this task, we manually identify the attributes of each search interface, and then compare them with the results of LEX. We evaluate the accuracy of LEX in two levels of granularity: *element level* and *attribute level*.

Table 1. Element-level accuracy of LEX

Domain	#elements	# elements whose label is correctly identified by LEX	Accuracy
Books	484	473	97.7%
Electronics	191	185	96.9%
Games	72	72	100%
Movies	275	258	93.8%
Music	240	237	98.8%
Toys	62	62	100%
Watches	258	258	100%
Overall	1582	1545	97.7%

Element level: A label is correctly extracted for an element if it matches the manually identified label. Table 1 shows the experimental results of our method on the element level accuracy. The overall accuracy of 1582 elements from 184 forms is over 97%. The element level accuracy only considers a single element but not the whole attribute.

Attribute level: An attribute consists of up to three aspects of information: the name/label of the attribute, the set of domain elements and the set of constraint elements. An attribute extracted by LEX matches a manually extracted attribute if they match on all three aspects. Table 2 shows the experimental results for attribute-level accuracy, where "#Man" denotes the number of attributes identified manually; "#LEX" denotes the number of attributes correctly extracted by LEX. The overall accuracy of 7 domains is over 95%. We can see that the majority of the failures are caused by mistakes in extracting attribute labels. Our examination revealed that most of these failures in attribute label extraction are caused by the presence of a single checkbox (*single-checkbox problem*). For example, in Figure 3, if the checkbox "Exact phase" were below the textbox, it would be hard for LEX to know whether or not the checkbox is part of the attribute "Title keywords".

Table 2. Attribute-level accuracy of LEX

Domain	#Man	# LEX	Accuracy	Errors		
				Label	Dom. elems	Const. elems
Books	370	351	94.8%	8	8	3
Electronics	146	137	93.8%	6	1	2
Games	63	63	100%	0	0	0
Movies	195	178	91.3%	11	1	5
Music	200	196	98%	2	2	0
Toys	59	59	100%	0	0	0
Watches	84	84	100%	0	0	0
Overall	1117	1068	**95.6%**	27	12	10

Table 3. Usefulness measurement of LEX heuristics

Domain	Rh1	Rh2	Rh3	Rh4	Rh5	Only Keep h3
Books	-2	0	0	-6	-8	-14
Electronics	-1	-10	0	-4	-9	-19
Games	0	-1	0	0	0	-2
Movies	0	0	0	0	0	-7
Music	0	-1	-3	0	-9	-1
Toys	0	0	0	0	-4	0
Watches	0	-6	0	0	-2	-6

Effectiveness of LEX heuristics:
LEX uses five different heuristics to discover the association between elements and labels (see Section 3.4). It would be interesting to find out the impact of each individual heuristic on the accuracy of LEX. To do so, we remove a particular heuristic and use the remaining heuristics to group related labels and elements. The relative importance of the remaining heuristics is not changed. Table 3 shows the experiment results. Column headed by "Rh#" indicates the number of attributes that are negatively affected when the #th heuristic listed in Section 3.4 is not used, compared to the results of using all heuristics. For example, for the books domain, when the first heuristic is removed, 2 more attributes are not correctly extracted compared to the results of using all heuristics. We also list the result when only the third heuristic (Distance) is used. Intuitively a label closest to an element is likely to be the attribute label and thus it seems reasonable to only use distance to associate labels and elements. The results in Table 3 indicate that, somewhat surprisingly, removing the third heuristic has little effect on the accuracy of LEX but keeping only the third heuristic would cause a large number of failures. In short, each individual heuristic contributes positively to the attribute extraction process and using all the heuristics increases accuracy.

Robustness of LEX:
To further evaluate the robustness of our approach, we carried out additional experiments using independently collected datasets. Two datasets are used for this purpose.

The first is the dataset from the MetaQuerier project [16, 17] (the work is closely related to ours). In this dataset, there are 106 search forms from 9 different domains (airfares, books, autos, jobs, music, movies, hotels, carRental and realestate). We run WISE-*i*Extractor on this dataset without making *any change* to WISE-*i*Extractor. The overall attribute-level extraction accuracy of our method is 92.5%, while the accuracy obtained based on the method in [16] is 85.9%. Clearly, our method is significantly more accurate than the method reported in [16]. The second dataset is from DeLa [15] that contains 27 search forms from 3 domains (books, cars and jobs). The overall attribute-level accuracy of our method on this dataset is 92.7%.

Effectiveness of extracting exclusive attributes:
We also evaluate the effectiveness of the statistical approach for identifying and extracting exclusive attributes. Table 4 shows the experimental results, where "#IE" denotes the number of search interfaces that have such attributes, "#Prog" for the number of such search interfaces that are correctly identified by our approach, "#Latts" for how many such attributes exist in those interfaces, "#Eatts" for how many such attributes are correctly extracted. Note that the "#LEX" in Table 2 includes the "#Eatts", which means without using this approach, the "#LEX" of Table 2 would lose "#Eatts" in each corresponding domain, and thus the accuracy of Table 2 would decrease accordingly. We can see that our approach is very effective for recognizing such attributes that appear in the elements.

Table 4. Accuracy of identifying & extracting exclusive attr.

Domain	# IE	# Prog	# Latts	# Eatts
Books	21	20	98	95
Electronics	2	1	7	5
Games	3	3	10	10
Movies	12	10	40	32
Music	11	11	38	38
Toys	1	1	2	2
Watches	0	0	0	0

5.3 Obtaining Attribute Meta-information

To evaluate the accuracy of obtaining attribute meta-information, we consider only attributes that are correctly identified by LEX. Table 5 shows our experimental results for each domain. "DT" denotes domain type, "VT" for value type, "U" for unit, "ER"

Table 5. Accuracy of deriving meta-information of attr.

Domain	# LEX	DT	VT	U	ER	DDC
Books	351	347	349	341	347	343
Electronics	137	347	136	137	137	137
Games	63	694	485	478	484	480
Movies	178	171	171	175	176	177
Music	196	1559	1141	1131	192	1137
Toys	59	3118	2282	2262	1336	2274
Watches	84	6236	4564	4524	2672	4548

for element relationship, "DDC" for differentiation of domain elements and constraint elements. For example, for the book domain, out of the 351 attributes considered, the domain types of 347 attributes are correctly identified. The results show that nearly all needed meta-information can be correctly identified using the proposed methods.

6 Related Work

The works reported in [9, 13, 16] are the most related to ours. The major differences between the three works and our LEX approach are as follows: (1) The approaches in [9, 13] are not completely *attribute-oriented*, i.e., they find labels for elements but not for attributes. In contrast, LEX is *attribute-oriented*. (2) Even though a more formal framework (it views search interfaces as a visual language) is used in [16], the grammar rules are actually defined in advance based on extensive manual observations of a large number of search interfaces. More importantly, as reported in Section 5, our experiments on the same dataset indicate that our method outperforms the method in [16] significantly. (3) The three works do not address how to extract exclusive attributes, which appear in many real search interfaces. Leveraging the knowledge from multiple interfaces in the same domain to help extract exclusive attributes is a unique feature of our approach. (4) Our solution is much more comprehensive for representing search interfaces than the three existing solutions. We not only model the search interfaces and extract attributes, but also identify more useful information implicitly existing in search interface schemas, such as relationships among elements and value type, for each attribute. Such information is quite important for precisely representing and understanding a search interface.

We also note that Ontobuilder [4] supports the automatic extraction of ontologies from Web search interfaces. However, the ontologies are limited to the properties of labels and elements themselves, other semantic/meta information such as data type is not revealed. Kushmerick [10] uses a Bayesian learning approach to classify Web search forms to a specific domain and predict a label for each element. However, the work does not address semantic/meta information on search interfaces.

7 Conclusions

In this paper, we proposed a schema model for representing form-based search interfaces of database-driven search engines. This model precisely captures the relationships between elements and labels in terms of logical attributes, as well as a significant amount of semantic/meta information on this type of search interfaces. The information in this model can be used to support many important Web applications.

We also presented our techniques for automatically constructing the schema for any search interface, including grouping labels and elements into logical attributes and deriving the semantic/meta information of such attributes. Such a comprehensive study of Web search interfaces has rarely been conducted in the literature. Our extensive experimental results showed that our techniques can achieve very high accuracy in automatically extracting form information. Although our solutions involve significant heuristics (just like other solutions [9, 13, 16]), our insight into Web search interfaces is unique and deeper.

In the future, we plan to apply data mining approaches to attribute extraction and analysis. We will also study the problem of constructing a complete schema for Web databases by combining the interface schema and the data schema reflected in the search result.

Acknowledgement. This work is supported by the following grants from NSF: IIS-0208574, IIS-0208434, IIS-0414981, IIS-0414939 and CNS-0454298.

References

1. S. Bergamaschi, S. Castano, M. Vincini, D. Beneventano. Semantic Integration of Hetero-geneous Information Sources. *Data & Knowledge Engineering*, 36: 215-249, 2001.
2. K. Chang, B. He, C. Li, M. Patel, and Z. Zhang. Structured Databases on the Web: Obser-vations and Implications. *SIGMOD Record*, 33(3), September 2004.
3. K. Chang and H. Garcia-Molina. Mind Your Vocabulary: Query Mapping Across Hetero-geneous Information Sources. In *SIGMOD Conference*, 1999.
4. A. Gal, G. Modica and H. Jamil. OntoBuilder: Fully Automatic Extraction and Consolida-tion of Ontologies from Web Sources. In *ICDE Conference*, 2004.
5. B. He and K. Chang. Statistical Schema Matching across Web Query Interfaces. In *SIGMOD Conference*, 2003.
6. B. He, T. Tao, and K. Chang. Clustering Structured Web Sources: a Schema-based, Model-Differentiation Approach. In *EDBT-ClustWeb workshop* 2004.
7. H. He, W. Meng, C. Yu, and Z. Wu. WISE-Integrator: An Automatic Integrator of Web Search Interfaces for E-commerce. In *VLDB Conference*, 2003.
8. H. He, W. Meng, C. Yu, and Z. Wu. Automatic Extraction of Web Search Interfaces for Interface Schema Integration. In *WWW Conference*, 2004.
9. O. Kaljuvee, O. Buyukkokten, H. Garcia-Molina, and A. Paepcke. Efficient Web Form Entry on PDAs. In *WWW Conference*, 2000.
10. N. Kushmerick. Learning to Invoke Web Forms. In *ODBASE Conference*, 2003.
11. A. Levy, A. Rajaraman, and J. Ordille. Querying Heterogeneous Information Sources Us-ing Source Descriptions. In *VLDB Conference*, 1996.
12. Q. Peng, W. Meng, H. He, and C. Yu. WISE-Cluster: Clustering E-Commerce Search En-gines Automatically. In *WIDM workshop*, 2004.
13. S. Raghavan and H. Garcia-Molina. Crawling the Hidden Web. In *VLDB Conference*, 2001.
14. W. Wu, C. Yu, A. Doan, and W. Meng. An Interactive Clustering-based Approach to Inte-grating Source Query interfaces on the Deep Web. In *SIGMOD Conference*, 2004.
15. J. Wang and F.H. Lochovsky. Data Extraction and Label Assignment for Web Databases. In *WWW Conference*, 2003.
16. Z. Zhang, B. He, and K. Chang. Understanding Web Query Interfaces: Best-Effort Parsing with Hidden Syntax. In *SIGMOD Conference*, 2004.
17. MetaQuerier:http://metaquerier.cs.uiuc.edu/formex

Temporal Ranking of Search Engine Results

Adam Jatowt[1], Yukiko Kawai[1], and Katsumi Tanaka[2]

[1] National Institute of Information and Communications Technology,
3-5 Hikaridai, Seika-cho, Soraku-gun, 619-0289, Kyoto, Japan
{adam, yukiko}@nict.go.jp
[2] Graduate School of Informatics, Kyoto University,
Yoshida-Honmachi, Sakyo-ku, 606-8501, Kyoto, Japan
ktanaka@i.kyoto-u.ac.jp

Abstract. Existing search engines contain the picture of the Web from the past and their ranking algorithms are based on data crawled some time ago. However, a user requires not only relevant but also fresh information. We have developed a method for adjusting the ranking of search engine results from the point of view of page freshness and relevance. It uses an algorithm that post-processes search engine results based on the changed contents of the pages. By analyzing archived versions of web pages we estimate temporal qualities of pages, that is, general freshness and relevance of the page to the query topic over certain time frames. For the top quality web pages, their content differences between past snapshots of the pages indexed by a search engine and their present versions are analyzed. Basing on these differences the algorithm assigns new ranks to the web pages without the need to maintain a constantly updated index of web documents.

1 Introduction

The Web has become the biggest information repository in the world, thus crawling the content of the Web takes a long time. Because web documents can change often, it is difficult to retrieve the freshest information. One strategy for coping with this problem is to customize the crawling patterns to match the frequency of changes to particular web pages. This works reasonably well for pages that change regularly and predictably, like news pages. However, the majority of web resources change in an arbitrary fashion. Thus, search engines cannot retrieve all recently modified content in real time and consequently contain older versions of web pages in their indexes. For example, according to one study, Google [11] crawls web documents with an average delay of one month [19]. This is unacceptable to users who require fresh and relevant information. They often cannot obtain information that is sufficiently fresh simply because the pages have not been crawled over frequently enough. Consequently, users may receive information that is out-of-date or already known to them, or that may even be no longer correct. Search engines generally calculate page ranks using cached versions of pages, which might be obsolete. Thus, the highest ranks may be assigned to the pages that are "popular" and relevant to the query topic but may not necessarily contain the freshest information.

M. Kitsuregawa et al. (Eds.): WISE 2005, LNCS 3806, pp. 43–52, 2005.

Ranking of pages, nowadays, is to large extent based on link structure. Algorithms like PageRank [5] help to order the Web and determine the importance of web documents on the basis of their in-link numbers. While such algorithms have been proven to be very effective for finding popularity and importance of documents, they are ineffective for detecting fresh information. It is not necessarily true that web documents with a large number of in-links have good temporal characteristics and consequently are kept up-to-date. There are many stale pages, i.e., pages that are rarely changed; yet they have high ranks assigned by search engines. Obviously, stale web pages are less likely to be interesting and may contain obsolete content with incorrect information. Documents can also be abandoned or their temporal characteristics might change, so that they become more static in terms of new content updates. By conventional link analysis we may not detect such pages because the number of links to the pages may change very slowly. However the decrease in the temporal quality of such web pages can be detected by our proposed system.

One way to determine which web pages are up-to-date and which are not is to analyze their content at several time points in relation to real world changes. High quality pages should have fresh content relevant to their topics. However, precisely determining what is new and up-to-date and what not for any arbitrary query would require computers containing a reliable and continuously up-dated external knowledge base about the world, which is still impossible with the current state of technology.

We thus take a simpler approach by analyzing how changes in web documents are related to the query to approximately estimate if pages are up-to-date and relevant to the query topic. First, we evaluate the temporal relevance of web pages during lengthy, previous periods and select the pages with the best temporal characteristics, i.e., the ones that are frequently changed and are on-topic. It is likely that these pages will also have fresh content later at the time of a query. Then, when a query is entered, we analyze the differences between the present versions of these pages and versions indexed by a search engine. Thus, our method attempts to detect inconsistencies between the state of web documents indexed by a search engine and the current state of web documents. This data is used to estimate the degree of modification needed to make the search engine rankings reflect the freshness and relevance of the content to the query. The rankings are modified accordingly, and the results are sent to the user.

Thus, our method enhances the rankings calculated by traditional search engines. By modifying the rankings based on temporal analysis, it helps the user retrieve fresh, relevant content. We assume here that search engines contain all past data that they have accumulated during crawling, so they can rank web pages in real time.

Another advantage of our approach is that by analyzing archives of web pages we estimate the general relevance of web documents. Thus, we can find whether web pages are devoted to the given topic or whether they just simply mention query words in some point of time in the context of different topic. It seems that currently used ranking algorithms like PageRank rely too much on measuring importance of web documents by link structure analysis and too little on the actual content. This is partially due to the fact that it is difficult for computers to understand the content of the page and its relevance degree to the query, when there is no metadata provided, without using costly natural language processing techniques. However, it often happens that for a given query we obtain results that are not exclusively related to the query topic. Instead we might get the pages that have high PageRank value and they just contain the query terms only in the search time. On the other hand, web documents that are devoted to the topic and contain always fresh and informative content that is relevant to the query may not have high ranks in the search engine results especially if they concern rare topics.

The next section discusses related research. Section 3 presents our method for temporal ranking of web pages, and Section 4 presents the results of experiments we conducted to evaluate the proposed method. We conclude with a short summary.

2 Related Research

Studies of the characteristics of the Web (e.g., [4,6]) have confirmed the common belief that the Web is a highly dynamic environment and have attempted to estimate the frequencies of web page changes or to predict their updating patterns. For example, more than 40% of web pages in the "com" domain are changed everyday [6].

Some web pages have adopted a push work style in which information about their updates is sent to interested users. This requires users to pre-select the web pages and submit specific requests to receive information about changes of possible interest. However, the majority of web pages still use the conventional pull work style in which users have to visit the appropriate sites each time they want to search for fresh data.

Several automatic change detection and monitoring systems have been proposed [8,13,3]. Most require the user to provide the URLs of target resources and to specify a notification method and several tracking parameters (monitoring frequency, types or locations of changes of interest, etc.). The well-known AIDE [8] uses the HTMLdiff algorithm to present different types of changes from archived web page versions in a graphical way. WebVigiL [13] is an information monitoring and notification system for detecting customized changes in semi-structured and unstructured documents. Finally, ChangeDetector [3] uses machine learning techniques for effectively monitoring entire web sites. The disadvantage of traditional change detection systems is that they require a user to identify beforehand potentially interesting web sites or the type of information that he or she wants to receive in the future.

Google News [10] is a popular automatic news retrieval system. It tracks more than 4000 news sources and displays the latest news related to a query. However, only news-type web pages are analyzed for fresh information. Thus, users receive fresh information from a limited number of news sources.

While there have been a few proposed modifications to the currently used ranking algorithms to incorporate the temporal dimension [1,2], there seems to be no easy way to maintain a fresh search engine index. One proposal was to use a distributed search engine that collects web pages locally [18]. While this could probably provide fresher information more quickly, it is unlikely that distributed search engines will soon replace the existing search engines.

The concept of continual queries was conceived to alleviate the impact of changing web content on information retrieval (e.g., [15,7]). Continual query systems guarantee the freshness of web pages by continuously monitoring them with appropriate frequencies. The crawling schedules of these systems are optimized to minimize resource allocation while keeping web pages as fresh as possible. Consequently, the responses to queries are more up-to-date and are generated at less cost. Our approach is different in that we examine changes in the contents of web documents over long time periods by using archived pages. Then we utilize these results in query time for ranking pages basing on the differences between their present versions and versions stored by search engines. Additionally, rather than estimating only the frequencies of the content changes of pages in the past, we also focus on the relevance of these changes to the query topic. Web pages modified frequently are considered "active" documents; however, changes that are not related to the query topic are usually of little value to the user.

3   Ranking Method

The basic schema of the system that is using our proposed algorithm is displayed in Figure 1. When a user enters a query, it is forwarded to a search engine, which returns a list of results. The system takes a certain number, N, of the top URLs. The number is limited since analyzing all pages for an arbitrary query would be too costly. Past versions of each of these pages are then retrieved from a web page archive. Since retrieving all available archived pages could be too time consuming, only those pages that match some specified time period are retrieved. The number of web pages and the length of the time period can be specified by the user.

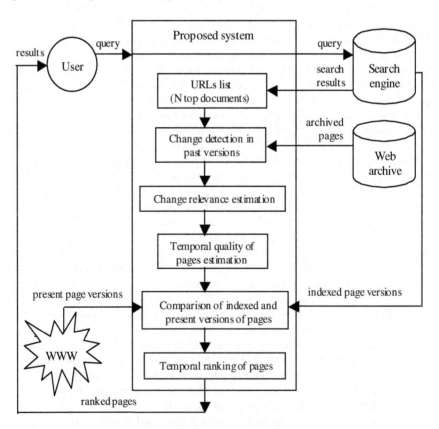

Fig. 1. Basic schema of the proposed system

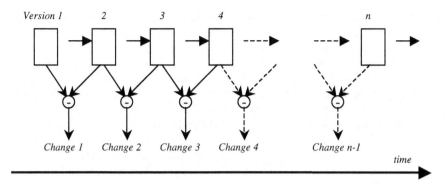

Fig. 2. Comparison of past web page versions to identify changes

The next step is to identify the changes in the past versions of documents. For simplicity, we assume that web documents have fixed structures. Since content changes are more important to users then other types of changes, like presentation or structural ones [9], only content changes are considered in the proposed method. HTML tags, links, and multimedia are discarded. As shown in Figure 2, consecutive versions of web pages are compared for changes. The change comparison is done at the sentence level. Sentences from every consecutive pair of versions of each web document are analyzed to identify added sentences. If a particular sentence appeared only in the later version, it is treated as an addition. To avoid detecting minor sentence modifications (e.g., a few changed words and grammatical corrections), a similarity comparison algorithm is used to examine the types of words and their order in the analyzed sentences. Analysis of the number and order of common words in each pair of sentences produces a similarity value for each sentence pair. A sentence is considered to be a changed one if it has a lower similarity value than some predefined threshold.

Through this comparison, previous additions to the web documents are detected. After these changes are extracted, standard text processing steps such as stemming and stop-word filtering are applied.

We want to find the relevance of changes to the topic represented by the query. To do so, first we employ vector-based representation of changed contents and the query topic. A vector is computed for the whole changed content in each web document version. Query vector is constructed from the query words issued previously by the user; however, it can be also expanded by adding terms related to the topic.

Although, a simple term frequency weighting method could be utilized here, we are using the weighting method shown in Equation 1. A word is weighted more highly the more frequently it occurs in the changed content of a past page version on the whole and also the more frequently it occurs in many different sentences in this changed content.

$$W_i = \frac{n^i}{n^{words} + 1} * \frac{N^{sen} + N^i}{N^{sen}} \tag{1}$$

Here, W_i is the weight of a word i in the changed part of a web page, n^{words} is the total number of words in the changed part, and n^i denotes the number of instances of the word i. N^{sen} is the number of sentences in the changed part, and N^i is the number of sentences containing the word i. Thus, the first part of Equation 1 is related to a term frequency of the word i, whereas the second one is related to its sentence frequency in the change of the page.

Next, the cosine similarities between each change vector and the query vector are computed. Additionally, we calculate the size of each change in relation to the size of the whole page and the time differences between consecutive page snapshots. All of this data is used to estimate a temporal quality value for each page. The formula for computing the temporal quality of a page is shown below.

$$TQ^n = \frac{1}{\sum_{j=1}^{j=n-1} \frac{1}{\left(T^{present} - T_j\right)}} * \sum_{j=1}^{j=n-1} \left(\frac{1}{\left(T^{present} - T_j^{past}\right)} * \frac{\cos(A_{(j,j+1)}^c, Q)}{\left(T_{j+1} - T_j\right)} * \left(1 + \frac{S_{(j,j+1)}^c}{S_j} \right) \right) \tag{2}$$

TQ^n is the measure of temporal quality of a page calculated over its n past versions, $A_{(j,j+1)}^c$ is the vector of added changes between the j and $j+1$ versions of the page, $\cos(A_{(j,j+1)}^c, Q)$ is the cosine similarity between vector $A_{(j,j+1)}^c$ and query vector Q, $S_{(j,j+1)}^c$ is the size of the change between the j and $j+1$ versions of the page, and S_j is the total size of the j version expressed as the number of words. Finally, T_j and T_{j+1} are the dates of the consecutive past versions of the page, and $T^{present}$ is the time when the query was issued. As shown by Equation 2, temporal quality depends on the relevance of its changed content to the query topic, on the size of the changes, and on the time differences between consecutive changes. Small changes are less likely to be as attractive as large changes if we assume the frequency of updating is constant. Additionally, the temporal quality of a page is higher if the page is usually modified relatively quickly. It also depends more on later changes than on older ones as the weight assigned to each change depends on its temporal distance from the present moment. Equation 2 is used to identify and discriminate slow-changing web documents as well as those that have changes not related to the query topic. The higher quality a page is, the greater the likelihood is that its actual content is fresh and relevant at the time of the query.

After the temporal qualities of the web pages have been estimated, the results from the search engine are analyzed again, and the dates of the last crawls of the candidate documents are checked. These dates are usually displayed close to a link to each URL on the search engine results page. Depending on the dates of last crawls and on the values of temporal qualities the system decides which web documents should be analyzed. If a candidate document has high temporal quality, and the date of the last crawl is quite old, the page is processed further. Thus, a page is considered for the next step of the algorithm if the result of multiplying its temporal quality value by the time elapsed since the last crawl is higher than some specified threshold value. In this way, only the pages that have highest probability of having new, relevant content at the time of the query are retrieved and analyzed. Thus, the cost of ranking is decreased.

The next step is to compare the indexed and present versions of the documents for changes. The indexed versions are extracted from a search engine database while the present versions are downloaded at the time of the query. Google [11], MSN Search [16] and other search engines offer cached document versions. This is done to provide page content when users cannot access a given web page. They can instead download the cached version of the document. Our algorithm uses the cached pages in order to compare how the web pages changed since the last crawl. We can see the difference between the state of the web pages seen at the present moment and the state seen by the search engine ranking mechanism. Thus, in this way the system can correct ranks assigned by search engines in case of some relevant information appearing or disappearing from a given web page.

When the present and indexed versions of the pages are compared, both addition and deletion type changes are extracted this time. If a sentence is found in the indexed page version and not in the present version, it is treated as a deletion. Additions mean that new content has been added that may or may not contain fresh information regarding the query. Deletions have an equally important, although negative, effect on the quality of the overall ranking. The present version of a page may not contain some piece of information related to the query because it was deleted since the last time the page was fetched. Or it cannot contain query word at all. In such cases, the user may have difficulty understanding the relationship between the content of the page and the query.

After we have found inserted and deleted sentences, we group them to form deleted and inserted change for each web document. For each type of change, we compute a vector using the weighting method in Equation 1: A_i and D_i denote the vectors of additions and deletions for page i.

To estimate the relevance of the changes to the query topic, we calculate cosine similarities between the query vector and the change vectors for each page. Calculation of the new rank is based on the cosine similarities, the time elapsed since the last crawl over the page, the rank assigned by the search engine, and the size of the changes (Equation 3).

$$R_i^{new} = \left[\frac{\cos(A_i, Q) - \alpha * \cos(D_i, Q) + 1}{\beta * \left(T^{present} - T_i^{indexed}\right) + 1} \right] * \left[1 + \gamma * \frac{N - R_i^{se} + 1}{N} \right] * \left[1 + \eta * \left(\frac{S_i^a}{S_i^{indexed}} + \mu * \frac{S_i^d}{S_i^{indexed}} \right) \right] \quad (3)$$

Here, R_i^{new} is the new ranking value of a page i, $cos(A_i, Q)$ is the cosine similarity between the vector of additions for the page and the query vector, and $cos(D_i, Q)$ is the cosine similarity between the vector of deletions and the query vector. R_i^{se} is the original rank assigned to the page by a search engine, $T_i^{indexed}$ is the time elapsed since the search engine indexed the page, and $T^{present}$ is the present time when the query is issued. S_i^a, S_i^d, and $S_i^{indexed}$ denote the number of words in additions, deletions, and in the indexed version of the page, respectively. Finally, $\alpha, \beta, \gamma, \eta, \mu$ are the weights used to adjust the effects of the features on the new ranking. Their values range from 0 to 1 for β, γ, η and -1 to 1 for α, μ.

The first part of Equation 3 shows how much the present version of a given page differs from its cached version in relation to the user's query and the time that has elapsed. We use the present time instead of the latest update time because the former means the time when the temporal ranking is being constructed. Using it enables us to determine the time difference between the current version of the page and the one indexed by the search engine. Additionally, the latter is not always available. The second part of Equation 3 takes into account the original ranking of the page in the search engine results. It enables a user to decide on the level of trust for the rankings decided by the search engine and to choose to which extent search engine ranks should be modified. Finally, the last part of Equation 3 depends on the sizes of both types of changes with respect to the size of the cached page.

By assigning suitable weights in Equation 3, we can obtain rankings from different viewpoints. Thus, it is possible to rank documents according to their additions similarity and deletions dissimilarity to the query vector, the time elapsed since the last crawl, the original search engine ranking, and the size of both types of changes. For example, we may look for documents that have large additions related to the query that were made shortly after the last crawl. Or we may search for documents that have both types of changes relevant to the query without considering the time difference between page versions.

Finally, the pages are sorted based on their new ranks. The final results include first the pages that had ranks computed by Equation 3 and later the rest of the pages from the whole set N of documents sorted by their temporal quality values (Equation 2). Then, the results are sent to the user. The original ranks assigned by the search engine are also displayed for each URL. Additionally, snippets of web page content in which the query words appear may also be shown.

4 Experiments

We implemented our method in Java 2.01 on a workstation with a Pentium M CPU (1.7 GHz) and 2.0 GB of RAM. We used a TomCat web server [20] and Porter Stemmer in Java [17]. Poorly written HTML code was repaired using the Java module of the JTidy HTML correction tool [14].

The past versions of web pages were obtained from the Internet Archive website [12]. Unfortunately, the pages provided were at least six months old, so we could not test the system using the latest page versions. We have retrieved past versions of web pages for the time frames of 6 months, one year and two years. For some relatively new pages that had not much history we analyzed up to the earliest page version available inside the given time frame. However, few such young pages appeared in the top results of the search engine results for the queries that we have used. Another problem was that some pages had more previous versions crawled by Internet Archive than others.

For simplicity, in our implementation, we have computed query vector using only query words so we did not expand the query vector by additional related terms.

We present here the results for two queries: "Indiana Jones" and "Japanese economy" that were issued to the Google search engine. We compared the results obtained using our method with results obtained from subjects. The subjects were asked to evaluate and rank the top ten web pages found by the search engine from the point of view of freshness and relevance. Table 1 shows the Spearman rank correlation coefficients for "Indiana Jones" query between the subject results and the search engine results, r_{ser}^{s}, and between the subject results and the proposed method results, r_{sys}^{s} for different time frames. It can be seen that our method achieves significantly higher correlation for all

Table 1. Spearman rank correlation coefficients for "Indiana Jones" query

Time frame	r_{ser}^{s}	r_{sys}^{s}
6 months	0.06	0.35
12 months	0.06	0.35
24 months	0.06	0.29

three time periods. For example, for the time frame equal to one year, the subjects judged "Welcome to TheRaider.net" (www.theraider.net) to be the page with the most relevant changes and fresh content related to the query among the top ten results and ranked it first. However, it was ranked sixth in the search engine results.

Table 2 shows results for the "Japanese economy" query. Similarly to Table 1 we can see that the results are slightly worse for longer time frames. This is probably due to the drift in topics of web pages for longer time periods.

Table 2. Spearman rank correlation coefficients for "Japanese economy" query

Time frame	r_{ser}^{s}	r_{sys}^{s}
6 months	0.23	0.78
12 months	0.23	0.78
24 months	0.23	0.63

5   Conclusions

In this paper we have investigated the temporal relevance issue of web pages and presented a novel method for fresh information retrieval from the Web basing on the search engine results. Our approach reorders the results returned by a web search engine so that the pages with fresher and relevant information are ranked higher. It does this by evaluating temporal characteristics and qualities of documents utilizing the archived versions of web pages. This enables identification of the documents that are more likely to contain fresh content that is relevant to the query topic. For such pages we examine the differences in present and indexed by the search engine versions of web documents. In our proposal the search engine does not have to maintain a continuously updated index of all web pages; rather it needs to fetch selected web documents at the time of query. Additionally, we find web documents related to the query topic not only at a single time point but also during a given time period. Such pages can be recommended to users interested in a given topic.

References

1. Amitay, E., Carmel, D., Herscovici, M., Lempel, R., and Soffer A.: Trend Detection Through Temporal Link Analysis. Journal of The American Society for Information Science and Technology, 55: 2004, 1–12
2. Baeza-Yates, R., Saint-Jean, F., and Castillo C.: Web Structure, Age and Page Quality. "String Processing and Information Retrieval", Springer, Lecture Notes in Computer Science (LNCS 2476) 117–130
3. Boyapati, V., Chevrier, K., Finkel, A., Glance, N., Pierce, T., Stokton, R., and Whitmer, C.: ChangeDetector™: A site level monitoring tool for WWW. Proceedings of 11th International WWW Conference. Honolulu, Hawaii, USA, 2002, 570-579
4. Brewington, E. B. and Cybenko, G.: How Dynamic is the Web? Proceedings of the 9th International World Wide Web Conference. Amsterdam, The Netherlands, 2000, 257-276

5. Brin, S. and Page, L.: The anatomy of a large-scale hypertextual web search engine. Proceedings of the 7th World Wide Web Conference, pages 107–117, 1998, Australia
6. Cho, J. and Garcia-Molina, H.: The Evolution of the Web and Implications for an Incremental Crawler. Proceedings of the 26th International Conference on Very Large Databases (VLDB). Cairo, Egypt, 2000, 200-209
7. Cho, J. and Ntoulas, A.: Effective Change Detection Using Sampling. Proceedings of the 28th VLDB Conference. Hong Kong, SAR China, 2002
8. Douglis, F., et al.: AT&T Internet difference engine: Tracking and Viewing Changes on the Web. World Wide Web, vol. 1 (1). Kluwer Academic Publishers, 1998, 27- 44
9. Francisco-Revilla, L., Shipman, F., Furuta, R., Karadkar, U. and Arora, A. Perception of Content, Structure, and Presentation Changes in Web-based Hypertext. Proceedings of the 12th ACM Conference on Hypertext and Hypermedia (Hypertext '01), Aarhus, Denmark, ACM Press, 2001, 205–214
10. Google News: http://news.google.com
11. Google Search Engine: http://www.google.com
12. Internet Archive: http://www.archive.org
13. Jacob, J., et al.: WebVigiL: An approach to just-in-time information propagation in large network-centric environments. Web Dynamics Book. Springer-Verlag, 2003
14. JTidy: http://jtidy.sourceforge.net
15. Liu, L., Pu, C., and Tang, W.: Continual Queries for Internet Scale Event-Driven Information Delivery. IEEE Knowledge and Data Engineering 11 (4). Special Issue on Web Technology, 1999, 610–628
16. MSN search: http://search.msn.com
17. Porter Stemmer in Java: http://www.tartarus.org/~martin/PorterStemmer/java.txt
18. Sato, N., Uehara, M., and Sakai, Y.: Temporal Ranking for Fresh Information Retrieval. Proceedings of the 6th International Workshop on Information Retrieval with Asian Languages. Sapporo, Japan, 2003, 116–123
19. Search Engine Statistics: Freshness Showdown, http://searchengineshowdown.com/stats/freshness.shtml
20. Tomcat Apache: http://jakarta.apache.org/tomcat/

Evaluation of Result Merging Strategies
for Metasearch Engines

Yiyao Lu[1], Weiyi Meng[1], Liangcai Shu[1], Clement Yu[2], and King-Lup Liu[3]

[1] Dept of Computer Science, SUNY at Binghamton, Binghamton, NY 13902
{ylu0, meng, lshu1}@Binghamton.edu
[2] Dept of Computer Science, U. of Illinois at Chicago, Chicago, IL 60607
yu@cs.uic.edu
[3] Webscalers, LLC, Lafayette, LA 70506
kliu@webscalers.com

Abstract. Result merging is a key component in a metasearch engine. Once the results from various search engines are collected, the metasearch system merges them into a single ranked list. The effectiveness of a metasearch engine is closely related to the result merging algorithm it employs. In this paper, we investigate a variety of resulting merging algorithms based on a wide range of available information about the retrieved results, from their local ranks, their titles and snippets, to the full documents of these results. The effectiveness of these algorithms is then compared experimentally based on 50 queries from the TREC Web track and 10 most popular general-purpose search engines. Our experiments yield two important results. First, simple result merging strategies can outperform Google. Second, merging based on the titles and snippets of retrieved results can outperform that based on the full documents.

1 Introduction

Metasearch engine is a system that provides unified access to multiple existing search engines. After the results returned from all used component search engines are collected, the metasearch system merges the results into a single ranked list. The major benefits of metasearch engines are their capabilities to combine the coverage of multiple search engines and to reach the Deep Web. A recent survey [2] indicates that the Web has about 550 billion pages and only about 1% of them are in the Surface Web while the rest are in the Deep Web. The coverage of each search engine is limited. For example, *Google*, has indexed about 8 billion pages currently. This provides the basis for increasing search coverage via combining multiple search engines. Documents in the Deep Web are not directly crawlable but are searchable through special search interfaces. Since metasearch engine utilizes other search systems, connecting to multiple Deep Web search engines is an effective mechanism to reach the Deep Web.

Sophisticated metasearch engines also perform *database selection*, which is to identify the most suitable component search engines to invoke for a given user query. If a metasearch engine has a large number of component search engines, then it is very inefficient to pass each user query to every component search engine due to the addi-

M. Kitsuregawa et al. (Eds.): WISE 2005, LNCS 3806, pp. 53–66, 2005.

tional time needed to invoke each search engine and to process the more results. In this case, database selection should be performed. In order to perform database selection, some information that can represent the main contents of each search engine is collected in advance. When a user query is received, the representative information is used to estimate the *usefulness* of each search engine with respect to this query, which is then used to determine if a search engine should be used to process this query. The above usefulness will be called *search engine score* in this paper. Many methods for database selection exist (see [12] for a survey of some methods) but will not be discussed in this paper. Search engine scores are used by some result merging techniques.

A straightforward way to perform result merging is to fetch the retrieved documents to the metasearch engine site and then to compute their similarities with the query using a global similarity function. This method is used in the *Inquirus* metasearch engine [10] as well in the approach in [20]. The main problem of this approach is that the user has to wait a long time before the results can be fully displayed. Therefore, most result merging techniques utilize the information associated with the search results as returned by component search engines to perform merging [12]. The difficulty lies in the heterogeneities among the component search engines. For example, some component search engines may return a local ranking score (some kind of similarity value) for each result while some don't. As another example, different search engines would rank the same set of documents differently since they adopt different ranking formulas and term weighting schemes.

In this paper, we experimentally evaluate and compare seven different result merging algorithms, five of them are either newly proposed in this paper or revised from existing ones. The main contributions of this paper are two folds. First, it proposes several new algorithms that reflect some fresh ideas about result merging. Second, it provides extensive experimental results to evaluate the effectiveness of newly proposed algorithms and compare them with the existing methods. Two important conclusions are observed from our experimental results. Utilizing the titles and snippets associated with search results can achieve better effectiveness than using the full documents. Moreover, a good result merging algorithm can help a metasearch engine significantly outperform the best single search engine in effectiveness.

The rest of the paper is organized as follows. Section 2 reviews various existing result merging approaches. In Section 3, we present five new result merging algorithms. Section 4 provides the experimental results. Section 5 concludes the paper.

2   Related Work

In the 1990s, most search engines reported the ranking scores of their search results. Therefore, many earlier techniques focused on normalizing the scores to make them more comparable across different search engines (e.g., [4, 16]). By this way, the results retrieved from different systems can be uniformly ranked by the normalized scores.

Nowadays, very few search engines report ranking scores, but it is still possible to convert the local ranks into local ranking scores. Borda Count [1] is a voting-based data fusion method applicable in the context of metasearch. The returned results are considered as the candidates and each component search engine is a voter. For each voter, the top ranked candidate is assigned n points (assuming there are n candidates), the second top ranked candidate is given $n - 1$ points, and so on. For candidates that are not ranked by a voter (i.e., they are not retrieved by the corresponding search engine), the remaining points of the voter (each voter has a fixed number of points) will be divided evenly among them. The candidates are then ranked in descending order of the total points they receive. Several more complex schemes using ranks to merge results are reported in [5] but they need a larger number of results (say 100) to be retrieved from each search engine and they need substantial overlap among the retrieved results from different search engines to work effectively.

In D-WISE [21], the local rank of a document (r_i) returned from search engine j is converted to a ranking score (rs_{ij}) by using the formula:

$$rs_{ij} = 1 - (r_i - 1) * S_{\min} / (m * S_j) \; , \tag{1}$$

where S_j is the usefulness score of the search engine j, $S_{\min}$ is the smallest search engine score among all component search engines selected for this query, and m is the number of documents desired across all search engines. This function generates a smaller difference between the ranking scores of two consecutively ranked results retrieved from a search engine with a higher search engine score. This has the effect of ranking more results from higher quality search engines (with respect to the given query) higher. One problem of this method is that the highest ranked documents returned from all the local systems will have the same ranking score 1.

Some approaches also take the search engine scores into consideration (e.g., [3, 7]). For example, the basic Borda Count method can be improved by adjusting the ranking score of a result by multiplying the points it receives with its source search engine's usefulness score so that the results from more useful search engines for the query are more likely to be ranked higher. However, estimating the search engine score usually requires some sample data to be collected from each component search engine beforehand (e.g., [1, 13, 17]). Thus, this type of approaches cannot be applied to situations where a search engine joins a metasearch engine on the fly, such as in the case where customized metasearch engines are created on demand [19]. In our work, we focus on the result merging approaches without collecting any sample data in advance.

Most of the current generation search engines present more informative *search result records* (SRRs) of retrieved results to the user. A typical SRR consists of the URL, title and a summary (snippet) of the retrieved document. As a result, the contents associated with the SRRs can be used to rank/merge results retrieved from different search engines. We are aware of only two works that utilize such SRRs. The work described in [8] is more about determining if a SRR contains enough information for merging so that the corresponding full document need not be fetched rather than a merging technique. The work reported in [13] is the most similar to our work in this paper. The available evidences that can be used for result merging are identified, such as the document title, snippet, local rank, search engine usefulness, etc. The algorithms based on different combinations of these evidences are proposed and their effectiveness is compared. However, their work is significantly different from ours in several aspects. First, while their metasearch system uses news search engines, we concentrate on general-purpose search engines. This makes our work more relevant to the current major metasearch engines as nearly all of them (e.g., Mamma.com, Dogpile.com, Search.com) use general-purpose search engines as their underlying components. Second, besides the title, snippet and the local rank of each retrieved document, some of our algorithms also consider the frequencies of query terms in each SRR, the order and the closeness of these terms, etc (see Section 3.2). On the other hand, publication date of each result is utilized in the algorithms in [13] but is not in ours because time is not as sensitive in the general web documents as in the news articles. Third, the datasets used are different. In [13], the dataset consists of the queries that are generated specifically for that work and the news items retrieved from the selected news search engines using these queries, while the dataset in our work consists of the queries used for the TREC Web Track and the documents retrieved from the 10 major general-purpose search engines using these queries. Fourth, titles and snippets of SRRs are used differently (different similarity functions are used) is these two approaches. Our experimental results indicate that our approach outperforms the best approach in [13] (see Section 4 for details).

Among all the proposed merging methods in [13], the most effective one is based on the combination of the evidences of document title, snippet, and the search engine usefulness. This method works as follows. First of all, for each document, the similarity between the query and its title, and the similarity between the query and its snippet are computed. Then the two similarities are linearly aggregated as this document's esti-mated global similarity. For each query term, its weight in every component search engine is computed based on the *Okapi* probabilistic model [14]. The *Okapi model* requires the information of document frequency (*df*) of each term. Since the *df* infor-mation cannot be obtained in a metasearch engine context, the *df* of the term t in search engine j is approximated by the number of documents in the top 10 documents returned by search engine j containing term t within their titles and snippets. The search engine score is the sum of all the query term weights of this search engine. Finally, the esti-mated global similarity of each result is adjusted by multiplying the relative deviation of its source search engine's score to the mean of all the search engine scores.

Major general purpose search engines have a certain amount of overlaps between them. It is very possible that for a given query, the same document is returned from multiple component search engines. In this case, their (normalized) ranking scores need to be combined. A number of fusion functions have been proposed to solve this prob-lem and they include *min, max, sum, average, CombMNZ*, and other linear combination functions [6, 11, 18].

3   Merging Algorithms

Algorithm 1: Use Top Document to Compute Search Engine Score (TopD)

This algorithm can be considered as a variation of the method described in [21] (see Formula 1). Let S_j denote the score of search engine j with respect to Q. The method in [21] needs the document frequency of every term to be collected in advance, while the *TopD* algorithm uses the similarity between Q and the top ranked document returned from search engine j (denoted d_{1j}) to estimate S_j. The rationale is that, in general, the highest ranked document is the most relevant to the user query based on the search en-gine's ranking criteria. Its content can reflect how "good" the search engine is with re-spect to the user query. Fetching the top ranked document from its local server will in-troduce some extra network delay to the merging process, but we believe that this delay is tolerable since only one document is fetched from each used search engine for a query.

For the similarity function, we tried both the *Cosine function* [15] and the *Okapi function* [14]. In *Cosine function*, the weight associated with each term in Q and d_{1j} is the *tf* weight [15] (we also tried *tf*idf* weight and the results are similar). The similarity between query Q and d_{1j} using *Okapi function* is the sum of the *Okapi weight* of each query term T. The formula is:

$$\sum_{T \in Q} w * \frac{(k_1 + 1) * tf}{K + tf} * \frac{(k_3 + 1) * qtf}{k_3 + qtf},$$

$$\text{with } w = \log \frac{N - n + 0.5}{n + 0.5} \text{ and } K = k_1 * ((1 - b) + b * \frac{dl}{avgdl}), \quad (2)$$

where *tf* is the frequency of the query term T within the processed document, *qtf* is the frequency of T within the query, N is the number of documents in the collection, n is the number of documents containing T, dl is the length of the document, and $avgdl$ is the average length of all the documents in the collection. k_1, k_3 and b are the constants with values 1.2, 1,000 and 0.75, respectively. Since N, n, and $avgdl$ are unknown, we use some approximations to estimate them. For $avgdl$, we used the average length of the documents we collected in our testbed (see Section 4.1), where the value is 1424.5 (words). We use Google's size to simulate $N = 8{,}058{,}044{,}651$. For each query term T in our testing queries, we submit it as a single-term query to *Google* and retrieve the number of documents returned as the value of n.

As mentioned before, the ranking scores of the top ranked results from all used search engines will be 1 by using Formula 1. We remedy this problem by computing an adjusted ranking score ars_{ij} by multiplying the ranking score computed by Formula 1, namely rs_{ij}, by S_j. If a document is retrieved from multiple search engines, we compute its final ranking score by summing up all the adjusted ranking scores.

Algorithm 2: Use Top SRRs to Compute Search Engine Score (TopSRR)

This algorithm is the same as the *TopD* algorithm except that a different method is used to compute the search engine score. When a query Q is submitted to a search engine (say search engine j), the search engine returns the search result records (SRRs) of a certain number of top ranked documents on a dynamically generated result page. In the *TopSRR* algorithm, the SRRs of the top n returned results from each search engine, instead of the top ranked document, are used to estimate its search engine score. Intuitively, this is reasonable as a more useful search engine for a given query is more likely to retrieve better results which are usually reflected in the SRRs of these results. Specifically, all the titles of the top n SRRs from search engine j are merged together to form a *title vector* TV_j, and all the snippets are also merged into a *snippet vector* SV_j. The similarities between query Q and TV_j, and between Q and SV_j are computed separately and then aggregated into the score of search engine j:

$$S_j = c_1 * Similarity(Q, TV_j) + (1 - c_1) * Similarity(Q, SV_j), \quad (3)$$

where $c_1 = 0.5$ and $n = 10$ are currently used in our work. Again, both the *Cosine similarity function* with *tf* weight and the *Okapi function* are used. In the *Okapi func-*

tion, the average document lengths (*avgdl*) of the title vector TV_j and the snippet vector SV_j are estimated by the average length of the titles and the snippets of the top 10 results on the result page. The values are 46.2 (words) and 163.6 (words), respectively.

Algorithm 3: Compute Simple Similarities between SRRs and Query (SRRSim)

Since each SRR can be considered as the representative of the corresponding full document, we may rank SRRs returned from different search engines based on their similarities with the query directly using an appropriate similarity function.

In the *SRRSim* algorithm, the similarity between a SRR R and a query Q is defined as a weighted sum of the similarity between the title T of R and Q and the similarity between the snippet S of R and Q:

$$sim(R,Q) = c_2 * Similarity(Q, T) + (1 - c_2) * Similarity(Q, S) , \qquad (4)$$

where, in the current implementation, $c_2 = 0.5$. Again both the *Cosine similarity function* with *tf* weight and the *Okapi function* are tried. The *avgdl* of title and snippet used in the *Okapi* weight is set to be 5.0 and 17.6, respectively, which are estimated based on the SRRs of the collected documents in our testbed. (The reason that the average lengths of individual titles and snippets are longer than those can be derived from the numbers given in Algorithm 2, i.e., 5 > 46.2/10 and 17.6 > 163.6/10, is because some result pages contain less than 10 results.) If a document is retrieved from multiple search engines with different SRRs (different search engines usually employ different ways to generate SRRs), then the similarity between the query and each such SRR will be computed and the largest one will be used as the final similarity of this document with the query for result merging.

Algorithm 4: Rank SRRs Using More Features (SRRRank)

The similarity function used in the *SRRSim* algorithm, no matter it is the *Cosine function* or the *Okapi function*, may not be sufficiently powerful in reflecting the true matches of the SRRs with respect to a given query. For example, these functions do not take proximity information such as how close the query terms occur in the title and snippet of a SRR into consideration, nor does it consider the order of appearances of the query terms in the title and snippet. Intuitively, if a query contains one or more phrases, the order and proximity information has a significant impact on the match of phrases versus just individual terms. As an example, suppose a user query contains two terms t1 and t2 in this order. Two documents d1 and d2 have the same length and they have the same numbers of t1 and t2 in it. In d1, t1 and t2 always occur together and t1 always appears in front of t2 while t1 and t2 are scattered all over in d2. The *Cosine function* or *Okapi function* will give d1 and d2 the same similarity value. However, intuitively, d1 should be a better match to the query than d2.

To better rank SRRs, we define five features with respect to the query terms. First, the number of distinct query terms appearing in the title and the snippet (NDT). Second, the total number occurrences of the query terms in the title and the snippet (TNT). These two features indicate the overlapping level between the query and the SRR. Generally speaking, the larger the overlap, the more likely they are relevant. Third, the locations of the occurred query terms (TLoc). There are three cases, all in title, all in snippet, and scattered in both title and snippet. This feature describes the distribution of the query terms in the SRR. In real applications, the title is more frequently associated with a returned result than the snippet (some search engines provide titles only). Therefore, title is usually given higher priority than the snippet. Fourth, whether the occurred query terms appear in the same order as they are in the query and whether they occur adjacently (ADJ). And finally, the window size containing distinct occurred query terms (WS). If all the distinct occurred query terms are located in the title or the snippet, it is the smallest number of consecutive words in the title or snippet that contains at least one occurrence of each occurred distinct query term; otherwise, the window size is infinite. The last two features represent how close the query terms appear in the SRR. Intuitively, the closer those terms appear in the SRR, the more likely they have the same meaning as they are in the query.

For each SRR of the returned result, the above pieces of information are collected. The *SRRRank* algorithm works as follows: first, all the SRRs are grouped based on the number of distinct query terms (NDT) in their title and snippet fields. The groups having more distinct terms are ranked higher. Second, within each group, the SRRs are further put into three sub-groups based on the location of the occurred distinct query terms (TLoc). The sub-group with these terms in the title ranks highest, and then the sub-group with the distinct terms in the snippet, and finally the sub-group with the terms scattered in both title and snippet. Finally, within each sub-group, the SRRs that have more occurrences of query terms (TNT) appearing in the title and the snippet are ranked higher. If two SRRs have the same number of occurrences of query terms, first the one with distinct query terms appearing in the same order and adjacently (ADJ) as they are in the query is ranked higher, and then, the one with smaller window size (WS) is ranked higher. After the above steps, if there is any tie, it is broken by the local ranks. The result with the higher local rank will have a higher global rank in the merged list. If a result is retrieved from multiple search engines, we only keep the one with the highest global rank.

Algorithm 5: Compute Similarities between SRRs and Query Using More Features (SRRSimMF)

This algorithm is similar to *SRRRank* except that it quantifies the matches based on each feature identified in *SRRRank* so that the matching scores based on different features can be aggregated into a numeric value. Consider a given field of a SRR, say title (the same methods apply to snippet). For the number of distinct query terms (NDT), its matching score is the ratio of NDT over the total number of distinct terms in the query (QLEN), denoted $S_{NDT} = NDT / QLEN$. For the total number of query terms (TNT), its matching score is the ratio of TNT over the length of title (i.e., the number of terms in the title), denoted $S_{TNT} = TDT / TITLEN$. For the query terms order and adjacency information (ADJ), the matching score S_{ADJ} is set to 1 if the distinct query terms appear in the same order and adjacently in the title; otherwise the value is 0. The window size (WS) of the distinct query terms in the processed title is converted into score $S_{WS} = (TITLEN - WS) / TITLEN$ (smaller WS leads to larger score). All the matching scores of these features are aggregated into a single value, which is the similarity between the processed title T and Q, using the following formula:

$$Sim(T,Q) = S_{NDT} + \frac{1}{QLEN} * (W_1 * S_{ADJ} + W_2 * S_{WS} + W_3 * S_{TNT}) \qquad (5)$$

This formula guarantees that titles containing more distinct query terms will have larger similarities.

For each SRR, the similarity between the title and the query ($Sim(T, Q)$) and the similarity between the snippet S and the query ($Sim(S, Q)$) are computed separately first and then merged into one value as follows:

$$Similarity = \frac{TNDT}{QLEN} * (c_3 * Sim(T,Q) + (1-c_3) * Sim(S,Q)) \qquad (6)$$

where $TNDT$ is the total number of distinct query terms appeared in title and snippet. By multiplying by $TNDT / QLEN$, we guarantee that the SRR containing more distinct query terms will be ranked higher.

A genetic algorithm based training method is used to determine the values of the parameters involved in this method. Among the testing queries, the odd numbered queries are used for the training. The optimal values of W_1, W_2, W_3 and c_3 found by the training are 0, 0.14, 0.41 and 0.2, respectively. $W_1 = 0$ means that the order and adjacency information is not useful for improving result merging in Algorithm 5. One possible explanation for this is that due to the small length of each title and snippet, the terms are already sufficiently close to each other to identify their meanings.

4 Experiments

4.1 Testbed

The purpose of this work is to evaluate and compare different result merging algorithms under the context of metasearch over the general-purpose search engines. So we select 10 most popular general-purpose search engines as the underlying component search engine. They are: *Google, Yahoo, MSN, Askjeeves, Lycos, Open Directory, Altavista, Gigablast, Wisenut,* and *Overture*. The reasons these search engines are selected are: (1) they are used by nearly all the popular general-purpose metasearch engines; (2) each of them has indexed a relatively large number of web pages; and (3) they adopt different ranking schemes. Even though we focus our work in the context of general-purpose search engines, the result merging algorithms we proposed in this paper are completely independent of the search engine type.

2002 TREC Web Track topics are used as the queries to collect the testbed from the selected search engines. Each web topic contains 4 parts: an index number, a title, a description and a narrative (see Figure 1 for an example). 2002 TREC Web Track has 50 topics indexed from 551 to 600. In this paper, for each topic, only the title part is used as a query to send to the search engines, because the titles are short, similar to most Internet queries submitted by real users. The average length of the titles of these 50 topics is 3.06. The description and the narrative describe what documents should be considered relevant to the corresponding topic. This information is served as the standard criteria for us to judge the relevancy of the collected result documents.

<num> Number: 551

<title> intellectual property

<desc> Description:

Find documents related to laws or regulations that protect intellectual property.

<narr> Narrative:

Relevant documents describe legislation or federal regulations that protect authors or composers

from copyright infringement, or from piracy of their creative work. These regulations may also be

related to fair use or to encryption.

Fig. 1. An Example TREC Query

Each query is submitted to every component search engine. For each query and each search engine, the top 10 results on the first result page are collected (some search engines may return less than 10 results for certain queries). Totally there are 4,642 result documents, excluding 42 broken links. This number corresponds to approximately 9.3 documents per query and per search engine. Information associated with each returned record is collected, including the URL, title, snippet and the local rank. Besides, the document itself is downloaded. The relevancy of each document is manually checked based on the criteria specified in the description and the narrative part of the corresponding TREC query. The collected data and the documents, together with the relevancy assessment result, form our testbed. The testbed is stored locally so it will not be affected by any subsequent changes from any component search engine.

4.2 Evaluation Criteria

Because it is difficult to know all the relevant documents to a query in a search engine, the traditional *recall* and *precision* for evaluating IR systems cannot be used for evaluating search/metasearch engines. A popular measure for evaluating the effectiveness of search engines is the *TREC-style average precision* (TSAP) [10]. In this paper, TSAP at cutoff N, denoted as *TSAP@N*, will be used to evaluate the effectiveness of each merging algorithm:

$$TSAP @ N = (\sum_{i=1}^{N} r_i) / N ,$$

(7)

where $r_i = 1/i$ if the i-th ranked result is relevant and $r_i = 0$ if the i-th result is not relevant. It is easy to see that *TSAP@N* takes into consideration both the number of relevant documents in the top N results and the ranks of the relevant documents. *TSAP@N* tends to yield a larger value when more relevant documents appear in the top N results and when the relevant documents are ranked higher. For each merging algorithm, the average *TSAP@N* over all 50 queries is computed and is used to compare with other merging algorithms.

4.3 Result Analysis

We first evaluated the average precision of each of the 10 component search engines used in our metasearching system. The results are reported in Table 1. Since for each query, we only collect the top 10 documents on the first result page from each search engine, we compute the effectiveness of each search engine at two N levels only, i.e., $N = 5$ and 10. It is easy to see that *Google* is the best performer, with *Altavista* and *Yahoo* close behind and others significantly behind.

Table 1. Retrieval Effectiveness of Component Search Engines

Seach Engine	TSAP@N	
	N = 5	N = 10
Google	*0.316*	*0.199*
Yahoo	0.308	0.194
MSN	0.265	0.164
Askjeeves	0.229	0.148
Lycos	0.224	0.145
Open Directory	0.091	0.051
Altavista	0.315	0.199
Gigablast	0.248	0.155
Wisenut	0.289	0.177
Overture	0.161	0.109

Six algorithms are compared and the results are listed in the Table 2. In addition to the five algorithms described in Section 3, the full document fetching method (**DocFetching**, see Section 1) is also included. Both the Cosine function and the Okapi function are considered. For each algorithm to be evaluated, we compute its *TSAP* at different N levels, where N = 5, 10, 20, and 30.

Table 2 shows that *TopD* and *TopSRR* algorithms are the least effective among all the merging algorithms evaluated. Their performances are close to that of the best single search engine (i.e., *Google*) for $N = 5$ and $N = 10$. This suggests that the local ranks of retrieved results do not contain enough information to achieve good merging.

We also find a large margin of differences in effectiveness between *Google* and the other four algorithms, including full document fetching method (Okapi). Table 3 shows the effectiveness of three merging algorithms, *SRRSim*, *SRRRank*, *SRRSimMF*, when Google is not a component search engine (i.e., only the other 9 search engines are used). The exclusion of Google did not noticeably impact the performance, probably because the results from *Google* are also retrieved by other search engines collectively. This experimental result shows that, while it is widely recognized that metasearch engines can increase search coverage, metasearching can improve the search effectiveness over a single search engine as well. One reason why metasearching may achieve better effectiveness is because different individual search engines often yield different relevant documents and a good result merging algorithm can rank more of these relevant documents higher than any single search engine.

Table 2. Retrieval Effectiveness Comparison

Algorithm		TSAP@N			
		N = 5	N = 10	N = 20	N = 30
TopD	Cosine	0.297	0.185	0.112	0.081
	Okapi	0.318	0.198	0.116	0.084
TopSRR	Cosine	0.314	0.194	0.112	0.084
	Okapi	0.311	0.193	0.115	0.084
SRRSim	Cosine	0.366	0.228	0.137	0.098
	Okapi	0.377	0.235	0.140	0.100
SRRRank		0.371	0.230	0.135	0.098
SRRSimMF		0.381	0.238	0.140	0.100
DocFetching	Cosine	0.271	0.177	0.108	0.080
	Okapi	0.338	0.217	0.131	0.094

Table 3. Effectiveness without Using Google

Algorithm	TSAP@N			
	N=5	N=10	N=20	N=30
SRRSim(Okapi)	0.381	0.236	0.139	0.099
SRRRank	0.370	0.230	0.134	0.097
SRRSimMF	0.381	0.237	0.139	0.099

Algorithms that perform merging based on the contents of SRRs (i.e., *SRRSim, SRRRank, SRRSimMF*) are the top performers among all the merging algorithms. They all outperform *Google* and the document fetching method significantly. It shows that the titles and snippets of SRRs contain good information about the contents of the corresponding documents. Overall, high quality snippets are generated by major general-purpose search engines. Moreover, because good merging algorithms using SRRs only can significantly outperform the document fetching based method, there is no need to fetch the full documents of the retrieved results for result merging. This means that by using SRRs for merging, not only can the merging process be sped up significantly, the effectiveness can also be improved, compared with using the full documents.

It is somewhat surprising that using the full documents yielded lower effectiveness than using the SRRs, but a careful analysis reveals a valid explanation for this phenomenon. Even though it is true that a full document has more information than its SRR, the information is not fully utilized by most similarity functions that are employed, including the *Cosine function* and the *Okapi function*. For example, neither of these two functions considers the proximity information of the query terms in a document. On the other hand, since titles and snippets are much shorter than the full documents, when they are used for similarity computations with a query, the proximity information is automatically taken into consideration. Furthermore, the search results returned by component search engines are obtained based on the full documents. In other words, the full documents have been used to gather the initial result sets and their SRRs are used for a second round of selection.

The best algorithm reported in [13] (**Rasolofo**) is also a SRR-based method. The main idea of this algorithm is summarized in Section 2. It is similar to Algorithm 3 (*SRRSim*) and the main differences between them are: (1) Rasolofo's algorithm uses search engine scores (which are computed based on the *Okapi model*) to adjust the similarity for each SRR while *SRRSim* does not do that. (2) Rasolofo's algorithm and *SRRSim* use different similarity functions to compute the similarity between a title/snippet and a query. While *SRRSim* uses the *Okapi function*, Rasolofo's algorithm uses $100000 * NQW \big/ \sqrt{|Q|^2 + |F|^2}$, where *NQW* is the number of query words that appear in the processed field (e.g., title or snippet), and |Q| and |F| are the lengths of the query and the processed field, respectively; if the above similarity is zero for a result, it is substituted by the *rank score* of the result, which is defined to be $1000 - R$, where R is the rank of the result given by the local search engine. We compared our three SRR-based algorithms, namely, *SRRSim*, *SRRank* and *SRRSimMF*, with Rasolofo. Since this method requires the information about the number of documents returned by every local search engine for each query to compute its search engine score and *Overture* does not provide this information, the comparison with *Rasolofo* is based on the results returned from the other 9 search engines. The results are reported in Table 4. It can be seen that all our algorithms outperform the *Rasolofo*'s algorithm. There are two possible reasons for this. First, the use of search engine scores to influence the ranking of SRRs may not be effective when high quality SRRs are generated by component search engines (more experiments are needed to confirm this conjecture). Second, the similarity function employed in *Rasolofo*'s algorithm for computing the similarities of titles and snippets with the query is not as good as the similarity functions or ranking method employed by *SRRSim* (*Okapi*), *SRRRank* and *SRRSimMF*. Our query-by-query comparison between *SRRSim* and the *Rasolofo*'s algorithm shows that *SRRSim* is better for 24 queries, worse for 14 queries and tied with *Rasolofo*'s algorithm for 12 queries.

Table 4. Comparison with Rasolofo's Approach

Algorithm	TSAP@N			
	N=5	N=10	N=20	N=30
SRRSim(Okapi)	0.377	0.235	0.140	0.101
SRRRank	0.372	0.230	0.136	0.098
SRRSimMF	0.380	0.237	0.139	0.100
Rasolofo	0.347	0.217	0.131	0.095

By comparing among the algorithms based on the contents of SRR, we found that the sophisticated ranking schemes employed by *SRRRank* and *SRRSimMF* fail to pay clear dividend over a much simpler scheme employed by *SRRSim* (*Okapi*). A possible reason is that because titles and snippets are already sufficiently short in terms of relating the meanings of the query terms in the SRRs, which makes the additional fine-tuning unnecessary.

5   Conclusions

In this paper, we reported our study on how to merge the search results returned from multiple component search engines into a single ranked list. This is an important problem in metasearch engine research. An effective and efficient result merging strategy is essential for developing effective metasearch systems. We experimentally compared 7 merging algorithms that utilize a wide range of information available for merging, from local ranks by component search engines, search engine scores, titles and snippets of search result records to the full documents. Ten popular general-purpose search engines and 50 TREC Web Track queries were used to perform the evaluation.

Our experimental evaluations yielded several interesting results. First, simple, efficient and easily implementable merging algorithms can outperform the best single search engine. This should help the cause of metasearch engine researchers/developers. Second, merging based on the titles and snippets of returned search result records can be more effective than using the full documents of these results. This implies that a metasearch engine can achieve better performance than a centralized retrieval system that contains all the documents from the component search engines. Third, a simply result merging algorithm can perform as well as more sophisticated ones. For example, the algorithm SRRSim that performs merging based on the weighted sum of the Okapi similarities of the title and snippet of each result with the query is as good as algorithms that take into consideration the order and proximity of query terms in the results.

A possible reason why the proximity and adjacency information of query terms in the title and snippet did not help improve effectiveness is due to the failure to distinguish different types of adjacency/proximity conditions. For example, named entities and other types of phrases (noun phrases, dictionary phrase, complex phrases, etc.) may need to be identified and dealt with differently. We plan to investigate this issue further in the near future.

Acknowledgement. This work is supported by the following grants from NSF: IIS-0208574, IIS-0208434, IIS-0414981, IIS-0414939 and CNS-0454298.

References

1. J. Aslam, M. Montague. Models for Metasearch. ACM SIGIR Conference, 2001, pp.276-284.
2. M. Bergman. The Deep Web: Surfing Hidden Values. White Paper of CompletePlanet. 2001. (Available at http://brightplanet.com/pdf/deepwebwhitepaper.pdf).
3. J. Callan, Z. Lu, W. Croft. Searching Distributed Collections with Inference Networks. ACM SIGIR Conference, 1995, pp. 21-28.
4. D. Dreilinger, A. Howe. Experiences with Selecting Search Engines Using Metasearch. ACM TOIS, 15(3), July 1997, pp.195-222.
5. C. Dwork, R. Kumar, M. Naor, D. Sivakumar. Rank Aggregation Methods for the Web. Tenth International World Wide Web Conference, pp.613-622, 2001.
6. E. Fox, J. Shaw. Combination of Multiple Searches. Second Text Retrieval Conference, Gaithersburg, Maryland, August 1994, pp. 243-252.

7. S. Gauch, G. Wang, and M. Gomez. ProFusion: Intelligent Fusion from Multiple, Distributed Search Engines. Journal of Universal Computer Science, 2(9), pp.637-649, 1996.
8. E. Glover and S. Lawrence. Selective Retrieval Metasearch engine. US Patent Application Publication (US 2002/0165860 A1), November 2002.
9. D. Hawking, N. Craswell, P. Bailey, K. Griffiths. Measuring Search Engine Quality. Information Retrieval Journal, 4(1): 33-59 (2001).
10. S. Lawrence, and C. Lee Giles. Inquirus, the NECi Meta Search Engine. Seventh International World Wide Web Conference, 1998.
11. J. Lee. Analyses of Multiple Evidence Combination. ACM SIGIR Conference, 1997
12. W. Meng, C. Yu, K. Liu. Building Efficient and Effective Metasearch Engines. ACM Computing Surveys, 34(1), March 2002, pp.48-84.
13. Y. Rasolofo, D. Hawking, J. Savoy. Result Merging Strategies for a Current News Metasearcher. Inf. Process. Manage, 39(4), 2003, pp.581-609.
14. S. Robertson, S. Walker, M. Beaulieu. Okapi at trec-7: automatic ad hoc, filtering, vlc, and interactive track. 7th Text REtrieval Conference, 1999, pp.253-264.
15. G. Salton and M. McGill. Introduction to Modern Information Retrieval. Mc-Graw Hill, 1983.
16. E. Selberg, and O. Etzioni. The MetaCrawler Architecture for Resource Aggregation on the Web. IEEE Expert, 1997.
17. L. Si, J. Callan. Using Sampled Data and Regression to Merge Search Engine Results. ACM SIGIR Conference, 2002, pp.19-26.
18. C. Vogt, G. Cottrell. Fusion via a Linear Combination of Scores. Information Retrieval, 1(3), 1999, pp.151-173.
19. Z. Wu, V. Raghavan, C. Du, M. Sai C, W. Meng, H. He, and C. Yu. SE-LEGO: Creating Metasearch Engine on Demand. ACM SIGIR Conference, Demo paper, pp.464, 2003.
20. C. Yu, W. Meng, K. Liu, W. Wu, N. Rishe. Efficient and Effective Metasearch for a Large Number of Text Databases. Eighth ACM CIKM Conference, 1999, pp. 217-224.
21. B. Yuwono, D. Lee. Server Ranking for Distributed Text Resource Systems on the Internet. International Conference on Database System For Advanced Applications, 1997, pp.391-400.

Decomposition-Based Optimization of Reload Strategies in the World Wide Web

Dirk Kukulenz

Luebeck University, Institute of Information Systems,
Ratzeburger Allee 160, 23538 Lübeck, Germany
kukulenz@ifis.uni-luebeck.de

Abstract. Web sites, Web pages and the data on pages are available
only for specific periods of time and are deleted afterwards from a client's
point of view. An important task in order to retrieve information from
the Web is to consider Web information in the course of time. Different strategies like push and pull strategies may be applied for this task.
Since push services are usually not available, pull strategies have to be
conceived in order to optimize the retrieved information with respect to
the age of retrieved data and its completeness. In this article we present
a new procedure to optimize retrieved data from Web pages by page decomposition. By deploying an automatic Wrapper induction technique a
page is decomposed into functional segments. Each segment is considered
as an independent component for the analysis of the time behavior of the
page. Based on this decomposition we present a new component-based
download strategy. By applying this method to Web pages it is shown
that for a fraction of Web data the freshness of retrieved data may be
improved significantly compared to traditional methods.

1 Introduction

The information in the World Wide Web changes in the course of time. New
Web sites appear in the Web, old sites are deleted. Pages in Web sites exist for
specific periods of time. Data on pages are inserted, modified or deleted. There
are important reasons to consider the information in the Web in the course
of time. From a client's point of view, the information that has been deleted
from the Web is usually no longer accessible. Pieces of information like old news
articles or (stock) prices may however still be of much value for a client. One
conceivable task is e.g. the analysis of the evolution of specific information, as
e.g. a stock chart or the news coverage concerning a specific topic. A Web archive
that mirrors the information in a specific Web area over a period of time may
help a client to access information that is no longer available in the 'real' Web.
A different aspect concerning information changes in the Web is to consider
information that appears in the future. *Continuous queries* in the Web may
help a client to query future states of the Web, similar to triggers in a database
context [11], [12]. There are different techniques available to realize such history
or future-based Web information analysis. In a push system a server actively

M. Kitsuregawa et al. (Eds.): WISE 2005, LNCS 3806, pp. 67–80, 2005.

provides a client with information. Information changes on a server may directly trigger the information of a 'passive' client [10]. In a distributed heterogeneous environment like the World Wide Web push services are difficult to realize and are usually not available. Pull systems on the other hand require an active client to fetch the information from the Web when it becomes available [7]. In contrast to push systems in a pull system the respective tool is usually not informed about the times of information changes. The pull system has to apply strategies in order to optimize the retrieved information with respect to the 'staleness' and the completeness of the information [4].

In this article we consider the problem of retrieving information from single Web pages that appears at unknown periods of time. By observing a Web page over a period of time we acquire certain aspects of the change characteristic of the page. This knowledge is used to optimize a strategy to access the information appearing on the page at future periods of time. The basic approach presented in this article is to decompose a Web page into segments. The 'change dynamics' of whole Web pages is usually very complex. However the change behavior of single segments is frequently relatively simple and the respective update patterns may easily be predicted as is shown by examples in this article. In the article we discuss different approaches to construct a segmentation of a Web page. We motivate the use of wrapper induction techniques for page decompositions. Wrappers are tools to extract data from Web pages automatically. Recently automatic wrapper induction techniques were introduced to learn a wrapper from a set of sample pages. The resulting wrapper is expressed by a common page grammar of the sample pages. We apply a modified wrapper induction process so that a wrapper is acquired from subsequent versions of the same page. Based on the resulting page grammar and the corresponding page segmentation technique we present a new reload strategy for information contained in Web pages. This new technique decreases the costs in terms of network traffic and optimizes the quality of the retrieved information in terms of the 'freshness' and the completeness of the data.

The paper is organized as follows:

After an overview of recent related research the contribution of this article is described. Section 2 gives an introduction into the theoretical background of wrapper induction techniques and the applied model for the dynamic Web. Section 3 describes a framework to define page changes based on page segmentation. The main contribution of this article, a new reload optimization strategy that is based on page decomposition, is presented in sections 4 and 5. In section 6, the decomposition-based change prediction is applied to Web pages. Section 7 summarizes the results and describes further aspects.

1.1   Related Research

The prediction of the times of information changes on a remote source plays an important role for diverse software systems like search engines, Web crawlers, -caches and Web archives. In these fields different prediction strategies were presented. [1] gives an introduction into problems related to optimal page refresh in the context of search engine optimization. In [4] and [13] the problem of minimizing the average level of 'staleness' of local copies of remote web pages is considered in the context of Web crawler optimization. The main basic assumption is usually an independent and identical distribution of time intervals between remote data changes. The series of update times is usually modeled by Poisson processes. In [3] an optimization of this approach is presented with respect to a reduction of the bias of the estimator. In a previous publication we considered the case that remote data change approximately deterministically and update times may be modeled by regular grammars [8]. The latter approach may only be applied to a fraction of Web data, the freshness of local copies may however be improved significantly. Similar questions are important in order to optimize *continuous queries* in the Web, i.e. standing queries that monitor specific Web pages [11], [12].

In the above publications a *change* of a Web page is usually defined as an arbitrary change in the HTML code of the page. However new approaches in the field of automatic Web data extraction may be applied to develop more precise definitions of Web changes. In [9] an overview of common approaches to extract data from the Web is given. The article presents a taxonomy of Web wrapping techniques and different groups of data extraction tools are identified as e.g. wrapper induction and HTML-aware, natural language- and ontology-based tools. A fully automatic approach in the field of HTML-aware wrapper induction is described in [5]. This technique is based on the assumption that there exist similar pages in the Web that may be regarded as created by the same grammar. The task is to estimate this common grammar based on page-examples. Based on the knowledge of the page grammar, data may be extracted automatically and insight into the function of certain page components, as e.g. lists, may be obtained. A further development of this approach accepting a more general class of HTML pages is presented in [2]. We apply a similar grammar inference approach in this work because successive page versions may frequently also be regarded as based on a single grammar.

1.2 Contribution

The main contribution of this article is a new strategy to reload remote data sources in the Web. In this article we consider only HTML content, however similar considerations may also apply to XML. In most previous publications about information changes in the Web a change is defined as an arbitrary modification of the respective HTML code of the page. In contrast to this for a more precise change definition we propose a decomposition of HTML pages based on automatically induced wrappers. The automatic wrapper induction is based on methods that were recently presented in the literature [5]. An extension of the respective methods is considered in order to learn wrappers by example pages that appear at subsequent and unknown periods of time. Based on a decomposition of pages we propose a method to analyze changes of Web pages. The main aspect considered in this article is a new strategy for the reload of remote data sources. The presented method is based on a decomposition step and is then based on a prediction of the times of remote changes that considers each component individually. We demonstrate in this article that for a fraction of Web data this decomposition based prediction may improve pull services in terms of the freshness of retrieved data.

2 Theoretical Background

2.1 Introduction to Automatic Wrapper Induction

The theoretical background concerning data extraction from the Web by automatic wrapper induction is similar to previous publications in this field [6], [5], [2]. We consider the fraction of pages on the Web that are created automatically based on data that are stored in a database or obtained from a different data source. The data are converted to HTML code and sent to a client. This conversion may be regarded as an encoding process. The encoding process may be regarded as the application of a grammar which produces HTML structures. We consider nested data types as the underlying data structure.

Given a set of sample HTML pages belonging to the same class of pages the task is therefore to find the nested data type of the source data set that was used to create the HTML pages. In the wrapper application phase it is the task to extract the respective source data instances from which the individual pages were generated. There exist different approaches for this task [5], [2]. In the following we summarize the approach in [5] which is used as a basis for the applied model in this work in section 2.2.

```
<html>
<a href="weath.html"> #PCDATA </a>
(<p><a href="conc.html">Concert</a></p>)?
<ul>
  (<li> <b> #PCDATA </b>
    (<p> #PCDATA </p>)+
  </li>)+
</ul>
</html>
```

Fig. 1. A common grammar of the pages in figure 2

Nested data types may be modeled by union-free regular grammars [5]. Let $\sharp$PCDATA be a special symbol and Σ an alphabet of symbols not containing $\sharp$PCDATA. A *union-free regular expression* (UFRE) is a string over the alphabet $\Sigma \bigcup \{\sharp\text{PCDATA}, \cdot, +, ?, (,)\}$ with the following restrictions. At first, the empty string ϵ and the elements of $\Sigma \bigcup \{\sharp\text{PCDATA}\}$ are UFREs. If a and b are UFREs, then $a \cdot b$, $(a)^+$ and $(a)?$ are UFREs where $a \cdot b$ denotes a concatenation, $(a)?$ denotes optional patterns and $(a)^+$ is an iteration. Further $(a)^*$ is a shortcut for $((a)^+)?$. In [6] it is shown that the class of union-free regular expressions has a straightforward mapping to nested data types. The $\sharp$PCDATA element models string fields, '+' models (possibly nested) lists and '?' models nullable data fields. For a given UFRE σ the corresponding nested type $\tau = type(\sigma)$ may be constructed in linear time. It is obvious that UFREs may not be used to model every structure appearing in the Web. It is however suitable for a significant fraction of Web data. Let $p_1, p_2, \ldots p_n$ be a set of HTML strings that correspond to encodings of a source data set $d_1, d_2, \ldots d_n$ of a nested type τ.

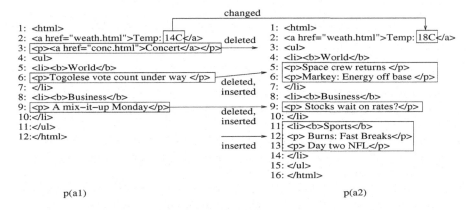

Fig. 2. The HTML sources of a Web page at two different points in time a_1 and a_2 with different kinds of changes like insertions, deletions and modifications

It is shown in [5] that the type τ may be estimated by inferring the minimal UFRE σ whose language $L(\sigma)$ contains the encoded strings $p_1, p_2, \ldots p_n$. In [5] a containment relationship is defined as $\sigma_a \leq \sigma_b$ iff $L(\sigma_a) \leq L(\sigma_b)$. The (optimal) UFRE to describe the input strings is the least upper bound of the input strings. [5] reduces this problem to the problem of finding the least upper bound of two UFREs. The grammar in figure 1 describes e.g. the pages in figure 2.

2.2 A Model for Data Changes in the Web

In contrast to the data model in the previous section where structurally similar pages appear at the same time in this article we consider page versions appearing at different time intervals. For this purpose a time stamp is attached to every page version. Let $u_i \in \mathbb{R}^+$ denote the point in time at which the ith update of a page occurs, where $0 \leq u_1 \leq u_2 \leq u_3 \leq u_4 \leq \ldots u_n \leq T \in \mathbb{R}^+, n \in \mathbb{N}$. The time span between the $i - 1^{st}$ and i^{th} update will be denoted by $t_i := u_i - u_{i-1}, i \in \mathbb{N}$. This is the 'lifetime' of a page version. The different page versions are denoted as $p(u_1), p(u_2), \ldots p(u_n)$. Let $a_1, a_2, \ldots a_m \in \mathbb{R}^+$ denote the points in time where reload operations of the remote source are executed, where $0 \leq a_1 \leq a_2 \leq a_3 \ldots \leq a_m \leq T$. The set of local copies of remote page versions $q(a_1), q(a_2), \ldots$ is obviously a subset of the remote page versions. For $t \in \mathbb{R}^+$ let $N^u(t)$ denote the largest index of an element in the sequence u that is smaller than t, i.e. $N^u(t) := \max\{n | u_n \leq t\}$. Let $A^u(t) \in \mathbb{R}^+$ denote the size of the time interval since the last update, i.e. $A^u(t) := t - u_{N^u(t)}$. If t is the time of a reload ($t = a_i$ for $i \leq m$), we denote $A^u(t)$ as the age of $q(a_i)$. The age of a local copy denotes how much time has passed since the last remote data update and thus how long an old copy of the data was stored although a new version should have been considered.

Finding an optimal reload strategy means that after each update of the remote data source, the data should be reloaded as soon as possible, i.e. the sum of ages $sumage := \sum_{i=1}^{m} A^u(a_i)$ has to be minimal. The number of reloads should be as small as possible. No change of the data source should be unobserved. The number of lost (unobserved) data objects will be denoted as $\sharp loss$ in the experiments.

One question considered in the following is the prediction of remote update times. For this purpose in this article we consider the special case that remote updates of page components are performed after deterministic time intervals. Let $Q := \{t_j | j \leq n \in \mathbb{N}\}$ denote the set of time intervals between updates of a page component. We assign a *symbol* $s_i, i \in \mathbb{N}_{\leq n}$ to every element of Q. We call the set of symbols $\Delta := \{s_i | i \leq n\}$ the *alphabet* of the sequence $(u_j)_{j \leq T}$.[1]

Let S denote a starting symbol, let $r_1, r_2, \ldots r_n$ denote terminals and the symbols $R_1, R_2, \ldots R_n$ non-terminals. In the following we refer to a regular grammar Γ corresponding to the non-deterministic finite automaton in figure 3 as a *cyclic regular grammar* [8]. In figure 3, 'R_0' is a starting state which leads to any of n states $R_1, \ldots, R_n$. After this, the list of symbols is accepted in a cyclic way. Every state is an accepting state. To abbreviate this definition we will use the notation: $(r_1 r_2 ... r_n)^{\circ} := \Gamma$.

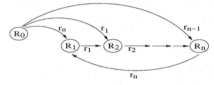

Fig. 3. Nondeterministic automaton corresponding to the grammar $(r_1 r_2 \ldots r_n)^{\circ}$

One problem is to find an optimal sequence $a_1, a_2, \ldots a_m$ in order to capture most of the data changes necessary to learn the wrapper which may be applied for a page decomposition as described in section 3. The set of local page versions $q(a_1), q(a_2), \ldots q(a_m)$ is the input set of 'positive examples' for the wrapper induction task. The basic problem concerning the wrapper induction is to find a basic schema for the page versions that appear at the considered URL. In [5] it is shown that the considered language is not only 'identifiable in the limit' but that a *rich set* of examples is sufficient to learn the grammar. This set of examples has a high probability of being found in a number of randomly chosen HTML pages. In this article we don't consider this problem in detail and assume in the experiments that a correct wrapper has been learned from previous page versions.

3   A Definition of Page Changes

3.1   Motivation

The question considered in this section is to find a description for changes in a Web page. An appropriate definition is necessary in order to acquire an understanding of the nature of changes. If e.g. a page provides a certain stock price

---

[1] Due to the size of the sampling interval and due to network delays intervals between updates registered at the client side are 'distorted'. The symbols are used to comprise registered intervals assumed to result from identical update intervals on the server side.

every minute and in addition provides news related to the respective company which appear about three times a day, it may be helpful to separate the two change dynamics in order to optimize e.g. a pull client.

3.2 Decomposition Strategies

There are different concepts for a segmentation of pages conceivable that are suitable for a change analysis of components. One approach is to consider the DOM (document-object-model) tree of a HTML page. Changes may be attached to nodes (HTML tags) in this tree. The problem with this strategy is that HTML tags are in general only layout directives and there may appear additional structures that are not clear by observing the HTML tag structure, as e.g. in the case of the inner list in figure 2 $p(a_2)$. A method to acquire additional information about the page structure is to consider a set of similar pages as described in section 2 and to determine the common grammar. This grammar may be used to decompose a page into segments as described below and to attach changes in a page to these segments.

3.3 Wrapper Based Change Definition

The decomposition-based time analysis is based on the estimated page grammar acquired from a sample set of pages as described in section 2. One notation for the page grammar is an Abstract-Syntax-Tree (AST) as shown in figure 4 for the pages in figure 2 which corresponds to the grammar in figure 1. By merging adjacent nodes or subtrees in the AST that have the same change dynamics, the AST may be tranformed into the *time-component-type* tree (TCT tree). The TCT-tree illustrated by the boxes in figure 4 shows the different time-components of the AST. A time-component is a node (or a set of adjacent

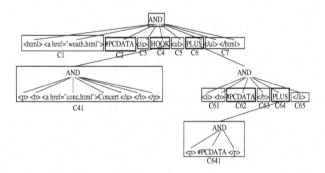

Fig. 4. Abstract-syntax-tree (AST) corresponding to the pages in figure 2. AND-nodes refer to tuples, PLUS-nodes refer to lists and HOOK-nodes refer to optional elements. Boxes framing AST-nodes denote time components (i.e. groups of nodes with a similar change characteristic). These groups constitute nodes of the TCT tree.

nodes in the AST that have the same time characteristic) and the respective subtrees. A *change of a component* requires a change in the node or the attached subtrees. Components that actually change in time, are marked by thick rectangles. Based on the TCT-tree different strategies to define page changes are conceivable. The *any-difference* method described above that considers an arbitrary change in the HTML source of a page is equivalent to considering only the root node of the TCT tree. More specific methods consider deeper levels of the TCT tree up to a certain depth. It is also conceivable that only specific nodes or subtrees of the TCT tree are considered, chosen e.g. manually by a user.

In order to analyze the change dynamics of a page over time it may not be sufficient to consider the TCT tree because nodes in the TCT tree may correspond to a number of instances of the respective type in real page instances. We will refer to the respective instance tree as the Time-Component-Instance-tree (TCI-tree).

Now we may finally define *changes* of a Web page. A (single) change c is a tuple $c = (node_{\in TCI}, t)$, where t is the time of the change. This change definition depends on the definition of the TCI tree, which itself is based on the decomposition by the grammar. The possible *causes* of changes depend on the position of the respective node in the TCI tree as described in the example below. A *change pattern* is a set of time series each of one is connected to a node in the considered TCI tree.

As an example the Web page in figure 2 may be considered. If the page change function is defined to consider the first level of the TCT tree (including level 0 an 1) the TCT tree has 7 nodes at level 1 similar to the corresponding TCI tree. Three of these nodes (C2, C4 and C6) actually change in the course of time. A change is detected if the string in element C2 is changed, if the optional element C4 appears, is modified or deleted or if a change in the list element C6 occurs, i.e. a list element is inserted, modified or deleted.

4   Component-Based Update Estimation

In this article we consider the special case that components of a specific Web page are updated deterministically. In order to model the update characteristics of each component we apply a cyclic regular grammar (fig. 3). In [8] a method to learn similar update characteristics of entire Web pages is presented. In this section we present a method to apply the respective algorithm to pages where not entire pages but page components change deterministically.

The input of this *Component-Update-Estimation-algorithm* are the target URL of the considered page and a wrapper of the respective page. In this algorithm the data source is reloaded after constant periods of time. In each cycle the data contained in page components are extracted by applying the wrapper. Based on the current and the previous data vector changes occurring in page components are registered. Based on detected changes of components the intervals between updates of specific components may be estimated.[2] The intervals are used to estimate symbols by a clustering process (section 2.2)[8]. Based on sequences of symbols associated to components the cyclic regular grammars (section 2.2) may be estimated. A termination criterion concerning the grammar estimation is applied to mark the grammar of a component as determined. This termination criterion may e.g. consider the number of times a new symbol is detected which has also been predicted correctly by a current grammar estimation.

Finally after the detection of the cyclic-regular grammar of each component the respective grammars are stored in a vector, which is denoted as *timeGrammarVector* in the following.

5   Download Optimization

The new download optimization strategy may now be described by the algorithm *Component-Based-Reload* in figure 5. The main aspect of the algorithm is

Component-Based-Reload(*wrapper*, *timeGrammarVector*, *URL***)**

```
1        set previous content = ∅
2        reload source(URL)
3        extract current content vector (wrapper)
4        copy current content vector to previous content vector

5        while ∃ component where phase not detected
6           reload source(URL)
7           extract current content vector (wrapper)
8           for each component: compare previous and current content
9           for each component: extract symbols(timeGrammarVector)
10          for each component: match phase(timeGrammarVector)
11          if phase of component j is determined
12              mark phase of component j as determined
13              start download thread for component j (timeGrammarVector)
14          wait(Δt)
15          copy current content vector to previous content vector
```

Fig. 5. The Component-Based-Reload-algorithm. For each component an independent reload-thread is started after a phase detection.

to determine the different 'phases'[3] of the components. If e.g. the cyclic regular grammar of a component is $(ababc)^*$ and we register a symbol a, the current state of the respective automaton is ambiguous. A sequence of successive symbols has

---

[2] Due to the finite sampling interval length, the interval length between updates is only an estimation.

[3] With the term 'phase' we denote the current symbol of the update characteristic of a component (fig. 3) and roughly the position in the respective interval.

to be considered in order to disambiguate the current state (symbol) of a component. In the algorithm in figure 5 the remote source is reloaded frequently from the considered URL (steps 2, 6). The data contained in the respective components are extracted applying the wrapper (step 3,7) and the contents is compared to the contents of previous component versions (step 8). By this method current symbols may be extracted and the symbols may be compared to the respective grammar in the time-grammar-vector (obtained from the grammar estimation algorithm) until the current symbol is unique. These steps are performed in steps 9 and 10 of the algorithm. If the phase of a component has been detected, in step 11 a download thread is started for this component that predicts further symbols of the respective component and performs reload operations. In particular in this reload strategy the remote source is loaded shortly before the expected remote change (as provided by the cyclic regular grammar of a component) and then by reloading the remote source with a high frequency until the change has been detected [8]. By this method a feedback is acquired that is necessary to compensate deviations of the registered update times of a remote source due to server and network delays. After the phase detection a number of threads is running performing reload operations that corresponds to the number of page components.

6 Experiments

6.1 Experimental Setup

The experiment consists of two basic stages. In the 'estimation' stage the change dynamics of a Web page is estimated by observation of the page over a period of time. This stage consists of four phases that are performed successively.

Phase 1: In the first phase the basic reload frequency for the wrapper induction and subsequent sampling processes is determined [8].

Phase 2: In this phase the wrapper is induced based on successive versions of the page. The estimated wrapper is subjected to a development in the course of time. A heuristic criterion is applied to terminate the induction process.

Phase 3: Based on the wrapper and the respective parser in this phase changes on the page are examined over a period of time. The result is a vector of component change series indicating, at which times a specific component changed in the considered period of time.

Phase 4: In this phase the detected change behavior of the page obtained in the previous step is examined. The result is a vector of update grammars of the different components (section 4).

In the second 'application' stage the knowledge about the page dynamics acquired in the previous stage is applied for the extraction of data in the course of time.

Phase 5: The data extraction algorithm considers each component independently. The 'phase' of the update pattern of each component has to be detected (section 5).

Phase 6: In this phase data are extracted by component-based reload requests.

6.2 Application Examples

In the experiments we apply artificial and real pages in order to demonstrate main benefits of the new method. In order to measure the quality of a reload strategy we consider the costs in terms of the number of reload operations (causing network traffic etc.), the number of lost data objects and the age of components (section 2.2). The steps of the procedure in section 6.1 are successively applied to a page and the respective results are demonstrated.

In a first example we consider the page http://www.sat.dundee.ac.uk/ pdus.html. This page contains links to images of different geostationary satellites. After the wrapper induction the final TCI graph has 117 leaf nodes all of which are related to links to specific satellite images in the page. Figures 6 and 7 show the result of step 3 of the procedure. The 'any-change' update detection in figure 6 shows a complex change pattern. After a grammar-based decomposition different components in figure 7 show however simple and deterministic update characteristics. The underlying process applied to generate the page automatically may easily be understood.

The change patterns obtained from step 3 of the experiment may be used to estimate the grammar vector in step 4 as described in section 4. The grammar vector is then used for the multi-phase detection (phase 5). As a visualization of phase 6 of the procedure, figure 8 shows the application of different reload strategies. In this experiment we consider only a fraction of the entire page, in particular the fraction consisting of the components c-38 and c-26 in figure 7 for reasons of simplicity. The superposition of the component's update patterns (c-38 and c-26) as depicted at the top of figure 8 reveals very close update operations. Because of a finite resolution in the estimation process due to network

Fig. 6. Detected changes of the Web page http://www.sat.dundee.ac.uk/ pdus.html by the 'any-change'-method over a period of 2 days and 7 hours

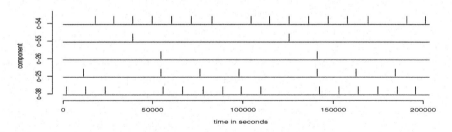

Fig. 7. Change dynamics of sample components of the Web page http://www.sat.dundee.ac.uk/pdus.html

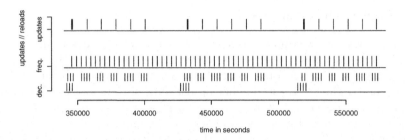

Fig. 8. Visualization of different reload strategies. The first graph ('updates') shows original updates. The second graph ('freq.') shows reloads applying a constant reload frequency. The third graph ('dec.') shows a decomposition based reload strategy where the data source consists of two components.

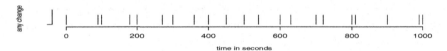

Fig. 9. Detected changes by the any-change method in the second example. No regularity in the change pattern may be observed.

delays etc. the superposed update pattern may not be regarded as a simple deterministic pattern. A quasi deterministic prediction as presented in [8] may therefore not be applied and only common constant-frequency sampling methods are applicable as depicted in the second graph ('freq.') in the center of figure 8. After a grammar based decomposition in phase 3 of the procedure the simple update characteristics of the components shown in figure 7 (c-38 and c-26) are revealed. After this decomposition step the different update characteristics of the components may be estimated and applied for the prediction of future updates of the remote source as shown in the third graph ('dec.') of figure 8. In this figure the reload operations triggered by the different components are depicted. In contrast to the constant-frequency reload strategy illustrated in the center of figure 8 ('freq.') it may be observed that reload operations are performed close to the points in time of remote update operations.

We present a second example to demonstrate the applicability of a grammar based decomposition in order to obtain a clear presentation of the update characteristics of a page. In this example an artificial page is considered that consists of two components. Each component is updated after a constant period of time (figure 10). The two update intervals are however slightly different (100 and 90 seconds). The superposition of the component's update patterns as registered by the 'any-change'-difference measure is shown in figure 9. Although the basic scenario is simple, the update characteristics of the page is quite complex and no regularities in the update pattern may be observed.[4] A prediction of future

---

[4] Regularities may obviously be observed at a larger time scale. However the length of periods may become arbitrarily large for more complex examples.

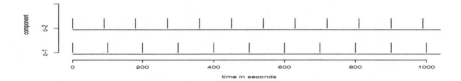

Fig. 10. Analysis of the change dynamics in the second experiment

Table 1. Comparison of the constant-frequency sampling and a decomposition-based reload strategy

		♯ downloads	♯ loss	$\overline{sumage}$ (seconds)
experiment 1	constant method	393	0	46157
	decomp. method	393	0	2903
experiment 2	constant method	654	0	130
	decomp. method	654	0	89

update times is hardly possible. After a grammar based decomposition the basic update characteristics of the components are easily revealed (figure 10). The decomposition-based reload is performed similar to the first example (figure 8).

Table 1 shows numeric results for the experiments described above. In order to compare the methods in this comparison the costs, i.e. the number of downloads triggered by a respective download strategy, is fixed. Since the quality parameters may be different for different components (if the decomposition-based method is applied) the values in table 1 constitute mean values with respect to all components. The table shows that the values for lost information are similar. The age of the data may be reduced significantly by the decomposition-based reload strategy.

7   Conclusion

In the article we presented a new reload strategy for Web information that is based on a decomposition of pages into functional segments. For the segmentation we applied automatic wrapper induction techniques. Successive versions of a Web page are used as sample pages for the wrapper induction process. By using artificial and real examples we showed that the quality of retrieved information may be improved significantly compared to traditional (sampling with constant frequency) techniques.

The (deterministic) change prediction based on page decomposition presented in this article is a method that may be applied only to a fraction of Web pages. If page components change statistically further optimization strategies have to be developed. However also in this case page decomposition may reveal new optimization strategies for client side data retrieval tools. A further research aspect is to achieve a higher degree of automatism, if e.g. different kinds of deterministic and statistic change characteristics are involved on a single page.

References

1. A.Arasu, J.Cho, H.Garcia-Molina, A.Paepcke, and S.Raghavan. Searching the web. *ACM Trans. Inter. Tech.*, 1(1):2–43, 2001.
2. Arvind Arasu, Hector Garcia-Molina, and Stanford University. Extracting structured data from web pages. In *SIGMOD '03: Proceedings of the 2003 ACM SIGMOD international conference on Management of data*, pages 337–348, New York, NY, USA, 2003. ACM Press.
3. Junghoo Cho and Hector Garcia-Molina. Estimating frequency of change. *ACM Trans. Inter. Tech.*, 3(3):256–290, 2003.
4. E. Coffman, Z.Liu, and R.R.Weber. Optimal robot scheduling for web search engines. *Journal of Scheduling*, 1(1):15–29, June 1998.
5. Valter Crescenzi and Giansalvatore Mecca. Automatic information extraction from large websites. *J. ACM*, 51(5):731–779, 2004.
6. S. Grumbach and G.Mecca. In search of the lost schema. In *ICDT '99: Proc. of the 7th Int. Conf. on Database Theory*, pages 314–331, London, UK, 1999. Springer-Verlag.
7. Julie E. Kendall and Kenneth E. Kendall. Information delivery systems: an exploration of web pull and push technologies. *Commun. AIS*, 1(4es):1–43, 1999.
8. D. Kukulenz. Capturing web dynamics by regular approximation. In X. Zhou et al., editor, *WISE 04, Web Information Systems, LNCS 3306*, pages 528–540. Springer-Verlag Berlin Heidelberg, 2004.
9. A. Laender, B. Ribeiro-Neto, A. Silva, and J. Teixeira. A brief survey of web data extraction tools. In *SIGMOD Record*, June 2002.
10. C. Olston and J.Widom. Best-effort cache synchronization with source cooperation. In *Proceedings of SIGMOD*, pages 73–84, May 2002.
11. S. Pandey, K.Ramamritham, and S.Chakrabarti. Monitoring the dynamic web to respond to continuous queries. In *WWW '03: Proc. of the 12th int. conf. on World Wide Web*, pages 659–668, New York, NY, USA, 2003. ACM Press.
12. M.A. Sharaf, A. Labrinidis, P.K. Chrysanthis, and K. Pruhs. Freshness-aware scheduling of continuous queries in the dynamic web. In *8th Int. Workshop on the Web and Databases (WebDB 2005), Baltimore, Maryland*, pages 73–78, 2005.
13. J. L. Wolf, M. S. Squillante, P. S. Yu, J. Sethuraman, and L. Ozsen. Optimal crawling strategies for web search engines. In *Proceedings of the eleventh international conference on World Wide Web*, pages 136–147. ACM Press, 2002.

An Ontological Approach for Defining Agents for Collaborative Applications

I.T. Hawryszkiewycz

Department of Information Systems, University of Technology, Sydney
igorh@it.uts.edu.au

Abstract. Collaboration has become important especially in knowledge intensive applications. Computer support systems for collaborative work on The Web, however, usually grow in an ad-hoc manner. The paper suggests two reasons for such an ad-hoc approach. One is a lack of methods to map collaborative requirements into collaborative workspaces. The other is that collaborative processes themselves change over time. The paper proposes a metamodel that provides an ontology to support collaborative process modelling and use these to define generic agents, which can assist users to set up and change collaborative workspaces. The metamodel itself integrates social, organizational and workflow semantics providing the ability to describe complex collaborative processes. The metamodel concepts and the corresponding agents are generic in nature and the paper will describe ways to map such generic concepts to specific domain applications.

1 Introduction

Collaborative systems have sometimes not been sustainable because of continuous changes required to the system. This in turn leads to extra burdens placed on users, who abandon systems and go back to alternate approaches, usually e-mail. One way to avoid this problem is to nominate a facilitator who will manage the change and facilitate interactions within collaborative workspaces. Another way, proposed here, is to facilitate collaboration by using software agents. These agents will assist users to setup and change applications. However, much of the work in collaborative systems concentrates on specific business processes (Iqbal, James, Gatward, 2003). Consequently supporting software agents must be specially developed. Such development can be expensive and this paper proposes ways to reduce this cost by proposing generic agents, which can customized to many applications. This paper proposes a generic metamodel to define a common ontology for collaboration to facilitate the development of generic agents for collaborative applications. The approach is identified in Figure 1.

The first step in Figure 1 is to identify generic concepts of collaboration by identifying real world phenomena across a wide range of collaborative applications. Our goal is to identify real world phenomena and express them as a metamodel that can be used to create conceptual models of specific applications. This follows the suggestion in (Shanks, Lansley, Weber, 2004), who propose composite objects that can be used to model higher level that those used in traditional methods such as E-R

M. Kitsuregawa et al. (Eds.): WISE 2005, LNCS 3806, pp. 81–94, 2005.

modeling. One aspect of this work has been to identify the semantic concepts that express real world phenomena in collaboration and integrate them into one metamodel to provide a general set of semantics to model collaborative processes. These metamodel concepts are then used to identify generic agents. There is a separate generic agent for each concept.

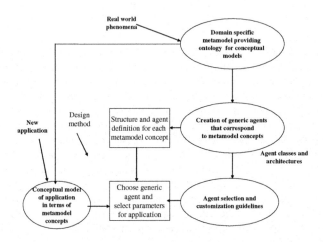

Fig. 1. Identifying Generic Agents

Applications can then be defined using the approach as shown in Figure 1. requires the definition of the concepts and creation of agents that use the ontology. These concepts are then used to develop conceptual models of new applications. The conceptual model includes a number of concepts with relationships between them. In a system design each object in the conceptual model identifies the corresponding generic agent to support it. The parameters of the agent are changed to suit the application. These agents are combined into a multi-agent architecture where connections between agents correspond to the relationships between objects in the conceptual model.

2 Collaborative Semantics

The proposed metamodel described in this paper has integrated the semantics of earlier developed models to create an integrated set of concepts to model collaborative processes (Hawryszkiewycz, 2005a). It combines social concepts, workflow systems and organizational activities within the same common framework.

The metamodel has evolved over a number of years and used both early results and has been tested in practice. It includes the semantics of previous models such as ConversationBuilder (Kaplan *et al.*, 1992) and Oval (Malone and Fry, 1992) but also includes concepts such as those found in Ariadne (Divitni and Simone, 2000), which concentrated on flexible coordination. It draws on concepts in social models such as those based on speech acts found in Action Workflow (Winograd and Flores, 1987) or activity theory (Kutti and Arvonen, 1992). It is also similar to the more goal-oriented support systems such as BCSW (2004) have been developed. Standards for collaboration have primarily concentrated on predefined workflows and evolved primarily through the workflow management systems coalition. In practice it has been used to develop conceptual models in applications, which included business networking (Hawryszkiewycz, 1996) and strategic planning (Hawryszkiewycz, 1997). The metamodel also supports the ideas of Carley and Gasser (1999) where each of the concepts can serve as a business agency in an intelligent business system.

In the first instance we combined community and work activities to create the set of concepts shown in Figure 1. Here each rectangle represents one concept and the links between them represent relationships between the concepts. Only the high level concepts and their relationships are shown. The central concept is the *activity*, which provides the space where people, here called *participants* take activity specified *roles* to collaborate in the production of a well-defined *artifact*. Each such role has clearly defined *responsibilities* to take *work-actions*. These concepts are sufficient to represent systems like ConversationBuilder (Kaplan, 1992) and Oval (Malone, 1992). Thus for example, one role may have the responsibility to change an artefact, whereas others may only be able to read the artefacts and comment on them. The model also indicates that each role assignment may have more than one responsibility. The semantics primarily centre on *participants* using known information to create new artifacts by continuous actions and interactions. Specific work-actions (such as updating a document) are taken by participants taking roles with assigned responsibilities.

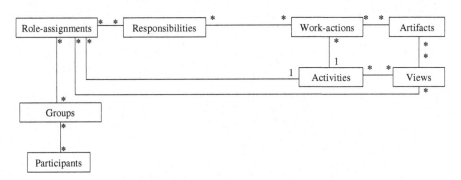

Fig. 2. Group semantics

The semantics shown in Figure 2 extend the earlier models to introduce the group concept and thus provide the ability to model independently coordinated but related groups. One group must be unaware of other groups in order to support independent collaborations within a larger framework. As an example, different and independent client groups are managed within the same organization. In education, this includes different lecture or study groups. However, the same person can participate in more than one group as is the case in many organizations. A further extension is associating access abilities to artefacts to specific roles.

The important constraint here is that activity is still the central concept but groups can be created independently of activities. This separates the social issues from organizational activities. At the same time it models the realistic situation where people can be part of different groups and thus informally transfer knowledge between these groups. Roles now have access to views and roles in the same activity can access different views thus giving more governance flexibility.

Figure 3 shows an example of using the concepts to describe a system. Here there are two activities – class 1 activity and class 2 activity. Each has a role of teacher and student. Each of these roles have defined responsibilities. These could be different for each activity. At the social side there are a large number of participants. Some are students and others are teachers. Participants can be assigned to both groups, for example 'Jill' is both a student and a teacher. The groups are then divided into sub-groups and each subgroup is assigned to a role. Thus 'Jill' is in subgroup 'class 2 teacher' where she is assigned the role of Class 2 teacher. 'Jill' is also a student in class 1.

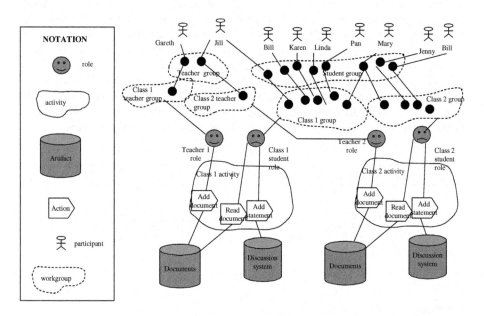

Fig. 3. An example of using the metamodel semantics

2.1 Extension to Work Processes – Emphasizing Emergent Processes

Figure 2 primarily concentrates on the social semantics of groups and their relationship to organizational activities. Process semantics were added to these social and organizational semantics. The semantics shown in Figure 4 now include the concept of *events*. Figure 4 also expands on Figure 3 in giving the names of relationships as well as their cardinality and whether they are mandatory or optional. This is either an initiation event or a completion event together with event-rules. Roles are authorized to initiate a completion event, once they have completed some work-item. The workflow rule defines the initiation event to be activated once a completion event has been initiated. The initiation event then notifies some other role that it must take some action.

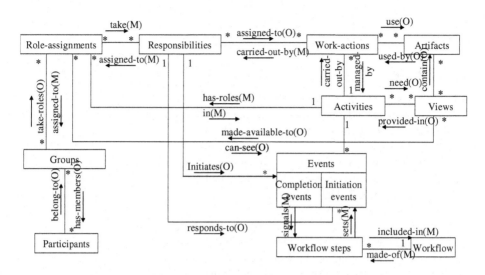

Fig. 4. Extending the Metamodel with events

Our goal now is to use the metamodel to define generic agent structure. The paper proceeds to do so this in a more formal way. It first defines the metamodel objects and the agent structures.

2.2 Formal Definitions of Metamodel Concepts

So far, we have described the semantics in informal ways. More formal definitions need to be based on ontology languages such as for example, OWL (Zuo, Zhou, 2003) or that described in WSML (Fensel, de Bruijn). In our description we separate the concepts from the relationships. Each of these have their methods. The concept methods apply to the concept only. The relationship methods apply to relationships only. The following skeleton structure is used in the definition:

```
concept <name>, '<description>':
 { {attributes: <attribute-name>},
   {methods: <method-name>: {permissions:<permission, role-name>}},
   {constraints},
 };
relationship <name>,'<description'>:
{{ source-name:<concept>, target-name: <concept>}
   {cardinality},
   {attributes: <attribute-name>},
   {methods: <method-name>: {permissions:<permission, role-name>},
   {communication: messages form source to target concept},}
   {constraints},
};
```

The distinction between concepts and relationships is important. The main goal of the concepts is to identify the contents and knowledge possessed by each concept.

The relationships on the other hand have the further puropose of defining communications between the concepts. These are defined in terms of messages.

Social Concepts

concept: participant, 'people involved in the system':
  {{attributes: (name, address, date-registered, expertise, group-coordinator <role>)};
    {methods: add-participant, delete participant}
  };
concept: group, 'groupings of people with similar characteristics'
  {{attributes: (date-created; rules: expertise-needed)},
    {methods: add-group, delete group}
  };
relationship: belongs-to, 'identifies groups that people belong-in'
  {{source-concept: <participant>, target-concept: <group>},
    {cardinality: can belong to many groups},
    {methods: request-membership, request-deletion}
    {attribute: date-assigned;}
  };
relationship: has-members, 'identifies people in a group'
  {{source-concept: <group>, target-concept: <participant>},
    {cardinality: group can have many participants},
    {methods: add-participant-to-group, delete-participant-from-group}
    {attribute: date-assigned;}
  };

Organizational Concepts

concept: role-assignment:
  {{attributes: (date-created: date)}
  {methods: create-assignment, delete-assignment}
  };
relationship: take-role:
  {{source-concept: <group>, target-concept: <role-assignment>}
  {methods: assign-group-to-role, delete-group-from-role}
    {cardinality: group can take many role assignments},
    {constraint rule – exclude group member if in groups (group set)}
  }
relationship: assigned-to:
  {{source-concept: < role-assignment >, target-concept: < group>}
  {methods: request-group-for-role, request-deletion-group-from-role}
    {constraint: }
  }
concept: activity:
  {{attributes: (date-created: date), (owner:<role>),(plan:<artifact>)}
  {methods: create-activity, delete activity}

2.3 Implementing the Metamodel

One proof of the value of a metamodel is in its instantiation, here the running LiveNet system. The current system operates with the metamodel shown in Figure 2. A screen shot of the newly formulated version of LiveNet is shown in Figure 5. This figure shows a workspace that supports a student group working on a case study. It shows artifacts that include a case study plan and milestones together with any discussions about them. It also includes the roles taken by students in the group.

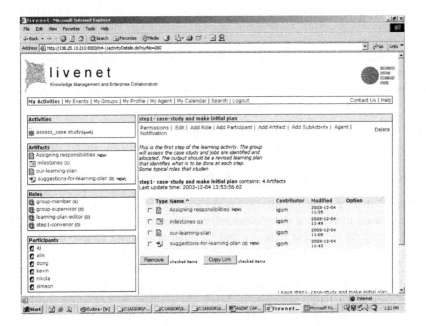

Fig. 5. Screen shot of LiveNet extension to design

3 Identifying Generic Agents

Software agents have been proposed for some time as necessary to support collaborative processes. Earlier Hattori and others (1999) proposed agent support for collaborative systems emphasizing workspace and personal agents. Their work suggested activity and personal agents and concentrated on loose groups exchanging information (Cummings, Butler, Kraut, 2002). Our metamodel extends this idea to collaborative systems, which include organizational and workflow components. We propose a richer set of agent classes (Hawryszkiewycz, Lin, 2003) to support collaborative work processes within organizational contexts. These are:

Activity agent – is set a goal and defines a plan to attain the goal. The plan requires tasks to be set up and monitored to realize parts of the goal. It initiates work-items to carry out the tasks.

Work-action agent – Carries out a specific task and reports to the activity agent. Arranges work in terms of role responsibilities. Can recommend specific collaborations such as a discussion, document management or notification service.

Role agent – determines the skills needed by the roles and finds participants with specific skills to carry out the role. The role agent finds such participants by interacting with a broker agent.

Group Agent – has as its goal to establish a group with common characteristics and share knowledge between them. Proactively, it can suggest that people join particular groups.

Personal agent – knows about a person's interests, responsibilities and commitments. Can maintain a person's schedules and keep track of their activities.

Artifact agent – possesses knowledge of how to structure a document and the skills needed to construct each part.

Connect (Broker) agent – knows domain-specific workspaces that can be specialized to selected goals.

The paper now illustrates ways to combine these agents into multi-agent architectures to support business processes.

3.1 Goal Structure for Defining Agents for Applications

The agent structure is predominantly made up of two sets of rules. One set are rules, which are used to create a new collaborative object and its associated agent. These include setting up the agent structure and its relationships. At a more detailed level, we use the usual reasoning model of agents and implement it using the three layer architecture (Muller, 1996) chosen from a number of alternative architectures (Wooldridge, 1999). Agents are used to achieve goals using plans defined by agent users. A plan is composed of event-condition-action rules, each of which specifies the actions to be executed when condition is true. The rules include managing the collaborative activities of the agent. Such rules are needed as each agent is part of a multi-agent structure and must communiucate with related agents. As an example Figure 6 illustrates a system made up of two activities – 'making claims' and 'assessing claims'.

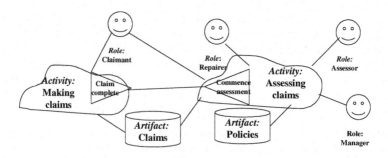

Fig. 6. A Model for Claims Processing

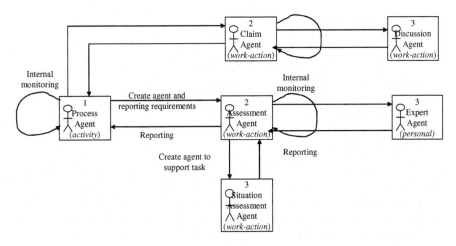

Fig. 7. Communication in a Multi-agent architecture

The corresponding agent structure is shown in Figure 7. The communication between agents can be described using sequence diagrams like that in Figure 8, which illustrate the messages between the agents. The agents would also get many of their messages from the collaborative system. In Figure 8 the claim processing agent receives a request to initiate a claim. Presumably this would come from a personal agent of the claimant. It then consults the claim form agent, which possesses the knowledge of different claims and nominates the claim type. The artifact agent contains the knowledge needed to complete the artifact. This knowledge is used by the activity agent to schedule the tasks. The goal here is to ensure that agents address particular aspects of organizational computational theory (Carley and Glasser, 1999) and hence can be flexibly customized to different processes.

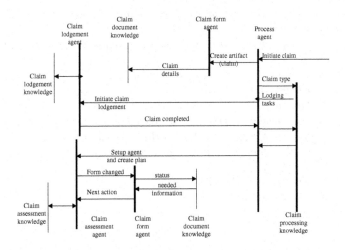

Fig. 8. Describing agent communication using sequence diagrams

3.2 Example Definitions

To describe agents we use a skeletal agent description language based on the metamodel ontology for illustrative purposes. Basically:

<agent-name>: uses corresponding metamodel concept;
    {relationships are implied by metamodel definition and are created by agents}
    <setting up goals>:
    <carrying-out goals>;
    <action-rules>:

The action rules in this case often emphasize changes to relationships based on the collaborative situation.   The general approach is to create concepts look at their relationships in the metamodel. The agent must then create all the mandatory relationships. As an example, the paper gives some very skeletal definitions of activity and work-action agents.

<activity-agent>

Goal: Set-up-activity;
Plan: for setting up activity.
Subgoal g1: create new activity-structure;
Plan: for creating a new activity;
  Sub-goal s1: determine activity owner;
Subgoal g2: set up required activity relationships;
  Plan: for setting-up activity relationships;
  sub-goal r1: determine needed roles:
  sub-goal r2: determine needed views;

Goal: Carry out activity;
Plan: for carrying out activity;
        Subgoal g1: initiate new work-actions;
                Rule: if completion-event on action   received then signal-event *('determine new-action');*
                        if completion-event requesting action received then signal-event *('start work');*
    Subgoal g2: determine if additional work- action is needed;
      Subplan: for identifying additional action:
                Rule: if message-received (artifact needs change 'a') and assigned-team-member has no 'a' knowledge then carry out learning-activity 'a';
                Rule: if message-received (artifact needs change 'a' and no team-member has 'a' knowledge and no learning-activity 'a' then get expert advice;
  Subgoal g3: get new expert advice;
Subgoal g4: make plan changes;

Goal: create management-view;
  create view;
  create artifact plan;
  create contains;

Goal: create role assignment;
Plan: for setting up role-assignment;
Sub-goal: create coordinator assignment;
Sub-goal: Create required role-assignment relationships;

<Work-action-agent>

<Roles>: coordinator (ability: report-progress),
　　　　member (ability: change-key-document)
<Artifacts>: plan, goal-specification, key-output.
<Actions>: create-work-action,
　　　　change-key-document, change-plan,
Goal: Complete work-action on time
Plan: for completing on time
　　　Sub goal g1: to determine if action is needed to *correctly assign responsibility*
　　　Sub goal g2: to determine if action needed *for work to proceed in a steady manner*
　　　Sub goal g3: to determine if action is needed to *improve interaction between team members*
　　　Sub goal g4: to determine if *team members are interacting*

　　Example of a subgoal definition follows:

　　　Sub goal g2: to determine if action needed *for work to proceed in a steady manner*
　　　Sub plan P2: for g2
　　　Rule R2: on timer alter if today is later than two days after last update and today is not after the task end date **then** take action A2
　　　Action A2: send the following message to participant in coordinator role "There seems to be no progress on the output document – should it be updated?"
　　　Rule R3:　　on timer alter if accesses larger than 15 and no updates to output artifact **then** action A3. (probably disagreement).
　　　Action A3: send the message to participants in team-member "You should begin to make changes to the output document"

The parameters here include various time criteria as well the definition of the output documents. These can be customized to a particular application. At a more detailed level, we use the three layer architecture (Muller, 1996) chosen from a number of alternative architectures (Wooldridge, 1999). Agents are used to achieve goals using plans defined by agent users. A plan is composed of event-condition-action rules, each of which specifies the actions to be executed when condition is true.

4　Customizing to Domain Applications

One kind of customization is to simply take each concept and relationship and set its parameters to the application. Thus for example we could customize the activity agent to the claims processing application shown in Figure 6 by taking the activity agent and naming it as claims lodgement, another activity agent as claims assessment and so on. The alternate is to customize at a higher level to particular application classes. In that case we need to define the generic agents in terms of domain specific terms. The two steps here are:

Step 1 – customize to the domain ontology
Step 2 – customize to domain application

4.1 Customizing to Domain Ontology

This usually involves identifying domain concepts and mapping them to collaborative concepts. As an example, we have earlier proposed a framework for composing flexible learning processes. The framework provides a taxonomy, or grammar, for describing leaning processes. The main elements, or learning process concepts, of such a grammar for the learning process include:

Learning environment, or where learning takes place. This may be a University of a person's place of work. It may be within a business process.
Learning goal, which describes what the process participant must learn,
Learning plan, which defines the sequence of learning activities to be followed to achieve the learning goal.
Learning activity, which describes a step of the learning plan; this may be create a report, evaluate a problem. Many such activities will in fact be engagements with other process components, in particular, process documents or process team members.
Subject metadata, which provides explicit references to information needed in the activity,
The learning method, which will be used in the learning step,
Support services provided for the learning method.

The general semantic here is that a learner specifies a learning goal. A plan, which is made up of a number of learning activities, is then constructed by the learner with assistance from an agent. Each activity has a learning subgoal and specifies the preferred learning method to be used by the learner. Wang (2005) defines a similar set made up of units (corresponding to our learning plans), activities (corresponding to our learning activities), and facilities (corresponding to our methods).

The conceptual framework can be used to identify some differences in learning in University and business environments. In University environments the learning goals are usually fairly broad and require plans composed of many activities. There are often fewer goals, for example, four goals corresponding to taking four subjects in a semester. In most business processes the learning goals would be of shorter duration but would occur more frequently and irregularly as new business issues arise. The mapping is to map the learning goal and plan to a managing activity, whereas learning activity can map either onto activities or work-actions depending on their complexity. The parameters here include various time criteria as well the definition of the output documents. These can then be customized to a particular application. More details can be found in (Hawryszkiewycz, 2005b).

5 Summary

The paper outlined the need for a metamodel to provide the ontology for collaborative business systems. The metamodel combined concepts from social, organizational and workflow aspects to develop an integrated model for representing collaborative business systems in organizational settings. The paper then described how the metamodel can be used to identify generic agents that can be adapted to collaborative business processes.

Acknowledgement

We wish to acknowledge the Australian Research Council for financial support for this project.

References

BCSW - http://bscw.fit.fraunhofer.de/ - last accessed 24 Sept. 2004.

Carley, K.M., and Gasser, L. (1999): "Computational Organizational Theory" in Chapter 7 "Computational Organization Theory" by KM Carley & L Gasser in "Multiagent Systems" Gerhard Weiss (Ed) MIT Press -- 1999

Chang, M.K. and Woo, C. (1984): "A Speech-Act-Based Negotiation Protocol: Design, Implementation, and Test Use" *ACM Transactions on Information Systems*, Vol. 12, No. 4, pp. 360-382.

Cummings, J.N., Butler, B. and Kraut, R. (2002): "The Quality of OnLine Social Relationships" Communications of the ACM, Vol. 45, No. 1, July, 2002, pp. 103-111.

Divitni, M. and Simone, C. (2000): "Supporting Different Dimensions of Adaptability in Workflow Modeling" Computer Supported Cooperative Work, Vol. 9, pp. 365-397.

Hawryszkiewycz, I.T., (1996): Support services for business networking, *Proceedings IFIP96*, Canberra, eds. E. Altman and N. Terashima, Chapman and Hall, London, ISBN 0-412-75560-2.

Hawryszkiewycz, I.T., (1997): A framework for strategic planning for communications support, *Proceedings of the Inaugural Conference of Informatics in Multinational Enterprises*, Washington, October, 1997, pp. 141-151

Hawryszkiewycz, I.T. and Lin, A .(2003): "Process Knowledge Support for Emergent Processes" Proceedings of the Second IASTED International Conference on Information and Knowledge Management, Scottsdale, Arizona, November, 2003, pp. 83-87.

Hawryszkiewycz, I.T (2005a): "A Metamodel for Modeling Collaborative Systems" Journal of Computer Information Systems, Vol. XLV, Number 3, Spring 2005, pp. 63-72.

Hawryszkiewycz, I.T. (2005b): "An Agent Framework for Learning Systems" Proceedings of the Fourth IASTED International Conference on Web-based Education, Grindelwald, pp. 142-147.

Hattori, F., Ohguro, T., Yokoo, M., Matsubara, S. and Yoshida, S. (1999): "Socialware: Multiagent Systems for Supporting Network Communities", Communications of the ACM, March, 1999, pp. 55-59.

Iqbal, R., James, A. and Gatward, R. (2003): " A Practical Solution to the Integration of Collaborative Applications in Academic Environment" http://www.inf.ethz.ch/personal/ignat/ECSCW03CEW/submissions/IqbalJames.pdf

Kaplan, S.M., Tolone, W.J., Bogia, D.P. and Bignoli, C. (1992): "Flexible, Active Support for Collaborative Work with ConversationBuilder" Proceedings of the CSCW'92 Conference, November 1992, Toronto, pp. 378-385.

Kutti, K., Arvonen, T. (1992): "Identifying Potential CSCE Applications by Means of Activity Theory Concepts: A Case Example" Proceedings of the CSCW'92 Conference, November 1992, Toronto, pp. 233- 240.

LiveNet – http://livenet4.it.uts.edu.au

Malone, T.W. and Fry, C. (1992): "Experiments with Oval: A radically Tailroable Tool for Collaborative Work" Proceedings of the CSCW'92 Conference, November 1992, Toronto, pp. 289-297.

Reyes, P., Raisinhani, S. and Singh, M., 2002, Global supply chain management in the telecommunications industry: the role of information technology in integration of supply chain entities, *Journal of Global Information Technology Management,* **5(2),** 48-67.

Shanks, G., Lansley, S., and Weber, R. (2004): "Representing Composites in Conceptual Modeling" Communications of the ACM, Vol. 43, No. 7, July, 2004, pp. 77-80.

Winograd, T., and Flores, F. (1987): "A Language/Action perspective on the design of cooperative work" Human Computer Interaction, 3, pp. 3-30.

Improving Web Data Annotations with Spreading Activation

Fatih Gelgi, Srinivas Vadrevu, and Hasan Davulcu

Department of Computer Science and Engineering,
Arizona State University, Tempe, AZ, 85287, USA
{fagelgi, svadrevu, hdavulcu}@asu.edu

Abstract. The Web has established itself as the largest public data repository ever available. Even though the vast majority of information on the Web is formatted to be easily readable by the human eye, "meaningful information" is still largely inaccessible for the computer applications. In this paper, we present automated algorithms to gather meta-data and instance information by utilizing global regularities on the Web and incorporating the contextual information. Our system is distinguished since it does not require domain specific engineering. Experimental evaluations were successfully performed on the TAP knowledge base and the faculty-course home pages of computer science departments containing 16,861 Web pages.

Keywords: Semi-structured data, spreading activation, semantic partitioning.

1 Introduction

Scalable information retrieval [1] based search engine technologies have achieved wide spread adoption and commercial success towards enabling access to the Web. However, since they are based on an unstructured representation of the Web documents their performance in making sense of the available information is also limited.

Our system that we present in this paper is capable of gathering meta-data and instances from attribute rich Web page collections. Figure 1 displays an example of a faculty home page that lists the attribute information such as publications, address and telephone. Our system utilizes the presentation regularities within the Web page to produce an initial meta-tagging of the Web page using a semantic partitioning algorithm [2, 3], and utilizes (i) the global regularities on the Web and (ii) the contextual information to refine the meta-tagging using a *spreading activation network (SAN) framework*.

Our system differs from the previous work by not requiring template drivenness and an ontology. Thus, we can not readily use previously developed wrapper induction techniques [4, 5, 6, 7] which require that the item pages should be template driven and ontology driven extraction techniques [8, 9, 10] which require that an ontology of concepts, relationships and their value types is provided apriori in order to find matching information.

M. Kitsuregawa et al. (Eds.): WISE 2005, LNCS 3806, pp. 95–106, 2005.

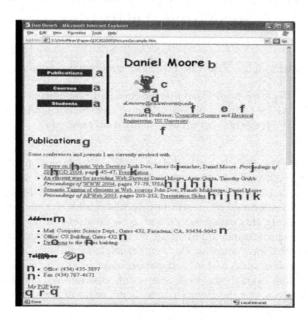

Fig. 1. An example of a Faculty home page. The labels in the page are marked with their corresponding path identifier symbols.

We will not discuss the details of our semantic partitioning algorithm in this paper, but more details about the algorithm can be found in [2, 3]. Initially our semantic partitioning algorithm also assigns ontological types to all labels based on their roles in the inferred group hierarchies using heuristic rules. The ontological type or the semantic role of a label can be either a concept (C), an attribute(A), a value (V) or nothing (N).

Presentation regularities on itself indeed won't be adequate for the semi-structured data such as web, thus the data generated by the semantic partitioning systems contain large amount of missing and incorrect annotations. For instance, in the example above *Daniel Moore, Electrical Engineering, Computer Science* and *US University* are all tagged as attributes instead of values as shown in Figure 2. The SAN framework is capable of reasoning with the meta-data reg-

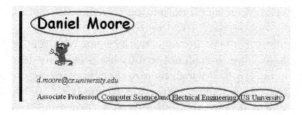

Fig. 2. The region from the facultys home in from the example in Figure 1. The circled labels are tagged incorrectly as attributes whereas they have to be values.

ularities in order to improve the accuracy of the ontological types of labels found within object attribute pages.

The rest of the paper is organized as follows. Section 2 explains the overview of our system and Section 3 presents discusses our SAN framework in detail. Section 4 presents complexity analysis of our algorithms and Section 5 provides experimental results on various data beds. Finally we conclude in Section 6 with some future directions of our work.

2 System Overview

In order to distinguish various roles of labels, we need a model of their "context" that is able to accurately predict the role of a label. The context of a label and its role can be determined by its associations with other labels. Hence, a suitable model for reasoning with contexts is a relational graph structure where the nodes correspond to labels with roles and weighted edges correspond to association strengths between nodes. Figure 3 illustrates a relational structure of the tagged labels and their association strengths. *Daniel Moore, Electrical Engineering, Computer Science* and *US University* are all weakly associated with the *Faculty* concept as attributes. The same set of value tagged labels are also strongly associated with the *Faculty* concept through *Publications* and *Contact Information* attributes.

In order to reason with the relational graph structures described above, we use the SAN [11, 12] which initializes tagged labels as nodes and their association strengths as weighted edges. Each label in the domain might have four nodes; label as a concept(C), an attribute(A), a value(V) or a nothing(N).

For each web page, SAN is activated with the nodes corresponding to the tagged labels of the page. Next, the energy spreads through the nodes proportional to their association strengths, which will also be propagated. The energy

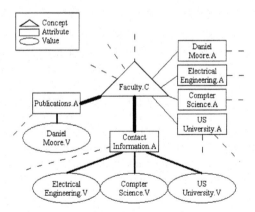

Fig. 3. A part of the graph of labels with roles and their association strengths are illustrated. Nodes with same roles have same shape. Each node has a label and its role which is concatenated at the end of the label (.C,.A,.V).

in the network will spread until it vanishes and then the activation levels of the nodes will be stabilized. Since the tagged labels are related to their associated neighbors as their context, it is expected that eventually the most activated role of each label will provide us with its context dependent correct role assignment.

For the above example, SAN was able to correct the roles of the mistagged attribute labels by iteratively spreading the energy through *Faculty.C* and then through *Publications.A* and *Contact Information.A*. Since the energy spreads proportional to the association strength eventually *Daniel Moore.V*, *Electrical Engineering.V*, *Computer Science.V* and *US University.V* will be activated more than their attribute nodes thus yielding the correct annotations.

The next section, formalizes the above SAN in details.

3   Technical Details

SAN works in three phases: *initialization*, *activation* and *inference*. The first phase is the construction of the relation graph and the remaining phases are for querying the graph. A *query* is the set of tagged labels in the web page. In the activation phase, the energies of the corresponding nodes in the query are initialized and SAN runs. The last phase is for collecting the roles of the labels in the query assigned by SAN.

3.1   Initialization

In the initialization phase the nodes and their association strengths are initialized. For the rest of the paper, we will use the formalism, $\mathcal{L}$ for the set of the labels in the domain, and l_i and r_i to express the label and role of a node i where $l_i \in \mathcal{L}$ and $r_i \in \{C, A, V, N\}$. In the network, the association strength w_{ij} between two nodes i and j is initialized using the following equation,

$$w_{ij} = w_{ji} = \frac{|l_i.r_i \leftrightarrow l_j.r_j|}{|l_i.r_i| + |l_j.r_j|},\tag{1}$$

where $|l_i.r_i|$ specifies the frequency of label l_i associated with the role r_i in the data, and $|l_i.r_i \leftrightarrow l_j.r_j|$ specifies the frequency of edges between $l_i.r_i$ and $l_j.r_j$ in the semantic hierarchies.

Although meta-data structures are hierarchical, i.e. with directed edges, we used undirected edges in our SAN model in order to enable energy spread to the neighboring context nodes as an average of their directed association strengths. Otherwise, for instance the attributes in the context wouldn't activate their corresponding concept. On the other hand, "being related" does not mean the hierarchical structure, but bi-directional relationship.

3.2   Activation

Each node i in SAN has an *activation level*, A_i and a *spreading energy*, S_i. In the activation phase, we use an iterative approach. For each Web page, we set the initial spreading energies of the nodes corresponding to the tagged labels of the page with their support. Then in each iteration the spreading energies spread to the neighbors with a decay factor α, which adjusts the total energy of the network to reduce in each iteration. Thus, it is guaranteed that the algorithm stops after a number of iterations, i.e., when the total spreading energy of the network becomes negligible. Initial values and recurrence formulas of A_i and S_i are given in the following:

$$A_i^{(0)} = 0$$
$$A_i^{(t+1)} = A_i^{(t)} + \sigma \sum_j \frac{w_{ij}.S_j^{(t)}}{\sum_k w_{jk}} \qquad (2)$$

for all nodes i in SAN and

$$S_i^{(0)} = \begin{cases} \frac{|l_i.r_i|}{|\mathcal{D}|} & \text{, if } l_i.r_i \in \mathcal{Q} \\ 0 & \text{, otherwise} \end{cases}$$
$$S_i^{(t+1)} = \alpha \sigma \sum_j \frac{w_{ij}.S_j^{(t)}}{\sum_k w_{jk}} \qquad (3)$$

where $|\mathcal{D}|$ is the number of Web pages in the domain, $\mathcal{Q}$ is the current query and iteration numbers are denoted by superscripts. σ is a normalization factor such as $\frac{1}{\sum_i \sum_j w_{ij}}$ or $\frac{1}{\max_i \{\sum_j w_{ij}\}}$. And, at a particular iteration t, the termination criterion for the activation is,

$$\sum_i S_i^{(t)} < \beta \qquad (4)$$

where β is a very small number.

3.3 Inference

In the inference phase, for each label of the Web page we determine the node with the highest activation levels to reassign its role. Formally, the role of a label l is,

$$r_{\arg\max_i \{A_i|l_i=l\}}. \qquad (5)$$

4 Complexity Analysis

In this section, we will show that the above SAN can be very efficiently implemented thus yielding a fast and scalable model.

Assuming there are n labels and m associations between labels, in the initialization phase requires only $O(n + m)$ time. For the rest of the analysis we will assume that we are working on a very large $n >> m$ which is reasonable for the web data. Hence, this phase has $O(n)$ time and memory complexity.

In the activation phase, suppose we have p web pages. Another issue is the number of iterations required per page. In each iteration, since the total activation decreases by a constant factor, α, then the number of iterations, k, will also be a constant. Finally, since SAN runs for each web page, the time complexity for all activations will be $O(pn)$.

5   Experimental Results

In this section we provide the details about the test beds we used in our experiments and present the results with these data sets. Precisions, recalls and f-measures given in the results are calculated regarding to the number of correctly and incorrectly tagged labels in the data. Experimental data and evaluation results are also available online at `http://cips.eas.asu.edu/ontominer_files/eval.htm`.

5.1   Setup

TAP Dataset: The TAP data set contains selected categories from TAP Knowledge Base 2 (TAP KB2) [13], including AirportCodes, CIA, FasMilitary, GreatBuildings, IMDB, MissileThreat, RCDB, TowerRecords and WHO. These categories alone comprise 9,068 individual Web pages and these Web pages are attribute-rich. We provide experimental results for this data set with our algorithms and compare them against the relations obtained by TAP.

CSEDepts Dataset: The CSEDepts data set consists of 60 computer science department Web sites, comprising 7,793 individual Web pages and 27,694 total number of labels. The computer science department Web sites are *meta-data-driven*, i.e., they present similar meta-data information across different departments. To demonstrate the performance of our meta-tagging algorithms, we created a smaller data set containing randomly chosen 120 Web pages from each of the *faculty* and *course* categories. We provide experimental results for this data set with our algorithms.

5.2   Preprocessing TAP Dataset

To test the SAN framework, we converted RDF files in the TAP knowledge base into triples then we applied distortions to obtain SAN inputs. SAN needs three files as inputs: (1) counts of tagged labels in the overall data, (2) tagged label pairs which are related (for the relational graph of SAN) such as (*concept, attribute*) or (*attribute, value*), and (3) sets of tagged labels for Web pages.

Regular Expression Processing: During the conversion we first split values into tokens and preprocessed the common types of values in the triples such as percentage, month, real number, currency etc... using simple regular expressions.

Distortion: For synthetic data, we considered real world situations and tried to prepare the input data as similar as possible to the data on the Web. There are two types of distortion: *deletion* and *role change*. Setting the distortion percentages for both deletion and role change first, we used the percentages as distortion probabilities for each tagged label in the Web page in our random distortion program.

   Over TAP data set, we prepared test cases for three kinds of distortions. In the first one, we only applied deletion with different percentages. In the second, similarly we only applied role changing. And the last one is the mixture of the previous two; we applied the same amount of deletions and role changes.

5.3 Experiments with the TAP Dataset

We present our results in two categories: (1) individual Web sites and (2) mixture Web sites. For both categories, SAN performed with 100% accuracy for distorted data with only deletions. The reason is, deletion does not generate ambiguity since the initial data is unambiguous. Thus, we found unnecessary to include them in the tables and figures.

Experiments with the individual Web sites provided us encouraging results to start experiments with mixture of Web sites as shown in that Tables 1 and 2. Table 1 displays SAN's performance of annotation on distorted data and Table 2 displays the final accuracies of Web sites which are initially distorted with

Table 1. SAN performance for individual Web sites. P, R and F stands for precision, recall and f-measure respectively.

Web sites	# of Web pages	Avg. # of labels per page	Distortion rates (role changes)											
			5%			20%			40%			60%		
			P	R	F	P	R	F	P	R	F	P	R	F
AirportCd.	3829	34	0.96	0.90	0.93	0.96	0.90	0.93	0.96	0.88	0.92	0.95	0.86	0.90
CIA	28	1417	0.96	0.85	0.90	0.92	0.82	0.87	0.81	0.74	0.77	0.47	0.43	0.45
FasMilitary	362	89	0.88	0.71	0.78	0.82	0.65	0.73	0.70	0.55	0.62	0.58	0.41	0.48
GreatBuild.	799	37	0.92	0.77	0.84	0.91	0.75	0.82	0.87	0.71	0.78	0.81	0.64	0.71
IMDB	1750	47	0.91	0.79	0.85	0.89	0.76	0.82	0.87	0.72	0.79	0.83	0.65	0.73
MissileThr.	137	40	0.99	0.96	0.98	0.98	0.94	0.96	0.97	0.92	0.94	0.81	0.77	0.79
RCDB	1637	49	0.98	0.91	0.94	0.95	0.88	0.92	0.91	0.85	0.88	0.84	0.77	0.80
TowerRec.	401	63	0.23	0.83	0.77	0.88	0.80	0.84	0.88	0.77	0.82	0.86	0.72	0.78
WHO	125	21	1.00	1.00	1.00	1.00	1.00	1.00	1.00	1.00	1.00	1.00	1.00	1.00
Overall	9068	200	0.87	0.86	0.89	0.92	0.83	0.88	0.89	0.79	0.84	0.79	0.69	0.74

Table 2. Label accuracies for individual Web sites

Web sites	Distortion rates (role changes)			
	5%	20%	40%	60%
AirportCodes	1.00	0.98	0.95	0.92
CIA	0.99	0.96	0.89	0.66
FasMilitary	0.99	0.93	0.82	0.65
GreatBuildings	0.99	0.95	0.88	0.78
IMDB	0.99	0.95	0.89	0.79
MissileThreat	1.00	0.99	0.97	0.87
RCDB	1.00	0.98	0.94	0.86
TowerRecords	0.99	0.96	0.91	0.83
WHO	1.00	1.00	1.00	1.00
Average	0.99	0.97	0.92	0.82

{5,20,40,60} percent role changes. Overall results show that even for 60% role changes SAN performed with 82% accuracy. The performance is usually better

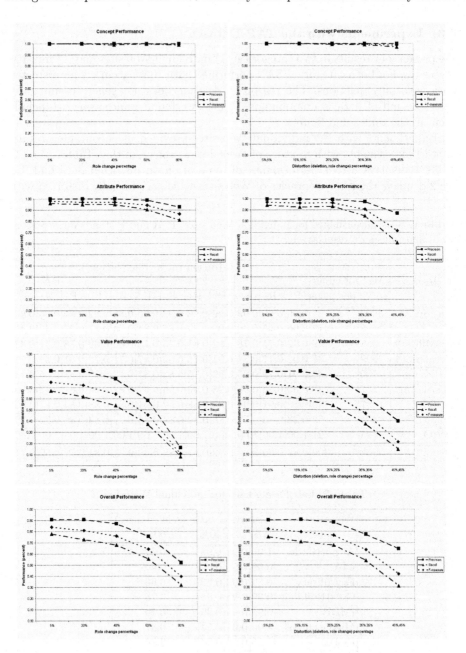

Fig. 4. SAN performance on mixed data for various distortion rates. In the left column, distortions are only role changes whereas in the right column, distortions include both deletions and role changes.

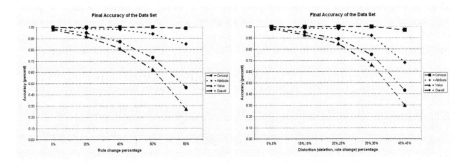

Fig. 5. Final label accuracies for different distortions. In the left figure, distortions are only role changes whereas in the right figure, distortions include both deletions and role changes.

with the Web sites containing large number of Web pages due to the high consistency and regularity among the Web pages. Another factor is the size of the tagged label set in the Web pages. The larger the set, the more difficult to keep context concentrated on the related roles in ambiguous data. That played the most important role for the low performance with *CIA* and *FasMilitary* Web sites and, high performance with *WHO* and *AirportCodes*.

In the experiments with mixture of Web sites, we tested SAN with {5,20,40,60,80} percent role changes and {(5,5),(15,15),(25,25),(35,35),(45,45)} percent (deletion, role change) distortions. Figures 4 and 5 show the performance of SAN in terms of concept, attribute and value accuracy, and the final Web site accuracy respectively. The overall performance for the mixture Web sites is slightly lower than the individual Web sites due to the fact that mixture Web sites initially have some ambiguities.

In conclusion, the overall results show that SAN can recover the TAP data up to 75% even with 60% and (35%,35%) distortion. the results are not surprising since the data set is template driven and also the relations are not complicated. Verifying the robustness of the system with template driven Web sites, next we will give the experimental results with a non-template driven data set.

5.4   Experiments with the CSEDepts Dataset

Recalling the motivating example, one can observe that labels in the faculty and course home pages of computer science departments are highly ambiguous. Many labels have different roles in different Web pages depending on the context.

In this experiment, we used the semantic partitioning algorithm to obtain initial annotations of the labels from Web pages. The initial annotations have low accuracy which is even eligible to provide enough statistics for SAN.

To compare our result, we used a simple but straightforward idea, named *majority measure*, to infer the role for each label by simply associating its majority role within the domain. The underlying assumption is that each label

Table 3. Comparison of annotations of the data using the initial semantic partitioner based method, the baseline majority method, and the spreading activation based method. P(C), R(C), F(C) denote the precision, recall and f-measure of the concept annotation. Similar notation is used for attributes (A), values (V) and nothing (N).

Method	Acc.	P(C)	R(C)	F(C)	P(A)	R(A)	F(A)	P(V)	R(V)	F(V)	P(N)	R(N)	F(N)
Courses													
Sem.Part.	57	0	0	0	64	42	50	61	75	76	21	90	37
Majority	63	50	0	7	69	48	55	72	83	77	31	85	48
SAN	81	83	94	88	82	86	83	91	80	85	44	85	62
Faculty													
Sem.Part.	62	50	0	4	51	44	47	65	80	71	34	31	32
Majority	62	7	0	2	62	51	56	64	85	73	56	35	42
SAN	83	86	95	90	74	83	79	93	79	86	60	84	69
Overall													
Sem.Part.	60	25	0	2	57	43	49	70	78	73	27	61	35
Majority	65	28	0	5	66	48	55	68	64	75	43	60	45
SAN	82	85	95	89	80	84	81	92	80	85	52	84	65

has a "unique role" in the domain. Although, this simple method improves the annotation accuracy slightly, the majority of the incorrect meta-data tags still remains weakly annotated as shown in the experimental results in Figure 6 and Table 3. Besides, we observed that the "unique role assumption" did not hold in many cases since labels might have different roles in different contexts. Figure 2 also demonstrates an example of such a case.

The individual f-measure values as shown in Figure 6 demonstrate that spreading activation based annotation achieves better performance in all the four different role annotations. The number of concept labels in the domain are fewer than other ontological types. Thus the lack of sufficient statistics for the concept annotation result in a surge in the increase of the f-measure for spreading

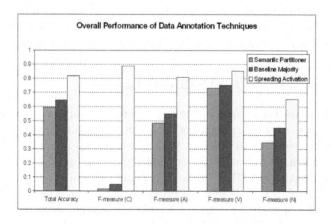

Fig. 6. Comparison of f-measure values for various data annotation techniques

activation, i.e., even though spreading activation corrects a few concept annotations, it is boosted because there are only a few number of concept labels. The f-measure for value annotation is the highest among all role annotations, as the semantic partitioner is able to annotate the values correctly in most cases and spreading activation is able to correct the remaining annotations.

These experimental results are obtained by comparing the data annotations of the algorithms to manually annotated data by eight human volunteers. The inter-human agreement on manual annotation was 87%, which indicates that the data annotations can be ambiguous and can be interpreted differently in various contexts. But our algorithms are able to perform well even in the presence of such ambiguity.

6   Conclusions and Future Work

In this paper, we have presented a system that can automatically gather and separate meta-data and their instances from various kinds of Web pages. The main focus has been on the SAN framework which is capable of reasoning on semi-structured data obtained from our semantic partitioning system. The novelty of the framework comes from spreading the energy of the contextual information thorough the overall relational graph to improve the annotations. That makes the system utilize the global regularities incorporating the contextual information.

Many research questions remain open for future work. We could identify the missing attribute labels of the values in the Web pages by identifying them using the contextual information in the spreading activation network. We could use the final annotations provided by the meta-tagging algorithm to bootstrap the semantic roles for the labels in the semantic partitioning algorithm, so it can perform the hierarchical grouping algorithm much more efficiently.

Acknowledgements. We would like to thank Rob McCool, Ramanathan V. Guha and their research group for providing us the TAP data set. We thank the reviewers of WISE for their helpful suggestions.

References

1. Ricardo Baeza-Yates and Berthier Ribeiro-Neto. *Modern Information Retrieval.* Addison Wesley, 1999.
2. Hasan Davulcu, Srinivas Vadrevu, Saravanakumar Nagarajan, and I.V. Ramakrishnan. Ontominer: Bootstrapping and populating ontologies from domain specific web sites. *IEEE Intelligent Systems*, 18(5), September 2003.
3. Srinivas Vadrevu, Saravanakumar Nagarajan, Fatih Gelgi, and Hasan Davulcu. Automated metadata and instance extraction from news web sites. In *The 2005 IEEE/WIC/ACM International Conference on Web Intelligence.* Compiegne University of Technology, France, 2005 (to appear).
4. Naveen Ashish and Craig A. Knoblock. Semi-automatic wrapper generation for internet information sources. In *Conference on Cooperative Information Systems*, pages 160–169, 1997.

5. Nickolas Kushmerick, Daniel S. Weld, and Robert B. Doorenbos. Wrapper induction for information extraction. In *Intl. Joint Conference on Artificial Intelligence*, pages 729–737, 1997.
6. Valter Crescenzi, Giansalvatore Mecca, and Paolo Merialdo. Roadrunner: Towards automatic data extraction from large web sites. In *Proceedings of 27th International Conference on Very Large Data Bases*, pages 109–118, 2001.
7. Arvind Arasu and Hector Garcia-Molina. Extracting structured data from web pages. In *ACM SIGMOD*, San Diego, USA, 2003.
8. Oren Etzioni, Michael Cafarella, Doug Downey, Stanley Kok, Ana-Maria Popescu, Tal Shaked, Stephen Soderland, Daniel S. Weld, and Alexander Yates. Web-scale information extraction in knowitall. In *Intl. World Wide Web Conf.*, 2004.
9. Fabio Ciravegna, Sam Chapman, Alexiei Dingli, and Yorick Wilks. Learning to harvest information for the semantic web. In *Proceedings of the 1st European Semantic Web Symposium*, Heraklion, Greece, 2004.
10. Stephen Dill, John A. Tomlin, Jason Y. Zien, Nadav Eiron, David Gibson, Daniel Gruhl, R. Guha, Anant Jhingran, Tapas Kanungo, Sridhar Rajagopalan, and Andrew Tomkins. Semtag and seeker: Bootstrapping the semantic web via automated semantic annotation. In *Twelth International Conference on World Wide Web*, pages 178–186, 2003.
11. A.M. Collins and E.F. Loftus. A spreading activation theory of semantic processing. *Psychological Review*, (82):407–428, 1975.
12. G. Salton and C. Buckley. On the use of spreading activation methods in automatic information. In *Proceedings of the 11th international ACM SIGIR conference on Research and development in information retrieval*, pages 147–160. ACM Press, 1988.
13. R.V. Guha and Rob McCool. Tap: A semantic web toolkit. *Semantic Web Journal*, 2003.

Semantic Partitioning of Web Pages

Srinivas Vadrevu, Fatih Gelgi, and Hasan Davulcu

Department of Computer Science and Engineering,
Arizona State University, Tempe, AZ, 85287, USA
{svadrevu, fagelgi, hdavulcu}@asu.edu

Abstract. In this paper we describe the *semantic partitioner* algorithm, that uses the structural and presentation regularities of the Web pages to automatically transform them into hierarchical content structures. These content structures enable us to automatically annotate labels in the Web pages with their semantic roles, thus yielding meta-data and instance information for the Web pages. Experimental results with the TAP knowledge base and computer science department Web sites, comprising 16, 861 Web pages indicate that our algorithm is able gather meta-data accurately from various types of Web pages. The algorithm is able to achieve this performance without any domain specific engineering requirement.

1   Introduction

The vast amount of data on the World Wide Web poses many challenges in devising effective methodologies to search and access the relevant information. Semantic Web attempts to address this problem by annotating the Web pages with contextual information so the data is uniform and can be shared across various communities. But the availability of such annotated Web pages is currently limited.

In this paper we present automated algorithms for gathering meta-data and their instances from collections of domain specific and attribute rich Web pages by annotating the labels with their semantic roles. Our system works without the requirements that (i) the Web pages need to share a similar presentation template or (ii) that they need to share the same set of meta-data among each other. Hence, we can not readily use previously developed wrapper induction techniques [1, 2] which require that the item pages should be template driven or the ontology driven extraction techniques [3, 4, 5] which require that an ontology of concepts, relationships and their value types is provided apriori in order to find matching information.

Consider the faculty home page in the example shown in Figure 1(a) that lists the attribute information in a detailed manner. Some of the attributes presented in the Web page are publications, address and telephone. Our system utilizes the presentation regularities within the Web page to annotate the labels in the Web page with their semantic roles, such as Concept (C), Attribute (A) and Value (V). This kind of annotation helps us in separating and gathering meta-data from Web pages, yielding to a powerful tool that can be utilized in various applications.

M. Kitsuregawa et al. (Eds.): WISE 2005, LNCS 3806, pp. 107–118, 2005.

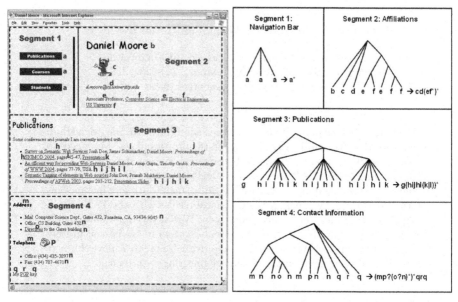

(a) Web page with Segments Marked   (b) Group Tree for each Page Segment

Fig. 1. (a) shows an example of a Faculty home page. The labels in the page are marked with their corresponding path identifier symbols. The page segments in the Web page are also marked as Segments 1 to 4. (b) shows the sequence of path identifiers, the regular expression inferred from it, and the corresponding group tree for each segment.

Unlike plain text documents, Web pages organize and present their content using hierarchies of HTML structures. Different logical blocks of content, such as taxonomies, navigation aids, headers and footers as well as various other information blocks such as indexes, are usually presented using different HTML structures. Furthermore, whenever an information block contains a list of items, then these items themselves are presented consecutively and regularly using repeating similar HTML substructures. Our semantic partitioning algorithm [6] can detect such repeating HTML substructures and organize the content into a *hierarchical content structure* consisting of *groups* of *instances*, while skipping HTML blocks that do not constitute a group. Our algorithm is *robust* in a well defined sense; it can accurately identify all groups and their instances even in the presence of certain presentation irregularities. The semantic partition algorithm requires no training and works automatically on each Web page.

The hierarchical organization of the content a Web page is useful in many scenarios. We can use such organization of the content annotate the labels of the page with semantic roles such as Concept (C), Attribute (A) and Value (V) by utilizing the context in which the Web page is obtained. For example, if we can organize the content in a Faculty home page, we would be able identify 'contact information', 'research interests', 'teaching', etc. as attributes of the concept 'Faculty', and we can identify the instances of these attributes as value labels.

Such kind of semantic tagging can then be used to empower an information retrieval system that can reason with the context and semantic labels, besides the plain bag of words. We can also use the semantically tagged Web pages to materialize a specialized information retrieval system for specific domains such as sports, restaurants, shopping and educational domains.

The key contributions and innovations of our semantic annotation algorithm can be described as follows:

- It performs extraction without the assumption that the input Web pages are template-driven. For example, we present experimental results with computer science faculty and course home pages which are not template-driven.
- It is domain independent and it does not require a previously engineered domain ontology.
- It effectively extracts and separates meta-data from the instance information in Web pages in a completely automatic fashion.

We currently do not align the extracted meta-data or instance information with any available ontology or knowledge structure. Various existing approaches developed for mapping and merging ontologies [7] can be utilized for this purpose. We also currently do not process plain text inside the Web pages, i.e., any text fragments that contain modal verbs. However, we hypothesize that the meta-data extracted from the attribute rich segments of the Web pages can be used to extract information from text with the help of natural language processing techniques [8].

The rest of the paper is organized as follows. Section 2 gives an overview of the related work. Sections 3, 4, 5, and 6 explain several phases in our semantic partitioning algorithm. Section 7 presents complexity analysis of our algorithms and Section 8 provides experimental results on various data sets. Finally we conclude in Section 9 with some future directions of our work.

2   Related Work

In this section, we present an overview of the related work from several areas and show how our system is different from them.

Template Based Algorithms: RoadRunner [9] works with a pair of documents from a collection of template generated Web pages to infer a grammar for the collection using union-free regular expressions. ExAlg [10] is another system that can extract data from template generated Web pages. ExAlg uses equivalence classes (sets of items that occur with the same frequency in every page) to build the template for the pages by recursively constructing the page template starting from the root equivalence class. TAP [11] is a system that extracts RDF triplets from template driven Web sites in order to generate a huge knowledge base that has a Web searchable interface. These algorithms are based on the assumption that the input Web pages are template driven in their presentation and are usually driven by standard meta-data. Our approach differs from all these approaches in that it does not require that the input Web pages are template driven and it can effectively handle noise.

Grammar Induction Based Algorithms: Grammar induction based systems employ a strong bias on the type and expected presentation of items within Web pages to extract instances. XTRACT [12] is such a system that can automatically extract Document Type Descriptors (DTDs) from a set of XML documents. It transforms each XML document as a sequence of identifiers and infers a common regular expression that serves as a DTD, using the Minimum Description Length (MDL) principle. Our pattern mining algorithm is different from these approaches and parses the given sequence in a bottom-up fashion and infers the grammar on-the-fly as it goes through the sequence multiple number of times.

Page Segmentation Algorithms: VIPS algorithm [13] is a vision-based page segmentation algorithm that is based on HTML based heuristics to partition the page into information blocks. Our page segmentation algorithm is similar to the VIPS algorithm in traversing the DOM (Document Object Model[1]) tree in top-down fashion, but our algorithm uses well-defined information theoretic methods in order to measure the homogeneity of the segment, whereas the VIPS algorithm is based on HTML heuristics.

3   Page Segmentation

A Web page usually contains several pieces of information [13] and it is necessary to partition a Web page into several segments (or information blocks) before organizing the content into hierarchical groups. In this section we describe our page segmentation algorithm that partitions given a Web page into flat segments.

The page segmentation algorithm relies on the DOM tree representation of the Web page and traverses it in a top-down fashion in order to segment the content of the page, which lies at the leaf nodes. We define a segment as a contiguous set of leaf nodes within a Web page. The algorithm aims to find *homogeneous segments*, where the presentation of the content within each segment is uniform. The algorithm employs a split-traverse based approach that treats all uniform set of nodes as homogeneous segments and further splits non-uniform nodes into smaller segments until each segment is homogeneous. The algorithm relies on the concept of *entropy* in order to determine whether a segment is homogeneous.

We define the notion of entropy of a node in a DOM tree in terms of the uncertainty in the root-to-leaf paths under the node. Our algorithm is based on the observation that a well organized or homogeneous system will have low entropy. We use this principle while traversing the DOM tree from root to leaf nodes in a breadth-first fashion, and split the nodes until each and every segment in the DOM tree is homogeneous.

Entropy is generally used to measure the uncertainty in the system. Hence if any random variable has low entropy, then there is less uncertainty in predicting

---

[1] http://www.w3.org/DOM/

the possible values that the random variable can take. In our case, we view each node as a random variable in terms of the root-to-leaf paths P_is under the node. We define a set of nodes in the DOM tree to be homogeneous if the paths in the random variable are uniformly distributed, and it is easy to predict the next path within the set.

Definition 3.1. *The path entropy* $H_P(N)$ *of a node* N *in the DOM tree can be defined as*

$$H_P(N) = -\sum_i^k p(i) \log p(i),$$

where $p(i)$ *is the probability of path* P_i *appearing under the node* N.

We use the concept of path entropy to partition the DOM tree into segments. The algorithm to partition a given Web page into segments is given in Algorithm 1. This algorithm is initialized with a vector of nodes containing just the root node of the DOM tree of the Web page. The *MedianEntropy* is calculated as the median of the path entropies of all the nodes in the DOM tree. Essentially we assume the nodes whose path entropy is less than the median entropy of all the nodes in the DOM tree to be homogeneous and output it as a pure segment. Otherwise, we traverse the children of the nodes in order to find the homogeneous segments. Our page segmentation algorithm is able to identify four segments in the Faculty home page as shown in Figure 1(a). Please note that we currently ignore any text fragments in the Web page that contains modal verbs as they add to the noise in identifying the patterns.

Algorithm 1. Page Segmentation Algorithm

PageSegmenter
Input: Nodes[], a node in the DOM tree
Output: A set of segments

```
1: for Each Subset S of Nodes[] do
2:    H_P(S) := Average Path Entropy of all nodes in S
3:    if H_P(S) ≤ MedianEntropy then
4:       Output all the leaf nodes under N as a new segment PS
5:    else
6:       PageSegmenter(Children(S))
7:    end if
8: end for
```

---

4   Inferring Group Hierarchy

Even though the page segmentation algorithm organizes the content in a Web page in terms of segments that present the content in a uniform fashion, each segment just contains a flat representation of the labels. In many scenarios, the content is usually represented a hierarchy of labels and we need to infer the hierarchy among the labels in order to properly depict the content structure. We define a *group* to be a contiguous collection of instances that are presented together in a Web page, where an *instance* is a repeating element of a group. Such a group hierarchy is helpful in organizing the content and determining the most general concept in the page and its attributes.

One possible way to achieve such hierarchical organization of the content is to work directly on the DOM tree in a top-down fashion [14]. But such approaches suffer from handling the noise in the leaf nodes and in successfully detecting the boundaries as look-ahead searching is expensive. An efficient alternative approach is to utilize the presentation information (embedded in their root-to-leaf tag path in the DOM tree) of the labels in order to infer a hierarchy among them. We transform each segment into a sequence of path identifiers of root-to-leaf paths of the leaf nodes and infer regular expressions from this sequence in order to extract patterns from them. For example, the path sequence corresponding to the Segment3 as marked in Figure 1(b) is $ghijhikhijhilhijhik$.

After the segment is transformed into a sequence of path identifiers, we extract patterns from it by inferring a regular expression. Our notion of regular expression contains four special operators: concatenation (.), kleene star (*), optional (?) and union (|). We build the regular expression for a given sequence by incrementally building it using bottom-up parsing. We go through the sequence several times, each time folding it using one of the four operators, until there are no more patterns left. The algorithm for building the regular expression from a sequence is described in Algorithm 2. The *InferRegEx* method is initialized for each segment in the page with its corresponding path sequence.

Once the regular expression is inferred from the sequence of path identifiers, every kleene star in the regular expression is treated as a group and its members are treated as instances of the group. For example, in Segment3 of the Web page in Figure 1(b), the regular expression $(hijhi(k|l))*$ is identified as a group which corresponds to the publications of the corresponding faculty member. The nested kleene star symbols are transformed into nested group hierarchies from the path sequence as shown in Figure 1(b).

5   Promotion

After grouping, the content of the Web page is organized into hierarchical group structures, but each of these group structures do not have any label. The labels for the groups, which we call as *group headers*, are important as they play a role in connecting the repeating set of instances with the corresponding concept or attribute label. For example, in a news Web page such as CNN, a group structure containing all the scientific articles cannot be of much use unless it is labeled as *Science* or *Sci/Tech* for indexing and searching purposes.

Bootstrapping the Promotion: In the grouping phase, all the leaf nodes that appear before the group are identified as candidate group headers and the goal of the promotion algorithm is to select the appropriate group header from these

Algorithm 2. Inferring Regular Expressions

InferRegEx(S)
Input: S, a sequence of symbols
Output: S, a new regex sequence of symbols

1: patternFound = true;
2: **repeat**
3:    patternFound = false;
4:    **for** len = 1:length(S)/2 **do**
5:      **for** i = 0:length(S) **do**
6:        currPattern := subseq(j, j+i);
7:        **if** ExtendPattern(currPattern, S, j+i+1) = true **then**
8:          ReplacePattern(currPattern, S);
9:          patternFound = true;
10:       **end if**
11:     **end for**
12:   **end for**
13: **until** patternFound = true
14: return S;
End of InferRegEx

ExtendPattern(P, S, startIndex)
Input: P, current pattern; S, a sequence of symbols; startIndex, the start index to look patterns for
Output: boolean, indicating whether the pattern is extended

1: **for** i = startIndex:length(S) **do**
2:    consensusString := IsMatch(currPattern, subseq(i,i+length(currPattern)));
3:    **if** consensusString $\neq$ *null* **then**
4:      currPattern := consensusString;
5:      ExtendPattern(currPattern, S, i+length(currPattern))
6:    **end if**
7: **end for**
End of ExtendPattern

IsMatch(P_1, P_2)
Input: P_1, first pattern; P_2, second pattern
Output: consensusString obtained by alining P_1 and P_2 or *null*

1: **if** EditDistance(P_1, P_2) $\leq \frac{MaxLength(P_1,P_2)}{3}$ **then**
2:    return Consensus(P_1, P_2)
3: **else**
4:    return *null*
5: **end if**
End of IsMatch

ReplacePattern(P, S)
Input: P, current pattern; S, a sequence of symbols
Output: none

1: replace all occurrences of the pattern P in the sequence S by a new symbol P'.
End of ReplacePattern

candidates for the group. These group headers are bootstrapped by promoting the label as the header whenever there is only one candidate for a particular group.

Frequent Label Based Promotion: Whenever similar Web pages from the same domain are available, we identify all the frequent labels in the domain from these similar pages and promote the closest frequent label that is present in the candidate headers of a group as the label for the group.

Naive Bayes Based Promotion: When many similar Web pages obtained from similar domains and from the same context are available, the candidate group headers can be used as a training data when deciding a label to promote as a group header for a group. In such scenarios, we use the words in the instances as features to train a Naive Bayes classifier and compute the likelihood of every candidate group header with a set of instances. Later we promote the closest one as the header for the group.

Path Consistent Labeling: Usually similar presentation templates are used to represent similar labels within the same Web page. Hence if one of those similarly presented labels is promoted with the above rules, then we promote all the other labels within the same Web page with the same presentation template on top of the next groups, whenever applicable.

The Figure 2 shows the final hierarchical content structure after promotion for the Web page shown in Figure 1. It can be noticed that the labels 'Daniel

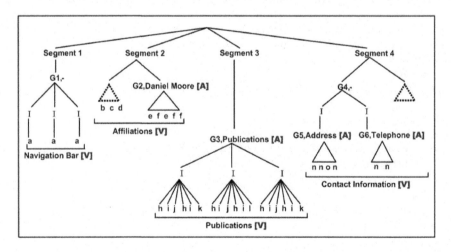

Fig. 2. The complete hierarchical structure of the Web page shown in Figure 1 after promotion. The group structures G1 through G6 with their respective promoted labels are shown in each page segment. The parts of the Web page that do not correspond to any group structure are shown with dotted triangles. The figure also illustrates meta tagging by annotating the labels with their corresponding semantic roles (C – concepts, A – attributes, V – values).

Moore', 'Publications', 'Address', and 'Phone Number' are promoted over the adjacent groups $G2$, $G3$, $G5$, and $G6$ as group headers. The groups $G1$ and $G4$ do not have any group headers as they did not have any candidate labels to promote over them.

6   Meta-tagging

After the group hierarchy has been found and the appropriate labels have been promoted on the groups, we have a powerful content structure that organizes the labels in the Web page in a uniform fashion. We utilize this content structure to annotate the labels in the Web page with meta-data tags.

In our annotation framework, we used four different tags: Concept (C), Attribute (A), Value (V), and None (N). A concept label is an abstract or symbolic tag that generally defines the context for a Web page. An attribute label is a property of a concept or the name of the relationship. A value label is an instance of the attribute relationship of a particular concept and a none label is tag that we use to denote a label that does not belong to any of these categories. The Figure 2 shows an example of the assignment of tags for the Web page shown in Figure 1(a). Within a certain context concept, we interpret all the group headers as attribute labels and the all the instance values as value labels of the corresponding attribute. Please note that this assignment of roles may not always be robust; for example, the label 'Daniel Moore' has been tagged as an attribute, but it is actually the name of the object that belongs the concept 'Faculty'. But the information present in the single Web page is not sufficient to find the correct semantic roles of the labels and approaches that utilize the global regularities within the domain [15] can be used to address this problem.

7   Complexity Analysis

In this section we analyze the computational complexity of our algorithms.

The page segmentation algorithm works directly on the DOM tree of the Web page in a top-down fashion and its complexity is $nlog(n)$, where n is the total number of nodes in the DOM tree. The group hierarchy inference phase iteratively goes through the path sequence in a bottom-up fashion until no more regular expressions are found. Assuming there are k nodes in the segment, the worst complexity of this phase is k^3. Since k is considerably smaller than the number of leaf-nodes in the Web page, this is reasonable for the Web. The promotion and labeling phases are linear in the number of nodes in the corresponding group.

8   Experimental Results

In this section, we describe the data we used in our experiments and provide the results and discussions for our experiments. In our experiments, we used two types of data sets: template driven ones and non-template driven

ones. Experimental data and evaluation results are also available online at
http://cips.eas.asu.edu/ontominer_files/eval.htm.

As the template driven data set, we selected the TAP[2] dataset, containing the categories AirportCodes, CIA, FasMilitary, GreatBuildings, IMDB, MissileThreat, RCDB, TowerRecords and WHO. These categories alone comprise 9,068 individual Web pages and these Web pages are attribute-rich. We provide experimental results for this data set with our algorithms and compare them against the relations obtained by TAP.

For the non-template driven category, we prepared our own data set which is composed of faculty and course home pages of 60 computer science departments, comprising 7,793 individual Web pages and 27,694 total number of labels. To demonstrate the performance of our meta-tagging algorithms, we created a smaller data set containing randomly chosen 120 Web pages from each of the *faculty* and *course* categories. We provide experimental results for this data set with our algorithms.

8.1   Experiments with the TAP Data Set

The Table 1 show the experimental results for the TAP data set using semantic partitioning algorithm. The algorithm achieves 100% accuracy with tagging the labels with the concept label. Since the TAP data set contains only one concept per page, the algorithm is able to easily identify the label. However, the algorithm suffers from low recall with tagging as attribute labels because some of the attribute labels are single valued and there is no group associated with them, and they are labeled as values. However the algorithm is able to tag with the attribute labels correctly whenever it does, as the precision is above 91%. As expected, the recall and precision numbers for the value label tagging are exactly opposite for the same reasons that many attribute labels are labeled as values.

Table 1. Experimental results with TAP data set using Semantic Partitioner algorithm. P(C), R(C), F(C) denote the precision, recall and F-measure of the concept annotation. Similar notation is used for attributes (A), values (V) and nones (N).

DomainName	P(C)	R(C)	F(C)	P(A)	R(A)	F(A)	P(V)	R(V)	F(V)
CIA	100	100	100	96	54	69	88	99	92
FAS Military	100	100	100	96	76	85	84	99	91
Great Buildings	100	100	100	95	61	74	88	99	93
Missile Threat	100	100	100	96	63	76	66	99	79
Roller Coster Database (RCDB)	100	100	100	78	52	46	84	91	88
Tower Records	100	100	100	75	69	72	62	55	58
WHO	100	100	100	100	94	97	85	100	92
Overall	100	100	100	91	67	74	79	92	85

---

[2] Home page is located at http://tap.stanford.edu

8.2   Experiments with the CSEDepts Data Set

Table 2 demonstrates that the initial annotations by the semantic partitioner algorithm achieves a reasonable overall accuracy around 60%. The F-measure for the concepts is very low because the number of concept labels in the domain are very few and they are ambiguously located along with the other attribute labels. However the algorithm is able to perform fairly accurately in annotating the attribute and value labels which is very vital because, these labels are the most frequent on the Web. The F-measure for value annotation is the highest among all role annotations, as the semantic partitioner is able to correctly identify the groups and thus identify the instances of the concept and attribute labels accurately.

Table 2. Results from CSEDepts Dataset. These results have been computed by manually evaluating the role assignments. P(C), R(C), F(C) denote the precision, recall and F-measure of the concept annotation. Similar notation is used for attributes (A), values (V) and nones (N).

Domain	P(C)	R(C)	F(C)	P(A)	R(A)	F(A)	P(V)	R(V)	F(V)	P(N)	R(N)	F(N)
Courses	0	0	0	64	42	50	61	75	76	21	90	37
Faculty	50	0	4	51	44	47	65	80	71	34	31	32
Overall	25	0	2	57	43	49	70	78	73	27	61	35

These experimental results are obtained by comparing the data annotations of the algorithms to manually annotated data by eight human volunteers. The inter-human agreement on manual annotation was 87%, which indicates that the data annotations can be ambiguous and can be interpreted differently in various contexts. But our algorithm is able to perform well even in the presence of such ambiguity.

9   Conclusions and Future Work

In this paper, we have presented algorithms to segment a Web page, organize the content of a Web page into a hierarchical content structure, and annotate the labels in the Web page with their semantic roles. The experimental results indicate that our algorithms were able to extract the meta-data and the instance information with high accuracy. In our future work, we identify the missing attribute labels to the values in the Web pages by identifying them using the contextual information. We plan to investigate the utility of our algorithms in extracting meta-data information for each group structure on the Web.

Acknowledgements. We would like to thank Rob McCool, Ramanathan V. Guha and their research group for sharing the TAP dataset with us. We also thank the reviewers of WISE for their suggestions.

References

1. Naveen Ashish and Craig A. Knoblock. Semi-automatic wrapper generation for internet information sources. In *Conference on Cooperative Information Systems*, pages 160–169, 1997.
2. Nickolas Kushmerick, Daniel S. Weld, and Robert B. Doorenbos. Wrapper induction for information extraction. In *Intl. Joint Conference on Artificial Intelligence (IJCAI)*, pages 729–737, 1997.
3. Fabio Ciravegna, Sam Chapman, Alexiei Dingli, and Yorick Wilks. Learning to harvest information for the semantic web. In *Proceedings of the 1st European Semantic Web Symposium*, Heraklion, Greece, 2004.
4. Stephen Dill, John A. Tomlin, Jason Y. Zien, Nadav Eiron, David Gibson, Daniel Gruhl, R. Guha, Anant Jhingran, Tapas Kanungo, Sridhar Rajagopalan, and Andrew Tomkins. Semtag and seeker: Bootstrapping the semantic web via automated semantic annotation. In *WWW*, pages 178–186, 2003.
5. Oren Etzioni, Michael Cafarella, Doug Downey, Stanley Kok, Ana-Maria Popescu, Tal Shaked, Stephen Soderland, Daniel S. Weld, and Alexander Yates. Web-scale information extraction in knowitall. In *Intl. World Wide Web Conf.*, 2004.
6. Guizhen Yang, Wenfang Tan, Saikat Mukherjee, I.V.Ramakrishnan, and Hasan Davulcu. On the power of semantic partitioning of web documents. In *Workshop on Information Integration on the Web*, Acapulco, Mexico, 2003.
7. N. Noy and M. Musen. Prompt: Algorithm and tool for automated ontology merging and alignment. In *Proceedings of the 17th Conference of the American Association for Artificial Intelligence (AAAI)*. AAAI Press, Menlo Park, US, 2000.
8. Marti A. Hearst. Untangling text data mining. In *Association for Computational Linguistics*, 1999.
9. Valter Crescenzi, Giansalvatore Mecca, and Paolo Merialdo. Roadrunner: Towards automatic data extraction from large web sites. In *VLDB*, pages 109–118, 2001.
10. Arvind Arasu and Hector Garcia-Molina. Extracting structured data from web pages. In *ACM SIGMOD*, San Diego, USA, 2003.
11. R.V. Guha and Rob McCool. Tap: A semantic web toolkit. *Semantic Web Journal*, 2003.
12. Minos Garofalakis, A. Gionis, R. Rastogi, S. Seshadri, and K. Shim. Xtract: A system for extracting document type descriptors from xml documents. In *ACM SIGMOD*, 2000.
13. Deng Cai, Shipeng Yu, Ji-Rong Wen, and Wei-Ying Ma. Vips: a vision-based page segmentation algorithm. Technical Report MSR-TR-2003-79, Microsoft Technical Report, 2003.
14. Soumen Chkrabarti. Integrating the document object model with hyperlinks for enhanced topic distillation and information extraction. In *WWW*, 2001.
15. Fatih Gelgi, Srinivas Vadrevu, and Hasan Davulcu. Improving web data annotations with spreading activation. In *The 6th International Conference on Web Information Systems Engineering (WISE)*, 2005.

A Formal Ontology Reasoning with Individual Optimization: A Realization of the Semantic Web

Pakornpong Pothipruk and Guido Governatori

School of ITEE, University of Queensland, Australia
pkp@itee.uq.edu.au, guido@itee.uq.edu.au

Abstract. Answering a query over a group of RDF data pages is a trivial process. However, in the Semantic Web, there is a need for ontology technology. Consequently, OWL, a family of web ontology languages based on description logic, has been proposed for the Semantic Web. Answering a query over the SemanticWeb is thus not trivial, but a deductive process. However, the reasoning on OWL with data has an efficiency problem. Thus, we introduce optimization techniques for the inference algorithm. This work demonstrates the techniques for instance checking and instance retrieval problems with respect to $\mathcal{ALC}$ description logic which covers certain parts of OWL.

1 Motivation

The *Semantic Web*, originated from an idea of the creator of the Web Tim Berners-lee [3], is an effort to bring back structure to information available on the Web. The structures are semantic annotations that conform to an explicit specification (called ontology) of the intended meaning of a piece of information. Thus the the Semantic Web contains implicit knowledge, and information on the Semantic Web is often incomplete since it assumes open-world semantics. In this perspective query answering on the Semantic Web is a deductive process [13].

A family of web ontology languages (OWL) based on *Description Logic* (DL) has been proposed as the languages to represent and reason with the Semantic Web. DL emphasizes clear unambiguous languages supported by complete denotational semantics and tractable/intractable reasoning algorithms [10]. Nevertheless, DL still faces problems when applied in context of the Web. One of them is the efficiency of query answering.

There are many works about DL reasoning optimization. However, most of them focus on DL-Tbox reasoning. In fact, DL-Abox reasoning, which is the basis for query answering over the Semantic Web, was seriously studied by some researchers recently. At present, there are only two prominent works for DL-Abox reasoning optimization, i.e., Instance Store [9] and RACER [8]. Instance Store uses a DL reasoner to classify Tbox and a database to store Abox. The database is also used to store a complete realization of the Abox. However, this approach only works with roll-free Abox. Thus an Abox reasoning over OWL or $\mathcal{SHOIQ}(\mathcal{D})$ will be reduced to an Abox reasoning over $\mathcal{ALCO}(\mathcal{D})$ without existential and universal quantifications, a very weak DL. Thus, this approach is inappropriate in practice. Another approach, RACER, proposes several optimization techniques for retrieval (an Abox reasoning), e.g., binary instance retrieval

M. Kitsuregawa et al. (Eds.): WISE 2005, LNCS 3806, pp. 119–132, 2005.

and dependency-based instance retrieval techniques. These techniques try to eliminate an individual, to be (SAT) tested, at-a-time.

Nevertheless, it would be better if we have another technique that can eliminate a chunk of individuals at-a-time from retrieval reasoning. Thus, we create optimization techniques that support this idea. In addition, we also introduce a novel optimization technique for instance checking, an Abox reasoning. We address the efficiency issue by a space partitioning and reduction approach.

2   Description Logic

The Semantic Web community implicitly adopted DL as a core technology for the ontology layer. One of the reasons behind this is that this logic has been heavily analyzed in order to understand how constructors interact and combine to affect tractable reasoning, see [4]. Technically, we can view the current Semantic Web, not including rule, proof and trust layers, as a DL knowledge base. Thus, answering a query posed on the Semantic Web (RDF and ontology layers) can be reduced to answering a query posed on a DL knowledge base, not taking into account low-level operations, such as name space resolution.

Description logic itself can be categorized into many different logics, distinguished by the set of constructors they provide. We focus on $\mathcal{ALC}$ description logic since it is the basis of many DL systems.

The language of $\mathcal{ALC}$ consists of an alphabet of distinct concept names **CN**, role names **RN**, and individual names **IN**, together with a set of constructors for building concept and role expressions [14].

Formally, a description logic knowledge base is a pair $\mathcal{K} = \langle \mathcal{T}, \mathcal{A} \rangle$ where $\mathcal{T}$ is a Tbox, and $\mathcal{A}$ is an Abox. The Tbox contains a finite set of axiom assertions. Axiom assertions are of the form

$$C \sqsubseteq D \mid C \doteq D,$$

where C and D are concept expressions. Concept expressions are of the form

$$A \mid \top \mid \bot \mid \neg C \mid C \sqcap D \mid C \sqcup D \mid \exists R.C \mid \forall R.C,$$

where A is an atomic concept or concept name in **CN**, R is a role name in **RN**, $\top$ (top or full domain) is the most general concept, and $\bot$ (bottom or empty set) is the least general concepts. The Abox contains a finite set of assertions about individuals of the form $a : C$ or $C(a)$ (concept membership assertion) and $(a,b) : R$ or $R(a,b)$ (role membership assertion), where a, b are names in **IN**.

The semantics of description logic is defined in terms of an interpretation $\mathcal{I} = (\Delta^{\mathcal{I}}, \bullet^{\mathcal{I}})$, consisting of a nonempty domain $\Delta^{\mathcal{I}}$ and an interpretation function $\bullet^{\mathcal{I}}$. The interpretation function maps concept names into subsets of the domain ($A^{\mathcal{I}} \subseteq \Delta^{\mathcal{I}}$), role names into subsets of the Cartesian product of the domain ($R^{\mathcal{I}} \subseteq \Delta^{\mathcal{I}} \times \Delta^{\mathcal{I}}$), and individual names into elements of the domain. The only restriction on the interpretations is the so called unique name assumption (UNA), which imposes that different individual names must be mapped into distinct elements of the domain. Given a concept name A (or role name R), the set denoted by $A^{\mathcal{I}}$ (or $R^{\mathcal{I}}$) is called the *interpretation*, or *extension*, of A (or R) with respect to $\mathcal{I}$.

The interpretation is extended to cover concepts built from negation ($\neg$), conjunction ($\sqcap$), disjunction ($\sqcup$), existential quantification ($\exists R.C$) and universal quantification ($\forall R.C$) as follows:

$$(\neg C)^{\mathcal{I}} = \Delta^{\mathcal{I}} \setminus C^{\mathcal{I}}$$
$$(C \sqcap D)^{\mathcal{I}} = C^{\mathcal{I}} \cap D^{\mathcal{I}}$$
$$(C \sqcup D)^{\mathcal{I}} = C^{\mathcal{I}} \cup D^{\mathcal{I}}$$
$$(\exists R.C)^{\mathcal{I}} = \left\{ x \in \Delta^{\mathcal{I}} \mid \exists y.\langle x,y \rangle \in R^{\mathcal{I}} \wedge y \in C^{\mathcal{I}} \right\}$$
$$(\forall R.C)^{\mathcal{I}} = \left\{ x \in \Delta^{\mathcal{I}} \mid \forall y.\langle x,y \rangle \in R^{\mathcal{I}} \rightarrow y \in C^{\mathcal{I}} \right\}$$

An interpretation $\mathcal{I}$ satisfies (entails) an inclusion axiom $C \sqsubseteq D$ (written $\mathcal{I} \models C \sqsubseteq D$) if $C^{\mathcal{I}} \subseteq D^{\mathcal{I}}$, and it satisfies an equality $C \doteq D$ if $C^{\mathcal{I}} = D^{\mathcal{I}}$. It satisfies a Tbox $\mathcal{T}$ if it satisfies each assertion in $\mathcal{T}$. The interpretation $\mathcal{I}$ satisfies a concept membership assertion $C(a)$ if $a^{\mathcal{I}} \in C^{\mathcal{I}}$, and satisfies a role membership assertion $R(a,b)$ if $(a^{\mathcal{I}}, b^{\mathcal{I}}) \in R^{\mathcal{I}}$. $\mathcal{I}$ satisfies an Abox $\mathcal{A}$ (written $\mathcal{I} \models \mathcal{A}$) if it satisfies each assertion in $\mathcal{A}$. If $\mathcal{I}$ satisfies an axiom (or a set of axioms), then we say that it is a *model* of the axiom (or the set of axioms). Two axioms (or two sets of axioms) are *equivalent* if they have the same models. Given a knowledge base $\mathcal{K} = \langle \mathcal{T}, \mathcal{A} \rangle$ we will say that the knowledge bases entails an assertion α (written $\mathcal{K} \models \alpha$) iff for every interpretation $\mathcal{I}$, if $\mathcal{I} \models \mathcal{A}$ and $\mathcal{I} \models \mathcal{T}$, then $\mathcal{I} \models \alpha$.

3   The Efficiency Issue

In DL, there are two standard types of queries allowed, i.e., boolean query and non-boolean query, which are in turn instance checking (or instantiation test) and retrieval Abox reasoning services respectively.

A boolean query $\mathcal{Q}_b$ refers to a formula of the form

$$\mathcal{Q}_b \leftarrow QExp,$$

where $QExp$ is an assertion about an individual, e.g.,

$$\mathcal{Q}_b \leftarrow Tom : (Parent \sqcap \exists hasChild.Employee)$$

The query will return one of the member of the boolean set $\{True, False\}$. $\mathcal{Q}_b$ will return $True$ if and only if every interpretation that satisfies the knowledge base $\mathcal{K}$ also satisfies $QExp$, and return $False$ otherwise.

A non-boolean query $\mathcal{Q}_{nb}$ refers to a formula of the form

$$\mathcal{Q}_{nb} \leftarrow QExp,$$

where $QExp$ is a concept expression, e.g.

$$\mathcal{Q}_{nb} \leftarrow Parent \sqcap \exists hasChild.Employee$$

In this case the query will return one of the member of the set $\{\bot, \mathcal{M}\}$, where $\bot$ refers to the empty set, and $\mathcal{M}$ represents a set of models $\{\mathcal{M}_1, \ldots, \mathcal{M}_m\}$, where each of them satisfies *QExp* with respect to the knowledge base $\mathcal{K}$. The query will return $\mathcal{M}$ if and only if there exists at least one such model, otherwise return $\perp$.

A non-boolean query (retrieval) can be trivially transformed into a set of boolean queries for all candidate tuples, i.e., retrieving sets of tuples can be achieved by repeated application of boolean queries with different tuples of individuals substituted for variables. However, answering a boolean query is in fact an entailment problem. For example, answering the boolean query:

$$\mathcal{Q}_b \leftarrow Tom : (Parent \sqcap \exists hasChild.Employee),$$

is the problem of checking whether

$$\mathcal{K} \models Tom : (Parent \sqcap \exists hasChild.Employee).$$

In a DL (supporting full negation, e.g., $\mathcal{ALC}$), boolean query or instance checking can be reduced to knowledge base satisfiability test: $\mathcal{K} \models C(a)$ iff $\mathcal{K} \cup \{\neg C(a)\}$ is unsatisfiable.

[5] gave a tableaux algorithm for solving $\mathcal{ALC}$ satisfiability problem with respect to a Tbox. They proved that their algorithm has EXPTIME-complete worst-case complexity. To the best of our knowledge, this is the latest known result of complexity proof for the $\mathcal{ALC}$ satisfiability problem with respect to a Tbox. Nevertheless, the ontology language OWL, in particular OWL-DL, of the Semantic web technology is based on $\mathcal{SHOIQ(D)}$ which is even more expressive than $\mathcal{ALC}$. Since the query answering is in fact an instance checking (or a retrieval reasoning service) which can be reduced to a satisfiability problem. It is easy to verify that the existing DL reasoning services are still not enough to be used solely with the Semantic web technology. One way to mitigate the problem is to optimize the algorithm even more. We propose an optimization technique for answering a query over a description logic knowledge base. This technique is coherent with nature of the Web in that it supports multiple-Abox environment, which corresponds to multiple data source environment in the Web.

4   Space Partitioning and Reduction Approach

This work focuses on finding an answer to the question: "How can we (efficiently) answer a query in a description logic, in particular $\mathcal{ALC}$, based-Semantic Web system, given single ontology $\mathcal{T}$, and multiple data sources $\mathcal{A}s$, examining the minimum number of data sources?". We refer to an Abox as a data source. Due to the space limitation, we present the result for boolean query only.

The idea of this section is based on the observation that $2^m > 2^n + 2^p$, where $m = n + p$ for $n, p > 1$. This means that if we can split the search space into independent parts, query the parts independently from each other, and combine the answers, then we have an improvement of the performance of the query system. This idea agrees with the understanding of the Semantic Web as a collection of sometime "unrelated" data sources. In addition we propose to attach to each data source a data source description (or source description), a compact representation of the content of the data page. This idea is similar to the intuition behind indexes in databases. In the same way that type of indexes is more or less appropriate for particular queries, source descriptions depend on the type of queries. On the other hand, as we will see in the rest of this section, the relationships among data sources are not influenced by queries. They are determined by the structure of the data itself.

4.1 The Knowledge Base

The intuition here is to associate to every Abox $\mathcal{A}$ a source description $SD(\mathcal{A})$, and to supplement the inference engine with information about the mutual dependencies of the Aboxes in the system, in order to determine which Aboxes are relevant and must be queried.

The first step is to associate to every Abox its domain.

Definition 1. *Given an Abox $\mathcal{A}$, let $H_{\mathcal{A}}$ be the Herbrand universe of $\mathcal{A}$ (i.e., the set of all the individual occurring in expression in $\mathcal{A}$). For any interpretation $\mathcal{I}$, $\Delta_{\mathcal{A}}^{\mathcal{I}}$, the domain of $\mathcal{A}$ is defined as follows:*

$$\Delta_{\mathcal{A}}^{\mathcal{I}} = \left\{ d \in \Delta^{\mathcal{I}} \mid a \in H_{\mathcal{A}} \wedge a^{\mathcal{I}} = d \right\}.$$

Definition 2 (Multiple Assertional Knowledge Base). *Given a set $\bar{\mathcal{A}}$ of Aboxes $\mathcal{A}_1, \ldots, \mathcal{A}_k$, i.e., $\bar{\mathcal{A}} = \{\mathcal{A}_1, \ldots, \mathcal{A}_k\}$ and a Tbox $\mathcal{T}$, the* multiple assertional knowledge base *is the knowledge base $\mathcal{K} = \langle \mathcal{T}, \mathcal{A} \rangle$, where $\mathcal{A}$ is the Abox obtained from the union of all the Aboxes in $\bar{\mathcal{A}}$, i.e., $\mathcal{A} = \mathcal{A}_1 \cup \mathcal{A}_2 \cup \ldots \cup \mathcal{A}_k$.*

A consequence of the above definition is that the interpretation domain of $\mathcal{A}$ is equivalent to the union of interpretation domains of the $\mathcal{A}_j$s ($\Delta_{\mathcal{A}}^{\mathcal{I}} = \bigcup_{1 \leq j \leq k} \Delta_{\mathcal{A}_j}^{\mathcal{I}}$). Since $C^{\mathcal{I}} \subseteq \Delta^{\mathcal{I}}$ by definition, thus, for arbitrary C, $C_{\mathcal{A}}^{\mathcal{I}} = \bigcup C_{\mathcal{A}_j}^{\mathcal{I}}$, for $j \in \{1, \ldots, k\}$ and $C_{\mathcal{A}_j}$ is the concept C that occurs in a concept membership assertion in $\mathcal{A}_j$.

4.2 The Algorithm

We approach the problem in 5 steps:

1. Determine dependencies among data sources, and group data sources which are dependent on each other together.
2. Associate each data source (or group of data sources) with a source description.
3. When one queries the knowledge base, exploit a procedure to find irrelevant data sources (or groups of data sources) with respect to the query, taking into account source descriptions and the query. Eliminate the irrelevant data sources (or groups of data sources) from query answering process, yielding a set of possible relevant data sources (or groups of data sources) to be queried.
4. For each remaining data source (or group of data sources) from the previous step, apply the existing query answering procedure to each of them, yielding answer from each of them.
5. Simply combine answers from the queried data sources (or group of data sources) together, since each data source (or group of data sources) is independent with the other.

Since a reasoning procedure for simple query answering in the fourth step exists [14], we will focus on other steps, which are in fact the steps of the data source space partitioning and reduction using source description.

The approach can be implemented by the following algorithm.

Algorithm 1. *partitioned_QA(query, $\mathcal{A}$):*

depset = {}
answer = False
for all $\mathcal{A}_m \in \bar{\mathcal{A}}$ **do**
        $AG(\mathcal{A}_m)$ = create_abox_graph($\mathcal{A}_m$)
end for
for all 2-combinations $\{\mathcal{A}_i, \mathcal{A}_j\}$ of $\mathcal{A}$ **do**
        if find_abox_dependency($AG(\mathcal{A}_i), AG(\mathcal{A}_j)$) = True **then**
                add dep($\mathcal{A}_i, \mathcal{A}_j$) to depset
        end if
end for
$\mathcal{A}^g$ = combine_dependent_abox($\mathcal{A}$,depset)
create_source_description($\mathcal{A}^g$)
for all $\mathcal{A}_h \in \mathcal{A}^g$ **do**
        if query_relevancy($SD(\mathcal{A}_h)$,*query*) = True **then**
                answer = answer $\vee$ instance_checking($\mathcal{A}_h$,*query*)
        end if
end for

First, since an Abox $\mathcal{A}_i$ can overlap with another Abox $\mathcal{A}_j$, we must consider multiple Aboxes at the same time. However, we will not treat all of the Aboxes as a single Abox, because, in this case, the associated reasoning is computational expensive. Consequently, we need some additional procedure to determine dependencies among Aboxes since we need to know which Aboxes should be considered together. In other word, we need to group dependent Aboxes together and treat them as a new single Abox consisting of multiple dependent Aboxes. To make this clear, we need to formally define the dependency between Aboxes in the context of Abox reasoning.

Firstly, we will introduce graph notation for an Abox.

Definition 3 (Abox Graph). *An Abox graph for an Abox $\mathcal{A}$, $AG(\mathcal{A})$, consists of a set N of nodes (vertexes), a set E of edges (arcs), and a function f from E to $\{(a,b) \mid a,b \in N\}$. Each edge, label ed R_i, represents exactly a role name of a role membership assertion $R_i(a,b) \in \mathcal{A}$. Hence, each node represents exactly one individual name. An Abox graph is a directed multigraph.*

The create_abox_graph function will produce an Abox graph $AG(\mathcal{A}_m)$ for each Abox $\mathcal{A}_m$. We will say that an Abox $\mathcal{A}$ is *connected* if its Abox graph $AG(\mathcal{A})$ is weakly connected (see its definition in any discrete mathematics textbook).

Definition 4 (Abox Dependency). *Given two connected Aboxes $\mathcal{A}_1$ and $\mathcal{A}_2$, where $\mathcal{A} = \mathcal{A}_1 \cup \mathcal{A}_2$; $\mathcal{A}_1$ and $\mathcal{A}_2$ depend on each other if the graph of Abox $\mathcal{A}$ is (weakly) connected, and independent otherwise.*

Proposition 1. *Let $\mathcal{A}_1$ and $\mathcal{A}_2$ be two independent Aboxes in multiple assertional knowledge base. Let $\Delta_{\mathcal{A}_1}^{\mathcal{I}}$ and $\Delta_{\mathcal{A}_2}^{\mathcal{I}}$ be the domains of $\mathcal{A}_1$ and $\mathcal{A}_2$, then:*

- $\Delta_{\mathcal{A}_1}^{\mathcal{I}} \cap \Delta_{\mathcal{A}_2}^{\mathcal{I}} = \emptyset;$
- *for any concept C, $C_{\mathcal{A}_1}^{\mathcal{I}} \cap C_{\mathcal{A}_2}^{\mathcal{I}} = \emptyset$, where $C_{\mathcal{A}_i}^{\mathcal{I}}$ is the extension of C in $\Delta_{\mathcal{A}_i}^{\mathcal{I}}$.*

If $\mathcal{A}$ is unconnected, i.e., $\mathcal{A}_1$ and $\mathcal{A}_2$ are independent on each other, then it means that $\mathcal{A}_1$ and $\mathcal{A}_2$ do not share any common node (individual) because Aboxes $\mathcal{A}_1$ and $\mathcal{A}_2$ are already connected by themselves. Thus, we can use Abox graphs to determine Abox dependency.

For any unordered pair of Aboxes $\{\mathcal{A}_i, \mathcal{A}_j\}$, we determine the Abox dependency between the two Aboxes ($\mathcal{A}_i$ and $\mathcal{A}_j$). According to the definition, Abox dependency can be detected using the connectivity of the Abox graph of $\mathcal{A}$, i.e., $AG(\mathcal{A})$, where $\mathcal{A} = \mathcal{A}_i \cup \mathcal{A}_j$. Thus, we can exploit any UCONN (undirected graph connectivity problem) algorithm for this purpose. The function find_abox_dependency$(AG(\mathcal{A}_i), AG(\mathcal{A}_j))$ returns True if two Aboxes $\mathcal{A}_i$ and $\mathcal{A}_j$ depend on each other, and False otherwise. If the function returns True, then we add dep$(\mathcal{A}_i, \mathcal{A}_j)$ to the set "depset", i.e., the set that stores dependency value of each pair of Aboxes. Then we virtually combine dependent Aboxes together as a group by the function combine_dependent_abox$(\mathcal{A}, depset)$. The Abox $\bar{\mathcal{A}}$ will become $\mathcal{A}^g$, i.e., the set of already-grouped Aboxes and ungrouped Aboxes. Each Abox in $\mathcal{A}^g$ is independent of each other.

Next, we need to show two things:

1. if two Aboxes depend on each other, then a DL reasoning service, in particular instance checking and retrieval, needs to take into account the two Aboxes together;
2. if two Aboxes are independent of each other, then a DL reasoning over the two Aboxes can be done separately over each of them.

The following theorem supports the last step in our approach. It provides the reason why we can simply combine the answer from each $\mathcal{A}_i \in \mathcal{A}^g$ together. In other words it states that the the instance checking (a query answering) problem over $\mathcal{A}^g$ can be reduced to separate instance checking problems over each $\mathcal{A}_i$.

Theorem 1 (Independent Abox and Instance Checking). *Given two connected Aboxes $\mathcal{A}_1$ and $\mathcal{A}_2$, where $\mathcal{A} = \mathcal{A}_1 \cup \mathcal{A}_2$, If $\mathcal{A}_1$ and $\mathcal{A}_2$ are independent on each other, then for any boolean query $\mathcal{Q}$ and Tbox $\mathcal{T}$, $\langle \mathcal{T}, \mathcal{A} \rangle \models \mathcal{Q}$ if and only if $\langle \mathcal{T}, \mathcal{A}_1 \rangle \models \mathcal{Q}$ or $\langle \mathcal{T}, \mathcal{A}_2 \rangle \models \mathcal{Q}$.*

Proof. First, we prove the only if direction, and we will assume that both $\mathcal{A}_1$ and $\mathcal{A}_2$ are consistent with $\mathcal{K}$, since if one of them is not then the theorem trivially holds.

Since $\mathcal{A}_1$ and $\mathcal{A}_2$ are *independent* on each other, by Proposition 1, we have $\Delta_1^{\mathcal{I}} \cap \Delta_2^{\mathcal{I}} = \emptyset$, where $\Delta_1^{\mathcal{I}}$ and $\Delta_2^{\mathcal{I}}$ are the domains of $\mathcal{A}_1$ and $\mathcal{A}_2$ respectively.

Suppose $\langle \mathcal{T}, \mathcal{A}_1 \rangle \not\models \mathcal{Q}$ and $\langle \mathcal{T}, \mathcal{A}_2 \rangle \not\models \mathcal{Q}$. These mean $\exists \mathcal{I}_1$ such that $\mathcal{I}_1 \models \mathcal{A}_1, \mathcal{I}_1 \models \mathcal{T}, \mathcal{I}_1 \models \neg \mathcal{Q}$, and $\exists \mathcal{I}_2$ such that $\mathcal{I}_2 \models \mathcal{A}_2, \mathcal{I}_2 \models \mathcal{T}$ and $\mathcal{I}_2 \models \neg \mathcal{Q}$. Note that $\mathcal{I}_1$ and $\mathcal{I}_2$ are arbitrary interpretations of $\mathcal{A}_1$ and $\mathcal{A}_2$ respectively with the only constraint of being interpretations of $\mathcal{T}$.

Since $\mathcal{A} = \mathcal{A}_1 \cup \mathcal{A}_2$ and $\Delta_1^{\mathcal{I}} \cap \Delta_2^{\mathcal{I}} = \emptyset$, we can create an interpretation $\mathcal{I}$ of $\mathcal{A}$ such that $\mathcal{I}$ is the union of the interpretation $\mathcal{I}_1$ of $\mathcal{A}_1$ and the interpretation $\mathcal{I}_2$ of $\mathcal{A}_2$ ($\mathcal{I} = \mathcal{I}_1 \cup \mathcal{I}_2$). More precisely, $\mathcal{I} = \langle \Delta^{\mathcal{I}}, \bullet^{\mathcal{I}} \rangle$ is defined as follows:

(i) $\Delta^{\mathcal{I}} = \Delta_1^{\mathcal{I}} \cup \Delta_2^{\mathcal{I}}$ because $\mathcal{A} = \mathcal{A}_1 \cup \mathcal{A}_2$, where $\Delta^{\mathcal{I}}$ is the domains of $\mathcal{A}$

(ii) For any constant a,

$$a^{\mathcal{I}} = \begin{cases} a^{\mathcal{I}_1} & \text{if } a \text{ occurs in } \mathcal{A}_1 \\ a^{\mathcal{I}_2} & \text{if } a \text{ occurs in } \mathcal{A}_2 \end{cases}$$

(iii) For any concept C, $C^{\mathcal{I}} = C^{\mathcal{I}_1} \cup C^{\mathcal{I}_2}$

(iv) For any role R, $R^{\mathcal{I}} = R^{\mathcal{I}_1} \cup R^{\mathcal{I}_2}$

Since $\Delta_1^{\mathcal{I}} \cap \Delta_2^{\mathcal{I}} = \emptyset$, then it is immediate to verify that $\mathcal{I}$ is indeed an interpretation, and $\mathcal{I} \models T$, since $\mathcal{I}_1 \models T$ and $\mathcal{I}_2 \models T$.

Since $\mathcal{I}_1 \models \neg Q$ and $\mathcal{I}_2 \models \neg Q$, from (iii), we can immediately verify $\mathcal{I} \models \neg Q$, i.e., $(\neg Q)^{\mathcal{I}} = (\neg Q)^{\mathcal{I}_1} \cup (\neg Q)^{\mathcal{I}_2}$, where $\mathcal{I}$ is the interpretation of $\mathcal{A}$. From (ii), (iii) and (iv), we can also infer that $(\mathcal{A})^{\mathcal{I}} = (\mathcal{A}_1)^{\mathcal{I}_1} \cup (\mathcal{A}_2)^{\mathcal{I}_2}$, i.e., $\mathcal{I} \models \mathcal{A}$.

Since $\mathcal{A}_1$ and $\mathcal{A}_2$ are assumed to be consistent by themselves, we only need to prove that there is no clash between $\mathcal{A}_1$ and $\mathcal{A}_2$. For an arbitrary concept C, by general definition in description logic, we get $C^{\mathcal{I}} \subseteq \Delta^{\mathcal{I}}$. In addition, we get $(\neg C)^{\mathcal{I}} = (\Delta^{\mathcal{I}} \setminus C^{\mathcal{I}}) \subseteq \Delta^{\mathcal{I}}$. Thus, for arbitrary C, $C^{\mathcal{I}_1} \subseteq \Delta_1^{\mathcal{I}}$ and $(\neg C)^{\mathcal{I}_2} \subseteq \Delta_2^{\mathcal{I}}$. Since $\Delta_1^{\mathcal{I}} \cap \Delta_2^{\mathcal{I}} = \emptyset$, therefore, $C^{\mathcal{I}_1} \cap (\neg C)^{\mathcal{I}_2} = \emptyset$, which infers that no clash can occur between $\mathcal{A}_1$ and $\mathcal{A}_2$.

Thus for the interpretation $\mathcal{I}$ of $\mathcal{A}$, we have $(\mathcal{A})^{\mathcal{I}} \neq \emptyset$ and $(\neg Q)^{\mathcal{I}} \neq \emptyset$, i.e., $\mathcal{I} \models \mathcal{A} \wedge \mathcal{I} \models \neg Q$ which is the definition of $\mathcal{A} \not\models Q$. Therefore, $\mathcal{A} \models Q$ only if $\mathcal{A}_1 \models Q$ or $\mathcal{A}_2 \models Q$ which infers $\langle T, \mathcal{A} \rangle \models Q$ only if $\langle T, \mathcal{A}_1 \rangle \models Q$ or $\langle T, \mathcal{A}_2 \rangle \models Q$.

For the if direction, we assume that either 1) $\langle T, \mathcal{A}_1 \rangle \models Q$ or 2) $\langle T, \mathcal{A}_2 \rangle \models Q$. In both cases, by monotonicity, we obtain $\langle T, \mathcal{A}_1 \cup \mathcal{A}_2 \rangle \models Q$ which is $\langle T, \mathcal{A} \rangle \models Q$.   □

In the second step of the approach, we associate each Abox (or group of Aboxes) with a source description, using create_source_description($\mathcal{A}^g$). A source description can be view as a surrogate of each data source. Surrogate refers to a brief representation of an information source that is designed to convey an indication of the information source's intent [7]. A good surrogate has two major properties: (1) it corresponds to some common understanding in the user's community, and (2) it can be organized in a way that is searchable.

Source descriptions are used to determine the relevancy of each Abox $\mathcal{A}_h \in \mathcal{A}^g$ with respect to a query. Source descriptions depend on the type of the query. For boolean queries, the source description of each Abox $\mathcal{A}_h \in \mathcal{A}^g$ can be a simple list of all individuals appearing in the Abox $\mathcal{A}_h$. The idea is if the query does not satisfy $SD(\mathcal{A}_h)$ (necessary and sufficient conditions), it is guaranteed that the query over Abox $\mathcal{A}_h$ will fail, i.e., it returns False. This is done by the function query_relevancy($SD(\mathcal{A}_h)$,query). This function returns False if the query does not satisfy $SD(\mathcal{A}_h)$, i.e., the Abox $\mathcal{A}_h$ is fully irrelevant to the query, and will contribute nothing to the answer of the query. The function works by extracting an individual from the query, then checking if it is in the source description $SD(\mathcal{A}_h)$ or not. If it is, then it queries the Abox $\mathcal{A}_h$, using normal boolean query answering procedure instance_checking($\mathcal{A}_h$,query).

This can be formalised as follows:

Definition 5. *Let $\mathcal{A}$ be an Abox, the boolean query source description for $\mathcal{A}$ ($SD_b(\mathcal{A})$) is the the Herbrand universe of $\mathcal{A}$, i.e., $SD_b(\mathcal{A}) = H_{\mathcal{A}}$.*

We can now prove soundness and completeness of the above choice of source descriptions.

Theorem 2 (Soundness and Completeness of Instance Checking Optimization).
Let Q be a boolean query. Let $A \not\sharp Q$ represents when query_relevance($SD_b(A), Q$) returns False, i.e., A is not relevant the query Q, and let $A\sharp Q$ represents otherwise. If $A \not\sharp Q$ then $\langle T, \bar{A} - \{A\} \rangle \models Q$ if and only if $\langle T, \bar{A} \rangle \models Q$.

Proof. Suppose $A \not\sharp Q$. This means $a \notin SD_B(A)$, where Q is $C(a)$.

First, we prove the only if direction. Suppose $\langle T, \bar{A} - \{A\} \rangle \models Q$. However, $\bar{A} - \{A\} \subseteq \bar{A}$. By monotonicity, we obtain $\langle T, \bar{A} \rangle \models Q$.

Therefore, $\langle T, \bar{A} - \{A\} \rangle \models Q$ only if $\langle T, \bar{A} \rangle \models Q$.

For the if direction, suppose $\langle T, \bar{A} \rangle \models Q$. We, then, prove by case.

Case 1: Q is a tautology. It is immediate to verify that $\langle T, \bar{A} - \{A\} \rangle \models Q$ is true.

Case 2: Q is not a tautology. From Lemma 1, we obtain $\langle T, A \rangle \not\models Q$. In addition, $\langle T, \bar{A} \rangle \models Q$ is equal to $\langle T, \bar{A} - \{A\} \cup \{A\} \rangle \models Q$. By Theorem 1, we get $\langle T, \bar{A} - \{A\} \rangle \models Q$ or $\langle T, A \rangle \models Q$. Since $\langle T, A \rangle \not\models Q$, we obtain $\langle T, \bar{A} - \{A\} \rangle \models Q$.

These cases cover all possibilities. Therefore, $\langle T, \bar{A} - \{A\} \rangle \models Q$ if $\langle T, \bar{A} \rangle \models Q$.

Therefore, if $A \not\sharp Q$ then $\langle T, \bar{A} - \{A\} \rangle \models Q$ if and only if $\langle T, \bar{A} \rangle \models Q$. □

Lemma 1. *Let Q be a boolean query $C(a)$. If $a \notin SD_B(A)$ and Q is not a tautology, then $\langle T, A \rangle \not\models Q$.*

Proof. Suppose $a \notin SD_B(A)$. By definition, this means $a \notin \Delta_A^I$. In other words, there is no a in A, i.e., $C(a)$ is definitely not in A. Supppose Q is not a tautology. At this state, we want to prove $\langle T, A \rangle \not\models C(a)$ which is equal to proving that $\langle T, A \rangle \cup \{\neg C(a)\}$ is satisfiable. Since $\langle T, A \rangle$ is consistent, $\langle T, A \rangle \cup \{\neg C(a)\}$ will be unsatisfiable only if either $C(a)$ is in A or $C(a)$ is a tautology. Since neither of them is true, $\langle T, A \rangle \cup \{\neg C(a)\}$ is satisfiable. Consequently, we prove $\langle T, A \rangle \not\models C(a)$.

Therefore, if $a \notin SD_B(A)$ and Q is not a tautology, then $\langle T, A \rangle \not\models Q$. □

Finally, in the last step we simply combine the answers together using disjunction. Again this step is justified by Theorem 1.

5   A Comprehensive Example

Suppose we have a knowledge bases $\mathcal{K} = \langle T, A \rangle$, where the data is distributed over four Aboxes, i.e., $A = A_1 \cup A_2 \cup A_3 \cup A_4$.

Suppose the Tbox T is a follows:

$T = \{Man \doteq \neg Female, Woman \doteq Human \sqcap Female, Man \doteq Human \sqcap Male,$

$\quad Mother \doteq Woman \sqcap \exists hasChild.Human, Father \doteq Man \sqcap \exists hasChild.Human,$

$\quad Parent \doteq Mother \sqcup Father, Organization \doteq Profit \sqcup Charity,$

$\quad Employee \doteq Human \sqcap \exists workAt.Organization,$

$\quad Profit \doteq Company \sqcup Partnership \sqcup SoleOwner Charity \doteq \neg Profit,$

$\quad CommunicationCompany \doteq Company \sqcap \exists provideService.CommunicationService,$

$\quad CommunicationService \doteq MobileService \sqcup TelephoneService \sqcup InternetService\}$

Suppose that the four Aboxes are as follows:

$\mathcal{A}_1 = \{Man(Tom), Man(Peter), Woman(Mary), SoleOwner(ThaiOrchid),$
$\quad hasChild(Tom, Peter), workAt(Peter, AIS), attend(Peter, MobileSys2003),$
$\quad hasChild(Tom, Mary), workAt(Mary, ThaiOrchid), studyAt(Mary, ITEE)\}$

$\mathcal{A}_2 = \{Department(ITEE), Faculty(EPSA),$
$\quad University(UQ), Conference(MobileSys2003), partOf(ITEE, EPSA),$
$\quad facultyIn(EPSA, UQ), locatedIn(UQ, Australia)\}$

$\mathcal{A}_3 = \{CommunicationCompany(AIS), Conference(MobileSys2003),$
$\quad CommunicationCompany(DTAC), locatedIn(AIS, Thailand),$
$\quad sponsor(MobileSys2003, AIS), sponsor(MobileSys2003, DTAC),$
$\quad hold(ITEE, MobileSys2003)\}$

$\mathcal{A}_4 = \{Charity(PinTao), CharityProject(MMM), CharityProject(TOLS),$
$\quad locatedIn(PinTao, Malaysia), propose(PinTao, MMM), propose(PinTao, TOLS)\}$

We simply create the Abox graph for each Abox, yielding four Abox graphs: $AG(\mathcal{A}_1)$, $AG(\mathcal{A}_2)$, $AG(\mathcal{A}_3)$, and $AG(\mathcal{A}_4)$. For every combination of two Aboxes of $\mathcal{A}$, we determine the Abox dependency between them using the find_abox_dependency function. The function will combine the two Aboxes together, and apply UCONN algorithm to the graph of the combined Abox.

If the graph is connected, then the two Aboxes depend on each other. We, then, add $dep(\mathcal{A}_i, \mathcal{A}_j)$ to the set depset as they are dependent, i.e., the function returns True. We get

$$depset = \{dep(\mathcal{A}_1, \mathcal{A}_2), dep(\mathcal{A}_1, \mathcal{A}_3), dep(\mathcal{A}_2, \mathcal{A}_3)\}$$

Since we know that $\mathcal{A}_1$ depends on $\mathcal{A}_2$, and also on $\mathcal{A}_3$, we virtually group them together, i.e., we will consider the data in both three Aboxes together. This is done by the combine_dependent_abox($\mathcal{A}$,depset) function. As a result we have $\mathcal{A}^g = \{\mathcal{A}_{123}, \mathcal{A}_4\}$, where $\mathcal{A}_{123} = \mathcal{A}_1 \cup \mathcal{A}_2 \cup \mathcal{A}_3$.

At this stage, we create source description for each Abox in $\mathcal{A}^g$, using the create_source_description($\mathcal{A}^g$) procedure:

- $SD(\mathcal{A}_{123}) = (AIS, Australia, DTAC, EPSA, ITEE, Mary,$
  $\quad MobileSys2003, Peter, Thailand, ThaiOrchid, Tom, UQ)$
- $SD(\mathcal{A}_4) = (Malaysia, MMM, PinTao, TOLS)$

Suppose, we have a boolean query $Tom : (Parent \sqcap \exists hasChild.Employee)$. For every $\mathcal{A}_h \in \mathcal{A}^g$, we determine relevancy with respect to the query, using the procedure query_relevancy($SD(\mathcal{A}_h)$,query). The procedure will extract "Tom" from the query, and search whether "Tom" is in $SD(\mathcal{A}_h)$ or not. In this case, "Tom" is in $SD(\mathcal{A}_{123})$, but not in $SD(\mathcal{A}_4)$. Consequently, we simply query $\mathcal{A}_{123}$, using the instance_checking($\mathcal{A}_h$, query) function. The result from instance checking test of the query in $\mathcal{A}_{123}$ is True. Thus, answer = False $\vee$ True = True, which is the same result as when we query the whole Abox $\mathcal{A}$.

6   Complexity Analysis

Each Abox Graph can be trivially generated in $O(n^2)$, where n is the number of assertions in Abox $\mathcal{A}$. The next part is Abox dependency determination. We need $k(k-1)/2$ comparisons (2-combinations) of unordered pair of Aboxes, where k is the number of Aboxes in $\mathcal{A}$. Each comparison needs UCONN algorithm. UCONN can be solved by DFS in $O(v^2)$, where v is the number of individuals in each Abox.

For source description, the create_source_description($\mathcal{A}^g$) procedure requires not more than $O(n^2)$ for all Aboxes, since it can be implemented using the quick sort algorithm. To determine the relevancy of an Abox to a query, we call the function query_relevancy($SD(\mathcal{A}_h)$,$query$) that operates in $O(n)$ for sequential search. Finally, we simply use the instance_checking($\mathcal{A}_h$,$query$) function to find the answer for each Abox, and simply combine the answer.

Till now, our space partitioning and reduction approach exploits at most PTIME algorithms in each part, i.e., the Abox dependency part and the source description part. Overall, our algorithm can be operated in PTIME, not including the instance checking part. Since the instance checking part is known to be solved in EXPTIME-complete, assuming P $\neq$ EXPTIME, the overall algorithm still operates in EXPTIME, but with a *reduced exponent*. The Abox dependency part will partition the search space, thus the exponent will be reduced if there are at least two partitions, e.g., the time complexity is reduced from 2^m to $2^n + 2^p$, where $m = n + p$. The source description part will further reduce the exponent if there are some Aboxes which can be eliminated from the process, e.g., the time complexity is reduced from 2^m to 2^q, where $q < m$.

7   The Extension

We intend to extend our work to non-boolean query answering (Abox retrieval) optimization. The space partitioning, Theorem 1, can be easily extended to cover Abox retrieval reasoning services. The main differences will be with the source description. Furthermore, we will investigate possible extensions of Theorem 1 to more expressive DLs.

In the nutshell, a source description of an Abox $\mathcal{A}$ for retrieval ($SD(\mathcal{A})$) consists of several types of source descriptions. In the basic setting, we shall have $SD^C(\mathcal{A})$ and $SD^R(\mathcal{A})$. $SD^C(\mathcal{A})$ is a set of *least common subsumer*s or *LCS*s of concepts appeared in concept membership assertions in the Abox $\mathcal{A}$. $SD^R(\mathcal{A})$ is a set of roles appeared in role membership assertions in the Abox $\mathcal{A}$. Let Q be a non-boolean query, C,D be concept expressions, and $\mathcal{A}_h$ be an Abox. The source description usage is different for each form of Q, for example:

- For the case $Q \leftarrow C$, $\mathcal{A}_h$ is relevant to Q if $\exists s \in SD^C(\mathcal{A}_h), Q \sqsubseteq s$
- For the case $Q \leftarrow C \sqcap D$, $\mathcal{A}_h$ is relevant to Q if $\mathcal{A}_h$ is relevant to C *and* $\mathcal{A}_h$ is relevant to D.
- For the case $Q \leftarrow C \sqcup D$, $\mathcal{A}_h$ is relevant to Q if $\mathcal{A}_h$ is relevant to C *or* $\mathcal{A}_h$ is relevant to D.
- For the case $Q \leftarrow \exists R.C$, $\mathcal{A}_h$ is relevant to Q if $R \in SD^R(\mathcal{A}_h)$ *and* $\mathcal{A}_h$ is relevant to C.
- For the case $Q \leftarrow \neg C$, $\mathcal{A}_h$ is relevant to Q if $\mathcal{A}_h$ is irrelevant to C.

These operations can be recursive. Hence, we can achieve a methodology for determine relevancy of the Abox $\mathcal{A}_h$ with respect to the arbitrary-formed non-boolean query Q. Note that the correctness of the above methodology follows from the independent Abox theorem, extended for non-boolean query.

8   Discussion and Related Works

The optimization approach presented in this work is based on the procedure normally adopted for deduction over a description logic knowledge base (the query answering process over such knowledge base is a deduction process). In particular we refer to the tableaux algorithm. Traditionally, tableaux algorithm was designed to prove the satisfiability problem. The main idea behind this algorithm is based on a notational variant of the first order tableaux calculus. In fact, a tableaux algorithm tries to prove the satisfiability of a concept expression C by demonstrating a nonempty model of C. It constructively builds a model for a given concept. The process of constructing a model proceeds by completing a constraint system [14], using a set of consistency-preserving completion (or expansion) rules. The process will continue if it can extend the existing constraint system. In $\mathcal{ALC}$ reasoning with $\mathcal{T}$ and $\mathcal{A}$, the process will proceed via a role membership assertion. The idea behind our work is to specify the condition where we guarantee that the reasoning process over $\mathcal{A}_1$ will never proceed to $\mathcal{A}_2$ if $\mathcal{A}_1$ and $\mathcal{A}_2$ are independent from each other. This optimization, in particular, the space partitioning part, can be seen as a divide-and-conquer technique. A general disadvantage of this kind of technique is the parts overlap. However, in this work we proposed a methodology to avoid overlapping part, thus, it does not suffer from such disadvantage of the divide-and-conquer technique.

Apparently, the major drawback of this approach is obviously the additional cost from Abox dependencies and source descriptions determination. But the cost is still in PTIME ($\subseteq$ PSPACE), as shown in previous section. One may argue that our space partitioning approach would support the reduction in apparent worst-case complexity for query answering, but at a high price in practice, in particular for a large knowledge base. However, this is not a scholarly argument, because the larger the knowledge base is, the less the relative cost is (recall that the normal query answering is in EXPTIME while the additional cost is in PTIME). Thus, our approach should behave well in practice. The only issue that we must give additional attention to is a design of effective Abox dependency information distribution, minimizing information exchange between nodes in the network, where each node represents an Abox. In addition, if the data pages do not change frequently, then there is no need to recompute the dependency of the Abox. In addition data source can be organised in indexes for fast retrieval.

This approach can be applied to a system which allows only one ontology (or Tbox). Though the Semantic Web technology tends to exploit multiple ontologies. In ontology-based integration of information area [15], we can divide the exploitation of ontology into 3 approaches: single-ontology approach, e.g., SIMS [2], multiple-ontologies approach, e.g., OBSERVER [11], and hybrid-ontology approach, e.g., COIN [6]. The multiple-ontologies approach requires additional mapping specifications between each pair of ontologies. Since such mappings are infact ontologies themselves [1], we need additional $n(n-1)/2$ ontologies for such an approach, where n is number of existing ontologies in the system. In hybrid-ontology approach, a global ontology and additional n mapping specifications (between global ontology and each local ontology) are required. Hence the single-ontology approach can be viewed as generalization of the other two approaches. Thus, we follow such approach. In addition, since the aim of our work is to study how to query multiple data sources, thus we do not need to add complexity arisen from ontology mapping in the last two approaches. Simple single-ontology approach, but not trivial for query answering, is enough. Note that we can extend our work to include multiple ontologies later when the research about ontology binding and ontology mapping and ontology integration is more mature.

This approach can be applied to a system which allows multiple data sources (or Aboxes). We can think of an Abox as an RDF document. In addition RDF databases try to partition RDF triples in disjoint graphs , where each graph can be understood as a data page of our approach. However, recent research has shown that there are several semantic problems when people tried to layer an ontology language, i.e., OWL, on top of the RDF layer [12]. Such problems stem from some features/limitations of RDF, e.g., no restriction on the use of built-in vocabularies, and no restriction on how an RDF statement can be constructed since it is just a triple. Thus, this implies that the ontology layer may be not compatible with the RDF layer of the Semantic Web. However, there is a work proposing additional layer on top of the RDF layer, i.e., RDF(FA) [12]. This layer corresponds directly to Aboxes, thus RDF(FA) may be very useful in the future.

There are few works related to our work, i.e., Instance Store [9] and RACER [8]. Both works propose retrieval optimization techniques. Hence, our approach seems to be the first approach for Abox instance checking optimization. Instance Store imposes an unnatural restriction on Abox, i.e., enforcing Abox to be role-free. This is a severe restriction since role names are included even for $\mathcal{FL}^-$ ($\mathcal{ALC}$ without atomic negation), a DL with limited expressive power. RACER proposes several innovative Abox reasoning optimization techniques. However, RACER allows single Abox, while our approach allows multiple Aboxes. Thus after we apply our techniques to reduce the reasoning search space, we can apply RACER techniques to reduce it further. Consequently, the approach taken in RACER seems to be complementary to ours. We will investigate the combination of our approach and RACER approach in the future.

Acknowledgements

This work was partially supported by the University of Queensland Early Career Researcher Grant no. 2004001458 on "A System for Automated Agent Negotiation with Defeasible Logic-Based Strategies".

References

1. J. Akahani, K. Hiramatsu, and K. Kogure. Coordinating heterogeneous information services based on approximate ontology translation. In *Proceedings of AAMAS-2002 Workshop on Agentcities: Challenges in Open Agent Systems*, pages 10–14, 2002.
2. Y. Arens, C. Hsu, and C. A. Knoblock. Query processing in the sims information mediator. *Advanced Planning Technology*, 1996.

3. T. Berners-Lee. *Weaving the Web : the Original Design and Ultimate Destiny of the World Wide Web by its Inventor*. HarperSanFrancisco, San Francisco, 1999.
4. F. M. Donini, M. Lenzerini, D. Nardi, and W. Nutt. The complexity of concept languages. In J. Allen, R. Fikes, and E. Sandewall, editors, *Proceedings of the Second International Conference on Principles of Knowledge Representation and Reasoning (KR-91)*, pages 151–162, Massachusetts, 1991.
5. F. M. Donini and F. Massacci. Exptime tableaux for $\mathcal{ALC}$. *Artificial Intelligence*, 124(1):87–138, 2000.
6. C. H. Goh. *Representing and Reasoning about Semantic Conflicts in Heterogeneous Information Sources*. PhD thesis, MIT, 1997.
7. A. Goodchild. *Database Discovery in the Organizational Environment*. PhD thesis, University of Queensland, 1998.
8. V. Haarslev and R. Möller. Optimization strategies for instance retrieval. In *Proceedings of the International Workshop on Description Logics (DL 2002)*, 2002.
9. I. Horrocks, L. Li, D. Turi, and S. Bechhofer. The instance store: Description logic reasoning with large numbers of individuals. In *International Workshop on Description Logics (DL 2004)*, pages 31–40, 2004.
10. D. L. McGuinness, R. Fikes, L. A. Stein, and J. Hendler. Daml-ont: An ontology language for the semantic web. In D. Fensel, J. Hendler, H. Lieberman, and W. Wahlster, editors, *Spinning the Semantic Web: Bringing the World Wide Web to its Full Potential*. MIT Press, 2003.
11. E. Mena, V. Kashyap, A. Sheth, and A. Illarramendi. Observer: An approach for query processing in global information systems based on interoperability between pre-existing ontologies. In *Proceedings of the 1st IFCIS: International Conference on Cooperative Information Systems (CoopIS '96)*, 1996.
12. J. Z. Pan and I. Horrocks. Rdfs(fa): A dl-ised sub-language of rdfs. In *Proceedings of the 2003 International Workshop on Description Logics (DL2003)*, 2003.
13. H. Stuckenschmidt. Query processing on the semantic web. *Künstliche Intelligenz*, 17, 2003.
14. S. Tessaris. *Questions and Answers: Reasoning and Querying in Description Logic*. PhD thesis, University of Manchester, 2001.
15. H. Wache, T. Vögele, U. Visser, H. Stuckenschmidt, G. Schuster, H. Neumann, and S. Hübner. Ontology-based integration of information - a survey of existing approaches. In *Proceedings of the IJCAI-01 Workshop: Ontologies and Information Sharing*, pages 108–117, 2001.

oMAP: Combining Classifiers for Aligning Automatically OWL Ontologies*

Umberto Straccia[1] and Raphaël Troncy[1,2]

[1] ISTI-CNR, Via G. Moruzzi 1, 56124 Pisa, Italy
{straccia, troncy}@isti.cnr.it
[2] CWI Amsterdam, P.O. Box 94079, 1090 GB Amsterdam, The Netherlands
raphael.troncy@cwi.nl

Abstract. This paper introduces a method and a tool for automatically aligning OWL ontologies, a crucial step for achieving the interoperability of heterogeneous systems in the Semantic Web. Different components are combined for finding suitable mapping candidates (together with their weights), and the set of rules with maximum matching probability is selected. Machine learning-based classifiers and a new classifier using the structure and the semantics of the OWL ontologies are proposed. Our method has been implemented and evaluated on an independent test set provided by an international ontology alignment contest. We provide the results of this evaluation with respect to the other competitors.

1 Introduction

The W3C recommendation of the *Resource Description Framework* (RDF) [22] and the *Web Ontology Language* (OWL) [19] languages is a new step towards the realization of the Semantic Web [4]. RDF aims to represent information and to exchange knowledge in the web, while OWL should be used to publish and share sets of terms called *ontologies*, supporting advanced web search, software agents and knowledge management. These languages are grounded on formal set-theoretic semantics, and specify meaning of concepts so that computers can process and understand them. They allow to infer new data from the knowledge already represented.

Ontologies are usually seen as a solution to data heterogeneity on the web [9]. An ontology is a way of describing the world: it allows to determine what kinds of things there are in the world, their characteristics, the relationships between them and more complex axioms [2]. Since a lot of efforts are deployed to provide hands-on support for developers of Semantic Web applications[1], with the online publishing of "best practices", it is expected now that more and more ontologies covering partially the same subjects will be available on the web. Indeed, this is already true for numerous complex domains such that the

---

* This work was carried out during the tenure of an ERCIM fellowship at CNR.

[1] W3C Semantic Web Best Practices and Deployment Working Group:
http://www.w3.org/2001/sw/BestPractices/.

M. Kitsuregawa et al. (Eds.): WISE 2005, LNCS 3806, pp. 133–147, 2005.

medical [11] or the multimedia domain [14]. In such a case, some entities can be given different names or simply be defined in different ways or in different languages. The semantic interoperability has then to be grounded in ontology reconciliation. The underlying problem is often called the "ontology alignment" problem [9], that we address in this paper.

Comparing ontologies is useful for various tasks. During the building phase of the taxonomies, it is likely that the designer has to reuse some pieces of existing ontologies, internally developed or found on the web. Alignment methods are also necessary for dealing with the evolution and versioning issue of the ontologies (track changes, detect inconsistencies, merge, etc.). These methods can then be used for reformulating queries: documents annotated with respect to a *source* ontology can be retrieved even if the query uses terms from a *target* ontology. In the same way, documents classified under different web directories can be retrieved by comparing the heterogeneous web classes they belong to.

In this paper, we focus on ontologies described in the same knowledge representation language (OWL) and we propose a general framework combining several specific classifiers for aligning them automatically. We introduce a new classifier that uses the semantics of the OWL axioms for establishing equivalence and subsumption relationships between the classes and the properties defined in the ontologies.

The paper is organized as follows. We briefly present in the next section the OWL language as well as its syntax. Readers who are already familiar with this language can skip this section. Then, we introduce in section 3 *oMAP*, a framework whose goal is to find automatically the best mappings (together with their weights) between the entities defined in the OWL ontologies. The final mappings are obtained by combining the prediction of different classifiers. We describe the set of classifiers used: terminological, machine learning-based and we present a new one, based on the structure and the semantics of the OWL axioms. We sketch in section 4 the implementation of our framework. We have evaluated our method on an independent test set provided by an international ontology alignment contest and we show our results with respect to the other competitors in section 5. We present an overview of other alignment methods in section 6. Finally, we give our conclusions and outline future work in section 7.

2   Preliminaries: OWL Overview

OWL is a new formal language, recommended by the W3C, for representing ontologies in the Semantic Web [19]. In the Semantic Web vision [4], ontologies are used to provide structured vocabularies that explicate the relationships between different terms, allowing automated processes (and humans) to interpret their meaning flexibly yet unambiguously.

OWL has features from several families of representation languages, including primarily Description Logics [1] and frames. OWL can declare classes, and organize them in a subsumption ("subclass") hierarchy. OWL classes can be specified as logical combinations (intersections, unions, complements) of other classes, or as enumerations of specified objects. In the same way, OWL can declare properties, organize them into a "subproperty" hierarchy, and provide domains and ranges for these properties. The domains of OWL properties are OWL classes while their ranges can be either OWL classes or externally-defined datatypes such as string or integer. OWL can state that a property is transitive, symmetric, functional or is the inverse of another property. OWL can express which objects (also called "individuals") belong to which classes, and what the property values are of specific individuals. Some axioms, such that the equivalence or disjointness between classes or the (in)equality between individuals, can be asserted. Finally, OWL is able to provide restrictions on how properties that are local to a class, behave. These restrictions may concern the type of all (or at least one) values of the property instances, or constrain their cardinality

Table 1. OWL Descriptions, Data Ranges, Properties, Individuals, and Data Values with examples (adapted from [12])

Abstract Syntax	DL Syntax	Example
Descriptions (C)		
A (URI reference)	A	Conference
owl:Thing	$\top$	
owl:Nothing	$\bot$	
intersectionOf($C_1\ C_2\dots$)	$C_1 \sqcap C_2$	Reference $\sqcap$ Journal
unionOf($C_1\ C_2\dots$)	$C_1 \sqcup C_2$	Organization $\sqcup$ Institution
complementOf(C)	$\neg C$	$\neg$ MasterThesis
oneOf($o_1\ \dots$)	$\{o_1,\dots\}$	{"WISE","ISWC",...}
restriction(R someValuesFrom(C))	$\exists R.C$	$\exists$ parts.InCollection
restriction(R allValuesFrom(C))	$\forall R.C$	$\forall$ date.Date
restriction(R hasValue(o))	$R:o$	date : 2005
restriction(R minCardinality(n))	$\geqslant n\ R$	$\geqslant 1$ location
restriction(R maxCardinality(n))	$\leqslant n\ R$	$\leqslant 1$ publisher
restriction(U someValuesFrom(D))	$\exists U.D$	$\exists$ issue.integer
restriction(U allValuesFrom(D))	$\forall U.D$	$\forall$ name.string
restriction(U hasValue(v))	$U:v$	series : "LNCS"
restriction(U minCardinality(n))	$\geqslant n\ U$	$\geqslant 1$ title
restriction(U maxCardinality(n))	$\leqslant n\ U$	$\leqslant 1$ author
Data Ranges (D)		
D (URI reference)	D	string
oneOf($v_1\ \dots$)	$\{v_1,\dots\}$	{"2004","2005",...}
Object Properties (R)		
R (URI reference)	R	location
Datatype Properties (U)		
U (URI reference)	U	title
Individuals (o)		
o (URI reference)	o	WISE
Data Values (v)		
v (RDF literal)	v	"Int. Conf. SW"

(i.e. they must be at least or at most a certain number of distinct values for this property) [12].

To illustrate this language, lets take a simple example on bibliographic data. A suitable bibliographic ontology, such as BibTeX, might represent the notions of book (e.g. monograph, proceedings) and part (e.g. chapter, article) that are reference entries; a journal or magazine should have a name, a publisher, a periodicity and contain some articles; a conference has a location and an organizer which is an institution that has an address, etc. The Table 1 summarizes the different constructs of the OWL language giving some examples within this domain. The first column gives the abstract syntax of OWL, the second, its equivalent in the Description Logics syntax, and the third some examples.

3   oMAP: A Framework for Automatically Aligning OWL Ontologies

This section introduces the *oMAP* framework for aligning automatically ontologies. Our approach is inspired by the data exchange problem [10] and borrows from others, like GLUE [6], the idea of combining several specialized components for finding the best set of mappings. The framework resumes partially the formalization proposed in [17] and extends the sPLMAP (*Schema Probabilistic Learning Mappings*) system to cope with the ontology alignment problem.

We draw in section 3.1 the general picture of our approach. Then, we detail several classifiers used to predict the *weight* of a possible mapping between two entities. These classifiers are terminological (section 3.2) or machine learning-based (section 3.3). Finally, we propose a classifier working on the structure and the formal semantics of the OWL constructs, thus using fully the meaning of the entities defined in the ontology (section 3.4).

3.1   Overall Strategy

Our goal is to automatically determine "similarity" relationships between classes and properties of two ontologies. For instance, given the ontologies in Figure 1, we would like to determine that an instance of the class Conference is likely an instance of the class Congress, that the property creator should subsume the property author, or that the class Journal is disjoint from the class Directions.

Theoretically, an ontology *mapping* is a tuple $\mathcal{M} = (\mathbf{S}, \mathbf{T}, \Sigma)$, where $\mathbf{S}$ and $\mathbf{T}$ are respectively the source and target ontologies, and Σ is a finite set of *mapping constraints* of the form $\alpha_{i,j}\ T_j \leftarrow S_i$, where S_i and T_j are respectively the source and target entities. The intended meaning of this rule is that the entity S_i of the source ontology is mapped onto the entity T_j of the target ontology, and the confident measure associated with this mapping is $\alpha_{i,j}$. Note that a source entity may be mapped onto several target entities and conversely. But, we do not require that we have a mapping for every target entity.

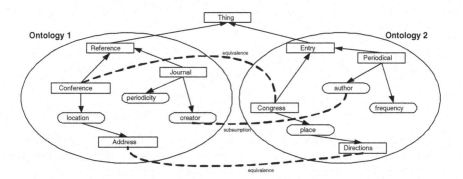

Fig. 1. Excerpt of two bibliographic ontologies and their mappings

Aligning two ontologies in *oMap* consists of three steps:

1. We form a possible set of mappings Σ, and estimate its quality based on the quality measures for its mapping rules;
2. For each mapping rule $T_j \leftarrow S_i$, we estimate its confidence $\alpha_{i,j}$, which also depends on the Σ it belongs to, that is, $\alpha_{i,j} = w(S_i, T_j, \Sigma)$;
3. As we cannot compute all possible sets Σ (there are exponentially many) and then choose the best one, we rather build iteratively our final set of mappings Σ using heuristics.

Similar to GLUE [6], we estimate the weight $w(S_i, T_j, \Sigma)$ of a mapping $T_j \leftarrow S_i$ by using different classifiers $CL_1, \ldots, CL_n$. Each classifier CL_k computes a weight $w(S_i, T_j, CL_k)$, which is the classifier's approximation of the rule $T_j \leftarrow S_i$. For each target entity T_j, CL_k provides a rank of the plausible source entities S_{i_k}. Then we rely on a priority list on the classifiers, $CL_1 \prec CL_2 \prec \ldots \prec CL_n$ and proceed as follows: for a given target entity T_j, select the top-ranked mapping of CL_1 if the weight is non-zero. Otherwise, select the top-ranked mapping provided by CL_2 if non-zero, and so on.

We present in the following several classifiers that have been used in our tests. It is worth noting that some of the classifiers consider the terminological part of the ontologies only, while others are based on their instances (i.e. the values of the individuals). Finally, we end this section by introducing a new classifier that fully uses the structure and the semantics of ontology definitions and axioms.

3.2 Terminological Classifiers

The terminological classifiers work on the name of the entities (class or property) defined in the ontologies. In OWL, each resource is identified by a URI, and can have some annotation properties attached. Among others, the `rdfs:label` property may be used to provide a human-readable version of a resource's name. Furthermore, multilingual labels are supported using the language tagging facility of RDF literals. In the following, we consider that the name of an entity is given by the value of the `rdfs:label` property or by the URI fragment if this property is not specified.

Same entity names. This binary classifier CL_N returns a weight of 1 if and only if the two classes (or properties) have the same name, and 0 otherwise:

$$w(S_i, T_j, CL_N) = \begin{cases} 1 & \text{if } S_i, T_j \text{ have same name,} \\ 0 & \text{otherwise} \end{cases}$$

Same entity name stems. This binary classifier CL_S returns a weight of 1 if and only if the two classes (or properties) have the same *stem*[2] (we use the Porter stemming algorithm [20]), and 0 otherwise:

$$w(S_i, T_j, CL_S) = \begin{cases} 1 & \text{if } S_i, T_j \text{ have same } stem, \\ 0 & \text{otherwise} \end{cases}$$

String distance name. This classifier CL_{LD} computes some similarity measures between the entity names (once downcased) such that the Levenshtein distance [3] (or edit distance), which is given by the smallest number of insertions, deletions, and substitutions required to transform one string into the other. The prediction is then computed as:

$$w(S_i, T_j, CL_{LD}) = \frac{dist_{Levenshtein}(S_i, T_j)}{\max(length(S_i), length(T_j))}$$

3.3   Machine Learning-Based Classifier

As we have seen in section 2, an ontology often contains some individuals. It is then possible to use machine learning-based classifiers to predict the weight of a mapping between two entities. The instances of an OWL ontology can be gathered using the following rules: we consider (*i*) the label for the named individuals, (*ii*) the data value for the datatype properties and (*iii*) the type for the anonymous individuals and the range of the object properties.

For example, using the abstract syntax of [12], let us consider the following individuals :

```
Individual (x₁ type (Conference)
        value (label "Int. Conf. on Web Information Systems Engineering")
        value (location x₂))
Individual (x₂ type (Address)
        value (city "New York city") value (country "USA"))
```

Then, the text gathered u_1 for the named individual x_1 will be ("Int. Conf. on Web Information Systems Engineering", "Address") and u_2 for the anonymous individual x_2 ("Address", "New York city", "USA").

---

[2] The root of the terms without its prefixes and suffixes.

[3] Levenshtein distance is named after the Russian scientist Vladimir Levenshtein, who devised the algorithm in 1965.

We describe in the following the typical and well-known classifier that we used in oMAP: the Naive Bayes [23].

Naive Bayes Text Classifier. The classifier CL_{NB} uses a Naive Bayes text classifier [23] for text content. Each class (or property) S_i acts as a category, and the instances are considered as bags of words (with normalized word frequencies as probability estimations). For each $(x, u) \in T_j$, the probability $Pr(S_i|u)$ that the value u should be mapped onto S_i is computed. In a second step, these probabilities are combined by:

$$w(S_i, T_j, CL_{NB}) = \sum_{(x,u)\in T_j} Pr(S_i|u) \cdot Pr(u)$$

Again, we consider the values as bags of words. With $Pr(S_i)$ we denote the probability that a randomly chosen value in $\bigcup_k S_k$ is a value in S_i. If we assume independence of the words in a value, then we obtain:

$$Pr(S_i|u) = Pr(u|S_i) \cdot \frac{Pr(S_i)}{Pr(u)} = \frac{Pr(S_i)}{Pr(u)} \cdot \prod_{m\in u} Pr(m|S_i)$$

Together, the final formula is:

$$w(S_i, T_j, CL_{NB}) = Pr(S_i) \cdot \sum_{(x,u)\in T_j} \prod_{m\in u} Pr(m|S_i)$$

If a word does not appear in the content for any individual in S_i $(Pr(m|S_i) = 0)$, we assume a small value to avoid a product of zero.

3.4 A Structural and Semantics-Based Classifier

Besides these well-known algorithms in information retrieval and text classification, we introduce a new classifier, CL_{Sem}, which is able to use the semantics of the OWL definitions while being guided by their syntax. It is used in the framework *a posteriori*, in so far as the weighted average of the predictions of all the other classifiers will serve as its input. In the following, we note with $w'(S_i, T_j, \Sigma)$ the average weight of the mapping $T_j \leftarrow S_i$ estimated by the classifiers of the previous sections, where S_i (*resp.* T_j) is a concept or property name of the source (*resp.* target) ontology. Note that in case the structural classifier is used alone, we set: $w'(S_i, T_j, \Sigma) = 1$. The formal recursive definition of CL_{Sem} is then given by:

1. If S_i and T_j are property names:

$$w(S_i, T_j, \Sigma) = \begin{cases} 0 & \text{if } T_j \leftarrow S_i \notin \Sigma \\ w'(S_i, T_j, \Sigma) & \text{otherwise} \end{cases}$$

2. If S_i and T_j are concept names: let assume that their definitions are $S_i \sqsubseteq C_1 \ldots C_m$ and $T_j \sqsubseteq D_1 \ldots D_n$, and we note $\mathcal{D} = \mathcal{D}(S_i) \times \mathcal{D}(T_j)^4$, then:

---

[4] $\mathcal{D}(S_i)$ represents the set of concepts directly parents of S_i.

$$w(S_i, T_j, \Sigma) = \begin{cases} 0 & \text{if } T_j \leftarrow S_i \notin \Sigma \\ w'(S_i, T_j, \Sigma) & \text{if } |\mathcal{D}| = 0 \text{ and } T_j \leftarrow S_i \in \Sigma \\ \frac{1}{(|Set|+1)} \cdot \left(w'(S_i, T_j, \Sigma) + \max_{Set} \left(\sum_{(C_i, D_j) \in Set} w(C_i, D_j, \Sigma) \right) \right) & \text{otherwise} \end{cases}$$

3. Let $C_S = (QR.C)$ and $D_T = (Q'R'.D)$, where Q, Q' are quantifiers $\forall$ or $\exists$ or cardinality restrictions, R, R' are property names and C, D are concept expressions, then:

$$w(C_S, D_T, \Sigma) = w_Q(Q, Q') \cdot w(R, R', \Sigma) \cdot w(C, D, \Sigma)$$

4. Let $C_S = (op\ C_1 \ldots C_m)$ and $D_T = (op'\ D_1 \ldots D_m)$, where the concept constructors op, op' in the concepts C_S, D_T are in prefix notation, op, op' are the concept constructors among $\sqcap, \sqcup, \neg$ and $n, m \geq 1$, then:

$$w(C_S, D_T, \Sigma) = w_{op}(op, op') \cdot \frac{\max\limits_{Set} \left(\sum\limits_{(C_i, D_j) \in Set} w(C_i, D_j, \Sigma) \right)}{\min(m, n)}$$

where:

- $Set \subseteq \{C_1 \ldots C_m\} \times \{D_1 \ldots D_n\}$ and $|Set| = \min(m, n)$,
- $(C, D) \in Set, (C', D') \in Set \Rightarrow C \neq C', D \neq D'$.

We give in the Table 2 the values for w_Q and w_{op} we used.

Table 2. Possible values for w_{op} and w_Q weights

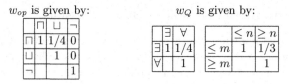

w_{op} is given by:

	$\sqcap$	$\sqcup$	$\neg$
$\sqcap$	1	1/4	0
$\sqcup$		1	0
$\neg$			1

w_Q is given by:

	$\exists$	$\forall$
$\exists$	1	1/4
$\forall$		1

	$\leq n$	$\geq n$
$\leq m$	1	1/3
$\geq m$		1

4   Implementation

Like we have seen in the section 3.1, our approach begins to form some possible Σ sets, for evaluating the weight of each mapping rules they contain. The generation of *all* possible Σ sets becomes quickly a critical issue since this number can be huge. We address this problem in the section 4.1. The $oMAP$ framework allows to align any OWL ontologies, represented in the RDF/XML syntax. Hence, it uses extensively the OWL API [3] and the Alignment API available in JAVA (section 4.2).

4.1   Reduction of the Space

Lets assume that the two ontologies to be aligned have the following characteristics: a source ontology S containing C_S classes, OP_S object properties and DP_S

datatype properties; and a target ontology $\mathcal{T}$ containing C_T classes, OP_T object properties and DP_T datatype properties. Theoretically, the number of all possible mapping rules is given by: $Nb\_rules = (C_S \cdot C_T) + (OP_S \cdot OP_T) + (DP_S \cdot DP_T)$. Then, the number of all possible Σ sets containing these mapping rules is given by: $Nb_\Sigma = 2^{Nb\_rules}$. To reduce the number of Σ sets to generate and then to evaluate, we make a first approximation: we consider only the Σ sets that contain exactly one mapping rule for each definition of classes, object properties and datatype properties of the source or the target ontology (see section 3.4 for the formal definition of these sets). The number of all possible Σ sets is then given by:

$$Nb_\Sigma = \frac{Max(C_S, C_T)!}{|C_S - C_T|!} \cdot \frac{Max(OP_S, OP_T)!}{|OP_S - OP_T|!} \cdot \frac{Max(DP_S, DP_T)!}{|DP_S - DP_T|!}$$

We reduce also the number of Σ sets to generate by taking into account the range of the datatype properties. A reasonable approximation is that a datatype property from the source ontology that has for range the datatype U_i cannot be align to another datatype property from the target ontology that has for range the datatype U_j if $U_i \cap U_j = \emptyset$ (for instance *string* and *integer*). We remind that the possible datatypes considered by OWL are the hierarchy provided by XML Schema.

Finally, we operate a third approximation which turns out to be, unsurprisingly, the more efficient for reducing the space search: a local maximum heuristic. When forming a Σ set, we consider firstly a class from the first ontology, and gather all the entities (classes and properties) involved in its closure definition. We do the same for each classes of the second ontology and we evaluate all these small Σ sets for retaining the best one. We iterate this process over all the classes. Additional criteria allow us to guarantee the convergence of our approach (i.e. the order of the classes considered has no significance).

4.2   The Alignment API

In order to exchange and evaluate results of alignment algorithms, [8] has proposed a simple yet extensible alignment format. In first approximation, an alignment is a set of pairs of elements from each ontology. More deeply, a relation between entities of the source ontology and entities of the target ontology can be characterized. This relation is not restricted to the equivalence relation, but can be more sophisticated operators (e.g. subsumption, incompatibility, or even some fuzzy relation). A strength denotes the confidence held in this correspondence. Finally, an arity allows to note if the mapping is injective, surjective and total or partial on both side.

An API[5] has been developed for this format, with a default implementation, which eases the integration and the composition of new alignment algorithms, the generation of transformations and axioms, and the alignment comparison. All the classifiers detailed in the section 3 have been implemented to be compatible with

---

[5] http://co4.inrialpes.fr/align/.

this API, thus easing their chaining. Therefore, our *oMAP* framework benefits from all the evaluation facilities for comparing our approach with other methods as we will see in the next section.

5   Evaluation

The problem of aligning ontologies has already produced some interesting works. However, it is difficult to compare theoretically the various approaches proposed since they base on different techniques. Hence, it is necessary to compare them on common tests. This was the goal of an International Ontology Alignment Contest (EON) [24] who has set up benchmark tests for assessing the strengths and weakness of the available tools (section 5.1). We present the metrics used (section 5.2), and evaluate thoroughly our new approach with respect to the other competitors of this contest (section 5.3).

5.1   The EON Ontology Alignment Contest

The EON "Ontology Alignment Contest"[6] has been designed for providing some evaluation of ontology alignments algorithms. The evaluation methodology consisted in publishing a set of ontologies to be compared with another ontology. The participants were asked to provide the results in a particular format (see section 4.2). Along with the ontologies, a reference alignment was provided [24].

The set of tests consisted in one medium OWL ontology (33 named classes, 39 object properties, 20 data properties, 56 named individuals, and 20 anonymous individuals) to be compared to other ontologies. This initial ontology was about a very narrow domain (bibliographic references). There were three series of tests [24]:

- *simple tests*: compare the reference ontology with itself, with another irrelevant ontology or the same ontology in its restriction to OWL-Lite;
- *systematic tests*: obtained by discarding some features of the initial ontology leaving the remainder untouched. The considered features were (names, comments, hierarchy, instances, relations, restrictions, etc.).
- *complex tests*: four real-life ontologies of bibliographic references that were found on the web and left untouched.

5.2   Metrics

Standard information retrieval metrics are used to assess the different approaches. Let R the set of reference alignments ($|R|$ its cardinality), and A the set of alignments obtained by a certain method ($|A|$ its cardinality). The definitions of *precision* and *recall* are then given by: $Precision = |R \cap A|/|A|$ and $Recall = |R \cap A|/|R|$. Precision measures then the ratio between the number

---

[6] http://oaei.inrialpes.fr/2004/Contest/.

of correct alignments and the number of all mappings found, while recall measures the ratio between the number of correct alignments and the total number of correct mappings that should be found. Traditional precision and recall are defined in a analogous way, but with equality as similarity measure. In addition, we also combine precision and recall in the *F-measure* and the *overall-measure*: $F = 2 \cdot precision \cdot recall/(precision + recall)$ and $O = recall \cdot (2 - 1/precision)$.

5.3   Results and Discussion

There were four teams entering the EON initiative (Stanford/SMI, Fujitsu, IN-RIA & UMontréal and Karlsruhe) [24]. Among the three test sets, the most difficult one was the last one with real world (but above all various heterogeneity). The first one was quite easy. The second set of test was indeed able to help identifying where the algorithms were more handicapped (especially when they were unable to match strings).

Table 3. Precision and recall of oMAP with respect to the other competitors of EON

algo	karlsruhe2		umontreal		fujitsu		stanford		oMAP	
test	*Prec.*	*Rec.*	*Prec.*	*Rec.*	*Prec.*	*Rec.*	*Prec.*	*Rec.*	*Prec.*	*Rec.*
101	n/a	n/a	0.59	0.97	0.99	1.00	0.99	1.00	1.00	1.00
102	NaN	NaN	0.00	NaN	NaN	NaN	NaN	NaN	NaN	NaN
103	n/a	n/a	0.55	0.90	0.99	1.00	0.99	1.00	1.00	1.00
104	n/a	n/a	0.56	0.91	0.99	1.00	0.99	1.00	1.00	1.00
201	0.43	0.51	0.44	0.71	0.98	0.92	1.00	0.11	0.96	0.23
202	n/a	n/a	0.38	0.63	0.95	0.42	1.00	0.11	0.93	0.14
204	0.62	1.00	0.55	0.90	0.95	0.91	0.99	1.00	0.92	0.81
205	0.47	0.60	0.49	0.80	0.79	0.63	0.95	0.43	0.73	0.48
206	0.48	0.60	0.46	0.75	0.85	0.64	1.00	0.46	0.91	0.43
221	n/a	n/a	0.61	1.00	0.98	0.88	0.99	1.00	1.00	1.00
222	n/a	n/a	0.55	0.90	0.99	0.92	0.98	0.95	1.00	1.00
223	0.59	0.96	0.59	0.97	0.95	0.87	0.95	0.96	1.00	1.00
224	0.97	0.97	0.97	1.00	0.99	1.00	0.99	1.00	1.00	1.00
225	n/a	n/a	0.59	0.97	0.99	1.00	0.99	1.00	1.00	1.00
228	n/a	n/a	0.38	1.00	0.91	0.97	1.00	1.00	1.00	1.00
230	0.60	0.95	0.46	0.92	0.97	0.95	0.99	0.93	1.00	1.00
301	0.85	0.36	0.49	0.61	0.89	0.66	0.93	0.44	0.94	0.25
302	1.00	0.23	0.23	0.50	0.39	0.60	0.94	0.65	1.00	0.58
303	0.85	0.73	0.31	0.50	0.51	0.50	0.85	0.81	0.90	0.79
304	0.91	0.92	0.44	0.62	0.85	0.92	0.97	0.97	0.91	0.91

Table 3 gives the *precision/recall*, and Table 4, the *F-measure/O-measure* of *oMAP* with respect to the other competitors. Clearly, during the presentation of the results at the EON workshop, there were two groups of competitors and clear winners, since it seems that the results provided by Stanford and Fujitsu/Tokyo outperform those provided by Karlsruhe and Montréal/INRIA. We have developed our framework after this contest but use the same benchmark tests in order to compare our approach with the current best alignments. At first sight, we should be in the first group. In fact, it can be considered that these constitute two groups of programs. The Stanford+Fujitsu programs are very different but strongly based on the labels attached to entities. For that reason they performed especially well when labels were preserved (i.e., most of the time). The Karlsruhe+INRIA systems tend to rely on many different features and thus to balance the influence of individual features, so they tend to reduce the fact that labels were preserved. Our mixed approach tend to success on both case even if we dispose yet of a large progression margin.

Table 4. F-Measure and overall-measure of oMAP with respect to the other competitors of EON

algo	karlsruhe2		umontreal		fujitsu		stanford		oMAP	
test	F	O	F	O	F	O	F	O	F	O
101	n/a	n/a	0.73	0.30	0.99	0.99	0.99	0.99	1.00	1.00
102	n/a	n/a	NaN	NaN	NaN	NaN	NaN	NaN	NaN	NaN
103	n/a	n/a	0.68	0.16	0.99	0.99	0.99	0.99	1.00	1.00
104	n/a	n/a	0.69	0.19	0.99	0.99	0.99	0.99	1.00	1.00
201	0.46	0.0-16	0.54	0.0-20	0.95	0.90	0.20	0.11	0.37	0.22
202	n/a	n/a	0.48	0.0-38	0.58	0.40	0.20	0.11	0.25	0.13
204	0.76	0.38	0.68	0.16	0.93	0.87	0.99	0.99	0.86	0.74
205	0.53	0.0-6	0.61	0.0-3	0.70	0.46	0.59	0.41	0.58	0.31
206	0.54	0.0-4	0.57	0.0-14	0.73	0.53	0.63	0.46	0.59	0.39
221	n/a	n/a	0.76	0.36	0.92	0.86	0.99	0.99	1.00	1.00
222	n/a	n/a	0.68	0.16	0.95	0.91	0.96	0.92	1.00	1.00
223	0.73	0.30	0.73	0.30	0.91	0.82	0.95	0.90	1.00	1.00
224	0.97	0.93	0.98	0.97	0.99	0.99	0.99	0.99	1.00	1.00
225	n/a	n/a	0.73	0.30	0.99	0.99	0.99	0.99	1.00	1.00
228	n/a	n/a	0.55	0.0-66	0.94	0.88	1.00	1.00	1.00	1.00
230	0.73	0.31	0.62	0.0-14	0.96	0.92	0.96	0.92	1.00	1.00
301	0.51	0.30	0.54	0.0-1	0.75	0.57	0.60	0.41	0.39	0.23
302	0.37	0.23	0.31	-1.0-20	0.47	0.0-35	0.77	0.60	0.74	0.58
303	0.79	0.60	0.38	0.0-60	0.51	0.02	0.83	0.67	0.84	0.71
304	0.92	0.83	0.51	0.0-17	0.89	0.76	0.97	0.95	0.91	0.82

6   Related Work

The alignment problem for ontologies, as well as the matching problem for schemas, has been addressed by many researchers so far and are strictly related. Some of the techniques applied in schema matching can be applied to ontology alignment as well, taking additionally into account the formal semantics carried out by the taxonomies of concepts and properties and the axioms of the ontology.

Related to schema matching are, for instance, the works [5, 6, 10, 16] (see [21] for a more extensive comparison). As pointed out above, closest to our approach is [10] based on a logical framework for data exchange, but we incorporated the classifier combinations (like GLUE) into our framework as well. GLUE [6, 5] employed a linear combination of the predictions of multiple base learners (classifiers). The combination weights are learned via regression on manually specified mappings between a small number of learning ontologies. The main improvement of our approach with respect to this system is then the structural classifier which is able to align two ontologies solely on their semantics, and without the presence of individuals.

Among the works related to ontology alignment, [7] propose to combine different similarity measures from pre-existing hand-established mapping rules. Besides the validity of these rules could be generally put into question, this method suffers from not being fully automatic. [18] has developed an interesting approach: from anchor-pairs of concepts that seem to be close (discovered automatically or proposed manually), their *hors-context* similarity are computed analyzing the paths in the taxonomy that link the pairs of concepts. This method has been implemented into the ANCHOR-PROMPT tool which has, until now, one of the best performance (see section 5.3). [9] have adapted works on similarity calculus for object-based knowledge representation languages to the Semantic Web languages. A global similarity measure taking into account all the features of the OWL-Lite language has been proposed, capable to treat both the circular definitions and the collections. For a complete state of the art on the numerous ontology alignment approaches proposed, see [15].

7   Conclusion and Future Work

As the number of Semantic Web applications is growing rapidly, many individual ontologies are created. The development of automated tools for ontology alignment will be of crucial importance. In this paper, we have presented a formal framework for ontology Matching, which for ease we call *oMap*. oMap uses different classifiers to estimate the quality of a mapping. Novel is the classifier which uses the structure of the OWL constructs and thus the semantics of the entities defined in the ontologies. We have implemented the whole framework and evaluated it on independent benchmark tests provided by the EON "Ontology Alignment Contest" [24] with respect to the other competitors.

As future work, we see some appealing points. The combination of a rule-based language with an expressive ontology language like OWL has attracted the attention of many researchers [13] and is considered now as an important requirement. Taking into account this additional semantics of the ontologies appear thus necessary. Additional classifiers using more terminological resources can be included in the framework, while the effectiveness of the machine learning part could be improved using other measures like the KL-distance. While to fit new classifiers into our model is straightforward theoretically, practically finding out the most appropriate one or a combination of them is quite more difficult. In the future, more variants should be developed and evaluated to improve the overall quality of *oMAP*. Furthermore, instead of averaging the classifier predictions, the appropriateness of each classifier could be learned via regression. These ideas are currently investigated since we are participating actively to the 2005 campaign of the Ontology Alignment Evaluation Initiative[7].

---

[7] http://oaei.inrialpes.fr/

References

1. Baader, F., Calvanese, D., McGuinness, D., Nardi, D., Patel-Schneider, P.F.: The Description Logic Handbook: Theory, Implementation, and Applications. Cambridge University Press, 2003.
2. Bachimont, B., Isaac, A., Troncy, R.: Semantic Commitment for Designing Ontologies: A Proposal. In 13th Int. Conf. on Knowledge Engineering and Knowledge Management (EKAW'02), Sigüenza, Spain, 2002, 114–121.
3. Bechhofer, S., Volz, R., Lord, P.W.: Cooking the Semantic Web with the OWL API. In 2nd Int. Semantic Web Conf. (ISWC'03), Sanibel Island, Florida, USA, 2003, 659–675.
4. Berners-Lee, T., Hendler, J., Lassila, O.: The Semantic Web. Scientific American, **284**(5), 2001, 34–43.
5. Dhamankar, R., Lee, Y., Doan, A., Halevy, A., Domingos, P.: iMap: discovering complex semantic matches between database schemas. In ACM SIGMOD Int. Conf. on Management of Data, Paris, France, 2004, 383–394.
6. Doan, A., Madhavan, J., Dhamankar, R., Domingos, P., Halevy, A.: Learning to Match Ontologies on the Semantic Web. The VLDB Journal, **12**(4), 2003, 303–319.
7. Ehrig, M., Staab, S.: QOM - quick ontology mapping. In 3rd Int. Semantic Web Conf. (ISWC'04), Hiroshima, Japan, 2004, 683–697.
8. Euzenat, J.: An API for ontology alignment. In 3rd Int. Semantic Web Conf. (ISWC'04), Hiroshima, Japan, 2004, 698–712.
9. Euzenat, J., Valtchev, P.: Similarity-based ontology alignment in OWL-Lite. In 15th European Conf. on Artificial Intelligence (ECAI'04), Valence, Spain, 2004, 333–337.
10. Fagin, R., Kolaitis, P.G., Miler, R.J., Popa, L.: Data Exchange: Semantics and Query Answering. In 9th Int. Conf. on Database Theory (ICDT'03), Sienna, Italy, 2003, 207–224.
11. Hahn, U., Cornet, R., Schulz, S. editors. KR-MED: 1st Int. Workshop on Formal Biomedical Knowledge Representation. Whistler, Canada, 2004.
12. Horrocks, I., Patel-Schneider, P.F., van Harmelen, F.: From SHIQ and RDF to OWL: The making of a web ontology language. Journal of Web Semantics, **1**(1), 2003, 7–26.
13. Horrocks, I., Patel-Schneider, P.F.: A proposal for an OWL rules language. In 13th Int. World Wide Web Conf. (WWW'04), New York, USA, 2004, 723–731.
14. Isaac, A., Troncy, R.: Designing and Using an Audio-Visual Description Core Ontology. In Workshop on Core Ontologies in Ontology Engineering at EKAW'04, Whittlebury Hall, Northamptonshire, UK, 2004.
15. KW Consortium: State of the Art on Ontology Alignment. Deliverable Knowledge Web 2.2.3, FP6-507482, 2004.
16. Madhavan, J., Bernstein, P.A., Rahm, E.: Generic schema matching with cupid. In 27th Int. Conf. on Very Large Data Bases (VLDB'01), Roma, Italy, 2001, 49–58.
17. Nottelmann, H., Straccia, U.: sPLMap: A probabilistic approach to schema matching. In 27th European Conf. on Information Retrieval (ECIR'05), Santiago de Compostela, Spain, 2005, 81–95.
18. Noy, N.F., Musen, M.A.: Anchor-PROMPT: Using non-local context for semantic matching. In Workshop on Ontologies and Information Sharing at IJCAI'01, Seattle, Washington, USA, 2001.
19. OWL, Web Ontology Language Reference Version 1.0. W3C Recommendation, 10 February 2004. http://www.w3.org/TR/owl-ref/

20. Porter, M.F.: An algorithm for suffix stripping. Program, **14**(3), 1980, 130–137.
21. Rahm, E., Bernstein., P.A.: A survey of approaches to automatic schema matching. The VLDB Journal, **10**(4), 2001, 334–350.
22. RDF, Ressource Description Framework Primer W3C Recommendation, 10 February 2004. `http://www.w3.org/TR/rdf-primer/`
23. Sebastiani, F.: Machine learning in automated text categorization. ACM Comuting Surveys, **34**(1), 2002, 1–47.
24. Sure, Y., Corcho, O., Euzenat, J., Hughes, T. editors. 3rd *Int. Workshop on Evaluation of Ontology-based Tools (EON'04)*, Hiroshima, Japan, 2004.

Semantic Web Technologies for Interpreting DNA Microarray Analyses: The MEAT System

Khaled Khelif[1], Rose Dieng-Kuntz[1], and Pascal Barbry[2]

[1] INRIA Sophia Antipolis, 2004 route des lucioles 06902 Sophia Antipolis, France
{khaled.khelif, rose.dieng}@sophia.inria.fr
[2] IPMC, 660 route des lucioles 06560, Sophia Antipolis, France
barbry@ipmc.fr

Abstract. This paper describes MEAT (Memory of Experiments for the Analysis of Transcriptomes), a project aiming at supporting biologists working on DNA microarrays. We provide methodological and software support to build an experiment memory for this domain. Our approach, based on Semantic Web Technologies, is relying on formalized ontologies and semantic annotations of scientific articles and other knowledge sources. It can probably be extended to other massive analyses of biological events (as provided by proteomics, metabolomics…).

1 Introduction

Most of our knowledge can be stored in documents published on the web, in databases or correspond to human interpretations of experimental results. This knowledge is essential for checking, validating and enriching new research work. But the large amount of data, either from sources that are internal or external to users' organisations make the efficient detection, storage and use of this(ese) knowledge(s) huge tasks. This is especially true for investigators manipulating huge amounts of biological data, such as those working with DNA microarray[1] experiments, where several hundreds of experimental conditions can be easily analysed against 100,000 probes, and are to be linked to thousands of scientific reports. Under these situations, biologists need helping tools suitable for the interpretation and/or validation of their experiments, which would ultimately facilitate the planning of further experiments.

The MEAT project presented in this paper aims at proposing solutions to address these needs.

1.1 Context

The technology DNA Microarray has been developed after the full sequencing of many genomes in order to get about gene functions under many different biological contexts. Typical microarray experiments can assess thousands of genes simultaneously. Thus, they provide a huge amount of information and present difficulties for a biologist, in particular when s/he has to validate and interpret the obtained results.

---

[1] http://www.gene-chips.com/

M. Kitsuregawa et al. (Eds.): WISE 2005, LNCS 3806, pp. 148–160, 2005.

The needs of biologists can be summarized as follows:

- *A view on related experiments*: trying to identify relations between experiments (local databases, on-line data...) and to discover new research paths and different perspective for exploration.
- *Support the validation of experimental results*: by searching in documents about the studied phenomenon information which argue, confirm or invalidate the biologist's assumptions; this requires rich annotations.
- *Support the interpretation of experimental results*: by identifying new/known relations or/and interactions between genes, cellular components and biological processes; this requires inference capabilities over the annotations.

MEAT has been developed in collaboration with biologists of the Nice Sophia Antipolis DNA Microarray platform (located at the IPMC[2] laboratory with the aim to provide an experiment memory for this domain: as such, it constitutes a specific case of corporate semantic web at the scale of a community.

1.2 Corporate Memory and Semantic Web

Currently, semantic web techniques can play a major role in knowledge management and in the building of a corporate memory.

In fact, ontologies can be used throughout knowledge representation and provide formal grounding for representing the semantics of the knowledge pieces and can guide the creation of semantic annotations constituting a set of all meta-level characterizations easing knowledge source description, evaluation, and access.

[7] proposes to materialize a corporate memory through a "corporate semantic web" by using ontologies to formalize the vocabulary shared by a community, and semantic annotations based on these ontologies to describe heterogeneous knowledge sources (textual corpora, databases,...) and facilitate their access via intranet/internet.

In our case this corporate semantic web is constituted of:

- Resources: databases of experiments, persons and articles which can come from internal sources such as specific documentation databases for each biologist or from external sources such as on-line documentation databases (e.g. Medline[3]).
- Ontologies: MeatOnto, which is a multicomponent ontology composed of 3 ontologies (cf. §3.1).
- Ontology-based semantic annotations: which describe experiments stored in the databases (results, interpretations) and knowledge extracted from scientific articles. These annotations can be generated manually (Annotation editor) or automatically (Text mining techniques).

2 Our Approach

Taking into account biologist's needs, we aimed at building an experiment memory for the DNA microarray domain.

---

[2] http://www.ipmc.cnrs.fr/
[3] http://www.ncbi.nlm.nih.gov/entrez/query.fcgi

We first made an inventory of different knowledge sources which would constitute this memory:

- MEDIANTE[4]: an information system for biochip experiments developed at IPMC. It supports the management of a microarray project from the design of the DNA probes to the storage of the results.
- Journal articles: for each biochip project, biologists constitute a textual corpus of papers concerning genes supposed a priori interesting for experiments. Of particular interest was the selection by the biologists of review articles, such as those provided by series or found on the web. Such a selection was useful, in the sense that it provided overviews of (a) specific field(s), written by a specialist of this field, and selected by another specialist (i.e. the biologist doing the microarray experiments). Our hypothesis was that such selection would decrease the number of contradictory points of view provided by wider approaches using the web scanning.
- Biologist's viewpoint: interpretation of results, connection/correlation of phenomena or experiments...

Figure 1, which summarizes the MEAT architecture, recapitulates the different stages of our approach:

1. *Construction of an ontology* which describes all kinds of resources used by biologists (experiments database, scientific papers, biomedical features); this stage produced the *MeatOnto ontology.*

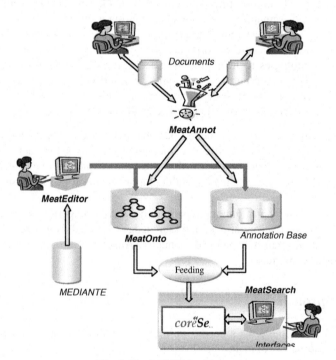

Fig. 1. The MEAT Architecure

---

[4] http://microarray.fr:8080/mediante/index

2. *Structuring knowledge contained in the MEDIANTE database* fields describing experiments in order to enable biologists to carry out searches, with the aim of finding similarities/correlations between experiments; this stage takes advantage of *semantic annotations based on MeatOnto.*
3. *Automation of the semantic annotation journal articles* interesting for experiments, using the MeatOnto ontology; for this, we designed and implemented the *MeatAnnot module.*
4. *Supplying the biologists with interfaces* to add new MeatOnto-based annotations on experiments or papers; this led to the implementation of *MeatEditor.*
5. *Facilitating the validation of experimental results* by proposing bibliographical searches guided by MeatOnto and by using the semantic annotations; this resulted in the *MeatSearch module.*
6. *Facilitating the interpretation of results* thanks to advanced inferences on semantic annotations which assist the explanation of a particular behaviour; this led to additional functionalities in the *MeatSearch* module.

In the following, we will present briefly MeatOnto (lack of space) and we will focus on MeatAnnot, the evaluation study on the generated annotations and MeatSearch with examples of use.

3 Meat Components

3.1 MEAT Ontologies: MeatOnto

MeatOnto is a modular ontology composed of 3 sub-ontologies, each dedicated to the description of a precise field:

- UMLS: the goal of the Unified Medical Language System project is to help health professionals and researchers to use biomedical information from a variety of different sources [12]. It consists of a metathesaurus which collects millions of terms belonging to the nomenclatures and terminologies defined in the biomedical domain and a semantic network which consists of 135 semantic types and 54 relationships, and it represents a high-level abstraction for the metathesaurus. To describe the biological domain (drugs, cells, genes, processes...), we chose UMLS, and we considered the UMLS semantic network as a general ontology: the hierarchy of semantic types can be regarded as a hierarchy of concepts and the terms of the metathesaurus as instances of these concepts.
- MGED: it was proposed by the MGED[5] group (Microarray Gene Expression Data) to describe microarray experiments [22] in order to facilitate the sharing of biochip experiment results. This ontology is used in MEAT to describe the experiments stored in MEDIANTE.
- DocOnto: we developed this ontology to describe metadata on papers (authors, source...) and on annotations (generated_by, validated_by...). This ontology describes the structure of papers (abstract, sentence, relation...) and it links documents to UMLS concepts (has_relation, speaks_about_genes...).

---

[5] http://www.mged.org/

The UMLS component was built automatically by a script translating the text format of the semantic network to an RDFS format and the DocOnto component was constructed progressively in order to cover our needs for the description of the knowledge contained in the scientific papers.

3.2 MeatAnnot

3.2.1 Generation of Annotations

In spite of its advantages, the creation of semantic annotations is a difficult and time-consuming process for biologists. Thus, we developed a system called MeatAnnot which, starting from texts (papers provided by biologists), allows to generate a structured annotation, based on MeatOnto, and describes the semantic content of this text.

MeatAnnot uses the NLP (Natural language processing) tools GATE[6], TreeTagger[11], RASP[2] and our own extensions dedicated to extract semantic relations and UMLS concepts. It processes texts and extracts interactions between genes and the others UMLS concepts.

So, for each sentence it detects an instance of UMLS relationship, it tries to detect the instances of UMLS concepts linked by this relationship and it generates an annotation describing this interaction (see more details in [13]).

The generation method breaks up into three steps described below:

Step1: Relation detection

In this step we used JAPE [6], a language based on regular expressions and allowing us to write information extraction grammar for texts processed by GATE. So, for each UMLS relation (such as interacts_with, expressed_in, disrupts...), an extraction grammar was manually created to extract all instances of this relation.

The example below shows a grammar which allows detection of instances of the semantic relation "Have an effect" with its different lexical forms in the text (e.g. has an effect, had effects, have a positive effect...).

```
{Token.lemme == "have"}|{SpaceToken}({Token.string == "a"}|{Token.string == "an"})?({SpaceToken})?
({Token.string == "additive"}|({Token.string == "synergistic"}|{Token.string == "inhibitory"}|{Token.string ==
"greater"}|{Token.string == "functional"}|{Token.string == "protective"}|{Token.string == "mono-
genic"}|{Token.string == "positive"})?({SpaceToken})?{Token.lemme == "effect"}
```

Step2: Term extraction

To extract terms, MeatAnnot uses the Tokeniser module of GATE and the TreeTagger. The tokeniser splits text into tokens, such as numbers, punctuation and words, and the TreeTagger assigns a grammatical category (noun, verb...) to each token.

After tokenizing and tagging texts, MeatAnnot uses an extraction window of four (four successive words are considered as a candidate term) and for each candidate term, if it exists in UMLS, MeatAnnot processes the following word, otherwise it decreases the size of the window till zero.

To interrogate UMLS, MeatAnnot uses the UMLSKS (KS: Knowledge Server). This server provides access and navigation in the UMLS metathesaurus and the UMLS semantic network. The answer received in XML format (if the term exists in UMLS) is parsed to obtain information about the term (semantic type, synonyms ...)

Step3: Annotation generation

In this step MeatAnnot uses the RASP module which assigns a linguistic role to sentence words (subj, obj ...) which allow to find out concepts linked by the relation. So for each relation, MeatAnnot verifies if its subjects and objects were detected as UMLS concepts and generates an annotation describing an instance of this relation.

The example below summarizes the process steps. Let us consider the sentence:

"In vitro assays demonstrated that only p38alpha and p38beta are inhibited by csaids."

First: by applying the extraction grammars on this sentence, MeatAnnot detects that it contains the UMLS relation *"inhibits"*.

Second: the table below describes the result of the term extraction phase:

Table 1. Term extraction results

Term	Semantic type	Synonyms
in vitro	Qualitative Concept	N/C
P38alpha	Gene or Genome	MAPK14 gene, CSBP1...
P38beta	Gene or Genome	MAPK11 gene, SAPK2...
Csaids	Pharmacologic Substance	Cytokine-Suppressant Anti-Inflammatory Drug

Third: MeatAnnot applies the RASP module on the sentence and parses the result to detect the different linguistic roles of words.

The result of RASP on this sentence is:

```
(|ncsubj| |demonstrate+ed:4_VVN| |assay+s:3_NN2| _)
(|clausal| |demonstrate+ed:4_VVN| |inhibit+ed:11_VVN|)
(|ncsubj| |inhibit+ed:11_VVN| |p38alpaha:7_NN2| |obj|)
(|ncsubj| |inhibit+ed:11_VVN| |p38beta:9_NN2| |obj|)
(|arg_mod| |by:12_II| |inhibit+ed:11_VVN| |csaid.+s:13_NN2| |subj|)
(|conj| _ |p38alpaha:7_NN2| |p38beta:9_NN2|)
(|mod| _ |p38alpaha:7_NN2| |only:6_RR|)
(|mod| _ |p38beta:9_NN2| |only:6_RR|)
```

p38alpha and *p38beta* are detected as the objects of the relation *inhibits* and *csaids* as its subject.

MeatAnnot generates an RDF annotation for these two instances and adds it to the paper annotation.

```
<m: Pharmacologic_Substance rdf:about='csaids#'>
  <m:inhibits>
      <m:Gene_or_Genome rdf:about='p38alpha#'/>
  </m:inhibits >
  <m:inhibits >
      <m: Gene_or_Genome rdf:about='p38beta#'/>
  </m:inhibits >
</m:Pharmacologic_Substance>
```

After text processing, MeatAnnot generates an RDF annotation describing all these interactions in the article and stores it in the directory containing the annotations of the other papers. These annotations can then be used, either in a bibliographical search or in a more complex IR (Information Retrieval) scenario such as searching interactions between genes or of genes with the other biomedical features.

3.2.2 Validation of Annotations

To validate our annotations we adopted a user-centered approach: we chose randomly a test corpus (2540 sentences) from the documents provided by biologists and we presented the suggestions proposed by MeatAnnot to biologists via an interface in order to evaluate their quality.

Since these annotations will be used in an IR context, we focused on classic IR quality measures for indexing and we adapted them to our case.

We noticed also that some suggestions were considered as correct but not useful to the biologists since they described a basic or vague knowledge. So, we introduced a new measurement called *usefulness* which measures the rate of useful suggestions.

Table 2. Measures for the quality of the annotations

	Measures
Precision	$\dfrac{\text{Nb suggestions correctly extracted}}{\text{Nb all suggestions extracted}}$
Recall	$\dfrac{\text{Nb suggestions correctly extracted}}{\text{Nb suggestions that should be extracted}}$
Usefulness	$\dfrac{\text{Nb useful suggestions extracted}}{\text{Nb suggestions correctly extracted}}$

Precision relates to the absence of noise (also called commission) in the extraction and *recall* relates to the absence of silence (also called omission).

Table 3. Quality of Meatannot suggestions

	Suggestion	Correct	Missing	Useful	Precision	Recall	Usefulness
Result	454	372	224	357	0,82	0,62	0,96

The second column describes the number of relations correctly extracted from texts. The difference with the number of suggestions proposed by MeatAnnot is due principally to the errors generated by the NLP tools (e.g. wrong grammatical category or linguistic role) and to the missing terms in UMLS (subject or object of a relation not found in UMLS). Nonetheless a good precision is obtained since 82% of the suggestions were correct.

The third column describes the number of relations not extracted by MeatAnnot, these missing suggestions are also due to the errors generated by the NLP tools and mainly to relations deduced by the biologist (when s/he reads the sentence) and which cannot be generated automatically.

Example of errors generated by the NLP tools:

"TRP gene, which belongs to the TRP-homolog group is expressed in neurons"

In this sentence where the relation "expressed_in" is detected, the RASP module suggests that *"which"* is the subject of the relation, so MeatAnnot does not generate the annotation because *"which"* is not an UMLS term and it losts the interaction between the *"TRP gene"* and *"neurons"*.

Example of missing relations:

"Upon interferon-gamma induction, after viral infection for example, a regulator of the proteasome, PA28 plays a role in antigen processing."

In this example, MeatAnnot extracts automatically the relation "PA28 plays_role antigen processing" but a biologist who reads this sentence can deduce, using his/her implicit knowledge, another relation which is "interferon-gamma have_effect PA28".

Finally, MeatAnnot has a good usefulness since 96% of correct suggestions are considered useful by biologists.

These results prove that MeatAnnot generates good quality annotations, an essential trait for a use in an information retrieval context.

3.3 Use of Annotations: MeatSearch

For enabling the biologists to use these annotations, we developed a tool called Meat-Search based on CORESE (Conceptual Resource Search Engine) [4][5] and composed of a set of GUI which allows users to ask queries on the annotation base.

MeatSearch translates the CORESE results to graphical or/and textual presentation (using adequate XSLT [3] style sheets) which is understandable by biologists. It also provides links to the sentence from which the annotation was extracted and to the document containing this sentence. This offers an interesting documentation on the annotations and this ability to trace the provenance is very useful for validation.

3.3.1 Use of CORESE

To formalize our ontologies and annotations, we chose RDFS [15] and RDF [14] languages, which are recommended by W3C, respectively to represent light ontologies and to describe web resources using ontology-based semantic annotations.

This choice enabled us to use the search engine CORESE which allows to:

- Navigate in the annotation bases taking into account the concept hierarchy and the relation hierarchy defined in the ontologies.
- Add rules which complete the annotation bases.
- Reason on the whole annotation base constructed from different and heterogeneous sources (papers, experiment database): it allows the biologist to deduce implicit and explicit knowledge about a gene.
- Use different levels of access (admin, public, group...) to the annotation base.
- Have different views on the annotations.

3.3.2 Examples of Use

CORESE proposes a query language for RDF very similar to SPARQL[6](currently under discussion as a w3c working draft); it enables to write queries constituted of a Boolean combination of RDF triples.

For example, the following query enables to retrieve all relations between a gene called "cav3.2" and a part of the human body:

```
select ?g ?r ?b where
?g    rdf:type    m:Gene_or_Genome
?g    =    'cav3.2'
?g    ?r    ?b
?b    rdf:type    m:Body_Part__Organ_or_Organ_Component
```

This query is generated automatically by MeatSearch and the result is formatted in a graphical representation (Figure 2) to facilitate its visualisation.

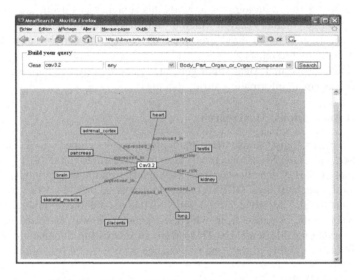

Fig 2. Result page of MeatSearch for the previous query

CORESE provides a rule language [4] which enables us to deduce new knowledge from existing one. The production rules are applied on the annotation base to complete it and to add more information in order to reduce the silence in the IR phase.

These rules are produced progressively by discussing with biologists.

An example of use of rule is:

"For each receptor which activates a molecular function, if this function plays a role in an organism function, the receptor can play the same role"

This rule is expressed as:

---

[6] http://www.w3.org/TR/rdf-sparql-query/

```
IF    ?r    rdf:type    m:Receptor
      ?r    m:activate    ?mf
      ?mf    rdf:type    m:Molecular_Function
      ?mf    m:play_role  ?of
      ?of rdf:type    m:Organism_Function
THEN
      ?r    m:play_role    ?of
```

A last example concerns the addition of metadata on an annotation so as to give more information on:

- The source of the resource: the biologist who provided the paper to annotate or the biologist who made the experiments.
- The source of the annotation: generated automatically by MeatAnnot vs. added/validated by a biologist.
- The general topic of the annotation: the different biologists may have different centers of interest about the same experiment.

The annotation below describes a paper provided by a biologist named Pascal and related to the lung development.

```
<do:paper rdf:about='http://www-sop.inria.fr/acacia/meat/lungrepair.pdf'>
    <do:providedBy>Pascal</do:providedBy >
    <do:relatedTo >
        <m: Organ_or_Tissue_Function rdf:about='lung_development #'/>
    </do:relatedTo >
    ....Annotation...
    <do:generatedBy>MeatAnnot</do:generatedBy>
    <do:validatedBy>Pascal</do:validatedBy>
    ...Annotation...
</do:paper>
```

MeatSearch uses these metadata to propose different views on the annotations base related to sources (annotation source), the context (general topic of the annotation) and the method of the annotation generation (automatically vs. manually).

Queries on these metadata are very useful for browsing the annotation base, for checking its coherence and for all the validation phase.

4 Conclusions

4.1 Discussion

In this paper, we presented a method based on semantic web technologies for building an experiment memory for the biochip domain. This method can be generalized to any life science domain (chemical domain, physical domain...), since they have the same needs such as the support for the validation and the interpretation of experiments results. In fact, the modules presented are reusable and rely on standard technologies. MeatAnnot is independent of NLP tools and can use any ontology.

Our approach proposes some solutions to problems raised in the final discussion of W3C Workshop on Semantic Web for Life Sciences [23]:

- Good quality of the annotations extracted automatically: MeatAnnot annotations.
- Adequate representation of the context: our metadata on annotations.
- Possibility of reasoning on annotations: CORESE enables such reasoning.
- Semantic web browsing: we offer an automatic association of semantics to the memory resources and we provide a user-interface support.

One originality of this work consists of (a) the integration of metadata on annotations which gives new ways of reasoning and more information on the annotation base, (b) the use of several technologies (such as NLP, Ontologies, Semantic annotations, CORESE) to provide a robust Corporate Semantic Web Application.

Finally, we think that an evaluation study on the generated annotations (as we propose in this paper) is necessary since this generation phase is expensive and often irreversible.

4.2   Related Work

The method on which MeatAnnot rests can be compared with (a) work using information extraction for the biology domain [21] and (b) work on the generation of semantic annotations for the semantic web [9]. In the domain of article mining in biology, statistical techniques and machine-learning algorithms has been proposed [20] for discovering interactions among genes from article abstracts in biology in the PubMed base. Our approach relying on linguistic tools differs from machine-learning-based approaches proposed by [1] [17]. It also differs from [8] that offers generation of annotations consisting of concept instances, in order to enrich the ontology: our approach allows the generation of semantic annotations based not only on concept instances but also on relation instances.

The couple MeatAnnot/MeatSearch generates and uses ontology-based semantic annotations extracted from texts. It offers an information retrieval system based on these annotations: this system has some similarities with Textpresso system proposed by [16]. Textpresso is an ontology-based information retrieval and extraction system for biological literature. It identifies terms (instances of the ontology concepts) by matching them against regular expressions and encloses them with xml tags. Textpresso also offers user interfaces to query these annotations. But Textpresso has the following drawbacks: (i) the annotation is embedded in the text, which makes difficult its reuse by other systems (while MeatAnnot generates an RDF annotation separate from the document), and (ii) it needs thousands of regular expressions to extract relevant terms (while in MeatAnnot, linguistic analysis performs the text matching task).

Relying on NLP techniques, MeatAnnot differs from semantic annotation systems that use a machine-learning based information extraction approach. These systems (for example S-CREAM [10] and MnM [24]) rely on manually annotated documents on which the method can be trained.

Relation extraction was studied by [19] that propose the CAMELEON method/system which allows the extraction of semantic relations between terms using linguistic patterns (For example "X is Indefinite_Article Y" for hypernomy relation). This method relies on morpho-syntactic regularity in texts and needs a pre-processing phase to define specific patterns for a domain.

Our method also uses patterns (JAPE grammar) to detect relations but it relies on an advanced syntactic analysis of texts (cf. use of linguistic roles) to extract terms linked by the relation. Methods like CAMELEON could be used in our system as complement to improve the relation extraction phase (for example when the system fails to assign the correct linguistic role in a sentence).

Finally, MeatSearch can also be compared with web reasoning systems [18] applied on corporate memory, since it integrates CORESE and enables advanced information retrieval and reasoning on annotations.

4.3 Further Work

As a further work, we will try to integrate a new module to MeatAnnot which takes into account graphics and tables in the papers. We will install a local version of UMLS and manage its evolution which implies the evolution of the annotations. Finally, we will create with biologists several scenarios of use with typical queries to facilitate the navigation in the annotation base.

Acknowledgements

We thank Remy Bars from Bayers Cropscience, the IPMC team working on microarray experiments and PACA[7] region which funds this work by regional grant.

References

1. Blaschke C. & Valencia A., Molecular biology nomenclature thwarts information-extraction progress. IEEE Intelligent Systems & their Applications, p. 73-76. (2002).
2. Briscoe, E. and J. Carroll (2002) Robust accurate statistical annotation of general text. In *Proceedings of the Third IC LR E,* Las Palmas, Gran Canaria. 1499-1504.
3. Clark J., "XSL Transformations (XSLT) Version 1.0," W3C Recommendation, http://www.w3.org/TR/xslt (November, 1999).
4. Corby, O., Faron-Zucker, C.: Corese: A Corporate Semantic Web Engine. In Workshop on Real World RDF and Semantic Web Applications - WWW'02 Hawaii. 2002.
5. Corby, O., Dieng-Kuntz R. Faron-Zucker, C., Querying the Semantic Web with the CORESE engine. ECAI'2004, Valencia, August 2004, IOS Press, p.705-709
6. Cunningham H., Maynard D., Bontcheva K. & Tablan V. (2002). GATE: A Framework and Graphical Development Environment for Robust NLP Tools and Applications. ACL'02.
7. Dieng-Kuntz R., Corporate Semantic Webs, To appear in Encyclopaedia of Knowledge Management, D. Schwartz ed., Idea Publishing Group, July 2005
8. Golebiowska J. & Dieng-Kuntz R. & Corby O., & Mousseau D. Building and Exploiting Ontologies for an Automobile Project Memory. .In Proc. of K-CAP, Canada. (2001)
9. Handschuh S. , Koivunen M., Dieng R. & Staab S., eds, Proc. of KCAP'2003 Workshop on Knowledge Markup and Semantic Annotation, Sanibel, Florida, October 26. (2003)

---

[7] http://www.cr-paca.fr/

10. Handschuh S., Staab S. and Ciravegna F. (2002), S-CREAM – Semi-automatic CREAtion of Metadata.The 13th International Conference on Knowledge Engineering and Management (EKAW 2002), ed Gomez-Perez, A., Springer Verlag
11. Helmut Schmid. 1994. Probabilistic part-of-speech tagging using decision trees. In Proceedings of International Conference on New Methods in Language Processing.
12. Humphreys BL, Lindberg DAB. The UMLS project: making the conceptual connection between users and the information they need. Bull Med Libr Assoc. 1993
13. Khelif K., Dieng-Kuntz R. - Ontology-Based Semantic Annotations for Biochip Domain, Proc. of EKAW 2004 Workshop on the Application of Language and Semantic Technologies to support KM Processes, U.K., 2004, http://CEUR-WS.org/Vol-121/.
14. Lassila O. and Swick R. (2001). W3C Resource Description framework (RDF) Model and Syntax Specification, http://www.w3.org/TR/REC-rdf-syntax/
15. McBride B.,"RDF Vocabulary Description Language 1.0: RDF Schema", W3C Recommendation, http://www.w3.org/TR/rdf-schema/ (February, 2004).
16. Muller, H.M., Kenny, E.E., Sternberg, P.W. (2004) Textpresso: an ontology-based information retrieval and extraction system for biological literature *PLoS Biol.*, 2, E309
17. Nédellec C., Bibliographical Information Extraction in Genomics. IEEE Intelligent Systems & their Applications, p.76-80, March/April. (2002)
18. Ohlbach H. J., Schaffert S. (eds) Workshop on Principles and Practice of Semantic Web Reasoning at The 20th ICLP, St Malo, France, 2004
19. Séguéla P. and Aussenac-Gilles N. (1999). Extraction de relations sémantiques entre termes et enrichissement de modèles du domaine. In IC'99, Paris, 79-88
20. Shatkay H., Edwards S. & Boguski M., Information Retrieval Meets Gene Analysis. IEEE Intelligent Systems & their Applications, p. 45-53. (2002)
21. Staab S., eds., Mining Information for Functional Genomics. IEEE Intelligent Systems & their Applications, p. 66-80, March-April. (2002)
22. Stoeckert, C.J., Jr and Parkinson H. (2003) The MGED ontology: a framework for describing functional genomics experiments. Comp. Funct. Genomics, 4, 127 132.
23. Summary Report - W3C Workshop on Semantic Web for Life Sciences. http://www.w3.org/2004/10/swls-workshop-report.html
24. Vargas-Vera M., Motta E., Domingue J., Lanzoni M., Stutt A. and Ciravegna F. (2002), MnM: Ontology Driven Semi-Automatic and Automatic Support for Semantic Markup, In Gomez-Perez A. and Benjamins R. eds, Proc. of the 13th International Conference on Knowledge Engineering and Knowledge Management EKAW 2002, Springer Verlag LNAI 2473, 379-391.

Extracting Global Policies for Efficient Access Control of XML Documents

Mizuho Iwaihara[1], Bo Wang[1], and Somchai Chatvichienchai[2]

[1] Department of Social Informatics, Kyoto University
[2] Department of Info-Media, Siebold University of Nagasaki
iwaihara@i.kyoto-u.ac.jp, wang@db.soc.i.kyoto-u.ac.jp,
somchaic@sun.ac.jp

Abstract. As documents containing sensitive information are exchanged over the Internet, access control of XML documents is becoming important. Access control policies can specify fine-grained rules to documents, but policies sometimes become redundant, as documents are restructured or combined during exchange. In this paper, we consider a new approach of optimizing access control policies, by extracting distribution information of given authorization values within XML data. The extracted information is called a global policy tree, and it can be utilized for minimizing the total size of policies as well as efficient query processing. We present a linear-time algorithm for minimizing policies utilizing global policy trees, and our evaluation results show significant improvement over existing work.

1   Introduction

XML is regarded as a standard language for information exchange over the Internet. As corporate and private sensitive data are stored and exchanged in XML documents, access control of XML is becoming important. A number of XML access control models are proposed in the literature [2][3][7] [10]. XACML [15] is an OASIS standard for access control of XML documents. Management of access control policies is an important issue, as modern privacy-aware systems offer functionalities for specifying policies to privacy information owners, resulting in a high volume of policies. Keeping non-redundant policies is an essential task for efficient policy management.

Compressed Accessibility Map (CAM)[19][20] is a space-efficient and time-efficient data structure for determining accessibility to nodes of XML document trees. A CAM is defined as a collection of access control rules (d, s) such that s defines accessibility (grant/deny) of a node, and d defines accessibility to the proper descendants of the node. A linear-time algorithm exists for constructing a minimum CAM.

The CAM approach can take advantages of locality of accessibility, such that one entire subtree of a document can be protected by a rule. The CAM approach is also suitable for specifying *instance-specific policies*, meaning that each instance node can have its own access control rule. This is useful for modeling fine-grained policies specified by the owners of privacy data, such as a patient chooses his/her own access control rule policies for his/her patient records, as pointed out in [1]. However, the CAM approach does not consider structural information of what collection of paths are involved in defining policies.

M. Kitsuregawa et al. (Eds.): WISE 2005, LNCS 3806, pp. 161–174, 2005.

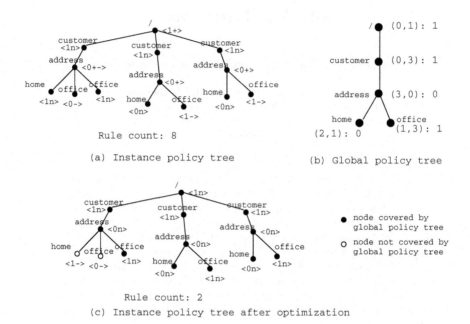

Fig. 1. Example of instance and global policy trees

Consider XML document trees shown in Fig. 1. Figure 1(a) is the tree structure of a document instance, where each node is labeled with its element name, such as customer, address, and name. The tree nodes are adorned with access control rules, represented by angular brackets. Here, 0 and 1 are access authorization values 'deny' and 'grant', respectively. The symbols '+', '-', '±', 'n' denote cascade modes, such that '+' means the authorization value is applied to the node itself and its descendants; namely the value is cascaded down. The symbol '-' means the value is applied only to the node and no cascaded value, while '±' means the value is imposed to the node itself, but the opposite value is cascaded down to its descendants. Finally, 'n' means no rule is defined at the node, and the cascaded value from its ancestor is adopted as the value for the node. For example, the node at the leftmost path '/customer/address/home' has a rule of type $\langle 1n \rangle$, meaning that access to the node is permitted, and the value 1 is cascaded from an ancestor of the node. We call XML document trees adorned with these access control rules *instance policy trees*. We call a node in a global policy tree a *global node* and a node in an instance policy tree an *instance node*.

Now consider finding a minimum set of rules for a given authorization value assignment to document nodes, by properly setting the cascade mode. Setting a rule of type $\langle 1+ \rangle$ can cover the descendants which have authorization value 1. The minimization can be done in linear time, by dynamic programming. Actually, the instance policy tree shown in Fig. 1 has minimum number of rules. This policy compression is proposed in the CAM model[19][20]. However, this compression is not optimum if the distribution of authorization values has some correlation with document structures. Consider the paths p_1 ='/customer/address/home' and p_2='/customer/address/office'. It is likely that most of users do not want their home addresses disclosed, and their office addresses can be public. These tendencies will be reflected to the statistic information such that for the nodes on path p_1, the number of nodes having value 0 is greater than the number of nodes having value 1, and the opposite tendency for path p_2. We can construct a *global policy tree* G from an instance policy tree I such that G contains all the paths of I, but each path appears to G only once. This technique is often called a structural summary, and extensively studied in the literature including dataguide[8]. But we add the following statistical information to a global policy tree: Each node f of G holds the node count $(count0, count1)$ such that $count0$ (resp. $count1$) is the number of nodes of I on the same path as f and has authorization value 0 (resp. 1). The global policy tree constructed from Fig. 1(a) is shown in Fig. 1(b). The statistical information of G can tell us that the majority of nodes on the path are inaccessible if $count0 > count1$, and accessible otherwise.

Global policy trees are much smaller than instance policy trees, and they can be utilized for policy compression as well as query optimization. For example, looking up a global policy tree G gives us the majority authorization value on a specified path. If the authorization value of an instance node is the same as that of the global policy tree node, we can omit a rule for the instance node. For example, by utilizing the global policy tree of Fig. 1(b), we can further reduce the policy size from 8 to 2, and obtain the instance policy tree of Fig. 1(c), and this is optimum.

The ratio of inaccessible nodes to accessible nodes on a path is useful for policy evaluation. Suppose that most of nodes on the path are inaccessible. Then a query on the path is permitted to a little number of nodes. In this case, policy evaluation before the query is advantageous. Furthermore, if $count1 = 0$ (resp. $count1 = 0$) holds on a path, then without accessing the instance policy tree we can conclude that a query to the path is denied (resp. granted).

In this paper, we present a linear-time algorithm for extracting global policy trees from instance policy trees, and a linear-time algorithm for minimizing policy sizes under the existence of global policy trees. We also show experimental results that our algorithm can achieve better compression results than the previous work of minimizing without global policy trees.

In the following, we survey related work. Access control policies are often formulated using XPath[18], where accessible/inaccessible parts of documents are specified as XPath expressions. In the statistic analysis approach[13], XPath queries to the XML database can be checked whether having intersection with access control policies. The result of statistic analysis of a query is either grant, deny, or indeterminate. In the grant case, the XML database is accessed to answer the query. In the deny case, query evaluation is terminated without accessing the XML database. In the indeterminate case, the XML database is accessed to retrieve necessary data to determine accessibility. QFilter[12] also follows this direction and constructs nondeterministic finite automata (NFA) for filtering out inaccessible parts. Pre-filtering and post-filtering are necessary before and after accessing XML databases.

Statical analysis of queries employed in these approaches are effective when accessibility can be determined only by comparing the query NFA and access control NFA. Such situations occur when policies are simple XPaths, such as '/customer/address'.

However, if path expressions of access control rules are more complex, such as containing predicates, it is often inevitable that database access is necessary. Furthermore, XPath-based policy specification is not suitable for instance-specific policies, since a larger subset of XPath queries, such as involving sibling axes, is necessary for policy specification. However, sibling axes are not allowed in the statical analysis. In our approach, policy NFA can be constructed from the statistical information of global policy trees, and the policy NFA can be utilized for static analysis and query translation. Also, global policy trees can provide probabilistic information, such as path selectivity, for query optimization.

The rest of this paper is organized as follows: In Section 2, we define a basic model of XML access control, and define global and instance policy trees. In Section 3, we present a linear-time algorithm for minimizing instance policy trees utilizing global policy trees. In Section 4, we show experimental results of minimizing access control policies, and Section 5 is a conclusion.

2   XML Access Control Rules

2.1   Instance Policy Tree

An XML document is denoted as $D = (N, E, r)$, where N is a labeled node set, E is a set of document edges, and $r \in N$ is the document root. Each node $n \in N$ has a content, denoted by $content(n)$, which consists of an element or attribute tag name and a text value. We do not distinguish elements and attributes, and we represent both by nodes.

We use the term *access control policy*, or simply *policy*, for a set of *access control rules*, or *rules*. Each rule of a node (owner node) has the following format:

$$\langle subject, privilege, decision, cascade \rangle$$

Here, $subject$ is a role[14] or user name, $privilege$ is either read or write, $decision$ is 1 (permit) or 0 (deny), $cascade$ is '+' or '-'. Here, '+' means that the decision value of the rule effect is cascaded down to the descendant nodes of the owner node e. On the other hand, '-' means no-cascade, and the decision is applied only to e. The no-cascade option '-' does not interfere with the cascade value descending from the parent of the owner node e. Namely, if the value of 0 or 1 is cascaded from the parent, then the same value is cascaded to the descendants of e, regardless of the value defined by the option '-'. On the contrary, the option '+' overrides the cascaded value from the parent and the value defined with '+' is cascaded down to the descendants of e. This way of resolving conflicting rules is called *descendant-take-precedence* or *most-specific-take-precedence*. There are three types of cascade values: 0, 1 and n (no value).

A policy can be partitioned into rule subsets where each subset consists of the same $subject$ and $priviledge$. For a fixed rule subset, we can define authorization function a from node set N to $\{0, 1\}$. We also use the abbreviations $\langle 0+ \rangle, \langle 1+ \rangle, \langle 0- \rangle, \langle 0+ \rangle$, which are combinations of the decision values $\{0, 1\}$ and the cascade options $\{+, -\}$. For example, $\langle 0+ \rangle$ means that a rule of authorization value $a(e) = 0$ and cascade option '+' is defined to node e. We use the symbol $\langle n \rangle$ to indicate that no rule is defined

Table 1. Symbols of cascade modes

Symbol	Semantics	# of rules
n	No rule for node e. The cascaded value from the parent of e is passed to e's descendants	0
+	Node e is assigned authorization value $a(e)$ and e'descendants receive $a(e)$ as the cascade value.	1
-	Node e is assigned value $a(e)$. The cascade value from e's parent is passed to e's descendants.	1
$\pm$	Node e is assigned cascade value $a(e)$, and the opposite value of $a(e)$ is cascaded to e's descendants.	2

to e. We also use the notations $\langle 0\pm \rangle$ and $\langle 1\pm \rangle$ as the combination of $\langle 0-\rangle\langle 1+\rangle$ and $\langle 1-\rangle\langle 0+\rangle$, respectively. Here, we assume that the first rule overrides the later rule. The rule $\langle 0\pm \rangle$ means that decision value 0 is defined to e, but value 1 is cascaded to the children of e. We assume two rules are counted for $\langle 0\pm \rangle$ and $\langle 1\pm \rangle$. The symbols of cascade options, and their costs (rule counts) are listed in Table 1.

The CAM model[19][20] uses a different system of rule types. The symbol s represents the node itself, and d represents (proper) descendants, and '+' is grant and '-' is deny. There are four rule types: $\langle s+, d+\rangle, \langle s+, d-\rangle, \langle s-, d+\rangle, \langle s-, d-\rangle$. The corresponding symbols in our system are: $\langle 1+\rangle, \langle 0\pm \rangle, \langle 1\pm \rangle, \langle 0+\rangle$, respectively. The reason of why we use a different system from the CAM model is that we need to add 'n' (no value) as a new cascade value, for introducing global policy trees. The CAM model always defines grant or deny as cascade value at each node, and 'n' no-value to cascade is not considered. On the other hand, in our system 'n' can be cascaded using the '-' option. The no-value works as *don't care* and plays an important role when a global policy tree is present.

As for the storage model of access control rules, we can choose from two approaches: One is to store rules separately from the documents, where each document node is assigned a unique identifier and rules for a node is looked up by using the identifier, in the same manner as the CAM model. Here, rules are grouped per user and per privilege. The other approach is to embed rules as a text value of an attribute of each node. In this paper, we do not discuss which approach is more advantageous. We rather focus on algorithms for compacting rules which work well for both approaches. We use the term an *instance policy tree* as a document tree adorned with access control rules, where rules may be stored at each node or separately from each node.

2.2 Global Policy Trees

In this section, we introduce the notion of global policy trees as as a structural summary of fine-grained accessibility of XML documents.

A *simple path* is an expression of the form $/e_1/e_2/\cdots/e_k$, where $e_i(i = 1,\ldots,k-1)$ is an element name and e_k is either element or attribute name, and the first slash '/' represents the document root. We use the notation p_e for the simple path from the root to node e, where the root should be clear from the context.

Let D be an XML document. To handle a collection of XML documents, we add a virtual root node and treat them as a single document. We define a *global policy tree* G of a document D such that G contains all the simple paths of D, and for each simple path p_f of G, G has only one node which satisfies p_f. Each node f of G has attributes $count0$ and $count1$ such that $count0$ (resp. $count1$) records the number of denied (resp. granted) nodes having the simple path p_f.

A global policy tree can be constructed from a given document D by the following simple linear-time algorithm:

Algorithm GlobalPolicy(D): Traverse D in preorder and for each encountered node e, create path p_e in G if it does not exist, and if $a(e) = 0$ then increment attribute $f.count0$, else increment attribute $f.count1$. Here, f is the sole node having the path p_e in G.

For each node f in G, we define the authorization value $a(f)$ as $a(f) = 0$ if $f.count0 < f.count1$ and otherwise $a(f) = 1$. Namely, $a(f)$ holds the majority of the authorization values of the nodes of D on the simple path p_f. The size of a global policy tree is significantly smaller than the original document. Global policy trees can be constructed regardless of existence of a DTD or schema.

Extracting tree-like structures from XML documents are discussed in XMILL[11], where *skeleton* of a document is extracted by reporting each simple path by the depth-first traversal, and the text value of each simple path is appended to a vector associated to each path. The original document can be reconstructed from the skeleton and the vectors. In the vector representation of XML data in [4], tree-like skeleton are compressed into DAGs, by sharing common subtrees. Both [11] and [4] propose XPath query evaluation on skeletons. Our approach of global policy trees is different from these previous works in the way that, we do not intend to reconstruct the original authorization assignment to the global policy tree, but we try to extract structural tendencies of authorization assignment to document trees, for policy tree compaction and query optimization. The original authorization assignment can be reconstructed from a global policy tree and an instance policy tree. Unlike skeletons for compression of the entire XML data, we only need to consider authorization values of 0 and 1, so that tendency information can be compactly extracted. We further discuss utilization of global policy trees in the following:

(**uniformity**) For a global policy tree G, assume that attribute $count0$ of a node f of G equals zero. Then there is no denied node that has simple path p_f. For example, from the global policy tree in Fig. 1(b), we find that the path '/customer' has no denied node, so we can conclude that accessing '/customer' is permitted without examining instance policy trees. Likewise, if the attribute $count1$ of g of G equals zero, then there is no accessible node that has simple path p_g. This uniformity information can be utilized for query evaluation and policy evaluation, in the way that if a query q is trying to access nodes on the path p_q, then we examine G and determine whether node g that matches p_q, and discover that if $count0$ value of node g equals zero, then all the nodes of D that match p_q are accessible, and if $count1$ value equals zero, then all the nodes of D that match p_q are inaccessible. In either case we can terminate policy evaluation without examining document instances or instance policy trees. The CAM approach[19][20] does not support utilizing extracted uniformity information and always needs to look up instance-level rules. Our approach of global policy trees can fill the gap between the static analysis approach and the CAM approach.

(**tendency**) Some document nodes may show inclination toward grant or denial authorization, even though they do not present uniformity. For example, the document tree in Fig. 1(a) shows that two out of three nodes on the path '/customer/address/home' are accessible, and one node on that path is inaccessible. This can be interpreted as most of customers do not want their home addresses being disclosed. But a minority of customers use their home addresses for contact. Such tendencies will be reflected to the global policy tree as the path p_{f1}= '/customer/address/home' has more inaccessible nodes than accessible nodes, namely, $p_{f1}.count0 > p_{f1}.count1$ holds. Such structural tendencies of authorization values can be utilized for compactly representing instance-specific rules. We record the majority authorization value to each node of a global policy tree, so that most common access control policies are covered by the global policy tree. Instance subtrees may have disagreement with the majority authorization values of the global policy tree. Therefore we create instance policy trees to cover nodes which have authorization values disagreeing with the corresponding nodes in the global policy tree. By creating instance policy trees only for deviation from the global policy tree, we can construct significantly compact policy representation.

3   Optimizing Instance Policy Trees

3.1   Issues in Total Optimization

Now we discuss constructing an instance policy tree which has minimum number of rules. We assume that instance policy tree I has priority over global policy tree G in authorization decision, so that if an authorization value is undefined in I, then the majority value of G is adopted. On the other hand, if an authorization value is defined at a node in I, then that value is adopted. This conflict resolution is called *instance-take-precedence*. By combining decisions from I and G, we can reconstruct the original access control policies.

If the authorization value of a node e of D is *covered* by the global policy tree G, that is, $a(e) = a(f)$ where f is a node of G having the same simple path as e, then there is no need to define an authorization value to e by the instance policy tree I. However, defining an authorization value to an instance node e is sometimes advantageous even if it overlaps with the global policy tree. For example, consider the instance policy tree depicted in Fig. 2. The global policy tree in Fig. 2(b) shows the majority authorization values 1, 1, and 0 for paths '/', '/a' and '/a/b', respectively. The instance policy tree in Fig. 2(a) has three instance nodes whose authorization value is 1 (depicted as 'o'), disagreeing with the global policy node on '/a/b'. Also there is an instance node which is a sibling of these three nodes but it has authorization value 0 (depicted as '•').

Now let us consider assigning optimum rules to these nodes. If we set a rule of type $\langle 1-\rangle$ to the three disagreeing nodes, we need three rules. On the other hand, if we set a rule of type $\langle 1+\rangle$ to the parent on '/a', then the rule can also cover the three nodes by cascade. However, this rule contradicts with the only node on '/a/b' which has value 0, thus we need to add one rule of type $\langle 0-\rangle$ to that node. But we can reduce the rule size

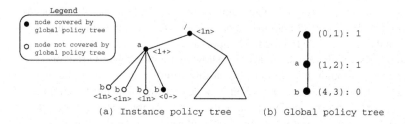

Fig. 2. Overlapping rules for covering disagreeing instance nodes

to two. Here, notice that the parent on '/a' has value 1, and hence it is already covered by the global policy tree. However, by adding an additional rule to the parent, we can reduce the rule size. Furthermore, the only node on '/a/b' having value 0 also needs the additional rule of type $\langle 0-\rangle$, since the cascade value from the parent contradicts with the global policy node. These overheads can be justifiable if the total instance policy tree size is reduced by taking such overheads. Although such complicating effects of rule settings exist, in the next subsection we show a linear-time algorithm for minimizing instance policy trees.

3.2 Algorithm InstancePolicy

First, we consider computing the following values for each instance node e in a bottom-up fashion.

1. $cost(x, e)$ is the minimum rule count for the instance subtree rooted at e. Parameter $x \in \{0, 1, n\}$ is the value cascaded from the parent of e. For example, $cost(0, e)$ represents the minimum rule size of the subtree when 'deny' is cascaded to e.
2. $rcas(x, e) \in \{0, 1, n\}$ is the authorization value which will be cascaded from e such that rules of size $cost(x, e)$ can be constructed by cascading $rcas(x, e)$. In the same manner as $cost(x, e)$, parameter $x \in \{0, 1, n\}$ is the value cascaded from the parent of e.

By computing the above functions $cost$ and $rcas$, we determine the rule type which gives the minimum number of rules for each subtree. We present algorithm InstancePolicy in Fig. 3. A sample of applying InstancePolicy to an instance policy tree is shown in Fig. 4. Here, $rcas$ values are shown in square brackets and $cost$ values are shown in curly brackets. The total rule count after optimization is three.

3.3 Timebound and Optimality of InstancePolicy

Theorem 1. Algorithm InstancePolicy computes an instance policy tree I from a document tree D in $O(|D|)$ time.

Proof. InstancePolicy consists of subroutines InstancePolicyBody and AssignPolicy. Both subroutines are called once. InstancePolicyBody traverses D in postorder, visiting

---

Algorithm InstancePolicy(D, G, e_r)
Input: An XML document D with root node e_r and a global policy tree G.
Output: An instance policy tree I.
Method:
/* Recursively apply subroutine InstancePolicy-Body to the subtree D_i rooted at a node e_i and obtain policy P_{D_i}. A rule is written to $rule(e_i)$. For a node in D, let $s(e)$ denote the unique node of the global policy tree G which has the same path as e.
*/
(1) InstancePolicyBody(D, e);
(2) AssignPolicy(D, n, e);
(3) return;

Algorithm InstancePolicyBody(D, e):
(1) if (e has children $\{e_1, \ldots, e_k\}$) then {
    for ($i = 1, \ldots, k$) {
      InstancePolicyBody(D, e_i); }
  }
(2) /* If e has no children, then let each Σ_i below be zero. */
  dcost0 := Σ_i cost(0, e_i); dcost1 := Σ_i cost(1, e_i);
  dcostn := Σ_i cost(n, e_i);
(3) /* In (3) and (4), compute cost0 (resp. cost1) for the cost of cascading 0 (resp.1) from e, when 0 is cascaded from e's ancestor. */
  if $a(e) = 1$ then {
    cost0 := dcost0 + 1; /* case of '−' */
    cost1 := dcost1 + 1; /* case of '+' */
  }
  else {
    cost0 := dcost0;   /* case 'n' */
    cost1 := dcost1 + 2; /* case of '±' */
  }
(4) if (cost0 = min(cost0,cost1)) then {
    rcas(0, e) := 0; cost(0, e) := cost0;
  }
  else {
    rcas(0, e) := 1; cost(0, e) := cost1;
  }
(5) /* Compute cost0 (resp. cost1) for the cost of cascading 0 (resp.1) from e, when 1 is cascaded from e's ancestor. */
  if ($a(e) = 1$) then {
    cost0 := dcost0 + 2; /* case of '±' */
    cost1 := dcost1;   /* case of 'n' */
  }
  else {
    cost0 := dcost0 + 1; /* case of '+' */
    cost1 := dcost1 + 1; /* case of '−' */
  }
(6) if (cost0 = min(cost0,cost1)) then {
    rcas(1, e) := 0; cost(1, e) := cost0;
  }

else {
  rcas(1, e) := 1; cost(1, e) := cost1;
}
(7) /* When cascading value from ancestor is 'n' */
  costn := dcostn;
  if ($a(e) <> a(s(e))$) then costn := costn +1;
  if ($a(e) = 1$) then {
    cost0 := dcost0 + 2;   /* case of '±' */
    cost1 := dcost1 + 1;   /* case of '+' */
  }
  else {
    cost0 := dcost0 + 1;   /* case of '+' */
    cost1 := dcost1 + 2;   /* case of '±' */
  }
(8) minc := min(cost0,cost1,costn);
  if (cost0 = minc) then {
    rcas(n, e) := 0; cost(n, e) := cost0;
  }
  else if (cost1 = minc) then {
    rcas(n, e) := 1; cost(n, e) := cost1;
  }
  else {
    rcas(n, e) := n; cost(n, e) := costn;
  }
(9) return;

Algorithm AssignPolicy(D, cas, e):
/* Using the rcas values computed by InstancePolicyBody, the following AssignPolicy determines the optimum rule for each node in a top-down fashion. The argument cas is the cascading value to node e.
*/
(1) if (cas = n) then {
    switch(rcas(cas,e)) {
    case 0 : if ($a(e) = 0$) then rule(e) := "+";
                    else rule(e) := "± ";
    case 1: if ($a(e) = 1$) then rule(e) := "+";
                    else rule(e) := "± ";
    case n: if ($a(e) = a(s(e))$) then rule(e) := "n";
                    else rule(e) := "-";
    }
  }
  else if (cas = rcas(cas,e)) then {
    if ($a(e) = $ cas) then rule(e) := "n";
    else rule(e) := "-";
  }
  else {
    if ($a(e) = $ cas) then rule(e) := "+";
    else rule(e) := "±";
  }
(2) /* Let node e's children be $\{e_1, \ldots, e_k\}$. */
  for ($i = 1, \ldots, k$)
    AssignPolicy(D, rcas(cas,e), e_i);
(3) return;

Fig. 3. Algorithm InstancePolicy

each node in D only once. Step (2) takes $O(|D|)$ time. Steps (3)-(9) take $O(1)$ per node. Notice that in Step (7) the global policy tree G is accessed by function $s(e)$. Since G is accessed in the same order of node labels as D, G is accessed in postorder and each evaluation of $s(e)$ takes $O(1)$ time. Combining those facts, we obtain that InstancePol-

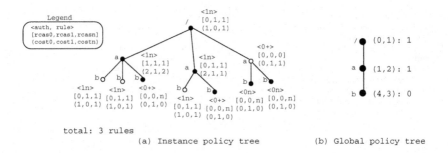

Fig. 4. Computing costs of each subtree by InstancePolicy

icyBody takes $O(|D|)$ time. AssignPolicy traverses D in preorder and processing each node takes $O(1)$ time.

Lemma 1. For a given node e in a document tree D, a global policy tree G, and a cascade value c to e in $\{0, 1, n\}$, InstancePolicyBody computes $cost(c, e)$ and $rcas(c, e)$ such that $cost(c, e)$ is the minium size of an instance policy tree I_e for the subtree D_e rooted at e such that I_e realizes the authorization assignment of D_e and the cascading value from e is $rcas(c, e)$.

Proof. We prove by induction on the size of subtree D_e.
(base case) When $|D_e| = 1$, e is a leaf node. In this case, $dcost0 = dcost1 = dcostn = 0$ is computed at Step 2. When value c cascading to e is 0, one rule of type '-' is needed if $a(e) = 1$, and no rule is necessary if $a(e) = 0$. The correct values of $cost(0, e) = 1$ for $a(e) = 1$ and $cost(0, e) = 0$ for $a(e) = 0$ are computed at Step 4. Likewise, when c is 1, the correct values of $cost(1, e) = 0$ for $a(e) = 1$ and $cost(1, e) = 1$ for $a(e) = 0$ are computed at Step 6. When c is n, if $a(e) = a(s(e))$ holds, namely e is covered by G, then no rule is necessary and $cost(n, e) = 0$, otherwise one rule is necessary and $cost(n, e) = 1$.
(inductive step) Suppose that the lemma holds for any node e such that $|D_e| \leq n(n \geq 1)$. Now consider a node e' such that $|D_{e'}| = n + 1$. Let the children of e' be $e_1, \ldots, e_k$. Here, $|D_{e_i}| \leq n$ holds. By the inductive hypothesis, InstancePolicyBody(D, e_i) at Step 1 computes the minimum tree size $cost(x, e_i)$ and the cascading value $rcas(x, e_i)$ from e_i, for each cascading value $x \in \{0, 1, n\}$ to e_i, $i = 1, \ldots, k$.

At Step 2, dcost0, dcost1 and dcostn are the sums of the instance policy tree sizes of the subtree rooted at $e_1, \ldots, e_k$, under cascading values 0,1,n *from* e', respectively. The sums dcost0, dcost1 and dcostn are minimum, since otherwise there should be a node e_i and a value x such that the minimum policy tree size is smaller than $cost(x, e_i)$, contradicting the hypothesis. The instance policy tree size at e' consists of one of dcost0, dcost1, and dcostn plus the rule size of the subtree root e'. Therefore it is now sufficient to prove that the selection of $rcas(c, e')$ is optimum.

At Step 3, for the case when $c = 0$ is cascaded to e', cost0 (resp. cost1) is computed as the cost of selecting 0 (resp. 1) as the cascading value from e'. Here, when $a(e') = 1$, since the cascading value to e' disagrees with $a(e')$, one rule of type '-' at e' is necessary to define authorization value 1 to e' (cost0), and one rule of type '+' is necessary to define authorization value 1 to e' and its descendants (cost1). When $a(e') = 0$ and the cascading value from e' is 0, no rule is necessary at e' (cost0). When $a(e') = 0$ and the cascading value to e' is 1, two rules ($\pm$) are necessary to define 1 to e' and 0 to e''s descendants(cost1). It is obvious that rules cannot be reduced any further. At Step 4, the cascading value which gives smaller cost is chosen as $rcas(0, e')$.

Likewise, Steps 5 and 6 compute $cost(1, e')$ and $rcas(1, e')$ for the case when $c = 1$ is cascaded to e'. We note that the case of cascading n from e' needs not to be considered, because the cascading value 0 or 1 is already cascaded to e' and n cannot be selected as the cascading value from e'.

Steps 7 and 8 are for the case where n is cascaded to e'. In this case, if authorization value $a(e')$ agrees with the corresponding node of G, then no rule is necessary for e'. In Steps 3-8, all the cases of cascading values from e' are tested and the minimum case is selected as $rcas(c, e')$, for each different cascading value $c = 0, 1, n$ to e'. Therefore minimality is proven.

Theorem 2. Given a document tree D and a global policy tree G, algorithm InstancePolicy computes an instance policy tree I which has minimum number of rules and realizes the given authorization assignment of D.

Proof. InstancePolicy calls InstancePolicyBody and AssignPolicy. In InstancePolicy-Body, $rcas(c, e)$ is computed for each $c \in \{0, 1, n\}$ and node e in D. By Lemma 1, a minimum instance policy tree can be constructed by configuring the cascade value to each node e to be $rcas(c, e)$, and this is done by AssignPolicy. Since the root of D has no parent, there is no cascading value to the root, and hence n should be selected as the cascading value to the root. In Step 1 of AssignPolicy, it is easily checked that rules are set to each node e to realize that the authorization value is $a(e)$ and the cascading value from e is $rcas(cas, e)$.

4 Performance Evaluation

4.1 Benchmark Data

In this section, we show experimental results of compressing instance policy trees by GlobalPolicy and InstancePolicy.

We used three real-life XML DTDs (document data types) for our evaluation: HL7 [9] is an XML standard for patient records of medical information, TravelXML[16] is a travel industry standard for order items, and VISA[17] is a standard for invoices of credit card information. HL7 has about 150 types of elements and about 200 types of attributes, and maximum tree height is 7. TravelXML has about 210 elements and no attribute, and maximum tree height is 5. VISA has about 350 elements and 610 attributes, and maximum tree height is 5. We randomly generated document instances for these DTDs. Each document size varies from 4KB to 20KB. We added two auxiliary attributes to each element to store the decision value and the rule type ('n', '+', '-', '$\pm$'). We carried out the succeeding experiments on a Windows XP PC with a 3.20GHz Pentium 4 CPU and 2GB memory. The algorithms are implemented using Java j2sdk1.4.2_05.

4.2   Uniform Distribution

Our first experiment is to compress uniformly distributed authorization values, meaning that randomly chosen instance nodes have value 1, and other instance nodes have value 0, where distribution of the nodes of value 1 is uniform in a document. We use control parameter γ as the percentage of nodes having value 0. The assumption of uniform distribution is disadvantageous for extracting global policy trees, since there will be little inclination to one of the authorization values for every simple path, and a significant percentage of nodes will have the opposite value from the majority, thus less nodes are covered by the global policy tree.

In Table 2, we show the reduction result for HL7, where 1,000 documents are generated with parameter $\gamma = 0.05, 0.25, 0.50, 0.75$, and 0.95. The column (b) is the number of rules before reduction, and the column (i) is the number of rules after reduction without using a global policy tree, which is equal to the result by the CAM method. The column (i)+(g) is the result by this paper (GlobalPolicy+InstancePolicy), where an extracted global policy tree is used. Even in this worst scenario, InstancePolicy (i+g) reduced the rules to 5 to 38 percent of the original, and this is 8 to 25 percent smaller than the method without global policy trees (i). The results for VISA and TravelXML were similar to HL7.

Table 2. Rule reduction for uniformly distributed data (HL7)

γ	5	25	50	75	95
(b) (rules)	37224	72243	72243	72243	72243
(i) (rules)	4804	19353	29995	19348	4666
(i+g) (rules)	3678	17528	27890	17748	3530
(i)/(b) (%)	6	26	41	26	6
(i+g)/(b) (%)	5	24	38	24	4
(i+g)/(i) (%)	76	90	92	91	75

γ (percentage of 0)
(b)   before minimization
(i)   instance only
(i+g)   instance + global

4.3   Zipf Distribution

Now consider the situation such that authorization value distribution has a certain correlation with location paths, such as most of the nodes on the path '/address/home' is inaccessible, while most of the nodes on the path '/address/ofice' is accessible. This is naturally modeled using Zipf distribution, such that the frequency P_n of occurrence of the nth ranked item is proportional to $1/n^\alpha$, where $\alpha > 0$. This distribution is described as a few occur very often while many others occur rarely. Zipf distributions are commonly observed in many kinds of phenomena, such as English word frequencies and web page access ranking.

We generated document instances as follows: Create an instance I where 50 percent of nodes have authorization value 0 and the other 50 percent of nodes have authorization value 1. We create $y = 1000/x^\alpha$ documents such that x nodes are randomly chosen and their authorization value is reversed. The parameter x is incremented from 1 until y is close to 1, and the parameter α is varied from 1 to 4.

Table 3. Rule reduction under Zipf distribution

(a) HL7
global policy tree size: 68 nodes

α	1	2	3	4
#documents	5472	1600	1194	1078
(b) (rules)	782496	228800	170742	154154
(i)(rules)	354966	103781	77449	69916
(i+g) (rules)	160541	46845	36095	33647
(i)/(b) (%)	45	45	45	45
(i+g)/(b) (%)	20	20	21	21
(i+g)/(i) (%)	45	45	46	48

(b) VISA
global policy tree size: 102 nodes

α	1	2	3	4
#documents	6052	1600	1194	1078
(b) (rules)	652196	436800	325962	294294
(i) (rules)	666068	176115	131433	118629
(i+g) (rules)	395198	107781	80400	73647
(i)/(b) (%)	40	40	40	40
(i+g)/(b) (%)	23	24	24	25
(i+g)/(i) (%)	59	61	61	62

(c) TravelXML
global policy tree size: 142 nodes

α	1	2	3	4
#documents	5746	1600	1194	1078
(b)(rules)	1103232	307200	229248	206976
(i)(rules)	454629	126524	94458	85322
(i+g) (rules)	151462	39026	31525	27388
(i)/(b) (%)	41	41	41	41
(i+g)/(b) (%)	13	12	13	13
(i+g)/(i) (%)	33	30	33	32

(b)   before minimization
(i)   instance only
(i+g)   instance + global

Tables 3(a), 3(b) and 3(c) show the reduction results for HL7, VISA and TravelXML, respectively. The sizes of global policy trees were actually very small. As we can see in the results of HL7, our method of extracting global policy trees (i+g) reduced the instance policy size to 20 - 21 percent of the original, improving the results of 45 percent by the previous approach (i). The results for VISA are 23 to 25 percent reduction by (i+g) against 40 percent reduction by (i), and the results for TravelXML are 12 to 13 percent reduction by (i+g) against 41 percent reduction by (i). Thus our method is twice to three-time better than the previous work, when authorization value distribution has a correlation with location paths.

5   Conclusion

In this paper, we proposed a method for extracting global policy trees from instance-level access control rules, and a sophisticated algorithm to compress access control policies utilizing global policy trees. The uniformity and tendency informations obtained from global policy trees can be utilized for efficient authorization decision as well as query optimization. The policy compression capability utilizing global policy trees surpasses the previous approach of compressing by instance policy trees only, and it is especially effective when instance-specific authorizations have a correlation with location paths. Our future work involves handling of document updates. In our framework, re-optimization of instance policy trees after an update will be kept to a local area of the instance policy tree, unless the update is massive and causes updates to the global policy tree.

References

1. R. Agrawal, J. Kiernan, R. Srikant, and Y. Xu, "Hippocratic Databases," Proc. VLDB 2002, pp. 143-154, Aug. 2002.
2. E. Bertino, S. Castano, E. Ferrari, M. Mesiti, "Specifying and Enforcing Access Control Policies for XML Document Sources," WWW Journal, vol.3, n.3, 2000.
3. E. Bertino, E. Ferrari, "Secure and selective dissemination of XML documents," ACM Trans. Inf. Syst. Secur. 5(3), pp. 290-331, 2002.
4. P. Buneman, B. Choi, W. Fan, R. Hutchison, R. Mann, S. Viglas, "Vectorizing and Querying Large XML Repositories," Proc. ICDE 2005, pp. 261–272, Apr. 2005.
5. S. Chatvichienchai, M. Iwaihara, and Y. Kambayashi, "Translating Content-Based Authorizations of XML Documents," Proc. 4th Int. Conf. Web Information Systems Engineering (WISE2003), pp. 103–112, Dec. 2003.
6. S. Chatvichienchai, M. Iwaihara, and Y. Kambayashi, "Authorization Translation for XML Document Transformation," World Wide Web: Internet and Web Information Systems, Kluwer, Vol. 7, No.1, pp. 111-138, Mar 2004.
7. E. Damiani, S. De Capitani di Vimercati, S. Paraboschi, P. Samarati, "A Fine-Grained Access Control System for XML Documents," ACM TISSEC, vol. 5, no. 2, 2002.
8. R. Goldman and J.Widom, "DataGuides: Enabling Formulation and Optimization in Semistructured Databases," In Proc. of VLDB, 1997.
9. HL7 Standards, http://www.hl7.org/library/standards_non1.htm
10. M. Kudo and S. Hada, "XML Document Security based on Provisional Authorization," Proc. 7th ACM Conf. Computer and Communications Security, pp. 87-96, 2000.
11. H. Liefke and D. Suciu, "XMILL: An XML Efficient Compressor for XML Data," Proc. ACM SIGMOD 2000.
12. B. Luo, D. Lee, W.-C. Lee, P. Liu, "QFilter: Fine-Grained Run-Time XML Access Control via NFA-based Query Rewriting," Proc. 13th ACM CIKM, pp. 543 - 552, 2004.
13. M. Murata, A. Tozawa, M. Kudo, S. Hada, "XML Access Control Using Static Analysis," Proc. ACM Conf. Computer and Communications Security, pp. 73–84, 2003.
14. R. Sandhu, E. Coyne, H. Feinstein, and C. Youman, "Role-Based Access Control Models," IEEE Computer, 29(2), pp. 38–47, 1996.
15. OASIS XACML Technical Committee, "eXtensible Access Control Markup Language (XACML) Version 2.0," http://www.oasis-open.org/committees/download.php/10578/XACML-2.0-CD-NORMATIVE.zip.
16. TravelXML: http://www.xmlconsortium.org/wg/TravelXML/TravelXML_index.html
17. VISA: http://international.visa.com/fb/downloads/commprod/visaxmlinvoice/
18. XML Path Language (XPath) Version 1.0, http://www.w3.org/TR/xpath
19. T. Yu, D. Srivastava, L. V. S. Lakshmanan, H. V. Jagadish, "Compressed Accessibility Map: Efficient Access Control for XML," Proc. 28th VLDB, pp. 478–489, 2002.
20. T.Yu, D. Srivastava, L. V. S. Lakshmanan, H. V. Jagadish, "A Compressed Accessibility Map for XML," ACM Trans. Database Syst. 29(2): 363-402, June 2004.

Querying and Repairing Inconsistent XML Data

S. Flesca, F. Furfaro, S. Greco, and E. Zumpano

D.E.I.S. - Università della Calabria, 87036 - Rende (CS), Italy
{flesca, furfaro, greco, zumpano}@deis.unical.it

Abstract. The problem of repairing XML data which are inconsistent and incomplete with respect to a set of integrity constraints and a DTD is addressed. The existence of repairs (i.e. minimal sets of update operations making data consistent) is investigated and shown to be undecidable in the general case. This problem is shown to be still undecidable when data are interpreted as "incomplete" (so that they could be repaired by performing insert operations only). However, it becomes decidable when particular classes of constraints are considered. The existence of repairs is proved to be decidable and, in particular, $\mathcal{NP}$-complete, if inconsistent data are interpreted as "dirty" data (so that repairs are data-cleaning operations consisting in only deletions). The existence of general repairs (containing both insert and delete operations) for special classes of integrity constraints (functional dependencies) is also investigated. Finally, for all the cases where the existence of a repair is decidable, the complexity of providing consistent answers to a query (issued on inconsistent data) is characterized.

1 Introduction

Since the adoption of XML as the new standard for representing and exchanging machine readable data on the Web, a great deal of attention has been devoted to the study of integrity constraints for XML data. Several types of constraints have been introduced, ranging from the simple reference mechanism provided by the ID/IDREF construct of DTD, to keys and foreign keys defined by XML Schema, as well as functional dependencies and several kinds of path constraint.

The relevance of managing integrity constraints for XML documents stems from several issues. First, the presence of integrity constraints is a certificate witnessing the consistency of data, and enriches the document semantics, defining correlations among data. Moreover, a large amount of XML data originates from object-oriented and relational databases, where several forms of integrity constraints may be defined. Therefore, equivalent XML constraints should be defined when these data are re-organized into XML documents, in order to avoid loss of information [20]. Finally, integrity constraints support the designing process of XML documents, allowing us to check data redundancy [4].

Most of works in this area mainly deal with either the definition of new forms of constraint specific for the XML data model [12], or with the validation of XML constraints [5, 11], or with the use of integrity constraints for designing XML repositories [17].

In this work we deal with a different issue regarding XML data and integrity constraints. We consider XML documents which are not consistent with respect to a DTD

M. Kitsuregawa et al. (Eds.): WISE 2005, LNCS 3806, pp. 175–188, 2005.

and a set of integrity constraints, and study the problem of repairing inconsistent documents by deleting "unreliable" portions of the document or adding new pieces of information which complete the document and make it satisfy integrity constraints.

Inconsistency of XML data often arises in practice, as XML documents are usually obtained by integrating information coming from different sources, and can be frequently updated. An example showing how data integration may cause inconsistency is given below.

Example 1. We are given two collections of books - stored in two object oriented databases - where each book object is univocally identified by the *isbn* value. Assume that each of the two collections is consistent with respect to this key constraint. Consider now the following piece of XML document, obtained by integrating the content of the two data sources. The information describing the first book is extracted from the first source whereas the information describing the second book is extracted from the second source.

```
<bib>
   <book isbn="0-451-16194-7">
      <title> A First Course in
              Database Systems
      </title>
      <author> Ullman </author>
      <author> Widom  </author>
      <publisher> Prentice-Hall
      </publisher>
   </book>
   <book isbn="0-451-16194-7">
      <title> A First Course
              in DB Systems
      </title>
      <author> Ullman </author>
      <publisher> Prentice-Hall
      </publisher>
   </book>
</bib>
```

```
<!ELEMENT bib (book+,publisher*)>
<!ELEMENT book (title,author+,
                publisher)>
   <!ATTLIST book isbn CDATA
                        #REQUIRED>
<!ELEMENT author #PCDATA>
<!ELEMENT title #PCDATA>
<!ELEMENT publisher #PCDATA>
```

The above document does not satisfy the key constraint, as the first and the second books have the same isbn attribute. □

The above example shows that, generally, the satisfaction of constraints cannot be guaranteed, even if the merged pieces of information are consistent when considered separately one from the other. Thus, in the presence of an XML document which must satisfy a DTD and a set of constraints, the issue of managing possible inconsistencies is relevant. This issue has been recently investigated for relational databases and several techniques based on the computation of repairs (minimal sets of insert/delete operations) and consistent answers have been proposed [3, 14]. However, these techniques cannot be easily extended to XML data, due to their complex structure and the different nature of constraints: in the XML context, meaningful constraints are defined on the structure of documents, and do not have an equivalent counterpart in the relational model. The document of the previous example can be repaired by performing the following minimal sets of update operations:

- deleting the book element with title "A First Course in Database Systems";
- deleting the book element with title "A First Course in DB Systems".

Generally, it is possible to repair a document in many distinct ways, thus generating several repaired documents. In repairing documents we prefer to apply minimal sets of changes to the original document, as for well known approaches proposed for relational databases. For instance, for the inconsistent document of Example 1 we do not consider the deletion of both the book elements as a repair: indeed, deleting only one of the elements suffices to get a consistent document.

In more detail, we consider three repairing strategies consisting in the computation of:

1. *(general) repairs*, defined as consistent sets of insert and delete operations,
2. *cleaning repairs*, where inconsistent documents are interpreted as "dirty" ones, so that they are repaired by only removing pieces of information,
3. *completing repairs*, where inconsistent documents are interpreted as incomplete, and are repaired by only adding data to the original document.

Moreover, we also study the problem of *consistent query answering* under the two classical forms of reasoning known as *possible* and *certain* semantics (or brave and cautious reasoning).

Contribution. The main contributions of this paper are the following:

- we formalize three classes of repairing strategies (general, cleaning, and completing);
- for each repairing strategy, we consider several forms of integrity constraints, including "traditional" ones (keys, foreign keys, etc.) and characterize the complexity of both determining the existence of a repair, and providing consistent answers to queries issued on inconsistent documents.

Organization. In Section 2 we introduce some basic notations and definitions used in the rest of the paper, and present the data model used for representing XML documents. In Section 3 we define several classes of constraints for XML data. We first introduce a general form of constraint, and then specialize it in order to express well known constraint classes (inclusion dependencies and functional dependencies) or sub-classes enabling feasible repairing strategies. Then, in Section 4, we formalize a framework for repairing XML documents which are not consistent with respect to a DTD and a set of integrity constraints, providing complexity results. In Section 5 we focus our attention on functional dependencies, analyzing the problem of using general repairs to make data consistent, and describe syntactic classes which make the repair feasible. The technical report [16] contains all proofs which have been omitted for space limitation and an algorithm computing repairs.

2   XML Trees and DTDs

Given an alphabet of nodes $\mathbb{N}$ and an alphabet of node labels Σ, a *tree* T over $\mathbb{N}$ and Σ is a tuple (r, N, E, λ), where $N \subseteq \mathbb{N}$ is the (partially ordered) set of nodes, $\lambda : N \to \Sigma$

is the node labelling function, $r \in N$ is the distinguished root of T, and $E \subseteq N \times N$ is the (acyclic and connected) set of edges. The set of leaf nodes of a tree T will be denoted as $Leaves(T)$. The set of trees defined on the alphabet of node labels Σ will be denoted as T_Σ.

Given a tag alphabet $\mathcal{E}$, an attribute name alphabet $\mathcal{A}$, a string alphabet Str and a symbol S not belonging to $\mathcal{E} \cup \mathcal{A}$, an *XML tree* is a pair $\mathcal{XT} = \langle T, \delta \rangle$, where: i) $T = (r, N, E, \lambda)$ is a tree in $T_{\mathcal{E} \cup \mathcal{A} \cup \{S\}}$ (i.e. $\lambda : N \to \mathcal{A} \cup \{S\} \cup \mathcal{E}$); ii) given a node n of T, $\lambda(n) \in \mathcal{A} \cup \{S\} \Rightarrow n \in Leaves(T)$; iii) δ is a function associating a (string) value to every leaf node n of T such that $\lambda(n) \in \mathcal{A} \cup \{S\}$. The symbol S is used to represent the #CDATA content of elements.

Definition 1. A DTD is a tuple $\mathcal{D} = (El, Att, P, M, rt)$ where: 1) $El \subset \mathcal{E}$ is a finite set of element names; 2) $Att \subset \mathcal{A}$ is a finite set of attribute names; 3) P is a mapping from El to *element type definitions*; 4) M is a mapping from El to *attribute lists*. 5) $rt \in El$ is the root element name. An element type definition is an expression α defined as follows: [1]

- $\alpha \to \alpha_1 \,\|\, \alpha_2$,
- $\alpha_1 \to (\alpha_1) \,\|\, \alpha_1 \,|\, \alpha_1 \,\|\, \alpha_1, \alpha_1 \,\|\, \alpha_1? \,\|\, \alpha_1* \,\|\, \tau$, where $\tau \in El$,
- $\alpha_2 \to \text{ANY} \,\|\, \text{EMPTY} \,\|\, S$.

An attribute list is a mapping from El to the powerset of Att. We say that $att \in Att$ is defined for τ if $\tau \in El$ and $att \in R(\tau)$.   □

In the following we consider only "well formed" DTDs, i.e DTDs which admit at least a finite document.

We say that a DTD $\mathcal{D}$ is *semi-deterministic* if in all its element type definitions the symbols "$|$", "?" and "$*$" are applied only to single elements (τ). For instance, the element type definition <!ELEMENT e (a,b) | (b,c)> cannot appear in a semi-deterministic DTD, whereas the element type definition <!ELEMENT e ((a | b), (b | c))> does.

The XML document introduced in Example 1 corresponds to the XML tree shown in Figure 1.

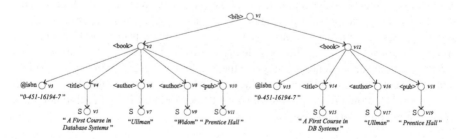

Fig. 1. The XML Tree corresponding to the document of Example 1

---

[1] The symbol $\|$ denotes different productions with the same left part. Here we do not consider *mixed content* of elements [13].

The internal nodes of the XML tree have a unique label, denoting the tag name of the corresponding element. The leaf nodes correspond to either an attribute or the textual content of an element, and are labelled with two strings: the first one denotes the attribute name (in the case that the node represents an attribute) or is equal to the symbol S (in the case that the node represents an element content), whereas the second label denotes either the value of the attribute or the string contained inside the element corresponding to the node.

A *path expression* is an expression of the form $p = ('/' \mid '//')s_1 \ldots ('/' \mid '//') s_m$ where $s_1, ..., s_{m-1} \in \mathcal{E} \cup \{*\}$, and $s_m \in \mathcal{E} \cup \mathcal{A} \cup \{S, *\}$. Given an XML tree $\mathcal{XT}$, a path on $\mathcal{XT}$ is a sequence $pt = [n_0, \ldots, n_k]$ of nodes on $\mathcal{XT}$ such that for each i in $1..k$, n_{i-1} is the parent of n_i.

Moreover, given a path expression $p = ('/' \mid '//')s_1 \ldots ('/' \mid '//')s_m$, pt *satisfies* p iff there exist a injective mapping μ associating each symbol s_i in p to a node n_j in pt such that μ satisfies the following conditions:

1. for each i in $1..m-1$, if s_i/s_{i+1} is in p then $\mu(s_{i+1})$ is a child of $\mu(s_i)$; otherwise, if $s_i//s_{i+1}$ is in p then $\mu(s_{i+1})$ is a child or a descendant of $\mu(s_i)$, and
2. for each i in $1..m$, $\lambda(\mu(s_i)) = s_i$ or $s_i = *$.

Let $p = ('/' \mid '//')s_1 \ldots ('/' \mid '//') s_m$ be a path expression, $\mathcal{XT}$ an XML tree and n a node of $\mathcal{XT}$. The application of p to n on $\mathcal{XT}$, denoted by $p(\mathcal{XT}, n)$, is defined as follows:

1. if $s_m \in \mathcal{A} \cup \{S\}$ then $p(\mathcal{XT}, n) = \{\delta(n_k) \mid \exists$ a path $pt = [n, \ldots, n_k]$ in $\mathcal{XT}$ satisfying $p\}$
2. if $s_m \in \mathcal{E}$ then $p(\mathcal{XT}, n) = \{n_k \mid \exists$ a path $pt = [n, \ldots, n_k]$ in $\mathcal{XT}$ satisfying $p\}$

3   XML Constraints

Throughout the paper we assume we are given an alphabet Var of variable names. A term τ is either a variable name, or a node identifier, or a string in Str. A term is said to be *ground* if it is not a variable name. A *path atom* is an expression of the form $[x_1]p[x_2]$, where p is a path expression, x_1 and x_2 are terms, and $x_1 \notin Str$. A path atom $[x_1]p[x_2]$ is said to be *ground* if x_1 and x_2 are ground.

Given an XML tree $\mathcal{XT}$, a ground atom $[x_1]p[x_2]$ is *true* w.r.t $\mathcal{XT}$ if $x_2 \in p(\mathcal{XT}, x_1)$, and *false* otherwise. A ground conjunction containing both path atoms and built-in atoms of the form $x\theta y$, where $\theta \in \{=, \neq, >, \geq, <, \leq\}$, is true w.r.t. to an XML tree $\mathcal{XT}$ if all paths and built-in atoms are true w.r.t. $\mathcal{XT}$. A conjunction of path and built-in atoms C is satisfiable w.r.t. an XML tree $\mathcal{XT}$ if there is a substitution σ for all variables in C such that $C\sigma$ is true w.r.t. $\mathcal{XT}$.

A conjunction of path and built-in atoms $C = [X_1]p_1[Y_1] \wedge \ldots \wedge [X_n]p_n[Y_n] \wedge U_1\theta_1 V_1 \wedge \cdots \wedge U_k\theta_k V_k$ is said to be *safe* if all variables in C are *range restricted*, i.e. if

- for every $[X_i]p_i[Y_i]$, either X_i is a constant (node identifier or a string), or there is some $[X_j]p_j[X_i]$ in C where X_j is range restricted;
- for every built-in term $U_i\theta_i V_i$ occurring in C, if θ_i is equal to " $=$ " then at least one of the two terms is range restricted; otherwise both U_i and V_i must be range restricted.

A safe conjunction of path atoms and built-in atoms is also said to be a *tree query*. A tree query C consisting in a single path will be also said to be a *path query*. The answer to a tree query C applied to an XML tree $\mathcal{XT}$, denoted by $C(\mathcal{XT})$, consists in the set of substitutions for the variables in C making C true in $\mathcal{XT}$, i.e. $Ans(C(\mathcal{XT})) = \{\sigma \mid XT \models C\sigma\}$.

Let us introduce some notation used in the rest of the paper. A rootless path formula is an expression of the form $p[y]$ where p is a path expression and y is a term. A rootless tree formula is an expression of the form $p(\Phi_1 \wedge \cdots \wedge \Phi_k)$ where Φ_i is a rootless path formula or a rootless tree formula and p is a path expression. A tree atom is an expression of the form $[x]T$ where T is a rootless tree formula and x is a term. An example of tree atom is: $[\texttt{root}]/\texttt{bib}(/\texttt{book}/\texttt{@isbn}[Y_1] \wedge /\texttt{book}/\texttt{@isbn}[Y_2])$, which corresponds to the conjunction $[\texttt{root}]/\texttt{bib}[Z] \wedge ([Z]/\texttt{book}/\texttt{@isbn}[Y_1] \wedge [Z]/\texttt{book}/\texttt{@isbn}[Y_2])$.

For the sake of brevity, in the following we shall denote with $[X]p_1[Z]p_2[Y]$ the conjunction $[X]p_1[Z] \wedge [Z]p_2[Y]$ and with $[X]p_1[Z](p_2[Y] \wedge p_3[W])$ the conjunction $[X]p_1[Z] \wedge [Z]p_2[Y] \wedge [Z]p_3[W]$.

Definition 2 (XML integrity constraint). An XML constraint is a formula of the form

$$(\forall X)[\Phi(X) \supset (\exists Y_1)\Psi_1(X, Y_1) \vee \ldots \vee (\exists Y_k)\Psi_k(X, Y_k)]$$

where $X, Y_1, \ldots, Y_k$ denote distinct sets of universally and existentially quantified variables, $\Phi(X)$ and $\Phi(X) \wedge \Psi_i(X, Y_i)$ ($\forall i \in [1..k]$) are safe conjunctions of built-in and tree atoms. □

An XML constraint is said to be *universally quantified* if existentially quantified variables refer only to node identifiers.

Example 2. The constraint that there must exist at least two books having different titles is expressed as

$$\forall(\texttt{X})[\,[\texttt{root}]/\texttt{bib}[\texttt{X}]) \supset \exists(Z_1, Z_2)(\,[\texttt{X}]/\texttt{book}/\texttt{title}/\texttt{S}[Z_1] \wedge [\texttt{X}]/\texttt{book}/\texttt{title}/\texttt{S}[Z_2] \wedge Z_1 \neq Z_2\,)\,]$$

□

XML integrity constraints can be used to express both inclusion and functional dependencies.

Definition 3 (Inclusion dependency). An inclusion dependency is a universally quantified XML constraint of the form $(\forall X)[\Phi(X) \supset \Psi(Y)]$ where $Y \subseteq X$, and $\Psi(Y)$ is a tree atom. □

Example 3. The following inclusion dependency states that, for each book, its publisher must appear in the list of publishers enclosed in the $\texttt{bib}$ element.

$$\forall(\texttt{X})[\,[\texttt{root}]/\texttt{bib}/\texttt{book}/\texttt{publisher}/\texttt{S}[\texttt{X}]) \supset [\texttt{root}]/\texttt{bib}/\texttt{publisher}/\texttt{S}[\texttt{X}]\,]$$

□

Definition 4 (Functional dependency). A functional dependency is an expression of the form $[root]P[Z_0]\Phi(Z_1, \ldots, Z_n, Y) \{W \rightarrow Y\}$, where $[root]P[Z_0]$ is a possibly empty path atom, $[Z_0]\Phi(Z_1, \ldots, Z_n, Y)$ is a tree atom, and $W = \{Z_{i_1}, \ldots, Z_{i_m}\}$ is a subset of $\{Z_0, \ldots, Z_n\}$. It defines the following universally quantified XML constraint:

$$\forall(Z_0', .., Z_n', Y', Z_0'', .., Z_n'', Y'')\,([root]P[Z_0'] \wedge [root]P[Z_0''] \wedge [Z_0']\Phi(Z_1', \ldots, Z_n', Y') \wedge$$
$$[Z_0'']\Phi(Z_1'', \ldots, Z_n'', Y'') \wedge Z_{i_1}' = Z_{i_1}'' \wedge \ldots \wedge Z_{i_m}' = Z_{i_m}'' \supset Y' = Y'') \qquad □$$

Example 4. The FD [root]/bib/book(/@isbn[Y] ∧ /title/S[W]) {Y → W}, stating that two books with the same isbn must have the same title, corresponds to the following constraint:

$$\forall(Y_1, Y_2, W_1, W_2)([\texttt{root}]/\texttt{bib/book}(/\texttt{@isbn}[Y_1] \wedge /\texttt{title/S}[W_1]) \wedge$$
$$[\texttt{root}]/\texttt{bib/book}(/\texttt{@isbn}[Y_2] \wedge /\texttt{title/S}[W_2]) \wedge Y_1 = Y_2 \supset W_1 = W_2)$$

The FD [root]/bib[Z]/book(/@isbn[Y] ∧ /title/S[W]) {Z, Y → W}, stating that two books of the same library having the same isbn must have the same title, corresponds to the constraint:

$$\forall(Z_1, Z_2, Y_1, Y_2, W_1, W_2)([\texttt{root}]/\texttt{bib}[Z_1]/\texttt{book}(/\texttt{@isbn}[Y_1] \wedge /\texttt{title/S}[W_1]) \wedge$$
$$[\texttt{root}]/\texttt{bib}[Z_2]/\texttt{book}(/\texttt{@isbn}[Y_2] \wedge /\texttt{title/S}[W_2]) \wedge$$
$$Z_1 = Z_2 \wedge Y_1 = Y_2 \supset W_1 = W_2)$$

The functional dependency [root]/bib/book[X]/@isbn[Y]{Y → X} informally presented in Example 1 states that there exists no pair of books with the same isbn value. □

4   Repairing Inconsistent XML Databases

In this section we present an approach to the problem of repairing XML documents which are inconsistent w.r.t. a DTD and a set of integrity constraints.

An inconsistent XML document can be repaired by deleting or inserting nodes (and, consequently, arcs). The insertion or deletion of a node both updates the structure of the XML tree and re-arranges the order relation among nodes. We distinguish between two basic update operations: 1) deletion of a node, and 2) insertion of a node as the next sibling of another node. The delete operation is represented as $-[x]a[y]$, where x is a node identifier, $a \in Att \cup El \cup \{S\}$, and y is either a node id or a string value, denoting the node to be deleted. The insertion of a new node is represented as $\langle + [x]a[y], z \rangle$, where i) x is node identifier, ii) a is a label, iii) y is either a node identifier or a value (y is a value if $a \in Att \cup \{S\}$; otherwise, it is a node identifier), and iv) z denotes the child of x which must immediately precede y ($\perp$ if y is inserted as first or unique child of x).

A set R of update operations for an XML tree $\mathcal{XT}$ is said to be *consistent* if the following conditions hold:

1. $-[x]a[y] \in R \Rightarrow \{-[y]b[w] \mid [y]b[w] is\,true\,w.r.t.\mathcal{XT}\} \subseteq R$, i.e. the deletion of a node implies the deletion of all descendant nodes;
2. $\{y \mid -[x]a[y] \in R\} \cap \{y \mid \langle +[x]b[y], z \rangle \in R$ or $\langle + [x]b[z], y \rangle \in R\} = \emptyset$, i.e. insertions cannot refer to deleted nodes.

Given a set of update operations R, we denote with R^+ the subset of all the insertions in R, and with R^- the set of all deletions in R. The application of a consistent set of updates R to an XML tree $\mathcal{XT}$, denoted by $R(\mathcal{XT})$, consists in the simultaneous application of the insertions in R^+ and the deletions in R^-.

Given two sets of update operations R_1 and R_2 we say that R_1 and R_2 are equivalent (written $R_1 \equiv R_2$) if R_1 is equal to R_2 up to a injective renaming of node identifiers. Moreover, we say that $R_1 \preceq R_2$ if $R_1^- \subseteq R_2^-$ or $R_1^- = R_2^-$ and $R_1^+ \subseteq R_2^+$. We say that $R_1 \sqsubseteq R_2$ if there exists a $R_2' \equiv R_2$ (not necessarily distinct) such that $R_1 \preceq R_2'$. Moreover and $R_1 \sqsubset R_2$ if $R_1 \sqsubseteq R_2$ and $R_1 \not\equiv R_2$.

Definition 5 (Repair). *Given an XML tree $\mathcal{XT}$, a DTD $\mathcal{D}$ and a set of integrity constraints $\mathcal{IC}$, a set of update operations R is said to be a repair for $\mathcal{XT}$ (with respect to $\mathcal{D}$ and $\mathcal{IC}$) if $R(\mathcal{XT}) \models \mathcal{IC}$, $R(\mathcal{XT})$ conforms $\mathcal{D}$ and $\nexists R' \sqsubset R$ such that $R'(\mathcal{XT}) \models \mathcal{IC}$ and $R'(\mathcal{XT})$ conforms $\mathcal{D}$.* □

Thus, a repair R for $\mathcal{XT}$ is a minimal set of consistent update operations which make $\mathcal{XT}$ consistent with respect to the set of integrity constraints $\mathcal{IC}$ and the DTD $\mathcal{D}$. The set of all repairs of an XML tree $\mathcal{XT}$ with respect to to a set of integrity constraints $\mathcal{IC}$ and a DTD $\mathcal{D}$ is denoted by $\mathbf{R}(\mathcal{XT}, \mathcal{D}, \mathcal{IC})$.

Repairs can be used to derive consistent scenarios of XML data. An interesting problem consists in computing queries with respect to repaired documents. As we can have more than one repair and, consequently, more than one repaired document, we consider two different types of consistent answer for queries.

Definition 6. Given a tree query Q, an XML document $\mathcal{XT}$, a DTD $\mathcal{D}$ and a set of integrity constraint $\mathcal{IC}$,

- the *possible (consistent) answer* to the query $Q(\mathcal{XT})$ is
$$\bigcup\nolimits_{R \in \mathbf{R}(\mathcal{XT}, \mathcal{D}, \mathcal{IC})} \{\sigma \mid R(\mathcal{XT}) \models Q\sigma\};$$

- the *certain (consistent) answer* to the query $Q(\mathcal{XT})$ is
$$\bigcap\nolimits_{R \in \mathbf{R}(\mathcal{XT}, \mathcal{D}, \mathcal{IC})} \{\sigma \mid R(\mathcal{XT}) \models Q\sigma\}.$$
□

Therefore, given a query $Q(\mathcal{XT})$, the *possible (consistent) answer* consists of the set of substitutions σ for the variables in Q such that $Q\sigma$ is true in some repaired document, while the *certain (consistent) answer* consists of the set of substitutions σ for the variables in Q such that $Q\sigma$ is true in all repaired documents.

Moreover, as the problem of deciding whether there exists a repair for an XML tree in the presence of general integrity constraints or (general) DTDs with restricted forms of constraints (e.g. inclusion and functional dependencies) is undecidable, we next consider restricted forms of repairs and constraints. More specifically, we consider the two types of repairs consisting of only deletions (called cleaning repairs) and only insertions (called completing repairs).

4.1   Cleaning XML Documents

We have presented a strategy for repairing possibly inconsistent XML data and shown that the problem of checking whether there exists a repair for an XML document is undecidable. Thus, we now consider a special class of repairs which can be used for "cleaning" inconsistent XML data. The process of cleaning possibly inconsistent data is based on the deletion of the portion of data which do not satisfy the DTD and the integrity constraints. The next result shows that, if we consider cleaning repairs instead of general repairs, the problem of deciding the existence of a repair becomes decidable.

Theorem 1. *Let $\mathcal{XT}$ be an XML tree, $\mathcal{D}$ a DTD and $\mathcal{IC}$ a set of constraints. The problem of checking whether there exists a repair R for $\mathcal{XT}$ such that $R = R^-$ is $\mathcal{NP}$-complete.* □

A second interesting problem consists in the recognition of repairs.

Theorem 2. *Let* $\mathcal{XT}$ *be an XML tree,* $\mathcal{D}$ *be a DTD,* $\mathcal{IC}$ *a set of constraints and* R *a set of update operations. The problem of checking whether* R *is a cleaning repair for* $\mathcal{XT}$ *is* $co\mathcal{NP}$-*complete.* $\square$

Example 5. Consider the XML document and DTD of Example 1, and the constraint

$$\forall(\mathtt{X}_1,\mathtt{X}_2,\mathtt{T},\mathtt{Y})([\mathtt{root}]/\mathtt{bib}(/\mathtt{book}[\mathtt{X}_1](/\mathtt{@isbn}[\mathtt{T}]\wedge/\mathtt{author}/\mathtt{S}[\mathtt{Y}])\wedge/\mathtt{book}[\mathtt{X}_2]/\mathtt{@isbn}[\mathtt{T}])\supset$$
$$[\mathtt{X}_2]/\mathtt{author}/\mathtt{S}[\mathtt{Y}]) \qquad\qquad \square$$

stating that two books having the same isbn values must contain the same sets of authors. There exists only one cleaning repair $R = \{\,\texttt{-}[v_0]/\texttt{author}[v_1],\ \texttt{-}[v_1]/\texttt{S}[\texttt{Widom}]\,\}$ where v_0 is the identifier of the first book and v_1 is the identifier of the second author in the first book. Since we have only one repair, possible and certain answer coincide. $\square$

Regarding the complexity of answering queries we have the following result.

Theorem 3. *Let* $\mathcal{XT}$ *be an XML tree,* $\mathcal{D}$ *be a DTD,* $\mathcal{IC}$ *a set of constraints and* Q *a ground tree query. Then*

- *checking whether there exists a cleaning repair* R *for* $\mathcal{XT}$ *such that* $R(\mathcal{XT}) \models Q$ *is* $\mathcal{NP}$-*complete,*
- *checking whether for all cleaning repairs* R *for* $\mathcal{XT}$ $R(\mathcal{XT}) \models Q$ *is* Π_2^p-*complete.*

$\square$

We point out that the above reported results are quite surprising as the complexity of query answering is complete in the first level of the polynomial hierarchy under brave reasoning and in the second level under cautious reasoning.

4.2 Completing XML Data

In this section we study the problem of repairing XML documents, whose information is assumed to be sound, by "completing" them. The process of completing a possibly inconsistent XML document is based on the insertion of data (nodes and arcs) which make the input XML tree consistent. This means that completing a document is equivalent to compute a repair consisting of only insert operations (hereafter called *completing repairs*). However, the undecidability results remain valid also considering completing repairs.

In the rest of this section we introduce some limitations on the form of integrity constraints and DTD which make the problem decidable.

Definition 7 (Basic integrity constraint). A basic integrity constraint is a universally quantified integrity constraint of the form

$$(\forall X)[\Phi(X) \supset \Psi_1(X) \vee \cdots \vee \Psi_n(X)]$$

where each $\Psi_j(X)$ is of the form $[X_1']P_1[X_1''] \wedge \cdots \wedge [X_k']P_k[X_k'']$ and P_i $(1 \le i \le k)$ is an attribute name or is equal to $\mathtt{S}$, or is of the form $/\tau/\mathtt{S}$. $\square$

Example 6. Consider the DTD of Example 1 and assume it is modified as follows

```
<!ELEMENT bib (book+, present, lent)>
<!ELEMENT present (title*)>
<!ELEMENT lent (title*)>
```

The below basic constraint states that every book in the library is either lent or present.

$$\forall(T, P, L)([\text{root}]/\text{bib}/\text{book}/\text{title}/S[T]) \land [\text{root}]/\text{present}[P] \land [\text{root}]/\text{lent}[L] \supset$$
$$[P]/\text{title}/S[T]\text{vee}[L]/\text{title}/S[T]]) \quad \square$$

In particular, we consider basic integrity constraints in presence of a semideterministic DTD. Complexity results are claimed in the following theorems.

Theorem 4. *Let $\mathcal{XT}$ be an XML tree conforming a semi-deterministic DTD $\mathcal{D}$ and $\mathcal{IC}$ a set of basic integrity constraints. The problem of checking whether there exists a repair R for $\mathcal{XT}$ such that $R = R^+$ is $\mathcal{NP}$-complete.* $\square$

Observe that the restrictions posed by semi-deterministic DTDs are not severe as documents could be restructured to satisfy such limitations. For instance, the DTDs used in this paper are all semi-deterministic. The next results introduce bounds for the complexity of answering queries.

Theorem 5. *Let $\mathcal{XT}$ be an XML tree conforming a semi-deterministic DTD $\mathcal{D}$, $\mathcal{IC}$ a set of basic constraints and R a set of update operations. The problem of checking whether R is a completing repair for $\mathcal{XT}$ is $co\mathcal{NP}$-complete.* $\square$

Theorem 6. *Let $\mathcal{XT}$ be an XML tree conforming a semi-deterministic DTD $\mathcal{D}$, $\mathcal{IC}$ a set of basic constraints and Q a ground tree query. Then*
- *checking whether there exists a completing repair R for $\mathcal{XT}$ such that $R(\mathcal{XT}) \models Q$ is Σ_2^p-complete,*
- *checking whether for all completing repair R for $\mathcal{XT}$ $R(\mathcal{XT}) \models Q$ is Π_2^p-complete.* $\square$

Example 7. Consider the XML document and DTD of Example 1 and the constraint of Example 5 (stating that two books with the same isbn must have the same sets of authors). There are two completing repairs: $R_1 = \{\langle + [v_{12}]/\text{author}[v_{20}], v_{14}\rangle, \langle + [v_{20}]/S[\text{Widom}], \bot \rangle\}$ and $R_2 = \{\langle + [v_{12}]/\text{author}[v_{20}], v_{16}\rangle, \langle + [v_{20}]/S[\text{Widom}], \bot \rangle\}$ where v_{12} is the identifier of the second book, v_{20} is a new node identifier, v_{14} is identifier of the title and v_{16} is the identifier of the existing author in the second book. The two repairs add a second author in different positions. The possible and certain answer to the query

[root]/bib/book(/title/S["A First Course of DB Systems"]$\land$/author/S["Widom"])

is *yes*, whereas the possible and certain answer to the query

[root]/bib/book(/title/S ["A First Course of DB Systems"] $\land$ /author/S[X])

is $\{\{X/\text{Ullman}\}, \{X/\text{Widom}\}\}$. $\square$

In the above example possible and certain answers coincide because there is only one repair. However, in the general case, the two types of query have different answers and different complexities.

We now introduce further restrictions on the form of constraints to achieve the tractability of the problem of computing repairs.

Definition 8 (Elementary integrity constraint). An integrity constraint is said to be *elementary* if it is both a basic integrity constraint and an inclusion dependency. □

The integrity constraint defined in Example 5 is an instance of elementary integrity constraint. The following results characterize the complexity of both deciding the existence of a completing repair and providing consistent answers in presence of elementary integrity constraints.

Theorem 7. *Let* $\mathcal{XT}$ *be an XML tree conforming a semi-deterministic DTD* $\mathcal{D}$ *and* $\mathcal{IC}$ *a set of elementary integrity constraints* $\mathcal{IC}$. *The complexity of checking whether there exists a completing repair R for* $\mathcal{XT}$ *is polynomial time in the size of* $\mathcal{XT}$. □

Theorem 8. *Let* $\mathcal{XT}$ *be an XML tree conforming a semi-deterministic DTD* $\mathcal{D}$, $\mathcal{IC}$ *a set of elementary constraints and R a set of insertions. The complexity of checking whether R is a completing repair for* $\mathcal{XT}$ *is polynomial time in the size of* $\mathcal{XT}$ *and R.* □

Theorem 9. *Let* $\mathcal{XT}$ *be an XML tree conforming a semi-deterministic DTD* $\mathcal{D}$, $\mathcal{IC}$ *a set of elementary constraints and Q a ground tree query. Then*
- *the complexity of checking whether there exists a repair R for* $\mathcal{XT}$ *such that* $R(\mathcal{XT}) \models Q$ *is polynomial time in the size of* $\mathcal{XT}$,
- *the complexity of checking whether* $R(\mathcal{XT}) \models Q$ *for all repairs R for* $\mathcal{XT}$ *is polynomial time in the size of* $\mathcal{XT}$. □

5   Repairing XML Data with Functional Dependencies

In this section we study the problem of computing general repairs for XML documents with general DTDs and functional dependencies. We start by characterizing the complexity of verifying if a set of functional dependencies is consistent with respect to a given DTD.

Theorem 10. *Let* $\mathcal{D}$ *be a DTD and* $\mathcal{FD}$ *a set of functional dependencies. The problem of checking whether there exists an XML document conforming* $\mathcal{D}$ *and satisfying* $\mathcal{FD}$ *is* $\mathcal{NP}$-*complete.* □

As the existence of a repair can be reduced to the problem of consistency checking, we have the following corollary.

Corollary 1. *Let* $\mathcal{XT}$ *be an XML tree,* $\mathcal{D}$ *a DTD, and* $\mathcal{FD}$ *a set of functional dependencies. The problem of checking whether there exists a repair for* $\mathcal{XT}$ *satisfying* $\mathcal{D}$ *and* $\mathcal{FD}$ *is* $\mathcal{NP}$-*complete.* □

As a consequence, the complexity of computing query answers is in the second level of the polynomial hierarchy.

Theorem 11. *Let* $\mathcal{XT}$ *be an XML tree,* $\mathcal{D}$ *be a DTD,* $\mathcal{FD}$ *a set of functional dependencies and Q a ground tree query. Then*
- *checking whether there exists a repair R for* $\mathcal{XT}$ *such that* $R(\mathcal{XT}) \models Q$ *is* $\mathcal{NP}$-*complete.*
- *checking whether* $R(\mathcal{XT}) \models Q$ *holds for all repairs R for* $\mathcal{XT}$ *is* $co\mathcal{NP}$-*complete.* □

Example 8. Consider the following XML document conforming the DTD reported on its right-hand side:

```
<cars>                            <!ELEMENT cars (car+)>
  <car cno="c1">                  <!ELEMENT car (policy?, garage+)>
    <policy pno="p1"/>            <!ATTLIST car cno CDATA>
    <garage>                      <!ELEMENT policy EMPTY>
      <name> Olympo </name>       <!ATTLIST policy pno CDATA>
      <city> Boston </city>       <!ELEMENT garage (name, city)>
    </garage>                     <!ELEMENT name PCDATA>
    <garage>                      <!ELEMENT city PCDATA>
      <name> Johnson </name>
      <city> Cambridge </city>
    </garage>
  </car>
</cars>
```

and the functional dependency $[root]\texttt{cars}/\texttt{car}[Z](/\texttt{policy}[X] \wedge /\texttt{garage}[Y]) \{Z, X \rightarrow Y\}$ saying that, if a car has a policy, then it can be repaired by only one garage. Otherwise, if no policy is associated to the car, then it can be repaired in more than one garage. The repairs for this document are the following: 1) deleting the `policy` element or 2) deleting the first `garage` element, or 3) deleting the second `garage` element.   □

We recall that for relational databases the problem is tractable. In particular, given a relational database $\mathcal{D}$ with functional dependencies $\mathcal{FD}$ and tuple Q, a repair for $\mathcal{D}$ satisfying $\mathcal{FD}$ always exists, and the problems of i) checking whether there exists a repair R for $\mathcal{D}$ such that $R(\mathcal{D}) \models Q$ and ii) checking whether $R(\mathcal{D}) \models Q$ holds for all repairs R for $\mathcal{D}$ are both polynomial.

Thus, we now consider a relevant subclass of functional dependencies for which the problem of computing certain answers and nondeterministically selected repairs is tractable.

Definition 9. Given a DTD $\mathcal{D}$, a functional dependency $[root]T\{X_1, ..., X_k \rightarrow Y\}$ is said to be *canonical* if all variables $X_1, ..., X_k$ cannot be associated with node identifiers and Y cannot be associated with either node identifiers or ID attributes.   □

Observe that this is a relevant class of constraints as it captures functional dependencies over relational databases. This means that in the translation of a relational scheme DS into a DTD $\mathcal{D}$, the functional dependencies over DS can be translated into canonical functional dependencies over $\mathcal{D}$.

It is also worth noting that while repairing strategies defined in the literature for relational databases allow us to insert or delete whole tuples [3, 14, 15], the techniques here considered allow us to update single values. This means that it is possible to repair an inconsistent relational database DB by translating it into an equivalent XML document $\mathcal{XT}$ and then repairing $\mathcal{XT}$, thus yielding finer grain repairs.

The following results define the complexity of computing repairs and consistent answers for canonical FDs and general DTDs.

Lemma 1. *Let $\mathcal{XT}$ be an XML tree, $\mathcal{D}$ a DTD D, and $\mathcal{CFD}$ a set of canonical functional dependencies. A repair for $\mathcal{XT}$ satisfying $\mathcal{D}$ and $\mathcal{CFD}$ always exists.*   □

Theorem 12. *Let $\mathcal{XT}$ be an XML tree, $\mathcal{D}$ a DTD and $\mathcal{CFD}$ a set of canonical functional dependencies. The complexity of computing a (non-deterministically selected) repair for $\mathcal{XT}$ is polynomial time.*   □

Theorem 13. *Let $\mathcal{XT}$ be an XML tree, $\mathcal{D}$ a DTD, $\mathcal{CFD}$ a set of canonical functional dependencies and Q a ground tree query. Then*

- *the problem of checking whether there exists a repair R for $\mathcal{XT}$ such that $R(\mathcal{XT}) \models Q$ is in $\mathcal{NP}$.*
- *the complexity of checking whether for all repairs R for $\mathcal{XT}$ $R(\mathcal{XT}) \models Q$ is polynomial time.*   □

6   Conclusions

We have studied the problem of computing consistent answers to queries and repairs for XML data which may be inconsistent with respect to a given DTD and a set of integrity constraints.

We have considered i) different types of repair, such as general repairs (containing both insert and delete operations), cleaning repairs (containing only delete operations) and completing repairs (containing only insert operations), ii) different DTDs such as general DTDs, semi-deterministic DTDs and documents without DTDs, and iii) several classes of constraints including general integrity constraints ($\mathcal{IC}$), inclusion dependencies ($\mathcal{ID}$), basic integrity constraints ($\mathcal{BIC}$), elementary integrity constraints ($\mathcal{EIC}$), functional dependencies ($\mathcal{FD}$) and canonical functional dependencies ($\mathcal{CFD}$). We have studied the computational complexity of i) checking whether a repair exists, ii) checking whether a set of insert and delete operations is a repair, iii) answering ground tree queries with respect to a repaired document (possible answer) and with respect to all repaired documents (certain answer). For completing repairs we have considered input XML documents conforming the associated DTD (otherwise no completing repair exists). The complexity results are reported in the following table where $= C$ means that the complexity is complete for the class C.

DTD type	Constraints	Repair type	∃ Repair	Ck. Repair	Poss. Ans.	Certain Ans.
DTD	$\mathcal{ID}+\mathcal{FD}$	General	Undecidable			
	$\mathcal{IC}$	General	Undecidable			
	$\mathcal{IC}$	Completing	Undecidable			
SD-DTD	$\mathcal{BIC}$	Completing	$= \mathcal{NP}$	$= co\mathcal{NP}$	$=\Sigma_2^p$	$= \Pi_2^p$
SD-DTD	$\mathcal{EIC}$	Completing	$\subseteq \mathcal{P}time$	$\subseteq \mathcal{P}time$	$\subseteq \mathcal{P}time$	$\subseteq \mathcal{P}time$
DTD	$\mathcal{IC}$	Cleaning	$= \mathcal{NP}$	$= co\mathcal{NP}$	$= \mathcal{NP}$	$= \Pi_2^p$
DTD	$\mathcal{FD}$	General	$= \mathcal{NP}$	$= co\mathcal{NP}$	$=\Sigma_2^p$	$= \Pi_2^p$
DTD	$\mathcal{CFD}$	General	$O(1)$	$\subseteq \mathcal{P}time$	$\subseteq \mathcal{NP}$	$\subseteq \mathcal{P}time$

References

1. Abiteboul, S., Hull, R., Vianu, V., *Foundations of Databases*, Addison-Wesley, 1994.
2. Abiteboul, S., Segoufin, L., Vianu, V., Representing and Querying XML with Incomplete Information, *Proc. of Symposium on Principles of Database Systems (PODS)*, Santa Barbara, CA, USA, 2001.
3. Arenas, M., Bertossi, L., Chomicki, J., Consistent Query Answers in Inconsistent Databases, *Proc. of Symposium on Principles of Database Systems (PODS)*, Philadephia, PA, USA, 1999.
4. Arenas, M., Libkin, L., A Normal Form for XML Documents, *Proc. of PODS Conf.*, 2002.
5. Arenas, M., Fan, W., Libkin, L., On Verifying Consistency of XML Specifications, *Proc. PODS Conf.*, 2002.
6. Arenas, M., Fan, W., Libkin, L., What's Hard about XML Schema Constraints? *Proc. of 13th Int. Conf. on Database and Expert Systems Applications (DEXA)*, Aix en Provence, France, 2002.
7. Buneman, P., Davidson, S. B., Fan, W., Hara, C. S., Tan, W. C., Keys for XML, *Comp. Networks*, Vol. 39(5), 2002.
8. Buneman, P., Davidson, S. B., Fan, W., Hara, C. S., Tan, W. C., Reasoning about keys for XML. *Inf. Syst.* 28(8), 1037-1063, 2003.
9. Buneman, P., Fan, W., Weinstein, S., Path Constraints in Semistructured Databases. *J. Comput. Syst. Sci.*, 61(2), 146-193, 2000.
10. Buneman, P., Fan, W., Weinstein, S., Path Constraints in Semistructured and Structured Databases, *Proc. of Symposium on Principles of Database Systems (PODS)*, Seattle, WA, USA, 1998.
11. Fan, W., Libkin, L., On XML integrity constraints in the presence of DTDs, *Journal of the ACM*, Vol. 49(3), 2002.
12. Fan, W., Simeon, J., Integrity constraints for XML. *J. Comput. Syst. Sci.* 66(1), 254-291, 2003.
13. Fernandez,. M., Robie, J., XML Query Data Model. *W3C Working Draft* http://www.w3.or/TR/query-datamodel/, 2001.
14. Greco, S., and Zumpano E., Querying Inconsistent Databases, *Proc. LPAR Conf.*, 2000.
15. Greco, G., Greco, S., Zumpano, E., A Logical Framework for Querying and Repairing Inconsistent Databases, *IEEE Trans. Knowl. Data Eng.* 15(6): 1389-1408, 2003.
16. Flesca S., Furfaro F., Greco, S., Zumpano, E., Querying and Repairing Inconsistent XML Data, *Thecnical Report*, 2005.
   Available at http://si.deis.unical.it/~flesca/XML-repairs.pdf.
17. Lee, M. L., Ling, T. W., Low, W. L., Designing Functional Dependencies for XML, *Proc. EDBT Conf.*, 2002.
18. Suciu, D., Semistructured Data and XML, *Proc. FODO Conf.*, 1998.
19. Vincent, M. W., Liu, J., Functional Dependencies for XML. *Proc. of 5th APWeb Conf.* 2003.
20. Yang, X., Yu, G., Wang G., Efficiently Mapping Integrity Constraints from Relational Database to XML Document, *Proc. of 5th ADIBIS Conf.* 2001.

Towards Automatic Generation of Rules for Incremental Maintenance of XML Views of Relational Data

Vânia Vidal[1], Valdiana Araujo[1], and Marco Casanova[2]

[1] Dept. Computação, Universidade Federal do Ceará, Fortaleza, CE, Brasil
{vvidal, valdiana}@lia.ufc.br
[2] Dept. Informática, PUC-Rio, Rio de Janeiro, RJ, Brasil
casanova@inf.puc-rio.br

Abstract. This paper first proposes a two-step approach to define rules for maintaining materialized XML views specified over relational databases. The first step concentrates on identifying all paths of the base schema that are relevant to a path of the view, with respect to an update. The second step creates rules that maintain all view paths that can be affected by the update. The paper then discusses how to automatically identify all paths in the base schema that are relevant to a view path with respect to a given update operation and how to create the appropriate maintenance rules.

1 Introduction

The eXtended Markup Language (XML) has quickly emerged as the universal format for publishing and exchanging data on the Web. As a result, data sources often export XML views over base data [7, 10]. The exported view can be either virtual or materialized. Materialized views improve query performance and data availability, but they must be updated to reflect changes to the base source.

Basically, there are two strategies for materialized view maintenance. Re-materialization re-computes view data at pre-established times, whereas incremental maintenance [1, 2, 12] periodically modifies part of the view data to reflect updates on local sources. Incremental view maintenance proved to be an effective solution.

Incremental view maintenance algorithms have been extensively studied for relational and object oriented views [3, 8, 11] and, more recently, for semi-structured views [1, 13] and XML views [5, 6, 8, 9]. It is worth nothing that the techniques of [8, 9] cannot be applied to the incremental maintenance of XML views of relational data. Also, in [5], the authors proposed two approaches for the incremental evaluation of ATGs [4], which is the formalism used for specifying the mapping between a relational schema and a predefined DTD. In their middleware system, an update monitor detects source updates and triggers the incremental algorithm to automatically propagate the changes to XML views.

In [15], we proposed an incremental maintenance strategy, based on rules, for XML views defined on top of relational data. The strategy has three major steps: (1) convert the base source schema to an XML schema, so that the view schema and the base source schema are expressed in a common data model [17]; (2) generate the set

M. Kitsuregawa et al. (Eds.): WISE 2005, LNCS 3806, pp. 189–202, 2005.

of view correspondence assertions by matching the view schema and the base source XML schema (the set of view correspondence assertions formally specify the mapping [21] between the view schema and the base source schema); and (3) derive the incremental view maintenance rules from the correspondence assertions.

Our solution has the following relevant characteristics, when compared with previous work:

- The views can be stored outside of DBMS.
- Most of the work is carried out at view definition time. Based on the view correspondence assertions, at view definition time, we are able to: (i) identify all source updates that are relevant to the view; and (ii) define the incremental view maintenance rules required to maintain the view with respect to a given relevant update. It is important to notice that the rules are defined based solely on the source update and current source state, and, hence, they do not access the materialized view. This is relevant when the view is externally maintained, because accessing a remote data source may be too slow.
- The incremental view maintenance rules can be implemented using triggers. Hence, no middleware system is required, since the triggers are responsible for directly propagating the changes to the materialized view.
- The incremental view maintenance rules do not require any additional queries over data sources to maintain the view. This is important when the view is maintained externally.

Incremental view maintenance rules are indeed a very effective solution to the problem of materialized view maintenance, but creating the rules can be an extremely complex process. So, one must construct tools that automate the rule generation process.

In this paper, we show that, based on the view correspondence assertions, one can generate, automatic and efficiently, all rules required to maintain a materialized view. Moreover, we formally justify that the rules thus generated correctly maintain the view.

The main contributions of the paper are twofold. First, we improved our mapping formalism in two aspects: (i) we formally specify the conditions for a set of correspondence assertions to fully specify the view in terms of the source and, if so, we show that the mappings defined by the view correspondence assertions can be expressed as XQuery view definitions; (ii) we propose an algorithm that, based on the view correspondence assertions, generates XQuery [19] functions that construct view elements from the corresponding tuples of base source. We note that other mapping formalisms are either ambiguous or require the user to declare complex logical mapping [21].

Second, we provide a formal framework to detect the view paths that are affected by a base update, and to define the rules required for maintaining a view with respect to a given base update. As we will show, this can be carried out automatic and efficiently using view correspondence assertions.

The paper is organized as follows. Section 2 reviews how to convert a relational schema into an XML schema. Section 3 presents our mapping formalism. Section 4 discusses how to specify XML view using correspondence assertions. Section 5 presents our approach for automatic generation of incremental view maintenance rules. Section 6 describes how to automatically identify the paths that are relevant to a view path with respect to an insertion, deletion or update on a base table. Finally, Section 7 contains the conclusions.

2 Mapping Relational Schema to XMLS⁺ Schema

We review in this section how to map a relational schema *R* into an XML schema **S**, using the mapping rules described in [17].

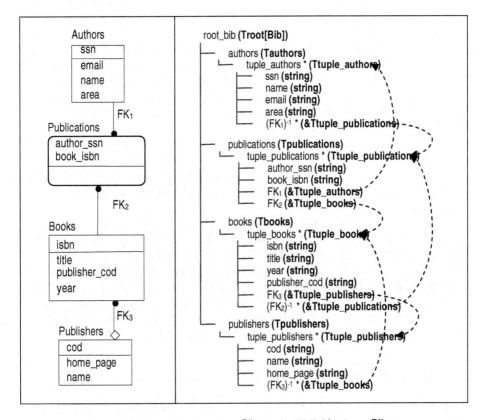

Fig. 1. The relational schema *Bib* and the XMLS⁺ schema **Bib**

Briefly, **S** has a root complex type, denoted Troot[**S**]. For each relation schemes R_i in *R*, Troot[**S**] contains an element R_i of type T_{Ri}. Note that the relation scheme and the XML element have the same name and will be used interchangeably. The complex type T_{Ri} contains a sequence of elements tuple_R_i of type Ttuple_R_i. For each attribute a of R_i of type t_a, the complex type Ttuple_R_i contains an element a of a built-in XML data type compatible with t_a. Finally, for each referential integrity constraint in *R*, the XML schema **S** contains a *key ref* constraint.

The mapping rules guarantee that the relational schema *R* and the XML schema **S** are semantically equivalent, in the sense that each database state of *R* corresponds to a XML document with schema **S**, and vice-versa.

We adopt a graphical notation, denoted XMLS⁺ for *Semantic XML Schema* [17], to represent the types of the XML schema **S**. Briefly, the notation represents the types of **S** as a tree, where type names are in boldface, "&" denotes references, "@" denotes attributes and "*" denotes that the element has minOccurs equal to zero and maxOccurs greater than one [20] (zero or more occurrences of the element). We say that an element *has multiple occurrence* when it has maxOccurs greater than one. Otherwise, it *has single occurrence*.

Fig. 1 shows graphical representations for the relational schema *Bib* and for the XML schema **Bib**. The root type Troot[**Bib**] contains an element for each relation in *Bib*. For example, the element authors, of typeTauthors, corresponds to the relation scheme authors. Tauthors contains a sequence of zero or more tuple_authors elements of type Ttuple_authors, which contains elements ssn, name, email and area. The constraint FK_3 of *Bib* is represented by two reference elements in **Bib**: Ttuple_books has a reference element, also labeled FK_3, with type &Ttuple_publishers (a reference to Ttuple_publishers); and Ttuple_publishers contains a reference element, labeled FK_3^{-1}, with type &Ttuple_books (a reference to Ttuple_books).

Let T_1 , ..., T_n be types of an XML schema. Suppose that T_k contains an element e_k of type T_{k+1}, for k=1,...,n-1. Then $\delta = e_1 /e_2 /.../e_{n-1}$ is a path of T_1, and T_n is the type of δ. If e_k has single occurrence, for k=1,...,n-1, then δ has single occurrence; otherwise, δ has multiple occurrences. For example, the path δ = books / tuple_books / FK_3 of Troot[**Bib**] has multiple occurrences.

In this paper, we assume that a XML document is represented as a directed graph, with nodes in the graph representing XML elements or attributes and edges representing parent-children relationships [14]. In what follows, we adopt an extension of XPath [18] that permits navigating through reference elements of XMLS schemas. For example, let σ be a XML document whose schema is **Bib**. The extended path expression document(σ) / books / tuple_books / FK_3 is defined by the following XQuery expression: { **For** $b **in** document($\sigma$) / Books / tuple_books, **For** $p **in** document($\sigma$) / publishers / tuple_publishers **where** $b / publisher_cod = $p / cod **Return** $p}.

3   Path Correspondence Assertions

Let **V** and **S** be XMLS schemas and T_v and T_s be complex types of **V** and **S**, respectively.

Definition 1: Let **e** be an element of T_v and δ be a path of T_s. We say that **e** is *compatible* with δ iff

i)   If **e** has single occurrence, then δ has single occurrence or is null.
ii) If **e** has multiple occurrences, then δ has multiple occurrences.
iii) If the type of **e** is an atomic type, then the type of δ is an atomic type.
iv) If the type of **e** is a complex type, then the type of δ is a complex type.

Definition 2: A *path correspondence assertion (PCA)* of **V** is an expression of the form $[T_v / e] \equiv [T_s / \delta]$, where **e** is an element of T_v and δ is a possibly null path of T_s such that **e** is compatible with δ.

Definition 3: Let T_v be a XML schema complex type and T_s be a XML schema type. Let **P** be a set of PCAs. We say that **P** *fully specifies* T_v *in terms of* T_s iff, for each element **e** in T_v:

i)   There is a single PCA of the form $[T_v / \mathbf{e}] \equiv [T_s / \delta]$ in **P**, called *the PCA for* **e** *in* **P**.

ii) Suppose that T_e is the type of **e** and T_δ is the type of δ. If T_e is complex, then **P** fully specifies T_e in terms of T_δ.

Definition 4: Let **P** be a set of PCAs that fully specify T_v in terms of T_s. Let \$v and \$s be instances of T_v and T_s, respectively. We say that \$v *matches* \$s *as specified by* **P**, denoted $\$v \equiv_P \$s$, iff, for any element **e** of T_v such that T_e is the type of **e** and $[T_v / \mathbf{e}] \equiv [T_s / \delta]$ is the PCA in **P** for **e** (which exists by assumption on **P**), we have that:

(i)   If δ is not Null, **e** has single occurrence and T_e is an atomic type then \$v/e = <e>\$s/\delta/text()</e>

(ii) If δ is not Null, **e** has single occurrence and T_e is a complex type then $\$v/e \equiv_p$ \$s/\delta

(iii) If δ is not Null, **e** has multiple occurrences and T_e is an atomic type then, for each \$a in \$v/e, there is \$b in \$s/\delta such that \$a=<e>\$b/text()</e> and, for each \$b in \$s/\delta, there is \$a in \$v/e such that \$a=<e>\$b/text()</e>

(iv) If δ is not Null, **e** has multiple occurrences and T_e is a complex type then, for each \$a in \$v/e, there is \$b in \$s/\delta such that $\$a \equiv_p \$b$ and, for each \$b in \$s/\delta, there is \$a in \$v/e such that $\$a \equiv_p \$b$

(v)   If δ is Null, then $\$v/e \equiv_p \$s$.

Based on Definition 4, the algorithm shown in Fig. 2 receives as input the types T_v and T_s, a set **P** of PCAs that fully specifies T_v in terms of T_s, and generates the function constructor $\tau[T_s \rightarrow T_v](\$s:T_s)$ such that, given an instance \$s of T_s, $\tau[T_s \rightarrow T_v](\$s)$ constructs the content for an instance \$v of T_v, such that $\$v \equiv_p \$s$.

Input: types T_v and T_s; set P of PCAs that fully specifies T_v in terms of T_s;
Output: function $\tau[T_s \rightarrow T_v](\$s:T_s)$ such that, given an instance \$s of T_s, $\tau[T_s \rightarrow T_v](\$s)$
               constructs the content of an instance of T_v as specified by the PCAs in P.
τ = "**declare function** $\tau[T_s \rightarrow T_v](\$s:T_s)$ { ";
For each element **e** of T_v where $[T_v / \mathbf{e}] \equiv [T_s / \delta]$, T_e is the type of **e**
            and T_δ is the type of δ **Do**
  In case of
    Case 1: If δ is not **Null**, e has single occurrence and T_e is an atomic type
          $\tau = \tau + $ "<e>\$s/\delta/text() </e> " ;
    Case 2: If δ is not **Null**, e has single occurrence and T_e is a complex type, **then**
          $\tau = \tau + $ "<e>$\tau[T_\delta \rightarrow T_e]$(\$s/\delta)</e>" ;
    Case 3: If δ is not **Null**, e has multiple occurrences and T_e is an atomic type, **then**
          $\tau = \tau + $ "{ **For** \$b **in** \$s/\delta **do return** <e>\$b / text() </e> }, " ;
    Case 4: If δ is not **Null**, e has multiple occurrences and T_e is a complex type, **then**
          $\tau = \tau + $ "{ **For** \$b **in** \$s/\delta **do return** <e> $\tau[T_\delta \rightarrow T_e]$(\$b) </e> }, " ;
    Case 5: If δ is **Null**, then $\tau = \tau + $ "<e>$\tau[T_s \rightarrow T_e]$(\$s) </e>, ";
  end case;
end for;
return τ }";

Fig. 2. Constructor Generation Algorithm

4 View Specification

In general, we propose to define a view with the help of a view schema, as usual, and a set of view correspondence assertions [16], instead of the more familiar approach of defining a query on the data sources. Without loss of generality, we assume that the type of the root element of a view has only one element which usually has multiple occurrences.

Let S be the XMLS schema of base relational source R. Recall that S has a root element Troot[S] and that, for each relation schemes R_i in R, Troot[S] contains an element R_i of type T_{Ri}. The complex type T_{Ri} contains a sequence of elements tuple_R_i of type Ttuple_R_i.

A *XML view*, or simply, a *view* over S is a triple V=<$\mathbf{V}$,Ψ,$\mathbf{P}$>, where:

i) $\mathbf{V}$ is a XMLS schema with a root element whose type is Troot[$\mathbf{V}$].
ii) Troot[$\mathbf{V}$] has only one element, e, which has multiple occurrences. Assume that e has type T_e.
iii) Ψ is an expression of the form [Troot[$\mathbf{V}$] / e] $\equiv$ [Troot[$\mathbf{S}$] / R_b / tuple_R_b [selExp]], where R_b is an element of Troot[$\mathbf{S}$] and selExp is a predicate expression [18], called a *global collection correspondence assertion*. Assume that tuple_R_b has type $T_{\text{tuple\_}Rb}$.
iv) $\mathbf{P}$ is a set of path correspondence assertions that fully specifies T_e in terms of $T_{\text{tuple\_}Rb}$.

The GCCA Ψ specifies that, given an instance σ_s of Troot[$\mathbf{S}$] and the value σ_v of V in σ_s, then, for any \$a in document(σ_v) / e, there is \$b in document(σ_s) / R_b / tuple_R_b [selExp] such that \$a $\equiv_P$ \$b and, conversely, for any \$b in document(σ_s) / R_b / tuple_R_b [selExp], there is \$a in document(σ_v) / e such that \$a $\equiv_P$ \$b.

Let **Bib** be the XML base source schema, shown in Fig. 1, **View_Bib** be a view over **Bib**, schematically shown in Fig. 3. Note that **View_Bib** has a root type Troot[**View_Bib**], with only one element, author$_v$, whose type is Tauthor$_v$. The global collection correspondence assertion matches the author$_v$ element of Troot[**View_Bib**] with a path from Troot[**Bib**]:

Ψ: [Troot[**View_Bib**] / author$_v$] $\equiv$ [Troot[**Bib**] / authors / tuple_authors [area="Database"]]

Ψ specifies that, given an instance σ_{bib} of Troot[**Bib**] and the value σ_{view_bib} of View_Bib in σ_{bib}, then:

σ_{view_bib} = <root_ view_bib > <u>For</u> \$a <u>in</u> document(σ_{bib})/authors/tuple_author[area= "Database"]
                    <u>return</u> <author$_v$>τ[$T_{\text{tuple\_authors}}\rightarrow T_{\text{author}v}$](\$a) </author$_v$>
        </root_ view_bib >

Fig. 3 shows the path correspondence assertions of View_Bib, which fully specifies Tauthor$_v$ in terms of Ttuple_authors. These assertions are generated by: (1) matching the elements of Tauthor$_v$ with elements or paths of the base type Ttuple_authors; and (2) recursively descending into sub-elements of Tauthor$_v$ to define their correspondence.

The function τ[$T_{\text{tuple\_authors}}\rightarrow T_{\text{author}v}$](\$a) returns the content of the author$_v$ element that matches the tuple_authors element \$a, as specified by Ψ_1 to Ψ_4. Functions τ[$T_{\text{tuple\_books}}\rightarrow T_{\text{book}v}$] and τ[$T_{\text{tuple\_publishers}}\rightarrow T_{\text{publisher}v}$] are likewise defined using Ψ_5 to Ψ_8 and Ψ_9 to Ψ_{11}, respectively:

declare function $\tau[T_{tuple\_authors} \rightarrow T_{authorv}]$ ($a as $T_{tuple\_authors}$){
    <ssn$_v$>{$a/ssn/text()}</ssn$_v$> <name$_v$>{$a/name/text()}</name$_v$>
    <email$_v$>{$a/ email/text()}</email$_v$>
    { **For** $b **in** $a / (Fk$_1$)$^{-1}$ / Fk$_2$ **return** <book$_v$><$\tau[T_{tuple\_books} \rightarrow T_{bookrv}]$($b) </book$_v$> } };

declare function $\tau[T_{tuple\_books} \rightarrow T_{bookv}]$ ($b as T_{tuple_books}){
    <isbn$_v$> {$b/ isbn /text()}</isbn$_v$><title$_v$> {$b/title/text() } </title$_v$>
    {**For** $p **in** b / FK_3$ **return** <publisher$_v$>$\tau[T_{tuple\_publishers} \rightarrow T_{publisherv}]$($p) </publisher$_v$>}},

declare function $\tau[T_{tuple\_publishers} \rightarrow T_{publisherv}]$($p as $T_{tuple\_publishers}$){
    <cod$_v$> {$p/cod/text()}</cod$_v$> <name$_v$> {$p/name/text()} </name$_v$>
    < home_page$_v$> {$p/ home_page/text()} </home_page$_v$ >}

As we have shown, the set of view correspondence assertions fully specify the view in terms of the data source, in the sense that the correspondence assertions of View_Bib (see Fig. 3) define a functional mapping from instances of the source schema **Bib** to instances of the view schema **View_Bib**.

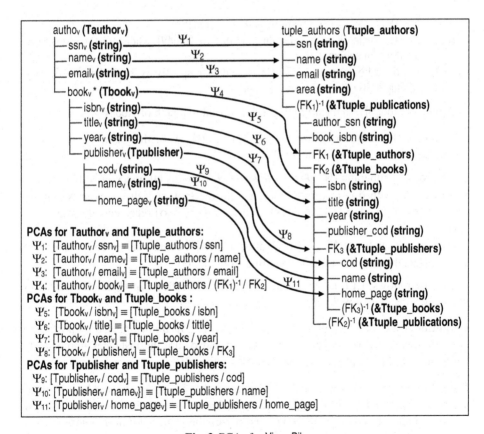

Fig. 3. PCAs for View_Bib

5   Automatic Generation of Rules

In this section, we first present a sequence of definitions and propositions, and then we discuss our approach for automatic generation of incremental view maintenance rules.

Let S be the XMLS schema of a base relational source R and V=<V, Ψ,P> be a view over S. Assume that the root type of V, Troot[V], contains a sequence of elements e of type T_e and that the GCCA Ψ is of the form:

$$\Psi: [\text{Troot}[V] / e] \equiv [\text{Troot}[S] / R_b / \text{tuple\_}R_b[\text{selExp}]]$$

Definition 5: A path δ_v of T_v is *semantically related* to a path δ_b of Ttuple_R_b, denoted $\delta_v \equiv \delta_b$, iff there are paths $\delta_{v_1},...,\delta_{v_n}$ in V and paths $\delta_{b_1},...,\delta_{b_n}$ in S such that $\delta_v = \delta_{v_1}/.../\delta_{v_n}$, $\delta_b = \delta_{b_1}/.../\delta_{b_n}$, $[T_v / \delta_{v_1}] \equiv [T_b / \delta_{b_1}] \in P$ and $[T_{v_i} / \delta_{v_{i+1}}] \equiv [T_{b_i} / \delta_{b_{i+1}}] \in P$, for $1 \le i \le n\text{-}1$.

Definition 6: A path δ_s of Troot[S] *is relevant to* a path of Troot[V] in the following cases:

Case 1. $\delta_s = R_b / \text{tuple\_}R_b$ is relevant to path e of Troot[V].
Case 2. $\delta_s = R_b / \text{tuple\_}R_b / a$ is relevant to path e of Troot[V], where a is an element or attribute in selExp.
Case 3.   Let δ_s and δ_v be paths of Ttuple_R_b and T_e, respectively, such that $\delta_v \equiv \delta_s$, then $R_b / \text{tuple\_}R_b / \delta_s$ is relevant to e / δ_v.

A path of Troot[S] *is relevant to* V iff it is relevant to a path of Troot[V].

Definition 7: Let σ be an instance of a type T, $G = (N, A)$ be the graph that represents σ, and let $\delta = e_1 /... / e_n$ be a path of T.

(i) $\mathcal{H}[\delta, \sigma]$ is a subgraph (N', A') of G, where N' contains all nodes in N that are visited when the path δ is traversed starting from the root, and all nodes in N that are descendents of a node $\$e_n$ in document(σ)/ $e_1 /... / e_n$. $\mathcal{H}[\delta, \sigma]$ represents the value of δ in σ.

(ii) $\mathcal{I}[\delta, \sigma]$ is a subgraph (N'', A'') of $\mathcal{H}[\delta, \sigma]$, where N'' contains all nodes in N that are visited when the path δ is traversed starting from the root.

In what follows, let μ be an update over a relation scheme of R, and U be a list of updates against the view V.

Definition 8: Let δ_s be a path of Troot[S]. We say that δ_s *can be affected by* μ iff there are instances σ and σ' of Troot[S] such that σ and σ' are the instances immediately before and after μ, respectively, and $\mathcal{I}[\delta_s, \sigma] \neq \mathcal{I}[\delta_s, \sigma']$.

Definition 9: Let δ_v be a path of Troot[V]. We say that δ_v *can be affected by* μ iff there are instances σ and σ' of Troot[S] such that σ and σ' are the instances immediately before and after μ, respectively, and σ_v and σ'_v are the values of V in σ and σ', respectively, and $I[\delta_v, \sigma_v] \neq I[\delta_v, \sigma'_v]$.

Proposition 1: A path δ_v of Troot[V] *can be affected* by μ iff there is a path δ_s of Troot[S] such that δ_s is relevant to δ_v and δ_s can be affected by μ .

Definition 10: We say that U *correctly maintains* V *with respect to.*μ iff, for any pair of instances of Troot[S], σ_s and σ'_s, if σ_s and σ'_s are the instances immediately before and after μ, respectively, σ_v and σ'_v are the values of V in σ_s and σ'_s, respectively, and $\sigma''_v = U(\sigma_v)$, then $\sigma''_v = \sigma'_v$, where $U(\sigma_v)$ returns the new value of view V after applying U to σ_v.

Definition 11: Let δ_v be a path of Troot[**V**]. We say that U *correctly maintains* δ_v *with respect to* μ iff, for any pair of instances of Troot[**S**], σ_s and σ'_s, if σ_s and σ'_s are the instances immediately before and after μ, respectively, σ_v and σ'_v are the values of V in σ_s and σ'_s, respectively, and $\sigma''_v = U(\sigma_v)$, then $\mathcal{H}[\delta_v, \sigma'_v] = \mathcal{H}[\delta_v, \sigma''_v]$.

Proposition 2: If U correctly maintains all paths δ_v of Troot[V] *with respect to* μ, then U *correctly maintains* V.

Proposition 3: Let $\delta_v = \delta_1 / \delta_2$ be a path of Troot[V]. Suppose that δ_1 can be affected by μ. If U correctly maintains δ_1 *with respect to* μ, then U correctly maintains δ_v.

In our approach, the process of generating the maintenance rules for V consists of the following steps:

1. Obtain the set $\mathcal{P}[\mu,V]$ of all paths δ_s such that: (i) δ_s is relevant to a path δ_v of Troot[V]; (ii) δ_s is affected by μ; and (iii) there is no path δ' such that δ' is a proper prefix of δ_s and $\delta' \in \mathcal{P}[\mu,V]$. $\mathcal{P}[\mu,V]$ denote the set of paths that are relevant to V with respect to a base update μ over S.

2. For each path δ_v of Troot[V] such that there is δ_s in $\mathcal{P}[\mu,V]$ such that δ_s is relevant to δ_v, generate the rule for maintaining δ_v with respect to μ. Note that, if $\mathcal{P}[\mu,V]=\emptyset$, then μ is not relevant to V and no rule is generated.

From Proposition 2, we have that the rules correctly maintain a view V iff they correctly maintain all paths of V. So, our strategy for proving that the rules created by the above process correctly maintain V with respect to an update μ consists in demonstrating that: (i) all updates generated by the rules correctly maintain all paths δ_v of Troot[V] that can be affected by μ; and (ii) all other paths cannot be affected by the updates generated by rules. From Propositions 1 and 3, we have to generate rules for maintaining each path δ_v such that there is δ_s in $\mathcal{P}[\mu,V]$ such that δ_s is relevant to δ_v, which are the paths corresponding to the rules generated in Step 2 above.

Let R be a relation scheme of base source R. Theorem 1 establishes sufficient conditions to compute the set $\mathcal{P}[\mu,V]$ when μ is an insertion or deletion over R, and Theorem 2, when μ is an update on attributes of R.

Theorem 1: Let μ be an insertion or deletion operation over R.

Case 1: Suppose that $R = R_b$. Then, we have $\mathcal{P}[\mu,V] = \{ R_b /\text{tuple}\_R_b \}$

Case 2: Suppose that $R \neq R_b$. Let δ_s be a path of Troot[**S**]. Then, a path $\delta_s \in \mathscr{P}[\mu,V]$ iff $\delta_s = R_b / \text{tuple\_}R_b / \delta_2 / FK_1^{-1} / \delta_1$, where δ_1 and δ_2 can be null, FK_1 is a foreign key of R, δ_s is relevant to V, and there is no path δ' such that δ' is a proper prefix of δ_s and $\delta' \in \mathscr{P}[\mu,V]$.

Theorem 2: Let μ be an update on an attribute a on R, and δ_s be a path of Troot[**S**].

Case 1: Suppose that $R = R_b$. Then, a path $\delta_s \in \mathscr{P}[\mu,V]$ iff
    Case 1.1: $\delta_s = R_b / \text{tuple\_}R_b / a$ where $R_b / \text{tuple\_}R_b / a$ is relevant to V.
    Case 1.2: $\delta_s = R_b / \text{tuple\_}R_b / FK / \delta_2$ where FK is a foreign key of R_b such that a is an attribute of FK, δ_s is relevant to V and there is no path δ' such that δ' is a proper prefix of δ_s and $\delta' \in \mathscr{P}[\mu,V]$.

Case 2: Suppose that $R \neq R_b$. Then, a path $\delta_s \in \mathscr{P}[\mu,V]$ iff
    Case 2.1: $\delta_s = R_b / \text{tuple\_}R_b / \delta / FK / a$ where δ can be null, FK is a foreign key that references R and δ_s is relevant to V.
    Case 2.2: $\delta_s = R_b / \text{tuple\_}R_b / \delta / FK^{-1} / a$ where δ can be null, FK is a foreign key of R and δ_s is relevant to V.
    Case 2.3: $\delta_s = R_b / \text{tuple\_}R_b / \delta_1 / FK / \delta_2$, where δ_2 can be null, FK is a foreign key of R such that a is an attribute of FK, δ_s is relevant to V and there is no path δ' such that δ' is a proper prefix of δ_s and $\delta' \in \mathscr{P}[\mu,V]$.
    Case 2.4: $\delta_s = R_b / \text{tuple\_}R_b / \delta_1 / FK^{-1} / \delta_2$, where δ_1 e δ_2 can be null, FK is a foreign key of R such that a is an attribute of FK, δ_s is relevant to V and there is no path δ' such that δ' is a proper prefix of δ_s and $\delta' \in \mathscr{P}[\mu,V]$.

Example 1: Consider the view **View_Bib** defined in Section 3 and let μ be the update of the attribute publisher_cod of the relation scheme Books.

From Case 3 of Definition 6, we have that δ = authors / tuple_authors / Fk_1^{-1} / Fk_2 / Fk_3, where FK_3 is a foreign key of Books, is relevant to view path author$_v$ / book$_v$ / publisher$_v$. From Case 2.3 of Theorem 2 we have that $\delta \in \mathscr{P}[\mu,\text{View\_Bib}]$.

Fig. 4 shows the rule for maintaining path author$_v$/ book$_v$/ publisher$_v$ with respect to μ. In this rule $view_bib represents the current instance of Troot[**View_Bib**], $new and $old represents the old and new state of the updated tuple_book element, respectively.

According to the rule, the updates required for maintaining author$_v$/ book$_v$/ publisher$_v$ reduce to: for each book$_v$ element in $view_bib / author$_v$ / book$_v$ that matches $new then:

i)   delete the sub-element publisher$_v$ that matches the element tuple_publishers in $old / FK_3 ;
ii) insert the sub-element publisher$_v$ that matches the element tuple_publishers in $new / FK_3.

The rule can be automatically generated based on the rule template shown in Fig. 5. This template should be applied in case where the relevant path satisfies conditions of Case 2.3 of Theorem 2.

The complete family of rule templates for insertion, deletion and update operation, covering all cases of Theorems 1 and 2, can be found in [16].

---

when UPDATE OF publisher_cod ON Books **then**
let \$vn **in** \$view_bib / authorv / bookv **where** \$vn / isbnv /text()= \$new / isbn/text()
for \$d **in** \$old / FK3 **do**
    let \$vn+1 **in** \$vn / publisherv **where** \$vn+1 / codv /text() = \$d / cod /text()
    delete \$vn+1 **as child of** \$vn;
for \$i **in** \$new / FK3 **do**
    \$c := <publisherv> τ [Ttuple_ublishers→ Tpublisherv] (\$i) </publisherv>
    insert \$c **as a child of** \$vn;

Fig. 4. Rule for maintaining path authorv / bookv / publisherv w.r.t μ

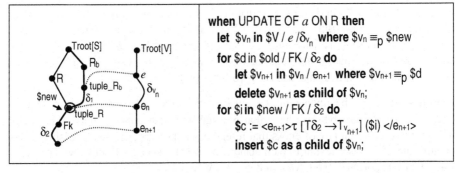

Fig. 5. Rule for maintaining the view V with respect to an update of an attribute a of R satisfying the following conditions: (i) R≠Rb and (ii) the path Rb / tuple_Rb / δ1/ FK / δ2 is relevant to path $e/\delta_{v_n}/v_{n+1}$ of Troot[V], where Fk is a foreign key of R and Rb /tuple_Rb / δ1 ≡p e/δ_{v_n} (Case 2.3 of Theorem 2)

6 Identifying Relevant Paths

In this section, let **S** be the XMLS schema of a base relational source R and R be a relation scheme of R. Let V=<**V**,**Ψ**,**P**> be a view defined over **S**. To automatically compute the set of all paths of Troot[**S**] which are relevant to V, we use the *relevant path tree* of V, denoted $\mathscr{T}$[**V**].

Fig. 6 shows the relevant path tree for the View_Bib defined in Section 3. For each path root,e_1,...,e_n in $\mathscr{T}$[**View_Bib**], there is a path e_1 / ... / e_n of Troot[**Bib**] which is a prefix of a path relevant to View_Bib, and vice-versa. If e_n is a solid node, then e_1 /.../ e_n is relevant to View_Bib. Hence, paths authors / tuple_authors and authors / tuple_authors / area are relevant to View_Bib, and the path authors is not relevant, since it is a prefix of the relevant path authors / tuple_authors.

Fig. 6 also shows the assertions that originated nodes and edges. For example, from the GCCA Ψ, paths authors / tuple_authors and authors / tuple_authors / area are relevant to View_Bib (cases 1 and 2 of relevant path). From Ψ and Ψ1, authors / tuple_authors / ssn is relevant to View_Bib (case 3). From Ψ and Ψ4, authors / tuple_authors / (Fk1)-1 / Fk2 is relevant to View_Bib (case 3).

The relevant paths for a given base update operation can be automatically identified using the relevant path tree, as we illustrate in the following examples.

Example 2: Let μ be an insertion or deletion on the relation scheme Publications. From $\mathscr{T}$[**View_Bib**], we have that the path δ = authors / tuple_authors / $(FK_1)^{-1}$/ FK_2, where FK_1 is a foreign key of Publications, is relevant to path $author_v$ / $book_v$ of Troot[**view_Bib**]. From Case 2 of Theorem 1, we have that $\delta \in \mathscr{P}$[μ,View_Bib].

Example 3: Let μ be an update of the attribute area of the relation scheme Authors. From $\mathscr{T}$[**View_Bib**], we have that δ = authors / tuple_authors / area is relevant to path $author_v$ of Troot[**view_Bib**]. From Case 1.1 of Theorem 1, we have that $\delta \in \mathscr{P}$[μ,View_Bib].

Example 4: Let μ be update of the attribute home_page of the relation scheme Publishers. From $\mathscr{T}$[**View_Bib**], we have that δ = authors / tuple_authors / $(FK_1)^{-1}$ / FK_2 / FK_3 / home_page, where FK_3 is a foreign key that references Publishers, is relevant to path $author_v$ / $book_v$ / $publisher_v$/ $home\_page_v$ of Troot[**View_Bib**]. From Case 2.1 of Theorem 2, we have that the path δ / home_page $\in \mathscr{P}$[μ,View_Bib].

Example 5: Let μ be update of the attribute publisher_cod of the relation scheme Books. From $\mathscr{T}$[View_Bib], we have that δ = authors / tuple_authors / $(FK_1)^{-1}$ / FK_2 / Fk_3, where FK_3 is a foreign key of Books that references Publishers such that publisher_cod is an attribute of Fk_3, is relevant to path $author_v$/ $book_v$/ $publisher_v$ of Troot[**View_Bib**]. From Case 2.3 of Theorem 2, we have that $\delta \in \mathscr{P}$[μ,View_Bib].

Given a view V, the full details of the algorithms to identify the set $\mathscr{P}$[μ,V], where μ is an insertion, deletion or update, can be found in [16].

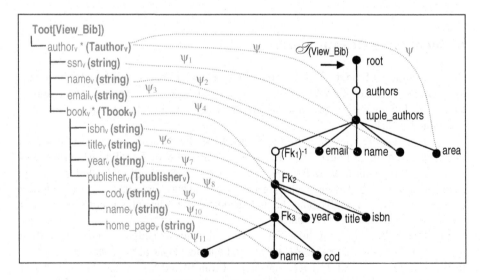

Fig. 6. Relevant Path Tree of View_Bib

7 Conclusions

We argued in this paper that we may fully specify a view in terms of the data source by using view correspondence assertions, in the sense that the assertions define a mapping from instances of the source schema to instances of the view schema.

We showed that, based on the view correspondence assertions, we can automatically and efficiently identify all view paths that can affected by a base update. Using view correspondence assertions, we can also define the rule required for maintaining a view path with respect to a given base update.

We notice that, in our approach, rules are responsible for directly propagating changes to the materialized view. Therefore, no algorithm for view maintenance is required. The effectiveness of our approach is guaranteed for externally maintained view because: (i) the view maintenance rule are defined at view definition time; (ii) no access to the materialized view is required; and (iii) rule execution does not require any additional queries over data source.

We are currently working on the development of a tool to automate the generation of incremental view maintenance rules. The tool uses a family of rule templates which are used to generate the specific rules for maintaining the view paths that can be affected by a given base updates. We have already defined the rules templates for most types of object preserving views.

References

1. Abiteboul, S., McHugh, J., Rys, M., Vassalos, V., Wiener, J.L.: Incremental Maintenance for Materialized Views over Semistructured Data. In Proceedings of the International Conference on Very Large Databases. New York City (1998) 38-49.
2. Ali, M.A., Fernandes, A.A., Paton, N.W.: Incremental Maintenance for Materialized OQL Views. In Proc. DOLAP (2000) 41–48.
3. Ali, M.A., Fernandes, A.A., Paton, N.W.: MOVIE: an incremental maintenance system for materialized object views, Data & Knowledge Engineering, v.47 n.2, p.131-166, November 2003.
4. Benedikt, M., Chan, C. Y., Fan, W., Rastogi, R., Zheng, S., Zhou, A.: DTD-directed publishing with attribute translation grammars. In VLDB, 2002.
5. Bohannon, P., Choi, B., Fan, W.: Incremental evaluation of schema-directed XML publishing, Proceedings of the 2004 ACM SIGMOD international conference on Management of data, June 13-18, 2004, Paris, France.
6. Byron Choi, Wenfei Fan, Xibei Jia, Arek Kasprzyk: A Uniform System for Publishing and Maintaining XML Data. VLDB 2004: 1301-1304.
7. Carey,M.J., Kiernan, J., Shanmugasundaram, J., Shekita, E.J., Subramanian, S.N.: XPERANTO: Middleware for Publishing Object-Relational Data as XML Documents. In The VLDB Journal(2000) 646–648.
8. Dimitrova, K., El-Sayed, M., Rundensteiner, E. A.: Order-sensitive view maintenance of materialized XQuery views. In ER, 2003.
9. Fa, Y., Chen, Y., Ling, T.W., Chen, T.: Materialized View Maintenance for XML Documents. WISE 2004: 365-371
10. Fernandez, M., Morishima, A., Suciu, D., Tan, W.: Publishing Relational Data in XML: the SilkRoute Approach. IEEE Trans on Computers, 44(4). (2001) 1–9.

11. Gupta, A., Mumick, I.S.: Materialized Views. MIT Press, 2000.
12. Kuno, H.A., and Rundensteiner, E.A.: Incremental Maintenance of Materialized Object-Oriented Views in MultiView: Strategies and Performance Evaluation. IEEE Transaction on Data and Knowledge Engineering, 10(5):768–792 (1998).
13. Suciu, D.: Query decomposition and view maintenance for query languages for unstructured data. In Proceedings of VLDB, pages 187--238, 1996.
14. Tian, F., DeWitt D.J., Chen J., Zhang, C.: The Design and Performance Evaluation of Alternative XML Storage Strategies. In SIGMOD (2002), vol. 31 5–10.
15. Vidal, V.M.P., Casanova, M.A, Araujo, V.S.: Generating Rules for Incremental Maintenance of XML Views of Relational Data. Proceedings of the 9th ACM International Workshop on Web Information and Data Management, WIDM 2003 139-146.
16. Vidal, V.M.P., Casanova, M.A., Araujo, V.S: Automatic Generation of Rules for the Incremental Maintenance of XML Views over Relational Data. Technical Report. Universidade Federal do Ceará, Janeiro, 2005.
17. Vidal, V.M.P., Vilas Boas, R.: A Top-Down Approach for XML Schema Matching. In Proceedings of the 17th Brazilian Symposium on Databases. Gramado, Brazil (2002).
18. World-Wide Web Consortium: *XML Path Language (XPath)*: Version 1.0 (November 1999). http:// www.w3.org/TR/xpath (visited on September 10th, 2005).
19. World-Wide Web Consortium: *XML Query Language (XQuery)*: Version 1.0 (November 1999). http://www.w3.org/TR/xquery/ (visited on September 10th, 2005).
20. World-Wide Web Consortium: XML Schema Part 0: Primer Second Edition (October 2004). http://www.w3.org/TR/xmlschema-0/ (visited on September 10th, 2005).
21. Yu, C., Popa, L.: Constraint-Based XML Query Rewriting For Data Integration. SIGMOD Conference 2004: Paris, France, June 2004, pp. 371-382.

A Methodological Approach for Incorporating Adaptive Navigation Techniques into Web Applications*

Gonzalo Rojas[1,2] and Vicente Pelechano[1]

[1] Technical University of Valencia, Camino de Vera s/n 46022 Valencia, Spain
[2] University of Concepcion, Edmundo Larenas 215 Concepcion, Chile
{grojas, pele}@dsic.upv.es

Abstract. The incorporation of Adaptive Navigation techniques into Web applications is a complex task. The conceptual specification of the navigation must consider the preferences and needs of users, as well as different implementation alternatives from the same navigational structure. However, there is a lack of methods that rule this integration. This work proposes a methodological approach that allow describing adaptive navigation characteristics of a Web application at a high abstraction level. We introduce a User Modelling process and a set of concepts that permit to incorporate two types of adaptive navigation techniques into the navigational description of a Web application. These techniques select and sort the links of a page, according to their relevance for a given user. The steps of the methodology are illustrated through a case study.

1 Introduction

The heterogeneous domain of potential users of Web applications asks developers to produce software solutions that meet individual information needs and preferences. Users must be provided with navigation capabilities that allow finding the relevant information in an easy and intuitive way. For this reason, the adaptivity of the navigation of a Web application is an issue that deserves special attention.

The introduction of Adaptive Navigation techniques into Web applications requires to consider the preferences and needs of information of the intended users, as well as to manage the needed expressiveness to model different alternatives of implementations for a unique navigational structure. However, there is a lack of methodological approaches that rule this integration. Research efforts made by Adaptive Hypermedia community have produced clearly defined adaptive navigation strategies and techniques, but they are mainly focused at late stages of the software development. At the same time, most of Model-Driven Web development proposals have hardly considered these concepts as part as a systematic process of software development.

---

* This work has been developed with the support of MEC under the project DESTINO TIN2004-03534 and cofinanced by FEDER.

M. Kitsuregawa et al. (Eds.): WISE 2005, LNCS 3806, pp. 203–216, 2005.

This work proposes a methodological approach that allows describing Web applications that include adaptive navigational techniques. Taking as an input an application requirement that requires an adaptation of the navigational hyperspace, it is possible to obtain a high-level description of the navigational structures and the adaptive techniques that allow fulfilling that requirement.

The adaptive navigation techniques that are introduced into the Web development process are defined at instance level, i.e., they are based on the relevance that instances of the domain concepts have to a given user. This strategy is a starting point for the introduction of more complex adaptive techniques.

Taking the OOWS Web development process [1] as a reference, the main contribution of this proposal can be summarized in the following points: (a) a User Modelling process, which contains application-relevant user characteristics and on which the adaptation of the navigation is based; (b) a set of concepts that augments the expressiveness of the OOWS Navigational Model, supporting the description of adaptive navigation techniques; and (c) conceptual descriptions of adaptive techniques that allow selecting and ordering links to domain concept instances, according to their relevance to a given user. These points are illustrated through a case study, which consists in an online bookstore.

The remainder of the paper is organized as follows: Section 2 presents an overview of the OOWS Modelling approach, focused on its Navigational Model. Section 3 describes the concepts introduced into OOWS method to support the adaptive navigation. In Section 4 we present the methodological approach for describing the adaptive navigation of Web applications. Section 5 describes the adaptive navigation techniques introduced into the OOWS process, presenting examples of their conceptual description and the resulting implementations. Section 6 presents a brief review of related works on conceptual modelling of Web applications with adaptive navigation features. Finally, Section 7 presents some conclusions and future works.

2   The OOWS Navigational Modelling Approach

OOWS (Object-Oriented Web Solution) method [1] is an extension of the OO-Method proposal for Automatic Code Generation [2], which allows describing the whole development process of Web applications. It is composed by five models: a *Class Diagram*, which defines the static structure of the system; *Dynamic and Functional models* that describe the system behaviour; and the *OOWS Navigational and Presentation Models*, which captures the navigational and presentation properties of the application, respectively.

The *OOWS Navigational Model* defines a set of *Navigational Maps*. Each map corresponds to a global view of the Web application for a given group of users. It is represented by a directed graph, whose nodes and arcs are *Navigational Contexts* and *Navigational Links*, respectively. Figure 1 shows a Navigational Map of an online bookstore and defined for a *Client* user type.

A Navigational Context is composed of a set of *Navigational Classes*, which represent class views with attributes and operations. Each context has one mandatory

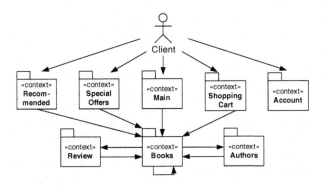

Fig. 1. Example of OOWS navigational map and the two types of navigational contexts

navigational class (*Manager Class*), and optional navigational classes that provide complementary information (*Complementary Classes*). Navigational classes are related through unidirectional binary relationships, called *Navigational Relationships*, which are classified into two types: (a) *Context Dependency Relationship* (dashed arrow), which represents a basic information recovery by crossing a structural relationship between classes; and (b) *Context Relationship* (solid arrow), which represents an information recovery plus a navigation to a target context. All these concepts are exemplified in Fig. 2.

Figure 2 shows the *Books* Navigational Context included in Fig. 1 and an example of its implementation. This context describes a page of a specific book of the bookstore. Frame 1 shows the main data of the book, retrieved from *Book* manager class; frames 2, 3 and 4 show data retrieved from the complementary classes, through navigational relationships.

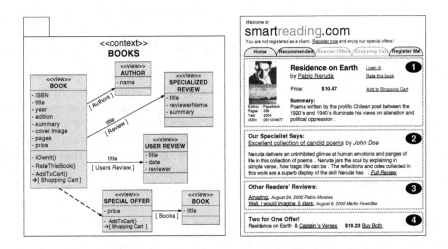

Fig. 2. Books navigational context for a web-based bookstore

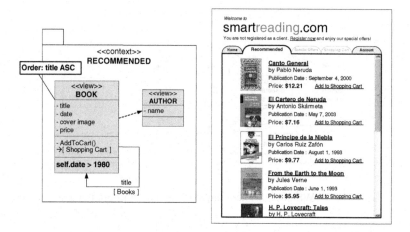

Fig. 3. Filter and Ordering Pattern of a navigational context

OOWS includes *Filters* and *Ordering Patterns* for selecting and ordering the displayed objects of a navigational class, respectively. Both structures are based on one or more attributes of the manager class. *Recommended* context of Fig. 3 includes a filter (lower section of *Book* class), which constrains the displayed books according to their *date* attribute values. An ordering pattern (left-side label) indicates that *Book* instances must be ordered in ascendant (ASC) order by *title* attribute.

The conceptual tools of the OOWS Navigational Model provide multiple alternatives for the navigational design of a web application. Distinct navigational maps and variants of the inner structure of their contexts (nodes) can be associated to different kinds of users. For this reason, this model is very suitable for the incorporation of adaptive features into its descriptions. The next section introduces some specific concepts that are needed to reach this goal.

3   Concepts for User Modelling and Adaptive Navigation

This section introduces a set of concepts for incorporating Adaptive Navigation techniques at instance level in OOWS-based Web applications. At first, we present the *Adaptive Navigation Requirement* concept, which rules the rest of the adaptivity modelling. Secondly, we define a *User Model proposal*, for describing the user characteristics on which the adaptation is based. Afterwards, we introduce the *Relevance* concept, which describes the importance that instances of domain concepts have for a given user. Finally, we introduce the *Adaptive Navigational Context* to describe the adaptive character of some contexts.

3.1   Adaptive Navigation Requirement

We define *Adaptive Navigation Requirements* as those functional requirements that consider navigational processes that are affected by the characteristics of a particular user. These requirements can be atomic or composed of simpler requirements. They can be described at distinct levels of granularity, according to the particular navigational structure involved in their fulfillment. In this work, we are focused on the definition of adaptive navigation requirements at *instance level*, i.e., those requirements whose implementation is achieved by applying adaptive navigation techniques over the instances of navigational classes.

3.2   A User Model Proposal

This proposal allow obtaining high level descriptions of the Web application's users for achieving the system adaptation, by defining the following diagrams:

User Stereotype Diagram. It consists on a hierarchy of groups of application users that are likely to share some features. The ordering of shared characteristics allows applying the same implementation of an adaptive technique to several users. Typical stereotypes are: skilled/novice users, child/young/adult clients.

Application-Dependent User Diagram. It includes the classes that describe those user's characteristics with some relation to the particular application domain. This is done in terms of attributes, operations and relationships of the introduced classes with the domain classes, as an overlay of the domain description (Class Diagram).

Navigational Behaviour Diagram. It describes the user's interaction with navigational structures of the application during a session. It is defined as an overlay of the conceptual structures specified in the Navigational Design, describing users in terms of their visits to a given navigational context, the activations of links (context relationships) and the operations they execute. Further information about this diagram can be found in [3].

3.3   Relevance

A *Relevance* property is defined to determine how relevant the domain concepts are for a given user. According to the adaptivity requirements, the developer describes this relevance in terms of the concepts included in the Application-Dependent User Diagram, by defining an OCL expression. This definition can be used for selecting and/or ordering the retrieved instances of the referred domain concept. For instance, in the e-bookstore application, the relevance of a B book for a C client can be described as (a) the number of instances of *Keyword* class related to B and also to books already purchased, owned, marked as favourite book, highly rated or visited by C; or (b) the number of visited relationships between C and *Book* instances that are related to the same *Author* instance related to B.

3.4   Adaptive Navigational Context

For supporting the adaptation, we describe a navigational context as *adaptive* or *non-adaptive*. An *Adaptive Context* receives data about the user that is currently accessing one of its instances (pages). This makes possible to determine the values for the user characteristics that are needed to implement the adaptation. Adaptive contexts are labelled with the *"thin-man"* symbol in their right upper corner. A *Non-Adaptive Context* only can receive domain information and its implementation is the same for any user.

4   A Methodological Approach for User Modelling and Adaptive Navigation Design

In this section, we introduce a method for defining Web Applications with Adaptive Navigation techniques at content level. This proposal assumes that the Requirements Elicitation stage is already accomplished. As an input, the methodology receives a set of application requirements that need the introduction of adaptive navigation features; the output is the conceptual description of the navigational solution to those requirements.

The defined steps of this methodology are exemplified by means of a case study (online bookstore). Specifically, we present the steps to describe the adaptive solution to the following requirement:

"The Page You Made": *the Web application includes a page that presents a set of recommended books to the user. These books must be thematically related to the books whose pages the current user has visited during a browsing session. The recommended items must be presented in a descendant order of closeness to the already visited books, selecting only the items that are more related to them.*

The steps of the proposed methodological approach are shown in Fig. 4 and described in the following subsections.

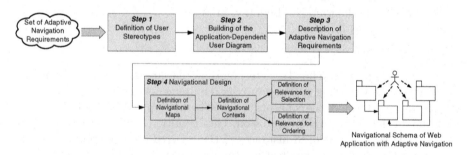

Fig. 4. Steps of the Methodology for Adaptive Navigation

4.1   Step 1: Definition of User Stereotypes

In the process of stereotypes specification, the developer must fulfil three tasks, which are adapted from the definition of user stereotypes made by Kobsa [4]:

(a) *Stereotypes identification*: according to the application requirements, the developer defines the subgroups of users that are relevant to the system.

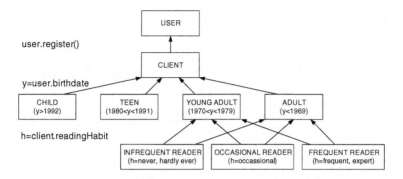

Fig. 5. Example of user stereotypes hierarchy

(b) *Stereotypes ordering*: the detected stereotypes are hierarchically ordered. This avoids redundancy in the definition of similar stereotypes, through the inheritance of shared attributes.

(c) *Identification of key user features*: the developer determines some key user features that describe the defined stereotypes, along with the values of these features that allow deciding the inclusion of users into each stereotype.

Figure 5 shows the user stereotype diagram for our case study (online bookstore). The most general stereotype is USER (anyone that accesses the bookstore); CLIENT stereotype describes those users that are registered (have executed the *register* operation). The rest of the stereotypes are classified by age groups (according to a *birthDate* attribute) and how frequent readers they are (through the qualitative *readingHabit* attribute).

4.2   Step 2: Building of the Application-Dependent User Diagram

The developer introduces the concepts that support the adaptive features of the application, by defining the *Application-Dependent User Diagram*. This diagram must include a *User* class and its corresponding subclasses, if needed. The diagram is completed by introducing the attributes and operations previously introduced in the stereotypes definition, and by defining other conceptual structures needed for the entire fulfillment of the adaptivity requirements.

Figure 6 shows the Application-Dependent User Diagram of the mentioned online bookstore. The developer has modelled the *Client* stereotype as a class of the diagram. For supporting the *"The Page You Made"* functionality, *hasVisited* relationship between *Book* and *Client* classes has been defined.

4.3   Step 3: Description of Adaptive Navigation Requirements

In this step, we describe the application requirements that include adaptive navigation features in terms of one or more atomic *adaptive navigation requirements*. This work is focused on the conceptual description of the solution to adaptive

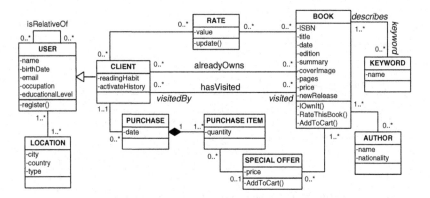

Fig. 6. Application Dependent User Diagram for an online bookstore

navigation requirements at instance level, which are described in terms of the concepts included into the Application-Dependent User Diagram and of the defined stereotypes. The structure of this description is:

(a) A *Domain Concept*, included in the Application-Dependent User Diagram, whose instances will be displayed in a Web page.
(b) A *Relevance concept for selecting* the instances to be shown, which is defined in terms of the concepts of the Application-Dependent User Diagram;
(c) A *Relevance concept for ordering* the instances to be shown, in terms of the concepts of the Application-Dependent User Diagram;
(d) The *User Stereotype* over whose users the requirement is applicable, from the User Stereotype Diagram;
(e) (optional) Additional *constraints on user attributes* that define a subset of the User Stereotype for which the requirement is valid. These attributes are selected from the Application-Dependent User Diagram.

For example, the "*The Page You Made*" functionality of the online bookstore can be described through the following atomic requirement (in italic, the concepts of the User Modelling step that are used):

(a) Instances of *Book* concept;
(b) Instances with at least three *Keyword* instances in common with items that current user *has visited*;
(c) Instances ordered by number of *Keyword* instances in common with items that current user *has visited*, in descendant order.
(d) For users belonging to *Client* stereotype.
(e) Users with at least one *visited Book* item

As it can be seen, this definition is based on the following concepts (see Figs. 5 and 6): *Client* stereotype; *Book*, *Keyword* and *Client* classes; and *hasVisited* relationships. The developer has decided to express the Relevance concepts for selecting and ordering the *Book* instances to be shown, by making use of the *Keyword* class, and has fixed a criterium for selecting those instances (at least *three keywords* in common with the already visited *books*).

4.4   Step 4: Navigational Design

Considering the description of adaptive requirements made in the previous step, the Navigational Design is accomplished through the following substeps:

Substep 1: Definition of Navigational Maps. One navigational map is defined for each user stereotype. In the definition of the set of navigational contexts, we propose to associate each adaptive navigation requirement at instance level to one navigational context. Along with the modularization of the adaptation modelling, this strategy allows identifying which are the navigational structures and the user characteristics that are involved in the fulfillment of the requirement.

Substep 2: Definition of Navigational Contexts. The inner structure of the defined navigational contexts is determined. The developer includes the navigational classes and relationships that are needed for implementing the adaptive requirement described in the previous step.

Substep 3: Introduction of Relevance Concept for Selecting Instances. For a given adaptive navigation requirement, the developer defines the *Relevance* concept that allow selecting the instances to be displayed from the corresponding context. This concept is included into an OCL expression and used as a filter into the manager class of the adaptive context, selecting the instances whose relevance value is greater than a given fix value. In the case of the *"The Page You Made"* functionality, the OCL expression that constrains the *Book* instances is expressed as follows:

```
self.keyword->select(k|user.visited.keyword=k)->size() >= 3
```

The left side of the expression corresponds to the *Relevance* concept for selecting instances, where `self` refers to the *Book* instance to be evaluated and `user` is the *Client* instance corresponding to the current user. As the corresponding adaptive navigation requirement states, this OCL expression selects those *Book* instances that are related with at least three *Keyword* instances to which the *Book* instances that the current user has visited are also related.

Substep 4: Introduction of Relevance Concept for Ordering Instances. The *Relevance* concept for ordering the retrieved instances is also described as an OCL expression and is introduced as the attribute considered by the Ordering Pattern of the adaptive context. In the example, the ordering pattern is based on the same concept of Relevance than the defined for selecting instances, applying a descendant order criterium, i.e., the most relevant book is placed on the top of the page. It is important to state that the Relevance concepts defined for selecting and for ordering instances are not necessarily the same.

5   Adaptive Techniques in the OOWS Navigational Model

There are multiple techniques of adaptive navigation which are implemented in existing Adaptive Hypermedia Systems. From the six groups of Adaptive

Navigation techniques identified by Brusilovsky [5], this work is focused on those groups that are mainly based on the relevance of domain concept instances to a particular user, i.e., on the introduced *Relevance* concept. These groups are:

(a) *Adaptive Link Hiding*: these techniques restrict the navigation space by hiding the links to pages that are irrelevant or forbidden to a certain kind of users. The *"hiding"* can be implemented, for instance, by deactivating or not showing the corresponding link anchor(s).

(b) *Adaptive Link Ordering*: these techniques sort the links of a given page, according to the user characteristics. For this, a criterium to emphasize some links from the others must be adopted, e.g., the closer to the top of the page the anchor link is displayed, the more important the target information is.

In this section, we present our proposal for describing two adaptive navigation techniques (one from each of the selected groups), by using the conceptual primitives of the OOWS Navigational Model and the concepts defined and used throughout the steps of the proposed method. These techniques are included in the substeps 3 and 4 of the Navigational Design and are applied to the Adaptive Navigational Contexts of a given map.

5.1 Link-Hiding for Navigational Class Instances

This technique allows hiding the links that retrieve those instances of a navigational class that are not relevant enough for the current user. Basing on the *Relevance for selecting instances* concept, the manager class of the context to be adapted is extended with a *filter*, which constrains the objects to be shown. This filter corresponds to the OCL expression for selecting instances defined in the *substep 3* of the Navigational Modelling step. For readability purposes, the OCL

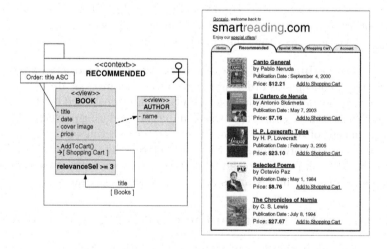

Fig. 7. Conceptual specification and implementation of Link-Hiding technique

definition of the *Relevance* concept can be represented in the graphical notation through the `relevanceSel` word.

As an example, we have applied the defined *Relevance* concept to the context of the *"Recommended"* functionality of Fig. 2. The conceptual description of this technique and its implementation are shown in Fig. 7. In comparison to the previous implementation, links to the *Book* instances maintain their alphabetical order, but those whose relevance for the user is less than 3 have been hidden.

5.2   Link-Ordering for Navigational Class Instances

This technique allows ordering the links to the instances of a navigational class, according to their relevance values for a given user. An *Ordering pattern* is assigned to the manager class of the corresponding adaptive context, ordering its instances by the values of the *Relevance for ordering instances* concept, in descendant or ascendant order. Figure 8 shows the application of this technique to the *"Recommended"* functionality.

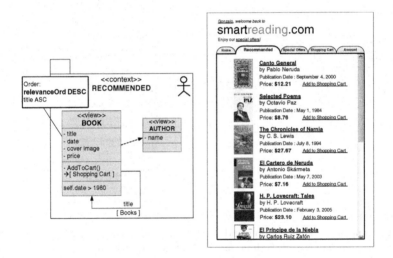

Fig. 8. Conceptual specification and implementation of Link-Ordering technique

In Fig. 8, the *Relevance* concept for ordering instances has been replaced by the `relevanceOrd` word. Links have been primarily ordered by their relevance value, in descendant order, and secondarily by their titles, in ascendant order. In this way, links to the most relevant instances are displayed closer to the top of the page. Instances with the same relevance value are alphabetically ordered.

5.3   Case Study: Navigational Solution

Finally, we can build the Adaptive Navigational Context that describes the *"The Page You Made"* functionality of the presented case study, by applying the two

Residence on Earth	Poetry	Chile	Nobel	Politics	Spanish
Canto General	X	X	X	X	X
El Cartero de Neruda	X	X			X
Lonely Planet Chile		X			
Octavio Paz Selected...	X		X	X	X
Selected Poems	X				X
The Complete Poems	X				

Poe's Tales of Mistery	Classics	USA	Children	Horror	Fantasy
El Príncipe de la Niebla				X	X
From the Earth to the Moon	X				X
H.P.Lovecraft: Tales		X		X	X
The Age of Innocence	X	X			
The Chronicles of Narnia	X	X	X		X
The Secret Garden	X		X		

Fig. 9. Example of *Book* instances to implement *"The Page You Made"* functionality

introduced adaptive navigation techniques. The tables of Fig. 9 show two books that a particular client has visited. In the first column, tables show those *Book* instances with at least one *Keyword* instance in common with the visited book. The other columns show the *Keyword* instances associated to the visited book and indicate (with "X") the other related *Book* instances.

Applying the two techniques, we obtain the conceptual description and implementation for the *"The Page You Made"* functionality, shown in Fig. 10.

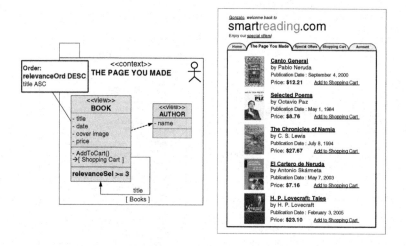

Fig. 10. Conceptual specification and implementation of the *"The Page You Made"* functionality, applying Link-Hiding and Link-Ordering techniques

The left side of Fig. 10 shows the resulting Adaptive Context. It has the same inner structure of the *"Recommended"* context, but considering the Relevance concepts for selecting and ordering instances for defining the *filter* and the *ordering pattern* of its manager class. The resulting implementation (Fig. 10, right) shows only those books that are more related to the previously visited in an descendant relevance order.

6 Related Work

Some existing Model-driven Web development methods have been increasing the expressiveness of their models to support adaptivity features. In the WebML adaptivity approach [6], a set of Event-Condition-Action rules allows the system to make adaptations of its navigational structure in reaction to link activations. The adaptivity proposal of OO-HDM [7] describes users inside the structural model, assigning roles and defining algorithms that implement different adaptive rules for distinct user profiles. The OO-H proposal [8] separates the static and the variable parts of the Web application, adapting the variable part. Even if the OOWS proposal considers implicitly the definition of adaptive rules, it describes the adaptive features at a higher abstraction level in terms of adaptive techniques, instead of making rule-based descriptions. In this way, we obtain adaptive descriptions that are closer to the adaptivity requirements, intuitive for the developer and with a more direct mapping to the final implementation.

The HERA approach [9] specifies the adaptivity by defining schema views on data for each model. The main difference with the HERA approach is that OOWS is object-oriented, providing a higher expressiveness in the functional dimension of the Web application. The UWE approach defines a reference model [10] that formally specifies the features of an adaptive hypermedia application, incorporating a user meta-model and an adaptation meta-model. These approaches make an important contribution to the introduction of adaptive features to Web Applications. However, there is a lack of methodological proposals that guide developers to integrate these concepts into the Web development process. An important exception is the AHDM Method [11], which includes a user modelling process within a methodology, but it does not consider the dependencies between the application functionalities and the modelled user characteristics. In our proposal, the conceptual description of the navigation of a Web application is strongly dependent on the user modelling phase, by introducing the Relevance concept, which is defined in terms of the relations between the user characteristics and the domain concepts.

7   Conclusions

This work has presented our methodological proposal for incorporating adaptive navigation techniques into the conceptual modelling of Web applications. We have introduced a User Modelling proposal, on which the conceptual description of the adaptive navigation features is based. We have augmented the expressiveness of a navigational model, introducing the required concepts to describe adaptive navigation techniques at instance level, at a high abstraction level. The flexibility of the OOWS navigational model makes possible that a non-adaptive specification can evolve into a diagram of an adaptive Web application, by using simple primitives.

In a previous work [3], we have defined adaptive navigation techniques at a greater granularity, adapting the accessibility of the entire navigational contexts and the visibility and presentation ordering of the complementary classes. One of the future works of this proposal is the incorporation of these techniques into this methodology. In the User Modelling approach, we need to define the rules that allow updating the Application-Dependent User Diagram from the information modelled by the Navigational Behaviour Diagram, i.e., the information of the actual interaction of the user with the application. This will allow to better describe the adaptation process for adaptive Web applications. Finally, we are working on the integration of this proposal in a CASE tool for generating Web applications. In this way, we will be able to capture the feedback of users from their interaction with the generated adaptive application.

References

1. Fons, J., Pelechano, V., Albert, M., Pastor, O.: Development of Web Applications from Web Enhanced Conceptual Schemas. In: Proceedings of ER 2003. LNCS 2813, Springer (2003) 232–245
2. Pastor, O., Gómez, J., Insfrán, E., Pelechano, V.: The OO-Method Approach for Information Systems Modeling: from Object-Oriented Conceptual Modeling to Automated Programming. Information Systems 26 (2001) 507–534
3. Rojas, G., Pelechano, V., Fons, J.: A Model-Driven Approach to include Adaptive Navigational Techniques in Web Applications. In: Proceedings of IWWOST 2005. (2005) 13–24
4. Kobsa, A.: User modeling: Recent work, prospects and hazards. In: Adaptive user interfaces: Principles and practice. North-Holland (1993) 111–128
5. Brusilovsky, P.: Adaptive Hypermedia. User Modeling and User-Adapted Interaction 11 (2001) 87–110
6. Ceri, S., Fraternali, P., Paraboschi, S.: Data-Driven, One-To-One Web Site Generation for Data-Intensive Applications. In: Proceedings of VLDB'99, Morgan Kaufmann (1999) 615–626
7. Rossi, G., Schwabe, D., Guimarães, R.: Designing Personalized Web Applications. In: Proceedings of WWW 2001. (2001) 275–284
8. Garrigós, I., Gómez, J., Cachero, C.: Modelling Dynamic Personalization in Web Applications. In: Proceedings of ICWE 2003. LNCS 2722, Springer (2003) 472–475
9. Frasincar, F., Houben, G.J., Vdovjak, R.: Specification Framework for Engineering Adaptive Web Applications. In: Proceedings of WWW 2002, Web Engineering Track. (2002)
10. Koch, N., Wirsing, M.: The Munich Reference Model for Adaptive Hypermedia Applications. In: Proceedings of AH 2002. LNCS 2347, Springer (2002) 213–222
11. Koch, N.: Towards a Methodology for Adaptive Hypermedia Systems Development. In: Proceedings of 6th Workshop ABIS-98. (1998) 49–60

A Web Service Support to Collaborative Process with Semantic Information*

Woongsup Kim and Moon Jung Chung

Computer Science and Engineering,
Michigan State University, East Lansing MI 48823, USA
{kimwoong, chung}@msu.edu

Abstract. Web services are introduced to deliver methods and technologies to help organizations link their software. However, existing web service standards based on WSDL limits web services' usefulness in collaborative process management. In this paper, we present a framework, WSCPC, that enables web service based collaborative process management in heterogeneous software environment. To facilitate web service based collaboration, we propose semantic service models and a web service extension that overcome limitations in current frameworks, and, hence, support complex level of communications needed for intensive collaboration in heterogeneous Virtual Enterprises environment. Through our semantic service models, organizational functionalities and capabilities are encapsulated and published as services. Collaborating partners can schedule, control, and monitor the relevant functionalities through WSCPC web services interactions model and web service extensions.

1 Introduction

A Virtual Enterprise (VE) is a temporary alliance of enterprises that come together to share resources for better responding to aggressive global competition, rapidly changing technologies and increasingly complex markets [1, 2, 3, 4]. In VE, organizations focus mainly on what they can do best, and turn to partnerships when they need to supplement internal abilities. Organizations participating in VE are generally managed by software systems running on heterogeneous computing environment, and must share process to bring new product on demand.

Web services are introduced to deliver methods and technologies to help organizations to link their software in order to support business partnership [5]. Web Services are software components that provide self-contained functionality via internet based interoperable interfaces with common description of their characteristics to be dynamically discovered, selected, and accessed. The term orchestration and choreography have been widely used to describe business process integration comprising web service based collaboration [6, 7].

However, both orchestration and choreography are based on WSDL which is represented by XML syntax and human targeted description, and, hence, they

---

* This work has been supported by the National Scientific Foundation (NSF). Grant No. DMI-0313174.

M. Kitsuregawa et al. (Eds.): WISE 2005, LNCS 3806, pp. 217–230, 2005.

expose limits to reflect dynamic nature in collaborative process management. For example, in design and manufacturing (D&M) domain, the parts designed by one partner may not match others due to complex product design and rapid technology changes [1]. Therefore, sufficient communication support to capture and understand process executions between various functional groups is required for timely exchange of process information and update of the relevant process information [8]. In addition, dynamic nature of process execution environment calls for flexible communicative behavior due to side effects specific to D&M domain [9]. However, current WSDL and web-service based integration protocols cannot provide such level of communications between various functional collaborative partners in product development stage [10].

In this paper, we present a framework, WSCPC (Web Service-based Collaborative Product Commerce), that enables collaborative process management using web services in heterogeneous software environment. To facilitate web service based collaborative process management, we propose semantic service model and web service extension that support complex level of communications needed for intensive collaboration in heterogeneous VE environment. Our semantic service model is based on grammatical approaches to avoid side effects caused from task dependency in collaborative process. Our models are also written in XML and OWL-S language, such that applications can understand the relevant process execution in heterogeneous environment. Therefore, collaborating partners can schedule, control and monitor the requisite functionalities within WSCPC framework.

The paper is structured as follows: Section 2 overviews our grammar-based approach and describes processes in service oriented collaboration. Section 3 proposes a semantic service models to facilitate collaboration in web services environment. Section 4 presents our WSCPC framework implementation based on our semantic service model. Section 4 also illustrates how our proposed service models support service-oriented collaboration. Case example that utilizes our semantic service model within WSCPC framework is illustrated in section 5. Section 6 concludes our contribution.

2   Grammar-Based Approach in Collaborative Process Management

A process is defined as ordering activities with a beginning and an end. A process involves sequence of steps that is initiated by an event, transforms information and materials, and produces output specifications [11]. In this paper, we consider a collaborative process as a process operated by multiple participants. Therefore, we consider four aspects to describe a collaborative process: states of the process execution, activities that are modeled as transition of states, functionalities represented as a set of operations, and providers that are associated with functionalities.

In a collaborative process environment, the main problem is side effects caused from task dependency in a process: one task in one organization affects the other tasks in other organizations. Thus, collaboration requires common process understanding of the relevant process execution and process reconfiguring ability under unforeseen effect of the relevant task execution. For this reason, we adopt grammar-based approach, Process Grammar [10, 12, 13], to model and implement collaborative process framework. In grammar based approach, detailed task descriptions can be abstracted into a simple, higher level task. In reverse, a higher-level logical task can be decomposed into a set of subtasks, evaluating current understanding of process execution and selecting the most appropriate sub process from the family of relevant alternative sub processes.

A production rule of Process Grammar is a substitution rule that permits alternatives representing a possible way of performing the task. A production rule allows a user to represent and manipulate a small number of abstract, higher-level tasks that can be expanded into detailed, executable alternatives. In collaborative environment, a production rule represents: 1) describing alternative sub processes given task specifications, and 2) describing status of sub task distribution and delegation to other participants in a VE.

Figure 1 illustrates the production rule used for a product casting process in design and manufacturing domain. The product casting process has a logical task 'Casting product', three input specs 'design requirement', 'Dies', and 'Trim Die', and 'Finished Product' as an output spec. We now consider three alternative processes as shown as (A), (B), and (C). Figure 1 (A) depicts a task delegation, while fig. 1 (B) and (C) shows two alternatives of possible task decomposition. In fig. 1, (B) represents Vacuum Die Casting process, and (C) illustrates High Pressure Die Casting process. Once a task is delegated, 'Casting Product' task is marked as 'Outsourcing' and engineers search the appropriate service provider.

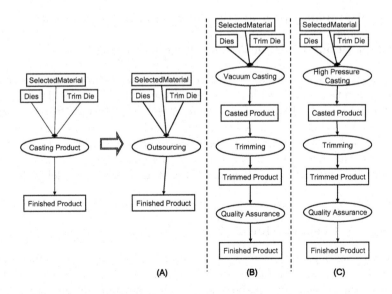

Fig. 1. An Example of Production Rule

When engineers decide to decompose 'Casting Product' task, they consider input specs, design constraints, and properties of each alternatives - i.e. property of vacuum Die Casting - in order to build the final process design.

3   Service Models for Collaborative Process Management

We define a service model that can be used for supporting web service based collaboration. The goal of service model is to provide a standardized way to understand distributed process specification and execution status, and hence overcome the limitations of web services in collaborative process management. Service models are composed of Semantic Service Description Model, Service Registry Model, and Service Interaction Model.

3.1   Semantic Service Description Model

Our service model employs grammar based approaches described in section 2, to describe process itself and its behavior. To realize such goal, we first identified five types of aspects needed for understanding others' process execution [14].

- **Functional aspect** describes how a process is decomposed into functional subsystems.
- **Behavioral aspect** depicts process control flow, i.e. when an activity is to be executed.
- **Informational aspect** concerns data exchanged during process execution between peers. Data can be either input/output specifications or activity execution status.
- **Organizational aspect** describes how a process is distributed to a group of participants.
- **Transactional aspect** depicts activity execution and sharing.

Considering those aspects, we defined and proposed three types of semantic service description model which is built on top of OWL-S [15]: Process Definition Model (PDM), Process Enactment Model (PEM), and Process Monitor Model (PMM) [16,17]. Process Definition Model describes functional and behavioral aspect, Process Monitor Model represents informational and organizational aspects, and Process Enactment Model characterizes transactional aspect. Detailed explanation on Semantic Service Description Model is described in [16,17].

3.2   Service Registry Model

To manage D&M process using web services, service providers should register their functional capabilities into a public registry, so that the service consumer may discover it if he needs collaboration. For this purpose, we propose a service registry model for registration and discovery of the semantics of services written on top of OWL-S [15]. The service consumer references the semantic information in the entries of service registry and compares the service type, the pre- and post-conditions and the input and output specifications of user's activities with the semantics presented. Pre- and post- conditions are used for maintaining consistency in distributed D&M process. A service requester is guaranteed certain qualities from the service provider before calling a service (pre-condition), and the service provider guarantees certain properties after the service returns outputs to the service requester (post-condition) [18]. Service provider posts pre-conditions to inform service requester of the requirements that service provider must satisfy to invoke the service. On the other hand, the service provider can describe the quality matrix of service execution in the post- condition entry. Service registry model also includes reference of Semantic Service Description Model of services such that service consumer can understand the expected service behaviors using OWL-S inference engine [16].

3.3   Service Interaction Model

Service Interaction Model is designed to assist service consumers during the service invocation, by controlling and guiding the invocation of the operations at each interaction step. Service interaction model represents communicative behaviors between partners in distributed and heterogeneous collaborative process management. As an elemental interaction model, we employ speech act theory [19], which is widely used in agent communication languages such as XLBC [20], KBML [21] and FBCL [22]. The interaction model is structured as a triple <intention, action, target>. Intention tells what semantic intention you have on the message. Intention is composed of request, propose, accept, reject, query, answer, assertion, and declare. Actions are classes that can be described using process enactment model and process definition model. That is, actions are classes that have some of functional, behavioral, and transactional aspects in section 3.1, neither informational nor organizational aspects. Target can be any object that companies want to mention during business interactions. Target can be anything instantiated such as output specs, operations to perform, message exchanged, etc. Target may use OWL, RDF or other standards specifications as long as there is description of language used. Service consumers can combine target and action to describe complex communicative behaviors in collaborative process management. We will discuss how the interaction model supports collaboration in section 4.2.

4   WSCPC Implementation

WSCPC is a collaborative engineering framework built on Java and Apache Axis. WSCPC utilizes the semantics of Process Grammar and OWL-S for process specification and manipulation, and hence manages D&M processes that are distributed over enterprises. Figure 2 illustrates WSCPC general architecture. WSCPC consists of the following basic components:

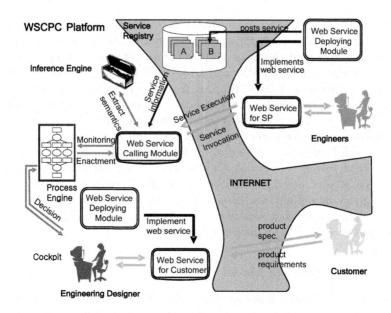

Fig. 2. WSCPC Framework Architecture

- **Process Engine (PE):** PE handles the process execution and maintains current status of execution.
- **Cockpit:** It is a JAVA applet, and provides a communications interface connecting users to PE. It transmits user's decision on process enactment to PE.
- **Web Service Module (WSM):** It connects PE with Web services, so PE can locate the suitable services for certain task through WSM, and invoke those services. WSM include OWL inference engine and captures user's actions and generates messages using interaction model. WSM also polls the invoked service, and captures runtime service execution through PMM. WSM is composed of two modules: Web Service Calling Module and Web Service Deploying Module. Web Service Calling Model provides functionalities such as service lookup via Service Registry, service invocation, and web service based communication with peers. Service execution information is also delivered to peers through this module. Web Service Deploying Module registers service capabilities into Service Registry and publishes invocable web service interace.
- **Service Registry:** Each collaborating organization individually has all the components except for Service Registry. However, Service Registry is shared among all the organizations. It stores the descriptions of Web services that specify the design and manufacturing capabilities, represented in PDM. The service registry includes the type of a service, input specification, output specification, pre- and post condition.

4.1   Building Partnership to Organize VE

When companies create partnerships with other companies by locating needed functionalities, they can locate appropriate companies through service representation described in service registry model [16]. In that case, companies should consider pre- and post- conditions and check if current task environment matches pre/post-condition of each alternative. If a suitable service is not available for a component, recursive service decomposition is invoked and the component is divided into more detailed sub functional components. Process Grammar [13, 23, 24] provides a way of representing and decomposing a process using production rule as seen in fig. 1.

4.2   Collaborative Process Enactment

Figure 3 illustrates web service invocation and the corresponding message exchanges in WSCPC collaborative process enactment. Once a service consumer decides outsourcing one of functional subsystems and locates a service, the consumer needs to create message to invoke the service. The service description is located in the partner's side linked by registry entry and service consumer fetches necessary information from there. The invocation message is composed of three components: *intention, action* and *target*. For example, to invoke a service request a message <*request, apply, service_name*> will be sent (fig. 3 (1)-(4)). *Apply* is a class defined in PEM [10]. Then the service provider understands the semantics of the received message (fig. 3 (5)). The service provider can either follow service consumer's action, or start negotiation steps based on local decision logic. In either case, service provider also creates a message with its communicational decision and behavior, and sends it (fig 3 (6)).

In WSCPC, the negotiation proceeds through direct contact between service consumer and service provider. Partners exchange messages using Service Interaction Model at each negotiation round. For example, a company can send message to initialize negotiation with <*request, rollback, price_B_of_target_A*>, where *roll-*

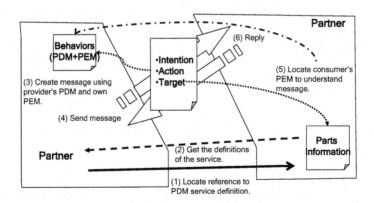

Fig. 3. Service Enactment Using Service Interaction Model

back is a class in PEM and $<price\_B\_of\_targe\_A>$ is written with OWL-S. Negotiation ends when a partner sends message $<accept, none, price\_C\_of\_target\_A>$.

4.3 Process Sharing Management

The platform neutral nature of Web services enables supporting concurrent and consistent access to heterogeneous software applications. Semantic integration to Web services brings up semantic based process sharing, where people continue to use their specialized applications but collaborative activities are shared with semantic information. In WSCPC framework, organizational and informational aspects are captured by PMM, and hence process sharing among multiple participants is possible through semantics in PMM class. Figure 4 shows how WSCPC supports process sharing with PMM. Once tasks are allocated to geographically dispersed service providers, Process Engine (PE) in WSCPC regularly polls the service execution status through Web Service Module (WSM). Once the query for service execution status comes into the service provider, current service execution status is fetched from software application tools, and sent to the service requester within messages based on our service interactive model. In fig. 4, the replying message is represented as $<answer, A, A_{status}>$, where A represent the task to be monitored and A_{status} describe A's execution status which is desribed in the form of PMM grounding. As PMM grounding is acceptable and understandable to all the participants, PE can translate it for the domain specific applications and update the task status information.

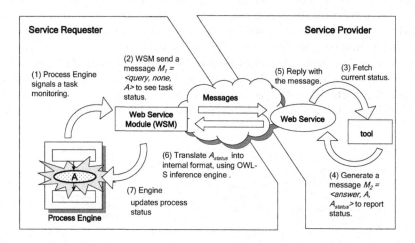

Fig. 4. Sharing Display for Concurrent and Consistent Collaboration

4.4 Web Service Extension

Collaboration requires supports for complex interactions among companies. For example, while D&M process is being enacted autonomously across the heterogeneous systems, companies may want to force certain decision modification to partners, or highlight problematic parts from the design spec before they start the outsourced task. However, Web Services are subject to several limitations that reduce their applicability to complex interactions. WSDL only supports the invocation of operations characterized by very specific signatures that fail to enable the peers to dynamically specify the realistic business interactions. Such characteristics in WSDL interface do not enable to specify the management of interactions between service consumer and provider.

To support interactions in service invocation, the ability of supporting interactive invocation must be defined and declared at WSDL. Appendix A shows a portion of WSDL declaration to support interactive service invocation. Given the public operational specifications in WSDL, the service provider informs the references of the service semantic description, pointing out where ontology of service description is located. Moreover, service providers should explicitly declare that their services support interactive invocation. Service consumers should prepare conversational input message from the declaration of interaction type. Appendix B shows an example of message to be exchanged. Service consumers locates where the service ontology is described, and builds messages with intention, desirable behaviors, and target object information. In this way, complex dialogue is enabled between service provider and consumers.

5   Case Study

In this section, we will discuss how WSCPC supports web service based collaboration. As an illustration of our work, we consider a case study [25] that describes a die casting process for thermoelectric fan housing. Figure 5 illustrates our case study - die casting process for thermoelectric fan housing - to test WSCPC implementation. The die casting process for thermoelectric fan housing can be decomposed into several sub tasks and each task can be distributed to different companies. From our case study, four companies are collaborating at a process startup, and each company has its own dedicated job, such as defining requirements, material selection, die making, and casting products. The left side of the arrow in fig. 5 shows the initial functional systems, while the right side illustrated task distribution result among the participating companies.

Tasks in the process are interdependent: one task in one company affects other companies' tasks. At the requirement setting stage, company A designs fan housing product. Based on a study [25], the key factors of product considerations are high thermal conductivity, uniform metal fill, free of porosity, and precise tolerance with "+/- 0.005". Ontology for the die casting process are defined with OWL, and design requirements are translated into XML, and sent to company B and C together as output specifications.

After A builds up output data and sends them to B and C, B needs to select the right materials for fan housing. B's selection is Aluminum 130 alloy among several alternatives. Company C starts die design process using A's design specs and B's material selections described in the output specifications. C's job is decomposed into subtasks: 'Design Dies,' 'MakeTrimDies,' and 'MakeDies.' Each

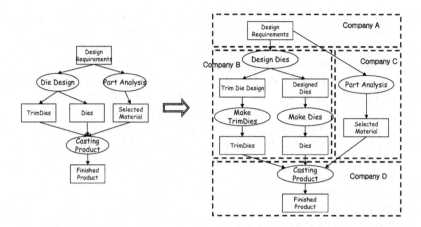

Fig. 5. A D&M Process Example

subtask owned by C can be decomposed into detailed subtasks with several alternatives. For example, 'DesignDies' task has several alternative processes such as 'vacuum assisted casting,' 'high pressure casting,' and 'semi-solid casting.' Figure 5 is an example of production rule of one alternative process 'Vacuum assisted casting' for 'DesignDies' task. In our scenario, company D is outsourcing 'casting product' and locating the right service provider. In order to outsource a 'casting products' job, the die casting manufacturing capabilities should be published and advertised in an understandable way such that every OEM can find the right provider satisfying design requirements. The manufacturer's capabilities are registered as an entry to semantic service registry in WSCPC framework. When company D decides to outsource 'casting product' task, the company defines the desired attributes for the product and searches service registry using such attributes. The manufacturing capability of a casting company will satisfy the query from company D, and then the service registry notifies that the casting company can match the 'casting product' requirements. Then company D evaluates attributes, starts negotiation if necessary, and outsources 'casting products' by invoking services.

Inter-organizational collaborations often encounter problems due to multiple local decision centers. Each company has its own local mechanism to decide how their tasks are executed. Such decisions affect other parties' decision due to side effects, and may result in overall failure. Therefore, decisions should be coordinated between various functional groups. For example, company B and C work and complete 'Part Analysis' and 'DieDesign' task respectively, and company D outsources its 'casting product'. Later, company D faces a design problem on the final product. The final product fails in mechanical stress testing. After certain diagnosis, D concludes that the product should be designed stronger and materials used in the product should be replaced. Company B then changes the material into a stronger one with minimum loss in thermal conductivity. This change affects the company C and

D's process execution since they are using A130 alloy selected by company B before. In such case, company C and D should rollback their task status by initializing their process execution. WSCPC is able to handle such situations by making service abortion and an immediate roll back. When company D faces failure and figures out the problem, company D builds message enforcing a rollback. Since the failure is guessed as a durability problem, Company D builds a message <*request, enforced_rollback, stressTest_failure*>, and invokes B's and A's interactive web services. Then B and C will figure out who will take responsibility for such problem. In this example, company B will try alternatives since the failure seems to be from material selection. B will create message <*accept, rollback, material_selection*> and send it to C and D, such that C and D avoid redundant works. B finds Zinc alloy ZA8 is the best alternative available. So B's decision is notified to C and D with <*declare, rollback, material$_{ZA8}$* >. After company D receives a roll back message, company D stops and suspends the service invocation. Company B's new selection then goes to company C and D and forces them to take adequate actions in a proper order. Company C will verify whether current die design fits for ZA8. Company D will check the selected casting company's capability for ZA8.

6 Conclusion

In this paper, we presented WSCPC, a framework supporting a web-service based process collaboration using semantic information. Until now a user utilizes web service semantics to quickly discover its collaborating counterpart and to make a decision on the fast changing customer requirement. In our research, we have extended web service semantics to describe communicational behaviors that can support efficient collaborative process management. We have implemented a prototype system using Java and OWL-S. For Web service implementation, we employ Tomcat Axis framework. We built a prototype system and tested a distributed die casting process making a simple product. Our contributions on collaborative process management and web service area are two-folds: 1) the separation of process definition and execution environment, avoiding side effects in process management, and 2) the overcoming of current web service limitations related to the lack of intensive communications, which are imperative in collaborative group working environment.

References

1. Lee, J.N., Kim, Y.G.: Exploring a Causal Model for the Understanding of Outsourcing Partnership. HICSS 2003. **268** (2003)
2. Floyd, T.D.: Winning the New Product Development Battle. New York: Institution of Electrical and Electronics Engineers. (1993)
3. O'Neill, D.A.: Offshore Outsourcing Takes Hold. Mortgage Bank. Dec (2003)

4. Terk, M., Subrahamanian, E., Kasabach, C., Prinz, F., Siewiorek, D.P., Smailagic, J., Stivoric, A., Weiss, L.: Rapid Design and Manufacture of Wearable Computers. Communications of the ACM, **38** (1996) 63-70

5. Mukhi, N.K. ,Plebani, P., Silva-Lepe, I.,Mikalsen, T.: Supporting Policy-driven Behaviros in Web Services: Experiences and Issues. presented at ICSOC'04. New York USA (2004)

6. Andrews, T., Curbera, F., Dholakia, H., Systems, S., Goland, Y., Klein, J., Leymann, F., Liu, K., Roller, D., Smith, D., Systems, S., Thatte, S., Trickovic, I., Weerawarana, S.: BPEL4WS. http://www-106.ibm.com/developerworks/webservices/library/ws-bpel/: IBM.

7. Weerawarana, S., Francisco, C.: Business Process with BPEL4WS: Understand-ing BPEL4WS, Part1. IBM Developer Works. (2002)

8. Williams, M.: Maximum cost reduction, minimum effort. Manufacturing Engineer-ing. **80** (2001) 179-82

9. Zeng, Y., Kwon, P., Pentland, B., Chahine, A.: A Grammar-Based Approach To Capturing and Managing Processes: An Industrial case study. Transactions of NAMRI/SME. **31** (2003) 555-562

10. Chung, M.J., Kim, W., Jung, H.S., Gopalan, R., Kim, H.: Service Model for Col-laborating Distributed Design and Manufacturing. WWW 2004 Workshop on Ap-plication Design, Development and Implementation Issues in the Semantic Web. New York NY (2004)

11. Herman, J.: The Impact of Ebusiness on Enterprise IT Management. Business Communications Review. (1999) 22-24

12. Chung, M.J., Kwon, P., Pentland, B.: Making Process Visible: A Grammartical Approach ot Managing Design Processes. ASME Transaction Journal of Mechani-cal Design. **124** (2002) 364-374

13. Baldwin R., Chung, M.J.: Design Methodology Management IEEE Computer. February (1995) 54-63

14. Henkel, M., Zdravkovic, J., Johannesson, P.: Service-Based Processes - Design for Business and Techonology. ICSOC'04. New York USA (2004)

15. Paolucci, M., Srinivasan, N., Sycara, K., Solanki, M., Lassila, O., McGuinness, D., Denker, G., Martin, D., Parsia, B., Sirin, E., Payne, T., McIlraith, S., Hobbs, J., Sabou, M., McDermott, D.: OWL-S. The OWL Services Coalition. (2003)

16. Chung, M.J., Kim, W., Jung, H.S., Kim, H.: A Service-oriented Framework for Collaborative Product Commerce. 8th International Conference on Computer Sup-ported Cooperative Work in Design (CSCWD 2004). Xiamen China (2004)

17. Chung, M.J., Kim, W., Jung, H.S., Kim, H.: Web Service Based Process Man-agement Model for Collaborative Product Commerce. 10th Interna-tional Confer-ence on Concurrent Enterprising. Seville Spain (2004)

18. Meyer, B.: Building bug-free o-o software: An introduction to design by contract: Object Currents. SIGS Publication. **1**(3) March (1996)

19. Shearle, J.: In direct Speech Act. Syntax and Semantics: Speech Acts. **3** (1975) 59-82

20. Heuvel, W.J.v.d., Maamar, Z.: Intelligent Web services moving toward a framework to compose. Communications of the ACM. **46** (2003)

21. Finin, T., Fritzson, R., McKay, D., McEntire, R.: KQML as an agent communica-tion language. the third international conference on Information and knowledge management. Gaithersburg Maryland United States (1994)

22. Weigand H., Heuval, W.J.v.d.: Meta-patterns for electronic commerce transac-tions based on the formal language for business communication (FLBC). Interna-tional Journal of Electronic Commerce. **2** (1999) 45-66

23. Chung, M.J., Jung, H.S., Kim, W., Gopalan, R., Kim, H.: A Framework for Collaborative Product Commerce Using Web Services. IEEE International Conference on Web Services (ICWS 2004). San Diego CA (2004)

24. Chung, M.J., Kwon, P., Pentland, B., Kim, S.: A process management system for collaborative manufacturing. IMECE'02, Symposium on Reconfigurable Manufacturing Systems, 2002 ASME International Mechanical Engineering Congress & Exposition. New Orleans Louisiana (2002)

25. _: Steel Founder's Society of America. www.sfsa.org (2004)

Appendix A: A WSDL Declaration for Interactive Communication

```
<definitions ..
  xmlns:pns="url_where_object_ontology_is_defined"
  xmlns:tns="url_where_intention_is_defined" ... />
  :
  :
<types>
  <schema ...>
    ...
    <complexType name="interaction">
      <element name="service:Intention" type="tns:#intention"/>
      <element name="service:Action" type = "anyType"/>
      <element name="service:Object" type = "pns:#object"/>
    </complexType>
  </schema>
</types>
  :
  :
<portType name="invokeEnactment">
  <operation name="enactment_operation" >
    <input message="invoking" type="interaction" />
  </operation>
</portType>
<service name="DieCastingService">
  <port name="invokeEnactment" bind-ing="tns:conversationBinding">
    <soap:address location="URL_of_Company_D"/>
  </port>
</service>
```

Appendix B: A Message Example Exchanged During Service-Oriented Collaboration

```
<service:conversation rdf:ID="message1">
  <service:hasIntention>
    <service:intention rdf:ID="intentionID">
     <service:parameterType rdf:about="#propose"/>
    </service:Intention>
    <service:Action rdf:ID="actionClass">
      <service:InvokeEnactment rdf:resource="consumerNS:#materialSelection"/>
      </service:Action>
    <service:Target rdf:ID="objectClass">
      <service:LogicalService rdf:about="providerNS:#Zinc"/>
      </service:Target>
  </service:hasIntention>
</service:conversation>
```

Server-Side Caching Strategies for Online Auction Sites

Daniel A. Menascé[1] and Vasudeva Akula[2]

[1] Department of Computer Science,
George Mason University, Fairfax, VA 22030, USA
menasce@cs.gmu.edu
[2] School of Information Technology & Engineering George Mason University,
Fairfax, VA 22030, USA
vakula@gmu.edu

Abstract. Online auction sites have very specific workloads and user behavior characteristics. Previous studies on workload characterization conducted by the authors showed that i) bidding activity on auctions increases considerably after 90% of an auction's life time has elapsed, ii) a very large percentage of auctions have a relatively low number of bids and bidders and a very small percentage of auctions have a high number of bids and bidders, iii) prices rise very fast after an auction has lasted more than 90% of its life time. Thus, if bidders are not able to successfully bid at the very last moments of an auction because of site overload, the final price may not be as high as it could be and sellers, and consequently the auction site, may lose revenue. In this paper, we propose server-side caching strategies in which cache placement and replacement policies are based on auction-related parameters such as number of bids placed or percent remaining time till closing time. A main-memory auction cache at the application server can be used to reduce accesses to the back-end database server. Trace-based simulations were used to evaluate these caching strategies in terms of cache hit ratio and cache efficiency.

1 Introduction

Online auctions are becoming an important segment of the e-commerce space with large players such as eBay and Yahoo!Auctions. It has been observed that web requests follow Zipf-like distributions and that this fact can be used to design caches that improve hit ratios [3]. That work was applied to web sites that mostly served static pages. E-commerce sites generate most of their pages dynamically. Our workload characterization work [1,10] of online auction sites also found evidences of Zipf distributions, and power laws in general. Our previous work also showed that the workload of online auction sites is substantially different from that of online retailers and uncovered a plethora of interesting findings that can be used, among other things, to improve the performance of online auction sites. These findings include i) A very large percentage of auctions have a relatively low number of bids and bidders and a very small percentage of

M. Kitsuregawa et al. (Eds.): WISE 2005, LNCS 3806, pp. 231–244, 2005.

auctions have a high number of bids and bidders. ii) There is some bidding activity at the beginning stages of an auction. This activity slows down in the middle and increases considerably after 90% of an auction's life time has elapsed. iii) Prices rise faster in the first 20% of an auction's life time than in the next 70% of its life time. However, after the age of an auction reaches 90%, prices increase much faster than in the two previous phases. iv) A relatively few users are responsible for winning the majority of auctions. v) A relatively few sellers are responsible for creating the majority of the auctions. vi) The majority of bids are placed by a relatively small number of unique bidders.

We rely on these facts to suggest that a main memory *auction cache* at the application server can save a significant number of accesses to a backend database and thus significantly reduce the server-side latency for both read and write requests at online auctions sites. We propose several cache placement and replacement policies. We conducted an experimental validation of our policies for various cache sizes using a trace derived from a data collection process in which an agent collected data for over 340,000 auctions from Yahoo!auctions. We measured the cache hit ratio and the cache efficiency. Our findings show that small caches can be quite efficient and are able to provide reasonably large hit ratios.

Significant work has been done in the area of web caching [5, 6, 13, 14]. Many conferences including IEEE's International Workshop on Web Content Caching and Distribution (WCW), already in its 10th installement, and the International World Wide Web Conference (WWW), started in 1994, have been some of the preferred venues for cache-related publications. A good collection of cache related information and resources is Brian Davidson's web site (www.web-caching.com/). In general, web caching work can be classified into browser caching, client-side proxy caching, network caching (as in Content Delivery Networks), and server-side caching. Our work falls into the realm of server-side caching and is specific to online auctions sites. The authors are not aware of any other auction-site specific caching study that uses real traces from a large production auction site.

The rest of this paper is organized as follows. Section two provides some background and definitions used throughout the paper and introduces in more detail the notion of an auction cache. Section three describes typical user behavior using a Customer Behavior Model Graph. The next section describes the cache placement and replacement policies studied here. Section five presents and discusses the results of our experiments. Finally, section six presents some concluding remarks.

2   Background

An open auction (i.e., one that is still in progress) is defined by several parameters including: opening time, t_o, closing time, t_c, and number of bids, $b(t)$, submitted up to time t. From these parameters, one can define $t_p(t)$, the percent remaining closing time at time t, as $[(t_c - t)/(t_c - t_o)] \times 100$.

The typical software architecture of an auction site is multitiered and is composed of three layers as indicated in Fig. 1. The first layer comprises web

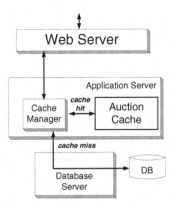

Fig. 1. Architecture of an online auction site

servers that handle the incoming HTTP requests and serve static HTML pages. Most pages served by an auction site are dynamically generated by an application server, which implements the site's business logic. The application server may need to access persistent data stored in a backend database server. An example is the processing of a request to view all bids for a given auction. The bid information comes from the database. The application server then generates an HTML page with the bid information. This page is passed back to the web server, which sends the page back to the browser.

The performance of online auction sites can potentially be improved if a fraction of the millions of auctions is cached in the main memory of the application server, thus avoiding most of the trips to the database. As indicated in Fig. 1, when the information about an auction can be found in the main memory cache of the application server, a *cache hit* occurs. Otherwise a *cache miss* occurs and the information about the auction has to be retrieved from the database. The auction cache can store the following information about an auction:

- Auction information: includes headline, textual description, names of the files that store thumbnail images and possibly larger images, number of bids, highest bid, highest bidder ID, bid increment, starting price, and seller ID.
- Bid history: all the bids placed for the auction. Each bid includes bidder ID, overall bid sequential number, bid price, and proxy flag (indicates if the bid was manually placed or if it was placed by an agent on behalf of the bidder).
- Seller information: specifies the seller of the auction and his/her rating information, number of auctions sold, and date since the seller has been a member of the auction site.

In this paper we are only concerned with transactions that can potentially be served by an auction cache. Therefore, we do not consider transactions such as auction creation, registration, and login. The transactions that may be served by the cache can be divided into read-only and write transactions. Read-only transactions include View Bid, View Auction Information, View Auction Details (e.g., description of items, warranty), View Seller Information and Ratings, and View Comments on the Seller. The main write transaction is Place Bid. There could be a problem executing write transactions at the cache without refreshing the database immediately. If a power failure occurs, the contents of the main memory cache could be lost and with it all updates (i.e., all bids on the cached auctions). However, large production e-commerce sites maintain multiple levels of backup power supplies. Typically, the servers have dual power supplies, from two separate power sources. There are multiple uninterrupted power supply (UPS) units that act as backup for these power supplies. In case of failure of these UPS units, or in cases in which the actual power supply is lost for a longer duration which can lead to the shutdown of UPS units, power generators act as backups for the UPS units. These generators can run for as long as the diesel supply lasts. So, power failures at popular e-commerce sites are extremely rare. Therefore, we assume that the auction cache survives power failures. This assumption assures that write transactions can be executed at the cache.

Failures due to software crashes are also possible. To cope with them, one may write a log of all write transactions at the application server in parallel with writing into the cache. A background process can be used to refresh the backend database at regular intervals from the log.

Most production auction sites have several web servers and several application servers. Therefore, each application server will have its own auction cache. To deal with problems of cache coherence we assume that any given auction can be cached at one and only one application server cache. This can be accomplished by identifying each auction by a unique id. Then, one can devise a function f that takes as input an auction's unique id and returns the id of one of the application servers. The id of the application server that handles requests for a given auction can be first sent in a cookie and returned in a cookie to the web server so that the request can be dispatched to the proper application server.

Auction sites have grown rapidly in the last couple of years, and recent statistics indicate that eBay carries about 50 million items for sale at any time on its site [7]. Yahoo!Japan carries 7.5 million items for sale [15]. We estimate that each auction, including its details, bids history and seller information, requires about 8KB of cache space. Thus, to cache 5% of all auctions, an auction site carrying 10 million items for sale would require $10,000,000 \times 0.05 \times 8KB = 4GB$ of main memory cache. This estimate does not include other items to cache, such as category names, state names, payment types and other static information to serve web requests quickly. Thus, for a caching scheme to be effective, it must provide a relatively high cache hit ratio for a reasonably small cache.

3   User Behavior

Users of an online auction site may invoke many different transactions during a session (i.e., a sequence of consecutive requests from a user during the same visit). We describe in what follows a typical user session using the Customer Behavior Model Graph (CBMG) defined by Menascé et al. [12]. Each node of

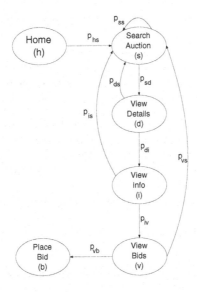

Fig. 2. Customer Behavior Model Graph (CBMG) for an online auction site

the graph represents a state in which a user may be during a session. Nodes of a graph are connected by directed arcs that indicate the possible transitions between states. Arcs are labeled with the probability that a transition between states occurs. Figure 2 depicts an example CBMG for an online auction site. Transactions that are not relevant to the cache are not shown. Transitions from each state to an Exit state are not shown for better readability. A CBMG can be used to determine the average number of visits per session to state i, V_i, as a function of the transition probabilities between states as shown in [12]. Applying this method to the CBMG of Fig. 2, yields the following equations.

$$V_s = p_{h,s} + p_{s,s}V_s + p_{d,s}V_d + p_{i,s}V_i + p_{v,s}V_v \tag{1}$$

$$V_d = p_{s,d}V_s \tag{2}$$

$$V_i = p_{d,i}V_d = p_{d,i}\, p_{s,d}V_s \tag{3}$$

$$V_v = p_{i,v}V_i = p_{i,v}\, p_{d,i}\, p_{s,d}V_s \tag{4}$$

$$V_b = p_{v,b}V_v = p_{v,b}\, p_{i,v}\, p_{d,i}\, p_{s,d}V_s \tag{5}$$

The value of V_s can be obtained by solving Eqs. (1)-(5):

$$V_s = \frac{1}{1 - (p_{s,s} + p_{d,s}p_{s,d} + p_{i,s}p_{d,i}p_{s,d} + p_{v,s}p_{i,v}p_{d,i}p_{s,d})} \tag{6}$$

The ratio between read and write transactions, RW, is given by $RW = (V_d + V_i + V_v)/V_b$. Using the values $p_{h,s} = 1.0$, $p_{s,s} = 0.8$, $p_{s,d} = 0.1$, $p_{d,i} = 0.55$, $p_{i,v} = 0.5$, $p_{v,s} = 0.75$, $p_{v,b} = 0.2$ $p_{d,s} = 0.4$, $p_{i,s} = 0.45$, yields a value of RW equal to 33.

4   Cache Placement and Replacement Policies

A cache placement policy determines if an auction should be placed in the cache and a cache replacement policy determines which auction should be removed from the cache if the cache is full and a new auction needs to be cached.

The following cache placement policies have been evaluated.

- ABn: this is an activity based policy. An auction accessed at time t is cached if $b(t) \geq n$ for that auction. For example the AB2 policy caches auctions with at least two bids already submitted at time t.
- PRTp: this is a percent remaining time policy. An auction is cached at time t if $t_p(t) < p$.
- H-AND-n-p: this a hybrid policy that caches an auction if both ABn and PRTp would cache it.
- H-OR-n-p: this is a hybrid policy that caches an auction if ABn or PRTp would cache it.

We consider the following auction replacement policies.

- AB: this replacement policy is only used in conjunction with the ABn placement policy. It removes the auction with the smallest number of submitted bids.
- PRT: this replacement policy is only used with the PRTn placement policy. It replaces from the cache the auction with the largest percent remaining time to close.
- AB-PRT: this replacement policy is used with both H-AND-n-p and H-OR-n-p. It removes the auction with the largest percent remaining time to close among the ones with the smallest number of bids.
- Least Recently Used (LRU): replaces the auction that has received a request further in the past. This is a standard replacement policy used in operating systems [4].
- Least Frequently Used (LFU): replaces the auction that has received the smallest percentage of requests among all auctions in the cache. This policy has been considered in the context of operating systems [4] and in the web in combination with LRU [9].

A caching policy is then specified by its cache placement and replacement policy. We use the naming convention <cache placement>:<cache replacement> to name the caching policies investigated here. For example, AB2:LRU means that AB2 is the cache placement policy and LRU the replacement policy.

If the cache size is unlimited (i.e., at least as large as the total number of auctions), the replacement policy does not matter since all auctions will always find a place in the cache. Also, in this case, one should cache all auctions. This means that placement policies such as PRT100, which is a "always cache" policy, are optimal.

Figure 3 shows a relationship between the various policies in the unlimited cache size case. An arrow from policy a to policy b indicates that the hit ratio for a is higher or the same as that of policy b in the unlimited cache size case.

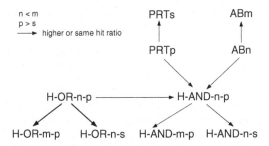

Fig. 3. Relation between placement policies for unlimited cache size

If the cache size is limited, there is a cost associated with evicting an auction from the cache since its state has to be refreshed in the backend database server. Also, an "always cache" policy may force a more popular auction than the incoming one out of the cache thus reducing the cache hit ratio.

5   Experimental Evaluation

The experimental evaluation of the policies described above was carried out with a trace-based simulation. The trace is derived from actual data collection performed for our previous workload characterization and closing time rescheduling work [1, 10, 11]. The data collection process was described in detail in these papers. We provide here a brief summary of the process. A data collection agent gathered a total of 344,314 auction items created during the month of January 2003, belonging to over two thousand categories, from the Yahoo!Auctions site. A total of 1.12 million bids were placed on these auctions.

For this paper we used three weeks worth of that data, which contains 210,543 auctions, and 156,074 bids on these auctions. Note that the data we collected only contains the auction creation and bid records for each auction. Thus, we do not have data on read-only requests (e.g., view bids, view seller info, view auction details). However, for the purpose of the simulation, we inserted thirty read requests in the trace before each bid to maintain a RW ratio compatible with the CBMG analysis of section 3.

We varied the cache size to assess the impact of the placement and replacement policies as the cache size changed. We report the cache size as a percent, P_c, of the total number of auctions N_a. Thus, a 5% cache size implies that 5% of the 210,543 auctions can be stored in the cache. The amount of main memory required per auction is around 8,000 bytes.

Each experiment used a combination of cache placement and cache replacement policy and computed the following metrics for different cache sizes:

- Cache hit ratio (H): percent of cacheable transactions that were served from the auction cache.
- Cache efficiency (ε): defined as the ratio $(H \times 100)/N_c$, where N_c is the average number of auctions in the cache. This number is computed, using

Little's Law [8], as the product of the average cache throughput (i.e., number of auctions that leave the cache divided by the duration of the experiment) and the average time spent in the cache per auction. The cache efficiency ε measures how much hit ratio one gets per cached auction on average.

Due to space limitations we only present a small subset of all graphs we generated in our simulations. A general observation seen from all graphs is that a relatively small cache, e.g., 4 to 5% of all auctions is enough to generate cache hit ratios of around 50 to 70%. Even very small caches of about 1% can generate cache hit ratios as big as 40%.

5.1   Results for ABn Placement Policies

Figure 4 displays the cache hit ratio for the AB1:AB, AB2:AB, and AB3:AB policies as a function of the percent cache size. The figure indicates that the three policies have almost the same cache hit ratio for very small cache sizes. However, as the cache size increases, AB1:AB outperforms AB2:AB, which outperforms AB3:AB, as discussed above. It can also be observed that the cache hit ratio increases much faster at the beginning for smaller cache sizes. It can also be observed that a cache size of 0.5% is sufficient to provide a cache hit ratio of about 35% for all three policies. It can also be seen that all three policies approach very fast their unlimited cache size performance. For example, the AB1:AB policy has a limiting hit ratio of 68.2%. Ninety nine percent of this value is achieved for a 4% cache size. Around 86% of the limiting performance of AB1:AB is obtained for a 2% cache size. While AB1:AB outperforms AB2:AB, which outperforms AB3:AB, the situation is reversed with respect to efficiency. For example, for a $P_c = 0.25\%$, the efficiency of AB1:AB is 0.078 while that of AB3:AB is 0.086.

Figure 5 shows a comparison among the replacement policies AB, LRU, and LFU when used in conjunction with placement policy AB1, the best in Figure 4.

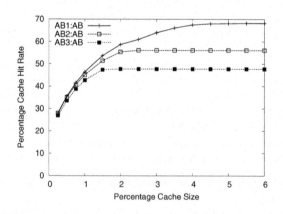

Fig. 4. Hit ratio for AB1:AB, AB2:AB, and AB3:AB

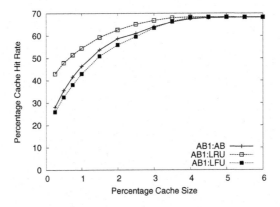

Fig. 5. Comparison among replacement policies AB, LRU, and LFU for placement policy AB1

As expected, for sufficiently large cache sizes, i.e., for $P_c > 4.5\%$ all three policies yield the same result. Smaller cache sizes distinguish the three policies with LRU being the best, followed by AB, and then by LFU. For example, for $P_c = 0.25\%$, LRU outperforms AB as a replacement policy by a 53% margin. In fact, AB1:LRU has a 43% hit ratio while AB1:AB has a 28.1% hit ratio for $P_c = 0.25\%$.

5.2 Results for PRTp Placement Policies

Figure 6 compares policies PRT10:PRT, PRT30:PRT, and PRT50:PRT. As was the case with the ABn placement policy, the increase in hit ratio is much faster for smaller caches. The unlimited cache size hit ratios for these policies are 18.6%, 32.2%, and 44.2%, respectively, and occurs for a value of P_c equal to 6%. The

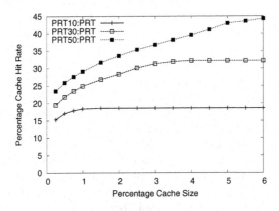

Fig. 6. Hit ratio for PRT10:PRT, PRT30:PRT, and PRT:50

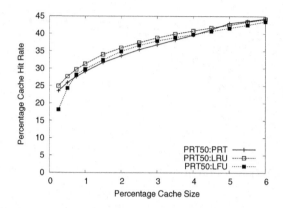

Fig. 7. Comparison among replacement policies PRT, LRU, and LFU for placement policy PRT50

difference in hit ratio is significantly reduced for smaller cache sizes. For example, for $P_c = 0.25\%$ the hit ratios for PRT10:PRT, PRT30:PRT, and PRT50:PRT, are 15.3%, 19.5%, and 23.5%, respectively. Figure 7 compares the effects of the PRT, LRU, and LFU replacement policies combined with the PRT50 placement policy. For a percent cache size of 6% all three replacement policies display similar results because the unlimited cache size behavior is already achieved at this point. For smaller cache sizes, LRU is slightly better than PRT, which is slightly better than LFU. The difference between these replacement policies when combined with PRT is not as marked as in the ABn case.

5.3   Results for the Hybrid Policies

We consider now policies of the type H-AND-n-p:AB-PRT in Fig. 8. The unlimited cache size behavior is achieved for much smaller cache sizes than in the ABn and PRTp cases ($P_c = 2.5\%$ instead of $P_c = 6.0\%$). As indicated in Fig. 3, one would expect that for large cache sizes, the following orders, from best to worst, to hold: i) H-AND-1-30 → H-AND-2-30 → H-AND-3-30; ii) H-AND-1-50 → H-AND-2-50. iii) H-AND-1-50 → H-AND-1-30. iv) H-AND-2-50 → H-AND-2-30. These relationships are confirmed in the graph of Fig. 8. However, Fig. 3 does not allow us to infer a relationship between H-AND-1-30 and H-AND-2-50. Our experiments indicate, as shown in Fig. 8, that H-AND-2-50 outperforms H-AND-1-30. For $P_c = 2.5\%$ the hit ratio of H-AND-2-50 is 15% higher than that of H-AND-1-30 and for a small cache of $P_c = 0.3\%$, the hit ratio of H-AND-2-50 is 20.0% higher than that of H-AND-1-30. This means that it is better to start caching earlier as long as the auction seems to be more popular. Figure 9 is similar to Fig. 8 except that a H-OR placement policy is used as opposed to a H-AND one. The H-OR policies provide higher hit ratios than their H-AND counterparts. We already knew that would be the case for unlimited cache sizes according to Fig. 3. For example, while H-AND-1-50:AB-PRT has a cache hit

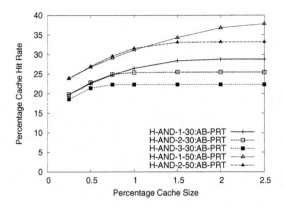

Fig. 8. Hit ratio for various HIT-AND-*n*-*p* policies

ratio of 37.8% for $P_c = 2.5\%$, H-OR-1-50:AB-PRT has a cache hit ratio of 59.0% for the same value of P_c. Consider now the same relationship for a small cache size of $P_c = 0.3\%$. The H-OR-1-50 policy outperforms the H-AND-1-50 one by a factor of 1.7.

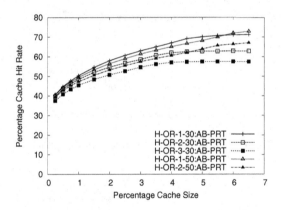

Fig. 9. Hit ratio for various HIT-OR-*n*-*p* policies

Another observation from Fig. 9 is that a large cache is required to achieve an unlimited cache size performance level ($P_c = 6.5\%$ as opposed to $P_c = 2.5\%$) when compared to the H-AND case. For the large cache sizes, the following relationships, which are in accordance with Fig. 3, can be observed (from best to worst): i) H-OR-1-50 → H-OR-2-50. ii) H-OR-1-30 → H-OR-2-30 → H-OR-3-30. iii) H-OR-1-50 → H-OR-1-30. iv) H-OR-2-50 → H-OR-2-30. It is interesting to note the crossovers between H-OR-1-50 and H-OR-1-30 and between H-OR-2-50 and H-OR-2-30. They show that for smaller cache sizes, the preferred policy is not the one that has the best performance for unlimited cache sizes.

5.4 Policy Comparisons

This section compares the best policies of each category—AB1:LRU, PRT50:LRU, H-OR-1-50:LRU, and H-AND-1-50:LRU—with respect to the cache hit ratio H and the cache efficiency ε. Figure 10 compares these policies with respect to H and shows that AB1:LRU and H-OR-1-50:LRU are very similar and far superior than PRT50:LRU and H-AND-1-50:LRU. AB1:LRU is slighty superior than H-OR-1-50:LRU for $0.25\% \leq P_c \leq 4.0\%$. For $P_c > 4.0\%$, H-OR-1-50:LRU has a higher hit ratio. Figure 11 compares the same policies in terms of cache efficiency. It can be seen that, for all four policies, ε decreases very fast as the cache size increases indicating that small caches are very effective because of the power law characteristics of auction workloads [1, 10]. In fact, the efficiency curves also follows a power law. For example, using regression on the AB1:LRU efficiency curve yields $\varepsilon = 0.001704/P_c^{0.703}$. As can be seen, AB1:LRU and H-OR-1-50:LRU have higher cache efficiency than the two other policies.

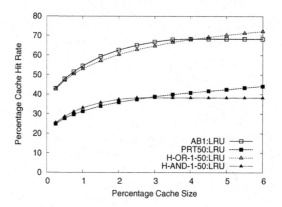

Fig. 10. Hit ratio comparison for various policies

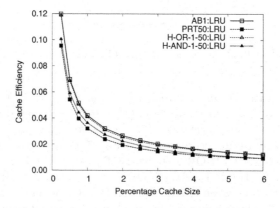

Fig. 11. Cache effectiveness comparison for various policies

6   Concluding Remarks

This paper proposed several cache placement and replacement policies and analyzed them through trace-based simulations using traces from a large production site. Some general observations from our analysis are: i) LRU is the cache replacement policy that outperforms the others when combined with any of the placement policies considered. For example, for $P_c = 0.25\%$, AB1:LRU outperforms AB1:AB by a 53% margin. ii) Hit ratios increase much faster for small cache sizes than for larger ones. For example, for the AB1:AB policy, an increase in cache size from 0.25% to 0.5% provides a 27% increase in hit ratio. An increase in cache size from 4% to 4.5% provides only a 0.7% increase in hit ratio. iii) The unlimited cache behavior can be obtained with cache sizes ranging from 2.5%, for H-AND policies, to around 6% for the other policies. iv) a relatively small cache, e.g., 4 to 5% of all auctions is enough to generate cache hit ratios of around 50 to 70% as is the case with the ABn policies. Even very small caches of about 1% can generate cache hit ratios as large as 40%. v) the H-OR-n-p policies provide a much better hit ratio than the H-AND-n-p ones. For example, while H-AND-1-50:AB-PRT has a cache hit ratio of 37.8% for $P_c = 2.5\%$, H-OR-1-50:AB-PRT has a cache hit ratio of 59.0% for the same value of P_c. vi) The H-OR policies have crossover points indicating that the best policy for unlimited cache sizes is not the best for smaller cache sizes. vii) AB1:LRU and H-OR-1-50:LRU are very similar and far superior than PRT50:LRU and H-AND-1-50:LRU. viii) AB1:LRU is slighty superior than H-OR-1-50:LRU for $0.25\% \leq P_c \leq 4.0\%$. For $P_c > 4.0\%$, H-OR-1-50:LRU has a higher hit ratio. ix) The cache efficiency decreases very fast as the cache size increases indicating that small caches are very effective because of the power law characteristics of auction workloads. In fact, the efficiency curves also follows a power law.

In summary, the performance of online auction sites can be significantly increased with very small caches (on the order of 1% of the millions of items being auctioned). These small caches are more effective than larger caches and produce more hits per cached auction. We are currently designing a comprehensive benchmark for online auctions based on our workload characterization of such sites. We are also implementing a testbed compliant with this benchmark and we will be using it to test the caching policies described in this paper.

References

1. Akula, V., Menascé, D.A.: An analysis of bidding activity in online auctions. 5th Intl. Conf. (EC-Web 2004), Zaragoza, Spain, Aug./Sept. (2004) 206–217
2. Bapna,R., Goes, P., Gupta, A.: Online auctions: insights and analysis. Comm. ACM. **44(11)** (2001) 42–50
3. Breslau, L., Cao, P., Fan, Li., Phillips, G., Shenker, S.:, Web Caching and Zipf-like Distributions: Evidence and Implications. INFOCOM (1), (1999), 126-134.
4. Coffman Jr., E.G., Denning, P.J.: Operating Systems Theory. Prentice Hall, Upper Saddle River, NJ (1973)

5. Davison, B. D.: The Design and Evaluation of Web Prefetching and Caching Techniques PhD Dissertation, Rutgers University, October (2002) URL: http://citeseer.ist.psu.edu/davison02design.html
6. Douglis, F., Davison, B. D. (eds) : Web Content Caching and Distribution Proc. 8th International Workshop. Kluwer, June (2004)
7. hardwarezone.com: 10,000 Ebay Enthusiasts to Gather For 10TH Anniversary Celebration. URL: www.hardwarezone.com/news/view.php?id=1576&cid=5, May 26 (2005)
8. Kleinrock, L.: Queuing Systems: Theory, Vol I. John Wiley & Sons, NY (1975)
9. Lee, D., Choi, J., Kim, J., Noh, S., Min, S.L., Cho, Y., Kim, C.: LRFU: A Spectrum of Policies that Subsumes the Least Recently Used and Least Frequently Used Policies. IEEE Trans. Computers 50(12): 1352-1361 (2001)
10. Menascé, D.A., Akula, V.: Towards workload characterization of auction sites. Proc. IEEE 6th Annual Workshop on Workload Characterization (WWC-6), Austin, TX, Oct. 27 (2003)
11. Menascé, D.A., Akula, V.: Improving the performance of online auction sites through closing time rescheduling. 1st Intl. Conf Quantitative Evaluation of Systems (QEST-2004), Enschede, the Netherlands, Sept. 27-30 (2004)
12. Menascé, D.A., Almeida, V.A., Fonseca, R., Mendes, M.: A methodology for workload characterization for e-commerce servers. ACM Conf. Electronic Commerce, Denver, CO, Nov. 3-5, (1999) 119-128
13. Pierre, G.: A Web caching bibliography, June (2000) URL : citeseer.ist.psu.edu/pierre00web.html
14. Yagoub, K., Florescu, D., Issarny, V., Valduriez, P.: Caching Strategies for Data-Intensive Web Sites. The VLDB Journal, (2000) 188–199. URL : citeseer.ist.psu.edu/yagoub00caching.html
15. Yahoo!Japan: Monthly Disclosure - March (2005 URL:http://ir.yahoo.co.jp/en/monthly/200503.html, April 8 (2005)

Maintaining Consistency Under Isolation Relaxation of Web Services Transactions

Seunglak Choi[1], Hyukjae Jang[2], Hangkyu Kim[1],
Jungsook Kim[3], Su Myeon Kim[2], Junehwa Song[2], and Yoon-Joon Lee[1]

[1] 371-1 Guseong-Dong, Yuseong-Gu, Daejeon, Korea
{slchoi, hkkim, yjlee}@dbserver.kaist.ac.kr
[2] 371-1 Guseong-Dong, Yuseong-Gu, Daejeon, Korea
{hjjang, smkim, junesong}@nclab.kaist.ac.kr
[3] 161 Gajeong-dong, Yuseong-gu, Daejeon, Korea
jungsook96@etri.re.kr

Abstract. For efficiently managing Web Services (WS) transactions which are executed across multiple loosely-coupled autonomous organizations, isolation is commonly relaxed. A Web services operation of a transaction releases locks on its resources once its jobs are completed without waiting for the completions of other operations. However, those early unlocked resources can be seen by other transactions, which can spoil data integrity and causes incorrect outcomes. Existing WS transaction standards do not consider this problem. In this paper, we propose a mechanism to ensure the consistent executions of isolation-relaxing WS transactions. The mechanism effectively detects inconsistent states of transactions with a notion of a *completion dependency* and recovers them to consistent states. We also propose a new Web services Transaction Dependency management Protocol (WTDP). WTDP helps organizations manage the WS transactions easily without data inconsistency. WTDP is designed to be compliant with a representative WS transaction standard, the Web Services Transactions specifications, for easy integration into existing WS transaction systems. We prototyped a WTDP-based WS transaction management system to validate our protocol.

1 Introduction

Major IT organizations such as Amazon, Google, and e-Bay have been migrating their interfaces for business partners to service-oriented architectures using the Web Services (WS) technology. Due to its flexibility and dynamicity, WS allows organizations to easily integrate services across different organizations as well as within organizations [9,10,11,12,13]. Such WS-based integrated applications should guarantee consistent data manipulation and outcome of business processes running across multiple loosely-coupled organizations. Thus, WS technologies should be extended to equip with transaction-processing functionalities.

There are three proposals for protocols to extend the WS with transaction processing capabilities, *i.e.,* Web Services Transactions specifications [6], Business Transaction Protocol (BTP) [7], and WS-CAF [8]. Also, commercial transaction management systems [17,18] have been developed implementing these protocols. For efficient

M. Kitsuregawa et al. (Eds.): WISE 2005, LNCS 3806, pp. 245–257, 2005.
© Springer-Verlag Berlin Heidelberg 2005

processing, these WS-based transaction protocols relax the *isolation property*[1] rather than use strictly-exclusive locking mechanisms such as the two-phase commit and the strict two-phase locking[2] [19]. In contrast to traditional transactions, WS transactions live long – *e.g.,* a few hours or days. Thus, if the strict locking mechanisms are used, an organization may not be able to access its resources even for a few days, until other organizations complete their works and release their resources. Relaxing the isolation property, an organization participating a transaction completes its work without concerning the status of other organizations' works. The organization releases its resources and continues its jobs for other transactions. In fact, most models for long-lived transactions proposed in literature [1,2,5,6,7,8,14] relaxed the isolation property.

In this paper, we argue that the isolation relaxation introduces a serious inconsistency problem. Consider a situation where a participant fails its transaction after releasing a shared resource and assume that other participants have already read the resource and proceeding their own transactions (see Section 2 for details). Such a situation implies that different participants hold different states of the same resource, resulting in a possibly serious inconsistency problem. Considering that WS transactions will get more and more prevalent, such a situation may occur quite frequently, being a major blocking factor for the WS transaction usage. However, existing WS transaction models and managing systems as well as the long-lived transaction models do not address this problem. After all, organizations have to solve the problems by themselves. However, the lack of pre-defined protocols among organizations makes it hardly possible since WS transactions are dynamically created across any Web services hosted by many loosely-coupled organizations.

We propose a mechanism to ensure the consistent executions of the isolation-relaxing transactions. The mechanism effectively identifies the transactions in an inconsistent state with a notion of a *completion dependency*. The notion is a relationship between two transactions in which one transaction's failure incurs the inconsistent state of other transaction. Once the inconsistent transactions are identified, the mechanism recovers those transactions to the previous consistent states and optionally further re-executes them. In the mechanism, a transaction should delay its completion until its related transactions are closed, *i.e.* they are guaranteed never to abort. Occasionally, the delayed completion incurs *circular waiting*, in which two or more transactions is waiting for the other to be completed and thereby no one can be completed. The mechanism provides a graph-based method to detect circular waiting and defines a condition to safely complete the involved transactions without inconsistency.

We also propose a new *Web services Transaction Dependency management Protocol* (WTDP). WTDP makes it possible for participants to identify and resolve occurrences of completion dependency. Upon its occurrence, using the protocol, participants automatically delivers related information to other participating organizations. Any changes affecting the status of the dependency are continuously monitored and processed, thus each organization is notified of the completion of related transactions when all the relevant dependencies are resolved. In addition, WTDP detects and resolves

---

[1] Isolation is one of the well-known transaction properties called ACID – Atomicity, Consistency, Isolation, and Duration.

[2] Those schemes maintain consistency through holding locks on all resources until the completion of a transaction. Thus, a resource cannot be released before all other resources are ready to be released.

circular waiting by a token-based approach, which is executed on dependency information distributed over multiple sites. Adopting the protocol, organizations do not need to concern the management of the dependencies. They only need to process transactions as they did according to the status notification of relevant transactions. In addition, being compliant with the de-facto WS transaction standards, WTDP can be easily implemented and deployed within existing WS transaction management systems.

The rest of this paper is organized as follows: Section 2 shows a motivating scenario of dependencies among WS transactions. In Section 3, we review related work and the WS Transactions specifications. Then, we propose a mechanism to guarantee consistent executions of transactions in Section 4, and WTDP in Section 5. Finally, we conclude our work in Section 6.

2 Motivating Scenario

Suppose there are five companies: furniture maker, wood distributor, steel distributor, lumber mill, and shipping company. The furniture maker manufactures furniture using both wood and steel which are supplied by the wood and steel distributors, respectively. The wood distributor buys wood from the lumber mill. Wood is delivered to the wood distributor by the shipping company. All the companies implement and use Web services for the above processes.

The wood distributor and the lumber mill agree on a vendor managed inventory (VMI) contract, which is an advanced inventory management technique [15]. Under the VMI contract, producers are responsible for managing and replenishing consumers' inventories. Thus, consumers can reduce the overhead of inventory management. In our scenario, the lumber mill and the wood distributor correspond to VMI producer and VMI consumer, respectively. The lumber mill therefore continuously checks the inventory of the wood distributor and delivers wood when the amount of wood in the inventory goes below an agreed level of stocks.

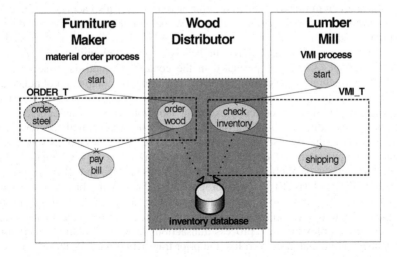

Fig. 1. The occurrence of dependency between two Web Services transactions

Figure 1 shows a snapshot of the internal process of three companies when the furniture maker receives a purchase order from a customer who needs 50 units of woods and steels. The furniture maker issues ordering transaction (ORDER_T) to acquire 50 units of wood and 50 units of steel. The wood order is processed and committed instantly, but the processing of steel order is delayed due to an internal problem of the steel distributor. At that moment, the lumber mill issues VMI transaction (VMI_T). It checks the inventory of the wood distributor and realizes that the total stock is less than the agreed amount of units (here 100 units). VMI_T automatically initiates supplying 50 units of wood. Let's assume that the order of 50 units of steel is aborted. Then, the supply of wood from the wood distributor to the furniture maker will be aborted. In that case, the wood distributor does not need the extra 50 units of wood any more. Thus, the supply of wood from the lumber mill to the wood distributor should be aborted instantly if possible.

In the level of transactions, VMI_T is said to be dependent upon ORDER_T; if ORDER_T fails, VMI_T should be aborted. By showing the intermediate value of the total stock (*i.e.* 50) to VMI_T, which is inherent due to the relaxation of isolation, the status of ORDER_T determines the status of VMI_T. ORDER_T and VMI_T are considered as completely independent transactions by current Web services transaction standards. There are no model to express the dependency and no protocols to handle such dependencies.

3 Related Work

3.1 Business Transaction Models

Several isolation-relaxing transaction models have been introduced since late 1980s. Garcia-Molina and Salem [1] addressed the performance problem of long-lived transactions. To alleviate this problem, they deal with a long-lived transaction (called *saga*) as a sequence of sub-transactions and permit each sub-transaction to be committed, irrespective of the commitment of other sub-transactions. They also addressed the concept of *compensation* to amend a partial execution. Weikum and Schek [2] proposed an open transaction model, in which a large transaction is decomposed into nested sub-transactions. These sub-transactions can be also committed unilaterally. A flexible transaction model [3,4,5] was proposed in the context of multi-database systems. It allows sub-transactions to be committed without waiting the completion of delayed sub-transactions. Note that all the transaction models above do not consider the inconsistency problem caused by concurrently executing isolation-relaxing transactions.

Nowadays, isolation-relaxing transaction models have been realized for business transactions under the Web services environment. The WS Transactions specifications [6] are a de facto standard of a framework and protocols to implement isolation-relaxing transactions on Web services, proposed by IBM, MS, and BEA. The Business Transaction Protocol (BTP) [7] was proposed by the OASIS business transactions technical committee, and also relaxes isolation of transactions. WS-CAF [8], proposed by Arjuna Technologies Limited et al., consists of three protocol layers which support long-running, complex business process transactions in which isolation relaxation is a basic concept. Note that, however, like the prior transaction models, these protocols do not handle the inconsistency problem of isolation-relaxing transactions.

3.2 WS Transactions Specifications

The WS Transactions specifications describe the framework for coordinating transactions running across multiple Web services. Since WTDP is designed as an extension of the WS Transactions specifications, we briefly review the specification to facilitate the understanding of WTDP.

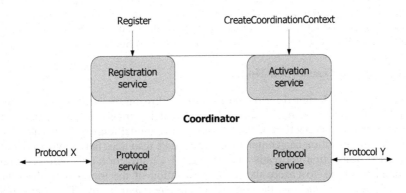

Fig. 2. Coordinator architecture

The specifications include the WS-Coordination specification, which defines an extensible framework (commonly called a coordinator) for providing protocols that coordinate the activities of distributed transactions. The specifications also provide two coordination types, WS-AtomicTransaction and WS-BusinessActivity, for simple short-lived transactions and complex long-lived business activities, respectively. By using those two specifications, the coordinator manages WS transactions. The coordinator consists of the following services, which is illustrated in Figure 2. All these services are provided as Web services.

- Activation service (specified in WS-Coordination) - operations that enable an application to create a coordination instance or context.
- Registration service (specified in WS-Coordination) - operations that enable an application and participants to register for coordination protocols.
- Protocol service (specified in WS-AtomicTransaction/BusinessActivity) - a set of coordination protocols.

When an organization wants to create a new WS transaction, it requests and receives a coordination context from its coordinator using the Activation service. The organization notifies all the participants of the WS transaction by forwarding the coordination context to them. Then, all the participants and the organization (WS transaction initiator) register their own transaction protocols, which are specified in the WS-AtomicTransaction/BusinessActivity specifications, to the coordinator using the Registration service. Then, the coordinator manages the transaction by exchanging messages with the transaction initiator and the participants via the Protocol service.

4 Consistency Maintaining

In this section, we present a mechanism to ensure the consistent executions of isolation-relaxing Web services transactions. In Section 4.1, we first briefly introduce an underlying transaction model on top of which our mechanism is built. We then formally define the completion dependency in Section 4.2, which is used to determine transactions affected by a given transaction's failure. In Section 4.3, we describe how to handle the dependency in Section 4.3. Finally, we discuss circular waiting which occurs when two or more transactions are waiting for other transactions to be ended, and also describe a scheme to resolve circular waiting in Section 4.4.

4.1 Underlying Transaction Model

Our mechanism is designed for the transactions following the business activity model of the WS-Transactions specifications. In that model, a transaction consists of multiple operations on a collection of Web services. The model relaxes the isolation property in that an operation can complete and release its resources before other operations in the same transaction are ready to complete. If a transaction fails before getting to the complete phase, to ensure the atomic execution of the transaction, the running operations are *cancelled*[3] and the completed ones are *compensated*. The compensation semantically undoes the effects of the completed operations.

4.2 Completion Dependency

We now introduce completion dependency between transactions. As shown in Section 2, a transaction may need to be cancelled according to the status of other transactions. The completion dependency is notated as $T_b \Rightarrow T_a$ when the successful completion of a transaction T_b is dependent upon the status of a transaction T_a. The completion dependency can be formally defined as follows:

Definition 1 (Completion dependency). Let us assume that there are two transactions T_a and T_b. The completion dependency $T_b \Rightarrow T_a$ occurs if O_j reads a value updated by O_i where $O_i \in T_a$ and $O_j \in T_b$.

In the above definition, we refer to T_a as a *dominant transaction* and T_b as a *dependent transaction*. We also refer to O_i as a *dominant operation* and O_j as a *dependent operation*. A dominant transaction determines whether its dependent transactions should be successfully ended or not. For instance, T_b should be cancelled if T_a fails, because the update on the data referenced by T_b has been cancelled.

4.3 Completion Dependency Handling

When a dominant transaction fails, there are two solutions, *redo* and *abort*, to handle its dependent transactions. The redo scheme re-executes a dependent transaction. This scheme first identifies the operations affected by the cancellation of data updates. It

---

[3] Cancellation and completion are the terms used in the document of WS transactions specifications and correspond to well-know transaction terms, abort and commit, respectively.

then compensates or cancels the identified operations depending on whether the operations has been completed or is running. Finally, it executes these operations again. Let us consider the example in Figure 3. Two transactions, T_1 and T_2, have a completion dependency $T_2 \Rightarrow T_1$, which occurs because an operation O_{22} of T_2 has read the value updated by the operations O_{11} of T_1. The operations, O_{21}, O_{22}, and O_{11} (colored by gray), have already been completed. We now assume that O_{12} fails and thereby O_{11} is compensated for ensuring the atomicity of T_1. The compensation nullifies the effect of the update of O_{11}. In this case, the redo scheme identifies O_{22} as an affected operation because it has read the cancelled update. The scheme also identifies O_{23}, which is a subsequent operation of the dependent operations ST_{22}. This is because O_{23} may have used the old output of O_{22}. Thus, O_{23} needs to cancel its execution and re-execute itself with the new output of O_{22}.

On the other hand, the abort scheme is to stop the execution of a dependent transaction and undo its data updates. The undo is done by compensating all completed operations and canceling all running operations. When applied to the above example, the scheme cancels O_{23} and compensates O_{21} and O_{22}.

Both schemes require some operations to be compensated. This compensation can recursively abort succeeding dependent transactions, which could result in a lot of transaction aborts. The redo scheme has lower possibility of the recursive compensation than the abort scheme. This is because, as mentioned above, the redo scheme needs to compensate only dependent operations and their following operations. In contrast, the abort scheme compensates all completed operations. In the example above, O_{21}, which is not compensated in the redo, is compensated in the abort. Hence, if applications allow re-executions of transactions, the redo scheme is more desirable.

As described so far, dependent transactions may need to be re-executed or aborted due to the failures of their dominant transactions. Thus, dependent transactions should delay the completion until their dominant transactions are all successfully ended.

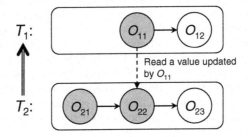

Fig. 3. An example of dependencies: $\Rightarrow$ denotes a completion dependency and $\rightarrow$ denotes precedence in an execution order of operations. Gray-colored circles indicate completed operations.

4.4 Circular Waiting

The delayed completion of dependent transactions can incur circular waiting in which each of two transactions is waiting for the other to be ended. For example, let us assume that two transactions T_1 and T_2 have completion dependencies in both directions, i.e. $T_1 \Rightarrow T_2$ and $T_2 \Rightarrow T_1$. After completing all their operations, T_1 and T_2 will be in a state of circular waiting; T_1 is waiting for T_2 to be ended, while T_2 is waiting for T_1 to be ended. Both T_1 and T_2 cannot be completed themselves. Meanwhile, the applications, which have issued T_1 and T_2, cannot proceed to their next tasks. Circular waiting is also possible when more than two transactions are involved (*e.g.* $T_1 \Rightarrow T_2 \Rightarrow T_3 \Rightarrow T_1$).

Fig. 4. A dependency graph which shows the state of circular waiting

To solve this problem, we need to be able to detect circular waiting. We construct a *dependency graph* where a node represents a transaction and an edge represents a completion dependency. Figure 4 shows the dependency graph for the example above. We say that a set of transactions is in a state of circular waiting if and only if its dependency graph has a cycle. This approach needs to build and maintain the dependency graphs across multiple Web services, which will be described in Section 5.4. If a cycle is discovered, the condition for the completions of the transactions in the cycle is changed. A transaction can complete if *all other transactions* in the same cycle are *ready* to complete. When such a condition is met, there is no possibility that transactions will be re-executed or aborted.

5   Web Services Transaction Dependency Management Protocol

5.1   Overview

In this section, we propose a new protocol called Web services Transaction Dependency management Protocol (WTDP). Our design goals of WTDP are to ensure interoperability and security, which are common and core requirements in Web services environments. Interoperability here means that WTDP-enabled coordinators and participants can seamlessly cooperate with existing ones not supporting WTDP. For this, WTDP is designed as an extension of the WS-BusinessActivity protocol, not requiring any modifications on the protocol. WTDP adds new services and their related messages which do not conflict with the existing protocols. Maintaining security is crucial in business transactions especially among different, loosely-coupled organizations. Completion dependencies can be interpreted as mission-critical information

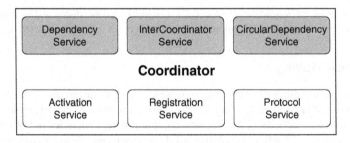

Fig. 5. Services at a coordinator: gray-colored ones are the services provided by WTDP

such as confidential contracts between organizations. WTDP makes such information to be stored at distributed coordinators, in which each coordinator manages only its involving completion dependencies. This policy prevents a coordinator to steal a look at other organizations' dependencies.

WTDP consists of three services, which are added to coordinators as shown in Figure 5. *Dependency service* is used by participants to inform their coordinators of dependency information whenever participants detect dependencies. *InterCoordinator service* is used to exchange dependency information among coordinators. Also, the ending status of dominant transactions such as failure or success is communicated among the coordinators of the transactions through an InterCoordinator service. *CircularDependency service* is used to detect and resolve circular waiting. A token-based approach is used to handle circular waiting over dependency information distributed over multiple coordinators. These services are defined in WSDL[4]. Each service uses one or more messages to communicate with the services of other coordinators. [16] includes the definitions of all services and messages.

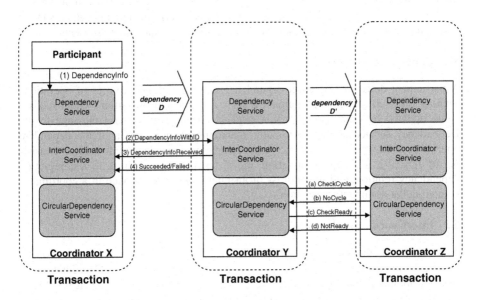

Fig. 6. The message flow of WTDP. There are two completion dependencies – D and D'. D is between transactions managed by coordinators X and Y. D' is between transactions of coordinators Y and Z.

Figure 6 shows WTDP messages and their flows. When a completion dependency D is detected at a participant site, it informs a dependent coordinator[5] of D by sending a DependencyInfo message (1). The dependent coordinator informs its dominant

---

[4] Web Services Description Language (WSDL) is a standard language for describing the operations and messages of network services.

[5] Throughout this paper, we refer to a coordinator instance managing a dependent transaction as a *dependent coordinator*. Likewise, we use a term called *dominant coordinator*.

coordinator by using a `DependencyInfoWithID` message (2). The dominant coordinator acknowledges the message by returning a `DependencyInfoReceived` message (3). Now, the dominant coordinator sends `Succeeded` or `Failed` messages to the dependent coordinator according to the completion status of the dominant transaction (4). The dependent coordinator can handle its transaction appropriately according to the completion status of the dominant transaction.

Meanwhile, the dominant transaction may additionally have a completion dependency D' with another transaction. In this case, the dependency relations may become a cycle. To determine if there is circular waiting, the dominant coordinator of D sends a `CheckCycle` message to the dominant coordinator of D' (a). The dominant coordinator of D' returns `NoCycle` if no cycle is found (b). Note that if a cycle exists, the `CheckCycle` message will finally be returned to the sender. If circular waiting is detected, the dominant coordinator sends a `CheckReady` message to its dominant coordinator to check whether all involved transactions are ready to be completed or not (c). Coordinators in the cycle return a `NotReady` message if their transactions are not ready to completed yet (d). This ready-check process is performed periodically. Detailed description of the messages and their flows are described in subsequent subsections.

5.2 Dependency Service

A participant detects completion dependencies by observing activities of operations running on itself. When a participant detects a dependent operation (which reads a value updated by other operation), it sends a `DependencyInfo` message to the Dependency service of the coordinator managing the transaction of the dependent operation. A `DependencyInfo` message contains dependency information consisting of IDs of a dominant transaction and a dependent transaction in a completion dependency relation, and the address of an InterCoordinator service in a coordinator managing the dominant transaction.

5.3 InterCoordinator Service

Four kinds of messages, `DependencyInfoWithID`, `DependencyInfoReceived`, `Succeeded`, and `Failed`, are transferred between InterCoordinator services of dominant and dependent coordinators. After receiving a `DependencyInfo` message from a participant, a dependent coordinator sends a `DependencyInfoWithID` message to its dominant coordinator. The `DependencyInfoWithID` message contains a dependency ID as well as dependency information included in the `DependencyInfo` message. The dominant coordinator replies to the dependent coordinator with a `DependencyInfoReceived` message, which is an acknowledgement that the `DependencyInfoWithID` message was received. The `DependencyInfoReceived` message also includes the address of the CircularDependency service of the dominant coordinator.

`Succeeded` and `Failed` messages are used by a dominant coordinator to inform its dependent coordinator of the completion status. If the dependent coordinator receives a `Succeeded` message, it can complete its dependent transaction. On the other hand, if the dependent coordinator receives a `Failed` message, it should abort or re-execute its dependent transaction as mentioned in Section 4.3.

5.4 CircularDependency Service

If a dominant transaction is further dependent on other transactions, there is a possibility that the dependency relations form a cycle. As mentioned in Section 4.4, the cycle means that circular waiting occurs. Thus, the dominant coordinator should detect such a *circular dependency*. The easiest way to detect circular dependencies would be maintaining information on all dependencies at a central single node. We can easily detect circular dependencies from consolidated information stored in the same memory space. However, this approach causes security problems. Completion dependencies can be interpreted as mission-critical information. Thus, it is better to manage this information at distributed points. We propose a token-based scheme that detects circular dependencies from completion dependency information distributed over multiple coordinators. The basic idea of this scheme is that we can recognize a circular dependency when a coordinator receives the token that was initiated by itself.

A CircularDependency service includes two messages, CheckCycle and NoCycle, to execute the token-based scheme. A CheckCycle message is a token which is traversed along coordinators. When a dominant coordinator receives a DependencyInfoWithID message, it initiates a new token with a unique ID. Then, the dominant coordinator sends the token to its every dominant coordinator. The token is recursively traversed along dependency relations. If the initiating coordinator receives the token initiated by itself, there must be a circular dependency.

If a dominant coordinator's transaction is not dependent on other transactions, the token traversal is stopped and the dominant coordinator responds with a NoCycle message to its dependent coordinator. The NoCycle is recursively sent to the dependent coordinator and eventually is arrived at the initiating coordinator. Only after receiving every NoCycle message from each dominant transaction, an initiating coordinator can guarantee that there are no circular dependencies.

Once a circular dependency is detected, we need to check whether all transactions in the cycle are ready to be completed as mentioned in Section 4.4. This checking is done in a very similar way as detecting circular dependencies. A coordinator which wants to complete its transaction initiates a CheckReady message. The initiating coordinator sends the CheckReady message to every dominant coordinator. The receiving coordinator forwards the CheckReady message to its every dominant coordinator if its transaction is ready to be completed. If the CheckReady message is returned to the initiating coordinator, it is guaranteed that all transactions in the cycle are ready to be completed. Thus, the initiating coordinator can complete its transaction and notifies its dependent coordinator of the successful completion.

If the receiving coordinator's transaction is not ready to be completed, it responds with a NotReady message to its dependent coordinator. The NotReady is recursively sent to the dependent coordinator and eventually is arrived at the initiating coordinator. Now, the initiating coordinator knows that some transactions in the cycle are not ready to be completed. Thus, it should wait for a while and re-initiate a CheckReady message.

5.5 Validating WTDP

To validate WTDP, we prototyped a WTDP-based WS transaction management system and implemented the scenario shown in Section 2 on the system. The design and implementation for the prototyped system is described in detail in [16]. Each company runs different Web services management systems on its own machine. In addition, different coordinators are assigned to different companies. All the Web services for the scenario and Web pages for user interface are implemented. The dependency between order transaction and VMI transaction is described by CDDL and loaded into the Wood distributor's CDD before running the scenario. The scenario runs correctly and the completion dependency is identified and its information is forwarded to relevant coordinators once it happens. Figure 7 shows a screen shot of our monitoring utility which is a part of our WTDP prototype. It displays the current status of completion dependencies of a coordinator using the relevant information stored in that coordinator. In the figure, a transaction initiated by the furniture maker – order transaction – and a transaction initiated by the lumber mill – VMI transaction – are displayed along with the completion dependency between them.

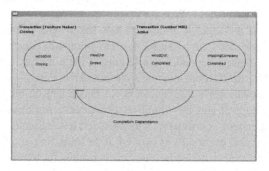

Fig. 7. A screen shot of the monitoring utility of the prototype system: two boxes mean two transactions; the furniture maker initiates the left transaction and the lumber mill initiates the right transaction. Although the right transaction has finished all its operations but it still waits for the closure of the left transaction since the operation labeled woodDist is not completed yet.

6 Conclusions

The isolation property of WS transactions is usually relaxed for a high level of concurrency. Relaxed isolation brought up the notion of completion dependency among transactions; when a transaction accesses intermediary results of another transaction, its completion depends on the completion status of the other. In this paper, we proposed a mechanism which guarantees the consistent executions of isolation-relaxing WS transactions. The mechanism effectively detects inconsistent states of transactions and recovers them to consistent states. We also proposed a dependency management protocol called WTDP. By employing the WTDP, organizations can save time and money in managing completion dependencies. Since WTDP is designed to incorporate with the WS transactions specifications, it can be easily deployed in existing WS-transactions-compliant transaction management systems.

References

1. Garcia-Molina and K. Salem. SAGAS. In Proceedings of ACM SIGMOD Conference, pages 249-259, 1987.
2. Weikum and H. J. Schek. Concepts and Applications of Multilevel Transactions and Open Nested Transactions. In A. Elmagarmid (ed.): Database Transaction Models for Advanced Applications, Morgan Kaufmann Publishers, pages 515-553, 1992.
3. A. K. Elmagarmid, Y. Leu, W. Litwin, and M. Rusinkiewicz. A Multi-database Transaction model for Interbase. In Proceedings of the 16th VLDB Conference, pages 507-518, 1990.
4. S. Mehrotra, R. Rastogi, H. F. Korth, and A. Silberschatz. A Transaction Model for Multi-database Systems. In Proceedings of the 12th International Conference On Distributed Systems, pages 56-63, June 1992.
5. A. Zhang, M. Nodine, B. Bhargava, and O. Bukhres. Ensuring Relaxed Atomicity for Flexible Transactions in Multi-database Systems. In Proceedings of ACM SIGMOD Conference, pages 67-78, 1994.
6. IBM, Microsoft, and BEA. Web Services Transactions Specifications. http://www-106.ibm.com/developerworks/webservices/library/ws-transpec/
7. OASIS. Business Transaction Protocol. http://www.oasis-open.org/committees/documents.php?wg_abbrev=business-transaction
8. Arjuna Technologies Ltd., Fujitsu Software, IONA Technologies PLC, Oracle Corp, and Sun Microsystems. Web Services Composite Application Framework (WS-CAF). http://developers.sun.com/techtopics/webservices/wscaf
9. R. Akkiraju, D. Flaxer, H. Chang, T. Chao, L.-J. Zhang, F. Wu, and J.-J. Jeng. A Framework for Facilitating Dynamic e-Business Via Web Services. In Proceedings of OOPLSA 2001 Workshop on Object-Oriented Web Services, Florida, USA, October 2001.
10. S. Tsur. Are Web Services the Next Revolution in E-commerce?. Proceedings of the 27th VLDB Conference, Roma, Italy, 2001.
11. F. Curbera, W. A. Nagy, and S. Weerawarana. Web Services: Why and How. In Proceedings of OOPLSA 2001 Workshop on Object-Oriented Web Services, Florida, USA, 2001.
12. S. Narayanan and S. A. McIlraith. Simulation, Verification and Automated Composition of Web Services. In Proceedings of WWW Conference, Honolulu, Hawaii, USA, 2002.
13. M. Pierce, C. Youn, G. Fox, S. Mock, K. Mueller, and O. Balsoy. Interoperable Web services for Computational Portals. In Proceedings of the IEEE/ACM SC2002 Conference, Baltimore, USA, November 16-22, 2002.
14. J. Eliot and B. Moss. Nested Transactions: An Approach to Reliable Distributed Computing. MIT Press, Cambridge, MA, 1985.
15. VMI process. http://www.vendormangedinventory.com
16. S. M. Kim, S. Choi, H. Jang, H. Kim, J. Kim, and J. Song. A Framework for Handling Dependencies among Web Services Transactions. Technical Report CS-TR-2004-207, KAIST.
17. Arjuna Technologies Ltd. ArjunaTS. http://www.arjuna.com/products/arjunats/ws.html
18. Choreology Ltd. Cohesions. http://www.choreology.com/products/index.htm
19. J. Gray and A. Reuter. Transaction Processing: Concepts and Techniques. Morgan Kaufmann Publishers.

Binding and Execution of Web Service Compositions

K. Vidyasankar* and V.S. Ananthanarayana**

Department of Computer Science,
Memorial University of Newfoundland,
St. John's, Newfoundland, Canada, A1B 3X5
vidya@cs.mun.ca, anvs@nitk.ac.in

Abstract. Web services enable the design, integration, composition, and deployment of distributed and heterogeneous software. While most syntactic issues in composition have been taken care of somewhat satisfactorily, several semantic issues remain unresolved. In this paper, we consider issues relating to binding and execution of composite services. A Web service composition or composite activity consists of a set of (basic or composite) activities with some ordering constraints. In general, an arbitrary collection of execution instances of the individual activities may not constitute an execution of the composite activity; the individual execution instances must be "compatible". In this paper, we propose (a) a simple formalism to express the compatibility requirements in a composition, and (b) a methodology for (i) the selection of a composite service provider for a composite activity and (ii) the selection of (other) service providers for the constituent activities of the composite activity, to ensure an execution of the composition satisfying the compatibility requirements.

1 Introduction

Web services enable the design, integration, composition, and deployment of distributed and heterogeneous software. Industry standards have been developed for description and invocation of the services, and for re-using them in compositions of higher level services. While most syntactic issues in composition have been taken care of somewhat satisfactorily, several semantic issues remain unresolved. In this paper, we consider issues relating to binding and execution of composite services.

A Web service composition or composite activity consists of a set of constituent (basic or composite) activities with some ordering constraints. The composition describes the program logic of an end user (or a composite service

---

* This research is supported in part by the Natural Sciences and Engineering Research Council of Canada Discovery Grant 3182.
** Work done while on leave from Department of Information Technology, National Institute of Technology Karnataka, Surathkal, INDIA, 575 025.

M. Kitsuregawa et al. (Eds.): WISE 2005, LNCS 3806, pp. 258–272, 2005.

provider) for executing a high level activity in terms of other, lower level, activities. The low level activities are generally intended to be executed by (other) service providers as services. Therefore the (present or future) availability of services is paramount for the choice and description of the activities in a composition. Thus, we can assume that the composition is designed such that there exist service providers to execute the activities in the composition.

Web service compositions can be classified broadly into two categories [1]. One is primarily for the end-user. We denote this *user* composition. The other is primarily for a composite service provider. We call this *provider* composition. The first type enables design of customized service that fits user requirements. It is typically executed *once*. The second type enables modular, hierarchical, development of highly complex software systems. A composite service of this type is intended to be used in several, varied, higher level compositions. For both types, the first stage is designing the composition using other services and the second stage is finding providers for the selected services and invoking the executions. Functional properties of the services and non-functional properties of the services and providers influence both stages of the composition, somewhat differently for each type. These stages may overlap. Thus, the composition may be *dynamic*. In this paper, we assume that a composition is given (*static composition*) and we consider the problem of finding service providers (*providers*, for short) for executing the composition (*dynamic binding*).

A (basic or composite) service is executed for specified values of input parameters and some constraints, collectively called *input constraints*, and the execution results in some values for output parameters and possibly new constraints, collectively called *output constraints*. Input constraints will usually affect the provider selection. A provider selected for a service is expected to execute the service satisfying the input constraints. Therefore, we assume that the input constraints for the composition are known before, and are used for, binding. We allow for the possibility that only some output constraints will be known before the execution, and others will be known only after the actual execution.

Execution of a composite activity involves execution of all its constituent activities. However, an arbitrary collection of execution instances of the individual activities may not constitute an execution of the composite activity; the individual instances must be "(mutually) compatible". Thus, providers must be selected such that they produce compatible executions of the composition.

We illustrate some of the compatibility requirements with an example.

Example 1: We consider flight reservations for a trip to New Delhi (India) from St. John's (Canada). Since there are no direct flights from St. John's to New Delhi, two flight segments, *Flt*-1 and *Flt*-2, are considered. Some of the ways these flights must be compatible are listed below.

R1. (Connection city) The destination of *Flt*-1 is the origin of *Flt*-2.

The connection city could be any place, for example, Toronto, London, New York, etc., such that flights are available from St. John's to this place, and from this place to New Delhi. The connection city may restrict the choice of airlines for the flights. For example, for *Flt*-2, the choices could be dictated by the following:

- Air Canada and Air India fly from Toronto to New Delhi;
- Lufthansa and United Airlines fly from New York to New Delhi;
- Air India and British Airways fly from London to New Delhi; etc.

R2. (Connection time) The connection time is at least 2 hours.

This could be the minimum time stipulated by the travel industry to complete the formalities of baggage transfer and passenger transfer.

R3. (Connection date) The arrival date of *Flt*-1 is the departure date of *Flt*-2.

This may be an user constraint, to avoid arranging overnight accommodation. However, if the airline provides the accommodation, the user may not object.

R4. (Connecting airport) The arrival airport of *Flt*-1 is the departure airport of *Flt*-2.

For example, if the connection city is New York, if *Flt*-1 arrives at JFK and *Flt*-2 leaves from Newark, then they are not compatible. This may be an user constraint: different airports may necessitate a visa to "enter" the U.S., whereas transit from the same airport may be allowed without a visa; the user may like to avoid applying for the U.S. visa.

R5. (Connecting airlines) The airlines of both the flights should be members of Star Alliance.

This is to get reward points for the air miles. (Air Canada, Lufthansa and United Airlines are some of the members of the Star Alliance.) ☐

This paper deals with mutual compatibility issues. (In the following, unless otherwise stated, by compatibility we mean mutual compatibility.) As illustrated in the example, several compatibility requirements may exist between activities and among the providers to be selected. We propose: (1) a simple formalism to express the compatibility requirements in a composition; and (2) a methodology for (a) the selection of a composite service provider for a composite activity and (b) the selection of (other) service providers for the constituent activities of the composite activity, to ensure an execution of the composition satisfying the compatibility requirements.

In Section 2, we discuss related work. The compatibility formalism is described in Section 3. A detailed example illustrating several aspects of binding and execution of composite services is given in Section 4. Section 5 deals with selections of a composite service provider and a composite service of that provider. Section 6 discusses how to achieve an execution of the composition satisfying the compatibility requirements. Section 7 discusses ways of guaranteeing a successful execution of the composite service. Section 8 concludes the paper.

2   Related Work

Web service composition has been discussed very widely in the literature. Extensive work has been done, and is being done, for the first stage of a composition, namely, mapping user requirements into individual services and putting them together. As stated earlier, our focus is on selecting service providers for, and executing, a given composition.

Considerable attention has been paid for the selection of services for the individual activities of a composition. The selection will be based on how well the requirements in the composition match the capabilities of provided services. Both the requirements and the capabilities need to be stated in as much detail as possible. Several syntactic and semantic details of functional and several non-functional properties have been considered [4, 9, 11, 12, 3].

Exact match between the requirements and the capabilities may not always be possible. Partial match is considered, in terms of *exact, plug in, subsumes* and *fail* in [11, 7], and as *equivalent-to, is-a* and *similar-to* in [2]. These issues are also discussed with respect to substitutability of one service with another (when a need arises) at some stage of the execution. They are referred to as compatibilities between services for executing the (same) activity, and *compatibility classes* containing substitutable services have been discussed. In this context, mutual compatibility property (that is, between services for different activities) is touched upon in terms of substituting one service for another in the context of the neighboring services (successors and predecessors) in the composition.

Some of the papers discussing mutual compatibilities (along with individual compatibilities) are the following. As design principles for composition of services, [12] introduces the concept of *service coupling* as the degree of interdependence between two component services and *service cohesion* as the degree of the strength of functional relatedness of the individual services within a composition. The design goals are to minimize coupling and to strengthen cohesion. [3] mentions three levels of service compatibility - syntactic, semantic, and policy level. Syntactic compatibility is with respect to the specifications, such as matching the output of one service with the input of the subsequent service. Semantic compatibility checks for adherence to domain-specific guidelines. The third refers to compatibility between the policies and rules that the providers of the services impose. In [9], mutual compatibility is referred to as *composability rules* that encompass both syntactic and semantic features of Web services. Further, they define *composition soundness* to determine added value obtained by the selection of a set of services for a composition. [8, 13] talk about added value obtained through composition, quality of service, etc.

[6] defines *input-output, interface* and *behavior* compatibilities. Behavior compatibility requirement includes the other two requirements and considers composition behavior. This notion has been expanded in [5] in two directions: *safety compatibility* and *liveness compatibility*. The first checks whether safety requirements have been implemented and the transitions of activities in the composition satisfy these requirements. Liveness compatibility ensures progress in execution.

3   Compatibility Formalism

In this section, we define a formalism to express the compatibility requirements among activities in a composition. Several kinds of compatibilities can be identified. We classify them broadly into three categories:

1. *Instance level*: For example, the value of an output parameter of one activity becomes the value of input parameter of another activity. An example is the connection city in Example 1.
2. *Activity level*: For instance, data types of an output parameter of an activity and an input parameter of another activity should be the same. An example of incompatibility is when the output is in inches but the input is in cms.
3. *Provider level*: The choice of a provider for one activity restricts the choice of providers for another activity. An example is the connecting airlines in Example 1.

The rationale behind our formalism is:

- A (mutual) compatibility requirement may involve two or more activities (or their instances or their providers). For simplicity, we restrict our attention to those between just two activities. Then we can use graphs with vertices corresponding to activities, and edges indicating compatibility requirements between their end vertices.
- Compatibility requirements do not necessarily dictate precedence relationship. For example, in Example 1, an instance of either *Flt*-1 or *Flt*-2 can be picked first and a compatible instance of the other flight can be looked for, with respect to any of the requirements. Therefore, we choose undirected edges, not directed ones.
- As we have seen in Example 1, there may be many compatibility requirements between two activities. Therefore, we associate a set of requirements with each edge. Each requirement can be stated as a predicate.

We start with the following definition.

Definition 1: For a composition C, the *one-level compatibility graph* $1\text{-}CG(C)$ is an undirected graph $G = (A, E, \chi)$ where vertices A correspond to activities in C, and edges E indicate compatibility requirements between their end points. With edge e, we associate a set $\chi(e)$ of compatibility requirements.   □

Thus, $1\text{-}CG$ describes the activities in one level (top level). The activities may be basic or composite. For a composite activity, say A_i, the user or the composer may have the knowledge of the constituent activities $\{a_{i1}, a_{i2}, ...\}$ of A_i, and may indicate compatibility requirements among them. Again, if a_{ij} is a composite activity, its component activities and compatibility requirements among them may be expressed too. This may go on for several levels. We like to be able to express this. Hence, we generalize our definition as follows.

Definition 2: (a) For a composition consisting of a single activity (and hence no mutual compatibility requirements), the *zero-level compatibility graph*, denoted $0\text{-}CG$, is a single vertex corresponding to that activity.

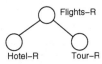

Fig. 1. India trip

(b) For a composition C, the *n-level compatibility graph* n-$CG(C)$, for $n \geq 1$, is an undirected graph $G = (A, E, \chi)$ where vertices A correspond to activities in C, each vertex is an m-CG, for $0 \leq m < n$, and at least one vertex is an $(n-1)$-CG. The edges indicate compatibility requirements between their end points (top level activities). With edge e, we associate a set $\chi(e)$ of compatibility requirements.

(c) A $CG(C)$ is an n-$CG(C)$ for some n.   □

Thus, some (not necessarily all) composite activities can be described in more detail (in "deeper" levels). Figure 1 shows a 1-CG for a composition that extends the composition of Example 1. It contains three activities flight-reservation *Flights-R* that includes segments *Flt*-1 and *Flt*-2 for the forward journey and similar segments *Flt*-3 and *Flt*-4 for the return journey, hotel-reservation *Hotel-R* in New Delhi, and a tour reservation *Tour-R* described in the next section. We consider the simple compatibility requirements that the dates of the hotel stay should correlate to the arrival and departure dates of the reserved flights in New Delhi, and the tour should be on one of the days the user stays in New Delhi. A 2-CG graph for the same composition is shown in Figure 6.

4   Binding and Execution of Service Composition – An Example

Next, we consider binding for a composite service and execution of that service. That is, we show (a) how compatibility graphs can be used to select a composite service provider (CSP) for a composite activity and (b) how that activity can be executed by the CSP satisfying compatibility requirements. We first introduce our methodology through an example. We formalize the concepts in subsequent sections.

Example 2: This is the tour in *Tour-R* mentioned earlier. This is a trip to Agra to visit Taj Mahal. The user may find that the following are some options available for Agra trip.

- Both one-day and two-days trips are available. One-day trip will cover visits to Taj Mahal and Agra Fort, and some shopping. Two-days trip will cover, in addition, Fateh Pur Sikri and a few other nearby attractions.
- Visit to Taj Mahal is possible in mornings, afternoons or evenings.
- Lunches are included in the trips, but they can be skipped.
- Two shopping locations are available, one near Taj Mahal and the other near Agra Fort.
- Wheel chair facility is available.

Suppose the user's requirements (or preferences) are: one-day trip; afternoon or evening, not morning, visit to Taj Mahal; shopping near Taj Mahal; and wheel chair access. Several tour companies offer one or both of one-day and two-days trips. One such company is Lovely-Agra. It offers three types of one-day tours: Morning-Taj; Afternoon-Taj; and Evening-Taj. Each type includes the same four activities, Taj Mahal visit T, Agra Fort visit F, lunch in restaurant L and shopping S, but in different orders, as illustrated in Figure 2.

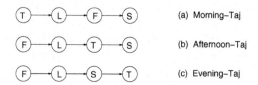

(a) Morning–Taj
(b) Afternoon–Taj
(c) Evening–Taj

Fig. 2. Lovely-Agra one-day tours

The company uses an already selected set of restaurants for lunch, one set near Agra Fort, denoted Fort-Restaurants, and the other near Taj Mahal, called Taj-Restaurants. The two shopping areas are denoted Fort-Shopping and Taj-Shopping. Using compatibility edges to denote vicinity (provider compatibility), the compatibility graphs that Lovely-Agra can guarantee are shown in Figure 3.

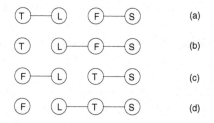

(a)
(b)
(c)
(d)

Fig. 3. Compatability graphs for Lovely-Agra tour company

In Figure 3, (a) and (b) are applicable to Morning-Taj, (c) and (d) for Afternoon-Taj, and (b), (c) and (d) for Evening-Taj tours. We call these provider compatibility graphs *PCGs*. (This and other terminology introduced below are defined formally in subsequent sections.)

We now describe the various steps in binding and execution.

S1. *Selecting a CSP for a composite service (that is, user selecting tour company):* The user requirements, stated above, can be represented by the compatibility graph H in Figure 4.

Fig. 4. User compatability graph for Taj Mahal trip

We call this user compatibility graph UCG. Then the binding process at this level involves selection of a provider such that the UCG is "covered by" a PCG of that provider. (Some other requirements, for example, wheel chair accessibility, have to be considered too.) In our example, H is a subgraph of both the graphs in Figures 3(c) and 3(d), which are applicable to both Afternoon-Taj and Evening-Taj. Hence Lovely-Agra can satisfy the user requirements. Then, the selection process would involve the user requesting a tour reservation for a particular date with Lovely-Agra, and Lovely-Agra accepting the reservation, thus guaranteeing an "execution" satisfying the user requirements. We will assume that this is done at time T_1. The tour company may not take any further steps at this time.

S2. *CSP selecting a (composite) service (that is, the tour company selecting a tour)*: As we have seen above, both 3(c) and 3(d) are appropriate for both Afternoon-Taj and Evening-Taj. The company chooses (perhaps checking with the user) one of them, say Figure 3(c) applied to Afternoon-Taj, some time, say at T_2, prior to the tour date and time. We call this tour 3(c)-Afternoon.

S3. *Selecting a service instance*: Several groups may be present for 3(c)-Afternoon. One of them, denoted 3(c)A, is selected for our user, say at time T_3. We will assume that selection of the tour 3(c)A includes assignments of a van with wheel chair facility and a tour guide.

S4. *Selecting providers for the constituent activities of the service instance*: In our case, the only remaining selection is a restaurant, say Res-A, (among Fort-Restaurants) for lunch, for the day of the tour, say at time T_4.

We note that it is likely that $T_1 \leq T_2 \leq T_3 \leq T_4$.   □

We describe the steps in detail in the following sections.

5   Selection of a Composite Service Provider and a Composite Service

In this section, we describe how a CSP can be selected for a composite activity C in a (user or higher level) composition, and then how a composite service can be selected by that CSP. Both the selections are based on compatibility graphs. Our proposal uses only the top level details of the composition, that is, 1-CG's. (Dealing with general n-CG's is left for future work.)

First, we introduce some terminology.

Definition 3: Let $G = (A, E, \chi)$ and $H = (A', E', \chi')$ be two compatibility graphs. We say that H *is covered by* G or G *covers* H, denoted $H \sqsubseteq G$, if (i) $A' \subseteq A$, (ii) $E' \subseteq E$ and the incidence relation of the edges is preserved, and (iii) for each edge e in E', $\chi'(e) \subseteq \chi(e)$. If $H \sqsubseteq G$ but $H \neq G$, then we say H *is properly covered by* G or G *properly covers* H and denote this as $H \sqsubset G$.   □

The compatibility graph of C reflecting the user requirements is called the *User Compatibility Graph (UCG)*. In general, a CSP can execute several (somewhat related) compositions. Each composition can be described by a compati-

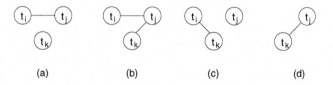

(a)   (b)   (c)   (d)

Fig. 5. Provider compatability graphs

bility graph. We call this a *provider compatibility graph (PCG)*. The set of such graphs, one for each composition that the CSP can execute, is denoted *PCG-set*.

Figure 5 shows such a set for activities t_i, t_j, and t_k. Among these graphs, we choose the maximal ones (with respect to covering), and group them into the *maximal PCG-set*, denoted *MPCG-set*. The graphs in Figure 5(b) and 5(c) constitute the *MPCG-set*. Then:

S1. CSP selection: A composite service provider P_C can be selected for a composite activity C, if the user compatibility graph for C is covered by some graph H in $MPCG\text{-}set(P_C)$, that is, if $UCG(C) \sqsubseteq H$.

For Agra-Trip by Lovely-Agra, *PCG-set* (and also *MPCG-set*) contains all the graphs in Figure 3.

The next step is the selection of a composite service by the CSP P_C.

S2. Composite service selection: Let H be a graph in $PCG\text{-}set(P_C)$ that covers $UCG(C)$. Then any composite service C' of P_C such that $CG(C')$ is H can be selected.

We note the following:

– H is from $PCG(P_C)$ for the composite service selection, whereas it is from $MPCG(P_C)$ for the CSP selection. This is because we presume that the *MPCG-set* will be smaller than *PCG-set*, and hence checking for covering of *UCG* will be faster.
– Several services of P_C may have the same CG's, as illustrated in Example 2.

Next, we have:

S3. Selection of a service instance: We allow for the possibility of several (pre-defined) instances of the composite service H. One of those instances can be selected.

Non-functional properties may play a role in this selection process. We do not address this aspect in this paper.

6   Compatible Executions

In this section, we consider execution of a composite service (instance) by a CSP using service providers for the constituent activities. Consider, for example, a composition consisting of two activities t_i and t_j with an edge e between them. Let ρ be a compatibility requirement in $\chi(e)$. We need to find providers, say P_1 for t_i, and P_2 for t_j, such that they produce instances of t_i and t_j that satisfy the requirement ρ. Three cases arise:

1. For any instance of t_j by P_2, P_1 may guarantee a compatible instance of t_i. Then P_2 can be executed first, and then (with the output constraints of t_j possibly contributing to the input constraints of t_i,) P_1 can be executed.
2. For any instance of t_i by P_1, P_2 may guarantee a compatible instance of t_j. Then P_1 can be executed first, and then (with the output constraints of t_i possibly contributing to the input constraints of t_j,) P_2 can be executed.
3. Compatible instances of t_i and t_j may have to be found by trial and error, doing some kind of exhaustive search. This responsibility can be assigned to P_C, the CSP executing C, or some other provider. This provider can get an instance of t_i by P_1, try for a compatible instance of t_j by P_2. If unsuccessful, execute P_1 again to get another instance of t_i, then try for a compatible instance of t_j by P_2 again, and so on.

That is, we suggest that *some service provider be given responsibility to satisfy the compatibility requirement*. In the above example, the responsibility for ρ is given to P_1 in case 1, P_2 in case 2, and P_C or some other provider in case 3. Then:

Binding for a composite activity: Binding for C should involve selection of service providers for each activity of C *and* for each compatibility requirement (of each compatibility edge) of the $CG(C)$.

Example 3: For the composition shown in Figure 6, considering the simple compatibility requirement stated earlier, between *Flights-R* and *Hotel-R*, that the dates of the hotel stay should correlate to the arrival and departure dates of the reserved flights in New Delhi, a provider P_F for *Flights-R* and a provider P_H for *Hotel-R* would suffice if either P_H can guarantee hotel for any days that P_F comes up with, or if P_F can find flights for any days that P_H can find accommodation, within the travel period stipulated by the user. In the case

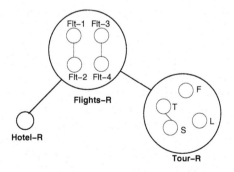

Fig. 6. User composition graph for India trip

where flights are not available every day and hotel accommodation is also not guaranteed for every day, a third provider who will check and find compatible flights and hotel reservations will be needed. (Again, this third provider could be P_C, the CSP, a travel agent in this example.) Similarly, the compatibility requirement between *Flights-R* and *Tour-R*, namely, Agra trip should be on one of the days the user stays in New Delhi, can be considered as the responsibility of *Tour-R* assuming that the tours are available every day.   □

We have allowed for several compatibility requirements to be associated with an edge. Different service providers may be selected for different requirements. For instance, in *Flights-R*, if two of the compatibility requirements between *Flt-1* and *Flt-2* were (*Flt-1* connects to *Flt-2* on the same day or overnight accommodation has to be provided) and (connection airport should be the same or transportation between the airports have to be provided), then one provider, say one of the airlines, may arrange accommodation, and another provider, say an inter-airport transit bus, can be used for transportation.

It is possible that P_1 and P_2 are the same. That is, both t_i and t_j are assigned to the same service provider P_1. Still, the compatibility requirements of e could be assigned to different providers. For example, a recreation complex and a hotel could be operated by the same provider, but the transportation between the two may be the responsibility of a rental car agency or a taxi company. However, in several situations, it may be reasonable to expect that P_1 takes responsibility for $\chi(e)$ also. That is, the provider selected for multiple activities takes care of the compatibility requirements among those activities. *This would be the added value provided by the CSP.*

Further on selection of CSP. A CSP can be selected for one or more activities of a composition and the compatibility requirements between those activities.

For example, for the composition with the compatibility graph of Figure 6, a travel agent Exotic Travels can be selected for *Flights-R, Hotel-R* and the compatibility requirement between them.

7   Guaranteeing a Composite Service Execution

When we bind a service provider for executing a service with certain input constraints, we expect that the provider can guarantee an execution of that service. This holds for a CSP also.

Consider again an execution of C by a CSP P_C. As stated earlier, P_C needs to find providers for each of the activities and the compatibility requirements of C. In general, to find a combination of providers that can produce compatible instances of activities, (at least a limited form of) exhaustive search may be required. This may be time consuming and, in theory, the execution may still fail due to unavailability of suitable providers. To be able to guarantee a successful execution, the CSP can pre-select a set of combinations of providers, on the basis of some exhaustive search done in advance, and choose one combination among them, appropriate for the given input constraints, for actual execution.

S4(a). Binding providers for executing a $CG(C)$ - Method 1: Let PS denote a set of providers that can be assigned to execute the activities and to be responsible for compatibility requirements of C. (That is, it contains one (not necessarily distinct) provider for each activity and each compatibility requirement.) Let $\mathcal{PS}$ denote a set of such provider sets $\{PS_1, PS_2, ...\}$. Then, binding for C amounts to selecting a PS_i from $\mathcal{PS}$.

Example 4: In Example 1, several instances of *Flt*-1 may have to be checked against several instances of *Flt*-2. In general, for each airline flying from St. John's, and for each destination that airline flies, possibility of connections from that destination to New Delhi has to be checked, again for different airlines. The search can be limited by pre-selection of provider sets like the following:

- {Air Canada (for both St. John's to Toronto, and Toronto to New Delhi flights)};
- {Air Canada (for St. John's to London), Hilton Airport hotel in London (for overnight accommodation), Air India (for London to New Delhi flight)}; and
- {Air Canada (for St. John's to New York Newark airport), Yellow Cab (for transportation from Newark to JFK), United Airlines (for New York JFK to New Delhi)}.

These combinations are pre-determined by the travel agent with the knowledge of the airlines schedules, transportation facility in New York and airport hotels in London. The travel agent will pick one of these sets appropriate to the input constraints. □

In this method, $\mathcal{PS}$ can be updated periodically by the CSP.

An alternate method is to have a collection of sets of providers for the individual activities and compatibility requirements of the composition graph, and select one provider for each activity and each requirement from the respective sets, again based on the input constraints.

S4(b). Binding providers for executing a $CG(C)$ - Method 2: Denoting provider sets for activities as $\mathcal{P}_i$'s and those for compatibility requirements as $\mathcal{P}_{\rho j}$'s, let $\mathcal{PC}$ denote $\{\mathcal{P}_1, \mathcal{P}_2, ..., \mathcal{P}_{\rho 1}, \mathcal{P}_{\rho 2}, ...\}$. Then, binding for C amounts to selecting a provider from each of $\mathcal{P}_i$ and $\mathcal{P}_{\rho j}$ in $\mathcal{PC}$.

Here, each set $\mathcal{P}_i$ and $\mathcal{P}_{\rho j}$ can be updated periodically by the CSP. In the special case where each compatibility requirement of an edge can be taken care of by the providers of either of the end vertices of that edge, this method requires just an assignment of a set of providers for each of the activities. In the above example, $\mathcal{P}_1$, for *Flt*-1, can be {Air Canada}, and $\mathcal{P}_2$, for *Flt*-2, can be {Air Canada, Air India, United Airlines} assuming that all the compatibility requirements can be taken care of by each of these airlines. Then the travel agent can pick one airline from $\mathcal{P}_1$ and one from $\mathcal{P}_2$. Here, contents of each $\mathcal{P}_i$ can be altered depending on the availability of airlines, for future bindings.

We note that each method provides different type of flexibility in the selection of service providers. It is also possible to have a scheme that combines both methods. Roughly, provider level and possibly even activity level compatibility requirements can be taken care of in such pre-selection, thus guaranteeing that the selected providers will succeed in executing C, whereas the instance level compatibilities still need to be ensured, perhaps by trial and error, by the selected providers, during execution.

8   Discussion

Execution of a composite service involves execution of the constituent activities satisfying certain compatibility requirements among them. This paper is concerned with issues relating to (mutual) compatibility requirements. In the following, we bring out the salient points of our contributions.

(1) Service descriptions need to encompass several semantic details in addition to syntactic ones for selecting appropriate services for the activities [4, 9, 3]. Our compatibility graph formalism adds to the semantic description of a composition or composite service. We note that there may be other, more elaborate, ways of expressing the compatibility requirements. We believe that our methodology for binding and execution is applicable to any such formalism.

(2) "Binding for a service" usually means selection of a service provider to execute that service. Accordingly, binding for a composite service involves selection of a composite service provider for executing that composite service. It is understood that, recursively, providers need to be selected for the constituent activities of the composite activity, and so on. In this work, we have brought out that the binding task (for composite activity) is still incomplete.

- We have suggested that service providers be identified explicitly for each compatibility requirement also, in addition to for each activity. This proposal is new. To our knowledge, this does not appear in the literature. We note that this idea has been advocated, implicitly, for certain (activity level) compatibility requirements in [10]. Services and hence service providers have been used to bridge "mismatch" between input and output types. For instance, inch-to-cm converters have been used, in an example, to convert the output of an activity in inches to input of another activity in cms. Our proposal allows for any type of compatibility requirement.
- We have identified two more stages of binding, after a CSP has been selected and before the providers for executing the composition are selected: (a) selecting a composite service; and (b) selecting an instance of that composite service, both by the CSP. Different (matching) algorithms can be designed for each of these.

(3) Again, binding for a (multi-level hierarchical) composite activity involves binding for its constituent activities and compatibility requirements at every level

of its composition. For guaranteed execution of a (static) composition, we may wish to select all necessary providers before starting the execution. This can be done one level at a time. That is, at each level of the composition, once providers are selected for all activities (and compatibility requirements) in that level, the execution in that level can start. We elaborate this aspect in the following. Consider a composition C consisting of activities A_1, A_2, etc. We need to find service providers for each A_i and each compatibility requirement involving A_i's. As soon as we find them, the execution of C can start. Suppose A_1 is a composite service, and P_1 is selected for A_1. Then, P_1 may have to employ service providers for its activities $a_1, a_2, ...$, and compatibility requirements between them. We stipulate that service providers for these be found *some time before* starting the execution of A_1, and not necessarily before starting the execution of the high level composition C. For example, in the user compatibility graph of Figure 6, as soon as providers are found for *Flights-R, Hotel-R* and *Tour-R*, the execution can start. That is, the reservations can be made by the respective providers and the user can even start the trip. The CSP for *Tour-R*, namely, Lovely-Agra, needs to bind providers for its activities T, F, L and S. This can be done some time before the tour starts, as illustrated in Example 2. Thus, we can deal with binding one level at a time. Therefore, our method scales well with any number of levels in the composition.

(4) We are able to strengthen the notion of "added value" offered by a CSP to include the property of satisfying compatibility requirements among the individual activities in the composite service, when all activities and responsibility for all compatibility requirements among them are assigned to the same CSP. [10] also argues that addition of services like inch-cm-converter increases the added value of a CSP employed for the main functionality.

(5) We have restricted our attention to static composition in this paper. We believe, and we have indicated in the paper, that such restriction is quite appropriate for provider compositions. With that restriction, we have concentrated on the guaranteed execution property which is a prominent requirement in several applications. (A typical example is e-Government applications.) Nevertheless, most of our proposals (user compatibility graph, provider compatibility graph, selection process for CSP, etc.) are useful in dynamic composition scenario also.

Compatibility requirements have been discussed widely in the literature. Many different compatibility notions have been proposed. We have mentioned a few of them in the section on related work. Many descriptions are vague and intuitive. Attempts are being made to define more precisely and classify them. Examples are syntactic, semantic, and policy level compatibilities of [3], and input-output, interface and behavior [6], and further safety and liveness [5] compatibilities. These classifications are orthogonal to each other. For example, some policy level requirements may relate to safety, and some others may related to interface compatibilities. Our classification as instance, activity and provider levels is orthogonal to each of the above. We cannot expect a single formalism and mechanism to take care of all compatibility requirements. Some requirements are accommodated through ontologies, some others by policy enforcements, etc. In this paper, we have addressed how, and when, to take care of (several) mutual compatibility requirements in Web service compositions.

Acknowledgement. It is a pleasure to thank Debmalya Biswas for many helpful suggestions that improved the presentation.

References

[1] Stanislaw Ambroszkiewicz: *enTish: An Approach to Service Composition*, Technologies for E-Services, 4th International Workshop on TES 2003, pp. 168–178.

[2] Valeria De Antonellis, Michele Melchiori, Barbara Pernici, and Pierluigi Plebani: *A Methodolgy for e-Service Substitutability in a Virtual District Environment*, 15*th* Int. Conf. Advanced Information Systems Engineering, 2003, pp. 552–567.

[3] Soon Ae Chun, Vijayalakshmi Atluri, Nabil R. Adam: *Policy-based Web Service Composition*, Proc. of the 14th Int. Workshop on Research Issues on Data Engineering: Web Services for E-Commerce and E-Government Applications (RIDE'04), pp. 85–92.

[4] A. Dogac, Y. Kabak, G. Laleci, S. Sinir, A. Yildiz, S. Kirbas, Y. Gurcan: *Semantically Enriched Web Services for the Travel Industry*, SIGMOD Record, Vol. 33, No. 3, pp. 21–27, 2004.

[5] Howard Foster, Sebastian Uchitel, Jeff Magee, Jeff Kramer: *Compatibility Verification for Web Service Choreography*, Proceedings of 2nd International Conference on Web Services (ICWS 2004), San Diego, pp. 738–741.

[6] Magnus Larsson, Ivica Crnkovic: *New Challenges for Configuration Management*, Proceedings of Ninth International Symposium on System Configuration Management, SCM-9, 1999, LNCS 1675, pp. 232-243.

[7] Mikko Laukkanen, Heikki Helin: *Composing Workflows of Semantic Web Services*, Proc. of the Workshop on Web-Services and Agent-based Engineering, 2003.

[8] Yutu Liu, Anne H.H. Ngu, Liangzhao Zeng: *QoS Computation and Policing in Dynamic Web Service Selection*, Proc. of the 13th Int. Conf. on WWW 2004, pp.66–73.

[9] Brahim Medjahed, Athman Bouguettaya, Ahmed K. Elmagarmid: *Composing Web Services on the Semantic Web*, The VLDB Journal 2003, pp. 333–351.

[10] Mihhail Matskin, Jinghai Rao: *Value-Added Web Services Composition Using Automatic Program Synthesis*, Proc. of Web Services, e-Business, and the Semantic Web workshop, Canada, 2002, LNCS 2512, Springer-Verlag, pp. 213–224.

[11] Massimo Paolucci, Takahiro Kawamura, Terry R. Payne, Katia Sycara: *Semantic Matching of Web Services Capabilities*, Proc. of the First Int. Semantic Web Conference 2002, LNCS 2342, pp. 333–347.

[12] Mike P. Papazoglou and Jian Yang: *Design Methodology for Web Services and Business Processes*, Proc. of TES 2002, LNCS 2444, pp. 54–64, 2002.

[13] Liangzhao Zeng, Boualem Benatallah, Marlon Dumas, Jayant Kalagnanam, Quan Z. Sheng: *Quality Driven Web Services Composition*, Proc. of the 12th Int. Conf. on WWW 2003, pp. 411–421.

Handling Transactional Properties in Web Service Composition

Marie-Christine Fauvet[1], Helga Duarte[1,*],
Marlon Dumas[2], and Boualem Benatallah[3]

[1] Joseph Fourier University of Grenoble, CLIPS-IMAG Laboratory,
BP 53, 38041 Grenoble Cedex 9, France
{Marie-Christine.Fauvet, Helga.Duarte}@imag.fr
[2] Centre for Information Technology Innovation, QUT,
GPO Box 2434, Brisbane QLD 4001, Australia
m.dumas@qut.edu.au
[3] School of Computer Science and Engineering, UNSW,
Sydney 2052, Australia
boualem@cse.unsw.edu.au

Abstract. The development of new services by composition of existing ones has gained considerable momentum as a means of integrating heterogeneous applications and realising business collaborations. Services that enter into compositions with other services may have transactional properties, especially those in the broad area of resource management (e.g. booking services). These transactional properties may be exploited in order to derive composite services which themselves exhibit certain transactional properties. This paper presents a model for composing services that expose transactional properties and more specifically, services that support tentative holds and/or atomic execution. The proposed model is based on a high-level service composition operator that produces composite services that satisfy specified atomicity constraints. The model supports the possibility of selecting the services that enter into a composition at runtime, depending on their ability to provide resource reservations at a given point in time and taking into account user preferences.

1 Introduction

Web services constitute a rapidly emerging technology that promises to revolutionise the way in which applications interact over the Web. Established organisations are discovering new opportunities to conduct business by providing access to their enterprise information systems through Web services. This trend has led to a paradigm known as Service-Oriented Computing (SOC) wherein information and computational resources are abstracted as (Web) services which are then interconnected using a collection of Internet-based standards.

* H. Duarte is financially supported by the European Union Programme of High Level Scholarships for Latin America (id. E03D13487CO) and the National University of Colombia.

M. Kitsuregawa et al. (Eds.): WISE 2005, LNCS 3806, pp. 273–289, 2005.

In this setting, the development of new services by composition of existing ones has gained considerable momentum as a means of integrating heterogeneous applications and realising business collaborations. The execution of a service obtained by composition, also known as a *composite service*, involves a series of interactions with the underlying *component services* in order to access their functionality. The logic of a composite service (also known as the *orchestration* model) determines, among other things, the interactions that need to occur, the order of these interactions, and the escalation procedures that should be triggered under specified exceptional situations (e.g. faults arising during the interactions). Importantly, the components of a composite service retain their autonomy, that is, they are free to enter into interactions with other services (whether composite or not).

Some services, for example in the area of electronic commerce, possess inherent transactional properties [1]. This is the case in particular of services associated with the management of resources with limited capacity (e.g. accommodation booking), the management of shared physical or human assets (e.g. short-term rental of equipment, hiring of professional services), or the sales of goods where demand tends to exceed supply (e.g. ticket sales services). In principle, these transactional properties can be exploited during service composition in order to fulfil constraints and preferences specified by the designer or the user of the composite service. At present however, the language and platforms supporting the development of transactional applications over (Web) services do not provide high-level concepts for : (i) expressing the transactional properties that composite services are required to fulfil; and (ii) automatically ensuring that these properties are fulfilled by exploiting the transactional properties of the underlying component services.

The aim of the work reported in this paper is to propose a model for the composition of Web services with transactional properties that takes into account the above requirements. Specifically, the paper focuses on ensuring atomicity properties. The main contribution of the paper is the definition of a service composition operator that exploits the atomicity properties and reservation functionality of the component services in order to ensure atomicity properties at the level of the resulting composite service. In particular, the operator supports the modelling of minimality and maximality constraints over the set of services entering into a transaction in the context of an execution of a composite service. Using the proposed model, it is possible to capture constraints such as "between X and Y component services must execute successfully up to completion or else no service must execute successfully up to completion" (i.e. up to the point where the underlying resource has been assigned to the composite service). For example, given four services A, B, C and D, the user of a service obtained by composition of these four services can specify that at least 2, but not more than 3 services among {A, B, C, D} must complete or none must complete, by setting the minimum and maximum bounds to 2 and 3 respectively. In addition, the proposed operator is parameterised so as to allow the end user to impose that certain domain-specific constraints and preferences are satisfied by the executions of the composite service.

The execution model underpinning the proposed composition operator relies on the *Tentative Hold Protocol* (THP) [2] to tentatively reserve the resources managed by the component services, as well as a variant of the Two-Phase Commit (2PC) protocol to perform the transaction once all the tentative reservations have been obtained. Note that this is not a fundamentally restrictive assumption, since tentative holds, as opposed to definite reservations do not force the service to lock a resource for a given client. So regardless of its atomicity properties (or absence thereof) the operations associated to THP can be implemented on any given service. This combination maximises the chances of achieving a successful transaction while avoiding blocking resources for relatively long periods of time. In addition, the execution model incorporates a runtime service selection mechanism, so that if a given component service is not able to provide a given resources, it can be replaced by another one among a set of candidate component services. This selection takes into account the constraints and preferences provided as parameter to the composition operator.

The remainder of the document is structured as follows. In Section 2 we frame the problem addressed in this paper and discuss related work. A scenario illustrating the proposed approach is then presented in Section 3. In Sections 4 and 5 we introduce the service composition model and the underlying execution model respectively. Finally, Section 6 draws some conclusion and discusses directions for future work.

2   Motivation and Related Work

The execution of composite services with transactional properties is generally based on long-lived complex distributed transactions that may involve compensation mechanisms. A significant number of transactional models have been proposed in various contexts, including database systems, cooperative information systems, and software configuration management [3, 4, 5, 6]. However, these models are not designed to address the following combination of challenges posed by the environment in which (Web) services operate:

- *Heterogeneity of transactional properties.* Whereas it is reasonable to assume that certain services will provide the operations required to participate in 2PC procedures and will expose these operations in a standardised manner as part of their interfaces, it is not realistic to expect that all services will do so. Some services will simply not provide transactional properties, or will provide them but not to the same level and in the same way as others. This may be due to purely technical issues (e.g. a given service provides operations corresponding to those required by 2PC but in a non-standard manner), or it may result from the choice of business model (e.g. the service provider is not willing to let clients lock its resources) or it may ensue from the inherent nature of a service (e.g. the notion of locks does not make sense for a given service). In addition, certain services will not offer the operations associated with 2PC, but may will instead offer compensation operations, possibly with associated costs like in the case of services for which the rights can be rescinded with associated penalties.

- *Limited duration of reservations and cost of compensation.* Even when a service does offer operations allowing it to participate in 2PC procedures (or when it offers compensation operations), it is crucial to minimise the duration between the two phases of the 2PC protocol (or to minimise the need for compensations to avoid the associated costs). In the field of electronic commerce for example, certain services only allow one to lock resources for a very limited period of time. This raises coordination problems when the number of services involved in a transaction is high and they need to be synchronised.
- *Need for dynamic service selection support.* The choice of services that will complete a given transaction may be performed dynamically (during the execution of the transaction) and hence it is not realistic to assume that this information will be known in advance. This is partly due to the fact that several services may offer the same functionality (or rather *capability*). Thus, when the execution of a given service fails during the first phase of the 2PC protocol, it is possible to replace it with another service providing the same capability so that the transaction can still proceed.

It is commonly accepted that traditional approaches for achieving transactions with ACID (*Atomicity, Consistency, Isolation, Durability*) properties are not suitable for long-running transactions like those found in the area of Web services, since it is not acceptable to lock a given resource managed by a service while work is being performed in parallel by other services and/or until locks for the resources managed by other services (which may end up refusing to grant these locks) are obtained. In addition, the 2PC protocol which is commonly used in distributed systems is not applicable in the context of composite service execution since this protocol assumes that all the partners participating in a transaction support the operations of preparation and validation essential to this protocol, and this assumption does not generally hold in the case of Web services as explained in the previous section. Furthermore, given the competing/substitutable (i.e. one or the other) relations that may exist between services that provide the same capability, it is appropriate not to restrict atomicity to the traditional all-or-none property, but instead to consider minimality and maximality constraints over the set of services that participate in a transaction as part of the execution of a composite service. Finally, integration issues need to be considered since the services participating in a composition may potentially each rely on a different type of transaction management system and/or expose its transactional operations in a different manner. This latter aspect is the main motivation for protocols such as *WS-Coordination* [7], *WS-AtomicTransaction* [8] which aim at defining standardised ways for services to interact with transactional coordinators in order to set up, join, and validate transactions.

In this paper we address the issues identified above by proposing a high-level operator that allows designers to compose sets of services (with or without transactional properties) and to specify atomicity constraints of the form *between X and Y component services must validate (i.e. complete their execution up to the validation phase), or else none of them should validate*. Such constraints are relevant in a broad range of applications, and in particular in electronic commerce applications as motivated in [9]. In addition to being parameterised by minimality and maximality constraints (i.e. variables X and Y in the statement above), the operator admits as parameters, restriction and preference functions that guide the (runtime) selection of services that are to participate in the selection of component services (among the pool of possible component services) as well as the replacement of services when some of the selected services fail to arrive up to the validation phase (e.g. because the resource that they manage is unavailable under the constraints captured by the composition).

The execution model associated with this composition operator relies on the THP protocol [2] to acquire tentative reservations on the resources managed by the component services and thus increase the probability of completing the transaction successfully with the subset of component services initially selected. A variant of the 2PC protocol is then used to complete the transaction. This variant takes into account the fact that some services do not provide the operations required by the 2PC protocol, i.e. services that do not provide atomicity properties, services for which atomicity is irrelevant, and services that offer compensation operations rather than supporting definitive reservations.

The THP protocol is intended to facilitate the automated coordination of multi-process business transactions. It is an open protocol operating over a loosely coupled architecture based on message exchanges between processes prior to a transaction. The idea is to allow a process to register an intention to acquire a resource managed by a service (i.e. a *tentative hold*) and from that point on, to be notified of changes in the availability of this resource. When the resource is definitely acquired by a process, a message is sent to all other registered processes to inform them that the resource is no longer available. This protocol thus allows processes to maintain up-to-date information regarding the ability for a set of resource management services to enter into a given transaction, thus maximising the chances that the transaction is successfully completed.

The idea of separating between a tentative reservation phase and a "definitive" reservation phase has previously been considered in the area of distributed component transactions. In [10] for example, a protocol similar to THP is employed during the so-called *negotiation* phase while the 2PC protocol is used to complete the transaction. This prior proposal differs from ours in at least two ways. Firstly, the proposed approach takes into account services that do not provide the operations required by the 2PC protocol. For a number of reasons as outlined above, such *non-transactional* services are numerous in the area of electronic commerce and business process management which are prominent application areas of SOC [11, 1]. Because of this, we do not use the traditional 2PC protocol but rather an extension of it. Secondly, our model allows designers to express maximality and minimality constraints over the set of services that are expected to go through the validation phase, as well as restriction and preference functions that are used to perform dynamic service selection. In contrast, the model put forward in [10] is limited to all-or-none transactions and does not take into account dynamic selection of the components entering into a composition.

The same comparative remarks apply to previously proposed web service transaction models based on THP and 2PC such as the one proposed in [12].

In [13] the authors present a multi-level model for service composition that covers the specification of composite services from the user-interface level of abstraction down to the implementation of transactional operations. However, this approach supports only "all or none" transactions whereas our model supports minimality and maximality constraints as discussed above. On the other hand, the model in [13] supports "all or none" executions of composite services that include sequentially ordered tasks. To achieve this, the model in [13] distinguishes tasks with different transactional characteristics, namely atomic, compensable and pivot tasks as defined in [11] and characterises a class of sequential arrangements of such tasks for which all or none execution can be guaranteed.

Another related work is [14], where a workflow-based approach is proposed to deal with workflow flexibility issues. This approach has a different scope than ours as it relies on transactions to enforce the atomicity of a set of modifications to be applied to a workflow specification.

3   Scenario

As a working and motivating example, we consider a scenario that arises when one wants to organise a meeting to be held at a given day. Potential participants must be invited, a room must be booked and catering must be arranged. To keep the example simple we assume the meeting to last only one day.

The organiser of the meeting determines that the meeting should be organised according to the following rules, which capture either restrictions or preferences:

- Restrictions: the person X should participate, consequently she has to be available at the given day, otherwise the meeting is postponed. To make sense, a minimum number of persons must participate (at least min but not more than max). Eventually the global cost (catering and room cost) cannot exceed a given budget.
- Preferences: the number of participants should be maximised and the global cost minimised.

For the sake of simplicity, both catering and room are arranged for an average number of people $((min+max)/2)$.

The organisation of the meeting succeeds only if all restriction rules given above are met, otherwise the meeting is cancelled. In addition, the organisation is done in a way that satisfies the preferences as much as possible.

To model this example, we define Meeting Organisation (MO in short) as a composite service type that captures the process of organising meetings as described above. MO relies on three other processes, each of which is modelled by a service type: Room for booking function rooms and Caterer for arranging food and drinks. The process of contacting participants to arrange a meeting is also modelled as a composite service type, namely Participant Invitation (PI in short).

The type PI results from the composition of service types each of which is associated to a potential participant's diary. Let pi be a service of type PI: services that compose pi have been selected in order to ensure pi to satisfy the restriction rules associated with it. pi's executions are performed as follows: pi processes requests to diary services hoping to obtain a successful booking at the given day. We assume here, that all diary services support the operations needed to manage such booking. When pi interacts with its service components, it does so according to their transactional properties and in a way that satisfies as much as possible the preferences defined at composition time by the designer. The outcome of this interaction process is to build a suitable set of diary services, such that each service in this set provides an operation to perform a booking on a given day (and possibly also other operations). If the resulting set contains X's diary and if its size is greater than min and less than max, then the service pi can complete successfully, otherwise it fails.

The service mo of type MO, responsible for organising the meeting, coordinates the execution of its component services: pi of type PI, r of type Room and c of type Caterer. r and c successfully complete only if they could be booked at the given day and if the total cost is less than the budget decided at design time. r and c have been chosen in order to minimise expenses.

4   Composition Model

This section introduces a composition model which aims at providing features for composing services and associating transactional properties to the resulting composite services. The proposed model handles the transactional properties of a composite service according to those exposed by the component services.

Our aim is not to define yet another model for Web service composition or another language for service description, but rather to abstract usual concepts used in many approaches (see for example [15, 16, 17]) and standards (see for example [18, 8, 19]). We introduce here an abstract notation that will enable some form of reasoning on transactional properties of Web services. In Section 4.1 we introduce an abstract data type-based notation for the purpose of Web service modelling. In Section 4.2 we then study a composition operator. Finally, Section 4.3 discusses transactional properties of services resulting from a composition.

4.1   Service Design

In the study reported here, we focus on Web services that offer resources to clients (e.g. flight tickets that can be purchased by customers). Interactions between the service that offers a resource and the clients interested in it, are usually encapsulated within a transaction. In the following we intend to characterise a Web service according to the properties of the transactions it can handle [11]:

– A service is said to be **atomic** (e.g. associated with the "all or nothing" semantics) when it provides the following operations: resource reservation (equivalent to the preparation phase of the 2PC protocol), cancellation, and validation.

- A service is **quasi-atomic**, when it supports a validation operation (i.e. an operation that performs the work involving the resource such as booking a flight seat), and a compensation function which undoes the effect of the validation (e.g. releasing the flight seat and applying a penalty).
- A service is defined as **non-atomic**, when the only operation it offers on resources is validation. It does not support neither (definite) reservation nor cancellation nor compensation.

In the sequel, we formally capture the notion of service and other related notions by describing a set of abstract types and operations. We adopt a functional style as it gives a high level and syntax-independent framework to describe types and operations. The following notations are used: T1 $\longrightarrow$ T2 stands for the type of all functions with domain T1 and range T2. {T} denotes the type of sets of T. The following functional specification introduces the Service abstract data type (ADT) and its elementary selectors.

type Service
  { *The type Service models an offer of a set of operations (e.g. books sells and buys).* *An instance of type Service models a software entity capable of providing* *these operations. Clients can access this entity using the operations it offers.*}
type Client
  { *An instance of the type Client models a customer (whether it is a person, an* *organisation or a service instance) who, after appropriate authentication, is* *allowed to access service instances.*}
property: Service $\longrightarrow$ {atomic, quasi-atomic, non-atomic}
  { *property(s) returns the transactional characteristic of service s (see Section 2).*}

With these conventions, the working example (see Section 3) can be formalised as follows:

Caterer: sub-type of Service
  { *An instance of Caterer represents an enterprise providing catering functions.*}
cost : Service, Resource, Client $\longrightarrow$ real
  { *cost(s, r, c) returns the price the customer c has to pay to purchase the resource* *r supplied by s.*}
Room: sub-type of Service
  { *An instance of Room represents an enterprise that proposes function rooms for rent.*}
Diary: sub-type of Service
D_1, ..., D_n: sub-types of Diary
  { *A Diary type D_i (i $\in$ [1..n]) is associated to each potential participant. We associate* *a type Diary to each potential participant. Doing so allows us to offer an homogeneous* *notation, even though there will not be more than a service associated to each type.*}
holder: Diary $\longrightarrow$ string
  { *holder(d) returns the name of d's holder.*}

Below we describe the operations supported by all services. The semantics of these operation is defined according to the transactional properties of the services. The following operations are provided by atomic services:

ReserveR, ReleaseR, ValidateR: Service, Resource, Client ⟶ boolean

> *{ReserveR (s, r, c) ⟺ resource r is reserved by service s for client c (this is a definite reservation as opposed to a tentative hold).}*
> *{ReleaseR (s, r, c) ⟺ client c has released resource r managed by service s. Pre-condition : ReserveR (s, r, c)}*
> *{ValidateR (s, r, c) ⟺ client c has definitely acquired resource r managed by s (Note: it is not mandatory for a client to reserve a resource first).}*

The operations provided by services whose executions are quasi-atomic are ValidateR introduced above and CompensateR describes below:

CompensateR: Service, Resource, Client ⟶ nil

> *{CompensateR (s, r, c) compensates the purchase by client c of resource r managed by service s.*

Finally, non-atomic services provide only one operation, namely ValidateR defined above.

4.2   Parallel Composition Operator

Composite service types can be built by using the parallel composition operator among others. As a first stage, and to focus on transaction issues we chose to limit the scope of this paper to parallel compositions only. Extending our approach to a set of operators (such as condition or sequence) is one of our further studies. Applying this operator to a set of service types with transactional properties defines a new composite service type whose transactional properties are derived from the types of the component services, at composition time.

It is worth noting that in this paper we do not consider sequential composition of services (e.g. dependencies imposing that a service must fully complete before another one can start). In order to support such control dependencies in the context of a transactional service composition model, techniques from the area of long-running database transactions and transactional business processes (see for example the concept of Sagas [20, 11]) would need to be incorporated. Dealing with such issues is outside the scope of this paper and integration in our model of a more complete set of composition operators is left as a direction for future work.

The parallel operator is parameterised by:

- The set of component service types {T1, T2, .., Tn}.
- The range of values for the number of component services which must successfully complete. This range is specified by the minimum and the maximum values (min ≤ max ≤ n), thereby offering more flexibility for executing the composition and increasing chances for it to successfully complete.
- Two functions: one Boolean function which specifies restrictions (e.g. *X must agree to participate*) and a scoring function that returns, for each potential instance of the composition, the score that the user wishes to maximise (e.g. *the number of participants in the case of the working example*).

To each service type Ti (i ∈ [1..n]) given as a parameter, is associated a set of potential service instances that may vary from an execution to another. For example, let us consider the service instances FrenchTable.com, PizzaSolutions.org and Doyles.org of service type Caterer accessible at a given time. At another time, some might no longer be reachable, and/or others might become accessible.

At an abstract level it is necessary to consider all potential sets of service instances that may enter in the composition. Such a set is called *option*. Let us consider the service instances {t1, t2, ..., tp} (p = 1, ..., n), this set of options is defined as follows (let us assume that type(s) returns the service type associated to s):

(1) $\|\{type(t1), type(t2), ..., type(tp)\}\| = p \wedge$
(2) $\{type(t1), type(t2), ..., type(tp)\} \subset \{T1, T2, .., Tn\}$

Rule (1) expresses that the component service types are distinct e.g. each service type is represented by one service instance. Rule (2) enforces that each service type is one of those given as a parameter. $\| E \|$ denotes the size of E.

The set of options is then reduced to contain only options that evaluate the restriction to true. Eventually, the score is calculated for each option and associated to it.

Summarising the discussion above, the parallel operator is formalised as follows:

Restriction: {Service} $\longrightarrow$ Boolean
Score: {Service} $\longrightarrow$ real
T1, .., Tn : sub-types of Service
// : {T1, .., Tn}, integer>0, integer>0, Restriction, Score, Client $\longrightarrow$ Service
  {*Let S = // ({S1, S2, .., Sn}, mi, ma, R, SC, c). S is a service type composed of service types, each belonging to {S1, S2, .., Sn}. Let s be a service of type S: an execution of s may lead to either a success or a failure. In the former case, among all options satisfying R, s is one that maximises SC. s is executed for the client c. mi $\neq$ 0 and ma $\geq$ mi. s is composed of at least mi service instances but not more and ma.* }

By using the operator specified above, the service type Participant Invitation (PI for short) introduced in the working example (see Section 3) can be described as follows:

Let $D_1, ..., D_n$ be the Diary service types of the n potential participants to the meeting. The following statement specifies the process of inviting participants for a meeting scheduled at time d: the person X must agree to attend the meeting, and at least 10 but not more then 15 persons must agree to attend as well:

PI $\longleftarrow$ // ({$D_1, ..., D_n$}, 10, 15, $\lambda o \cdot \exists x \in o$, holder(x) = X, $\lambda o \cdot \| o \|$, c)

c is the client who made the request, holder being a function that applies to diaries, $\lambda o \cdot \exists x \in o$, holder(x) = X is a Boolean function that evaluates to true if and only if o (a composition option) contains X's diary. The score associated to each option is its size (e.g the number of participants, to be maximised).

In this expression, the number of service instances entering in the composition is bounded by 10 and 15, therefore relaxing the "all or nothing" rule associated to executions of the composed service: the execution is successful even if the number of participants that complete does not reach 15, as soon as this number is greater than 10.

PI is then used as a component type in the expression defining MO (Meeting Organisation):

MO $\longleftarrow$ // ({PI, Caterer, Room}, 3, 3,
$\quad$ λo • cost(o.Caterer, client(o.PI), (min(o.PI)+max(o.PI))/2)
$\quad$ + cost(o.Room, client(o.PI), (min(o.PI)+max(o.PI))/2)) $\leq$ b,
$\quad$ λo • $-$(cost(o.Caterer, client(o.PI), (min(o.PI)+max(o.PI))/2))
$\quad$ + cost(o.Room, client(o.PI)), (min(o.PI)+max(o.PI))/2)),
$\quad$ client(o.PI))

o being an option, o.Caterer (respectively o.Room and o.PI) returns the service, instance of type Caterer (respectively Room and PI), that participates in o.

min(o.PI) (respectively max(o.PI)) returns the lower bound (respectively the upper bound), used as parameters in the expression given to specify PI and which define the range of values for the number of component services which must successfully complete. The function described by the first lambda expression specifies the restriction. The global cost (e.g. calculated by the means of the second lambda expression) specifies the preference, it is calculated for each option o. The opposite of the resulting value (which is a negative number) forms the score associated to o. Both minimum and maximum values are set to 3: to successfully complete, an option must be composed of exactly 3 components, each of which must successfully complete. For instance, if X does not participate, the service Participant Invitation (PI) fails, and MO must then propagate this failure to the two other services by using the cancellation operation associated to the 2PC protocol.

4.3   Transactional Properties of a Service Composition

It is important to note that when min $\geq$ 2, the minimality constraint implies an atomicity constraint. For example, when min = 2, either at least two component services must successfully complete, or none must complete. This means that the situation where only one out of the two components completes can not arise. To enforce this constraint, each option must necessarily contain at least min services which are either atomic or quasi-atomic. The resulting composite service will itself provide the operations associated to the 2PC protocol (preparation, cancellation and validation). The implementation of these operations relies on the operations provided by the component services participating in the composition. The mapping between operations offered by the composite service and those provided by its components is defined by the execution model detailed in the next section.

On the other hand, min = 1 does not entail any atomicity constraint. The resulting composite service may be atomic, quasi-atomic or non-atomic depending on the properties of the component services in the selected option. The first situation arises when all participants of the selected option are atomic and provide preparation, validation and cancellation operations. Similarly, when all participants are quasi-atomic, the composite service is then capable of offering a compensation operation. In other cases, the resulting composite service is non-atomic. Note that the option to be selected is not known in advance since it depends on the evaluation of the restriction and scoring functions, and therefore in this situation it is not possible to know at composition time whether the resulting composite service will be atomic, quasi-atomic, or non-atomic. In other words, the exact transactional nature of the composite service can only be known at runtime.

In this paper, we do not consider the possibility of deriving the transactional properties of composite service at runtime (i.e. we restrict the model to design-time derivation). Deriving such properties at runtime (as opposed to design time) will necessarily imply that the set of operations supported by a service (e.g. its interface) can dynamically evolve, since atomic services do not have the same set of operations as quasi-atomic or non-atomic. In contrast, in the context of Web services, the interface of a service is statically defined at design time and exposed as a WSDL document (among other languages) when the service is published. Hence, composite services for which $min = 1$ are considered to be non-atomic.

5   Execution Model

This section presents the execution model associated to the operator previously introduced. The execution of a composite service is carried out in two steps:

(1) Options exploration: the procedure *selection/reservation* is meant to build so-called *service composition options*, each of which is composed of a set of component services that together satisfy the restrictions specified by the designer. This process involves identifying which services will participate in an option. A service is selected only if a tentative reservation has been successfully obtained (according to the Tentative Hold Protocol). In addition, each option must satisfy the minimality and maximality constraint as well as the restriction function. Each option is then associated with its score (which reflects the designer/user preferences) and the set of options is then sorted in descending order by score. This step is detailed in Section 5.1.

(2) Execution phase: the procedure *execution/validation* considers the options built during the first step and ordered according to their score (from the higher to the lower score). Each option is considered in turn and its execution is attempted (see Section 5.2).

In [21] we detail an architecture and the associated algorithm which implement the process summarised above.

5.1   Dynamic Selection Process

An important feature of our approach is that the services that will participate in a given execution of a composite service are selected at runtime rather than this choice being hard-coded in the specification of the composite service. Most of the time, several services can be of the same service type, in the sense that they provide the same capability, and are thus interchangeable except for the fact that they may possess different non-functional properties for which the values may vary over time (e.g. cost, location). This feature is similar to the one provided by the concept of "service community" defined in the SELF-SERV service composition system [15, 22].

In our approach we push this idea further: during the execution of a composite service, tentative hold requests are sent to several instances of the same service type. As a result, reservations are obtained from several of these services (which are interchangeable), thereby enabling the execution framework to defer, until validation time, the choice of the instance of a given service type (called a *instance service*) that will participate in the composition.

The selection of services is performed in two steps. First, a thread is created for each of the service types passed as parameters to the operator. Threads are meant to seek potential services supporting the THP protocol and offering the capabilities corresponding to the service type they are associated to.

The second step aims at building the set of all options according to the composition specification. For each of the options built in this way, the restriction function must evaluate to true (i.e. it must satisfy the domain-specific constraints). In addition, each option must contain at least mi component services but not more than ma, where mi and ma are parameters of the composite service. Moreover, if mi's value is two or more, then at least mi services in each option must be atomic or quasi-atomic, otherwise satisfying the atomicity constraint cannot be achieved. This is because non-atomic services do not provide neither a preparation nor a compensation operation which is necessary to ensure atomicity of the composite service execution (i.e. to ensure that at least mi services validate successfully or no service validates successfully). The only operation supported by non-atomic services is validation and the outcome of this operation is not under the control of the composite service: when the validation operation is invoked on a service, the service may either complete its execution successfully (and thus the associated resource is definitely acquired) or it may complete unsuccessfully (meaning that the associated resource could not be acquired).

At the end of the second step, resources associated to services which do not belong to any option and which have been reserved (in the sense of the THP protocol) are released.

Subsequently, the scoring function is evaluated for each composition option. The set of options is then sorted in descending order according to the option's score and the resulting list is passed on to the execution/validation phase described in the next section.

5.2   Execution Process

The second phase aims at executing and validating the services involved in one of the options identified in the previous phase. Options are considered in turn starting with the option with the highest score. For each option, the corresponding transaction is executed as explained below. If the execution of the selected option completes successfully (up to and including the validation phase) then the process stops and the composite service execution is considered to have completed with success. If on the other hand the transaction fails, then the next option in the list is considered. The process continues until either an option has completed successfully, or all the options have been exhausted. In the latter case, the composite service execution is considered to have failed.

All along this phase, the coordination module dynamically updates the list of options. Specifically, when unavailability notifications are received by the coordination module from the component services, meaning that the corresponding resources are no longer available as per the rules of the THP protocol, all options relying on such unavailable services are withdrawn from the list of options. In particular, if a notice of unavailability concerns an option which is in the process of being executed, the corresponding transaction is cancelled (provided that it is still in the "preparation" phase). As the time passes, the score associated to an option may change, thereby modifying its ranking. Studying the evolutions of options over time is out of the scope of this paper, although we acknowledge that studying this issue could lead to identifying various optimization possibilities. The aim here is merely to provide an execution semantics for the composition operator and so, possible optimisations are not considered.

Each option is executed as follows. The transaction manager sends first a *prepare* message to each atomic service in the option (as per the 2PC protocol). If the number of atomic services that positively acknowledges this request (i.e. services that return a message with a "ready" status) is enough to achieve the minimality constraint, then a *validate* message is sent to all the component services (again as per the 2PC protocol), this time including both atomic and non-atomic services. If on the other hand the number of atomic services which acknowledge positively does not reach the required minimum, the validation cannot complete; hence, a *cancel* message is sent to all the atomic services that acknowledged positively thereby releasing the resources reserved during the preparation phase. However, all tentative reservations made during the first phase described Section 5.1 are kept until the end of the execution process, once all the composition options have been tried. Of course, if at a given point during the execution it is found that a given service does not appear in any of the options that have not yet been tried, then the THP on this service may be released.

Quasi-atomic services are treated in a similar way as atomic services, except that during the "preparation" phase of the composite service execution they are sent a *validate* message, as opposed to a *prepare* message. This is because quasi-atomic services do not provide a preparation operation (they only provide two operations: validation and compensation). Following the *validate* request, a quasi-atomic service may reply with either a *success* or a *fail* message. For the purpose of satisfying the minimality constraint, a quasi-atomic service that replies with a *success* message is equated to an atomic service that replies with a *ready* message at the end of the preparation phase. If later on, cancellation of the transaction is necessary because not enough atomic/quasi-atomic services are available to complete the transaction, then a *compensate* message will be sent to all quasi-atomic services that replied with a *success* message during the preparation phase (this is seen as equivalent to sending a *cancel* request to an atomic service). Since quasi-atomic services do not provide a validation operation, they do not get involved in the validation phase of 2PC.

Non-atomic services are considered as extra participants: each non-atomic service that validates during the validation phase is seen as a bonus on top of the atomic/quasi-atomic services, and they can be included in the transaction so long as the number of component services that validate does not exceed the maximum threshold specified for the composite service.

6 Conclusion

We have presented a composition model for Web services. The model aims at exploiting transactional properties of services which enter in a composition in order to ensure transactional properties on the composite service. The proposed model approach overcomes some key limitations of existing models as identified in Section 2:

Support for heterogeneous transactional properties. The model allows atomic, quasi-atomic, and non-atomic services to be involved in a composition. If an atomicity constraint is specified on the composite service, a certain minimum number of atomic and quasi-atomic services must participate in the composition, but otherwise, atomic, quasi-atomic and non-atomic services can be composed in arbitrary ways.

Provision for limited duration of reservations and cost of compensations. The model aims at (1) maximising the chances of acquiring the resources managed by the selected services during the preparation phase of the 2PC protocol, but without blocking these resources for long periods of time (in the case of atomic services); (2) reducing the risk of having to perform compensations on services because not enough other resources are obtained (in the case of quasi-atomic services); and (3) optimising the chances of acquiring the desired resources (in the case of non-atomic services). To achieve this, the model relies on the Tentative Hold Protocol for placing tentative resource reservations during the execution of the composite service before engaging in the final stage of the transaction.

Support for dynamic selection and substitution. The parallel composition operator which lies at the core of the proposed model does not apply to individual services but rather to service types, that is, sets of substitutable services that provide the same capability. In this way, the operator provides direct support for service selection. Moreover, the operator is parameterised by a restriction and a scoring (i.e. preference) function which guide the selection of composition options.

In order to give a semantics to the composition operator, we have defined an execution model based on an algorithm which explores all composition options that satisfy the minimality and maximaility constraints and the restriction function in order to identify which options maximise the scoring function [21].

In this paper, we focused on atomicity constraints, and more specifically on service coordination under such constraints. In order to be applicable in a broad range of setting, the proposed basic model needs to be extended in at least two directions:

- *Data mediation*: a composite service's data model depends on those of its component services. The composition operator must be extended so as to allow the designer to define the data model of the resulting composite service as well as the dependencies between the data model of the composite service and those of the components. This could be achieved by using, for instance, mediation and reconciliation functions.
- *Control dependencies*: so far we have only considered parallel execution of services (at which point only tentative holds are obtained). Services are then synchronised at validation time, at which point an attempt is made to acquire the underlying resources definitely. In practice however, sequential dependencies may be imposed over the execution of the services that enter in a composition (e.g. service A must complete its execution before service B can start). In order to take into account such dependencies, we plan to extend the model presented here based on the principles of well-known transactional process models such as Sagas [20], which rely on the compensation capabilities of quasi-atomic services.

References

1. Baïna, K., Benatallah, B., Casati, F., Toumani, F.: Model-driven web services development. 16th International Conference on Advanced Information Systems Engineering (CAISE'04), Riga, Latvia. Springer-Verlag **3084** (2004)
2. Roberts, J., Srinivasan, K.: Tentative hold protocol. http://www.w3.org/TR/{tenthold-1,tenthold-2} (2001)
3. Elmagarmid, A.K., ed.: Database Transactions Models for Advanced Applications. Morgan Kaufmann Publishers (1990)
4. Gray, J., Reuter, A.: Transaction Processing: concepts and Tecniques. Morgan Kaufmann Publishers (1993)
5. Alonso, G., Casati, F., Kuno, H., Machiraju, V.: Web Services. Concepts, Architectures and Applications. Springer Verlag (2003)
6. Papazoglou, M.: Web services and business transactions. Technical Report 6, Infolab, Tilburg University, Netherlands (2003)
7. Cabrera, F., Copeland, G., Cox, B., Freund, T., Klein, J., Storey, T., Langworthy, D., Orchard, D.: Web service coordination, ws-coordination. http://www.ibm.com/developerworks/library/ws-coor/ (2002) IBM, Microsoft, BEA.
8. Cabrera, F., Copeland, G., Cox, B., Freund, T., Klein, J., Storey, T., Thatte, S.: Web service transaction, ws-transaction. http://www.ibm.com/developerworks/library/ws-transpec/ (2002) IBM, Microsoft, BEA.
9. Si, Y., Edmond, D., H. M. ter Hofstede, A., M., D.: Property propagation rules for prioritizing and synchronizing trading activities. In: CEC, IEEE International Conference on Electronic Commerce (CEC 2003), Newport Beach, CA, USA, IEEE Computer Society (2003) 246–255

10. Arregui, D., Pacull, F., Riviere, M.: Heterogeneous component coordination: The clf approach. In: EDOC, 4th International Enterprise Distributed Object Computing Conference (EDOC 2000), Makuhari, Japan, IEEE Computer Society (2000) 194–2003

11. Hagen, C., Alonso, G.: Exception handling in workflow management systems. Software Engineering, IEEE Transactions on **26** (2000) 943–958

12. Limthanmaphon, B., Zhang, Y.: Web service composition transaction management. In Schewe, K.D., Williams, H., eds.: ADC. Volume 27 of CRPIT., Database Technologies 2004, Proceedings of the Fifteenth Australian Database Conference, ADC 2004, Dunedin, New Zealand, Australian Computer Society (2004)

13. Vidyasankar, K., Vossen, G.: A multi-level model for web service composition. Technical report, Dept. of Information Systems, University of Muenster (2003) Tech. Report No. 100.

14. Halliday, J., Shrivastava, S., Wheater, S.: Flexible workflow management in the OPENflow system. In: EDOC, 5th IEEE/OMG International Enterprise Distributed Object Computing Conference, IEEE Computer Society Press, USA (2001) 82–92

15. Benatallah, B., Dumas, M., Maamar, Z.: Definition and execution of composite web services the self-serv projet. IEEE Computer Society Technical Committee on Data Engineering Bulletin **25** (2002)

16. Mikalsen, T., Tai, S., Rouvellou, I.: Transactional attitudes: Reliable composition of autonomous web services. In Workshop on Dependable Middleware-based systems (WDMS 2002) (2002) Washington, D.C., USA.

17. Dalal, S., Temel, S., Little, M., Potts, M., Webber, J.: Coordinating business transactions on the web. IEEE Internet Computer Society Journal **7** (2003) 30–39

18. for the Advancement of Structured Information Standards OASIS, O.: Business transaction protocol - btp. http://www.oasis-open.org/ (2002)

19. Andrews, T., Curbera, F., Dholakia, H., Goland, Y., Klein, J., Liu, K., Roller, D., Smith, D., Thatte, S., Trickovic, I.: Business process executions langage for web services. version 1.1. http://www.ibm.com/developerworks/library/ws-bpel (2003) BEA, IBM, Microsoft, SAP AG, Siebel Systems.

20. Garcìa-Molina, H., Salem, K.: Sagas. In: Proc. of the ACM SIGMOD International Conference on Management of Data, San Francisco, CA, USA (1987) 249–259

21. Fauvet, M.C., Duarte, H., Dumas, M., Benatallah, B.: Handling transactional properties in web service composition. Technical report, CLIPS-IMAG, Joseph Fourier University of Grenoble (2005) http://www-clips.imag.fr/http://www-clips.imag.fr/mrim/User/marie-christine.fauvet/Publis/wise05_full.pdf.

22. Benatallah, B., Sheng, Q.Z., Dumas, M.: The SELF-SERV Environment for Web Services Composition. IEEE Internet Computing (2003) IEEE Computer Society.

XFlow: An XML-Based Document-Centric Workflow

Andrea Marchetti, Maurizio Tesconi, and Salvatore Minutoli

CNR, IIT Department, Via Moruzzi 1, I-56124, Pisa, Italy
{andrea.marchetti, salvatore.minutoli, maurizio.tesconi}
@iit.cnr.it

Abstract. This paper aims at investigating on an appropriate framework that allows the definition of workflows for collaborative document procedures. In this framework, called XFlow and largely based on XSLT Processing Model, the workflows are described by means of a new XML application called XFlowML (XFlow Markup Language). XFlowML describes the document workflow using an agent-based approach. Each agent can participate to the workflow with one or more roles, defined as XPath expressions, based on a hierarchical role chart. An XFlowML document contains as many templates as agent roles participating to the workflow. The document workflow engine constitutes the run-time execution support for the document processing by implementing the XFlowML constructs. A prototype of XFlow has been implemented with an extensive use of XML technologies (XSLT, XPath, XForms, SVG) and open-source tools (Cocoon, Tomcat, mySQL).

1 Introduction

The problem of processing documents has long been recognized to be a critical aspect in the enterprise productivity ([3], [6], [7], [8], [9]). The management of documents becomes more difficult when it involves different actors, possibly in a decentralized working environment, with different tasks, roles and responsibilities in different document sections.

Many enterprise day-to-day operations can be viewed as a series of steps involving the filling out of appropriate forms by different actors, sometimes with a concurrent processing. We can expect that implementing an effective system that supports these forms flows will result in considerable cost savings for enterprises. We propose a solution based on a complete independence between workflow definition and workflow engine which supports the management of simultaneous document workflows by largely using XML technologies.

2 Overview: Definitions, Concepts, Terminology

Before illustrating our approach, we give some remarks on the terminology used.

A *workflow* is "the automation of a business process, in whole or part, during which documents, information or tasks are passed from one participant to another for action, according to a set of procedural rules".

M. Kitsuregawa et al. (Eds.): WISE 2005, LNCS 3806, pp. 290–303, 2005.
© Springer-Verlag Berlin Heidelberg 2005

As *Document-centric Workflow* or *Document Workflow* (DW) we refer to a particular workflow in which all activities, made by the agents, turn out to documents compilation. It can be viewed as the automation and administration of particular documents procedures ([1],[3],[9]). In other words, a DW can be seen as a process of cooperative authoring where the document can be the goal of the process or just a side effect of the cooperation.

Through a DW, a document life-cycle is tracked and supervised, continually providing document compilation actions control. In this environment a document travels among *agents* who essentially carry out the pipeline receive-process-send activity. There are two types of agents: *external agents* are human or software actors which perform activities dependent from the particular DW, and *internal agents* are software actors providing general-purpose activities useful for any DW and, for this reason, implemented directly into the system. An external agent *executes* some processing using the document content and possibly other data, *updates* the document inserting the results of the preceding processing, *signs* the updating and finally *sends* the document to the next agent(s).

Figure 1 illustrates a generic document workflow diagram where external and internal agents cooperate exchanging documents according to defined procedural rules.

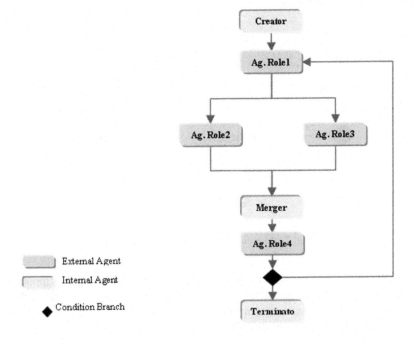

Fig. 1. A generic document workflow

Internal agents perform general functionalities such as *creating* a document belonging to a particular DW, populating it with some initial data, *duplicating* a document to be sent to multiple agents, *splitting* a document and sending partitions to different agents, *merging* duplicated documents coming from multiple agents, *aggregating* document fragments, *terminating* operations on the document.

3   Document Workflow Framework

Our document workflow framework is based on document-centric model where all the activities, made by the agents, turn out to document compilation.

During its life the document passes through several phases, from its creation to the end of its processing. The state diagram in figure 2 describes the different states of the document instances. At the starting point of the document instance life cycle there is a creation phase, in which the system raises a new instance of a document with several information attached (such as the requester agent data). The document instance goes into *pending* state. When an agent gets the document, it goes into *processing* state in which the agent compiles the parts of his concern. If the agent, for some reason, doesn't complete the instance elaboration, he can save the work performed until that moment and the document instance goes into *freezing* state. If the elaboration is completed (submitted), or cancelled, the instance goes back into *pending* state, waiting for a new elaboration.

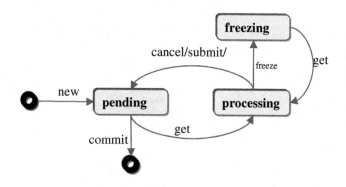

Fig. 2. State diagram of a document instance

The *DW engine* has the task of managing all the functionalities to support agent activities. In order to design a *DW engine* independent from the single DW, it's necessary to isolate the information of each DW inside an XML document. We will see in detail the essential components necessary to describe a DW.

Summarizing, the *DW framework* is composed of three parts:

- The DW Environments (Agents participating to the DW)
- The DW Engine
- The DW Data (DW descriptions + Documents created by the DW)

3.1 Document Workflow Description

The description of a DW can be seen as an extension of the XML document class. A class of documents, created in a DW, share the schema of their structure, as well as the definition of the procedural rules driving the DW and the list of the agents attending to the DW. Therefore, in order to describe a DW, we need four components:

- a *schema* of the documents involved in the DW;
- the agent roles chart, called *role chart*, i.e. the set of the external and internal agents, operating on the document flow. Inside the role chart these agents are organized in roles and groups in order to define who has access to the document. This component constitutes the DW environment;
- a *document interface description* used by external agents to access the documents. This component also allows to check the access to the document resource;
- a *document workflow description* defining all the paths that a document can follow in its life-cycle, the activities and policies for each role.

Furthermore the system for keeping track of document instances history (including the agents that manipulated the document) and document state during its whole flow path needs respectively a *Log* and *Metadata* component. The Metadata component represents the document current state. Every time a document changes its state (see Figure 1) the Metadata is first saved into Log component and then updated. These last two documents are produced automatically by the DW engine. For each component we define a declarative language, using XML. Hence, each document belonging to a DW, during all its life-cycle ,will be associated with six documents, as indicated in figure 3.

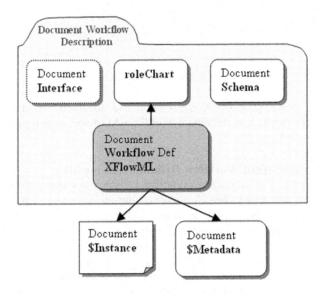

Fig. 3. Document Workflow Description

3.1.1 Document Schema (XML Schema)

Document schema describes the structure and the data-types of the documents participating to the flow. *Document schema* will be described using XML Schema.

3.1.2 Document Interface (XForms, Web Service)

This document describes, for each agent role, the interface to the document. The *document interface* for *external human agents* relies upon Web Modules technologies [2], and *external software agents* make use of Web Services technologies (WSDL, SOAP). In the first solutions we adopted XForms technology, promoted by W3C.

3.1.3 Role Chart: Agent Role Declaration

The *role chart* is an XML document containing the description of all actors (agents) that participate to the workflow. Each actor has a *role* and a *unique identifier*. Roles are organized in the role chart hierarchically. Each agent can participate to the workflow with one or more roles, therefore it can appear in one or more role chart positions. The role chart schema is depicted in figure 4.

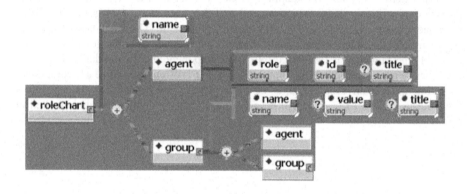

Fig. 4. The Role Chart Schema

Finally the *document workflow description* is a document based on a new XML application (XFlowML Xml document workFlow Markup Language) suitably defined for this purpose.

3.1.4 XFlow: Document Workflow Definition (XFlowML)

For the definition of a language to describe complex document flows we analyzed several syntaxes and approaches. A possible solution was to use a notation similar to concurrent languages, using statements like fork and join to describe flows. Another choice was to describe the document flow from the *point of view of the agents*. To describe a document flow it is sufficient to accurately describe all the agents and all the operations any agent can perform on the document instance. This way of describing the flow resembles XSL syntax, where actions performed by various agents are similar to the templates to apply to the elements of an XML document. Our basic decision to *represent flows as XML documents*, led us to choose the second option, since with XML, due to its intrinsic hierarchical notation, it is more straightforward to represent lists rather than graphs (other approaches which emphasize the role of XML can be found in [4], [5], [10], [11], [12]). Taking as a simple example the generic flow depicted in Figure 1, we will have to supply as many descriptions as the agents roles involved in the process. For instance, in the description of the external agent with role1 (*Ag. Role1*), we must specify that it can receive documents from *Creator* or *Ag.Role4*, and send it to *Ag.Role2* and *Ag.Role3*. Figure 5 shows both the graphical representation and the XML notation of the Agent Role1.

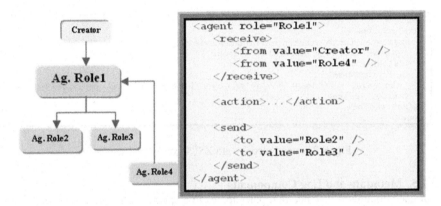

Fig. 5. Description of Agent Role1 (see Fig.1)

To describe document flow we adopted a XML dialect, called XFlowML, largely based on XSL-Syntax.

A XFlowML document is composed of a list of *internal* or *external* `agents`. Each `agent` has a mandatory attribute `role`, containing a XPath expression referring to the *rolechart*. Other optional attributes specify if the agent has to sign the document (`sign`), and the maximum time the agent is allowed to keep the document (`timeout`).

When an agent requests a document, the DW Engine matches the agent's role on XFlow document and processes the three section: receive, action and send.

In the `receive` section the `from` elements identify from which agent roles the document can be received. The roles of the agents are coded as XPath expressions. The `receive` section is optional because it's necessary only to verify if the agent can really receive the current document.

In the `action` section there are one or more `permission` elements defining the access policies to the document fields.

The `send` section contains all the possible receivers of the document. The document can be sent simultaneously to several agents by using a sequence of `to` elements.

In order to increase the flexibility and power of the language, thus allowing for an easy definition of more complex DWs, we introduced the conditional `<if>` and

<choose> statements which adopt the XSLT syntax and can be specified in any agent section (i.e. receive, action, send). Test attributes can contain any XPath expression which returns a Boolean, and it is possible to refer document *Metadata* or document *instance*. For distinguishing the referred document the 'test' XPath expression will begin with two different prefixes: respectively $Metadata and $Instance.

A typical use of these conditional statements is in send element, when we have to send the document to two different agent depending on the value of a document field previously filled out (see Figure 6).

```
<send>
  <xsl:choose >
    <xsl:when test="$instance//financeReview[approved='true']">
      <to select="//agent[@role='manager']"
    <xsl:when>
    <xsl:otherwise>
      <to value = "//agent[@role='employee'][@id=$instance//employee/@id]">
    <xsl:otherwise>
  </xsl:choose>
</send>
```

Fig. 6. The send section with XSLT conditional statements

3.1.5 Metadata and Log Components

For each document instance that participates to a specific DW, additional information (that we have called metadata) is stored together with information needed to reconstruct the document history (Log) that consists of all the document transitions during its processing, including information about actors involved. Log permits to undo actions. Every time a document is submitted by an agent, the differences with the previous version of the document are generated and saved. Only when the document life cycle is completed and it is archived all this data is deleted.

3.2 The Document Workflow Engine (DWE)

The document workflow engine constitutes the run-time support for the DW, it implements the *internal agents,* the support for *agent's activities*, and some *system modules* that the external agents have to use to interact with the DW system. Also, the engine is responsible for two kinds of documents useful for each document flow: the *documents system logs* and the *documents system metadata.*

3.2.1 Agent's Activities Support

These are the two modules, called *Sender* and *Receiver*, supporting the activities of sending to, and receiving from the current agent1.

The *Sender* has to prepare and send the document (identified by an URN) requested by an external agent. It checks the agent rights, verifies if the document instance is still available, analyzes/interprets the workflow description to generate an adapted

---

[1] The name of these modules are given with the point of view of DWE.

document, using the agent's role and access rights to determine which are the parts of the stored document to be included (using XForms for a human agent and SOAP for a software agent).

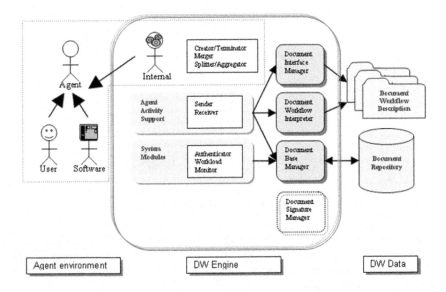

Fig. 7. Document Workflow Framework

The *Receiver* gets the document from the handling agent in consequence of a submit, freeze or cancel command. It determines the roles of the next agents to whom the document must be sent.

Both modules use the *DW Interpreter* which transforms the XFlow document into a XSLT stylesheet. The generated stylesheet is applied to the Rolechart document producing the role agent's activities.

4 Case Study: A Travel Request

To illustrate the usefulness of our system, a case study is set up and briefly outlined.

One typical activity in a research institute is the participation in conferences or seminars. In this case, the employee (researcher) must obtain the proper authorization, involving the approval of the office manager, administrative verification, and final approval by the director.

In terms of workflow, this consists of filling out several mandatory fields (such as purpose, destination, duration and dates of the trip and estimated daily traveling allowance) by the employee. Some employee's data, such as name and division can be pre-filled by the application.

Then the document must be approved by the office manager and by the administration.

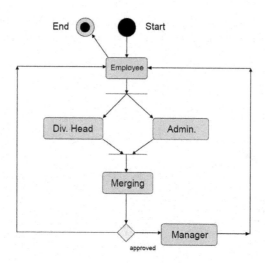

Fig. 8. Travel Request Graph

These two activities are independent and can be performed concurrently, therefore the document is duplicated in different copies, each one sent to the appropriate actor. Afterwards the document is properly recomposed from the merging agent and sent to the director for authorization.

Here each actor involved fills out a different part of the form. The method used to visualize the document consists of an adaptive user interface that shows the fields to be filled out.

Note that the Administration is actually a role, designating a set of individuals who can perform the task, while each of the other actors is a specific person.

4.1 Travel Request Flow Description

In order to describe this flow it's necessary to create a schema as well as a rolechart and a xflow document.

4.1.1 The Rolechart Document

A rolechart document contains all the agents organized by groups and roles. The roles are: employee, division head, administrator and manager.

Let's suppose that in our firm ACME there is only the division "Foo" where George is the division head and Bob is the only employee. Two employees work in administration. The manager of ACME's firm is Alice. Figure 9 describes this situation.

4.1.2 The XFlow Document

The travel request graph is codified in xflow document. It's organized in 5 sections corresponding to the 5 agents roles: employee, division head, administration employee, merging (internal agent necessary for merging the document coming from division head and administration, see Figure 8) and the manager.

```
<?xml version="1.0" encoding="iso-8859-1" ?>
- <roleChart xmlns:xsi="http://www.w3.org/2001/XMLSchema-instance"
    xsi:noNamespaceSchemaLocation="RoleChartSchema.xsd" name="ACME">
  - <group name="System">
      <agent role="Merging" id="m0" />
    </group>
      <agent role="Manager" id="m1" title="ACME manager">Alice</agent>
  - <group name="Administration">
      <agent role="Employee" id="m2" title="Finance reviewer">David</agent>
      <agent role="Employee" id="m3" title="Finance reviewer">Martha</agent>
    </group>
  - <group name="Division" value="Foo">
      <agent role="DivisionHead" id="m4" title="Foo division head">George</agent>
      <agent role="Employee" id="m5" title="Foo employee">Bob</agent>
    </group>
  </roleChart>
```

Fig. 9. Rolechart document

In the figure 10 we can see the *send* section of the "Employee" agent. In this section it is declared that a document submitted by an Employee can follow two paths. If the document has just been created, it will be duplicated and sent to an administration employee and to the division head of the employee, otherwise the document will be archived because the process is completed.

```
<?xml version="1.0" encoding="iso-8859-1" ?>
- <xflow xmlns:xsl="http://www.w3.org/1999/XSL/Transform" xmlns:xslOut="http://www.w3.org/1999/XSL/Transform">
  - <agent role="$rolechart//agent[@role='Employee']">
    + <receive>
    + <action>
    - <send>
      - <xsl:choose>
        - <xsl:when test="$metadata//sender[.='creator']">
            <to value="/group[@name='Administration']/agent[@role='Employee']" />
            <to value="/group[@name='Division'][@value='{$Instance//division}']/agent[@role='DivisionHead']" />
          </xsl:when>
        - <xsl:otherwise>
            <to value="end" />
          </xsl:otherwise>
        </xsl:choose>
      </send>
    </agent>
  + <agent role="$rolechart//agent[@role='DivisionHead']">
  + <agent role="$rolechart//agent[@role='Employee'][ancestor::group[@name='Administration']]">
  + <agent role="$rolechart//agent[@role='Merging']">
  + <agent role="$rolechart//agent[@role='Manager']">
  </xflow>
```

Fig. 10. XFlow document

5 Implementation Overview

5.1 The Client Side: External Agent Interaction

Our system is currently implemented as a web-based application where the human external agents interact with system through a web browser. All the human external agents attending the different document workflows are the users of the system. Once authenticated through user/psw (Fig. 11A) the user accesses his/her workload area (Fig. 11B) where the system lists all his/her pending documents sorted by flow.

The system shows only the flows to which the user has access.

From the workload area the user can browse his/her documents and select some operations such as:

- select and process a pending document (Fig. 12C)
- create a new document partly filled with his/her data.
- display a graph representing a DW of a previously created document, highlighting the current position of the document (Fig. 12D). This information is rendered as an SVG image.

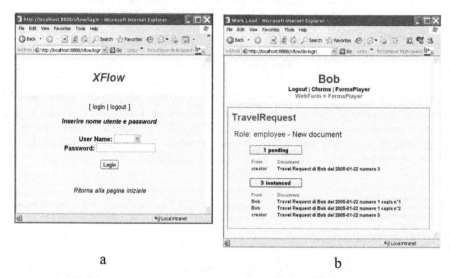

Fig. 11. Some screenshots of XFlow

The form used to process the documents is rendered with XForms (See Fig. 12C). XForms can communicate with the server by means of XML documents and is

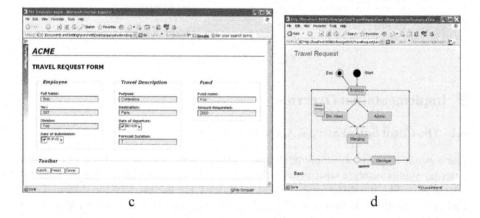

Fig. 12. Some screenshots of XFlow

capable of displaying the document with a user interface that can be defined for each type of document. XForms is a recommendation of the W3C for the specification of Web forms. In XForms the description of how the form is displayed is separated from the description of what the form must do, so it is easy to use different type of views depending on the platform and on the document. A browser with XForms capabilities will receive an XML document that will be displayed according to the specified template, then it will let the user edit the document and finally it will send the modified document to the server.

5.2 The Server Side

The server-side is implemented with Apache Tomcat, Apache Cocoon and MySql. Tomcat is used as the web server, authentication module (when the communication between the server and the client needs to be encrypted) and servlet container. Cocoon is a publishing framework that uses the power of XML.The entire functioning of Cocoon is based on one key concept: component pipelines. A pipeline is composed by a series of steps, which consists of taking a request as input, processing and transforming it, and then giving the desired response. The pipeline components are generators, transformers, and serializers. A Generator is used to create an XML structure from an input source (file, directory, stream ...) A Transformer is used to map an input XML structure into another XML structure (the most used is XSLT transformer). A Serializer is used to render an input XML structure into some other format (not necessarily XML)

MySql is used for storing and retrieving the documents and the status of the documents.

There are some modules that allow the interaction with the user agents.

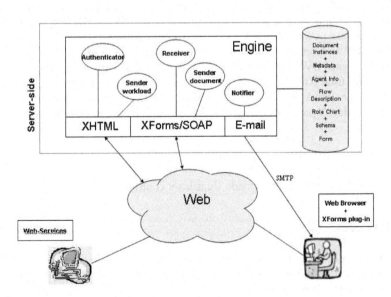

Fig. 13. The overall system architecture

The *Authenticator* and *WorkloadSender* modules use XHTML to display data. The *Receive* and *Sender Document* modules use XForms to exchange XML document with human agents and the SOAP protocol to exchange documents with software agents. (fig. 13).

Each software agent is implemented as a web-service and the WSDL language is used to define its interface. The *Notifier* is used to alert an agent when some document needs to be processed in a short time (deadline) and optionally when a new document is inserted in his work list.

6 Conclusion

In this paper we have described a framework to define a workflow for collaborative document procedures. It is based upon a complete independence between workflow definition and engine, and supports the simultaneous processing of collaborative documents.

The benefits arising from the usage of this system include:

- interoperability/portability deriving from using XML technologies;
- concurrent documents workflows support;
- reduction of the cost of documents processes, through the e-documents processing and distribution;

XML is a suitable technology for representing not only data/documents but also to describe the document workflow logic. XFlowML is the XML application defined to describe a document workflow.

We have defined a model to describe DW based on three XML documents (schema, rolechart and xflow) that allows an easy description of many DW.

We have implemented a DW engine interpreting XFlowML documents, by using Cocoon, a very powerful middleware, to develop XML prototypes.

The DW engine implemented is heavily based on XML technologies (XSLT, XPath, XForms, SVG) and open-source tools (Cocoon, Tomcat, mySQL).

We have used Xforms technology to create dynamic user interfaces.

Our future work will focus on extension of the DW engine with new internal agents and development of a distributed framework based on mobile agents.

Acknowledgments

Thanks to Tatiana Bacci who made significant contributions.

References

1. A. Marchetti, S. Minutoli, P.Lazzareschi, and M.Martinelli. *A System for Managing Documents in a Step by Step Process*. In Proc. XML World Euro Edition, 26-28 March 2001, Amsterdam-Holland.
2. M. Tesconi, A. Marchetti, S. Minutoli, F. Ronzano, Web Forms T.R. IIT TR-09/2005 April 2005.

3. R. Krishnan, L. Munaga, and K. Karlapalem. *XDoC-WFMS: A Framework for Document Centric Workflow Management System.* In Proc. 20th International Conference on Conceptual Modeling – ER 2001, 27-30 Springer Verlag, November 2001, pp. 348-362, ISBN:3-540-44122-0.

4. L. Aversano, G. Canfora, A. De Lucia, P. Gallucci. *Integrating document and workflow management tools using XML and web technologies: a case study.* In Proc. Sixth European Conference on Software Maintenance and Reengineering, 11-13 March 2002, Budapest – Hungary, pp. 24-33.

5. P. Ciancarini, R. Tollksdorf, F. Zambonelli. *Coordination Middleware for XML-Centric Applications.* In Proc. 16th ACM Symposium on Applied Computing – SAC2000, 10-14 March 2002, Madrid, Spain.

6. G. Kappel, S. Rausch-Schott, S. Reich, W. Retschitzegger. *Hypermedia document and workflow management based on active object-oriented databases.* In Proc. of the Thirtieth Hawaii International Conference on System Sciences, Vol. 4, 7-10 Jan. 1997, pp. 377-386.

7. L. Baresi, F. Casati, S. Castano, M.G. Fugini, I. Mirbel, B. Pernici. *WIDE Workflow Development Methodology.* In Proc. of the International Joint Conference on Work activities Coordination and Collaboration, 1999, San Francisco, California, United States, pp. 19 – 28, ISBN: 1-58113-070-8.

8. F. Casati, M. G. Fugini, I. Mirbel, B. Pernici. WIRES: *A Methodology for Developing Workflow Applications.* In Requirements Engineering Journal, Springer Verlag Press., Vol. 7, Num. 2, 2002, pp. 73-106.

9. D. Georgakopoulos, H. Hornick and A. Sheth. *An Overview of Workflow Management: from Process Modelling to Workflow Automation Infrastructure.* In Distributed and Parallel Database Journal, Kluwer Academic Publishers Press., Vol. 3, Num. 2, April 1995, pp. 119-152.

10. A. Tripathi, T. Ahmed, V. Kakani, S. Jaman. *Implementing Distributed Workflow Systems from XML Specifications.* Department of Computer Science, University of Minnesota, May 2000. Available at http://www.cs.umn.edu/Ajanta/publications.html

11. R. Tolksdorf, Marc Stauch *Using XSL to Coordinate Workflows* Kommunikation in Verteilten Systemen 2001 127-138

12. R. Tolksdorf *Workspaces: A Web-Based Workflow Management System* IEEE Internet Computing September 2002 v.6 n.5 p.18-26

Optimization of XSLT by Compact Specialization and Combination

Ce Dong and James Bailey

NICTA Victoria Laboratory,
Department of Computer Science and Software Engineering,
The University of Melbourne, VIC 3010, Australia
{cdong, jbailey}@cs.mu.oz.au

Abstract. In recent times, there has been an increased utilization of server-side XSLT systems as part of e-commerce and e-publishing applications. For the high volumes of data in these applications, effective optimization techniques for XSLT are particularly important. In this paper, we propose two new optimization approaches, Specialization Combination and Specialization Set Compaction, to help improve performance. We describe rules for combining specialized XSLT stylesheets and provide methods for generating a more compact specialization set. An experimental evaluation of our methods is undertaken, where we show our methods to be particularly effective for cases with very large XML input and different varieties of user queries.

1 Introduction

The standardized, simple and self describing nature of XML makes it a good choice for arbitrary data sources representation, exchange and storage on World Wide Web [15]. The eXtensible Stylesheet Language Transformation (XSLT) standard [5] is a primary language for transforming, reorganizing, querying and formatting XML data. In particular, use of server-side XSLT is an extremely popular technology [27] for processing and presenting results to user queries issued to a server-side XML database (e.g. google map, google search, Amazon Web services, and the ebay developer program).

Although faster hardware can of course be used to improve transformation speed, server-side XSLT transformations can still be very costly when large volumes of XML and large size XSLT stylesheets are involved (e.g. an XSLT transformation based on a 1000MB XML document and a relatively simple XSLT stylesheet can take up to 128 minutes [23]). Techniques for the optimization of such transformations are therefore an important area of research [12].

In previous work [9], we proposed an optimization method for XSLT programs based on the well known technique of program specialization [1, 18, 20], called *XSLT Template Specialization* (XTS) [9]. The underlying idea is that server-side XSLT programs are often written to be generic and may contain a lot of logic that is not needed for execution of the transformation with reference to given user query inputs (such inputs are passed as parameters to the XSLT program at run-time, often using forms in web browser). For example, a customer of an online XML based department store

M. Kitsuregawa et al. (Eds.): WISE 2005, LNCS 3806, pp. 304–317, 2005.
© Springer-Verlag Berlin Heidelberg 2005

might pass a query with several query terms to an XSLT program, referring to a 'Computer' with particular requirement of 'CPU'. The department store server-side XSLT program may contain logic which is designed to present other different kinds of merchandise (e.g. 'Desk'), but they are not needed for this user query. Given knowledge of the user input space, it is instead possible to automatically (statically) create different specialized versions of the *Original XSLT* program, that can be invoked in preference to the larger, more generic version at runtime. Important savings in execution time and consequently response time improvement were clearly shown by the experimental results [9].

The effectiveness of the XTS optimization technique is restricted to generating specializations only for *strong interconnection queries* [6], which are queries whose terms refer to XML tags that are 'close' to each other in the XML-tree (we further describe the concept of *interconnection* in section 2.1). In this paper, we present a new method, that is able to handle *weak interconnection queries*, whose query terms refer to XML tags that can be 'far apart' from each other in the XML-tree. Such *weak interconnection queries* are common in the real world [6]. Our method is called *Specialization Combination* (SC) and intuitively, it constructs specializations that cover *disconnected* sub-graphs of the DTD.

An additional challenge faced by specialization based optimization, is the potentially large number of specializations that may need to be created to cover the anticipated user queries (e.g. based a 100 template *Original XSLT*, hundreds, or even thousands of specializations might be generated). Such a large specialization set can increase the cost of searching for and finding an appropriate specialization, when the server-side system responds to the user query at run-time. In this paper, we also present an approach called *Specialization Set Compaction* (SSC), that balances the *user query coverage*, *search cost* and *transformation cost* for sets of specializations, and generates a more *Compact Specialization Set* (CSS), that is more suitable for use at run-time.

Our contributions in this paper are two optimization methods suitable for use with specialized XSLT programs:

- *Specialization Combination* (SC), which combines XSLT specializations together in order to handle *Weak Interconnection Queries*.
- *Specialization Set Compaction* (SSC), which produces a *Compact Specialization Set,* that reduces the specialization search space and allows quicker selection of a specialization at run-time.

Experimental results demonstrate the ability of these techniques to yield speedups of up to 40%. We are not aware of any other work, which uses similar concepts to *Specialization Combination* (SC) and *Specialization Set Compaction* (SSC), for improving the performance of XSLT programs.

The remainder of this paper is as follows. We first review some basic concepts in section 2. Then, in section 3 we describe the process of *Specialization Combination* (SC). Next, in section 4, we propose the approach of *Specialization Set Compaction* (SSC) and in section 5 overview the optimization processes of SC and SSC. In section 6, we present and discuss our experimental evaluation of the techniques. Related work is surveyed in section 7 and in section 8, we conclude and discuss future work.

2 Background

We begin by briefly reviewing some useful concepts. We assume basic knowledge of XML and XSLT [5, 21, 22].

2.1 DTDs, DTD-Graph and Interconnection of Query Terms

A DTD provides a structural specification for a class of XML documents and is used for validating the correctness of XML data. A DTD-Graph is a data structure that summarizes the hierarchical information within a DTD. It is a rooted, node-labeled graph, where each node represents either an element or an attribute of the DTD, and the edges indicate element nesting [9, 14]. The nodes in a DTD-Graph can be thought of as corresponding to either XML tags, or XSLT template *selection patterns*, or user query terms. An example of a DTD and its corresponding DTD-Graph is shown in Fig.1.

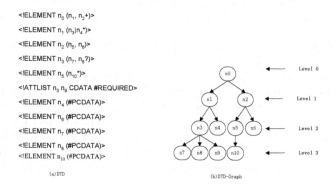

Fig. 1. DTD and corresponding DTD-Graph

Based on the kinds of different DTD-Graph structures, XML documents can be classified into four types [17]: i) *Broad-Deep* XML, ii)*Narrow-Deep* XML iii)*Broad-Shallow* XML and iv)*Narrow-Shallow* XML. Our new techniques (SC and SSC) will be evaluated on XML datasets having these different kinds of structures (discussed in section 6).

A user query for a server-side XSLT system consists of one or more query terms (modeled as nodes in the DTD-Graph). It can be expressed as $q = \{term_1, term_2, \ldots term_n\}$ $(n >= 1)$. A query, which consists of terms (nodes) such that every pair of terms is separated by at most 2 edges in the DTD-Graph, is defined as a *strong interconnection query*. Otherwise, it is a *weak interconnection query*. In our online department store example, query q_1 (expressed as q_1={Computer, CPU}), would be a *strong interconnection query* if 'CPU' was a child node of 'Computer' in the DTD-Graph. Whereas, query q_2 (expressed as q_2={Computer, CPU, Desk}), would be a *weak interconnection query* if, additionally, 'Computer' and 'Desk' were sibling nodes under a 'Merchandise' node (the 'Desk' node is 3 edges far from 'CPU' node) in the DTD-Graph.

Weak interconnection queries are reasonably prevalent when the user asks for data from different sub-structures of the XML tree, and they cannot be ignored in the real-world [6]. According to our online department store example, a customer may quite possibly buy a desktop 'Computer' (i.e. with Pentium IV 'CPU') and a matched 'Desk' together in one purchase. Many other similar examples exist.

2.2 XSLT Templates, Server-Side XSLT

An XSLT program consists of a set of templates. Execution of the program is by recursive application of individual templates to the source XML document [22]. XSLT stylesheets can be designed using three principal styles [22]: i)*Push* style, ii)*Pull* style and iii) *Hybrid* style. We will use these different styles of XSLT when constructing test cases in our experimental evaluation (described in section 7).

Server-side XSLT is a popular solution for data exchange and querying on the Web. It is often deployed for e-commerce, e-publishing and information service applications. A problem that can occur in the use of server-side XSLT is that, when a generic XSLT program is designed, it is able to handle a broad range of possible user inputs. At run-time, given specific user query inputs, much of the logic of this generic XSLT program may not be required. This results in increased run-time, since extra logic may be required for XPath evaluation and template matching [22].

2.3 XSLT Template Specialization Technique (XTS)

Our previous work, using the *XSLT Template Specialization* (XTS) technique, automatically creates a set of specializations offline and selects an appropriate minimum cost XSLT from the specialization set at run-time, to respond to the user query input.

The XTS technique is not effective at generating specializations for *weak interconnection queries*. This is because the specialization principles for the XTS technique, generate an XSLT specialization by grouping together templates (represented as nodes in DTD-Graph), that correspond to a collection of nodes in a *connected* sub-graph of the DTD-Graph. This *connected* sub-graph can obviously be big, if two existing nodes (query terms) that need to be covered are 'far apart' (weakly connected) to each other. Specializations generated based on this sub-graph can consequently be 'overweight', since they can contain templates that need not be involved in answering the *weak interconnection query*. Consequently, the transformation time is potentially slower. Therefore, instead of forming *specializations* that correspond to a (potentially large) *connected* sub-graph of the DTD-Graph, we would like to form specializations that correspond to a smaller, *disconnected* sub-graph of the DTD-Graph. This is the motivation behind our method of *Specialization Combination* (SC). Small (*connected*) specializations are combined together to form a new (*disconnected*) specialization, instead of using 'overweight' specializations or even the *Original XSLT*, to execute the transformation for the *weak interconnection query*.

Another problem which can arise, is that the number of specializations that are generated as a result of specialization combination may be very large. This enlarged specialization set takes more time to search, when a given specialization needs to be identified at run- time in response to a user query. To resolve this problem, we have developed the method of *Specialization Set Compaction* (SSC), to reduce the size of the specialization set.

3 Specialization Combination

Assume we have a log file mechanism associated with the server-side XSLT system, which, at run-time, can record information about user queries and the corresponding specializations that can be used to answer them. If using the XTS technique, it is likely that the log file will indicate that some queries (*weak interconnection queries*) need to be handled by the *Original XSLT* or 'overweight' specializations. In other words, the optimization effectiveness of the XTS technique is degraded when *weak interconnection queries* are passed to the system. In this section, we propose a method called *Specialization Combination* (SC), to combine pertinent specializations together, instead of using the *Original XSLT* or 'overweight' specializations, to deal with the *weak interconnection queries*. This saves execution time. Suppose we already have the specialization set that was generated based on the XTS technique. Call this the *Primary Specialization Set* (PSS). The process of combining the specializations for a specific *weak interconnection query* can now be described as follows (we demonstrate using an example across all steps):

- Step_1: For each query term of a *weak interconnection query*, we list all specializations in the *Primary Specialization Set* (PSS), which can handle this query term. Suppose q is a *weak interconnection query* which consists of query terms t_1 and t_2, (expressed as $q=\{t_1,t_2\}$) and term t_1 can be handled by specializations s_1 or s_2 and term t_2 can be handled by specializations s_3 or s_4. We generate the specialization set list as: $\{s_1$ or $s_2\} \rightarrow t_1$, $\{s_3$ or $s_4\} \rightarrow t_2$.
- Step_2: Generate all possible specialization combinations which can 'cover' all query terms for a specific *weak interconnection query*. Based on the example above, we generate the combinations $\{s_1s_3\}$, $\{s_1s_4\}$, $\{s_2s_3\}$ and $\{s_2s_4\}$. At a high level, the details of the generation process are: 1) place templates from different specializations into one <xsl:stylesheet> element, 2) place the contents from all repeated templates into one template and delete the redundant templates; 3)delete the redundant content in each template.
- Step_3: Re-calculate the cost for each combined specialization according to some cost model (any cost model is permitted here. We use a simple one, details not included due to space restrictions)

We add all the generated combined specializations to the *Primary Specialization Set* (PSS) to form the new *Refined Specialization Set*, (hereafter referred to as RSS).

4 Specialization Set Compaction

An RSS may turn out to be very large, if the XTS technique and SC techniques are applied to an *Original XSLT* having many templates. The server-side XSLT system may therefore take a lengthy time to search and select an appropriate *specialization* in answer to a given user query. Even though indexing methods can be applied to speed up the *specialization* searching, many *specializations* that have never been useful for answering any user query, might still have to be scanned at run-time. Deleting the non-invoked *specializations* from the RSS is not necessarily a good idea for forming a more compact specialization set. This is because non-invoked *specializations* may still be good candidates for inclusion, since even though they may not have the smallest cost, they can still cover a relatively large number of query terms. Accordingly, we propose a novel approach, *Specialization Set Compaction* (SSC), to produce a *compact specialization set* which has the minimum total cost, given an expected query set with some estimated distribution.

4.1 Query Set and Refined Specialization Set

Assuming the existing query log has the records of queries issued to the server, then, we can generate summary data listing the distinct queries and their corresponding probabilities. This related data is shown in Fig.2.(a), where QS denotes the *query set*, each q_i denotes a *distinct* query, and each p_i denotes its corresponding *probability* of being issued. The *Refined Specialization Set* (RSS) generated by the *Specialization Combination* (SC) technique is shown in Fig.2.(b), where s is used to denote an individual specialization and s_{orig} denotes the *Original XSLT,* which is selected by the specialized server-side XSLT system to process any queries that cannot be handled by any single *specialization*.

$$QS = \{q_1, q_2, q_3 \ldots q_i \ldots q_n\} \quad \begin{matrix} p_1, p_2, p_3 \ldots p_i \ldots p_n \\ \uparrow \ \uparrow \ \uparrow \ \ \uparrow \ \ \uparrow \end{matrix}$$

$$RSS = \{s_{orig}, s_1, s_2, \ s_3 \ldots s_{m-1}\}$$

(a) Query Set

(b) Refined
Specialization Set

Fig. 2. Query Set and Refined Specialization Set

4.2 Time Cost Analysis

There are two aspects that determine the runtime cost of answering a user query: i)searching and selecting the appropriate *specialization* from the RSS (this time cost is denoted as T_s), ii) executing the XSLT transformation to generate the answer (this time cost is denoted as T_e). Hence, the total processing time T is equal to $T_s + T_e$.

The average T_s depends on the size of the RSS. It can be described as T_s=d|RSS| (|RSS| denotes the cardinality of *Refined Specialization Set* (RSS) and *d* represents the relationship between |RSS| and T_s, which varies according to the specialization search strategy).

T_e is defined as T_e=Time_Exe(q,s) (s∈ RSS and the function Time_Exe() is used to measure the transformation time for query q using specialization s). If s is a single specialization, which can cover all query terms in q, then the value for Time_Exe(q,s) is expected to be finite . However, if s can not cover all query terms in q, the value of Time_Exe(q,s) is considered to be ∞. Additionally, s_{orig} is the *Original XSLT,* which can cover all possible legal queries and the value of Time_Exe(q, s_{orig}) is always finite.

4.3 The Compact Specialization Set

The *Compact Specialization Set* (CSS) is a subset of RSS and is required to be small, so it does not take too much time to search through. Also, each element in the CSS should have relatively low cost and be applicable to a lot of situations (query terms). We wish to choose a CSS that minimizes the value of the following formula:

Formula_1:

Total_Time(CSS) =Total_Searching_Time(CSS)+Total_Execution_Time(CSS)

$$= \sum_{i=1}^{n} p_i * [d|CSS| + Min_{s \in CSS} (Time\_Exe(q_i,s))]$$

- $d|CSS|$:: T_s, the time spent on finding a minimum cost specialization from CSS to handle q_i
- $Min_{s \in CSS} (Time\_Exe(q_i,s))$:: T_e, the minimum time spent on executing s ($s \in$ CSS) to answer q_i.
- $d|CSS| + Min_{s \in CSS} (Time\_Exe(q_i,s))$:: T, the total time for processing q_i based on CSS
- $p_i * [d|CSS| + Min_{s \in CSS} (Time\_Exe(q_i,s))]$ :: The time spent for processing the distinct query q_i, which has the probability p_i, based on CSS.

- $\sum_{i=1}^{n} p_i * [d|CSS| + Min_{s \in CSS} (Time\_Exe(q_i,s))]$ :: the total time for processing

all distinct queries $(q_1,q_2,...q_n)$ in QS based on the CSS

4.4   Generate an Approximation of the Compact Specialization Set

In generating the CSS, if the RSS is not too large, we can generate all subsets of it and choose the one which has the minimum Total_Time according to Formula_1. However, this method is impossible if the RSS is a large set. For example, an RSS with 100 *specializations* has 2^{100} subsets.

It is well known that the query distribution of Web based searching applications is asymmetrical [15]. A small number of distinct queries account for most searches (i.e. have high summed probability (sum(p_i))). Using this knowledge, we can dramatically reduce the search space. Our method is related to the well known problem of computing the transversals of a hypergraph or the vertex cover problem [11]. It consists of the following steps:

- Step_1: Sort the distinct queries in QS according to descending probabilities and create a list of specialization sets (LSS), where each specialization set in LSS consists of all *specializations* which can cover the corresponding query q_i in QS. Also, for each specialization set of LSS, we order the elements in ascending cost from left to right. Step_1 is described in Fig.3.(a)

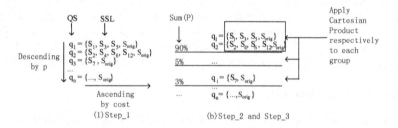

Fig. 3. Steps of Specialization Set Compaction

- Step_2: Slice the LSS horizontally into different groups, according to a predefined threshold list of descending sum (p_i). Specifically, we slice the LSS into 5 groups and define the required values of sum (p_i) for each group respectively as 90%, 5%, 3%, 1.5% and 0.5%. This predefined threshold list of sum(p_i) is defined based on analysing the *user query set* and must obey the following two policies : i) distinct queries with high probability must be grouped in the first slice and ii) sum(p_i) of the first slice should be big enough to cover most of user queries (e.g. 90%). For the groups with small sum (p_i), we only keep several (e.g. 1 or 2) of the leftmost *specializations* of each specialization set and omit (delete) other the other relatively bigger cost *specializations*, since they have low probabilities and only have a small impact on the final result.
- Step_3: Apply a *Cartesian-Product* operation, to each sliced group of specialization sets and generate new specialization sets such that every set can cover all the distinct queries in that group. Step_2 and step_3 are illustrated in Fig.3.(b).
- Step_4: For each group, select the set which has the minimum value of Total_Time, by evaluating all candidates using Formula_1.
- Step_5: Combine all of the specialization sets selected by step_4 into one set and delete the redundant *specializations*. Thus, we obtain the final approximation of *Compact Specialization Set* (CSS).

If we want to obtain a more accurate result, we can also make a second round *Cartesian-Product* on the specialization sets generated by step_3. Then test the result sets one by one based on Formula_1 to choose the minimum set as final CSS.

5 Overview of Compact Specialization and Combination

We overview our techniques in Fig.4. We can see that in the static environment, the system generates the *Primary Specialization Set* (PSS) based on the *Original XSLT* using the specialization principles of the XTS technique and then applies the approach of *Specialization Combination* (SC) to generate the RSS. Next, the *Specialization Set Compaction* (SSC) technique produces the *Compact Specialization Set* (CSS) as the final output. At runtime, our server-side XSLT system uses an XSLT specialization index to select the best (lowest cost) individual *specialization* in the *Compact Specialization Set* (CSS) for responding to the user query (The *Original XSLT* is retained

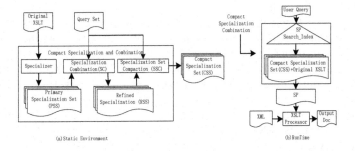

Fig. 4. Overview of Compact Specialization and Combination

as a member of the *Compact Specialization Set* (CSS) for handling any new queries which can not be handled by any *specialization*). We can repeat the process of *Compact Specialization and Combination* (SC plus SSC), based on the latest data of the query set (QS) (e.g. every month), to increase the accuracy of the *Compact Specialization Set.*

6 Experimental Results

We choose XSLT and XML test cases by considering the different XSLT design styles [22] and different XML DTD-Graph structures [17] (mentioned in section 2.1 and 2.2). Specifically, *shakespeare.xml* (*Broad-Deep* structure), is used as the XML input data source for *XSLBench1.xsl* (*Push* style XSLT), *XSLBench2.xsl* (*Pull* style XSLT) and *XSLBench3.xsl* (*Hybrid* style XSLT). The *brutal.xml* (*Narrow-Deep* structure) is the XML input data source of *brutal.xsl*, and *db8000.xml* (*Broad-Shallow* structure) is the XML input of *db.xsl*.

Experimental results were generated for two different XSLT processors: i)Xalan-j v2.6, ii) Saxon v8.3, and two different system environments (hardware&OS): i) Dell PowerEdge2500 (two P3 1GHz CPU and 2G RAM running Solaris 8(X86)), ii) IB-MeServer pSeries 650 (eight 1.45GHz CPU, 16GB RAM, running AIX5L 5.2).

To simulate the user query inputs, we stipulate that each query should consist of 1-3 terms [15]. Then, based on the possible query term space for each XSLT, we randomly generate three different query sets, QS_1, QS_2, and QS_3, each containing 1000 queries and a specific percentage of *weak interconnection queries*. (i.e. QS_1 consists of 100 WIQs and 900 SIQs, QS_2 consists of 300 WIQs and 700 SIQs, and QS_3 consists of 500 WIQs and 500 SIQs.)

Also, in order to simulate the asymmetrical query distribution of Web applications [15] (mentioned in section 4.4), we stipulate that 10% of the queries cover 90% of the probability space.

The following is a description of our testing methodology for each XSLT:

- Generate the *Primary Specialization Set* (PSS) based on the *Original XSLT stylesheet,* using different *specialization principles* (described in section 2.3) with possible values of parameter k being (1, 2, 3…).
- Test the *Primary Specialization Set* (PSS) using the XTS technique for different query sets (QS_1, QS_2 and QS_3) respectively and record the average processing time for each.
- Generate the *Refined Specialization Set* RSS_i (i=1,2,3), based on the *Primary Specialization Set* (PSS) and the query set QS_i (i=1,2,3), using the technique for *Specialization Combination* (SC)
- Test the *Refined Specialization Set* RSS_i (i=1,2,3), using the query set QS_i (i=1,2,3) and record the average processing time across RSS_1, RSS_2 and RSS_3.
- Generate the *Compact Specialization Set* CSS_i (i=1,2,3), based on the *Refined Specialization Set* RSS_i (i=1,2,3) and corresponding query set QS_i (i=1,2,3), using the technique of *Specialization Set Compaction* (SSC).

- Test the *Compact Specialization Set* CSS_i (i=1,2,3) based on the corresponding query set QS_i (i=1,2,3) and record the average processing time among CSS_1, CSS_2 and CSS_3.

In Table.1 below, we illustrate the sizes of the various specialization sets (based on different query sets QS_1, QS_2 and QS_3), generated by the different optimization approaches (XTS, SC and SSC) for each XSLT test case. The specialization reduction (percentage) between the *Specialization Set Compaction* technique and the *Specialization Set Refining* technique is shown under column (Avg|RSS|-Avg|CSS|)/Avg|RSS|)*100% in Table.1 as well.

Table 1. The number of specializations generated by different approaches

	|PSS|	|RSS|	|CSS|	$\dfrac{\text{Avg } \mid \text{RSS} \mid - \text{Avg} \mid \text{CSS} \mid}{\text{Avg } \mid \text{RSS} \mid}\%$
XSLBench1	52	75	33	84.00%
		124	27	
		177	32	
XSLBench2	72	96	27	75.00%
		144	26	
		189	35	
XSLBench3	68	91	20	79.00%
		144	21	
		192	25	
brutal	38	57	19	72.65%
		84	22	
		117	23	
db	42	63	21	74.25%
		94	20	
		125	23	

The optimization performance of our new techniques is effective and encouraging. We provide the comparison of processing time and corresponding time saving (compared to *Original XSLT*) between different optimization approaches in Table.2.

The value under column 'Orig' is the average transformation time using the *Original XSLT* stylesheet, the value under column 'T_e' is the XSLT execution time; the value under column 'T_s' is the time used to search for an appropriate *specialization* from the relevant specialization set (PSS, RSS or CSS); the value under column 'T' is the total processing time, $T=T_e+T_s$; the value under column 'S%' is the percentage of processing time saved for the optimization approach compared with the *Original XSLT*, S%=(((Orig-T)/Orig)*100)%. All processing time in Table.2 is expressed in seconds and computed based on 1000 user queries.

These results illustrate that, firstly, that our new approaches, *Compact Specialization Combination* (SC+SSC), can effectively improve the server-side XSLT processing time compared to the *Original XSLT* and the XTS optimization technique (our previous work). The saving of processing time is due to i) the use of combined specializations, instead of the *Original XSLT* or 'overweight' *specializations*, to handle *weak interconnection queries* and consequently save XSLT execution time (T_e) and ii) the use of *Compact Specialization Set* (CSS) to reduce the search space and save the *specialization* searching time (T_s) at runtime.

Secondly, the *Specialization Combination* (SC) technique is more effective for improving the XSLT execution time (T_e) for query sets which have a higher number of *weak interconnection queries*. Moreover, *Specialization Set Compaction* (SSC) inherits the advantage of dealing with *weak interconnection queries* from the SC technique and is more effective at reducing the specialization search time (T_s) for the larger specialization set.

Table 2. The processing time(seconds) and time saving(%)

	Orig	Query Set	XTS (based on PSS)				SC (based on RSS)				SSC (based on CSS)			
			Te	Ts	T	S%	Te	Ts	T	S%	Te	Ts	T	S%
XSLBench1	4993	QS1	3010	372	3382	32%	2312	536	2848	43%	2422	236	2658	47%
		QS2	3248	372	3620	27%	2374	887	3261	35%	2478	193	2671	47%
		QS3	3519	371	3890	22%	2349	1266	3615	28%	2499	229	2728	45%
		Avg				27%				35%				46%
XSLBench2	5735	QS1	3831	515	4346	24%	2414	686	3100	46%	2530	195	2724	52%
		QS2	4081	512	4593	20%	2889	1030	3918	32%	2892	186	3078	46%
		QS3	4252	513	4766	17%	2672	1351	4023	30%	2726	250	2976	48%
		Avg				20%				36%				49%
XSLBEnch3	5467	QS1	3580	461	4041	26%	2492	651	3143	43%	2604	143	2747	50%
		QS2	3827	460	4287	22%	2623	1030	3652	33%	2717	150	2868	48%
		QS3	4156	463	4619	16%	2550	1373	3923	28%	2598	179	2777	49%
		Avg				21%				35%				49%
brutal	2678	QS1	1803	272	2075	23%	1388	408	1796	33%	1468	135	1603	40%
		QS2	1979	278	2257	16%	1403	601	2004	25%	1517	157	1674	37%
		QS3	2164	269	2433	9%	1394	837	2231	17%	1502	164	1666	38%
		Avg				16%				25%				38%
db	3228	QS1	2110	300	2410	25%	1608	450	2058	36%	1819	150	1969	39%
		QS2	2287	302	2590	20%	1627	672	2299	29%	1837	143	1980	39%
		QS3	2474	298	2773	14%	1590	894	2484	23%	1794	167	1961	39%
		Avg				20%				29%				39%

Thirdly, our new technique, *Compact Specialization and Combination* (SC+SSC), can be applied to XSLT designed in the three different styles (*Push* style, *Pull* style and *Hybrid* style) and XML documents designed in different structures (*Broad-Deep*, *Narrow-deep* and *Broad-Shallow* DTD-Graph structures). It is more effective for XML designed in the *Broad-Deep* DTD-Graph structure, since i) the query terms of a *weak interconnection query* for a *Broad-Deep* XML database might be more 'far apart' than *Narrow* or *Shallow* XML and the *specialization* (generated with our previous XTS technique) used to handle the *weak interconnection query* might be more 'overweight' and so the combined *specialization* can save relatively more execution time; ii)the larger specialization set might be generated based on the *Broad-Deep* XML database compared with *Narrow* or *Shallow* XML, and the technique of *Specialization Set Compaction* (SSC) can prune relatively more search space. *Compact Specialization and Combination* is not applicable for small XSLT stylesheets and the *Narrow-Shallow* XML, since too few specializations are able to be generated.

We conducted all the above tests using the Xalan XSLT processor as well. The experimental results were similar to that for Saxon (Table.2).

7   Related Work

To the best of our knowledge, there is no other previous work, which considers *Specialization Combination* or *Specialization Set Compaction* for optimizing server-side XSLT programs. Extensive study has been done specialization for various kinds of programs [1, 18, 20]. A partial evaluator for inductively sequential functional logic programs has been proposed by M. Alpuente and M. Hanus et al in 1999 [1]. S. Helsen and P.Thiemann presented their framework for offline partial evaluation for call-by-value functional programming languages in 2004 [18]. The main difference on specialization between the XSLT scenario and functional or logic programs is that XSLT is data intensive and, usually, a data schema (DTD or XML-schema) is provided. XSLT and XQuery based optimization have been considered in [16, 19, 28, 31]. Z. Guo, M. Li et al in 2004[16] use a streaming processing model to transform an XML document to other formats without using extra buffer space. However, some strong restrictions on the XSLT syntax and design are made, limiting the applicability. S. Jain, R. Mahajan and D. Suciu proposed several optimization techniques in their paper about *translating XSLT to SQL* in 2002 [19]. Their method leverages the use of a relational database. The XSLT transformation tuning method was represented by L. Villard, N. Layaida, in their paper about *incremental transformation framework* in 2002 [28]. X. Zhang, K. Dimitrova, L. Wang and et al, in 2003, proposed an XQuery optimization based on query rewriting using materialized views [31]. Our optimization method, differs from [16, 19, 28, 31], since it focuses on XSLT stylesheets and uses statistics from query logs. It can be applied regardless of XSLT processor and hardware&OS platform. XPath or XML index based query optimization has been considered in a large number of papers [2, 8, 26]. The research proposed by S. Abiteboul and V. Vianu in 1997 [2] focuses on local information expressed in the form of path constraints for optimization of path expression queries. A declarative, optimizable query language XML-QL, is presented by Deutsch and M. Fernandez et al in 1999 [8], Li and Moon propose a new system for indexing and storing XML data on a numbering schema for elements in 2000 [26]. The DTD-Graph mentioned in this paper is similar to the Dataguide structure described by Goldman and Widom in 1997 [14].

8   Conclusion and Future Work

In this paper, we have proposed two new approaches: *XSLT Specialization Combination* (SC) and *XSLT Specialization Set Compaction* (SSC), for the task of optimizing server-side XSLT transformations. We have shown that *Compact Specialization and Combination* (SC +SSC) significantly outperform the *Original XSLT* transformation and the method of our previous work (XTS). Based on the technique of SC, the system can process and optimize not only *strong interconnection queries*, but also another very important class of user queries, *weak interconnection queries*. Moreover, based on the technique of *Specialization Set Compaction* (SSC), we reduce the size of the *Refined Specialization Set* (RSS) and, practically, generate an approximate *Compact Specialization Set* (CSS) to further improve performance.

Our experimental results showed that these new approaches provide more effective optimization (saving about 40-50% in processing time compared with the *Original XSLT*) for server-side XSLT transformation. As part of our future work, we plan to investigate extending our methods and algorithms to handle further XSLT syntax, such as the wider use of built-in templates, and functions within *construction patterns*.

Acknowledgment

This work is partially supported by National ICT Australia. National ICT Australia is funded by the Australian Government's Backing Australia's Ability initiative, in part through the Australian Research Council.

References

[1] M. Alpuente and M. Hanus.: Specialization of inductively sequential functional logic programs. In *Proceedings of the fourth ACM SIGPLAN international conference on Functional programming table of contents*. (1999) 273 – 283.

[2] S. Abiteboul and V. Vianu.: Regular path queries with constraints. In *the 16th ACM SIGACT-SIGMOD-SIGSTART Symposium on Principles of Database Systems*, AZ (1997)

[3] T. Bray, J. Paoli, and C. M. Sperberg-McQueen, and E. Maler.: W3C Recommendation. Extensible Markup Language (XML) 1.0 (2000)

[4] C.Y. Chan, P. Felber, M. Garofalakis, and R. Rastogi.: Efficient Filtering of XML Documents with XPath Expressions, Proceedings of *Intl' Conference on Data Engineering*, San Jose, California (2002) 235-244

[5] J. Clark.: W3C recommendation. XSL Transformations (XSLT) version 1.0. (1999)

[6] S. Cohen, Y. Kanza and Y. Sagiv.: Generating Relations from XML Documents. In *Proceedings of ICDT 2003'*, Italy (2003) 285-299

[7] A. Deutsch and V. Tannen.: Containment and integrity constraints for XPath. In *Proc. KRDB 2001*, CEUR Workshop Proceedings 45 (2003)

[8] A. Deutsch, M. Fernandez, D. Florescu, A. Levy and D. Suciu.: A query language for XML. In *Proc.of 8th Int'l. World Wide Web Conf.* Toronto, Canada (1999) 1155-1169

[9] C. Dong and J. Bailey.: Optimization of XML Transformations Using Template Specialization. In *Proc.of The 5th International Conference on Web Information Systems Engineering (WISE 2004)*, Brisbane, Australia (2004) 352-364

[10] C. Dong and J. Bailey.: The static analysis of XSLT programs. In *Proc.of The 15th Australasian Database Conference*, Vol.27, Pages 151-160, Dunedin, New Zealand (2004)

[11] T. Eiter and G. Gottlob. Identifying the Minimal Transversals of a Hypergraph and Related Problems. *SIAM Journal of Computing* 24(6) (1995) 1278-1304.

[12] W. Fan, M. Garofalakis, M. Xiong, X. Jia.: Composable XML integration grammars. In *Proceedings of Thirteenth ACM conference on Information and knowledge management*. Washington, D.C., USA (2004) 2-11

[13] M. Gertz, J. Bremer.: Distributed XML Repositories: Top-down Design and Transparent Query Processing. *Technical Report CSE-2003-20*, Department of Computer Science, University of California, Davis, USA (2003)

[14] R. Goldman and J. Widom.: Enabling query formulation and optimization in semi-structured database. *Proc. Int'l Conf on VLDB*, Athens, Greece (1997) 436-445
[15] Google Gulde. http://www.googleguide.com
[16] Z. Guo, M. Li, X. Wang, and A. Zhou.: Scalable XSLT Evaluation, In *Proc. of APWEB 2004*, HangZhou, China (2004) 137-150
[17] http://www.datapower.com/xmldev/xsltmark.html
[18] S. Helsen and P.Thiemann.: Polymorphic specialization for ML. *ACM Transactions on Programming Languages and Systems (TOPLAS) archive*. 26(4) (2004) 652-700
[19] S. Jain and R. Mahajan and D. Suciu (2002): Translating XSLT Programs to Efficient SQL Queries. *Proc. World Wide Web 2002*, Hawaii, USA (2002) 616-626
[20] N. Jones.: An Introduction to Partial Evaluation. *ACM Computing Surveys*. (1996) 28(3)
[21] M. Kay.: Saxon XSLT Processor. http://saxon.sourceforge.net/
[22] M. Kay.: Anatomy of an XSLT Processor.
       http://www-106.ibm.com/developerworks/library/x-xslt2/ (2001)
[23] P. Kumar.: XML Processing Measurements using XPB4J (2003)
[24] C. Laird.: XSLT powers a new wave of web.
       http://www.linuxjournal.com/article.php?sid=5622 (2002)
[25] D. Lee, W. Chu.: Comparative analysis of six XML schema languages. *ACM SIGMOD Record archive Volume 29, Issue 3*. ACM Press, New York, NY, USA (2000) 76–87
[26]]Q. Li, B. Moon.: Indexing and querying XML data for regular path expressions. In *Proc. Int'l Conf on VLDB*, Roma, Italy (2001) 361-370
[27]]S. Maneth and F. Neven.: Structured document transformations based on XSL. In *Proceedings of DBPL'99*, Kinloch Rannoch, Scottland (2000) 80-98
[28] L. Villard, N. Layaida.: An incremental XSLT transformation processor for XML document manipulation. *Proc. World Wide Web 2002*, Hawaii, USA (2002) 474-485
[29] [29]World Wide Web Consortium. XML Path Language(XPath) Recommendation.
       http://www.w3.org/TR/xpath
[30] M. Weiser: Programmers use slices when debugging. In *Communications of ACM*, Volume 25, Issue 7, 446 – 452 (1982)
[31] X. Zhang, K. Dimitrova, L. Wang, M. E. Sayed, B. Murphy, B. Pielech, M Mulchandani, L. Ding and E. A. Rundensteiner.: RainbowII: multi-XQuery optimization using materialized XML views. In *Proceedings of the 2003 ACM SIGMOD international conference on Management of data*, San Diego, California, USA (2003) 671-685

Extracting Web Data Using Instance-Based Learning

Yanhong Zhai and Bing Liu

Department of Computer Science, University of Illinois at Chicago,
851 S. Morgan Street, Chicago, IL 60607
yzhai, liub@cs.uic.edu

Abstract. This paper studies structured data extraction from Web pages, e.g., online product description pages. Existing approaches to data extraction include wrapper induction and automatic methods. In this paper, we propose an instance-based learning method, which performs extraction by comparing each new instance (or page) to be extracted with labeled instances (or pages). The key advantage of our method is that it does not need an initial set of labeled pages to learn extraction rules as in wrapper induction. Instead, the algorithm is able to start extraction from a single labeled instance (or page). Only when a new page cannot be extracted does the page need labeling. This avoids unnecessary page labeling, which solves a major problem with inductive learning (or wrapper induction), i.e., the set of labeled pages may not be representative of all other pages. The instance-based approach is very natural because structured data on the Web usually follow some fixed templates and pages of the same template usually can be extracted using a single page instance of the template. The key issue is the similarity or distance measure. Traditional measures based on the Euclidean distance or text similarity are not easily applicable in this context because items to be extracted from different pages can be entirely different. This paper proposes a novel similarity measure for the purpose, which is suitable for templated Web pages. Experimental results with product data extraction from 1200 pages in 24 diverse Web sites show that the approach is surprisingly effective. It outperforms the state-of-the-art existing systems significantly.

1 Introduction

Web data extraction is the problem of identifying and extracting target items from Web pages. It is important in practice because it allows one to integrate information or data from multiple sources (Web sites and pages) to provide value-added services, e.g., customizable Web information gathering, comparative shopping, meta-search, etc.

In this paper, we focus on regularly structured data which are produced by computer programs following some fixed templates. The contents of these data records are usually retrieved from backend databases, and then converted to HTML documents by programs and published on the Web. One such example

M. Kitsuregawa et al. (Eds.): WISE 2005, LNCS 3806, pp. 318–331, 2005.
© Springer-Verlag Berlin Heidelberg 2005

is the product description pages. Each merchant who sells products on the Web needs to provide a detailed description of each product. Fig.1 shows an example page. One may want to extract four pieces of information from this page, product name, product image, product description, and product price, for comparative shopping. Note that each of the items is marked with a dash-lined box in Fig.1. We call each required piece of information a *target item* (or simply *item*).

Fig. 1. An example product description page

Existing research on Web data extraction has produced a number of techniques ([1, 2, 3, 4, 5, 6, 7, 8, 9, 10]). The current dominate technique is wrapper induction based on inductive machine learning. In this approach, the user first labels or marks the target items in a set of training pages or a list of data records in one page. The system then learns extraction rules from these training pages. The learned rules are then applied to extract target items from other pages. An extraction rule for a target item usually contains two patterns [11, 8]: a prefix pattern for detecting the beginning of a target item, and a suffix pattern for detecting the ending of a target item. Although there are also automatic approaches to extraction based on pattern finding, they are usually less accurate and also need manual post-processing to identify the items of interest. In Sec.2, we discuss these and other existing approaches further.

A major problem with inductive learning is that the initial set of labeled training pages may not be fully representative of the templates of all other pages. For pages that follow templates not covered by the labeled pages, learnt rules will perform poorly. The usual solution to this problem is to label more pages because more pages should cover more templates. However, manual labeling is labor intensive and time consuming (still no guarantee that all possible templates will be covered). For a company that is interested in extracting all product information from most (if not all) merchant sites on the Web for comparative shopping, this represents a substantial work. Although active learning helps [12], it needs sophisticated mechanisms.

In this paper, we propose an instance-based learning approach to data extraction that is able to deal with this problem effectively. In classic instance-based learning, a set of labeled instances (more than 1) is stored first (no induction learning is performed). When a new instance is presented, it is compared with the stored instances to produce the results. The approach is commonly used in classification. The most popular instance-based learning methods are *k-nearest neighbor* and *case-based reasoning* [13]. However, we cannot directly apply these classic approaches because we will still need an initial set of many labeled instances, and thus will have the same problem as inductive learning.

We propose a different instance-based method that is more suitable to data extraction from Web pages. It does not need an initial set of labeled pages. Instead, the algorithm can begin extraction from a single labeled page. Only when a new page cannot be extracted does the page need labeling. This avoids unnecessary labeling and also ensures that all different templates are covered.

We believe that instance-based learning is very suitable for structured data extraction because such Web data are presented by following some fixed layout templates (see Fig.1). Pages from the same template can be extracted using a single page instance of the template.

The key to our instance based learning method is the similarity or distance measure. In our context, it is the problem of how to measure the similarity between the corresponding target items in a labeled page and a new page. Traditional measures based on the Euclidean distance or text similarity are not easily applicable in this context because target items from different pages can be entirely different. We propose a natural measure that exploits the HTML tag context of the items. Instead of comparing items themselves, we compare the tag strings before and after each target item to determine the extraction. This method is appropriate for templated pages because a template is essentially reflected by its sequence of formatting tags. Our technique works as follows:

1. A random page is selected for labeling.
2. The user labels/marks the items of interest in the page.
3. A sequence of consecutive tags (also called *tokens* later) before each labeled item (called the *prefix string* of the item) and a sequence of consecutive tags after the labeled item (called the *suffix string* of the item) are stored.
4. The system then starts to extract items from new pages. For a new page d, the system compares the stored prefix and suffix strings with the tag stream of page d to extract each item (this step is involved and will be clear later). If some target items from d cannot be identified (i.e., this page may follow a different template), page d is passed to step 2 for labeling.

We have implemented an extraction system, called IDE (*Instance-based Data Extraction*) based on the proposed approach. The system has been tested using 1200 product pages from 24 Web sites. Our results show that IDE is highly effective. Out of the 1200 pages, only 6 pages were not extracted correctly, and only one of the items in each page was extracted incorrectly. For most Web sites, the user only needs to label 2-3 pages. We also compared IDE with the FETCH [14] system, which is the commercial version of the state-of-the-art research system Stalker [11, 8, 15, 12]. Our results show that IDE outperforms FETCH in our experiments. Our proposed approach is also efficient.

2   Related Work

The closely related works to ours are in the area of wrapper generation. A wrapper is a program that extracts data items from a Web site/page and put them in a database. There are two main approaches to wrapper generation. The first approach is wrapper induction (or learning), which is the main technique presently. The second approach is automatic extraction.

As mentioned earlier, wrapper learning works as follows: The user first manually labels a set of training pages or data records in a list. A learning system then generates rules from the training pages. These rules can then be applied to extract target items from new pages. Example wrapper induction systems include WIEN [6], Softmealy [5], Stalker [8, 15, 12], BWI [3], WL^2 [1], and etc [9]. A theoretical study on wrapper learning is also done in [16]. It gives a family of PAC-learnable wrapper classes and their induction algorithms and complexities.

WIEN [6] and Softmealy [5] are earlier wrapper learning systems, which were improved by Stalker [11, 8, 15, 12]. Stalker learns rules for each item and uses more expressive representation of rules. It does not consider ordering of items but treat them separately. This is more flexible but also makes learning harder for complex pages because local information is not fully exploited. Recent research on Stalker has added various active learning capabilities to the system to reduce the number of pages to be labeled by the user. The idea of active learning is to let the system select the most useful pages to be labeled by the user and thus reduces some manual effort.

Existing systems essentially learn extraction rules. The rules are then used directly to extract each item in new pages. Our work is different. Our technique does not perform inductive learning. Instead, it uses an instance-based approach. It can start extraction from a single labeled page. Although [17] can learn from one page (two for single-record pages), it requires more manual work because if the system does not perform well the user who monitors the system needs to change some system thresholds.

In recent years, researchers also studied automatic extraction, i.e., no user labeling is involved. [18] proposes a method for finding repetitive patterns from a Web page, and then uses the patterns to extract items from each object in the page. [19] shows that this technique performs unsatisfactory in extraction. [20, 21, 7] propose two other automatic extraction methods. However, these automatic methods are less accurate than the systems that ask the user to label training pages. Manual post-processing is also needed for the user to identify what he/she is interested in. In [10], a more accurate technique is proposed based on tree matching. However, it is only for list pages (each page contains multiple data records). [22, 19] propose some techniques for finding data objects or data records. However, they do not perform data extraction from the records.

Another related research is information extraction from text documents [23, 24, 2, 3, 4, 25, 26]. Our work is different as we mainly exploit structural information in a Web page for extraction, which requires different techniques. Finally, a number of toolkits to facilitate users to build wrappers are reported in [27, 28, 29].

3   Instance-Based Extraction

We now present the proposed approach. As mentioned earlier, given a set of pages from a Web site, the proposed technique first (randomly) selects a page to ask the user to label the items that need to be extracted. The system then stores a certain number of consecutive prefix and suffix tokens (tags) of each item. After that, it starts to extract target items from each new page. During extraction, if the algorithm is unable to locate an item, this page is given to the user to label. This process goes on until all the pages from the given site have been processed. Below, Sec.3.1 presents the overall algorithm and the page labeling procedure. Sec.3.2 presents the similarity measure used for extraction. Sec.3.3 presents an efficient algorithm for implementation.

3.1   The Overall Algorithm

Let S be the set of pages from a Web site that the user wants to extract target items from. Let k be the number of tokens in the prefix or suffix string to be saved for each target item from a labeled page. In practice, we give k a large number, say 20. The setting of this value is not important because if it is too small, the system can always go back to the labeled page to get more tokens. Fig.2 gives the overall algorithm.

```
Algorithm (S, k)              // S is the set of pages.
1. p = randomSelect(S);       // Randomly select a page p from S
2. Templates = <>;            // initialization
3. labelPage(Templates, p, k);        // the user labels the page p
4. for each remaining page d in S do
5.     if  ¬(extract(Templates, d)) then
6.         labelPage(Templates, d, k)
7.     end - if
8. end- for
```

Fig. 2. The overall algorithm

In line 1, the algorithm randomly selects a page p from S. This page is given to the user for labeling (line 3). A user-interface has been implemented for the user to label target items easily. Variable *Templates* (line 2) stores the templates of all labeled pages so far. For example, in the page of Fig.1, we are interested in extracting four items from a product page, namely, *name, image, description* and *price*. The template (T) for a labeled page is represented as follows: $T = < pat_{name}, pat_{img}, pat_{description}, pat_{price} >$

Each pat_i in T consists of a prefix string and a suffix string of the item i(also called the *prefix-suffix pattern* of i). For example, if the product image is embedded in the following HTML source:

```
...<table><tr><td> <img> </td><td></td>...
```

then we have:

$pat_{img}.prefix$ = `<<table ><tr><td>>` $pat_{img}.suffix$ = `<</td><td></td>>`

Here, we use $k = 3$ (in our experiments, we used $k = 20$, which is sufficient).

In this work, we treat each page to be labeled as a sequence of tokens. A token can be any HTML element, a HTML tag, a word, a punctuation mark, etc. Not all kinds of tokens before or after a target item will be saved as a part of the prefix or suffix string. All tags and at most one word or punctuation mark right before (or after) the target item are regarded as part of the prefix (or suffix) string. Basically, we mainly rely on HTML tags to locate each target item.

After page p is labeled by the user, the algorithm can start extraction from the rest of the pages (lines 4-8). The extraction procedure, extract() (line 5), extracts all the items from page d.

To label a page, the user marks the items to be extracted in the page. This procedure is given in Fig3. A user-interface makes this process very easy. Basically, only mouse clicks on each target item are needed.

A requirement for the first page p is that it must contain all target items. The reason for this requirement is that if there is one or more missing items in this page, the extraction system will not know that additional items are needed. Selecting such a page is not difficult as most pages have all target items. Another important issue is the handling of missing items (see below).

Procedure labelPage(*Templates, p, k*)
1. The user labels all the required items in page p;
2. $T = <>$;   *// initialization*
3. **for** each required item i **do**
4.   **if** item i does not exist in page p **then**
5.   insert $\emptyset$ into T at the right end;
6.   **else**
7.   prefix = extract k prefix tokens before item i in p;
8.   suffix = extract k suffix tokens after item i in p;
9. T = insert *<prefix, suffix>* into T at the right end;
10.   **end - if**
11. **end - for**
12. **if** p has missing item(*s*) **then**
13.   *Templates* = insert T into *Templates* at the end;
14. **else**
15.   *Templates* = insert T into *Templates* before any template with missing item(*s*);
16. **end - if**
17. output all the labeled items in p;

Fig. 3. Labeling a page p

T is a new template that stores the prefix and suffix strings of every item in page p. In lines 12-13, if page p has missing items, we put T at the end of *Templates*, which stores all the templates of labeled pages. This is to ensure that it will not be used before any other template is used to extract a page.

3.2   The Similarity Measure

The key to instance-based learning is the similarity or distance measure. In our context, it is the problem of measuring whether an item in the new page (to be extracted) is similar to or is of the same *type* as a target item in a labeled page. As indicated earlier, we do not compare the items themselves. Instead, we compare their prefix and suffix strings. The score is the number of marches.

Definition 1. *(prefix match score): Let $P =< p_1, ..., p_k >$ be the prefix string of an item in a labeled page and $\mathcal{A}$ be the token string of page d (to be extracted). A sub-string of $\mathcal{A}(=< a_1, ...a_i, a_{i+1}, ..., a_{i+h}, ..., a_n >)$ matches P with a match score of $h(h \leq k)$, if $p_k = a_{i+h}, p_{k-1} = a_{i+h-1}, ..., p_{k-h-1} = a_{i+1}$, and ($p_{k-h} \neq a_i$ or $h = k$)*

Definition 2. *(suffix match score): Let $P =< p_1, ..., p_k >$ be the suffix string of an item in a labeled page and $\mathcal{A}$ be the token string of page d (to be extracted). A sub-string of $\mathcal{A}(=< a_1, ...a_i, a_{i+1}, ..., a_{i+h}, ..., a_n >)$ matches P with a match score of $h(h \leq k)$, if $p_1 = a_{i+1}, p_2 = a_{i+2}, ..., p_h = a_{i+h}$, and ($p_{h+1} \neq a_{i+h+1}$ or $h = k$)*

Note that the match starts from the right for the prefix match, and the left for the suffix match. Fig.4 shows an example. Assume that we saved 5 tokens `<table><tr><td><i><b>` in the prefix string of item *price* from a labeled page. The HTML source of a new page d to be extracted is shown in the box of the figure. From the figure, we see that there are 4 sub-strings in d that have matches with the prefix string of *price*. These are shown in four rows below the prefix string. The number within () is the sequence id of the token in page d. "-" means no match. The highest number of matches is 5, which is the best *match score* for this prefix string. The best score can also be computed for the suffix string.

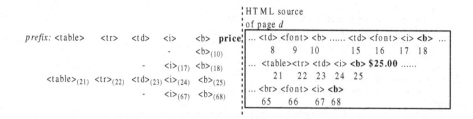

Fig. 4. Example 1 - Prefix matching

3.3   The Extraction Algorithm

We now discuss the extraction algorithm based on *match scores*. Note that in this paper, we are interested in extracting target items from pages that focus on a single object per page, not a list of objects per page due to one of our practical applications. A similar algorithm can be designed for list pages (we plan to do this in our future work).

The basic idea of the algorithm is as follows: For a new page d to be extracted, we try to use each labeled page (represented as a template of prefix and suffix strings) to extract the required items from d. Using the prefix and suffix strings of each item i, we can compute the prefix and suffix match scores of every item in page d. If a particular item j in d has a unique best match score (≥ 1) for both the prefix and suffix strings of a target item i in a template, item j is regarded as i's corresponding item in d and is extracted. After item j is extracted from d, we use the token strings of d before j and after j to identify and extract the remaining items. This process continues recursively until all items are extracted or an item cannot be extracted (which indicates that page d needs labeling). The detailed algorithm is more involved for efficiency reasons. This algorithm has the following characteristics:

1. In determining which item to extract, the system does not choose the item with the highest (prefix or suffix) match score among all items. Instead, it chooses the item with the unique best match score for the item in d.
2. There is no pre-specified sequence of items to be extracted. For example, the user is interested in 4 items from each page. The ordering of items in the HTML source is: *image, name, price,* and *description*. If at the beginning we are able to find item *price* uniquely in the page, we then start from price and search forward to find item *description* and search backward to find item *image* and *name*. In searching for the remaining items, the same approach is used. The final extraction sequence of items may be the one in Fig.5.
   This method has a major advantage. That is, we can exploit local contexts. It may be the case that from the whole page we are unable to identify a particular item. However, within a local area, it is easy to identify it.
3. Ordering of items is exploited in extraction as shown above.

Fig.6 gives the extraction control procedure, which basically tries each saved template T in *Templates*. T contains the prefix and suffix strings of each item in a previously labeled page. d is the page to be extracted. If using a template T, all the items can be extracted with the procedure *extractItems()* (line 2), it returns true (line 4) to indicate that page d is successfully extracted. If none of the template in *Templates* can be used to extract page d, the procedure returns

```
... image ... name .... price ... description
     2        3        1        4      - extraction sequence
```

Fig. 5. An example item extraction sequence

Procedure extract(*Templates, d*)
1. **for** each template *T* in *Templates* **do**
2.   **if** extractItems(*T, d, 1, end_id*) **then**
3.   output the extracted items from *d*;
4.   return **true**
5.   **end-if**
6. **end-for**
7. return **false**;

Fig. 6. The extraction control procedure

false to indicate that page *d* cannot be extracted using any previous *T*. "1" is the sequence id number of the first token of page *d*, and *end_id* is the sequence id of the last token of page *d*. These two id's tell extractItems() where to locate the target items. Note that each token has a sequence id, which enables the algorithm to find every token quickly.

The extractItems() procedure is given in Fig. 7. It takes 4 parameters, which have the same meanings as those in procedure extract(). *start* and *end* are the start and end token id's, which defines a region in *d* to look for target items.

In line 1 of Fig.7, we scan the input stream of page *d*. From lines 2-6, we try the prefix string in pat_i of each item *i* to identify the beginning of item *i*. If token *t* and its predecessors match some tokens in the prefix string (line 3),

Procedure extractItems(*T, d, start, end*)
1.   **for** each token *t* of *d* in sequence from *start* to *end* **do**
2.   **for** each *pat_i* in *T* **do**
3.   **if** $pat_i \neq \varnothing$ **and** *t* and its predecessors match some prefix tokens in *pati.prefix* **then**
4.   record the string of id's of the matching tokens
5.   **end-if**
6.   **end-for**
7.   **end-for**
8.   **if** an item *i*'s beginning can be uniquely identified **then**
9. idB_i = the id of the immediate token on the right of the prefix string of item *i*;
10.   **if** idE_i = find the ending of item *i* between idB_i and *end* **then**
11.   extract and store item *i*;
12.   **if** before(*T, i*) is not empty **then**
13.   **if** (extractItems(before(*T, i*), *d, start, idB_i*)) **then**
14.   return **false**
15.   **end-if**
16.   **end-if**
17.   **if** after(*T, i*) is not empty **then**
18.   **if** (extractItems(after(*T, i*), *d, idE_i, end*)) **then**
19.   return **false**
20.   **end-if**
21.   **end-if**
22.   **else** return **false**
23.   **end-if**
24.   **elseif** every target item may be missing **then**   //indicated by $\varnothing$ in every element of *T*
25.   do nothing   // items are not in the page
26.   **else** return **false**
27. **end-if**
28. return **true**

Fig. 7. The extractItems procedure

we record the sequence id's of the matching tokens (line 4). $pat_i \neq \emptyset$ means that item i is not missing. Let us use an example in Fig.4 to illustrate this part. 5 tokens `<table><tr><td><i><b>` are saved in the prefix string of item *price* from a labeled page (assume we have only one labeled page). After going through lines 1 to 7 (Fig.7), i.e., scanning through the new page, we find four `<b>`'s, two `<i><b>` together, but only one `<table><tr><td><i><b>` together. We see that the beginning of *price* can be uniquely identified (which is done in line 8 of Fig. 7) because the longest match is unique.

The algorithm for finding the ending location of an item (line 10 in Fig. 7) is similar to finding the beginning. This process will not be discussed further.

After item i is extracted and stored (line 11), if there are still items to be extracted before or after item i (line 12 and 17), a recursive called is made to extractItems() (line 13 and 18). idB_i and idE_i are the sequence id's of the beginning and the ending tokens of item i.

Extraction failures are reported in lines 14, 19, 22 and 26. Lines 24 and 25 say that if all target items to be extracted from *start* to *end* may be missing, we do nothing (i.e., we accept that the page does not have these items).

The functions before() and after() obtain the prefix-suffix string patterns for items before item i and after item i respectively. For example, currently T contains prefix-suffix string patterns for items 1 to 4. If item 3 has just been extracted, then before(T) should give the saved prefix-suffix string patterns for items 1 and 2, and after(T) gives the saved prefix-suffix patterns of item 4.

Finally, we note that in lines 13 and 18 of Fig.7, both the *start* and *end* id's should extend further because the prefix and suffix strings of the next item could extend beyond the current item. We omit this detail in the algorithm to simplify the presentation.

4 Empirical Evaluation

Based on the proposed approach, we built a data extraction system called IDE. We now evaluate IDE, and compare it with the state-of-the-art system FETCH [14], which is the commercial version of Stalker (the research version Stalker is not publicly available). Stalker improved the earlier systems such as WIEN, Softmealy, etc. The experimental results are given in Tab.1. Below, we first describe some experimental settings and then discuss the results.

Web sites used to build IDE: We used pages from 3 Web sites in building our system, i.e., designing algorithms and debugging the system. None of these sites is used in testing IDE.

Test Web sites and pages: 24 e-commerce Web sites are used in our experiments[1]. From each Web site, 50 product description pages are downloaded. All

---

[1] We did not use the archived data from the RISE repository (http://www.isi.edu/info-agents/RISE/) in our experiments because the data in RISE are mainly Web pages that contain a list of objects per page. Our current technique is designed to extract data from pages that focus on a single object per page, which are important for comparative shopping applications.

the sites and pages are selected and downloaded by a MS student who is not involved in this project. See Tab.1 for our test Web sites.

From each product page, we extract the name, image, description and price for the product as they are important for many applications in Internet commerce, e.g., comparative shopping, product categorization and clustering.

Evaluation measures: We use the standard precision and recall measures to evaluate the results of each system.

Experiments: We performed two types of experiments on FETCH:

1. The training pages of FETCH are the pages being labeled by the user using IDE. These pages are likely to follow different templates and have distinctive features. Thus, they are the best pages for learning. However, they give FETCH an unfair boost because without IDE such pages will not be found. Tab.1 shows the results of FETCH and IDE in this setting.
2. Use the same number of training pages as used by IDE. However, the training pages are randomly selected (this is the common situation for inductive learning). In this case, FETCH's results are much worse (see Tab.2).

Tab.1 shows the results for experiment 1. Before discussing the results, we first explain the problem descriptions used in the table:

- miss: The page contains the target item, but it is not found.
- found-no: The page does not contain the target item, but the system finds one, which is wrong.
- wrong: The page has the target item, but a wrong one is found.
- partial err.: The page contains the target item, but the system finds only part of it (incomplete).
- page err.: It is the number of pages with extraction errors (any of the 4 types above).

We now summarize the results in Tab 1.

1. IDE is able to find all the correct items from every page of each Web site except for Web site 4. In site 4, IDE finds wrong product images in 6 pages. This problem is caused by irregular tags used before the image in many pages. This site also requires a high number of labeled pages which shows that this site has many irregularities. The FETCH system also made many mistakes in this site.
2. For 15 out of 24 Web sites, IDE only needs to label one or two pages and find all the items correctly.
3. We compute precision and recall in term of the number of items extracted. We also give a page accuracy value, which is computed based on the number of pages extracted correctly, i.e., every target item in these pages is extracted correctly.

	Recall	Precision	Page accuracy
IDE:	99.9%	99.9%	99.5%
FETCH:	95.7%	97.8%	82.5%

Table 1. Experiment 1 results

Site	No.of labeled pages	IDE					FETCH				
		miss	found-no	wrong	partial err.	page err.	miss	found-no	wrong	partial err.	page err.
1 alight	2	0	0	0	0	0	1	0	0	0	1
2 amazon	5	0	0	0	0	0	13	2	1	0	15
3 avenue	2	0	0	0	0	0	1	0	0	0	1
4 bargainoutfitters	8	0	0	6	0	6	0	0	9	0	9
5 circuitcity	2	0	0	0	0	0	1	0	0	3	4
6 computer4sure	4	0	0	0	0	0	4	0	0	0	4
7 computersurplusoutlet	1	0	0	0	0	0	0	0	0	0	0
8 dell	7	0	0	0	0	0	3	0	0	0	3
9 gap	2	0	0	0	0	0	0	0	0	1	1
10 hp	2	0	0	0	0	0	1	0	7	13	21
11 kmart	3	0	0	0	0	0	0	0	0	0	0
12 kohls	5	0	0	0	0	0	1	0	0	0	1
13 nike	1	0	0	0	0	0	0	0	0	0	0
14 officemax	3	0	0	0	0	0	24	0	7	9	38
15 oldnavy	2	0	0	0	0	0	0	0	0	5	5
16 paul	2	0	0	0	0	0	0	0	0	0	0
17 reebok	2	0	0	0	0	0	11	0	0	0	11
18 sony	5	0	0	0	0	0	0	0	1	7	8
19 shoebuy	1	0	0	0	0	0	5	0	0	26	31
20 shoes	2	0	0	0	0	0	0	0	0	1	1
21 staples	5	0	0	0	0	0	0	0	10	0	10
22 target	2	0	0	0	0	0	24	0	0	1	25
23 victoriasecret	2	0	0	0	0	0	0	0	0	14	14
24 walmart	2	0	0	0	0	0	9	0	0	0	9
Total	72	0	0	6	0	6	98	2	25	80	212

Tab. 2 summarizes the results of experiment 2 with FETCH, which is the normal use of FETCH. A set of pages is randomly selected and labeled (the same number of pages as above). They are then used to train FETCH. The recall value of FETCH drops significantly, and so does the page accuracy. IDE's results are copied from above.

Table 2. Experiment 2 results

	Recall	Precision	Page accuracy
IDE	99.9%	99.9%	99.5%
FETCH	85.9%	96.8%	46.0%

Time complexity: The proposed technique does not have the learning step as in FETCH and thus saves the learning time. The extraction step is also very efficient because the algorithm is only linear in the number of tokens in a page.

5   Conclusions

This paper proposed an instance-based learning approach to data extraction from structured Web pages. Unlike existing methods, the proposed method does not perform inductive learning to generate extraction rules based on a set of user-labeled training pages. It thus does not commit itself pre-maturely. Our algorithm can start extraction from a single labeled page. Only when a new page cannot be extracted does the page need labeling. This avoids unnecessary page labeling, and thus solves a major problem with inductive learning, i.e., the set of labeled pages is not fully representative of all other pages. For the instance-based approach is to work, we proposed a novel similarity measure. Experimental results with product data extraction from 24 diverse Web sites show that the approach is highly effective.

Acknowledgments

This work was partially supported by National Science Foundation (NSF) under the grant IIS-0307239. We would like to thank Steve Minton of Fetch Technologies for making the FETCH system available for our research.

References

1. Cohen, W., Hurst, M., Jensen, L.: A flexible learning system for wrapping tables and lists in html documents. In: The Eleventh International World Wide Web Conference WWW-2002. (2002)
2. Feldman, R., Aumann, Y., Finkelstein-Landau, M., Hurvitz, E., Regev, Y., Yaroshevich, A.: A comparative study of information extraction strategies. In: CICLing '02: Proceedings of the Third International Conference on Computational Linguistics and Intelligent Text Processing. (2002) 349–359
3. Freitag, D., Kushmerick, N.: Boosted wrapper induction. In: Proceedings of the Seventeenth National Conference on Artificial Intelligence and Twelfth Conference on Innovative Applications of Artificial Intelligence. (2000) 577–583
4. Freitag, D., McCallum, A.K.: Information extraction with hmms and shrinkage. In: Proceedings of the AAAI-99 Workshop on Machine Learning for Informatino Extraction. (1999)
5. Hsu, C.N., Dung, M.T.: Generating finite-state transducers for semi-structured data extraction from the web. Information Systems **23** (1998) 521–538
6. Kushmerick, N.: Wrapper induction for information extraction. PhD thesis (1997) Chairperson-Daniel S. Weld.
7. Lerman, K., Getoor, L., Minton, S., Knoblock, C.: Using the structure of web sites for automatic segmentation of tables. In: SIGMOD '04: Proceedings of the 2004 ACM SIGMOD international conference on Management of data. (2004) 119–130
8. Muslea, I., Minton, S., Knoblock, C.: A hierarchical approach to wrapper induction. In: AGENTS '99: Proceedings of the third annual conference on Autonomous Agents. (1999) 190–197
9. Pinto, D., McCallum, A., Wei, X., Croft, W.B.: Table extraction using conditional random fields. In: SIGIR '03: Proceedings of the 26th annual international ACM SIGIR conference on Research and development in informaion retrieval. (2003) 235–242
10. Zhai, Y., Liu, B.: Web data extraction based on partial tree alignment. In: WWW '05: Proceedings of the 14th international conference on World Wide Web. (2005) 76–85
11. Knoblock, C.A., Lerman, K., Minton, S., Muslea, I.: Accurately and reliably extracting data from the web: a machine learning approach. (2003) 275–287

12. Muslea, I., Minton, S., Knoblock, C.: Active learning with strong and weak views: A case study on wrapper induction. In: Proceedings of the 18th International Joint Conference on Artificial Intelligence (IJCAI-2003). (2003)
13. Mitchell, T.: Machine Learning. McGraw-Hill (1997)
14. : (Fetch technologies, http://www.fetch.com/)
15. Muslea, I., Minton, S., Knoblock, C.: Adaptive view validation: A first step towards automatic view detection. In: Proceedings of ICML2002. (2002) 443–450
16. Kushmerick, N.: Wrapper induction: efficiency and expressiveness. Artif. Intell. (2000) 15–68
17. Chang, C.H., Kuo, S.C.: Olera: Semi-supervised web-data extraction with visual support. In: IEEE Intelligent systems. (2004)
18. Chang, C.H., Lui, S.C.: Iepad: information extraction based on pattern discovery. In: WWW '01: Proceedings of the 10th international conference on World Wide Web. (2001) 681–688
19. Lerman, K., Minton, S.: Learning the common structure of data. In: Proceedings of the Seventeenth National Conference on Artificial Intelligence and Twelfth Conference on Innovative Applications of Artificial Intelligence. (2000) 609–614
20. Arasu, A., Garcia-Molina, H.: Extracting structured data from web pages. In: SIGMOD '03: Proceedings of the 2003 ACM SIGMOD international conference on Management of data. (2003)
21. Crescenzi, V., Mecca, G., Merialdo, P.: Roadrunner: Towards automatic data extraction from large web sites. In: VLDB '01: Proceedings of the 27th International Conference on Very Large Data Bases. (2001) 109–118
22. Embley, D.W., Jiang, Y., Ng, Y.K.: Record-boundary discovery in web documents. In: SIGMOD. (1999)
23. Bunescu, R., Ge, R., Kate, R.J., Mooney, R.J., Wong, Y.W., Marcotte, E.M., Ramani, A.: Learning to extract proteins and their interactions from medline abstracts. In: ICML-2003 Workshop on Machine Learning in Bioinformatics. (2003)
24. Califf, M.E., Mooney, R.J.: Relational learning of pattern-match rules for information extraction. In: AAAI '99/IAAI '99: Proceedings of the sixteenth national conference on Artificial intelligence and the eleventh Innovative applications of artificial intelligence conference innovative applications of artificial intelligence. (1999) 328–334
25. McCallum, A., Freitag, D., Pereira, F.C.N.: Maximum entropy markov models for information extraction and segmentation. In: ICML '00: Proceedings of the Seventeenth International Conference on Machine Learning. (2000) 591–598
26. Nahm, U.Y., Mooney, R.J.: A mutually beneficial integration of data mining and information extraction. In: Proceedings of the Seventeenth National Conference on Artificial Intelligence and Twelfth Conference on Innovative Applications of Artificial Intelligence. (2000) 627–632
27. Hammer, J., Garcia-Molina, H., Cho, J., Crespo, A., Aranha, R.: Extracting semistructured information from the web. In: Proceedings of the Workshop on Management fo Semistructured Data. (1997)
28. Liu, L., Pu, C., Han, W.: Xwrap: An xml-enabled wrapper construction system for web information sources. In: ICDE '00: Proceedings of the 16th International Conference on Data Engineering. (2000) 611
29. Sahuguet, A., Azavant, F.: Wysiwyg web wrapper factory (w4f). In: WWW8. (1999)

PRoBe: Multi-dimensional Range Queries in P2P Networks*

O.D. Sahin, S. Antony, D. Agrawal, and A. El Abbadi

Department of Computer Science,
University of California at Santa Barbara,
Santa Barbara, CA 93106, USA
{odsahin, shyam, agrawal, amr}@cs.ucsb.edu

Abstract. Structured P2P systems are effective for exact key searches in a distributed environment as they offer scalability, self-organization, and dynamicity. These valuable properties also make them a candidate for more complex queries, such as range queries. In this paper, we describe PRoBe, a system that supports range queries over multiple attributes in P2P networks. PRoBe uses a multi-dimensional logical space for this purpose and maps data items onto this space based on their attribute values. The logical space is divided into hyper-rectangles, each maintained by a peer in the system. The range queries correspond to hyper-rectangles which are answered by forwarding the query to the peers responsible for overlapping regions of the logical space. We also propose load balancing techniques and show how cached query answers can be utilized for the efficient evaluation of similar range queries. The performance of PRoBe and the effects of various parameters are analyzed through a simulation study.

1 Introduction

Peer-to-peer (P2P) systems are a popular paradigm for exchanging data among users in a decentralized manner. Currently P2P systems efficiently support exact key lookups in addition to offering properties such as scalability, decentralization, self-organization, and dynamic node insertion and departure. These valuable properties also render them a candidate for more complex queries, such as range queries. Several techniques have been proposed for supporting range queries over a singe attribute. Our goal here is to develop a scheme for supporting range queries over multiple attributes. Some example applications that can benefit from a P2P architecture that supports multi-dimensional range queries are as follows: Resource discovery in Grid Computing [1, 2], publish/subscribe systems [3], multiplayer games [4], multi-dimensional data sharing in P2P networks [5], and P2P databases [6, 7].

In this paper, we describe PRoBe (P2P Range Queries over Multiple Attributes using Hyper-Boxes), a P2P architecture that supports range queries

---

* This research was supported in parts by NSF grants CNF 04-23336, IIS 02-23022, and IIS 02-20152.

M. Kitsuregawa et al. (Eds.): WISE 2005, LNCS 3806, pp. 332–346, 2005.

over multiple attributes. PRoBe maps data items onto a multi-dimensional logical space. This space is divided into non-overlapping hyper-rectangular zones and each zone is maintained by a peer in the system. Each range query also corresponds to a hyper-rectangle in the logical space and is answered by contacting all the peers whose zones intersect with the query.

Supporting range queries in a P2P system introduces several challenges. Most of the existing systems that are designed for exact key lookups rely on hashing data items. Since hashing destroys locality, we cannot hash data items. In order to support range queries we distribute data based on their values. This distribution, however, may lead to skewed distribution of data in the system because most real world data sets tend to be skewed. Hence we need to employ load-balancing techniques to prevent peers from overloading. We also discuss the utilization of cached query answers for the efficient computation of future range queries. We propose a mapping that enables peers to advertise their cached results and to locate the cached results that are similar to a given query.

The rest of the paper is organized as follows. Section 2 surveys the related work. The design of PRoBe is explained in Sect.3. We describe techniques for load balancing and incorporating caching into the system in Sect.4. Experimental results evaluating different aspects of PRoBe are presented in Sect.5. Section 6 concludes the paper.

2   Related Work

Structured P2P systems impose a certain structure on the overlay network and control the placement of data. For example, Distributed Hash Tables (DHTs) [8, 9, 10, 11] hash both peers and objects onto a logical space and assign each object to a peer dynamically. They offer very efficient exact key lookups, which is logarithmic or sublinear in the number of peers. However, hashing prevents DHTs from supporting range queries. Several studies address this problem and support range queries over a single attribute by distributing the data tuples based on their attribute values and using explicit techniques to balance the load over the peers [12, 13, 14]. These load balancing techniques are based on redistributing data items among peer pairs and changing the locations of peers in the logical space, and they achieve constant degree of imbalance ratio among the peers. Another structured P2P system, Skip Graphs [15, 16], supports range queries over a single attribute by organizing the peers into a distributed skip list structure based on their key values. To support range queries, PePeR [17] assigns domain intervals to peers, whereas the inverse Hilbert curve is used for mapping the attribute domain to a d-dimensional CAN space in [1]. Data structures for prefix search in P2P networks are described in [18, 19].

Recently interest has increased to support multi-dimensional range queries. Ganesan et al. [20] investigate two approaches: *1) SCRAP* maps both data items and queries from higher dimensions to 1 dimension with space filling curves and then uses existing schemes for routing [15, 16] and load balancing [12], *2) MURK* uses a multi-dimensional logical space to distribute data items among peers and to identify peers with data relevant to queries. Mercury [4] creates a separate overlay for each attribute. Range queries are forwarded to a single hub based on node-count histograms constructed through a sampling mechanism. MAAN [2] and Squid [21] map multi-dimensional objects to the Chord identifier space using uniform locality preserving hashing and Hilbert curve, respectively. SkipIndex [22] partitions the space into regions and maintains them in a Skip Graph using their split histories.

PRoBe is built on top of MURK as it uses a logical space for data distribution, routing and query answering. In contrast to MURK, it also proposes and evaluates techniques for load balancing and investigates the issue of using cached results. A number of techniques have been proposed for load balancing in DHTs [23, 24, 13], but they are not directly applicable to PRoBe since they rely on hashing and require a one dimensional identifier space. The idea of using cached results for efficient evaluation of future queries in a P2P environment have been explored in the context of range queries [25, 26, 27], OLAP queries [28], and conjunctive lookups [29].

Orthogonal to our work, P2P systems have also been used for more complex functionality such as sharing relational data and query processing [6, 7, 30, 31]. The adaptations of popular spatial index methods, such as R-trees and quad-trees, for a P2P setting have been devised [32, 33], but these methods still rely on certain statically fixed parameters.

3   The Design of PRoBe

To support range queries over multiple attributes, PRoBe organizes peers into a multi-dimensional logical space, similar to that used by CAN [9]. The dimensionality of this space is set to the number of *range attributes*, i.e., attributes over which range predicates can be specified[1]. Each dimension corresponds to an attribute and is bounded by the domain of the corresponding attribute.

The logical space is divided into non-overlapping rectangular regions called *zones*. Each peer in the system is assigned a zone and is responsible for maintaining the data items mapped to its zone. When a data item is inserted into the system, it is mapped to the point corresponding to its values for the range attributes. Figure 1(a) shows a 2-dimensional logical space corresponding to two range attributes: A_x with domain $[100 - 200]$ and A_y with domain $[0 - 80]$. The space is partitioned among 7 peers, P_1 to P_7. A data item with $A_x = 150$ and $A_y = 35$ is thus mapped to point $P(150, 35)$ and assigned to peer P_4. When a new peer P_n joins the system, it contacts an existing peer P_e in the system. P_e then splits its zone into two in such a way that both halves contain the same number of data items and assigns one half to the new peer. In Fig.1(b), peer P_8 joins the system and contacts peer P_4, which then splits its zone and hands over one half to P_8. For routing in the system, each peer keeps information (zone coordinates and IP addresses) about its neighbors in the logical space. During

---

[1] We assume that the number of range attributes is known at initialization time, or, in the worst case, all attributes can be considered range attributes.

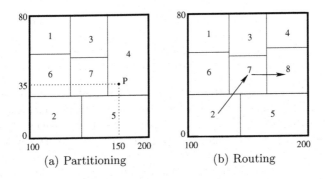

(a) Partitioning   (b) Routing

Fig. 1. Management of the Logical Space

routing, each intermediate hop forwards the message to the neighbor closest to the destination. Figure 1(b) shows the path for a message routed from P_2 to P_8.

Range Queries

A range query specifies ranges over a subset of the range attributes. If it does not specify any range for a range attribute, then the domain of that attribute is used as the corresponding range predicate. Notice also that equality predicates are just a special case where the lower and upper bounds of a range are equal. Each range query then corresponds to a hyper-rectangle in the logical space, which will be referred to as the *query box*. Figure 2(a) illustrates two range queries Q_1 and Q_2, where $Q_1 = \{(116 < A_x < 160) \wedge (20 < A_y < 40)\}$ and $Q_2 = \{A_x > 185\}$.

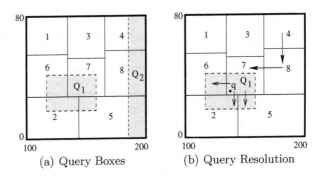

(a) Query Boxes   (b) Query Resolution

Fig. 2. Multi-Dimensional Range Queries

Since the data items and range queries are directly mapped onto the logical space, locality is preserved and the range queries can be answered by only visiting the peers with relevant data. All data items that are mapped to a point inside the query box satisfy the query and have to be returned. Thus answering a range query requires contacting all *candidate peers*, i.e., peers whose zones overlap with the query box. The query answering occurs in two phases in the following order:

1. **Routing:** The query is routed from the initiator to a peer whose zone intersects the query box.
2. **Retrieval:** The query is forwarded to all candidate peers, which in turn identify and return qualifying data items.

When routing the query, the initiator sets the destination to the center of the query box. Each peer that receives the query during routing checks if its zone overlaps with the query box. As soon as the query reaches a peer in the query box, the routing ends and that peer initiates the query retrieval. In the retrieval phase, each peer that receives the request passes over the data items it is assigned and returns those that satisfy the query to the query initiator. It also forwards the retrieve request to its neighbors whose zones intersect with the query box. Hence every peer in the query box will receive the query and all qualifying data items will be returned. In Fig.2, peer P_4 initiates query Q_1 and sends it towards the center of the query box, i.e., point q. When the query reaches peer P_7, which is the first peer whose zone overlaps with the query box, the retrieval phase begins and the query is forwarded to candidate peers P_2, P_5, and P_6. These four peers then identify the data items matching the query and return them to peer P_4.

4   Improvements

4.1   Load Balancing

Most of the load balancing algorithms proposed for structured P2P systems cannot be used for PRoBe because:

- They rely on hashing, but PRoBe does not hash data,
- They require peers to hand over their partitions to their neighbors, however PRoBe uses a multi-dimensional logical space so it is not always possible to find a neighbor that can be used for merging zones.

Thus we use a load balancing scheme based on *virtual servers* [23]. The basic idea is to allow a peer to manage multiple zones rather than a single zone. These zones are called virtual peers. The load balancing scheme works by allowing peers to start and stop virtual peers depending on the load distribution. When a peer P finds that the ratio between the load of the most loaded peer it knows of and its own load has crossed some fixed threshold T, it initiates the load redistribution process. First, peer P hands over its virtual peers to the peers responsible for the neighboring zones. The neighbor with the least load is used for handover. Then P splits the load with the most loaded peer such that after splitting their loads are nearly equal. This is achieved by transferring some virtual peers from the most loaded peer to P and if necessary splitting a virtual peer into two by dividing it across the current splitting dimension of the virtual peer. The splitting dimension for a virtual peer is chosen cyclically among all dimensions. A similar scheme is followed when the load of a peer is above T when compared to the least loaded peer.

A peer joins the system by splitting the load with the most loaded peer it can find. This splitting is similar to the load distribution process explained above. The load balancing scheme depends on a peer knowing the most loaded peer in the system. This can be achieved either by maintaining a separate 1-dimensional index on the load values [14, 12] or by polling random peers periodically about their load [13].

4.2 Sharing Cached Results

Caching is a widely used technique in databases for improving query processing performance. It is also used in P2P systems mainly for improving routing and lookup performance. For example, peers can cache the identity of other peers that are the recipient of messages or that return good lookup results. In PRoBe, we use caching for efficient evaluation of range queries. The idea is that if the answer of a range query is already computed and cached by a peer, then future range queries asking for similar ranges can benefit from that result. Note that the peers usually keep the answers of their range queries locally for a while. In such a data sharing environment, it is a realistic assumption that peers are also willing to share their cached results with others. These cached answers then can be used for efficiently evaluating future queries [25, 26, 27].

To facilitate the sharing and retrieval of cached results, PRoBe allows peers to share their cached results similar to the way they share data items. A cached result is mapped to the center point of the corresponding query box in the logical space. Thus whenever a peer wants to share its cached result for a given query, it sends an advertise message towards the center point of the query box and the peer responsible for that point then stores the identifying information, i.e., the range of the cached result and the address of the peer sharing it.

The query answering scheme presented in Sect.3 should be modified accordingly to consider cached results. A range query is still destined towards the center of the query box. However, now the routing does not stop when it reaches a zone intersecting the query box, instead the query is routed all the way to the destination peer P_d that is responsible for the center point. P_d then checks the advertised cached results it maintains and tries to locate a cached result that can be used for evaluating the query answer, i.e., a result that has a high overlap with the query range. If such a result is found, P_d contacts the caching peer so that it returns the matching portion of the cached result to the querying peer. P_d also generates sub-queries for the remaining parts of the query and forwards them to the corresponding peers. Thus the sub-queries are answered from the system, whereas the result for the rest of the query is obtained from the peer sharing the cached result.

This scheme uses the heuristic that if two queries are similar, then the centers of their query boxes will be close. However it is possible that the centers of two similar queries can map to different peers. The accuracy of the scheme can be increased by advertising the cached results for multiple points (e.g., k different points on the diagonal of the query box) and having P_d also ask its immediate neighbors for overlapping cached results upon receiving a query. Additionally, in order to avoid stale results, caching peers periodically refresh their results and stop sharing a result after a certain time period. Thus the advertised cached results are removed from the system if they are not refreshed (for example when the caching peer leaves the system or stops sharing the result). Using a cached result is usually more efficient since all the results are obtained from a single peer. However the result might not be very accurate because there might have been matching data items inserted or removed after the cached result was computed. Thus the querying peer specifies in its query whether it is willing to accept cached results. For example, it might prefer not to use cached results if the accuracy of the query result is crucial.

5   Experiments

We implemented a simulator in C++ to understand the various aspects of PRoBe. The domain of each attribute is set to $[0, 10000)$, thus the data space is a hyper-cube of side length 10000. We run each experiment using a uniform dataset and a skewed dataset, and report the results for both datasets. The uniform dataset is created by selecting data values uniformly at random from the corresponding attribute domain. In the case of skewed dataset, each attribute value is picked from a standard normal distribution, i.e., with mean 0 and standard deviation 1, and then scaled to the attribute domain as follows. It is mapped to the $[-5,5)$ interval using modular arithmetic, multiplied by 1000 and added 5000. The insertion of data objects and peers into the system are interleaved such that on the average one peer is inserted per 50 data objects. Queries are performed once all data and peer insertions are complete. All queries are hyper-cubes of specified coverage and they are uniformly spread over the data space. Query coverage is defined as the ratio of the volume of the query box to the volume of the data space. Each query is initiated at a random peer. We study different aspects of the system by varying three main system parameters, namely, the number of attributes (dimensions), query coverage, and the number of peers in the system. In the experiments where the number of dimensions is not varied, we use 2 and 4 dimensions as representative dimensions. Similarly coverages of 10^{-5} and 10^{-2} are used as representative query coverages. Unless otherwise stated, the number of peers in the system is 10000 and the load balancing algorithm is turned on. However caching is not used by default and is studied separately to isolate the effects of caching from other parameters of the system. For more efficient routing, whenever a peer has virtual peers, it considers the neighbors of all its zones to forward messages.

5.1   Response Time

Response time is the time interval between the time a range query was issued by a peer and the time the first result is received in response. We measure the number of hops taken by the query message from the querying peer to the first candidate peer and use it as an approximation for response time. This cost is

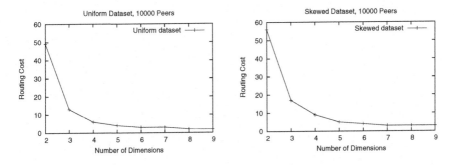

Fig. 3. Dimensionality vs. Routing Cost

referred to as the *routing cost*. Even though the number of hops may not always be an accurate measure in an Internet scale dynamic system, for the purpose of simulation and for understanding the nature of range query processing by the system it is a reasonable assumption.

Figure 3 shows that the routing cost decreases with increasing dimensions. That is because the number of neighbors per peer increases with the increased number of logical space dimensions, and thus there are more alternatives to forward the message at each intermediate hop. The routing is efficient for both datasets when the dimensionality is greater than 3. However the routing cost for lower dimensions (for 2 and 3 dimensions) is high. Therefore there is a need for an enhanced routing scheme for lower dimensions. A generalization of the long distance pointer scheme used in one dimensional schemes might mitigate this problem. For example, [20] suggests using random pointers and pointers based on building a one dimensional index on the centroids of zones to speed up routing. [34] discusses and evaluates different schemes for selecting long distance pointers. Similarly, [35] shows that it is possible to achieve $O(logN)$ routing performance in CAN by keeping neighbor pointers at different granularities (Each peer keeps $O(logN)$ routing information in this case).

While CAN divides the zones evenly between peers during joins, the expected routing cost is $O(dN^{1/d})$. In our case the partitioning is with respect to load and hence the data space is unevenly divided among the peers. We experimentally measure the impact of uneven partitioning on the routing cost by varying the number of peers. The results are shown in Fig.4. For 4 dimensions, the system scales well as the routing cost increases slowly with the increasing number of peers. However for 2 dimensions the rate of increase is higher. As already discussed, routing in 2 dimensions can be improved using long distance pointers.

As seen in Fig.3 and Fig. 4, the routing cost is higher for the skewed dataset. That is because there are more zones in the system due to our load balancing scheme, which creates virtual peers to cope with the data skew. The efficiency of the load balancing scheme will be investigated in Sect.5.4. For the skewed dataset in Fig.4, there is an unexpected increase in the routing cost in 2 dimensions around 8000 peers. That is because the number of virtual peers created in the

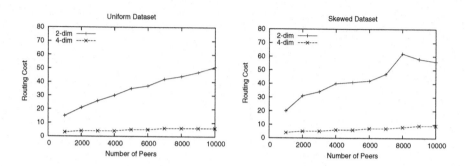

Fig. 4. Number of Peers vs. Routing Cost

case of 8000 was relatively fewer. Note that a peer uses the neighbors of all its virtual zones while deciding the next hop during routing for efficiency.

5.2   Retrieval Time

Retrieval time is the total time spent in the retrieval phase, which begins once the query reaches a candidate peer. We use the number of peers that are visited to retrieve the results as an approximation of the retrieval time. This is referred to as the *retrieval cost*. We first vary the number of dimensions from 2 to 9 and measure the change in the retrieval cost. The results are shown in Fig.5 for two different coverages of 10^{-5} and 10^{-2} (y-axis is in log scale). It can be seen that the space partitioning scheme is afflicted by the well-known curse of dimensionality. The performance degrades rapidly with increasing number of dimensions. The inefficiency is particularly acute for high coverage.

We also measure the effect of the number of peers and query coverage on the retrieval cost. Figure 6 plots the retrieval cost against the number of peers. The retrieval cost increases almost linearly with increasing number of peers. The effect of query coverage is shown in Fig.7. The performance is excellent for low coverages and is acceptable for coverages up to $O(10^{-3})$. Beyond this, performance rapidly degrades. This inefficiency is more pronounced in higher

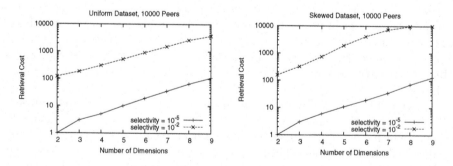

Fig. 5. Dimensionality vs. Retrieval Cost

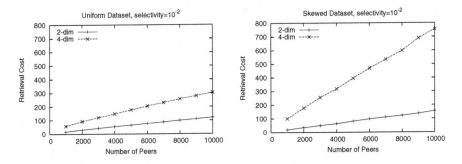

Fig. 6. Number of Peers vs. Retrieval Cost

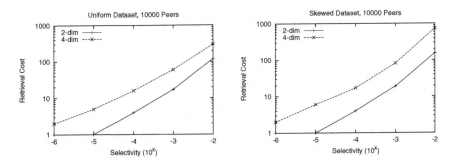

Fig. 7. Coverage vs. Retrieval Cost

dimensions which limits the utility of PRoBe for higher dimensions. However queries of high coverage can be efficiently cached as shown in Sect.5.5. Note that the query coverage affects only the retrieval cost since the routing scheme is independent of the query coverage.

5.3   Maintenance Cost

In order to maintain the overlay network, a peer has to know all its neighbors and send heartbeat messages periodically. This is necessary for routing, recovering from peer failures, and processing range queries. Thus we use the maximum number of neighbors for any peer and the average number of neighbors over all peers as measures of the maintenance cost.

In Fig.8, the maintenance cost is plotted against the number of peers. For both datasets the average number of neighbors remain constant with increasing number of peers. However due to the uneven partitioning of the zones, the numbers are greater than the expected value $O(2d)$ [9]. The number of neighbors for the skewed dataset is slightly higher than that of the uniform dataset. The maximum number of neighbors shows a slightly uneven behavior with increasing number of peers especially for the skewed dataset. This can also be explained by the uneven partitioning of the space.

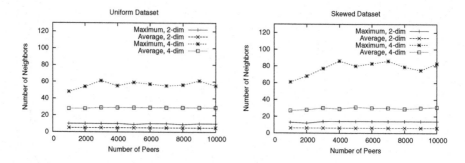

Fig. 8. Number of Peers vs. Number of Neighbors

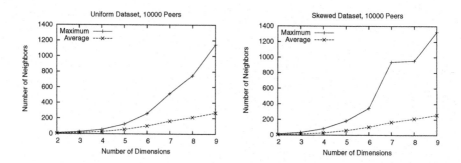

Fig. 9. Dimensionality vs. Number of Neighbors

Figure 9 depicts the number of neighbors as a function of the number of dimensions. The average number of neighbors per peer is low and increases rather slowly with increasing dimensions. However the maximum number of neighbors for the skewed dataset shows an uneven behavior with increasing dimensions. In spite of the uneven behavior two characteristics can be observed from the graphs for both datasets. The maximum number of neighbors is considerably higher than the average number of neighbors and the maximum number of neighbors degenerates to a very high cost for dimensions greater than 6. This is the price paid for the uneven partitioning of the space.

5.4   Load Balancing

The efficiency of the load balancing scheme is shown in Fig.10. The graph shows the corresponding number of peers for different values of storage load, i.e., the number of data objects assigned. In all runs, the load threshold is set to 4 and new peers join the system by splitting the highest loaded peer. Thus the load balancing scheme bounds the ratio of load between the maximum loaded peer to the minimum loaded peer to 4. In the case of uniform dataset, there are no virtual peers created. That is because the the load in the system is already balanced without the intervention of the dynamic load balancing scheme. As seen from

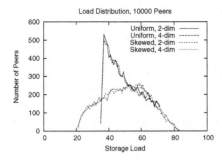

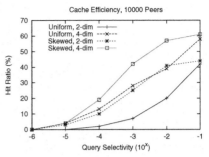

Fig. 10. Load Distribution   **Fig. 11.** Efficiency of Caching

the graph, most peers have load around 40 and the ratio of maximum load to minimum load is around 2. The dynamic scheme, however, effectively balances the load for the skewed dataset. In this case, there is one virtual peer per peer on the average, and the ratio of maximum load to minimum load is slightly less than 4 (For both dimensions, the maximum and minimum load are 83 and 21, respectively). Additionally, for both datasets, changing the dimensionality from 2 to 4 does not affect the load distribution.

5.5   Caching Efficiency

The efficiency of the caching protocol is shown in Fig.11. These results are obtained by running 10000 queries for different coverages. The y axis shows the percentage of the query volume covered by the local cached result that has the highest overlap with the query box. The percentage of results fetched from cache hits increases steadily with increasing query coverage. This can be readily explained since the amount of overlap between different queries is higher for high coverage queries. In all cases, the cache hit percentage rises to more than 40% for query coverage of 10^{-1}. The results are higher for the skewed dataset due to large zones in sparse regions of the space. For a given dataset, the cache hit behavior with respect to increasing coverage is similar for 2 dimensions and 4 dimensions. Additionally, for any given coverage, the cache hit percentage is higher for 4 dimensions.

5.6   Discussion

From the experiments we conclude that:

1. PRoBe is best suited for low dimension and low coverage applications. For such applications, it provides excellent performance with low maintenance costs. It also scales well with increasing number of peers, which is an important criterion for dynamic P2P systems.
2. The routing performance is good for high dimensions. However a long distance pointer scheme is necessary for acceptable routing performance in low dimensions. The CAN-like routing alone is inefficient for low dimensions.

3. For high coverage queries in higher dimensions, PRoBe almost degrades to broadcasting among all peers (Figure 5). This suggests that for P2P systems for which these kind of queries are important a super-peer based broadcast architecture would be more efficient.
4. The above inference is further strengthened by high maintenance cost for higher dimensions. This can be reduced in exchange for less efficient performance by mapping higher dimensions to a lower dimensional logical space.
5. For high coverage queries, the base scheme is not very efficient. However when combined with caching, large portions of the query results can be answered from cached results of earlier queries. This is due to the high overlap between queries of high coverages.

6   Conclusions

In this paper, we have discussed the design and evaluation of PRoBe that efficiently supports range queries over multiple attributes in a P2P environment. PRoBe is based on a multi-dimensional logical space that is partitioned among participating peers, and also implements techniques for load balancing and sharing cached range query results.

There are several future directions we want to pursue. We plan to analyze how PRoBe compares to other schemes. We want to investigate routing improvements to accomplish more efficient routing in the system by keeping more routing information at peers. We will also explore the possibility of implementing a fully dynamic and decentralized tree-like index structure that efficiently supports range queries.

References

1. Andrzejak, A., Xu, Z.: Scalable, efficient range queries for grid information services. In: P2P. (2002) 33–40
2. Cai, M., Frank, M., Chen, J., Szekely, P.: Maan: A multi-attribute addressable network for grid information services. In: GRID. (2003) 184–191
3. Gupta, A., Sahin, O.D., Agrawal, D., El Abbadi, A.: Meghdoot: Content-based publish/subscribe over p2p networks. In: Middleware. (2004) 254–273
4. Bharambe, A.R., Agrawal, M., Seshan, S.: Mercury: supporting scalable multi-attribute range queries. In: SIGCOMM. (2004) 353–366
5. Tang, C., Xu, Z., Dwarkadas, S.: Peer-to-peer information retrieval using self-organizing semantic overlay networks. In: SIGCOMM. (2003) 175–186
6. Halevy, A.Y., Ives, Z.G., Suciu, D., Tatarinov, I.: Schema mediation in peer data management systems. In: ICDE. (2003) 505–516
7. Kementsietsidis, A., Arenas, M., Miller, R.J.: Mapping data in peer-to-peer systems: Semantics and algorithmic issues. In: SIGMOD. (2003) 325–336
8. Stoica, I., Morris, R., Karger, D., Kaashoek, M.F., Balakrishnan, H.: Chord: A scalable peer-to-peer lookup service for Internet applications. In: SIGCOMM. (2001) 149–160

9. Ratnasamy, S., Francis, P., Handley, M., Karp, R., Shenker, S.: A scalable content-addressable network. In: SIGCOMM. (2001) 161–172
10. Zhao, B.Y., Huang, L., Stribling, J., Rhea, S.C., Joseph, A.D., Kubiatowicz, J.D.: Tapestry: A global-scale overlay for rapid service deployment. IEEE Journal on Selected Areas in Communications **22** (2004) 41–53
11. Rowstron, A., Druschel, P.: Pastry: Scalable, distributed object location and routing for large-scale peer-to-peer systems. In: Middleware. (2001) 329–350
12. Ganesan, P., Bawa, M., Garcia-Molina, H.: Online balancing of range-partitioned data with applications to peer-to-peer systems. In: VLDB. (2004) 444–455
13. Karger, D.R., Ruhl, M.: Simple efficient load balancing algorithms for peer-to-peer systems. In: SPAA. (2004) 36–43
14. Crainiceanu, A., Linga, P., Machanavajjhala, A., Gehrke, J., Shanmugasundaram, J.: P-Ring: An index structure for peer-to-peer systems. Technical Report TR2004-1946, Cornell University (2004)
15. Aspnes, J., Shah, G.: Skip graphs. In: SODA. (2003) 384–393
16. Harvey, N.J.A., Jones, M.B., Saroiu, S., Theimer, M., Wolman, A.: SkipNet: A scalable overlay network with practical locality properties. In: USITS. (2003)
17. Daskos, A., Ghandeharizadeh, S., An, X.: PePeR: A distributed range addressing space for peer-to-peer systems. In: DBISP2P. (2003) 200–218
18. Awerbuch, B., Scheideler, C.: Peer-to-peer systems for prefix search. In: PODC. (2003) 123–132
19. Ramabhadran, S., Ratnasamy, S., Hellerstein, J.M., Shenker, S.: Brief announcement: prefix hash tree. In: PODC. (2004) 368–368
20. Ganesan, P., Yang, B., Garcia-Molina, H.: One torus to rule them all: multi-dimensional queries in p2p systems. In: WebDB. (2004) 19–24
21. Schmidt, C., Parashar, M.: Enabling flexible queries with guarantees in p2p systems. Internet Computing Journal **8** (2004) 19–26
22. Zhang, C., Krishnamurthy, A., Wang, R.Y.: SkipIndex: Towards a scalable peer-to-peer index service for high dimensional data. Technical Report TR-703-04, Princeton University (2004)
23. Rao, A., Lakshminarayanan, K., Surana, S., Karp, R., Stoica, I.: Load balancing in structured p2p systems. In: IPTPS. (2003) 68–79
24. Byers, J., Considine, J., Mitzenmacher, M.: Simple load balancing for distributed hash tables. In: IPTPS. (2003) 80–87
25. Gupta, A., Agrawal, D., El Abbadi, A.: Approximate range selection queries in peer-to-peer systems. In: CIDR. (2003) 141–151
26. Kothari, A., Agrawal, D., Gupta, A., Suri, S.: Range addressable network: A p2p cache architecture for data ranges. In: P2P. (2003) 14–22
27. Sahin, O.D., Gupta, A., Agrawal, D., El Abbadi, A.: A peer-to-peer framework for caching range queries. In: ICDE. (2004) 165–176
28. Kalnis, P., Ng, W.S., Ooi, B.C., Papadias, D., Tan, K.L.: An adaptive peer-to-peer network for distributed caching of OLAP results. In: SIGMOD. (2002) 25–36
29. Bhattacharjee, B., Chawathe, S., Gopalakrishnan, V., Keleher, P., Silaghi, B.: Efficient peer-to-peer searches using result-caching. In: IPTPS. (2003) 225–236
30. Huebsch, R., Hellerstein, J.M., Lanham, N., Loo, B.T., Shenker, S., Stoica, I.: Querying the Internet with PIER. In: VLDB. (2003) 321–332
31. Ng, W., Ooi, B., Tan, K., Zhou, A.: PeerDB: A p2p-based system for distributed data sharing. In: ICDE. (2003)

32. Mondal, A., Lifu, Y., Kitsuregawa, M.: P2PR-Tree: An R-Tree-based spatial index for peer-to-peer environments. In: P2P&DB. (2004) 516–525
33. Tanin, E., Harwood, A., Samet, H.: A distributed quadtree index for peer-to-peer settings (short paper). In: ICDE. (2005)
34. Sahin, O.D., Agrawal, D., El Abbadi, A.: Techniques for efficient routing and load balancing in content-addressable networks. In: P2P. (2005) 67–74
35. Xu, Z., Zhang, Z.: Building low-maintenance expressways for p2p systems. Technical Report HPL-2002-41, HP Laboratories Palo Alto (2002)

An Infrastructure for
Reactive Information Environments

Rudi Belotti, Corsin Decurtins, Michael Grossniklaus, and Moira C. Norrie

Institute for Information Systems, ETH Zurich, 8092 Zurich, Switzerland
{belotti, decurtins, grossniklaus, norrie}@inf.ethz.ch

Abstract. We introduce the concept of reactive information environments and a general infrastructure for experimentation with such systems. Its asynchronous state-based processing model is described along with the architectural requirements and main components of our infrastructure. These include a general context engine coupled together with a web publishing platform. An application for a public news service is used to motivate the requirements, explain the processing model and show how an application is implemented using the platform.

1 Introduction

Developments in mobile and ubiquitous computing have led to increasing demands for information systems that can adapt to users and their situations. Tools and technologies to support concepts such as multi-channel access, adaptive interfaces, context-awareness and multi-modal interaction abound. Yet it seems that each of these represents only one step along a path leading us away from traditional information system architectures based on the simple request-response model of processing towards a notion of *reactive information environments* that react to many forms of stimuli and deliver information in various formats and places. Processing will no longer be based purely on the synchronous request-response model, but rather on asynchronous state-based models.

We present the architectural requirements of such systems and a general infrastructure developed for experimentation with reactive information environments. To motivate the requirements of such a system and explain its operation, we use an example of a community news and awareness service that adapts the set of articles on public displays to the group of users currently present in the environment. Since the users do not interact with the system in a command-based way, the system itself has to decide which tasks to execute at what time and the most appropriate information to be displayed. It needs to keep track of the environment and the users within it, as well as news updates. A general context engine coupled with a content publishing system is responsible for delivering the right information to one or more channels as and when required.

We begin in Sect. 2 with a look at how this notion of reactive information environments has evolved and relates to various developments in information system technologies. In Sect. 3, we present the architecture and main components of the system. Sect. 4 describes the context engine and Sect. 5 content

M. Kitsuregawa et al. (Eds.): WISE 2005, LNCS 3806, pp. 347–360, 2005.

publication. Details of the control flow of the entire system are presented in Sect. 6. Concluding remarks are given in Sect. 7.

2   Background

Since the outset of information systems, the demands made on these systems have changed constantly. The requirement for structured data once led from file-based storage to the first hierarchical databases and early path-based query languages. Demands for more flexibility and performance resulted in the relational model together with its well-defined algebra and the necessity for more advanced data models gave rise to the entity-relationship (ER) model and its many variants. Although specialist application domains such as Computer-Aided Design (CAD) have motivated the development of object-oriented database management systems (OODBMS), relational databases are still considered the state-of-the-art in contemporary information systems.

In the midst of this extensive evolution, however, at least one aspect has stayed the same. Interaction with a database has until recently been based purely on the paradigm of request and response, or, client and server, respectively. With the advent of the World Wide Web, new requirements needed to be considered that also affected the manner in which clients interacted with databases. Early approaches of supporting web-based access to databases were witnessed in the OODBMS O_2 [1]. Other reactions to this new requirement of Web access were also found in well-known commercial systems such as Oracle [2] with the first version of Oracle Web Server released in 1995. Although the importance of the web for information systems was accepted early on, the Internet has continued to spawn new demands ever since.

Probably the most important of these demands has been the requirement to manage ever larger web-sites within a database. Several research projects have acknowledged this requirement and provided valuable solutions to it. The Strudel [3] project approached the problem with StruQL a query language that allows the declarative specification of web-sites. Building on database modelling techniques, the WebML [4] project was among the first to extend traditional data models for the creation of data-intensive web-sites. Their long lasting endeavour in the field of model-based approaches has led to a collection of models and tools that together form a CASE suite for web engineering. The Hera [5] project also takes a model-driven approach. However, the Hera approach is not based on a traditional data model but rather on technologies and standards that have been developed by the World Wide Web Consortium (W3C), such as XML, RDF [6] and OWL [7]. Finally, projects such as UML-based Web Engineering (UWE) [8] and W2000 [9] introduced powerful modelling languages based on UML that allow the specification of both the data and behaviour of a web information system. In the meantime, industry has also been aware of the challenges and lived up to them by developing a multitude of content management systems.

While most of these approaches focused on web-sites represented in HTML, the Internet has moved on to become a platform that uses several presentation channels to deliver information. Most of the projects mentioned above reacted to that development and at some point integrated support for multi-channel access. Adapting to different presentation channels is only one form of adaptation and over time other dimensions of adaptation have gained importance and a general notion of context-awareness emerged. This has led to numerous projects seeking to provide a uniform way of expressing the state of a client when issuing a request to a database server and allowing the information system to react to that state. While still retaining the basic architecture of request and response, the response in these systems is influenced by context that may be decoupled from the request. The same query asked at various points in time may return completely different results as the context of the client or the server changes.

Various components, frameworks and toolkits for the acquisition, management and provision of context information have been proposed, e.g. Context Toolkit [10]. An infrastructure that aims more at the provision of an integrated platform is Gaia [11] which uses a virtual machine metaphor and abstracts all kinds of distributed and mobile devices for input, output, storage, processing etc. into a meta-operating system. Applications are based on an extended version of a Model-View-Control (MVC) approach. The components of the application are mobile and mapped dynamically to devices and resources that meet the requirements specified by the application at runtime. In the area of information systems WebML has been extended to support the notion of context [12]. In [13], we describe how context and content information can be integrated to build a highly adaptive content management system.

Ubiquitous computing is another domain that calls for highly context-aware and distributed architectures. Instead of synchronous request and response, there is a demand for systems that autonomously deliver information asynchronously depending on the context of the environment. Research projects such as the Multichannel Adaptive Information Systems (MAIS) project [14] address these new requirements with the development of infrastructures that can adapt to constantly changing requirements, execution contexts and user needs. The MAIS project has produced a number of results in the domains of service registries, personal databases and adaptive user interfaces, to name only a few. We also believe that reactive information environments are the foundation for supporting ubiquitous and mobile applications.

To illustrate the requirements of such systems and the solution that we propose, we will use the example of AwareNews, a context-aware and ambient news visualisation system. The aim of the application is to promote community awareness by integrating community news into a global news service. The news displayed depends on the set of user currently present and their profiles, with the goal of encouraging communication as well as keeping users informed.

3 Architecture

The SOPHIE platform is a research project that aims at the integration and consolidation of the various proposals for adaptive, multi-channel and context-

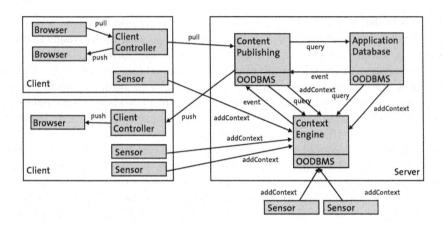

Fig. 1. SOPHIE Architecture Overview

aware information systems into a generic platform for reactive information environments. We put special emphasis on reactiveness and proactivity of the information environment as this is quite a novel concept in the area of web-based information systems. In this section, we present the overall architecture of the SOPHIE platform along with its core components and their integration.

Figure 1 shows an overview of the architecture. On the client side, the system consists of various user interface components, such as web browsers, voice engines or mobile devices. On the server side, the SOPHIE platform integrates a context engine, a content publishing framework and an application database. The context engine is backed up by various sensors (hardware and software) that provide contextual information about the physical and virtual environment. These sensors can be on the client side, for instance mounted on a mobile device, or embedded in the environment, such as for example a light barrier.

The server components have all been implemented using object-oriented database technologies since notions of modularity, extensibility and the integration of behaviour were central to the system. Further, both system and application metadata are represented as objects, enabling a common shared metamodel for the components. The OODBMS comes with a set of predefined models and metamodels to aid application development, e.g. the user model. These can be extended and completed according to the requirements of the application. Since data and metadata are represented objects, information about system concepts such as types and associations can be extended and modified using the same techniques as for user data. In AwareNews, the application database has information about news articles and their classification into categories etc. The predefined user model was extended to include an AwareNews-specific user profile and preferences of the individual users such as their preferred languages and news categories.

The *context engine* is responsible for managing contextual information about all application entities, including the physical and virtual environment of all users and the location and state of devices that deliver information to them. The information is acquired by *physical sensors* in the environment. For example, in AwareNews, we use physical sensors to detect the presence of people in a certain area of a room and to identify them. The messages on a display are then adapted according to the profiles of the users currently present. In addition to the physical sensors, software components and applications can also serve as *software sensors* providing contextual information about entities in the virtual environment of the application.

The application database and the context engine, together with the OODBMS on which they were implemented, were developed within our research group in previous projects and required only slight modifications to integrate them into the SOPHIE platform. However, the remaining server component, the content publishing framework, was based on a general web-publishing framework that required more significant modifications to adapt it to an asynchronous state-based model from a traditional request-response model.

The content publishing framework includes a content model with information about the publication of application data, as well as a publishing process based around the separation of content, structure, presentation and view. It already supported a lot of the features required for a reactive information environment such as multi-channel delivery and context-awareness. While the core of the original web publishing framework supported a very flexible and generic concept of request and response that enabled it to be used more or less in its original form, as described later in Sect. 5, some parts at the periphery of the system had to be adapted to support reactiveness and the proactive delivery of content.

The client components were also greatly affected by the requirements of reactiveness and proactivity. Traditionally, desktop web browsers have been used as thin clients for access to information systems. With the evolution towards multi-channel and multi-modal interfaces, other browser components such as voice engines, mobile phones and PDA browsers, and even paper interfaces [15], have been incorporated into information system architectures. However, these components are all based on the traditional request-response model and cannot be used in their current form for a reactive information environment. We therefore propose an additional, integrating component on the client side, the *client controller*. This component acts as an HTTP proxy for the client-side components and serves as a gateway for all of the communication between a client and the server. In addition to the proxy functionality, the client controller also serves as an HTTP server for callbacks from the server, enabling the standard client-server configuration to be reversed and the server side to make requests to the client side, for example, in order to push content to the user.

The actual implementation of the server components was based on OMS, an OODBMS which implements the OM model [16]. Whereas the details of the OM model and OMS system are not important here, we believe that the use of a semantically expressive object data model as the foundation for the infrastructure is important, especially with respect to the integration of the various components and services.

In summary, the architecture of the SOPHIE platform presented in this section provides the basis for a flexible, model-based implementation of reactive information environments. It incorporates components such as the context engine and the content publishing framework which have proven to be very powerful through their generality. It also provides a high degree of flexibility with respect to interactional control flows, supporting not only traditional request-response interaction, but also more reactive patterns such as the pushing of content based on internal events of the application.

4   Context Engine

The context engine provides abstractions and general mechanisms for the acquisition and management of context information which allows context information to be presented to the other components of the SOPHIE infrastructure in a uniform and generic way. In contrast to other context frameworks, such as the Context Toolkit [10], the SOPHIE context engine is based on an expressive data model, which structures the context information and provides semantics for the values. Being database-driven, the context engine can work directly with the system's knowledge base. It is composed of different layers that we describe below.

The *context acquisition* layer includes a general definition of sensors that acquire context information from the physical and virtual environment. The information from the sensors is processed by components of this layer and stored in so-called context elements. For example, a physical sensors can be used to recognise persons in an AwareNews room. When a new user is detected, a software sensor can decide on the language to be used to present information on public displays based on their preferred language or a common language if more than one users is present.

In the next layer, *context augmentation*, existing context elements are associated with application objects that are concerned with the current context. The context elements can also be augmented through accumulation or combination with other data sources by means of software sensors. Examples are the computation of average values, as in the case of temperatures (both over a history of values or values from multiple sensors) or the mapping of user identifiers such as RFID tags or identification badges [17] to actual user objects stored in a user database. This layer is responsible for the conversion of the data coming from the sensors to valuable information that is related to existing objects.

Context-aware applications can query the context model and thus have access to all of the context elements. Another possibility for accessing the context model is the *event notification* layer. An application can register for certain events on specific context elements. For example, the publishing platform of AwareNews can register for changes to language context in order to present the news in the best language for the users currently viewing the public display. The context engine will send an event to the publishing platform if this context element changes. The application entities that want to be notified of an event can provide a notification endpoint, for example, in the form of a web service.

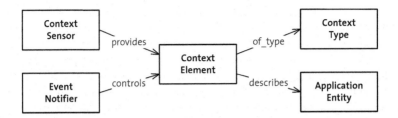

Fig. 2. Context Model

Figure 2 depicts the relationships between the components of the context engine. Each component of the context engine is typed. The type definitions provide a general abstraction of the component and provide parameters that allow the instantiation of concrete components. For example, you can define a sensor type describing a class of person-recogniser sensors connected through the USB port. In this case, the USB port represents the parameter required at the time of definition of the real sensor. In order to connect a new sensor that recognises the current users in the room, you need to instantiate a new sensor object of the corresponding type by passing the appropriate parameters as the ID of the USB port to which the person recogniser is connected.

```
contextType ctx_users {
      users: set of user;
};
context users_in_lab: ctx_users describes awarenews:student_lab;
sensorDriver user_sensor(usb_port: integer): ctx_users;
sensor user_recogniser: user_sensor(3) provides users_in_lab;
contextType ctx_lang {
      language: string;
};
context lang: ctx_lang describes awarenews:display;
sensorDriver lang_sensor(users: ctx_users): ctx_lang;
sensor lang_selector: lang_sensor(users_in_lab) provides lang;
```

Fig. 3. Context Definition Statements

Figure 3 illustrates the definitions for the example of the person-recogniser and language detector using our Context Definition Language (CDL). This language provides a simple means of defining metadata for the context engine. First we define a *context type* ctx_users, which characterises the users currently in an AwareNews room. This context type can be used to instantiate a context describing the presence of users in a given room. The context declaration links the set of users to an application concept, here the room awarenews:student_lab. Finally, sensors need to be defined to acquire the identity of the users. A sensor definition comprises both a declaration of the sensor type and an instantiation of a sensor. In our example, with the `sensorDriver` statement, we define an abstract class of user sensors that can be connected to arbitrary USB ports. Then, with the `sensor` statement, we create a concrete person-recogniser that is plugged into USB port 3 and provides data for the context element `users_in_lab`. We define another context type `ctx_lang` which characterises the AwareNews' display properties and instantiate a context `lang` that describes the language used to present the information. A sensor driver is then defined which takes the `users_in_lab` context and extrapolates the appropriate language for the current set of users. Finally, we define the sensor instance that provides the context `lang`. More details on the context engine of SOPHIE and its interworking with applications can be found in [13, 18].

When we design context-aware applications, we have to define clearly the basic application functionality and the context-aware functionality. There is one main difference between these two classes of functionality. The basic application features are always available and completely predictable since they make no use of context information. On the other hand, it is important to notice that context-aware functionality could be restricted if the relevant context information is not available at the time of a request. Moreover, context-aware functionality is dynamically adapted at runtime and could be difficult to predict. This unpredictability could also lead to different responses to the same user's request because of changes in context. Considering the special properties of the context-aware functionality, we must therefore classify and handle it in a special way.

The contribution of the context engine in the field of reactive information environments resides in offering a general model for context information and also a standard component that allows the information system to manage the context and adapt to it accordingly. The adaptation mechanism is implemented in the application. The notification mechanism of the context engine is implemented using traditional database methods and triggers, combined with filters to ensure notification of only relevant changes.

5   Content Publication

Delivering content to the applications built on the SOPHIE platform is the task of the integrated content publishing system displayed in Fig. 1. For SOPHIE, we use our own content management system XCM [19] which is also based on the OM model and thus shares the same semantics as the application database and context engine. The content publishing system provides support to applications requiring features typical of content management such as user management, workflows, personalisation, multi-channel delivery and multi-format objects. At the core of the system is the clear separation of the notions of content, structure, presentation and view.

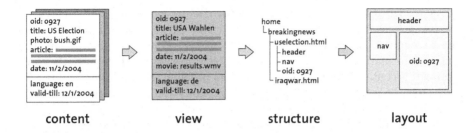

content   view   structure   layout

Fig. 4. Publishing Process

The process of publishing information illustrated in Fig. 4 is defined by the following course of action. First, the system selects the appropriate content requested by the client. As the same content often needs to be delivered in different variations, the system supports "multi-variant objects" [20]. which are content objects with multiple context-dependent variants. These content variants are of the same type and are described in the system with a set of characteristics. Each characteristic specifies a content dimension and a value for that dimension e.g. dimension `language` and value `english`. The set of dimensions is specified by the application. Using the information from context engine and request, the content publishing system determines the most appropriate variant by matching this information to the characteristics of the variants.

Personalisation is achieved through the concept of view objects which define the properties of content objects to be published. As with views in relational systems, these can be used to aggregate content semantically linked together by references. The personalised content objects are incorporated into a tree-like hierarchy using the metadata stored in the structure objects and based on a component and container model. A component corresponds to a content object forming a leaf of the structure tree and containers can contain components or other container objects. Finally, the layout stored in presentation objects is applied to the structure tree, thereby producing the final representation. We use XML as a natural representation of the structure tree and hence XSLT as the language used by the presentation objects.

As with content, all other basic concepts of the system—view, structure and presentation—can be annotated and described by characteristics. Hence views, structure and presentation can be customised for different users and devices as well as content. The strength in this approach lies in the fact that our system does not specify what annotations have to be made. It only provides the capabilities to store and manage characteristics and match them according to the current context. By allowing for very fine-grained descriptions of data and metadata, our approach is also able to reduce complexity and redundancy as only the information that really varies from one context to another has to be managed. These requirements are not met by current systems as they mostly focus on multi-lingual aspects only, ignoring other useful dimensions to describe objects completely.

As described in [13], our system uses the context engine not only as a client, but also acts as a software sensor that delivers context information back to the context engine. The content management system is able to provide valuable context information, such as what the user is browsing and how busy they are. Storing this context information, gained from profiling the user's interaction with the system, back into the context component allows other applications that share the same context engine to profit from this information.

Traditionally, content publishing systems react to explicit requests only. Reactive information environments such as the SOPHIE platform break with this tradition and move towards asynchronous interaction. We solved this problem by allowing clients to register with the content publishing system for content that is pushed from the server to the client. As mentioned before, the client controller that manages communication on behalf of the client is itself an HTTP server. Hence, if the context engine triggers the content publishing system in the case of a particular event, it can communicate with all registered client controllers and send updated content to these clients. The existing flexibility of the system meant that few modifications were necessary to move away from the traditional paradigm of request and response and integrate the system as a component in a reactive information environment.

6   Control Flow

Traditionally, interaction with web-based information systems has been based on a simple request-response model at both the level of user interaction and the technical level where interaction is matched directly to the HTTP protocol. The user request corresponds to an HTTP request and the response of the system to an HTTP response. Thus, we can say that interaction is based on a serial dialogue between the user, represented by a client application such as a web browser and the application. This corresponds to a very simple control flow model in which actions are always initiated by the user on the client side and the application on the server side only passively reacts to these actions. The integration of multi-channelling or context-awareness into web information systems has not changed this basic interaction model. Content might be delivered through multiple channels, but the interaction model is still based on request-response. Usually context information is only used passively, i.e. it is used to alter and adapt content and services of the information system but does not initiate any actions in the system. Figure 5 shows a simplified sequence diagram of a request-response based on interaction with a context-aware content publishing system.

Proactivity is an important requirement for ubiquitous and mobile systems. Applications have to be able to initialise an interaction or dialogue and push information to the user solely upon internal conditions of the system and without an explicit request from the user. These internal conditions can be based on application data, publication data or contextual information. For example, in AwareNews, the creation of a breaking news article in the application database can trigger the publication of this article to all users. Contextual information

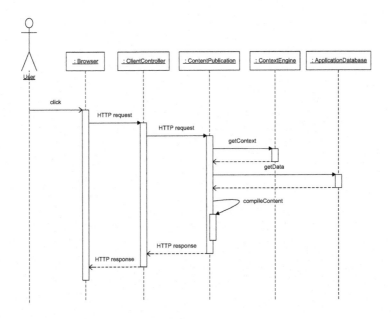

Fig. 5. Request-response based content publishing

such as the location of a user can also be used to trigger the publication of information. A user entering a room can trigger the display of some information on an ambient screen. Statistical information and access patterns could be used to trigger actions. For example, if a particular story in the AwareNews system is requested frequently within a certain time period, it becomes a "hot story" and will be pushed to interested users. Figure 6 shows the sequence diagram of content publishing initiated by the context engine and pushed to the user interface without any interaction by the user.

The OODBMS provides conventional database triggers on various operations on objects, such as creation, update or deletion. When the trigger is fired, the registered handler can execute arbitrary functionality in the system. Time triggers are also supported and these can be configured to fire at a specific point in time. Both types of triggers can be used to initialise arbitrary operations in the system, such as an interaction with a user. Further the Context Engine also provides the concept of *context events*, as described in Sect. 4. Context events can occur upon modification of context elements in the engine. They are propagated to all notification listeners that have been registered for the specific events. These notification listeners can in turn be used to trigger any functionality of the system based on the contextual information.

On the user interface and interaction level, the request-response model is thus extended to a model where responses can also be sent without a preceding request. An interaction of user and application, represented through client and server, respectively, can be initialised not only by the user, but also by the

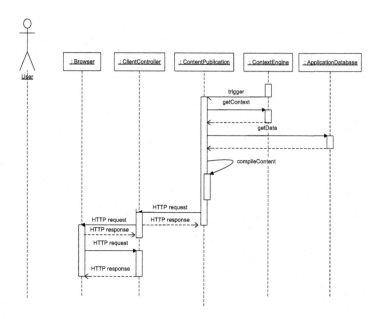

Fig. 6. Context-triggered content pushing

application. On the technical level, we still use the request-response based HTTP protocol for communication between the distributed components of the system as we did not want to abandon what has become a defacto standard. However, whereas HTTP request and interaction requests were congruent in traditional web-based information systems, we now have to make a clear distinction between the two. HTTP requests and responses still have to come in pairs, but one interaction response, for instance the pushing of some content to the client, could be mapped to an HTTP request-response pair that originates at the server instead of the client or even multiple HTTP request-response pairs.

For the pushing of information to the client, we have can use the following technique. The client, represented by the gateway component mentioned in Sect. 3, also acts as an HTTP server and provides a callback for this mechanism. The exact address of the callback is managed by the server side as contextual information. If the server side now wants to push content to the client side, it compiles a URL that can later be used by the client to request this content. In the case of the breaking news example, this might be a simple article request URL with the particular identifier of the news article. The server now makes an HTTP request to the callback that corresponds to the user who is supposed to receive the content. This information can be looked up in the context engine. The content URL that was compiled previously is passed as a parameter of the HTTP request. The client replies to the HTTP request with an empty response and, as a side-effect, makes an HTTP request for the URL that it has just received from the server and receives the correct response with the breaking news article content. For obvious reasons, this callback has to be protected by state-of-the-art authentication and authorisation mechanisms.

The advantage of this approach is that it requires minimal changes to an existing web-based information system with a traditional request-response approach. The system only has to be extended with the callback mechanism on the client side as well as the content publishing trigger on the server side. The disadvantage is that we need two HTTP calls to publish the content. Alternatively, the server can also send the content for the client directly in the first HTTP request. The client again replies with an empty HTTP response, but the second HTTP request from the client to the server is unnecessary. As a side-effect to the callback, the client does not have to initiate a new HTTP request, but can instead present the content directly to the user.

7 Conclusions

We have presented a platform that supports the development of information systems that can react to various forms of events in the user environment and control a variety of information channels. The platform was implemented through the integration of existing components for context-awareness and content publishing and we describe how these can be coupled with an application database and client controllers. We believe that this work represents an important step towards the development of general infrastructures for the support of ubiquitous and mobile information systems.

In contrast to a number of projects with similar aims in the field of ubiquitous computing, we adopted a metamodel-driven approach to the development of our system. As a result, our system is more flexible than other frameworks in terms of generality and extensibility and also has greater support for component reuse. In addition, it ensures greater semantic consistency due to the underlying semantic metamodels.

References

1. Bancilhon, F., Delobel, C., Kanellakis, P.C., eds.: Building an Object-Oriented Database System, The Story of O2. Morgan Kaufmann (1992)
2. Oracle Corporation: Company Web Site (1999-2005) (http://www.oracle.com/).
3. Fernandez, M.F., Florescu, D., Kang, J., Levy, A.Y., Suciu, D.: STRUDEL: A web-site management system. In: Proc. Intl. ACM SIGMOD Conference on Management of Data, Tucson, Arizona, USA (1997) 549–552
4. Ceri, S., Fraternali, P., Bongio, A., Brambilla, M., Comai, S., Matera, M.: Designing Data-Intensive Web Applications. The Morgan Kaufmann Series in Data Management Systems. Morgan Kaufmann (2002)
5. Houben, G.J., Barna, P., Frasincar, F., Vdovjak, R.: Hera: Development of semantic web information systems. In: Proc. Intl. Conference on Web Engineering (ICWE), Oviedo, Spain (2003) 529–538
6. World Wide Web Consortium (W3C): Resource Description Framework (RDF) (2005) (http://www.w3.org/RDF/).

7. World Wide Web Consortium (W3C): Web Ontology Language (OWL) (2005) (http://www.w3.org/2004/OWL/).
8. Koch, N., Kraus, A.: The expressive power of UML-based web engineering. In: Proc. Intl. Workshop on Web-oriented Software Technology (IWWOST), Málaga, Spain (2002) 105–119
9. Baresi, L., Garzotto, F., Paolini, P.: Extending UML for modeling web applications. In: Proc. Intl. Hawaii Conference on System Sciences (HICSS), Big Island, Hawaii, USA (2001)
10. Dey, A.K., Abowd, G.D., Salber, D.: A conceptual framework and a toolkit for supporting the rapid prototyping of context-aware applications. Human-Computer Interaction (2002) 97–166
11. Román, M., Hess, C., Cerqueira, R., Ranganathan, A., Campbell, R.H., Nahrstedt, K.: Gaia: A middleware infrastructure for active spaces. IEEE Pervasive Computing 1 (2002) 74–83
12. Ceri, S., Daniel, F., Matera, M.: Extending WebML for modeling multi-channel context-aware web applications. In: Proceedings of MMIS'2003, International Workshop on Multichannel and Mobile Information Systems, Rome, Italy (2003) 34–43
13. Belotti, R., Decurtins, C., Grossniklaus, M., Norrie, M.C., Palinginis, A.: Interplay of content and context. Journal of Web Engineering 4 (2005)
14. Pernici, B., The MAIS Team: Mais: Multichannel adaptive information systems. In: Proc. Intl. Conference on Web Information Systems Engineering (WISE), Rome, Italy (2003) 303–308
15. Norrie, M.C., Signer, B.: Switching over to paper: A new web channel. In: Proc. Intl. Conference on Web Information Systems Engineering (WISE), Rome, Italy (2003)
16. Norrie, M.C.: An extended entity-relationship approach to data management in object-oriented systems. In: Proceedings of ER'93, 12th International Conference on the Entity-Relationship Approach, Arlington, USA (1993)
17. Want, R., Hopper, A., Falcão, V., Gibbons, J.: The Active Badge location system. Technical Report 92.1, Olivetti Research Ltd. (ORL), 24a Trumpington Street, Cambridge CB2 1QA (1992)
18. Belotti, R., Decurtins, C., Grossniklaus, M., Norrie, M.C., Palinginis, A.: Modelling context for information environments. In: Proc. Intl. Workshop on Ubiquitous Mobile Information and Collaboration Systems (UMICS), CAiSE, Riga, Latvia (2004)
19. Grossniklaus, M., Norrie, M.C.: Information concepts for content management. In: Proc. Intl. Workshop on Data Semantics in Web Information Systems (DASWIS), WISE, Singapore, Republic of Singapore (2002)
20. Norrie, M.C., Palinginis, A.: Versions for context dependent information services. In: Conference on Cooperative Information Systems (CoopIS), Catania-Sicily, Italy (2003)

LoT-RBAC: A Location and Time-Based RBAC Model

Suroop Mohan Chandran and J.B.D. Joshi

Department of Information Sciences and Telecommunications, University of Pittsburgh

Abstract. Recent growth in location-based mobile services has introduced a significant need for location and time-based access control to resources. High mobility of the users and services in the emerging mobile applications in particular make the issue of controlling who can access what information and resources from which locations a daunting challenge. Several RBAC based models have been proposed that attempt to capture the location based and/or time-based access control requirements in various applications. However, they have limited flexibility and granularity. In this paper, we propose a Location and Time-based RBAC (LoT-RBAC) model to address the access control requirements of highly mobile, dynamic environments to provide both location and time based control.

Keywords: location based access, role based access, temporal constraint.

1 Introduction

With the recent developments in location sensing, mobile computing and wireless networks, location-based services are increasingly becoming a part of everyday life. While location-based services are being considered as a killer application for emerging mobile and wireless networks, there are increasing demands placed on the need to provide controlled access to information at various levels of sensitivity, importance or relevance to mobile users based on the location of the users and the time of request. Furthermore, with the increasing volume of available information and resources, access control management to ensure that information and resources are available to only the authorized users have become more crucial. An access control model that ensures confidentiality, integrity and availability of information and resources based on the location and time contexts associated with the users and resources is critical for the success of emerging mobile applications. Several existing work deals with access control based on users' location context [1, 2, 11, 14, 15, 16, 17, 19, 20, 21, 23] and time context [3, 4, 5, 7, 9]. While some works ([10, 14, 15]) address both time and location based access requirements using an RBAC approach, they have limited expressive power. Use of RBAC has been attributed to its maturity as a promising approach to address fine-grained access requirements [8]. A key weakness of the existing models facilitating location-based access is that location is associated primarily with users only. For instance, the GEO-RBAC model, which possibly is the most expressive location based RBAC model, proposed by Bertino *et al.* [2], assumes that users can use a role only from a particular location, and the role and its permissions are predefined for that location. This assumption renders it

M. Kitsuregawa et al. (Eds.): WISE 2005, LNCS 3806, pp. 361–375, 2005.

inadequate for capturing fine-grained location based access control requirements in mobile applications.

In this paper, we present a comprehensive location and time based RBAC (LoT-RBAC) model that subsumes and significantly extends the expressivity of the existing location and/or time based models. A unique distinction we make in this paper is that while the notion of time is uniform over all the entities of the RBAC model - users, roles, permissions - a location context may be different for each. Hence, users at a given location may be restricted to assume a role that is enabled in a specific location to access objects that reside in a particular location. Such an approach is needed to address emerging mobile and peer-to-peer (P2P) applications where mobile devices are involved in collaborative multi-domain interactions. The proposed LoT-RBAC model uses a more fine-grained spatial model including detailed location hierarchy and the notion of relative locations, and is integrated with the fine-grained logic and event-based temporal constraint specification framework of the recently proposed GTRBAC model [3]. In our model, location context for user indicates the location of the mobile device the user is using to access information or resource. Role location is also defined by the location of the mobile device in which the role is enabled or activated. For instance, if a user wants to allow his friends to access his files in his mobile PC in a P2P interaction only when he is in the office, he can define a role that is enabled only when he is in the office and assign it to his colleagues.

The paper is organized as follows. In Section 2, we discuss motivation for a fine-grained location and time-based access control model in mobile environments and present the related work. In Section 3, we present a spatial model for the LoT-RBAC model. In Section 4, we present the formal LoT-RBAC model. In Section 5, we present the basic events and triggers of the LoT-RBAC model and an illustrative example to show how policies can be specified in the LoT-RBAC model. In Section 6, we give an illustrative example and in Section 7 we present our conclusions and some future work.

2 Motivation and Related Work

Location based technologies have become essential components of personalized, ubiquitous computing environments, and hence pervade all types of environments ranging from active office, healthcare services, to entertainment and information services that provide information related to travel, weather, etc. The following example illustrates a need for associating a location context with each of the RBAC entities.

Example 1: Consider a hospital environment, where only a consulting physician has authorized access to his patients' records. Assume that while at a mall, a patient has a stroke. The sensor based system he is wearing detects the stroke and requests the Mall's system (MS) to seek out a doctor in the near proximity to provide help. Dr. Smith happens to be nearby. He has enabled certain roles in his mobile system that someone can assume in an emergency situation to access his credentials. Assume that the MS engages in a trust-based negotiation with Dr. Smith's mobile system to access and verify his credentials. After the required verification, the MS alerts the doctor and provides access to the patient's status information. Dr. Smith attends to the patient and after some basic treatment arranges for an ambulance, which is equipped with state-of-the-art equipments. The ambulance system (AS) continuously monitors the patient's detailed health status and also retrieves his medical records from the hospital. The hospital system (HS), detects location of the AS, continuously reads the patient's current status, and prepares for attending the situation once the patient reaches the hospital. At this time, the attending doctor may be in the ambulance or may be driving in a car to attend to the patient in the hospital. If the doctor is in the ambulance, he will be authorized to access the patient's records in the hospital as well as an access to the controls in the AS to allow him to efficiently attend to the patient's needs. If he is in his own car, he may be given access to the medical records (by the HS) and patient status (by the AS) but not the permission to operate ambulance equipments.

From the example, we observe that the location context can be associated with users, roles and objects independently. The context association is dependent on the location of the mobile device that (1) acts as a user's agent in accessing information from another system, thus providing the location context for the user, or (2) provides a service controlled by an RBAC mechanism, hence providing the location context for the roles of the policy and/or the objects in the device that are being accessed by users from another system. While this is a representative example, much more fine grained requirements can be expected in location-aware healthcare services, location-aware games, mobile grid environments and mobile P2P interactions. The requirements particularly arise when there are significant interactions among mobile systems with diverse access policies. While multiple policies raise significant secure interoperation challenges [24], we believe they can be effectively addressed only after we a have a very fine-grained location based access control model that can be applied in individual systems.

Several works exist in the literature related to context-based RBAC [10, 11, 14, 18, 21], including those that capture time and location based access [1, 2, 3, 9, 15, 17]. The first significant time-based RBAC model was proposed by Bertino *et al.* in [9], which was later generalized and comprehensively extended to role hierarchies and to the specification of SoDs, cardinality constraints in the GTRBAC model [3, 4, 5, 7]. In [14], an RBAC model is presented for ubiquitous environments that can capture physical and logical contexts including location. Covington *et al.* [10] use environmental roles that embeds context information on roles; however, no formal semantics is provided. An engineering approach to construct contextual constraints is presented in [11]; however, the work does not explore fine-grained location or time based policies. Bertino *et al.* [2] has recently proposed the GEO-RBAC model with a spatial model based on the OpenGIS environment. A significant aspect of the GEO-RBAC model includes (1) its specification of role schema that are location-based, and (2) the separation of role schema and role instances to provide different authorizations for different logical and physical locations. The Spatial RBAC model [1], allows specification of SoDs, but does not completely address the idea of location constraints that are not SoDs. The proposed model subsumes existing location and time-based models and supports much more fine-grained semantics.

3 Location Context Model

A comprehensive spatial model is needed to capture all the necessary spatial details for a location-based access control model. In this section, we present a spatial model that we will use to develop the location based RBAC model. The following definitions capture the basic notion of the location context.

Definition 1 (Physical, logical location): *We define a* physical position *$pos \in \Re^3$ and a* physical location *$ploc = \{pos_1, pos_2, .., pos_n\}$, where $n > 0$. A* logical location *lloc characterizes a set of physical locations, with a given application-specific property.*

As the definition indicates, physical locations are collections of points in a three dimensional geometric space. In this paper, we are not concerned about how the physical locations are represented or computed; for instance, a physical location could be represented as a collection of the end points of a bounded polygon, or a point and the radius (for a circle), etc. Further, the physical location could be a point (*i.e*, it is a singleton set) or can have multiple dimensions. We assume that there exist distinct names that map to an underlying geometric representation based on the location sensing/processing interface that generates the geometric details of the physical location. In addition to determining access rights based on the physical location of a user, they may be determined based on the logical location of a user [2, 20]. A logical location is an abstract notion that characterizes possibly many physical locations. For instance, *City, Baggage Claim Area, EntertainmentVenues*, etc., are logical locations that can have multiple actual instances. Instances of *City* may include all the cities on earth. In the example scenario 1, *"Patient's home"* may be used as a logical location to define where Sara should be located to assume a particular role in the hospital system. The notion of the *logical location* has been addressed in existing literature in various forms, such as *spatial realms* in [20], and a *spatial feature type* in [2]. Based on the real world scenarios, we observe that a logical location may have multiple subtypes and multiple super types. The *subtype* relation implicitly captures the *containment* relation that can exist among the physical instances of the logical locations, as we show in the next definition. We use *loc* to represent either a logical or physical location. For every location, we define the set of positions exterior to the location as loc^+, interior to the location as loc^- and on the boundary as $loc^°$, similar to the convention used in [13]. Two locations may be related in several ways, as captured in the following definition and illustrated in Example 1.

Definition 2 (Relationships between/among location contexts): *Let LLOC and PLOC be the sets of logical and physical locations respectively.*

(a) *We define the following relations*
   subtype: *$LLOC \rightarrow 2^{LLOC}$: a logical location may have multiple subtypes,*
   supertype: *$LLOC \rightarrow 2^{LLOC}$: a logical location may have multiple super types,*
   instance: *$LLOC \rightarrow 2^{PLOC}$: a logical location may have a set of instances,*
   type: *$PLOC \rightarrow 2^{LLOC}$: a physical location may have multiple location types*
(b) *Given two locations, they may be related by* contains, overlaps, equals, meets *and* disjoint *relationships as defined in Table 2 [2, 13].*

(c) *instance$_{ploc}$: PLOC x LLOC → 2^{PLOC}: defines the instances of a logical location bounded by a physical location.*

(d) *The properties listed in Table 2 hold.*

Example 2: As an illustrative example, consider the partially detailed map of the country *ABC*, given in Figure 1. The country *ABC* is composed of three states *A*, *B* and *C*. The cities A_1, A_2, A_3 and A_4 are in state *A*, and city B_1 is in state *B*. Lake L_1 is right in the center of the country and covers all three states. Thus we have four logical locations – *Country*, *State*, *City* and *Lake*; and ten physical locations – *ABC*, *A*, *B*, *C*, A_1, A_2, A_3, A_4, B_1 and L_1. We formally define the locations in Figure 2.

Table 1. Relations between two locations

Relation	Semantics(physical location)	Semantics (logical location)
loc_1 contains loc_2	$contains(ploc_1, ploc_2)$ → $(ploc_2^- \subset ploc_1^-) \land (ploc_2^\circ \subset ploc_1^-)$	$contains(lloc_1, lloc_2)$ → $(\forall ploc_2 \ (ploc_2 \in instance(lloc_2)$ → $(\exists ploc_1, \ ploc_1 \in instance(lloc_1) \land contains(ploc_1, ploc_2)))$
loc_1 overlaps loc_2	$overlaps(ploc_1, ploc_2)$ → $(ploc_2^- \cap ploc_1^- \neq \varnothing) \land (ploc_2^\circ \cap ploc_1^\circ \neq \varnothing) \land (ploc_2^+ \neq ploc_1^+)$	$overlaps(lloc_1, lloc_2)$ → $(\forall ploc_2 \ (ploc_2 \in instance(lloc_2)$ → $(\exists ploc_1, \ ploc_1 \in instance(lloc_1) \land overlaps(ploc_1, ploc_2))) \land (\forall ploc_1 \ (ploc_1 \in instance(lloc_1) \rightarrow (\exists ploc_2, ploc_2 \in instance(lloc_2) \land overlaps(ploc_1, ploc_2)))$
loc_1 equals loc_2	$equals(ploc_1, ploc_2)$ → $(ploc_1^+ = ploc_2^+) \land (ploc_1^- = ploc_2^-) \land (ploc_1^\circ = ploc_2^\circ)$	$equals(lloc_1, lloc_2)$ → $(\forall ploc_2 \ (ploc_2 \in instance(lloc_2) \rightarrow (\exists ploc_1, ploc_1 \in instance(lloc_1) \land equals(ploc_1, ploc_2))) \land (\forall ploc_1 \ (ploc_1 \in instance(lloc_1) \rightarrow (\exists ploc_2, ploc_2 \in instance(lloc_2) \land equals(ploc_1, ploc_2)))$
loc_1 meets loc_2	$meets(ploc_1, ploc_2)$ → $(ploc_2^\circ \cap ploc_1^\circ \neq \varnothing) \land (ploc_2^- \cap ploc_1^- = \varnothing)$	$meets(lloc_1, lloc_2)$ → $(\forall ploc_2 \ (ploc_2 \in instance(lloc_2) \rightarrow (\exists ploc_1, ploc_1 \in instance(lloc_1) \land meets(ploc_1, ploc_2))) \land (\forall ploc_1 \ (ploc_1 \in instance(lloc_1) \rightarrow (\exists ploc_2, ploc_2 \in instance(lloc_2) \land meets(ploc_1, ploc_2)))$
loc_1 is disjoint with loc_2	$disjoint(ploc_1, ploc_2)$ → $(ploc_2^- \cap ploc_1^- = \varnothing) \land (ploc_2^+ \cap ploc_1^+ = \varnothing) \land$	$disjoint(lloc_1, lloc_2)$ → $(\forall ploc_1, ploc_2 \ ploc_1 \in instance(lloc_1) \rightarrow (\exists ploc_2, ploc_2 \in instance(lloc_2) \land disjoint(ploc_1, ploc_2)))$

Table 2. Properties of *instance*, *subtype* and *contains* relations

	Property
1	$(lloc_1 \in subtype(lloc_2)) \leftrightarrow (lloc_2 \in supertype(lloc_1))$
2	$(lloc_1 \in subtype(lloc_2)) \land (lloc_2 \in subtype(lloc_3)) \rightarrow (lloc_1 \in subtype(lloc_3))$ (*Transitivity*)
3	$(lloc_1 \in supertype(lloc_2)) \land (lloc_2 \in supertype(lloc_3)) \rightarrow (lloc_1 \in supertype(lloc_3))$ (*Transitivity*)
4	$(ploc_1 \in instance(lloc_1)) \land (lloc_1 \in subtype(lloc_2)) \rightarrow (ploc_1 \in instance(lloc_1))$
6	$(ploc_1 \in instance_{ploc}(lloc_1, ploc_2)) \rightarrow (ploc_1 \in instance(lloc_1)) \land (contains(ploc_2, ploc_1))$

Fig. 1. Example Map of ABC

PLOC = {*ABC*, *A*, *B*, *C*, *L₁*, *A₁*, *A₂*, *A₃*, *A₄*, *B₁*, *b₁ Sports Bar*, *c₁ Football Stadium*, *c₂ Diner*}

LLOC = {*Country, State, City, Lake, Sports Center, Football Stadium, Dining Spot*}

subtype(Sports Center) = {*Football Stadium*}; *supertype(Football Stadium)* = {*Sports Center*}

instance(Country) = {*ABC*}, *type(ABC)* = {*Country*}; *instance(State)* = {*A, B, C*}; *type(x)*={*State*}, for all *x*∈ {*A, B, C*}

instance(City) = {*A₁, A₂, A₃, A₄, B₁, C₁*}; *type(x)* = {*City*}, for all *x* ∈ {*A₁, A₂, A₃, A₄, B₁, C₁*}

instance(Sports Center)={*b₁ Sports Bar*}, *instance(Football Stadium)*={*c₁ Football Stadium*};

instance(Dining Spot)={*b₁ Sports Bar, c₂ Diner*}; *type(b₁ Sports Bar)* = {*Sports Center, Dining Spot*};

type(c₁ Football Stadium) = *Football Stadium*, *type(c₂ Diner)* = {Dining Spot}; *instance_{ploc}(A, City)* = {*A₁, A₂, A₃, A₄*}

contains(ABC, A), *contains(ABC, B)*, *contains(ABC, C)*; *contains(A, A₁)*, *contains(A, A₂)*, *contains(A, A₃)*, *contains(A, A₄)*, *contains(B, B₁)*, *contains(ABC, L₁)*

overlaps(A, L₁), *overlaps(B, L₁)*, *overlaps(C, L₁)*

meets(A, B), *meets(B, C)*, *meets(A, C)*; *meets(A₁, A₂)*, *meets(A₂, A₃)*, *meets(A₃, A₄)*, *meets(A₁, A₃)*, *meets(A₁, A₄)*, *meets(A₂, A₄)*

disjoint(A₁, B₁), *disjoint(A₂, B₁)*, *disjoint(A₃, B₁)*, *disjoint(A₄, B₁)*; *disjoint(L₁, A₁)*, *disjoint(L₁, A₂)*,

---

Fig. 2. Formal Representation of locations in map of ABC

3.1 Relative Location

In many mobile application scenarios, it is relevant to specify policies according to relative locations with respect to some reference location. For instance, we can define a physical or logical relative location as "10 miles east from the Fountain" and "6 miles near a Shopping Mall." Furthermore, in mobile applications, it may be important to specify reference point to be moving. For instance, while driving a car, the policy may specify that the users within 10 miles of your vehicle can assume a role in your device, for instance, to access your music files.

Definition 3 (Relative Location): *A relative location rloc is a tuple (loc_{ref}, d, dir); i.e., rloc corresponds to physical location(s) that is d units in direction dir. Furthermore,*

- $loc_{ref} \in \{ploc, lloc, \overrightarrow{lloc}\} \cup location(ent)$, *where* $\overrightarrow{lloc}$ *denotes that the reference location can be in motion; location(ent) denotes the location(s) of an application entity ent.*
- *dir can be a physical or logical value that corresponds to 1, 2 or 3-dimensional space.*

Furthermore, we define function instance$_r$(rloc) which generates a set of physical points for the relative location rloc.

The displacement can be expressed in physical units such as miles, kilometers, etc. (1-dimension) or units such as blocks, floors, (3-dimension). It can also be expressed in logical units such as "two blocks," "two floors", etc. The direction can be geometric directions such as "East", "x degree North-East", or logical direction, such as "around/inside [building]", "along [I-376]" etc. Logical directions may have specific real world semantics or may be application specific. For example, a relative location $rloc=$ ($\overrightarrow{car}$, 5 *miles, around*), indicates the moving location of size 5 miles centered on the "car".

3.2 Location Hierarchy

We earlier introduced location feature *subtype, instances* of logical locations and *contains* relation that relates different locations. These all give rise to natural location hierarchies, which may be used to design role hierarchies. We differentiate such location hierarchy as physical, logical and hybrid location hierarchies, as defined next.

Definition 4 (Location Hierarchy Relations): *Let PLOC and LLOC be a set of physical and logical locations, we define location hierarchy relations,* $\succ_{ploc}, \succ_{lloc}$ *and,* $\succ$, *in Table 3*

Table 3. Location hierarchy Relations

Location Hierarchy	Type	Semantics
$\succ_{ploc}$	Physical location hierarchy	$(ploc_1 \succ_{ploc} ploc_2) \rightarrow contains(ploc_1, ploc_2),$ *and* $(ploc_1 \succ_{ploc} ploc_2) \wedge (ploc_2 \succ_{ploc} ploc_3) \rightarrow (ploc_2 \succ_{ploc} ploc_3)$
$\succ_{lloc}$	Logical location hierarchy	$(lloc_1 \succ_{lloc} lloc_2) \rightarrow subtype(lloc_2, lloc_1),$ *and* $(lloc_1 \succ_{lloc} lloc_2) \wedge (lloc_2 \succ_{lloc} lloc_3) \rightarrow (lloc_2 \succ_{lloc} lloc_3$ $lloc_1 \succ_{lloc} lloc_2 \rightarrow (instance(lloc_2) \subset instance(lloc_1))$
$\succ$	Hybrid location hierarchy	$(ploc \succ lloc) \rightarrow \forall pl,((pl \in instance(lloc)) \rightarrow contains(ploc, pl)),$ $(lloc \succ ploc) \rightarrow ploc \in instance(lloc),$ $(ploc_1 \succ lloc_1) \wedge (lloc_1 \succ_{lloc} lloc_2) \rightarrow (ploc_1 \succ lloc_2),$ $(lloc_1 \succ ploc_1) \wedge (ploc_1 \succ_{ploc} ploc_2) \rightarrow (lloc_1 \succ ploc_2),$

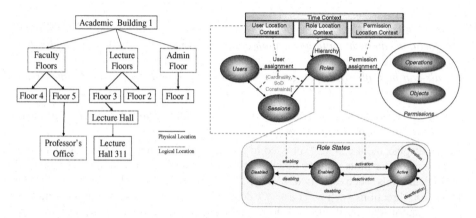

Fig. 3. Example Location Hierarchy   **Fig. 4.** The LoT-RBAC Model

Example 3: Let PLOC = {*Academic Building* 1, *Floor* 1, *Floor* 2, *Floor* 3, *Floor* 4, *Floor* 5, *Lecture Hall* 311}, and LLOC = {*Faculty Floors, Lecture Floors, Admin Floors, Lecture Hall* and *Professor's Office*}. These can form the hierarchy given in Fig. 4. and the following hold: *contains(Academic Building* 1, *Faculty Floors)*, *contains(Academic Building* 1, *Lecture Floors)*; *contains(Academic Building* 1, *Lecture Floors)*, *contains(Floor* 3, *Lecture Hall)*; *contains(Floor* 5, *Professor's Office)*; *instance(Faculty Floors)* = {*Floor* 4, *Floor* 5}, *instance(Lecture Floors)* = {*Floor* 2, *Floor* 3}; *instance(Admin Floor)* = {*Floor* 1; *Lecture Hall* 311 ∈ *instance(Lecture Hall)*

4   The LoT-RBAC Model

We use the spatial model described in Section 3 to extend the basic RBAC model to construct a fine grained LoT-RBAC model. The GTRBAC introduced the notion of role being in three states: *enabled, disabled* and *active*. Enabled roles can be activated (goes to active state) by an authorized user whereas the disabled role cannot be. To allow these state changes based on time, the GTRBAC model uses enabling, assignment and activation events. We adapt this to LoT-RBAC and allow the enabling, assignment and activation or roles to be determined by the location context. Figure 4 depicts the LoT-RBAC model and shows that location and time constraints apply to role enabling, assignment and activation.

4.1   Location Context, Status Predicates

As mentioned earlier, each entity of the RBAC model can have its own location context. We use loc_u as the location (pos_u as the exact position) of the user u; loc_r as the location (pos_r as the exact position) of role r and loc_p as the location (pos_p as the exact position) of permission $p = (op, obj)$. Note $p = (op, obj)$ represent operation op on object obj and loc_p actually is determined by the location of obj. We first discuss about location context for different RBAC entities, followed by the event and trigger framework for the location time based RBAC model.

Definition 5 (Location of user, role and permission): *We define the following to capture the location context information associated with each user, role or permission:*

- $LOC_u \subseteq LOC$ *be the locations of the users in U and user_lc:* $U \to 2^{LOC_u}$
- $LOC_p \subseteq LOC$ *be the locations of the permissions in P and perm_lc:* $P \to 2^{LOC_p}$
- $LOC_r \subseteq LOC$ *be the locations of the roles in R and role_lc:* $R \to 2^{LOC_r}$

Typically, in simple application we can expect $loc_u = loc_p = loc_r$. However, we believe there are scenarios where there may be a need to define policies where the user pool, the server that has RBAC policies and the objects and resources are in different locations. For instance, different military teams may be deployed in different countries around the world; there may be military headquarters that are spread within the US housing the servers that the teams may need to use. While identity based authorization is crucial, it may need to also verify that the user is located in a particular location before he is authorized to assume a crucial role to access required information. Based on these location domains for users, roles and permission, we define the status predicates as shown in Table 4 to capture what the state of the RBAC system is, with given location contexts and time. For instance, state predicate *enabled(r, pos_r, t)* indicates that the role is enabled in position *pos_r*, at time *t*. The subscripts indicate whether the position parameter is associated with the user, role or permission. Column 2 defines the evaluation domain for each argument of the predicate. As user location defines where the user is, it can be used to define from where he can assume a particular role. Similarly, the permission location information can be used for defining where the object should be for it to be assigned to a role. Similarly, role location information can be used to define where a role is enabled and hence can be activated by authorized users, as shown by the following definitions.

Definition 6 (Location contexts for Role Enabling and Assignment): *Let* LOC_u, LOC_r *and* LOC_p *be the locations associated with the user u, role r and permission p, as defined in Definition 5. The location contexts are defined as follows:*

Table 4. Location Contexts

Location Context	Notation	Semantics
User-Role Assignment/Deassignment	*u_assign_lc*	$U \times R \to 2^{LOC_u \times LOC_r}$ s.t. $\forall (loc_u, loc_r) \in u\_assign\_lc\ (u, r) \to u\_assigned(u, r, loc_u, loc_r)$
	u_deassign_lc	$U \times R \to 2^{LOC_u \times LOC_r}$ s.t. $\forall (loc_u, loc_r) \in u\_deassign\_lc(u,r) \to \neg u\_assigned(u,r,loc_u, loc_r)$
Permission-Role Assignment/Deassignment	*p_assign_lc*	$U \times R \to 2^{LOC_r \times LOC_r}$ s.t. $\forall (loc_p, loc_r) \in p\_assign\_lc\ (r, p) \to p\_assigned(r, p, loc_p, loc_r)$
	p_deassign_lc	$U \times R \to 2^{LOC_r \times LOC_r}$ s.t. $\forall (loc_p, loc_r) \in p\_deassign\_lc(r, p) \to \neg p\_assigned(r,p,loc_p, loc_r)$
Role Enabling	*r_enable_lc*	$R \to 2^{LOC_r}$ s.t. $\forall loc_r \in p\_assign\_lc\ (r, p) \to enabled(r, loc_r)$
	r_disable_lc	$R \to 2^{LOC_r}$ s.t. $\forall loc_r \in p\_deassign\_lc\ (r, p) \to \neg enabled(r, loc_r)$

Next, we introduce the location expressions that are used to specify constraints for LoT-RBAC. The temporal expression is adopted from the GTRBAC model [3].

Definition 7 (Location and Time Specification):

1. *Location Expression: Let l_expr_x be a location expression and MAP be a function that generates the physical positions for l_expr_x; i.e, $MAP(l\_expr) = \{pos_1, ...pos_n\}$. We define l_expr_x in Table 5 ([x] indicates that x is optional).*
2. *Time Expression: Let t_expr be the time expression defined as follows [3]:*
   - $t\_expr_1 = D$ *is a duration of time instants*
   - $t\_expr_2 = (I, P)$ *is a periodic interval, such that, $I = $ [begin, end], with begin and end indicating distinct time points.*

   $$P = \sum_{i=1}^{n} O_i.C_i \triangleright x.C_d, \text{ where } C_d, C_i \text{ are calendars, } O_1 = \text{all and } O_i \in 2^N \cup \{\text{all}\}.$$

Calendars are of the form Years, Months, Days and Hours, with hours being the finest in granularity. The $\triangleright$ symbol separates the set of starting points defined using C_i, from the duration of each period defined using C_d.

Table 5. Status Predicates

Predicate(s_t)	Evaluation Domain (DOM)	Semantics
P:permission set, R:role set, U:user set, S:set of sessions, T:time instants, LOC_u, LOC_r, LOC_p: Location contexts and $r \in R$, $p \in P$, $u \in U$, $s \in S$, $t \in T$,		
enabled(r, pos_r, t)	$R \times LOC_r \times T$	*r is enabled at pos_r at t*
U_assigned(u, r, pos_u, pos_r, t)	$U \times R \times LOC_u \times LOC_r \times T$	*u at pos_u is assigned to r at pos_r at t*
P_assigned(p, r, pos_r, pos_p, t)	$P \times R \times LOC_r \times LOC_p \times T$	*p is assigned to r at pos_r at t when object is at pos_n*
Can_activate (u, r, pos_u, pos_r, t)	$U \times R \times LOC_u \times LOC_r \times T$	*u at pos_u can activate r at pos_r at t*
Can_acquire (u, p, pos_u, pos_p, t)	$U \times P \times LOC_u \times LOC_p \times T$	*u at pos_u can acquire p at t when object is at pos_n*
R_can_acquire (u, p, r, pos_u, pos_r, pos_p, t)	$U \times P \times R \times LOC_u \times LOC_r \times LOC_p \times T$	*u at pos_u can acquire p through r at position pos_r at t when object is at position pos_p*
Can_be_acquired(p, r, pos_p, pos_r, t)	$P \times R \times LOC_p \times LOC_r \times T$	*p can be acquired through r at pos_r at t when object is at pos_n*
active(r, pos_r, t)	$R \times LOC_r \times T$	*r is active at pos_r at t*
U_active(u, r, pos_u, pos_r, t)	$U \times R \times LOC_p \times LOC_r \times T$	*r at pos_r is activated by u at pos_u at t*
us_active(u, r, s, pos_u, pos_r, t)	$U \times R \times S \times LOC_u \times LOC_r \times T$	*r is active in a session s at pos_r created by u at pos_u at t*
acquires(u, p, pos_u, pos_p, t)	$U \times P \times LOC_u \times LOC_p \times T$	*u at pos_u acquires p at t when object is at pos_n*
R_acquires(u, p, r, pos_u, pos_r, pos_p, t)	$U \times P \times R \times LOC_u \times LOC_r \times LOC_p \times T$	*u at pos_u acquires p through r at pos_r at t when object is at pos_n*
S_acquires(u, p, s, pos_u, pos_p, t)	$U \times P \times S \times LOC_u \times LOC_p \times T$	*u at pos_u acquires p in session s at t when object is at pos_n*
rs_acquires(u, p, r, s, pos_u, pos_r, pos_n, t)	$U \times P \times R \times S \times LOC_u \times LOC_r \times LOC_p \times T$	*u at pos_u acquires p through r at pos_r at t when object is at pos_n in a*

Example 4: Some examples of the usage of above expressions are as follows:

a) $l\_expr_1 = (\{Restaurants, Movie\ Theaters\})$, will map to all restaurants and movie theaters. $l\_expr_1 = (Pittsburgh, \{Restaurants, Movie\ Theaters\})$ will map to *Restaurants* and *Movie Theaters* in *Pittsburgh*.

b) $t\_expr_2 = [6/1/2005, 12/31/2005,$ all.$Days+ 9.Hours+ \triangleright 12.Hours$, maps to all the time instants for every day between 9am and 9pm, for the interval starting on 1st of June, 2005 and ending on 31st December, 2005.

Table 6. Location Expressions

Form	Conditions	MAP(l_expr)
$l\_expr_1=$ "$([ploc_x,]LLOC_y)$"	$ploc_x \in PLOC$ and $LLOC_y \subseteq LLOC$	$\cup ploc_j, s.t.\ lloc_i \in LLOC_y \wedge ploc_j \in instance(lloc_i)$, or $\cup ploc_j, s.t.\ lloc_i \in LLOC_y \wedge ploc_j \in instance(lloc_i) \wedge contains(ploc_x, ploc_j)$
$l\_expr_2=$ "$([lloc_x], LOC_y)$"	$lloc_x \in LLOC$ and $PLOC_y \subseteq PLOC$	$\cup ploc_j, s.t.\ ploc_i \in PLOC_y$, or $\cup ploc_j, s.t.\ lloc_i \in LLOC_y \wedge ploc_j \in instance(lloc_i) \wedge contains\ (ploc_x, ploc_j)$
$l\_expr_3=$ "$([LOC_x], RLOC_y)$"	$RLOC_y = \{rloc_1, rloc_2, ..., rloc_n\}$	$\cup ploc_k, s.t.\ loc_i \in LOC_u \wedge rloc_i \in RLOC_y \wedge ploc_k \in relative\_instance(rloc_j) \wedge contains(loc_i, ploc_k)$

5 Events and Triggers

We adopt the GTRBAC framework to specify the location and time constraints by extending the notions of events and triggers [7]. We consider only simple events. Role events are associated with the RBAC model, like role activation, permission assignments etc. Location events represent a mobile entity's arrival/entry to or departure/exit from a location.

Definition 8 (Simple Events): *Given $u \in U, r \in R, p \in P$ and $s \in S$, the following are the simple events:*   (a) enable$_R$ (or disable$_R$) *r*,   (b) assign$_U$ (or deassign$_U$) *r* to *u*, (c) assign$_P$ (or deassign$_P$) *p* to *r*; (d) *u* activates (or deactivates) *r*.

We can now define contextual triggers on the model, specified with respect to the location and time. Although this has been done before [1, 2, 7], we would like to stress here that we take a different approach by assuming that locations can be associated with the user, the role and the object (or permissions). A location-based (or time-based) trigger is defined as a location (or time) event that causes a status event to occur.

Definition 9 (Triggers): *Given a simple event E, time intervals π_i and τ_j, duration time expression t_expr_2, and a location expression l_expr, then a trigger is defined as:*

$(E_1$ in $\pi_1)$ op$_1$ ... op$_{m-1}$ $(E_m$ in $\pi_m)$ op $_m$ $(C_1$ in τ_1 for $t\_expr_{2,1})$ op$_{m+1}$...
op$_{m+n-1}$ $(C_n$ in τ_n for $t\_expr_{2,n}) \rightarrow pr$:$E$ after $[\Delta t \mid l\_expr]$ for$[\Delta d \mid l\_expr]$,

- E_is are simple event expressions or run time requests; C_is are GTRBAC status expressions,
- pr:E is a prioritized event expression with priority pr.
- Δt is the duration between the firing of the trigger and the occurrence of the event E, and Δd is the duration for which the event E remains valid.
- l_expr is as defined in Table 4, but typically it is a relative location.

Table 7 lists LoT-RBAC constraint expressions based on Definitions 8 and 9. Priority of an event is specified as *pr*. For lack of space, we refer readers to [3] for more details.

Table 7. Constraint Expressions for Location and Time

Constraint Categories	Constraints		Expression
Location and Periodicity Constraint	User-role assignment		$([t\_expr_1], [l\_expr_x], pr:\text{assign}_U/\text{deassign}_U \ r \text{ to } u)$
	Role enabling		$([t\_expr_1], [l\_expr_x], pr:\text{enable}/\text{disable } r)$
	Role-permission assignment		$([t\_expr_1], [l\_expr_x], pr:\text{assign}_P/\text{deassign}_P \ p \text{ to } r)$
Location and Duration Constraints	User-role assignment		$([(t\_expr_x, t\_expr_{2,U}],[l\_expr_x], pr:\text{assign}_U/\text{deassign}_U \ r \text{ to } u)$
	Role enabling		$([(t\_expr_x, t\_expr_{2,R}], [l\_expr_x], pr:\text{enable}/\text{disable } r)$
	Role-permission assignment		$([(t\_expr_x, \qquad t\_expr_{2,P}], \qquad [l\_expr_x], pr:\text{assign}_P/\text{deassign}_P \ p \text{ to } r)$
Location and Duration Constraints on Role Activation	Total active role duration	Per-role	$([[t\_expr_x], \quad t\_expr_{2,active}, \quad [l\_expr_x], \quad [t\_expr_{2,default}], pr:\text{active}_{R\_total} \ r)$
		Per-user-role	$([(t\_expr_x], t\_expr_{2,uactive}, [l\_expr_x], u, pr:\text{active}_{UR\_total} r)$
	Max role duration per activation	Per-role	$([(t\_expr_x], t\_expr_{2,max}, [l\_expr_x], pr:\text{active}_{R\_max} \ r)$
		Per-user-role	$([(t\_expr_x], t\_expr_{2,umax}, [l\_expr_x], u, pr:\text{active}_{UR\_max} r)$
Location and Cardinality Constraint on Role Activation	Total no. of activations	Per-role	$([(t\_expr_x], [l\_expr_x], N_{active}, [N_{default}], pr:\text{active}_{R\_n} r)$
		Per-user-role	$([(t\_expr_x], [l\_expr_x], N_{uactive}, u, pr:\text{active}_{UR\_n} r)$
	Max. no. of concurren	Per-role	$([(t\_expr_x], [l\_expr_x], N_{max}, [N_{default}], pr:\text{active}_{R\_con} r)$
		Per-user-role	$([(t\_expr_x], [l\_expr_x], N_{umax}, u, pr:\text{active}_{UR\_con} r)$
Trigger	$(E_1 \text{ in } \pi_1) \text{ op}_1 \dots \text{ op}_{m-1} (E_m \text{ in } \pi_m) \text{ op}_m (C_1 \text{ in } \tau_1 \text{ for } {}_tt\_expr_{2,1}) \text{ op}_{m+1}\dots \text{ op}_{m+n-1}$ $(C_n \text{ in } \tau_n \text{ for } t\_expr_{2,n}) \to pr:E \text{ after } [\Delta t \mid l\_expr_3] \text{ for } [\Delta d \mid l\_expr_3]$		
Constraint Enabling	$pr:\text{enable}/\text{disable } c$ where $c \in \{([t\_expr_2 \mid l\_expr_3], t\_expr_{2,x}, pr:E), (C), ([t\_expr_2 \mid l\_expr_3], C)\}$		
Location and Run-time Requests	Users' activation request		$(s:(\text{de})\text{activate } r \text{ for } u \text{ after } [\Delta t \mid l\_expr_3]))$
	Administrator's run-time request		$(pr:\text{assign}_U/\text{de-assign}_U \ r \text{ to } u \text{ after } [\Delta t \mid l\_expr_3])$
			$(pr:\text{enable}/\text{disable } r \text{ after } [\Delta t \mid l\_expr_3])$
			$(pr:\text{assign}_P/\text{de-assign}_P \ p \text{ to } r \text{ after } [\Delta t \mid l\_expr_3])$
			$(pr:\text{enable}/\text{disable } c \text{ after } [\Delta t \mid l\_expr_3])$

6 Illustrative Example

Example 5: Here the physical locations are the {*Shopping Mall$_1$, Hospital$_1$, Ambulance$_1$*} and the logical locations are {*Shopping Mall, Hospital, Ambulance*}. We also define two relative locations to depict proximity to the ambulance and hospital. We define above a generic policy from which the policies of the *EmergencyDoctor, Ambulance* and *Hospital* are derived. Constraint expressions have been defined to control access to patient information by the *Hospital* and the *Doctor* roles. The Hospital should be allowed to access the patient monitoring information from the ambulance only when the ambulance is close to the hospital. Since the hospital maintains the records themselves, there is no condition for it to access patient information. The *Emergency Doctor* can view patient monitoring information as long as the user is within 0.5 miles of the *Ambulance*. The *Emergency Doctor* can operate equipment in the Ambulance only when he is located in the *Ambulance*. A trigger has been defined to enable the *Emergency Doctor* role for the doctor, whenever the Shopping Mall System asks to verify the doctor's credentials. It is assumed that the verification tales place only when there is an emergency situation. Location contexts have been defined for the *Hospital, Ambulance, Emergency Doctor* and *Shopping Mall* roles. Note that *Shopping Mall* role has a context only within the Shopping Mall.

$PLOC$ = {*Shopping Mall$_1$, Hospital$_1$, Ambulance$_1$*},
$LLOC$ = {*Shopping Mall, Hospital, Ambulance*}
$rloc_1$ = (*Ambulance$_1$*, 0.5 *miles, around*), $rloc_2$ = (*Hospital, 5 miles, around*)

U = {*ShoppingMall$_1$_System, Hospital$_1$_System, Doctor$_1$, Ambulance$_1$*}
R = {*ShoppingMall_System, Hospital_System, Ambulance, EmergencyDoctor*}

P =
⌈ *accessPatientRecords* = (*Read, PatientRecords*)
│ *monitorPatient* = (*monitor, Patient*)
⟨ *operateAmbulance* = (*Operate, AmbulanceEquipment*)
│ *accessPatientStatus* = (*Read, PatientStatus*)
⌊ *verifyDoctorCredentials* = (*check, Credentials*)

ShoppingMall$_1$_System_lc = {*Shopping Mall*},
Hospital$_1$_System_lc = {*Hospital$_1$*},
Doctor$_1$_lc = {*ShoppingMall$_1$, Ambulance$_1$, Hospital$_1$*}
ShoppingMall_System_lc = {*Shopping Mall*},
Hospital_System_lc = {*Hospital$_1$, Ambulance*},
Ambulance_lc = {*Ambulance*},
EmergencyDoctor_lc = {*Ambulance, Hospital$_1$*}

Constraint Expressions:
($rloc_1$, assign *accessPatientStatus* to *EmergencyDoctor*);
($rloc_2$, assign *accessPatientStatus* to *Hospital*);
(*Ambulance*, assign *operateAmbulance* to *EmergencyDoctor*)

Triggers:
assign *verifyDoctorCredentials* to *Shopping Mall* in [11am, 1pm]
→ enable *EmergencyDoctor* for 6 *hours*

r_enable_lc(Shopping_Mall_System) = {*Shopping Mall*},
r_enable_lc(Hospital_System) = {*Ambulance, Hospital*}
r_enable_lc(EmergencyDoctor) = {*Ambulance, Hospital,*
                          Shopping Mall},
r_enable_lc(Ambulance) = {*Ambulance, Shopping Mall*}

u_assign_lc(ShoppingMall$_1$_System, Shopping Mall) = {*Shopping Mall$_1$*}
u_assign_lc(Hospital$_1$, Hospital) = {*Ambulance, Shopping Mall*},
u_assign_lc(Doctor$_1$, EmergencyDoctor) = {*Ambulance, Hospital$_1$*},
u_assign_lc(Ambulance$_1$, Ambulance) = {*Ambulance*}

p_assign_lc(accessPatientRecords, EmergencyDoctor) = {*Ambulance, rloc$_1$*},
p_assign_lc(operateAmbulance, EmergencyDoctor) = {*Ambulance*};
p_assign_lc(accessPatientStatus, EmergencyDoctor) = {*Ambulance, rloc$_1$*},
p_assign_lc(accessPatientStatus, Hospital_System) = {*rloc$_2$*},
p_assign_lc(verifyDoctorCredentials, Hospital_System) = {*Hospital$_1$*},
p_assign_lc(verifyDoctorCredentials, Ambulance) = {*Ambulance, rloc$_1$*};
p_assign_lc(verifyDoctorCredentials, ShoppingMall_System) = {*Shopping Mall*},
p_assign_lc(monitorPatient, Ambulance) = {*Ambulance*},

accessPatientRecord_lc = {*Hospital, Ambulance, rloc$_1$*},
OperateAmbulance_lc = {*Ambulance*}
accessPatientStatus_lc = {*Hospital1, Ambulance, rloc$_1$*},
monitorPatient_lc = {*Ambulance*},
verifyDoctorCredentials_lc = {*Hospital, Ambulance*},

Fig. 5. Formal Expressions for Illustrative Example

7 Conclusions and Future Work

We have proposed a comprehensive location and time based access control model for mobile application environments by extending the GTRBAC model in [3, 4, 5, 7].

The proposed model LoT-RBAC uses a fine-grained spatial model which extends the currently existing approaches to modeling both physical and logical location hierarchy. A novelty of our approach is that the spatial model captures fine grained location hierarchy semantics and associates location context to individual user, role or permission. The LoT-RBAC modeling framework provides elaborate specification of location and time constraints for access control. Our current work is being extended in several directions. One direction is to implement the proposed model, which is being currently pursued. Similarly, we will be working on location-sensitive content and location privacy, both of which are issues of great concern today. Based on the work in [3].

References

1. Hansen F., Oleshchuk V., "*Spatial Role-Based Access Control Model for Wireless Networks*", 2003 IEEE 58th Vehicular Technology Conference, 2003. VTC 2003-Fall. 6-9 Oct. 2003, Volume 3, Page(s):2093 – 2097
2. Bertino, E., Catania, B., Damiani, M.L. and Persasca, P., "*GEO-RBAC: A Spatially Aware RBAC*". in 10th Symposium on Access Control Models and Technologies (SACMAT'05), (2005).
3. Joshi, J.B.D., Bertino, E., Latif, U. and Ghafoor, A. "*A generalized temporal role-based access control model*". IEEE Transactions on Knowledge and Data Engineering, 17 (1). 4-23, 2005
4. Joshi, J.B.D., Bertino, E. and Ghafoor, A. "*Analysis of Expressiveness and Design Issues for a Temporal Role Based Access Control Model*" IEEE Transactions on Dependable and Secure Computing (accepted).
5. Joshi, J.B.D., Bertino, E. and Ghafoor, A., "*Formal Foundations for Hybrid Hierarchies in GTRBAC*". ACM Transactions on Information and System Security (under review).
6. Joshi, J. B. D., Bertino , E., Ghafoor , A.., "*Temporal hierarchy and inheritance semantics for GTRBAC*", 7th ACM Symposium on Access Control Models and Technologies. Monterey, CA, June 3-4, 2002.
7. Joshi , J. B. D., Bertino E., Shafiq B., Ghafoor A., "*Dependancies and Separation of Duty Constraints in GTRBAC*", 8th ACM Symposium on Access Control Models and Technologies. Como, Italy, June 2-3, 2003.
8. Sandhu, R., Coyne, E.J., Feinstein, H. L., Youman. C. E., "*Role-based access control models*". IEEE Computer 29(2), IEEE Press, 1996,p 38-47.
9. Bertino, E., Bonatti, P. A., Ferrari, E., "*TRBAC: A temporal role-based access control model*". ACM Transactions on Information & System Security, 4(3), Aug.2001, p.191-233.
10. Covington, M.J., Long, W., Srinivasan, S., Dev, A.K., Ahamad, M., Abowd, G.D., "*Securing context-aware applications using environment roles*", in Proceedings of the sixth ACM symposium on Access control models and technologies ACM Press, Chantilly, Virginia, United States 2001 10-20
11. Strembeck, M., Neumann, G., "*An integrated approach to engineer and enforce context constraints in RBAC environments*", ACM Transactions on Information and System Security (TISSEC) Volume 7, Issue 3 (August 2004) Pages: 392 - 427
12. Ferraiolo, D. F., Sandhu, F., Gavrila, S., Kuhn D. R., Chandramouli, R., "*Proposed NIST standard for role-based access control*", ACM Transactions on Information and System Security (TISSEC) Volume 4, Issue 3, August 2001.

13. Erwig, M, Schneider, M., *"Spatio-Temporal Predicates"*, IEEE Transactions on Knowledge and Data Engineering, 14 (4). 881-901, 2002
14. Corradi, A., Montanari, R., Tibaldi, D., *"Context-based Access Control in Ubiquitous Environments"*, Proceedings. Third IEEE International Symposium on Network Computing and Applications, 2004. (NCA 2004). 30 Aug.-1 Sept. 2004 Page(s):253 – 260
15. Fu, S. Xu, C.-Z, *"A Coordinated Spatio-Temporal Access Control Model for Mobile Computing in Coalition Environments"*, Proceedings. 19th IEEE International Parallel and Distributed Processing Symposium, 2005. 04-08 April 2005 Page(s):289b - 289b
16. Wedde, H. F., Lischka, M., *"Role Based Access Control in Remote and Ambient Spaces"*, in Proceedings of the ninth ACM symposium on Access control models and technologies ACM Press, YorkTown Heights, New York, United States 2004 21-30
17. Jiang, H., Elmagarmid, A. K., *"Spatial and temporal content-based access to hypervideo databases"*, The VLDB Journal (1998) 7: 226–238, Springer-Verlag, 1998
18. Wang, W., *"Team-and-Role-Based Organizational Context and Access Control for Cooperative Hypermedia Environments"*, Proceedings of Hypertext '99: Returning to our diverse roots (Darmstadt, Germany 1999). ACM Press, 37-46
19. Atluri, V., Chun, S. A., *"An Authorization Model for Geospatial Data"*, IEEE Transactions on Dependable and Secure Computing, Vol. 1, No. 4, October-December 2004
20. Narayanan, A. K., *"Realms and States: A Framework for Location Aware Mobile Computing"*, Proceedings of the 1st International Workshop on Mobile Commerce, Rome, Italy, Pages: 48 – 54, 2001
21. Kumar, A., Karnik, N., Chafle, G., *"Context-Sensitivity in Role-based Access Control"*, ACM SIGOPS Operating Systems Review, Volume 36 , 3: 53 – 66, 2002
22. Thomas, R. K., *"Team-based Access Control (TMAC): A Primitive for Applying Role-based Access Controls in Collaborative Environments"*, Proceedings of the second ACM workshop on Role-based access control, Fairfax, Virginia, United States, Pages: 13 - 19, 1997
23. Zhang, G., Parashar, M., *"Dynamic Context-aware Access Control for Grid Applications"*, Proceedings of Fourth International Workshop on Grid Computing, 17 Nov. 2003 Page(s):101 – 108
24. Joshi, J.B.D., *"Access-control language for multidomain environments"*, IEEE Internet Computing, Volume 8, Issue 6, Nov.-Dec. 2004 Page(s):40 - 50

Document Re-ranking by Generality in Bio-medical Information Retrieval

Xin Yan[1], Xue Li[1], and Dawei Song[2]

[1] School of Information Technology and Electrical Engineering,
University of Queensland, ITEE, University of Queensland, QLD 4072, Australia
{yanxin, xueli}@itee.uq.edu.au
[2] Knowledge Media Institute, The Open University,
Walton Hall, Milton Keynes, MK7 6AA, United Kingdom
dawei_song2005@hotmail.com

Abstract. Document ranking is an important process in information retrieval (IR). It presents retrieved documents in an order of their estimated degrees of relevance to query. Traditional document ranking methods are mostly based on the similarity computations between documents and query. In this paper we argue that the similarity-based document ranking is insufficient in some cases. There are two reasons. Firstly it is about the increased information variety. There are far too many different types documents available now for user to search. The second is about the users variety. In many cases user may want to retrieve documents that are not only similar but also general or broad regarding a certain topic. This is particularly the case in some domains such as bio-medical IR. In this paper we propose a novel approach to re-rank the retrieved documents by incorporating the similarity with their generality. By an ontology-based analysis on the semantic cohesion of text, document generality can be quantified. The retrieved documents are then re-ranked by their combined scores of similarity and the closeness of documents' generality to the query's. Our experiments have shown an encouraging performance on a large bio-medical document collection, OHSUMED, containing 348,566 medical journal references and 101 test queries.

Keywords: Generality, Relevance, Document Ranking.

1 Introduction

Document ranking is a fundamental feature for information retrieval (IR) systems. In general, an IR system ranks documents based on how close or relevant a document is to a query. In traditional models such as vector space model, documents are represented by vectors of keywords. The relevance is computed based on similarity (often defined by functions such as cosine or inner product) between the document and the query vectors.

Due to information explosion and popularity of WWW information retrieval, however, the sufficiency of using relevance alone to rank documents has been questioned by the generality retrieval problem.

M. Kitsuregawa et al. (Eds.): WISE 2005, LNCS 3806, pp. 376–389, 2005.

On one hand, information explosion somehow increases not only the quantity of information but also the variability. For instance, consider a topic for general AIDS information in PubMed[1], a medical searching service. Thousands of documents may be retrieved in a wide range such as treatment, drug therapy, transmission, diagnosis and history. User may need to have a holistic view on the topic by first reading some general and conclusive documents to find something reasonably related to their information needs. This is a challenge to the traditional relevance based document ranking since it cannot help user to sort out the relevant documents which are also general in content.

Moreover, the growing popularity of WWW information retrieval makes domain-specific information retrieval open to the public. For example there are human identified and labeled documents about patient education available in PubMed. Other patient education materials are separately maintained on WWW such as MedicineNet[2]. Easy-to-understand and jargon free information is needed by user with little domain knowledge. However, current ranking mechanism does not focus on this perspective.

Based on the concerns of generality retrieval, we argue that the factor "generality" should be taken into account in document ranking process. We need to consider both document and query generality, which separately refers to how general it is for a document/query to describe a certain topic. The goal of this research is to improve the query performance of domain specific (bio-medical literature in this paper) information retrieval by re-ranking retrieved documents on generality.

A novel ontology based approach to the calculation of generality is developed via analyzing the semantic cohesion of a document. The documents are then ranked by a combined score of relevance and the closeness of documents' generality to the query's. Experiments have been conducted on a large scale bio-medical text corpus, OHSUMED, which is a subset of MEDLINE collection containing 348,566 medical journal references and 101 test queries. Our approach has demonstrated an encouraging improvement on performance.

The remainder of this paper is organized as follows: Section 2 presents related work. Our methods to re-rank documents on generality are proposed in Section 3. Section 4 reports the experimental results. Section 5 finally concludes the paper and addresses future research directions.

2   Related Work

To the best of our knowledge, the previous studies on generality in IR literature [1], [2], [3], [4], [5] focus on two different aspects: query generality (i.e. query scope) and content-based document generality. Since our proposed re-ranking method is a process comparing the closeness of document's generality scores to the queries, it is necessary to review both literatures.

---

[1] http://pubmed.gov
[2] http://www.medicinenet.com

2.1 Query Generality

The studies [2], [3], [4] about query generality mainly focus on the overall generality of retrieval rather than the generality of individual documents. Van Rijsbergen [4], [3] regarded query generality as "a measure of the density of relevant documents in the collection". Derived from Van Rijsbergen's definition, Ben He [2] defined query generality as follows:

$$\omega = -log(\frac{N_Q}{N}) \qquad (1)$$

where N_Q is the total number of documents containing at least one query term and N is the total number of documents in the collection.

However, because of the content variability of retrievals, it is not sufficient to quantify the query generality purely based on the statistical methods. Let's consider two topics T_1 and T_2. T_1 requires literature reviews about AIDS, T_2 requires reviews about SARS, a newly discovered disease. In PubMed, a boolean query to get all the review articles about "AIDS" may result in 7650 documents. Whereas, there are only 220 review articles about "SARS". Moreover, the term "SARS" appears in 3394 references but "AIDS" appears in 108439. Is the query for T_1 more general than T_2? The answer is probably "no", because "SARS" is a new disease which has less related documents in collection than "AIDS".

2.2 Document Generality

The studies about document generality aim at finding approaches to rank general documents more closely to the query. Allen [1] argued that user has needs to know whether a document retrieved is general or concrete. Document generality was defined as the mean generality of terms in the documents. The generality of 64 words was determined. Those words were used to form a reference collection. Half of the words in the collection were regarded as general and the other half as concrete. Joint entropy measure was used to verify that general terms were more related to each other than concrete terms. Thus. through the relatedness computation between the terms in documents and those 64 terms in the reference collection, the generality of terms in the documents could be calculated.

However, some problems still remain unsolved. First, in [1], the generality of documents was judged manually for the purpose of evaluation. However, for dealing with large collections, this is obviously not practical. Secondly, not only the statistical term relatedness, but also the semantic relationships between terms need to be taken into account. Sometimes general terms may have low relatedness if they are not in a same domain. In the area of bio-medical information retrieval, for example, a stomach medicine may be semantically related to a skin medicine in terms of their generality. However, they may not have a statistical relatedness simply due to no co-occurrence in the text corpus. Thirdly, how to apply generality ranking to improve IR performance has not been discussed. Moreover, we need to consider how to combine the relevance ranking with generality ranking. User does not want a document with high generality but very low relevance to query.

The study of subtopic retrieval [5] addressed that there is a need (e.g literature survey) to find documents that "cover as many different subtopics of a general topic as possible" [5]. The subtopic retrieval method solved two problems we referred above. Firstly, a new evaluation framework was developed to evaluate the performance of re-ranking. The subtopic recall and precision can be calculated for every retrieved document since the human assigned subtopic labels are available for those documents in TREC interactive track. Documents with high generality will have a good balance between subtopic recall and subtopic precision. This framework avoids the human judgement of document generality. Secondly, the relevance ranking has been considered when re-ranking documents by generality.

There are still some major differences between the study of subtopic retrieval [5] and our proposed approach.

1. We assume that the relevance judgment of a document in OHSUMED collection is independent to that of the others. In the study of subtopic retrieval, relevance between two documents may depend on which document user will see in the first time.
2. Semantics inherent in the documents is considered in our research. We measure the ontology based semantic relationships of concepts in document in order to compute generality. In the study of subtopic retrieval, only statistical methods were used.

3   Proposed Approach

In this section, we first define our research problem and give the intuition of our solution, followed by the detailed computational methods.

The research problem is defined as: given a ranked list of documents R retrieved by a query Q, find R' so that documents in R' are ordered by both their relevance to Q and the closeness of their generality to Q's.

We approach the generality ranking problem from two perspectives. The first is to consider the query generality. We believe that generality ranking depends on both query generality and document generality. To a specific query (i.e., a query with low generality), it is not proper to simply rank general documents higher than the specific ones. The second is to consider the semantics in documents. For instance, a stomach medicine is not statistically but semantically same as a skin medicine in terms of their generality.

A query can be regarded as a short document. So in the same way a query is to be computed for its generality as if a document. Then the documents are re-ranked by comparing the closeness of documents' generality scores to the query's.

On the other hand, the semantics of documents can be computationally gripped in terms of ontology. In our work, we use bio-medical documents together with an ontology database called MeSH hierarchical structure (or MeSH tree) in bio-medical domain. Our purpose is to compute generality of text by considering the semantic properties and relations of terms appearing in the MeSH tree. For example, stomach medicine and skin medicine both belong to "Chemicals and Drugs" no matter how different their usages are. Here we regard the terms in text which can be found in MeSH ontology as domain specific concepts or MeSH concepts. The terms in text which cannot be found in MeSH ontology are referred to non-ontology concepts.

We introduce cohesion as a key feature of generality. When there is a focused topic or theme discussed in a document, the terms are closely correlated in a certain context. The cohesion of a document is regarded as a computation of the associations between the concepts found in the MeSH tree. It reflects the frequencies of the associated concepts that appear in the MeSH ontology. The more closely the concepts are associated, the more specific the document is.

In following subsections, we will describe the MeSH hierarchical structure and propose a method to identify MeSH concepts from text. We then present our approach to computational generality of documents.

3.1   MeSH Hierarchical Structure

All the headings used to index OHSUMED documents are well organized in a hierarchical structure namely MeSH tree. Figure 1 is a fragment of the MeSH tree.

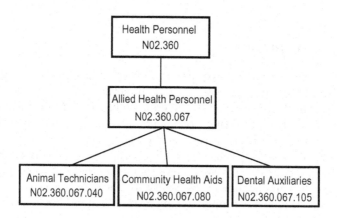

Fig. 1. A Fragment of MeSH tree

The MeSH terms are numbered and organized based on a broader/ narrower relationships in the tree. In this example, the heading "Allied Health Personnel" is a kind of "Health Personnel" and "Community Health Aides" is a kind of occupation under "Health Personnel".

Moreover, MeSH provides entry terms which may act as synonyms of a certain heading. In the given document example, the heading "Allied Health Personnel" has following entry terms: "Allied Health Personnel", "Allied Health Paramedics", "Paramedical Personnel", "Specialists, Population Program" and

"Paramedics". With entry terms, it is possible to take advantage of semantic relation between terms to identify synonyms.

3.2   Concept Identification Algorithm

In order to use MeSH ontology to extract the semantic relations between terms, the MeSH concepts in the text corpus must be recognized. The proposed algorithm of concept identification aims to allocate a single word or a compound(noun) from the corpus as a concept in the MeSH tree.

The major problem that the algorithm is concerned about is: a part of a compound term may match with a MeSH concept. For example, the compound "Plant Viruses" contains the term "Viruses". If we stop the concept identification process after a match of "Viruses" in the MeSH tree is found, then "Plant" will be mistakenly regarded as a term not in domain ontology. Indeed, "Plant Viruses" is also a MeSH concept. We solve the problem by introducing the conceptual marking tree (CMT) that is derived from the MeSH tree. The structure of a node in CMT is shown in Figure 2. A concept C is a sequence of terms $\{T_1 \ldots T_n\}$, where n is the length of C. The occurrence information of individual terms are stored separately in the cells of an array. In cell T_i, $0 \leq i \leq n$, we use P_i to store a set of position values $\{p_{i1} \ldots p_{im}\}$, where m is the term frequency of T_i in a document. p_{ij} $(0 \leq j \leq m)$ is the term position of the jth occurrence of T_i. The term position p_{ij} indicates that there are $(p_{ij} - 1)$ terms before T_1 from the beginning of a document.

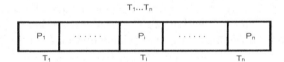

Fig. 2. Data Structure of a Node in CMT

There are 3 steps to perform the conceptual marking for a document.

1. Pick up a term t which is the k-th term counted from the beginning of the document (initially $k = 0$).
2. Locate t in CMT.
3. Assign the position value k to p_{ij} in P_i. j will be increased by one automatically when a new element is added to P_i.
4. Increase k by one, then go to step 1.

For example, the following is a one-sentence document just containing one sentence:

Over 390 individual descriptions of plant viruses or virus groups are provided.[3]

---

[3] http://www.dpvweb.net/dpv/index.php

In this example, "plant viruses" and "viruses" are all MeSH concepts. We assume that stemming has been done so that "viruses" can be identified as "virus". After the CMT is created for this document, the concept "plant viruses" in CMT have two cells, T_1 = "plant", T_2 = "viruses". $p_{11} = 6$, $p_{21} = 7$, $p_{22} = 9$. The concept "viruses" has one cell T_1 = "viruses" where $p_{11} = 7$, $p_{12} = 9$.

After marking CMT, if it is always true that $p_{(i-1)j} = p_{(i)j} + 1$ $(1 \leq i \leq m)$, then the concept C is identified as a candidate concept at its jth occurrence in the document. If in the same place of the document, no other candidate concepts can be found with more compound terms than concept C, then C is identified as the concept at its jth occurrence in the document. For the above example, we may find that the MeSH concept "viruses" may be identified as the candidate concept in position 7 and 9. However, the concept "plant viruses" has $p_{11} = p_{21} + 1$. Furthermore, it has two constituent terms but the concept "viruses" only has one. Thus it is "plant viruses" rather than "virus" which is identified as the concept at position 6.

3.3   Document Cohesion

With MeSH hierarchical structure (tree), it is possible to retrieve the semantic distance between MeSH concepts according to their positions in tree.

We introduce the concept of document cohesion which is a state or quality that the elements of a text (e.g. clauses) "tend to hang together" [6]. The intuition of our approach is based on a hypothesis that document with less cohesion would be more general. Consider the following two definitions of Severe Acute Respiratory Syndrome (SARS). Definition 1 comes from an FAQ page of Centers for Disease Control and Prevention (CDC) [4] under a section namely "what everyone should know". Definition 2 is an official definition from the Department of Health in Hong Kong [5]. Obviously, definition 1 is more general than definition 2.

1. Severe Acute Respiratory Syndrome(SARS) is a viral respiratory illness that was recognized as a global threat in March 2003, after first appearing in Southern China in November 2002.
2. Severe Acute Respiratory Syndrome(SARS) is a viral respiratory infection caused by a coronavirus (SARS-CoV).

In definition 2, four MeSH concepts can be identified: "Severe Acute Respiratory Syndrome", "respiratory infection", "coronavirus" and "SARS-CoV". In definition 1, "Severe Acute Respiratory Syndrome" and "China" are identified as MeSH concepts.

What makes definition 1 be more general than definition 2? We found that there is stronger cohesion in definition 2 than in definition 1. In other words, concepts in definition 2 are more strongly associated than those in definition 1. "Severe Acute Respiratory Syndrome" is a kind of "respiratory infection" in terms of MeSH ontology. Moreover, "SARS-CoV" is a kind of "coronavirus".

---

[4] http://www.cdc.gov/ncidod/sars/faq.htm
[5] http://www.info.gov.hk

However, in definition 1, there is not a direct relationship between 'Severe Acute Respiratory Syndrome" and "China" in terms of the MeSH ontology.

Following the above observations, it seems that the document generality is somehow related to document cohesion. The higher a document's degree of cohesion, the lower its generality. In our research, the degree of document cohesion is inversely proportional to the mean semantic distance of all the pairs of concepts in document. The calculation of semantic distance is based on the Leacock-Chodorow similarity [7] function which measures the shortest path between two concepts in the MeSH tree. We adopt Leacock-Chodorow similarity and propose our algorithms to compute cohesion.

$$Cohesion(d_i) = \frac{\sum_{i,j=1}^{n} Sim(c_i, c_j)}{Number of Associations}, \ where \ n > 1, \ i < j \qquad (2)$$

$$Sim(c_i, c_j) = -log\frac{len(c_i, c_j)}{2D} \qquad (3)$$

$$Number of Associations = \frac{n(n - 1)}{2} \qquad (4)$$

In Equation 2, n is the total number of MeSH concepts in a document d_i. $Sim(c_i, c_j)$ is a function computing the Leacock-Chodorow semantic similarity by using the shortest path $len(c_i, c_j)$ between c_i and c_j in the MeSH tree. $Number of Associations$ is the total number of associations among different MeSH concepts, which is defined in Equation 4.

In Equation 3, D is the maximum MeSH tree depth. In our experiments, D is 11. The scope of Equation 2 is $[0, -log(\frac{1}{22})]$. As to a document without any MeSH concepts or with only one MeSH concept, its document cohesion is 0. For a documents with strongest associations among all the concepts within the document, its cohesion is $-log(\frac{1}{22})$, the maximum value.

3.4   Document Generality

We give Equation 5 for calculating document generality. In Equation 5, $DG(d_i)$ denotes the generality of a document d_i.

$$DG(d_i) = \frac{1}{Cohesion(d_i) + 1} \qquad (5)$$

The query generality computation is similar to the computation of document generality. The difference between them is that we take Equation 1, with a new name Statistical Query Generality (SQG) as an option for query generality calculation.

$$QG = \frac{SQG}{Cohesion(Q) + 1} \tag{6}$$

In Equation 6, QG is the query generality. The calculations of query cohesion is the same as document cohesion.

However, we believe that it is better to give high ranks to those documents whose generality are close to the queries'. For example, it is not suitable to give high ranks to the review or introduction papers on "malignant pericardial effusion" for the query "best treatment of malignant pericardial effusion in esophageal cancer". Thus, we rank the documents by comparing the closeness of documents' generality scores to the query's. In this research the generality closeness between query Q and document d_i is computed as the absolute value of the difference between $DG(d_i)$ and QG.

3.5   Combining Relevance and Generality

As an important step in our proposed approach, we consider both the document relevance and generality. Here we treat information retrieval system as a black box. Through the query submitted as input, the output of the black box is a ranked list where documents are scored. Let $RScore(d_i)$ denote the relevance score given to a ranked document d_i and QG is the query generality. The final score considering both document relevance and generality is given in the following formula.

$$Score(d_i, Q) = RScore(d_i)^\alpha * e^{-|DG(d_i)-QG|^\beta} \tag{7}$$

α and β are parameters for a well tuned performance.

4   Experiments and Evaluations

4.1   Data Set

Our experiments are designed based on the OHSUMED corpus, which is a subset of Medline and contains 348566 medical references. There are a number of fields in a reference, such as title, abstract, author, source and publication type. In our research, we use title and abstract only. The following is a fragment of a sample document in OHSUMED collection, where

- .I Sequential Identifier
- .U MEDLINE identifier (UI)
- .T Title (TI)
- .P Publication type (PT)
- .W Abstract (AB)
- .A Author (AU)
- .S Source (SO)

```
.I 1
.U 87049087
.S Am J Emerg Med 8703; 4(6):491-5
.T Refibrillation managed by EMT-Ds: incidence and
outcome without paramedic back-up.
.P JOURNAL ARTICLE.
.W Some patients converted from ventricular
fibrillation to organized rhythms by
defibrillation-trained ambulance technicians (EMT-Ds)
will refibrillate before hospital arrival.
......
.A Stults KR; Brown DD.
```

4.2 Queries

In OHSUMED there are 106 topics and their relevance judgments made by novice physicians. Each topic has two parts: the patient information and the physician's information need. In this research, 106 test queries are formed by combining both parts for each of the 106 topics. In addition, queries 8, 28, 49, 86, and 93 are dropped for there are no relevant documents identified for them. Therefore, a total number of 101 test queries are used in our experiments.

There are queries apparently asking for review information. The following eight review-type queries are selected to test the effect of query generality.

- No.4 reviews on subdurals in elderly
- No.11 review article on cholesterol emboli
- No.17 RH isoimmunization, review topics
- No.31 chronic pain management, review article, use of tricyclic antidepressants
- No.34 review article on adult respiratory syndrome
- No.54 angiotensin converting enzyme inhibitors, review article
- No.105 review of anemia of chronic illness
- No.106 HIV and the GI tract, recent reviews

4.3 Baseline and Pre-processing

In our experiments, Lucene[6] is used as the baseline IR system to index and retrieve the titles and abstracts of documents in OHSUMED collection. All terms are filtered by the SMART 571 stop word list and stemmed using the Porter stemming algorithm. The MeSH concepts are identified by using our conceptual marking tree algorithm.

---

[6] http://lucene.apache.org/java/docs/index.html

4.4   Evaluation Methodology

In our experiments, the baseline system is used to retrieve 1000 documents for each test query. We then cover all three possible cases where query generality, document generality and SQG are used solely or together in a reasonable manner. Those three cases are derived from our proposed Equation 5, 6 and 7 for re-ranking the documents retrieved by the baseline.

Case One: DG. The first case is to re-rank documents without considering query generality. The scoring function (Equation 7) is changed to Equation 8:

$$Score(d_i, Q) = RScore(d_i)^\alpha * DG(d_i)^\beta \qquad (8)$$

α and β are parameters for a well tuned performance.

Case Two: DG+QG+SQG. The second case is to re-rank documents by considering both document generality and query generality with SQG. This option exactly consists of Equation 5, 6 and 7.

Case Three: DG+QG-SQG. The third case is to re-rank documents by considering both document generality and query generality without SQG. The Equation 6 is changed to Equation 9 to remove SQG. Equation 9 is then used for calculating QG in Equation 7.

$$QG = \frac{1}{Cohesion(Q) + 1} \qquad (9)$$

4.5   Performance Indicators

The performance of re-ranking are measured in two ways. Firstly we compare the precision and recall of re-ranking with the original ranking given by baseline system for all the 101 test queries. Secondly, we check if all the review type queries get larger improvement in term of average precision.

4.6   Evaluations

Table 1 gives detailed precisions of each algorithm at different recall levels averaged over 101 test queries. In Table 2, we show the performance of the algorithms on the review type queries. The mean average precision ("MAP" in the tables) and the percentages of improvement in MAP ("%" in the tables) are summarized.

It seems a general case that DG+QG+SQG and DG+QG-SQG improve the query performance for the 101 queries over the baseline. However, DG degrades overall query performance slightly. Therefore, it is more effective to re-rank documents based on the closeness between document and query generality rather than considering document generality alone.

Table 1. Detailed Precision-Recall Comparisons

R	Baseline	DG	DG+QG+SQG	DG+QG-SQG
0	0.6369	0.6311	**0.6512**	0.6366
0.1	0.4071	**0.4110**	**0.4139**	**0.4089**
0.2	0.3239	0.3222	**0.3281**	**0.3263**
0.3	0.254	0.2480	**0.2635**	**0.2644**
0.4	0.1963	0.1942	**0.1985**	**0.2024**
0.5	0.1679	**0.1681**	**0.1689**	0.1675
0.6	0.1396	0.1364	0.1389	0.1372
0.7	0.088	0.0873	**0.0884**	**0.0893**
0.8	0.0544	0.0537	0.0543	0.0542
0.9	0.0223	0.0221	**0.0224**	0.0218
1	0.0018	0.0018	**0.0019**	0.0017
MAP	0.1849	0.1834	**0.1883**	**0.1873**
%		-0.81%	**1.84%**	**1.30%**

Table 2. Precision Improvement on Review Type Queries

QNo.	Baseline	DG	DG+QG+SQG	DG+QG-SQG
4	0.0821	0.0450	**0.0824**	0.0375
11	0.0741	0.0712	**0.1046**	**0.0936**
17	0.0021	0.0020	0.0021	**0.0023**
31	0.1522	0.1415	**0.1542**	**0.1544**
34	0.0193	**0.0198**	0.0188	0.0164
54	0.1099	**0.1125**	0.1025	**0.1181**
105	0.2950	**0.3003**	0.2926	0.2789
106	0.0085	0.0053	**0.0121**	0.0066
MAP	0.0929	0.0872	**0.0962**	0.0885
%		-6.14%	**3.55%**	-4.76%

Unlike documents, queries are normally very short. Consequently there is less information involved in the computation of query cohesion, which in turn may not be sufficient enough to reflect query generality. SQG is therefore an important complementary component for effectively measuring query generality. This is demonstrated by the fact that the DG+QG+SQG, which takes SQG into account, always performs better than DG+QG-SQG.

In summary, as both document generality and query generality with SQG are considered, DG+QG+SQG performed the best to benefit generality retrieval.

Moreover, Table 2 shows the better performance of the DG+QG+SQG algorithm on review type queries. There is an encouraging 3.55% improvement over the baseline. We performed a dependent t-test (Paired Two Sample for Means) which compares the paired precisions between the baseline and the DG+QG+SQG algorithm over different queries in Table 2. With a $p-value$ less than 0.05, it turns out that the improvement is significant. This also verifies our motivation discussed in Section 1 that the generality retrieval happens more often for review type queries from non-domain-expert user.

5   Conclusions and Future Work

In this paper, we studied a generality retrieval problem in bio-medical area where document ranking is based not only on relevance but also on generality. Traditional document ranking methods are insufficient for generality retrieval because they are depends on relevance only. This paper argued that the "generality" is an important complement to the traditional relevance based ranking. The intuition is that when search results are returned by IR system, user, especially non-domain-expert user, may expect to see the general and conclusive documents on the top of the list, so that they can first have an overview on the topic rather than going into the specific technical details directly.

We have proposed a novel ontology-based approach in biomedical IR to re-rank the retrieved documents via generality. Our approach is distinct as to make use of the MeSH ontology structure in bio-medical domain in order to compute the generality from statistical as well as semantic perspectives. Moreover, query generality and document generality were both considered in our proposed re-ranking algorithms. Documents are scored and re-ranked by a combination of their relevance to query and the closeness of documents' generality to the query's. Experiments have been conducted on a large corpus namely OHSUMED. Our approach shows an improved query performance and encourages us to pursue the further investigation. Our approach can also be easily generalized into other domains provided that the domain specific ontologies are available.

We plan to study other factors for ranking document by generality. So far we have considered quantifying only the semantic relationships amongst MeSH concepts in order to calculate the document cohesion. In our further study we will explore other features of document generality and incorporate the relationships between general and domain-specific concepts via statistical approaches, such as term co-occurrence counts.

Acknowledgments

The work reported in this paper has been funded in part by the Co-operative Centre for Enterprise Distributed Systems Technology (DSTC) through the Australian Federal Governments CRC Programme (Department of Education, Science and Training).

References

1. Allen, R.B., Wu, Y.: Generality of texts. In: Proceedings of the 5th International Conference on Asian Digital Libraries: Digital Libraries: People, Knowledge, and Technology. (2002) 111–116
2. He, B., Ounis, I.: Inferring query performance using pre-retrieval predictors. In: 11th Symposium on String Processing and Information Retrieval, Padova, Italy (2004) 43–54

3. Plachouras, V., Cacheda, F., Ounis, I., Rijsbergen, C.v.: University of glasgow at the web track: Dynamic application of hyperlink analysis using the query scope. In: In Proceedings of the 12th Text Retrieval Conference TREC 2003, Gaithersburg (2003)
4. Van Rijsbergen, C.J.: Information Retrieval. London; Boston: Butterworths (1979)
5. Zhai, C., Cohen, W.W., Lafferty, J.: Beyond independent relevance: Methods and evaluation metrics for subtopic retrieval. In: Proceedings of the 26th annual international ACM SIGIR conference on Research and development in informaion retrieval. (2003) 10–17
6. Morris, J., Hirst, G.: Lexical cohesion computed by thesaural relations as an indicator of the structure of text. Computational Linguistics **17** (1991) 21–48
7. Leacock, C., Chodorow, M.: Combining local context and wordnet similarity for word sense identification. In: Fellbaum. (1998) 265C283

Representing and Reasoning About Privacy Abstractions

Yin Hua Li[1] and Salima Benbernou[2,*]

[1] CSE, UNSW, Sydney, Australia
yinhual@cse.unsw.edu.au
[2] LIRIS, UCB Lyon I, France
sbenbern@liris.univ-lyon1.fr

Abstract. The emerging next generation Web technologies offer tremendous opportunities for automating information management in a variety of application domains including office tasks, travel, and digital government. One of the main challenges facing effective automation is privacy. Verifying the correct usage of collected personal data is a major concern for both individuals and organizations. In this paper, we present a framework for reasoning about privacy models including provider's privacy policies and user's privacy preferences. More specifically, we use a Description Logic (DL) based notation to specify privacy abstractions. We provide a formalization of matching user's privacy preferences against provider's privacy policies using DLs' reasoning mechanisms. We have implemented a Privacy Match Engine(PME) which is based on RACER.

1 Introduction

Semantic web services paradigm aims at building upon semantic Web and Web services technologies to enable automatic discovery, access, combination, and management of web services [4]. Web services allow software entities to be described, advertised, discovered and accessed through XML based standard languages and protocols [3]. When services are described and interact in a standardized manner, the task of developing complex services by composing other services is simplified. The reason is that the cost of reconciling differences in communication protocols and interfaces in heterogeneous systems is reduced. However, semantic interoperability is still an open and challenging issue because services are typically developed by different teams/organizations. Semantic Web services focus on providing machine understandable representation of services characteristics and capabilities to provide support for automatically discovering, composing and managing services. Clearly, this paradigm is promising, nevertheless many of its objectives, including automatic service discovery, remain futuristic visions partially because of the difficulties created by services autonomy and heterogeneity, especially in complex and dynamic environments. Another challenge faced by the success of semantic web services paradigm is privacy. Services may need to collect, store, process and share information about their users(e.g.,

---

* This work was completed during her visiting UNSW.

M. Kitsuregawa et al. (Eds.): WISE 2005, LNCS 3806, pp. 390–403, 2005.

Car Rental service may need service requestors to provide their driver license information). Information processing and sharing must preserve the privacy of these individuals [17, 18, 19, 20, 21, 7, 6].

Our work in this paper is to study privacy issues in Web serivce. Our long term objective is to ground the automation of several privacy related interoperability activities (e.g., understanding similarities and differences between privacy policies, verifying whether services can interact with each other at privacy level). We argue that representing privacy abstractions using high-level notations that are endowed with formal semantics can lead to use similar techniques to those provided in models analysis and management in schema integration [8] and service protocols interoperability [5].

This paper reports on preliminary results in this project. We use a Description Logic (DL) based notation to specify privacy abstractions including privacy preferences and privacy policies. We provide a formalization of matching preferences against policies using DLs' reasoning mechanisms over privacy vocabularies. The choice of a description logic based formalism is motivated by several factors. First, we want to build upon our previous work in the area of web services discovery [1]. Second, DLs provide effective trade-offs between expressive power and efficient reasoning. Indeed, DLs have heavily influenced the development of some semantic web ontology languages (e.g., DAML-OIL or OWL [4]). Third, the existing DL-based technologies(e.g., subsumption) can be used to match user's privacy preference against service provider's privacy policy.

Due to the fact that Platform for Privacy Preference(P3P) is the most significant effort underway to enable users to gain more control and a sense of control over what information a Website collects, currently many Websites specify their privacy practices in P3P. We hence provide an algorithm to map a P3P policy to policy terminology; then we focus on the specific problem of how DL-based technology can be used for checking the compatibility between P3P privacy policies and users' privacy preferences. In order to make the semantics of privacy vocabularies and the relationship between these vocabularies applicable to the matching procedure, we provide domain-specific privacy ontologies which work as knowledge bases.

The remainder of this paper is organized as follows: Section 2 overviews the basic concepts of description logics. Section 3 focuses on the representation of privacy concepts using a DL-based notation. Section 4 describes the formalization of matching privacy preferences against privacy policies in the context of P3P and overview our implememtation. Section 5 gives concluding remarks.

2 Description Logics Background

Description Logics(DLs)[12] are a family of logics that were developed for modeling complex hierarchical structures and providing a specialized reasoning engine to perform inferences on these structures. The main reasoning mechanisms (e.g., subsumption and satisfiability) are decidable for main description logics[9]. Recently, DLs have heavily influenced the development of the semantic web lan-

Table 1. Syntax and semantics of some concept-forming constructors

Constructor name	Syntax	Semantics
concept name	P	$P^{\mathcal{I}} \subseteq \Delta^{\mathcal{I}}$
top	$\top$	$\Delta^{\mathcal{I}}$
bottom	$\bot$	$\emptyset$
conjunction	$C \sqcap D$	$C^{\mathcal{I}} \cap D^{\mathcal{I}}$
disjunction	$C \sqcup D$	$C^{\mathcal{I}} \cup D^{\mathcal{I}}$
primitive negation	$\neg P$	$\Delta^{\mathcal{I}} \setminus P^{\mathcal{I}}$
universal quantification	$\forall R.C$	$\{x \in \Delta^{\mathcal{I}} | \forall y : (x,y) \in R^{\mathcal{I}} \rightarrow y \in C^{\mathcal{I}}\}$
existential quantification	$(\exists R.C)$	$\{x \in \Delta^{\mathcal{I}} | \exists y | (x,y) \in R^{\mathcal{I}} \wedge y \in C^{\mathcal{I}}\}$

guages. For example, DAML+OIL, the ontology language used by DAML-S, is an alternative syntax of a very expressive Description Logic[10]. Description logics represent domain of interest in terms of *concepts*(unary predicates) which characterize subsets of the objects(*individuals*), and *roles*(binary predicates) which denote binary relationships between individuals. Concepts are denoted by expressions formed by means of special constructors. Examples of DL constructors considered in this paper are:

- the top concept($\top$) and the bottom concept($\bot$);
- concept conjunction($\sqcap$), e.g., the concept description *parent $\sqcap$ male* denotes the set of fathers (i.e., male parents);
- concept disjunction($\sqcup$), e.g., the concept description *father$\sqcup$mother* denotes the set of parents (i.e., a father or a mother);
- the universal role quantification($\forall R.C$), e.g., the description $\forall child.male$ denotes the set of individuals whose children are all male;
- the number restriction constructors $(\geq n \ R)$ and $(\leq n \ R)$, e.g., the description $(\geq 1 \ child)$ denotes the set of parents who have at least one child, while the description $(\leq 1 \ Leader)$ denotes the set of individuals that cannot have more than one leader.

The various description logics differ from one to another based on the set of constructors they allow. Table 1 shows all constructors of $\mathcal{ALC}$ which is the extension of $\mathcal{AL}$ by union and full existential quantification. The language $\mathcal{AL}$(attributive language) has been introduced in [11].

The semantics of a concept description is defined in terms of an interpretation $\mathcal{I} = (\Delta^{\mathcal{I}}, \cdot^{\mathcal{I}})$, which consists of a nonempty set $\Delta^{\mathcal{I}}$, the domain of the interpretation, and an interpretation function $\cdot^{\mathcal{I}}$, which assigns a set $P^{\mathcal{I}} \subseteq \Delta^{\mathcal{I}}$ to each concept name $P \in \mathcal{C}$ and a binary relation $R^{\mathcal{I}} \subseteq \Delta^{\mathcal{I}} \times \Delta^{\mathcal{I}}$ to each role name $R \in \mathcal{R}$. Additionally, the extension of $\cdot^{\mathcal{I}}$ to arbitrary concept descriptions is defined inductively as shown in the third column of Table 1. Based on this semantics, subsumption and equivalence are defined as following.

Let C and D be concept descriptions:

- C is *subsumed by* D(denoted as $C \sqsubseteq D$) iff $C^{\mathcal{I}} \subseteq D^{\mathcal{I}}$ for all interpretation $\mathcal{I}$
- C is *equivalent to* D(denoted as $C \equiv D$) iff $C^{\mathcal{I}} = D^{\mathcal{I}}$ for all interpretation $\mathcal{I}$

The *intentional* descriptions contained in a knowledge base built using a description logic is called *terminology*. The kind of terminologies we consider in this paper are defined below.

Definition 1. *(terminology) Let A be a concept name and C be a concept description. Then $A \doteq C$ is a concept definition. A terminology $\mathcal{T}$ is a finite set of concept definitions such that each concept name occurs at most once in the left-hand side of a definition.*

A concept name A is called a defined concept in the terminology $\mathcal{T}$ iff it occurs in the left-hand side of a concept definition in $\mathcal{T}$. Otherwise A is called an atomic concept. An interpretation $\mathcal{I}$ satisfies the statement $A \doteq C$ iff $A^{\mathcal{I}} = C^{\mathcal{I}}$. An interpretation $\mathcal{I}$ is a *model* for a terminology $\mathcal{T}$ if $\mathcal{I}$ satisfies all the statements in $\mathcal{T}$. In the sequel, we assume that a terminology $\mathcal{T}$ is *acyclic*, i.e., there is no cyclic dependencies between concept definitions.

3 Representing Privacy Concepts Using Description Logics

In this section, we first introduce main privacy concepts and then show how they can be described using description logics. The main motivations behind using DLs are twofold:

- Providing a declarative framework, endowed with formal semantics, for representing privacy abstractions.
- Using DL-based reasoning techniques to automate privacy related interoperability activities (e.g., matching privacy preference against privacy policy, understanding similarities and differences between privacy policies, verifying whether services can interoperate at privacy level).

3.1 Privacy Abstractions

As personal information becomes more accessible, precautions must be taken to protect against the misuse of the information. For example, a client opening an account in a bank may provide some personal information (e.g., name, address) with the understanding that bank employees are authorized to access information only when they need it to maintain client accounts; and the bank will not give the clients' personal information to marketing service providers for the purpose of offering new services. On the other hand, organizations want the ability to define a comprehensive description of a website's practices(*Privacy policies*) that is located on the site itself and may be easily accessible by clients. Privacy policies inform consumers about how organizations collect and use their personal information and serve as a basis for consumer browsing and transaction decisions. Generally speaking, the following privacy abstractions can be used to describe both provider privacy policies and user privacy preferences [13, 19]:

- PersonalData: stating what customer's personal information will be collected (e.g., user's home postal address);
- User: stating who can use the collected data (e.g., the company uses the purchase data);
- Purpose: declaring what purposes the collected-data will be used for(e.g., purchase)

Table 2. Example of a privacy statement

PersonalData	UserName, UserEmail, UserHomePostal
Purpose	Current, Contact
User	SamePolicies
Retention	$(\leq 180 \ day)$

- Retention: describing how long the data referenced in the PersonalData will be retained(e.g., the data will be kept until the purchase transaction finishes)

Table 2 shows an example illustrating how such abstractions can be used to describe a privacy statement. Such a statement may be used to describe a service provider privacy policy. This statement describes that user's name, email address and home postal address will be collected and used by the service provider to complete the current activity (e.g., purshasing a book) and to contact an individual for the promotion of a product or a service; those collected information may be delivered to legal entities who use the data on their own behalf under the same practices (*User= SamePolicies*); those collected user information will be retained for less than half year (*Retention=* $(\leq 180 \ day)$) before they are destroyed. Note that, same abstractions are also useful for a user to specify his/her preferences (i.e., contraints on how user data should or should not be used). Usually, a provider policy or user preferences are described using a set of privacy statements.

In order to let service providers and service requestors in the same domain understand each other from privacy point of view, it is necessary to provide common privacy vocabularies (e.g., meaning of *User=SamePolicies*). These vocabularies are domain-specific. Figure 1 is an example of personal data ontology for e-bookshop domain.

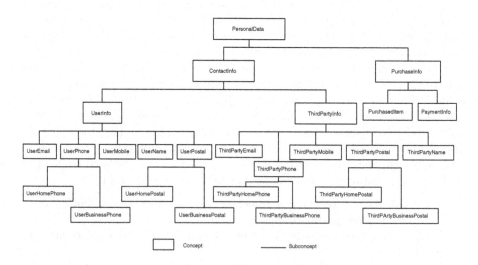

Fig. 1. Personal Data ontology for e-bookship domain

3.2   Declarative Representation of Privacy Abstractions

We propose to describe a privacy statement as DL defined concept. For example, the statement, shown in Table 2, can be mapped to concept S, where

$$S \doteq \exists has\_Data.(UserName \sqcap UserEmail \sqcap UserHomePostal)$$
$$\sqcap \exists has\_Purpose.(Current \sqcap Contact) \sqcap \exists has\_User.SamePolicies$$
$$\sqcap has\_Retention(\leq 180\ Day)$$

Given such formal descriptions of privacy statements, DL-based reasoning mechanism can then be applied in matching preference against policy. For example, subsumption can be used to test whether a statement S_1 is more specific than a statement S_2. However, as mentioned before, privacy policies and user preferences are usually described as a set of privacy statements. Hence, we propose to describe both privacy policy Po and user preferences Pr as DL terminology $\mathcal{T}_{Po}$ and $\mathcal{T}_{Pr}$ respectively. Then, in order to provide support for privacy analysis, management and matchmaking, we need to extend DL-based reasoning techniques to deal with terminologies rather than only concepts. The following definition extends the notion of subsumption to terminologies.

Definition 2. (Subsumption between terminologies) *Let $\mathcal{T}_1$ and $\mathcal{T}_2$ be two terminologies. Then we say that $\mathcal{T}_1$ is subsumed by $\mathcal{T}_2$, denoted as $\mathcal{T}_1 \sqsubseteq \mathcal{T}_2$, iff for every defined concept S_1 in $\mathcal{T}_1$, there exists a defined concept S_2 in $\mathcal{T}_2$ such that $S_1 \sqsubseteq S_2$.*

As a concrete example, we present in the next section how P3P policies and preferences can be mapped into DL terminologies and show how the reasoning mechanism can be used to match user's privacy preferecnce against provider's privacy policy in this context. It should be noted, in addition to subsumption and equivalence, other non-standards DL reasoning techniques such as computing difference between two concepts, computing least common subsumers [12] can also be very useful in studying interoperability of services at privacy layer.

4   The Case of P3P

P3P, developed by the World Wide Web Consortium(W3C), provides a standardized, XML-based policy specification language that can be used to specify an organization's privacy practices [14, 15]. P3P has two parts: Privacy Policy and Privacy Preference [14, 15]. Following we discuss both of them.

4.1   Declarative Representation of Privacy Policy

A P3P privacy policy includes a sequence of *STATEMENT* elements. A *STATEMENT* groups together a PURPOSE element, a RECIPIENT element, a RETENTION element and a DATA-GROUP element (e.g., Table 3 is an example of P3P privacy policy). Even though there are some other optional elements(e.g., < ENTITY >< CONSEQUENCE >) in P3P policies, these optional elements have no effect on the match and are not considered here. The algorithm **MapPolicy** shows

Table 3. Example of a P3P Policy *Po*

```
<POLICY>
    <STATEMENT>
        <PURPOSE><current/><contact/></PURPOSE>
        <RECIPIENT><ours><same/></RECIPIENT>
        <RETENTION><stated_purpose/></RETENTION>
        <DATA-GROUP>
            <DATA ref="\#user.home_info.postal"/> </DATA>
        </DATA-GROUP>
    </STATEMENT>
    <STATEMENT>
        <PURPOSE><contact  required="opt_in"/></PURPOSE>
        <RECIPIENT><ours/></RECIPIENT>
        <RETENTION><business_practise/></RETENTION>
        <DATA-GROUP>
            <DATA  ref="user.home_info.online.email"/>
        <DATA-GROUP>
    </STATEMENT>
    <STATEMENT>
        <PURPOSE>
            <individual_decision required="opt_in"/>
            <admin/><develop/>
        </PURPOSE>
        <RECIPIENT><ours/></RECIPIENT>
        <RETENTION><business_practise/></RETENTION>
        <DATA-GROUP>
            <DATA ref="\#dynamic.miscdata">
                <CATEGORIES><purchase/><CATEGORIES>
            </DATA>
    </STATEMENT>
</POLICY>
```

how to map a P3P policy into a privacy policy terminology. More specifically, each statement of policy is mapped to a defined concept in the terminology. For example, the P3P privacy policy *Po* given in Table 3 is mapped into terminology T_{Po} depicted in Table 4. There are three statements in *Po*, hence T_{Po} consists of three concepts S_1, S_2 and S_3, and each concept is corresponding to a statement.

4.2 Declarative Representation of Privacy Preference

P3P also proposes a language, called APPEL(A P3P Preference Exchange Language 1.0), for users to express their privacy preferences. Users' APPEL privacy preferences are organized as a set of rules and each rule has two components, rule behavior and rule body. Rule body consists of a set of statements.

Each element(e.g., PURPOSE) in APPEL statements has a *connective* attribute which defines the logical operators of the language. There are 6 connec-

---

Algorithm 1. MapPolicy (skeleton)

Require: A P3P policy P.
Ensure: A terminology $\mathcal{T}_P = \emptyset$.
1: **for all** statement $SinP$ **do**
2:    Let $PurP$, $User$, Ret and $Data$ be four concept names
3:    $PurP := \exists has\_Purpose.(p_1 \sqcap \ldots \sqcap p_m)$, for all the purposes p_j, with $j \in [1,m]$, that appear in S
4:    $User := \exists has\_User.(r_1 \sqcap \ldots \sqcap r_n)$, for all the recipients r_j, with $j \in [1,n]$, that appear in S
5:    $Ret := \exists has\_Retention.(t_1 \sqcap \ldots \sqcap t_l)$, for all the retention periods t_j, with $j \in [1,l]$, that appear in S
6:    $Data := \exists has\_Data.(d_1 \sqcap \ldots \sqcap d_k)$, for all the data element or category d_j, with $j \in [1,k]$, that appear in the data group of S
7:    generate a new concept C_S in $\mathcal{T}_P$ defined as follows:
8:    $C_S \doteq PurP \sqcap User \sqcap Ret \sqcap Data$.
9:    $\mathcal{T}_P = \mathcal{T}_P \cup C_S$.
10: **end for**

Table 4. A terminology $\mathcal{T}_{Po}$ obtained from the policy Po

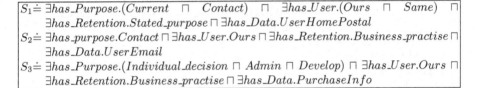

$S_1 \doteq \exists has\_Purpose.(Current \quad \sqcap \quad Contact) \quad \sqcap \quad \exists has\_User.(Ours \quad \sqcap \quad Same) \quad \sqcap$
$\exists has\_Retention.Stated\_purpose \sqcap \exists has\_Data.UserHomePostal$
$S_2 \doteq \exists has\_purpose.Contact \sqcap \exists has\_User.Ours \sqcap \exists has\_Retention.Business\_practise \sqcap$
$\exists has\_Data.UserEmail$
$S_3 \doteq \exists has\_Purpose.(Individual\_decision \sqcap Admin \sqcap Develop) \sqcap \exists has\_User.Ours \sqcap$
$\exists has\_Retention.Business\_practise \sqcap \exists has\_Data.PurchaseInfo$

---

tives, $or, and, non\_or, non\_and, or\_exact$ and and_exact. The semantics of these connectives are:

- *or*: a successful match is achieved if at least one contained expressions can be found in the policy;
- *and*: a successful match is achieved if all of the contained expressions can be found in the policy;
- *non_or*: a successful match is achieved if none of the contained expressions can be found in the policy;
- *non_and*: a successful match is acheived if at least one of the contained expressions cannot be found in the policy;
- *or_exact*: a successful match is achieved if one or more of the contained expressions can be found in the policy and the policy only contains elements appeared in the rule;
- *and_exact*: a successful match is achieved if all of the contained expressions can be found in the policy and the policy contains only elements appeared in the rule

In our approach, each APPEL preference Pr is mapped into a preference terminology $\mathcal{T}_{Pr}$ using an algorithm similar to the one used for mapping policies. The

Table 5. Example of an APPEL privacy preference P_r

```
<appel: RULESET>
    <appel:RULE behaviour="request">
        <P3P:POLICY>
            <P3P:STATEMENT>
                <P3P:PURPOSE appel:connective="or">
                    <P3P:current/> <P3P:contact/>
                </P3P:PURPOSE>
                <P3P:RECIPIENT appel:connective="and-exact">
                    <P3P:ours/> <P3P:same/>
                </P3P:RECIPIENT>
                <P3P:DATA-GROUP appel:connective="and">
                    <P3P:DATA ref="#user.home_info.phone"/>
                </P3P:DATA-GROUP>
            </P3P:STATEMENT>
            <P3P:STATEMENT>
                <P3P:PURPOSE appel:connective="and-exact">
                    <P3P:current/><P3P:individual-decision/>
                </P3P:PURPOSE>
                <P3P:DATA-GROUP appel:connective="or-exact">
                    <P3P:DATA ref="#dynamic.miscdata."/>
                        <P3P:CATEGORIZE><purchase></P3P:CATEGORIZE>
                </P3P:DATA-GROUP>
            </P3P:STATEMENT>
        </P3P:POLICY>
    </appel:RULE>
</appel: RULESET>
```

Table 6. A terminology $\mathcal{T}_{Pr}$ obtained from the preference Pr

$R_1.Behaviour$	$\doteq$	$request$
$R_1.S_1.purpose.connective$	$\doteq$	DL
$R_1.S_1.purpose.description$	$\doteq$	$\exists Has\_Purpose.(Current \sqcup Contact)$
$R_1.S_1.user.connective$	$\doteq$	and_exact
$R_1.S_1.user.description$	$\doteq$	$\exists Has\_Recipient.(Ours \sqcap Same)$
$R_1.S_1.data.connective$	$\doteq$	DL
$R_1.S_1.data.description$	$\doteq$	$\exists Has\_Data.UserHomePhone$
$R_1.S_2.purpose.connective$	$\doteq$	and_exact
$R_1.S_2.purpose.description$	$\doteq$	$\exists Has\_Purpose.(Current \sqcap Individual\_Decision)$
$R_1.S_2.data.connective$	$\doteq$	or_exact
$R_1.S_2.data.description$	$\doteq$	$\exists Has\_Data.PurchaseInfo$

P3P preference shown in Table 5 is mapped into the preference terminology in Table 6.

4.3 Matchmaking

According to P3P, all rules in APPLE privacy preference are evaluated with respect to the provider's privacy policy in the order they appear. Once a rule evaluates to be true, the corresponding behaviour is returned and rule evaluation ends. Only if all statements in a rule can find a matched statement in the P3P policy, then the P3P policy can be considered as compatible with the rule.

Algorithm 2. DataMatching algorithm(skeleton)

Require: $(S_j.data.connective,\ S_j.data.description)$, S(a subset of $\mathcal{T}_{Po}$) and personal data ontology

1: **for all** concept S_i in S **do**
2:     match=False
3:     **if** $S_j.data.connective \equiv DL$ **then**
4:       **if** $S_i.Data \sqsubseteq S_j.data.description$ **then**
5:         match=True
6:       **end if**
7:     **end if**
8:     **if** $S_j.data.connective \equiv or\_exact$ **then**
9:       **if** $S_j.data.description \sqsubseteq S_i.Data$ **then**
10:         match=True
11:       **end if**
12:     **end if**
13:     **if** $S_j.data.connective \equiv and\_exact$ **then**
14:       **if** $S_i.Data \equiv S_j.data.description$ **then**
15:         match=True
16:       **end if**
17:     **end if**
18:     **if** $S_j.data.connective \equiv non\_or$ **then**
19:       **if** all concepts C in $S_j.data.description$, $S_i.Data \sqsubseteq C$ is false **then**
20:         match=True
21:       **end if**
22:     **end if**
23:     **if** $S_j.data.connective \equiv non\_and$ **then**
24:       **if** Existing one concept C in $S_j.data.description$,$S_i.Data \sqsubseteq C$ is false **then**
25:         match=True
26:       **end if**
27:     **end if**
28:     **if** match==False **then**
29:       remove S_i from S
30:     **end if**
31: **end for**

We implement the P3P matching mechanism in discription logic context. The **DataMatching** algorithm shows how DLs techniques are used to match data element of a preference rule statement against the data element of the policy statement.

4.4 Implementation Status

We have implemented a DL-based Privacy Match Engine(PME) in Java. The architecture, which is shown in Figure 2, consists of user GUI, match model,

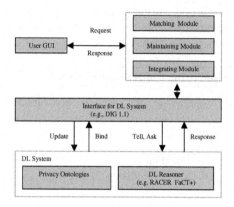

Fig. 2. Architecture of the matching engine

the functional interface for DL system, privacy ontologies and DL reasoner. We choose RACER version 1.7.24 for Windows[23] to be the DL reasoner, and DIG 1.1[22], defined by the Description Logic Implementation Group(DIG), to be the DL functional interface. We define domain-specific privacy ontologies and represent them in DIG 1.1 concept language.

The Statement handler defines how to wrap DL-based statement into DIG concepts which are represented in DIG's Tell language, and how a DL-based statement is organized as human readable information for display. The Policy handler and the Preference handler deal with policy and preference respectively. The Matching handler defines how to establish the connection between DIG 1.1 and RACER, how to load the knowledge base, how to match preference terminology against the policy terminology.

Users can interact with the match model(e.g., specify the knowledge base) via user GUI. The user GUI has three sub-windows. The preference window(top left) shows the preference information, while the policy window(top right) shows the policy information. The matching result window(bottom) displays the matching result. If the returned behavior is *request*, then the result window discribes which rule in the preference is successfully matched against the policy. Otherwise if the returned behaviour is *block*, then the discription for those unsuccessfully matched rules whose behavior is *request* are presented in the result window. These information could be used by the requestor to refine his/her preference. Figure 3 is a snapshot of scenario whose returned action is *request*, while Figure 4 is a snapshot of scenario whose returned action is *block*.

All requestors who concern their disclosed personal information would like to provide as less personal information as possible in order to access a certain service. Sometimes they need to make a trade-off between disclosing personal information and accessing the service. If the service request is often blocked, it may mean that the preference is too strict and may need to be refined. In this case, more detail information about the matching outcome(e.g., which rule

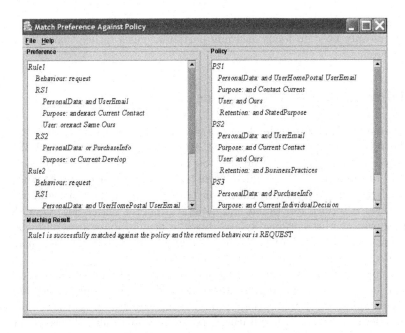

Fig. 3. The returned behaviour is request

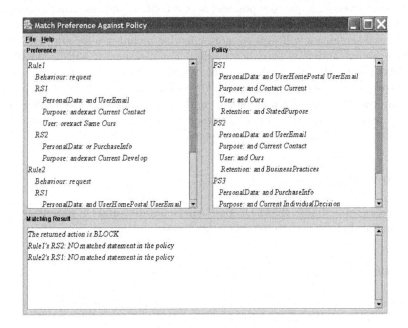

Fig. 4. The returned behaviour is block

statement is always unsuccessfully matched) is useful. Using these information, requestors only need to focus on some particular rules rather than all rules in the preference.

5   Discussion and Conclusions

Current mainstream web technology has serious limitations with respect to meeting the privacy challenge. For example, standardization efforts(e.g., P3P) rely on representation languages that are too low-level and consequently not suitable for automating activities such as matchmaking, replace-ability and compliance. Semantic Web services efforts such as OWL-S focus on providing generic constructs for service functional and general property ontologies. They do not consider privacy abstractions. Related work in the database area[13] focuses on providing database support(e.g., query language, automated enforcement) for efficient management of privacy abstractions.

Our approach builds upon existing ontology description languages to develop support for the declarative representation and reasoning about privacy abstractions techniques. The framework presented in this paper is one of the components of a broader framework for facilitating services interoperability[2]. We plan to use the preliminary results presented in this paper as a basis for studying interoperability of services at policy layer. There can be several policy models at different abstraction levels(e.g., privacy policies, access control policies, trust negotiation policies). Abstracting such models using high-level notations that are endowed with formal semantics will lead to more effective techniques for automating key interoperability activities in policy models. For instance, it will be possible to automate compatibility analysis(e.g., compare two privacy models and verify if the corresponding services can interact), replaceability analysis (compare privacy models of two service providers to understand similarities and differences), and compliance analysis (compare different kinds of policy specifications for the same service to verify if they are consistent).

Acknowledgement

The authors would like to thank Dr. Boualem Benatallah and Dr. Farouk Toumani for their very helpful and constructive discusses.

References

1. Boualem Benatallah, Mohand-Said Hacid, Alain Leger, Christophe Rey and Farouk Toumani, *On Automating Service Discovery*, VLDB Journal (to appear).
2. Karim Baïna, Boualem Benatallah, Hye-young Paik, Farouk Toumani, Christophe Rey, Agnieszka Rutkowska, and Bryan Harianto, *WS-CatalogNet: An Infrastructure for Creating, Peering, and Querying e-Catalog Communities*, Demonstration, Proceedings of the 30th VLDB Conference, Toronto, Canada, 2004.

3. G. Alonso, F. Casati, H. Kuno, V. Machiraju, *Web Services: Concepts, Architectures, and Applications*, Springer Verlag. 2004.
4. http://www.w3.org/2001/sw/webont/.
5. B. Benatallah, F. Casati, and F. Toumani, *Analysis and Management of Web Services Protocols*, ER'04, Shanghai, China. 2004.
6. A. Rezgui, A. Bouguettaya, M. Eltoweissy,*Sem WebDL: A privacy-preserving Semantic Web infrastructure for digital libraries*, International Journal on Digital Libraries, 4(3):171 - 184, Nov 2004
7. A. Rezgui, A. Bouguettaya, M. Eltoweissy,*A Reputation-Based Approach to Preserving Privacy in Web Services*, Technologies for E-Services, 4th International Workshop, September 2003
8. Bernstein, P.A., *Applying Model Management to Classical Meta Data Problems*, Proc. CIDR 2003, pp. 209-220
9. Francesco M. Donini, Maurizio Lenzerin, Daniele Nardi and Andrea Schaerf, *Reasoning in Description Logics*, (CSLI) Publications, pp191-236, 1996
10. Ian Horrocks, *Reasoning with Expressive Description Logics: Theory and Practices*, CADE 2002
11. M. Schmidt-Schau and G. Smolka,*Attributive concept descriptions with complements*, Articial Intelligence, 48(1):1-26, 1991
12. F. Badder, D. Calvanese, D. McGuinness, and editors D. Nardi and P. Patel-Schneider, *The Description Logic Handbook. Theory, Implementation and Applications*, Cambridge University Press, 2003
13. Rakesh Agrawal, Jerry Kiernan, Ramakrishnan Srikant, yirong Xu, *Implementing P3P Using Database Technology*, Proc. of the 19th Int'l Conference on Data Engineering, Bangalore, India, March 2003
14. L. Cranor, M. Langheinrich, M. Marchirio, *A P3P Preference Exchange Language 1.0*, w3C working draft Feburary 2001
15. L. Cranor, M. Langheinrich, M. Marchirio, *The Platform for Privacy Preference 1.0 Specification*, W3C Recommendation, April 2002
16. W. Stufflebeam, A. I. Anton, Q. He and N. Jain,*Specifying privacy policies with P3P and EPAL: Lessons Learned*, 3rd ACM Workshop on privacy in Eletronic Society, Oct, 2004
17. P. Ashley, S. Hada, G. Karjoth and M. Schunter, *E-P3P Privacy Policies and Privacy Authorization*, Proc. of the workshop on Privacy in the Electronic Society(WPES'02). Washington D.C.Novermver 21, 2001
18. P. Ashley, S. Hada, G. Karjoth, C. Powers and M. Schunter,*Enterprise Privacy Authorization Language(EPAL 1.1) Specification*, IBM Research Report, http://www.zurich.ibm.com/security/enterprise-privacy/epal
19. P. Ashley, S. Hada, G. Karjoth, C. Powers and M. Schunter,*From Privacy Promises to Privacy Management: A New Approach for Enforcing Privacy Throughout an Enterprise*, Proc. of the ACM New Security Paradigms Workshop, 2002
20. A. I. Anton, E. Bertino, N. Li and T. Yu,*A Roadmap for Comprehensive Online Privacy Policy*, CERIAS Tech Report 2004-47
21. K. Bohrer, S. Levy, X. Liu and E. Schonberg, *Individualized Privacy Policy Based Access Control*
22. Sean Bechhofer, *The DIG Description Logic Interface: DIG/1.1*
23. *http://www.sts.tu-harburg.de/ r.f.moeller/racer*

Conceptual Query Refinement: The Basic Model

Nenad Stojanovic

Institute AIFB, University of Karlsruhe, 76128 Karlsruhe, Germany
nst@aifb.uni-karlsruhe.de

Abstract. In this paper we present a novel approach for the refinement of Boolean queries by using ontologies. We introduce a conceptual model for defining user's queries, whih enables that the disambiguation (and consequently the refinement) of a query can be performed on the level of the meaning of a query. In that way the refinement process results in a set of meaningful, conceptual extensions of the initial query. Moreover, since a query is represented as a set of logic formulas, the query refinement process can be modeled as an inference process. It opens a palette of additional services that can enrich the query refinement process, like cooperative answering.

1 Introduction

A very important characteristic of an information retrieval process is its exploratory nature since a user is usually unfamiliar with the content of the information repositories and he often has ill-defined information needs. In order to avoid making an over-specified "long" query that retrieves zero results (i.e. a failing query), the user starts searching with a short query and tries to exploit the repository in several subsequent refinement steps. Moreover, he starts searching by assuming what can be the right information, but often, by exploring the resulting answers, he redefines what he is actually searching for.

In the nutshell of this exploratory process is the process of expanding or redefining the initial query in order to obtain more relevant results – the so-called query refinement process. However, existing methods for query refinement seem to be inadequate for real-world usage [1], since they usually return a long list of refinements, which is hard to process manually. Indeed, recent experimental studies of interactive query refinement have shown that only one third of the terms derived from document relevance feedback is identified by users as useful for refining their queries [2]. In other words, users are overloaded with refinement information, similarly to overloading with search results in an information retrieval task.

The main cause of the problem is an insuficient definition of the notion of relevance: a term is considered relevant for the refinement if it appears frequently in relevant documents. Obviously, such a definition covers only the syntax level of relevance, since the context in which these terms appear (i.e. their meaning) is not at all treated. Consequently, a lot of irrelevant refinements for the particular user's information need will be generated, since it is possible that a candidate term appears very frequently in relevant documents but not in the context of the query terms. Indeed, existing query refinement methods take only the document-centred view on

M. Kitsuregawa et al. (Eds.): WISE 2005, LNCS 3806, pp. 404–417, 2005.

the problem, without taking into account query characteristics, i.e. semantic relationships between refinement terms and the user's need (i.e. the user's query). An example of these relationships is how a query refinement term contributes to the disambiguation of the meaning of the query. Such a measure is very important, since an ambiguous query covers a lot of information needs, whereas usually only one need is relevant for the user. Therefore, the evaluation of the conceptual context, which a refinement term appears in, is needed.

In this paper we present an approach that resolves the query refinement task on the conceptual level, the so-called conceptual query refinement. In order to deal with the meaning of a Boolean query, we develop an ontology that defines the conceptual space in which a query can be interpreted, so that the query refinement process is performed on the level of the query model (i.e. meaning of a query). It that ensures the relevance of generated refinements for a user's information need. For example, in this space it is possible to determine which of the query terms introduce the most ambiguity in the query. Moreover, since a query is represented as a set of logic formulas, the query refinement process is modeled as an inference process. The logic-based nature of the refinement enables a variety of additional services that enrich the query refinement process like cooperative answering i.e. resolving from failing queries. In that way our approach goes beyond refinement of a user's query toward the refinement of the user's information need. The approach is based on the Librarian Agent Query Refinement Process we defined in our previous work on query refinement [3].

Due to lack of space, we omit in this paper evaluation studies that can be found in [4]. These studies have shown how a traditional full-text search engine can benefit from applying semantic technologies, since the instantiated conceptual model, needed for our approach, is built bottom-up from text documents.

The paper is organized as follows: In Section 2 we present the conceptual model, which we base our approach on. In Section 3 we present the approach itself. In Section 4 we present the most important work related to this research. Section 5 contains some concluding remarks.

2 Conceptual Query Model

2.1 The Model

The main problem in analysing a Boolean (i.e. keyword-based) query is the lack of a conceptualisation in which the meaning of the query can be interpreted. For example, if a user posts the query "knowledge and management", then there are several interpretations of the symbol "knowledge" regarding the user's information need. For example, a user might be interested in: (i) knowledge management (as a subtype of management, i.e. "management of knowledge"), (ii) management knowledge (as a subtype of knowledge, i.e. "knowledge about management"), (iii) management and knowledge (as an arbitrary relation between management and knowledge). In order to account the problem of query ambiguity more formally, we have defined a conceptual model for describing the interpretation(s) of a query. It is presented in the form of an ontology in Fig. 1. The model can be treated as an extension of the meaning triangle, a paradigm frequently used for describing the role an ontology plays in communication. The main task of the model is to represent the possible intensions (regarding information search) a user might have by specifying such a query.

The interpretation of a query depends on the interpretations of individual query terms. The interpretation of a query term can be defined through its relations with other terms (c.f. Fig. 1, concept *Relation*). The interpretation of a query is then defined through the interpretation of these relations in various contexts (c.f. Fig.1, concept *Context*) whereas these contexts are organized hierarchically (c.f. Fig. 1, relation *isPartOf*). Since the meaning of a query is built hierarchically, the relationships should be established between *Relations* concepts as well (c.f. Fig. 1, *fromRelation, toRelation*). Therefore, a meaning of a query is represented as a context that encompasses (hierarchical) relations between query terms.

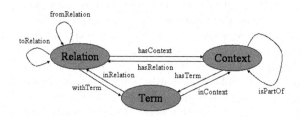

Fig. 1. Ontology for query interpretation

A meaning of a query represents an information need that can be assigned to the given query. For example, if a user posts the query $query_1$= "knowledge, management, quality" a possible meaning "quality *regarding*[1] knowledge management" can be in the given model represented as a set of statements:

Context($query_1$), *Relation*(rel_1), *Term*("knowledge"), *Term*("management"), *Term*("quality"), *inRelation*("knowledge", rel_1), *withTerm*(rel_1, "management"), *Relation*(rel_2), *inRelation*("quality", rel_2), *toRelation*(rel_1, rel_2).

Such a meaning can be represented in short as: rel_2("quality", rel_1("knowledge", "management")). This is called a query model. Note that a query might have several meanings, i.e. it can be mapped into several query models.

By introducing this conceptual model of a keyword-based query, the query refinement process can be seen as the refinement of a query model. Indeed, for a query (q_1, q_2, ... q_n), where q_i i=1, n are query terms, several query models can be built and for each of them several refinements can be generated. Fig. 2 illustrates this process. Therefore, by using a conceptual representation of a query, a refinement is not represented just as a bug of words, but rather as a structure with an implicitly represented meaning. It will enable a user to better understand the refinements and to focus on semantic relevant ones.

---

[1] The word "regarding" is just a placeholder for a connection between the term "quality" and the phrase "knowledge management". The crucial point in building the meaning of a query is that instead of treating the query as a bag of words, some relations between query terms are established. In this case, terms "knowledge" and "management" are related to each other and as a whole to the term "quality".

Query	Query Models	Query Model Refinements
$(q_1, q_2, ... q_n) \rightarrow$	$rel_x(q_1, ... (rel_w(q_{n-1}, q_n))...) \rightarrow$	$rel_x(q_1, ... (rel_w(q_{n-1}, rel_{w+1}(q_n, q_x))...)$
		$\rightarrow rel_x(q_1, ... (rel_w(rel_{w+1}(q_{n-1}, q_x), q_n))...)$
		...
	$\rightarrow rel_{x1}(q_1, ... (rel_{w1}(q_{n-1}, q_n))...) \rightarrow$	$rel_{x1}(q_2, ... (rel_{w1}(q_1, rel_{w1+1}(q_n, q_x))...)$
		$\rightarrow rel_{x1}(q_2, ... (rel_{w1}(rel_{w1+1}(q_1, q_x), q_n))...)$
	...	...

Fig. 2. Basics of the conceptual query refinement: (i) a query is interpreted as a conceptual model and (ii) the refinement is performed on these models

2.2   Relation and Context

A lot of relations can be established between two terms, for example between the terms *"process"* and *"workflow"*: "a *process* is executed by a *workflow*" or "a *process* optimises a *workflow*" or "a *process workflow* is a type of *workflow*". From the point of view of defining the meaning of a term, the exact naming of relations can be replaced by introducing types of relation, which a term belongs to. Indeed, from the conceptual point of view, two terms are either in a *specialization* relation (*Specialize*) (i.e. a term specializes the meaning of another term, like "process + workflow = process workflow"), in a *modification* relation (*Modify*) (i.e. a term modifies the meaning of another term, like a "process executed by a workflow") or in a *co-occurrence* relation (*Co-occurrence*) (i.e. two terms just appear together in a context, without a direct influence on each other, like "... Process is described using a model, which can be found in the literature about workflows"). Note that this classification corresponds to analyses regarding the frequently used query refinement "patterns", which show that 90% of the changes users make in subsequent refinements of a query are the specialization or modification (in the sense we defined above) of the query [5]. The remaining ten percent can be treated as adding just co-occurring terms. Therefore, our conceptual model reflects the users' refinement behaviour quite well.

It is clear that in an information repository there are lots of meanings in which a query term can appear. In the case that a query contains several query terms only terms that appear together (regarding the conceptual model: in the same *Context*) can be treated as relevant ones. The structure of contexts is determined by the syntactic organisation of documents in the infor mation repository, i.e. a Context can be a noun phrase[2], a sentence, or a paragraph, which corresponds to the way a human captures the relatedness between two terms. It means that two semantically related query terms should appear together in the context of two noun phrases, sentences or paragraphs that are located close to each other, respectively.

Fig. 3 presents the above mentioned extensions of the model: There are three types of relations: *Specialize*, *Modify* and *Cooccurrence*. There are three types of contexts: *NounPhrase*, *Sentence* and *Paragraph*[3] which are related with the *isPartOf* relation.

---

[2] In linguistics a noun phrase is a phrase whose Head is a noun. For example, in the sentence "Semantic knowledge management is a new topic", the phrase "semantic knowledge management" is a noun phrase. The term "management" plays the role of the Head.

[3] Due to lack of space the context "Paragraph" will be not treated here.

The relationship *neighbour* between two contexts describes their collocation. A *Term* can play the role of a *head* in a noun phrase.

Finally, by using these typing of relations a conceptual model of a query $(q_1, q_2, \ldots q_n)$ is represented as a statement in the form $\mathbf{rel}_{x1}(q_1, \ldots (\mathbf{rel}_{xi}(q_{n-1}, q_n))\ldots)$, whereas $\mathbf{rel}_{xi} \in \{Specialize, Modify, Cooccurrence\}$. For example, for the query (business, knowledge, management), the model *Modify*("business", *Specialize*("knowledge", "management")) represents an information need for "business *regarding* knowledge management", whereas the model *Specialize*(*Specialize*("business", "knowledge"), "management")) represents a need for "business knowledge management", as the management of the business knowledge.

Note that the aim of this conceptual model is not to generate a natural language expression of a query, but rather to define some relations between query terms that should help a user to specify the meaning of the query more precisely. The query refinement process will be based upon these relations.

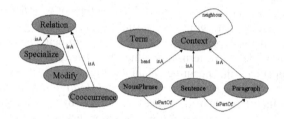

Fig. 3. Entities of the Conceptual Model used in this paper

2.3 Axioms

The main advantage of using an ontology for modelling a domain is the possibility to express knowledge about the domain in the form of axioms. When used in the reasoning process, these axioms support the derivation of new knowledge regarding the particular state of affairs. This knowledge can be used (1) for eliminating inconsistent information (consistency checking) and (2) for the further reasoning about the problem at hand. In order to support these two processes we define two types of axioms. Below we present several examples of consistency checking axioms. The second type of axioms will be presented in the next sections, where the particular steps of our query refinement process are elaborated.

Axioms (a selection):

$\forall c_1, r_1 \; hasContext(r_1, c_1) \leftarrow Relation(r_1) \wedge Context(c_1) \wedge hasRelation(c_1, r_1).$
$\forall c_1, t_1 \; inContext(t_1, c_1) \leftarrow Term(r_1) \wedge Context(c_1) \wedge hasTerm(c_1, t_1).$
$\forall r_1, c_1 \; NounPhrase(c_1) \leftarrow Specialize(r_1) \wedge hasContext(r_1, c_1)$
$\forall r_1, c_1 \; Sentence(c_1) \leftarrow Modify(r_1) \wedge hasContext(r_1, c_1)$

These axioms are used in the process of building (instantiating) the conceptual model for a given query. As mentioned above, this model supports the interpretations of the meaning of the query, by establishing relations between query terms and other terms from the information repository. Since the queries are typically very short (in average 2-4 terms), it is possible that there are several interpretations of a query regarding the given information repository. The presented model enables to determine not only how ambiguous a query is, but moreover, which part(s) of the query contribute most to this ambiguity, e.g. the query term that is completely isolated from the rest of the query terms. Further, the model supports an analysis of the requirements for the disambiguation of the query, e.g. how to find links between an isolated part of the query and the rest of the query. Therefore, the model serves as a backbone for the query refinement process, what is the topic of the next section.

3 Conceptual Query Refinement Process

As a general workflow for performing query refinement we use the Librarian Agent Query Refinement Process described in [3]. Very briefly, the goal of the Librarian Agent Query Refinement process is to enable a user to efficiently find results relevant for his information need, even if the query does not match perfectly his information need so that either a lot of irrelevant results and/or only a few relevant results are retrieved. The process consists of three phases: potential ambiguities (i.e. misinterpretations) of the initial query are firstly discovered and assessed (cf. the so-called *Query Ambiguity Discovery* phase). Next, the suitable query refinements are generated in order to decrease the accounted ambiguities (cf. the so-called *Refinements Derivation* phase). Finally, the recommendations for refining the given query are ranked according to their relevance for fulfilling the user's information need and according to the possibility to disambiguate the meaning of the query (cf. the so-called *Refinements Ranking* phase). In the next three subsections we describe these three phases for our Conceptual query refinement approach.

3.1 Phase1: Query Ambiguity Discovery

Since the goal of the query refinement process is to decrease misinterpretations of a query, the first step in this phase is to discover interpretations (query models) that can be assigned to the query. The second step is to assess them in order to determine which of them can be treated as misinterpretations.

Generate Interpretations of a Query

As we already mentioned, a meaning of a query (i.e. an interpretation) is defined through the relations that can be established between query terms, i.e. for a query $(q_1, q_2, \ldots q_n)$ a meaning is defined as

$$\textbf{rel}_{x1}(q_1, \ldots (\textbf{rel}_{xk}(q_{n-1}, q_n))\ldots), \text{ whereas } \textbf{rel}_{xi} \in \{Specialize, Modify, Cooccurrence\}.$$

Since a user posts a query against an information repository in order to satisfy his information need, an interpretation of the query should emerge from that repository. However, an information repository contains plain text, which represents, in the first instance, linguistic information, like: there is a sentence, there is a verb, there is a noun phrase, etc. Therefore, in order to build the meaning of a query, one has to process this information and derive conceptual relations between query terms.

Since our approach is ontology-based, we can formalize procedural knowledge needed for the extraction of the conceptual relations in a set of axioms. As an example we mention only one such an axiom here:

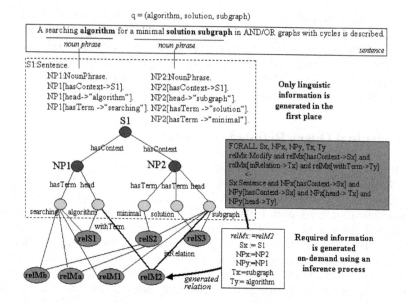

Fig. 4. Illustration of the inference-based approaches for generating relations between terms. The presented axiom derives the relation relM2. All other relations (relXY) are generated in an analogous way. As a logical language we use Flogic [6]. The syntax of the language is obvious: 1) **A:Class** means that the instance A belongs to the concept Class, i.e. Class(A) and 2) **A[rel->C]** means that there is a relation instance between A and C, i.e. rel(A, C), 3) **Class1::Class2** means that Class1 is a subconcept of the Class2.

Axiom1.1: Deriving relation *Specialize* between two terms

$\forall t_1, t_2, r_1, c_1$ *Specialize*$(r_1) \wedge$ *inRelation*$(t_1, r_1) \wedge$ *withTerm*$(r_1, t_2) \wedge$ *hasContext*(r_1, c_1)
$\leftarrow$ *Term*$(t_1) \wedge$ *Term*$(t_2) \wedge$ *inContext*$(t_1, c_1) \wedge$ *inContext*$(t_2, c_1) \wedge$ *NounPhrase*$(c_1) \wedge$ *head*(c_1, t_2),
where   predicate *NounPhrase(a)* denotes that a is a noun phrase
         predicate *head(a, b)* indicates that b is the head of the noun phrase a.

This axioms means that each term in a noun phrase is the specialisation of the head of that noun phrase. However, during the execution of this axiom a set of other axioms (e.g. consistency checking axioms) can be evaluated and new information will be derived, so that more relevant results will be produced. Beside the compactens of the knowledge representation, this is another advantage of this inference-based approach.

We have defined about 20 axioms that formalize procedural knowledge needed for extracting these three types of relation between terms. Note that we are discovering only relations that are related to query terms and not doing the formalization of all sentences in all documents.

The very first phase in generating a query's interpretation is the shallow NLP[4] processing of the results of the query. It results in the set of noun phrases, related to query terms, which are placed in a particular context (sentence, paragraph). Moreover

---

[4] We use existing NLP open source packages for this purpose, like Text2Onto (text2onto.semanticweb.org).

the relations (order) between noun phrases are discovered as well. Therefore, the linguistic processing creates the initial fact base that is used as a knowledge base in the inference process, that is the second phase in the interpretation process. Figure 4 illustrates this process.

The query models are built using the mentioned set of axioms. Since the task of this processing is to determine the most plausible interpretation of the query, a complete set of query models is generated. However, our logic-based approach enables the automation of this process. Indeed, we can define logic queries for generating abstract query models that will result in the concrete instances of the model. It means that we need one logic query to derive a query model.

We illustrate this process for a query with three query terms:

For a query (q_1, q_2, q_3) the generic set of models is as follows: $\{\mathbf{rel_x}(q_1, \mathbf{rel_y}(q_2, q_3)), \mathbf{rel_x}(q_2, \mathbf{rel_y}(q_1, q_3)), \mathbf{rel_x}(q_3, \mathbf{rel_y}(q_1, q_2))\}$, where $\mathbf{rel_x}, \mathbf{rel_y} \in \{Specialize, Modify, Cooccurrence\}$.

In Flogic, the logic query for deriving the model $\mathbf{rel_x}(q_1, \mathbf{rel_y}(q_2, q_3))$ looks like:

$$\text{FORALL } \mathbf{rel_{xx}}, \mathbf{rel_{yy}} <- q_1[\text{inRelation} -> \mathbf{rel_{xx}}] \text{ and } q_2[\text{inRelation} -> \mathbf{rel_{yy}}] \text{ and }$$
$$\mathbf{rel_{yy}}[\text{withTerm} -> q_3] \text{ and } \mathbf{rel_{xx}}[\text{toRelation} -> \mathbf{rel_{yy}}] \text{ and } \mathbf{rel_{xx}}{:}\mathbf{rel_x} \text{ and } \mathbf{rel_{yy}}{:}\mathbf{rel_y}. \quad (1)$$

This query produces all instances of the query model $\mathbf{rel_x}(q_1, \mathbf{rel_y}(q_2, q_3))$. Note that performing this logic query causes evaluation of several axioms for deriving relations we gave above.

The main advantage of the inference process is that it introduces an abstraction level that enables focusing only on important terms, i.e. only information relevant for a user's query will be generated.

Regarding complexity, for a query with n-terms there are $(n!)/2$ queries in the form: $\mathbf{rel_x}(q_1, \mathbf{rel_y}(q_2, \ldots \mathbf{rel_z}(q_{n-1}, q_n)\ldots))$. However, as we already mentioned, the average length of web queries is beetween 2 and 4, which makes the approach efficient for a realistic searching scenario. For example, for n = 4, there are in total 48 possible query model forms.

Calculate Ambiguity

Interpretations of a Query Term

As we already mentioned, the meaning (interpretation) of a query term can be defined through the relations with other terms. It is clear that the number of such relations indicates the diversity in the interpretation of a query term. We define two functions to assess this interpretability, whereas each of these functions has two forms since the used relations are not symmetric, i.e. the meaning of the relation $rel(a, b)$ is different from $rel(b, a)$ for $rel \in \{Specialize, Modify, Cooccurrence\}$. For example, the relations $Specialize(\text{"knowledge"}, \text{"management"})$ and $Specialize(\text{"management"}, \text{"knowledge"})$ have different interpretations, as we already illustrated at the beginning of this section.

$TermInterpretability(t, term_x, r\_type, first) = \{x| \; r\_type(x) \wedge inRelation(t, x) \wedge withTerm(x, term_x)\}$

$TermInterpretability(t, term_x, r\_type, second) = \{x| \; r\_type(x) \wedge inRelation(term_x, x) \wedge withTerm(x, t)\}$

$TermInterpretabilityTotal(t, r\_type, first) = \{x| \; \exists y \in T \; r\_type(x) \wedge inRelation(t, x) \wedge withTerm(x, y)\}$

$TermInterpretabilityTotal(t, r\_type, second) = \{x| \; \exists y \in T \; r\_type(x) \wedge inRelation(y, x) \wedge withTerm(x, t)\}$,

where $\qquad\qquad\qquad\qquad\qquad\qquad\qquad\qquad\qquad\qquad\qquad\qquad\qquad\qquad\qquad\quad$ (2)

$r\_type \in \{Specialize, Modify, Cooccurrence\}$, $t \in Q_x$ (the set of query terms), $term_x \in T$ (the set of all terms that can be found in the given repository).

The first function (*TermInterpretability*) calculates all relations of the type r_type between t and *term*. The second function (*TermInterpretabilityTotal*) calculates all relations of the type r_type related to t.

For example, regarding Fig. 4, *TermInterpretabilityTotal*(subgraph, *Specialize*, *first*) = {relS2, relS3}, if we assume that relSx depicts a *Specialize* relation.

In order to ensure the completeness of the calculation (i.e. to find all possible relations of the given type), each of these formula is calculated using the inference process. For example, the set of r_type_x relations between terms t and t_x can be calculated using the following FLogic query:

$$TermInterpretability(t, t_x, r\_type_x, first) := \qquad\qquad (3)$$

FORALL $\mathbf{rel_x}$ <- $\mathbf{rel_x}::r\_type_x$ and $\mathbf{rel_x}$[inRelation -> t] and $\mathbf{rel_x}$[withTerm -> t_x].

Interpretation of a Query

Since we assume that a query represents a user's information need, the notion of the interpretation of the query is related to a plausible meaning that can be assigned to a query as a whole. Consequently, the ambiguity of a query is defined through the number of interpretations of a query.

However, the crucial question is how to define a "plausible meaning" that can be assigned to a query. As we already mentioned, the meaning of a query is captured by the relations between query terms, where the "plausibility" is defined by the support that this meaning gets in the information repository (i.e. how many instances of this relation exist). In order to do that we define function $RelationSet(\mathbf{rel_x}(a, b))$ that returns the set of relations of type $\mathbf{rel_x}$ established between a and b, as follows:

$$RelationSet(\mathbf{rel_x}) = \{\begin{array}{l} \text{if } \mathbf{rel_x} := r\_type_x(q_p, q_n) \\ TermInterpretability(q_p, q_n, r\_type_x, first) \\ \text{if } \mathbf{rel_x} := rel_x(t, rel_z) \\ \{x | \exists y \in RelationSet(rel_z)\ rel_x(x) \wedge inRelation(t, x) \wedge toRelation (x, y) \\ \text{if } \mathbf{rel_x} := rel_x(rel_z, t) \\ \{x | \exists y \in RelationSet(rel_z)\ rel_x(x) \wedge fromRelation(t, x) \wedge withTerm(x, y)\} \\[6pt] \text{if } \mathbf{rel_x} := rel_x(rel_y, rel_z) \\ \{x | \exists y \in RelationSet(rel_y)\ \exists z \in RelationSet(rel_z)\ rel_x(x) \wedge fromRelation(y, x) \\ \wedge toRelation (x, z) \} \end{array}$$

where:

$\mathbf{rel_x} := rel_x(t, rel_z)$ depicts that relation $\mathbf{rel_x}$ is defined between a term t and a relation rel_z

$\mathbf{rel_x} := rel_x(rel_y, rel_z)$ depicts that relation $\mathbf{rel_x}$ is defined between two relations

For example, regarding Fig. 4:

$RelationSet(Specialize$("solution", "subgraph")) = $TermInterpretability$("solution", "subgraph", *Specialize*, *first*) = {relS3}.
$RelationSet(Modify$(searching, (*Specialize*("minimal", "subgraph"))={relMa, relMb}.

The task of this measure is to compare the interpretability that a query term has in the repository and the interpretation that is assigned to it in a particular query model.

Relation Interpretability (*RelationInterpretability*, *RelationInterpretabilityTotal*) can be defined in a analogous way to the query interpretability (2). Due to lack of space we omit these formulas, as well as the corresponding queries, like (3).

So far, in order to discover the meaning of a query, we analysed only query terms. However, if we consider the query as an approximation of a user's information need, it seems to be sound to assume that the structure of the query is a valuable source for determining the meaning of the query. Indeed, a query is produced in a cognitive process that should be (implicitly) reflected in the structure of the query. We use the following heuristic in order to reflect this process: "A user does not order query terms arbitrarily, but rather in a meaningfull way". Indeed, the order of query terms can indicate the meaning. For example, the need that caused the query "quality system reengineering" (e.g. quality for system reengineering) seems to be different from the need that caused the query "system quality reengineering" (e.g. system for quality reengineering).

In order to take this into account we have defined a new function *OrderImportance* as a combinaton of the distance between query terms (first factor) and the order between them (second factor):

$$
OrderImportance(\mathbf{rel_x}, Q) = \{
$$

$1/\lvert dist(q_p, q_n, Q)\rvert * 1/(1\text{-sign}(dist(q_p, q_n, Q)))$,	if $\mathbf{rel_x} := rel_x(q_p, q_n)$
$1/\lvert dist(t, termL(rel_z), Q)\rvert * 1/(1\text{-sign}(dist(t, termL(rel_z), Q)))$,	if $\mathbf{rel_x} := rel_x(t, rel_z)$
$1/\lvert dist(t, termR(rel_z), Q)\rvert * 1/(1\text{-sign}(dist(t, termL(rel_z), Q)))$,	if $\mathbf{rel_x} := rel_x(rel_z, t)$
$1/\lvert dist(termR(rel_y), termL(rel_z), Q)\rvert * 1/(1\text{-sign}(dist(termR(rel_y), termL(rel_z), Q)))$	if $\mathbf{rel_x} := rel_x(rel_y, rel_z)$

where:

$\mathbf{rel_x} := rel_x(q_p, q_n)$ depicts that relation $\mathbf{rel_x}$ is defined between two query terms,

$dist(q_p, q_n, Q)$ represents the distance between q_p and q_n in query Q. E.g. $dist(\text{"system"}, \text{"reengineering"}, \text{"system quality reengineering"}) = 2$.

$$
termL(rel_z) = \{ \begin{array}{ll} q & \text{if } rel_z := rel_x(q, rel_y) \\ termL(rel_y) & \text{if } rel_z := rel_x(rel_y, q) \text{ or } rel_z := rel_x(rel_v, rel_y) \end{array}
$$

$$
termR(rel_z) = \{ \begin{array}{ll} q & \text{if } rel_z := rel_x(rel_y, q) \\ termR(rel_y) & \text{if } rel_z := rel_x(rel_v, rel_y) \text{ or } rel_z := rel_x(q, rel_y) \end{array}
$$

$$
sign(a) = \{ \begin{array}{ll} 0, & \text{for } a \geq 0 \\ -1 & \text{for } a < 0 \end{array}
$$

The function sign is required for describing the reverse order of terms in the query and in a query model. For example, *OrderImportance*(*Specialize*("reengineering", "system"), "system quality reengineering") = $(1/2)*(1/(1-(-1)))$ = $1/4$. Note that, regarding complexity, this operation can be very easily performed.

Finally, by taking into account all above mentioned factors the plausibility of an interpretation (query model) is a combination of the (i) support (number of instances) of its relations (i.e. all parts of the query model), (ii) the type of relations and (iii) the order-importance for each relation:

Plausibility($\mathbf{rel_1}(q_1, \mathbf{rel_2}(q_2, \ldots \mathbf{rel_n}(q_n, q_{n+1})\ldots)), Q) =$

$\prod_{i=1,n} Card(RelationSet(\mathbf{rel_i})) * RelImportance(\text{Type}(\mathbf{rel_i})) * OrderImportance(\mathbf{rel_i}, Q)$, where

Card(a) is the function that retrives the number of elements in the set a,

RelImportance represents the strength of defining a meaning by using a type of relations. Obviously, the *Specialize* relation is the strongest one.

$$RelImportance(Type(\mathbf{rel}_i)) = \{ \begin{array}{ll} p & \text{for Type}(\mathbf{rel}_i) = Specialize \\ q & \text{for Type}(\mathbf{rel}_i) = Modify \\ r & \text{for Type}(\mathbf{rel}_i) = Cooccurrence, \end{array}$$

where $p > q > r$. In experiments we use $p = 3$, $q = 2$, $r = 1$.

Therefore, *Plausibility* represents a kind of estimation that a query model corresponds to the user's information need expressed in a query. Moreover, the *Plausibility* can be used for assessing the gap between the user's information need and the corresponding query: if the query model that corresponds to the information need has low plausibility (relatively to other query models from the same query) then the user fails to express his need in a clear manner in the given query. It means that a lot of irrelevant resources are retrieved in the retrieval process, i.e. the precison of the retrieval is rather low. In this situation, the system should make suggestions for modifying parts of query in order to meet the user's information need.

The set of query models for a query is generated automatically, whereas the level of the plausibility is defined for each of them. Regarding complexity, note that just one logic query of the above mentioned form (1), is required to determine all query models for a given order of variables and the plausibility values for all of them. Therefore, for a query of 4 query terms, 48 queries in total are required to complete this calculation.

3.2 Phase 2: Inferring Refinements

The main advantage of building the conceptual model of a query is the possibility to reason about the refinement process, i.e. to define refinements not on the basis of the (syntactic) co-occurrence between terms, but rather on their semantic co-acting. In that way the refinement can be defined as an improvement of the meaning of the query and not only as a pure syntactical change in the query. For example, the query ("algorithm", "subgraph") can be syntactically extended as ("algorithm", "subgraph", "solution") or conceptually refined as *Modify*("algorithm", *Specialize*("solution", "subgraph")), which can be interpreted as "algorithm" *regarding* "solution subgraph".

The main assumption is that a user is not familiar with the information repository and he needs help to explore it. Note that even if a user exactly knows that he is interested in "solution subgraphs", the definition of such a request on the syntax level, i.e. the query "solution subgraph", does not enable semantic searching since the resources about "solution direct subgraph" will not be found. By deriving the meaning and representing it conceptually in the refinement process (i.e. *Specialize*(solution, subgraph)) such syntactical varieties will be abstracted.

Moreover, the quantification of the plausibility of query models enables reasoning not only on the possible refinements, but moreover on the role that these refinements might have with respect to the meaning of the query. It means that each added term has well-defined relations to other query terms. Consequently, each possible refinement can be quantified according to the "increase" in the meaning of the query, i.e. how that refinement contributes to decreasing the ambiguity of the query.

One of the main problems for traditional query refinement approaches is that they produce a lot of refinements, whereas a (large) part of them is completely irrelevant for the query. In order to resolve this problem, our approach uses a reasoning process in order to guarantee the relevance of the generated refinements, i.e. for each refinement there is a logic explanation why it is generated and which role it plays for clarifying the meaning of the query.

Since the elementary building block for defining meaning is a relation between two terms $rel_x(q_a, q_c)$, we define the refinement process on relations. More specifically, we have defined two inference patterns that drive the refinement process: *termRefinement* and *relationRefinement*, whereas *termRefinement* refines a term, as an argument of a relation (i.e. q_a or q_c) and *relationRefinement* refines a relation as a whole (i.e. $rel_x(q_a, q_c)$).

For the first pattern, *termRefinement*, there are two forms whereas each of them corresponds to a combination of the term and a new query term:

termRefinement(q_a):   1. $rel_{xx}(q_a, XX)$ 2. $rel_{xx}(XX, q_a)$,

where rel_{xx} is a new relation, XX is a new query term.

This pattern represents narrowing the interpretation of a query by specifying more details about the context given by query terms, like *Modify*("algorithm", "subgraph") ----> *Modify*("algorithm", *Specialize*("solution", "subgraph")). The natural language interpretation is: "algorithm *regarding* subgraph" is refined into "algorithm *regarding* solution subgraph".

For the second pattern, *relationRefinement*, there are two forms whereas each of them corresponds to a combination of the relation and a new query term:

relationRefinement($rel_x(q_a, q_c)$): 1. $rel_{xx}(XX, rel_x(q_a, q_c))$ 2.$rel_{xx}(rel_x(q_a, q_c), XX)$.

It represents narrowing the interpretation of a query by extending the context in which query terms are considered, like *Specialize*("solution", "subgraph") ---> *Modify*("algorithm", *Specialize*("solution", "subgraph")). The natural language interpretation is "solution subgraph" is refined into "algorithm *regarding* solution subgraph".

The formal description of these refinement patterns looks like:

termRefinement(q_a):=
        FORALL q_x, rel_{xx} <- (q_a[inRelation -> rel_{xx}] and rel_{xx}[withTerms -> q_x]) or
        (q_x[inRelation -> rel_{xx}] and rel_{xx}[withTerms -> q_a])
relationRefinement(rel_x):=
        FORALL q_x, rel_{xx} <- (rel_{xx}[fromRelation -> rel_x] and rel_{xx}[withTerms -> q_x]) or
        (rel_{xx}[toRelation -> rel_x] and q_x[inRelation-> rel_{xx}])

Therefore, for an elementary relation $rel_x(q_a, q_c)$ there are six refinements (two for each entity: two query terms + one relation term = six refinements).

$rel_x(q_a, q_c)$ -> 1. $rel_x(rel_{xx}(q_a, XX), q_c)$ 2. $rel_x(q_a, rel_{xx}(q_c, XX))$ 3. $rel_x(rel_{xx}(XX, q_a), q_c)$
        4. $rel_x(q_a, rel_{xx}(XX, q_c))$ 5. $rel_{xx}(XX, rel_x(q_a, q_c))$ 6. $rel_{xx}(rel_x(q_a, q_c), XX)$

Moreover, for a query that consists of n query terms and m relations there are (m+n)*2 refinements in total. Since the number of query terms in a real scenario is small, the complexity of this process is not critical.

3.3 Phase 3: Ranking of Refinements

As we already mentioned, a user's query can be mapped into the several query models and each query model can produce a lot of refinements. Therefore some ranking of the query models and the refinements should be performed in order to retain the effectiveness of the proposed method. Indeed, for each query model a level of the confidence with the user's information need is expressed through the *Plausibility* factor. The ranking depends on the (i) plausibility of the given query model (evaluated through the function *Plausability*), (ii) the strength of the relation that defines the minimal context for the refinement (evaluated trough *RelationSet*), (iii) the type of the relation that is refined (measured using *RelImportance*), (iv) the type of the relation in which a new term is added (measured using *RelImportance*) and (v) the increase in the disambiguation of the term/relation that is directly refined. The last parameter represents the ratio between the number of relations of a type that include a query term (i.e. relation) and the number of these relations when the query refinement term is added. Obviously, if the ratio is larger the increase in meaning is larger. Due to lack of space we omit here the formal definition of this parameter (*RelationInterpretabilityRatio*).

Regarding complexity, note that in this step no inference is performed. Moreover, all data are already precalculated in the previous two phases of the refinement process. In order to make this calculation even more feasible we take only the first n (n<10) query models that correspond to the most plausible interpretations of the query, i.e. that have the biggest values for the *Plausibility* parameter.

4 Related Work

The use of co-occurrence statistics to automate the discovery of semantic relationships among terms has a long history in Information Retrieval and Computational Linguistic [7]. The INSTRUCT term clustering technique [8] identifies keyword stems which are most similar to the query term stem. The morphological expansion [9] calculates a measure of string similarity (measured in trigrams) between a selected query stem and each of the stems in the dictionary file of the database. Then, in both cases, the system displays the twenty most similar stems to the user who chooses one to be added to the query. Strzalowski [10] utilized a broader notion of dispersion in a formula to compare the specificity of semantically related terms for the automatic construction of lexical domain maps. The REALIST hyperterm system [11] made an on-line database of phrases available to end-users for interactive query formulation. More recently, the terminological feedback is used for improving performance of a query refinement system. Paraphrase Search Assistant [12] exploits the tendency for key domain concepts within results sets to participate in families of semantically related lexical compounds. However, our approach differs from the above presented ones by introducing the conceptual level, which is used for the analysis of a user's query. It enables a more efficient refinement process. Moreover, our inference-like searching is a unique feature, as well as the cooperativeness enabled by it. The important difference is the process-driven nature of our approach, especially the existence of the refinement ranking phase.

5   Conclusion

This paper presented a novel approach for the refinement of Boolean queries by using semantic technologies. We introduced a conceptual model for defining user's queries, which enables the resolution of the query disambiguation on the semantic level, i.e. on the level of the meaning of a query. Consequently, the query refinement is performed as an inference process and provides opportunities for more semantic-enabled services. The main advantage for a user is that the refinements' set contains only refinements whose role in clarifying the meaning of the query is clear. Moreover, due their conceptual nature, the refinements are represented as meaningful patterns that can be directly compared to the user's information need. The presented method has been implemented in a real information portal, which illustrates the scalability of the approach.

Acknowledgments. Research for this paper was partially financed by EU in projects "SEKT" (IST-2003-506826) and "KnowledgeWeb" (507482).

References

1. Campbell, I., "The ostensive model of developing information needs", Ph.D. Thesis, University of Glasgow, 2000.
2. Efthimiadis, N., "Interactive query expansion: a user-based evaluation in a relevance feedback environment", Journal of the American Society for Information Science, v.51 n.11, pp. 989-1003, Sept. 2000.
3. Stojanovic, N., "On Modelling Cooperative Retrieval Using an Ontology-based Query Refinement Process" 23rd International Conference on Conceptual Modeling (ER2004), Shanghai, China, 2004
4. Stojanovic, N., Ontology-based Information Retrieval: Methods and Tools for Cooperative Query Answering, PhD thesis, University of Karlsruhe, 2005
5. Bruza, P. D., Dennis, S., "Query Reformulation on the Internet: Empirical Data and the Hyperindex Search Engine", in Proceedings of RIAO'97, pp. 500-509, 1997.
6. Kifer, M., Lausen, G., Wu, J. "Logical Foundations of Object-Oriented and Frame-Based Languages", J.ACM 1994
7. Jinxi X., Croft, W. B., "Query expansion using local and global document analysis", in Proceedings of the 19th annual international ACM SIGIR conference on Research and development in information retrieval, pp.4-11, Zurich, Switzerland, 1996.
8. Wade, S. J., Willett, P., "INSTRUCT: A Teaching Package for Experimental Methods in Information Retrieval", III. Browsing, Clustering and Query Expansion. Program. 1988; 22(1): 44-61. ISSN: 0033-0337; CODEN: PRGMBD., 1988.
9. Freund, G. E., Willett, P., Online Identification of Word Variants and Arbitrary Truncation Searching Using a String Similarity Measure", Information Technology: Research and Development, 1(3): 177-187. ISSN: 0144-817X; CODEN: ITRDDE, 1982.
10. Strzalkowski, T., "Building a lexical domain map from text corpora", COLING94, 1994.
11. Ruge, G., Schwarz, C., Thurmairet, G., "A Hyperterm System based on Natural Language Processing", International Forum on Information and Documentation, 1990.
12. Anick, P.G., Tipirneni, S., "The Paraphrase Search Assistant: Terminological Feedback for Iterative Information Seeking", SIGIR 1999, pp. 153-159, 1999.

Peer-to-Peer Technology Usage in Web Service Discovery and Matchmaking*

Brahmananda Sapkota[1], Laurentiu Vasiliu[1], Ioan Toma[2],
Dumitru Roman[2], and Chris Bussler[1]

[1] Digital Enterprise Research Institute, Galway
[2] Digital Enterprise Research Institute, Innsbruck
{firstname.lastname}@deri.org

Abstract. This paper presents a dynamic and scalable mechanism for discovery of semantically enriched descriptions of Web services. By employing Web Service Modeling Ontology (WSMO) as the underlying framework for describing both user requests and Web services, and combining it with the usage of Peer-to-Peer technology in this context, a scalable, distributed, dynamic and flexible discovery mechanism is obtained. A use case scenario is presented for supporting the viability of such a mechanism.

1 Introduction

A combination of Web services and Peer-to-Peer (P2P) technologies have potential to be an effective means for solving business integration problems (e.g. data consistency, discovery, validation, etc) due to their distributed nature and interoperability features. In the research communities, work is underway looking for such a combination [2], [3], [14]. A P2P network of Web service registries has been proposed in [2] whereas [3] provides an infrastructure dealing with P2P scalability issues at the cost of topology maintenance. The P2P approach taken in [2] is vulnerable to a single point of failure as it uses a single central server to index all Web service registries.

In this paper, we propose a combination of Web service and P2P technologies for supporting communication between different Web service platforms such as WSMX [4] and IRS-III [5] thereby addressing the aforementioned problems during service discovery and matchmaking. Such a combination can support scalability, maximize search recall; enable dynamic and distributed Web service discovery and matchmaking at a minimum maintenance cost. In addition, unlike other approaches (e.g., [2], [14], [15]) it avoids the problem of single point of failure. The distributed Web service discovery is supported by a goal decomposition algorithm. The aforementioned goals are validated through a real-life business process integration use case.

The rest of the paper is structured as follows: Section 2 and Section 3 provide a short overview of Web services and P2P technologies. Section 4 gives an insight to the general solution achieved by combining these technologies. Section 5 takes this

---

* This material is based upon works supported by the EU funding under the DIP project (FP6 – 507483) and the ASG project (FP6 – 004617) and by the Science Foundation Ireland under Grant No. SFI/02/CE1/I131.

M. Kitsuregawa et al. (Eds.): WISE 2005, LNCS 3806, pp. 418–425, 2005.

further focusing on service discovery and Section 6 presents a real use case. Section 7 describes related work and Section 8 concludes the paper suggesting future work.

2 Web Services

Web services [17] have added a new level of functionality to the current Web by taking a first step towards seamless integration of distributed software components using web standards. Nevertheless, current Web service technologies around Simple Object Access Protocol (SOAP), Web Service Definition Language (WSDL) and Universal Description, Discovery and Integration (UDDI) operate at a syntactic level and, therefore, they still require human interaction to a large extent [7]. This limits the scalability and greatly curtails the added value envisioned with the advent of Web services.

Recent research aimed at making Web content more machine-processable under the common term Semantic Web [18] are gaining momentum, particularly in the context of Web service usage. Here, semantic markup shall be exploited to automate the tasks of Web service discovery, composition and invocation, thus enabling interoperation between them with minimum human intervention. In this context, WSMO [6] aims to describe relevant aspects related to general services, with the ultimate goal of enabling the (total or partial) automation of the tasks involved in both inter- and intra-enterprise integration. In this paper, we commit to the use of WSMO for describing Web services because of the enriched semantic capabilities it provides.

3 Peer-to-Peer Computing

P2P technology is known to be a simple to administer and powerful to compute technology. Functionally, P2P technology comes in three different forms, namely: *pure-P2P*, where each participant has equal role; *hybrid-P2P*, where some of the nodes act as a central server and provide search facilities; and *server based-P2P*, where a dedicated server indexes control information but the data flow is between participants [8].

A P2P system functions through the interaction between 'neighbours' thus avoiding central control and the single point of failure. This interaction is defined through the algorithms that enforce the topology and the roles of the participants. Each participant can store/access other participant's data, if needed, with or without knowing its origin. If a participant fails, other participants can take over rebuilding the system. P2P technology also allows load distributing among participants.

4 Peer-to-Peer Enabled SWS Platforms

In order to discover a service that satisfies a requester's goal, multiple Web services may have to be consulted, since a single Web service may not be able to fully satisfy a requester's goal. Therefore, Web services need to be able to communicate with each other which can be made possible by the use of P2P technology because of their: distributed nature; scalability, flexibility and manageability characteristics; ability to deal with data, protocol, and machine heterogeneity.

4.1   SWS Platforms in Peer-to-Peer Networks

Several Semantic Web Service (SWS) platforms, e.g. WSMX, IRS-III, etc, emerged along with the SWS technology. The interconnection between these SWS platforms is desired and needed to deal with complex business process integration problems. On a small scale, these SWS platforms can communicate by registering themselves with each other as Semantic Web services. However, scalability becomes an issue when the number of these platforms grows. Through the combination of P2P and SWS technologies, these platforms can be discovered dynamically. Since pure-P2P does not scale, we adapt hybrid P2P topology for connecting these platforms together.

Our adapted hybrid P2P network is similar to the Super-node based P2P network as described in [10]. However, in our P2P network nodes are described semantically and the Super-node is a relative concept. Therefore, a node S that is seen as Super-node from neighbour X can be seen as 'normal' node from neighbour Y. The network evolves dynamically electing such Super-nodes and the requests are processed among these Super-nodes enabling load balancing and failure recovery.

4.2   Clustering SWS Platforms

In order for a system to be practically compelling, it needs to be efficient. In the context of this paper, a system is efficient if maintenance cost is low and the system is quick to execute requests. To achieve this efficiency, clustering of SWS platforms based on similar Web service description is proposed in Figure 1. A cluster consists of at least one Super-node. Each cluster is maintained and managed by one of the Super-nodes, which is chosen dynamically based on its availability, processing power, storage capacity, etc. We call this Super-node the cluster *manager*. It indexes the Web services registered with its cluster and facilitates communication within and between clusters. A cluster *manager* can become a member of another cluster.

The following algorithm, inspired by [13], is used for selecting the cluster *manager*, where availability α, available storage ζ, and processing power ω are the metrics used for evaluation of Super-nodes.

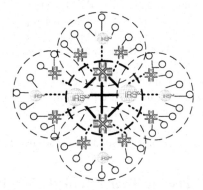

```
1. initialize candidate set to null
2. for all S in cluster C
3.    if S_α ≥ (1/n)ΣⁿS_α, candidate ∪ {S_α}
4. for all K in candidate
5.    if K_ζ ≥ (1/n)ΣⁿK_ζ candidate ∪ {K_ζ}
6. for all L in candidate
7.    if L_ω ≥ (1/n)ΣⁿL_ω candidate ∪ {L_ω}
8. for all M in candidate
9. return best M.
```

Fig. 1. SWS Platforms in Service Clusters

best implies: highest availability, largest storage, and highest processing power amongst others. If no such node exists, the one with highest availability is chosen.

A cluster may not have a *manager* if all of its members are *manager* of other clusters. Such a cluster is called a *super-cluster*. In Figure 1, this notion is indicated by a thick dotted circle. The user's goals are always executed in the *super-cluster*. This significantly reduces the total number of invocations required to execute a request. When a new member joins the network but no similar service cluster exists, then it creates new cluster, becomes its *manager* and notifies *super-cluster* of its existence.

4.3 Goal Decomposition

The complexity of the user initiated goal can vary from simple to difficult. In the latter case goal decomposition is necessary because of several reasons such as: the information required to evaluate the user goal is distributed; the goal consists of unrelated concepts; it requires mutually exclusive service composition; the goal can be executed only partially; etc. Thus, based on Ontologies O defining the goal G, it is decomposed into sub goals g_i such that $\cup g_i = G$. The following algorithm gives a set of sub goals:

```
1. initialize sub-goal sg, to null         where,
2. for each i of c ∈ pc(G)
3.    for each a of i                       i = instance,
4.       if |elem(a of i)|> minCard(a)      C = set of Concepts defined in
5.          sg ∪ (createGoal (a of i))      O; c ∈ C,
6.       else sg ∪ (createGoal(i of c))     a = attribute,
7. return sg                                sg = set of sub-goals
```

The operator $pc(G)$ returns all the concepts used in G, the operators *elem* (a) and *minCard* (a) return all the value elements of attribute a, and their required minimum cardinalities respectively, The operation *createGoal* creates sub-goal using the same formalism used in goal G.

4.4 Service Invocation in Clustered Network

In our clustered network of SWS platforms, a backend-application requests for a service through one of the known SWS platforms which then executes it. The invocation is successful if a matching Web service is found locally. It is pending if a no matching Web service is found locally, but some Super-nodes are yet to be consulted. If the invocation is pending, the *manager* of the relevant cluster is consulted in an attempt to successfully resolve the invocation. The result of this successful invocation ends up at the initiating backend-application. If all Super-nodes are invoked and the invocation is still pending, it is deemed unsuccessful. Invocation through Super-nodes thus reduces the number of calls required to satisfy a user's goal.

5 Discovery and Matchmaking in P2P

This section describes how efficient and effective the discovery and matchmaking can be in a hybrid P2P network of SWS platforms. We concentrate on the services provided by a P2P network to the SWS platforms only. Explanation on discovery and matchmaking is out of the scope of this paper but for illustration purposes basic characteristics of both Web service discovery and matchmaking processes are presented.

5.1 Discovery

The process of obtaining a set of services which can possibly fulfill a user request is called Service Discovery. At a conceptual level, we employ the framework presented in [9] as the high level methodology for Web service discovery, which in turn, will make use of a P2P architecture, to gain greater scalability. The Web service discovery is done based on matching abstracted goal descriptions with semantic annotations of web services. The whole P2P architecture will deal specifically with the Web service discovery i.e. *semantic-based approaches* to web service discovery.

In a real-life scenario, there can be a huge number of requests for web services. Processing large numbers of requests in a single SWS platform will introduce the scalability issues. Therefore, the processing task needs to be distributed which can be made possible by connecting SWS platforms in a P2P network. Similarly, knowledge of the availability of a particular Web service will become visible (indirectly) to all participants in the P2P network. It is important to note that service composition may require fulfilling the requester's goal which can be achieved by decomposing the goal, executing these sub-goals at neighbouring SWS platforms, obtaining partial services, and finally composing them.

5.2 Matchmaking

The process of identifying the Web service from a collection of 'similar' Web services that 'fully' satisfies the requester's goal is called matchmaking. In SWS platforms matchmaking is done by evaluating the user's goal against the capabilities of the Web services registered with these SWS platforms. The mechanism outlined in [9] will be used for the purpose of matchmaking. The process seems simple but is quite complicated in reality. Web services whose capabilities are specified in a language other than English, for instance, might have a better deal but may never be considered. However, such heterogeneity can be resolved by using data mediators.

In the event of matchmaking in the P2P network of SWS platforms, the request will always be evaluated locally first. In the case of partial-match or no-match, the request will be forwarded to the cluster *manager* that will then execute the request in order to find out the local match. While doing so, if the matchmaker component is over loaded, the request will be forwarded to another member of the same cluster. Thus, use of P2P technology in Web service technology will enable load balancing.

6 Case Study

The Super-node based P2P network in our case study is shown in Figure 2. The *managers* of AirService, TrainService, BusService, and HotelService clusters are forming a *super-cluster*, which is indicated by the centre circle. The clustered network shown in Figure 2 is invisible to the service requester and it is created over time. Therefore, a service requester can contact any of the members of the network to initiate a TravelPlan request.

The goal in this example is that the requester is looking for a cheap round trip holiday plan with the following constraints: the trip originates in Galway and its ends in Bucharest; it should include a visit to and at least one night's stay in Dublin, Amsterdam and Geneva; the trip should cost $\leq$ € 1500 including accommodation; the duration of the trip should be $\leq$ 3 weeks. Following is the WSMO description of this goal:

```
wsmlVariant _"http://www.wsmo.org/wsml/wsml-syntax/wsml-rule"
namespace { "http://example.org/goals#",
 dc    _"http://purl.org/dc/elements/1.1#",
 wsml _"http://www.wsmo.org/wsml/wsml-syntax#",
       loc  _"http://www.wsmo.org/ontologies/location#",
       tr   _"http://example.org/tripPlanOntology"}
goal_"http://example.org/tripPlanGalwayBucharest"
importsOntology { _"http://example.org/tripPlanOntology",
                  _"http://www.wsmo.org/ontologies/locationOntology"}
capability
postcondition
 definedBy //User wants a holiday trip
 ?planTrip [ planRequester hasValue ?planRequester,
            item hasValue ?plan ] memberOf tr#tripplan
 and
 ?plan[ trip hasValue ?trip ] memberOf tr#trip
 //A round trip: Galway to Galway with stop over in: Dublin, Amsterdam, Geneva, Bucharest
  and
 ?trip [ origin hasValue loc#Galway,
          destination hasValue loc#Galway,
          stopOvers hasValue {loc#Dublin,loc#Amsterdam,loc#Geneva,loc#Bucharest},
          accomodation hasValue ?accomodation,
          travel hasValue ?travel,
          duration hasValue ?tripDuration ] memberOf tr#trip
 and
 ?accomodation [ numberOfNights hasValue ?numberOfNights,
            location hasValue {loc#Dublin,loc#Amsterdam,loc#Geneva,loc#Bucharest},
            price hasValue ?accomodationPrice ] memberOf tr#accomodation
 and
 ?travel [ transportation hasValue ?transportation,
       price hasValue ?travelPrice ] memberOf tr#travel
 and // The total numebr of nights is thus ≥ 3
 ?numberOfNights ≥ 3
 and //The duration of the trip should be less than 3 weeks/21 days
 ?tripDuration < 21
 and //accommodation + transportation should be less than 1500 euro:
 (?accomodationPrice + ?travelPrice) < 1500
```

Let us follow the execution of the requester's goal submitted to one of the SWS platforms in figure 2. Initially, a goal is presented to the SWS platform number 1. As the goal consists of unrelated sub-goals and the goal receiver is a member of TrainService cluster, the goal cannot be fully discovered and matched. Therefore, the goal is forwarded to its cluster *manager*; numbered 2 in Figure 2. The goal is decomposed by the *manager* of the TrainService using the algorithm defined in section 4.3, and the following sub-goals are obtained: *tripGalwayDublin, tripDublinAmsterdam, tripAmsterdamGeneva, tripGenavaBucharest, hotelDublin, hotelAmsterdam, hotelGeneva,* and *hotelBucharest* where the trip is a round trip. The trip sub-goals are

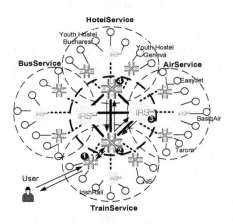

Fig. 2. Service Discovery and Matchmaking

forwarded to the AirService and BusService cluster *manager* and are also evaluated locally. The accommodation-related goals are forwarded to the HotelService cluster *manager*. Every cluster *manager* performs their respective task and returns the result to the *manager* of the TrainService cluster. The results received from other *managers* are merged and a set of potential TravelPlan are obtained by TrainService cluster manager. The result is further filtered according to the user constraints to obtain a minimal result set. The cheapest cost plan is selected and is presented to the requester.

7 Related Works

The combination of P2P and Semantic Web service technologies for allowing better service discovery and matchmaking has recently attracted the attention of different research communities. In [14] an interesting solution for combining semantic descriptions of services and P2P technologies is described. This approach is based on DAML-S, for service description and *pure-P2P* as underling network architecture. A DAML-S matchmaker is used to match a request against services registered with one peer. The choice of technology made this approach vulnerable to: a) scalability due to query flooding; b) the use of DAML-S for service description inherits the drawbacks of this model [19]. Our approach is different to [14], as we do not use *pure-P2P* technology and our approach is guided by the much richer WSMO framework.

Semantic technologies are used as well in METEOR-S approach ([2], [15]) where a P2P network of semantically enriched UDDI registries is envisioned. Requests are created by populating a predefined user request template. P2P network of registries envisioned in METEOR-S suffers from single point of failure problem as there is a single entry point for requests to enter the network. In this context, our approach is features co-op between nodes, is faster, and is more scalable. The discovery mechanism presented in [16] also suffers from the same problems because of thee choice of unstructured P2P technology. It limits the discovery scope by using TTL (Time To Live) so the best services may not be discovered. In our Supernode based P2P approach, the discovery of the best service available in the network is possible. A generic algorithm for goal decomposition and for selecting a cluster manager is presented which can be extended or adapted to the requirements of the applications.

8 Conclusions and Future Works

In this paper we presented a mechanism for merging two different technologies that are designed to achieve the same goals. This combination opened up a new horizon in the area of Semantic Web services thereby supporting distributed, dynamic and scalable Web service discovery and matchmaking. We illustrated the use of a load balancing mechanism and scalable co-operation between the SWS platforms.

The example presented in this paper reflected the benefits of this combination by enabling greater load balancing, quicker discovery of Web services, requiring less invocations, and better scalability than other similar approaches. In the next step we intend to further consolidate our work with SWS platforms by providing 'fully' semantic description of the functional properties of each node in the network and refine the implementation towards this direction.

References

1. Garofalakis, J., Panagis, Y., Sakkopoulos, E., Tsakalidis, A.: Web Service Discovery Mechanisms: Looking for a Needle in a Haystack?", International Workshop on Web Engineering, Santa Cruz (2004).
2. Verma, K. , Sivashanmugam, K. , Seth, A. , Patil, A.: METEOR-S: A Scalable P2P Infrastructure of Registries for Semantic Publication and Discovery of Web Services, Journal of Information technology and Management, (2004).
3. Schlosser, M., Sintek, M., Decker, S., Nejdl, W.: A Scalable and Ontology-Based P2P Infrastructure for Semantic Web Services, Second International Conference on Peer-to-Peer Computing (P2P '02), (2002).
4. Web Service Execution Environment (WSMX), *http://www.wsmx.org*, (2005)
5. Domingue, J., Cabral, L., Hakimpour, F., Sell, D., Motta, E.: A platform and Infrastructure for Creating WSMO-based Semantic Web Services, In Proceedings of the WSMO Implementation Workshop (WIW 2004), Frankfurt, (2004).
6. Roman, D., Lausen, H., Keller, U.: Web Service Modeling Ontology-Standard (WSMO), WSMO-Working Draft, DERI, (2005). available at: http://www.wsmo.org/TR/d2/v1.2/
7. Alesso, H.P., Smith, C.F.: Developing Semantic Web Services, A.K. Peters, Massachusetts, (2004).
8. Schollmeier, R.: A Definition of Peer-to-Peer Networking for the Classification of Peer-to Peer Architecture and Applications, In Proceedings of the First International Conference on Peer-to-Peer Computing (P2P '01), (2001).
9. Keller, U., Lara, R., Polleres, A., Toma, I., Kifer, M., Fensel, D.: WSMO Web Service Discovery, WSMO Working Draft v0.1, DERI, (2004).
10. Yang, B., Garcia-Molina, H.: Designing a Super-Peer Network, In Proceedings of the 19th International Conference of Data Engineering (ICDE), Banglore, (2003)
11. Cimpian, E., Mocan, A., Roman, D., Scharffe, F., Scicluna, J.: WSMO Mediators, WSMO Working Draft v0.1, DERI, (2005).
12. Mocan, A., Cimpian, E.: WSMX Data Mediation, WSMX Working Draft v0.2, DERI, (2005).
13. Sapkota, B.: Design of a Peer-to-Peer Protocol for AmbientDB, Masters Thesis, University of Twente, the Netherlands, (2003).
14. Paolucci, M., Sycara, K. P., Nishimura, T., Srinivasan, N.: Using DAML-S for P2P discovery. In ICWS, (2003).
15. Patil, A. A. , Oundhakar, S. A., Sheth, A. P. , Verma, K.: METEOR-S Web Service Annotation Framework. In Proceedings of Thirteenth International World Wide Web Conference Proceedings, (2004).
16. Banaei-Kashani, F., Chen, C.-C., Shahabi, C.: WSPDS: Web Services Peer-to-Peer Discovery Service. In Proceedings of the International Conference on Internet Computing, (2004).
17. Alonso, G., Casati, F., Kuno, H., Machiraju., V.: Web Services, Springer, (2003).
18. Berners-Lee, T., Hendler, J., Lassila., O.: The Semantic Web. Scientific American, (2001).
19. Lara, R., Roman, D., Polleres, A., Fensel, D.: A Conceptual Comparison of WSMO and OWL-S. In proceedings of European Conference on Web Services (ECOWS 2004), Erfurt, Germany, (2004).

A Contract-Based Approach for Monitoring Collaborative Web Services Using Commitments in the Event Calculus

Mohsen Rouached, Olivier Perrin, and Claude Godart

LORIA-INRIA-UMR 7503,
BP 239, F-54506 Vandœuvre-lès-Nancy Cedex, France
{mohsen.rouached, olivier.perrin, claude.godart}@loria.fr

Abstract. Web services (WS) are gaining popularity for supporting business interactions in cross-organisational distributed business processes. However, current WS specifications mostly concentrate on syntactic aspects. Because multiparty collaborations in business involve complex and long-lived interactions between autonomous partners, their behaviour must be specified to ensure the reliability of the collaboration.

This paper presents an event-based framework associated with a semantic definition of the commitments expressed in the event calculus, to model and monitor multi-party contracts. This framework permits to coordinate and regulate Web services in business collaborations, by allowing detection of actual and imminent violations.

Keyword: Service Monitoring, Collaboration and Coordination, Event Calculus, Commitments.

1 Introduction

Web services are gaining popularity for supporting reusable business processes across distributed and heterogeneous environments. They are well suited to support cross-organisational interactions because such interactions require tighter communication between organizations while preserving their individual processes and practices as an element of their competiveness. However, Web services specifications mostly concentrate on lower levels and do not offer high-level abstractions to accomodate variations in service invocations and business process models.

On the other hand, business contracts seems to be an interesting technology for inter-organisational collaborations, and as such, they are increasingly taking a central role in the context of virtual entreprises. They provide a flexible way to define a protocol, which when formally defined, can be analyzed and checked. Moreover, contracts can be encoded outside the organizations, and this is interesting as most of the organizations demands are oriented towards more transparency, autonomy, and preservation of the corporate knowledge. Therefore, for reliability and efficiency, a contract could be mapped onto a number of

M. Kitsuregawa et al. (Eds.): WISE 2005, LNCS 3806, pp. 426–434, 2005.

more formalized modeling concepts which can be used to facilitate its integration with cross-organisational business processes and other enterprise systems. This includes contract monitoring features and dynamic updates to the processes and policies associated with contracts.

This paper presents our contract-based approach which makes use of business contracts for regulating Web services to support the cross-organisational nature of collaborations and to integrate contract management services into the overall business processes between organizations. It consists of:

- an event-based framework to model and monitor multi-party contracts, which permits to organizations to fulfill their needs of externalisation and autonomy,
- a commitment-based formalisation of contract clauses since commitments are now widely recognized as a satisfying representation for the interaction in multi-partners business processes,
- and a representation of commitments in terms of the Event Calculus [KS86] predicates, as Event Calculus is a formal language with well defined semantics providing an efficient mean for temporal abstractions.

The paper is organized as follows. Section 2 describes our event-based model, and shows how to express contract events in the Event Calculus. In section 3, we present the event-based monitoring for e-contracts. We explain our strategy for expressing contract clauses in terms of commitments in the Event Calculus. Section 4 discusses the related work. In section 5, we give a running example. Finally, section 6 concludes the paper and presents some future directions.

2   An Event-Based Model for e-Contracts

Using events for modeling contracts appears to be interesting, and this interest comes mostly from their effects in terms of changes that are produced by the execution operations. Indeed, specifying and detecting events play an important role in the process of analyzing, monitoring, and visualizing the behaviour of each party involved in the e-contract. Relevant events need to be recorded. After conflicts between contractual parties, these records can be used as evidence to determine what happened and to specificy the responsibilities.

2.1   Specifying Composite Events

In order to provide a computational model for events, we use the Event Calculus [KS86] which is a calculus that allows for specifying some state at particular time-points for time-varying properties (called fluents). The concepts used are inspired from the first order logic, and we find four types of objects:

- $\mathcal{A}$(variables $a, a_i, \ldots$): events, or actions,
- $\mathcal{F}$(variables $f, f_i, \ldots$): fluents, the value of fluents is time-dependent,
- $\mathcal{T}$(variables $t, t_i, \ldots$): timepoints,
- $\mathcal{X}$(variables $x, x_i, \ldots$): domain objects.

The Event Calculus also defines five basic predicates:

(1) $Happens(e,t)$: event e occurs at timepoint t,
(2) $HoldsAt(f,t)$: fluent f is true at timepoint t,
(3) $Initiates(e,f,t)$: if e occurs at t, then f is true and not released at $t+1$,
(4) $Terminates(e,f,t)$: if e occurs at t, then f is false and not released at $t+1$,
(5) $t1 < t2$: this is the standard order relation for time, $t1$ precedes $t2$.

Then, the last two axioms are *Clipped* and *Declipped*, and their definitions are: $Clipped(t1,f,t2) = \exists(a,t)[Happens(a,t) \wedge (t1 <= t < t2) \wedge Terminates(a,f,t)]$. This means that fluent f is no more true (terminated) between times $t1$ and $t2$. Respectively, we have: $Declipped(t1,f,t2) = \exists(a,t)[Happens(a,t) \wedge (t1 <= t < t2) \wedge Initiates(a,f,t)]$. This means that fluent f is true (initiated) between times $t1$ and $t2$.

With these definitions, it is easy to treat concurrent actions, as different *Happens* can refer to the same timepoint. Given this property, we can deduce that two events (with their corresponding timepoints) can be totally ordered based on the ordering of their timepoints (and predicate 5).

In our event-based mechanism, a timepoint denoted t_s of a distributed composite event e is the supremum of the set of timepoints of the constituent primitive events collected when the composite event occurs.

Temporal Orders. Let $e1$ and $e2$ be any primitive events. The temporal order of these two events is defined as follows:

1. $Happens(e1,t1)$ is said to be happen *before* $Happens(e2,t2)$ if $t1 < t2$.
2. $Happens(e1,t1)$ is said to be *concurrent* with $Happens(e2,t2)$ if $t1 = t2$.
3. $Happens(e1,t1)$ is said to be happen *after* $Happens(e2,t2)$ if $t1 > t2$.

Disjunction. The meaning of disjunction is that as soon as one of the two events occurs, the disjunctive event occurs. Disjunction of two events $e1$ and $e2$ is denoted $disj(e1,e2)$. Formally:

$$disj(e1,e2)(t) = Initiates(e_2, raised, t) \Longleftarrow Happens(e_1,t)$$
$$\vee Initiates(e_1, raised, t) \Longleftarrow Happens(e_2,t)$$

Conjunction. The meaning of a conjunction is that two events must both occur before the conjunctive event occurs, but that the order of occurrence, and any overlap of occurrence, is not relevant. Conjunction of two events $e1$ and $e2$ is denoted $conj(e1,e2)$. Formally:

$$conj(e1,e2)(t) = Initiates(e_3, raised, t) \Longleftarrow$$
$$Happens(e_1,t_1) \wedge Happens(e_2,t_2) \wedge t \geq sup(\{t_1,t_2\})$$

Sequence. Sequence is said to be strict, i.e. one event must have occurred before the next event in the sequence. Sequence of two events $e1$ and $e2$ is denoted $seq(e1,e2)$, and is defined as follows:

$$seq(e1, e2)(t) = Happens(e_2, t_2) \Longleftarrow Happens(e_1, t_1) \wedge (t_2 > t_1)$$

It is possible that after the occurrence of $e1$, $e2$ does not occur at all. To avoid this situation, we must appropriately use definite events, such as absolute temporal event or the end of the activities execution.

Negation. The meaning of a negation is that an event $e1$ does not occur in a closed interval formed by $e2$ and $e3$. It is denoted by $neg(e1, e2, e3)$. Formally:

$$neg(e1, e2, e3)(t) = \forall t_2 \in [t_1, t_3],$$
$$Happens(e_1, t_1) \wedge Happens(e_3, t_3) \wedge \neg Happens(e_2, t_2)$$

Temporal Iteration. A periodic event is a temporal event that occurs periodically. It is denoted by $P(e1, d, e2)$ where $e1$ and $e2$ are arbitrary events and d is a time slot. $e1$ occurs for every d in the interval $]e1, e2]$. Formally:

$$P(e1, d, e2)(t) = \exists t_1, (\forall t_2 \in [t_1, t], t =$$
$$t_1 + i * d \ for \ some \ i)(Happens(e1, t_1) \wedge \neg Happens(e2, t_2)$$

If the constraint "$e1$ occurs only once $e2$ occurs" exists, the previous definition becomes:

$$P(e1, d, e2)(t) = \exists t_1, (t > t_1)(Happens(e1, t_1) \wedge (Happens(e2, t)))$$

Of course, it is possible to combine different operators. For instance, $disj(e1, seq(e2, e3))$ represents a composite event which occurs as a result of the disjunction of $e1$ and the sequence of $e2$ and $e3$.

3 Event-Based Monitoring for e-Contracts

To determine whether an execution of a contract is correct, we must represent not only the behavior of the different parties but also the evolution of the contractual relationships among them. These contractual relationships are naturally represented through commitments which permit to capture the obligations of one party to another. The time factor is an important element in the representation of a commitment, and to formally express a commitment, it is necessary to find a representation able to handle temporal constraints. A richer representation of the temporal content of commitments will make them more suitable for representing real situations of business contracts which commonly involve many clauses and have subtle time periods of reference. The representation of temporal properties for commitments usually use some branch of the Temporal Logic [Tl90]. However, as we are interested in analyzing and checking multi-party contracts, the monitoring mechanism needs a high level of externalisation and temporal abstraction. That is why we rely on the use of the Event Calculus introduced so far. Thus, in our monitoring model, we view each action in the contract as an operation on commitments. Then, we develop an approach for formally representing and reasoning about commitments in the Event Calculus. Therefore, we can specify the content of the contract throught commitments of each party. Contract parties create commitments and manipulate them as a result of performing actions through the contract clauses. Further, by allowing preconditions to be associated with the initiation and termination of contract activities, different commitments can be associated with these activities to model the interactions among parties. Conceptually, these interactions are governed by the rules mentioned in the contract clauses.

In our approach, we are using three types of commitments as defined in [Sin99]: (1) a *base-level commitment* denoted $C(p1, p2, c)$ which stipulates that party $p1$ becomes responsible to party $p2$ for statisfying condition c, i.e, c holds sometime in the future,(2) a *conditional commitment* denoted $C_c(p1, p2, c1, c2)$ stipulates that if the condition $c1$ is satisfied, $p1$ will be committed to bring about condition $c2$, and (3) a *persistent commitment* denoted $C_p(p1, p2, A(c))$ is defined as a commitment from party $p1$ to party $p2$ to ensure that condition c holds on all future time points (operator $A(c)$).

Then, deontic clauses can be defined in terms of operations on commitments. The main step consists of specifying deontic constraints including specification of roles and their permissions, obligations and prohibitions using both commitments axioms and Event Calculs axioms [Sha97]. Thus, prohibitions (F), permissions (P), and obligations (O) can be rewritten as follows:

Prohibitions: a prohibition is used to express that an action is forbidden to happen for a party. If a party is prohibited to bring out a proposition p, then it has a commitment to ensure that p never holds.

$$Create(F(p1, p2, p), p2, C(p2, p1, A(\neg p)))$$

Permissions: by considering permissions as negations of prohibitions, we obtain that a party $p1$ is permitted to bring about a proposition p if it has not been prohibited from it. Permission is given by party $p2$.

$$Release(P(p1, p2, p), p1, C(p2, p1, A(\neg p)))$$

Obligations: an obligation is a prescription that a particular behaviour is required. It is fulfilled by the occurrence of the prescribed behaviour. To express that a proposition p is compulsory for a party, we use the permission's expression presented so far. Among deontic logic rules defined in [MW93], we find the following rule that establishes a relationship between permission (P) and obligation (O):

$$P(p) \longleftrightarrow \neg(O(\neg p))$$

From this rule we deduce the following relation

$$O(p) \longleftrightarrow \neg(P(\neg p))$$

As such, using commitments and event calculus, obligations are defined as:

$$Create(O(p1, p2, p), p2, C(p2, p1, A(p)))$$

Given these formal specifications of contract clauses, we can specify the content of business contracts through the partners commitments. Indeed, the specification of a contract is seen as a set of *Initiates* and *Terminates* clauses that define which activities pertaining to the contract are initiated and terminated by each party. Then, the contract execution consists of performing a set of actions that will take place at specific timepoints, that is, a set of *Happens* clauses along with an ordering of the timepoints specified in the contrat rules.

4 Running Example

As a running example, we use a business contract established for buying and selling books on the Internet. Its idea was inspired from the Netbill protocol introduced by Sirbu in [Sir98]. The contract's execution begins with a customer (BR) requesting a quote for some desired books, followed by the purchaser (BP) sending the quote. If the customer accepts the quote, then the purchaser delivers just the book's abstract and waits for an electronic payment order (EPO). After receiving the EPO, the purchaser forwards the EPO and the book to an intermediation server, which handles the funds transfer. When the funds transfer completes, the intermediation server sends a receipt back to the purchaser. As the last step, the purchaser forwards the receipt to the customer to communicate the reception date. Here, we focus on a contract that involves the customer and the purchaser and we try to formalise its operations using commitments in the event calculus. First, we define the fluents used in this contract protocol.

- **Fluents**
  - request(i): a fluent meaning that the customer has requested a quote for item i.
  - books(i): a fluent meaning that the purchaser has delivered the book i.
  - pay(m): a fluent meaning that the customer has paid the agreed upon amount m.
  - receipt(i): a fluent meaning that the purchaser has delivered the receipt for item i.
- **Commitments**
  - $C_c(CT, MR, books(i), pay(m))$ means that the customer is willing to pay if he receives the books.
  - $promiseBooks(i, m) = C_c(MR, CT, accept(i, m), books(i))$ means that the purchaser is willing to send the goods if the customer promises to pay the agreed amount.
  - $promiseReceipt(i, m) = C_c(MR, CT, pay(m), receipt(i))$ means that the purchaser is willing to send the receipt if the customer pays the agreed-upon amount.

After identifying fluents and commitments necessary for the contract's execution, we look now at how the commitments among contract parties evolve during this phase.

1. When the books are sent at time $t1$, the fluent $books(i)$ is initiated. Further, by $Create(sendBooks(i,m), BP, promiseReceipt(i,m))$, the commitment $C_c(BP, BR, pay(m), receipt(i))$ is created. So now the books have been delivered, and the purchaser is willing to send the receipt if the customer pays. Formally, we have:
   - $HoldsAt(books(i), t1)$ since we have
     $Initiates(sendBooks(i,m), books(i), t)$.
   - $HoldsAt(C_c(GP, GR, pay(m), receipt(i)), t2)$ after executing
     $Create(sendBooks(i,m), GP, promiseReceipt(i,m))$. (1)
2. By sending the EPO at time $t2 > t1$, the customer initiates the fluent $pay(m)$ at time $t3$. This ends the commitment $C_c(BP, BR, pay(m), receipt(i))$ and creates the commitment $C(BP, BR, receipt(i))$. Since no event occurred to terminate $books(i)$, it continues to hold. Formally, we have:
   - $HoldsAt(pay(m), t3)$ since $Initiates(sendEPO(i,m), pay(m), t)$ was initiated. (2)
   - $HoldsAt(C(BP, BR, receipt(i)), t3)$ by using (1) and (2).
   - $\neg HoldsAt(C_c(BP, BR, pay(m), receipt(i)), t2)$ by using (1) and (2). (3)
3. At time $t3 > t2$ the happens clause $Happens(sendReceipt(i), t3)$ is applicable, which initiates the fluent $receipt(i)$. This discharges the commitment $C(BP, BR, receipt(i))$ and then it will be terminated. Thus, we reach the stage where the purchaser has delivered the books and the receipt, and the customer has paid.
   - $HoldsAt(receipt(i), t4)$ by using
     $Initiates(sendReceipt(i,m), receipt(i), t)$
   - $\neg HoldsAt(C(BP, BR, receipt(i)), t4)$ by using (3).
4. Thus, at time $t4 > t3$, the following holds:
   $HoldsAt(books(i), t4) \wedge HoldsAt(pay(m), t4) \wedge HoldsAt(receipt(i), t4)$.

As such, given a business contract composed of obligations, permissions, and prohibitions, we have formalized these prescriptions using commitments. Then, by exploiting the strengths of the event calculus to specify business interactions rigorously, we showed how these commitments enabled Web service interactions will produce more flexible and reliable business process models.

5   Related Work

Because of the autonomy and decentralization of the participants, specifying and managing Web services interactions can be challenging. Conventional techniques fall into one of two extremes, being either too rigid or too unstructured. Our contract-based approach using commitments takes the middle path, emphasizing the coherence desired from the activities of autonomous decentralized entities, but allowing the entities to change their services in a controlled manner, which enables them to achieve progress in a dynamic and unpredictable environment. Below we discuss some approaches that are related to our work.

Traditionally, business contracts have been specified using formalisms such as finite state machines, or Petri Nets, that only capture the legal orderings of actions. However, since the semantic content of the actions is not captured, the participants can not handle unexpected situations at runtime. To remedy this, our approach relies on the use of commitments and the Event Calculus. Commitments have been studied before [Cas95] but have not been used for business contract specification. One of the problems with the use of commitments is ensuring that Web services would not be able to retract them with no consequences. Sandholm et al. [SL01] describe various mechanisms for decommitting that would prevent prevent agents (in our case Web services) from decommitting at will. On the other side, the Event Calculus has been theoretically studied, but has not been used for modeling commitments or commitment-based specification. Denecker et al. [DMB92] use the Event Calculus for specifying process protocols using domain propositions to denote the meanings of actions. Then, contracts in distributed environments should respect the partners autonomy and enable them to interact flexibly to handle exceptions and contract breaches.

Paper [FSSB04] studied the automated performance monitoring of contracts, in terms of tracking contract state. In order to facilitate state tracking, the authors define an XML formalization of the Event Calculus, ecXML. This language is used to describe how a contract state evolves, according to events that are described in the contract. However, the contract monitoring and the composite event specification were not dressed.

Flores and Kremer [FK02] develop a model to specify conversation protocols using conversation policies. As in our approach, Flores and Kremer model actions as creating and discharging commitments. However, they only model base-level commitments, whereas our approach accommodates conditional commitments and reasoning rules for these commitments.

A common pattern of the related works discussed above is that all of them are in the direction of the system administration, but not business process automation and Web services regulation. The different domains have different requirements for monitoring. In our work, the Web services regulation requires semantic level monitoring, rather than system level monitoring. To achieve this goal, our e-contract monitorability relies on a purely event-based paradigm allowing a complete separation of the coordination aspects and functionality aspects which was not expressed in the works listed so far.

6   Conclusion and Future Work

This paper presents an approach to regulate and monitor collaborative Web services. We have described our solution to the problem of integrating contracts as part of cross-organisational collaborations. This solution consists of an event-based framework, associated with a semantic definition of the commitments expressed in the Event Calculus, to model and to manage multi-party contracts. First, we have developed a methodology to specify and detect composite events in busines contracts. Second, we have detailed a method to express deontic contract clauses using commitments in the Event Calculus. Finally, the related work was discussed.

In our future work, we plan to test our solution in existing Web services architectures such as ebXML or RosettaNet. This would help us to determine the expressive power of the model and its acceptability by contract domain experts and practitioners. Another alternative is to study correctness requirements in business process protocols, and then express them in terms of commitments and Event Calculus predicates.

References

[Cas95]   C. Castelfranchi. Commitments: From individual intentions to groups and organizations. In *Proceedings of the International Conference on Multiagent Systems*, pages 41–48, 1995.

[DMB92]   M. Denecker, L. Missiaen, and M. Bruynooghe. Temporal reasoning with abductive event calculus. In *Proceedings of the 10th European Conference and Symposium on Logic Programming (ECAI)*, pages 384–388, 1992.

[FK02]   R. A. Flores and R. C. Kremer. To commit or not to commit: Modeling agent conversations for action. *Computational Intelligence 18(2)*, pages 120–173, 2002.

[FSSB04]   A. D. H. Farrell, M. Sergot, M. Salle, and C. Bartolini. Using the event calculus for the performance monitoring of service-level agreements for utility computing, WEC 2004.

[KS86]   R. Kowalski and M. J. Sergot. A logic-based calculus of events. *New generation Computing 4(1)*, pages 67–95, 1986.

[MW93]   J. Ch. Meyer and R. J. Wieringa. *Deontic Logic in Computer Science: Normative Systems Specification*, chapter Deontic Logic: A concise Overview. John Wiley and Sons, 1993.

[Sha97]   M. Shanahan. Solving the frame problem: A mathematical investigation of the commen sence law of inertia. In *Cambridge: MIT Press*. 1997.

[Sin99]   M. P Singh. An ontology for commitments in multiagent systems: Toward a unification of normative concepts. In *Artificial Intelligence and Law 7*, pages 97–113. 1999.

[Sir98]   M. A. Sirbu. Credits and debits on the internet. In *Huhns and Singh,1998*, pages 299–305. 1998. Reprinted from IEEE Spectrum, 1997.

[SL01]   T. Sandholm and V. Lesser. Leveled commitment contracts and strategic breach. *Games and Economic Behavior*, 35:212–270, 2001.

[Tl90]   Temporal and Modal logic. Temporal and modal logic. In *Theoretical Computer Science. Amsterdam: North-Holland*, pages 995–1072. 1990.

Asynchronous Web Services Communication Patterns in Business Protocols

Marco Brambilla, Giuseppe Guglielmetti, and Christina Tziviskou

Politecnico di Milano, Dipartimento di Elettronica e Informazione,
Via Ponzio 34/5, 20133 Milano, Italy
{mbrambil, tzivisko}@elet.polimi.it, giuseppeg@libero.it

Abstract. Asynchronous interactions are becoming more and more important in the realization of complex B2B Web applications, and Web services are at the moment the most innovative and well-established implementation platform for communication between applications. This paper studies the existing business protocols for Web services interactions, compares their expressive power, extracts a set of patterns for implementing asynchrony, studies the trade-offs and the typical usage scenarios of the various patterns, and finally proposes a sample application that has been implemented based on these patterns. The application has been designed using a high-level modeling language for Web applications, thus showing that the studied patterns can be applied at a conceptual level as well as directly at implementation level.

1 Introduction

The Web is more and more consolidating as the primary platform for application development; the advent of Web services has contributed to establishing the Web as the ubiquitous technical platform for implementing B2C and B2B applications. In such context, asynchronous interactions are becoming more and more important: (i) when service time is expected to be either too long to make it comfortable to wait for a response or not predictable, because of the interactive nature of the application; (ii) when users may not be continuously online; (iii) when strict reliability and performance requirements are imposed.

Since Web services are at the moment the most innovative and well-established implementation platform for communication between applications, their interactions are currently studied [16, 2]. Actually, the business world has shown growing interest in achieving loosely coupled, message based interaction's forms for its Web application using Web Services [11]. Web service-specific standards for composition, orchestration and choreography, such as BPEL4WS, WSCI and WS-CDL, are outside the scope of this work, since they work at a much lower level. They do not explicitly address asynchronous mechanisms, although they provide the basic primitives that enable asynchronous implementations.

Other authors address the asynchrony problem by means of patterns. In particular, [16] presents a set of patterns very similar to our proposal. The main differences are: they propose a message queue pattern, they do not consider factory and acknowledge patterns, and they address the problem at a very lower level, by focusing on the design

M. Kitsuregawa et al. (Eds.): WISE 2005, LNCS 3806, pp. 435–442, 2005.

of the software for implementing the interactions. In [5], powerful patterns are presented, integrated with business logic: timers and data values are used to control multilateral interactions. Our approach is instead oriented to high-level design of the interactions, focusing only on the communication between B2B partners. Other pattern-based approaches exist in [1], but they are either at the very implementation level, or simple scenarios without motivating the various patterns.

The paper is organized as follows: Section 2 presents a set of protocols for asynchronous Web services interactions; Section 3 presents the patterns that can be extracted from the protocols, while Section 4 compares the protocols' expressive power based on these patterns; Section 5 presents the implementation experience using a high-level modeling language for Web applications, namely WebML [6, 11] extended with Web services primitives [14], and finally Section 6 concludes.

2   Protocols

Various standards have appeared that support interactions among Web services. In this section we present six protocols that have gained acceptance for general use or in specific contexts. Indeed, some of them, like RosettaNet and IHE, are targeted to specific fields (e.g., industry or medical fields), while others, like ebXML, consist of complete specifications of business interactions.

RosettaNet [10] is a non-profit business consortium of more than 400 leading companies in Information Technology, Electronic Components, Solution Providers, and Semiconductor Manufacturing. It provides standardization of: the business documents, the sequence of documents exchange, and the attributes that determine the service quality. The *RosettaNet Implementation Framework* defines the packaging, routing and transport of the messages in a secure and reliable way.

Integrating the Healthcare Enterprise (IHE) [8] is a proposal for integration of existing standards, like HL7 and DICOM, in the healthcare environment in order to effectively share patient information across systems. The IHE Technical Framework specifies the workflow-based exchanges of messages among systems.

The XML Common Business Library (xCBL) [13] is the standardization proposal from CommerceOne for documents definition. It specifies in XML the most common documents to be exchanged in B2B e-commerce scenarios, their contents and their semantics. The Electronic Business using eXtensible Markup Language (ebXML) [7] by UN/CEFACT and OASIS provides XML specifications for the exchange of business data, from a workflow perspective. The coordination protocol of the possible process scenario is built from the intersection of the partners' process specifications.

Asynchronous Service Access Protocol (ASAP) [3] is the proposal of OASIS for the integration of asynchronous services across the Internet. The asynchrony is based on the creation of an instance of the accessed service, called Instance, and an on-purpose Web service (Factory) used to monitor and control the state of the Instance services. The Open Grid Services Architecture (OGSA) [9] is the standardization effort by the Global Grid Forum, built upon Web services technologies for the description, discovery, invocation and management of Grid resources. The implementation of the architecture model takes place on the Open Grid Services Infrastructure.

3 Extraction of Patterns

From the analysis of the considered standards, we can identify some common communication configurations between the involved partners. Two orthogonal aspects emerge: acknowledge mechanisms and interaction patterns.

3.1 Acknowledgement Mechanisms

In asynchronous communications receiving a response sent by the service provider acknowledging receipt of a request can be useful: this kind of acknowledgement is tied to the business logic of the communication and is independent to the acknowledgement returned by the transport protocol. We can identify three types of business logic acknowledgement: (i) request without acknowledgement; (ii) request followed by synchronous acknowledgement; and (iii) request followed by asynchronous acknowledge.

3.2 Interaction Patterns

The other aspect emerged from the analysis of the protocols concerns the interaction patterns between the partners involved in the communication. In the rest of this section, we briefly describe the six asynchronous patterns that have been identified, and we present their semantics, general features, and typical usage scenarios.

Callback Pattern. This pattern is a very general communication method: a request is made to the provider and a response is sent back to the requester when it is ready. In Fig. 1(a), the client submits a request to the service, and then proceeds with its own execution. When the response is completed, the service provider sends it to the requester. Since callback is the most important pattern for asynchronous interactions, some proposals for supporting callback already exist: (i) WS-Callback [15], which defines a SOAP Callback header and a WSDL definition for it; a Callback header becomes necessary when the Web Service is asynchronous and the reply-to address is unknown at deployment time. (ii) WS-Addressing [4] provides transport-neutral mechanisms to identify Web service endpoints and to secure end-to-end endpoint identification in messages, also in case of intermediate nodes processing.

Publish/Subscribe Pattern. The Publish/Subscribe pattern allows information distribution to a group of partners. Fig. 1(b) depicts the behaviour of the client that is interested to receive notifications periodically by the published service. The client submits a subscription request to the service and continues its process execution. Whenever information needs to be notified to the client, the service provider sends a message response to him.

Polling Pattern. This pattern may be used as an alternative to the Callback pattern when the client cannot implement a Web service to accept the callback of his request. It allows the client to send a request to the service (Fig. 1c), to continue with the process execution and to periodically request the response from the service provider.

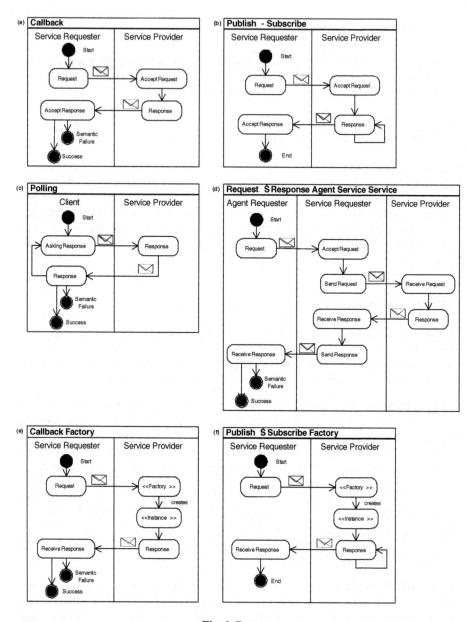

Fig. 1. Patterns

Request Response Agent Service Pattern. The Request Response Agent Service pattern may be seen as an extension of the Callback pattern when the requester cannot interact directly with the service provider. This configuration is depicted in Fig. 1 (d): the agent requester sends its request to the service requester and continues its computation; the service requester forwards the request to the service provider in an asynchronous way. When the response is ready, the service provider sends it to the service requester that, in its turn, forwards it to the agent requester. One of the main advantages of this pattern consists in a more strict-decoupling between agent requester and service provider, thanks to the intermediate layer of the service requester. A variant of this pattern exists which allows the service provider to accept the identity of the agent requester and send the response directly to him.

Callback Factory Pattern. The Callback factory pattern has the same usage of the previously presented Callback pattern but the request is processed by a service instance dedicated to the present interaction. The lifetime of the service instance is dynamically controlled by the Factory service. In Fig. 1 (e), the client sends a request to the Factory service and continues its process execution. The Factory service creates an instance of a service dedicated to fulfil that request. Once the response is ready, the service instance sends it to the requester. The Factory service will terminate the instance when the whole interaction is completed. Therefore, this pattern allows every requester to enjoy a dedicated service for unlimited time.

Publish/Subscribe Factory Pattern. The Publish/Subscribe factory pattern is similar to the previously described Publish/Subscribe pattern. The server requester submits a subscription request to the factory service and continues its process execution. The factory service creates a new instance dedicated to that subscription. Whenever information needs to be notified to the client, the service instance sends a message response to it (Fig. 1 (f)). Like the Callback factory, this pattern creates a dedicated service to the client, so that further requests may be fulfilled by that instance.

These six asynchronous patterns can be used in conjunction with the three types of acknowledgement presented in Section 3.1, according to the needs. Indeed, these two aspects are orthogonal, and can be combined at wish.

4   Comparison of the Protocols

In this section, we offer a very simple expressive power comparison between the business protocols introduced in Section 2. In particular, we present the patterns supported by each protocol and explain the mere realizability of patterns due to the very diverse characteristics and targets of the various standards. Therefore, any other way for comparing them would be rather unfeasible. For each protocol, Table 1 registers the existence (+ sign), or the absence (– sign) of the studied patterns.

Table 1. Patterns support in the existing standards

	RosettaNet	XCBL	ebXML	IHE	OGSA	ASAP
Callback	+	+	+	+	+	-
Publish – Subscribe	-	-	+	-	+	-
Polling	-	-	+	-	-	-
Request Response Agent Service	+	-	-	-	-	-
Callback Factory	-	-	-	-	+	+
Publish Subscribe Factory	-	-	-	-	+	-

As we can see from the table, Callback is the pattern supported by most of the protocols. This is justified by the fact that business interactions are mostly based on request-response message exchanges and less on other architectures. Moreover, Callback is the simplest asynchronous pattern, which constitutes the basis of asynchrony itself. Thus, business protocols like RosettaNet, xCBL and ebXML implement this pattern and give less importance to the others. In more details, RosettaNet and xCBL are focused on the documents specification and use the traditional request-response pattern for the messaging specification. IHE is another standard where business documents are more important than the messaging techniques, and therefore, it is limited to the Callback pattern. On the other hand, ebXML is the standard that supports the largest number of patterns. It provides a complete business framework that supports even publish-subscribe and polling patterns.

The Factory patterns are supported only by OGSA and ASAP. ASAP assumes the Factory pattern as the basis for every asynchronous interaction, thus making it the main philosophy of the protocol. The main reason for OGSA for implementing a Factory pattern stands in the fact that several instances of a Grid service exist at the same time only after respective client requests. After terminating its interactions, every resource may be released and be ready for a new request. The mechanism supported by the Factory patterns can dynamically control such interactions in the grid.

5   Pattern Modeling in WebML

WebML is a conceptual language for specifying Web applications developed on top of database content described using the E-R model. A WebML schema consists of hypertexts (site views), expressing the Web interface (pages) used to publish or manipulate the data specified in the underlying E-R schema. Pages enclose content units, representing atomic pieces of information to be published from an underlying entity. Pages and units can be connected with links to express a variety of navigation effects. Besides content publishing, WebML allows specifying predefined or customized operations: the creation and modification of entity instances, the creation of relationship instances, the filling of a shopping cart, and so on.

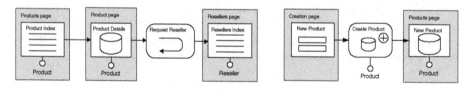

Fig. 2. WebML site view diagram featuring pages, units, operations and Web services

In order to exemplify WebML, we describe the purchase process of goods performed through the interaction of the buyer and the supplier on the Web. In the hypertext diagram of Fig. 2, the buyer selects a product from an index and look at the product details (Product page). To describe Web services interactions, appropriate WebML units have been devised [14] that correspond to the WSDL type description of Web services. In Fig. 2, once the user navigates from the Product page, a request is made (outgoing message) to the Web service in order to gather all the suppliers of the selected product. After the response is constructed (incoming message), the user visualizes all the sellers of the

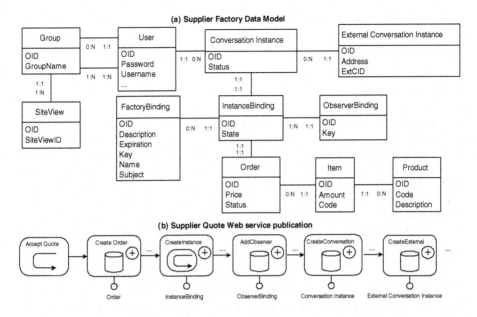

Fig. 3. Callback factory pattern: Supplier data model and Web service publication

product (Resellers page). Other WebML Web service units correspond to publishing primitives (Fig. 3), since they allow the application to stand and wait for incoming messages. Finally, in the seller's site, the Creation page (Fig. 2) allows the seller to create a new product through a form and visualize its attributes.

Fig. 3(a) describes the data model of the application for the Supplier, realized using the callback factory pattern. User's related data is kept into the User, Group and Site-View entities. The Conversation Instance and External Conversation Instance entities represent the way in which correlation in exchanged messages is realized in WebML: a user participates in a Conversation Instance and each Conversation Instance may be correlated to one or more External Conversation Instances and be connected to application data. The External Conversation Instance contains the Conversation ID that the remote partner internally uses (ExtCID) and the URL of the partner (Address). This model allows to couple different ID mechanisms for different partners. The entities Factory Binding, Instance Binding, and Observer Binding represent the way in which the factory scheme is implemented based on ASAP [3] metadata description. Factory Binding entity contains all the data needed to identify the factory service and is connected to zero or more Instances. Each Instance represents the instance of the web service created on demand by the factory. It is connected to one or more Observers, to Conversation Instance and to application data.

Fig. 3(b) illustrates the Web service published by the Supplier. For the sake of simplicity, in the presented WebML diagram we do not represent (1) the connection operations that create associations between objects (we use [...]), and (2) data and connect units required for the complete context retrieval of the conversation. The Supplier factory publishes a solicit-response service unit to accept orders to be quoted. Whenever an order arrives, the order is recorded in the database, a new instance of service is created and part of the data of the Buyer is recorded in an observer binding; then a new conversation is created and the remaining part of data of the Buyer are recorded in an external conversation instance.

6 Conclusions

This work presented our study of various business standards for asynchronous interactions. We extracted a set of interaction patterns, and we provided some evaluations and typical usage scenarios for each of them. Our main contribution consists in describing asynchronous interaction between Web services with a high level of abstraction, and then providing implementation experiments of the patterns. Based on these patterns, expressive power of the existing standards has been compared. Identified patterns are also useful in process design, since they provide certified solutions to important problems. The analysis of patterns advantages and drawbacks highlighted that Callback is the most suitable pattern for business transaction, together with full-fledged acknowledgment mechanisms. Each standard usually provides the patterns required for its specific target, but Callback patterns are supported almost everywhere. In the last part of the paper, a simple running case gives an overview of our experience: we modeled the interactions in WebML [6], and we demonstrated the patterns by using the WebRatio [12] CASE tool.

References

1. Adams, H., Asynchronous operations and Web Services. IBM http://www-106.ibm.com/developerworks/library/ws-asynch1/index.html
2. Alonso, G., Casati, F., Kuno, H., Machiraju, V., Web Services - Concepts, Architectures and Applications. Springer Verlag, October 2003.
3. ASAP site http://www.oasis-open.org/committees/tc_home.php?wg_abbrev=asap.
4. Bosworth, A., Web Services Addressing. http://msdn.microsoft.com/ws/2003/03/
5. Service Interaction Patterns site http://www.serviceinteraction.com.
6. S. Ceri, P. Fraternali, A. Bongio, M. Brambilla, S. Comai, M. Matera. Designing Data-Intensive Web Applications. Morgan-Kaufmann, Dec. 2002.
7. Electronic Business Using eXtensible Markup (ebXML) site http://www.ebxml.org/.
8. Integrating the Healthcare Enterprise (IHE) site http://www.ihe.net/.
9. Open Grid Service Architecture (OGSA) site http://www.globus.org/ogsa/.
10. RosettaNet site http://www.rosettanet.org/.
11. WebML site http://www.webml.org/.
12. WebRatio site http://www.webratio.com/.
13. xCBL site http://www.xcbl.org/.
14. Manolescu, I., Brambilla, M., Ceri, S., Comai, S., Fraternali, P., Model-Driven Design and Deployment of Service-Enabled Web Applications, TOIT, 5 (3), August 2005.
15. Orchard, D., WS-CallBack http://dev2dev.bea.com/webservices/WS-CallBack-0_9.html
16. Yendluri P., Web Services Reliable Messaging, http://webservices.org/
17. Zdun, U., Voelter, M., Kircher, M., Remoting Patterns: Design Reuse of Distributed Object Middleware Solutions. IEEE Internet Computing, Nov-Dec 2004.

Towards the Automation of E-Negotiation Processes Based on Web Services - A Modeling Approach[*]

Stefanie Rinderle[1,**] and Morad Benyoucef[2]

[1] Dept. DBIS, University of Ulm, Germany
rinderle@informatik.uni-ulm.de
[2] School of Management, University of Ottawa, Canada
benyoucef@management.uottawa.ca

Abstract. E-Negotiation is the process of conducting negotiations between business partners using electronic means. The interest in e-negotiation is motivated by its potential to provide business partners with more efficient processes, enabling them to draft better contracts in less time. Most of today's e-marketplaces support some form of e-negotiation. Numerous attempts are being made to design e-marketplaces that support more than one negotiation protocol. The main problem in designing these e-marketplaces is the lack of a systematic approach. In our view, the e-marketplace enforces negotiation protocols and therefore should make them available for consultation by humans and for automation by software agents. Separating the protocols from the e-negotiation media is a step towards a configurable e-marketplace. In this paper we address the requirements for modeling e-negotiation protocols. Then we adopt the Statechart formalism as a modeling language and provide descriptions of five commonly used e-negotiation protocols. Finally, we discuss how we move from these Statechart descriptions of the protocols to modeling the interactions between the e-marketplace participants using a web service orchestration language.

1 Introduction

Contracts are the basis for creating business relationships between organizations. A possible sequence of contract operations includes: (1) the establishment phase where the parties negotiate the terms of the contract; and (2) the performance phase where the contract is monitored and enforced [1]. The recent developments of electronic means for communication and collaboration between business partners led to the emergence of electronic contracting (e-contracting) as an alternative to manual contracting. By integrating their IT infrastructures with those of their partners, traditional businesses move a step closer towards becoming real e-businesses.

---

[*] This work was conducted as part of a SSHRC funded project on Electronic Negotiations, Media, and Transactions for Socio-Economic Transactions.

[**] This research work was conducted during a post doctoral stay at the School of Management, University of Ottawa, Canada.

We believe e-contracting to be a cornerstone in that integration. Electronic negotiation (e-negotiation) is defined as the process of conducting negotiations between business partners using electronic means. The interest in e-negotiation is motivated by its potential to provide business partners with more efficient processes, enabling them to arrive at better contracts in less time. The research community recognizes three categories of e-negotiation systems [2]: (1) negotiation support systems assist users with communication and decision-making activities; (2) negotiation software agents replace users in their communication and decision-making activities; and (3) e-negotiation media provide a platform that implements a negotiation protocol. There are two categories of e-negotiation media: servers which implement multiple protocols, and applications which implement a single protocol. Traditionally, applications have dominated negotiation design, but lately, the importance of servers has increased, and a need for configurable servers is being felt [3]. Attempts were made to design configurable e-negotiation media to support more than one negotiation protocol. They were partially successful, but they were designed in an ad-hoc manner. Some of these attempts were: the AuctionBot [4] which supports the configuration of various auctions; GNP [5] which separates auction specifications from the logic of the server, and eAuctionHouse [6] which allows for the configuration of auctions with the help of an expert system. Recently, Kersten et al. [7] designed a configurable negotiation server that supports bargaining, based on a process model which organizes negotiation activities into phases; and a set of rules that govern the processing, decision-making, and communication. The main problem in designing e-negotiation media is the lack of a systematic approach. Indeed, to this day, design has been a trial-and-error process. We propose a new model for configurable e-negotiation systems in which "e-negotiation media" is the electronic marketplace (e-marketplace) where human and software participants meet to negotiate deals. We refer to "negotiation software agents" as automated negotiation systems. In our model, automated negotiation systems provide a framework for the existence of software agents. The e-marketplace enforces negotiation protocols, and therefore should make these protocols available for consultation (by humans), and for automation purposes (by automated negotiation systems). Separating the protocols from the e-negotiation media is a first step towards a configurable e-marketplace. Separating negotiation strategies from protocols will also give flexibility to the design of automated negotiation systems. The design of e-marketplaces will have a direct effect on the design of automated negotiation systems. Fig. 1 clarifies this model.

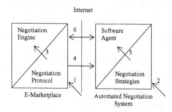

Fig. 1. Model for Configurable e-Marketplaces and Automated Negotiation Systems

(1) Negotiation protocols are designed, formally specified, and made available to the e-marketplace. (2) Negotiation strategies are designed, formally specified, and made available to the automated negotiation system. (3) The e-marketplace configures the negotiation based on the protocol. (4) The automated negotiation system obtains the protocol from the e-marketplace and uses it (5) along with the negotiation strategies to configure the software agent. (6) Automated negotiation takes place. In this paper we only detail the e-marketplace part of the framework. The other part will be elaborated in future publications.

The first objective of this paper is to investigate and assess various formalisms for specifying negotiation protocols, suggest a set of requirements for a formalism that enables configurable e-marketplaces, and select and apply a formalism that satisfies the requirements.

Businesses are moving towards exposing their services on the web, hoping to interact more efficiently with their partners and to achieve high levels of automation at lower cost. The second objective of this paper is to propose a service oriented architecture (SOA) for our model. According to Kim and Segev [8] web services are the most appropriate way to deploy e-negotiation systems for the following reasons: (1) relationships between negotiating partners are dynamic therefore run-time binding is preferable to design-time binding; (2) negotiation is part of procurement, therefore interoperability with internal and external IT systems is important; and (3) web services provide a standardized and flexible integration technology that no organization can afford to ignore if it wants to interact with its partners. Web services provide the means for software components to communicate with each other on the web using XML. A web service describes itself (using WSDL), can be located (using UDDI), and invoked (using SOAP). A SOA will permit, for instance, an online auction to be deployed on the e-marketplace, and located and invoked through the web by a distant Automated Negotiation System. A web services orchestration language will be used to describe the negotiation process on the e-marketplace. The paper is organized as follows: In Section 2 we propose a set of requirements for a formal specification of e-negotiation protocols and assess different formalisms based on these requirements. Section 3 presents Statechart models for five commonly used e-negotiation protocols. In Section 4 we provide an approach towards the implementation of e-negotiation processes within a SOA. In Section 5 we discuss related work and close with a summary and an outlook in Section 6.

2   Requirements for Modeling E-Negotiation Protocols

In this section we state and discuss a set of requirements for describing[1] e-negotiation protocols using common business process modeling formalisms. We proceed in two steps by first summarizing general requirements for business process modeling and then by discussing special requirements in the context of mod-

---

[1] Throughout the paper we interchangeably use the terms formal description, modeling, and representation for the same purpose.

eling e-negotiation protocols. Based on this, different formalisms are assessed. Finally we select the formalism that best meets our requirements.

2.1   General Requirements for Business Process Modeling

There are different formalisms for modeling business processes, e.g., Petri Nets or Statecharts. General requirements for comparing these formalisms are:

Expressiveness/Completeness: A first important requirement is the expressive power of the formalism; i.e., which constructs (e.g., sequences, parallel branchings, loops) are supported by the respective formalism. Intensive research has been spent on this question within the workflow patterns project (www.workflowpatterns.com). Important workflow patterns have been identified and commercial workflow systems as well as standard formalisms have been compared to each other regarding their support of these patterns [9]. Like other formalisms (e.g., Petri Nets), Activity Diagrams and Statecharts support the majority of the standard workflow patterns and even some which are typically not supported by commercial Workflow Management Systems (WfMS) [10].

Formalization/Verification: It is very important to precisely define the syntax and semantics of a formalism for business process modeling in order to be able to detect modeling errors or inconsistencies (e.g., deadlock causing cycles) at design-time. Petri Nets, for example, provide a sound mathematical foundation such that their dynamic behavior can be examined at design-time. Statecharts as defined in [11] also have a formal specification and a precise operational semantics which enables the use of standard verification methods [12].

Automation: In many projects the modeling of business processes comes prior to their automation within, for example, a WfMS. In this case the choice of a business process modeling formalism may also be dependent on whether the processes can be directly executed (e.g., using Petri Nets) or whether or not there exists a mapping to an executable formalism. In the context of process execution within a SOA (which is a major goal within the e-negotiation application domain [8]), the orchestration of web services has become very important. Therefore it is beneficial to use a formalism for which a mapping to a web service orchestration language, for instance the Business Process Execution Language for Web Services (BPEL4WS), can be found. Examples of such model-driven approaches include mappings from Statecharts or Activity charts to BPEL4WS [13, 14].

2.2   Specific Requirements for Modeling E-Negotiation Protocols

In addition to these general requirements there are also requirements which are especially important in the context of describing e-negotiation protocols.

Design for Reactive Systems: When modeling e-negotiation protocols it is often required to express situations in which the system is waiting for a message (e.g., making a new offer). From this two important requirements can be derived: (1) the modeling formalism should allow to model wait states [10] as well as (2) the sending and receiving of messages. In contrast to many other modeling formalisms Statecharts fulfill both requirements [10]. Statecharts are transition systems where arcs are labeled by Event-Conditions-Action rules. If the Statechart is in a given state then it waits (see (1) above) until a certain event under a certain condition triggers an action and the system transits to another state. Such events may be sending or receiving messages (see (2) above).

Understandability/Compactness: In order to increase user acceptance, business process models should be easy to understand. In particular, models of e-negotiation protocols should be compact and clear. [12] argues that, for instance, Statecharts are perceived by users as being more intuitive and easier to learn than alternative business process modeling formalisms such as Petri Nets. In contrast with activity-oriented formalisms, Statecharts usually lead to much more compact process models as we know from comparative studies. In summary Statecharts meet all the requirements discussed in this section. In particular the compact and understandable representation of the e-negotiation protocols has convinced us to select this formalism for our approach.

3 Statechart Models for Five Commonly-Used E-Negotiation Protocols

In this section we provide Statechart models for five commonly-used e-negotiation protocols. We will not discuss the details of the Statechart models since they are self-explanatory. Understandability (see Section 2.2.2) is one of the man requirements of the description formalism. Since the language is complete these models can be modified as needed. Generic templates can also be provided to be used as building blocks for new negotiation protocols.

Fixed Price: The Statechart depicted in Fig. 2a) describes the fixed price sale. This protocol (also called the "take-it-or-leave-it" protocol) is a special case of e-negotiations where there is no exchange of offers and counter-offers. A unique offer is created by an "offer to sell" message from the seller which can either be accepted by a buyer or can be withdrawn by the seller to close the negotiation.

English Auction: Fig. 2b) shows the Statechart description of the English auction protocol. Each buyer receives an update message containing the bid submitted by a rival buyer and can respond to it with a counter-bid. The auction is closed after a certain time. We modeled this by using the hierarchical state *Auction closed* which contains the final states *Deal* and *No Deal*[2]. There is a deal if there is at least one bid and the last bid exceeds the reserve price [15].

Dutch Auction: Dutch auctions are often used to sell perishable goods such as vegetables or airplane seats where the seller starts with a high price and

---

[2] In our models final states are recognized by the absence if outgoing edges.

gradually decreases this price [16]. The Statechart depicted in Fig. 2c) reflects a Dutch auction for an arbitrary number of items, i.e., buyers can specify how many items they will purchase at the current price.

Bargaining: The bargaining protocol is a two-party negotiation model since both the seller and the buyer can make offers. As can be seen from Fig. 2d) the initial offer is made by the seller. Note that there may be other variations where, for example, initial offers from the buyer are also possible. In order to keep the number of states low we parameterized the offer messages such that we can distinguish between a regular counter-offer and a final offer.

Double Auction: Within a double auction (cf. Fig. 2e) buyers and sellers are bidding at the same time. A match between a seller's and buyer's bid implies a deal. We represented the matchmaking within a clearing phase which is again modeled by using the hierarchical state Auction closed.

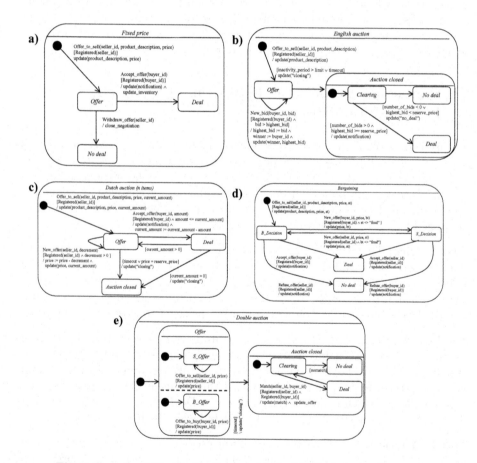

Fig. 2. Statechart Models for Commonly-Used E-Negotiation Protocols

4 Implementation Within a Service-Oriented Architecture

In this section we introduce our approach towards the automation of e-negotiation processes within a SOA.

4.1 Why Use a Service-Oriented Architecture?

As pointed out in [8] it is crucial to provide automated e-negotiation systems in order to build flexible inter-organizational supply chain systems. Traditionally, e-negotiation processes have been carried out by humans registering themselves at certain web pages, placing bids and making offers through fill-in forms, and receiving counter-offers of other participants by updating the respective web pages. One major drawback of this human-centered way of e-negotiation is that the underlying processes are not explicitly modeled but only kept within the human minds. The next step towards automated e-negotiation systems was achieved through software agents which acted as participants in the e-marketplace. In this approach the e-negotiation processes are still not described in an explicit manner. Though they are no longer kept in the human minds they are now hard-coded within the implementation of the software agents. This, in turn, raises important problems regarding the flexibility of the systems in question. Reason is that each process change taking place results in modifying the software agent code. Therefore, on the one hand, an adequate solution for the automation of e-negotiation processes has to be based on the separatio5n of process logic and program code of the invoked applications as realized, for example, in WfMS. On the other hand, a very important requirement for the automation of e-negotiation processes is the adequate support of interoperability between the partner processes in the e-negotiation application domain. In order to meet this requirement, the dynamic invocation of web services within a SOA is the most appropriate approach [8]. Using a SOA also supports the interoperability between internal and external systems of the particular partners. This is crucial since e-negotiation processes are generally part of larger procurement or sales processes [8]. Generally, within a SOA a service provider registers a web service offering a certain functionality (e.g., placing a bid) with a service broker. If a service requester is searching for a certain service it can find the corresponding web service by asking the service broker. The service broker provides a link to the service provider to which the requester can bind. The communication between the parties involved is based on SOAP. Since web services themselves are stateless web service orchestration languages have been developed in order to compose web services into long-running processes. One example for such web service orchestration languages is BPEL4WS. Going back to our Statechart description of e-negotiation protocols and considering a SOA implementation for such protocols it is clear that we need to model the interactions between participants in a given e-negotiation protocol. A web service orchestration language is the obvious solution in this case. The following section provides the BPEL4WS processes for the English and Dutch auction.

4.2 Web Service Orchestration for E-Negotiation Processes

Fig. 3a) depicts the BPEL4WS process model for the English auction. In order to illustrate our approach we use an abstract visualization here. The English auction process is initiated if the e-marketplace receives an "offer-to-sell" message from the seller (activity type receive). Using a switch construct a conditional branch is inserted afterwards in order to check whether the seller is registered or not. If so, an update broadcast message is sent using an invoke activity. The bidding phase is modeled using a while construct. The e-marketplace waits until it receives a "new bid" message from the buyer. After checking the registration, the e-marketplace assigns the new highest bid and sends an update broadcast message including the current highest bid to all participants. If the while loop is terminated by a timeout or by exceeding the inactivity period an update message is sent to all participants indicating that the auction has been closed. Finally, depending on whether there is a deal or not a respective update message is sent to all. Note that in a concrete implementation we precisely distinguish between the different message types. For the sake of understandability we used an abstract update broadcast message type in Fig. 3a). Finding a mapping between the parameterized event messages used within the Statechart models (cf. Fig. 2) and the messages sent within the BPEL4WS processes is one important challenge of our future work.

To initiate a Dutch auction the same BPEL4WS pattern (a receive activity waiting for an "offer to sell" from the seller plus a switch construct checking the registration) can be used as in the English auction (cf. Fig. 3b). Find-

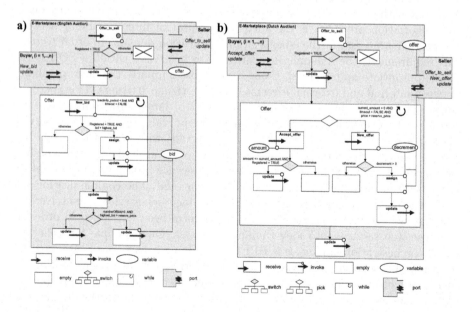

Fig. 3. Web Service Orchestrations for English and Dutch Auction

ing such patterns is important in order to provide generic e-negotiation protocol templates within the service-oriented e-marketplace. These templates may then be modified and mapped to BPEL4WS processes. The initial phase is followed by a while loop. Here the e-marketplace waits until either a buyer sends an "accept offer" message or the seller sends a "new offer" message. This is modeled using a pick construct. After the auction is closed by terminating the while loop an update broadcast message including all necessary information is sent.

5 Discussion

In [15] different price negotiation protocols such as fixed price sale or the Dutch auction are described using finite state machines. The authors aim at discovering common elements, such as basic activities, within auction services in order to provide a design for an auction software. Though finite state machines are a formally founded formalism, Statecharts provide additional constructs (e.g., hierarchical states) which make them better suited for the modeling of e-negotiation protocols. Rolli and Eberhart [17] propose a reference model for describing and running auctions as well as an associated three-layered architecture which is prototypically implemented using a BPEL4WS editor. The processes are then executed within a Java environment. The definition of a reference model and an associated architecture is important. However, it remains unclear how the auction processes are fed into the system. Apparently they are modeled manually using BPEL4WS which might be a complex task for users in general. Therefore our approach of providing generic Statechart models for auction protocols which can then be automatically mapped to web service orchestrations is complementary to the approach proposed by Rolli and Eberhart. Kim and Segev [8] also follow an approach for establishing a web-service enabled e-marketplace. The authors provide a Statechart description for one e-negotiation protocol and the corresponding BPEL4WS process. In this paper we adopt the idea of providing understandable models for e-negotiation protocols and to automate them within a SOA. In [18] e-negotiation protocols are modeled using the Petri Net formalism. Special focus is put on the modeling of attributes which reflect the different strategies the participants in the e-negotiation might adopt. In this paper we focus on the understandability of e-negotiation protocols and therefore we use Statecharts instead of Petri Nets. We also address the question of automating the e-negotiation processes within a SOA afterwards. Chiu et al. [19] present an interesting approach for developing e-negotiation plans within a web services environment. The authors provide meta models for e-contract templates and e-negotiation processes which can be used to set up the concrete e-negotiation processes within a web service environment. Though this approach is generic we believe that providing (generic) e-negotiation templates (i.e., Statechart models) to users which can be individually modified and immediately mapped onto executable web service orchestrations is more intuitive and user-friendly.

6   Summary and Outlook

In this paper we introduced Statechart models for five commonly-used e-negotiation protocols. For that we first systematically elaborated the requirements for modeling e-negotiation protocols and select the Statechart formalism as the most appropriate one. We discussed the importance of automating the corresponding e-negotiation processes within a service-oriented environment in order to meet the flexibility and interoperability requirements of the e-negotiation application domain. In order to illustrate our ideas we presented the web service orchestrations for the English and the Dutch auctions which were executed in a web service environment. In the future we will work on formalizing a mapping between the Statechart models of the e-negotiation protocols and the corresponding web service orchestrations. Based on this mapping it will be possible to provide generic e-negotiation protocol templates to users which are understandable and adaptable. If such a protocol template is chosen and possibly adapted it can be immediately mapped to a BPEL4WS process and then executed in a web-service enabled e-marketplace. This will increase user acceptance and application of e-negotiations and e-marketplaces in practice.

References

1. Goodchild, A., Herring, C., Milosevich, Z.: Business contracts in B2B. In: Workshop on Infrastructures for Dynamic B2B Service Outsourcing. (2000)
2. Bichler, M., Kersten, G., Strecker, S.: Towards a structured design of electronic negotiations. GDN **12** (2003) 311–335
3. Neumann, D., Benyoucef, M., Bassil, S., Vachon, J.: Applying the MTL taxonomy to state of the art e-negotiation systems. GDN **12** (2003) 287–310
4. Wurman, P., Wellman, M., Walsh, W.: The michigan internet auctionbot. In: Autonomous Agents. (1998) 301–308
5. Benyoucef, M., Keller, R., Lamouroux, S., Robert, J., Trussart, V.: Towards a generic e-negotiation platform. In: Re-Technologies for Inf. Syst. (2000) 95–109
6. University of Washington: The eAuctionHouse (2002)
7. Kersten, G., Law, K., Strecker, S.: A software platform for multi-protocol e-negotiations. Technical report, An InterNeg Research Report 04/04 (2004)
8. J.B. Kim, Segev, A.: A web services-enables marketplace architecture for negotiation process management. Decision Support Systems. **40** (2005) 71–87
9. Aalst, W., Hofstede, A., Kiepuszewski, B., Barros, A.: Workflow patterns. DPD **14** (2003) 5–51
10. Dumas, M., Hofstede, A.: UML activity diagrams as a workflow specification language. In: UML'02. (2001) 76–90
11. Harel, D.: Statecharts: A visual formulation for complex systems. Scientific Computer Programming **8** (1987) 231–274
12. Muth, P., Wodtke, D., Weienfels, J., Kotz-Dittrich, A., Weikum, G.: From centralized workflow specification to distributed workflow execution. JIIS **10** (1998) 159–184
13. Baina, K., Benatallah, B., Casati, F., Tournani, F.: Model-driven web service development. In: CAiSE'04. (2004) 290–306

14. Mantell, K.: From UML to BPEL. Model-driven architecture in a web services world. Technical report, IBM Research (2003)
15. Kumar, M., Feldman, S.: Business negotiations on the internet. Technical report, IBM Research (1998)
16. Kumar, M., Feldman, S.: Internet auctions. Technical report, IBM Research (1998)
17. Rolli, D., Eberhart, A.: An auction reference model for describing and running auctions. In: Wirtschaftsinformatik. (2005)
18. Simon, C., Rebstock, M.: Integration of multi-attributed negotiations within business processes. In: BPM'04. (2004) 148–162
19. Chiu, D., Cheung, S., Hung, P., Chiu, S., Chung, A.: Developing e-negotiation support with a meta-modeling approach in a web services environment. Decision Support Systems 40 (2005) 51–69

Modeling of User Acceptance of Consumer E-Commerce Website

Rui Chen

State University of New York at Buffalo,
Buffalo, NY 14260
ruichen@buffalo.edu

Abstract. As the consumer e-commerce market grows intensively competitive, the capability of a website to capture consumers and to be accepted has been recognized as a critical issue. The user acceptance of a website not only brings immediate business opportunities, it also casts great impact on future return and loyalty buildup of the consumer. This paper is intended to explore the measurement of consumer acceptance of e-commerce website. By synthesizing previous research into a coherent body of knowledge and by recognizing the roles of contingency factors, we develop a new e-commerce website acceptance model that examines the website success. The model is extended from Garrity & Sanders Model and is expected to shed light on website design practice.

1 Introduction

The growth of the World Wide Web and its user groups has paved a way to the rise of web-based consumer e-commerce. Web-based information system represents a new frontier for business trying to establish an on-line presence by establishing virtual store, which exists in the cyberspace and offers merchandise and services [1], [2]

Though prior IS researches have presented a variety of measurements for e-commerce website success, the research contribution is still limited and insufficient. The sales volumes suggest that consumer e-commerce websites remain incapable of capturing business opportunities as sales are extremely low despite of a long growth period [3]. Therefore, it is of high priority of researchers to fully explore the major factors that influence the consumer acceptance of the websites.

Extended from Garrity & Sanders Model [4], the proposed model measures the user acceptance by assessing task support satisfaction, interface support satisfaction, user satisfaction, the fit between tasks and designs, trust, self-efficacy, and user intention to use the website. We expect this paper to bring a better understanding of the system design and management so that the website can efficiently capture online users and business opportunities.

The rest of the paper is organized as follows. Section 2 presents literature review and the theoretical background of consumer e-commerce acceptance models. Section 3 presents the research model and hypotheses. Section 4 concludes the paper with a discussion of future research.

M. Kitsuregawa et al. (Eds.): WISE 2005, LNCS 3806, pp. 454–462, 2005.
© Springer-Verlag Berlin Heidelberg 2005

2 Review of Consumer E-Commerce Acceptance Literature

The majority of existing consumer e-commerce website success models have originated from the research in general IS success models. We provide a detailed discussion of the prevailing IS success models and their influences on the development of consumer e-commerce website studies.

2.1 Technology Acceptance Model (TAM) and Extensions to Consumer E-Commerce

A web site is, in essence, an information technology. As such, online purchase intentions may be explained in part by the Technology Acceptance Model (TAM) [5], [6], [7]. TAM, as in Figure 1, is at present a preeminent theory of technology acceptance in IS research. Many empirical tests have shown that TAM is a parsimonious and robust model of technology acceptance [8], [9], [10]. The major determinants are the perceived usefulness and perceived ease of use, contributing to user behavior intention which later leads to actual system use. TAM has been widely adopted into the study of consumer e-commerce and proved to be successful [11], [12], [13].

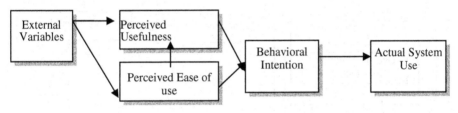

Fig. 1. Technology Acceptance Model

However, the external variables which impact the perceived usefulness and perceived ease of use are not fully explored in the TAM. Therefore, TAM is limited in its impact on website design practices.

2.2 DeLone and McLean Model and Extensions to E-Commerce

The DeLone and McLean Model (D&M) [14], [15] is based on the communications research of Shannon and Weaver [16] and the Information Influence Theory [17]. In the D&M Model, construct "system quality" measures technical success and "information quality" measures semantic success. In addition, "user satisfaction", "individual impacts", and "organizational impacts" measure system success when the system "use" is executed. The D&M model has been validated by the researchers [18], [19] and been adopted for the analysis on consumer e-commerce [20], [21]. The D&M Model is shown in Figure 2.

However, researchers have commended on the difficulty of applying the model to specific research contexts [14]. In addition, the D&M model does not recognize the impact of contingency factors on system quality and information quality. Contingency literatures [22], [23] implies that elements such as individual traits, purchasing task characteristics, and cognitive believes may influence the online customers with their decision making or purchasing behaviors.

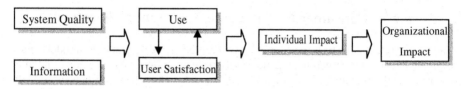

Fig. 2. DeLone and McLean Model 1992

2.3 Garrity and Sanders Model and Extensions to E-Commerce

Garrity and Sanders [4], [24] extended the DeLone & McLean model of user satisfaction by identifying four major factors such as task support satisfaction, decision support satisfaction, interface satisfaction, and quality of work-life satisfaction. The model is illustrated in figure 3.

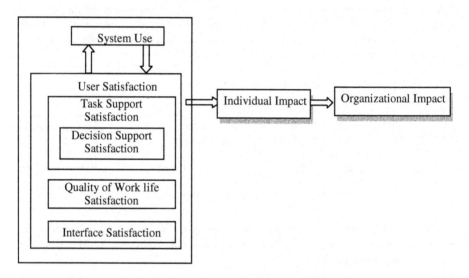

Fig. 3. Garrity and Sanders Model of IS Success

G&S Model measures the fit with the system, the user, and the task and is in consistent with the TAM. Task support satisfaction and interface satisfaction are closely related to Davis' perceived usefulness dimension and perceived ease of use dimension. This model has been successfully adopted into consumer e-commerce studies [24], [25].

3   Research Model and Hypotheses

To measure user acceptance of e-commerce website and to bring practical implications to the system design, we present the following research model as in Figure 4. The model is extended from the G&S model by substantializing the satisfaction constructs with design principles and contingency factors.

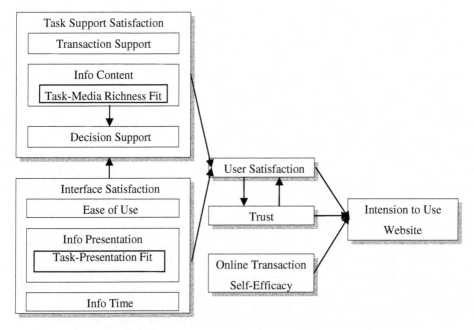

Fig. 4. Consumer's Acceptance of E-Commerce Model

3.1 Task Support Satisfaction

Prior research about e-commerce success suggests the important role of task support in user online purchasing activities. Failure in task support may result in rejections to the website for a user.

Transaction Support. Transaction support assesses the website's capacity to facilitate user's purchase transactions. Tang et al. [26] defines e-commerce transaction as "a means to conduct particular commercial activities using the global digital E-commerce infrastructure." Transaction involves a flow of activities towards online purchasing. Example activities are such as "searching for product", "managing shopping cart", "filling the payment", "submitting the order", and "tracking order status". To support such transactions, the website information system is expected to provide a complete set of transaction procedures and tools for users. An incomplete, flaw, or unreliable transaction support, on the other hand, suggests a low level of task support satisfaction. Hence, we propose the following hypothesis.

   H1: Transaction support has a positive impact on task support satisfaction

Decision Support. A consumer e-commerce website can be decomposed into numerous tasks, subtasks, and decisions [24]. Many of the purchasing tasks and subtasks can be categorized as intellectual or decision support based. Decision support measures the support provided by the web site in facilitating user decision making process. Unlike the transaction support which is required by every e-commerce website, the decision support is an optional design option. The value added through decision support helps users make purchasing decisions and finish purchasing tasks at efficiency and qualities. Hence, we propose the following hypothesis.

H2: Decision support has a positive impact on task support satisfaction

Information Content. Information content [27] is geared towards providing users with accurate, relevant, and complete information, thereby addressing the problem of irrelevant information in web systems.

It has been noticed that information quality should always be considered in terms of "use-based data quality" [28]. This highlights the fit between the task characteristics and the information richness [29]. In the context of consumer e-commerce, rich media are high in (a) the possibility of instant feedback, (b) the ability to convey multiple cues, and (c) the use of natural language to convey subtleties and nuances etc. As information requirement of uncertainty and equivocality are inherent in non-routine online purchasing tasks, a high level of support in media richness are suitable, on contrary to routine purchases where low volume of information and lean median are recommend.

Information content helps convey business critical information to online consumers for purchasing tasks. Therefore, the quality of information content influences the task support satisfaction of users. Meanwhile, the information content is relevant to the quality of decision support. Accurate, relevant, and complete information enhance the efficiency of decision making. Hence, we propose the following.

H3: Information content has a positive impact on the task support satisfaction

H4: Information content has a positive impact on decision support

3.2 Interface Satisfaction

Interface satisfaction measures consumers' evaluation of the website interface design in terms of information presentation, webpage navigability, ease of use and efficiency of interaction with the website [24]. Interface design facilitates the communication between online users and the website in information sharing and interaction.

Ease of Use. In the context of consumer e-commerce, ease of use includes website format design, facilitated browsing, and accessing speed etc [30]. Low level of ease of use may contribute to lower usability of the system and introduces unnecessary difficulty for users to operate the website and navigate through the web pages. As such, we propose the following hypothesis.

H5: Ease of Use has a positive impact on interface satisfaction

Information Presentation. Information presentation concerns about presentation issues in terms of interface structure, information packaging, and information accessibility that are geared towards enhancing users' cognition, thereby addressing the hypermedia problem of cognitive overhead [27].

Though the interface design is critical to the website success, the suitability of the prevalent information formats in supporting various online shopping tasks remains unknown. Using the cognitive fit theory as the theoretical framework, the fit between information presentation format and online consumer tasks are investigated. Research findings suggest that the level of fit greatly influences on consumers' online shopping performance and perceptions of shopping experience [31]. E.g., list format is found to support browsing tasks and the matrix format facilitates searching tasks [31].

Consequently, the task-information presentation fit is considered an integrated part of information presentation.

H6: Information presentation has a positive impact on interface satisfaction

Information Time. Information time dimension provides users with control over temporal aspects of their actions. The design features related to information time construct grant users with the sense of temporal orientation and addresses the critical hypermedia problem of disorientation in e-commerce systems. The features in this dimension help users easily control their activities and make navigation at efficacy. The design concern for information time, therefore, enhances the interface usability and increases the user interaction with website systems. Thus, we propose the following hypothesis.

H7: Information time has a positive impact on interface satisfaction.

Prior research findings suggested that interface satisfaction may lead to improved task support satisfaction. Design improvements in interface increase the usability of the website system and the transaction support as a result. Meanwhile, interface design of better information presentation and control helps users with the decision making process. It is found that the perception of information quality is also closely related to the interface design. Poor information presentation and usability reduce the user perception of the information content quality. Hence, we propose the following hypothesis.

H8: Interface satisfaction has a positive impact on task support satisfaction

3.3   Online Transaction Self-efficacy

In the domain of consumer e-commerce where transaction activities are the core of business interest, Kim and Kim developed online transaction self-efficacy [32]. Kim and Kim suggested that consumers are more likely to purchase on a website over which they have confidence about purchasing exactly the item they want. The more self-efficacious consumers are with online purchasing activities, the more favorable expectation they are likely to have, and the more they are likely to use the website. Therefore, online transaction self-efficacy may contribute to users' intention to use a website.

H9: Web self-efficacy has a positive impact on user intention to use website

3.4   User Satisfaction

Satisfaction is widely accepted as a major indicator of the system success and adoption. Doll and Torkzadeh [33] defined end-user computing satisfaction as "the affective attitude towards a specific computer application directly." Prior research suggested that low level of user satisfaction with an information system may cause users to abandon the technology [34], [35]. In addition, Paul et al. [36] indicated that user satisfaction is directly related to system use. Therefore, we propose that the similar relationship still hold in the context of consumer e-commerce.

H10: User satisfaction has a positive impact on user intention to use website

From the organizational view, an information system is a complex set of interacting subsystems designed to provide a product or service to a customer. This view lead to three different dimensions of IS success: task support satisfaction, decision making satisfaction, and interface satisfaction. These subgroups of satisfaction contribute to an overall user satisfaction suggested by Garrity and Sanders [4]. In the context of consumer e-commerce where the website is constructed as an information of hypermedia technologies and information, we propose that the similar relationships hold.

H11: Task support satisfaction has a positive impact on user satisfaction
H12: Interface satisfaction has a positive impact on user satisfaction

3.5 Trust

The consumer e-commerce poses new challenges to the online purchasing as risk becomes a concern. Unlike the conventional buying-selling process, consumers have limited information concerning about the website and the vendor; this, in turn, introduces the uncertainty and risk of online purchasing such as Internet fraud, credit card theft, and privacy leakage. The level of risk inherent in consume e-commerce, however, is offset by the degree to which trust is maintained by online customers. Trust reduces the uncertainty and risk perceived by users and, consequently, enhances the perception about the website and leads to higher satisfaction. Higher user satisfaction, in turn, brings favorable attitude toward the website with its products and services which may lead to higher trust on the website.

H13: Trust toward the website has a positive impact on user satisfaction
H14: User satisfaction has a positive impact on trust towards the website

Trust also plays a key role in purchasing processes where consumers look for credential qualities of goods or services. It is considered as a potential antecedent of user intention to use [37], [38], [39]. Therefore, we propose the following hypothesis.

H15: Trust has a positive impact on user intention to use website

4 Conclusion and Future Work

This paper presents a conceptual framework to assess consumer acceptance of e-commerce websites. It stresses on the roles of contingency factors and pinpoints potential areas for development in consumer website design. As suggested, a website which achieves the fit between varying purchasing tasks and media richness and presentation, recognizes user individual traits, and provides users with sufficient support and control power may reach success and to be accepted.

The future work may include the validation of research model and examination of hypotheses. An experiment design is suitable for the validation purpose and structural equation modeling may be employed for statistical inference.

References

1. Hoffman, D.L., Kalsbeek, W.D., Novak, T.P.: Internet and Web Use in the U.S. Communications of the ACM **39** (1996) 36-46
2. Yesil, M.: Creating the Virtual Store: Taking Your Web Site from Browsing to Buying. John Wiley & Sons (1996)
3. Johnson, C.: The Growth of Multichannel Retailing. (2003)

4. Garrity, E.J., Sanders, G.L.: Dimensions of Information Systems Success. In: Khosrowpour, M. (ed.): Information Systems Success Measurement, Vol. 1. Idea Group Publishering, Hershey, PA (1998) 13-45
5. Davis, F.D.: Perceived Usefulness, Perceived Ease of Use, and User Acceptance of Information Technology. MIS Quarterly (1989) 319-340
6. Davis, F.D.: User Acceptance of Information Technology: System Characteristics, User Perceptions and Behavioral Impacts. International Journal of Man-Machine Studies 38 (1993) 475-487
7. Davis, F.D., Bagozzi, R.P., Warshaw, P.R.: User Acceptance of Computer Technology: A Comparison of Two Theoretical Models. Management Science 35 (1989) 982-1003
8. Adams, D.A., Nelson, R.R., Todd, P.A.: Perceived Usefulness, Ease of Use, and Usage of Information Technology: A Replication. MIS Quarterly 16 (1992) 227-247
9. Chin, W.W., Todd, P.A.: On the Use, Usefulness, and Ease of Use of Structural Equation Modeling in MIS Research: A Note of Caution. MIS Quarterly 19 (1995) 237-236
10. Gefen, D., Straub, D.W.: Gender Differences in the Perception and Use of E-Mail: An Extension to the Technology Acceptance Model. MIS Quarterly 21 (1997) 389-400
11. Benslimane, Y., Plaisent, M., Bernard, P.: Apply the Task-Technology Fit Model to WWW-based Procurement: Conceptualization and Measurement. 36th Hawaii International Conference on System Sciences, Hawaii (2003)
12. Klopping, I.M., McKinney, E.: Extending the Technology Acceptance Model and the Task-Technology Fit Model to Consumer E-Commerce. Information Technology, Learning, and Performance Journal 22 (2004) 35-48
13. Dishaw, M.T., Strong, D.M.: Extending the Technology Acceptance Model with Task-Technology Fit Constructs. Information & Management 36 (1999) 9-21
14. DeLone, W.H., McLean, E.R.: The DeLone and McLean Model of Information Systems Success: A Ten-Year Update. Journal of Management Inforation Systems 19 (2003) 9-30
15. DeLone, W.H., McLean, E.R.: Information Systems Success: The Quest for the Dependent Variable. Information Systems Research 3 (1992) 60-95
16. Shannon, C.E., Weaver, W.: A Mathematical Model of Communication. University of Illinois Press, Urbana-Champaign (1949)
17. Mason, R.O.: Measuring Information Output: A Communication Systems Approach. Information & Management 1 (1978) 219-234
18. Rai, A., Lang, S.S., Welker, R.B.: Assessing the Validity of IS Success Models: An Empirical Test and Theoretical Analysis. Information Systems Research 13 (2002) 50-69
19. Seddon, P.B., Kiew, M.Y.: A Partial Test and Development of the DeLone and McLean Model of IS Success. In: I., D.J., Huff, S.L., Munro, M.C. (eds.): International Conference on Information Systems. Association for Information Systems, Atlanta, GA (1994) 99-110
20. DeLone, W.H., McLean, E.R.: Measuring e-Commerce Success: Applying the DeLone and McLean Information Systems Success Model. International Journal of Electronic Commerce 9 (2004)
21. Molla, A., Licker, P.S.: E-Commerce Systems Success: An Attempt to Partially Extend and Respecify the Delone and Maclean Model of IS Success. Journal of Electronic Commerce Research 2 (2001) 131-141
22. Myers, B.L., Kappelman, L.A., Prybutok, V.R.: A Comprehensive Model for Assessing the Quality and Productivity of the Information Systems Function: Toward a Theory for Information Systems Assessment. In: Garrity, E.J., Sanders, G.L. (eds.): Information System Success Measurement. Idea Group Publishing, Hershey (1998) 94-121
23. Van den Hooff, B., Groot, J., De Jonge, S.: Situational Influences on the Use of Communication Technologies. Journal of Business Communication 41 (2005) 4-27

24. Garrity, E.J., Glassberg, B., Kim, Y.J., Sanders, G.L., Shin, S.K.: An Experimental Investigation of Web-based Information Systems Success in the Context of Electronic Commerce. Decision Support Systems **39** (2005) 485-503
25. Lu, J.: A Model for Evaluating E-Commerce Based on Cost/Benefit and Customer Satisfaction. Information Systems Frontiers **5** (2003) 265-277
26. Tang, J., Fu, A.W., Veijalainen, J.: Supporting Dispute Handling in E-Commerce Transactions, a Framework and Related Methodologies. Electronic Commerce Research **4** (2004) 393
27. Kim, Y.J., Kishore, R., Sanders, G.L.: From DQ to EQ: Understanding Data Quality in the Context of E-Business Systems. Decision Support Systems (2003)
28. Orr, K.: Data Quality and Systems Theory. Communications of the ACM **41** (1998) 66-71
29. Rice, R.E., Grant, A.E., Schmitz, J., Torobin, J.: Individual and Network Influences on the Aadoption and Perceived Outcomes of Electronic Messaging. Social Networks **12** (1990) 27-55
30. Lu, Z., Lu, J., Zhang, C.: Website Development and Evaluation in the Chinese Tourism Industry. Networks and Communication Studies **16** (2002) 191-208
31. Hong, W., Thong, J., Y L, Tam, K.Y.: The Effects of Information Format and Shopping Task on Consumers' Online Shopping Behavior: A Cognitive Fit Perspective. Journal of Management Information Systems **21** (2004) 149
32. Kim, Y.H., Kim, D.J.: A Study of Online Transaction Self-Efficacy, Consumer Trust, and Uncertainty Reduction in Electronic Commerce Transaction. 38th Hawaii International Conference on System Science (2005)
33. Doll, W.J., Torkzadeh, G.: The Measurement of End-User Computing Satisfaction. MIS Quarterly **12** (1988) 259-274
34. Bailey, J.E., Pearson, S.W.: Development for a Tool for Measuring and Analyzing Computer User Satisfaction. Management Science **29** (1983) 530-545
35. Benson, D.H.: A Field Study of End-User Computing: Findings and Issues. MIS Quarterly **7** (1983) 33-45
36. Paul, S., Seetharaman, P., Ramamurthy, K.: User Satisfaction with System, Decision Process, and Outcome in GDSS Based Meeting: An Experimental Investigation. 38th Hawaii International Conference on System Science (2004)
37. Chiravuri, A., Nazareth, D.L.: Consumer Trust in Electronic Commerce: An Alternative Framework Using Technology Acceptance. Americas Conference on Information Systems 2001 (2001)
38. Chircu, A., Davis, G., Kauffman, R.: Trust, Expertise and Ecommerce Intermediary Adoption. 6th Americas Conference on information Systems (2000)
39. Pavlou, P.A.: Consumer Acceptance of Electronic Commerce: Integrating Trust and Risk with the Technology Acceptance Model. International Journal of Electronic Commerce **7** (2003) 101

A Collaborative Recommender System Based on User Association Clusters

Chein-Shung Hwang and Pei-Jung Tsai

Dept. of Information Management, Chinese Culture University, 55, Hwa-Kang Road,
Yang-Ming-Shan, Taipei, Taiwan 111, R.O.C.
cshwang@faculty.pccu.edu.tw, g9214004@ms2.pccu.edu.tw

Abstract. The ever-increasing popularity of the Internet has led to an explosive growth of the sheer volume of information. Recommender system is one of the possible solutions to the information overload problem. Traditional item-based collaborative filtering algorithms can provide quick and accurate recommendations by building a model offline. However, they may not be able to provide truly personalized information. For providing efficient and effective recommendations while maintaining a certain degree of personalization, in this paper, we propose a hybrid model-based recommender system which first partitions the user set based on user ratings and then performs item-based collaborative algorithms on the partitions to compute a list of recommendations. We have applied our system to the well known *movielens* dataset. Three measures (precision, recall and F1-measure) are used to evaluate the performance of the system. The experimental results show that our system is better than traditional collaborative recommender systems.

1 Introduction

The ever-increasing popularity of the Internet has led to an explosive growth of the sheer volume of data. However these high dimensional and heterogeneous data sources are often too large or complex to analyze using the classical or manual approaches. Many researchers [1-5] have developed various techniques to deal with the information overload problem. Among them, the most prevalent approach is utilizing the search engines which help users locate their desired information using keywords. Search engines provide limitedly personalized services by returning a list of information that matches users' search queries. However, the amount of returned information is still too huge for a user to actually absorb it. Furthermore, the search results are highly depends on search skill mastery. Another possible technique is to provide a personalized recommender system that automatically builds user profiles to suggest information which best match users' interests. One of the most successful and widely used recommender techniques is *collaborative filtering* (CF) [3-7]. CF models can be built based on users or items. User-based CF finds other users that have shown similar tastes to the active user and recommends what they have liked to him. However, they suffer from serious scalability problems. Some potential solutions to the problems are to adopt the clustering [8, 9] or dimensionality reduction techniques [10]. Although these approaches can speed up the recommendation engine, they tend to degrade the result of recommendations.

M. Kitsuregawa et al. (Eds.): WISE 2005, LNCS 3806, pp. 463–469, 2005.

Item-based CF suggests items that are most similar to the set of items the active user has rated. Since the relationships between items are relatively static, item-based approaches can be implemented by first computing the item relationship model and then providing a quick recommendation. Although several researches [6, 7] have shown that item-based approaches provide more accurate recommendations than user-based approaches, globally computed item-to-item relationships may not be able to provide truly personalized information. A possible approach can be done by first exploring a sufficiently large neighborhood of similar users and then apply item-based approaches using this subset [6].

Association rule algorithms were introduced in [11, 12] and often applied in market basket analysis. They analyze how the items purchased by customers are associated. An example of such associations might be that 60% of customers that purchase *milk* may also purchase *bread*. Association rules are good in representing item affinity where each item is present only a small fraction of the transaction and presence of an item is more significant than the absence of the item. Han et al. [13] proposed a new clustering method using association rules and hypergraph partitioning (ARHP) for grouping related items in transaction-based databases. This method is able to provide high-quality results even when data are sparse or in high dimensional space. This is particularly true for collaborative filtering domains.

In this paper, we propose a hybrid model-based recommender system by integrating ARHP and item-based CF. Initially, the ARHP is used to cluster closely related users into groups. Each cluster holds users with similar historical ratings data and represents a potential neighborhood. Next, the item-based CF is performed to provide a list of recommendations based on the user neighborhoods. Sect. 2 provides a brief overview of related collaborative filtering algorithms and applications. Sect. 3 describes each task of the proposed system. Sect. 4 discusses our experimental results. The final section provides some conclusions and the directions of future work.

2   System Architecture

The main goal of our study is to propose a recommender system that can provide efficient and effective recommendations while maintain a certain degree of personalization. To accomplish this, we employ a hybrid model-based approach by combining ARHP and item-based CF techniques. The proposed system consists of three main modules: AC Module (Association Clustering Module), NF Module (Neighborhood Formation Module), and RC Module (Recommendation Module).

The AC module uses the ARHP algorithm to find the user association clusters. User association clusters capture the affinities among users and form potential and reliable user neighborhoods. Based on the ratings matrix and the user clusters, the NF module uses an item-to-item approach to find the relationship among items for each cluster. The RC module first produces a set of candidate items from each cluster based on the item relationships and the ratings history of the active user, and then provide a top-N recommendation list by integrating those candidate sets based on the similarities between the active user and each cluster.

2.1   Association Clustering Module

In the AC module, we use the ARHP algorithm proposed by Han et al. [13] to cluster similar users based on the ratings matrix. ARHP first constructs a weighted hypergraph representing the relations among different users. A hypergraph $H = (V, E)$ consists of a set of vertices V representing the users and a set of hyperedges E representing related users. The hyperedges are determined by using the association rules algorithm [12]. The frequent itemsets that satisfy a minimum support become the candidate hyperedges. The weight of each candidate hyperedge $e \in E$ is computed by averaging the confidence of the underlying strong association rules.

$$weight(e) = \frac{\sum_{l \in L_e} conf(l)}{|L_e|}, \quad conf(l) \geq min\_conf \tag{1}$$

Where L_e is the set of all possible strong association rules with respect to the vertices in hyperedge e and $|L_e|$ is the number of L_e. The final hyperedges are selected by removing those that are subsets of other hyperedges. After creating a hypergraph, the hypergraph partitioning algorithm hMETIS [14] is then used to find the partitions of related users.

To be implemented in AC module, the input ratings matrix must be first converted into a Boolean format. We map the numerical ratings into two categories: *like* (1) and *dislike* (0) according to whether the rating of each item is greater than a predefined threshold μ (we let $\mu = 3$ in our case). The Boolean rating r_{jk}^b of user u_j for item i_k is defined as follows.

$$r_{jk}^b = \begin{cases} 1, & if \quad r_{jk} >= \mu \\ 0, & if \quad r_{jk} < \mu \\ \perp, & if \quad r_{jk} = \perp \end{cases} \tag{2}$$

Where the value r_{jk} stands for the initial rating of user u_j for item i_k. We then convert the Boolean ratings matrix into transactions where each user corresponds to an "item" and each item rated by users corresponds to a "transaction". The ARHP is then implemented based on the converted transaction datasets.

2.2 Neighborhood Formation Module

In NF module, we use an item-based approach [7] to compute the item similarity matrix. As the computation of similarities between each pair of items is over the whole users, the personalized information may be lost. One way to solve this problem is to first compute the neighborhood of each user and then applies item-based approach based on those clusters separately. However, this approach involves extensive computations and large amounts of storage, which make it technically infeasible. The motivation behind our model is to exploit the advantages of the item-based approach while maintaining a degree of personalization by utilizing the idea of shared neighborhoods. More specifically, instead of computing the item similarity over the whole users or build a similarity matrix for each user, we will only consider the similarity computations over the user clusters obtained from the AC module. Thus, for each user cluster C, there is an associated similarity matrix M^C which contains the similarity value m_{jk}^C standing for the similarity between two items i_j and i_k.

$$m_{jk}^C = \left(\sum_i \frac{r_{ij} \cdot r_{ik}}{\sqrt{\sum_i r_{ij}^2} \sqrt{\sum_i r_{ik}^2}} \right) \tag{3}$$

Where r_{ij} and r_{ik} are the ratings that item i_j and i_k have been given by user u_j, and $u_i \in C$. For each item i_j, we only store the similarities of the l most similar items to item i_j and zero out the rest 1. As stated in [7], there is a trade-off between performance and quality for choosing the value of l. A small value of l will lead to higher efficiency but lower quality. From the experimental evaluation by [7], a small value between 10 and 30 is suggested. In all of our experiments, l is set to 20.

2.3   Recommendation Module

RC module is an on-line process. As a user (active user) u_a interacts with the system, his ratings history is compared with each cluster profile to capture the similarities between them. The user-cluster similarity between u_a and cluster C_k can be computed as follows.

$$sim(u_a, C_k) = \sum_i \frac{r_{ai} \cdot r_i^{C_k}}{\sqrt{\sum_i r_{ai}^2} \sqrt{\sum_i (r_i^{C_k})^2}} \tag{4}$$

The computation is over all the items that have been rated by u_a. $r_i^{C_k}$, the average of user ratings for item i_i in C_k, can be defined as:

$$r_i^{C_k} = \frac{\sum_{u_j \in C_k} r_{ji}}{|C_k|} \tag{5}$$

To recommend a new item i_p for a user, we need to look at the items that have been purchased or rated by the user and find out whether the new item is within their l most similar neighbors. Only those rated items that have item i_p in their l most similar neighbors are taken into account. Therefore, for each unrated item i_p of user u_a, the recommendation score from each cluster C_k is then computed as:

$$score(i_p, C_k) = \sum_i r_{ai} \cdot m_{ip}^{C_k} \tag{6}$$

Where r_{ai} represents the rating of user u_a for item i_i and $m_{ip}^{C_k}$ is the similarity value between item i_i and i_p with respect to cluster C_k. Those items whose recommendation score satisfies a minimum recommendation score are selected as a candidate recommendation set representing the contribution from cluster C_k to item i_p.

We believe that each cluster should contribute to the computation of recommendation score for an item. The more similar a cluster is, the more contributive it should be. Therefore, the final recommendation score of item i_p is now computed based on its recommendation score in each cluster and the similarity between active user and that cluster.

$$score(i_p, u_a) = \sum_k sim(u_a, C_k) \cdot score(i_p, C_k) \tag{7}$$

Finally, all unrated items are sorted in non-increasing order with respective to the final score, and the first N items are selected as the Top-N recommended set.

3 Experimental Evaluation

3.1 Data Sets

We use the *movielens* dataset collected by the GroupLens Research at the University of Minnesota. It contains 100,000 ratings from 943 users for 1628 movies. Each user has rated at least 20 movies, and each movie has been rated at least once. The original data set was converted into a new user-movie matrix R that had 943 rows (i.e. 943 users) and 1682 columns (i.e. 1682 movies). We employ the 5-fold cross-validation approach. First, we randomly divide the dataset into five groups. Then we run five rounds of tests, each time choosing one group of data as test data and the other four groups as training data. The training set is used to generate the recommendation model. For each transaction in the test data, we randomly select 10 non-zero entries and delete the rest. Our recommender system is then evaluated by comparing the Top-N recommendations it makes, given the test data, with the set of deleted items.

3.2 Evaluation Metrics

We use *precision* and *recall*, two commonly used performance measures in the information retrieval community, to evaluate the quality of a recommendation. Precision is the fraction of recommended movies that the user really likes. Recall is the fraction of interesting movies that are recommended. More precisely,

$$precision = \frac{correctly\_recommende\,d\_movies}{total\_recommende\,d\_movies} \tag{8}$$

$$recall = \frac{correctly\_recommende\,d\_movies}{total\_movies\_liked\_by\_users} \tag{9}$$

However, there is always a trade-off between precision and recall. Increasing the number of recommended movies will reduce the precision and increase the recall. To balance both measures, we use another measure $F1$ metric that gives equal weight to precision and recall and is given as

$$F1 = \frac{2 \times recall \times precision}{recall + precision} \tag{10}$$

We compute each metric for each individual user and the overall average value for the test data is taken as measures of the quality of the recommendation.

3.3 Performance Results

We compare the ARHP scheme to the classic *k-means* scheme for providing good clusters for the item-based algorithms. Recall that, in the proposed recommender system, the item similarity matrix is computed based on the neighbors in the same cluster. To evaluate the sensitivity of different cluster sizes, we fix the recommendation number to 10 and perform an experiment with different cluster number of 3, 5, 10, 15 and 20. Table 1 shows the results for *precision, recall* and *F1*, for different cluster sizes created by ARHP and *k-means* schemes. All three measures improves as the number of clusters increases but they reach the maximum performance at $k = 10$ and any further increment makes no better or even worse results. However, the overall performance ARHP scheme is superior to that of *k-means* scheme.

Table 1. Comparison of our model with *k-means* approach for different values of k

k	The proposed hybrid model			k-means-based approach		
	Precision	Recall	F1	Precision	Recall	F1
3	0.409	0.114	0.178	0.396	0.102	0.162
5	0.410	0.115	0.179	0.405	0.105	0.167
10	0.420	0.120	0.186	0.411	0.110	0.173
15	0.415	0.114	0.178	0.407	0.108	0.171
20	0.409	0.111	0.174	0.405	0.104	0.166

Table 2. Comparison of our model with traditional item-based approach and user-based approach

N	The proposed hybrid model			Traditional item-based approach			Traditional user-based approach		
	Prec.	Recall	F1	Prec.	Recall	F1	Prec.	Recall	F1
5	0.460	0.064	0.112	0.390	0.044	0.079	0.409	0.048	0.086
10	0.420	0.120	0.186	0.368	0.081	0.133	0.376	0.083	0.135
15	0.393	0.158	0.225	0.351	0.115	0.173	0.348	0.110	0.167
20	0.375	0.193	0.255	0.336	0.145	0.202	0.333	0.141	0.198
30	0.342	0.255	0.292	0.309	0.198	0.241	0.304	0.185	0.230
40	0.317	0.305	0.311	0.289	0.247	0.266	0.287	0.231	0.256
50	0.304	0.355	0.327	0.276	0.284	0.280	0.271	0.267	0.269

We also compare the quality of the recommendations with the traditional item-based and user-based approaches (i.e., the cluster size = 1) for different recommendation numbers. We fix the cluster number to 10. Table 2 lists the comparisons of *precision, recall*, and *F1* between our model and the traditional approaches. As expected, when the number of recommendations increases, the *precision* drops smoothly but the *recall* improves gradually. In all cases, the recommendation quality of our model is much better than that of these two traditional approaches.

4 Discussion and Future Work

In this paper we have presented a hybrid model-based approach for the collaborative filtering problem which combines user clustering (based on association rule and hypergraph partitioning algorithms) with item-based CF algorithms. Our key idea is to provide a higher degree of personalization by performing neighborhood search in a highly related user subset of the whole ratings database. The experimental results show that our approach is superior to that of the *k-means*-based approach. Also the recommendation quality can be improved using the ARHP partitioning scheme.

Our empirical evaluation is based on the ratings database with explicit votes. In the near future, we plan to extend this work to other domains such as web pages in which data is often implicit and continuous. In particular, we need to develop a new CF algorithm that is able to deal with the viewing time of a web page. This can be done through the use of fuzzy logic. The idea borrowed from [15] is under investigation.

References

1. Beheshti Jamshid, Browsing through public access catalogs. Information Technology & Libraries, Vol. 11, No. 3, Library and Information Technology Association (1992) 220-228
2. Ji-Rong Wen, Jian-Yun Nie, and Hong-Jiang Zhang, Clustering user queries of a search engine. In Proceedings of Conference on World Wide Web, ACM Press (2001) 162-168
3. Daniel Billsus and Michael J. Pazzani, Learning collaborative information filters. In Proceedings of ICML, Morgan Kaufmann Publishers Inc. (1998) 46-53
4. Lyle H. Ungar and Dean P. Foster, Clustering methods for collaborative filtering. In Proceedings of Workshop on Recommendation Systems, AAAI Press (1998) 59-62
5. Bardul M. Sarwar, George Karypis, Joseph A. Konstan, and John T. Riedl, Analysis of recommendation algorithms for e-commerce. In Proceedings of ACM EC, ACM Press (2000) 158-167
6. Bardul M. Sarwar, George Karypis, Joseph A. Konstan, and John T. Riedl, Item-based collaborative filtering recommendation algorithms. In Proceedings International WWW Conference, ACM Press (2001) 285-295
7. Mukund Deshpande and George Karypis, Item-based top-N recommendation algorithms. ACM Transactions on Information Systems, Vol.22 No.1, ACM Press (2004) 143-177
8. Miyahara, K. and Pazzani, M., Collaborative Filtering with the Simple Bayesian Classifier. In Proceeding of Pacific Rim International Conference on Artificial Intelligence, Springer-Verlag (2000) 679-689
9. Mark O'Connor and Jon Herlocker, Clustering items for collaborative filtering. In Proceedings of Workshop on Recommendation Systems, AAAI Press (1999)
10. Bardul M. Sarwar, George Karypis, Joseph A. Konstan, and John T. Riedl, Application of Dimensionality Reduction in Recommender System -- A Case Study. In ACM Web Mining for E-Commerce Workshop, ACM Press (2000)
11. R. Agrawal, T. Imielinski and A. Swami, Mining Associations between Sets of Items in Large Databases. In Proceedings of the ACM-SIGMOD International Conference on Management of Data, ACM Press (1993) 207-216
12. R. Agrawal and R. Srikant, Fast algorithms for mining association rules. In Proceedings of the 20th VLDB, Morgan Kaufmann Publishers Inc.(1994) 487-499
13. Eui-Hong Han, George Karypis, Vipin Kumar, and Bamshad Mobasher, Clustering based on association rule hypergraphs. In Proceedings of SIGMOD Workshop on Rreseach Issues in Data Mining and Knowledge Discovery, Springer US (1997) 9-13
14. George Karypis and Vipin Kumar, Multilevel hypergrph partitioning: Application in VLSI domain. IEEE Transaction on VLSI Systems, Vol. 7, IEEE Computer Society (1999) 69-79
15. Stefano Aguzzoli, Paolo Avesani and Brunella Gerla, A logical framework for fuzzy collaborative filtering. In Proceedings of The 10th IEEE International Conference On Fuzzy Systems, IEEE Computer Society (2001) 1043-1046

Space-Limited Ranked Query Evaluation
Using Adaptive Pruning

Nicholas Lester[1], Alistair Moffat[2], William Webber[2], and Justin Zobel[1]

[1] School of Computer Science and Information Technology,
RMIT University, Victoria 3001, Australia
[2] Department of Computer Science and Software Engineering,
The University of Melbourne, Victoria 3010, Australia

Abstract. Evaluation of ranked queries on large text collections can be costly in terms of processing time and memory space. Dynamic pruning techniques allow both costs to be reduced, at the potential risk of decreased retrieval effectiveness. In this paper we describe an improved query pruning mechanism that offers a more resilient tradeoff between query evaluation costs and retrieval effectiveness than do previous pruning approaches.

1 Introduction

Ranked query evaluation against a document collection requires the computation of a *similarity score* for each document in the collection, and then the presentation of the r highest-scoring documents, for some user-specified value r. For an introduction to the area, see Witten et al. [1999].

The most efficient way to evaluate such similarity formulations is to use a pre-computed *inverted index* that stores, for each term that appears in the collection, the identifiers of the documents containing it. The *pointers* in the *postings list* for a term also include any ancillary information that is required, such as the frequency of the term in the document. *Term-ordered* query evaluation strategies take one term at a time, and, for every document containing that term, incorporate the per-document contribution of the term into the document's *accumulator*, a temporary variable created during evaluation of a query. However, in typical applications much of this computation is ultimately wasted, as is a great deal of memory. For example, in web searching tasks $r = 10$ answer documents are usually required, but a full set of accumulators on a collection of $N = 25,000,000$ documents requires perhaps 100 MB, a non-trivial amount of space.

Query *pruning* heuristics seek to bypass some or all of the unnecessary computation, by eliminating low-scoring documents from answer contention at a relatively early stage in the process. In this paper we examine query pruning heuristics that have been proposed in previous literature, and show that, as the size of the document collection grows, they have flaws that render them ineffective in practice. We then propose a new *adaptive pruning* mechanism that avoids those failings. A target number of accumulators is chosen beforehand; as each list is processed, existing low-scoring accumulators are discarded and, depending on estimates of available space that are computed adaptively, new accumulators can be added. The new mechanism allows relatively tight

M. Kitsuregawa et al. (Eds.): WISE 2005, LNCS 3806, pp. 470–477, 2005.

control over the size of the set of accumulators, and at the same time provides a high level of agreement between the pruned ranking and the equivalent unrestricted ranking. The actual number of accumulators can be reduced to less than 1% of the number of documents without appreciable loss of effectiveness.

2 The Quit and Continue Strategies

Using a *document-sorted* index, the natural strategy for ranked query evaluation is to process the lists corresponding to the query terms in turn, from shortest (describing the rarest term) to longest (describing the commonest). The similarity of a given document is the sum of the contributions made by each of the query terms that occur in the document. Each term potentially contributes a partial similarity to the weight of each document in the collection; hence, because the postings lists are processed in term order rather than document order, the partial similarities need to be stored in some temporary form as the computation proceeds. As each postings list is processed, the accumulator A_d is updated for each document d that contains the term. Once all lists are processed, the accumulators may be normalized by the document length. Then the top r values are extracted for presentation to the user.

For a query involving a common term, a large proportion of the indexed documents could be expected to end up with a non-zero accumulator, meaning that at face value the most appropriate way to store them is in an array indexed by document number d. However, for large collections the processing of such an array is a severe bottleneck, as its sheer size acts as an impediment to the simultaneous evaluation of multiple queries. It is therefore attractive to limit the number of accumulators in some way using a query pruning mechanism.

Probably the best-documented of the previous schemes are the *quit* and *continue* methods of Moffat and Zobel [1996]. In the *quit* strategy, a target number L of accumulators is chosen. Initially the set A of accumulators is empty. Each postings list I_t is processed in turn; for each document $d \in I_t$, if A_d is present in the set A it is updated, otherwise a new accumulator A_d is created. At the end of each list, the *quit* strategy checks whether the number of accumulators created so far exceeds L; if so, processing is terminated. We call this the *full* form of *quit*, as each list is completely processed.

A shortcoming of *quit-full* is that the target L may be dramatically exceeded by the time the end of a list is reached. We refer to this as *bursting* the set of accumulators. For example suppose that L is 10,000, the first list contains 1,000 entries, and the second one contains 1,000,000 entries – entirely plausible numbers in the context of web queries on web data. Then the number of accumulators created will be around 1,000,000. An alternative is the *part* form of *quit*, where the number of accumulators is checked after every posting. The accumulator target will be complied with in a strong sense, but documents with higher ordinal identifiers are much less likely to be granted an accumulator, and are thus much less likely to be returned as the answer to a query.

A greater problem is that with *quit* the more common terms will in many cases not contribute to the accumulators at all, leading to substantial reduction in effectiveness for smaller accumulator targets. This issue is addressed by the *continue* strategy. Once the target L is reached, no more accumulators can be created, but processing of postings lists continues, so that existing accumulators are updated. With *continue*, much smaller targets give reasonable effectiveness; Moffat and Zobel [1996] report that *continue-full* with L set to around 1%–5% of the total number of indexed documents gives retrieval effectiveness (measured in any of the usual ways) not worse than $L = \infty$.

We report experiments with *continue-full* in this paper, showing, in contrast, that it is rather less successful. The difference in outcomes arises because some of the conditions assumed in the earlier work no longer apply. In particular, the queries used by Moffat and Zobel had dozens of terms (the work was completed in a universe in which web search engines did not exist, document collections were maintained by editors, and users had university degrees), which typically had a relatively broad mix of f_t values, meaning that the likelihood of significant bursting was low.

The *continue* and *quit* strategies were not the first approaches used for pruning ranked query evaluation. Earlier methods include those of Smeaton and van Rijsbergen [1981], Buckley and Lewit [1985], Harman and Candela [1990], and Wong and Lee [1993]; however, these approaches are not likely to be effective in the context of current collections and system architectures. Other ranked query evaluation strategies are based on *frequency-sorted* indexes [Persin et al., 1996] and *impact-sorted* indexes [Anh et al., 2001]. These representations allow fast ranked querying, but Boolean querying becomes harder to support. Inclusion of new documents is also complex. Hence, there remain contexts in which it is appropriate to maintain postings lists in document-sorted order. It is these environments that we assume in this paper.

3   A New Approach: Adaptive Pruning

The objectives of any strategy for pruning the memory usage or computation of query evaluation are threefold: it should treat all documents in the collection equitably; it should be resistant to the "bursting" effect that was noted above; and at any given point in time it should allocate accumulators to the documents that are most likely to feature in the final ranking. Note, however, that compromise is necessary, since any scheme that processes whole postings lists before changing state risks bursting, and any scheme that makes significant state changes part way through a list cannot treat all documents equitably. The third requirement is also interesting. It suggests that a pruning mechanism must be willing to rescind as well as offer accumulators to documents.

In our proposed strategy, postings lists are again processed in decreasing order of importance, as assessed by the term weight component of the similarity heuristic. But at the commencement of processing of the list I_t for term t, a threshold value v_t is estimated, as a lower limit on an accumulator contribution that needs to be exceeded before any occurrence of t is permitted to initialize an accumulator.

When a pointer and accumulator coincide, a new accumulator score is computed, by applying the update generated by that pointer. But no accumulator is retained in A unless its value exceeds the current value of v_t, the numeric contribution that arises from (for this term) a corresponding within-document frequency hurdle of h_t. Thus current accumulators that do not exceed the hurdle requirement are removed from A in the merge; new accumulators are created only if they have strong support indicated by $f_{d,t} \geq h_t$; and, even when a pointer updates a current accumulator, the revised value is

Algorithm 1. Processing ranked queries

Input: a set of query terms t, their document frequencies f_t, their collection frequencies F_t, their postings lists I_t, and an accumulator limit L.

1: assign $A \leftarrow \{\}$
2: **for** each term t, in increasing order of F_t **do**
3:     use L, $|A|$, F_t, and the previous threshold v_t to establish an new threshold v_t
4:     **for** each document d in $A \cup I_t$ **do**
5:       **if** $d \in I_t$ **then**
6:         calculate a contribution c using F_t and $f_{d,t}$
7:       **else**
8:         assign $c \leftarrow 0$
9:       **if** $d \in A$ **then**
10:         assign $c \leftarrow A_d + c$
11:       **if** $c \geq v_t$ **then**
12:         assign $A_d \leftarrow c$ and $A \leftarrow A \cup \{A_d\}$
13:       **else if** $d \in A$ **then**
14:         assign $A \leftarrow A - \{A_d\}$
15:       pause periodically to reevaluate v_t, tracking the current size of A, and the rate at which it has been changing relative to the target rate of change

Output: a set of approximately L accumulator values, not yet normalized by document length

---

allowed to stay as a candidate only if it exceeds the current v_t. That is, the combination of v_t (as a similarity score) and h_t (as a corresponding $f_{d,t}$ threshold) act as a "scraper", that removes low-value candidates from A and replaces them by any new high-valued accumulators represented by the current list.

Algorithm 1 summarizes this process. The set of accumulators A and I_t are both lists sorted by document number, and are jointly processed in a merge-like operation.

The critical component is that of setting, for each term's list I_t, a minimum value h_t on $f_{d,t}$ scores that are to be allowed to create an accumulator. The threshold h_t should be set so that it changes as little as possible during the processing of I_t (the equity principle); and so that at the end of I_t, the number of accumulators is reasonably close to target L (the principle of using the available accumulators wisely). Setting h_t (and hence v_t, which is directly related to h_t) too low means that too many new accumulators will get created from term t, and not enough old ones get reclaimed, making the total number of accumulators grow beyond L. On the other hand, setting h_t too high means that plausible candidates from I_t get denied, and equally plausible candidates from A get unnecessarily discarded, resulting in a pool of fewer than L candidates being made available to the final ranking process. Another way of looking at v_t is that as far as possible it should be set at the beginning of the processing of I_t to a value that would be equal, were no pruning at all taking place, to the Lth largest of a complete set of accumulators at the end of processing I_t.

At the beginning of processing, if a term cannot possibly cause the accumulator limit to be exceeded because $|A| + f_t \leq L$, then h_t is set to one, and every document in I_t without an accumulator is allocated one.

Once the accumulator target is under threat by a term for which $|A| + f_t > L$ (potentially even the first query term, if $f_t > L$), a larger h_t is derived. If the entries

---

Algorithm 2. Adaptively estimate the thresholding parameter for a term

---

Inputs: a set of accumulators A, a term t, and an accumulator target L

1: assign $startA \leftarrow |A|$
2: assign $p \leftarrow f_t/L$
3: **if** this is the first term that risks exceeding L accumulators **then**
4:      assign $h_t \leftarrow \max\{f_{d,t} \mid d \in \text{the first } p \text{ pointers in } I_t\}$
5: **else**
6:      assign h_t to be the $f_{d,t}$ frequency corresponding to the previous value of v_t
7: assign $s \leftarrow h_t/2$
8: **while** pointers remain in I_t **do**
9:      process pointers through until the pth as described in Algorithm 1, using h_t as a term frequency threshold, and the corresponding v_t as an accumulator value threshold
10:     assign $predict \leftarrow |A| + (f_t - p) \times (|A| - startA)/p$
11:     **if** $predict > \theta L$ **then**
12:         assign $h_t \leftarrow h_t + s$ and recalculate v_t
13:     **else if** $predict < L/\theta$ **then**
14:         assign $h_t \leftarrow h_t - s$ and recalculate v_t
15:     assign $p \leftarrow 2p + 1$
16:     assign $s \leftarrow (s + 1)/2$

---

in each list I_t were homogeneous, a sampling approach could be used to select h_t, and that value could be used for the whole list. Unfortunately, postings lists are rarely homogeneous – term usage can change dramatically from one end of a collection to another, and factors such as document length can also have a significant bearing.

Algorithm 2 shows an adaptive estimation process that addresses these problems. The philosophy is that it is acceptable to adjust h_t as each list is being processed, provided that the bulk of each list is handled using values that do not differ too much; and that, conversely, if big shifts in h_t become necessary, they should be made in such a way that as few as possible of the list's pointers are treated unfairly. The objective is to end the processing of this term with L accumulators. However it is impossible to hit such a target exactly, so a tolerance θ is allowed, and any arrangement in which $L/\theta \leq |A| \leq \theta L$ is tolerable. A typical value might be $\theta = 1.2$.

In Algorithm 2 the first step is to record, using variable *startA*, the number of accumulators at the commencement of processing this term. After some number p of the f_t pointers in I_t have been processed, the change in the size of the set A is clearly $|A| - startA$. Extrapolating forwards over the remaining $f_t - p$ pointers in I_t allows calculation of a quantity *predict*, the number of accumulators expected if the remainder of the list I_t is homogeneous with respect to the part already processed. If *predict* is higher than θL, it is time to increase h_t and v_t so as to reduce the rate at which A is growing; and, if *predict* is less than L/θ, then h_t and v_t should be decreased.

Increases and decreases to h_t are by an amount s, which is initially large relative to h_t, but halves at each evaluation until it reaches one. At the same time, the intervals p over which h_t is held constant are doubled after each reevaluation. The initial interval p is set to f_t/L, namely, the interval over which (if I_t were homogeneous) one accumulator might expect to have been identified. Taking h_t to be the maximum $f_{d,t}$ identified in the first p pointers is thus a plausible initial estimate.

4   Evaluation Methodology

The standard method for evaluating a retrieval mechanism is via a controlled text collection, a set of queries, and a set of partial or full relevance judgments that indicate which of the documents are relevant to which query. For example the NIST TREC project has created several such resources; see trec.nist.gov. In addition, a range of effectiveness metrics have been defined, with mean average precision (MAP) perhaps the most widely used [Buckley and Voorhees, 2000]. In the experiments here we make use of the 426 GB TREC GOV2 collection, which contains approximately 25 million web documents; and the short queries associated with query topics 701–750. In terms of scale, our experimentation is thus realistic of whole-of-web searching using a document distributed retrieval system on a cluster of 100 computers [Barroso et al., 2003].

Another interesting question that arises is how to count accumulators, and what type of averaging is appropriate over a query stream. The obvious possibilities would be to take the absolute maximum requirement over the stream; or to take the average of the per-query maximums. But both of these have drawbacks, and do not accurately reflect what it is that we wish to quantify, namely, the amount of memory in a parallel query handling system that is required on average by each query thread. Instead, we measure the *time-averaged accumulator requirement* over the query stream, by tracking the number of active accumulators throughout the processing, and disregarding query boundaries. Queries that have a high accumulator load for an extended period are then accurately counted, since they contribute through more of the time intervals.

5   Experiments

Table 1 shows the result of applying the two variants of the *continue* strategy to web-scale data using short web-like queries, and compares their performance to the adaptive

Table 1. Retrieval effectiveness scores, using TREC topics 701–750 (short queries) the GOV2 collection, retrieval depth $r = 1,000$, and a language model with Dirichlet smoothing [Zhai and Lafferty, 2004]. Numbers reported are mean average precision (MAP), and the time-averaged number of accumulators required to process the query stream. A full evaluation of each query leads to a MAP of 0.240.

Target ('000)	continue-part		continue-full		adaptive pruning	
	Actual ('000)	MAP	Actual ('000)	MAP	Actual ('000)	MAP
1	1.0	0.045	237.9	0.235	1.5	0.150
2	2.0	0.065	238.9	0.235	3.2	0.179
4	4.0	0.093	252.4	0.235	5.8	0.202
10	10.0	0.126	260.3	0.235	13.0	0.215
20	19.9	0.142	372.1	0.235	26.5	0.228
40	39.8	0.141	478.7	0.235	47.7	0.233
100	98.5	0.170	533.7	0.235	121.1	0.237
200	194.1	0.194	599.9	0.237	214.7	0.239
400	373.8	0.212	1,590.6	0.239	395.5	0.240
1,000	845.3	0.221	2,862.0	0.240	900.0	0.240

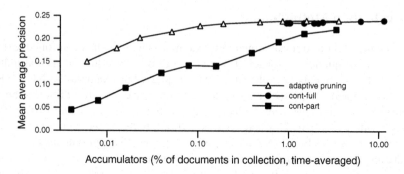

Fig. 1. Efficiency-effectiveness tradeoffs in different pruning techniques. The new adaptive pruning approach provides a clearly superior combination of high retrieval effectiveness with accurate management of memory use.

pruning regime described in Section 3. The control knob in these experiments is the target number of accumulators, shown in the first column. The next three pairs of columns show respectively the *continue-part* mechanism, the *continue-full* mechanism, and the new method. The time-averaged number of accumulators used for the *continue-part* combination is always within the target (and less than the target is some cases because some queries cannot support even 20,000 accumulators), so in that sense *part* is a useful technique. But the loss of retrieval effectiveness compared to full evaluation is acute. We also experimented with the two *quit* versions, and confirmed that they are faster, but yielded even worse effectiveness scores for the same level of accumulator usage.

The next pair of columns demonstrate why the retrieval is so bad with *part* – the actual number of accumulators required just to equitably complete the processing of the boundary term is enormously bigger than the accumulator target. That is, in the *part* strategy only a small fraction of the boundary term gets processed before the target is reached, and documents early in the collection are greatly favored. On the other hand, fully processing the boundary term can give good retrieval effectiveness – especially with the *continue* strategy – but causes the accumulator set to burst.

The final pair of columns show the new method. In all cases the time-averaged accumulator requirement is close to the target value L. More interesting is the retrieval performance – with as few as 100,000 accumulators, just 0.4% of the size of the collection, very good MAP results are obtained.

Figure 1 shows the same data graphically, but with average memory space presented as a ratio of accumulators to documents in the collection. The two variants of the *continue* approach provide bookends to performance, with the *full* version requiring very large numbers of accumulators, irrespective of the target L, but providing high effectiveness; and the *part* version tightly bounding the number of accumulators, but sacrificing retrieval effectiveness as measured by MAP.

6   Conclusions

The adaptive pruning method presented here combines the strengths of the two *continue* approaches and eliminates their weaknesses, in that the number of accumulators can be reasonably controlled to a specified target, and for a given accumulator consumption, retrieval effectiveness is excellent. Adaptive query pruning is a useful technique that allows memory usage to be tightly controlled, even when carrying out search operations on web-scale document collections.

Acknowledgment. This work was supported by the Australian Research Council.

References

V. N. Anh, O. de Kretser, and A. Moffat. Vector-space ranking with effective early termination. In W. B. Croft, D. J. Harper, D. H. Kraft, and J. Zobel, editors, *Proc. 24th Annual International ACM SIGIR Conference on Research and Development in Information Retrieval*, pages 35–42, New Orleans, LA, Sept. 2001. ACM Press, New York.

L. A. Barroso, J. Dean, and U. Hölzle. Web search for a planet: The Google cluster architecture. *IEEE Micro*, 23(2):22–28, Mar. 2003.

C. Buckley and A. F. Lewit. Optimization of inverted vector searches. In *Proc. 8th Annual International ACM SIGIR Conference on Research and Development in Information Retrieval*, pages 97–110, Montreal, Canada, June 1985. ACM Press, New York.

C. Buckley and E. M. Voorhees. Evaluating evaluation measure stability. In N. J. Belkin, P. Ingwersen, and M.-K. Leong, editors, *Proc. 23rd Annual International ACM SIGIR Conference on Research and Development in Information Retrieval*, pages 33–40, Athens, Greece, Sept. 2000. ACM Press, New York.

D. K. Harman and G. Candela. Retrieving records from a gigabyte of text on a minicomputer using statistical ranking. *Journal of the American Society for Information Science*, 41(8): 581–589, Aug. 1990.

A. Moffat and J. Zobel. Self-indexing inverted files for fast text retrieval. *ACM Transactions on Information Systems*, 14(4):349–379, Oct. 1996.

M. Persin, J. Zobel, and R. Sacks-Davis. Filtered document retrieval with frequency-sorted indexes. *Journal of the American Society for Information Science*, 47(10):749–764, Oct. 1996.

A. Smeaton and C. J. van Rijsbergen. The nearest neighbour problem in information retrieval. In C. J. Crouch, editor, *Proc. 4th Annual International ACM SIGIR Conference on Research and Development in Information Retrieval*, pages 83–87, Oakland, California, May 1981. ACM Press, New York.

I. H. Witten, A. Moffat, and T. C. Bell. *Managing Gigabytes: Compressing and Indexing Documents and Images*. Morgan Kaufmann, San Francisco, second edition, 1999.

W. Y. P. Wong and D. K. Lee. Implementations of partial document ranking using inverted files. *Information Processing & Management*, 29(5):647–669, Sept. 1993.

C. Zhai and J. Lafferty. A study of smoothing methods for language models applied to information retrieval. *ACM Transactions on Information Systems*, 22(2):179–214, Apr. 2004.

Automated Retraining Methods for Document Classification and Their Parameter Tuning

Stefan Siersdorfer and Gerhard Weikum

Max-Planck-Institute for Computer Science, Germany
{stesi, weikum}@mpi-sb.mpg.de

Abstract. This paper addresses the problem of semi-supervised classification on document collections using retraining (also called self-training). A possible application is focused Web crawling which may start with very few, manually selected, training documents but can be enhanced by automatically adding initially unlabeled, positively classified Web pages for retraining. Such an approach is by itself not robust and faces tuning problems regarding parameters like the number of selected documents, the number of retraining iterations, and the ratio of positive and negative classified samples used for retraining. The paper develops methods for automatically tuning these parameters, based on predicting the leave-one-out error for a re-trained classifier and avoiding that the classifier is diluted by selecting too many or weak documents for retraining. Our experiments with three different datasets confirm the practical viability of the approach.

1 Introduction

Automatic document classification is useful for a wide range of applications such as organizing web, intranet, or portal pages into topic directories, filtering news feeds or mail, focused crawling on the web or in intranets, and many more. In some applications, the availability of good training data for the classifier is the key bottleneck. As an example, consider a personalized or community information tool that uses thematically focused crawling [10, 29] to build and maintain a directory or index for browsing, search, or recommendations.

To overcome the training bottleneck, semi-supervised learning techniques could be applied. In our given setting, the classifier could be bootstrapped by training it with whatever explicitly class-labeled training data are available and used for making decisions about the classes of previously unseen, unlabeled test documents retrieved by the crawler. These decisions would have a certain degree of uncertainty, depending on the classifier's statistical learning model. However, some of the test documents are usually accepted for their corresponding classes with high statistical confidence, and these could then be selected for retraining the classifier, now with considerably more training documents. Obviously, this simple idea does not provide a robust solution, for the automatically selected, additional training data may also increase the classifier's uncertainty and may eventually lead to an unintended topic drift. In this paper we address the issue of how to make such a semi-supervised classifier robust and practically viable.

There are various approaches, like Transductive SVM, EM-iterated Bayesian Classifiers, or Co-Training [30, 23, 7], that successfully use information from ini-

M. Kitsuregawa et al. (Eds.): WISE 2005, LNCS 3806, pp. 478–486, 2005.

tially *unlabeled* documents to improve classification results. However these methods come with parameters, which have a crucial influence on the quality of the classification results and need to be *tuned manually* on a per application basis.

To this end we propose a retraining algorithm that performs *automatic parameter tuning*. When our method considers adding a batch of initially unlabeled documents to the training set, it predicts the resulting improvement (or degeneration) of the classifier's accuracy by performing a leave-one-out validation. The training set is extended, by selecting the unlabeled documents with highest classification confidence and then retraining the classifier, only as long as the predictor expects an improvement. To avoid extensive leave-one-out validations, which are resource-intensive, the predictor invokes the validation merely after a certain number of iterations and rather uses a spline interpolation technique for less expensive estimation.

A particularly subtle but important point in this procedure is that one should often select different numbers of positive and negative samples for retraining, depending on the ratio in the underlying corpus. In the case of a focused Web crawler, usually a much larger fraction of negative (i.e., thematically uninteresting) documents is seen and may lead to a wrong classifier bias unless such corrective steps are taken.

The novel contributions of this paper are the following:

1. We develop a robust, practically viable procedure for automated retraining of classifiers with careful selection of initially unlabeled documents.
2. We perform comprehensive experiments that evaluate our retraining procedure against state-of-the-art semi-supervised classification methods like EM-iterated Bayesian classifiers, Transductive SVMs, and Spectral Graph Transduction.

Related Work. There is a considerable prior of work on classification using unlabeled data (also called semi-supervised learning), see [26] for an overview. Naive Retraining where new documents with highest classification confidence are iteratively added to the training set, is, e.g., described in [10]; but these methods perform often worse than the underlying base learning method. A more enhanced EM (Expectation Maximization)-based variant for Bayesian Classifiers is proposed in [23] and applied to text classification. For Transductive SVM [15, 30] and Semi-Supervised SVM [5] unlabeled samples are taken into account (opposite to standard SVM) in a modified optimization problem (standard SVM cannot use unlabeled samples at all). Co-training [7] splits the feature space into conditionally independent dimensions and performs retraining on the corresponding classifiers. Recent graph-based semi-supervised learning algorithms work by formulating the assumption that nearby points, and points in the same structure should have similar labels [18, 31, 16]. In [6] semi-supervised learning is combined with ensemble classification methods. An approach for the case that only positive (and no negative) training data plus unlabeled data are available is described in [20]. In [3] semi-supervised learning is used for text summarization; in [32] a retraining method with user feedback as a stopping criterion is used for image retrieval. However, to our knowledge, none of these methods deals with the problem of automatically tuning their parameters.

The issue of asymmetric distribution of documents among different classes is addressed, e.g., in [19, 8, 13], and the problem of automated parameter tuning has been considered in the field of machine learning, e.g., in [17], but, to our knowledge, not in the context of retraining.

2   Technical Basics

Classifying text documents into thematic categories usually follows a supervised learning paradigm and is based on training documents that need to be provided for each topic. Both training documents and test documents, which are later given to the classifier, are represented as multidimensional feature vectors. In the prevalent bag-of-words model the features are derived from word occurrence frequencies, e.g. based on tf*idf feature weights [4, 22]. Often feature selection algorithms are applied to reduce the dimensionality of the feature space and eliminate "noisy", non-characteristic features, based on information-theoretic measures for feature ordering (e.g., relative entropy or information gain).

Feature vectors of topic labeled text documents (e.g., capturing $tf \cdot idf$ weights of terms) are used to train a classification model for each topic, using probabilistic (e.g., Naive Bayes) or discriminative models (e.g., SVM). Linear support vector machines (SVMs) construct a hyperplane $w \cdot x + b = 0$ that separates the set of positive training examples from a set of negative examples with maximum margin δ. This training requires solving a quadratic optimization problem whose empirical performance is somewhere between quadratic and cubic in the number of training documents [9]. For a new, previously unseen, (test) document d the SVM merely needs to test whether the document lies on the "positive" side or the "negative" side of the separating hyperplane. The decision simply requires computing a scalar product of the vectors w and d. SVMs have been shown to perform very well for text classification (see, e.g., [12, 14]).

Unlike the inductive SVM setting, for Transductive SVM (TSVM) [15, 30], a hyperplane is computed that separates *both* taining and (unlabeled) test data with maximum margin.

The most widely used technique for empirically estimating the classifier quality is *cross-validation* [22] on a set of independent data samples with known topic memberships (aka. class labels). The partitioning is systematically varied by dividing the overall data into k groups and investigating each of the k choices for using one group as test data and the other $k - 1$ groups for training; the empirical results are finally averaged over all choices. An important variation is *leave-one-out validation* [22]. Here the n documents of a data collection are divided by the ratio $(n - 1) : 1$. Both methods are also popular for predicting a classifier's quality. Leave-one-out prediction is more accurate than prediction based on cross-validation but requires training the classifier n times, unless special properties of the classifier's underlying model could be exploited.

In this paper we consider only binary classifiers that make a decision for a single topic, based on positive and negative training examples.

3   Retraining and Its Parameter Tuning

3.1   A Simple Base Algorithm

Consider a training set T and a set of unlabeled data U. We can perform retraining by iteratively building a classifier C on T, classifying the documents in U and adding the documents with the highest classification confidence, p positively and n negatively classified documents in one iteration. Classification confidence could be estimated, e.g., by the distance from the separating hyperplane in the SVM case or by the probability of accepting a document for a class.

This algorithm provides us with a tradeoff. On one hand, a higher number of training examples could potentially improve the classification accuracy; on the other hand, there are potentially incorrectly labeled documents among the automatically labeled training docs U_{pos} and U_{neg}, which can dilute the training set. The algorithm thus has two important tuning parameters:

1. the number m of iterations
2. the ratio p/n between new positively classified and negatively classified docs used for retraining

In the following we show how we can automatically tune these parameters. Note that the total number of selected documents for each retraining step, $r := p + n$ could be considered as an additional tuning parameter. However, we can simply choose it sufficiently small to be on the conservative side.

3.2   Tuning the Number of Iterations

Because of the tradeoffs mentioned above, a higher number of iterations do not necessarily imply a lower error. Our idea now is to approximate this error curve on the test set U by an estimated error curve.

For a retraining step we can build an error estimator by performing leave-one-out validation of the current classifier C on the original training set T_0, i.e., the part of the training set that consists of the manually labeled documents (which are correct with perfect confidence).

For a set of sample estimates

$$\{(i_0, estError(i_0)), \ldots, (i_l, estError(i_l))\}, \tag{1}$$

where the i_j values are the iteration numbers and $estError(i_j)$ is the estimated error, we can now approximate the overall error curve by fitting the sample estimates.

There are various approaches to this curve fitting. In our experiments we obtained good performance using cubic splines. Cubic splines are used in many areas, e.g., bio medicine, signal processing, and computer graphics [11, 24, 27]. In our experiments we also tested other approaches like linear splines, and error estimation by the less time consuming k-fold-cross-validation instead of leave-one-out.

Having approximated the error estimation curve $S(x)$, we choose the retraining classifier C in the iteration i with minimum $S(i)$. Choosing the number of supporting points for the fitting is an efficiency issue. The more supporting points the better the approximation but the higher the overall cost for computing the estimator values.

The classifier can be optimized in the same way for other quality measures like the F-measure (the harmonic mean of precision and recall).

3.3 Tuning the Ratio of Positive and Negative Samples

For an effective classification the training set should be an appropriate representation of the test set. For binary classification, it is especially helpful if the ratio between positive and negative documents is approximately the same for the test and the training set. For example, Bayesian classifiers take the prior class probabilities explicitly into account. For SVM a badly proportionalized training set can also lead to a disadvantageous bias [8]. The assumption of having a training set with the same ratio ratio of positive and negative documents as a test set is not at all self-guaranteed or easy to satisfy in practice. Typically a human, collecting training documents, would rather choose roughly the same number of documents for each class, even if there are significant (but a priori unknown) differences in the real world.

The idea is to overcome this problem by adjusting the training set such that it better represents the test set. To do so, in each iteration of our retraining algorithm we approximate the ratio between positive and negative documents by applying the current classifier to the set of initially unlabeled data U_0 (test data). Among a small number r of new retraining documents we choose the number of positive and negative documents, n and p, such that the difference between the overall ratio of positive and negative training docs and the estimated ratio on the unlabeled data is minimized.

More formally let t_{pos} be the number of positive, t_{neg} be the number of negative training documents in the current iteration, v_{pos} be the number of unlabeled documents classified as positive by the current classifier C, and v_{neg} be the number of documents classified as negative. Then we choose the number of *newly* added positive and negative documents for retraining, p and n, such that the ratio $(t_{pos} + p) : (t_{neg} + n)$ between the overall number of positive and negative training documents provides the best approximation for the ratio $v_{pos} : v_{neg}$ of positive and negative test documents estimated by the current classifier:

$$p = \arg \min_{x \in \{0,...,r\}} \left| \frac{t_{pos} + x}{t_{neg} + r - x} - \frac{v_{pos}}{v_{neg}} \right| \qquad (2)$$

and

$$n = r - p \qquad (3)$$

3.4 The Enhanced Retraining Algorithm

With the parameter tuning methods described above, our retraining algorithm now works as follows: We retrain as long as documents for retraining are available. In each retraining iteration we add a small number r of documents to the

```
Input: training set T = T_0; set of unlabeled Data U = U_0; stepsize

set of classifiers C-Set = empty
set of supporting points Support-Set = empty
iteration number i = 0;
while (U is not empty) do
    build classifier C on T; add (i,C) to C-Set
    estimate p and n \\as described above; classify U
    U_pos := top-p positively classified docs
    U_neg := top-n negatively classified docs
    T = T + U_pos + U_neg ; U = U - U_pos - U_neg
    if (i mod stepsize = 0)
        estimate error estError of C by leave-one-out on T_0
        add (i,estError) to Support-Set
    i++


compute interpolating curve S on Support-Set \\as described above
choose j which minimizes S(i)
return Classifier c from C-Set with iteration number = j
```

Fig. 1. Enhanced Retraining Algorithm

training set, determining the ratio between new positive and negative training documents as described in Section 3.3. Every *stepsize* iterations we compute and save an error estimator. We apply curve fitting to the estimated error, and choose the classifier corresponding to the minimum estimated error (see Section 3.2.).

The pseudo code in Figure 1 summarizes our modified retraining algorithm.

4 Experiments

Setup. We performed a series of experiments with real-life data from the following sources: 1) The Newsgroups collection at [1] with 17,847 postings collected from 20 Usenet newsgroups such as 'rec.autos', 'sci.space', etc. 2) The Reuters collection [21] with 21,578 newswire articles; 12,904 of them are subdivided into categories ('earn', 'grain', 'trade', etc.). 3) The Internet Movie Database (IMDB) at [2] with short movie descriptions from 20 topics according to particular movie genres ('drama', 'horror' etc.). Only 34,681 movies were considered that have a unique genre.

For every data collection we considered each class with at least 300 documents. We obtained 20 classes for Newsgroups, 8 for Reuters and 9 for IMDB. For each class we randomly chose 100 documents as positive training examples and 100 negative examples from all other classes. For testing we considered two cases: 1) the symmetric case: we chose equal numbers of positive and negative test documents for each class (200 per class), and 2) the asymmetric case: we chose the number of positive and negative test documents in a ratio of 1 : 6 (i.e., 200:1200).

In all experiments, the standard bag-of-words model [4] (using term frequencies to build L1-normalized feature vectors, stemming with the algorithm of Porter [25], and deletion of stopwords) was used for document representation. We used binary classifiers so as to recognize documents from one specific topic against all other topics; this setup was repeated for every topic.

For each data collection we computed the macro-averaged error (i.e., the average ratio of incorrectly classified documents to the number of test documents) along with the 95 percent confidence interval and the macro-averaged F1 value (the harmonic mean of precision and recall).

Results. We compared the following classification methods:

1. Standard linear SVM (**SVM**)
2. Standard linear TSVM. Here the fraction f of unlabeled examples to be classified into the positive class is a selectable parameter. As default setting we used the ratio between the positive and the negative examples in the training data. (**TSVM**)
3. Linear TSVM where the ratio f between positive and negative test documents was set according to the SVM classification (Method 1) on the test documents. (**TSVM+est**)
4. The augmented EM-iterated Bayesian classifier with weighting of the unlabeled data as described in [23]. Here we determined the weighting parameter λ by leave-one-out validation (considering the values between 0 and 1 with a step width of 0.2), choosing the λ with the lowest estimated error. (**EM-Bayes**)
5. Spectral Graph Transduction as described in [16] (**SGT**)
6. Our retraining approach with linear SVM (Method 1) as the underlying base classifier and 10 new retraining documents per iteration and
   (a) error/F1 prediction by leave-one-out estimation invoked after every 10 iterations and cubic spline interpolation (**RetCsplL1o**)
   (b) error/F1 prediction by leave-one-out estimation invoked after every 10 iterations, linear spline interpolation (**RetLsplL1o**)

Method	Newsg. avg(error)	IMDB avg(error)	Reuters avg(error)	Newsg. avg(F1)	IMDB avg(F1)	Reuters avg(F1)
SVM	0.097 ± 0.0035	0.246 ± 0.0075	0.075 ± 0.0049	0.726	0.481	0.783
TSVM	0.364 ± 0.0056	0.401 ± 0.0086	0.362 ± 0.0089	0.434	0.376	0.437
TSVM+est	0.096 ± 0.0035	0.249 ± 0.0075	0.076 ± 0.0049	0.728	0.475	0.78
EM-Bayes	0.202 ± 0.0047	0.267 ± 0.0077	0.093 ± 0.0054	0.596	0.498	0.75
SGT	0.216 ± 0.0048	0.329 ± 0.0082	0.167 ± 0.0069	0.543	0.402	0.606
RetCsplL1o	**0.077 ± 0.0031**	0.207 ± 0.0071	**0.058 ± 0.0043**	**0.749**	0.497	**0.818**
RetCsplCv	0.08 ± 0.0032	0.211 ± 0.0071	0.059 ± 0.0044	0.749	0.496	0.817
RetLsplL1o	0.081 ± 0.0032	0.212 ± 0.0071	0.058 ± 0.0043	0.744	0.49	0.813
RetLsplCv	0.083 ± 0.0032	0.209 ± 0.0071	0.06 ± 0.0044	0.744	0.491	0.812
RetCv	0.084 ± 0.0032	**0.204 ± 0.007**	0.059 ± 0.0044	0.745	**0.499**	0.816

Fig. 2. Macro-averaged Results for **Asymmetric** Test Set: Baseline and Retraining Methods

(c) error/F1 prediction by 5-fold cross-validation invoked after every 10 iterations and cubic spline interpolation (**RetCsplCv**)

(d) error/F1 prediction by 5-fold cross-validation invoked after every 10 iterations and linear spline interpolation (**RetLsplCv**)

(e) error/F1 prediction by 5-fold cross-validation invoked after every iteration - and no interpolation (**RetCv**)

For SVM and TSVM we used the popular *SVMlight* implementation [14] with parameter C = 1000 (tradeoff between training error and margin). For the Spectral Graph Transductor we used the *SGTlight* implementation with parameterization as desribed in [16].

The average results for asymmetric test sets are shown in Figure 2 (best values in boldface). For lack of space, results for the symmetric case are omitted here; they can be found in [28]. The main observations are: In the asymmetric test case, our retraining algorithm clearly provides the best performance on all three datasets. For example, on the IMDB data, which is the hardest test case in terms of the absolute accuracy that was achievable, we reduce the error from approximately 25-27 percent (for SVM and TSVM with estimator and for EM-iterated Bayes) to 20.7 percent, quite a significant gain. The very bad performance of standard TSVM can be explained by the big gap between the parameter f, estimated on the training set, and the real ratio between positive and negative documents in the asymmetric test set.

As we regard the asymmetric test case, significantly more unacceptable test documents than acceptable ones, as the far more realistic setting (e.g. in focused crawling, news filtering, etc.), we conclude that the newly proposed retraining method is the clear winner and outperforms the previously known state-of-the-art algorithms by a significant margin.

An extended version of this paper is available as a technical report [28].

References

1. The 20 newsgroups data set. *http://www.ai.mit.edu/ jrennie/20Newsgroups/*.
2. Internet movie database. *http://www.imdb.com*.
3. M.-R. Amini and P. Gallinari. The use of unlabeled data to improve supervised learning for text summarization. In *SIGIR '02*, pages 105–112. ACM Press, 2002.
4. R. Baeza-Yates and B. Ribeiro-Neto. *Modern Information Retrieval*. Addison Wesley, 1999.
5. K. P. Bennett and A. Demiriz. Semi-supervised support vector machines. In *NIPS 1999*, pages 368–374. MIT Press, 1999.
6. K. P. Bennett, A. Demiriz, and R. Maclin. Exploiting unlabeled data in ensemble methods. In *SIGKDD*, pages 289–296. ACM Press, 2002.
7. A. Blum and T. Mitchell. Combining labeled and unlabeled data with co-training. *Workshop on Computational Learning Theory*, 1998.
8. J. Brank, M. Grobelnik, N. Milic-Frayling, and D. Mladenic. Training text classifiers with SVM on very few positive examples. *Technical Report MSR-TR-2003-34*, *Microsoft Corp.*, 2003.

9. C. Burges. A tutorial on Support Vector Machines for pattern recognition. *Data Mining and Knowledge Discovery*, 2(2), 1998.
10. S. Chakrabarti. *Mining the Web: Discovering Knowledge from Hypertext Data.* Morgan-Kauffman, 2002.
11. E. Chen and C. Lam. Predictor-corrector with cubic spline method for spectrum estimation in compton scatter correction of spect. *Computers in biology and medicine, 1994, vol. 24, no. 3, pp. 229, Ingenta.*
12. S. Dumais and H. Chen. Hierarchical classification of Web content. *SIGIR*, 2000.
13. H. Guo and H. L. Viktor. Learning from imbalanced data sets with boosting and data generation: the databoost-im approach. *SIGKDD Explorations, 30 - 39, 2004.*
14. T. Joachims. Text categorization with Support Vector Machines: Learning with many relevant features. *ECML*, 1998.
15. T. Joachims. Transductive inference for text classification using support vector machines. In *ICML'99, 200 - 209*, 1999.
16. T. Joachims. Transductive learning via spectral graph partitioning. In *ICML*, pages 290–297, 2003.
17. R. Kohavi and G. John. Automatic parameter selection by minimizing estimated error. In *Machine Learning*, 1995.
18. B. Krishnapuram, D. Williams, Y. Xue, A. Hartemink, L. Carin, and M. Figueiredo. On semi-supervised classification. In *NIPS*. MIT Press, 2005.
19. M. Kubat and S. Matwin. Addressing the curse of imbalanced training sets: One-sided selection. In *ICML'97, Nashville, TN, U.S.A., 179-186*, 1997.
20. W. S. Lee and B. Liu. Learning with positive and unlabeled examples using weighted logistic regression. In *ICML'03, Washingtion USA*, 2003.
21. D. D. Lewis. Evaluating text categorization. In *Proceedings of Speech and Natural Language Workshop*, pages 312–318. Defense Advanced Research Projects Agency, Morgan Kaufmann, Feb. 1991.
22. C. Manning and H. Schuetze. *Foundations of Statistical Natural Language Processing.* MIT Press, 1999.
23. K. Nigam, A. McCallum, S. Thrun, and T. Mitchell. Text classification from labeled and unlabeled documents using em. *Machine Intelligence*, 39(2/3), 2000.
24. E. Okanla and P. Gaydecki. A real-time audio frequency cubic spline interpolator. *Signal processing, 1996, vol. 49, no. 1, pp. 45, Ingenta.*
25. M. Porter. An algorithm for suffix stripping. *Automated Library and Information Systems*, 14(3).
26. M. Seeger. Learning with labeled and unlabeled data. *Tech. Rep., Institute for Adaptive and Neural Computation, University of Edinburgh, UK*, 2001.
27. C. Seymour and K. Unsworth. Interactive shape preserving interpolation by curvature continuous rational cubic splines. *Appl. Math. 102 (1999), no. 1, 87–117.*
28. S. Siersdorfer and G. Weikum. Automated retraining methods for document classification and their parameter tuning. In *Technical Report MPI-I-2005-5-002, Max-Planck-Institute for Computer Science, Germany,* http://www.mpi-sb.mpg.de/~stesi/sources/2005/report05retr.pdf, 2005.
29. S. Sizov, M. Biwer, J. Graupmann, S. Siersdorfer, M. Theobald, G. Weikum, and P. Zimmer. The BINGO! system for information portal generation and expert Web search. *Conference on Innovative Systems Research (CIDR)*, 2003.
30. V. Vapnik. *Statistical Learning Theory.* Wiley, New York, 1998.
31. D. Zhou, O. Bousquet, T. N. Lal, J. Weston, and B. Schölkopf. Learning with local and global consistency. In *NIPS*. MIT Press, 2004.
32. Z. Zhou, K. Chen, and Y. Jiang. Exploiting unlabeled data in content-based image retrieval. In *ECML'03, Pisa, Italy*, 2004.

NET – A System for Extracting Web Data from Flat and Nested Data Records

Bing Liu and Yanhong Zhai

Department of Computer Science,
University of Illinois at Chicago,
851 S. Morgan Street, Chicago, IL 60607
{liub, yzhai}@cs.uic.edu

Abstract. This paper studies automatic extraction of structured data from Web pages. Each of such pages may contain several groups of structured data records. Existing automatic methods still have several limitations. In this paper, we propose a more effective method for the task. Given a page, our method first builds a tag tree based on visual information. It then performs a post-order traversal of the tree and matches subtrees in the process using a tree edit distance method and visual cues. After the process ends, data records are found and data items in them are aligned and extracted. The method can extract data from both flat and nested data records. Experimental evaluation shows that the method performs the extraction task accurately.

1 Introduction

Structured data objects are an important type of information on the Web. Such objects are often data records retrieved from a backend database and displayed in Web pages with some fixed templates. This paper also calls them *data records*. Extracting data from such data records enables one to integrate data from multiple sites to provide value-added services, e.g., comparative shopping, and meta-querying.

There are two main approaches to data extraction, wrapper induction and automatic extraction. In wrapper induction, a set of data extraction rules are learnt from a set of manually labeled pages [5, 8, 9, 14]. However, manual labeling is labor intensive and time consuming. For different sites or even pages in the same site, manual labeling needs to be repeated because different sites may follow different templates. For large scale web data extraction tasks, manual labeling is a serious drawback.

For automatic extraction, [1, 4, 6] find patterns or grammars from multiple pages containing similar data records. Requiring an initial set of pages containing similar data records is, however, a limitation. [6] proposes a method that tries to explore the detailed information pages behind the current page to segment data records. The need for such detailed pages behind is a drawback because many data records do not have such pages or such pages are hard to find. [3] proposes a string matching method. However, it could not find nested data records. A similar method is proposed in [11]. [7] and [15] propose some algorithms to identify data records, which do not extract data items from the data records, and do not handle nested data records. Our previous

M. Kitsuregawa et al. (Eds.): WISE 2005, LNCS 3806, pp. 487–495, 2005.

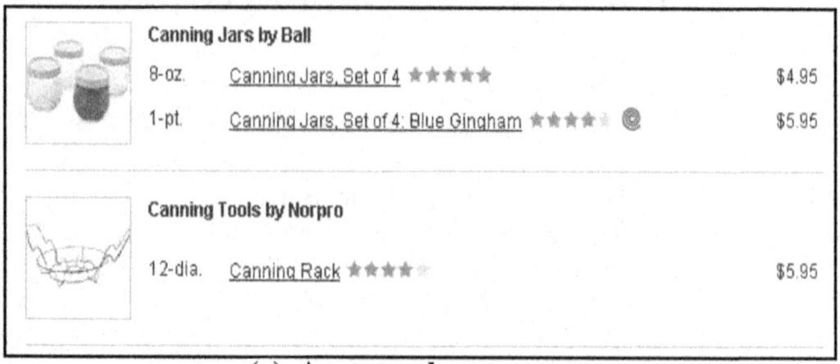

(a). An example page segment

image 1	Canning Jars by Ball	8-oz	Canning Jars, Set of 4	*****	$4.95
image 1	Canning Jars by Ball	1-pt	Canning Jars, Set of 4; Blue Gingham	****	$5.95
image 2	Canning Tools by Norpro	12-dia	Canning Rack	****	$4.95

(b). Extraction results

Fig. 1. An example page and the extraction results

system DEPTA [13] is able to align and extract data items from data records, but does not handle nested data records.

This paper proposes a more effective method to extract data from Web pages that contains a set of flat or nested data records automatically. Our method is based on a tree edit distance method and visual cues. It is called NET (*N*ested data *E*xtraction using *T*ree matching and visual cues). Given a Web page, it works in two main steps:

1. Building a tag tree of the page. Due to erroneous tags and unbalanced tags in the HTML code of the page, building a correct tree is not a simple task. A visual based method is used to deal with this problem.
2. Identifying data records and extracting data from them. The algorithm performs a post-order traversal of the tag tree to identify data records at different levels. This ensures that nested data records are found. A tree edit distance algorithm and visual cues are used to perform these tasks.

Experimental evaluation shows that the technique is highly effective.

2 Problem Statement

Fig. 1a gives an example page segment that contains two data records. In this segment, the first data record has two nested data records, i.e., the same type of products but different sizes, looks, prices, etc.

Our task: Given a Web page that contains multiple data records (at least two), we discover the underlying data records, extract the data items in them and put the data in a relational table. For Fig. 1a, we aim to produce the table in Fig. 1b. Due to space limitations, we omitted the red spot in Fig. 1a. Note that "image 1" and "Canning Jars by Ball" are common for the first and the second rows due to nesting.

3   Building the Tag Tree

In a Web browser, each HTML element is rendered as a rectangle. Instead of using nested tags (which have many errors) in the HTML code to build a tag tree, we build a tag tree based on the nested rectangles (see [13] for more details).

1. Find the 4 boundaries of the rectangle of each HTML element by calling the embedded parsing and rendering engine of a browser, e.g., Internet explorer.
2. Detect containment relationships among the rectangles, i.e., whether one rectangle is contained inside another. A tree can be built based on the containment check.

4   The Proposed Algorithm

Before presenting the algorithm, we discuss two observations about data records in Web pages, which simplify the extraction task. The observations were made in [7].

1. A group of data records that contains descriptions of a list of similar objects are typically presented in a contiguous region of a page and are formatted using similar HTML tags, e.g., the data records in Fig. 1a.
2. A group of similar data records being placed in a region is reflected in the tag tree by the fact that they are under one parent node, although we do not know which parent (the algorithm will find out). In other words, a set of similar data records are formed by some child sub-trees of the same parent node.

These observations make it possible to design a tree based method for data extraction.

The basic idea of our proposed algorithm is to traverse the tag tree in post-order (or bottom-up). This ensures that nested data records are found at a lower level based on repeating patterns before processing an upper level. For example, in Fig. 1a, the following two nested data records are found first at a lower level:

| 8-oz | Canning Jars, Set of 4 | ***** | $4.95 |
| 1-pt | Canning Jars, Set of 4; Blue Gingham | **** | $5.95 |

Then at an upper level, all the data records are found as shown in Fig. 1b. The overall algorithm NET is given in Fig. 2.

Algorithm NET(*Root*, *T*)
1   Traverse(*Root*, *T*);
2   Output().

Traverse(*Node*, *T*)
1   **if** Depth(*Node*) => 3 **then**
2   **for** each *Child* ∈ *Node.Children* **do**
3   Traverse(*Child*, *T*);
4   Match(*Node*, *T*);

Fig. 2. The overall NET algorithm

Line 1 of Traverse() says that the algorithm will not search for data records if the depth of the sub-tree from *Node* is 2 or 1 as it is unlikely that a data record is formed with only a single level of tag(s). Match() is the procedure that performs tree matching on child subtrees of *Node* (see below). T is a threshold for a match of two trees to

Match(*Node, T*)
1   *Children = Node.Children*;
2 **for** each *ChildF* in *Children* **do**
3   **for** each *ChildR* in *Children* = *Children* – {*ChildF*} **do**
4   **if** TreeMatch(*ChildF, ChildR*) > *T* **then**
5   AlignAndLink();
6   **if** all items in *ChildR* are aligned and linked **then**
7   *Children = Children* – {*ChildR*}
8 **if** some alignments have been made **then**
9   PutDataInTables(*Node*);
10   GenPrototypes(*Node*);

Fig. 3. The Match procedure

Simple_Tree_Matching(*A, B*)
1. **if** the roots of the two trees *A* and *B* contain distinct symbols or there is a visual
     conflict between *A* and *B*
2. **then** return (0);
3. **else** m:= the number of first-level sub-trees of *A*;
4. n:= the number of first-level sub-trees of *B*;
5.   Initialization: $M[i, 0]$:= 0 for $i = 0, ..., m$;
                      $M[0, j]$:= 0 for $j = 0, ..., n$;
6.   **for** $i = 1$ to m **do**
7.   **for** $j = 1$ to n **do**
8. $M[i,j]$:=max($M[i,j\text{-}1], M[i\text{-}1, j], M[i\text{-}1, j\text{-}1]+W[i, j]$);
           where $W[i,j]$ = Simple_Tree_Matching(A_i, B_j)
9.   return ($M[m, n]+1$)

Fig. 4. The simple tree matching algorithm

be considered sufficiently similar. Output() in NET() outputs the extracted data to the user in relational tables (as a page may have multiple *data areas* with different structured data, and data in each area are put in a separate table). Note that some simple optimization can be performed to the NET algorithm. For example, if *Child* does not have any data item, e.g., text, image, etc, Traverse() may not be performed on *Child*.

The Match procedure is given in Fig. 3. TreeMatch() matches two child subtrees under *Node* (line 4). In lines 2 and 3, we set TreeMatch() to be applied to every pair of child nodes, which ensures all necessary data item matches are captured. AlignAndLink() aligns and links matched data items (leaf nodes) (line 5). The details of these procedures are given below.

PutDataToTable() extracts the matched data items and puts them in tables. This will be discussed below together with GenPrototypes(). Note that PutDataToTable() does not output the final results, which is done by Ouput() (line 2 of NET() in Fig. 2).

Tree Matching: TreeMatch()

TreeMatch() uses a tree edit distance or matching algorithm. Since a list of data records form repeated patterns, this procedure basically finds such tree patterns.

In this work, we use a restricted tree matching algorithm, called *simple tree matching* (STM) (Yang 1991). STM evaluates the similarity of two trees by producing the maximum matching through dynamic programming with complexity $O(n_1 n_2)$, where n_1 and n_2 are the sizes of trees A and B respectively.

Let A and B be two trees and $i \in A$, $j \in B$ are two nodes in A and B respectively. A *matching* between two trees in STM is defined to be a mapping M such that for every pair $(i, j) \in M$ where i and j are non-root nodes, (parent(i), parent(j)) $\in M$. A *maximum matching* is a matching with the maximum number of pairs.

Let $A = <R_A, A_1, A_2,..., A_m>$ and $B=<R_B, B_1, B_2,..., B_n>$ be two trees, where R_A and R_B are the roots of A and B, and A_i, B_j are the ith and jth first-level sub-trees of A and B respectively. When R_A and R_B match, the maximum matching between A and B is $M_{A,B}+1$ ($M_{A,B}$ is the maximum match between $<A_1, A_2,..., A_m>$ and $<B_1, B_2,..., B_n>$).

In the Simple_Tree_Matching algorithm in Fig. 4, the roots of A and B are compared first (line 1). If the roots match, then the algorithm recursively finds the maximum matching between first-level sub-trees of A and B and save it in W matrix (line 8). Based on the W matrix, a dynamic programming scheme is applied to find the number of pairs in a maximum matching between two trees A and B.

Note that we add a visual based condition in line 1. That is, we want to make sure that A and B has no visual conflict. For example, based on the visual information, if the width of A is much larger than that of B, then they are unlikely to match. Due to space limitations, we are unable to present all the rules that we use here. These rules help to produce better match results and also to reduce the computation significantly.

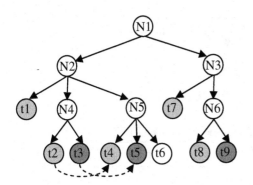 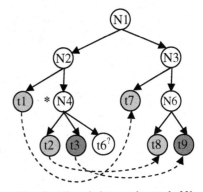

Fig. 5. Aligned data nodes under N2 are linked   **Fig. 6.** Aligned data nodes underN1 are linked

Align Matched Data Items: AlignAndLink()

AlignAndLink() aligns the data items after tree matching. We simply trace back in the M matrices to find the matched/aligned items in the two trees. When there is more than one match for a node that gives the maximum result, we choose the one appearing the earliest in the tree. This performs well (visual information may also be used).

All the aligned data items are then linked. The links are directional, i.e., an earlier data item will point to its next matching data item. Fig. 5 gives an example, where ti represents a terminal (data item) node, and Nj represents a tag node. Since NET performs post-order traversal, at the level N4-N5, t2-t4 and t3-t5 are matched (assume they satisfy the match condition, line 4 of Fig. 3). They are aligned and linked (dash lines). N4 and N5 are data records at this level (nested in N2). t6 is optional.

PutDataInTables(*Node*)
1 *Children* = FindFirstReturnRest(*Node.Children*); // find the first child node of a data area
   and return all child nodes from it onward
2 *Tables* = { };   // multiple data areas may exist under *Node*
3 *DataTable* = create a table of suitable size; // store data items
4 *Row* = 0;   // *DataTable* row that a data item will be inserted in
5 **for** each *Child* in *Children* in sequence **do**
6   **if** *Child* has aligned data items **then**
7   **if** a link to *Child* exists from an data item in an earlier column **then** // a variable
            can keep track of the current column
8   *Row* = *Row* + 1;
9   **for** each data item *d* in *Child* **do**
10   **if** *d* does not have in-coming link **then**
11   add a new column and insert *d* in *Row*;
12   **else** Insert *d* in *Row* and the same column as the data item with an out-going
               link pointing to *d*.
13   **else**   *Tables* = *Tables* ∪ {*DataTable*};
14   **if** no aligned data in the rest of *Children* nodes **then**
15   exit loop
16   **else** *DataTable* = create a table of suitable size;
17   *Row* = 0;

Fig. 7. The PutDataInTables procedure

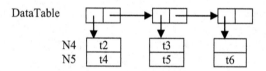

Fig. 8. DataTable for N4 and N5 (children of N2)

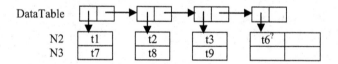

Fig. 9. DataTable for N2 and N3 (children of N1)

t1	t2	t3	
t1	t4	t5	t6
t7	t8	t9	

Fig. 10. Final output (children of N1)

At the level of N2-N3, TreeMatch() will only match N4 subtree and N6 subtree. We see that t2-t8 and t3-t9 are linked. t1 and t7 are also linked as they match (Fig. 6).

The subtree at N5 is omitted in Fig.6 because N5 has the same structure as N4. N4 is marked with a "*" in Fig. 6 as it is turned into a prototype data record by GenProto-types(). Note that t6 is inserted into N4 as an optional node, denoted by "?". A prototype represents a standard/typical data record containing the complete structure so far. We may not be able to use the first data record (e.g., N4) directly because it may not contain some optional items, which may cause loss of data items in upper level matches. Note also that a prototype may consist of multiple child nodes (not just one as N4) as a single data record may consist of multiple child nodes. To produce the prototype, in general we need to perform multiple alignments of data records [13]. However, we use a simpler method based on the extracted data (see below).

Put Data in Tables and Generate Prototypes: PutDataInTables() and
GenPrototypes()
PutDataInTables (Fig. 7) puts the linked data items in tables (as there may be more than one data areas with different structures). A table here (*DataTable* in Fig. 7) is a linked list of one dimensional arrays, which represent columns. This data structure makes it easy to insert columns in appropriate locations for optional data items.

The basic idea of the algorithm is as follows: All linked data items are put in the same column (line 9-12). A new row is started if an item is being pointed to by another item in an earlier column (line 7). For example, for node N2 in Fig. 5 this procedure produces the *DataTable* in Fig. 8. For node N1 in Fig. 6, it produces the *DataTable* in Fig. 9. Here we only use *N4, but not N5 (in Fig. 5). PutDataInTables() is a linear algorithm.

After putting data in tables, producing prototypes from each table is fairly simple. GenPrototypes() follows the tree structure based on the first data record (e.g., N4 in Fig. 5) and inserts those tree paths representing optional items not in the first data record, but in other data records. The optional items are clear from the table because they occupy some columns that do not have data items in the first data record. In the example of Fig. 9, $t6^?$ is added to N4 as an optional item which gives *N4 (the prototype). In Fig. 6, we can also see that $t6^?$ is attached to *N4.

Output Data and Prototypes: Output()
Output() outputs the final data tables, which are tables not covered by any upper level tables. For example, Fig. 10 shows the final table for the tree in Fig. 5. Note that the nested data are expanded and included. The procedure also outputs the final prototypes that can be used to extract data from similar pages from the same site.

5   Empirical Evaluation

This section evaluates NET. We compare it with the most recent system DEPTA [13], which does not find nested data records. We show that for flat data records, NET performs as well as DEPTA. For nested data records, NET also performs very well. Our experimental results are given in Table 1.

Column 1 lists the site of each test page. Due to space limitations, we could not list all of them here. The number of pages that we used in our experiments is 40. The first 32 pages (without nesting) are from DEPTA. The last 8 pages all contain nested data records. We did not collect more nested pages for testing because such pages are relatively rare and quite difficult to find.

Columns 2 and 4 give the numbers of data items extracted wrongly (Wr.) by DEPTA and NET from each page respectively. In x/y, x is the number of extracted results that are incorrect, and y is the number of results that are not extracted. The tree similarity threshold is 0.7, which is the default of our system and is used in all our experiments. Columns 3 and 5 give the numbers of correct (Corr.) data items extracted by DEPTA and NET from each page respectively. Here, in x/y, x is the number of correct items extracted, and y is the number of items in the page.

Table 1. Experimental results

URL	DEPTA		NET	
	Wr.	**Corr.**	**Wr.**	**Corr.**
Without Nesting				
http://accessories.gateway.com/	0/0	15/15	0/0	15/15
http://google1-cnet.com.com/	0/0	180/180	0/0	180/180
http://google-zdnet.com.com/	0/0	80/80	0/0	80/80
...	...	...	...	...
http://sensualexpression.com/	0/0	12/12	0/0	12/12
http://www.shopping.com	0/0	35/35	0/0	35/35
http://www.tigerdirect.com/	0/0	70/70	0/0	70/70
Recall	97.15%		98.99%	
Precision	99.37%		98.92%	
With Nesting				
http://froogle.google.com/	12/0	124/136	0/0	136/136
http://www.cooking.com/	0/15	48/63	1/0	62/63
http://www.kmart.com/	38/0	0/38	0/0	38/38
http://www.rei.com/	45/26	32/103	2/0	101/103
http://www.sonystyle.com/	78/23	0/101	0/0	101/101
http://www.target.com/	0/43	36/79	0/0	79/79
http://www.walmart.com/	50/0	28/78	0/0	78/78
http://www1.us.dell.com/	189/0	32/221	0/0	221/221
Recall	36.63%		99.63%	
Precision	42.13%		100%	

From the table, we can observe that without nesting the results of DEPTA and NET are both accurate. With nesting, NET is much better. DEPTA still can correctly extract some data items because not all data records in the pages have nested records. The precision and recall are computed based on the extraction of all pages.

6 Conclusions

In this paper, we proposed a more effective technique to perform automatic data extraction from Web pages. Given a page, our method first builds a tag tree based on visual information. It then performs a post-order traversal of the tree and matches subtrees in the process using a tree edit distance method and visual cues. Our method enables accurate alignment and extraction of both flat and nested data records. Experimental results show that the method performs data extraction accurately.

Acknowledgements

This work was partially supported by National Science Foundation (NSF) under the grant IIS-0307239.

References

1. Arasu, A. and Garcia-Molina, H. Extracting Structured Data from Web Pages. *SIGMOD'03,* 2003.
2. Buttler, D., Liu, L., Pu, C. A fully automated extraction system for the World Wide Web. *IEEE ICDCS-21*, 2001.
3. Chang, C. and Lui, S-L. IEPAD: Information extraction based on pattern discovery. *WWW'10*, 2001.
4. Crescenzi, V. Mecca, G. Merialdo, P. Roadrunner: towards automatic data extraction from large web sites. *VLDB'01*, 2001.
5. Kushmerick, N. Wrapper induction: efficiency and expressiveness. *Artificial Intelligence*, 118:15-68, 2000.
6. Lerman, K., Getoor L., Minton, S. and Knoblock, C. Using the Structure of Web Sites for Automatic Segmentation of Tables. *SIGMOD'04*, 2004.
7. Liu, B., Grossman, R. and Zhai, Y. Mining data records from Web pages. *KDD'03*, 2003.
8. Muslea, I., Minton, S. and Knoblock, C. A hierarchical approach to wrapper induction. *Agents'99*, 1999.
9. Pinto, D., McCallum, A., Wei, X. and Bruce, W. Table extraction using conditional random fields. *SIGIR'03*, 2003.
10. Reis, D. Golgher, P., Silva, A., Laender, A. Automatic Web news extraction using tree edit distance, *WWW'04*, 2004.
11. Wang, J.-Y., and Lochovsky, F. Data extraction and label assignment for Web databases. *WWW'03*, 2003.
12. Yang, W. Identifying syntactic differences between two programs. *Softw. Pract. Exper.*, 21(7):739–755, 1991.
13. Zhai, Y and Liu, B. Web data extraction based on partial tree alignment. *WWW'05*, 2005.
14. Zhai, Y and Liu, B. Extracting Web data using instance-based learning. To appear in *WISE'05*, 2005.
15. Zhao, H., Meng, W., Wu, Z., Raghavan, V., Yu, C. Fully automatic wrapper generation for search engines. *WWW'05*, 2005.

Blog Map of Experiences: Extracting and Geographically Mapping Visitor Experiences from Urban Blogs

Takeshi Kurashima, Taro Tezuka, and Katsumi Tanaka

Department of Social Informatics, Graduate School of Informatics,
Kyoto University, Yoshida-Honmachi, Sakyo-ku, Kyoto 606-8501, Japan
{ktakeshi, tezuka, tanaka}@dl.kuis.kyoto-u.ac.jp
http://www.dl.kuis.kyoto-u.ac.jp/

Abstract. The prevalence of weblogs (blogs) has enabled people to share the personal experiences of tourists at specific locations and times. Such information was traditionally unavailable, except indirectly through local newspapers and periodicals. This paper describes a method of spatially and temporally obtaining specific experiences by extracting association rules from the content of blog articles. For example, we can read about visitors' activities and evaluations of sightseeing spots. By geographically mapping their experiences, the proposed system enables observation of tourist activities and impressions of specific locations, which can often be more diverse than local guidebooks and more trustworthy than advertisements.

1 Introduction

The prevalence of weblogs enables the observation of personal experiences, specific to location and time. Such information was traditionally unavailable, except indirectly through local newspapers and periodicals. One characteristic of blogs is that the moment they are written, they are stored as attributes. This enables the extraction of the writers' experiences during a specific time period. When combined with the extraction of geographic keywords (geo-coding of blogs) from the articles, tourist experiences, related to a specific place and time can be obtained. For example, in spring many people go out and see the flower blossoms. At famous sight-seeing spots, they are likely to try out local specialties. These are actual experiences, unlike commercially prepared tourist guides or media reports. This kind of information is particularly valuable to potential tourists and marketing analysts, interested in local trends. Recently, some services have allowed users to map their blog articles to spatial locations. However, such systems are not yet widespread, and most of the location-specific personal experiences are stored separately on individual blog sites. Existing search engines do not provide satisfactory results because the search results for specific location names are often a vast collection of blog articles, and it is unrealistic to read them all. In addition, many of the articles contain only generic information about the location,

M. Kitsuregawa et al. (Eds.): WISE 2005, LNCS 3806, pp. 496–503, 2005.

and not the writer's personal experience. In this paper, we describe a system for extracting local and temporal experiences by mining spatially and temporally specific association rules from blog articles. The system enables people to learn about the experiences of others, specific to location and time period.

2   Related Work

2.1   Blog Mining

Kumar et al. discussed blog link structures and proposed *time graphs* and *time-dense community tracking* to represent the growth of blog communities and a way to track changes within communities [1][2]. Bar-Ilan examined links between blogs and their postings and obtained statistics [3]. However, these analyses focused only on the relationships between blogs, and were not targeted at the content of the blog articles. Bar-Ilan's survey also pointed out that personal information and self-expression are becoming important aspects in blogs. Okumura et al. proposed a system that collects blog articles and presents aggregated results [4]. Unlike our system, *blogWatcher* does not perform spatial aggregation. Avesani et al. proposed a system which aggregates blog articles on specified topics [5]. Their work was mainly focused on aggregating user reviews on products.

2.2   Spatial Blogs

There have been various services that unify geographic information with blogs. DC Metro Blogmap and nyc bloggers provide services that link one's personal blogs to metro maps. Users of these services can find bloggers related to specific area in the city [6][7]. Uematsu et al. proposed *Ba-log*, in which users upload blog contents using cellular phones equipped with cameras and GPS extensions [8]. WorldKit is a toolkit for creating map based applications on the Web, and it has been applied to a blog mapping service also [9]. However, these services require manual registrations, and the automatic extraction of knowledge from blog articles is not performed.

2.3   Association Rule Mining

Association rules are patterns in relational data, which can be expressed as $X \Rightarrow Y$, where X and Y indicates sets of expressions with a certain attribute having a specific value [10]. Two factors, *support* and *confidence*, determine the value of each association rule. *Support* is the ratio where one tuple contains both X and Y of all the tuples in a data set and is expressed as, $sup(X \Rightarrow Y)$. *Confidence* is the ratio of tuples containing Y in tuples containing X. *Confidence* is expressed as $conf(X \Rightarrow Y)$.

In extracting association rules, the minimum confidence (MCV) and support values (MSV) are set as thresholds. Association rules with a higher confidence rate than MCV and a higher support rate than MSV are extracted as important rules. The APRIORI algorithm described by Agrawal et al. enabled the extraction of the association rule from large data sets in practical time [11].

3   Experience Extraction

The aim of this paper is to describe the extraction of tourists' real life experiences. These experiences are written while the memories are still fresh and with an honesty often lacking in commercially written pieces, although not all sentences in blog articles describe real-life experiences. In order to extract actual experiences, we extract sentences that refer to actions. After that, we are mining spatially and temporally specific association rules from blog articles because tourist's real life experiences is local and temporal. The *antecedent* of the association rules is place and time, and the *consequent* is verb and noun. The following subsections describe each of steps of the extraction.

3.1   Blog Collection

Blog articles are collected using generic blog search engines, provided by blog hosting services. These hosting services provide the search results in RSS metadata. RSS is an RDF rich site summary that consists of titles, summaries, date, and other attributes. The system collects articles by following these steps:

1. Set location names as search queries.
2. Send queries to generic blog search engine
3. Retrieve search results in RSS.
4. Extract title, content, links, and date from RSS.
5. Store in the blog database.
6. Wait for set amount of time, and repeat from (2).

3.2   Morphological Analysis and Database Insertion

From the collected articles, transaction sets are extracted. The surrounding text of a location name is first extracted from the blog content. The extracted text is divided into sentences and then into morphemes. This process is language dependent and is discussed in more detail in the implementation section. Then the sentences are converted into a *transaction*. The scheme is as follows.

$T = (date, geo, noun_1, ..., noun_n, verb_1, ..., verb_m)$
T: Transaction.
date: Date attribute of the blog article containing the sentence.
geo: Location name found in the sentence.
$noun_i$: ith noun in the sentence.
$verb_i$: ith verb in the sentence.

3.3   Refinement 1: Extraction of Verbs Referring to Actions

In order to extract only the rules that are related to user experiences, the transaction database must be refined. In general, sentences can be divided into the three groups listed below.

1. Do statements (ex. *I saw autumn leaves.*)
2. Become statements (ex. *The autumn leaves turned yellow.*)
3. Be statements (ex. *Autumn leaves are beautiful.*)

Sentences are categorized into these groups, based on their verbs. Experiences are most closely related with the do statements, because these sentences indicate user action. Therefore, we only use transactions that contain verbs that are used in do statements.

3.4   Refinement 2: Elimination of Verbs Indicating Movements

Actions that do not take place in the specified location are eliminated. For example, verbs such as "go" or "come" do not indicate actions that take place at the specified location. Instead, these indicate movement toward the location. Therefore, transactions containing these verbs are eliminated from the transaction database.

3.5   Association Rule Mining

The association rules are extracted using the APRIORI algorithm. There are three types of rules that we can extract.

Type 1: [Time, Location name] ⇒ [Verb]
Type 2: [Time, Location name, Verb] ⇒ [Noun]
Type 3: [Time, Location name] ⇒ [Verb, Noun]

Other rules, such as those between nouns, are eliminated because they do not match our purpose of extracting spatially and temporally specific experiences.

3.6   User Interaction

The extracted association rules are presented as a *summary* to the user's request. The user query consists of a combination of four attributes: location name, time, action, and object. Some typical combinations are described below.

Case 1: Query = Space, Time   Search Result = Action
In this case, the user wants to know about typical activities taking place at a specific place during a specific time period. For example, the user can input "Kyoto city,April".

Case 2: Query = Space, Time, Action   Search Result = Object
In this case, the user wants to know the object of specified activities taking place at a specific place and time. For example, the user can input terms, such as "Kyoto city, April, Eat".

Case 3: Query = Space, Time   Search Result = Action, Object
In this case, the user wants to know about typical activities taking place at a specific place and time period, as well as the object of the action.

Then the user can view the set of original articles and read about the writer's experiences in more detail by making a click on a link. The user can also access to the extracted living experiences through a map interface. A mock-up image of the visual interface is shown in Figure 1.

Table 1. Case3 summary

Location name:	Date:
[rank] Verb1:conf([Location name,Date] ⇒ [Verb])	
Object1:conf([Location name,Date,Verb] ⇒ [Noun])	
Object2:conf([Location name,Date,Verb] ⇒ [Noun])	
[rank] Verb2:conf([Location name,Date] ⇒ [Verb])	
Object1]:conf([Location name,Date,Verb] ⇒ [Noun])	
Object2:conf([Location name,Date,Verb] ⇒ [Noun])	

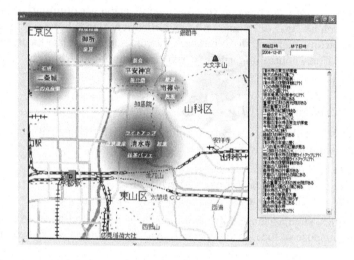

Fig. 1. Visual user interface for browsing actual experiences

4   Implementation

Based on the algorithm described in the previous section, we implemented a prototype system, the Blog Map of Experiences, which extracts and summarize actual experiences from blog articles. The next section describes the implementation details. A system configuration is shown in Figure 2.

4.1   Blog Collection and Morphological Analysis

Our implementation collects blog articles from "goo blog"[12] and "livedoor blog"[13]. Both are typical blog hosting services in Japan. Location names used as search queries were taken from digitized residential maps provided by Zenrin Ltd.[14] The collected blogs were stored into the MySQL database [15].

Morphological analysis of the blog articles was performed, using the Chasen morphological analyzer [16]. Chasen divides sentences into words and estimates their parts of speech. The results are then stored in the transaction database.

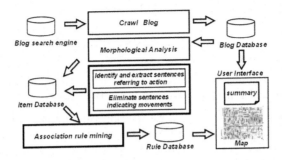

Fig. 2. system configuration

4.2 Refinement of Transactions and Association Rule Mining

The collection of verbs referring to actions was obtained from the lexical database of the Japanese Vocabulary System [17]. It categorizes verbs into tree structure, and verbs referring to actions are grouped into one top-level category.

We then manually listed verbs that indicate movements. For example, verbs such as "go", "come", and their synonyms were among the list. Transactions containing these verbs were eliminated, since their original sentences are likely be describing the motions toward the location, rather than the actions at the location. The latter is what we want to extract and present to the users. As a preprocessing of the association rule mining, time attribute of the transactions were grouped by month, so that the resulting association rules have higher support values. Finally, APRIORI algorithm was used for the association rule mining.

In our implementation, we extracted Type 1 and Type 2 rules discussed in the previous section. The result of a preliminary experiment showed that Type 3 rules contain too much noise and could not be used without further improvements in the refinement methods. The precisions of these rules were around 10 percent.

The extraction of Type 2 rules is performed in two steps. First, Type 1 rules are extracted and a set of typical verbs for the given place name is obtained. Second, Type 2 rules are extracted for the pairs of the given place name and the extracted typical verbs. The pseudocode for this process is the following.

> Define a set of place names $P = p_1, p_2, ..., p_n$.
> For $i = 1$ to n do
>   Obtain m association rules $p_i \rightarrow v$,
>   in the decreasing order of the support value.
>   Obtain the set of verbs $V_i = v_{i1}, v_{i2}, ..., v_{im}$
>   For $j = 1$ to m do
>   Obtain k association rules $p_i, v_{ij} \rightarrow n$,
>   in the decreasing order of the support value.
>   Store k rules.
>   Done
> Done

The result was stored into the rule database.

5 Evaluation

In this section, we evaluate two refinement algorithms proposed in the previous section, as listed below.

Refinement 1: Identify and extract sentences refering to actions.
Refinement 2: Eliminate sentences indicating movements.

We first apply the conventional association rule mining method (APRIORI algorithm) and obtain results. We then calculate the precision for different sizes of the extracted rules. We then apply two refinement algorithms, and observe if they improve the precision.

We performed experiments using two major blog hosting services in Japan, goo and livedoor [12][13]. The target locations were 20 popular sightseeing spots in Japan, and we collected 500 blog articles for each. First, Type1 rules are extracted, and top j rules are obtained in the decreasing order of the *support* value. Second, Type2 rules are also extracted each of the verbs which are the *consequent* of the Type1 rules. We obtained top 10 nouns which are the *consequent* of the Type2 rules. We evaluated the extracted pairs of verbs and nouns. Table 2 is the average results of precisions. The results show that the combination of Refinement 1 and 2 improves the resulting rule set.

Table 2. The average Precision of the extracted association rules

top j result	Size of experiences	Assoc.rules:unrefined	Refine.1	Refine.1+Refine.2
3	30	0.007	0.083	0.216
5	50	0.058	0.111	0.221
10	100	0.087	0.131	0.182

6 Existing Problems

There are still several remaining problems in our system. One is that the system cannot handle synonyms yet. Another is that it does not consider dependency between terms. There is still some ambiguity regarding whether the noun extracted using the association rule is really the object of the action. Our future plans include applying dependency analysis to extract the objects of the action more precisely.

7 Conclusion

In this paper, we described a system for extracting actual experiences related to a specific location and time period. Association rules between place, time, action, and objects aggregate the user experiences expressed in blog articles. We have implemented a system that allows users to search actions or objects using specified places and times. The results verified that the system could successfully extract actions and objects.

Acknowledgments

This work was supported in part by the Japanese Ministry of Education, Culture, Sports, Science and Technology under a Grant-in-Aid for Software Technologies for Search and Integration across Heterogeneous-Media Archives, a Special Research Area Grant-In-Aid For Scientific Research (2) for the year 2005 under a project titled Research for New Search Service Methods Based on the Web's Semantic Structure (Project No, 16016247; Representative, Katsumi Tanaka), and the Informatics Research Center for Development of Knowledge Society Infrastructure (COE program by Japan's Ministry of Education, Culture, Sports, Science and Technology).

References

1. R. Kumar, J. Novak, P. Raghavan and A. Tomkins, On the bursty evolution of blogspace, Proceedings of the 12th International World Wide Web Conference, pp. 568-576, 2003
2. R. Kumar, J. Novak, P. Raghavan and A. Tomkins, Structure and evolution of blogspace, Communications of the ACM, 47(12) pp. 35-39, 2004
3. J. Bar-Ilan, An outsider's view on 'topic-oriented' blogging, Proceedings of the Alternate Papers Track of the 13th International World Wide Web Conference, pp. 28-34, 2004
4. M. Okumura, T. Nanno, T. Fujiki and Y. Suzuki, Text mining based on automatic collection and monitoring of Japanese weblogs, The 6th Web and Ontology Workshop, The Japanese Society for Artificial Intelligence, 2004
5. P. Avesani, M. Cova, C. Hayes and P. Massa, Proceedings of the WWW2005 2nd Annual Workshop on the Weblogging Ecosystem: Aggregation, Analysis and Dynamics, Chiba, Japan, 2005
6. nyc bloggers, http://www.nycbloggers.com/
7. DC Metro Blogmap, http://www.reenhead.com/map/metroblogmap.html
8. D. Uematsu, K. Numa, T. Tokunaga, I. Ohmukai and H. Takeda, Ba-log: a proposal for the use of locational information in blog environment, The 6th Web and Ontology Workshop, The Japanese Society for Artificial Intelligence, 2004
9. worldKit, http://www.brainoff.com/worldkit/index.php
10. D. J. Hand, H. Mannila and P. Smyth, Principles of Data Mining (Adaptive Computation and Machine Learning), 425p, MIT Press, 2001
11. R. Agrawal and R. Srikant, Fast algorithms for mining association rules in large databases, Proceedings of the 20th International Conference on Very Large Data Bases, pp. 487-499, 1994
12. goo blog, http://blog.goo.ne.jp
13. livedoor blog, http://blog.livedoor.com/
14. Zenrin Co.,Ltd, http://www.zenrin.co.jp/
15. MySql, http://www.mysql.com/
16. Chasen, http://chasen.aist-nara.ac.jp/index.html
17. Japanese Vocabulary System, http://www.ntt-tec.jp/technology/C404.html
18. Geolink Kyoto, http://www.digitalcity.gr.jp

Reliable Multicast and Its Probabilistic Model for Job Submission in Peer-to-Peer Grids

Peter Merz and Katja Gorunova

University of Kaiserslautern, Dept. of Computer Science, Germany
{pmerz, gorunova}@informatik.uni-kl.de

Abstract. We present an efficient algorithm for job submissions in Peer-to-Peer (desktop) grids based on limited multicasts. Our approach combines the advantages of two overlay architectures: Chord-like structured networks and unstructured networks with epidemic communication. To predict the multicast properties and to optimize its distribution schedule, we present a probabilistic model of the process of information propagation within the overlay. We show the efficiency and the fault-tolerance of our proposed method and demonstrate the high accuracy of the predictive model.

1 Motivation

To utilize the computational power of modern desktop PCs, desktop grids have been proposed for automated deployment of computational tasks to idle machines in computer networks. To avoid a central management of these systems and to enable scalability on wide area networks, it is promising to use peer-to-peer (P2P) overlays as a basis for desktop grids. P2P grids require efficient mechanisms for job distribution: if the job is comprised of several independent tasks, the goal is to find a certain number of peers willing to participate in the computation. The process of finding idle peers can be considered as a multicast in the overlay that terminates as soon as a job-dependent number of peers have agreed to join the computation. Ideally, the multicast should reach the desired fraction of peers very fast and with low message complexity. In this paper, we discuss a reliable, failure-tolerant hybrid method for multicast distribution in P2P grids. Our approach combines the advantages of regular (non-redundant) and epidemic (redundant) multicast distribution schemes. Furthermore, we introduce the probabilistic model to predict the properties of the multicast distribution for optimal scheduling.

2 Related Work

Various aspects of grid computing were intensively studied in last years in the context of P2P grids: network design (e.g. [21, 11, 20]), utilization of distributed resources [4, 10], or load balancing [15]. In contrast to analogous systems with client/server design (e.g. SETI@Home [1]), fully decentralized solutions provide higher failure tolerance and better scalability. Many proposed systems make use of simple multicast distribution mechanisms like flooding; the important disadvantage of this method is the extremely high redundancy of multicast messages [19].

M. Kitsuregawa et al. (Eds.): WISE 2005, LNCS 3806, pp. 504–511, 2005.

For structured P2P architectures like Chord [21] or CAN [18], special multicast distribution methods were proposed that make use of regular network design. For example, the multicast algorithm for Chord introduced in [6] has minimal message complexity and spreads very fast over the network. The partitioning of the network address space into equal-sized slices for multicast distribution was considered in [8]. It is not surprising that regular methods consistently outperform the flooding [3]. However, the problem of fault tolerance and multicast robustness was, up to now, not intensively discussed in the context of such distribution schemes.

Unstructured P2P networks with epidemic communication [11] distribute multicast information by periodically contacting some randomly chosen neighbors (infection). Epidemic multicast (also known as gossip, or rumor mongering) performs the distribution by a significantly lower number of messages than aggressive flooding [7, 17, 13]. Although this method has probabilistic guarantees for reaching all nodes [5, 9], it is slower than other approaches and has substantially higher message complexity than 'regular' distribution schemes. For efficiency reasons, the multicast distribution can be limited to the depth or lifetime. For instance, in the rumor mongering scenario, the node stops propagating the rumor after several forwarding attempts to other nodes that have already seen it [5]. Unfortunately, these solutions usually provide no a priori prediction for multicast distribution behavior (e.g. in the sense of optimal scheduling).

3   System Architecture

3.1   Self-organizing Structure

Our framework uses Chord [21] as the base model. Every peer maintains an (incomplete) database about the rest of the network. This database contains entries (e.g. addresses) on some other peers (neighbors) together with timestamps of the last successful contact to that neighbor. Additionally, every node n_i is associated with an address value $adr(n_i) \in [0..adrMax]$ (e.g. using SHA-1 as base hash function). For any two nodes n_x and n_y, the distance in the circular address space can be defined as follows:

$$dist(n_x, n_y) = (adr(n_y) - adr(n_x) + adrMax)_{mod(adrMax)} \qquad (1)$$

Every node stores in its neighbor list (finger table) addresses of some other nodes nearest to 'ideal' positions in the address space. Analogously to finger tables in Chord, we consider positions with distances 2^k from node's address as optimal neighbor locations for that node. Each entry in the neighbor list is associated with a timestamp of the last known successful contact to that neighbor. The finger table is initialized when the node joins the network using chord-like address lookups. Later, the nodes periodically contact randomly chosen neighbors to exchange and to refresh local neighbor lists. Failure or leave of a peer does not require any administration at all. The failed address is guaranteed to be removed from all neighbor lists at latest after the specified TTL delay (when its timestamp is outdated).

3.2   Multicast

The multicast can be started by every node in the network. The basic idea follows [6]: each node that is involved into multicast distribution halves its sending interval after

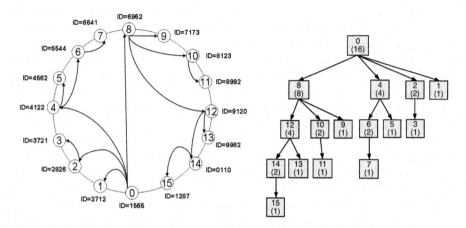

Fig. 1. Regular multicast and its distribution tree

every contact. The notification message contains the information to be multicasted, and a *limit* argument. This *limit* is used to restrict the forwarding space of a receiving node. When a node n_i receives the multicast message, it picks from its neighbor list the neighbor n_m nearest to the middle between its own address and *limit*: $middle = adr(n_i) + 0.5 \cdot dist(n_i, limit)$ and sends to n_m the multicast message with *limit* argument (in other words, n_m then must forward the multicast between its address and *limit*). The node n_i itself continues the multicast distribution within an interval between its address and $adr(n_m) - 1$. This distribution scheme forms a spanning tree covering all the nodes in the system. In the rest of the paper, we will refer to this method as 'regular' multicast distribution. Figure 1 shows the multicast tree for the sample network with 16 nodes.

In the failure-free environment, each node will receive the multicast message exactly once. However, the failure of any non-leaf node node blocks the multicast distribution within the subtree under this node. In our example (Figure 1), the failure of node 8 would make the entire branch with nodes 9..15 unreachable. On the other hand, even in the scenario with 50% node failures at least one-third of the neighbors in any neighbor list do not fail [12], which means that the network remains connected and the multicast could potentially reach all remaining nodes.

Motivated by this observation, our algorithm aims to combine the regular and the epidemic distribution schemes. All nodes that have received the multicast, periodically forward the multicast message to their randomly chosen neighbors as part of epidemic communication. In contrast to the regular scheme, the forwarding space of epidemic multicast is not restricted in any way.

4   The Predictive Model

The behavior of the meta algorithm can be modelled as the combination of two components: the regular multicast distribution, and the epidemic multicast spreading. In this paper, we restrict our model to the most important case with node failures. The modelled problem can be formally stated as follows. Initially, the network consists of N nodes with stabilized neighbor lists of certain length l. The addresses of nodes are assumed to be randomly distributed in the (sufficiently large) address space of size R. Before the multicast starts, some number of nodes X fail. Without loss of generality, we may assume that each node in the network fails with probability X/N. We assume that the stabilization of the network is substantially slower than the multicast progress; the dead neighbors remain in neighbor lists of other nodes.

In the considered model, we assume the knowledge about two global properties of the network: its size N and the number of failed nodes X. The simple estimator for N can be constructed using the average distance between neighbors in the ring (approximated by the distance to the node's first successor). The parameter X can be estimated from node's observations on failures within its neighbor list. These values can be exchanged between nodes as part of epidemic contacts. Advanced estimation techniques, e.g. using distributed hash sketches [2] [16], can be used as well.

4.1   The Regular Multicast Model

First, we can estimate the effect of the failure of the randomly chosen node n_i in the network. The node n_i has any possible position in the distribution tree with probability $1/N$ and fails with probability X/N. This node will be reached by the broadcast only when all of its predecessors in the distribution tree do not fail. When n_i resides on depth level u from the root of the distribution tree, this probability equals

$$Prob(\text{all } u \text{ predecessors of } n_i \text{ alive}) = \left(1 - \frac{X}{N}\right)^{u-1} \qquad (2)$$

When the node n_i with distribution interval that contains m nodes fails, it makes its $m - 1$ children unreachable. However, some of these $m - 1$ children may themselves fail, too. Since the nodes fail independently, the probability that exactly k nodes of $m - 1$ fail, can be estimated by the binomial formula:

$$Prob(k \text{ of } m - 1 \text{ fail}) = \binom{m-1}{k} \left(\frac{X}{N}\right)^k \left(1 - \frac{X}{N}\right)^{m-1-k} \qquad (3)$$

The expected number $Q(m - 1)$ of unreached live nodes under n_i can be estimated by summation over all possible k:

$$Q(m - 1) = \sum_{k=0}^{m-1} Prob(k \text{ of } m - 1 \text{ fail}) \cdot (m - 1 - k) \qquad (4)$$

Each node n_i that must distribute the multicast within an interval that contains m nodes, would split this interval into disjoint sub-intervals with $1, 2, .., m/2$ nodes and would have $log_2 m$ children in the distribution tree (the maximum depth of the multicast spanning tree is $log_2 N$). In our example from Figure 1, the node 8 For example, the distribution interval of node 8, including this splits its interval into sub-intervals with 1, 2, and 4 nodes and has $log_2 8 = 3$ children (nodes 9, 10, 12). The number of children on the depth level d from the node n_i can be recursively computed as

$$F(d,m) = \begin{cases} log_2 m, & d = 1 \vee m = 1 \\ \sum_{k=0}^{log_2 m - 1} F(i-1, 2^k), & d > 1 \wedge m > 1 \end{cases} \tag{5}$$

Using (5), the total number of children on multiple depth levels $1..k$ can be computed as

$$F^*(k,m) = \sum_{d=1}^{k} F(d,m) \tag{6}$$

Using (4) and (6), we estimate the expected total number of unreached live nodes on any number of depth levels $1..k$, $k \le log_2(m)$ by $Q(k, m-1)$ using:

$$Q(k, m-1) = Q\left(F^*(k,m)\right) \tag{7}$$

Using (2) and (4), we estimate the expected number of live nodes that become unreachable when n_i fails on level u from root and having the distribution interval with m nodes:

$$K(u,m) = \begin{cases} Q(m-1)\left(1 - \frac{X}{N}\right)^{u-1} \frac{1}{N}, & u > 0 \\ 0, & u = 0 \end{cases} \tag{8}$$

The average number of live nodes in that one failed node n_i in the tree makes unreachable can be estimated by summation over all its possible positions of n_i in the tree:

$$K^*(u,m) = \begin{cases} K(u,m) + \sum_{j=0}^{log_2 m - 1} K^*(u+1, 2^j), & m > 1 \\ 0, & m = 1 \end{cases} \tag{9}$$

When the failure rate X/N is known, the number of unreached live nodes in the whole distribution tree by failure of X nodes can be estimated as

$$E(\text{alive unreached}) = X \cdot K^*(0, N) \tag{10}$$

Replacing in (8) the total number of unreached live children (4) by depth-limited number of unreached live children (7), we obtain estimators for intermediate multicast distribution steps.

4.2   The Epidemic Multicast Model

The result of (10) is the input for the second part of the multicast distribution model, the epidemic spreading. Within each interval between epidemic contacts I_{COM}, every node contacts one of its neighbors and may be contacted by some other nodes. According to the push+pull multicast distribution scheme, we assume that both types of contact are used for multicast distribution. Thus, within each interval I_{COM}, our model should consider two cases: a) the node n_j contacts a previously infected node n_1, and b) the node n_j itself is contacted by a previously infected node n_2.

Let a and b be the total numbers of not yet infected and infected live nodes in the network. At the beginning of epidemic multicast distribution, $a = X \cdot K^*(0, N)$ and $b = N - X - a$.

a) The node n_j contacts another node n_1, randomly chosen from its neighbor list, once a period I_{COM}. The probability to obtain the multicast from n_1 equals the probability that n_1 is already infected $Prob(infected) = b/N$. Consequently, $P(\neg \text{pull infected}) = 1 - b/N$.

b) The node n_j is contacted by other node n_2. We notice that n_2 can contact n_j only when its address is in the neighbor list of n_2. In other words, the address of n_j must be the first successor of some 'optimal' finger address from the neighbor list of n_2. The expected interval between adjacent nodes in the address space of dimensionality R with N participating peers is R/N. Thus, when the finger of n_2 points to some address in the interval of width R/N before n_j, this node is expected to be the first successor and would qualify for the neighbor list of n_2. Since the intervals of $l = log_2(N)$ fingers are expected to be disjoint, there are $l \cdot (R/N)$ positions of n_2 in the address space such that n_j comes into its neighbor list. The probability for n_2 to have one of these addresses is $l \cdot (R/N)/R = l/N$. The probability for n_j to be chosen by n_2 for the next contact from its neighbor list of length l equals $l/N \cdot 1/l = 1/N$. Therefore, $Prob(\neg \text{push infected}) = 1 - 1/N$. Assuming that all epidemic contacts are independent, the probability for n_j to be infected within interval I_{COM} by at least one of b infected nodes (and the resulting expected total number of infected nodes after I_{COM}) can be estimated as

$$b_{new} = b + a \cdot Prob(infected) = b + a \cdot \left(1 - \left(1 - \frac{1}{N} \right)^b \cdot \left(1 - \frac{b}{N} \right) \right) \quad (11)$$

The further modelling of the epidemic multicast distribution can be continued in an iterative manner by substituting of b_{new} and $a_{new} = N - X - b_{new}$ as new input values for the next step.

5   Experiments

In [14], we have shown positive results in systematical experiments on failure tolerance, distribution speed, and message complexity for the proposed multicast distribution in comparison with its base methods. We will not repeat this here and will instead focus on the prediction quality of the proposed theoretical model. Our experiments were focused on goodness of prediction for the multicast spreading. We have systematically simulated the most critical failure scenarios of the dynamic behavior in P2P networks (an significant amount of peers leaves the network within a short period of time). In our evaluations, we simulated the network architecture with following properties:

- number of participating peers: 1024;
- interval between epidemic contacts I_{COM}: 2000 time units; higher values lead to a greater gain of the meta method compared to the 'pure' epidemic multicast;
- average network delay for message delivery: 100 time units.

To illustrate the behavior of multicast distribution in dynamically changing overlay networks, the multicast was initiated in every model at multiple fixed timepoints. Each experiment was repeated 30 times with randomization factors: the order of contacts between nodes, refreshing of neighbor lists, failure points, etc. To analyze the statistical significance of deviations between predicted and observed values, we also computed 95% confidence intervals for our experimental series.

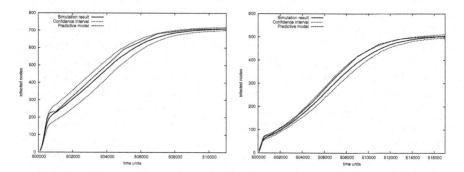

Fig. 2. Job distribution progress in the network with 30% node failures (left) and 50% node failures (right)

Figure 2 shows the multicast distribution for models where 30% or 50% of nodes randomly leave the network within a short period of time, but stay still in the neighbor lists of other nodes as the dead neighbors. It is notable that the predictive model captures the multicast behavior with high accuracy. Moreover, in most cases the deviation of predicted results from simulation model is not statistically significant. It can be also observed that with a growing number of unavailable nodes, the regular multicast reaches significantly lesser nodes. The amount of nodes that are reached in the meta method by the epidemic distribution becomes higher.

6   Conclusion and Future Work

In this paper, we discussed a new multicast distribution algorithm for heterogenous P2P networks. Our hybrid approach combines the advantages of two architectures: Chord-style regular networks and random epidemic networks. The advantages of the proposed approach are higher failure tolerance, faster multicast distribution and better message complexity compared to the base methods. Furthermore, we introduced the probabilistic predictive model for optimal multicast scheduling that captures the multicast behavior with high accuracy.

The modelling of further application scenarios (node joins, simultaneous joins / leaves) is subject of our future work. Furthermore, we are interested in statistical estimations for job distribution with redundancy in order to improve guarantees for job completion.

References

1. D. Anderson, J. Cobb, E. Korpela, M. Lebofsky, and D. Werthimer. SETI@home: An Experiment in Public-Resource Computing. *Communications of the ACM*, 45(11), 2002.
2. M. Bawa, H. Garcia-Molina, A. Gionis, and R. Motwani. Estimating aggregates on a peer-to-peer network. *Tech. Report, Computer Science Dept., Stanford University*, 2003.
3. M. Castro, M. Jones, A. Kermarrec, A. Rowstron, M. Theimer, H. Wang, and A. Wolman. An Evaluation of Scalable Application-level Multicast Built Using Peer-to-Peer Overlays, 2003.
4. A. Chakravarti, G. Baumgartner, and M. Lauria. The Organic Grid: Self-Organizing Computation on a Peer-to-Peer Network. In *Proceedings of the International Conference on Autonomic Computing (ICAC '04)*, New York, 2004.
5. A. Demers, D. Greene, C. Hauser, W. Irish, J. Larson, S. Scott, S. Shenker, H. Sturgis, D. Swinehart, and D. Terry. Epidemic algorithms for replicated database management. *6th Annual ACM Symposium on Principles of Distributed Computing (PODC'87)*, 1987.
6. S. El-Ansary, L.O. Alima, P. Brand, and S. Haridi. Efficient Broadcast in Structured Peer-to-Peer Networks. *International Workshop on Peer-to-Peer Systems (IPTPS)*, 2003.
7. O. Escalante, T. Perez, J. Solano, and I. Stojmenovic. RNG-based Searching and Broadcasting over Internet Graphs and Peer-to-Peer Computing Systems. *Technical report, Universidad Nacional Autónoma de México, IIMAS*, 2002.
8. A. Gupta, B. Liskov, and R. Rodrigues. One Hop Lookups for Peer-to-Peer Overlays. *Ninth Workshop on Hot Topics in Operating Systems (HotOS)*, 2003.
9. I. Gupta, A. Kermarrec, and A. Ganesh. Efficient epidemic-style protocols for reliable and scalable multicast. *IEEE Intl. Symp. Reliable Distributed Systems (SRDS)*, 2002.
10. R. Gupta and A. Somani. CompuP2P: An Architecture for Sharing of Computing Resources In Peer-to-Peer Networks With Selfish Nodes. In *Proc. of the Second Workshop on the Economics of P2P Systems*, Harvard University, 2004.
11. M. Jelasity, M. Preuss, and B. Paechter. A scalable and robust framework for distributed applications. *Proceedings of the IEEE Congress on Evolutionary Computation (CEC)*, 2002.
12. D. Liben-Novll, H. Balakrishnan, and D. Karger. Analysis of the evolution of peer-to-peer systems. *Annual ACM Symposium on Principles of Distributed Computing*, 2002.
13. M. Lin, K. Marzullo, and S. Masini. Gossip versus Deterministically Constrained Flooding on Small Networks. In *DISC: International Symposium on Distributed Computing*, 2000.
14. P. Merz and K. Gorunova. Efficient Broadcast in P2P Grids. *CCGrid, International Symposium on Cluster Computing and the Grid*, 2005.
15. A. Montresor. A Robust Protocol for Building Superpeer Overlay Topologies. In *Proceedings of the 4th International Conference on Peer-to-Peer Computing*, Zurich, Switzerland, 2004. IEEE.
16. N. Ntarmos and P. Triantafillou. Hash Sketches over DHTs. *Tech. Report 2004/12/06, Computer Technology Institute, University of Patras*, 2004.
17. M. Portmann and A. Seneviratne. Cost-effective broadcast for fully decentralized peer-to-peer networks. *Computer Communications*, 26(11):1159–1167, 2003.
18. S. Ratnasamy, P. Francis, M. Handley, R. Karp, and S. Shenker. A scalable content addressable network. *Tech. Report TR-00-010, Berkeley, CA*, 2000.
19. M. Ripeanu, A. Iamnitchi, and I. Foster. Mapping the Gnutella Network. *IEEE Internet Computing*, 2002.
20. M. Schlosser, M. Sintek, S. Decker, and W. Nejdl. HyperCuP - Shaping Up Peer-to-Peer Networks. 2002.
21. I. Stoica, R. Morris, D. Karger, F. Kaashoek, and H. Balakrishnan. Chord: A Scalable Peer-To-Peer Lookup Service for Internet Applications. *ACM SIGCOMM*, 2001.

Peer-Sensitive ObjectRank
– Valuing Contextual Information in Social Networks

Andrei Damian, Wolfgang Nejdl, and Raluca Paiu

L3S Research Center / University of Hanover,
Deutscher Pavillon, Expo Plaza 1, 30539 Hanover, Germany
{damian, nejdl, paiu}@l3s.de

Abstract. Building on previous work on how to model contextual information for desktop search and how to implement semantically rich information exchange in social networks, we define a new algorithm, *Peer-Sensitive ObjectRank* for ranking resources on the desktop. The new algorithm takes into account different trust values for each peer, generalizing previous biasing PageRank algorithms. We investigate in detail, how different assumptions about trust distributions influence the ranking of information received from different peers, and which consequences they have with respect to integration of new resources into one peer's initial network of resources. We also investigate how assumptions concerning size and quality of a peer's resource network influence ranking after information exchange, and conclude with directions for further research.

1 Introduction

Due to the boom of web search engines and powerful ranking algorithms like Google PageRank, Web search has become more efficient than PC search. The recent arrival of desktop search applications, which index all data on a PC, promises to increase search efficiency on the desktop. Even with these tools, searching through our personal documents is inferior to searching the documents on the web, though.

The main problem with ranking on the desktop comes from the lack of links between documents, the foundation of current ranking algorithms (in addition to TF/IDF measures). By gathering semantic information from user activities, from the contexts the user works in we build the necessary links between documents. This context information can then be shared between peers in a social network, providing another important source of context information which can be integrated into the local context network of a peer. In this case, however, it is very important to distinguish between items received from different peers of the social group, to take their different background, experience or reliability into account. *Peer-sensitive ObjectRank*, as defined and investigated in this paper, describes how to do just that.

As motivating scenario, let us consider our L3S Research Group context and within this group, Bob, Alice and Tom as three members who exchange information. We assume that Bob mails Alice a document which he sent to the DELOS Workshop. As Bob is one of the authors and therefore has already all the important context for the paper, in this first email, Alice will not only receive the article, but also its immediate context relevant for the research group. From the references included, Alice decides that two of them are of particular interest for her and she sends back an email to Bob requiring

M. Kitsuregawa et al. (Eds.): WISE 2005, LNCS 3806, pp. 512–519, 2005.

additional information about those. As an answer, she receives from him the associated context information, containing the references that Bob has already downloaded. So the context information will be exchanged progressively, from the immediate context to the more distant one. Tom also sends Alice an email, containing a paper on ranking algorithms. From all the papers referenced by it, Tom has read three of them, so that the corresponding context will also include these references.

Bob and Tom play different roles in the L3S research group: Bob is a professor, while Tom is a Ph. D. student. This translates into different levels of trust on Alice's scale, which means that Bob will be higher ranked than Tom, or other authors not known to her. Additionally, the recommendations Alice receives from Bob are more important for her than those received from Tom.

In the next section we provide an overview on how to represent and exchange contextual information based on RDF metadata and specify how to model importance and influence between resources in such a contextual information graph. In Section 3 we discuss how this information is used to rank these resources at a peer and how our ranking algorithm - *Peer-Sensitive ObjectRank* - can take different trust values for the peers participating in the social network into account. In Section 4 we analyse in detail the influence of different trust distributions on the ranking algorithm. We conclude with a short summary and further research issues to be explored.

2 Representing Context and Importance

Motivation. Context information describes all aspects important for a certain situation: ideas, facts, persons, publications, and many more, including all relevant relationships as well as interaction history. Current desktop search prototypes fall short of utilizing any desktop specific information, especially context information, and just use full text index search. In our scenario we clearly need to use additional context information, and specifically want to exploit the *CiteSeer, Browsing* and *Desktop contexts*. A detailed description of these contexts can be found in [3] and [5].

Scenario specific annotation ontologies. For creating the ontologies describing the contexts we are focusing on [3, 5] we use two different shapes: circles and rectangles in order to designate classes and class attributes respectively. We use classes whenever we want to attach importance/rank to entities, attributes otherwise. In addition to the information which resources are included in a specific context, we also want to know how important or valuable these resources are. We therefore have to specify how to express this information, in order to use it for ranking search results.

Authority transfer annotations. Annotation ontologies describe all aspects and relationships among resources which influence the ranking. The identity of the authors, for example, influences our opinion of documents so "author" should be represented explicitly as a class in our publication ontology. We also have to specify how importance of one resource influences the importance of another resource. To do this, we build upon a recent variation of PageRank, ObjectRank [1], which has introduced the notion of authority transfer schema graphs. These graphs extend ontologies by adding weights and edges in order to express how importance propagates among the entities and resources inside the ontology. These weights and edges represent the authority transfer annotations, which extend our context ontologies with the information we need to compute ranks for all instances of the classes defined in the context ontologies.[1]

3 Peer-Sensitive ObjectRank

Our contextual information graphs not only add additional information to the resources on our desktop, they also connect them. This makes it possible to use link-based algorithms like PageRank to enhance ranking in addition to the usual TF/IDF-based methods. In this section we will revisit ObjectRank [1] which can build upon our annotation ontologies to provide PageRank-based ranking for our linked desktop resources and then generalize it to take different trust values for the peers in a social network into account - important for supporting reliable information sharing in such a network.

3.1 PageRank / ObjectRank

Link-based algorithms like PageRank base their computation of rankings on the link structure of the resources, in our case specified by our annotation ontologies and the corresponding metadata. Rank computation is then done using the well-known Page-Rank formula:

$$r = d \cdot A \cdot r + (1 - d) \cdot e \tag{1}$$

The random jump to an arbitrary resource from the data graph is modelled by the vector e. A is the adjacency matrix which connects all available instances of the existing context ontology on one's desktop. When instantiating the authority transfer annotation ontology for the resources existing on the users' desktop, the corresponding matrix A will have elements which can be either 0, if there is no edge between the corresponding entities in the data graph, or the value of the weight assigned to the edge determined by these entities, in the authority transfer annotation ontology, divided by the number of outgoing links of the same type. According to the formula, a random surfer follows one of the outgoing links of the current page, with the probability specified by d, and with a probability of $(1-d)$ he jumps to a randomly selected page from the web graph. The r vector in the equation stores the ranks of all resources in the data graph, computed iteratively until a certain threshold is reached. [5] presents an example on how this computation is done.

3.2 Peer-Sensitive ObjectRank

Motivation. In our distributed scenario each user has his own contextual network/ context metadata graph and for each node in this network the appropriate ranking computed by the algorithm, as previously described. When sharing resources within the social network, we also exchange the contextual information associated with these resources. This, of course, translates into different ranking values for the items existing on the desktop. If a user receives resources from several members of his interest group, for which he has different levels of trust, he would like to have higher rank values for the items received from his most trusted neighbours.

---

[1] In contrast to ObjectRank, we do not compute a keyword-specific ranking, but a global one.

Biasing on Peers. The key insight in taking different trust values for different peers into account is that we can represent different trust in peers by corresponding modifications to the e vector. Specifically, we will modify it in a way such that the resources received from highly trusted members have a higher probability to be reached through a random jump than the resources received from less trusted peers. In our formula, this means that the e vector has high values for the positions corresponding to items received from important neighbours, and lower values for the other ones.

In order to be able to create such a "peer-sensitive jumping vector", we have to keep track of the provenance of each resource. We introduce the following notions:

$$originates(r_i, P_n) = \begin{cases} 1 \text{ , if } r_i \text{ is in the original set of resources of peer } P_n \\ 0 \text{ , otherwise} \end{cases}$$

$trust(P_i, P_j) \in [0, 1]$, which represents the trust value of peer P_i for peer P_j.

With these definitions, we can now specify how the e vector is computed:

$$e_k(P_i) = max_{j=0}^{N}\{trust(P_i, P_j) \cdot originates(r_k, P_j)\},$$

where N is the total number of peers. This says, that for peer P_i, the probability to jump to the resource r_k is equal to the highest trust value of peer P_i for those peers where this resource originated from. The new formula still guarantees the convergence of our ranking algorithm: it preserves the Markov property of the graph, i.e. each resource can be reached from any other resource. It is a generalization of PageRank biasing, as the e vector now contains more than two different values: basically, for each peer, we have a different value (thus the name *"Peer-Sensitive ObjectRank"*).

Assumptions on Trust Distributions. Based on these definitions, it is obviously important to investigate which influence trust has, if it has any and if so, how much. Besides, which difference does it make for ranking if we consider different trust distributions? We will investigate these issues for different kinds of social networks, and focus on the situation when the peers from a social network have merged all their resources to compare the initial rankings and the rankings after the merge. We will analyze situations where: a) peers have the same trust in one another, b) trust values are evenly distributed (linear distribution) and c) trust is unevenly distributed (powerlaw distribution).

4 Evaluation

4.1 General Experiment Setup and Hypotheses

For the general experiment setup we consider n peers that are part of the same interest group and have different numbers of resources on their desktops. For allocating resources to peers, we build the article set of all the papers published at the Semantic Web related tracks of the following conferences: WWW1999, WWW2000, WWW2001, WWW2002 as well as to ECDL2000 and SWWS2001.

For each peer i, we select an initial set of papers and starting from this set, we consider all their references. For each article we query the CiteSeer database and get additional information (authors, conference, PageRank, references). From all references of a paper we select the top k articles based on their PageRank values and allocate to each peer a percentage of these. We call the percentage of the top ranked articles each peer receives the *accuracy* of the peer. In addition we allocate to the peers a certain $fill\_in$ percentage from the other articles. We repeat the resource selection mechanism described above until we have collected the number of resources we want to allocate to that peer.

Based on the generated resource sets we compute for each peer i the ACP_i adjacency matrix (AuthorsConferencesPapers). After all resources have been exchanged, all peers will have all articles. The matrix for the union of all resources stored on the peers' desktops is generated appropriately.

Our experiments are intended to investigate the following hypotheses: a) powerlaw trust distribution makes peers "consultancy resistant", i.e. more reluctant to highly value resources received from other peers and b) bigger peers influence smaller peers based on their larger and therefore more influential network of resources. The first hypothesis will be tested mainly through our first experiment, the second hypothesis by the second experiment. An additional hypothesis was that the second effect is stronger than the first one. The next subsections will show whether these hypotheses are true or false and will discuss what we can conclude from the results.

4.2   Experiment I - Consequences of Trust Distributions

Setup. We considered a set of three peers, all being members of the same interest group and having approximately the same number of resources on their desktops: peer 0 has 95 papers, peer 1 has 97 papers and peer 2 has 93 papers and the corresponding authors and conferences. We computed the rankings for all resources initially existing at each peer. The results were sorted in descending order of their rank values. We compared the values for the top 10 best ranked resources (tables 1 and 2).

In our experiment we consider the situation where the peers exchange all the resources they have, so that after a while everybody will have everything. Identical resources coming from different peers appear only once in the resulting data graph, but we keep track of the sources from which each resource originated. In order to be able to see the influence of the trust biased rank computation, we first computed the initial rankings for the merged graph, after all peers have exchanged everything. This rank computation is basically pure ObjectRank computation.

For the next step of our experiment we computed again for each peer the rankings for the whole graph of resources, this time taking different trust values into account. We considered a list of trust values following a linear and a powerlaw distribution respectively. For all computations we assumed that each peer has 100% trust in itself and lower trust values for the other peers.

Results. Some of the results we obtained for this experiment are summarized in tables 1 and 2. Table 1 presents the top 10 highest ranked resources initially computed for peer 0. In the columns labelled "Powerlaw Ranks" and "Linear Ranks", for resources originally appearing at peer 0, we include the ranks we obtained for a rank computation with biasing on a powerlaw trust distribution and a linear trust distribution respectively. The "Merged Ranks" column contains the ranks of the initial resources after peer 0's resources have been merged with all the resources of the other peers. Table 2 has the same structure and presents the results for peer 2.

Discussion. The results we obtain for peer 0 when using a powerlaw trust distribution show a strong resistance against new publications. Peer 0's top 10 initial rankings remain the same with the powerlaw trust distribution and the results indicate that peer 0 integrates not the highest ranked publications from the others, but the ones best connected to his initial network. On the 20th place, peer 0 integrates the resource with the 20th highest rank from peer 1. This is also understandable since peer 0 uses the highest trust value for itself (100%), 25% and 11% trust for peers 1 and 2, respectively. This behaviour is similar in the case of peer 1 and 2.

The linear trust distribution is similar to powerlaw in resistance, though here the rank of others seems to be more important than in the powerlaw case. The 20th highest place in the rank hierarchy is occupied by the resource initially appearing on the 1st place in the top 20 initial rank list of peer 1. Peer 0 assigns 60% trust for peer 1 and 40% trust for peer 2. The same effect can be seen at peers 1 and 2: peer 1 integrates the first ranked resources from peer 0 and peer 2, the resource coming from peer 0 appearing before the resource originating at peer 2. This can be explained not only by the fact that peer 1 assigns 60% trust to peer 0 and 40% to peer 2, but also by the fact that peer 0 has better resources than peer 2, according to the accuracy they use when selecting the references of a paper. For peer 2, the top 20 highest ranked resources include a new resource, which originally appeared after the best 20 ranked resources. This new resource is a conference: its rank has increased since peer 2 received more papers presented at this conference.

Table 1. Exp. 1: Rankings for Peer 0

Ranks				Resource
Powerlaw	Linear	Merged	Initial	
1	1	3	1	ITTALKS...
3	3	7	2	A Framework...
2	2	6	3	Integrating...
9	10	> 10	4	MSL: A Model...
4	4	8	5	Pickling...
5	5	9	6	Evolution of...
8	8	> 10	7	Forward...
7	7	> 10	8	The Case...
6	6	> 10	9	Study On...
10	> 10	> 10	10	Semantic Web..

Table 2. Exp. 1: Rankings for Peer 2

Ranks				Resource
Powerlaw	Linear	Merged	Initial	
1	1	1	1	PowerBookmarks:...
2	2	2	2	EDUTELLA:...
3	3	5	3	Logical...
4	4	4	4	Implementation...
5	5	> 10	5	An Improved...
6	6	> 10	6	Automating...
9	10	> 10	7	Squeal:...
7	8	> 10	8	Accessing...
8	9	> 10	9	Simplified...
> 10	> 10	> 10	10	Translating...

4.3 Experiment II - Consequences of Initial Resource Distributions

Setup. We considered six peers, all members of the same social network, having different numbers of resources following a powerlaw distribution. Like in the previous experiment, we investigated how trust can influence the rankings of the resources existing on one's desktop, so we run the experiment for linear and powerlaw trust distributions.

Results. For analysing the effects of trust biasing we will present the results only for peer 0 (with 300 papers) and peer 5 (with 5 papers) (tables 3, 4 and 5). Table 3 shows the peer 0's highest top 10 ranked resources for an ObjectRank computation with biasing on a powerlaw trust distribution. We compare these rankings with the ranks we obtain for the rank computation on the merged data graph and with the ones we obtain when biasing on a linear trust distribution. For peer 5 we compare the ranks of the top 10 resources for a powerlaw trust biased rank computation with the merged and initial ranks, and also the "Linear Ranks" with the merged and initial ranks.

518   A. Damian, W. Nejdl, and R. Paiu

Table 3. Exp.2: Rankings for Peer 0

Merged	Initial	Powerlaw	Resource
1	1	1	PowerBookm...
2	2	2	ITTALKS:...
3	3	3	The Semantic...
4	4	4	EDUTELLA:...
5	5	5	XML-GL:...
6	6	6	Accessing...
7	7	7	Extension of...
8	8	8	Automating...
9	9	9	Integrating...
10	10	10	Keys for...

Table 4. Exp.2: Rankings for Peer 5 (Powerlaw Trust Distribution)

Merged	Initial	Powerlaw	Resource
5	1	1	XML-GL:...
> 10	3	2	A Query...
> 10	7	3	SWWS2001...
> 10	6	4	ECDL 2000...
> 10	2	5	Learning...
> 10	> 10	6	SemWeb...
> 10	9	7	Steffen S...
> 10	8	8	Alexander...
> 10	> 10	9	SEBD...
> 10	> 10	10	Dan S...

Table 5. Exp. 2: Rankings for Peer 5 (linear Trust Distribution)

Merged	Initial	Linear	Resource
1	> 10	1	PowerBookm...
2	> 10	2	ITTALKS:...
5	1	3	XML-GL:...
3	> 10	4	The Semantic...
4	> 10	5	EDUTELLA:...
> 10	7	6	SWWS2001...
6	> 10	7	Accessing...
> 10	3	8	A Query...
> 10	6	9	ECDL 2000...
9	> 10	10	Integrating...

Discussion. We observed that peer 0's initial ranks are identical to the ranks computed after resource merging. Rankings computed with a linear as well as with a powerlaw trust distribution are the same as the initial rankings (Table 3). The reason is that peer 0 had already most of the resources contained in the merged data graph. It is obvious in this case that trust biasing plays no role, peer 0's rankings remaining unchanged. The situation is totally different for peer 5. This peer has initially only 5 papers, plus a certain number of authors and conferences. Even when computing the new rankings for the merged data graph, its original rankings change dramatically. With a powerlaw trust distribution, peer 5 seems to be resistant to new resources. When biasing on a linear trust distribution, peer 5's ranks change considerably in comparison to the initial rankings (Table 5). Only a few of the resources still appear in the top 20 new reranked list of resources. Things are different when comparing the new rankings with the initially merged rankings (table 5). With one exception, all resources from the top 20 linear ranks also appear in the top 20 merged rank list, though in a new order.

5   Related Work

The idea of biased ranking has first been explored in topic-sensitive PageRank. [6] builds a topic-oriented PageRank, starting by computing off-line a set of 16 PageRank vectors, biased on each of the 16 main topics of the Open Directory Project. At query time, the vectors are combined based on the topics of the query to form a composite PageRank score for pages matching the query. [2] presents a generalization of this approach.

An interesting search and retrieval system for finding semantic web documents on the web is Swoogle [4]. Their ranking scheme uses weights for the different types of relations between Semantic Web Documents (SWD) to model their probability to be explored. This mainly serves to rank ontologies or instances of ontologies. In our approach we have instances of a fixed ontology and the weights for the links model the users' preferences.

On the aspect of desktop search, [5] presents another way of making use of the contextual information existing on the users' desktops, exploring how semantically rich complex recommendation structures, represented as RDF graphs, can be exchanged and shared in a distributed social network. The interest groups are specified with the aid of an extended FOAF vocabulary. The recommendations transport the shared context information as well as ranking information, as described in the annotation ontologies.

The idea of personalized ranking is exploited in [7]. Their personalized search engine built on Google's Web API, redirects the search keywords to Google and retrieves the search results. The system dynamically creates a user profile, by recording the "clickthrough data", which implicitly collects the user's feedback to infer her interests. Based on the user profile and on the result items' semantic meanings in WordNet, the system re-ranks Google search results. The re-ranking is computed differently to the approach described in this paper and is based on the computation of the semantic similarity between result items and user profile.

6   Conclusions and Further Work

This paper presented and analysed a new variant of the PageRank algorithm, called *Peer-Sensitive ObjectRank*, for ranking resources on the desktop, which takes into account different trust values, generalizing previous biasing PageRank algorithms. We performed several experiments and the results confirm the two hypotheses we made in the beginning: powerlaw trust distributions make peers consultancy resistant and bigger peers influence smaller peers.

Several further research questions are worth to be investigated. The first one is how to handle and defend against malicious peers sending bad quality resources. Second, we are interested in investigating the case where one user is member of several interest groups, and exchanges information with members of these groups. Then the user would like to have different trust values for the same peer based on the topic under which a certain resource received from this peer is classified. Finally, we want to investigate in more detail additional aspects which might influence Peer-Sensitive ObjectRank values, such as specific connectivity properties of the context graphs available on the desktop.

References

1. A. Balmin, V. Hristidis, and Y. Papakonstantinou.   Objectrank: Authority-based keyword search in databases. In *VLDB*, Toronto, Sept. 2004.
2. P. Chirita, W. Nejdl, R. Paiu, and C. Kohlshuetter. Using odp metadata to personalize search. In *SIGIR*, Salvador, Aug. 2005.
3. P. A. Chirita, R. Gavriloaie, S. Ghita, W. Nejdl, and R. Paiu. Activity based metadata for semantic desktop search. In *ESWC*, Heraklion, Greece, May 2005.
4. L. Ding, T. Finin, A. Joshi, R. Pan, R. S. Cost, Y. Peng, P. Reddivari, V. C. Doshi, and J. Sachs. Swoogle: A search and metadata engine for the semantic web. In *Proceedings of the 13th ACM Conference on Information and Knowledge Management*, Washington, DC, Nov. 2004.
5. S. Ghita, W. Nejdl, and R. Paiu. Semantically rich recommendations in social networks for sharing, exchanging and ranking semantic context. In *ISWC*, Galway, Nov. 2005.
6. T. Haveliwala. Topic-sensitive pagerank. In *WWW*, May 2002.
7. G. Huang and W. Liu. An online adaptive method for personalization of search engines. In *WISE*, Australia, Nov. 2004.

Automatic Performance Tuning for J2EE Application Server Systems

Yan Zhang[1], Wei Qu[1] and Anna Liu[2]

[1] School of Information Technologies,
The University of Sydney,
Sydney NSW 2006 Australia
{yanzhang, wequ3946}@it.usyd.edu.au
[2] Microsoft Australia,
North Ryde NSW 2113 Australia
annaliu@microsoft.com

Abstract. Performance tuning for J2EE application server systems is a complex manual task. This is unfortunately a necessary task in order to achieve optimal performance under dynamic workload environment. In this paper, we present our architecture and approach for implementing autonomic behavior in J2EE application server systems. Our experimental results demonstrate the feasibility and practicality of our architecture and approach in automatic performance tuning of J2EE application server systems.

1 Introduction

J2EE-based application servers are popular server-side solutions for many Web-enabled e-business applications. They offer a highly declarative design and deployment model, and various software components that aim to ease the development of complex Internet-based applications. However, there is much manual performance tuning that needs to be done in order to achieve scalable, high-performance J2EE applications [1, 2]. The task of such performance tuning is not only very difficult and time-consuming but also error-prone [3]. In addition, the workloads of e-business sites tend to vary dynamically and exhibit short-term fluctuations [20], even if the system is tuned well at one point in time, it will show poor performance at other times. That is, a statically configured system will perform poorly in the time-varying workloads as present in typical e-business environment. The end result is that systems performing badly will frustrate customers. Customers will leave this site and move to other sites with better performance [4].

Autonomic computing [5], which derives its name from the autonomic nervous system, seeks to bring automated self-configuring, self-healing, self- optimizing and self-protecting capabilities into computing systems. The development of autonomic computing systems has attracted much research efforts. Our work is targeted at automating the performance tuning of J2EE Application Servers, which belongs to the self-configuration and self-optimization aspects. The goals of our work are to free the administrator from manually setting "knobs" that can have serious impact on

M. Kitsuregawa et al. (Eds.): WISE 2005, LNCS 3806, pp. 520–527, 2005.

performance and to make application server minimize response time for its applications while not being conservative and rejecting excessive requests.

The rest of this paper is organized as follow. Section 2 introduces our solution architecture and discusses a specialization of a generic control system model for the purpose of automatic performance tuning in J2EE application servers. Section 3 describes our performance tuning strategy. Section 4 presents our implementation and experimental results. Section 5 reviews related work. Finally, conclusions and plans for future work are presented in section 6.

2 Self-configuration and Self-optimization Solution Architecture

2.1 Control System Model

In general, a control system is composed of controller and controlled system, shown in Fig. 1. [14]. The controller can control the controlled system via feed-forward control strategy or feedback control strategy. With a feed-forward control strategy, regulation is determined based on the input to the controlled system. With a feedback control strategy, regulation is determined based on the comparison of the difference between a desired objective and measured output delivered by the controlled system.

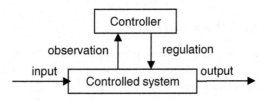

Fig. 1. Generic control system

2.2 Solution Architecture for Enabling Autonomic J2EE Application Server

In the context of our work, the "controlled system" is the J2EE application server systems and the "controller" provides dynamic performance regulation.

As shown in Fig. 2, the Data Collector component is to obtain observations. It collects real-time performance data which will be further processed by Data Processor to obtain average response time or throughput values etc. These real-time performance data stored in the database will be used by other components. The Predictor component uses the performance data to predict future workloads to help the Decision Maker component to proactively deal with the time-varying workloads. The Comparator component will compare the difference between the real-time performance data such as response time and Service Level Agreement (SLA). The Decision Maker component applies some algorithm based on the result from Predictor, Comparator and SLA to choose an appropriate performance tuning strategy in the Knowledge Base. The Tuner component will translate the strategy into actions and inject the actions into the application server to realize the configuration strategy to attain the system performance requirements.

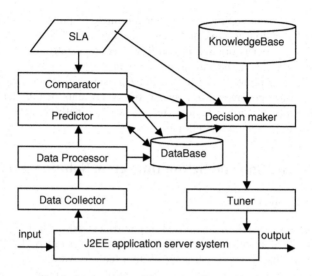

Fig. 2. Automated performance tuning architecture

3 Performance Tuning Strategy

3.1 A Performance Tuning Scenario

Our research is based on JBoss application server. JBoss is used in our research because it is freely available, and is also representative of the commercial J2EE products in terms of functionality and architecture. Being open source, it also means that we can readily instrument the J2EE application server code.

According to our experimental results [15, 16], thread pool size in EJB container has the most significant effect on the whole system performance. In JBoss application server, the corresponding parameter is MaxPoolSize. The effect of MaxPoolSize on response time is shown in Figure 3 and Figure 4. (The testbed will be described in section 4.1)

Our experimental results show that there exists optimal MaxPoolSize value for certain workload. As shown in the figures, if MaxPoolSize is too small, it would take much time for clients to wait in the queue to be accepted by the server thread. If MaxPoolSize is too large, it increases the contention on application resources and databases which degrades performance. The above figures also verified that different workload has different optimal value of MaxPoolSize. In this scenario, when the client number is 200, the optimal value of MaxPoolSize is 80, while client number is 400, the optimal value of MaxPoolSize is 200. It indicates that the performance can be optimized if the MaxPoolSize can be configured dynamically. Unfortunately, current application servers are static and have no runtime optimization mechanism. In addition, configuring and reconfiguring current application servers involve a shutdown and a restart of the system. Therefore the corresponding mechanisms need to be developed to achieve optimized performance requirement.

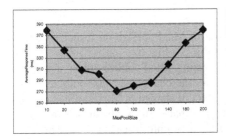

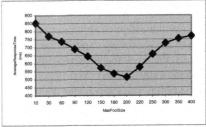

Fig. 3. Client number: 200   **Fig. 4.** Client number: 400

3.2 Automated Performance Tuning with Qualitative Knowledge

To solve the above optimization problem, we utilize the rich semantics and features in existing fuzzy logic and fuzzy control systems theory [17].

As shown in Fig. 3 and Fig. 4, the MaxPoolSize in JBoss application server has a concave upward effect on the response time. Therefore, response time can be minimized via a gradient descent procedure. We have set up a set of fuzzy rules to adjust MaxPoolSize. Due to space limitation we provide two of them as follows:

if Change-In-MaxPoolSize is Medium Negative and Change-In-ResponseTime is Medium Positive then Next-Change-In-MaxPoolSize is Medium Positive.

if Change-In-MaxPoolSize is Medium Positive and Change-In-ResponseTime is Medium Positive then Next-Change-In-MaxPoolSize is Medium Negative.

The above rules can be proven by Lyapunov method [18] that can converge to the optimal MaxPoolSize value at steady state.

As for fuzzy membership function, we choose triangular shaped functions in our rule base other than Gaussian shaped membership functions due to the more computational simplicity of the triangular shaped functions.

In fuzzy control systems, because of the ability of generating smoother control surfaces, the *Center of Gravity (COG)* method [17] is frequently used. Therefore, we choose COG in defuzzification.

4 Implementation and Experimental Results

The technical challenges in implementation have been thoroughly discussed in our previous paper [4]. For the data collector and tuner components, we have so far successfully implemented them with ease through the use of JMX [19] API provided in JBoss application server. The fuzzy control algorithm in the Decision Maker component is implemented in Java.

4.1 Experimental Testbed

Our experimental testbed consists of one dual-processor Windows 2000 server PC running JBoss application server and Oracle 8.1.7 Database server, and one Windows 2000 server PC running synthetic workload generator. The machines are connected over 100MB/s switched LAN. We use Stock-OnLine benchmark [15], which is a simulation of an on-line stock-broking system.

4.2   Experimental Results

To show the effect of dynamic configuration of MaxPoolSize on response time, we conduct the following experiments shown in Fig. 5 – Fig. 6.

Fig.5 displays the effect of dynamic adjusting MaxPoolSize under a stationary workload (400 clients). The upper chart shows the change of MaxPoolSize with the time varying. The chart under it shows the effect of change of MaxPoolSize on the response time given 400 clients. We can observe that with the dynamic configuration support, the MaxPoolSize keeps increasing from 10 until it reaches 200, which is the neighborhood of its optimal value. Due to the stochastic nature of computing systems, the optimal value of MaxPoolSize under 400 clients is not absolute. In our experimental environment, it is in the neighborhood of between 180 and 200. After such configuration, the performance of the system was improved by approximately 37%. We can also see that our automated configuration mechanism can help to determine the optimal value of MaxPoolSize without exhaustive human testing.

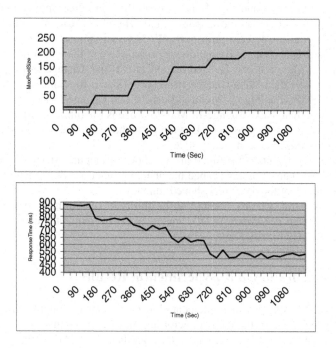

Fig. 5. The effect of change of MaxPoolSize on response time under 400 clients

Fig.6 displays the effect of change of MaxPoolSize on response time under different workload. Firstly, the MaxPoolSize is set to be 10 and the client generator generates 200 clients that simultaneously perform operations. Then, at around 900 seconds, we add more 200 clients. The upper chart shows the change of MaxPoolSize with the time varying. The chart under it shows the effect of change of MaxPoolSize on the response time under different workload. We can observe that when client number is 200, the MaxPoolSize starts at 10 and keeps increasing until it converges to a value that results in a much lower mean and variance of response time. Around 900 seconds, the response time dramatically increases due to the more clients coming. Once again, the MaxPoolSize is increased until it converges to the value that results in a much lower mean and variance of response time. It reveals that our dynamic configuration mechanism can improve performance and can adapt to changes in workloads without human intervention.

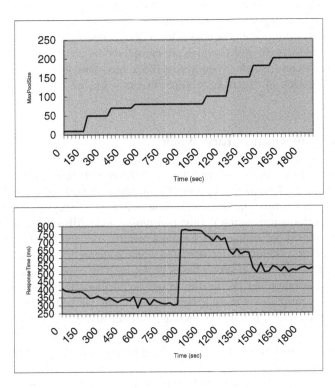

Fig. 6. The effect of change of MaxPoolSize on response time under different workloads

5 Related Work

To the best of our knowledge, there has been little previous work on automatic performance tuning for J2EE application servers. [3] tries to find good application server configurations via empirical approach. However, they only provide a rule of thumb to manually configure application servers. And there is also no framework devised for J2EE application server reconfiguration. The framework proposed by [8] focuses on J2EE applications and the application adaptation is still performed by a human manager. General framework for self-manage systems is presented in [12]. Our research work aligns with this framework, employing monitoring and knowledge-based configuration mechanisms, targeting J2EE application server systems.

There are some commercial products like [13], providing scaling management. However, no work is targeted at per node level. we focus on individual application server system which is complemented with Clustering/Scaling work.

Two main approaches have been employed in software configuration. One is queuing theoretic approach. The other one is control theoretic Approach. [10] employs queuing models, while [6], [7], [9] and [11] employ control theory. Queuing theory is a widely used conceptual framework in which computing systems are viewed as networks of queues and servers. It has proven quite effective at modeling the steady-state behavior of computing systems. Unfortunately, queuing models become complicated if dynamics are considered. The results from Queue model are steady-state results and do not include transient effects which are considered by control theory. Control theoretic approach can treat the system as a black box, thus is not affected by system complexity or lack of expert knowledge. In our work, we employ control theoretic approach.

6   Conclusions and Future Work

J2EE application server systems play the key roles in web-based enterprise distributed systems. Their performance is of utmost importance in building distributed systems. Failure to meet the performance requirements can lead to entire system failure. However, their performance tuning is time consuming and skills intensive. In this paper, we have presented our architecture for implementing autonomic behavior in J2EE application server systems. It incorporated control theoretic approach. A prototype based on JBoss application server has been set up. Our experimental results demonstrated the feasibility and practicality of our architecture and approach in automatic performance configuration management. In the future, we will aim to incorporate additional configuration parameters into our model and set up more configuration strategies for those additional configuration parameters. A more sophisticated decision mechanism will be set up to choose the appropriate strategy and resolve any conflicting choices.

The ultimate goal of our self-configuration architecture is to eliminate manual configuration and re-configuration effort, and to enable system self-optimization and self-configuration.

Acknowledgements

We acknowledge Commonwealth Scientific and Industrial Research Organization (CSIRO) Australia for the support of this work.

References

1. IBM: IBM WebSphere Application Server Advanced Edition Tuning Guide, Technical report, 2001.
2. JBoss: http://www.jboss.org/

3. Raghavachari, M., Reimer, D., and Johnson, R. D.: The Deployer's problem: Configuring Application Servers for Performance and Reliability. In Proceedings of the 25th International Conference on Software Engineering (ICSE' 03), 2003.
4. Zhang, Y., Liu, A., and Qu, W.: Software Architecture Design of an Autonomic System. In Proceeding of the Fifth Australasian Workshop on Software and System Architectures. April 13 and 14, 2004, Melbourne, Australia.
5. IBM.: Autonomic Computing. http://www.research.ibm.com/autonomic/manifesto/autonomic_computing.pdf, 2001.
6. Li, B., and Nahrstedt, K.: A control-based middleware framework for quality of service adaptations, IEEE J. on Sel. Areas in Comms. Vol. 17, No. 9, September 1999, pp1632-1650.
7. Abdelzaher, T., and Bhatti, N.: Web Server QoS Management by Adaptive Content Delivery, Proceedings of Seventh International Workshop on Quality of Service, 1999.
8. Diaconescu, A., Mos, Adrian., and Murphy, J.: Automatic Performance Management in Component Based Software Systems. In Proceeding of IEEE International Conference on Autonomic Computing (ICAC'04), New York, 2004.
9. Gandhi, N., Hellerstein, J. L., Parekh, S. and Tilbury, D. M.: Managing the Performance of Lotus Notes: A control Theoretic Approach, in Proceedings of 27th International Computer Measurement Group Conference, 2001.
10. Menascé, D. A., Barbará, D., and Dodge R.: Preserving QoS of E-commerce Sites Through Self-Tuning: A Performance Model Approach. In Proceedings of 2001 ACM Conference on E-commerce, Tampa, FL. October 2001, ACM, NewYork (2001), pp224-234.
11. Russell, L. W., Morgan, S. P. and Chron, E. G. Clockwork: A new movement in autonomic systems, IBM SYSTEMS JOURNAL, VOL 42, NO 1, 2003, pp77-84.
12. Kephart, J. O., and Chess, D. M.:The Vision of Autonomic Computing, IEEE Computer, January 2003, pp41-50.
13. http://www.wilytech.com/
14. William L. B.: Modern control theory 3rd ed., Englewood Cliffs, N.J., Prentice Hall, c1991.
15. CSIRO: CSIRO Middleware Technology Evaluation Series: Evaluating J2EE Application Servers version 2.1, 2002.
16. Zhang, Y., Liu, A., and Qu, W.: Comparing Industry Benchmarks for J2EE Application Server: IBM's Trade2 vs Sun's Ecperf, In Proceeding of the twenty-sixth Australian Computer Science Conference (ACSC2003), Adelaide, Australia, 2003.
17. Driankov, D., Hellendoorn, H., and Reinfrank, M.: An Introduction to Fuzzy Control. Springer-Verlag, 1993
18. Khalil, H. K.: Nonlinear Systems, MacMillan, New York, 1996
19. Lindfors, J., Fleury, M. and The JBoss Group, LLC.: JMX: Managing J2EE with Java Management Extensions. Sams, 2000.
20. Menascé, D. A., Almeida, V. A. F., Riedi, R., Pelegrinelli, F., Fonseca, R., and Meira W.: In Search of Invariants for E-Business Workloads. In Proceeding of Second ACM Conference on Electronic Commerce, Minneapolis, October 17-20, 2000.

Xebu: A Binary Format with Schema-Based Optimizations for XML Data

Jaakko Kangasharju, Sasu Tarkoma, and Tancred Lindholm

Helsinki Institute for Information Technology,
PO Box 9800, 02015 TKK, Finland
Tel: +358 50 384 1518, Fax: +358 9 694 9768
jkangash@hiit.fi, sasu.tarkoma@hiit.fi, tancred.lindholm@hiit.fi

Abstract. XML is currently being used as the message syntax for Web services. To enable small mobile devices to use Web services, this XML use must not be too resource-consuming. Due to several measurements indicating otherwise, alternate serialization formats for XML data have been proposed. We present here a format for XML data designed from the ground up for the mobile environment. The format is simple, yet gives acceptable document sizes and is efficiently processable. An automaton-based approach gives further improvements when full or partial schema information is available. We provide performance measurements verifying these claims and also consider some issues arising from the use of an alternate XML serialization format.

Keywords: XML and Semi-structured Data, Web Services, Mobile Environment, XML Serialization Format, Binary XML.

1 Introduction

The use of XML has increased quite rapidly in the last few years, because it is a standard format for representing structured data. However, due to this ubiquity, XML is now even becoming used in areas where its designers never intended it to be. Our research is focused on the use of XML as a syntax for messaging in the mobile environment, typically in the context of SOAP.

Existing measurements of SOAP messaging performance indicate that marshaling and unmarshaling of typed data causes a significant loss in performance [1] and that latencies in wireless networks can be a significant cause of low performance [2]. This paper is mostly concerned with the verbosity and processor strain caused by the XML format, both of which have been found problematic in traditional industries moving towards SOAP use [3].

A natural idea is to replace the XML serialization format with something else that is compatible with XML. This concept is often referred to as "binary XML", and the recent final report of the World Wide Web Consortium's XML Binary Characterization (XBC) Working Group [4] details requirements for such a format and lists several existing formats.

M. Kitsuregawa et al. (Eds.): WISE 2005, LNCS 3806, pp. 528–535, 2005.

This paper presents our format, called Xebu[1], which we use as a part of an XML-based messaging system of a mobile middleware platform. Our analysis of the format requirements [5] mirrors the Web Services for Small Devices use case of the XBC group [6]. Our additions are the requirements for some schema evolvability and special-purpose data encoding.

The main interesting feature of Xebu is that it requires less coupling between communicating peers than many other formats. While our default implementation retains state between XML messages in a stream, the format degrades gracefully in the case where state cannot be retained. In addition, if this state gets corrupted, it will be re-built gradually as new messages are processed instead of in one step immediately after corruption. Xebu also allows optimizations when a schema for messages is available, and these optimizations are designed to let the schema evolve in common ways without invalidating existing processors.

We describe the basic tokenization of Xebu in Section 2. Our model for schema-based enhancements is discussed in Section 3 and the actual implementation is described in Section 4. Section 5 presents performance measurements of our format and some others. Finally, Section 6 gives our conclusions and plans for future work.

2 Basic Format

We view an XML document as a sequence of events [7], and serialize it event by event. The serialization of a single event starts with a one-byte discriminator that identifies the event type and contains flag bits indicating how to process the rest of the event. This is followed by the strings applicable to the event type.

Similarly to other formats, such as Fast Infoset [8] and XBIS [9], we define a (one-byte) token for each string when it first appears in an event, and then use the token on later appearances. In contrast to other formats, the token value is given explicitly in the serialized form at definition time, which reduces the coupling between serialization and parsing by making the tokenization policy only concern the serializer. Therefore a token replacement algorithm does not need to be standardized to be interoperable. Furthermore, if the token mapping on the parser falls out of sync, it is sufficient for the serializer to invalidate tokens assigned after the last known good state instead of duplicating the parser's current state.

Since the typical case is that a single namespace has many associated local names and a namespace-name pair many attribute values, the token for a name includes its namespace and the token for a value includes both namespace and name. In this way, e.g., a repeated complete attribute or element name is replaced by a single token instead of having separate tokens for each string. In contrast to Fast Infoset, Xebu tokenizes namespace URIs instead of namespace prefixes.

All strings are serialized in a length-prefixed form. This is the length in bytes according to the encoding defined in the document start event. Use of length prefixes does not sacrifice streamability, since, as with XML, text content can be given in chunks by the application. Unlike in XML, in Xebu these chunks are explicit in the serialized

---

[1] The implementation is available at http://www.hiit.fi/fuego/fc/download.html.

form because of the length prefix. We also encode common data types directly in binary format, as this is more efficient in at least some cases.

3   Schema Optimization Concepts

In many cases when doing XML messaging, a complete or partial schema for the messages is available. In the case of SOAP the high-level structure is always available, and often schema information for some headers or the body is also specified. To be properly considered schema-aware [10], a serialization format needs to exploit the structure present in the schema to achieve its optimizations, and not just to recognize the defined names.

We construct two *omission automata*, *encoding* (EOA) for the serialization and *decoding* (DOA) for the parsing side, that process the XML event sequence one event at a time. The EOA will omit some events from its input, which the DOA is able to reinsert back into its output. As this technique is based on the event sequence representation, it is not Xebu-specific; it only requires that events be distinguishable in serialized form even if some are omitted.

Both automata are structurally similar. Each has a start state, from which the processing of a document begins. Transitions of each are labeled with an event and a type, and a state transition happens when the event label of a transition matches the event from the sequence being processed. The event may contain wildcards, so there can be several matching transitions. In these cases there is always the most specific transition that is the one selected.

Transitions in the EOA are of two types, out and del. The former of these outputs the event of the transition while the latter omits it. In the DOA, transitions can be of three types. A read transition is the most typical one. A peek transition is used to transfer from state to state without consuming the event from the sequence. Finally, a promise transition is used when the event is typed content. This will cause the DOA to inform the type of the data, so the parser can interpret it. A promise transition is always followed by a read transition for the decoded typed content event.

Edges in the DOA also carry two lists of events, the push list and the queue list. The events that the DOA passes upwards on a transition are first the transition's push list, then the event if it is a read transition, and finally the queue list. Any events of del transitions on the EOA side therefore need to appear in push or queue lists so that they get reinserted back into the sequence.

Each state in both automata also has a default transition to itself that is taken if no other transitions match the current event. These default transitions pass the events unmodified through the automata, which means that unexpected events are passed through as such. Hence it is possible to, e.g., add elements and attributes not present in the schema and still use automata of the old schema without problems.

An example RELAX NG [11] schema fragment of an element containing a typed value and its transformation into an EOA and a DOA are shown in Fig. 1. Each edge is labeled with its corresponding event and type. The EOA will omit the element start, the type attribute, and the element end, which the DOA's push and queue lists insert back. Fig. 2 shows an XML fragment that matches this schema fragment, and its processing.

Schema fragment: `element ns:age { xsd:int }`

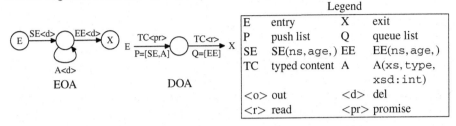

Fig. 1. Example transformation from schema to automata. Default transitions of the automata are not shown.

XML fragment	`<ns:age xs:type="xsd:int">29</ns:age>`			
Event sequence	SE(ns,age,) A(xs,type,xsd:int) TC(xsd,int,29) EE(ns,age,)			
EOA processing	`del`	`del`	`out`	`del`
Produced fragment			%0C%1D	
DOA processing	`promise TC`	`push[SE(ns,age,), A(xs,type,xsd:int)]`		
	`read TC(xsd,int,29)`	`queue[EE(ns,age,)]`		
Result sequence	SE(ns,age,) A(xs,type,xsd:int) TC(xsd,int,29) EE(ns,age,)			

Fig. 2. Example processing of an XML fragment

The serialized fragment consists of two bytes (shown in URL-encoded form): a type tag and the value of the integer.

4   Omission Automata Implementation

The automata are constructed recursively from an abstract syntax tree of a RELAX NG schema [12]. Each piece of supported[2] RELAX NG syntax produces a *subautomaton* and *entry* and *exit points* for it. The entry and exit points are states for the EOA and edges for the DOA, and are used by higher layers to build their own subautomata.

In general, the construction of a subautomaton for an element cannot determine whether the start and end events can be omitted, since it does not know the context in which the automaton is used. Because of this, each subautomaton has two entry and exit points, the *known* and *unknown* points. The higher-level construction will select the known points when it is certain that the subautomaton will be used, e.g., if it is the second item in a group construct. The unknown points will be selected when this is uncertain, e.g., when the subautomaton is a part of a choice construct.

The full generic handling of an element with a known name is shown in Fig. 3 in similar format as in Fig. 1. The box labeled M refers to the subautomaton built from the content of the element. In the figure the k and u subscripts refer to the known and unknown entry and exit points, while the M superscripts denote M's entry and exit

---

[2] The interleave operator is not processed, and recursive elements are treated as errors.

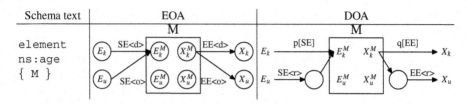

Fig. 3. Generic handling of an element. The p and q indicate a lengthening of the corresponding list (push or queue) from the appropriate end (front or back).

points. On the DOA side only the modifications made to existing edges are shown, i.e., the additions to the push and queue lists. The DOA side has also inserted two states internal to the subautomaton. If these states are not used, they will get removed at the end when we reduce the automata to those states that are mutually reachable from the start state.

The star, i.e., a sequence of indeterminable length, requires additional handling. If what follows the star could be interpreted as included in it, omitting all events in between would make it impossible to determine this. Therefore any subautomaton built from a star is marked an *open* one. An element wrapped around an open subautomaton always has its end event inserted, so that the end of the star can be determined.

Existing approaches for schema optimizations include BiM for MPEG-7 [13] and Fast Web Services [14]. Like our approach, BiM uses automata that are driven by XML events. It achieves a higher level of compactness due to its bit-oriented nature, but at the same time requires a more rigid conformance to the schema than Xebu does. Fast Web Services, on the other hand, leverages existing work in structured data representation by mapping XML Schemas to ASN.1 schemas [15]. Like BiM, this is also tightly coupled to the schema, especially when the recommended Packed Encoding Rules are used.

5   Performance Measurements

There are several considerations on measuring a format for mobile devices. While document size is important, due to constrained memory and the use of battery it is also necessary to have fast and low-memory processing combined with a small implementation footprint.

We conducted measurements on a desktop machine and two mobile phones. The desktop machine had a 3 GHz Intel Pentium 4 processor, 1 GB of main memory, running Debian GNU/Linux 3.1. All of the measured processors are implemented in the Java programming language; we used Sun Microsystems's Java 2 Runtime Environment 1.5.0 as the Java platform and set its maximum heap size to 256 MB. The mobile phones were a Nokia 3660 and a Nokia 7610.

Our test data is a 698-message sequence from an event notification system that uses SOAP as its message format. Full schema information for the notifications was available and was utilized to generate omission automata. For XML we measured the performance of both Apache Xerces and kXML, the latter of which is designed especially for Java MIDP devices. We also measured the Fast Infoset [8] binary XML format. For

Table 1. Comparison of different XML serialization formats

Format	Size (B)	Size (%)	Serialization				Parsing				Foot (KB)
			Time (ms)	Thr (1/s)	DB (ms)	Mem (KB)	Time (ms)	Thr (1/s)	DB (ms)	Mem (KB)	
Xerces	3033	100.0	0.45	2201	0.13	39.77	0.76	1315	0.13	113.23	502.9
XercesZ	675	22.3	0.74	1356	0.14	42.45	0.87	1144	0.13	114.22	–
FI	1689	55.7	0.35	2825	0.13	13.88	0.48	2072	0.13	37.63	191.8
FIZ	687	22.7	0.62	1608	0.13	17.67	0.55	1833	0.13	39.11	–
kXML	3033	100.0	1.06	941	0.15	141.23	0.93	1078	0.14	73.69	29.1
XebuF	1304	43.0	0.53	1874	0.15	55.51	0.83	1198	0.18	58.48	–
XebuFZ	695	22.9	0.93	1079	0.15	56.04	0.91	1094	0.18	60.14	–
Xebu	807	26.6	0.45	2230	0.15	38.63	0.76	1309	0.17	50.87	52.1
XebuFS	493	16.3	0.56	1794	0.14	38.92	0.79	1264	0.18	55.78	–
XebuS	493	16.3	0.42	2357	0.15	34.52	0.77	1299	0.18	47.13	87.7

the mobile phone we measured a 10-message sequence to avoid memory problems; the only processors available for that platform were kXML and Xebu.

Table 1 shows the measurement results on the desktop machine. The main implementations are Xerces, FI (for Fast Infoset), kXML, and Xebu. These are suffixed with Z to indicate the use of gzip on the serialized form. Xebu measurements use two other suffixes: F (for forget) indicates that token mappings were not preserved from one message to another and S indicates that omission automata were used. Both total processing time and throughput are reported. Included in the processing time is data binding, which is also reported separately. The footprint, consisting of all Java classes loaded by our experiment, is reported for each distinct system[3]. Memory consumption did not vary between measurements, and the time deviations were all between 0.01 and 0.02 ms.

Xebu's main advantages are in message size and footprint. While FI's processing efficiency is higher, this appears to come at the cost of a complex implementation. Furthermore, the use of prefixes for tokenization in FI contributes to its higher throughput on serialization. The gzip results indicate that the local nature of the tokenization in Xebu and FI has no significant effect on the more global analysis performed by gzip. The similarities in data binding speeds are explained by our test data, which has only integers as typed content. A quick experiment verified that date and floating point values are encoded and decoded by Xebu at 2–3 times the speed of the normal string encoding specified for XML.

Table 2 shows the measurements results on the phones. The footprint measurement is after obfuscation with Proguard, and standard deviations are reported, as they varied more in this case. The kXML implementation performs much better, indicating that the Java virtual machines differ significantly. The data binding of Xebu appears problematic on the 3660, but otherwise the results are consistent with each other. Omission automata appear to provide more benefits in this case, probably due to their more static nature.

We note that if schema information can be assumed, coupling can be reduced by not preserving the token mappings without any loss (and even some gain on the mobile

---

[3] Non-Xebu formats do not include marshaling code; this is 7.6 KB on the desktop and 4.8 KB on the phones.

Table 2. XML serialization comparison on a mobile phone

Format	Serialization				Parsing				Foot
	Time (ms)	Thr (1/s)	DB (ms)	Mem (KB)	Time (ms)	Thr (1/s)	DB (ms)	Mem (KB)	(KB)
7610									
kXML	56.0±3.1	17.9	6.3±2.8	23.2±3.3	134.0±5.5	7.5	9.1±3.1	50.5±2.8	16.3
Xebu	60.0±5.1	16.7	8.1±3.6	33.1±2.2	134.1±4.4	7.5	10.8±3.0	50.9±3.5	22.0
XebuS	45.0±4.1	22.2	6.4±5.0	25.5±2.0	123.7±6.7	8.1	10.1±4.9	49.4±5.1	44.3
3660									
kXML	250.0±6.4	4.0	7.5±4.0	8.1±0.3	527.5±2.9	1.9	15.6±3.6	29.3±3.0	–
Xebu	211.1±15.6	4.7	19.2±7.4	22.9±2.5	503.8±43.9	2.0	33.9±8.4	30.7±4.1	–
XebuS	159.5±7.6	6.3	20.9±7.9	18.6±0.3	406.9±11.9	2.5	30.3±9.4	25.7±0.3	–

phones) in performance. The footprint increase could be mitigated by having generic automata that would drive the transitions based on a data structure. Furthermore, only one such structure per schema would be needed, and the only required per-message information would be the automaton state. We estimate that the generic automata would take approximately 10 kilobytes (5 kilobytes obfuscated), and the automata of our measurements would take an additional 10 kilobytes.

6   Conclusions and Future Directions

In this paper we presented Xebu, a binary serialization format for XML data designed for the mobile environment. Xebu achieves an acceptable level of compactness without sacrificing either processing efficiency or simplicity of implementation. The design explicitly takes into account the loosely coupled nature of Web services.

Our approach of modeling an XML document as a sequence of events and then deriving the format and optimizations through this has proved to be useful. Schema-based automata are easier to describe and implement in terms of abstract sequences instead of byte sequences. Further, the abstract sequence provides a natural view of XML for mobile messaging applications, as we argue elsewhere [7], bridging the serialization and application use cleanly.

The low-level nature of event sequences also enables integration with most existing XML applications. The event sequence can be easily mapped to data models expected by them, and our XML processing system already includes SAX interfaces for the binary format. In the future we intend to explore whether exposing the binary tokens to applications would provide performance gains.

A major consideration in messaging systems will be security features, such as Web Services Security [16]. These rely on mutual understandability of the bytes being transmitted, so the above data model compatibility is not sufficient. Furthermore, using bridges to translate between binary and XML at the edge of the fixed network is not possible, since translation is not possible for encrypted content, and it would also invalidate signatures. Finding an interoperable solution that can be adopted piecewise will be important in the future.

References

1. Juric, M.B., Kezmah, B., Hericko, M., Rozman, I., Vezocnik, I.: Java RMI, RMI tunneling and Web services comparison and performance analysis. ACM SIGPLAN Notices **39** (2004) 58–65
2. Laukkanen, M., Helin, H.: Web services in wireless networks — what happened to the performance? In Zhang, L.J., ed.: Proceedings of the International Conference on Web Services. (2003) 278–284
3. Kohlhoff, C., Steele, R.: Evaluating SOAP for high performance applications in capital markets. Journal of Computer Systems, Science, and Engineering **19** (2004) 241–251
4. World Wide Web Consortium: XML Binary Characterization. (2005) W3C Note.
5. Kangasharju, J., Lindholm, T., Tarkoma, S.: Requirements and design for XML messaging in the mobile environment. In Anerousis, N., Kormentzas, G., eds.: Second International Workshop on Next Generation Networking Middleware. (2005) 29–36
6. World Wide Web Consortium: XML Binary Characterization Use Cases. (2005) W3C Note.
7. Kangasharju, J., Lindholm, T.: A sequence-based type-aware interface for XML processing. In Hamza, M.H., ed.: Ninth IASTED International Conference on Internet and Multimedia Systems and Applications, ACTA Press (2005) 83–88
8. Sandoz, P., Triglia, A., Pericas-Geertsen, S.: Fast infoset. On Sun Developer Network (2004)
9. Sosnoski, D.M.: XBIS XML infoset encoding. In: W3C Workshop on Binary Interchange of XML Information Item Sets, World Wide Web Consortium (2003)
10. Pericas-Geertsen, S.: Binary interchange of XML infosets. In: XML Conference and Exposition, Philadelphia, USA (2003)
11. Organization for the Advancement of Structured Information Standards: RELAX NG Compact Syntax. (2002)
12. Organization for the Advancement of Structured Information Standards: RELAX NG Specification. (2001)
13. Niedermeier, U., Heuer, J., Hutter, A., Stechele, W., Kaup, A.: An MPEG-7 tool for compression and streaming of XML data. In: IEEE International Conference on Multimedia and Expo. (2002) 521–524
14. Sandoz, P., Pericas-Geertsen, S., Kawaguchi, K., Hadley, M., Pelegri-Llopart, E.: Fast Web services. On Sun Developer Network (2003)
15. International Telecommunication Union, Telecommunication Standardization Sector: Mapping W3C XML Schema Definitions into ASN.1. (2004) ITU-T Rec. X.694.
16. Organization for the Advancement of Structured Information Standards: Web Services Security: SOAP Message Security 1.0. (2004)

Maintaining Versions of Dynamic XML Documents

Laura Irina Rusu[1], Wenny Rahayu[2], and David Taniar[3]

[1,2] LaTrobe University, Department of Computer Science and Computer Engineering,
Bundoora, VIC 3086, Australia
lirusu@students.latrobe.edu.au, wenny@cs.latrobe.edu.au
[3] Monash University, School of Business Systems, Clayton, VIC 3800, Australia
David.Taniar@infotech.monash.edu.au

Abstract. The ability to store information contained in XML documents for future references becomes a very important issue as the number of applications which use and exchange data in XML format is growing continuously. Moreover, the contents of XML documents are dynamic and they change across time. However, storing all document versions in an XML data warehouse would introduce a high level of redundancy. Nevertheless the ability to store XML documents together with their different versions across time is often required.

Our paper proposes a novel approach for storing changes of dynamic XML documents in time with less overhead so earlier versions can be easily queried. We show how our proposed *consolidated delta* is built, with steps and rules of the algorithm involved and we demonstrate the efficiency of the versioning approach in terms of storage and retrieval using some test data.

1 Introduction

The eXtensible Markup Language (XML) is continually evolving as a standard of representation and exchange of information on the web. Two major features of concerns in XML are: (i) the text format of XML documents, which needs fewer resources to be processed and do not require specific database tools to be accessed *and* (ii) the great extensibility of XML structure which allow users to change the document tailored to their own needs (for example the ability to create new elements to store a new type of information).

In this context, building efficient data warehouses to store the growing amount of data represented in XML format became an important problem to solve, for both research and industry people.

We identified at least two types of XML documents which could be included in a presumptive XML data warehouse: *static XML documents*, which do not change their contents and structures (e.g. an XML document containing the papers published in a certain proceedings book) and *dynamic XML documents*, which change their structures or contents based on certain business processes (e.g. the content of an on-line store might change hourly depending on customer behavior).

While the first category of XML documents was the subject of intense research in recent years, with various methods for storing and mining them being developed, there is still work to be done in finding efficient ways to store dynamic XML documents. The goal is to eliminate the possible redundancies introduced by storing

M. Kitsuregawa et al. (Eds.): WISE 2005, LNCS 3806, pp. 536–543, 2005.

successive highly similar versions of the documents without loss of important information. At the same time, the XML warehouse should allow the ability to get or query earlier versions of the document when necessary.

In this paper, we are focusing on how to store the changes of dynamic XML document as efficient as possible, using a format that is easy to interpret and to query in order to get the necessary data.

2 Related Work

A change-centric management of versions in an XML warehouse was first introduced by the authors of [3]. They calculate a *delta* document as the difference between two consecutive versions of an XML document. Also, the authors introduce the notion of *completed delta,* which contains more information than a regular *diff* document and works both forward and backward, being able to reverse the D_{i+1} version of the document to the D_i version. In their proposal, the warehouse stores the initial version of the analyzed XML document together with the all completed deltas calculated in time, arguing that this model is able to successfully solve different versioning requests. The same team at INRIA proposed XyDiff algorithm, as a published free tool [5] which compares two versions of an XML file and creates a delta document that describes all changes that occurred between the first version and the second version of the document. The authors argue that XyDiff is a very fast algorithm, supporting very large files (10+ Mb).

Another change detection algorithm, X-Diff, was proposed by the authors of [1], who argue that an unordered tree model is much appropriate for most database applications. They develop a methodology to detect changes in XML documents by integrating specific XML structure characteristics with standard tree-to-tree correction techniques. Experimental results show a better performance of X-Diff in terms of speed but only for small or medium documents. For larger documents XyDiff performs better.

In the present paper we present a novel approach for storing changes of dynamic XML documents in a format which eliminate the possible redundancies and allows for versioning at any time.

The rest of the paper is structured as follows: in Section 3 we present the problem specifications and our proposal, Section 4 describes the building consolidated delta algorithm, in Section 5 we present the algorithm for versioning using the consolidated delta, Section 6 contains an evaluation of our proposal, based on the test results so far and finally, in Section 7, we conclude the paper, with some proposals for future research work.

3 Problem Specification

One of the existing approaches, currently used in the industry for determining changes between two versions of an XML document or between two different XML documents is the DeltaXML tool [4]. It compares two versions V_i and V_{i+1} of an XML document and builds a new XML document, called *completed delta,* which contains changes detected between versions. If one of the versions *and* the completed delta are stored in a XML data warehouse, the other version can be calculated by applying / reversing changes from the completed delta document.

Inside the delta document as build by [4], any update, insertion, deletion of a child element determines the delta to be set as "modified" for the parent. The issue is, in case of documents which are constantly changing in time, we might need to store all the completed deltas and at least one of the initial or final XML documents, to be able to get a historic version. Considering a pair of versions of the same XML document (e.g. the D_i version at the time T_i and D_{i+1} version at the time T_{i+1}), we have to keep one of the two versions and calculate Δ_i (as difference between D_i and D_{i+1}), in order to be able to get the other version when necessary.

Maintaining the same logic, suppose we have n versions of the same document at n time stamps, T_1, T_2, ...T_n. If we are at the T_n moment and we want, for example, to get the T_3 version, we need to determine each intermediate version D_i , $3<i<n-1$, by reversing changes contained in Δ_i (calculated and stored earlier) on the D_{i+1} document (see Figure 1).

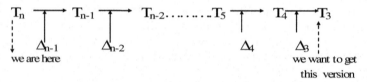

Fig. 1. Solving historical versioning in the existing methods

The immediate and major *drawbacks* of this series of transformations suggested by the existing versioning methods are mainly two: (a) we need to keep all the delta documents, and this may cause redundancy in case of elements or parts of the document changing often; (b) we have to run a specific algorithm for many times (*n-3* in our example) to recreate, one by one, all the previous versions of the document based on the information contained in the intermediate deltas; this is the most important drawback, as we are time-stressed and in most of the cases we might not be interested in getting every time the same intermediate parts of the documents which had not been changed during T_i- T_n period of time.

Our paper proposes a storage method for multiple versioned XML documents which overcome the above mentioned drawbacks, i.e. eliminates the redundancy as much as possible and allows for getting an earlier version of the document in a straight manner.

4   A Proposed Approach: The Consolidated Delta

Our proposed approach, *the consolidated delta*, will mainly consider the changed parts of the documents when versioning, not worrying much about the unchanged parts.

The main idea is to build a single (consolidated) XML delta document (called CΔ further in the paper), containing all changes supported by the versioned XML document in the period of time $T_1 - T_n$, by introducing a new temporal element (<stamp>) to store the changes at each timestamp for each altered element. To get a high speed in building the consolidated delta, we assign unique identifiers to elements in the initial XML document and store the maximum ID value. When new elements are inserted in a following version, they will receive IDs based on the existing maximum ID, so at any time all the elements will be unique identified and we will be able to track their changes.

In order to get the consolidated delta for a sequence of versions of an XML document, we start from the initial document (D_1 version, at the time T_1) and for each version D_i at the time T_i perform as follows:

- assign unique identifiers for the new inserted elements in the D_i version;
- compare the current version D_i with the previous one D_{i-1};
- for each changed element in the D_i version, we insert in the consolidated delta a new child element, named <stamp>, with two attributes: (a) "time" , which contain the T_i value (e.g. month, year etc) and (b) "delta" , which contain one of *modified, added, deleted* or *unchanged* values, depending on the change detected at the time T_i;
- remove the D_{i-1} version from the data warehouse, as it can be anytime recreated using the consolidated delta. The D_1 version of the XML document (i.e. the initial one) will be included in the initial consolidated delta;
- keep the D_i version in the data warehouse, until a new version arrives or until a decision to stop the versioning process is taken; remove Di from data warehouse after the last run of the consolidated delta algorithm;
- at the end of the process, whenever the series of XML transformations/versions stops, we will store in the warehouse just one document, i.e. the consolidated delta, as it contains enough historical information to allow for versioning.

In order to get an easy to interpret structure of the consolidated delta, we set some *rules* to be observed during the building steps:

- *Rule 1* – if all the children are unchanged, the parent is unchanged; if a parent is "unchanged" at the time Ti, its children are not stamped for that particular time stamp; they will be easily rebuilt from the existing previous versions of their parents;
- *Rule 2* – if any of the children is either modified or deleted or inserted, the parent is modified; if a parent is "modified" at the time Ti, all its children will be stamped, each with their own status, i.e. *modified, inserted, deleted* or *unchanged*;
- *Rule 3* - if a parent is "deleted" at the time Ti, all its children will be deleted, so they will not appear in the consolidated delta for that particular time stamp or for any time stamp after that.

The algorithm will be repeated for all pair of consecutive versions or any time a new version is added; at the end of the process the consolidated delta will contain the initial XML document and all the historical changes.

We have considered the speed issue so we tried to reduce as much as possible the presumptive slow areas of the algorithm. For example when the algorithm finds that an element was deleted, all the children elements would be marked as deleted as well, so we keep an open list to store all possible "deleted" children, to not be unnecessarily checked again by the algorithm. Similarly, during step two, we check the new version of the document to find the new inserted elements, based on the unique identifiers applied and keep a list will all possible parent elements modified by the insertions. Finally, during step three, the modified elements are stamped in the consolidated delta with the time of modification and delta type. In this way, we loop only once through both old and new version of the XML document checking for changes and once through the consolidated delta.

Our proposal – the consolidated delta – is not just another way of storing the XML changes over a period of time. The first major improvement which can be easily noticed is that all the temporal changes are now organized and grouped in the same delta document, smaller in size than the sum of the regular (or completed) deltas which could be determined between each two versions (see Section 6 for evaluation tests). Furthermore, we solve a very important issue, which has not been solved by the previous research work, i.e. the redundancy of information in case of consequently modified elements. In our proposed approach, for a particular timestamp only the new value of a modified element is stored the consolidated delta, while the earlier values can be determined by interrogating the history of the element timestamps, eliminating the double recording of old and new value which was an issue for the authors of [3].

5   Using the Consolidated Delta to Perform Versioning

Suppose we are at the moment T_n in time (see Figure 2) and we want to determine the effective look for the XML document at a moment Ti, where i<n (i=3 in the example in Figure 2).

Using the consolidated delta, we do not need to recreate the entire set of intermediate documents from T_n to T_i ($T_n \rightarrow T_{n-1}$, $T_{n-1} \rightarrow T_{n-2}....T_{i+1} \rightarrow T_i$). Instead, we query the consolidated delta for the elements which have <stamp> elements with T_i value of "time" attribute.

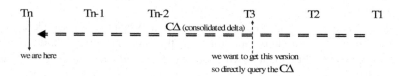

Fig. 2. Using consolidated delta to get an earlier version of an XML document

Certainly, this query will not return at once the entire structure and content of the XML document at the moment T_i - this would be an ideal output. We still have to query backward the history of certain elements, but only for a limited number, i.e. the unchanged ones, as the modified or inserted elements will contain the actual values at the time T_i.

5.1 An Overview of the Versioning Algorithm

When an earlier version is required, the consolidated delta $D\Delta$ document is scanned starting from the root and for each element we determine if the delta attribute has one of the {*modified, deleted, added* or *unchanged*} values, building, in the same time, the required D_i version of the document, as follows:

- delta has the *modified* value - if the element is a complex one (has children), we analyze the changes for each of its children elements; they may have *modified, deleted, added* or *unchanged* value, as well; if the element is not a complex one, we take its value;
- delta has the *inserted* value - if it is a complex element, all its children were inserted, too, so we take their values as they are returned for the T_i time stamp; if it is not a complex one, we take its value;
- delta has the *deleted* value - from building the consolidate delta rules (Rule 3) we know that if the parent element was deleted (together with its children) at the time T_i, the consolidated delta will contain the *deleted* value for the delta and no children details; consequently, the element will not appear in the built version document;
- delta has the *unchanged* value - a complex unchanged element does not include its unchanged children (Rule from building the consolidated delta), so if we find an *unchanged* element we will query backwards, for each of the T_{i-1}, T_{i-2} etc timestamps changes, until we get to a version with non-*unchanged* delta attribute or until we get to the initial D_1 version of the document (included in the consolidated delta as a starting point;

The improved speed is obvious as we may indeed need to enquiry for earlier changes but only for some of the elements, not for all of them. In this case, the number of operations involved is anyway much smaller than entirely re-creating all the (n-3) intermediate documents.

6 Experimental Evaluation of the Proposed Approach

To evaluate the proposed approach we measured the consolidated delta obtained from successive versions of the same XML documents of various sizes, i.e. 10kB, 20kB, 63kB, 127kB and 509kB, data being downloaded from the SIGMOD dataset [8]. We built a number of versions for each type of document by using a changes simulator, created by us, which takes as input the D_i version and returns a modified D_{i+1} version, where the desired percentages of deletions, insertions and modifications can be controlled through a user-friendly interface and elements to be changed are randomly chosen.

We discovered that in case of small documents, the size of the consolidated delta grows very quickly for small values of change percentages, but maintains less than 40% even for 5% deletions, insertions or modifications and we got similar results for larger documents.

In Figure 3 we show how the consolidated delta performs during 10 successive versions of a medium sized XML document (127kB), applying random 3% changes.

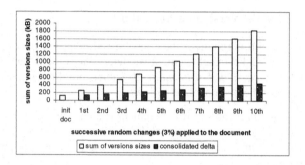

Fig. 3. Dynamic of the consolidated delta during 10 successive changes of a medium sized XML document (127kB)

As it can be noticed, the consolidated delta grows much more slowly than the sum of versions sizes, at the end of the process (in our test example) we got less than 25% volume of data stored in the XML data warehouse than if we would had stored all 10 versions of the document. Our experiments show very good performances for versions of larger documents and for bigger percentages of changes, as well.

Other test results show a very good scalability of the consolidated delta algorithm, its size growing equally when same percentages of changes are applied to different sizes of XML documents. This means some predictions can be done for large dynamic XML documents, based on the results obtained after running the algorithm on a smaller version of the same document. As we mentioned earlier in the paper, the consolidated delta contains from the beginning the initial document, so *it will be the single XML document stored in the data warehouse*, with enough information to allow versioning and other types of data extraction at any time. In this context, the test results we got are excellent if we consider both: (i) the huge reduction of amount of XML data stored for future references and (ii) the ability to obtain any earlier version of the XML document using only the developed consolidated delta.

7 Conclusions and Future Work

In this paper we present a novel approach for storing the changes which affect an XML documents during a period of time. We represent the temporal changes of an XML document grouped in a *consolidated delta,* showing how earlier versions of the document can be determined, based only on the information contained in this delta. Based on the test results so far, we believe this method successfully solves both issues, i.e. storage of dynamic XML documents without redundancy and easier versioning. The proposed framework was validated only against test data, i.e. multiple versions of XML documents containing simulated changes, so in future we intend to experiment our proposed framework on a warehouse containing real web XML documents which have been changing over time, to prove its efficiency for real world applications.

References

[1] Wang, Y., DeWitt, D.J., Cai, J.Y., X-Diff: An Effective Change Detection Algorithms for XML Documents, Proceed.of the 19th Intl.Conf.on Data Engineering (ICDE'03), 2003

[2] Zhao, O., Bhowmick, S., Mohania, M., Kambayashi, Y., Discovering Frequently Changing Structures from Historical Structural Deltas of Unordered XML, Proceed. of CIKM'04, November 2004, US

[3] Marian, A., Abiteboul, S., Cobena, G., Mignet, L., Change-Centric Management of Versions in an XML Warehouse, VLDB Journal, 2001, pp. 581-590

[4] DeltaXML, Monsell EDM Ltd, www.deltaxml.com

[5] Cobena, G., Abiteboul, S., Marian, A., XyDiff Tools – Detecting Changes in XML Document", http://www-rocq.inria.fr/ gemo/XyDiff/

[6] Chen, L., Bhowmick, S., Chia, L.T., Mining Association Rules from Structural Deltas of Historical XML documents, Proceed. of PAKDD 2004, Springer-Verlag LNAI 3056, pp.452-457, 2004

[7] Zhao, O., Bhowmick, S., Mandria, S., Discovering Pattern-Based Dynamic Structures from Versions of Unordered XML Documents, Proceed. of DaWaK 2004, LNCS 3181, pp.77-86, Springer-Verlag, 2004

[8] www.cs.washington.edu/datasets - SIGMOD XML dataset

[9] Garofalakis, M., Rastogi, R., Seshadri, S., Shim K., Data Mining and the Web: Past, Present and Future, Proceed.of WIDM 99, Kansas, US, ACM 1999

[10] Mignet, L., Barbosa, D., Veltri, P., The XML Web: a First Study, Proceed.of WWW 2003, Budapest, Hungary, ACM

[11] Chien, S.Y., Tsotras, V.J., Zaniolo, C., Zhang D., Storing and Querying Multiversion XML Documents using Durable Node Numbers, Proceed.of the 2nd Intl. Conf. on Web Information Systems Engineering (WISE), Kyoto, Japan, 2001

Identifying Value Mappings for Data Integration: An Unsupervised Approach

Jaewoo Kang[1], Dongwon Lee[2], and Prasenjit Mitra[2]

[1] NC State University, Raleigh NC 27695, USA
[2] Penn State University, University Park PA 16802, USA

Abstract. The Web is a distributed network of information sources where the individual sources are autonomously created and maintained. Consequently, syntactic and semantic heterogeneity of data among sources abound. Most of the current data cleaning solutions assume that the data values referencing the same object bear some textual similarity. However, this assumption is often violated in practice. "Two-door front wheel drive" can be represented as "2DR-FWD" or "R2FD", or even as "CAR TYPE 3" in different data sources. To address this problem, we propose a novel two-step automated technique that exploits statistical dependency structures among objects which is invariant to the tokens representing the objects. The algorithm achieved a high accuracy in our empirical study, suggesting that it can be a useful addition to the existing information integration techniques.

1 Introduction

As the Web has become the primary vehicle of information dissemination and exchange, we witness increasing numbers of databases published on the Web. No individual website, however, can satisfy the information needs of all applications. Useful information is often scattered over multiple sites. Thus, information integration across diverse sources is essential. Integrating such heterogeneous Web sources often involves two related subtasks: 1) reconciling structural heterogeneity of data by mapping schema elements across the data sources and 2) resolving semantic heterogeneity of data by mapping data instances across the tables. The first task is commonly referred to as the *schema matching* problem [1, 2, 3] (see [4] for survey) and the second, as the *object mapping* problem [5, 6, 7, 8, 9, 10, 11, 12, 13, 14].

The object mapping problem discussed in previous literature typically refers to the problem of finding duplicate tuples within or across the tables to be integrated. Virtually all previously proposed work assume the data values in each corresponding columns are drawn from the same domain or at least they bear some textual similarity that can be measured using a string distance algorithm (e.g., edit distance, Jaccard). However, this assumption is often challenged in practice where sources use various different representations for describing their data. This problem poses a substantial challenge to the existing object mapping techniques. We name this problem as the *value mapping* problem.

M. Kitsuregawa et al. (Eds.): WISE 2005, LNCS 3806, pp. 544–551, 2005.

In order to address the value mapping problem, in our previous work [15], we introduced an iterative and interactive framework where the system incrementally builds the mapping through iteration while incorporating the user feedback. In this work we propose an unsupervised technique that can automatically produce a highly accurate subset of mappings which can serve as the seed mappings for the subsequent iterative mapping process. The proposed technique can work as a stand-alone process as well as a preprocessor generating seed mappings in our iterative framework. It works in two steps as follows. In the first step, it constructs a statistical model that captures the correlations between all pairs of values in each table to be matched. In the second step, the constructed models are aligned such that the distance between the two models is minimized. The alignment with the minimum distance is returned as the mapping. In what follows, we formally define the problem and give the solution overview.

Problem Definition. We have two tables: the source table, S, with columns, $s_1, ..., s_n$, and its corresponding target table, T, with columns, $t_1, ..., t_n$. We focus on the value mapping problem in this paper and assume schema matching is done beforehand using existing solutions [4]; that is, the column mapping $f : s_i \rightarrow t_j$ is given. Also, the domain and range of a column c_i is denoted as $D(c_i)$ and $R(c_i)$, respectively. Then, formally, we consider the following as the **Value Mapping Problem**:

> For a pair of corresponding columns, s_i and t_j, where $f : s_i \rightarrow t_j$, find a bijective value mapping function $g : D(s_i) \rightarrow R(t_j)$ that maps two values representing the same real-world object.

Solution Overview. Our value mapping algorithm finds mappings using co-occurrence information gathered from tables without interpreting individual values. Two values are said to *co-occur* if they occur in the same row. A *co-occurrence model* captures the co-occurrence of the values in a table. An example of a simple co-occurrence model is a co-occurrence matrix. The rows and columns of it represent the set of unique values in the table, and the entries represent the co-occurrence counts of the corresponding value pairs. Our algorithm consists of two-steps: (1) the first step, **Table2CoocurrenceModel()**, takes two table instances as input and produces corresponding co-occurrence models, and (2) the second step, **ModelMatch()**, using the co-occurrence models, produces the value mapping between the two models (i.e., a set of matching value pairs). Typically, the models are matched based on a distance metric. The distance metric captures how similar a value from one table is to another value from the other table. Optimizing on the distance metric over all pairs of matched values gives us the bijective mapping from values in one table to those in another.

In this paper we make the following contributions:

1. We present the value mapping problem as an important problem in information integration that is a real and hindering problem in practice.
2. We propose a matching framework that does not rely on the syntactic similarity of values and thus applicable to many different domains, even including domains to which the system has not previously been exposed.

Table 1. University Employee Tables

Name	Gender	Title	Degree	Status	Name	Gender	Title	Degree	Status
J. Smith	M	Professor	Ph.D.	Married	S. Smith	F	Emp10	D7	SGL
R. Smith	F	T.A.	B.S.	Single	T. Davis	M	Emp3	D3	SGL
B. Jones	F	T.A.	M.S.	Married	R. King	M	Emp10	D7	MRD
T. Hanks	M	Professor	Ph.D.	Married	A. Jobs	F	Emp3	D2	MRD

(a) Table X (a) Table Y

Table 2. Value-row matrix and Co-occurrence matrix of Table X

	row_1	row_2	row_3	row_4
v1:M	1	0	0	1
v2:F	0	1	1	0
v3:Professor	1	0	0	1
v4:TA	0	1	1	0
v5:Ph.D	1	0	0	1
v6:M.S	0	0	1	0
v7:B.S	0	1	0	0
v8:Married	1	0	1	1
v9:Single	0	1	0	0

	v1	v2	v3	v4	v5	v6	v7	v8	v9
v1	2	0	2	0	2	0	0	2	0
v2	0	2	0	2	0	1	1	1	1
v3	2	0	2	0	2	0	0	2	0
v4	0	2	0	2	0	1	1	1	1
v5	2	0	2	0	2	0	0	2	0
v6	0	1	0	1	0	1	0	1	0
v7	0	1	0	1	0	0	1	0	1
v8	2	1	2	1	2	1	0	3	0
v9	0	1	0	1	0	0	1	0	1

(a) Value-Row Matrix T_1 (b) Co-occurrence Matrix C_1

3. The proposed algorithm can complement many existing algorithms as it utilizes different types of information that is not commonly used in the existing algorithms. The prediction result (i.e., mapping) produced by our algorithm can be combined with the results produced by other existing methods in order to improve the accuracy of the mapping.

2   Step 1: Modeling Co-occurrence Relation

We introduce the following co-occurrence models that can be used in the first step of our algorithm, **Table2CooccurrenceModel()**.

Simple Vector Model. Consider tables in Table 1. Suppose we want to find the value mapping between terms used in three columns, *Gender*, *Title*, and *Degree* across the two tables. One simple solution is to use frequencies of values such that values appearing more often correspond to each other while values appearing less often correspond to each other. This approach, however, may not work when values are evenly distributed (e.g., *Gender*) or when the frequencies of several values in a column are very similar. To remedy this problem, *Simple Vector Model* considers pair-wise term frequencies.

We first generate a "value-row" matrix for each table instance as shown in Table 2. Table 2(a) shows a value-row matrix T_1 generated from tables X. A column vector of T_1 corresponds to a matching row in table X, and a row vector of T_1 encodes occurrences of the corresponding value in each row of table X.

For example, T_1("M", row_1) is 1 because "M" occurs in row_1 of table X. The value-row matrix T_2 of Table Y can be constructed similarly. With the value-row matrix, one can easily calculate pair-wise co-occurrences by taking product of a matrix T_i and its transpose T_i^T: $C_i = T_i \times T_i^T$.

This co-occurrence matrix C_i captures pair-wise value co-occurrences between all pairs of values in the corresponding table. Table 2(b) shows the co-occurrence matrix C_1 for table X. The co-occurrence matrix, C_2, for table Y can be constructed similarly. Now let us assume that value mappings of three columns are known as follows: $Gender(M \rightarrow M, F \rightarrow F)$, $Status(Married \rightarrow MRD$, $Single \rightarrow SGL)$, and $Degree(Ph.D \rightarrow D7, M.S \rightarrow D3, B.S \rightarrow D2)$. Given such mappings and the co-occurrence matrices, how can one find the remaining value mappings (e.g., the ones between the values in the $Title$ columns?)

We could, perhaps, first align the rows and columns of C_1 and C_2 according to the known mappings, and then, for each term vector (row) in C_1, try to find the closest term vector from C_2 by comparing only the parts that we know are correctly aligned. For example, suppose we are trying to find a value in table X that corresponds to "Emp10" in table Y. First we take the term vector of "Emp10" from C_2 (not shown): $C_2($"Emp10"$) = [1\ 1\ 2\ 0\ 2\ 0\ 0\ 1\ 1]$. The third and fourth entries are for "Emp10" and "Emp7" for which we do not know the correct mapping across the tables; so we ignore them and keep only entries for known values as follows: $C_{2a}($"Emp10"$) = [1\ 1\ 2\ 0\ 0\ 1\ 1]$. Then, if we measure the typical Euclidean distances between $C_{2a}($"Emp10"$)$ and the two term vectors corresponding to the terms "Professor" and "TA" from C_1, we get 2 for the "Emp10-Professor" pair and 2.83 for the "Emp10-TA" pair, suggesting that the "Emp10-Professor" pair is a better match.

One way to improve the performance of this scheme is to weight terms according to their *information content*. That is, rare terms carry more weights when they co-occur than terms that occur frequently (e.g., "male" or "female"). In this work, we use a standard inverse document frequency weighting [16]. The weighted value-row matrix is defined as follows: $T(i,j) = 1 - \frac{k}{N}$, if term i occurs in row j, or 0 otherwise, where k is the number of rows where term i occurs and N is the total number of rows in the table. Note that when term i occurs in all rows, $T(i,j)$ is 0 for all j. We incorporated the weighting scheme in all the models for our experimentation, but have not weighted the examples in this paper to retain their simplicity.

Co-occurrence Matrix Model. One straightforward extension of the simple vector model is to compare two co-occurrence matrices as a whole rather than limiting the focus to only vector-wise comparisons. This approach works as follows. We compute the distances between the two co-occurrence matrices while we permute the second matrix, and find the permutation that minimizes the distance between the two matrices. The algorithm then returns the permutation as the proposed mapping.

Latent Semantic Model. *Latent Semantic Indexing* (LSI) [16] is an information retrieval technique introduced to address the inherent difficulty of handling semantic heterogeneity in traditional inverted-index based text indexing schemes. For example, if a user asks for documents about "human computer interface," then traditional inverted-index based techniques with term overlap measures will fail to return documents that using "HCI" instead of its full wording because the query terms are not appearing in these documents. LSI tries to overcome this shortcoming by exploiting the co-occurrence information. For example, if "HCI" frequently co-occurs with "user" and "interaction" and the "user" and "interaction" co-occur frequently with "human computer interface", it may implies that "HCI" and "human computer interface" are semantically relevant.

LSI uses *Singular Value Decomposition* (SVD) for its co-occurrence analysis. SVD decomposes a value-row matrix T into the product of three distinct matrices: $T = U \times S \times V^T$, where S is a diagonal matrix that contains singular values in a decreasing order, and U and V are orthogonal matrices that contain corresponding left and right singular vectors (principal components), respectively.

An interesting property of SVD is that we can use it to reduce the noise in the model. Data from databases often contain errors due to various reasons. These errors result in very small singular values occurring in the diagonal of matrix S. We can eliminate the effect of these errors by throwing away the small singular values, thereby reducing the dimensionality of U and V. The side effect of this dimensionality reduction is that the resulting model captures indirect multi-level co-occurrence patterns which are not apparent in the original co-occurrence matrix. The *Latent Semantic Model* is built upon this result. Using SVD, co-occurrence matrix C_1 can be calculated as follows: $C_1 = T_1^k \times (T_1^k)^T$ where T_1^k is a best rank-k approximation of T_1 obtained by $U \times S \times V^T$ using only top k principal components and singular values (see [17] for more details).

3   Step 2: Matching Models

Matching process for the Simple Vector Model is relatively easy as the matching problem naturally reduces to a linear assignment problem (e.g., bipartite-graph matching problem). We use the Hungarian method [18] to solve the linear assignment problem.

For both the co-occurrence matrix model and the latent semantic model, we use the Hill-climbing algorithm to align the models being matched. It optimizes on the Euclidean distance between the models to find the matches. The Hill-climbing algorithm is a greedy approach such that it moves, in each state transition, to a state where the most improvement can be achieved. A state represents a permutation that corresponds to a mapping between the two graphs. We limit the set of all states reachable from one state in a state transition, to a set of all permutations obtained by one swapping of any two nodes in the current state. The algorithm stops when there is no next state available better than the current state. As we can see, the Hill-climbing algorithm is non-deterministic; depending on where it starts, even for the same problem, the final states may differ. In our experiments, we ran the Simple Vector Model first, and then ran the Hill-climbing algorithm using the result of the Simple Vector Model as its starting point.

4   Validating the Framework

Set-up: We implemented our two-step matching algorithm using Matlab 6.5. Experiments were performed using a machine running Windows XP Professional with 2.4Ghz Pentium 4 and 1 GB of memory. We ran our tests using census data tables obtained from the website U.S. Census Bureau[3]. We used two state-census-data files, "CA" and "NY", in our experiments. The CA table contains approximately 10,000 tuples and NY table contains about 7,500 tuples. Each table has 18 columns; there exists a one-to-one correspondence between the columns across the tables. There are small numbers of low frequency values (11, out of total of 641 unique values from both the tables) that appear only in one side of the tables, either in NY or CA; we ignore them because in this work, we limit our focus to the problems where one-to-one correspondences exist between the values to be mapped. We use the precision to measure the effectiveness of various algorithms as follows: $Precision = \frac{\#\ of\ correct\ mappings\ by\ an\ algorithm}{\#\ of\ true\ mappings}$. The number of true mappings is the total number of mappings we know exist from our encoding process. We then divide the number of correct mappings produced by an algorithm in testing by this number (#of true mappings) to calculate the precision. We iterated the tests 20 times at each data point with random samples of 6,500 tuples chosen from each table, and averaged the results. For comparison, we implemented five variations: Simple Vector Model (SVM), Co-occurrence Matrix Model (CMM), and three Latent Semantic Models with ranks 20, 40 and 60 (LSM-20, LSM-40, LSM-60, respectively).

Experiments: Figure 1(a) presents the results of mapping between the two OCCU (occupation code) columns across the tables. We ran the experiment while incrementally adding more columns (whose mappings between the values are known) to the tables in each step. The left-most data point (x=1) in Figure 1(a) represents the precision of the matching where only the two OCCU columns were given to the algorithm. All five algorithms that we compared yielded almost identical results on the first data point because no co-occurrence information is available to exploit.

The second data point (x=2) shows the results of the test where we compared the same OCCU pairs, but with extra information of mappings between OCCUMG pairs, i.e., the correct mappings of OCCUMGs are given to the algorithms. The precisions of the algorithms improved to around 78% from 18%. Note that the OCCUMG column contains the codes of major occupation groups while OCCU contains detailed occupation codes. It is very likely that significant amount of information about the contents of the OCCU column is captured in the contents of the OCCUMG column.

As shown in Figure 1(a), the match precision reached almost 100% at the third data point (x=3) for all but Latent Semantic Model with dimension 20 (LSM-20), after taking the third column (INDU) into account. It appeared that the added information given from the two extra columns was just enough for finding the correct mapping for all 45 unique values between the two OCCU columns. Figure 1(b)

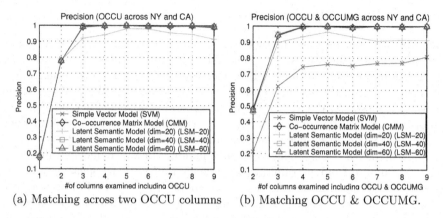

(a) Matching across two OCCU columns   (b) Matching OCCU & OCCUMG.

Fig. 1. Precision graphs

shows a similar result from the experiment where the mappings of the two columns (OCCU and OCCUMG) are unknown. In this test, the performance of SVM deteriorated significantly while the other matrix models sustained.

In addition to the two graphs reported in this paper, we performed additional tests with up to seven unknown columns. Throughout the test, LSM-60 was the best performer while CMM was a close second. There was no severe performance degradation among the top performing algorithms. LSM-60 achieved slightly over 70% accuracy in the seven column unknown test. We also compared the computational complexity of the algorithms. CMM was the slowest among all, taking more than 400 seconds to finish the seven column mapping test (with all extra columns used). On the other hand, LSMs showed a stable performance over the course of tests, taking only 60 seconds to finish the same test. This result is quite striking because both LSM and CMM run the same Hill-climbing algorithm to align the models. Moreover, LSM has an additional cost of doing Singular Value Decomposition (SVD) while CMM does not. We speculated that the noise canceling helped speed up the Hill-climbing process by smoothing the gradient search space of the Hill-climbing algorithm.

5   Related Work and Conclusion

Our "value mapping" problem is closely related to the object mapping problem, which is also known as various names in diverse contexts: e.g., record linkage [19,11], citation matching [10,20], identity uncertainty [10], merge-purge [5], duplicate detection [6,7], and approximate string join [8,9]. Common to all these is the problem to find similar objects (e.g., values, records, tuples, citations). Although different proposals have adopted different approaches to solve the problem in different domains, by and large, they focus on syntactic similarities of objects under comparison. On the other hand, our value mapping solutions can identify mappings where two objects have little syntactic similarity. To cope with such difficulties, we proposed to explore statistical characteristics of objects such as co-occurrence frequency. We believe our algorithms can complement many existing object mapping algorithms as it exploits information that is not used by the existing algorithms.

References

1. Kang, J., Naughton, J.F.: "On Schema Matching with Opaque Column Names and Data Values". In: ACM SIGMOD, San Diego, CA (2003)
2. Andritsos, P., Miller, R.J., Tsaparas, P.: Information-theoretic tools for mining database structure from large data sets. In: ACM SIGMOD. (2004)
3. Dhamankar, R., Lee, Y., Doan, A., Halevy, A.Y., Domingos, P.: "iMAP: Discovering Complex Mappings between Database Schemas". In: ACM SIGMOD. (2004)
4. Rahm, E., Bernstein, P.A.: "A survey of approaches to automatic schema matching". VLDB J. **10** (2001)
5. Hernandez, M.A., Stolfo, S.J.: "The Merge/Purge Problem for Large Databases". In: ACM SIGMOD. (1995)
6. Sarawagi, S., Bhamidipaty, A.: "Interactive Deduplication using Active Learning". In: ACM SIGMOD. (2002)
7. Ananthakrishna, R., Chaudhuri, S., Ganti, V.: "Eliminating Fuzzy Duplicates in Data Warehouses". In: VLDB. (2002)
8. Gravano, L., Ipeirotis, P.G., Koudas, N., Srivastava, D.: "Text Joins for Data Cleansing and Integration in an RDBMS". In: IEEE ICDE. (2003)
9. Cohen, W.W.: "Integration of Heterogeneous Databases Without Common Domains using Queries based on Textual Similarity". In: ACM SIGMOD. (1998)
10. Pasula, H., Marthi, B., Milch, B., Russell, S., Shpitser, I.: "Identity Uncertainty and Citation Matching". In: Advances in Neural Information Processing Systems. MIT Press (2003)
11. Winkler, W.E.: "The State of Record Linkage and Current Research Problems". Technical report, US Bureau of the Census (1999)
12. Chaudhuri, S., Ganjam, K., Ganti, V., Motwani, R.: "Robust and Efficient Fuzzy Match for Online Data Cleaning". In: ACM SIGMOD. (2003)
13. Bilenko, M., Mooney, R.J.: "Adaptive Duplicate Detection Using Learnable String Similarity Measures". In: ACM KDD, Washington, DC (2003)
14. Doan, A., Lu, Y., Lee, Y., Han, J.: "Object Matching for Data Integration: A Profile-Based Approach". In: Workshop on Info. Integration on the Web. (2003)
15. Kang, J., Han, T.S., Lee, D., Mitra, P.: "Establishing Value Mappings using Statistical Models and User Feedback". In: ACM CIKM. (2005)
16. Deerwester, S.C., Dumais, S.T., Landauer, T.K., Furnas, G.W., Harshman, R.A.: "Indexing by Latent Semantic Analysis". J. of the American Society of Information Science **41** (1990) 391–407
17. Golub, G.H., van Loan, C.F.: "Matrix computations". The Johns Hopkins University Press (1999)
18. Kuhn, H.W.: "The Hungarian Method for the Assignment Problem". Naval Research Logistics Quarterly **2** (1955) 83–97
19. Fellegi, I.P., Sunter, A.B.: "A Theory for Record Linkage". J. of the American Statistical Society **64** (1969) 1183–1210
20. McCallum, A., Nigam, K., Ungar, L.H.: "Efficient Clustering of High-Dimensional Data Sets with Application to Reference Matching". In: ACM KDD, Boston, MA (2000)

Relaxing Result Accuracy for Performance in Publish/Subscribe Systems

Engie Bashir and Jihad Boulos

Department of Computer Science, American University of Beirut,
P.O.Box 11-0236 Riad El-Solh, Beirut, Lebanon
{engie.bashir, jihad.boulos}@aub.edu.lb

Abstract. Since the evaluation of XPath expressions is highly dependent upon their size and navigational structures that include ancestor-descendant relationships (*"//"*) and wildcard steps (*"/*"*), we introduce a novel and complementary approach to optimizing XPath queries by rewriting and minimizing such structural occurrences. This rewriting approach depends upon the existence of a statistical schema, which we derive from a set of pre-processed XML documents. However, an imprecision in the schema extraction may lead to a loss of accuracy in the results. Through experimentation and analysis, we validate the scalability and efficiency of our approach.

1 Introduction

We present in this paper a scheme for rewriting XPath queries in Publish/subscribe systems [2] that can enhance the performance of such systems. Publish/Subscribe systems offer valuable functionalities for both publishers and subscribers; however, they exhibit some characteristics that may degrade their performance and throughput to unacceptable levels. First, the data streaming into the system may be unbounded and arriving at an unpredictable rate. Second, the number of subscribers may be unlimited, and hence the number of subscriptions may be quite high.

Different optimization approaches have been considered to resolve these issues and they have been proved to be quite successful. Most approaches (*e.g.* [1][3][5][8]) have exploited commonalties in the prefix of XPath queries, and some others (*e.g.* [6]) focused on query indexing. Most Publish/Subscribe systems face performance and memory bottlenecks when handling a large number of queries over a fast stream of XML documents, especially if these queries include unspecified contents or structures (*i.e.* "*" and "//" in the XPath queries) that need to be matched on recursively defined elements. This imprecision in queries is mostly due to the subscriber's lack of knowledge about the structure of documents that need to be matched, or alternatively the non-existence of schemas for the streaming XML documents.

This lack of a schema has led us to exploit and capture the possible existence of an implicit schema for streaming documents to rewrite some XPath queries. The rewriting mechanism would minimize the number of wildcards and ancestor-descendant relationships found in XPath queries.

M. Kitsuregawa et al. (Eds.): WISE 2005, LNCS 3806, pp. 552–559, 2005.

If a schema exists for streaming XML documents, XPath query rewriting is straightforward and simple. On the other hand, if no schema exists, a schema must be extracted [4] from a sufficiently large number of streamed XML documents. Unfortunately, rewriting some XPath expressions according to an extracted XML schema of past-processed XML documents might introduce a certain error rate when missing some matches on subsequent streaming documents. This problem is the direct result of missing elements in past-processed documents, which ultimately leads to building non-perfect schemas. Therefore, some rewritten queries might not match parts of some newly streaming documents.

Section 2 presents some background. In Section 3, we describe our solution approach. Experimental results are presented in Section 4 and then we give a brief conclusion and some ideas for future work in the last Section.

2 Preliminaries

In this paper, we are mostly concerned with SAX, since we consider large streaming documents. We also consider a subset of XPath expressions that contains elements, wildcards ("*"), child ("/"), ancestor-descendant relationships ("//"), and branches or predicates ("[...]"). Although our implementation can handle a larger grammar, the following grammar is the portion that mostly incorporates our target rewriting part of XPath:

$$ E \quad \rightarrow \quad E/E \mid E//E \mid E[E] \mid label \mid * \tag{1} $$

2.1 Different Phases

Our optimization scheme is divided into three phases: schema extraction from a stream of XML documents; query rewriting for a set of XPath expressions; and XML document matching against these rewritten XPath expressions.

XML Schema Extraction: The issue here is to derive a statistical XML schema from a collection of streaming XML documents. This schema is represented as an XML document that preserves relationships, hierarchy, and most importantly the frequencies of arrivals of XML elements. These frequencies make the error rate in rewritten queries controllable.

Problem Statement: Given a set of XML documents $D = \{d_1, d_2, \ldots, d_s\}$, we need to compute the XML schema S such that: $\forall <e> \ldots </e>$ in S with frequency f, $\exists <e> \ldots </e>$ in f documents in D such that $children(e, d_i) \subseteq children(e, S)$.

XPath Rewriting: The major component in our approach is to rewrite XPath expressions by minimizing the occurrences of wildcards and ancestor-descendant relationships. Thus, we focus on replacing location steps l that are of the forms: "/*" and "//a". These replacements take place according to a derived schema

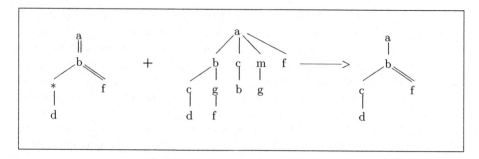

Fig. 1. $Tree(p) + Tree(\mathcal{S}) \rightarrow Tree(ep_1)$

and a user-provided precision tolerance rate. Each replacement may introduce an error rate $\mathcal{E}(l)$.

Problem Statement: Given an XPath expression $p \in P$ where $p = l_0...l_n$, a tolerated error rate η, and a derived XML Schema $\mathcal{S}$, we need to find the set (including a singleton) of XPath expressions $EP = \{ep_1, ep_2, ..., ep_k\}$ equivalent to p such that $\sum_{i=1}^{n} \mathcal{E}(l_i) \leq \eta$.

Example: Given an XPath expression $p = "/a//b[//f]/*/d"$ and an XML Schema $\mathcal{S}$ in Fig. 1. The equivalent XPath expression $ep_1 = "/a/b[//f]/c/d"$ is generated.

Efficient Filtering of XML Documents: The problem of matching XML documents against XPath expressions has been addressed by several researchers ([1][3][8][5][6]). In our case, we are going to use both the set of rewritten queries and the set of original ones to compare and validate the performance and precision of the former against the latter. We next formalize this problem.

Problem Statement: Given a set of XPath expressions $P = \{p_1, p_2, ..., p_n\}$ and a stream of XML documents $D = \{d_1, d_2, ..., d_s\}$, we need to compute for each document $d_i \in D$, the set of XPath expressions that match d_i.

3   Solution Approach

In this Section, we introduce our approach of rewriting a set of XPath expressions in a streaming environment. We first provide an overview of our system's architecture. We then give a detailed description of the three major components of our system: the XML Schema Extraction (XSExtract), the Query Rewriter, and the Query Matcher.

3.1   System Architecture

Our system is divided into three major components that cooperate to produce higher throughput, while keeping a target error rate under control. The first component is called once for a set of streaming XML documents and extracts

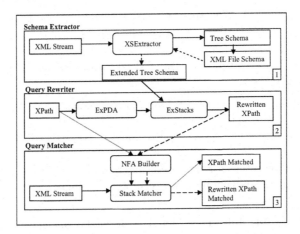

Fig. 2. System architecture

an approximate schema for this set along with some other statistics. The second component is called to rewrite the queries in a set of XPath queries according to the schema extracted using the first component. The third component builds an NFA for the rewritten set of queries. These three components constitute the compile-time part of our system. The run-time part, called Stack Matcher, is executed once for every newly streaming XML document. A general overview of these components is given in Figure 2.

3.2   XML Schema Extractor

XSExtractor is responsible for extracting a schema from a set of streaming XML documents. The derived schema reflects the hierarchy and frequency of arrivals of each XML element. It also preserves relationships among these elements. This schema has three models of representation: a Tree Model (TM), an XML File Model (XML-FM), and an Extended Tree Model (ETM). These models are semantically equivalent, but have different structures which facilitate different uses.

Tree Model: Our TM is a schema model intended to summarize the structure and content of streaming XML documents. It also tracks the frequency of arrivals of each XML element.

Definition: The TM is a tree $T(V, E)$ where each node $v_i \in V$ corresponds to an XML element, and $edge(v_i, v_j) \in E$ represents the parent-child relationship between v_i and v_j. Every node $v_j \in V$ has the following attributes:

- $element(v_j)$: the XML element name.
- $count(v_j)$: the frequency of arrivals of the element.
- $level(v_j)$: the depth of an element where $level(v_j) = level(v_i) + 1$.

TM extraction is driven by the $startElement(a, attrs, d)$ and $endElement(a, d)$ events of the SAX handler on a set of XML Streams.

XML File Model: The XML-FM is another schema model for XML documents. To build an XML-FM, a TM is transformed into an XML document to represent the extracted schema.

The XML-FM is derived from the TM according to the following mapping: Let $v_i = Root(T)$, then:

- transform $element(v_i)$ to its corresponding "start" and "end" tags as denoted by $<v_i> \ldots </v_i>$,
- transform $count(v_i)$ to an attribute $count = count(v_i)$ to be added to the start tag,
- repeat the above steps for the set of direct children $C = \{v_j \in V \mid \exists\ edge(v_i, v_j) \in E\}$ and recursively nest the results accordingly.

Extended Tree Model: This model is derived from the XML-FM and is intended to be consumed by the Query Rewriter. It is an extended representation of the TM where every node in the tree holds additional information about its descendants.

Definition: ETM is a tree $T'(V', E')$ where each node $v_i' \in V'$ corresponds to an XML element and $edge(v_i', v_j') \in E'$ represents the parent-child relationship between v_i' and v_j' in the XML schema file. Every node $v_j' \in V'$ has the following attributes:

- $element(v_j')$: the XML element name.
- $count(v_j')$: the frequency of that element arrivals.
- $level(v_j')$: the depth of element v_j' where $level(v_j') = level(v_i') + 1$.
- $descendants(v_j')$: the set of descendants $D_j = \{d_{j_1}, d_{j_2}, \ldots, d_{j_n}\}$ of v_j' such that $(\forall\ d_{j_h} \in D_j, 1 \leq h \leq n \Leftrightarrow \exists\ v_k' \in V' \mid element(v_k') = d_{j_h})$ and the following two frequencies are collected:
  - $count(d_{j_h}, l)$: the arrivals frequency of descendant d_{j_h} at relative levels $l = level(v_k') - level(v_j')$ where $1 \leq l \leq max$.
  - $count(d_{j_h})$: the arrivals frequency of descendant d_{j_h} at all levels where $level(v_k') > level(v_j')$.

Given the above attributes, we define the following terms:

- let $P_{v_k', l} = Pr(v_k' \mid v_j', l)$ denote the probability of an XML element v_k' at level l given that it is a descendant of element v_j' where $1 \leq l \leq m$, $(m = max)$.
- let $P_{v_k'} = Pr(v_k' \mid v_j')$ denote the probability of v_k' at all levels given that it is a descendant of v_j', i.e., $P_{v_k'} = \Sigma_{l=1}^{m} Pr(v_k' \mid v_j', l)$.

3.3   Query Rewriter

As its name indicates, this component takes a set of XPath expressions $P = \{p_1, p_2, \ldots, p_n\}$, each accompanied by a tolerated error rate η_i, and rewrites them in simpler forms without violating η_i for each p_i. The rewriting is accomplished by an Extended Push (ExPush) machine through matching each query separately against an ETM schema, and according to a set of rewriting rules presented next.

Rewriting Rules: The idea behind rewriting is to minimize the occurrences of ancestor-descendant ("//") and wildcard ("*") steps. This is done through the eventual application of the following set of rewriting rules:

- replace a parent-descendant relationship in an XPath expression p_i (e.g., "a//b") with a set of at most $m = max$ wildcard location steps (e.g., "a/* /.../*/b") for each <b> found to be a descendant of <a> in the derived schema and such that $level(b) - level(a) \leq m$ and $\Sigma_{l=1}^{m} 1 - Pr(b \mid a, l) \leq \eta_i$.
- replace a wildcard step ("/*") with a location steps (e.g., "/a") where <a> is found to be the proper replacement of "*" in the derived schema.

Extended Push Machine: The ExPush machine is a modified PDA. The purpose of an ExPush machine is to rewrite an XPath expression, $p = l_0 l_1 \cdots l_n \mid p \in P$ where each location step $l_j = /e_j \mid //e_j$, while it is being matched against an ETM schema. When it exhausts the input of the schema, the ExPush machine returns as set of equivalent XPath expressions $EP = \{ep_1, ep_2, \ldots, ep_k\}$. The main change from a normal PDA is that it has multiple, extended, and linked stacks to operate on instead of just one. These chained stacks (ExStacks), each with its extensions (i.e., additional parameters), hold information on the rewritten queries. The second change is that the ExPush machine accepts as input the nodes of the ETM.

3.4 Preliminary Theoretical Analysis

Given an XPath expression $p = l_0 l_1 \ldots l_n \mid p \in P$, a tolerated error rate η, and a derived ETM schema ($\mathcal{S}$) with nesting degree N, each $l_j = /e_j \mid //e_j$ is associated with $h_j = N - level(e_{j-1})$. Rewriting p might introduce a loss of precision $\mathcal{E}$ whose upper bound is η. This imprecision is added to α, an expectation value that is estimated at schema extraction time, and indicates the maximum error rate of an XML schema with respect to subsequent streaming documents. $\mathcal{E}$ is computed in the following manner:

$$\mathcal{E} = \sum_{j=0}^{n} \mathcal{E}(l_j) + \alpha \qquad (2)$$

where $\mathcal{E}(l_j) = \begin{cases} \sum_{l=m+1}^{h_j} Pr(e_j \mid e_{j-1}, l), & \text{if } l_j = //e_j \text{ and } \mathcal{E}(l_j) \leq \eta_i \\ 0, & \text{otherwise.} \end{cases}$

In case $\mathcal{E}(l_j) \neq 0$, the tolerated error rate η is updated to $\eta = \eta - \mathcal{E}(l_j)$ while making sure that $\eta \geq 0$.

Thus, the loss of precision is introduced through two factors. The first factor occurs due to the replacement of descendant axes according to the derived schema. The second factor α is due to the variation and randomness introduced by newly arriving elements in the schema. This factor is unpredictable, yet it depends on the learning phase or schema extraction.

3.5　Query Matcher

This component is a YFilter-like system [3]. It is modeled with two sub-components: the NFA Builder and the Stack Matcher. It is a stand-alone component in our framework, and hence it is independent from the EXtract and Query Rewriter components. Thus, any matching system (*e.g.*, [6],[8]) can replace YFilter and perform the desired task.

4　Experimental Results

We compare here the performance and the accuracy of the rewritten queries against the original ones. Our goal is also to detect the behavior of the rewriting mechanism with its different parameters. Our experiments are based on both real and synthetic data sets. We use the NASA ADC XML Repository [7]— which we call hereafter NASA—as a real data set and generate a synthetic data set (Random) using an XML document generator that we developed ourselves. Table 1 provides some information on both data sets.

Table 1. Characteristics of the Experimental Data Sets

	NASA	Random
Number of documents for extracting a schema	15	75
Number of documents for matching	120	300
Average size of a document (KB)	7.85	0.35
Maximum number of Levels	6	7
Number of distinct elements	58	27

Our experiments are classified into two categories: *Descendant* and *Wildcard*. Each category examines two metrics: performance and accuracy (always 100% when no rewriting is considered). These two metrics are collected from a set of XML documents when matched against the original queries (referred to hereafter as WNR) and the rewritten queries (referred to hereafter as WR). In the following, and due to space limitations, we present only one result for the descendant category.

Varying Descendant Probability and Error Rate: This experiment examines the impact of varying the descendant axes probability on a set of 3,000 XPath expressions. Thus, the performance and the accuracy are measured on sets of XPath expressions that are classified as follows: with no rewriting (WNR), with rewriting/no tolerated error (WR: $\eta = 0$) , with rewriting/0.2 tolerated error (WR: $\eta = 0.2$), and with rewriting/0.4 tolerated error (WR: $\eta = 0.4$). Fig. 3 shows the results of this experiment. From the figure we can see that we have almost an order of magnitude better performance on the NASA data with rewriting with a negligible loss of accuracy.

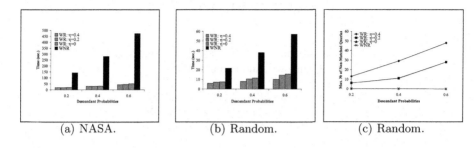

(a) NASA.   (b) Random.   (c) Random.

Fig. 3. Varying Descendant Probability and Error Rate

5   Conclusion

This paper presented the results of simplifying the structure of XPath expressions through the reduction of wildcards (" * ") and ancestor-descendant axes ("//"); this process of query rewriting facilitates the evaluation of these rewritten queries over streaming data. Our future work will focus mainly on extending this work to XQuery.

References

1. Altinel M., and Franklin M. J.: Efficient Filtering of XML Documents for Selective Dissemination of Information. VLDB 2000.
2. Eugster P., et al.: The Many Faces of Publish/Subscribe Environments. ACM Computing Surveys, pp. 114-131, 2003.
3. Fischer, P., et al.: YFilter: Efficient and Scalable Filtering of XML Documents. ICDE 2002.
4. Garofalakis, M., et al.: XTRACT: A System for Extracting Document Type Descriptors from XML Documents. Sigmod 2000.
5. Green, T. J., et al.: Processing XML Streams with Deterministic Finite Automata. ICDT 2003.
6. Gupta A., and Suciu D.: Stream Processing of XPath Queries with predicates. Sigmod 2003.
7. NASA ADC XML Repository Homepage. Available from http://www.cs.washington.edu/research/xmldatasets/data/nasa/nasa.xml. 2001.
8. Peng F. and Chawathe S.: XPath Queries Streaming Data. Sigmod 2003.

Using Non-random Associations for Predicting Latency in WANs*

Vladimir Zadorozhny[1], Louiqa Raschid[2], Avigdor Gal[3],
Qiang Ye[1], and Hyma Murthy[2]

[1] University of Pittsburgh, Pittsburgh, PA
[2] University of Maryland, College Park, MD
[3] Israel Institute of Technology, Haifa, Israel

Abstract. In this paper, we propose a scalable performance management tool for Wide Area Applications. Our objective is to scalably identify non-random associations between pairs of *individual Latency Profiles (iLPs)* (i.e., latency distributions experienced by clients when connecting to a server) and exploit them in latency prediction. Our approach utilizes *Relevance Networks (RNs)* to manage tens of thousands of *iLPs*. Non-random associations between iLPs can be identified by topology-independent measures such as correlation and mutual information. We demonstrate that these non-random associations do indeed have a significant impact in improving the error of latency prediction.

1 Introduction

Wide area applications (WAAs) utilize a WAN infrastructure, e.g., the Internet, to connect a federation of hundreds of servers, typically content providers, with tens of thousands of clients. Servers provide services that may range from simple downloads of digital content to complex Web services with multiple interchanges between client and server. It is expected that WAA must scale to millions of client and server pairs. A significant challenge in deploying WAA is that of scalable performance management for large numbers of clients. The unpredictable behavior of a dynamic WAN [11, 13] results in a wide variability in access latency (end-to-end delay). There has been extensive research in the networking literature to develop metrics and models to predict latencies. The UCBerkeley SPAND Project [13] established techniques for shared passive information gathering, where performance data is gathered for all requests. Their techniques gathered large amounts of low level data and is not scalable to large numbers of clients and servers or to continuous monitoring. There has been research on route aggregation based on IP prefixes exchanged via the Border Gateway Protocol (BGP) as well as research to exploit BGP information for intelligent routing and to monitor and predict performance [3, 5]. The *Network Weather Service*, NWS [15, 16] is a tool that provides dynamic resource performance forecasts for wide area networks and for the computational grid. More recently, Ganglia [12] has developed promising techniques for scalable performance monitoring for clusters and the grid. Commercial solutions, *e.g.*, Keynote and Appliant [1, 2] have addressed performance issues for the WAN. However,

---

* This research is supported by NSF Grants IIS0219909 and EIA0130422.

M. Kitsuregawa et al. (Eds.): WISE 2005, LNCS 3806, pp. 560–568, 2005.

they are typically based on proprietary technology and are not designed to be scalable to a federation of autonomous servers. Further, the focus of these products is to monitor traffic, bandwidth, or server utilization for (possibly limited number of) servers, so as to identify performance bottlenecks and improve or ensure quality of service for some specific applications or services. Global Network Positioning (GNP)[7] present an approach to the round-trip transmission and propagation delay prediction problem. It is based on modeling the Internet as a geometric space (e.g. a 3-dimensional Euclidean space) and characterize the position of any host in the Internet by a point in this space such that the distance between any two hosts can be predicted with high accuracy by the output of the distance function evaluated on the hosts coordinates.

While such prediction models are both accurate and valuable, their primary objective was understanding the behavior of wide area networks. It was not to develop techniques for scalable performance monitoring of large numbers of clients and servers. This motivates the need for a complementary methodology based on passive performance gathering that does not rely as heavily on complete (and perhaps expensive) knowledge of the underlying network topology and network behavior. In [18, 17, 9], we proposed *latency profiles* as a conceptual model to characterize the behavior of sources over a WAN. Latency profiles (LPs) are time-dependent latency distributions that capture the changing latencies clients experience when accessing a server. Latency profiles can be utilized to predict latencies that clients should expect in response to requests, using historical data and recurrent behavior patterns. However, in the presence of hundreds of servers and tens of thousands of clients, managing millions of latency profiles cannot scale.

In this paper, we propose a management tool to provide scalable performance monitoring of tens of thousands of LPs, and to complement network-topology based prediction models. We propose information theoretic and statistical measures such as mutual information and correlation to determine non-random associations among groups of iLPs. Individual We propose *Relevance Networks* (RN) technique in order to determine non-random associations in a large collection of iLPs and to determine how to group them into *aggregate latency profile (aLP)*. Relevance networks represent clusters of non-randomly associated iLPs with a similarity measure above certain threshold. As will be seen in the paper, our technique is based on constructing RN using MI, or Correlation as a similarity measure, and determining the changes to the number of identifiable networks, associations, etc., as the MI or Correlation threshold is modified. A representative latency profile for an aggregate will then be maintained. Whenever a request for service arrives, a prediction will be based on the representative latency profile. We demonstrate that higher MI and Correlation are typically associated with low prediction error. RNs can also be used as a visualization technique that provides a birds eye view of aggregate performance patterns that would have been difficult to obtain using network topology and characteristics alone. The visualization technique of the RN can be used to change the threshold and identify groups of clients and servers with a large number of associations versus clients and servers with a sparse number of associations between them. It allows us to observe both stable patterns and unstable network patterns. A pattern is stable if for a range of MI or Correlation threshold, the number of associations or the number of RNs does not change significantly. An unstable pattern characterizes network areas where as the MI or Correlation threshold is changed, there is a major change in the number of associations or RNs. Using experimental data collected over the CNRI Handle testbed [14] and the PlanetLab testbed [8], we empirically show that there is a considerable amount of non-random associations between iLPs. We demonstrate that the physical topology characteristic of same server combined with these non-random associations of high correlation or high mutual information can play a significant role in latency prediction.

2   Wide Area Performance Monitoring, Latency Profiles and Relevance Networks

Figure 1 presents a WAA performance monitoring architecture. There are three types of nodes, namely clients, content servers, and performance monitors (PMs). Clients continuously download data from content servers and passively construct individual Latency Profiles (iLPs). Given a client c and a server s, an iLP characterizes the end-to-end delay for a request from server s. Due to the stochastic nature of the network, iLP is a random variable represented as a latency probability distribution. PMs manage large collections of iLPs; this is done by aggregating iLPs into a smaller number of aggregate Latency Profiles (aLPs); PMs then manage some number of aLPs and the associated iLPs. Clients consult PMs to obtain a prediction. The scope of an aLP is depicted in Figure 1 by ellipses, where each ellipse contains clients and servers for each an iLP can be constructed. It is worth noting that some aLPs overlap, to illustrate a situation in which a single client (or server) belong to one aLP for some servers (clients) and to another aLP for other servers (clients).

The number and placement of PMs should maximize scalability of performance monitoring by reducing the number of $aLPs$ to be monitored and maintained. It should also minimize uncertainty in latency estimation by increasing the number of aLPs. We construct an aLP by grouping $iLPs$ with similar characteristics that are non-randomly associated with each other; this will ensure that the grouping will benefit the prediction ability of the aLP. For this grouping, we rely on information theoretic and statistical similarity measures computed for the pair-wise association of iLPs. We utilize two similarity measures, namely *mutual information* [10] and *correlation* [6]. A higher mutual information (or correlation) between two $iLPs$ means that these $iLPs$ are non-randomly associated. Conversely, a mutual information of zero means that the joint distribution

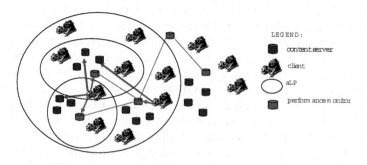

Fig. 1. WAA monitoring architecture based on performance profiles

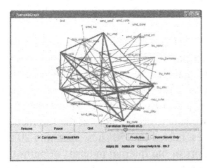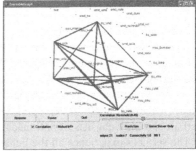

Fig. 2. Examples of Correlation Relevance Networks

of iLPs holds no more information than their individual distributions. In general, there is no straightforward relationship between correlation and MI [4]. While correlation captures linear dependence, mutual information is a general dependence measure.

We propose *Relevance Networks* (RN) as a management tool to analyze and visualize meaningful relationships among iLPs. Consider a graph where the nodes represent iLPs. The RN based methodology computes pair-wise measures of the non-random associations (correlation or mutual information), for all iLP pairs. We then choose a threshold for the measure, either for correlation or mutual information. An edge exists in the graph only if the pair-wise measure exceeds the threshold.

Thus, there is an edge in the graph between 2 nodes if the corresponding iLPs indeed have some non-random association. The tool can highlight clusters of iLPs whose relationship to each other is "stronger" as defined by the threshold and the measure. Such clusters are called *Relevance Networks*. Figure 2 gives an example of correlation RNs generated by our experimental prototype for two increasing threshold values and the Handle data. Each node is a client-server pair (*e.g.*, pubs-qew) and an edge between two nodes represents a non-random association. The thickness of an edge reflects the strength of the association. As we increase the threshold, only the *strongly associated* RNs survive. Such RNs can be used to construct an aLP.

Thus, RNs help in determining how *strongly associated* is a cluster, compared to the entire graph, or to other clusters, by observing the changes of the RN, as the threshold is changed. In addition, RNs can also provide a birds-eye view of potential aLPs. Observing how the threshold increase impacts characteristics of the Relevance Networks (*e.g.*, number of edges and number of connected components), one can generate a set of iLP relationships and aggregate strongly related iLPs. One outcome of this approach is that it provides us with a natural quality estimation of both aLPs (aggregate only above certain threshold), and the whole group of candidate LPs (sensitivity to threshold increase). Such management features are not provided by network based prediction models.

After constructing an aLP from a set of iLPs, we can improve the prediction of an iLP by using observations of other iLPs within the aLP. For the example presented in this section we demonstrate that the non-random association within an aLP can be used to improve latency prediction; we do so by using latency estimations using conditional expectation (CE) [6].

3   Experiments

The experimental data was collected over *CNRI Handle* testbed [14] and *PlanetLab* testbed [8]. CNRI Handle protocol is an emerging IETF/IRTF standard that provides a global name service for use over WANs. We gathered latency data over CNRI Handle testbed during December 2003. We report on the performance of 22 clients (2 each on 11 client ASes) accessing 10 servers, yielding 220 *iLPs*. PlanetLab [8] is a globally distributed wide area testbed for deploying various network services at the Internet scale. PlanetLab currently consists of 350 machines, hosted by 150 sites, spanning 20 countries. The services experience all the behaviors of the Internet in terms of paths taken, latency, available bandwidth, connection properties, network presence and geographical location. All the PlanetLab machines run a common software package. Our experiment gathered latency data in Summer 2004 for approximately 1600 *iLPs*.

First we demonstrate the utility of Relevance Networks to identify strong non-random associations between iLP pairs. We computes pair-wise MI and Correlation values for all iLP pairs. Each iLP pair represents an edge in a complete $iLPs$ relationship graph. We produce a sequence of such graphs by varying the MI and correlation thresholds, starting from $th = 0$ with fixed increments. For each such threshold, we modify the iLP relationships graph by discarding edges with $MI < th\ (Corr < th)$. Each transformation generates a group of connected subnetworks. The subnetworks correspond to the MI or Correlation Relevance Networks with respect to a given threshold. We also maintain several metrics of the RNs representing the associations among the iLP pairs, for self-assesment. The metrics include the number of associations (edges that surpass the threshold), the number of participating nodes, the number of relevance networks and the connectivity (a ratio of the number of edges that surpassed the threshold to the number of all possible edges). Figure 3 illustrates two of these four metrics for different values of the MI threshold for CNRI Handle dataset.

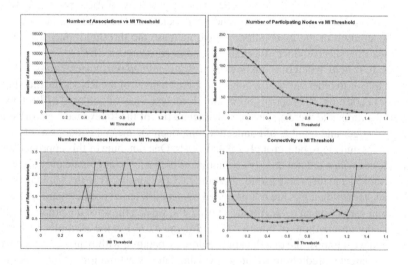

Fig. 3. Characteristics of MI Relevance Networks as a Function of MI Threshold

Our experiments demonstrated that a considerable amount of non-random associations between latency profiles exist. When comparing MI RNs and Correlation RNs, it seems that the latter provides more useful aLPs than the former. With correlation we were able to achieve a reasonable number of aLPs, that contain most of the iLPs. For the same number of iLPs, MI provides a single relevance network, that with most likelihood will reduce the accuracy of prediction.

Now we report results on predicting latency. For this experiment we considered only aLPs that includes two iLPs (iLP pairs) selected using MI and correlation relevance networks considered above. First we plotted MI and correlation vs. the average relative error of prediction for complete MI and correlation relationship graphs for all iLP pairs (Figure 4). We observe a strong dependency of prediction quality on MI and correlation between latency profiles. We also observe that variability of the relative error is considerable. We found that major part of prediction errors is in a good range. However, considerable number of prediction errors are large. Meanwhile, practically all of the large prediction errors spread over areas of low MI (< 0.4) and low correlation (< 0.2). We use this last observation to conclude that latency estimation that avoids choosing representative iLP with low MI value and a low correlation efficiently eliminates large estimation errors.

Figure 5 plots the distribution of the average relative estimation error for PlanetLab data set. We observe that while the Average Relative Estimation Error ranges considerably, it is fairly low over all pairs. For approximately 60% of the pairs, the error is

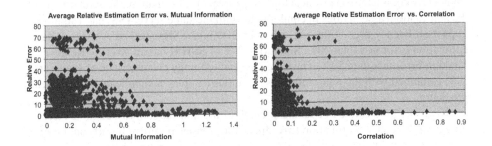

Fig. 4. Average Prediction Error vs MI and Correlation (CNRI Handle dataset)

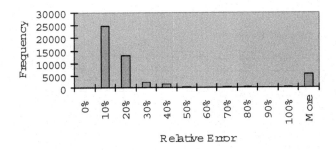

Fig. 5. Distribution of Average Relative Estimation Error (PlanetLab dataset)

from 0-30%; it ranges from 30 to 100% for some 30% of the pairs and for 10% of the pairs it exceeds 100%. To explain the low relative error, we postulate that the PlanetLab overlay is associated with a well provisioned physical network infrastructure. The capacity of the physical network may therefore have the most impact on latency and there is less impact due to points of congestion, etc. Further, most of the servers on the PlanetLab overlay are dedicated to PlanetLab and the workload on the server (measured during our experiments) was low and also unvarying over time/day. We have confirmed this by validating that for many iLPs on Planetlab, the variation of latency across time/day for the experiment period is small; hence the Relative Error of Prediction is also small.

We now address the 40% of iLP pairs with a greater Average Relative Estimation Error. We investigate the impact of physical topology, e.g., same server (SS), as well as non-random association metrics, e.g., high correlation (HC) and high mutual information (HMI) and how they can be exploited to identify those cases where the Average Relative Estimation Error may be improved through the choice of a suitable iLP pair. We group the 30,000 PlanetLab iLP pairs as follows: **All** (all iLP pairs); **SS** (all iLP pairs that share the same server); **SSHC** (all iLP pairs that share the same server and have relatively high correlation); **SSHM** (all iLP pairs that share the same sever and have relatively high MI). A quantile plot of the Average Relative Estimation Error for each of the groups is reported in Figure 6. We observe that the **SS** group has slightly less error compared to **All**. The lack of impact of network topology, e.g., same server (SS) in improving the prediction error is notable, since it indicates that in many situations, one cannot rely completely on physical topology for latency estimation. We further note that the non-random associations in combination with the same server (SS) has a significant impact on latency prediction. For example, 100% of **SSHC** has an Average Relative Estimation Error less than 20%. Similarly, 99% of **SSHM** has an Average Relative Estimation Error less than 50%. Thus, the physical topology characteristic of same server (SS) combined with the non-random associations can play a significant role in latency prediction.

Next we demonstrate that as the strength of the non-random associations increase, the Average Relative Estimation Error further decreases. Figure 6 reports on the Average Relative Estimation Error for all iLP pairs in SS, separating them by the range of the mutual information (MI) measure. We observe that as mutual information increases, the prediction error decreases. For SS iLP pairs with MI > 0.5, 82% of the errors are

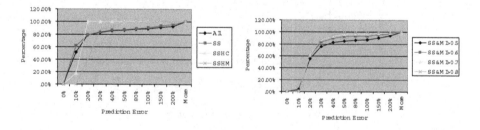

Fig. 6. Impact of Various Associations on Relative Estimation Error (PlanetLab dataset)

less than 50%, whereas with MI > 0.8 all errors are below 50%. The graphs for different Correlation ranges within SS group demonstrated similar performance.

4 Conclusion

To summarize, the physical topology characteristic of same server (SS) combined with the non-random associations can play a significant role in latency prediction. While high MI or correlation alone does not always improve prediction, in conjunction with the same server (SS), they can be exploited. Finally, physically topology alone, e.g., same server (SS) could not always be relied on to improve latency prediction.

We are implementing our methods in a prototype, allowing the generation and testing of aggregate latency profiles. We plan to use more advanced prediction techniques such as Neural Networks and Web Prediction Tool [19], to fully utilize prediction power of aggregate latency profiles.

References

1. *http://www.appliant.com/default.asp.*
2. *http://www.keynote.com/services/html/product_lib.html.*
3. B. Krishnamurthy and J. Wang. On network-aware clustering of web clients. In *Proc. SIG-Comm*, pages 97–110, 2000.
4. W. Li. Mutual information functions versus correlation functions. *Journal of Statistical Physics*, (60), 1990.
5. Z. Mao, C. Cranor, F. Douglis, M. Rabinovich, O. Spatscheck, and J. Wang. A precise and efficient evaluation of the proximity between web clients and their local dns servers, 2002.
6. W. Mendenhall and T. Sincich. *Statistics for Engineering and the Sciences*. Macmillan Publishing, 1985.
7. Eugene Ng Ng and Hui Zhang. Towards global network positioning. *Proceedings of ACM SIGCOMM Internet Measurement Workshop*, 2001.
8. The planetlab home page. http://www.planet-lab.org/.
9. L. Raschid, H.-F. Wen, A. Gal, and V. Zadorozhny. Latency profiles: Performance monitoring for wide area applications. In *Proceedings of the Third IEEE Workshop on Internet Applications (WIAPP '03)*, San Jose, CA, June 2003.
10. F. Reza. *An Introduction to Information Theory*. McGraw-Hill, 1961.
11. D. Rubenstein, J. Kurose, and D. Towsley. Detecting shared congestion of flows via end-to-end measurement. *Proceedings of the ACM SIGMETRICS Conference*, 2000.
12. F. Sacerdoti, M. Katz, M. Massie, and D. Culler. Wide area cluster monitoring with ganglia. *Proceedings of the IEEE Cluster 2003 Conference*, 2003.
13. M. Stemm, S. Seshan, and R. Katz. A network measurement architecture for adaptive applications. In *Proceedings of IEEE InfoComm*, 2000.
14. S. Sun and L. Lannom. Handle system overview. *IRDM/IRTF Draft, 2001, http://www.idrm.org/idrm_drafts.htm*, 2001.
15. M. Swany and R. Wolski. Multivariate resource performance forecasting in the network weather service. *Proceedings of SC02*, 2002.
16. R. Wolski. Dynamically forecasting network performance to support dynamic scheduling using the network weather service. *Proc. of the 6th High-Performance Distributed Computing Conference*, 1997.

17. V. Zadorozhny, A. Gal, L. Raschid, and Q. Ye. Wide area performance monitoring using aggregate latencyprofiles. *Proceedings of the International Conference on Web Engineering*, 2004.
18. V. Zadorozhny, A. Gal, L. Raschid, and Q. Ye. Arena: Adaptive distributed catalog infrastructure based on relevance networks. *Proceedings of the International Conference on Very Large Data Bases*, 2005.
19. V. Zadorozhny, L. Raschid, T. Zhan, and L. Bright. Validating an access cost model for wide area applications. *Proceedings of the International Conference on Cooperative Information Systems (CoopIS 2001)*.

An Online Face Recognition System Using Multiple Compressed Images over the Internet[1]

Hwangjun Song[1], Sun Jae Chung[2], and Young-Ho Park[3]

[1] Dept. of Computer Science and Engineering, POSTECH, Korea
[2] School of Electronic and Electrical Engineering, Hongik University, Korea
[3] School of Electronics and Electrical Engineering, Sangju National University, Korea

Abstract. In this work, we propose an effective online face recognition system over the error-prone Internet. The proposed system uses multiple JPEG-compressed images to improve the recognition rate, and image compression and resizing to reduce the transmission delay and the processing delay. Furthermore, the robustness is improved by effective packetization of compressed image data. First of all, we examine the face recognition rate in terms of quantization parameter and image size, and then implement the effective multiple-image-based face recognition system. Finally, experimental results are provided to show the performance comparison with existing algorithms over the error-prone Internet environment.

1 Introduction

The demand of automatic face recognition has been increasing rapidly for various applications such as security, authentication, access control, and video indexing /browsing, etc. It has been an active research area in bio-informatics, and many efficient algorithms have been proposed so far. In general, face recognition algorithms can be classified into four categories, i.e. template matching approach, statistical classification approach, syntactic approach, and neural network approach [1]. Due to relatively low computational complexity and efficient performance, PCA-related methods of statistical classification approach such as PCA [2, 3], KPCA (Kernel PCA) [4, 5, 6, 7] and 2D-PCA (2-dimensional PCA) [10] have been widely employed. In recent years, effective face recognition algorithms using a compressed image have been proposed [11, 12]. They are based on JPEG (joint photographic expert group) compressed image and hidden Markov model, and recognition process is performed in the DCT (discrete cosine transform) domain.

We present an online face recognition system over the error-prone Internet that consists of a server and many network-connected clients. In this scenario, each client extracts the features and transmits them to the remote server for the recognition. The client may be a camera or a mobile computing device with image capturing function.

---

[1] This research was supported by the MIC(Ministry of Information and Communication), Korea, under the HNRC-ITRC(Home Network Research Center) support program supervised by the IITA(Institute of Information Technology Assessment).

M. Kitsuregawa et al. (Eds.): WISE 2005, LNCS 3806, pp. 569–576, 2005.

Generally speaking, since image needs a large amount of data compared with the text data, image compression is essential for the online applications over the Internet. But, compression can degrade the image quality, which may deteriorate the performance of the face recognition system. Hence, we need an effective trade-off between compressed image data size and face recognition rate. Basically, KPCA and 2D-PCA are employed as a component in the proposed online system although any other face recognition algorithms including 2D-HMM algorithms are employed. First of all, we examine the face recognition rates of KPCA and 2D-PCA in terms of compressed image quality and image size. Based on the observation, we implement an efficient real-time online face recognition system and test its performance over the Internet.

2 Proposed Online Face Recognition System

The main idea of the proposed system is based on the fact that face recognition rate can be improved if more information is available at the remote server. Hence, one unique feature of the proposed system is to use multiple images in order to improve the recognition rate, make use of image compression/resizing so as to reduce the time delay, and effectively packetize the compressed image data to be robust to packet loss over the error-prone Internet. In this scenario, client captures several images, detects the facial area in the images, and then resizes/compresses images to reduce the transmission delay over the Internet and the processing delay at the server. The recognition process is done in the spatial domain at server, and then the recognition result is sent back to the client.

To detect the face part, down-sampling is fulfilled to reduce computational complexity and noise. And candidate regions are rapidly extracted after low-pass filtering the image in order to decrease high-frequency component (filtering/re-sampling). Now compensation technique is needed since the appearance of the skin-tone color depends on the lightning condition (light compensation). For the extraction of face region, the corrected red, green, and blue color components are then nonlinearly transformed into the YCbCr color space (color space transformation). The skin-tone pixels which are detected using an elliptical skin model in the transformed space are grouped into face candidates (skin color detection). If a face candidate has facial features such as eyes, the candidate is extracted [8, 9]. It is summarized in Figure 1. This detection algorithm is adopted in our system.

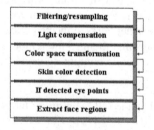

Fig. 1. Flow-chart of face detection algorithm

Now, the detected face part is compressed by the still image compression standard JPEG. In this section, ORL (Olivetti Research Laboratory) face database (40 Classes with 10 images, their image size is 92*112) is used to determine the control parameters of the proposed system, and five images for each class are employed for training. The main spec. of the server is Pentium-4 1.8GHz and 1G-RAM, and every experimental data in the followings is measured at this computer.

2.1 Face Recognition Rate w.r.t. Compression Ratio and Image Size

First of all, we need to consider the relation between face recognition rate and compressed image quality. Although the subjective quality of compressed images is seriously degraded as shown in Figure 2 and the amount of data greatly decreases as the QP (quantization parameter) of JPEG becomes larger, it is however observed that the face recognition rate is almost independent of the quantization parameter when the image size is 92*112. It can be understood when we see the distances among training images, the original input image and the compressed input image. The distance between the original input image and the compressed input image increases as the quantization parameter becomes larger as expected. However, these values are relatively very small compared with the distance among the original images and training images. Hence the effect of compression is negligible and the face recognition rate is not decreased. Consequently, the image data size can be remarkably reduced without the degradation of face recognition rate at the server.

Now, we study the relation between face recognition rate and image size because the image size is related to not only the transmission delay but also the recognition processing delay and the training time at the server. In this work, the image size is reduced by wavelet-based low pass filtering, i.e. low-low band image is used. We define the image size (S_R) by

$$S_R = \frac{S_{origin}}{4^R},$$

where S_{origin} is the size of original image and R is an integer. For example, $R=0$ means that the image is the original image and the image size is a quarter of the origin image size when $R=1$. The required database training time and the recognition processing time are exponentially decreased as the image size becomes smaller (The time includes the JPEG decoding time.) as shown in Figure 3. On the other hand, the face recognition rate is almost constant when $R \leq 4$ but decreases very fast when $R > 4$ as shown in Figure 4. The reason is that the number of eigen-faces decrease as the image size becomes smaller and thus dimension and magnitude of coefficient vector decrease. Consequently, the effect of compression becomes dominant and thus the face recognition rate decreases.

Face recognition rates of KPCA and 2D-PCA are given in (a) and (b) of Figure 4 when quantization parameter and image size change simultaneously, respectively. Based on this observation, quantization parameter and image size are set to 10 and 3, respectively. At this point, the face recognition rate is not deteriorated while the data size and the processing time are significantly decreased.

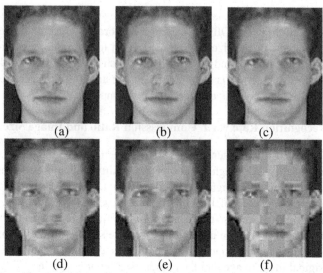

Fig. 2. Visual quality comparison of compressed images with respect to quantization parameters: (a) origin image, (b) QP=5, (c) QP=10, (d) QP=15, (e) QP=20, (f) QP=25, and (g) QP=30

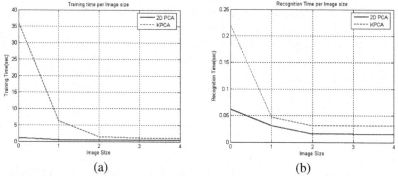

Fig. 3. Recognition rate and processing time with respect to image size and QP: training processing time, and (b) recognition processing time

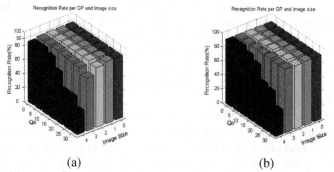

Fig. 4. Recognition rate with respect to image sizes and quantization parameters: KPCA and (b) 2D-PCA

2.2 Majority-Making-Decision Rule Based on Multiple Images

Now, we propose a face recognition algorithm using multiple images to improve the recognition rate. The recognition rate is improved by the majority-making-decision rule when multiple images are available, i.e. we decide that the class is a correct one when more than half of received images match a class at the server. Then, the theoretical face recognition rate P_m is calculated by

$$P_m = \sum_{k=\lfloor n/2 \rfloor}^{n} \binom{n}{k} p_s^k (1-p_s)^{n-k},$$

where n is the number of the input images, P_s is the average face recognition rate when a image is used, $\binom{n}{k}$ is the number of possible combinations when k elements are selected from n elements, and $\lfloor x \rfloor$ is the greatest integer number that is smaller than x. For example, when P_s is 0.94, 3 images are transmitted and majority-making-decision-rule is employed, P_m is about 0.99.

We examined several odd number-image cases for the easy decision: 3, 5 and 7-image cases, etc. The performance of the proposed algorithm is compared with those of KPCA and 2D-PCA. Actually P_m almost saturates at $n=5$ when P_s is greater than about 0.7 in above equation. Based on the observation, 5-image case is adopted in the proposed system. Finally, image size, quantization parameter and the number of images of the proposed system are set to 3, 10, and 5, respectively. It is observed that the face recognition rate is considerably increased with low processing delay and reduced data size. And we implemented robust face recognition system with these parameters. During the transmission, compressed images are encapsulated into different packets. Hence we can still obtain a reasonable recognition rate even though some packets are lost while those of existing algorithms may be significantly decreased when some packets are lost in either the frequency domain or the spatial domain.

3 Experimental Results

The experiment over the Internet is carried out with our Hong-ik DB (300 Classes with 14 images, the size is 160*120) in error-prone Internet environment, and the architecture of the implemented system is shown in Figure 5. The proposed algorithm is compared with KPCA, 2D-PCA and 2D-HMM [12] based on JPEG compressed image. During the experiment, recognition time, training time, amount of transmitted data and recognition rate are exploited as performance measures.

Packet loss is sometimes inevitable over the current Internet since only best-effort service is supported. Although packet loss may be recovered by retransmission in transport layer or application layer, the delay is increased. By the experimental result, we show that the proposed algorithm is more robust to the packet loss over the error-prone Internet. During the transmission, the data are equally partitioned into 5 packets, and then transmitted to the remote server. In the case of 2D-HMM, overlap, state and mixture are set to 25%, 7*7 and 3, respectively. When one of 5 packets is lost

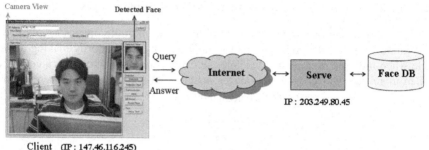

Fig. 5. Architecture of the proposed online face recognition system

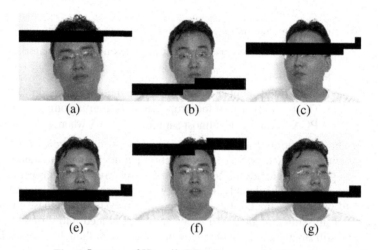

Fig. 6. Images of Hongik DB when a packet loss occurs

Table 1. Performance comparison in the case of no packet loss (Test images are Hongik DB)

		Existing Algorithms			Proposed Algorithm	
		KPCA	2D-PCA	2D-HMM	based on KPCA	based on 2D-PCA
Recognition Rate		78.5	91.4	91.3	92.6	95.7
Amount of Data		19200	19200	4200	3610	3610
Processing Time	Training (sec)	1.8 (hours)	21.0	63	0.69	4.8
	Recognition (sec)	49.5	0.42	2.7	41.2	0.35

during the transmission, the received images are shown in Figure 6 and the performance is summarized in Table 1 and 2. Even though the existing algorithms show the good performance in the case of no packet loss, recognition rates of KPCA, 2D-PCA, and 2D-HMM are seriously degraded to 43.2%, 54.1%, and 18.4%, respectively when only one packet is dropped. Especially, the performance of 2D-HMM is seriously degraded under the error-prone environment since it is very sensitive to packet loss. On the other hand, the proposed system can keep the recognition rate in the tolerable range in the spite of the lost packets. It is observed that the difference becomes more obvious as the rate of lost packets increases.

Table 2. Performance comparison when a packet loss occurs (Test images are Hongik DB)

	• Existing Algorithms			• Proposed Algorithm	
	KPCA	2D-PCA	2D-HMM	based on KPCA	based on 2D-PCA
Recogntion Rate	43.2	54.1	18.4	84.3	90.2

4 Conclusion

We have presented an effective online face recognition system over the error-prone Internet. By considering the relation between the recognition rate and the image compression/resizing, we implemented an effective online face recognition system and explained the relation analytically by comparing distances in the vector space spanned by eigen-faces. Furthermore, we have shown that the proposed multiple-image-based face recognition system can effectively enhance the face recognition rate. Especially, the proposed online system has showed the superior performance over the error-prone Internet environment. Thus, the proposed system is expected to efficiently work in the noisy wireless environment. Although the proposed system is based on PCA-related methods in this paper, the main idea of the proposed system may be combined with any other face recognition algorithms including 2D-HMM algorithms.

References

1. A. K. Jain, R. W. Duin, and J. Mao, "Statistical pattern recognition: a review," IEEE Trans. on Pattern Analysis and Machine Intelligence, Vol. 22, No. 1, pp. 4-37, Jan. 2000.
2. Zhujie, Y. L. Yu, "Face Recognition with Eigen-faces," IEEE International Conference on Industrial Technology, pp. 434 -438, Dec. 1994.
3. M. A. Turk , A. P. Pentland, "Eigen-faces for recognition," Journal of cognitive neuroscience, Vol.3, No.1, pp. 71-86, 1991.
4. Y. Zhang and C. Liu, "Face recognition using kernel principal component analysis and genetic algorithms," IEEE Workshop on Neural Networks for Signal Processing, Sept. 2002.
5. K. I. Kim, S. H. Park, H. J. Kim, "Kernel Principal Component Analysis for Texture Classification," IEEE Signal Processing Papers, Vol. 8 No. 2, pp. 39 -41, Feb. 2001.
6. M. H. Yang, N. Ahuja, and D. Kriegman, "Face recognition using kernel eigen-faces," IEEE International Conference on Image Processing, Vol. 1, pp. 10-13, Sept. 2000.
7. J. Zhang, Y. Yan and M. Lades, "Face Recognition: Eigen-face, Elastic Matching, and Neural Nets," Proceeding of the IEEE, Vol. 85, No. 9, pp. 1422-1435, 1998.
8. R. Hsu, M. Abdel-Mottaleb, and A. K. Jain, "Face detection in color images," IEEE Transactions on Pattern Analysis and Machine Intelligence, Vol. 24 , No. 5, pp. 696-706, May 2002.

9. K. Sobottka and I. Pitas, "Segmentation and tracking of faces in color images," the Second International Conference on Automatic Face and Gesture Recognition, pp. 236 -241 Oct. 1996.

10. J. Yang, D. Zhang, A. F. Frangi and J. Yang, "Two-dimensional PCA: a new approach to appearance-based face representation and recognition," IEEE Transactions on Pattern Analysis and Machine Intelligence, Vol. 26 , No. 1, pp. 131-137, Jan. 2004

11. S. Eickeler, S. Muller, and G. Rigoll, "Recognition of JPEG compressed images based on statistical methods," Image and Vision Computing, Vol. 18, pp. 279-287, March 2000.

12. http://www.intel.com/research/mrl/research/opencv/

The Information Market: Its Basic Concepts and Its Challenges*

P. van Bommel, B. van Gils, H.A. Proper,
M. van Vliet, and Th.P. van der Weide

Institute for Computing and Information Sciences, Radboud University Nijmegen,
Toernooiveld 1, 6525 ED Nijmegen, The Netherlands, EU
{P.vanBommel, B.vanGils, E.Proper, M.vanVliet, Th.P.vanderWeide}@cs.ru.nl

Abstract. This paper discusses the concept of information market. The authors of this paper have been involved in several aspects of information retrieval research. In continuing this research tradition we now take a wider perspective on this field and re-position it as a market where demand for information meets supply for information. The paper starts by exploring the notion of a market in general and is followed by a specialization of these considerations in the information market, where we will also position some of the existing work[1].

1 Introduction

Our modern day western societies are dominated by computerized information systems. Despite being incredibly useful for many tasks, computers have not (yet) solved the problem of dealing with large collections of information. The apparent rise of the Web has resulted in a in a multiplication of the information available to people around the globe. Even more, this information is available in many forms and formats which makes life rather difficult for the average user who shops around to discover information resources that fulfill his or her information needs. These developments have shifted the attention of information retrieval research away from "stand alone" collections to information retrieval on the Web [1].

When the Web matured it, on its turn, gave birth to e-commerce. Given the abundance of information available via the Web, an important part of the commodities traded on the Internet are actually "carriers" of information. This brings us to the focus of this paper. This paper proposes to look at the exchange of information on the Internet as an *Information Market*, where demand and supply of information meet. As such, this paper aims to mark a transition from a traditional view on information retrieval to an *Information Market Paradigm*.

This paper is not concerned with developing yet another approach to match demand and supply of information, but rather with an attempt of fundamentally

---

* The investigations were partly supported by the Dutch Organization for Scientific Research (NWO). We would like to thank the reviewers for their usefull suggestions wich resulted in many improvements of this article.
[1] An extended version of this paper can be found http://osiris.cs.kun.nl/~basvg/pubBvG.php

M. Kitsuregawa et al. (Eds.): WISE 2005, LNCS 3806, pp. 577–583, 2005.

understanding the workings of the *Information Market*. We focus on the elaboration of *Information Market*, which we regard as a follow up to *Information Retrieval*.

2   Markets

Our generalized perspective on markets as presented here is partially based on the concept of economic markets, in particular on the field of micro-economics. We will, however, adopt the point of view that markets deal with *exchange* in general. As such, we consider economic markets to be a specific class of markets dealing with the trading of goods, services and *money*. Economic markets assume the existence of some form of currency to serve as a universal trading unit. In our study of markets, we generalize from these requirements. Nevertheless, our considerations are indeed inspired by literature on economic theories. Our considerations are primarily based on [2, 3, 4] as well as introspection.

2.1   Traded Assets

In our view, two main classes of *assets* can be traded on a market: *Ownership of entities* and *Execution of services* (which can be split further into *transformation of entities* and *reduction of uncertainty*). Even though one may hold the position that in the case of markets dealing with physical goods, it are the physical goods which are the entities being traded, we take the view that what is *actually* traded is the *ownership* of these entities. Trading entities on a market can, in our view, only be discussed if these entities can be regarded as being *owned* by some participant in the market. Trading an entity involves a *change* of ownership. In the next section we will discuss some information market pendants of these classes of services. Let us now explore markets in more detail.

2.2   Transactions

Let p_1 and p_2 be two participants of the market, and let a_1 and a_2 be two assets that are on offer by these two respective participants. The participants may decide to trade these assets, leading to a *transaction*.

In economic markets, one is used to referring to participants as either being a *selling* or a *buying* participant. In our view, the notion of selling and buying can only be defined relative to a specific asset that is involved in the transaction. In the example given above, one could state that participant p_1 sells asset a_1 to participant p_2, making p_1 the selling and p_2 the buying party. By the same token, however, one could state that participant p_2 sells asset a_2 to p_1. We argue that there is nothing wrong with this duality.

It is only our day-to-day use of the terms *sell* and *buy* in the context of the *economic markets* that have lead to a uni-directional view on selling and buying. The "pre-occupation" of economic market with the role of *money* as a universal means of trading has produced this default interpretation of seller and buyer.

The sales of an asset by a participant to another participant, will be referred to as a trans*actand*. Let t be a transactand, then we will use $t : s \xrightarrow{a} b$ to denote the fact that in transactand t participant s sells asset a to participant b. The (two) participants in a transactand are given by the function $\mathsf{Participants}(t) = \{s, b\}$. Similarly, the buyer and seller 'role' within a transactand are given by $\mathsf{Buyer}(t) = b$ and $\mathsf{Seller}(t) = s$ respectively. A transaction can now be regarded as being a set of transactands. If T is a transaction, then we can define: $s \xrightarrow{a} b \in T \triangleq \exists_{t \in T} \left[t : s \xrightarrow{a} b \right]$. The set of participants involved in a transaction are defined as: $\mathsf{Participants}(T) \triangleq \bigcup_{t \in T} \mathsf{Participants}(t)$. As a rule we will require:

[IM1] $t_1, t_2 \in T \wedge t_1 : s \xrightarrow{a} b \wedge t_2 : s \xrightarrow{a} b \Rightarrow t_1 = t_2$

In other words, the involved participants and asset uniquely determine the transactand in a transaction. Even more so, a participant can not play the buyer and seller role in one single transactand:

[IM2] $\forall_{t \in T} \left[\mathsf{Seller}(t) \neq \mathsf{Buyer}(t) \right]$

There is usually some *benefit* to the participants of a transaction, even though this may be an *'artificial'* benefit such as holding on to one's life in the case of a *you're money or your life* situation. As such, a transaction is not just any set of transactands; each participant in a transaction must both receive and pay an asset:

[IM3] $\forall_{p \in \mathsf{Participants}(T)} \exists_{t_1, t_2 \in T} \left[\mathsf{Seller}(t_1) = p \wedge \mathsf{Buyer}(t_2) = p \right]$

Also, transactions are assumed to be 'singular' in the sense that participants of a transaction play the buyer and seller role exactly once. We presume the participants of the market to behave in a goal-driven manner. These goals might be explicit in the reasoning of the participants, but may also be more implicit and based on emotions. We assume $\mathcal{GL}$ to be the set of possible goals a participant may have, and $\mathcal{PA}$ of participants on the market and $\mathcal{ST}$ of states a participant may hold. A state, in this context, is defined to be the present satisfaction (of a searcher) with regard to the goals in $\mathcal{GL}$. Let the function: $\mathsf{Id} : \mathcal{ST} \to \mathcal{PA}$ identify which states belong to which participant. Given the state s of a participant $\mathsf{Id}(s)$, we can view the satisfaction of the goals which the participant (in a certain state!) may have as a function: $\mathsf{Satisfaction} : \mathcal{ST} \times \mathcal{GL} \to [0..1]$.

The consumption of some asset by a participant in a transaction, will result in a change of state of that participant. If T is a transaction, and s is a participant state, then $s \ltimes T$ is the state which results after the participation of $\mathsf{Id}(s)$ in transaction T. We require the resulting state to belong to the original participant and the participant to be a participant of the transaction:

[IM4] $\mathsf{Id}(s) = \mathsf{Id}(s \ltimes T)$

[IM5] $\mathsf{Id}(s) \in \mathsf{Participants}(T)$

We will use $t : s_1 \xrightarrow{a} s_2$ as an abbreviation for: "In transactand t, participant $\mathsf{Id}(s_1)$ in state s_1 sells asset a to participant $\mathsf{Id}(s_2)$ in state s_2":

[IM6] $t : s_1 \xrightarrow{a} s_2 \ \Rightarrow\ t : \mathsf{Id}(s_1) \xrightarrow{a} \mathsf{Id}(s_1)$

The set of states involved in a transaction is identified as:

$$\mathsf{States}(T) \triangleq \left\{ s_1 \ \middle| \ \exists_{s_2,a} \left[s_1 \xrightarrow{a} s_2 \in T \ \lor \ s_2 \xrightarrow{a} s_1 \in T \right] \right\}$$

2.3 Costs and Benefits

The actual benefit of an asset is difficult to measure. This also makes it hard for participants to assess whether they wish to purchase/consume the resource or not: the only way to assess the true benefit is by consuming it! We presume that the benefits of an involvement in a transaction can be defined as the positive impact on the satisfaction levels of a participant:

$$\mathsf{Benefit}(s,T) \triangleq \lambda_{g \in \mathcal{GL}}.\mathrm{MAX}(\mathsf{Satisfaction}(s \ltimes T, g) - \mathsf{Satisfaction}(s, g), 0)$$

The costs of an involvement in a transaction can be defined as the negative impact on the satisfaction levels of a participant:

$$\mathsf{Cost}(s,T) \triangleq \lambda_{g \in \mathcal{GL}}.\mathrm{MAX}(\mathsf{Satisfaction}(s, g) - \mathsf{Satisfaction}(s \ltimes T, g), 0)$$

Given a relative prioritization of the different goals, a weighed level of satisfaction could be computed. Let $\mathsf{Priority} : \mathcal{ST} \times \mathcal{GL} \to [0..1]$ therefore be a function which identifies the level of priority a participant (in a specific state) gives to the specified goal. We presume the priority function to be a distribution totaling to one for each of the states:

[IM7] $\forall_{s \in \mathcal{ST}} \left[\sum_{g \in \mathcal{GL}} \mathsf{Priority}(s, g) = 1 \right]$

With this weighing function, we can define the overall satisfaction as follows: $\mathsf{Satisfaction}(s) \triangleq \Sigma_{g \in \mathcal{GL}} \mathsf{Satisfaction}(s, g) \times \mathsf{Priority}(s, g)$. The (micro)economic assumption of rational behavior can now be reformulated as follows: if two people are in the same *state* (i.e. have the same level of satisfaction) and the same goal, then actually executing a transaction will have the same cost/benefit for these players. An increment in satisfaction does not have to be a *hard* goal such as the quantity of possession, but could also be a *soft* goal such as social esteem or appreciation by friends. It seems sensible to presume that the level of satisfaction of all participants of a transaction should not decrease:

[IM8] $\forall_{s \in \mathsf{States}(T)} [\mathsf{Satisfaction}(s) \leq \mathsf{Satisfaction}(s \ltimes T)]$

2.4 Value Addition

Given some tradable asset, it may be possible to increase the value of this asset by means of a transformation. From the perspective of some participant (state) the transformation may, or may not, be value adding. If a is an asset, and $S(a)$ is the asset which results after performing some transformation S to it, then the added value of performing S to a, in the *context* of a participant in state s and a transaction T, can be defined as: $\mathsf{AddedValue}(S,a)[s,T] \triangleq \mathsf{Satisfaction}(s \ltimes T) - \mathsf{Satisfaction}(s \ltimes T^a_{S(a)})$, where $T^a_{S(a)}$ is the transaction which differs from T *only* in that all transactands involving a have been changed to involve $S(a)$. More formally:

$$R^a \triangleq \left\{ s_1 \xrightarrow{a} s_2 \mid s_1 \xrightarrow{a} s_2 \in T \right\}$$

$$A^a_{a'} \triangleq \left\{ s_1 \xrightarrow{a'} s_2 \mid s_1 \xrightarrow{a} s_2 \in T \right\}$$

$$T^a_{S(a)} \triangleq (T - R^a) \cup A^a_{S(a)}$$

An obvious example is the market for antiquities such as paintings. It is unlikely that intermediaries will 'transform' the painting itself. They do, however, add value in the sense of an appraisal, insurrance etcetera.

3 Particularities of the Information Market

3.1 The Assets

In accordance to [5] the entities traded on the information market are dubbed *information resources*, or *resources* for short. In the context of the Web, an information resource can be defined as [6]: any entity that is accessible on the Web and which can provide information to other entities connected to the Web. A definition which truly supports the open character of the net. Examples of information carriers included are: web pages free text databases, traditional databases and people's e-mail addresses. Note that even though the trading is about information resources, it are actually different levels of ownership/usage rights that are traded. Quite often, the resources will actually be available for free. That is to say, the amount of Euros one has to hand over in exchange is close to zero. As we will see below, the costs/benefits of information resource involves more than the amount of money that is handed over. In addition to trading of ownership/usage of information sources, services pertaining to these information sources are traded as well. Such services may include transformation of an information resource's storage format or translation of an information resource from one language to another. Information resources and related services are not the only assets traded on the market. Producers (and transformers) of information resources will only do so if they have a reason. In other words, there must be some flow of assets back to the producers. This backward flow will have to originate from the consumers of the information resources. This flow could consist of money, but could equally well deal with intangible assets such as intellectual esteem, personal achievement, social standing, etc.

3.2 Transactions

A future consumer of an information resource should have a need for information. This need for information can be caused by a number of reasons. At the moment we distinguish between two types of goals: *increment of knowledge* and *change of mood*. The former corresponds to a situation where someone finds that they are lacking some information/knowledge.

Collectively, one can refer to these two types of goals as *cognitive* goals. In addition to a cognitive goal, a consumer of information will have some *operational goal* as well. This latter goal relates to the tasks the consumer has/wants to perform. These tasks may put requirements (such as timeliness) on the information consumption (and searching!) process. For example, timeliness is a good reason for turning to a (good) search engine when searching for some specific information.

3.3   Costs and Benefits

The costs and benefits of an information resource are particularly difficult to measure. We shall adopt a multi-dimensional view on measuring the potential benefit of a resource. The utility domain deals with the information that may be provided by a resources and the timeliness. The structure domain is concerned with the form (report, painting, movie, audio) and format (PDF, MP3) of a resource. Lastly, the emotion domain deals with the emotional effect (pretty/inspiring) that a resource may have when it is "consumed". This benefits-taxonomy can be used to explore the potential benefits of resources in diverse situations. For instance, in case of art the emotional benefit is likely to be more important than in the case of technical reports, for searchers using a WAP or I-mode based connection the structural aspects are likely to be of high importance.

The costs associated to a resource also fits the above discussed multidimensional domain. For a searcher these costs would, for example, include: *Utility*: the costs of actually obtaining the resource such as search costs (time and money), costs for the Web-connection etc; *Structure*: the amount of disk space needed to store the information resources at a convenient location, computing capacity needed to display the information resource, etc; and *Emotion*: the costs associated to actually conceiving the resource (i.e. the cognitive load associated with interpreting and understanding the resource. These are costs from the informational domain. For a publisher these costs would, for instance, include: *Utility*: the costs associated to creating the resource such as time and effort; *Structure*: the costs associated to storing the resource such as disk space, as well as required computing power in creating the resource; and *Emotion*: Intellectual energy needed to create the contents of the resource. This may also be referred to as cognitive load [7].

3.4   Value Addition

Value addition on the information market may be achieved by the earlier discussed services, such as: (1) transformation of an information resource's storage format, (2) translation of an information resource from one language to another,

(3) aiding searchers in articulating/formulating their specific need for information, and (4)matching demand for information to supply of information. Traditionally, information retrieval focuses on (4) with extensions towards (3). In our opinion, theories are needed to underpin all services that enable the working (value addition) of the information market. Such theories will need to take the goals of all participants of the market into consideration.

4 Conclusion

At the start of this paper we discussed how an evolution can be observed moving beyond the traditional information retrieval paradigm to an information market paradigm. We have provided a discussion on the general notion of a market where assets are traded. This was then narrowed down to information resources, leading to an information market.

At present, we are working on a more fundamental understanding of markets in general and information markets in particular. Based on these insights, we will evolve our existing theories for different aspects of information retrieval. We expect that models for goal-driven reasoning of participants on the information market will in particular be fruitfull in improving the workings of the information market. Most importantly, we expect this to be most helpful in the retrieval of relevant information by by searchers in the information market. This, however, requires a thorough and fundamental understanding of the goals of the participants on the market and how the traded information resources may contribute towards these goals, i.e. what their costs/benefits are with regards to these goals.

References

1. Desai, B.: Supporting Discovery in Virtual Libraries. Journal of the American Society for Information Science **48** (1997) 190–204
2. Sarkar, M., Butler, B., Steinfield, C.: Cybermediaries in electronic marketspace: Toward theory building. Journal of Business Research **41** (1998) 215–221
3. Shannon, C., Varian, H.: Information Rules, a strategic guide to the network economy. Harvard Business School Press, Boston, Massachusetts, USA (1999)
4. Varian, H.: Intermediate Microeconomics, a modern approach. 4th edn. Norton, New York, USA (1996)
5. Gils, B.v., Proper, H., Bommel, P.v.: A conceptual model for information suppy. Data & Knowledge Engineering **51** (2004) 189–222
6. Proper, H., Bruza, P.: What is Information Discovery About? Journal of the American Society for Information Science **50** (1999) 737–750
7. Bruza, P., Dennis, S., McArthur, R.: Interactive internet search: keyword directory and query reformulation mechanisms compared. In: Proceedings of the 23rd Annual ACM Conference of Research and Development in Information Retrieval (SIGIR'2000), Athens, Greece, EU, ACM Press (2000)

List Data Extraction in Semi-structured Document

Hui Xu, Juan-Zi Li, and Peng Xu

Department of Computer Science and Technology,
Tsinghua University, Beijing, P.R. China, 100084
{xuhui, ljz, xp}@keg.cs.tsinghua.edu.cn

Abstract. The amount of semi-structured documents is tremendous online, such as business annual reports, online airport listings, catalogs, hotel directories, etc. List, which has structured characteristics, is used to store highly structured and database-like information in many semi-structured documents. This paper is about list data extraction from semi-structured documents. By list data extraction, we mean extracting data from lists and grouping it by rows and columns. List data extraction is of benefit to text mining applications on semi-structured documents. Recently, several methods are proposed to extract list data by utilizing the word layout and arrangement information [1, 2]. However, in the research community, few previous studies has so far sufficiently investigated the problem of making use of not only layout and arrangement information, but also the semantic information of words, to the best of our knowledge. In this paper, we propose a clustering based method making use of both the layout information and the semantic information of words for this extraction task. We show experimental results on plain-text annual reports from Shanghai Stock Exchange, in which 73.49% of the lists were extracted correctly.

1 List Data Extraction

List data extraction is the task of extracting data from lists in documents and grouping by rows and columns, namely presenting as a table. Extracting data from list is a necessary component in semi-structured document processing and mining. It has two major challenges: how to select the separators to identify the data items of each list item and how to process missing data items in some list items.

We formalize list data extraction as a clustering problem. We take all the data types contained in the list to indicate the clusters, data items in each list item as the data to be clustered, so that list data extraction can be automatically accomplished by clustering the data items. We perform list data extraction in two procedures:

(1) **Separator Selection.** We assume that for each structured list, there is only one separator and select the punctuation which appears more often than others in a structured list and appears nearly the same times in each list item to be separator, for which MISD (Mean Value Inverted Standard Deviation) is defined, and then use the separator to identify the data items from the list.

(2) **Clustering Based List Extraction.** We first rank the salient phrases in all data items to indicate similar lexical pattern [3], then cluster the data items into several

M. Kitsuregawa et al. (Eds.): WISE 2005, LNCS 3806, pp. 584–585, 2005.

clusters using a clustering algorithm taking into account some constraints such as that the data items in the same list item should be clustered according to the order in which they are arranged in the list item, etc. In order to make use of semantic information, text and pattern similarities are defined to calculate the phrase similarity as the distance between two clusters, where the score obtained from the salient phrase ranking is used. The Multiple Layer Recursive Matching algorithm is applied to define the pattern similarity of phrases [4]. Clusters indicate columns of the list and rows can be identified according to the order of data items in the list.

2 Experimental Results

We carried our experiment on plain-text annual reports from Shanghai Stock Exchange. Totally, 110 annual reports were collected and 166 lists were found from them for the experiment. We applied the proposed extraction algorithm on the 166 lists. Table 1 shows the data set and the experimental results.

Table 1. Data Set and Experimental Results

Annual Reports	Lists Found	Correctly Extracted Lists	Extraction Accuracy
110	166	122	73.49%

3 Conclusion

In this paper, we have proposed a clustering approach to list data extraction, and not only the layout and arrangement information but also the semantic information is used. Our experimental results indicate that the proposed clustering based method performs effectively in the experimental data, in which 73.49% of the lists were grouped by rows and columns correctly.

As future work, we plan to make further improvement on the accuracy. We also want to investigate the recognition of lists in semi-structured documents.

References

1. Kristina Lerman, Craig Knoblock, Steven Minton. Automatic Data Extraction from Lists and Tables in Web Sources. Proc. ATEM 2001, IEEE Press, USA, pp. 34~41.
2. Shona Douglas and Matthew Hurst. Layout and language: Lists and tables in technical documents. In Proceedings of the ACL SIGPARSE Workshop on Punctuation in Computational Linguistics, pages 19-24, 1996.
3. Hua-Jun Zeng,Qi-Cai He,Zheng Chen,Wei-Ying Ma and Jinwen Ma. Learning to Cluster Web Search Results. Proceedings of the 27th annual international conference on Research and development in information retrieval, 2004.
4. Von-Wun Soo, Chen-Yu Lee, Chung-Cheng Li, Shu Lei Chen and Ching-chih Chen. Automated Semantic Annotation and Retrieval Based on Sharable Ontology and Case-based Learning Techniques. Proceedings of the 2003 Joint Conference on Digital Libraries. 2003 IEEE.

Optimization Issues for Keyword Search over Tree-Structured Documents

Sujeet Pradhan[1] and Katsumi Tanaka[2]

[1] Kurashiki University of Science and the Arts, Kurashiki, Japan
`sujeet@soft.kusa.ac.jp`
[2] Kyoto University, Kyoto, Japan
`ktanaka@i.kyoto-u.ac.jp`

Abstract. In this paper, we discuss one of several optimization issues regarding our algebraic query model for keyword search over tree-structured documents. In particular, we focus on the properties of a class of filters. The filters in this class not only restrict the size of query results, but also are capable of reducing the cost of query processing.

1   Introduction

Keyword search over tree-structured documents has drawn a growing amount of attention in recent years, particularly since the advent of document standards such as XML. Our earlier work[1] proposed query model supported by *selection* and *join* operations; the two primary operations in traditional database systems.

Given a query (a set of keywords) and a document, the basic idea of our query model is to return a set of relevant fragments in the document as the answer. These fragments are computed by joining smaller fragments in which the specified keywords appear. However, in doing so, the answer set may also contain potentially irrelevant fragments. For example, although the fragment in Figure 1 (b) is a potentially relevant answer fragment, users may find the fragment Figure 1 (c) irrelevant since it consists of a large number of document portion in which none of the query keywords appear. Application of selection predicates, or simply *filters*, is an effective means of discarding such irrelevant fragments. As shown in Figure 2, several useful filters can be considered for restricting the size of a query result.

2   Key Issue

The key issue, however, is whether or not an arbitrary selection predicate can also help optimize query processing. One of the main principles for query optimization in conventional database systems is to perform *selection* as early as possible[2]. If we are to follow the same principle, we must ensure that *selection* can indeed be pushed down in the query evaluation tree; that is even if we perform *selection* ahead of *join*, we are still guaranteed to obtain the same desired result. Unfortunately, this commutativity between *selection* and *join* cannot be achieved for all types of filters. Only a class of filters having a certain property allows selection operation to be pushed down in the query tree.

M. Kitsuregawa et al. (Eds.): WISE 2005, LNCS 3806, pp. 586–587, 2005.

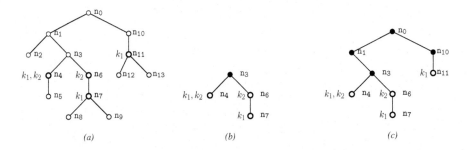

Fig. 1. (a) A document tree and (b) a relevant answer (c) and a potentially irrelevant answer to the query $\{k_1, k_2\}$

3   Class of Filters for Optimization

The required property that a filter must possess for optimization is that if a fragment f satisfies a selection predicate P, then all sub-fragments of f also satisfies P. In other words, if a filter P has this property, then for any fragment not satisfying P, none of its super-fragment too can satisfy P. Obviously, both the filters in Figure 2 possess this property and therefore fall in this class of filters. There may be several other filters having this property and the list may be endless. However, our intention is not to create such a list but to formalize this idea so that a sound theoretical framework can be provided for query optimization.

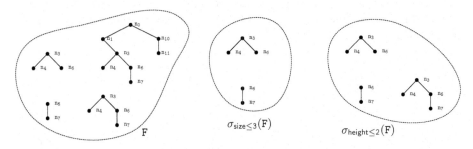

Fig. 2. Filters for restricting the size of the resulting set. F denotes a set of fragments and size ≤ 3 and height ≤ 2 are examples of selection predicates.

Our future work with deal with formal theories and several other optimization issues.

References

1. S. Pradhan and K. Tanaka. Retrieval of relevant portions of structured documents. In *Proc. 15th Int'l Conf. of Database and Expert Systems Applications*, pages 328–338. Springer-Verlag, Aug-Sep 2004.
2. J. D. Ullman. *Principles of Database and Knowledge-Base Systems Vol. II*. Computer Science Press, 1989.

Semantic Integration of Schema Conforming XML Data Sources

Dimitri Theodoratos[1], Theodore Dalamagas[2], and I-Ting Liu[1]

[1] Dept. of CS, NJIT
{dth, il2}@njit.edu
[2] School of EE and CE, NTUA
dalamag@dblab.ece.ntua.gr

A challenging problem in Web engineering is the integration of XML data sources. Even if these data sources conform to schemas, they may have their schemas and the correspongind XML documents structured differently.

In this paper, we address the problem of integrating XML data sources (a) by adding semantic information to document schemas, and (b) by using a query language that allows a *partial specification* of tree patterns. The semantic information allows the grouping of elements into the so called *schema dimensions*.

Our approach allows querying data sources with different schemas in an integrated way. Users posing queries have the flexibility to specify structural constraints fully, partially or not at all. Our approach was initially developed for arbitrarily structured data sources [1]. Here, we show how this approach can be applied to tree-structured data sources that comply to schemas.

We consider XML data sources that conform to DTDs. The DTD of an XML data source can be represented as a *schema tree* whose nodes are labeled by the elements of the DTD and the edges denote element-subelement relationships. An example of a schema tree S_1 for a DTD is shown in Figure 2. Abbreviations for the names of the elements are shown in Figure 1.

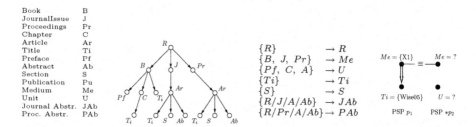

Book	B
JournalIssue	J
Proceedings	Pr
Chapter	C
Article	Ar
Title	Ti
Preface	Pf
Abstract	Ab
Section	S
Publication	Pu
Medium	Me
Unit	U
Journal Abstr.	JAb
Proc. Abstr.	PAb

$$\{R\} \rightarrow R$$
$$\{B, J, Pr\} \rightarrow Me$$
$$\{Pf, C, A\} \rightarrow U$$
$$\{Ti\} \rightarrow Ti$$
$$\{S\} \rightarrow S$$
$$\{R/J/A/Ab\} \rightarrow JAb$$
$$\{R/Pr/A/Ab\} \rightarrow PAb$$

Fig. 1. Abbrv   **Fig. 2.** Schema tree S_1 **Fig. 3.** Dim. set $\mathcal{D}_1$ **Fig. 4.** Query

The nodes of a schema tree may share common features. This semantic information allows the partitioning of the nodes into sets which are called *schema dimensions*. The semantic interpretation of the nodes is provided by the user. Figure 3 shows a partition of the nodes of S_1 of Figure 2 into a dimension set $\mathcal{D}_1$. The name of a set of nodes follows the $\rightarrow$.

M. Kitsuregawa et al. (Eds.): WISE 2005, LNCS 3806, pp. 588–589, 2005.

Queries are formed on dimension sets. A query on a dimension set provides a (possibly partial) specification of a tree pattern (PSTP). This query pattern is formed by a set of graphs of annotated schema dimensions called *partially specified paths (PSPs)*. The edges of PSPs are ancestor ($\Rightarrow$) or child ($\rightarrow$) relationships. A query also involves *node sharing expressions* denoted by an edge labeled by $\equiv$. This tree pattern is to be matched against an XML document of a data source. A node sharing expression forces nodes from different PSPs to be shared. Figure 4 shows an example of a query on $\mathcal{D}_1$.

We introduce *schema dimension graphs* (a) to guide the user in formulating queries, (b) to check queries for satisfiability, and (c) to support the evaluation of queries. Schema dimension graphs abstract the structural information of a schema tree based on the semantic equivalences of nodes defined by the dimension set.

A PSTP query can be computed by identifying a set of (completely specified) tree-pattern queries. Tree-pattern queries are constructed using schema dimension graphs. They are used to generate XPath expressions to be evaluated on the XML documents in the data sources.

In our data integration approach, we assume that a global set of schema dimension names is fixed and used among the different data sources to be integrated. Each data source creates its own *local* schema dimension graph. In addition, a *global* schema dimension graph is created that merges the dimension graphs of the different data sources. The global dimension graph is used to guide user query formulation and to identify queries that are globally unsatisfiable (that is, unsatisfiable with respect to the global schema dimension graph). A query issued against an integrated system is specified on the global set of schema dimensions. Its answer is the collection of its answers on every local data source. Figure 5 shows the different steps of the evaluation of a query in an integration system.

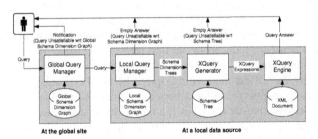

Fig. 5. Evaluation of queries in an integration system

References

1. D. Theodoratos, T. Dalamagas, A. Koufopoulos and N. Gehani. Semantic Querying of Tree-Structured Data Sources Using Partially Specified Tree Patterns. In *Proc. of the 14th Conference on Information and Knowledge Management (CIKM'05)*, 31st Oct - 5th Nov, Bremen, Germany, 2005.

Extract Salient Words with WordRank for Effective Similarity Search in Text Data

Xiaojun Wan and Jianwu Yang

Institute of Computer Science and Technology,
Peking University, Beijing 100871, China
{wanxiaojun, yangjianwu}@icst.pku.edu.cn

Abstract. We propose a method named WordRank to extract a few salient words from the target document and then use these words to retrieve similar documents based on popular retrieval functions. The set of extracted words is a concise and topic-oriented representation of the target document and reduces the ambiguous and noisy information in the document, so as to improve the retrieval performance. Experiments and results demonstrate the high effectiveness of the proposed approach.

Similarity search in text data is to find documents similar to a target document (query document) in the corpus and return a list of similar documents to users. It is widely used in recommender systems in library or web applications, such as Google and CiteSeer.IST. Various text retrieval functions are employed in this task and the standard cosine metric is the most popular one. Previous research [1, 2] focuses on performing similarity search in a semantic concept space instead of the original term space. In this paper, we propose an approach to effectively perform similarity search in text data in two steps: salient word extraction and document retrieval. In the first step, a small number of salient words are extracted from the target document with the novel WordRank method. In the second step, we use the extracted words instead of the full document as the query to retrieve similar documents based on popular retrieval functions. Those noise effects in the target document, which stem from the presence of a large number of words unrelated to the overall topic in the medium to large size document, are reduced in the first step and so the retrieval performance is expected to be improved.

The proposed WordRank method is inspired by the TextRank method [3]. It takes into account the semantic relatedness between words and is able to extract the most salient and representative words from the target document as query words. The semantic relatedness between words is computed based on the electronic lexical database-WordNet. The basic idea underlying the WordRank method is the mutual reinforcement principle widely employed in many graph-based algorithms, e.g. PageRank, HITS and Positional Function. In the graph, when one vertex links to another one, it is basically casting a weighted vote for that other vertex. The higher the total weight of votes that are cast for a vertex, the higher the importance of the vertex. Moreover, the importance of the vertex casting the vote determines how important the vote itself is, and this information is also taken into account by the ranking model.

M. Kitsuregawa et al. (Eds.): WISE 2005, LNCS 3806, pp. 590–591, 2005.
© Springer-Verlag Berlin Heidelberg 2005

The WordRank method goes as follows:

First we have to build a graph that represents the text and interconnects words with meaningful relations to enable the application of graph-based ranking algorithms. We denote the graph as $G=(V,E)$ with the set of vertices V and set of edges E. V contains all words in the text except those stop words. The edges in E are undirected and weighted. Two vertices are connected if their corresponding words are semantically related. The semantic similarity value is assigned as the weight of the corresponding edge. Figure 1 shows a sample graph.

Then each vertex in the constructed graph is assigned with an initial score of the normalized $tf*idf$ value of the corresponding word. The ranking algorithm formulated as follows is run on the graph for several iterations until it converges.

$$WS^{k+1}(V_i) = WS^0(V_i) + d * \sum_{v_j \in neighbor\ (v_i)} \frac{w_{ji}}{\sum_{v_k \in neighbor\ (v_j)} w_{jk}} WS^k(V_j) ,$$

where $WS^k(V_i)$ represents the score of vertext V_i at iteration k, $WS^0(V_i)$ represents the initial score of vertext V_i and w_{ji} represents the weight of the edge between vertex V_j and V_i. $neighbor(V_i)$ is the set of vertices that has a edge with V_i. d is a damping factor and usually set to 0.85. Once a final score is obtained for each vertex in the graph, vertices are sorted in reversed order of their score. A few top words in the ranking are selected as query words.

In order to evaluate the effectiveness of the proposed approach, we performed experiments on TDT (topic detection and tracking) data and Web data. The proposed two-step approaches with different retrieval functions (i.e. the standard cosine metric, the vector space model with pivoted document length normalization, and the Okapi BM25 model) were compared with the traditional retrieval approach in which all words except stop words in the target document were used as the query. The WordRank method for word extraction was compared with the baseline tf-based and tfidf-based word extraction methods. The number of extract words varied from 5 to 30 in the experiments.

The results demonstrate that 1) The proposed two-step approaches perform much better than the traditional approaches based on the original target document, which shows that the set of extracted words does reduce the noise effects in the target document; 2) The Okapi BM25 model is the best one to retrieve similar documents in the proposed two-step approach; 3) The WordRank method has a better ability to extract salient words to represent the target document than the baseline tf-based method and tfidf-based method.

References

1. Aggarwal, C. C., Yu, P. S.: On effective conceptual indexing and similarity search in text data. In Proceedings of IEEE ICDM'01, (2001) 3-10
2. Brants, T., Stolle, R.: Finding similar documents in document collections. In Proceedings of LREC-2002, Workshop on Using Semantics for Information Retrieval and Filtering (2002)
3. Mihalcea, R., Tarau, P.: TextRank: bringing order into texts. In Proceedings of Proceedings of the 2004 Conference on Empirical Methods in Natural Language Processing (2004)

Intensional P2P Mappings Between RDF Ontologies

Zoran Majkić

University of Maryland, College Park, USA

We consider the Peer-To-Peer (P2P) database system with RDF ontologies and with the semantic characterization of P2P mappings based on logical views over local peer's ontology. Such kind of virtual-predicate based mappings needs an embedding of RDF ontologies into a predicate first-order logic, or at some of its sublanguages as, for example, logic programs for deductive databases. We consider a peer as a local epistemic logic system with its own belief based on RDF tuples, independent from other peers and their own beliefs. This motivates the need of a semantic characterization of P2P mappings based not on the extension but on the *meaning* of concepts used in the mappings, that is, based on intensional logic. We show that it adequately models robust weakly-coupled framework of RDF ontologies and supports decidable query answering. The approach to use conventional first order logic (FOL) as the semantic underpinning for RDF has many advantages: FOL is well established and well understood. We will consider an RDF-ontology as finite set of triples $< r, p, v >$, where r is a *resource* name (for class, an instance or a value), p is a *property* (InstanceOf or Property in RDF, or Subclass or Property in RDFS), and v is a value (which could also be a resource name). We denote by $\mathcal{T}$ the set of all triples which satisfy such requirements.

Definition 1 (Logic embedding of RDF-ontology). *We define the logic embedding as a mapping* $\mathcal{E} : \mathcal{T} \rightarrow \mathcal{L}$, *where* $\mathcal{L}$ *is FOL with a domain D, such that:*

1. Case when $p = Subclass$: $\mathcal{E}(< r, Subclass, v >) = r'(x) \leftarrow v'(x)$
where r', v' *are unary predicates for the subject and object of a triple respectively, and* x *is a variable over a domain D.*
2. Case when $p = InstanceOf$: $\mathcal{E}(< r, InstanceOf, v >) = r'(v) \leftarrow$
where r' *is an unary predicate for the resource of the RDF triple.*
3. Case when $p \notin \{InstanceOf, Subclass\}$:

$$\mathcal{E}(< r, p, v >) = (r'(x) \wedge v'(y)) \leftarrow p'(x, y), \quad \textit{if } r, v \textit{ are classes;}$$
$$= r'(x) \leftarrow p'(x, v), \quad \textit{if } r \textit{ is a class and } v \textit{ is an instance or value;}$$
$$= v'(y) \leftarrow p'(r, y), \quad \textit{if } v \textit{ is a class and } r \textit{ is an instance or value;}$$
$$= p'(r, v) \leftarrow, \quad \textit{if } r \textit{ and } v \textit{ are instances or values;}$$

where p' *is a binary predicate assigned to the property name p, and* r', v' *are unary predicates assigned to the subject and the object classes of a triple.*

The peer database in this framework is just the logic theory, defined as union of the RDF-ontology FOL-embedding $\mathcal{E}(\mathcal{O})$ and a number of views defined over it (they constitute a virtual user-type interface). Such embedding of an RDF-ontology, together with its view-extension can be used as mean for intensional mapping with other peer databases in a Web P2P networks, and has the following nice properties:

M. Kitsuregawa et al. (Eds.): WISE 2005, LNCS 3806, pp. 592–594, 2005.

1. The FOL embedding of standard RDF-ontology together with views corresponds to the definite logic program, thus the database model of such RDF peer database has a *unique* Herbrand model: consequently, the query answering from peer databases with RDF-ontology and views is very efficient (polynomial complexity).

2. The defined views can be materialized and there are efficient algorithms for maintenance of RDF views when a new RDF triples are inserted in a peer database, when some of them are deleted, or modified.

3. The possibility to transform original RDF based peer database into the more expressive, but *decidable*, FOL sublanguages, is important if we want to add also integrity constraints over a peer database ontology (for example, in the simplest case, the key constraints over a view). In that case we are able to parse the original RDF structures into a deductive predicate-based database. In such way we are able to rich the full expressive power of standard relational Data Integration Systems.

Let P_i and P_j be the two different peer databases, denominated by 'Peter' and 'John' respectively, and $q_1(\mathbf{x})$, $q_2(\mathbf{x})$ be the concepts of "the Italian art in the 15'th century" with attributes in $\mathbf{x}$.

The with*weakly-coupled* semantics mappings between peers [1, 2, 3], where each peer is completely independent entity, which has not to be directly, externally, changed by the mutable knowledge of other peers, is based on the *meaning* of the view-based concepts:

1. The knowledge of other peers can not be directly transferred into the local knowledge of a given peer.

2. During the life time of a P2P system, any local change of knowledge must be independent of the beliefs that can have other peers. The *extension* of knowledge which may have different peers about the same type of real-world concept can be very different.

'John' can answer only for a part of his own knowledge about Italian art, and not for a knowledge that 'Peter' has. Thus, when 'query-agent' asks 'John' about this concept, 'John' responds only by the facts known by himself (*known*) answers, and can tell to query-agent that, probably, also 'Peter' is able to answer. It is the task of the *query-agent* to reformulate the request to 'Peter' in order to obtain other (*possible*) answers.

We can paraphrase this by the kind of *belief-sentence*-mapping '*John believes that also Peter knows something about Italian art in the 15'th century*'. Such belief-sentence has *referential* (i.e., extensional) *opacity*. In this case we do not specify that the knowledge of 'John' is included in the knowledge of 'Peter' (or viceversa) for the concept 'Italian art in the 15'th century', but only that this concept, $q_1(\mathbf{x})$, for 'John' (expressed in a language of 'John') *implicitly corresponds* to the 'equivalent' concept, $q_2(\mathbf{x})$, for 'Peter' (expressed in a language of 'Peter'). More about intensional equivalence of concepts, and query-answering in such P2P systems, can be find in [4].

References

1. Z. Majkić, "Weakly-coupled P2P system with a network repository," *6th Workshop on Distributed Data and Structures (WDAS'04), July 5-7, Lausanne, Switzerland*, 2004.
2. Z. Majkić, "Massive parallelism for query answering in weakly integrated P2P systems," *Workshop GLOBE 04, August 30-September 3,Zaragoza, Spain*, 2004.
3. Z. Majkić, "Weakly-coupled ontology integration of P2P database systems," *1st Int. Workshop on Peer-to-Peer Knowledge Management (P2PKM), August 22, Boston, USA*, 2004.
4. Z. Majkić, "Intensional logic and epistemic independency of intelligent database agents," *2nd International Workshop on Philosophy and Informatics (WSPI 2005), April 10-13, Kaiserslautern, Germany*, 2005.

Meta-modeling of Educational Practices for Adaptive Web Based Education Systems

Manuel Caeiro-Rodríguez, Martín Llamas-Nistal, and Luis Anido-Rifón

University of Vigo, Department of Telematic Engineering,
C/ Maxwell S/N E-36310, Spain
{Manuel.Caeiro, Martin.Llamas, Luis.Anido}@det.uvigo.es

Abstract. This paper proposes a component-based architecture for adaptive Web-based education systems that support a particular kind of EML models. Our work is concerned with the development of an EML meta-model to provide an enhanced support for the modeling of collaborative practices. The proposal is based on the identification of perspectives.

1 Introduction

Educational technology has been used for decades to support and automate a variety of "educational practices". These different educational practices have been supported by Web-based technologies to some extend, although constructivist and socio-cultural related approaches are not well solved. A main problem remains: current Web-based educational systems are based on implicit assumptions about instruction that constrain the way teaching and learning may proceed, hindering the development of certain pedagogical approaches.

During the last few years, there has been an intense effort to solve this situation trying to separate technology from instructional and pedagogical issues. As result, Educational Modeling languages (EMLs) [1] [2] [3] were proposed to allow the learning design (modeling) of educational practices. These languages are focused on the coordination of the entities involved in educational practices, describing what should be done by learners and instructors, the features of learners that will participate, the resources and services available in the educational scenario, the order in which tasks are proposed, etc. EMLs are intended to be used by educational designers (e.g. a course author, a teacher) to model educational practices (e.g. a course, a lesson, a lab practice). Eventually, these models will be supported by appropriate computational systems to provide the intended practices through their execution.

2 Architecture

We have developed an EML to support the modeling of collaborative practices based on a set of well-defined and separated perspectives [4] [5]. We also are developing a component-based architecture for the development of adaptive Web-based education systems based on the perspectives identified. The proposed architecture (cf. figure 1) follows a typical three-tier scheme:

M. Kitsuregawa et al. (Eds.): WISE 2005, LNCS 3806, pp. 595–596, 2005.
© Springer-Verlag Berlin Heidelberg 2005

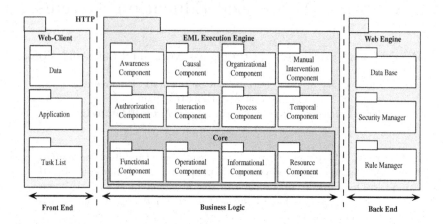

Fig. 1. Main components of the proposed architecture

- The *Web Engine* plays the role of the back-end tier, providing backup and supporting functionalities to the business logic tier.
- The *EML Execution Engine* is the logic-tier responsible for managing and controlling the elements involved in the educational practices in accordance with the learning designs (education models). This engine determines the activities that can be performed by each participant, the tools and resources available in each activity environment, the conditions to use such tools and interact with other participants, etc. All this management and control functionality is considered in separate components in accordance with the perspectives identified in [5]. This design localizes the changes required to tailor an educational feature to the component that implements it.
- The *Web Client* provides the front-tier to support participant interaction. It is devoted to present the available activities, tools and information.

Acknowledgements

This work was supported by *Xunta de Galicia* grant PGIDIT02PXIC32202PN.

References

1. Rawlings, A., van Rosmalen, P., Koper, R., Rodrguez-Artacho, M., Lefrere, P.: Survery of Educational Modelling Languages (EMLs), CEN/ISSS WS-LT (2002)
2. Koper, R.: Modeling units of study from a pedagogical perspective The pedagogical metamodel behind EML, Open University of the Netherlands (2001)
3. IMS Global Learning Consortium: IMS Learning Design Information Model. (2003)
4. Caeiro-Rodríguez, M., Llamas-Nistal, M., Anido-Rifón, L.: Modeling Group-based Education. A Proposal for a Meta-Model. Accepted for publication ER (2005)
5. Caeiro, M., Llamas, M., Anido, L.: Towards a Benchmark for the Evaluation of LD Expressiveness and Suitability. JiME Special Issue on Learning Design (2005)

An On-line Intelligent Recommendation System for Digital Products Using Fuzzy Logic

Yukun Cao, Yunfeng Li, and Chengliang Wang

Department of Computer Science, Chongqing University, Chongqing, 400044, P.R. China
marilyn_cao@163.com

Abstract. Developing an intelligent recommendation system is a good way to overcome the problem of products information overload. We believe that the personalized recommendation system should be build according the special features of a certain kind of products, thereby forming professional recommendation systems for different products. In the paper, we propose a system for digital products, such as laptop, digital camera, PDA, etc. The approach utilizes fuzzy logic to retrieve optimal products based on the consumer's current preferences from the system-user interactions. Experimental results show the promise of our systems.

1 System Architecture

A good way to overcome the product information overload on Internet is to develop intelligent recommender systems. As there is a great deal of products on Internet, it is impossible to recommend all kinds of products in one system. We believe that the personalized recommendation system should be build according the special features of a certain kind of products, thereby forming professional recommendation systems for different products. In the approach, we present a fuzzy-based recommender system for those products that a general consumer does not buy very often, especially for digital products, such as laptop, cell phone, digital camera, video games computer and so on. The mechanism for the most ideal alternative combination to suit consumer's needs is summarized as follows.

To help consumers easily express their judgments, and domain experts easily evaluate product features, the seven linguistic sets:(1) Very Low (0,1,2), (2) Low (1,2,3), (3) Medium Low (2,3,4), (4) Medium (3,4,5), (5) Medium High (4,5,6), (6) High (5,6,7), (7) Very High (6,7,8), are allowed to describe one's subjective judgment, and each term could be quantified with a triangular fuzzy number. The proposed system analyzes a consumer's current requirements and finds out the most ideal products for him.

The system inquires some qualitative questions according the consumer's job, hobby and other aspects what consumer is concerted about. Through answering those questions, each consumer could be represented by a triangular fuzzy number vector of consumer need $\tilde{R} = (\tilde{r}_1, \tilde{r}_2, \cdots, \tilde{r}_n)$, where the *ith* element is the answer of *ith* question. A product is assembled by some critical components, and each critical component has its own technical features. Therefore *ith* component could be represented as a triangu-

M. Kitsuregawa et al. (Eds.): WISE 2005, LNCS 3806, pp. 597–598, 2005.

lar fuzzy number vector of feature functional values $\tilde{F}_i = (\tilde{f}_i^1, \tilde{f}_i^2, \cdots, \tilde{f}_i^n)$, where each element is the rate of a technical feature of the component. Because different technical feature has different influence on the capability of a component, a feature weight vector $\overline{W}$ is assigned to the feature functional vector. Then we could calculate the component capability value $\tilde{p}_i = \left(p_i^1, p_i^2, p_i^3 \right)$ of a component by the equation

$p_i^k = \sum_{j=1}^n \left(f_i^{jk} \times w_i^j \right)$. The component capability vector $\tilde{P} = (\tilde{p}_1, \tilde{p}_2, \cdots, \tilde{p}_n)$ is composed by the quantitative capability values of all components, what represents the quantitative ability of the critical components.

As the qualities of critical components are the key factors in the capability of a laptop, each qualitative need of a certain consumer is correlative to a number of critical components of a laptop. Therefore, assume that the interrelated components of *ith* need are represented by a component capability vector $\tilde{P}_i = \left(\tilde{p}_i^1, \tilde{p}_i^2, \cdots, \tilde{p}_i^n \right)$. And an ability weight vector $\overline{V}$ is assigned to the component capability value vector. Hence we could measure the synthetical capability value $\tilde{q}_i = \left(q_i^1, q_i^2, q_i^3 \right)$ of a laptop about the *ith* customer need by the equation $q_i^k = \sum_{j=1}^n \left(p_i^{jk} \times v_i^j \right)$. Based on the previous method, a vector $\tilde{Q} = (\tilde{q}_1, \tilde{q}_2, \cdots, \tilde{q}_n)$ is obtained, what denotes the synthetical capability values of a laptop. The *ith* fuzzy number $\tilde{q}_i$ in the vector represents the integrative ability of a product for the *ith* qualitative need $\tilde{r}_i$ of a consumer.

Based on the previously obtained vectors $\tilde{R}$ and $\tilde{Q}$ respectively representing the quantified consumer needs and the synthetical abilities of a product, we could calculate the fuzzy near compactness of the two fuzzy number vectors. For each laptops in the product database, the synthetical capability vector and its fuzzy near compactness with the consumer need vector could be calculated based on the previous method. And the smaller near compactness denotes the higher synthetic similarity to the qualitative needs of a certain consumer, i.e. the laptops with smaller near compactness are the ideal alternatives for the customer.

2   Experiment and Conclusions

In the experiment, fifteen laptops in all 138 laptops are recommended to the customer, according the fuzzy near compactness value between the consumer qualitative need and the product synthetical capability. Furthermore, 7 consumers use our experimental system and give their opinion about it. The average of *precision, recall and F1* measures are 83.82%, 87.57%, 85.39%, respectively. Experimental results have shown the promise of our systems. And the system isn't only applied to e-commerce as an assistant system, but could be an independent system for the real-life business.

Consensus Making on the Semantic Web: Personalization and Community Support

Anna V. Zhdanova and Francisco Martín-Recuerda

DERI - Digital Enterprise Research Institute, University of Innsbruck, Innsbruck, Austria
{anna.zhdanova, francisco.martin-recuerda}@deri.org

Abstract. We propose a framework for ontology-based consensus making, which is grounded on personalization and community support. Corresponding software is designed to be naturally deployed in community Web environments.

1 Introduction and Related Work

For facilitation of information delivery and application interoperation, the Semantic Web extends the current Web with machine-processable, commonly understood and shared evolving data and metadata, i.e., ontologies. Specification and support of processes leading to ontology sharing are the problems to resolve for making the Semantic Web approach practically applicable.

Collaboration Tool Support. Many existing ontology editing tools provide collaborative ontology construction facilities to ontology engineers. Among the examples of such tools are Protégé, OntoEdit, KAON, Ontolingua, Tadzebao and APEKS.

Distributed Construction of Consensual Knowledge. Many ontology building methodologies do not explicitly address the problem of consensus making. The methodologies addressing consensus making problem (e.g., CO4 and DILIGENT) mainly introduce editors/moderators responsible for specific ontology parts and collecting inputs from the community.

Ontology Views. Similar to database views that provide a specific visualization of part of the database instances, the ontology view approaches (e.g., in KAON and Protégé) exploit the idea of views in ontologies. Users can reach easier an agreement about the structure and instances of an ontology, as views facilitate visualization of the data to each particular need.

Here modeling of a consensus framework is performed with a personalization and community support perspective, adhering to the requirements of dynamicity, heterogeneity and the original ontology bases integrity maintenance. Current consensus-making solutions often ignore these principles and normally incur additional costs specifically for consensus making.

2 Consensus Framework

2.1 Consensus Process

As for the current Web, numerous contributors are expected to be involved in creation and evolution of the Semantic Web. Therefore, users/contributors, communities and

M. Kitsuregawa et al. (Eds.): WISE 2005, LNCS 3806, pp. 599–600, 2005.

distributed online content provide the ground for consensus making. We specify the consensus process via actions of individual users and interactions across communities and platforms.

We model *consensus* as a result of a reiterating process with the following steps:

1) Creation or creation with reuse of an ontology or data item(s) that are estimated as highly relevant by an individual.

2) Discovery of relevance of created or created with reuse items to other individuals The discovery process consists of the following steps:

a. Ranging communities and individuals as more and less relevant to an individual, e.g., depending on presentation of external ontology items in the individual and community profiles, dynamics and tendency in the evolution of individual and community profiles.

b. Reception of information on individual and community actions, e.g., as a summary starting from more relevant communities and individuals to less relevant communities and individuals. Information on similar actions (e.g., efforts that can bring benefit via making alignment) and complementing actions (which can influence or be influenced by actions of an individual) is of special importance for estimating relevance.

3) Returning to step (1) with estimation of relevance renewed by a discovery process.

2.2   Implementation

The consensus framework is implemented in the People's portal, a community Semantic Web portal infrastructure providing ontology management facilities to the community members [4]. The infrastructure is built as a Java application, employing Jena 2 [2] and Ontology alignment API [3]. The People's portal is applied to the DERI intranet [5] and a Semantic Web community associated with the KnowledgeWeb NoE [1].

3   Conclusions

Involvement of a broad stratum of Web users and enabling communities to regulate their own ontology evolution processes are advantages of the proposed consensus making solution. We are interested in further employment of the developed consensus framework and its tool support in real-life scenarios on community Web portals.

Acknowledgements. The work is partly funded by the European Commission under the NoE KnowledgeWeb (IST-2004-507482) and IP DIP (IST-2004-507483).

References

1. knowledgeweb on the people's portal. URL: http://people.semanticweb.org, 2005.
2. J. Carroll, I. Dickinson, C. Dollin, D. Reynolds, A. Seaborne, and K. Wilkinson. Jena: Implementing the Semantic Web recommendations. In *Proc. of WWW*, pages 74–83, 2004.
3. J. Euzenat. An API for ontology alignment. In *Proc. of ISWC*, pages 698–712, 2004.
4. A. V. Zhdanova. The People's Portal: Ontology management on community portals. In *Proc. of the FOAF workshop*, pages 66–74, 2004.
5. A. V. Zhdanova, R. Krummenacher, J. Henke, and D. Fensel. Community-driven ontology management: DERI case study. In *Proc. of Int. Conf. on Web Intelligence*, 2005.

Dictionary-Based Voting Text Categorization in a Chemistry-Focused Search Engine

Chunyan Liang, Li Guo, Zhaojie Xia, Xiaoxia Li, and Zhangyuan Yang

Key Laboratory of Multiphase Reactions, Institute of Process Engineering,
Chinese Academy of Sciences, 100080 Beijing, China
cyliang@home.ipe.ac.cn

A chemistry-focused search engine, named ChemEngine, is developed to help chemists to get chemical information more conveniently and precisely on Internet. Text Categorization is used in ChemEngine to facilitate users' search. The semantic similarity and noisy data in chemical web pages make traditional classifier perform poorly on them. To classify chemical web pages more accurately, a new text categorization approach based on dictionary and voting is proposed and integrated into the ChemEngine.

In the dictionary-based approach, the terms in a chemical dictionary are first extracted by the longest substring matching algorithm from a document to intensify the chemical concepts. Then, after indexing, the LSI is adopted to produce the final concept space, and the categories are assigned to the test page using kNN algorithm.

We constructed a chemistry-focused dataset (ChIN-Page) using a subset of the web pages indexed in ChIN (http://chin.csdl.ac.cn), a comprehensive chemistry resource directory. Each page of it is classified into one or more categories of a three level hierarchical topic structure which has total 341 categories. The descriptive and complementary information assigned by ChIN editors to web pages are used to generate another dataset (ChIN-SK).

The baseline method using traditional kNN and the proposed dictionary-based approach were run on the datasets. To observe the effects of the descriptive information of web pages on the classifier performance, ChIN-SK training set is used as train data (ChIN-SK->ChIN-Page), and is also combined with ChIN-Page train set together as train data (ChIN-SK+ChIN-Page->ChIN-Pag) to predict the pages in ChIN-Page test set. The optimal micro-average F1 results are shown in Fig.1 (Left). We can observe that Dictionary-based method performs better than the baseline on all the datasets. The results also show that the performance on the description information in ChIN-SK is superior to that on the web pages in ChIN-Page. It is because that ChIN-SK has more intense chemical concepts than ChIN-Page.

Worse performance is surprising observed when using the training sets in ChIN-Page and ChIN-SK together to predict the test pages in ChIN-Page. The cause of the problem is probably that the entropy of the heterogeneous training data is increased. So, a voting method is introduced to try to solve this problem. In the voting method, the dictionary-based classifier is firstly done respectively using the training set of ChIN-SK and that of ChIN-Page to predict the pages in ChIN-Page test set. Then the resultant categories are used as voted categories to obtain the final categories. The results (Fig. 1 Right) show that the voting method is more effective than the baseline.

M. Kitsuregawa et al. (Eds.): WISE 2005, LNCS 3806, pp. 601–602, 2005.

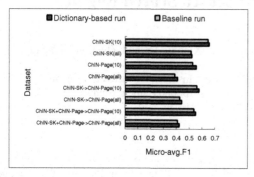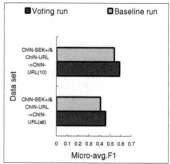

Fig. 1. Comparison figures (Left: baseline and dictionary-based method; Right: baseline and dictionary-based voting method.)

The dictionary-based voting classifier has been integrated into ChemEngine. All of the documents in ChIN-SK and ChIN-Page are used to train the classifier, and then the web pages indexed in ChemEngine are assigned into the hierarchical topic structure. The relation between the pages and the categories is preliminarily stored in the background database. A subject tree representing the hierarchical category structure is offered in addition to a normal result list when a user submits a query to ChemEngine. Once the user clicks a node of the tree, the corresponding pages of the category will be selected from the origin result list. We can observe the acute reduction of the result number when a category is chosen to refine the search. It helps user to get the needed information more easily and quickly (Fig. 2).

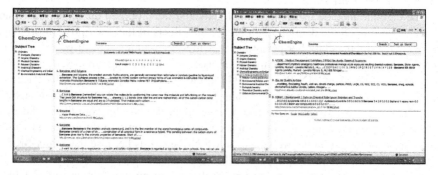

Fig. 2. Screen shots of the query results page of ChemEngine (Left: all results of query "benzene"; Right: results in the "Environmental Analytical Chemistry" category of query "benzene")

Text categorization of the domain-specific web pages into a hierarchical topic structure is a difficult issue. The proposed dictionary-based voting classifier can effectively improve the categorization performance as shown above, and can supply fairly accurate classification results to satisfy users' need when applied in ChemEngine, the chemistry-focused search engine.

This research is part of Internet chemistry-focused search engine project supported by a grant of Natural Science Foundation of China (project No. 20273076).

An Approach to Securely Interconnect Geo Web Services

Adrian Spalka and Stefan Schulz

Dept. of Computer Science III, University of Bonn,
Römerstr. 164, 53117 Bonn, Germany
adrian@iai.uni-bonn.de

1 Introduction

Web Services play a growing role in the geographic community. Efforts to establish a Spatial Data Infrastructure (SDI) are coordinated by the Open Geospatial Consortium (OGC). However, as the infrastructure gets established, and more content providers wish to offer their products, questions of security arise.

Geographical services often stand to gain tremendously from composition and delegation of requests, where one piece of data is constructed from several sets of data, using different sources. However, current standards by the OGC regulate only message transfers, without taking considerations of access control, security and privacy into account.

For the purposes of our examination, we start with the parties business model, and derive security requirements from it. We understand the business model of a node as its 'mode of business', ie, the conditions under which the node offers its services. These conditions include access control, payment and demands on the messaging environment, for example confidentiality guarantees for provided data.

2 Node Roles

We consider four types of node-roles. For the sake of simplicity, we examine only pure roles, but not mixed-role nodes[1].

- **Requester** nodes are 'application proxies'. They are the ultimate source of requests and destination of replies.
- **Broker** nodes provide no data of their own, but collect and delegate requests to other nodes. They may provide authorisation, and portal-like functions.
- **Data-Source** nodes are leafs in the network graph, which provide geographical data. They never delegate requests.
- **Cut-Broker** nodes are similar to Broker nodes in delegating requests, but they do not communicate both the origin of the request to the nodes they invoke and the origin of the data to the Requester. These nodes consider these ultimate origins their business secrets.

---

[1] Such as a Broker who has a local cache of data, thereby becoming a Data-Source as well.

M. Kitsuregawa et al. (Eds.): WISE 2005, LNCS 3806, pp. 603–604, 2005.

3   A Business-Orientated Security Model

We propose a two-phased protocol to address the issues presented. We assume that each node is capable of formulating its access restrictions and messaging parameters in a machine-readable format. Moreover, neither data possession nor the access constraints on any particular piece of data can be considered confidential in our model.

In the first phase, a discovery request is send to one or more nodes, requesting information about data possession and access restrictions. Using this information, a second request is formed, which includes the necessary credentials for each node.

Data delivery can be subject to security demands all by itself. A particular node may only deliver data to requests who provide a complete trustworthy path to itself, and even then only in encrypted form, while some customers may be interested only in data which is certified with a digital signature.

Credentials can be demanded and provided by any node, with broker nodes always communicating the as-yet-unsatisfied demands to their calling node. Each node has a set of credentials necessary to gain access to a piece of data, and a set of credentials it grants to correctly authorised users. This Grant-Set can be used to satisfy demands issued by further delegates. For example, a Broker node might possess a bulk customer pass to some service, enabling it to buy data at discount price. The proof of this agreement would be added to the request by that Broker, enabling access to data at reduced costs. Since only unsatisfied credential demands are communicated, this agreement does not become visible to the customer.

Cut-Brokers, by virtue of not communicating path information to either side of themselves, can only claim to have found data if they would not need further credentials to gain access. Otherwise, they would expose information [2] to across themselves, which would violate their role.

---

[2] The credentials, or the credential demands.

Automatic Keyword Extraction by Server Log Analysis

Chen Ding[1], Jin Zhou[1], and Chi-Hung Chi[2]

[1] Department of Computer Science, Ryerson University, 350 Victoria St.,
Toronto, ON, Canada M5B 2K3
{cding, j3zhou}@ ryerson.ca
[2] School of Software, Tsinghua University, Beijing, China 100084
chichihung@mail.tsinghua.edu.cn

Abstract. Traditionally, keywords are extracted from full texts of a document. While in the web environment, there are more sources we can use to provide a more complete view of a web page's contents. In this paper, we propose to analyze web server logs to extract keywords of entry pages from anchor texts and query terms, and propagate these terms along user access paths to other linked pages. The major benefit of this method is that temporal changes could be reflected in extracted terms, and it is more about a user's viewpoint on page's contents instead of author's.

1 Automatic Keyword Extraction from Server logs

On the web, the server log of a web site provides a rich source of information about how users access the web site. A study by Chi et al. [1] tried to find a list of weighted keywords to represent the information scent of a well-traveled path. Inspired by their work, in this study, we are trying to use the server log analysis to extract keywords which could represent a web page's contents from web site users' viewpoints. It is observed [2] that queries submitted to search engines and anchor texts on hyperlinks could be taken as comments on page contents from users. We believe that both types of keywords could represent page contents, and by combining them, we can get a more complete view of page contents.

In this study, the main purpose of server log analysis is to get query terms and anchor texts linking to entry pages, and find access paths starting from these entry pages. Our basic data element is defined as "referrer session". A referrer session is a consecutive sequence of web page accesses in a single user visit, in which the referrer field of entry page is not empty. We use heuristics to decide when a new session starts and when a session should be discarded. A new user starts a new session; if the time between two consecutive requests is larger than a pre-defined threshold (e.g. 20 minutes), a new session starts; if the duration of a session is larger than a pre-defined threshold (e.g. 1 hour), it means a new session starts; if the referrer does not appear in accessed URLs of current session, a new session starts; if the referrer of the entry page is empty, or there is only one request in current session, this session is discarded.

If referrer is a search engine result page, it is quite straightforward to get the query terms from referrer URL. Otherwise, keywords would be extracted from anchor texts.

M. Kitsuregawa et al. (Eds.): WISE 2005, LNCS 3806, pp. 605–606, 2005.

We use anchor window instead of anchor text to extract keywords, and we filter out those non-content terms before continuing with any further processing.

After keywords are extracted for entry pages, they could be propagated along access paths which are recorded in referrer sessions. The weight of keywords in entry page is defined as 1. The weight of keywords in other pages is determined by the degree of association between two linked pages, and the decay factor. The association degree could be measured by whether the anchor text is on the initial topic, the content similarity between two pages, session duration, and user access recency.

2   Experiment Results

We ran our keyword extraction algorithm on monthly server logs from our department web site. In Table 1, we show a list of web pages, their keywords in decreasing order based on server log analysis, and keywords extracted from full text of web pages. The term in italic is the common term of two extraction approaches.

Table 1. Sample Web Pages and Their Ranked Keywords

URL of web page	Keywords from logs	Keywords from full text
/scs/news.shtml	ryerson university *tony* *cellini* what new scs	*tony* engineering computer science *cellini* center church street
/~mkolios/	*kolios* pcs213 ryerson mkolios pcs125	physics michael *kolios* ultrasound therapy chair academic
/~eharley/cps125/cmf4f .html	cps125 course management form cps 125 2004 hamelin	hr week chapter lab assignment tba program grade mark

By checking actual pages, we could see that most of keywords extracted from server log analysis could accurately represent page's contents. Server-log based keywords are more general terms on page's contents and more representative, while full-text based keywords provide more detailed information. Overlap between the two is low. By running experiments on more logs, it shows that our approach could also capture the temporal changes.

References

[1] E. H. Chi, P. Pirolli, K. Chen, and J. Pitkow, Using information scent to model user information needs and actions on the web, In *Proceedings of the ACM CHI Conference on Human Factors in Computing Systems (SIGCHI)*, 2001.
[2] N. Eiron, and K. S. McCurley, Analysis of anchor text for web search, In *Proceedings of the 26th Annual International ACM SIGIR Conference on Research and Development in Information Retrieval (SIGIR)*, 2003.

Approximate Intensional Representation of Web Search Results

Yasunori Matsuike, Satoshi Oyama, and Katsumi Tanaka

Department of Social Informatics, Graduate School of Informatics, Kyoto University,
Yoshida-Honmachi, Sakyo-ku, Kyoto 606-8501, Japan
{matsuike, oyama, tanaka}@dl.kuis.kyoto-u.ac.jp
http://www.dl.kuis.kyoto-u.ac.jp/

1 Introduction

In this paper, we propose the notion of the "Approximate Intensional Representation (abbrieviated by AIR)" for Web search result. Intuitively, an AIR for a user query q is another query q' such that the search result (Web pages) is approximately represented by the query expression q'. The purpose of the AIR is to support users to understand the outline of the searched Web pages in a form of query.

2 Creation of Approximate Intensional Representation

We propose that an AIR for a given keyword query q is the combination of keywords by using the logical operator "AND" and "OR" another keyword such that without using q. Let q be the query that the user used, and Ans(q) be the Web page set for retrieval results by using the query q. A logical expression q' of keywords such that Ans(q') is approximately equal to Ans(q), where Ans(q) and Ans(q') denote the set of retrieved Web pages by the query q and q', respectively.

The algorithm to derive an appropriate AIR for a given query q is as follows:

1. Get the keyword set by morphologically analysing the texts of retrieved Web pages obtained by using q
   - The retrieval query q is not included in keyword set.
2. Create Elements by combining some keywords in the keyword set with "OR". The n-th Element is described as E_n.
   - Add keywords to E_n with OR to increase the precision to Ans(q).

$$E_n = k_n(0) \vee k_n(1) \vee \cdots \vee k_n(m)$$

   - Finish adding keywords when evaluation exceeds a fixed threshold.
3. Create AIR q' by combining Elements with "AND".
   - Add Elements to q' with AND to increase the recall to Ans(q).

$$q' = E_x \wedge E_{x+1} \wedge \cdots \wedge E_{x+y-1}$$

M. Kitsuregawa et al. (Eds.): WISE 2005, LNCS 3806, pp. 607–608, 2005.

608   Y. Matsuike, S. Oyama, and K. Tanaka

We illustrate the derivation of an AIR for a given query q= "Ichiro" as follows. Since there may exist multiple candidates q$\prime$, we introduce the notion of the precision rate and the recall ratio of the AIR q$\prime$. The q$\prime$ that has higher degree of both the recall and the presicion is more appropriate AIR. We use the Harmonic mean to the evaluation of AIR. The function of Harmonic mean is as follows.

$$H(q\prime) = \frac{1+1}{\frac{1}{\frac{Ans(q \land q\prime)}{Ans(q)}} + \frac{1}{\frac{Ans(q \land q\prime)}{Ans(q\prime)}}} \tag{1}$$

If the q$\prime_1$ is evaluated in higher degree than q$\prime_2$, q$\prime_1$ is more appropriate to the AIR for a given query q.

$$q\prime_1 = Suzuki \land baseball \land (Seattle \lor Mariners)$$
$$q\prime_2 = Suzuki \land (MVP \lor baseball) \land (Safeco \lor Mariners)$$

3 Query Modification Using AIR

The AIR q$\prime$ for a user query q is the combination of several keywords with a logical operator. Therefore it can be used for further query modifications.

We propose three ways of applying q$\prime$ for further query modifications, "Refinement", "Expansion", and "Panoramic View". The following are the examples of these query modifications for a user query q= "Ichiro" and its AIR q$\prime$ = $Suzuki \land baseball \land (Seattle \lor Mariners)$.

⟨ **Refinement** ⟩ If a user wants to refine the content of page set Ans(q), he or she can use the query "q$\prime\prime$ = $q \land q\prime$".
    Ex.) q$\prime\prime$ = $Ichiro \land (Suzuki \land baseball \land (Seattle \lor Mariners))$
⟨ **Expansion** ⟩ When a user is not interested in some keywords in q$\prime$, he or she can remove the keyword which he or she is not interested in from q$\prime$.
    Ex.) q$\prime\prime$ = $Suzuki \land (Seattle \lor Mariners)$
⟨ **Panoramic View** ⟩ If a user wants to grasp the big picture about Ans(q), he or she can use such query using several q$\prime$ as "q$\prime\prime$ = $q\prime_h \lor q\prime_i \lor q\prime_j$".
    Ex.) q$\prime\prime$ = $(Suzuki \land baseball \land (Seattle \lor Mariners)) \lor ((MVP \lor baseball) \land (Safeco \lor Mariners))$

4 Conclusion

In this paper, we proposed the approach that generated AIR that briefly expressed what content retrieved Web pages contained. We also described query modification that used generated AIR.

Acknowledgment

This work was supported in part by the Japanese Ministry of Education, Culture, Sports, Science and Technology under a Grant-in-Aid for Software Technologies for Search and Integration across Heterogeneous-Media Archives, a Special Research Area Grant-In-Aid For Scientific Research (2) for the year 2005 under a project titled Research for New Search Service Methods Based on the Web's Semantic Structure (Project No, 16016247; Representative, Katsumi Tanaka).

A Unique Design for High-Performance Decentralized Resources Locating: A Topological Perspective

Xinli Huang, Fanyuan Ma, and Wenju Zhang

Department of Computer Science and Engineering,
Shanghai Jiao Tong University, Shanghai, P.R. China, 200030
{huang-xl, fyma, zwj03}@sjtu.edu.cn

Abstract. In this paper, we propose a unique protocol for high-performance decentralized resources locating, focusing on building overlays with good topological properties. Our protocol operates with only local knowledge, yet results in enlarged search scope and reduced network traffic, by better matching the heterogeneity and the physical topology, which is also justified by simulations.

1 Introduction and Contributions

To tackle the scalability problem of decentralized resources locating (the most common and pervasive application to date [1]) in unstructured overlay networks, we eye our viewpoint on the topological properties and develop novel techniques to make sure the resultant overlay topologies possess the following desirable properties: (a) low diameter, (b) connectedness, (c) capacity-sensitive node degree self-sustaining, and (d) better exploitation of underlying physical topology.

The main contribution of this paper is a unique topology-constructing protocol which, if obeyed by every peer, results in stronger guarantees on the above mentioned topological properties. The protocol is especially attractive for applications of large-scale high-performance decentralized resources locating.

The rest of the paper is organized as follows: in Section 2 we present the key ideas of our unique protocol design, in a very brief way due to space limitation. We give the main experimental results in Section 3 and conclude the paper in the last section.

2 The Key Ideas of Our Unique Design

The key ideas of our protocol are summarized below as a set of rules applicable to various situations that a peer may find itself in.

```
//Upon a peer P joining the network
Connect itself to k nodes, chosen from the current buffer of the
nearest neighbor it can reach, at descending node-stability ranks.
Here k is computed proportional to P's capacity, and we assume that
every existing peer maintains a buffer containing a list of nodes.

//Upon one of P's neighbors leaving the network
Connect to a random node R in the buffer with a probability propor-
tional to C_R/D_P-R, where C_R is the capacity of R, and D_P-R is the physi-
cal proximity between P and R.
```

M. Kitsuregawa et al. (Eds.): WISE 2005, LNCS 3806, pp. 609 – 610, 2005.

```
//Buffer Updating Scheme
When a peer U reaches the upper limit of node degree according to its
capacity, it is replaced in the buffer by a node L with only lower-
limit degree. Here L is found by a breadth-first search rule.

//Better-Neighbor Selection Strategy
Select a better neighbor following a greedy strategy: the node with
(1) smaller distance of underlying network, and then (2) higher node
capacity will be considered as better neighbor.
```

3   Simulation Results

Compared with Gnutella [2] and the similar protocol proposed in [3], our protocol results in much fewer duplicate messages (see Fig.1), larger search space (also see Fig.1), and smaller underlying network distance to nodes within a given radius (see Fig.2), which shows significant system performance gains of our unique design.

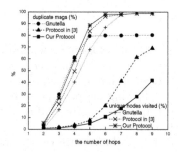
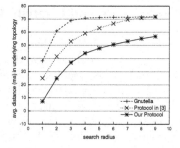

Fig. 1. The percentage of duplicate messages and the percentage of unique nodes visited

Fig. 2. The avg. underlying network distance to nodes as a function of a given search radius

4   Conclusions

The unique protocol we proposed in this paper provably results in significant performance gains of both enlarged search scope and reduced traffic load, by explicitly guaranteeing the desirable topological properties like connectedness, low diameter, exploitation of the node heterogeneity, and matching of the underlying topology.

References

1. John Risson, et al. "Survey of Research towards Robust Peer-to-Peer Networks: Search Methods", Technical Report, UNSW-EE-P2P-1-1, University of New South Wales, 2004
2. Gnutella website. http://gnutella.wego.com/
3. G. Pandering, P. Raghavan, and E. Upfal. "Building Low-Diameter Peer-to-Peer Networks", IEEE Journal on Selected Areas in Communications, 21(6), Aug. 2003, 995-1002

Searching the Web Through
User Information Spaces

Athanasios Papagelis[1] and Christos Zaroliagis[1,2]

[1] Department of Computer Engineering and Informatics,
University of Patras, 26500 Patras, Greece
[2] Computer Technology Institute, P.O. Box 1122, 26110 Patras, Greece
papagel@ceid.upatras.gr, zaro@ceid.upatras.gr

During the last years web search engines have moved from the simple but inefficient syntactical analysis (first generation) to the more robust and usable web graph analysis (second generation). Much of the current research is focussed on the so-called *third generation* search engines that, in principle, inject "human characteristics" on how results are obtained and presented to the end user. Approaches exploited towards this direction include (among others): an alteration of PageRank [1] that takes into account user specific characteristics and bias the page ordering using the user preferences (an approach, though, that does not scale well with the number of users). The approach is further exploited in [3], where several PageRanks are computed for a given number of distinct search topics. A similar idea is used in [6], where the PageRank computation takes into account the content of the pages and the query terms the surfer is looking for. In [4], a decomposition of PageRank to basic components is suggested that may be able to scale the different PageRank computations to a bigger number of topics or even distinct users. Another approach to web search is presented in [2], where a rich extension of the web, called semantic web, and the application of searching over this new setting is described.

In this work we depart from the above lines of research and propose a new conceptual framework for representing the web and potentially improving search results. In particular, the new framework views the web as a collection of web-related data collected and semi-organized by individual users inside their information spaces. These data can be explicitly collected (e.g., bookmarks) or implicitly collected (e.g., web-browsing history). Our approach is based on the observation that users act as small crawlers seeking information on the web using various media (search engines, catalogs, word-of-mouth, hyperlinks, direct URL typing, etc). They tend to store and organize important-for-them pages in tree-like structures, referred to as *bookmark collections*, where the folder names act as tags over the collected URLs. This method of organizing data helps people to recall collected URLs faster, but can also be used as a kind of semantic tagging over the URLs (the path to the URL can be perceived as different ways to communicate the URL itself). This information constitutes part of the user's *personal information space* and it is indicative of his interests. One might argue that people do not collect bookmarks or that they do not organize them in any reasonable manner. However, as our experiments show, people indeed collect and organize bookmarks under certain patterns that follow power law distributions.

M. Kitsuregawa et al. (Eds.): WISE 2005, LNCS 3806, pp. 611–612, 2005.

The proposed framework has been materialized into a hybrid peer-to-peer system, which we call *Searchius* (`http://searchius.ceid.upatras.gr`), that produces search results by strictly collecting and analyzing bookmark collections and their structures. Conceptually, Searchius can be positioned somewhere between search engines and web catalogs.

Searchius can be easily expanded and updated in an ad-hoc manner through asynchronous connections initiated by end-users. It can overcome shortcomings of algorithms based on link analysis (e.g., web islands), where information unreferenced by other sites is not being indexed. Moreover, Searchius is not capital intensive, since it concentrates on a small portion of the data that typical search engines collect and analyze. However, the collected data is of the highest interest for users. To order pages by importance, Searchius uses an aggregation function based on the preference to pages by different users, thus avoiding the expensive iterative procedure of PageRank. This allows for efficient implementations of several personalization algorithms. Finally, the way people organize their bookmarks can be used to segment the URL space to relative sub-spaces. This property can be exploited to provide efficient solutions to additional applications, including the construction of web catalogs and finding related URLs. Note that Searchius does not collect any personal data from end-users.

We have also conducted an extensive experimental analysis of the characteristics of bookmark collections and a comparative experimental study with Google to measure the quality of the search results. Our experiments with a collection of bookmark sets from 36.483 users showed that: (i) people collect and organize bookmarks in ways which follow power law distributions; (ii) there are diminishing returns on the rates that (distinct) URLs and search keywords are discovered; (iii) the number of bookmarks that a given URL has accumulated is linear to the number of users; (iv) important URLs are discovered early on the database construction phase; and (v) there is a consistently significant overlap between the results of Searchius and those produced by Google. More details on the experimental results as well as on Searchius can be found in [5].

References

1. S.Brin, R.Motwani, L.Page, and T.Winograd. What can you do with a web in your pocket. In Bulletin of the IEEE Computer Society Technical Committee on Data Engineering, 1998.
2. R.Cuha, R.McCool, and E.Miller. Semantic Search. In Proc. *World Wide Web Conference*, 2003.
3. T.Haveliwala. Topic Sensitive Page Rank. In Proc. *World Wide Web Conference*, 2002.
4. G.Jeh and J.Widom. Scaling Personalized Web Search. In Proc. *World Wide Web Conference*, 2003.
5. A. Papagelis and C. Zaroliagis. Searching the Web through User Information Spaces. CTI Tech. Report TR 2005/09/01, September 2005.
6. M. Richardons and P. Domingos. The Intelligent Surfer: Probabilistic Combination of Link and Content Information in Page Rank. Volume 14. MIT PRess, Cambridge, MA, 2002.

REBIEX: Record Boundary Identification and Extraction Through Pattern Mining

Parashuram Kulkarni

Yahoo Research and Development Centre, #9, M.G Road,
560028 Bangalore, Karnataka, India
parshu@yahoo-inc.com

Abstract. Information on the web is often placed in a structure having a particular alignment and order. For example, Web pages produced by Web search engines, CGI scripts, etc generally have multiple records of information, with each record representing one unit of information and share a distinct visual pattern. The pattern formed by these records may be in the structure of documents or in the repetitive nature of their content. For effective information extraction it becomes essential to identify record boundaries for these units of information and apply extraction rules on individual record elements. In this paper I present REBIEX, a system to automatically identify and extract repeated patterns formed by the data records in a fuzzy way, allowing for slight inconsistencies using the structural elements of web documents as well as the content and categories of text elements in the documents without the need of any training data or human intervention. This technique, unlike the current ones makes use of the fact that it is not only HTML structure which repeats, but also the content matter of the document which repeats consistently. The system also employs a novel algorithm to mine repeating patterns in a fuzzy way with high accuracy.

1 System Architecture

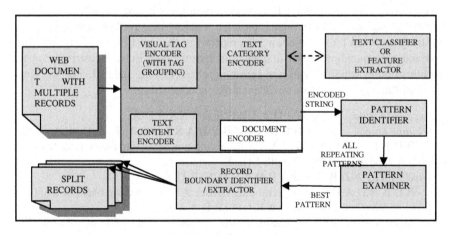

Fig. 1. REBIEX System Architecture

M. Kitsuregawa et al. (Eds.): WISE 2005, LNCS 3806, pp. 613–615, 2005.
© Springer-Verlag Berlin Heidelberg 2005

2 Document Encoder

The document encoder performs the function of identifying text elements of interest and representing the document as a string of encoded symbols. (a) *Visual Tag Encoding*, HTML tags which affect the visual appearance of text are translated to a character representation. (b) *Text Category Encoding*, Text classifiers are used to gather domain specific information about text elements and use this information to represent each text element by the class to which they belong. (c) *Text Content Encoding,* The text content of each element is represented as a unique character by taking a hash value of the text string to capture repetitions of text common to all records.

<table><tr><td><H2>Software Engineer</H2> </td></tr><tr><td><b>Location : </tb></td>
<td> Sunnyvale, CA, USA </td></tr><tr><td>Responsibilities of this job include ......The
candidate should have strong communication skills ....</td></tr><tr><td><b>Email resume to :
</b> </td><td><a href="mailto:resumes@yahoo.com">resumes@yahoo.com</a> </td></tr>
</table><table> <tr><td> <H2>System Administrator</H2> </td></tr> <tr><td> <b>Location
: </b> </td><td>Bangalore, IND </td></tr><tr><td>Reponsibilities of this job include ......The
candidate should have strong communication skills, ... </td></tr><tr><td><b>Email resume
to : </b> </td><td> <a href="mailto:resumes@yahoo.com"> resumes@yahoo.com </a>
</td></tr></table>

Encoded String: H, **T**, B, *1*, **L**, **D**, B, *2*, A, H, **T**, B, *1*, **L**, **D**, B, *2*, A
Tag Encoding(H = <Hn>, B = <B>, A = <A>), *Text Category Encoding* (T = Job Titles, L = Locations, D = Job Descriptions), *Text Content Encoding* (1 = "Location:", 2 = "Email Resume to :")

3 Pattern Identifier

The Pattern Identifier algorithm iterates over the encoded string with comparison window length increasing by 1 in each pass until the window length reaches half the encoded string length. Within each pass the window is moved by one place and the substring enclosed by the window is compared to the substrings already seen in the pass and corresponding repeat frequency is incremented. Equal Substrings constituting consecutive windows and non repeating characters are deleted. The working of the algorithm is shown below on an example encoded string.

Encoded String: B B B D B D A T Z B B D A S S B D A
Window length 1: **B** B̶ B̶ **D B D A** T̶ Z̶ **B** B̶ **D A S** S̶ **B D A** (B=6, D=4, A=3, S=2)
=> B D B D A B D A S B D A (By removing non repeating chars T, Z, S and consecutively repeating chars of length 1 (B, S)
Window length 2: **B D** B̶ D̶ **A B D A B D A** (B̲ ̲D = 4)
=> B D A B D A B D A (By removing consecutively repeating chars of length 2)
Window length 3: **B D A** B̶ D̶ A̶ B̶ D̶ A̶ (B̲ D̲ A̲ = 3)
=> B D A (By removing consecutively repeating chars of length 3) => Empty string (By removing non repeating chars B, D, A)
Resulting Patterns: (BDA) -> 3, (BD) -> 4, (B) -> 6, (D) -> 4, (A) -> 3, (S) -> 2

4 Pattern Examiner

Pattern Examiner determines that repeating pattern which represents the record boundary by employing thresholds and calculating an overall score based on the following measures. (a) Pattern Length, which is the number of encoded characters in the pattern (b) Pattern Frequency, which is the number of times a pattern repeats (c) Pattern Text Element Regularity, which is the consistency with which the records identified by a pattern have the same number of elements, as the standard deviation of the number of text elements in records corresponding to the pattern (d) Pattern Text Coverage, which is the content covered by the records identified by a pattern in a document. Ideally, a pattern should have large length, large frequency, high regularity (low standard deviation) and high coverage.

5 Record Boundary Identifier and Extractor

Upon successful discovery of the best pattern in the encoded document symbol sequence, the extractor searches the document and marks the record boundaries signified by decoding and matching text elements. The beginning and end of each unit of information corresponds to the beginning and end characters/symbols of the discovered pattern.

6 Experiments and Results

The *Accuracy (A)* of the system is defined as the ratio of the number of data records for which boundaries were marked correctly to the number of total data records present in all the pages which were marked valid. The *Recall(R)* of the system is defined as the ratio of the total number of multi record pages that were marked valid to the total number of multi record pages supplied to the system.

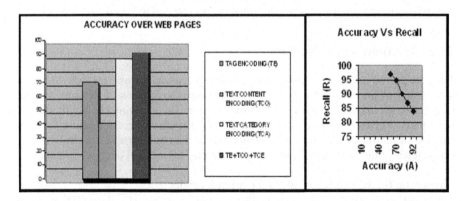

Fig. 2. Accuracy of REBIEX using different methods of encoding on web pages from various domains and the Accuracy vs. Recall graph

Discovering the Biomedical Deep Web

Rajesh Ramanand and King-Ip Lin

Department of Computer Science, The University of Memphis, Memphis TN 38152
rramannd@memphis.edu, davidlin@memphis.edu

Abstract. The rapid growth of biomedical information in the *Deep Web* has produced unprecedented challenges for traditional search engines. This paper describes a new Deep web resource discovery system for biomedical information. We designed two hypertext mining applications: a *Focused Crawler* that selectively seeks out relevant pages using a *classifier* that evaluates the relevance of the document with respect to biomedical information, and a *Query Interface Extractor* that extracts information from the page to detect the presence of a Deep Web database. Our anecdotes suggest that combining focused crawling with query interface extraction is very effective for building high-quality collections of Deep Web resources on biomedical topics.

1 Project and System Overview

This research tackles two issues: Firstly, a lot of information on the web does not have an explicit URL and is not indexed by traditional search engines. This information is stored in content rich databases that are collectively called the Deep Web [3]. Our system aims to identify these Deep Web databases. Secondly, domain-specific web portals are growing in importance, as they improve usability. Our goal is to build a system that can discover sources for biomedical information in the deep web, while automatically maintaining and updating the information. We choose the biomedical domain for our system due to its importance and the lack of existing portals that contains extensive information on it (especially those available from the Deep Web).

The system has three main components: a *classifier* which makes judgments on pages crawled to decide on link expansion, a *focused crawler* [*1*] with dynamically changing priorities governed by the classifier, and a *query interface extractor* [2] which uses information from the page to determine the presence of a deep web database.

2 Experiments and Results

The core part of our experiments is to validate our reasons for using a focused crawler as opposed to a traditional crawler and to measure the success of determining deep web databases that contain biomedical information. The experiments are divided into three parts: 1) Determine the right parameters for the classifier, 2) Measure the effectiveness of the focused crawler to find biomedical data quickly and efficiently, and 3) Locate query interfaces in relevant pages to identify biomedical deep web databases.

Measuring the Effectiveness of the Focused Crawler

The classifier was trained on a biomedical corpus [4] using TFIDF to produce an accuracy of 90.4% and an F-measure of 94.1% which indicates that the system identifies

M. Kitsuregawa et al. (Eds.): WISE 2005, LNCS 3806, pp. 616–617, 2005.

most positives and negatives accurately but does have a few false results as well. The most crucial evaluation of our focused crawler is to measure the rate at which relevant biomedical pages are acquired, and how effectively irrelevant pages are filtered off from the crawl.

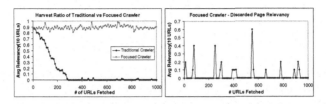

Fig. 1. Rate of harvesting relevant biomedical pages & relevancy of discarded pages

Starting with the same URLs, it can be seen that the traditional crawler quickly loses its relevancy. On the other hand, the focused crawler steadily continues to locate relevant biomedical pages. About 70% to 90% of all pages retrieved are biomedical in nature. The figure on the right shows that only 3.2% of the biomedical pages were missed during the focused crawl. It shows that by performing a focused crawl we are discarding very few pages that would actually be relevant.

Discovering Deep Web Databases
A Decision Tree classifier was trained using a sample set of data containing query interfaces to Deep Web databases. A decision tree was used mainly because of its expressive power. The trained classifier was then tested on all pages identified as biomedical and the system achieved an accuracy of 98% with an F-measure of 92% which shows the effectiveness of this approach.

3 Conclusion

We showed that a focused crawler is a powerful way to discover biomedical information in the deep web. The focused crawler uses a classifier to learn the specialization from a known biomedical data set, and then explores the web, guided by a starting set of biomedical URLs. It filters at the data acquisition level giving the system the ability to crawl to a greater depth and refresh sources easily. Query interfaces on the page were then used to determine Deep Web databases using a Decision Tree classifier.

References

1. S. Chakrabarti, M. Van den Berg and B. Dom: Focused crawling: A new approach to topic-specific web resource discovery. Computer Networks (1999) 31(11—16):1623-1640
2. K. Chang, B. He and Z. Zhang: Toward Large Scale Integration: Building a MetaQuerier over Databases on the Web. Proceedings of the Second Conference on Innovative Data Systems Research (2005) 44-55
3. S. Raghavan and H. Garcia-Molina: Crawling the Hidden Web. Proceedings of the 27th International Conference On Very Large Databases (VLDB) (2001) 109-118.
4. BioMed Central Corpus. http://www.biomedcentral.com/info/about/datamining/. Last accessed Sept 10th, 2005.

A Potential IRI Based Phishing Strategy

Anthony Y. Fu, Xiaotie Deng, and Wenyin Liu

Dept of Computer Science, City University of Hong Kong,
83 Tat Chee Ave., Hong Kong SAR., China
anthony@cs.cityu.edu.hk, csdeng@cityu.edu.hk,
csliuwy@cityu.edu.hk

Abstract. We anticipate a potential phishing strategy by obfuscation of Web links using Internationalized Resource Identifier (IRI). In the IRI scheme, the glyphs of many characters look very similar while their Unicodes are different. Hence, certain different IRIs may show high similarity. The potential phishing attacks based on this strategy are very likely to happen in the near future with the boosting utilization of IRI. We report this potential phishing strategy to provoke much further dissections of related counter measures.

Keywords: Internet security, Anti-phishing, Internationalized Resource Identifier (IRI).

1 Introduction

Phishing webpages are webpages forged to mimic the webpages of certain real companies offering Internet transactions in order to spoof end users to leak their private information. It is a popular way for phishers to use visually and semantically similar URIs and similar webpages to spoof people. Unwary Internet users who are induced to access phishing webpages could be deceived to expose their bank accounts, passwords, credit card numbers, or other important information to the phishers.

In this paper, we report a potential phishing attack that depends on the utilization and popularization of Internationalized Resource Identifier (IRI) [2], as could be a quite severe problem. We also anticipate provoking a series of related further dissections on the potential flaw of IRI on the anti-phishing aspect.

2 IRI Based Phishing Strategy

Rapid evolution of the Internet requires advanced security developments to make it safe. It is not an over claim if we say it is unimaginable if the Internet is not available. However, the Internet is still not mature, and its development is an endless process. In the very beginning, people use IP address directly to access a webpage or other Internet resources. Later, uniform resource identifiers (URI) [1], which are ASCII based, are used to locate or access a webpage or other Internet resources. With the popularization of the Internet, people speaking languages other than English are demanding to use a

M. Kitsuregawa et al. (Eds.): WISE 2005, LNCS 3806, pp. 618–619, 2005.

unified representation of internet resource identifiers to locate the information resources, while URI has its inborn deficiency for this purpose. It uses ASCII and can represent a set of very limited number of readable characters. IRI is such a standard proposed as a complement of URI. An IRI is a sequence of characters chosen from the Unicode [4], which could be used instead of URIs to identify resources. However, the utilization of IRI could bring in severe, potential phishing attacks, since the Universal Character Set (UCS)[4] covers almost all characters in the word for information exchanges, in which a lot of visually similar characters and semantically similar characters co-exist. Fig. 1 shows some of the similar characters to "a".

Fig. 1. Similar characters of "a" in Arial Unicode MS Font (adapted from UC-SimList [3])

It is very easy for phishers to spoof users by replacing characters in a target IRI with similar ones. Although a phishing IRI looks very similar or exactly the same with a target one, they are definitely different in coding level, and people could be victims of this kind of scams without knowing what is happening. Hence, this kind of phishing attacks is very likely to happen in the near future.

3 Conclusion and Future Work

An IRI based potential phishing strategy is reported in this paper. Phishers may use visually and semantically similar characters in UCS to mimic IRIs of real webpages. Various methods can be used to detect this kind of phishing attacks. As a following up research, we consider nondeterministic finite automaton (NFA) to be a possible counter measure of this kind of phishing attacks.

Acknowledgement

We thank Dr. Felix Sasaki from University of Bielefeld for his useful discussion and suggestions.

References

1. T. Berners-Lee., R. Fielding., L. Masinter, *RFC 3986: Uniform Resource Identifier (URI): Generic Syntax*, The Internet Society (2005), Jan. 2005.
2. M. Duerst, M. Suignard, *RFC 3987: Internationalized Resource Identifiers (IRIs)*, The Internet Society (2005), Jan. 2005.
3. A. Y. Fu, http://www.cs.cityu.edu.hk/~anthony/AntiPhishing/IRI, Jun. 2005
4. The Unicode Consortium, http://www.unicode.org/

Multiway Iceberg Cubing on Trees

Pauline LienHua Chou and Xiuzhen Zhang

School of CS & IT, RMIT University, Australia
{lchou, zhang}@cs.rmit.edu.au

Abstract. The Star-cubing algorithm performs multiway aggregation on trees but incurs huge memory consumption. We propose a new algorithm MG-cubing that achieves maximal multiway aggregation. Our experiments show that MG-cubing achieves similar and very often better time and memory efficiency than Star-cubing.

1 Introduction

Since the introduction of the CUBE operator [4], the computation of iceberg cubes, or *iceberg cubing*, has attracted much research. Iceberg cubes are cubes consisting of aggregates satisfying an aggregation constraint [1]. The tree structure has been proposed for iceberg cubing [5]. Bottom-up, represented by H-cubing [5], and top-down, represented by Star-cubing [6], aggregation strategies on trees have been developed. It has been shown that Star-cubing achieves better efficiency in general. But a prominent weakness of Star-cubing is its consumption of memory. We propose the MG-cubing algorithm to address this issue in Star-cubing. Extended description of MG-cubing and comparison with Star-cubing are presented in [3].

2 MG-Cubing: Top-Down Multiway Cubing

The G-tree is compression of the input data and is used for iceberg cubing. A common path starting from the root collapses the tuples with common dimension-values.

Observation 1. *On a G-tree, the aggregate in each node is the aggregate for the group with dimension-values on the path from the root to the node.*

MG-cubing achieves maximal simultaneous aggregation: all group-bys represented on a G-tree are computed. The group-bys that are not represented on the G-tree are computed by removing one dimension each time to construct sub-G-trees.

To compute a data cube on dimensions A, B, C, D, and E, without pruning $2^{5-1} = 16$ trees need to be constructed, where A is the common prefix dimension for all sub-trees of the ACDE-tree, namely ADE, ACE and AE. Assuming an anti-monotone aggregation constraint for iceberg cubing [1], if some (A) group fails the constraint it can be pruned from further computation.

M. Kitsuregawa et al. (Eds.): WISE 2005, LNCS 3806, pp. 620–622, 2005.

Observation 2. *Given an ordered list of n dimensions d_1, ..., d_n and a G-tree T formed by removing dimension d_k, $1 < k < n$, d_1, ..., d_{k-1} are the common prefix dimensions for group-bys to be computed on T and all its sub-trees.*

We conducted experiments to examine the performance of tree-based algorithms. Bottom-up G-cubing is a baseline for comparison [3] with MG-cubing and Star-cubing. The US Census (ftp://ftp.ipums.org/ipums/data/ip19001.Z), US Weather (http://cdiac.ornl.gov/ftp/ndp026b/SEP85L.DAT.Z), and artificial TPC-R (http://www.tpc.org/tpcr/) datasets were used. The time and memory efficiency of the algorithms is shown in Figure 1.

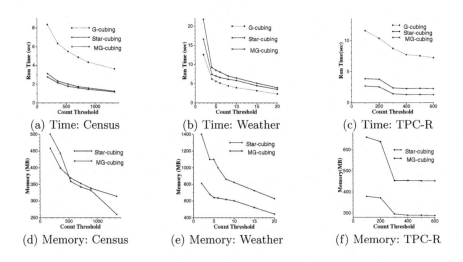

(a) Time: Census   (b) Time: Weather   (c) Time: TPC-R

(d) Memory: Census   (e) Memory: Weather   (f) Memory: TPC-R

Fig. 1. Tree-based iceberg cubing algorithms

3   Conclusions

We have proposed the iceberg cubing algorithm MG-cubing. It achieves maximal simultaneous aggregation. Our experiments confirm that MG-cubing very often has better time and memory efficiency than the state-of-the-art algorithm Star-cubing.

References

1. K. Beyer and R. Ramakrishnan. Bottom-up computation of sparse and iceberg cubes. In *SIGMOD'99*.
2. L. Chou and X. Zhang. Computing complex iceberg cubes by multiway aggregation and bounding. In *DaWak'04 (LNCS 3181)*.
3. L. Chou and X. Zhang. Multiway iceberg cubing on trees. Technical Report TR-05-4, School of CS IT, RMIT University, 2005.

4. J Gray *et al.* Data cube: a relational aggregation operator generalizing group-by, cross-tab, and sub-totals. *Data Mining and Knowledge Discovery*, 1(1), 1997.
5. J Han, J Pei, G Dong and K Wang. Efficient computation of iceberg cubes with complex measures. In *Proceedings of SIGMOD'01*.
6. D. Xin, J. Han, X. Li and B. W. Wah. Star-cubing: computing iceberg cubes by top-down and bottom-up integration. In *VLDB'03*.

Building a Semantic-Rich Service-Oriented Manufacturing Environment

Zhonghua Yang[1], Jing-Bing Zhang[2], Robert Gay[1],
Liqun Zhuang[2], and Hui Mien Lee[1]

[1] Information Communication Institute of Singapore,
School of Electrical and Electronics Engineering,
Nanyang Technological University, Singapore 639798
[2] Singapore Institute of Manufacturing Technology (SIMTech), Singapore 638075
eZhYang@ntu.edu.sg

Abstract. Service-orientation has emerged as a new promising paradigm for enterprise integration in the manufacturing sector. In this paper, we focus on the approach and technologies for constructing a service-oriented manufacturing environment. The service orientation is achieved via *virtualization* in which every thing, including machines, equipments, devices, various data sources, applications, and processes, are virtualized as standard-based Web services. The virtualization approach is based on the emerging Web Services Resource Framework (WS-RF). A case study of virtualizing an AGV system using WS-RF is described. The use of Semantic Web Services technologies to enhance manufacturing Web services for a semantic-rich environment is discussed, focusing on OWL-S for semantic markup of manufacturing Web services and OWL for the development of ontologies in the manufacturing domain. An enterprise integration architecture enabled by Semantic Web service composition is also discussed.

1 Introduction

Service-oriented architecture (SOA) has emerged as a new promising paradigm for building loosely coupled, standard-based and Web-enabled distributed applications and systems. SOA is an architectural style for building software applications that use services available in a network such as the Web, and the concept of services refers to as network-enabled entity delivered over the Web using XML-based technologies. *Services* provide the highest level of abstraction and support the right kind of programming model for open distributed systems in the following ways:

- Services are network-enabled components with well-defined interfaces that are implementation-independent.
- Services are self-contained to offer functionality as defined in interfaces. Services can be dynamically discovered and their consumptions are by message exchange; Consumers are not concerned with how these services will execute their requests.

M. Kitsuregawa et al. (Eds.): WISE 2005, LNCS 3806, pp. 623–632, 2005.

- Services are loosely coupled, only thin message-level connection exists, and thus more independent.
- Composite services can be built from aggregates of other services, providing the ability to choreography their behaviors so that the local policies can be applied autonomously and yet creates a coherent cross enterprise processes.

SOA provides a new opportunity for solving long-standing problems in industry and enterprises, for example, the notorious integration problem. In a nutshell, the integration problem can be viewed as a problem of service integration or service composition. This in turn imposes a new challenge of building a service-oriented environment. In this paper, we focus on the approach and technologies for constructing a service-oriented manufacturing environment. The service orientation is achieved via *virtualization* in which every thing, including machines, equipments, devices, various data sources, applications, and processes, are virtualized as standard-based Web services. The virtualization approach is based on the emerging Web Services Resource Framework (WS-RF). We illustrate how WS-RF is used to virtualize an AGV system as Web services.

The full potentials of service-oriented environment can be fulfilled by enhancing it with semantics, creating a semantic-rich environments. We leverage Semantic Web technologies for this purpose, and use OWL-S for semantic markup of manufacturing Web services and OWL for the development of ontologies in the manufacturing domain.

2 Service-Oriented Architecture for Manufacturing

The overall semantic-enhanced service-oriented architecture is shown in Figure 1. Fundamental to the service orientation is the *virtualization layer*. Via a virtualization, all manufacturing systems to be integrated are exposed as Web services, and they can offer their services and functionality in a standard Web service environment. The emerging WS Resource Framework provides a standardized way for the virtualization [3]. Using WS-RF, manufacturing resources will be modeled as a WS-Resource which is the combination of the Web Service and the stateful resource. The ultimate objective of virtualization is the construction of a service-oriented manufacturing environment, and all services are hosted in a standard Web service platform. The basic Web service infrastructure (SOAP-WSDL-UDDI) is augmented with Business Process Execution Service to support automated business process execution. This is the *Web services infrastructure layer*.

All the Web services, newly developed manufacturing services or those from the virtualization, will be enhanced with domain specific semantic information. The emerging Semantic Web standards provide the Web services infrastructure with the semantic interoperability that integration needs. It provides formal languages and ontologies, most notably OWL [6] and OWL-S [5], to reason about service description and capability. A Semantic Web service is a Web Service whose description is in a language that has well-defined semantics. The description is therefore unambiguously computer interpretable and facilitates maxi-

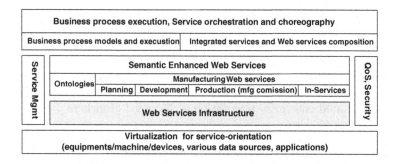

Fig. 1. A service oriented architecture for manufacturing

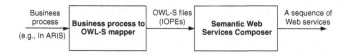

Fig. 2. Business process realization via Semantic Web services composition

mal automation and dynamism in Web service discovery, selection, composition, negotiation, and invocation. This feature provides the sound technical foundation for achieving automated integration. In a way, Semantic Web transforms the Web service infrastructure into repository of computer manipulatable data with rich semantics (*Semantic-enhanced Web services layer*). The significance of this architectural design is that we obtain a semantic rich Web services environment and the semantics marked up in OWL-S are readily processable by autonomous agents.

Within a semantic-rich environment, we must develop *service-oriented requirements* ready for service realization. This is a process of transforming business processes into *service processes*. As shown in Figure 2, first, the requirements of enterprise are modeled as business processes. The essence of business process modeling is to create a *virtualized enterprise* (VE) which represents a coherent, integrated (and interoperated) business process for achieving enterprise's ultimate strategic business goals. The those parts of business processes that are IT-enabled will be realized using Web services processes. When leveraging OWL-S based approach for service composition, business process is transformed into OWL-S service process with Input, Output, Precondition and Effects (IOPE) specified. A Semantic Web services composer will take OWL-S files as input and generate a set of Web services that realize the business process [10].

In a service-oriented approach to enterprise integration, Web services become an integral part of the enterprise IT landscape, and, as such, are vital resources to enterprises. Managing such a service-oriented environment is critical for enterprises that use Web services to automate and integrate various internal functions, and deal with partners and clients electronically. We adopt the OASIS service management standards (i.e., WSDM) including two aspects: (1) Management

Using Web Services and (2) management of the Web services resources via the former [7]. In addition, the emerging Web standard technologies can be used for security and Quality of Services (QoS). These two aspects are functionally orthogonal (Figure 1).

In the remainder of the paper, we focus on how to create a semantic-rich service-oriented environment. The Semantic Web services based composition to achieve automated enterprise integration is discussed elsewhere [9].

3   Service-Orientation Via Virtualization

As emphasized previously, fundamental to realizing service-oriented enterprise integration is *virtualization*, creating a service-oriented environment. Every thing in a considered environment (machine, devices, equipments, data sources, processes and applications) is required to be virtualized as a Web services offering their services and functionality in a standard Web service environment.

The benefits and advantages of service virtualization is well-documented [2]. Virtualization enables consistent resource access across multiple manufacturing systems and environments. Virtualization also enables mapping of multiple logical resource instances onto the same physical resource and facilitates management of resources within/across enterprises based on composition from lower-level resources. Further, virtualization lets us compose basic services to form more sophisticated services-without regard for how these services are implemented. Virtualizing services also underpins the ability to map common service semantic behavior seamlessly onto native systems and facilities.

It is argued that although Web service's behavior is defined solely by the message exchanges through the interface description supported by the service, the external observable behavior implies the existence of a *stateful resources* that are used and manipulated in the processing of a Web service request message. Particularly in manufacturing setting, many resources (machine and equipment, inventory state, process state) have a strong notion of *state* that resources are in. Nonetheless, Web services are generally *stateless*. It is important to identify and standardize the patterns by which state is represented and manipulated, so as to facilitate the construction and use of interoperable services. Web Service Resource Framework (WS-RF), currently under standardization by OASIS, defines a generic and open framework for modeling and accessing stateful resources using Web services [8]. It provides a standard based approach for creation, addressing, inspection, and lifetime management of stateful resources. WSRF is a promising approach to virtualization. A WS-Resource is the combination of a Web service and a stateful resource on which it acts, and thus a WS-Resource is a virtualized representation of a stateful resource accessible using Web services. A WS-Resource has various properties. The values of these properties define the state of the resource. The change of a property value, the state changes. WS-RF relies on WS-Addressing, especially, *EndpointReference*, to specify the location of a particular WS-Resource in URI. EndpointReference is a pointer to the Web service associated with the WS-Resource.

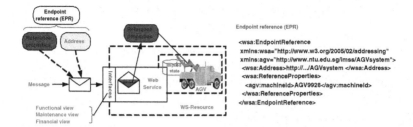

Fig. 3. AGV as a WS-Resource

As an illustration of virtualization based on WSRF, we consider a physical AGV (Automatic Guided Vehicle) system. An Automated Guided Vehicle system is a material handling system in which driverless, battery-powered carts are moved by means of Laser, Optical or Electronic guidance. The vehicles themselves may be towing vehicles, fork lifts, pallet trucks, or unit load carriers.

When virtualized as Web services, they can offer different views of the AGV, such as Physical, Operational, Performance, and Financial view [1]. The view represents an abstraction of the physical system (Figure 3). The views of an AGV are defined in WS-ResourceProperty [4]. The resource properties document type is associated with a Web service's WSDL 1.1 portType definition, and thus provides the declaration of the exposed resource properties of the WS-Resource[4]. In fact, the declaration of the WS-Resource's property represents a particular view or projection on the WS-Resource's state.

The virtualization takes the following steps.

Defining the Resource Properties

The properties of the AGV system are defined using XML schema. A change in state requires a change in one or more of these property values, and vice-versa.

```
<xsd:schema
  targetNamespace="http://www.ntu.edu.sg/agvviews"    ... >
  <!-- Resource properties doc declaration -->
  <xsd:element name="PhysicalAGVViewProperties">
    <xsd:complexType>
      <xsd:sequence>
        <xsd:element ref="tns:AGVID"/>
        <xsd:element ref="tns:AGVType"/>
        <xsd:element ref="tns:GuidanceType" />
        <xsd:element ref="tns:LoadHeight"/>
        <xsd:element ref="tns:LoadDiameter" />
        <xsd:element ref="tns:MaximumLoad" />
        <xsd:element ref="tns:MinimumLoad"/>
        ...
      </xsd:sequence>
    <xsd:complexType>
```

Adding the Resource Property Declaration to WSDL of the Web Services

Now we've created the representation of the stateful resource (the AGV system in a physical view), but to actually create the WS-Resource, we have to tie it to the service using the WSDL file, that is, the actual stateful resource is added to the file and associated it with the Web service:

```
<!-- WSDL for AGV Web services -->
<?xml version="1.0" encoding="UTF-8"?>
<definitions name="AGVsystem"
 xmlns:tns="http://www.ntu.edu.sg/agvviews"
 xmlns:wsa="http://.../ws/2004/03/addressing"
 xmlns:wsrp="http://.../wsrf-WS-ResourceProperties.xsd" ... >
<types>
 <xsd:schema
  <!-- property representation above added here-->
 ...
```

Defining the Type of the WS-Resource

Next, we can establish the association of the resource properties document with the portType as defined in the WSDL. This association defines the type of the WS-Resource added to the WSDL file as follows:

```
<!-- Association of resource properties document
     to a portType -->
<wsdl:portType name="PhysicalAGVView"
   wsrp:ResourceProperties=
     "tns:PhysicalAGVViewProperties" >
...
</wsdl:portType>
```

Notice that the important part of the portType is the wsrp:ResourceProperties attribute. That attribute specifies that any operations the Web service performs are performed on a particular type of AGVsystem resource, as defined by a PhysicalAGVViewProperties element which is defined in the schema. The combination of that stateful resource and that Web service is the *WS-Resource*. As seen from above, this combination is actually merging the Web service and (resource) properties into a WSDL file.

Create a Reference to an Actual WS-Resource Instance

In order to actually operate or manipulate on the WS-Resource, we must create a reference to an actual WS-Resource instance in the WSDL file:

```
...
<types>
 <xsd:schema targetNamespace="..."
```

```
xmlns:xsd="http://www.w3.org/2001/XMLSchema">
<xsd:import namespace= "http://
      schemas.xmlsoap.org/ws/2004/03/addressing"
   schemaLocation="WS-Addressing.xsd" />

<xsd:element name="createAGV">
  <xsd:complexType/>
</xsd:element>

<xsd:element name="createAGVResponse">
  <xsd:complexType><xsd:sequence>
  <xsd:element ref="wsa:EndpointReference"/>
   </xsd:sequence>
  </xsd:complexType>
</xsd:element>
...
```

Notice the difference from the WSDL file with no WS-Resource in that the service returns an *EndpointReference* that points to the newly created WS-Resource.

Defining the Messages and Operations for the Web Services

The WSDL description of *message* and *operation*is done similarly to what is done with no WS-Resource.

```
...
<message name="CreateAGVRequest">
  <part name="request" element="tns:createAGV"/>  </message>
<message name="CreateAGVResponse">
  <part name="response"
        element="tns:createAGVResponse"/>
</message>
...
<portType name="PhysicalAGVView"
    wsrp:ResourceProperties= "tns:PhysicalAGVViewProperties" >
  <operation name="createAGV">
    <input message="tns:CreateAGVRequest"
      wsa:Action= "http://.../CreateAGV" />
    <output message="tns:CreateAGVResponse"
      wsa:Action="http://.../CreateAGVResponse" />
  </operation>
</portType>
...
```

Manipulating the Property Values

Requesting the value of a property is a simple matter of constructing the appropriate SOAP message. For example, the basic SOAP message to request the value of the MaximumLoad property would look something like this:

```
<SOAP-ENV:Envelope  xmlns:SOAP-ENV="http://.../soap/envelope/"
  xmlns:wsrp=""http://docs.oasis-open.org/wsrf/.../
    wsrf-WSResourceProperties..-01.xsd">
  <SOAP-ENV:Header>...</SOAP-ENV:Header>
  <SOAP-ENV:Body>
    <wsrp:GetResourceProperty
        xmlns:agvProp="http://.../AGVsystem">
             agvProp:MaximumLoad
    </wsrp:GetResourceProperty>
  </SOAP-ENV:Body>
</SOAP-ENV:Envelope>
```

When the AGVsystem is created, the Web services returned an endpoint reference that pointed to the newly created WS-Resource. We can take that information and add it to the Header of the SOAP message.

```
<SOAP-ENV:Envelope
  xmlns:SOAP-ENV="http://.../soap/envelope/"
  xmlns:wsrp=""http://docs.oasis-open.org/wsrf/.../
                     wsrf-WSResourceProperties..-01.xsd">
  <SOAP-ENV:Header>
    <wsa:Action>
       http://..oasis../.../WS-ResourceProperties/GetResourceProperty
    </wsa:Action>
    <wsa:To SOAP-ENV:mustUnderstand="1">
       http://.../AGVsystem </wsa:To>
      <AGVId>SAT9928</AGVIdId>
  </SOAP-ENV:Header>
  <SOAP-ENV:Body>... </SOAP-ENV:Body>
</SOAP-ENV:Envelope>
```

The wsa:Action element is not part of the original endpoint reference; it changes depending on how it is used. In this case, we're using the GetResourceProperty action. The wsa:To element takes the value from the wsa:Address in the endpoint reference, and any wsa:ReferenceProperty values are included directly in the Header.

WS-RF defines operations that allow you to get and set various resource properties using Web service operations: SetResourceProperties, Update, or remove a property completely, delete, among others.

Once a stateful resource is virtualized as a WS-Resource, we can manipulate the resource using the Web services associated with the resource. Very often, WS-Notification is used to obtain notifications of various events (e.g., state changes). WS-Notification is a family of specifications that define a standard way for Web service clients to *subscribe* to a particular topic and receive notification of various events.

In addition to equipments and machines, other logical resources such as data sources, workflow, applications, and systems can be virtualized in a similar way. Furthermore, the sensible use of technologies in these specifications, the sophisticated stateful Web services can be developed.

4   A Semantic-Rich Environment

The service-oriented environment can be enhanced with rich semantics using Semantic Web technologies. Two core technologies are crucial for creating semantic rich environments: ontologies (upper ontologies and domain ontologies) and standard languages for developing ontologies.

Manufacturing knowledge exists in all aspects of manufacturing and can be captured at the different levels of generality. The corresponding ontologies typically include *domain ontology, value chain ontology*, and *product life cycle ontology*. A domain ontology classifies the most general information that characterizes an entire domain. For example, a domain ontology would include general information about products, manufacturing techniques and tools, and so forth, applicable across the entire manufacturing domain. A value chain ontology include the general information about entire value chain involved in a certain manufacturing sector (semiconductor, for example). A product life cycle ontology are more specific information for a life cycle of a product and covers activities for implementation of production planning and control (product design, process design, layout design, production plan and scheduling plan), including information about all relevant kinds of objects, properties, and relationships for that product. These manufacturing ontologies are developed using OWL.

In order to bring semantics to Web services, a standard approach is to use OWL-S, a OWL-based Web service upper ontology, and domain ontologies (also in OWL) as shown in Figure 4. Due to space constraints, the illustration of semantic markup for manufacturing Web services is omitted.

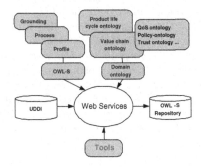

Fig. 4. OWL-S: an upper ontology for Semantic Markup for Web Services

5   Conclusion

In this paper, we discussed the Web standard-based approach and technologies for constructing a service-oriented manufacturing environment. The service orientation is achieved via *virtualization* using the emerging Web Services Resource Framework (WS-RF). A practical AGV system was used as an illustration example. We emphasize that the more full potential of a service-oriented environment can be fulfilled if it is enhanced with semantics. The Semantic Web standard based techniques for bringing Semantics to Web services and thus creating a semantic rich environment were discussed in the paper.

This work is part of ongoing project of enterprise integration which adopts a Semantic Web Services approach [9]. The key notions of the project are constructing a service-orientation environment via virtualization which is further semantically enhanced using OWL-based domain ontologies and OWL-S service ontology and then achieving automated service integration via software agents.

References

1. Michael C Dempsey. *Automated guided vehicle control systems: design application and selection.* Society of Manufacturing Engineers Publication, 1986.
2. Ian Foster, Carl Kesselman, Jeffrey M. Nick, and Steven Tuecke. Grid Services for Distributed System Integration. *IEEE Computer*, 35(6):37–46, June 2002.
3. Steve Graham, Anish Karmarkar, Jeff Mischkinsky, Ian Robinson, and Igor Sedukhin. *Web Services Resource (WS-Resource) V1.2.* OASIS, 9 December 2004.
4. Steve Graham and Jem Treadwell (Eds.). *Web Services Resource Properties (WS-ResourceProperties) v1.2.* OASIS WSRF TC, 10 June 2004.
5. David Martin, Mark Burstein, and Jerry Hobbs *et al.* *OWL-S: Semantic Markup for Web Services.* W3C Member Submission, 22 November 2004.
6. Deborah L. McGuinness and Frank van Harmelen (Eds.). *OWL Web Ontology Language Overview* . W3C Recommendation, 10 February 2004.
7. Igor Sedukhin (Ed.). *Web Services Distributed Management: Management of Web Services.* OASIS Standard, 1.0 edition, March 9 2005.
8. WSRF TC. *OASIS Web Services Resource Framework (WSRF).* OASIS, http://www.oasis-open.org/committees/tc_home.php?wg_abbrev=wsrf, 2004.
9. Zhonghua Yang, Robert Gay, Chunyan Miao, Jing-Bing Zhang, and Zhiqi Shen. Automating Integration of Manufacturing Systems and Services: A Semantic Web Services Approach. In *Proceedings of the 31st Annual Conference of the IEEE Industrial Electronics Society*, Raleigh, North Carolina, USA, 6-10 November 2005.
10. Zhonghua Yang, Jing Bing Zhang, Jiao Tao, and Robert Gay. Characterizing Services Composeability and OWL-S based Services Composition. In *The 4th International Conference on Grid and Cooperative Computing*, Beijing, China, November 30-December 3 2005. Lecture Notes in Computer Sciences, Springer-Verlag. (To appear).

Building a Semantic Web System for Scientific Applications: An Engineering Approach

Renato Fileto[1,3], Claudia Bauzer Medeiros[1], Calton Pu[2], Ling Liu[2], and
Eduardo Delgado Assad[3]

[1] Institute of Computing, University of Campinas,
Caixa Postal 6176, Campinas, SP, 13081-970, Brazil
{fileto, cmbm}@ic.unicamp.br
[2] College of Computing, Georgia Institute of Technology,
801 Atlantic Drive, Atlanta, GA, 30332-0280, USA
{lingliu, calton}@cc.gatech.edu
[3] Embrapa – Brazilian Agricultural Research Agency,
Av. Dr. Andre Torsello, 209, Campinas, SP, 13083-886, Brazil
{fileto, assad}@cnptia.embrapa.br

Abstract. This paper presents an engineering experience for building
a Semantic Web compliant system for a scientific application – agricultural zoning. First, we define the concept of ontological cover and a set
of relationships between such covers. These definitions, based on domain
ontologies, can be used, for example, to support the discovery of services
on the Web. Second, we propose a semantic acyclic restriction on ontologies which enables the efficient comparison of ontological covers. Third,
we present different engineering solutions to build ontology views satisfying the acyclic restriction in a prototype. Our experimental results unveil
some limitations of the current Semantic Web technology to handle large
data volumes, and show that the combination of such technology with
traditional data management techniques is an effective way to achieve
highly functional and scalable solutions.

1 Introduction

POESIA (Processes for Open-Ended Systems for Information Analysis) [4, 5]
pursues the Semantic Web vision [1, 13] to bring about solutions for resources
discovery and composition on the Web. The foundations of POESIA are: (1)
Web services to encapsulate data sets and processes; (2) workflow technology to
manage complex processes; and (3) domain ontologies to drive the description,
discovery and composition of resources. POESIA's mechanisms for composing
Web services appear in [5], and its methods for tracking data provenance and
support data integration appear in [6].

This paper focuses on the design and implementation challenges of handling
domain ontologies in POESIA. In particular, it points out the obstacles met in
loading and using domain ontologies in application programs, and describes the
solutions implemented in a prototype. Rather than forcing applications to deal

M. Kitsuregawa et al. (Eds.): WISE 2005, LNCS 3806, pp. 633–642, 2005.

with large, cumbersome ontologies, we propose ontology views satisfying the acyclic restriction to enable efficient automated means to discover and compose Web services based on domain specific knowledge. In these ontology extracts, one can determine the relative order of ontology terms by directed graph traversal or just one string comparison, instead of using inference engines, for example.

The experimental results of our implementation effort give an insight on the limitations of the current Semantic Web technology, when faced with applications using large data sets. The combination of Semantic Web standards and tools with conventional data management techniques provides more efficiency and scalability than the solutions based purely on Semantic Web technologies.

2   Motivating Application: Agricultural Zoning

This research has been inspired by the need of versatile tools to support scientific applications on the Web, and more specifically the development of decision support systems for agriculture. One example of an application in this domain is *agricultural zoning* – a scientific process that classifies the land in a given geographic region into parcels, according to their suitability for a particular crop, and the best time of the year for key cultivation tasks (such as planting, harvesting, pruning, etc). The goal of agricultural zoning is to determine the best choices for a productive and sustainable use of the land, while minimizing the risks of failure. It requires looking at many factors such as climate, regional topography, soil properties, crop requirements, social and environmental issues.

Typically, this kind of application involves intricate data processing activities across different organizations. Agricultural zoning relies on data from a variety of heterogeneous sources, including sensors that collect data on physical and biological phenomena (e.g., weather stations, satellites, and laboratory automation equipment). These data may be stored in a variety of databases, with different spatial, temporal and thematic scopes. Domain experts combine these data, in multiple steps of a multi-institucional process, in order to produce, for example, maps showing the suitability of the lands of a particular state for planting soybeans in different periods of the year.

3   Solution Context

POESIA relies on Web services [2] to encapsulate data sets and processes, so that Web standards and protocols ensure interoperability among different platforms. Ontologies, which can also be published and looked up through Web services, play another key role in POESIA. They provide a shared conceptualization to drive the description, discovery and composition of distributed resources.

3.1   General Architecture

Figure 1 illustrates the general architecture of a POESIA supporting system. In the right bottom corner, it shows the three kinds of POESIA servers connected

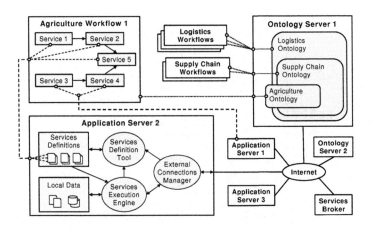

Fig. 1. POESIA's architecture

through the Internet: application servers, ontology servers, and service brokers. An *Application Server* maintains a local data set and a collection of service definitions that provide external access to local resources. Mechanisms for creating composite services are specified and managed by means of workflows, so that arbitrarily complex processes can be built from other processes [5].

An *Ontology Server* offers encapsulated access to a set of ontologies about different domains (e.g., agriculture, logistics), with adaptation means for particular application needs, including the extraction of ontology views. A *Services Broker* is a catalog of resources that centralizes the discovery of services using ontology views. The sharing of an ontology view among application servers and service brokers enables the semantic-driven discovery and composition of services.

3.2   An Ontology for Agriculture

As part of the effort to implement and validate POESIA, we have developed an ontology to support agricultural zoning. This ontology is divided in *dimensions* – ontology portions referring to particular agricultural concerns and disconnected from each other. Figure 2 illustrates the `Territory` dimension, depicting 3 layers of geographic data that refer to independent territorial partitions: political divisions, ecological regions and hydrological basins. These layers have `Country`, `Eco Region` and `Macro Basin` as their respective top classes.

Each rectangle in Figure 2 represents a *class*. Edges ending with a diamond represent *specialization relations* (of type IS_A) – the class at the diamond side is a subclass of the class in the other end of the edge. *Aggregation relations* (of type PART_OF) are represented by edges with a black circle on the side of the class playing the constituent role. Other dimensions of the agriculture ontology (e.g., `Agricultural Product`) are also represented with the basic constructs described above.

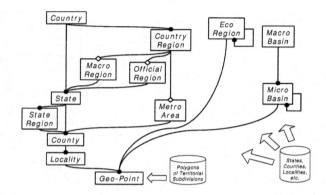

Fig. 2. The Territory dimension

4   Using the Domain Ontology

A POESIA ontology view has the form of a directed acyclic graph Σ, whose nodes refer to terms that can be concepts (e.g., Country) or instances of concepts (e.g., Country(Brazil)). The directed edges of Σ refer to semantic relations between terms (instantiation, specialization or aggregation). Edges are oriented from the general to the instantiated, specialized or constituent terms. These semantic relations induce a partial order among the terms [5], determined by the relative positions of these terms in the ontology graph. Imposing the acyclic restriction preserves the semantic contents of the original ontology, because it requires removing just inverse relations (e.g., remove generalizations while maintaining the corresponding specialization relations). Figure 3 shows a POESIA ontology view, where instances of some classes from the ontology dimension of Figure 2 appear in the right bottom corner.

4.1   The Encompass Relation, Ontological Covers and Service Scope

Let t and t' be two terms of an ontology view Σ. We say that t *encompasses* t', denoted by $t \models t'$, if and only if there is a path in Σ leading from t to t', i.e., a sequence of instantiations, specializations and/or aggregations relating t to t'.

The encompass relation is transitive – if Σ has a path from t to t' and another path from t' to t'', then Σ has a path from t to t''. In the right bottom corner (Territory dimension) of the view in Figure 3, for example, Country(Brazil) $\models$ State(RJ) and State(RJ) $\models$ State(RJ).County(Valena). The string State(RJ).County(Valena) represents the path to the term County(Valena) in Rio de Janeiro State.

An *ontological cover* is a tuple of terms taken from different dimensions of an ontology view. For instance, the ontological cover [Orange, Country(Brazil)] is a tuple of terms from two dimensions of a POESIA view of the agricultural ontology – Agricultural Product and Territory.

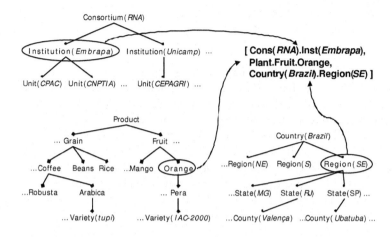

Fig. 3. An ontological cover in the agriculture ontology

An ontological cover attached to a Web service plays the role of metadata, describing the utilization scope of that service. We thus define the *service scope* as the transitive closure of the nodes reachable from the terms of the onto-logical cover associated with a particular service. Hence, the ontological cover [Orange, Country(Brazil)], when attached to a Web service providing access to agricultural production data, indicates that data from that service refer to the production of Oranges in Brazil. Figure 3 illustrates the composition of an ontological cover in which the term Institution(Embrapa) expresses the utilization scope in the Organization dimension, Orange in the Product dimension and Country(Brazil).Region(SE) in the Territory dimension.

4.2 Relations Between Ontological Covers and Services Discovery

The *encompass* relation between terms gives rise to corresponding relations between ontological covers. For simplicity, let us consider that an ontological cover has exactly one term for each dimension[1]. Given two ontological covers, $OC = [t_1, \cdots, t_n]$ and $OC' = [t'_1, \cdots, t'_n]$ $(n \geq 1)$, where $t_i \in OC$ and $t'_j \in OC'$ are terms from the same ontology view Σ, OC and OC' may be disjoint or satisfy one of the following relations.

Overlapping: OC *overlaps* OC' if and only if:
1. $\forall\, t \in OC : \exists\, t' \in OC'$ such that $t \models t' \lor t' \models t$
2. $\forall\, t' \in OC' : \exists\, t \in OC$ such that $t \models t' \lor t' \models t$

Encompassing: $OC \models OC'$ if and only if:
1. $\forall\, t \in OC : \exists\, t' \in OC'$ such that $t \models t'$
2. $\forall\, t' \in OC' : \exists\, t \in OC$ such that $t \models t'$

---

[1] Multiple terms referring to the same dimension are considered in [4, 5].

Equivalence: $OC \equiv OC'$ if and only if:
  1. $\forall\, t \in OC : \exists\, t' \in OC'$ such that $t \models t'$
  2. $\forall\, t' \in OC' : \exists\, t \in OC$ such that $t' \models t$

Overlap is bidirectional and the weakest of these relations. The *encompass* relation, on the other hand, only accepts encompassing relations between terms in one direction. The *equivalence* relation requires that each pair of terms taken from the two ontological covers reciprocally encompass each other. Finally, two ontological covers are *disjoint* if they do not overlap each other in at least one dimension, i.e., there is a term in one of the covers that does not encompass neither is encompassed by any term of the other cover.

The *encompass*, *overlap* and *equivalence* relations between ontological covers are *reflexive* and *transitive*, and the two latter are also *symmetric*. The transitiveness of these relations induces a partial order among ontological covers referring to the same ontology.

Services discovery can be understood as an ontology based query. More specifically, a service discovery request is stated as a query specified in the same way as an ontological cover, i.e., as a collection of terms from a POESIA ontology view. The query processing corresponds to investigating relations between the query and the service scopes, all of which are expressed by ontological covers. The services satisfying a query q are those whose ontological covers overlap q.

5   Engineering Considerations: Design and Implementation

Our ontology for agriculture has been built with Protg [9], an open-source graphic tool for ontology construction. POESIA's current implementation accepts ontologies in the RDF format [11] exported by Protg.

The acyclic restriction imposed on ontology views enables more efficient algorithms for comparing ontological covers than using, for example, inference engines to process a full ontology. Thus, our engineering solution to handle ontologies in POESIA involves three aspects: (i) use views tailored for particular applications, thereby reducing the number of terms and relations to be handled; (ii) restrict these ontology views to directed acyclic graphs (DAGs) or trees, in order to enable efficient algorithms to check relations between ontological covers; (iii) adopt a procedural approach to ontology management, backed by databases to attain persistence and scalability.

Our view extracting algorithm is analogous to that of [8], as it works by traversing the ontology graph. The view specification consists of three sets: starting classes, intermediate classes and properties (semantic relationships) to traverse. The algorithm traverses the class and instances hierarchy from the starting classes, including in the view only the classes, instances and properties contained in the view specification. The classes and properties of the view specification must ensure the acyclic restriction.

OntoCover, our prototype Java package for building ontology views, uses the Jena toolkit [15] to parse and handle RDF statements. The RDFS (RDF-Schema) file delineates the classes, subclasses and properties of an ontology, with tags marking the classes and properties of the view specification described above. The RDF file, on the other hand, contains the instances of those classes and their respective properties. Jena loads RDF/RDFS files in memory or in a database management system (DBMS) and allows navigation in the RDF triples through the Jena API or the RDQL query language [12]. The DBMS provides persistence and scalability for large ontology specifications.

We construct an ontology view by using Jena in two steps: (1) load in RAM the RDFS that specifies the ontology view; and (2) manipulate this RDFS specification via Jena API to generate the view, considering three alternatives for getting the many instances of the ontology classes to include in the view:

RAM: use Jena to parse RDF specifications from files into an auxiliary data structure in RAM, manipulated via the Jena API to build the view tree;

DB RDF: use the Jena API to handle ontology instance data stored in PostgreSQL [10] as RDF triples;

DB Conventional: take instances from a PostgreSQL database that contains one table per ontology class.

The database schema used by Jena to store RDF triples in the DBMS – for the DB RDF strategy – appears in [15]. The schema employed by the DB Conventional strategy to maintain the Territory dimension instances (for our experiments) is the one presented in Figure 2, regarded as an entity-relationship diagram, i.e., when each rectangle represents an entity and each edge represents a 1:N relationship, with the diamond or black circle in the N side.

6   Performance Evaluation

6.1   Comparing Ontological Covers on Ontology Views

Using views with the acyclic restriction, one can efficiently determine semantic relations between ontology terms. In a tree-like ontology view, determining if a term t encompasses another term t' reduces to checking if the string representing the path from a root o of the view to t is the head of the string representing the path from o to t'. Therefore, the problem is solved by just one string comparison. In a DAG-like view, one can use graph search algorithms to determine if there is a path from t to t'. These algorithms run in linear time for the ontology views used in agricultural zoning applications, because these views have the number of edges (semantic relations) proportional to the number of nodes (terms).

6.2   View Construction

Given our engineering option for ontology views satisfying the acyclic restriction, the bottleneck has been the memory and time necessary for extracting the views. Therefore, we focused our experiments on this part of the solution, comparing the alternatives described in Section 5 for managing ontologies stored as RDF/RDFS files and relational databases.

Our experiments used the ontology described in Section 3.2. Instances for the `Territory` dimension of this ontology were provided by IBGE (Brazilian Institute of Geography and Statistics), yielding an ontology view graph with more than 15000 nodes, to allow experiments with large volumes of data. These experiments ran on Linux (Red Hat 8), in a 1.6 GHz Pentium IV machine, with 512 megabytes of RAM.

Figure 4 presents the results of some experiments on constructing tree-like views of the agriculture ontology, with chunks of increments of 1000 nodes, as shown in the X-axis. The Y-axis represents the time to build the view (Figure 4(a)) or the memory use (Figure 4(b)). We compare the strategies described in Section 5; namely, `RAM`, `DB RDF` and `DB Conventional`. For the `RAM` strategy, we consider the time to parse RDFS and RDF, plus the time to build the tree by handling these RDF specifications in memory. `DB RDF` and `DB Conventional`, on the other hand, rely on the efficiency of a DBMS to manage large data sets in persistent memory. These strategies only load RDFS as a whole in memory, and query individual instances of the ontology in a PostgreSQL database modeled as RDF triples (`DB RDF`) or as a conventional schema (`DB Conventional`). The memory use is the peak of memory allocation for loading the necessary RDF/RDFS triples and build the view.

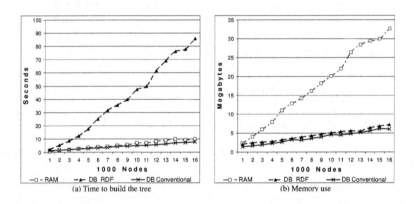

(a) Time to build the tree   (b) Memory use

Fig. 4. Comparing alternative schemes for generating ontology views

The running time measurements of Figure 4(a) show that `DB Conventional` is the fastest strategy. `RAM` is slightly slower than `DB Conventional` for large data sets, because of the burden of parsing RDF files, as opposed to efficiently taking instances from an indexed database via queries. `DB RDF` is by far the slowest alternative. This bad performance is probably due to the way RDF breaks the data about each instance – one RDF triple for each field value – leading to additional levels of indirection. Another advantage of `DB Conventional` over the other two strategies is that it uses a secondary index on the label values to order the position of sibling nodes in the ontology view. This ordering facilitates browsing the ontology view in the user's interface.

Figure 4(b) shows that the RAM strategy consumes the largest amount of memory. Both DB Conventional and DB RDF are more economical, because they do not require the construction of intermediate data structures in memory and take advantage of a database to load large sets of instances. DB Conventional is slightly more economical than DB RDF, perhaps due to Jena's housekeeping procedures for memory management. Therefore, the DB Conventional strategy is both fast and economical in terms of memory consumption.

7   Related Work

The Semantic Web [1, 13] foresees a new generation of Web based systems, taking advantage of semantic descriptions to improve the functionalities of current syntax-based data processing, and provide enhanced facilities in semantic aware open-ended information systems. Although much research effort has been directed to Semantic Web issues, few studies yet address engineering challenges, domain-specific issues, and the impact of ontology structure and ontology size, for example, on system design and performance.

The need for mechanisms to handle ontologies for semantic Web applications is recognized and addressed in [3, 8, 14, 7]. Dameron et al. [3] analyze some categories of ontology manipulation facilities necessary in a semantic Web infrastructure. They propose an architecture for offering facilities such as generation of ontology views, mapping between ontologies and reasoning, via Web services. Noy et al. [8] formalize the specification of ontology views by traversal – the same strategy employed in our prototype. Different mechanisms to express ontology views, such as using set operators on sets of classes and properties and restructuring hierarchies of classes are described in [14, 7]. Our traversal scheme is simpler and adherent to the POESIA approach and our applications.

8   Conclusions

This paper has considered implementation issues for loading, adapting and using domain ontologies for service discovery and composition on the Web. The main contributions are: (1) carrying out facilities adhering to the Semantic Web in a scientific application for the agricultural domain; (2) introducing the mechanism of ontological cover and a set of well defined relations among such covers to describe and recover services according to domain specific knowledge; (3) using ontology views with the acyclic restriction to enable the efficient manipulation of domain ontologies in applications. By using ontology views satisfying the acyclic restriction, we reduce a semantic problem (relating terms in an ontology), to a syntactic one (graph traversal or string comparison), without loss of semantic information. Our experimental results point out some shortcomings of current Semantic Web tools to handle large data volumes on producing ontology views, and we provide solutions to overcome these limitations. Though these results were presented in the context of a case study in agriculture, they apply to several domains and a wide class of applications that can benefit from the use of ontology views to manage data and services on the Web.

Acknowledgments. Authors from Campinas University were partially supported by Embrapa, CAPES, CNPq and projects MCT/PRONEX/SAI and CNPq/WebMaps. Authors from Georgia Tech were partially supported by two grants from the Operating Systems and ITR programs (CISE/CCR division) of NSF, by a contract from the SciDAC program of DoE, a contract from the PCES program (IXO) of DARPA, a faculty award and a SUR grant from IBM. Lauro Ramos Venncio has supplemented the experiments described on Section 6.

References

1. T. Berners-Lee, J. Hendler, and O. Lassila. The semantic web. *Scientific American*, May 2001.
2. F. Casati and U. Dayal (editors). Special issue on web services. *IEEE Data Engineering Bulletin*, 25(4), 2002.
3. O. Dameron, N. F. Noy, H. Knublauch, and M. A. Musen. Accessing and manipulating ontologies using web services. In *Intl. Semantic Web Conference (ISWC), Semantic Web Services Workshop*, 2004.
4. R. Fileto. *The POESIA Approach for Integrating Data and Services on the Semantic Web*. PhD thesis, Inst. of Computing, Campinas University, Brazil, 2003.
5. R. Fileto, L. Liu, C. Pu, E. D. Assad, and C. B. Medeiros. POESIA: An ontological workflow approach for composing web services in agriculture. *The VLDB Journal*, 12(4):352–367, 2003.
6. R. Fileto, C. B. Medeiros, L. Liu, C. Pu, and E. D. Assad. Using domain ontologies to help track data provenance. In *Proc. Brazilian Symposium on Databases*, pages 84–98, 2003.
7. A. Magkanaraki, V. Tannen, V. Christophides, and D. Plexousakis. Viewing the semantic web through RVL lenses. In *Intl. Semantic Web Conference (ISWC)*, pages 96–112, 2003.
8. N. F. Noy and M. A. Musen. Specifying ontology views by traversal. In *Intl. Semantic Web Conference (ISWC)*, pages 713–725, 2004.
9. N. F. Noy, M. Sintek, S. Decker, M. Crubezy, R. W. Fergerson, and M. A. Musen. Creating semantic web contents with Protg-2000. *IEEE Intelligent Systems*, 16(2):60–71, 2002.
10. PostgreSQL. http://www.postgresql.org/ as of September 2003.
11. W3C's Resource Description Framework (RDF). http://www.w3.org/RDF/ (as of October 2003).
12. W3C's RDF Query Language (RDQL). http://www.w3.org/Submission/RDQL/ (as of November 2004).
13. W3C's Semantic web Activity. http://www.w3.org/2001/sw/ (as of July 2004).
14. R. Volz and D. Oberlea nd R. Studer. Implementing views for light-weight web ontologies. In *Intl. Database Engineering and Applications Symp. (IDEAS)*. IEEE Computer Society, 2003.
15. K. Wilkinson, C. Sayers, and H. Kuno. Efficient RDF storage and retrieval in Jena2. In *Proc. Intl. Workshop on Semantic Web and Databases*, pages 131–150. Humboldt-Universitt, 2003.

A SOAP Container Model for e-Business Messaging Requirements

Hamid Ben Malek and Jacques Durand

Strategic Planning Dept, Fujitsu Software Corporation, Sunnyvale CA 94085, USA
hmalek@us.fujitsu.com, jdurand@us.fujitsu.com

Abstract. e-Business software vendors need to accommodate several standards involved in the various functions of a messaging endpoint. Vendors also need to quickly rollout the next version of a messaging protocol by reusing as much as possible of the common software. Increasingly in an e-Business context, several versions of a messaging standard will have to be concurrently operated by business partners. The current platforms for Web service or SOAP offer little support to the above. We have designed SPEF (SOAP Profile Enabling Framework) to address these engineering and business challenges. SPEF allows for coordinating the processing of SOAP modules that implement different standards (security, reliability, etc.). It has been designed as a lightweight messaging framework that behaves as a container for functional plug-ins. Message processing (either for sending or receiving) amounts to a workflow among such plug-ins. The framework relies heavily on open-source software for the basic functions common to various messaging profiles. The paper reports on the resulting integration and on experimenting with SPEF on existing SOAP standards.

1 Introduction

e-Business software vendors need to accommodate various messaging standards, e.g. different Web services WS-I profiles, as well as other forms of messaging over SOAP (e.g. ebXML). For this, diverse combinations of a few Web services standards (security, addressing, reliability, choreography) need be supported, along with specific header extensions. Vendors also need to quickly roll-out the next version of a messaging protocol, with enough reuse in software components so that the entire cycle from prototyping, to development and QA is short. Finally, over a multi-partners deployment like in a supply-chain, upgrades to the next version of a messaging protocol are likely to be done in a non coordinated way. This is the case for a large manufacturer dealing with many suppliers, but also increasingly of upper-tier small suppliers dealing with several customers. The current platforms for Web service or SOAP offer little support to address these engineering challenges. However, the layer of basic functions that are necessary to enable these variants and extensions of the SOAP protocol, is fairly stable and known: persistence, XML processing, monitoring, workflow of SOAP headers. SPEF (SOAP Profile Enabling Framework) was designed at Fujitsu Software to

M. Kitsuregawa et al. (Eds.): WISE 2005, LNCS 3806, pp. 643–652, 2005.

support the rapid development of SOAP-based messaging protocols - called here
SOAP profiles - by coordinating this layer of basic functions and allowing for
plug-ins that are protocol-specific.

2   Some e-Business Requirements

2.1   Support for Multiple Versions of a Messaging Protocol

Versions of messaging standards are seldom backward compatible. Gateways
based on SOAP 1.2 will generally not support SOAP 1.1 messages, and vice-
versa. ebXML Messaging V2 was incompatible with V1, and V3 will not be
compatible with V2. In spite of this diversity of modes of SOAP-based messaging, e-Business partners need to constantly maintain interoperability through
upgrades of their messaging middleware. Yet it is very unlikely that all partners
will upgrade simultaneously to the same version. As a result, it is becoming critical for an e-Business product to be able to run multiple versions of the same
SOAP-based messaging standard.

2.2   Support for Multiple SOAP Profiles

Even within the space of SOAP-compliant protocols, it is likely that e-Business
messaging will remain heterogeneous, i.e. involving several variants of messaging
protocols or "profiles" - either as specific header extensions, or as WS-I profiles.
This is because SOAP messaging in the e-Business domain involves a collection
of SOAP specifications, such as WS-Security, WS-addressing, WS-Reliability,
etc. . ... It is likely that decisions on which ones of these profiles or protocols should
be used, will be made at the level of a user community, such as participants in a
particular supply-chain. As supply-chains consolidate, being able to run several
messaging profiles becomes an e-Business software requirement.

2.3   Support for Monitoring and Management

Monitoring - and more precisely business activity monitoring or BAM - has
been recognized as a key function for the new generation of business process
management products. An increasing part of the business activity is reflected in
e-Buisness exchanges. Logging and auditing of data and messages by the messaging infrastructure and/or the B2B products is not sufficient. It is desirable or
even critical that IT administrators have a near real-time notification of troubles,
and that they be able to manage and tune the e-Business gateway.

2.4   Support for Many Databases

SOAP-based gateways often use message persistence for various reasons, from
basic store-and-forward functions to support for some quality of service features
such as security and reliability, or auditing for legal purposes. In order to scale

up to the heavy load of some e-Business scenarios, a full-fledged commercial database is needed. If only one type of database is supported, the gateway product would be limited and tied to a specific vendor's platform. As a result, a portable and scalable gateway will need to support several databases.

3   SPEF: A Functional Overview

As a vendor of e-Business software, Fujitsu has addressed the above requirements in the form of an architecture design for SOAP-based gateways that we call "SOAP Profile Enabling Framework", or SPEF. This framework speeds up the implementations of SOAP profiles, and also represents a run-time container for these profiles, allowing several of these to run concurrently.

In this paper, we will use the term "integrator" for any implementor who leverages SPEF API for developing a messaging gateway.

3.1   Design Principles

A Light-Weight Design: SOAP-based standards are better served when implemented by light-weight containers (versus middleware heavy duty application servers). The messaging aspect of the collaboration between separate parties should not involve the whole IT system of each party. For example using a heavy duty middleware application server to manage the messaging aspect of the collaboration is not a reasonable alternative and most of the time it is limitative. To play the messaging part, each party will have to use a separate component that is light-weight and that can be deployed in front of the firewall. This approach is aligned with SOA architecture principles which recommend light-weight containers for the SOAP messaging communication between parties and services.

A Design Based on Open Source: Products supporting SOAP-based protocols are more likely to be well received and welcomed by the worldwide community of users and companies willing to do e-Business. SOAP-based protocols are open standards developed at Oasis, WS-I, and W3C. Open Source and Open Standard usually go hand in hand, but for SOAP-based standards there are even more compelling reasons for open source implementations, namely composability. Composing the various SOAP-based standards is not an easy task, and if the products implementing these standards are in binary form only or proprietary, it would be more difficult to reconcile different implementations of these various SOAP-based standards.

A Container API for Plug-Ins: SPEF container provides an API for plug-in integrators. For example, in order to write a new plug-in for SPEF, an integrator would simply use SPEF plug-in API which allows SPEF and the plug-in to communicate in both directions. The plug-in can also leverage other SPEF API in order to reuse all the built-in functionalities in SPEF. Any third party functionality can also be used as a SPEF plug-in by simply wrapping it up using SPEF plug-in API.

3.2   Orchestration of SOAP Processors

SPEF supports the coordination and workflow of the various SOAP functions used to process the messaging features. An explicit representation of this processing is critical for ensuring proper control on this coordination as well as for meeting the rules and business policies of a company. There are unfortunately no specifications or manuals on how to orchestrate SOAP processors in the most general case. The only use-case scenario that is known and implemented by various products is the pipeline processing where the processors are chained in a linear workflow. All SOAP runtime stacks are built and implemented according to the pipeline processing model of the message, where general workflow orchestration is considered to happen behind services and not between services. Recent specifications (such as WS-choreography) are attempting to remedy to this issue, however they are limited in scope. Other orchestration efforts such as WS-BPEL, WS-CAF have targeted the business process layer (coordinating several Web services invocations) but they fall short of addressing the lower layer of the processing of each message individually. Although only the pipeline processing is supported in current SOAP stacks, a framework such as SPEF improves on this processing model by adding an explicit representation of controls, and by easing the deployment and configuration of SOAP processors.

3.3   Persistence Framework

SPEF provides a persistence framework, based on Hibernates 2.0[1]. This persistence framework allows a developer to interact with 16 relational database servers without writing SQL or JDBC code. The interaction with database servers is done in object-oriented approach. The developer need not have an advanced knowledge about Hibernates to use the persistence framework, because all the configuration and mapping files are hidden from the developer and are already provided by SPEF framework.

3.4   XML Binding Framework

SPEF provides an XML Utility library to marshal/unmarshal objects to/from xml. The XML library is based on CastorXML framework, and hides the mapping files from the integrator. By using the XML utility, a integrator can marshal Java objects to XML and unmarshal them back from XML documents using a simple API, without resorting to SAAX, DOM, JDOM, or any other XML parsing tools. This speeds up the development since the integrator does not have to write many parsing classes for XML. The integrator need not learn about CastorXML or any other XML binding framework, since the XML utility class, provided by *SPEF* API, offers a clean and simple API and hides configuration details.

---

[1] See http://www.hibernate.org/ for more information on Hibernate.

3.5 Monitoring and Administration

Since *SPEF* application server is built using JMX as its backbone, an integrator will not need to write management consoles to manage his/her application. By just writing the application components as MBeans and deploying them on *SPEF*, management client tools can be used to manage and change the properties of the application at runtime. This is because JMX is the standard technology in the Java platform for performing management/monitoring operations. JMX also has many other benefits such as being protocol agnostic (that is, HTTP, SMTP, JINI, IIOP, RMI could all be used as the transport protocol to communicate with a JMX agent.

3.6 Workflow Support

A built-in linear template of activities mechanism is supported in *SPEF*. One can specify the sequence of activities by declaring them in a configuration file. These will be executed one after the other when processing a given SOAP message. This provides a way of customizing and changing the processing behavior of the engine. A linear template (made of a linear sequence of activities) is sufficient for most implementations, including WS-Reliability, ebMS, Web Services Security, etc... If, however, a integrator wants to execute non-linear workflow templates (with conditions, splits and joins), one can write a custom class that inherits from the "`org.oasis.spef.spp.Processor`" class, and override the processing behavior by calling an existing workflow system for example.

4 Internal Concepts

SPEF is a light-weight[2] messaging gateway based on MX4J[3]. The microkernel consists of an MBean[4] server capable of deploying MBeans from various directories that are declared in its configuration file. SOAP Profiles implementations (such as WS-Reliability, ebMS, WSS, etc...) could be implemented in the form of MBeans and then deployed on SPEF.

4.1 Plug-Ins

A SPEF plug-in is either a SPEF service or an SPP (SOAP Profile Processor). A SPEF service is just a collection of MBeans performing together some work. A SPEF service is declared using an XML configuration file[5]. An SPP represents

---

[2] As a comparison between SPEF, Tomcat, and JBoss: SPEF is about 15 MB, Tomcat is about 25 MB (documentation excluded), and JBoss about 118 MB.

[3] MX4J (http://www.mx4j.org) is an open source implementation of JMX specifications.

[4] An "MBean" stands for "Managed Bean". As EJB (Enterprise JavaBeans) are the base components of the EJB specification, MBeans are the base components of the JMX specification. To learn more about JMX, see its homepage at http://java.sun.com/products/JavaManagement.

[5] See http://mx4j.sourceforge.net/docs/ch06.html#N10BA6 for an example of such an XML configuration file.

a SOAP processor such as an ebMS2 processor, a WS-Reliability processor, or a WSS processor for example. The work performed by an SPP consists of a series of tasks that are all declared inside one XML configuration file. As an example, the following listing provides a sample of such a configuration file for a WSS processor:

```
<?xml version="1.0" encoding="UTF-8"?>

<processor-config name="Processors:name=wss-1.0" version="1.0">
   <Client-handleRequest>
       <task class="org.oasis.wss.SenderTask" enabled="true"/>
   </Client-handleRequest>

   <Client-handleResponse>
       <task class="org.oasis.wss.ReceiverTask" enabled="true"/>
   </Client-handleResponse>

   <Service-handleRequest>
       <task class="org.oasis.wss.ReceiverTask" enabled="true"/>
   </Service-handleRequest>

   <!-- Uncomment if you want security on the response message -->
   <Service-handleResponse>
       <!--
       <task class="org.oasis.wss.SenderTask" enabled="true"/>
       -->
   </Service-handleResponse>
</processor-config>
```

4.2   Clusters

An SPP (SOAP Profile Processor) is played by the Processor MBean object. A single Processor MBean instance can process SOAP messages and provide a profile support to the exchange of SOAP messages. However, there are circumstances where one would want to run multiple instances of SPPs (instances of the Processor MBean object) at the same time. For example, one reason for doing so would be the case of multi-versioning where each SPP instance is can process only one version a given SOAP profile. One would group a collection of these instances (Processor MBean instances) and declare them to form a cluster.

There are various reasons why a cluster is useful. Some of these reasons are the following:

- To run multiple versions of the same SOAP profile within a given cluster.
- The cluster can provide a common set of services/resources that can be shared by all the SPPs that are member of it, instead of replicating these services in every SPP. For example, if each SPP needs to have an HTTP

SPEF Runtime

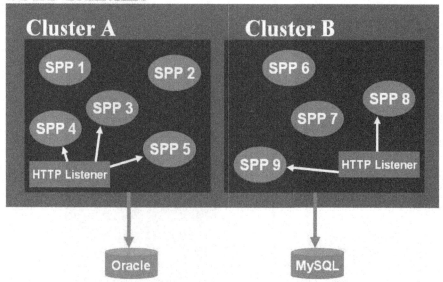

Fig. 1. *SPEF* Clustering: A cluster provides access to a relational database server, as well as an HTTP listener that could be used by certain SPPs that need to have their own address

listening port, it would be more appropriate to have a cluster offering this kind of service and that all the SPPs within that cluster could share the HTTP port, insteaf of each SPP creating its own HTTP server socket to listen on a different port.

A cluster is represented by the Cluster MBean object. By clustering, we simply mean a set of SPPs that are running at the same time and declared to be part of the same cluster (by having their "clusterName" property referring to the same Cluster MBean). Load balancing between the SPPs members of the same cluster is not implied. It can however be the case in future versions.

SPEF is not limited in having only one single cluster. *SPEF* can run multiple clusters at the same time (Clusters run in the same JVM). Each cluster containing many SPPs. Each SPP may implement a different version of a given SOAP profile specification. All the SPPs within the same cluster use the same relational database server. The picture in figure 1 illustrates this.

4.3   Message Workflow

An SPP (an instance of the Processor MBean class) can be viewed as an configurable workflow engine. By empty, we mean that the engine does not have a hard-coded processing behavior. Its processing is determined by which "workflow template" it will execute. It is the workflow template that contains the

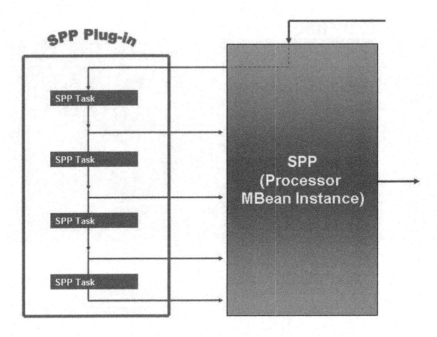

Fig. 2. SPP Internal Structure

processing path to follow. The worflow template that the engine can execute is rather very simple compared to templates used by workflow products. However, even though the template is simple, it is flexible enough to accomodate many SOAP profiles. Figure 2 illustrates the template structure that can be executed by the Processor MBean's engine:

The template consists of a sequence of activities, one after another (an ordered linear sequence of activities). The engine (a Processor MBean instance) executes these activities one after the other in the order they are layed out. These activities are called "SPP tasks". However, not all of the SPP tasks need be executed. Each SPP task has the right to decide whether the processing of the SOAP message should continue by the next SPP task in the chain, or whether the engine should not execute the remaining SPP tasks.

Each activity (an SPP task) can work on a SOAP message that is wrapped by an object called "PMessage" ("Processed Message"). The engine (a Processor MBean instance) passes an instance of the PMessage class to an SPP task. If an SPP task wants the engine to not continue executing the remaining SPP tasks, it would signal this to the engine by setting the "Continue" property of the PMessage to false:

```
pMessage.setContinue(false);
```

The SPP finishes the processing of a SOAP message when the PMessage instance is either processed by all the SPP tasks in the template or when the "continue" property of the PMessage instance is set to false by one of the SPP tasks in the template. In this case, the SPP would return back the PMessage instance object to the *SPEF* handler residing in the Web Service runtime stack. The template is part of what we refer to as an *SPEF* plug-in. This template is described in XML in the configuration file of the SPP.

The coordination between SPP tasks can be done via the PMessage. For example, decision to skip a task or branch to another can be decided by setting a certain custom property on the PMessage object (this of course implies that various tasks are written by the same implementor and therefore the tasks would know how to correctly interpret the meaning of these custom properties that are set on the PMessage object). This kind of workflow would obviously be hardcoded in the tasks code (versus a more general workflow defined in some exterior template that is executed by a workflow engine).

5   Experience Report

SPEF has been used to implement three SOAP-based OASIS messaging standards: ebXML Messaging V2.0, and Web services augmented with WS-Reliability 1.1 and WSS (Web Services Security version 1.1). Each of these SOAP profiles largely reused framework functions (database persistence, XML binding and parsing, API for SOAP manipulation, monitoring and configuration support) that would have had to be separately implemented otherwise, or duplicated. (idea of the size of plug-in code written, vs code reused?) In addition, although the message reliability protocols are different in both, some plug-ins can be reused (message resending mechanism). As a result, the three SOAP profiles (ebMS-2, WS-Reliability-1.1, and WSS) have been implemented in a relatively short time. The following gives an estimate of the size of each component:

- SPEF native code is of modest size. It consists of 81 classes that make up a jar file of 181 KB.
- The third party libraries that are leveraged by SPEF (such as MX4J, Hibernate, Log4J, Axis, Jetty, CastorXML, SOAP API) make the bulk of the SPEF package. For example:
  - Hibernate is about 4.07 MB of size
  - CastorXML is about 1.5 MB of size
  - MX4J is about 1.26 MB of size
  - Jetty is about 4.88 MB of size
  - SOAP API (JavaMail, JAXP-RPC, SAAJ, DOM) is about 2.22 MB of size
- WS-Reliability plug-in is about 103 KB of size. If WS-Reliability were implemented as standalone (that is without the reuse of SPEF functionalities), its real size would have been at least 500 KB. The same thing applies for WSS plug-in and for ebMS-2 plug-in.

6   Conclusion

e-Business gateway vendors are facing a particular challenge. On one hand, there is a trend to commoditize the messaging function, because it is heavily reliant on standards and because in an e-Business context, fostering adoption among a wide spectrum of users – from SMEs to large retailers or manufacturers – is most important. This certainly reduces the opportunities to build a business model on this type of product. On the other hand, the emerging e-Business networks (those using the Internet protocols) create new challenges such as those described here: integration of standards, quick roll-out, running multiple SOAP profiles and multiple versions of a profile - which require an innovative design. SPEF is an answer to these challenges, the value of which resides in a 2-level integration framework capable of reusing code and libraries in:

 - an enabling layer based on a versatile integration of open-source libraries that support the common basic functions
 - a profiling layer, allowing the coordination of processors (plug-ins) that define a SOAP profile, some of these also available on the open-source market.

References

1. WS-I. *Basic Security Profile 1.0.*
   http://www.ws-i.org/deliverables/workinggroup.aspx?wg=basicsecurity
2. W3C.   *"SOAP Version 1.2 Part 2: Adjuncts"*, *W3C Recommendation.*
   http://www.w3.org/TR/2003/REC-soap12-part2-20030624/
3. W3C. *"SOAP Version 1.2 Part 1: Messaging Framework"*, *W3C Recommendation.*
   http://www.w3.org/TR/soap12-part1/
4. developerWorks, D.F.Ferguson and Al.   *"Secure, Reliable, Trans-acted Web Services: Architecture and Composition"*.   http://www-128.ibm.com/developerworks/webservices/library/ws-securtrans/index.html
5. WS-Reliable Messaging TC, OASIS Standard.   *"WS-Reliability 1.1"*.
   http://www.oasis-open.org/committees/download.php/9330/WS-Reliability-CD1.086.zip
6. WS-Security TC, OASIS Standard. *"WS-Security: SOAP Message Security 1.0"*.

An Empirical Study of Security Threats and Countermeasures in Web Services-Based Services Oriented Architectures

Mamoon Yunus and Rizwan Mallal

Crosscheck Networks, Research & Development,
25 Thurston Road, Newton, MA 02464, USA
{mamoon, rizwan}@crosschecknet.com
http://www.crosschecknet.com

Abstract. As enterprises deploy Services Oriented Architecture (SOA), Web Services Security and Management has become the cornerstone of successful architectures. The greatest potential of Web Services is through re-usability and flexibility. This required flexibility in turn leads to significant security and management challenges. Enterprises migrating to SOA face security challenges such as malicious and malformed SOAP messages parser vulnerabilities and Denial of Service attacks over Web Services. Discovering Web Service Vulnerabilities and Compliance Violations and establishing countermeasure policies for Web Services security threats across large enterprises need to be addressed through standards-based products. This paper explores typical Web Services implementations, threat identification methods, and countermeasures against Web Services vulnerabilities.

1 Introduction

The corporate business environment is constantly evolving, increasing the demand for new and improved business applications. One of the major factors driving this demand is the need to reduce the overhead costs of conducting business. The streamlining process of a corporation's business is achieved through interoperable and reusable application integration interface and efficient trading partner interaction. This model is the basis of Service Oriented Architecture (SOA) paradigm.

1.1 Evolution of Services Oriented Architecture

The principles of the SOA paradigm are not new. The goal to move away from a monolithic software architecture to a more modular and interoperable software architecture has always been one of the key principles of SOA. SOA paradigm was applied to DCOM or Object Request Brokers based on the CORBA specification in the 1990s. However, the SOA paradigm never established a solid foothold because of interoperability issues in the CORBA specifications.

Today the SOA paradigm is again being applied to business application development and integration. However, this time SOA is gaining foothold in the enterprise market because of Web Services. Web Services based SOAs are enabling businesses

M. Kitsuregawa et al. (Eds.): WISE 2005, LNCS 3806, pp. 653–659, 2005.

to build and streamline their applications through a standard set of technologies and protocols [1].

1.2 The Base Web Services Stack

Web Services describe a standard way of integrating applications using SOAP, WSDL and UDDI open standards over any protocol. The Web Services Stack is the collection of standards-based protocols that is used to define, locate and implement messaging between applications. Figure 1 illustrates a Web Services stack. The Web Services Stack is comprised of four areas: service transport, messaging, service description, and services discovery. Web Services are independent of the communication layer and may use communication protocols, such as HTTP, HTTPS, JMS, SMTP, FTP, and IIOP for transporting messages between networked applications.

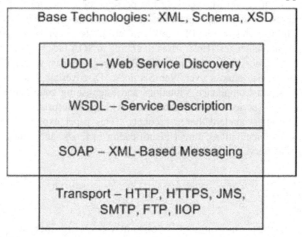

1.3 The Web Services Security Problem

The emergence of Web Services-based SOA has ushered in a new era of business application development and deployment. As Web Services are being deployed to increase reusability, interoperability and flexibility across business applications, a new threat vector has opened up. The fact that business application are now Web Services enabled allows a hacker to attack any of these applications using a standard set of technologies such as WSDL and SOAP/XML [2]. It is no longer imperative for the hacker to possess detailed knowledge of a business application's platform or its architecture to start probing for weaknesses. The flexibility and wealth of information offered by a WSDL file about a specific Web Service is sufficient for any savvy hacker to start subversive techniques. The TCP/IP protocol had became the de-facto standard of the hosts in the 1990s which had made it easier for hackers to find common vulnerabilities across all hosts since they shared a standard network protocol. Similarly, SOAP/XML is the standard messaging protocol of Web Services-based applications, thus enabling hackers with malicious intent to easily identify common vulnerabilities across disparate applications.

The problem is further exacerbated by the fact that the new threat vector introduced by Web Services is not plugged by the existing firewalls. Current state of the art network firewalls are designed to protect networks and hosts by restricting connections [3]. These network firewalls fall short of plugging the gap that has been opened by Web Services enabled applications. Later in this paper, we will mention some innovative firewalls that are addressing this new threat vector.

Another factor, which makes Web Services more enticing for hackers to attack, is the fact that business applications usually carry information that has monitory value. Hackers today are increasingly crafting more focused attacks with a potential for profit [4]. A hacker with malicious intent would rather spend time on a exploiting a specific Web Service that might yield some profit rather than releasing malware to disrupt Web Services on the Internet, which might only yield notoriety. Profit is the primary motivator for cyber criminals to launch sophisticated attacks against a specific application service and Web Services is no exception.

2 Web Services Threat Vector

Web Services offers a new threat vector for existing application exploits such as viruses, worms and spyware as well as exposes a new class of parser exploits. In this section, we present an example of each category: viruses riding over Web Services and a simple parser Denial of Service (DoS) exploit. These examples serve as a sample for a broader Web Services Threat that includes numerous emerging threats such as SQL injection over Web Services, Parameter Tampering, Schema poisoning, and Coercive Parsing that will be published in subsequent papers by the authors.

2.1 Viruses, Worms, and Spyware over Web Services

One of the most significant new threat vectors comes with SOAP with Attachments (SwA), a standard that enables any complex content to be wrapped within a SOAP message and sent over internet protocols such as HTTP, HTTPS and SMTP [5]. The use of SwA is being widely adopted in a variety of industries such as finance, insurance, healthcare and manufacturing.

For example, insurance companies are improving medical claims processing by replacing inefficient and expensive physical transfer of patient MRI scans and X-Ray images with published Web Service that use SOAP with Attachments. The health care providers consume these Web Services and electronically send SOAP with Attachments right from their internal document management systems.

Similarly, the Manufacturing and Semiconductor industry use standards such as ebXML and RossettaNet for integrating their supply and demand chains [6]. These standards are flexible enough to enable email-based protocols such as SMTP to be used for integrating small businesses with larger enterprises. Large manufactures typically place frequent orders with dozens of suppliers. The order management process includes message exchanges such as purchase orders and invoices over Web Services. With no central control over small businesses, this flexibility of integration exposes the large enterprises to mal-ware over such standards.

Malware that can readily exploit SwA include viruses, worms and spy ware. Viruses and worms are pieces of computer code written with the intention of disrupting a host or a network from performing normal operations. A virus attempts to spread from device-to-device infecting host machines as it attaches itself to other programs or files [7]. Viruses may damage hardware, software or information on a host machine. A worm, like a virus, is designed to replicate from host to host, but unlike viruses, worms generally spread without human interaction and distribute complete copies of itself across the network [8]. A worm typically consumes host resources or network bandwidth causing the host machine or an entire network to stop responding.

Unlike viruses and worms, spyware does not seek to destroy the host machine or disrupt a network. Spyware function is to go undetected and provide valuable information in a stealth fashion [9]. Spyware is a type of software that is placed on a host machine surreptitiously as either an invisible file or as a disguised as a legitimate file. Once a host device, spyware tries to capture and control key aspects of the target device and turn them into means of gathering information.

Through SwA, malicious attachments such as viruses, worms, and spyware can readily make their way into and enterprise over the Web Services channel. As enterprises exposes their internal systems for deep integration with their supply and demand chains, messages such as SwA arrive within large enterprises over a variety of protocols such as HTTP, HTTPS and SMTP. These messages then propagate to their final destinations typically using an Enterprise Service Bus (ESB) over JMS-based queues such as MQ Series, Tibco EMS and or Sonic MQ. It is highly likely that a SOAP/XML message will move over 2-3 transport protocols before arriving at its final destination. This protocol flexibility with the provisions of Content-based routing for QoS, increases the risk profile of SOAP with Attachments by opening the door to malicious attachments over a variety of protocols.

In the following sample SOAP with Attachment, the second MIME boundary includes a base64-encoded attachment. The attachment is a benign test virus Eicar used to test the availability of a virus engine.

```
-------=_MIME_boundary
Content-Type: text/xml; charset=UTF-8
Content-Transfer-Encoding: 8bit
Content-ID: SwAStart@crosschecknet.com
Content-Location: Echo.xml

<?xml version="1.0" encoding="utf-8"?>
<soap:Envelope
xmlns:soap=http://schemas.xmlsoap.org/soap/envelope/
xmlns:xsi=http://www.w3.org/2001/XMLSchema-instance
xmlns:xsd=http://www.w3.org/2001/XMLSchema
xmlns:s0="http://qa.crosschecknet.com/ws">

<soap:Body>
<s0:Echo>
<s0:Buf>hello world</s0:Buf>
</s0:Echo>
</soap:Body>
</soap:Envelope>
-------=_MIME_boundary
Content-Type: text/plain
Content-Transfer-Encoding: base64
Content-ID: Eicar-Virus.virus.txt@crosschecknet.com
Content-Location: Eicar-Virus.virus.txt
```

WDVPIVA1QEFQWzRcpYNTQoUF4pN0NDKTd9JEVJQ0FSLVNUQU5EQVJEL
UFOVE1WSVJVUy1URVNULUZJTEUhJEgrSCoNCg0K
------=_MIME_boundary-

Typical enterprise networks have virus, worms and spyware scanning products
such as McAfee, Symantec and Trend Micro's products installed to protect IT assets.
Such products rely on scanning content against an updated database of virus signatures. Typical malware scanners are useless if the content is present in an encrypted
fashion. A well-crafted virus attack over SOAP with Attachments would encrypt the
virus. Such malware would flow undetected within the network. The risk of such
attack vectors is mitigated by deploying specialized SOAP/XML-aware Firewall such
as Forum System's XWall™. Such best-of-breed Web Services Firewalls can first
decrypt the attachments in the SOAP messages before running a full malware scan on
the attachments.

2.2 Denial of Services Attacks

XML and Web Services are structured and self-describing. The messages are serialized and de-serialized during the message exchange process between applications.
When an application receives a message, its parser typically takes the text format of
the messages and creates a structure right away or uses a callback mechanism to retrieve the data from the message blob.

In a simple denial of service attack, a hacker can test the boundary of a data type
such as an integer by sending data that exceeds the numerical limit of that data type.
Integer overflow likely can cause denial of service as a result of buffer overrun or
logic error, especially in C/C++ code [10]. With a publicly available WSDL in hand,
the data types of all input parameters of an operation are human readable and well

WSDL   http://localhost:9090/MathService.asmx?WSDL
Service   TestService
Operation   Divide
Test Case   Divide_4
Request URL   http://localhost:9090/MathService.asmx

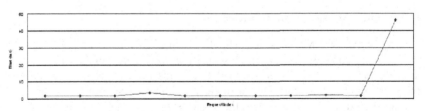

Log Index	Request Bytes	Response Bytes	HTTP Response	Time (ms)	Success
1	342	351	200	1.80	True
2	343	351	200	1.70	True
3	344	352	200	1.60	True
4	345	353	200	3.40	True
5	346	354	200	1.70	True
6	347	355	200	1.60	True
7	348	356	200	1.60	True
8	349	357	200	1.70	True
9	350	358	200	1.90	True
10	351	359	200	1.70	True
11	352	1427	500	46.50	False

defined.   In the example below, a *MathService* is published with an operation *Divide* that takes two integers *a* and *b*, and presents the results to the client.   The test is run with *b=7* and *a=1-to-10,000,000,000* ramping up by a factor of 10 between iteration values.   Excluding the last iteration, all divisions are successful with an average roundtrip response time is 1.87 ms.   The last iteration fails with a ~2400% spike in response time to 46.50 ms.

The last iteration value of 10,000,000,000 exceeds the limit of a 32-bit integer, which is 2,147,483,647.   A value that exceeds the inherent limit of a 32-bit integer would cause an exception in the receiving application.   Such an exception has to be handled by the application and its parser.   With a wide array of parsers and different exception handling styles, such exceptions can pose a serious denial of service threat to the application.   The threat may be simply excessive resource consumption (2400% increase in our test), or in extreme cases parser and application crashes.

3   Best Practices for Threat Mitigation

Web Services are being deployed enterprise wide, both for internal and external system-to-system communication.   A number of applications such as the Oracle 10g platform, BEA WebLogic come pre-packaged with parsers.   Developer are typically oblivious to the parser internals, they focus on building desired functionality, and later running automatic WSDL generation tools that produce interface definitions consumed by client application.   Weakness in programming methods are rapidly proliferated internally and externally through published WSDLs.   Even with the strictest developer governance rules, the involvement of contractors and high developer turnover within large enterprise typically results in weak enforcement of governance rules.   The weak governance enforcement in turn results in large exposures that are even more significant now with the emergence of Web Services where deep internal systems expose their sensitive interfaces using WSDLs.   However, enterprises are now reducing such risks by deploying SOAP/XML-aware firewalls that do deep content inspection and filtering of both incoming and outgoing messages.

3.1   Incoming Message Countermeasures

Incoming SOAP or XML messages should be checked for payload size, data types, and malicious content.   At different security enforcement points within a Service Oriented Architecture, message payload thresholds need to be set and enforced to protect the applications from Denial of Service attacks.   Similarly, strong data-type checking should be enforced so that the values sent to the applications are within the defined limits of the data-type within that message.   A large number of WSDLs generated contain string types with no buffer limits.   Such limits need to be set and enforce centrally.   Similarly malicious content carried over Web Services need to be identified using Web Services firewalls with integrated malicious code scanners.

3.2   Outgoing Message Countermeasures

Outgoing SOAP or XML messages or responses may contain verbose fault messages. SOAP offers an elegant fault handling mechanism; however, if not properly implemented, application developers inadvertently return verbose stack traces that expose internal application sub-components. Armed with information from stack traces over SOAP/XML, hackers can readily exploit know vulnerabilities of application sub-components. Since exception handling is rooted in programming skills and styles, it is imperative for an enterprise to centralize and decouple sensitive information returned from applications to a Web Services Firewall. This is critical for outward facing applications that have publicly available WSDLs. Additional sensitive keywords such as Credit Card Numbers or Social Security Numbers may be prevented from leaking from an enterprise over SOAP responses by enforcing content inspection filters that use regular expression to search for such keywords in the response messages.

3.3 Web Services Firewall

Web Services Firewalls from vendors such as Forum Systems, Checkpoint, Microsoft, NetContinuum and Network Engines have become an essential commodity within a Service Oriented Architecture. Such firewalls act as deep content inspectors. Such firewalls discover WSDLs from UDDI registries or manually load them. The administrator then configures a number of security policies, such as restricting message size, tightening schemas to prevent parameter tampering, and scanning messages for malicious content such as SQL injection, viruses, spyware, or worms. Addition policies that prevent small but deeply nested nodes in a message provide additional threats prevention for parsers from Denial of Service attacks. One of the most significant threat mitigation policies provided by Web Service Firewalls is to control the responses leaving the enterprise. Such firewall policies provide response filters that prevent damaging information such as stack traces or sensitive information such as credit card numbers from leaking from an enterprise. With Web Services Firewalls deployed, enterprises mitigate their Web Services Threat exposure and ensure that their Service Oriented Architecture provides privacy and information leak prevention.

References

1. Ed Ort, Service-Oriented Architecture and Web Services: Concepts, Technologies, and Tools. Sun Developer Network, April, 2005.
2. W3C, Web Services Description Language (WSDL) 1.1, http://www.w3.org/TR/wsdl, March 2001
3. Martin G. Nystorm, North Carolina State University: Securing Web Services, March 2004
4. Associated Press, *www.securitypipleine.com*, June 2005.
5. W3C, SOAP Messages with Attachments, http://www.w3.org/TR/SOAP-attachments, December 2000
6. RosettaNet Press, Industry Standard Facilities Product Material Composite Exchange, http://www.rosettanet.org/, May 31ˢᵗ 2005
7. Brad Griffin, An Introduction to Viruses and Malicious Code, Part One: Overview, http://www.securityfocus.com, Nov 2000
8. Jose Nazario, The Future of Internet Worms, Black Hat Proceedings, 2001 Las Vegas
9. Sachin Shetty, Introduction to Spyware Keyloggers, www.securityfocus.com , March 2005
10. Michael Howard, David LeBlanc and John Viega, 19 Deadly Sins of Software Security, McGraw-Hill, 2005

Collaborative End-Point Service Modulation System (COSMOS)

Naga Ayachitula, Shu-Ping Chang, Larisa Shwartz, and Surendra Maheswaran

IBM Thomas J Watson Research Center,
Hawthorne, NY 10532
{nagaaka, spchang, lshwart, suren}@us.ibm.com
http://www.research.ibm.com/

Abstract. Many diverse end point devices require high levels of interoperability to effectively manage services and applications. This paper attempts to provide a comprehensive framework for classifying services and offers a building-block approach that uses service as a basic unit for end-point interactions and collaboration. This paper presents a layered architecture of service classification that can be leveraged for facile and an effective adoption of new services and the orchestration of existing services. Today, a vast variety of services and agents exist in the market place and new ones are constantly created at a faster pace than ever. Initiated earlier, the move to a common open service platform for service collaboration conforming to standards like Open Service Gateway initiative (OSGi), Open Mobile Alliance Device Management (OMA DM) etc., expands the capabilities and service delivery for service providers and device manufacturers. Common end point device platform management functions include, but are not limited to, service collaboration, configuration, and inventory and software management services. A common service platform will make the services on the device interoperable with a broader range of applications, services, and transport and network technologies. Solutions available today use a single service for data connectivity, transport service mechanism, etc and therefore, by means of this tight coupling, risk limiting the service provider capabilities. Choosing to support multiple technologies enables service providers to support more types of services on device. However, the complexities arising from adoption of interoperability require taxonomy of services for effective service collaboration with existing services.

1 Introduction

When web services have appeared on the information technologies horizon some time ago, it captivated the technology gurus by it's' ubiquity and interoperability, and promised to the business world fast return-on-investment since required technology was already accepted by the most of industrial world. SOAP, HTTP and XML where going to do a magic allowing companies and individuals to make their digital resources available worldwide in a short period of time and with minimal cost. [1]

Today web services technology delivered on the assurances of the early stages; it is proven to provide robust, scalable, secure, manageable service infrastructures for

M. Kitsuregawa et al. (Eds.): WISE 2005, LNCS 3806, pp. 660–668, 2005.

governments, financial institutions, service providers, telecommunication companies, and a world of other global industries. Web services are deployed using a combination of registries and interface descriptions to create discoverable, self-describing units of functionality that can be invoked and combined dynamically. An introduction of the SOA facilitated the composition of services across disparate pieces of software, making possible rapid application integration, multi-channel access to applications, including fixed and mobile devices, etc, spurring a formation of new strategic solutions. The challenges, of course, remain. [2]

Not the smallest is scalability. Available today's solutions use a single service for data connectivity, transport service mechanism and such, therefore creating condition of limited scalability. Introduced in this paper, Collaborative End-Point Service Modulation System (COSMOS) offers an ability to exploit end-point resources such as hardware for storage; processing or data capture for instance compact flash memory, CPUs, thus making a solution more scalable.

Another issue of high importance is reliability. What happens when a Web Service host goes off-line temporary? Or for example, a mobile client becomes unreachable? COSMOS deploys local caching and processing to enable operation during periods of no network connectivity or intermittent network connectivity.

Currently web services positioned to be published for many software systems and applications across multiple organizations' IT environments. Now an orchestration engine can be used to create more complex interaction patterns in extensive business process flows. Orchestration added a strategic importance to the web services. Having distributed to client orchestration engine allows expanding scope of the services available to a client tremendously. [4] In a simple peer-to-peer (P2P) architecture, let's define K as a number of types of services, n1....nk - number of providers for each type of services;   while suppose that on server this types of services are combined by servers composition into categories c1,... ,cl and categories provide partition on the set 1,..,K. From client point of view under modular services architecture total number of variants will be $\prod_{j=1..K} n_k$. In the case of categorized services approach number of the possible variants for the client will be l.

The paper is structured as follows: Section 2 gives an overview of OSGi™ specification that COSMOS leverages as a service collaboration platform and as a Service Management Framework. Section 3 describes COSMOS proof-of-concept prototype implementation that is being developed here at IBM Research. Section 4 on Control Services, Section 5 on Processing Services, and Section 6 on Persistent Store are described. Section 7 details all the different layers of service connectors for collaboration. Section 8 and 9 concludes the paper and presents issues for further research.

2   OSGi as a Service Collaboration Platform for COSMOS

COSMOS leverages the OSGi specification as a service collaboration platform. The OSGi™ specifications define a standardized, component oriented, computing environment for networked services.[5] Adding an OSGi Service Platform to a networked device, adds the capability to manage the life cycle of the software components in the device from anywhere in the network. Software components can be installed, updated, or removed on the fly without having to disrupt the operation of the device. Software components are libraries or applications that can dynamically discover and use other components. Software components can be bought off the shelf or are developed in house. The OSGi Alliance has developed many standard component interfaces that are available from common functions like HTTP servers, configuration, logging, security, user administration, XML, and many more. Compatible implementations of these components can be obtained from different vendors with different optimizations.

For the purposes of this paper, we used IBM's OSGi implementation called IBM Service Management Framework™ hereby referred as SMF. COSMOS can be deployed on other OSGi implementations as well without any design or code changes, and SMF was purely a choice to work with, for the proof of concept. The Service Management Framework (SMF) is used for building and deploying these open standards-based, Internet-connected applications and services [8]. For OSGi devices, such as Windows 32 devices, WinCE devices etc. software is distributed as OSGi bundles. An OSGi bundle is comprised of Java classes and other resources which together can provide functions to device owners and provide services and packages to other bundles. A bundle is distributed as a JAR file. An OSGi bundle contains the resources and information to implement zero or more services. These resources can be class files for the Java programming language and other data, such as html files, help files, and icons. A manifest file describes the contents of the jar file and provides information about the bundle. The manifest file uses headers to specify parameters that are needed to install and activate a bundle. There could be dependencies on other resources, such as Java packages, other bundles, that must be available to the bundle before the bundle can run. The dependencies for these packages are resolved prior to starting a bundle. A special class in the bundle acts as the bundle activator. The class is instantiated and invoked to start and stop methods, which are used to start or stop the bundle. Clean-up operations can be performed when the bundle is stopped. Once a bundle is started, the functions and services are exposed to other bundles.

The administrator places the bundle on a content server, and then uses the Device Manager [7] console to register the software with Device Manager [7] so that it is available for distribution to devices with a software distribution job. A software distribution job can be created to distribute the software to target devices in device classes that support OSGi bundles.

3 COSMOS Architecture

The goals of COSMOS architecture design are openness; modularity, scalability and a platform to extend for future service integration. In order for architecture to be open, all its interfaces must be documented via explicitly published APIs (Application Programming Interfaces) or standardized XML (extensible markup language) based structures. In COSMOS this is achieved through service registry and service discovery.

To achieve modularity, the platform architecture must be isolatable to a specific set of modules and services. The architecture must be scalable and allow for one or more levels of analysis to be distributed to other computer systems. It must be extensible in order to allow for improvements or changes to analysis algorithms or components to be deployable entirely within the appropriate analysis layers and modules without requiring modification of the entire system. COSMOS is designed precisely for this purpose. Figure 2 below depicts the basic building module for COSMOS.

Service Management Framework

Administration

Registered Services

Registered Services ↑	Owner Bundle
com.ibm.osg.service.metatype.MetaTypeService	file:bundlefiles/metatype.jar
com.ibm.osg.service.osgiagent.EventService	file:bundlefiles/osgiagentservlet.jar
com.ibm.osg.service.osgiagent.InventoryService	file:bundlefiles/Win32AgentExt.jar
com.ibm.osg.service.osgiagent.OSGiAgentService	file:bundlefiles/osgiagent.jar
com.ibm.osg.webapp.WebApplicationService	file:bundlefiles/webhttpservice.jar
com.ibm.osg.webcontainer.listeners.HttpSettingListener	file:bundlefiles/webhttpservice.jar
com.ibm.pvc.wea.wealog.WeaLogService	file:bundlefiles/wealogservice.jar
javax.xml.parsers.DocumentBuilderFactory	file:bundlefiles/MicroXML.jar
javax.xml.parsers.SAXParserFactory	file:bundlefiles/MicroXML.jar

Fig. 1. Service Management Framework Registered Services at the end-point

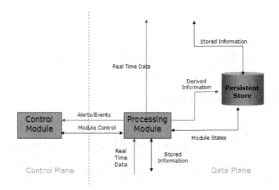

Fig. 2. Base Service Connector Module for COSMOS

4   Control Service Module

As in any other system's design, there are two planes for the building module: the
control plane and the data plane. In the control plane, there is only one control service
module which interacts with the processing service module for managing configuration, reset, states inquiry, etc.   The Control service module also accepts alerts or
events from the processing service module for signaling attention and remediation
required operations. Control service modules can be structured hierarchically so as to
manage signal distribution to the overall solution and simultaneously collect alarms
and events for analysis. Figure 3 depicts a control plane structured this way.

The interface between the processing service module (PM) and the control service
module (CM), however, is normally specific to the control service module/ processing

service module pair. The higher level control along the hierarchy should be standardized for certain operations such as reset, armed/set, etc. and simple feedback from the processing service module could carry the same output format. However, most sophisticated events or alerts need XML typed communication to provide their semantics to the control plane operation or to search the service registry.

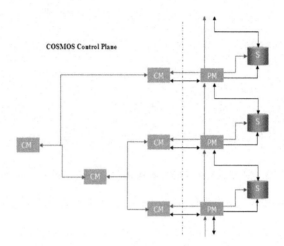

Fig. 3. Hierarchical Control Service Modules

5 Processing Service Module

Processing service Module (PM) provides the analytic mechanism/algorithm for sensor service data processing which on one hand has real time streaming data coming in and at the same time real-time modified data stream going out from it to feed the next module or service. Processing service Module (PM) could also access derived information stored by other PMs in previous processing stage for its analytic wok. Under the same token, PM could store derived information to its persistent store for deeper processing by other PM. The data format of the real time sensor data input and output need to be well documented for easy integration with other building blocks. PM also use its persistent store, if necessary, for its state preservation. This, however, is not necessarily standardized.

6 Persistent Store

The persistent store records the derived information from the Processing service Module (PM). The format of the stored data needs to be standardized and published for other PM's to use. This goal could be achieved by offering data access APIs and define output data formats from the API. This is typically achieved by registering to the OSGi service registry so that other services could discover this information by looking up at the service registry. It is obvious that with above building blocks, a sequential collaboration operational model and a parallel collaboration operational model could be easily achieved as depicted by figure 4, correspondingly. However, any real utilization of such a building structure would most likely be a mixture of the two. It is unpractical to standardize data with different complexities in content and semantics. It would end up with a standard so complex then its processing becomes extremely difficult. Therefore, COSMOS proposed a layered architectural approach for the sensor based data processing and collaboration in the following sections.

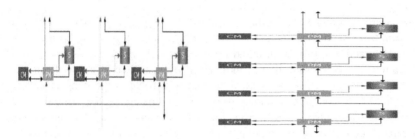

Fig. 4. Sequential and Parallel Execution Mode of Service Collaboration

7 The Modulated Service Architecture

COSMOS is a modular component based and layered service architecture. The efficiency of such architecture has been proven in earlier implementations. We will consider an example from video surveillance systems. The COSMOS architecture has been modulated into five layers, each with clearly defined functions and capabilities. Each layer can have services provided by different service providers.

7.1 Sensors and Effector's Services Layer

This can sometimes be the connector layer which defines the service component interaction with the physical device of the sensor and its connection to the sensor based system. The processing unit at this layer converts the sensor's raw signal into its digital representation in real time. Different sensors can have their own processing units at the physical layer. However, this digitalization requires clear definition for processing at the data layer. The sensors are not necessarily connected to physical devices but can be services that talk to a particular component, such as network elements, operating system components, application components or some other services on the end-point. In an extreme approach, services may also be even on a different endpoint. The sensor services are typically monitoring services that can gather data and information. The Effectors services can control change, or alter configuration and data of the component or service with which it interacts.

7.2 Data Services Layer

The data services layer is responsible for combining received digital representation from the physical layer into a particular pattern aggregating bits together to form bytes, providing boundary mark for data group, etc. The storage requirements of this layer depends on the sensor type or the whether there is a requirement to preserve original raw data. A real time stream is then delegated to the upper service layer, the adaptor services layer. If persistent storage is used, this data is also available for upper layer processing.

7.3 Adaptor Services Layer

Adaptors are typically services that can transform, aggregate, refine and classify information from the underlying data services. Processing units at this layer are responsible for extracting information based on policies from the lower layers of services. For example, in video surveillance monitoring, typical facts that can depend on the raw data source are attributes such as object identification, moving direction, and speed, etc. There could be several processing units receiving the same data but extracting different patterns and information details. Some processing units could use previously stored data in the data layer for analysis. In short, this layer provides the function for major data extraction to form the known patterns. Most deduced results at this layer are stored in persistent repository for further analysis.

7.4 Integration Services Layer

This layer integrates information through service collaboration and reasoning. Multiple extracted data facts provided by the adaptor layer are integrated. It receives inputs and data from the adaptor layer, mainly the stored and arranged data from adaptor layer for reasoning and integration of different features to produce a recognizable pattern that will either trigger an alarm or have no effect. The Integration layer can receive output from more than one adaptor layer sources to form even more knowledge regarding the sensor information. Consider the example of a vehicle approaching the train tracks during a foggy night. In this situation the camera surveillance sensor is ineffective. However, another sensor may detect the ground vibrations produced by the vehicle, triggering an appropriate response by the system.

7.5 Arbitration Services Layer

The Integration Layer and the Arbitration Layer have different knowledge sources. In our example of the surveillance camera, the Integration layer handles almost all known attributes of the local sensor system. But the arbitration layer will use not only the output of the Integration layer but also knowledge sources outside the end-point for further deep analysis. For instance, a high speed approaching vessel to the shore could be indicated by the Integration layer as an obvious threat. But the Arbitration layer could consult a naval image database server and analyze planned activity logs and identify the approaching vessel as our own vessel conducting planned exercise and ignore the alarm. This kind of intelligence is very important in the sensor based system since it ensures the production of practical and reliable results.

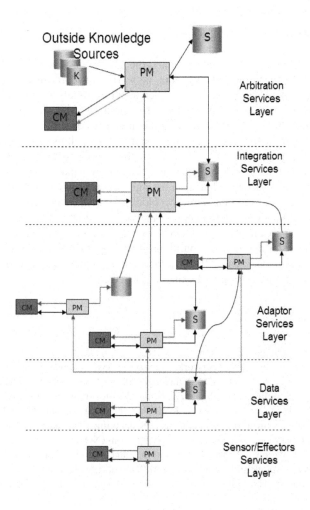

Fig. 5. Service collaboration layers

8 Future Directions and Outlook

COSMOS can receive provisioning requests or CBE (Common Base Events) events and correlate using light-weight event correlation engines. Policies can be enforced by a policy engine like ABLE to adapt to user, system or enterprise policies. A policy engine can exhaustively list conditions and specify the corresponding actions that need to be taken.[6] Planning for Provisioning using planning frameworks like Planner4J based on ABLE can define and solve a planning problem, viz., action, state, problem, domain and plan, and their reference implementations that can be further reused and extended.

9 Conclusion

The recent technology advances enhance the ability of service providers to use increasingly extensive service stacks (data, network, transport, monitor etc.) to be interactive to, recognize and correlate in order to allow timely response. These systems also improve the efficiency and reduce the operating cost of service infrastructure. The COSMOS design allows new systems and services developed using innovative architectural approaches, and new components or algorithms to achieve revolutionary advances in capabilities without locking the whole system down as a whole. COSMOS design utilizes emerging utility computing capabilities to defray costs and lower the risk of over-dependence on a single service provider. With COSMOS layered architecture and modular building blocks , it is now possible to integrate automated service provider decision support that allows other service providers to deploy their services easily and quickly. COSMOS provides a comprehensive framework for classifying services and offers a building-block approach that uses service as a basic unit for end-point interactions and collaboration for easy and effective adoption of new services and orchestration of existing services.

References

[1] Web Services Standards section.
http://www.ibm.com/developerworks/views/webservices/standards.jsp.
[2] Paul S. Clarke Hidden SOA Challenges, Enterprise Architect, December 13, 2004
http://www.ftponline.com/ea/magazine/winter2004/columns/workingmodel/pclarke/.
[3] A. Keller, J. Hellerstein, J.Wolf, K.-L.Wu, and V. Krishnan. The CHAMPS System: Change Management with Planning and Scheduling. Proceedings of the 9th IEEE/IFIP Network Operations and Management Symposium (NOMS'2004), Apr. 2004.
[4] IBM Corporation. IBM Orchestration and Provisioning Automation Library
http://www.developer.ibm.com/tivoli/workflow/validate.html
[5] OSGi Alliance. The OSGi Service Platform - Dynamic services for networked devices
http://www.osgi.org
[6] K. Appleby, S.B.Calo, J.R. Giles, K.W.Lee. Policy-based automated provisioning. IBM Systems Journal, Vol. 43, No. 1, 2004 page 121.
[7] IBM Corporation. WebSphere Everyplace Device Manager
http://www-306.ibm.com/software/pervasive/ws_everyplace_device_manager/support/
[8] IBM Corporation. IBM Service Management Framework.
http://www-306.ibm.com/software/wireless/smf/features.html

A Process-Driven e-Business Service Integration System and Its Application to e-Logistics Services

Kwanghoon Kim[1] and Ilkyeun Ra[2]

[1] Collaboration Technology Research Lab.,
Department of Computer Science, Kyonggi University
kwang@kyonggi.ac.kr
http://ctrl.kyonggi.ac.kr
[2] Distributed Computing and Networking Lab.,
Department of Computer Science and Engineering,
University of Colorado at Denver
ikra@carbon.cudenver.edu
http://www.cudenver.edu/~ikra

Abstract. In this paper, we introduce a process-driven e-Business service integration (BSI) system, which is named 'e-Lollapalooza', and has been successfully developed through a functional extension of the ebXML technology. It consists of three major components - Choreography Modeler coping with the process-driven collaboration issue, Runtime & Monitoring Client coping with the business intelligence issue and EJB-based BSI Engine coping with the scalability issue. This paper particularly focuses on the e-Lollapalooza's implementation details supporting the ebXML-based choreography and orchestration among the engaged organizations in a process-driven multiparty collaboration for e-Logistics and e-Commerce services. Now, it is fully deployed on an EJB-based middleware computing environment, and operable based upon the ebXML standard as an e-Business process management framework for e-Logistics process automation and B2B choreography. Finally, we describe an application of the e-Lollapalooza system to the purchase order and delivery processes in a cyber-shopping mall run by a postal service company.

Keywords: e-Business Service Integration System, B2B Choreography and Orchestration, e-Business Process Management, ebXML Standard, CPP/CPA, BPSS, e-Logistics, e-Commerce.

1 Introduction

In recent, the business process management and web services and their related technologies have been swiftly adopted and hot-issued in the real world, and they are becoming excellent topics for proliferating and hyping in the information technology market. This atmosphere is becoming a catalyst for triggering explosion of the so-called process (business process) driven e-Business service

M. Kitsuregawa et al. (Eds.): WISE 2005, LNCS 3806, pp. 669–678, 2005.

integration domains, such as the electronic logistics, electronic procurement, value-chain management, and supply chain management technologies. However, those process driven e-Business service integration models are a little different from the traditional B2B model of e-Commerce in terms of the shape of behaviors among organizations in collaboration. That is, in the traditional B2B e-Commerce model, only dual-party (buyer/seller) organizations collaborate along with the direction of CPA/CPP of ebXML, which is established through agreement between the participating parties. So, without any further modification, the ebXML technology is unable to be directly fit into those process-driven applications of the e-Business service integration domains.

So, in this paper, we try to extend the ebXML technology's functionality and implement it in order to cope with especially the rapidly increasing trade volumes issue (the scalability issue) and the traceable and monitorable business processes and services issue (the business intelligence issue). For the sake of the scalability issue, we adopt the EJB (enterprize java beans) framework approach to implement a e-Business service integration system, and we newly implement a functionality providing the traceable and monitorable business processes and services for the business intelligence issue. Based on these issues and considerations, we have completed the development of a process-driven e-Business service integration system, which is named 'e-Lollapalooza[1]'. Conclusively, we describe the implementation details of e-Lollapalooza system and its application that is an outstanding example to demonstrate how well the e-Lollapalooza system works in the e-Logistics and e-Commerce markets.

In the next section, we present the backgrounds and related works that have been done in the literature. And in the continued sections, we describe the details of the e-Lollapalooza system such as the overall system architecture and components, process-driven e-Business collaboration model, choreography modeling tool, runtime & monitoring client, and the EJB-based e-Business service integration engine, respectively. Finally, we introduce an application example that the e-Lollapalooza systems on collaborative organizations orchestrate for conducting the order and delivery process of a cyber-shopping mall.

2   Related Works

We, in this paper, are particularly interested in the B2B e-Commerce automation technologies. As a matter of fact, in order to accomplish the total process automation for B2B e-Commerce, it is necessary for the workflow and BPM technology to be integrated, as a platform, with major four contributory technologies: object-orientation, EAI, web service, and XML technology. So, there might be two possible approaches, as we can imagine, to deploy a total process automation entity for B2B e-Commerce - open e-business framework (ebXML) and closed e-business framework (inter-organizational workflow and BPM [13]) approaches. The open e-business means that the business contractors or partners of the B2B

---

[1] In the Webster's dictionary, "one that is extraordinarily impressive; also: an outstanding example".

e-business can become anyone who are registered in the registry/repository, in contrast to that they are predetermined in the closed framework approach. We concluded that the former is more reasonable approach for the process-driven e-Business service integration domain.

We would characterize ebXML as an open e-business framework, because it is targeting on opening a business contract between universal organizations unknown each other. The ebXML is a set of specifications that enable to form a complete electronic business framework. Suppose that the Internet is the information highway for e-businesses, then the ebXML can be thought of as providing the on-ramps, off-ramps, and the rules of the road. [3] And, it is proposed by a joint initiative of the United Nations (UN/CEFACT) and OASIS, which are developed with global participation for global use. This partnership brings a great deal of credibility to ebXML being representative of major vendors and users in the IT industry and being supported from leading vertical and horizontal industry groups including RosettaNet, OTA (Open Travel Alliance) and many others. Membership in ebXML is open to anyone, and the initiative enjoys broad industry support with hundreds of member companies, and more than 1,400 participants drawn from over 30 countries.[11]

We would not describe the details of ebXML [3] in here, but adopt the basic concept and mechanism of ebXML as an e-business service agent of e-Lollapalooza providing process-related information to the e-business service entities over organizations. As you know, the ebXML is hardly applicable to e-Logistics management or supply chain management framework, at which our e-Lollapalooza is targeting, without any modifications, because it is basically proposed for e-business contracts between two parties (buyer and seller), each of which corresponds to an organization in collaboration. That is, the concept of business process being accepted in the ebXML domain is completely different from the concept in the process-driven e-Business integration domain. So, we try to extend its functionality so as to be reasonably adopted in the domain.

3   e-Lollapalooza: e-Business Service Integration System

In this section, we at first define the basic concept of the process driven e-Business service integration (BSI) model that is a little different from the traditional dual-party B2B model of e-Commerce in terms of the shape of behaviors among organizations in collaboration. And we describe the functional details of the e-Lollapalooza system, such as its overall system architecture and its major components (EJB-based engine, e-business service integration process modeler and monitoring client), that is extended from the ebXML basic functionality and implemented so as to cope with especially the rapidly increasing trade volumes issue and the traceable and monitorable business processes and services issue.

3.1   The Process-Driven e-Business Service Integration Model

The process-driven e-business service integration model is the specifications of business contracts and of how to integrate the business services between organi-

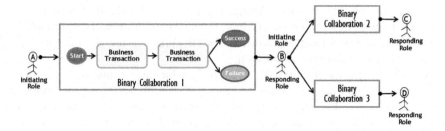

Fig. 1. A Process-driven e-Business Service Integration Model

zations that are engaged in a process-driven multiparty collaboration. Fig. 1 shows a typical example of the process-driven e-business service integration model. The model consists of three dual-party collaborations (Binary Collaboration 1 ∼ 3) that have a certain type of control-precedence relationships, each other, such as sequential, disjunctive or conjunctive relationship, according to the business contracts of the organizations in multiparty collaboration. And the dual-party collaboration is specified by the activity flow diagram, in which each activity represents a business transaction. Also, each organization (Organization A ∼ D) has associated to either the initiating role or the responding role, or both of the roles like Organization B.

Additionally, each dual-party collaboration in the model is represented by the ebXML specifications. The ebXML's information models define reusable components that can be applied in a standard way within a business context, and enable users to define data that are meaningful to their business and also maintaining interoperability with other business applications. Also, the ebXML messaging service specification defines a set of services and protocols that enables electronic business applications to exchange data. The specification allows any level of application protocols including common protocols such as SMTP, HTTP, and FTP to be used. The Collaborative Partner Agreement defines the technical parameters of the Collaborative Partner Profiles (CPP) and Collaborative Partner Agreements (CPA). This captures critical information for communications between applications and business processes and also records specific technical parameters for conducting electronic business.

3.2   Overall System Architecture of e-Lollapalooza

This section shortly concentrates on architectural requirements and components in terms of designing the e-Lollapalooza business service integration system. The e-Lollapalooza has the different runtime (enactment) architecture from the conventional ebXML-based business service integration systems' in terms of the process structure. We have conceived a particular conceptual architecture and its functional implementation suitable for the process-driven e-business service integration model and applications, such as electronic logistics, e-supply chain management, and process-driven e-commerce.

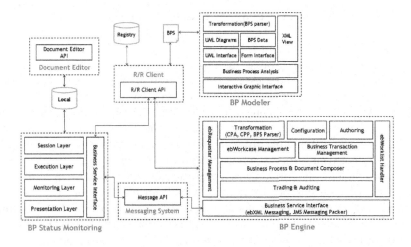

Fig. 2. Overall System Architecture and Components

With considering some advanced system-level requirements, such as interoperability, scalability, and extensibility, we developed the system that provides the basic functionality for defining, enacting and monitoring those process-driven e-Business service choreography and integration models. The overall system architecture and components are illustrated in Fig. 2. As shown in the figure, the e-Lollapalooza consists of three major architectural components - the BP modeler, the BP enactment engine, and the BP status monitor. These components asynchronously communicate each other through the messaging system, and the models defined by the modeler are registered into the registry through the registry/registration component.

The e-Lollapalooza system's design principle is summarized as followings:

- Basically the system is based upon the ebXML's framework for supporting a business collaboration and choreography between partner companies of the business integration services.
- Also, it is possible for the system to be deployed as a type of ASP (Application Service Provider) system in order to support business choreographs among small-sized business partners that are too small to be affordable to maintain a system.
- The conceptual architecture of the system is called ebworkcase-based architecture that is newly proposed in this paper.
- The system is implemented by using the the enterprize java beans (EJB) framework approach of Sun's J2EE.
- The communication mechanism of the system uses the EJB's JMS messaging technology and the ebXML's messaging technology as well.
- The BP status monitoring component of the system provides the runtime client functionality, too.

3.3   The e-Lollapalooza Business Process Enactment Engine

The functional architecture of the e-Lollapalooza's business process enactment part consists of business process monitoring and runtime client, business service integration engine, and message transfer system that supports communication services between enactment engines through firewall secured communication channels. All of these components are deployed on EJB framework. So, the communication between the monitoring client and the enactment engine is simply done through the EJB simple object access protocol. However, The communication services between business service integration engines, each of which resides in each of collaborative organizations, are performed through the JMS-based message transfer system. So, a serial of payloads for business contracts has to be wrapped by JMS message formats, and be transferred to each of the underlining engines. The details of the monitoring client is explained in the next section, and this section is dedicated to the description of the enactment engine.

Inside of the business service integration engine is structured as shown in Fig. 3. Especially, in order for the e-Lollapalooza system to be satisfied with the scalability requirement, we have proposed a new conceptual architecture that is called ebWorkcase-based enactment architecture. The ebWorkcase means a name of object that is instantiated for dealing with its corresponding business service integration case in the real-world. So, it is reflecting data structure of business choreography that contains collaboration process, transaction activity and the execution order that is composing an ebXML-based and process-driven e-business service integration model. It also is based upon the CPA XML schema defined in ebCCP to support collaborations between partner companies by parsing transaction CPA, analyzing business process specification, and monitoring CPA execution status and progress reports. The ebRequester deals with a serial of requests that informs ebWCM (ebXML Workcase Manager) creation or remove at the beginning of transaction, and the ebWCM manages the created ebWorkcase instances such as enacting instances, changing requested status information, and interacting with the monitoring clients. Table 1 shows the detail information and properties of the major functions performed by the ebWorkcase objects — Business Collaboration, Business Transaction, and Choreography within Collaboration.

We have adopted an incremental (spiral) approach of the software development methodology in designing and implementing the e-Lollapalooza system. So, at first we extract a set of usecases of the engine by considering the requirements. The usecases are the followings:

1. *Business process management request usecase* - It takes in charge of the member and administrator roles by handling the requests of starting a collaboration process, and also receiving administrator's process control requests and process start requests.
2. *Process control usecase* - It controls processes so that administrators are able to handle process creation, start, suspension, resumption, termination and completion.

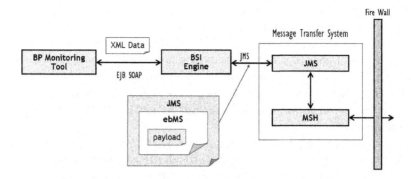

Fig. 3. The Architecture of the e-Lollapalooza BSIS's Engine

Table 1. Properties of the Major Functions handled by the BSIS's Engine

Business Collaboration	Business Transaction	Choreography within Collaboration
MultiPartyCollaboration: *name, Partners*	BusinessTransaction: *name, isGauranteedDeliveryRequired, precondition, postCondition, beginsWhen, endsWhen, pattern, activities, requester, responder*	BusinessState: *collaboration, entering, exiting*
BusinessPartnerRole: *performs, transitions, collaboration*	BusinessAction: *name, IsAuthorizationRequired, IsNonRepudiationRequired, isNonRepudiationOfReceiptRequired, timeToAcknowledgeReceipt, isIntelligibleCheckRequired*	Transition: *onInitiation, conditionGuard, conditionExpression, in, out*
Performs: *performedBy, authorizedRole*	RequestingBusinessActivity: *timeToAcknowledgeAcceptance, transaction, documentEnvelope*	Start
AuthorizedRole: *name, isInitiator, performers, from, to, collaboration*	RespondingBusinessActivity: *transaction, DocumentEnvelope*	CompletionState
BinaryCollaboration: *name, timeToPerform, precondition, postCondition, beginesWhen, endsWhen, pattern, role, states, usedBy, transitions*	DocumentFlow	Success: *conditionExpression*
BusinessActivity: *name, from, to*	DocumentSecurity: *IsAuthenticated, IsConfidential, isTamperProof*	Failure: *conditionExpression*
BusinessTransactionActivity: *timeToPerform, inConcurrent, isLegallyBinding, uses*	DocumentEnvelope: *isPositiveResponse, requesting, BusinessDocument, attachment*	Fork : *name*
BusinessCollaborarionActivity: *uses*	BusinessDocument: *name, conditionExpression, documentEnvelope, attachment*	Join: *name, waitForAll*
	Attachment: *name, mimeType, specification, version, documentEnvelope, businessDocument*	

3. *Active business process monitoring usecase* - It provides a set of services for the active business process's status inquiries.

4. *Transaction documentation send-receive processing request usecase* - It handles the requests from members to send-receive transaction documents through enactments of workitems in the worklist handler.

5. *Business process documentation send-receive usecase* - It deals with sending/receiving business process documents by making their relevant information messages.

6. *Registry retrieve usecase* - The registry stores CPAs, business process documentations, and business processes through the registration procedure.

7. *To engine database save usecase* - It handles for the engine to store the processes' statuses and the registry's contents.

8. *Exception handling usecase* - It deals with engine's malfunctions that take place during sending or receiving letters or transaction documents.

9. *Audit data save usecase* - It treats all traces of the engine's enactment history by keeping its audit logs.

Based on the usecases, we extract a set of classes and their relationships for the engine. The classes consist of BSI, ebRequester, ebWorklistHandler, ebWorkcaseManager, ebWorkcase, ebWorkcaseThread, BPS, CPA, BinaryCollaboration, and ProcessDrivenCollaboration. If ebRequester receives a business process instance creation and beginning request from the business process interface (BSI), then ebWorkcaseManager parses its corresponding BPS and CPA by retrieving from the registry. And also by considering the business process's collaboration type (binary collaboration or multiparty collaboration), it creates its instance of ebWorkcase through ebRequester. The ebRequester is basically inherited from the SessionBean of EJB Framework, and delivers process creation and start requests to ebWorkcaseManager through ebWorkcaseManagerHome. Finally, in Fig. 4 we show a captured screen of the business transaction flow status that is monitored and provided by the engine.

3.4   An Application of the e-Lollapalooza: e-Logistics for the Postal Cyber-Shopping Mall

An e-Logistics application of the process-driven inter-organizational business service integration model, to where the e-Lollapalooza BSI system has applied, has been developed. The process-driven inter-organizational choreography processes between the cyber-shopping mall and the postal service company are modeled by the e-Lollapalooza choreography modeling system, and are also integrated and serviced by the BSI engine systems that are installed on both of these two companies. Due to the page limitation, we would just introduce the web site, here. Now, the whole application programs of the e-Logistics example including contract and order document forms are fully available on the web site, http://www.cnit.com.

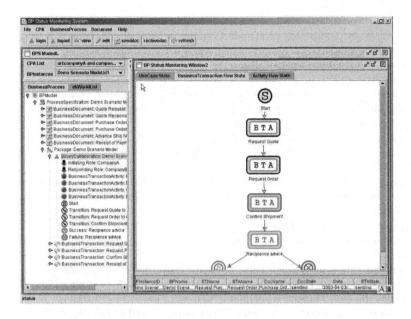

Fig. 4. The Operational Example of the e-Lollapalooza BSIS's Monitor: Business Transaction Flow Status

4   Conclusions

So far, we have described the implementation details of the e-Lollapalooza process-driven inter-organizational business service integration system. And it is targeting on the process-driven e-business service integration markets, such as e-Logistics, e-SCM, e-Procurement, and e-Government, that require process-driven multi-party collaborations of a set of independent organizations. Through the modeling tool, a set of process-driven choreography models, which specify not only the dual-party collaboration but also the process-driven multi-party collaboration between organizations, are defined and transformed into the ebXML-based specifications, and finally the e-Lollapalooza e-business service integration (BSI) system is able to enact and control the choreography models. As our further research works, we are going to apply the e-Lollapalooza system to the various fields of the cross-organizational e-business processes and service integrations markets.

References

1. UN/CEFACT and OASIS - ebXML Registry Information Model v1.0, May (2001)
2. UN/CEFACT and OASIS - ebXML Registry Services Specification v1.0, May (2001)
3. UN/CEFACT and OASIS - Enabling Electronic Business with ebXML, December (2000)
4. Madhu Siddalingaiah: Overview of ebXML, Sun Microsystems, August (2001)

5. Haruo Hayami, Masashi Katsumata, Ken-ichi Okada: Interworkflow: A Challenge for Business-to-Business Electronic Commerce, Workflow Handbook 2001, WfMC, October (2000)
6. The JAVATM 2 Enterprise Edition Developer's Guide, Version 1.2.1, Sun Microsystems, May (2000)
7. Enterprise JavaBeans Programming, Revision A.1, Sun Microsystems, May (2000)
8. Fosdick, H.: The Sociology of Technology Adaptation, Enterprise System Journal, September (1992)
9. Kwang-Hoon Kim, Clarence A. Ellis: A Framework for Workflow Architectures, University of Colorado, Department of Computer Science, Technical Reports, CU-CS-847-97, December (1997)
10. Dong-Keun Oh, Kwang-Hoon Kim: An EJB-Based Database Agent for Workflow Definition, Journal of Korean Society for Internet Information, Vol.4, No.5, December (2001)
11. Kwang-Hoon Kim, Clarence A. Ellis: Performance Analytic Models and Analyses for Workflow Architectures, Information Systems Frontiers, Vol. 3, No. 3, (2001) 339–355
12. Sung-Su Sim, Kwang-Hoon Kim: Workcase based Very Large Scale Workflow System Architecture, Porceedings of Korea Database Society, October (2002)
13. Haruo Hayami, Masashi Katsumata, Ken-ichi Okada: Interworkflow: A Challenge for Business-to-Business Electronic Commerce, Workflow Handbook 2001, WfMC, October (2000)
14. Dogac, A., Tambag, Y., Pembecioglu, P., Pektas, S., Laleci, G. B., Kurt, G., Toprak, S., Kabak, Y.: An ebXML Infrastructure Implementation through UDDI Registries and RosettaNet PIPs, ACM SIGMOD International Conference on Management of Data, Madison, Wisconsin, USA, June (2002)
15. Jae-Gak Hwang, Se-Won Oh, ,Yong-Jun Lee: e-Logistics Integration System based on ebXML specifications, Proceedings of the Conference of Korea Information Science Society, Vol 29, No 2, October (2002)
16. Dong-Keun Oh, Jong-Mi Chun, Jung-Sun Hong, Se-Won Oh, Jae-Gak Hwang, Yong-Jun Lee, Kwang-Hoon Kim: ebXML-Based e-Logistics Workflow Engine Architecture, Proceedings of the Conference of Korean Society for Internet Information, Vol 3, No.3, November (2002) 348–351

BPM and SOA: Synergies and Challenges

Thomas Woodley[1] and Stephane Gagnon[2]

[1] CGI Group, Inc., eBusiness and CRM Solutions, 1350 Rene-Levesque,
Montreal, Canada
Thomas.woodley@cgi.com
[2] New Jersey Institute of Technology, School of Management,
Newark, NJ 07102, USA
gagnon@njit.edu

Abstract. While BPM and SOA have evolved independently, there is an inevitable symbiotic relationship between them. As well, a SOA can be developed using various service formats, whether unique Web Services, orchestrated services using the Business Process Execution Language (BPEL), or other service providers. A SOA promotes the creation of highly accessible, loosely coupled, discrete business services. For greatest reach, BPM consumes and leverages such services, tying them together to solve and streamline broad business challenges. Not surprisingly however, there are certain considerations while designing a SOA to support BPM. Certain service designs align well within a BPM solution or strategy, while others can cause significant headaches for an overall BPM solution. Conversely, SOA with BPM layered on top can become an entirely different value proposition as compared to SOA alone. As a backbone for SOA components, BPM can integrate important functionalities to extend the value of the SOA investment. Similarly, BPM can provide a platform for SOA service management. We will explore the interdependencies between BPM and SOA, and will provide practical guidance on how to make each implementation mutually supportive, extending the reach and value of each. We will also discuss whether SOA alone can provide the business service functionality required for BPM solutions of the future, or if other complementary architectures may also have a role to play.

1 Introduction

BPM (Business Process Management) and SOA (Service Oriented Architecture) are two IT concepts that have received almost unprecedented attention in the last few years. A 2004 Gartner survey of CIOs indicated that 43 percent of IT investment in the subsequent three years would address business process improvement. Similarly, there is virtual unanimity among IT analysts that SOA is transforming and enabling advancements in enterprise architecture as never seen before.

There is a broad and fascinating intersection between BPM and SOA – one which offers both promise, and caveats for each. The SOA promotes the creation of highly accessible, loosely coupled, business-oriented services, as well as end-to-end, fully orchestrated services using such standards as the Business Process Execution Language (BPEL). As such, a SOA can provide exactly the types of enterprise artifacts

M. Kitsuregawa et al. (Eds.): WISE 2005, LNCS 3806, pp. 679 – 688, 2005.

that BPM is designed to consume and integrate, for the broader purpose of streamlining diverse business processes. In addition to leveraging the SOA, BPM can in turn serve as both a backbone and a platform for SOA constructs, and BPM design methodologies can be extremely useful in helping to define and design target business services and their orchestration.

Despite all the obvious synergy between BPM and SOA, it is important to understand that BPM creates a unique type of service consumer – quite different than that of a standalone application, or a service-to-service utilization of SOA. This distinctiveness is so great that certain service designs can become unusable in an enterprise BPM solution, whether due to the messaging model, the interface specifications, the available transport protocols, or other concerns.

This paper provides an introduction to these issues, and approaches them from two angles. On one hand, we discuss how BPM can be used to improve SOA execution. We will review the key strengths of BPM and how these are compatible within a service environment. On the other hand, we will explore how SOA can be used to develop BPM solutions. Our goal will be to identify the strength of a service approach, and find valuable levers to improve the design and execution of business processes.

2   Leveraging BPM for SOA

While SOA can enable stronger and cheaper benefits for BPM, BPM meets a broad swath of needs not satisfied easily in a pure service environment. These needs go beyond purely technical capabilities, and extend to the practices, methodologies and tools provided by BPM. In fact, while SOA exists as a concept, BPM actually represents a market with configurable tools – a difference that has important implications for the synergy between the two.

Fundamentally, BPM is a means to narrow the "execution gap" between business needs and IT delivery capabilities. This gap can be viewed in a variety of ways. Most commonly, this gap is understood as a time delay between the moment of clarity on the business need, and IT's ability to provide a solution which meets the need. Alternatively, this gap can be viewed as a "mind share" gap. That is, how directly and reliably is the business need translated into an IT deliverable? Are there unwritten and undocumented translation steps between the client's defined need, and the actual implementation of the solution? Finally, this execution gap can speak to IT's ability to monitor, refine and redeploy the business solution after it is first deployed – an "improvement gap."

2.1   The Time Gap

Business services change very slowly, while business processes change rapidly. For example, there is always be a need to perform customer verifications, send shipping orders, and prepare invoices However, products themselves, and customers themselves, and the processes that integrate them come and go quite rapidly.

This fundamental difference between business services and business processes has implications for each. Notably, services should be built without overtones of process, while business processes should focus on process rules, and de-emphasize service interpretation. If this domain respect is maintained, BPM can dramatically reduce the time gap in a number of ways.

First, BPM solutions become an automation backbone, orchestrating the invocation of disparate business services based on business process rules, in parallel to other standards such as BPEL. For example, if a new product is introduced, a new ordering process can be stitched together using existing business services, and the business rules that govern the new order process. As a by product, if process sequences or rules change over time, BPM tools provide flexible, and configuration-oriented (i.e. not code-based) ways of updating and redeploying the process. For example, in our ordering application, from a process definition perspective, it would be a fairly simple matter to insert a customer credit check without disrupting the existing model.

Second, the many out-of-box features of existing BPM tools allow for the integration of functions that would otherwise become major custom deliverables. Workflow screens and solutions – servicing the manual steps required in a BPM solution – are very simple to add in an integrated BPM solution. Most BPM tools also provide some rules capability which will facilitate the reuse of process rules across models. Again, this is not something typically or easily done in a pure service environment.

2.2 The "Mind Share" Gap

BPM products offer exciting improvements enabling better collaboration between system teams and their clients. All BPM pure-play products provide modeling capabilities which provide a clear visual depiction of processes, along with interpretive cues. Many of these products even argue that the users themselves can design and configure processes through the BPM tool. While the mind share gap can only be *fully eliminated* if the business users themselves configure and code their own processes, the ability to model and design collaboratively removes many of the unknowns from traditional implementation processes.

Beyond the visual modeling, some BPM tools allow developers and their clients to go even further – whether through business rules environments, meta-data repositories, scripting environments, or other techniques – to try to validate the process implementation against the true requirements. These tools can also be used in testing the proper orchestration of services in BPEL processes, especially ensuring integrity in port mapping and proper data formats between integrated SOA and BPM solutions.

It is also important to note another trump card that that BPM tools bring to the drawing board: workflow features built on sophisticated organizational models. BPM tools are built to support the workflow requirements of the BPM solution, to allow the designer to model the allocation of manual workflow tasks appropriately across business teams. This is a huge plus when trying to narrow the mind share gap. Development and business teams can use a common (and action-able) vocabulary to model the interaction. And second, development teams are able to avoid building a complex, usually incomplete, and ultimately inflexible custom solution.

2.3 The Continuous Improvement Gap

BPM tools offer impressive process feedback mechanisms and continuous improvement models to ensure optimal implementation of both business processes and business services. Here, the BPM solution plays an important role as implementation platform, providing monitoring and management capabilities otherwise usually vacant from a pure service environment. This platform role of the BPM solutions enables a number of important advantages.

First, BPM tools continue to come out with successively stronger tools to monitor and manage both process and service usage. While this monitoring can occur on an ad hoc basis, it can also be tied to SLAs, with feedback mechanisms into BAM or other BAM-like tools. Scalability is also something that is best managed at a platform level, and many BPM tools provide built-in features to enable fail-over capabilities across available service points.

Second, simulation and optimization are features of BPM tools which are difficult to realize otherwise. Here, BPM tools enable the configuration of load levels, response times, and probability paths to see where process and service bottlenecks will occur. Load levels seen in production only during crises can be simulated prior to deployment to ensure the broader solution is prepared to manage peak loads. Once system weaknesses are understood, BPM tools can be configured to allocate platform resources to meet the most critical need..

2.4 BPM Practices and SOA

Beyond the coupling, de-coupling, recombining, and re-configuring, the actual practices and methodologies used to define BPM solutions will also often provide guidance and value to the enterprise SOA strategy. Some organizations have taken to creating Process Integration Centers (PICs) or similar teams to coordinate the strategy for process prioritization, automation and optimization. As they drive the successful implementation of BPM solutions, they will also have a big role to play in the selection and management of the enterprise SOA.

One of the first roles played by the PIC (or whoever is driving process automation in the enterprise) is the analysis of the opportunities. Core and highly-used IT assets – e.g. customer information, inventory information, etc. – will likely be areas of initial focus for any corporate architecture team. However, the PIC will, in addition, bring a process-centric perspective to the analysis. As such, it will assess the relative demand for key services and processes, and channel further development accordingly.

Thus, in this way service opportunities are identified, and their fit into the corporate architecture is strategically planned. In addition, the PIC should drive the communications on service development and availability. Business and IT organizations should be kept informed of the available services, and the value created.

Beyond the internal service planning, the PIC must also keep its eye on external providers, whether service providers, or standards organizations. For example, if we enhanced our order management system to check customer credit, we may find ourselves looking for a reliable credit service available on the Internet. Obviously, managing the access and usage of this service is not a task to leave to developers. Similarly, in implementing the shipping quote steps of our order management system, the PIC would probably want to find industry quote interface and interaction standards to guide the BPM-to-service design.

Finally, the PIC would need to help define standards and prototypes, both for the BPM solutions implemented, and for the services they invoke. Such initiatives do much to prevent a mismatch between SOA implementations, and the BPM solutions they should strive to support.

3   Leveraging SOA for BPM

Designing a BPM solution on a SOA must be done with the same vigilance as any other software platform. To guide our analysis, Fig. 1 summarizes the constraints and priorities imposed by a BPM solution. From these constraints and priorities, we will extract guidelines for a corresponding service design. Above these constraints, however, are two other implicit constraints that will be addressed: the need for a true loosely-coupled design under BPM, and the realities of coarse-grained service design.

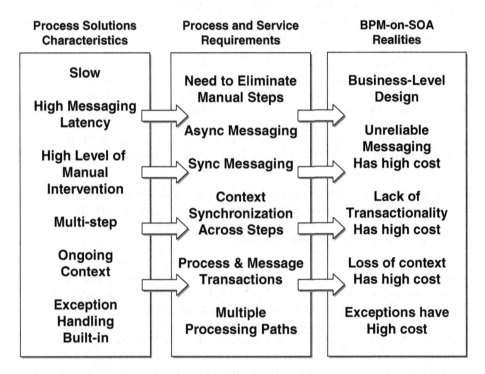

Process Solutions Characteristics	Process and Service Requirements	BPM-on-SOA Realities
Slow	Need to Eliminate Manual Steps	Business-Level Design
High Messaging Latency	Async Messaging	Unreliable Messaging Has high cost
High Level of Manual Intervention	Sync Messaging	
Multi-step	Context Synchronization Across Steps	Lack of Transactionality Has high cost
Ongoing Context	Process & Message Transactions	Loss of context Has high cost
Exception Handling Built-in	Multiple Processing Paths	Exceptions have High cost

Fig. 1. This figure indicates how the peculiarities of a BPM ("Process") solution (left-most column) drive BPM-to-service requirements (center column), which in turn have implications for the ultimate BPM-on-SOA solution (right-most column)

3.1   Loose-Coupling in a BPM Context

Ideally, loose coupling is achieved through maximal use of open standards, such as WSDL, XML and SOAP for Web services. This applies to BPM solutions too, even though they are usually intranet solutions and there might be the tendency to downplay the need to adhere to open standards. For example, even with the best of intentions, a "simple" customer verification service can inadvertently be deployed with an interface requiring lots of "shared knowledge" between client and service. Soon, every business process has its own custom-built customer verification service.

Unfortunately, it is easy to be fooled into thinking a design is loosely-coupled when, in fact, a very high degree of coupling has been designed into the interface.

Vinoski [3] suggests that designers take three views when considering Web service design. The "bottom up" view – the one most often used by developers – looks at the mechanics of the implementation, and provides a view of how readily a service can exposed in a SOA. Most design shops stop after assessing the "bottom up" view. The "top down" view is one that the PIC should apply, and is one that gains greater importance for a BPM solution. Here, the intent is to understand the broad enterprise need for the service, and how best to define it in the SOA. Better to define the interface contract first, and then design the service against the interface. Finally, the "message-focused" view analyzes the target service from the perspective of the messages received and sent by the service.

If designers use only the "bottom up" view, they will usually provide an implementation that is locked somehow to the underlying IT asset. This will happen when the designer mistakes a component for a service, and finishes by exposing a class rather than an interface. This can often happen when designers and developers rely blindly on an automated tool to define a contract. Yet even when the designer is careful to limit the shared information to an interface, and use open standards, an RPC-style of SOAP message will probably not provide the independence between client and service that the designer wants. Bakker [1] describes the following drawbacks of RPC-style SOAP messages:

- Use of methods, parameters and return values as described in the SOAP message which must be shared/coded between the client and the service.
- A fairly rigid request/reply message pattern which is usually provided through a synchronous HTTP implementation

The best choice for loosely-coupled services in a BPM solution is to use "document-style" Web services. Here, the service's SOAP message contains an XML document. In this case, the primary function of the WSDL is simply to wrap the XML message payload. An XSD describes the message for the service consumer, thus minimizing the direct link between the service interface and its implementation. Note also that a document-style Web service may offer other advantages for a BPM solution e.g. easier asynchronous implementation; or greater facility to carry context in the messaging.

While document-style Web services are more complex then their RPC-style counterparts, it is important to note that the complexity lies in the messaging infrastructure, and is not embedded directly in the core service functionality. Thus, once the messaging infrastructure is established, the incremental cost of building document-style Web services drops.

Few environments can boast an exclusively open standards-based SOA. BPM solutions will undoubtedly be glued to proprietary and/or custom service interface here and there. Nevertheless, as much as possible, the amount of data that must be explicitly shared between BPM client and its supporting service must be minimized, or the service endangers its reuse and longevity within the BPM vision.

3.2 Coarse-Grained from a BPM Perspective

The term "coarse-grained" is very frequently used when describing SOA and its favored implementation, Web services. More so perhaps than with other technologies,

BPM solutions require this "coarse grained" business-level implementation. Natis [2] suggests that the best service interface "represent a complete business function" so that the interaction between client and service does not need to be "chatty." For example, in the context of an inventory reservation step within a typical order management process, this might imply that the service not only verify inventory, but reserve it for each line item – all in one invocation. Indeed, separate invocations to verify and then reserve inventory, by order line item would certainly be far too "chatty" for a robust BPM client.

It is usually recommended that services be designed to be stateless – all information being passed in the service invocation. This enables better load balancing and easier failover. Interestingly, given this "coarse-grained" view of services, it is difficult to envision many services that could be implemented synchronously. Certainly it would be difficult to find a transport that could deal with the latency of verifying and reserving inventory for 60 order line items. Fortunately, if coarse-grained services are fated to favor asynchronous implementation, this isn't necessarily a bad fit for a BPM client. Nevertheless, the asynchronous design must be carefully crafted to ensure that the BPM solution has its reliable messaging, without hindering its scalability.

3.3 Transactions in BPM-on-SOA Solutions

Transactions will be a challenge for long-running processes for a long time to come. Standards for transactional behavior for services, or for automated processes are either nascent, or non-existent. Even as these key standards (e.g. WS-Transactions) move up the Standards Maturity Model, BPM solutions will continue to depend on legacy-based services which were established long prior to the (future) acceptance of these standards.

Fig. 1 presents both the dire need for, and the difficulty of providing reliable support for transactions in automated business processes and their supporting services. But if the standards are "not there yet," a pragmatic alternative must be pursued – one which confidently grapples with all exceptions, and moves the end-to-end process inexorably to completion. This inevitably puts an onus both on the service design vision, and the BPM solution. Nevertheless, once such a vision is operational, it is far preferable than managing a flaky and easily-desynchronized business process.

Before moving to the discussion of these new process and service design techniques, it is useful to clarify briefly what is meant by several key terms: process transactions, service transactions, and process desynchronization.

Process Transactions. A process transaction offers the ability to commit or rollback the component steps of an automated business process based on the end-to-end progress (the "context") of the overall process. Thus, for example, if a "transaction context" existed in an order management process, then if the invoice were not approved at the invoice approval step, the prior step of inventory reservation could be rolled back, and the reserved inventory would once again become available.

Service Transactions. A capability for service-oriented transactions would require that a service client be able to commit or roll back the result of a service invocation. Process transactionality inescapably requires that all implicated services also support transactions. Thus, to support the transaction example mentioned in the above paragraph, the inventory reservation service (invoked by the BPM solution) would need to support transactions: committing or rolling back the inventory reservation with the appropriate signal from the transaction manager.

Process Desynchronization. Without support for transactions, a process and its support services can become desynchronized – with dismal consequences. Using again the order management process example, suppose that the order entry system were weak, and that an order arrived with a line item that was no longer carried in inventory. The order management process is well under way – the customer is expecting the order to be shipped within hours – but the inventory service can simply reply, "Inventory reservation request denied." Thus, the process instance is stuck in a state of de-synchrony with one of its supporting services.

3.4 Grappling with Exceptions and Errors

There are varied causes and remedies for process exceptions, so this section can only hope to provide some general guidelines for BPM and service design. There are several possible scenarios.

If designers have already implemented reliable messaging, the issues that arise in the solution could simply be business exceptions, e.g. the customer verification failed – the customer is insolvent. In this case, the BPM solution should contain transitions and activities which terminate the order management process appropriately. If this is not the case, the business process component of the solution has been badly designed.

Alternatively, an issue might arise where a service returns an indeterminate exception – an "Other error" type response. First of all, this is an indication of poor service exception management. Nevertheless, the BPM solution should provide mechanisms to avoid the unnecessary termination of the process. This could be done by pushing the exception out to a workflow screen for manual intervention, and the possibility of resubmission.

Or again, a true system error might occur. This could occur because of a failure somewhere among the layers of the onion, e.g. the BPM Web layer is down, or the messaging server is unavailable, or the service's Web layer is down, or the service's supporting class throws an untrapped error, etc. Here again, the BPM solution should provide mechanisms to avoid unnecessary termination of the process. If, for instance, inventory is reserved for an order, but the order management process aborts at a later step in the process, the business runs the risk of holding inventory for an order that will never be shipped. Nevertheless, this impact pales in comparison to the danger that the customer will never receive his order.

As suggested above, there is every reason to avoid aborting an automated process in mid-course, both from the perspective of the business process, and from the perspective of the supporting services. Given the difficulty of implementing transactional behavior, there are a few options to "force complete" the process. Of course, whatever the completion, it should satisfy the transactional requirement of "consistency" – leaving the BPM solution and its supporting services synchronized.

Issuing "compensating transactions" is a technique which has gained traction in BPM circles. For example, the Business Process Management Notation (BPMN) itself provides a nomenclature for such design. Briefly, since transactional support in services is so uncommon, BPM solutions can be designed to invoke a service to undo the result of some previous step. In essence, it's like a hard-coded roll back. For example, using again the order management process example, if inventory had been reserved, but the order could note be completed, the BPM solution could be designed such that a second invocation of the inventory service could be performed. This second call would un-reserve the previously reserved inventory. Of course, enterprise services would need to be designed in light of this requirement to support compensating transactions.

Optionally, the BPM solution can always be designed to push errors out to a workflow screen for operations staff to review. This is an option of last resort, but it is still preferable to aborting the end-to-end process, and leaving enterprise assets in an inconsistent state. Yet pushing the issue out to workflow for manual intervention is not always the best option. Operations staff will need to have tools to address the workload. Such tools might include, 1) access to process context data, to update process information on the fly (e.g. update a product id on an order line item), or 2) ability to invoke a service (e.g. via a Web screen) to resync enterprise assets to align with the state of a running process instance.

4 Conclusion

We explored the potential of using BPM and SOA together in process-centric application development. Our analysis was guided by the constraints and priorities typical of such applications, allowing us to map a number of opportunities and challenges for BPM-on-SOA solutions (summarized in Fig. 1).

On one hand, we found that BPM can help improve the execution of SOA projects and solutions. Process-centric tools can be used to rapidly develop, publish, and orchestrate services. They can also help ensure greater coherence between a SOA solution and its overarching processes, especially by automating the validation of port mapping and data formats. Process monitoring and management, which are key features of most BPM suites, can also be leveraged to support the continuous improvement of service-based applications. Finally, BPM methodologies, along with Process Integration Centers (PICs), can stimulate the application of the SOA by clearly identifying high value, high impact processes to consume, publish, and/or orchestrate services.

On the other hand, the SOA offers extensive potential to build new BPM-on-SOA solutions. Such principles as loose-coupling, if applied using a comprehensive approach (along with PICs), can provide valuable guidance in selecting the right services to consume/publish/orchestrate, and in fine-tuning its interfaces. Another principle, coarse-grained services, is well in line with the BPM tradition of managing an array of functional operations. These principles are also related to emerging SOA standards for transaction management, which have the potential of strengthening BPM if they are properly aligned with process synchronization requirements. These standards can also be used to improve how BPM solutions deal with errors and exception, and help automate compensating processes.

Overall, together BPM and SOA form a more complete solution environment than apart. Architects of process-centric applications should consider their synergies, despite the idiosyncrasies of existing BPM and SOA operating platforms.

Indeed, future work is needed to develop a complete platform and approach for BPM-on-SOA. Vendors of both technologies must build more integrated suites that fully blend their respective strengths, especially to alleviate one another's weaknesses. These new BPM-on-SOA suites, going well beyond the mere introduction of Web Services in BPM suites, should be linked to new development methods that closely blend BPM traditions with SOA standards and implementation techniques. As such, while several issues remain to be addressed, there is excellent potential for both approaches to converge in a single solution and implementation environment.

References

1. Bakker, L.: Business Integration Journal. Not all Web Services Fit into an SOA: Why some Web Services are Better for an SOA than others. May, 2005. Thomas Communications, Inc. (2005)
2. Natis, Y.: Business Integration Journal. Service-Oriented Architecture (SOA) Ushers in the Next Era in business Software Engineering. May, 2004. Thomas Communications, Inc. (2004)
3. Vinoski, S.: Business Integration Journal. Debunking the Myths of Service Orientation. April, 2005. Thomas Communications, Inc. (2005)

Web Performance Indicator by Implicit User Feedback - Application and Formal Approach

Michael Barth[1], Michal Skubacz[2], and Carsten Stolz[3]

[1] Ludwig-Maximilian-Universität, München, Germany
barth@pst.ifi.lmu.de
[2] Siemens AG, Corporate Technology, Germany
michal.skubacz@siemens.com
[3] University of Eichstätt-Ingolstadt, Germany
carsten.stolz@ku-eichstaett.de

Abstract. With growing importance of the internet, web sites have to be continously improved. Web metrics help to identify improvement potentials. Particularly success metrics for e-commerce sites based on transaction analysis are commonly available and well understood. In contrast to transaction based sites, the success of web sites geared toward information delivery is harder to quantify since there is no direct feedback of the user.

We propose a generic success measure for information driven web sites. The idea of the measure is based on the observation of user behaviour in context of the web site semantics. In particular we observe users on their way through the web site and assign positive and negative scores to their actions. The value of the score depends on the transitions between page types and their contribution to the web site's objectives.

To derive a generic view on the metric construction, we introduce a formal meta environment deriving success measures upon the relations and dependencies of usage, content and structure of a web site.

1 Introduction

An Internet presentation is essential for almost all companies. But a web site is not creating value by itself. It has to offer utility to its users. The business models behind a corporate web site can range from offering contact possibilities or information to purchasing or selling products and services. Due to a growing realistic judgement about the possibilities of Internet technology, companies focus on the return they generate by their web sites.

This return can be calculated straightforward on web sites, selling products or services. The utility on those transaction oriented web sites can be derived from the monetary value of the transactions. Many metrics to evaluate a transaction based web site have been developed and are well understood. In section 2 we give a state of the art overview of web metrics.

Web sites without transactions lack this evaluation possibility. In this approach we will concentrate on non-transactional web sites. We subsume them

M. Kitsuregawa et al. (Eds.): WISE 2005, LNCS 3806, pp. 689–700, 2005.

under the term *information driven web sites*. The main reason why there are no satisfactory success measures is the lack of explicit feedback of the users on the successfulness of their sessions.

1.1 Developing Metrics for Information Driven Web Sites

To overcome the missing user feedback problem, we propose to approximate an implicit user feedback. In our approach described in section 3 we make an estimation of the user feedback by analysing his behaviour on the web site under consideration of the semantics of the web site. Having the clickstreams in the semantics of the web site, we evaluate each click of a user in respect to its contribution to fulfilling the web site's objectives.

In section 5 we demonstrate the applicability of our metric to a corporate web site. After demonstrating the construction and evaluation of the metric on a example, we deem it necessary to describe our approach with a formal model in section 6. This model of a meta environment describes the relations of usage, content and structure within a web site and it is focused on evaluation.

2 Existing Metrics

A general overview of web metrics is provided by Dhyani [3], NetGenesis [8] and Schwickert[10]. The most recent study about existing web metrics as been performed by Calero in [2].

2.1 Transaction Based Success Measures

The user intention and by extention the web site's success can be easily measured if the user completes a transaction on an e-commerce site. On transaction based web sites a variety of success measures have been developed.

The user declares her intentions as soon as he is willing to pay for a product and purchases it, revealing also the monetary value or utility to the user. If a purchase is conducted on a web site, this makes the success measurement straightforward and allows deeper analysis of the whole purchase process.

NetGenesis [8] show how different measures can describe the customer life cycle. From **reach, acquisition, conversion** and **retention** a customer can reach **loyalty** status. Other metrics like **abandonment, attrition** and **churn** describe the migration of users.

2.2 Information Provision Based Success Measures

Success measures for information driven web sites are rare. The problem to identify user intention is described by Pather [9] in a conceptual study to evaluate user satisfaction by gap measurement, but no metrics are developed.

Most approaches combine structural, content and usage data to uncover the user intention. Heer and Chi propose in [5] a way to discover user interest by clustering usage and content data. Heer and Chi continued their research on web site usability in [5]. Like we did in [11, 13] Jin et al. [6] analyse and compare usage data and content in order to discover hidden semantic information. Barnard and Wesson outline three measurements to evaluate the usability of a web site in [1]: **effectiveness** for the users determining their tasks, **efficiency** measures the time it took the users to complete their tasks and **satisfaction**, inquired from the user by questionnaire.

In [13] we compare the user's web site perception with the intentions of the web author, identifying inconsistencies between both user and web author, resulting in an indicator for improvements in web site design. This allows a qualitative but not success oriented judgement.

Summarising the existing success based metrics for information driven web sites, the utility of a quantification of the web site's success is considerable.

3   Web Success Metric for Information Driven Web Sites

The **effectiveness** of an information driven web site depends on successfully leading the user to pages providing information. The **efficiency** depends on leading the user to the desired content.

We distinguish between pages **navigational pages**, helping the user to find information and navigating the web site, and **content pages**, providing the sought after content. As can be seen in figure 1, we first describe the effectiveness measure, combining page content in 3.1 and page characteristics derived from link information in 3.2. As second part we describe the efficiency measure in 3.3.

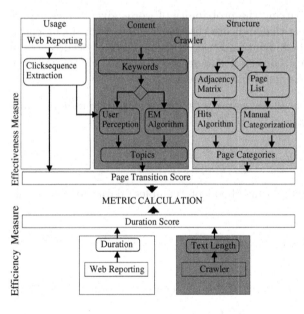

Fig. 1. process

3.1   Content and Topic Change

Aiming to estimate the user's focus, important information comes from the content of the pages he visited.

The understanding of textual or other pieces of information depends on the understanding of the recipient. Thus leaving the topic identification up to every user, author or analyst. Semantic information can be provided by the author directly via a Semantic Web, taxonomies or ontologies. In [13] we have proposed a user perceived topic identification. Since this approach mixes usage and content of a web site, we now want to present a purely content based topic identification in order provide a more generic evaluation metric.

Topic Identification Algorithm. As we have shown in [11] the application of a probabilistic topic identification. We use a crawler to extract the text from all web pages and calculate the text length, remove stop words and apply stemming.

We create a matrix consisting of the web pages and the extracted key words and use it as input for the clustering algorithm. By clustering key words we are trying to identify topics. In other words, we consider word classes (topics) $\{z_j\}_{j=1}^L$, and model the likelihood of a document d (web pages) as follows,

$$p(\mathbf{w}_d) = \prod_w \left(\sum_z p(w|z, \beta)p(z|\theta_d) \right)^{n_{d,w}} \tag{1}$$

where β are parameters specifying the probability of words given topics, θ_d are document-specific parameters that indicate the topics mixture for document d, $\mathbf{w}_d$ is the word list of this document and $n_{d,w}$ is the number of occurrences of word w in $\mathbf{w}_d$. Then given a corpus of documents $d = 1, \ldots, n$, we have the following EM algorithm to estimate the parameters:

- E-step: for each document d, we estimate the posterior distribution of topics given each word w in it:

$$p(z|w, d) = \frac{p(w|z, \beta)p(z|\theta_d)}{\sum_z p(w|z, \beta)p(z|\theta_d)} \tag{2}$$

- M-step: we maximise the log-likelihood of "complete data" for the whole corpus:

$$\sum_d \sum_{\mathbf{z}} \left(\prod_w p(z|w, d) \log \prod_w \left(p(w|z, \beta)p(z|\theta_d) \right)^{n_{d,w}} \right) \tag{3}$$

with respect to parameters β and $\{\theta_d\}_{d=1}^N$, which gives rise to

$$\beta_{i,j} = p(w_i|z_j) \propto \sum_d n_{d,w_i} p(z_j|w_i, d) \tag{4}$$

$$\theta_{j,d} = p(z_j|d) \propto \sum_w n_{d,w} p(z_j|w, d) \tag{5}$$

We perform the E-step and M-step iteratively and at the convergence obtain the final estimate of $p(w|z)$ and $p(z|d)$. The meaning of these two parameters can be explained as follows:

- $p(w|z)$ indicates the probability of occurrence of word w given topic z. The algorithm groups semantically related words into topics and thus explores the semantic relations between words. Intuitively, if several words often occur together, these words are likely to be associated with one topic.
- $p(z|d)$ indicates the probability of topic z for document d.

3.2   Page Categories

An important part in creating a measurement is to judge whether the user followed a link in the desired or wrong direction. This gives clues about if he had found what he was looking for or not.

In [12] we distinguish between navigational and content pages. A navigation page should lead the user as fast and intuitively as possible to the desired content. Both page categories have to be judged differently. We evaluate the transitions between both categories creating a matrix of every possible category transition.

Table 1. Page Category Transition Rating

		Destination				
		Home	Sitemap	Search	Content	Sess. End
Start	Home	−	−	−	+	−
	Sitemap	−	−	−	+	−
	Search	−	−	−	+	−
	Content	−	−	−	+	0

Table 2. Web Page Duration Rating

	short d.	long d.
Navigation	+	−
Content	−	+

The pages dedicated to guiding the user through the web site are *Home, Search Page and Sitemap*. The content pages represent the major part of a web site and need further attention by identifying topics of the content pages and the topic transition per click in order to quantify successful transitions, see section 3.1. Due to the fact that the last page view can not be evaluated (see section 3.3), we assign a value of 0 to all click sequences *page → end*.

Incorporating HITS Algorithm of Kleinberg [7] for calculation of hub and authority scores, we achieve an alternative generic page categorisation. Ding et al [4] provide further analysis of the HITS algorithm. For this scoring the web graph is considered to be directed, therefore only links are considered and not client side options like back-buttons. This would result in an undirected graph, since each edge in the graph would have an oppositely directed edge resulting from the back-button usage.

For each web page p_i is assigned a hub score y_i and an authority score x_i. Like Kleinberg points out [7], a good authority is pointed to by many good hubs and a good hub points to many good authorities. The authority and hub scores are obtained, by iteratively updating equation 6

$$x_i = \sum_{j:e_{ij} \in E} y_i, \ y_i = \sum_{j:e_{ij} \in E} x_i \qquad (6)$$

3.3 Duration

Having described the above measure for effectiveness, measures for efficiency will focus on evaluating the time it took the users to complete their tasks.

The time necessary to perceive, read and understand textual information depends apart from design issues mainly on the length of the text. We characterise the interest of an user in a given content page by calculating the time spent per word. By contrasting this value to the average time spent on all words for all users, we can get a feel for where a user's focus is acknowledged, and where not.

Table 2 assigns bonus values to long durations on content pages and negative penalty values to navigational pages and vice versa for short durations. In order to make all durations comparable we normalise all values as described in the following section 4.

The duration of the last click in a user session is not measurable since we do not receive any further user actions after the last click.

We can measure the time between the user's actions, which means clicks, but it is technically not possible to measure either the amount of attention the user payed to the web page content or whether he read the content at all. It is generally only possible to achieve this with any accuracy under controlled conditions.

In case of tabbed browsing, allowed by a newer generation of browsers, the duration and sequence does not necessarily resemble the sequence and duration the user is reading the content.

4 Construction of the Metric

Effectiveness Measures. We begin with the calculation of the effectiveness measures described in 3.1. First we extract the textual information from the web pages with the help of a crawler. After cleaning the data we determine the number of topic clusters and apply standard clustering methods to identify groups of related web pages.

Now we have all the information needed to construct the transition matrix assigning values to each possible click. The basic value for each click is derived from the categories of the source and destination pages, as described in table 1. The multiplication factors are directly derived from the transition table.

Definition 1 (Transition Type). *Let τ be a transition within the web site and T the associated transition table. The transition type χ_τ is defined as*

$$\chi_\tau = 1 * sign(T_{i,j}) \qquad (7)$$

where i is the source type of τ, and j the destination page type.

The next aspect we want to capture in the metric is the type of transitions occurring between web pages bearing content. We want to emphasise transitions which stay within a topic, and deemphasise transitions between topic areas. Having assigned values to each page category transition, the transitions between content pages are evaluated in greater detail. We calculate the distance between all possible content page transitions based on the comparison of both topics. In other words we calculate a similarity measure by comparing the topic affiliation of all pages.

Normalisation. Instead of using continuous values as gained from the distance between individual pages, we determine a transition to be significant or not. A significant transition distance would signify a change in topic, while an insignificant shift would leave the user perusing the same general topic area. Since we want a web site to guide a user quickly to the content he desires, we introduce a characterisation of this topic change.

Definition 2 (Transition Weight). *Let τ be a transition between content pages. The effectiveness of a transition is captured by an assigned weight factor μ_τ.*

$$\mu_\tau = \begin{cases} negligible\ topic\ shift & \Rightarrow 1 < \mu_\tau \\ significant\ topic\ shift \Rightarrow 0 < \mu_\tau < 1 \end{cases} \tag{8}$$

The evaluation of the degree of topic change is performed by regarding all occurring topic transitions and comparing them with the topic transition in focus. Any change larger than x is considered significant, while any change smaller would leave the user within the to same general topic.

Definition 3 (Efficiency Factor). *Let τ be a transition within the web site. We have the duration d_τ and the text length l_τ of the source page. We also maintain the global average of all users reading a word δ_{word}:*

$$\delta_{word} = \frac{\sum\limits_{\forall \tau} d_\tau}{\sum\limits_{\forall \tau} l_\tau} \tag{9}$$

The efficiency ϕ of a transition τ can now be characterised with respect to δ_{word}
for content $\xrightarrow{\tau}$ content :

$$\phi_\tau = \begin{cases} 0 < x < 1 & \delta_{word} > \delta_{word}^\tau \\ 1 < x & \delta_{word} < \delta_{word}^\tau \end{cases} \tag{10}$$

for navigation $\xrightarrow{\tau}$ content:

$$\phi_\tau = \begin{cases} 0 < x << 1 & , if\ \delta_{word} < \delta_{word}^\tau \\ 1 << x & , if\ \delta_{word} > \delta_{word}^\tau \end{cases} \tag{11}$$

With the help of the defined characteristics, we can now construct our metric. Since the metric reflects how well a web site guides a user to the content he seeks, we refer to the metric as the Guidance Performance Indicator.

Definition 4 (Guidance Performance Indicator). *We determine the effectiveness of a session σ with $\sigma = \{\tau_1, \tau_2, \ldots \tau_m\}$ by combining the transition type χ_τ, transition weight μ_τ and transition efficiency ϕ_τ for each transition $\tau \in \sigma$.*

$$Our Approach GPI_\sigma = \sum_{i=1, \tau_i \in \sigma}^{|\sigma|} \chi_{\tau_i} * \mu_{\tau_i} * \phi_{\tau_i} \tag{12}$$

5   Case Study and Evaluation

We analyse usage data from a corporate web site dealing with financial products and services.

Web Page Assessment. One application of the GPI is to evaluate and compare web pages. We regard two navigation pages and one content page as comparison, since one GPI value of its own reveals no user feedback. Both navigation pages are search pages, namely the simple search and the advanced search offering more selection possibilities.

Table 3 shows the absolute GPI values. In order to compare the GPI values of pages with different traffic density, we contrast their average GPIs per click. The negative average GPI per click for the simple search page can have several reasons. Users need more time to find a relevant search result within all search results or the search leads to information not of interest to the user. Whereas the Advanced Search reached a positive GPI by leading users faster to desired information. This is a reasonable result, since more selection criteria allow better search results. But 443 times the simple search was used compared to 75 times usage of advanced search. A recommendation could be to replace the simple search with the advanced search.

Session Assessment. Table 4 shows two sample sessions. Both users have each accessed a search page and have been directed to a content page. According to the GPI the web site provided better guidance in the first instance. It took the second user (who was accessing the simple search page) two clicks to reach a content page, which he left after a short duration and retreated to the home

Table 3. GPI: Example pages

	GPI	clicks	GPI/clicks
Search	-350,5	443	-0.79
Adv. Search	14,9	75	0.20
Product	775,5	1193	0,65

Table 4. GPI: Example Sessions

	GPI$_1$	GPI$_2$	GPI$_3$	total
Home→Adv.Search→ Content→Content	-1.1	1.7	1.5	2.1
Search→Search→ Content→Home	-1.2	1.44	-1.4	-1.1

page. The negative GPI reflects the assumption that this user did not find what he was looking for.

This evaluation shall be expanded to different kind of information driven web sites. We also work on calibrating the metric with artifical data.

6   Meta Environment for Web Success Metrics

6.1   Domain Analysis

Conception. The web site author and the user face each other. Only indirectly we can get hold of this by their artefacts. On part of the author we can analyse the web site, on part of the user, we can observe the click sequence of a session. In package *SiteStructure* in figure 2 the web site is represented mainly by the pages (*Page*) and their directed connections (*Links*), resembling vertices and edges they build a directed graph. The clickstream, as list of *SessionItems* defined in package *SessionStructure* can be derived from navigating through the web site. A concrete session resembles a path through the web site graph. Artefacts arising from bookmarks, direct prompting of the URL, use of the back button in the browser or tabbed browsing, have the effect, that all pages within a site can be the successor of each page. Therefor we regard a complete graph and use the physical character of a link to distinguish between *internal, external* and *virtual* links.

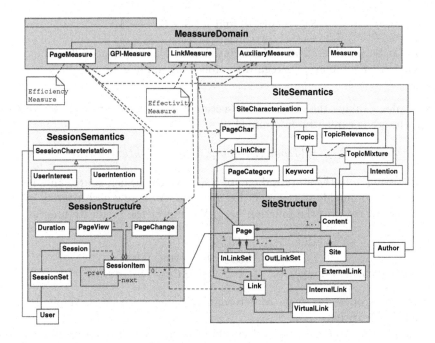

Fig. 2. Meta Environment

Describing the page view by a link with literal character z and a web site as set of all reachable pages Σ, we get the *Clickstream* as string out of the set of all strings over this alphabet $\omega \in \Sigma^*$. We now can principally define measures on this alphabet, a single literal character, strings and substrings, that are calculable directly on the set or inductively by ω.

In particular we introduce new semantic terms essential for calculating the measures, but not directly available from the web site or from session data. In figure 2 we subsume them under superclass *Characterisation*. For classification of structural elements, one can derive sets of one or more elements from the respective semantical term.

6.2   Evaluation of Structural Elements

On the highest level of abstraction we consider a structural element and its characterisations, being interested in the measure they apply to. Thus with:

$$
\begin{aligned}
\text{Measure} &\quad M \in \mathcal{M} \\
\text{Charcterization} &\quad \mathcal{C} \in \mathcal{C}_{Set} \\
\text{Structural Element} &\quad s \in \mathcal{S}
\end{aligned}
$$

for each structural domain $\mathcal{S}$, in respect of a distinct characterisation $\mathcal{C}$ out of the set of characterisations $\mathcal{C}_{Set}$, we are looking for a function μ, that evaluates each element with:

$$[\![\mathcal{S}]\!]_{\mathcal{C}_x} = \mu(s,c) \text{ and } \mu : \mathcal{S} \times \mathcal{C}_x \longrightarrow M$$

μ can be considered as weight function of the relation of domain $\mathcal{S}$ and codomain $\mathcal{C}$. Exemplary, we regard the following application:

Example.   Taking the categories of section 3 as example for a characterisation $\mathcal{C}_{Cat}$, the set is explicitly determined by

$$\mathcal{C}_{Cat} = \{Home, Sitemap, Search, Content, \bot\}$$

We assign $\bot$ to the start and end of a session, since their source and destination is located outside of the regarded web site. Assigning each page to exactly one category, requires the function μ_{Cat}. We expect the predicate function:

$$
\begin{aligned}
\mu_{Cat} : \mathcal{S} \times \mathcal{C}_{Cat} &\to M_{bool} \\
\text{with: } M_{bool} = \mathbb{B} &= \{\text{true}, \text{false}\}
\end{aligned}
$$
$$\text{which is unique, so: } \forall s \in \mathcal{S} : |\{c \in \mathcal{C}_{Cat} : \mu_{Cat}(s,c)\}| = 1$$

In 3 we propose two ways to determine the page categories: Manually or by the HITS Algorithm.

The *Transition Rating* defined in table 1 is intuitively comprehendible in the context of the metric explanation in section 3. Formally considered, this is a complex process, including miscellaneous definitions and assumptions.

Transition Rating is an additional characterisation (by a single element set) evaluating a *Link* $l \in \mathcal{L} \subset \mathcal{S}$ of a web site. The codomain of the one digit function $\mu_{tr} : \mathcal{L} \rightarrow M_{tr}$ is determined deliberately by $M_{tr} = \{-1, 0, 1\}$. We only know the clicked Link, but we need the categorisation of start and target page for the evaluation. Therefor we introduce a navigational function to get access to the site structure:

Link:	$l \in \mathcal{L} \subset \mathcal{S}$
Page:	$p \in \mathcal{P} \subset \mathcal{S}$
Predecessor Page:	$pred : \mathcal{L} \rightarrow \mathcal{P}$
Successor Page:	$succ : \mathcal{L} \rightarrow \mathcal{P}$

By means of this function we can determine the start and target page of a link. For a particular page the related category has to be determined by μ_{Cat}.

determine category: $\kappa : \mathcal{P} \times \left(\mathcal{P} \times \mathcal{C}_{Cat} \rightarrow \mathbb{B}\right) \longrightarrow \mathcal{C}_{Cat}$

with: $\kappa\left(p, \mu_{Cat}\right) = \bigcup_{\mu_{Cat}(p,c)} c \in \mathcal{C}_{Cat}$

The table structure becomes directly apparent in the last auxiliary function ν, used for the definition of μ_{tr}:

$$\mu_{tr}(l) = \nu\left(\kappa(pred(l), \mu_{Cat}), \kappa(succ(l), \mu_{Cat})\right)$$

with $\nu : \mathcal{C}_{Cat} \times \mathcal{C}_{Cat} \rightarrow M_{tr}$
(defined by table 1)

6.3   Benefits

Approaching the task by this formal analysis, results in precise separation of certain aspects like functions, algorithms, assumptions and deliberate specifications, which grants a high quality of the defined measure. This approach allows reuse of present techniques, reduces redundant definitions and helps to calibrate different measures mutually. By adherence of this abstract methodology we obtain affirmation of the measure's reliability, information about error sources and insufficient definitions of domains and codomains.

Consequences for Our Approach.   We outlined a formal meta model for measure definition in our domain. This formal reflection showed assumptions hidden in our problem's initial definition. By example, the user's interest in topics is not considered explicitly, or we assume time spent on a page is used for reading content. These issues may be considered by auxiliary measures also derived by our formal model. We are looking forward to advances in measure techniques according to our methodology.

7   Conclusion

Though there are numerous general metrics to measure web site usability and success available, those including user feedback are limited to analysing transaction based e-commerce web sites. Therefore we have introduced a new metric geared towards assessing the success of information driven web sites. We approach the challenge of making user feedback available without enquiring the user directly, by analysing their behaviour on the web site and particularly visited content. By modelling desired user behaviour patterns, our metric assigns positive as well as negative values according to the perceived success of a user session.

This success metric for information driven web sites does not provide absolute measures about the generated value or utility. Rather it can be used as a valuable indicator, to identify inefficiently working web pages. With help of the GPI metric a web site editor can discover important elements in the website structure and content, which influence user behaviour. For example attractive content presentation, positive web site design or misleading navigation. Monitoring the development of the metric over time can reveal user acceptance of the web site and reactions to changes in content and design. The GPI can be applied to all kind of web sites and can be adjusted to specific web site characteristics by fine tuning of the transition matrix.

The presented formal model provides a precise comprehension of terms, measures and methods and prepares for future extensions.

References

1. L. Barnard and J. L. Wesson. Usability issues for e-commerce in south africa: an empirical investigation. pages 258–267, 2003.
2. C. Calero, J. Ruiz, and M. Piattini. A web metrics survey using wqm. In *Web Engineering, 4th International Conference, ICWE 2004, Munich, Germany, Proceedings*, pages 147–160. Springer, 2004.
3. Dhyani, D.;Keong NG, W.;Bhowmick, S.S. A survey of web metrics. *ACM Computing Surveys*, 34(4):469–503, December 2002.
4. C. Ding, H. Zha, X. He, P. Husbands, and H. Simon. Link analysis: Hubs and authorities on the world wide web. Technical report, LBNL Tech Report 47847, 2002.
5. J. Heer and E.H. Chi. Separating the swarm: Categorization methods for user sessions on the web. *ACM*, 2002.
6. X. Jin, Y. Zhou, and B. Mobasher. Web usage mining based on probabilistic latent semantic analysis. *KDD 2004*, pages 197–205, 2004.
7. J. M. Kleinberg. Authoritative sources in a hyperlinked environment. *Journal of the ACM*, 46(5):604–632, 1999.
8. NetGenesis. E-metrics business metrics for the new economy. www, 2000.
9. S. Pather, G. Erwin, and D. Remenyi. Measuring e-commerce effectiveness: a conceptual model. *SAICSIT '03*, pages 143–152, 2003.
10. A. C. Schwickert and P. Wendt. Controlling kennzahlen fuer web sites. Arbeitspapiere WI 2, Justus-Liebig-Universitt Gieen, 8 2000.
11. C. Stolz, V. Gedov, K. Yu, R. Neuneier, and M. Skubacz. Measuring semantic relations of web sites by clustering of local context. In *LNCS: Proc. Int. Conf. Web Engineering, ICWE 2004, Munich*, pages 182–186. Springer, 2004.
12. C. Stolz, M. Viermetz, M. Skubacz, and R. Neuneier. Guidance performance indicator - web metrics for information driven web sites. In *IEEE Intl. Conf. Web Intelligence 2005, Proc.*, 2005.
13. C. Stolz, M. Viermetz, M. Skubacz, and R. Neuneier. Improving semantic consistency of web sites by quantifying user intent. *LNCS: Proc. Int. Conf. Web Engineering, ICWE 2005, Sydney*, 2005.

Discovering the Most Frequent Patterns of Executions in Business Processes Described in BPEL

Benoit Dubouloz[2] and Candemir Toklu[1]

[1] Siemens Corporate Research (SCR), Princeton NJ 08540, USA
Candemir.Toklu@siemens.com
[2] Swiss Federal Institute of Technology Lausanne (EPFL),
1015 Lausanne, Switzerland
Benoit.Dubouloz@epfl.ch

Abstract. Emerging Business Process Management Systems (BPMS) are revolutionizing the way enterprises address inter-/intra- company process integration and business IT alignment problems. BPMS is becoming the tool of choice for process lifecycle management. Continuous process improvement is the key focus of process lifecycle management. To carry out this task effectively process designers need a deep understanding of the process behavior. They will need efficient mining algorithms that deliver pertinent and valuable information on all executed instances of a complex process. We propose an algorithm that mines the frequent paths of execution for processes described in BPEL by extending the formalism that has been proposed for mining frequent patterns in a workflow.

1 Introduction

Web services have recently emerged as a powerful abstraction of the application component interface and business service definition. Service Oriented Architecture (SOA) is gaining momentum for the definition of today's information systems. Business Process Management systems (BPMs) utilize SOA architecture to empower companies with a complete solution for process management. BPM systems provide the capability to manage the complete lifecycle of processes, to discover, design, deploy, execute, interact with, operate, optimize and analyze end to end processes, and finally to do it at the level of business design, not technical implementation.

BPM systems start with mapping the processes and designing improvements based on the process performance data collected. There is a huge body of literature on process improvement methodologies such as Six Sigma, TQM, QFD, QS9000, ISO9000, etc. Systematic collection of runtime process performance data and the tools for bottleneck diagnosis are starting to receive attention [4]. We believe that process analysis is one of the key steps in realizing continuous process improvement. Our work will provide the process designers with a technology to help them with their process analysis tasks.

M. Kitsuregawa et al. (Eds.): WISE 2005, LNCS 3806, pp. 701–710, 2005.

BPEL4WS (BPEL in short) [11], Business Process Execution Language for Web Services, has emerged as an XML based description to enable web services composition. It allows the definition of complex processes using web services invocation as basic activities. Process access is exposed as standard web services.

BPMS vendors are already building powerful graphical tools for designing business processes in BPEL. When the process description is deployed in a BPMS, instances are created on demand and all the activities and communications are logged. These logs can then become the basis for process analysis and optimization. One key tool process designers need for process optimization is finding the most executed sequence of activities or patterns of executions. In this paper, we propose a novel framework on top of a frequent pattern mining algorithm [1]. It supports the mining of nearly any BPEL 1.1 compliant process.

It will empower the process designer with critical information to identify redundant duplicate or non value add steps by discovering frequently occuring:

- sub patterns - sub patterns containing a given activity
- paths from start to end - paths from start to end containing a given activity
- multiple processes sub patterns mining

1.1   Related Work

The work in this paper focuses on extracting critical information to help process owners better assess and reengineer processes. More specifically we focus on processes described in BPEL in order to gather information from the large data set represented by the process execution logs.

Data mining is usually defined as the analysis of large observational data sets to find unsuspected relationships and to summarize the data in novel ways that are both understandable and useful for the data owner [2].

Very interesting work has been done in mining interaction logs to derive work-flow models. According to [4], the goal of process mining is to collect data at run-time to support workflow design and analysis. Gathered information can be used in discovery, design and analysis step. Message exchanged between legacy applications can be analyzed to discover process models thus facilitating the discovery and design steps. The process maps gathered by analyzing message exchange for a deployed process greatly helps to asses the process and enables Delta analysis, i.e., the detection of discrepancies between the designs constructed in the design phase and the actual execution [4].

Powerful algorithms have been proposed to address the discovery of process maps from recorded execution events[4]. InWoLvE [3] is a workflow mining system that has been refined to enable a interactive workflow mining [5]. Recently, a new approach based on genetic algorithm has been proposed to address the problems many process mining algorithm are facing: concurrency, duplicate activities, hidden activities, non-free-choice constructs, and the fact that real life logs contains noise [6]. In [7], 3 levels of abstraction are proposed in the context of Web Service Interaction Mining (WSIM).

While the aforementioned algorithms and frameworks focus on discovering process maps from event logs, our work is based on another approach where the workflow schema is the starting point, not the result [1]. Although traditional process mining gives valuable information for the process discovery activities, process designers look for performance data in redesigning the processes. In addition, finding patterns and paths that are never executed in the real-life is certainly useful for redesigning the process. Finding non executed patterns or paths could help the process designer to optimize his process.

Furthermore much more efficient algorithms can be developed for supporting the redesign and analysis activities if the process map is accurately known. Taking into account the very large number and size of the process execution logs, process analysis for finding the most frequent paths of executions will require effective algorithms as well.

The work in this paper is an extension of the state of the art process mining framework developed by Greco, et. al., from University of Calabria, Italy [1]. To the best of our knowledge, this work is the first targeting the mining of graphs with constraints imposed by the structures of workflow schemes and instances. In this framework, the workflow execution logs are analyzed contextually and comparatively on the basis of the process map to find frequent patterns of activities, thus discovering useful knowledge [1]. They have shown that their algorithm, based on novel mining techniques, outperforms traditional data mining algorithms, even though they are suitably reengineered to work with workflow instances. Other interesting mining approach have been proposed for mining frequent trees in a forest and are active research subject [10].

The meaning of the terms process mining and workflow mining is often used in contradictory ways. In this paper, process mining refers to the analysis of execution logs to find frequent patterns and paths of executions.

1.2 Contribution

By providing a framework enabling the mining of BPEL processes by state of the art graph mining algorithm, we are able to deliver highly valuable information to process designers for process improvement. The contribution of this paper is providing a mapping of BPEL process definition and process instance execution logs to a graph representation where a fast mining algorithm [1] can then be employed to find the most frequent patterns and paths of execution. We have built a prototype implementation of our solution to test it in real life situations where all the execution logs come from a running BPEL engine. The software implemented for this work can easily be extended to handle other workflow description languages like XPDL and be integrated to other production environments utilizing process engines.

2 Workflow Abstract Model

The algorithm we extend in our work [1] is based on a control flow graph model. The model named as *Workflow Abstract Model* (WAM) does not incorporate compensation and assumes non iterative executions. This model aims at providing a rigorous framework on top of which the mining algorithm is developed.

A WAM graph is a tuple composed of a finite set of activities, an acyclic relation of precedence among activities, a start activity and a set of final activities. Each activity is assigned one of 3 natural number values, IN, OUTmin, OUTmax referring to the number of incoming links, the minimum number of outgoing links and maximum number of outgoing links respectively. Activities are classified in two categories, *and-join* that can be executed only after all its predecessors are completed and *or-join* that can be executed as soon as one predecessor is completed. Arcs are labeled in three ways depending whether the source node is a full fork, a deterministic fork or an exclusive fork. Fig. 1.b shows the graph representation in the WAM of the BPEL process described in Fig. 1.a.

W-find, the first algorithm proposed in [1] relies on the notion of elementary weak pattern, pattern of activities that are enforced to be executed with some activity [1]. An elementary week pattern or ew-pattern, is the graph ws-closure ($<\{a\},\{\}>$). Where a ws-closure is defined as a graph where every and-join node must contains all his parents and every node that is a deterministic fork must contain all it's or-join childrens.

The initialization phase constructs the set of elementary weak patterns and the set of frequent arcs from the instances log. Each process instance log is represented as a WAM graph. The algorithm then iterates through all frequent elementary weak patterns and tries to add frequent arcs and frequents elementary weak patterns to each elementary weak pattern of the initial set.

By transforming the BPEL process description and the BPEL logs according to the workflow abstract model, we are able to use the w-find algorithm on bpel described processes. The BPEL process description file is used to derive the WAM graph of the process from which the ew-patterns are generated. The process instance logs are also transformed into WAM graphs before being sent to the algorithm input.

3   BPEL Mapping to Workflow Abstract Model

Only a subset of the BPEL elements is represented in the WAM model. There is no need to represent structured elements like flows, scope or while since the semantic of their construct can be expressed by the link type and node type of the WAM. This has two advantages, first to reduce the number of operations and data size for the algorithm and secondly to make the needed log information smaller and inter-operable with log data gathered by capturing message exchanges on the network. Fig. 1.b shows the mapping of the BPEL process described on Table. 1.a to the WAM model.

Due to its origin in two different workflow language, BPEL inherit a block structure process representation from XLANG and a graph oriented representation from WSFL. The mapping of BPEL processes to the abstract workflow schema proposed in [1] is not a trivial task. The workflow abstract model is a Directed Acyclic Graph (DAG) and the algorithm input data structure consists of two matrixes for the workflow schema: the matrix of arcs or the adjacency matrix, defining the precedence relation between nodes and the matrix of nodes

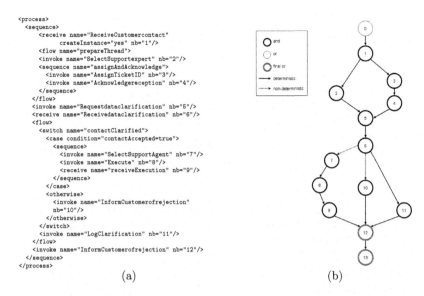

```
<process>
  <sequence>
    <receive name="ReceiveCustomercontact"
             createInstance="yes" nb="1"/>
    <flow name="prepareThread">
    <invoke name="SelectSupportexpert" nb="2"/>
    <sequence name="assignAndAcknowledge">
      <invoke name="AssignTicketID" nb="3"/>
      <invoke name="Acknowledgereception" nb="4"/>
    </sequence>
    </flow>
    <invoke name="Requestdataclarification" nb="5"/>
    <receive name="Receivedataclarification" nb="6"/>
    <flow>
      <switch name="contactClarified">
        <case condition="contactAccepted=true">
          <sequence>
            <invoke name="SelectSupportAgent" nb="7"/>
            <invoke name="Execute" nb="8"/>
            <receive name="receiveExecution" nb="9"/>
          </sequence>
        </case>
        <otherwise>
          <invoke name="InformCustomerofrejection"
                  nb="10"/>
        </otherwise>
      </switch>
      <invoke name="LogClarification" nb="11"/>
    </flow>
    <invoke name="InformCustomerofrejection" nb="12"/>
  </sequence>
</process>
```

(a)   (b)

Fig. 1. (a) Excerpt from the example process described in BPEL. (b) Example of BPEL to WAM mapping.

which contains the nodes of the workflow abstract model. Each Instance log is also represented as a graph with those two data structures. The matrix of nodes is constructed by extracting the nodes that constitute a basic activity. BPEL assign, invoke, receive, reply, empty, terminate, onAlarm, onEvent and while are represented as nodes in the WAM graph. The precedence relationships between nodes are discovered by a method illustrated in Fig. 2.

The notion of precedence between nodes is found with a recursive algorithm determining the predecessors and the type of the relation for a given node. It consists of two steps, the first determining the predecessors from the block structure of BPEL the second determining the predecessors from the directed graph structure. An example of the predecessors determination for the block structure is shown in Figure 2.

Artificial Start and End. Without modifying the semantic of the process, an artificial start and end node are added to the graph at the end of the mapping phase. In BPEL, multiple start activities are allowed to express the possibility that any one of a set of required inbound messages can create the process instance because the order in which these messages arrive cannot be predicted [11]. The start activities that haven't been selected as the one creating the instance will still wait for incoming messages and will be executed in the already created process instance. If one is interested to express the fact that a process can be started by only one of a set of activities prohibiting the further execution of other concurrent start activities, the BPEL pick construct can be used. The artificial start activity will have different links depending on the type of start activity and those start activities may be of different type if they are concurrent receive

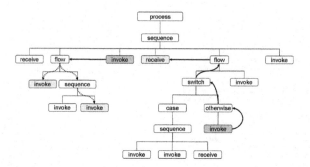

Fig. 2. Example of adjency matrix construction. In light gray the predecessor of the nodes in dark gray. The solid arrows represent the find preceding method while the dashed arrows the find preceding in.

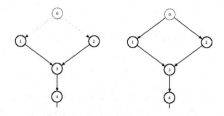

Fig. 3. Multiple starts: pick and receive. Left figure represent a pick construct while the figure on the right represent a receive construct.

activity or message event of a pick activity. This is illustrated in Fig. 3. The end activities must also be taken care of since not all BPEL end activities may need to be executed in a process where switch constructs appears. Thus deciding if the type of the link between the end activities and the artificially added end activity will depends on the presence of choices in the parent activities of the treated end activity.

Loop Handling. The while element is an interesting construct since it is an important factor for the process variability. The mining of loops can be classified into four different meaningful categories.

- One could be interested by the graphical perspective only and look at the most executed path followed in the loop body independently of the number of iteration.
- Another way to look at loops would be to consider only the path generated at the end of the loop execution.
- The third and fourth way to consider loops is an extension of the two identified case where loops are first differentiated by the number of iteration and in a second time by discriminating either by the frequent paths or the graphical perspective.

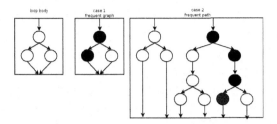

Fig. 4. Two basic loops semantic

Fig. 4 illustrates the difference between graph and path generation perspectives.

We support the first case, defining the while constructs as node of the main process graph and considering each loops iteration as instances of a process defined by the loop body. We are interested by the graphical perspective and mine the process defined by the loop body with the instances being the loop iteration. In the near future, we will implement the second aspect of loops where the path generated most frequently in the overall loop execution is of interest.

In our implementation, we are only interested by the graphical representation of loops and thus represent the while, onAlarm and onEvent inside an event handler as a node in the WAM graph. If this node is frequent, the loop body is mined for frequent graphical paths. For better analysis, the frequent loop body is substituted to the loop body in the final graph result. Although not presented, the event handling is implemented the same way as loops. In this case, events are treated as loop iteration.

Error and Compensation Handling. Error and compensation handling add a lot of variability to the process. In our mapping, they are handled by adding the possible arcs and node they may generate to the WAM. Each BPEL element represented in the WAM graph may generate an error and thus has an outgoing link to the error handler or the process termination. The result is that the solid links in the WAM graph disappear. Indeed the next step of an activity can be either the activity defined by the control flow or the error handling activity. Compensation handler are added to the WAM graph as a possible continuation of the scope or activity they are associated with.

3.1 Eliminating Elementary Weak Patterns

Optimization can be done by reducing the number of weak pattern the algorithm generates in the initialization phase. The number of ew-patterns can be pruned, taking into account the restriction imposed by the BPEL process structure. Not all BPEL constraint can be made explicitly in the WAM. Pruning the not allowed to happen elementary weak patterns reduce the algorithm computation and data input size. In the example of activity precedence being described by BPEL links. Advantage can be taken by restricting the ew-patterns to the set of all possible combination of the allowed transition and join condition. See Figure 5.

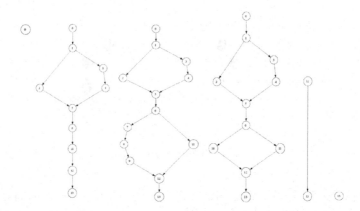

Fig. 5. EW-patterns generated during the initialization phase of the algorithm applied to mining the process shown in Fig. 1.b It is clear that ew-pattern 2 (0,1,2—3,4,5,6,11,12,13) can be removed from the set of ew-patterns since it is not allowed to happen by the BPEL process description that states that node 11 must appear in the process

3.2 Experiments

We have tested the algorithm against processes running on a BPEL 1.1 compliant process engine. ActiveBPEL process engine is a powerful open-source BPEL engine [8]. It provides SOAP API to access the engine functions and a graphical administrative web front-end enabling the visualization of process instances.

The input for the algorithm, the BPEL process description and the execution logs, are gathered through ActiveBPEL SOAP API. For mining the process deployed in the ActiveBPEL engine, the logs produced by the engine had to be mapped to a suitable format. We convert the ActiveBPEL logs using the same

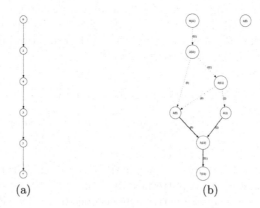

(a)   (b)

Fig. 6. Experiment Results. (a) Executed path for support 9/11. (b) Annotated process schema.

steps as for the transformation of BPEL process definition into WAM graphs. The implementation of a common XML log format is discussed in section 4.1.

We successfully applied the algorithm to the loan approval process [9] to find the most frequent patterns and paths of execution. Fig. 6b shows the most executed path for a minimum support of 9/11, whereas Fig. 6a shows the annotated WAM graph after the mining. In these figures each circle denotes an activity in the process, and the number inside the circle denotes the activity number. Each number within the parenthesis inside each circle in Fig. 6b corresponds to the number of executions of the given arcs and nodes. Out of 11 executions of the process 9 went through the approver activity (activity #3).

4   Conclusion

We strongly believe that companies will need efficient algorithms to extract knowledge from logged execution of BPEL processes. With BPEL being more and more widely adopted and accepted as the standard for web service orchestration, companies will amass huge sets of data logs. Extremely valuable information for analyzing and redesigning processes can be extracted from data logs. Gathering this information in an efficient way will be an issue for big systems dealing with thousands of instance logs. In this paper we extend a robust and efficient workflow mining algorithm to support the mining of BPEL processes and demonstrate preliminary experimental results.

4.1   Further Work

Multiple interacting process mining is our ultimate goal. Ongoing work extends our framework to support the mining of frequent patterns of execution between multiple interacting BPEL processes. Interacting BPEL processes can be aggregated into more general process definition. The goal of mining frequent patterns and path across interacting BPEL processes is to find unexpected relations between independent processes for optimizing the overall system.

In the near future, we intend to test and benchmark our solution on large data sets. We also plan to support the XML workflow log format proposed in [4]. Having a standard log format would enable easier integration of the framework with different BPEL engines for which a translation to this format is already available.

Another interesting direction would be to investigate the possibility to get the algorithm data directly from the message exchange between processes instead of getting the logs from BPEL engines. This would have the advantage of having a BPEL engine agnostic algorithm without having to write adapters to convert instance logs. But the lack of internal BPEL Information only available in the engine log will be a major issue.

Acknowledgments

We thank the authors of Mining and Reasoning on workflows [1] who where kind enough to share their source code.

References

1. Gianluigi Greco, Antonella guzzo, Giuseppe Manco, Domenico Sacca: Mining and Reasoning on Worflows. IEEE Transcation on knowledge and data engineering, vol. 17, no. 4. (April 2005)
2. Karl Aberer: Distributed Information Systems. LSIR EPFL. (2004)
3. Joachim Herbst, Dimitris Karagiannis: Workflow mining with InWoLvE. Daimler-Chrysler, University of Vienna. Computers in Industry archive Volume 53 , Issue 3. (April 2004) 245 - 264
4. W.MP. van der Aalst, B.F. van Dongen, J.Herbst, L.Maruster, G. Schimm, and A.J.M.M. Weijters: Workflow Mining: A survey of Issues ans Approaches. Eindhoven University of Technology, DaimlerChrysler, OFFIS. (2002)
5. Markus Hammori, Joachim Herbst and Niko Kleiner: Interactive Workflow Mining. DaimlerChrysler, University of Ulm. LNCS Volume 3080/2004. (June 2004) 211 - 226
6. A.K. Alves de Medeiros, A.J.M.M. Weijters and W.M.P. van der Aalst: Using Genetic Algorithms to Mine Process Models: Representation, Operators and Results. Eindhoven University of Technology. (2004)
7. Schahram Dustdar, Robert Gombotz and Karim Baina: Web Services Interaction Mining. Technical University of Vienna. (September 2004)
8. ActiveBPEL. ActiveEndpoints,. http://www.activebpel.org/.
9. Loan Approval Demo. ActiveBpel.
   http://www.activebpel.org/docs/samples/loan_approval/doc/index.html.
10. Mohammed J. Zaki: Efficiently Mining Frequent Trees in a Forest. Rensselaer Polytechnic Institute. (2002)
11. Business process execution language for Web Services specification V1.1. OASIS specification. (5 May 2003)

CONFIOUS[*]: Managing the Electronic Submission and Reviewing Process of Scientific Conferences

Manos Papagelis[1,2], Dimitris Plexousakis[1,2], and Panagiotis N. Nikolaou[2]

[1] Institute of Computer Science, FORTH, Heraklion, Greece
papaggel@ics.forth.gr
[2] Computer Science Department, University of Crete, Heraklion, Greece
pnikol@csd.uoc.gr

Abstract. Most scientific communities have recently established policies and mechanisms to put into practice electronic conference management, mainly by exploiting the Internet as the communication and cooperation infrastructure. Their foremost objective is to reduce the operational and communication costs but to maintain high quality reviewing and the fairness of the evaluation process. Interestingly, we report on experience gained by an implemented system named Confious. Confious [8] is a state-of-the-art management system that combines modern design, sophisticated algorithms and a powerful engine to help the program committee (PC) Chair to effortlessly accomplish a number of complicated tasks and carry out the necessary activities to produce the proceedings of a scientific conference. We are principally interested in (a) describing the workflow dynamics of a real-world scientific process, (b) identifying the main concerns of the person in charge of the conference organization, (c) providing mechanisms that enable the efficient management and monitoring of the overall coordination process.

1 Introduction

In the last few years, the need of systems for collaboration support has expanded, leading to their growing application in organizational, communication, and cooperation processes. At the same time, the World-Wide Web (WWW), by now the most popular service over the Internet, evolves rapidly, from a simple, read-only data sharing system, as it was a few years ago, to a universal, distributed platform for information exchange. Furthermore, the WWW has recently been perceived as an attractive base suitable to support extensive online cooperative work. Therefore, an interest arises for researchers to study technical, business and social impacts of collaboration systems and for engineers to put into practice functional implementations of sophisticated services that operate worldwide and employ distributed data, servers, and end-users [3]. However, usually an integration of the most recent technology with existing organizational practices remains challenging.

---

[*] Confious comes up as the combination of the words *Conference and Nous*, where *Nous* is the Greek word for Mind. Therefore, Confious may be interpreted as the Conference Mind.

M. Kitsuregawa et al. (Eds.): WISE 2005, LNCS 3806, pp. 711–720, 2005.
© Springer-Verlag Berlin Heidelberg 2005

In this paper, we attempt to integrate two themes of practice and research: the functional and organizational issues with the algorithmic and implementation aspects of building online collaboration systems. We do so by specifying and implementing a system that exploits the Internet infrastructure as the cooperation medium to support the process of submission and evaluation of scientific documents. More precisely, we identify the activities that typically have to be performed by a number of people widely distributed all over the world in order to submit, select, and prepare the set of papers to be published in the proceedings of a conference [4].

The foremost motivation of our work is based on the observation that most scientific communities and organizations are looking for establishing policies and mechanisms to put into practice electronic conference management [2, 6]. Their main objective is to minimize the organizational efforts but maintain high the quality of accepted papers and the fairness of the selection process. This process commonly involves a number of activities and user roles and presents interesting coordination issues to study. In view of the fact that "coordination is the management of dependencies" [1], the coordination of a conference may well be regarded as the management of the dependencies that arise during the submission and reviewing process. These processes are sufficiently familiar to most scientists, who normally participate to conferences as authors, PC members, or PC chairs.

Interestingly, we report on experience gained by the development of a real-world system named *Confious*. *Confious* [8] is a state-of-the-art management system that combines modern design, sophisticated algorithms and a powerful engine to help a program committee chair to effortlessly accomplish a number of complicated tasks and carry out the necessary activities to produce the proceedings of a scientific conference. In our study we are primarily interested in:

- Describing the workflow dynamics of an essential scientific process
- Identifying the main concerns of the PC chair during the conference
- Providing mechanisms that enable the efficient management of the process

Confious may well be regarded as an example of a general class of services, in which either some from a set of documents need to be picked up according to an evaluation process or in which a composite document has to be produced as the result of a workflow of activities enacted by several people.

2   Dynamics of a Workflow System

Confious is in principle a document management and evaluation system, in which a number of user roles interact to carry out a scientific process by enacting a number of complicated tasks. Usually, these systems are referred to as workflow management systems. In this section, we try to identify the dynamics of a workflow system in Confious by defining *user roles* and *chronological dependencies*.

2.1   User Roles

There are four user roles that interact in Confious, each of which is described below.

- Program Committee Chair (or PC Chair), which is in charge of the enactment, coordination and monitoring of the necessary tasks.

- Senior Program Committee Member (or Meta-Reviewer), which supervises the reviewing process and makes recommendations for the final decision.
- Regular Program Committee Member (or Reviewer), which evaluates the overall quality of a paper that usually falls in his or her area of expertise.
- Contact Person (or Author), which submits documents of recent research.

2.2 Chronological Dependencies

In order to coordinate the overall process we have identified chronological dependencies that may allow or forbid the execution of specific tasks at a particular moment. We do so by defining independent, self-described chronological phases that determine the tasks and actions that are acceptable in particular time fragments. Even if, in general, these phases occur in a chronological order, they may overlap, thus allowing specific tasks to be executed in parallel. Mind that some phases in Confious are optional and may be omitted. The whole process may as well be separated in four meta-periods; *setup, submission, reviewing* and *publishing* periods. Fig. 1 illustrates the chronological dependencies of these phases in form of a Gantt Graph, where the horizontal axe is a time scale. Phases are better described below.

Setup Phase: The PC Chair provides functional information about the conference.

Invitation Phase: The PC Chair sends invitation letters to reviewers and meta-reviewers asking them whether they are willing to participate in the reviewing phase.

Abstract Submission Phase: Authors register to the system and submit abstracts and other useful information of their contribution.

Bidding Phase: Reviewers are asked to read the submitted abstracts and bid for papers that would prefer to review.

Full Paper Submission Phase: Authors submit a full paper of their contribution.

Assignment Phase: The PC Chair assigns papers to reviewers either automatically or manually taking into account specific constraints.

Reviewing Phase: Reviewers evaluate the quality of the papers assigned to them.

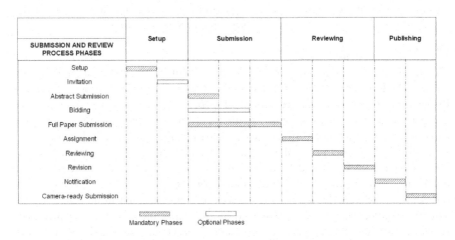

Fig. 1. Chronological dependencies of the phases that are defined in Confious

Revision Phase: The PC Chair, meta-reviewers and reviewers participate in a virtual PC meeting in order to decide on the set of papers to be accepted.

Notification Phase: The PC Chair communicates the final decision to authors.

Camera-ready Submission Phase: Authors of accepted papers submit a camera-ready copy of their contribution.

3   Identifying the PC Chair's Main Concerns

In this section, we try to identify the main concerns of the PC chair during the submission and reviewing process and subsequently to describe specific techniques and design policies we have followed to facilitate their efficient accomplishment. These concerns are methodically discussed in the following paragraphs.

3.1   Efficient Identification of Potential Conflicts of Interest

One of the main concerns of the PC Chair is to identify members of the program committee that may have a conflict of interest in reviewing a specific paper. Such occasions may arise in several ways, the most popular of which are that:

    a.   Scientists usually submit papers to a conference that they serve as reviewers.

    b.   PC members are usually associated with authors of submitted papers, either because they are occupied in the same institute or project or because they have co-authored an article in the past.

Even if both cases are officially authorized, they may offend the confidentiality of the review process and seriously affect the conference's overall reputation. In Confious, we have tried to efficiently identify and manage potential conflicts of interests that may exist in the review process between reviewers and papers. Additionally to the intentional definition of conflicts by users, we have designed mechanisms that recommend potential conflicts according to *"same institute appointment"* or *"previous co-authorship appointment"* techniques.

Same Institute Appointment

This technique tries to identify PC members and authors of submitted papers that are occupied in the same institute. Consequently, a potential conflict of interest may arise between a PC member and a submitted paper. The method is based on string comparison of their email accounts. Actually, a gradual string matching algorithm is applied that compares the different parts of the email accounts. The formula may as well consider the level of accuracy to be applied. In this way, the expected conflicts may be narrowed or broadened according to the precision that is required in each conference. For example, in an international conference, it may be of interest to find out conflicts between reviewers and authors that are occupied in the same institute. This information is more often indicated by the same suffix in their email accounts. However, such conflicts may be of less interest in the case of a national conference. The technique is better illustrated in Fig. 2.

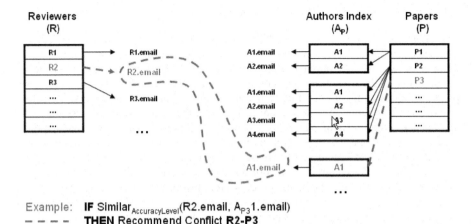

Example: **IF** Similar$_{AccuracyLevel}$(R2.email, A$_{P3}$1.email)
- - - -   **THEN** Recommend Conflict **R2-P3**

Fig. 2. Recommendations of Conflicts based on "Same Institute Appointment"

Previous Co-authorship Appointment

This technique tries to identify pairs of PC members and authors of submitted papers that have co-authored one or more papers in the past. Consequently, a potential conflict may arise between a PC member and a submitted paper. The dataset employed for this identification purpose comes from a co-authorship index, as it has been compiled by DBLP Library [7]. Actually, for each conference only a small part of the DBLP co-authorship index is required. Subsequently, we scan the set of papers authors and the set of reviewers' co-authors to identify matches that define potential conflicts. Matches are based on string comparison of their first and last names. The technique is better illustrated in Fig. 3.

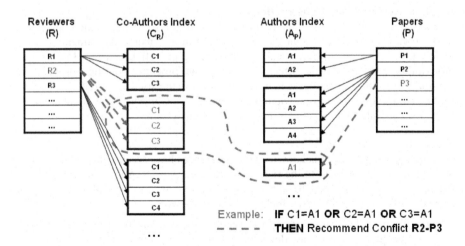

Example: **IF** C1=A1 **OR** C2=A1 **OR** C3=A1
- - - -   **THEN** Recommend Conflict **R2-P3**

Fig. 3. Recommendations of Conflicts based on "Previous Co-authorship"

3.2   Reliable Assignment of Papers to Reviewers

The peer review process requires that every paper be independently reviewed by a number of reviewers. However, in the last years the number of submissions and the number of reviewers of popular conferences has evidently increased [2]. Considering the diversity of the reviewers' research interests and the range of topics that submitted papers cover is almost impossible to manually assign papers to reviewers. Therefore, one of the most agonizing and critical tasks that a PC Chair needs to carry out is the appropriate assignment of papers to reviewers. Actually, PC members are regularly pleased to review papers that match their interests, so the correct assignment may as well affect the overall quality of the reviews delivered.

In Confious, PC Chair has the option to assign papers either automatically or manually. The most advantageous process includes an automatic assignment by the system followed by manual adjustment of assignments by the PC chair. The automatic assignment algorithm takes into account the following constraints:

- *Matches between paper topics and reviewer interests*: Reviewer interests are matched to paper topics so as to improve the assignment precision.
- *Bids of reviewers to specific papers*: During the bidding phase, reviewers may express their *high, neutral* or *low* interest to be assigned specific papers and therefore to favor their chances to review or avoid them.
- *Conflicts of interest between PC members and papers*: Conflicts of interest prohibit the assignment of specific papers to specific reviewers.
- *Workload Balance*: Papers need to be normally distributed between reviewers.

3.3   High Quality of the Reviews Communicated to Authors

In this paragraph, we present two features that are enabled in Confious to make the reviewing process flexible and to help maintain the quality of the reviews high.

Dynamic Review Form Construction

One of the main drawbacks of the majority of electronic software for the management of the reviewing process is that they do not permit a dynamic customization of the review form. As a result, they usually employ static predefined forms. However, this inflexibility may negatively affect the evaluation process. Confious provides the possibility to either construct a new review form or customize a predefined review form. This is one of the most advantageous features of Confious, as it is not supported by almost any other known conference management system.

Hierarchical Reviewing

Organizing committees of acknowledged conferences have recently employed a meta-review process, additional to the regular review process, to ensure that the quality of the reviews communicated to authors is as decent as possible. Meta-reviews are carried out by meta-reviewers, which role is usually twofold:

a.   To provide a summary of the regular reviews and the rational behind the acceptance or rejection decision by pointing out comments of reviewers.

b.   To monitor the reviewing process, identify problematic reviews, such as incomplete and weakly argued ones, and ask from reviewers to update them.

Therefore, Confious, by enabling a hierarchical reviewing process, helps PC chairs to obtain better control over the quality of the reviews communicated to the authors, by boosting part of their overall responsibility to meta-reviewers. This is certainly beneficial to authors that receive more constructive comments and may also affect the conference's overall reputation.

3.4 Making Correct Decisions Efficiently

One of the most challenging, as well as time-consuming tasks that the PC chair is in charge of is to decide on the sets of papers that are going to be accepted and the set of papers that are going to be rejected. Actually, it is hard to reduce the results of several reviews into a single meaningful score because when papers are ordered numerically, there may often be some high ranked papers that are rejected, and some low ranked papers that end up being accepted [5]. Moreover, the decisions are made even more efficiently if papers with comparable evaluations are grouped together and when conflicted evaluations are identified as early as possible.

In Confious, the papers are first classified in five meaningful classes and then the papers of each class are ordered according to the average score of their several individual overall evaluations. Due to the classification, a much more meaningful ordering occurs that evidently facilitates the decision making.

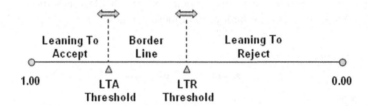

Fig. 4. LTA-threshold and LTR-threshold are employed to classify papers

To define these classes we employ two thresholds; the LTA-threshold and the LTR-threshold, which are better illustrated in Fig. 4. The former defines the lower bound over of which an evaluation is considered positive, while the latter defines the upper bound below of which an evaluation is considered negative. Both thresholds may be adjusted by the PC chair to meet specific requirements. Therefore, the following classes may be defined:

- *Leaning to Accept*: The reviews are either over the LTA-threshold or below the LTA-threshold but over the LTR-threshold, and their normalized average score is over the LTA-threshold, which indicates a "leaning to accept" paper.
- *Border Line*: The reviews are either over the LTA-threshold or below the LTA-threshold but over the LTR-threshold, and their normalized average score is between the LTA-threshold and the LTR-threshold, which indicates a "border line" paper. Some of these papers are going to be accepted.
- *Leaning to Reject*: The reviews are either below the LTR-threshold or over the LTR-threshold but below the LTA-threshold, and their normalized

average score is below the LTR-threshold, which indicates a "leaning to reject" paper.

- *Conflicted Reviews*: There is at least one review over the LTA-threshold and at least one review below the LTR-threshold, which indicates that there is probably a conflict in the reviewers' evaluation and therefore further investigation is required.
- Incomplete Reviews: There are missing reviews for this paper.

4 System Overview

Confious is a web information system that is based on the client-server model, where many clients may connect to and interact with the server. On the server side it follows the *3-tier* architecture which distinguishes between *presentation*, *business* and *data* logic layers. Each logic layer has been implemented around a number of self-determining engines so as to smooth the development process and to facilitate its future extension. Each engine is consisted of a number of modules, which are responsible for the execution of specific tasks. Our main objective is to design an as much as possible extensible architecture that may push the complete functionality and complexity of specific tasks to independent, re-usable, easily invoked, effortlessly developed and efficiently executed components. Fig. 5 illustrates this architecture, while a brief description follows for each of these engines.

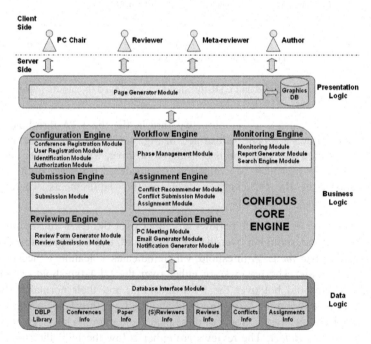

Fig. 5. Modular 3-Tier Architecture of Confious

Configuration Engine: It consists of four modules; one that handles conference details, one that enables user profiling, one for user and conference identification and one for secure login procedure.

Submission Engine: It consists of one module that handles the abstract, full and camera-ready paper submissions. It also encapsulates the functionality of an upload manager to handle the submitted files.

Assignment Engine: It consists of three modules; one that handles the assignment of papers to reviewers, one for defining explicit conflicts and one that handles automatic recommendation of potential conflicts.

Reviewing Engine: It consists of two modules; one that enables the dynamic construction of the review form and one that enables the submission of reviews.

Workflow Engine: It consists of one module that coordinates the multiple dependencies throughout the submission and reviewing process.

Communication Engine: It consists of three modules; one that enables the virtual PC meeting, one that handles the email based communication, and one that enables the customization, compilation and delivery of the notification letters to authors.

Monitoring Engine: It consists of three modules; one that enables monitoring functionality, one that creates printable reports on useful statistics, and one that enables the access of specific papers according to predefined criteria or keywords.

Other Modules: There also exist two self-determining modules; one that is responsible for the compilation and delivery of the dynamic web pages and one that enables the straightforward portability of the system to another DBMS.

5 Conclusions

In order to support scientific committees to efficiently manage the submission and evaluation process of a conference, we have designed and implemented *Confious*, a state-of-the-art conference management system. Confious provides mechanisms for efficient management of scientific data, intelligent identification and analysis of constraints during the reviewing process, enhanced monitoring and better communication. While loosely related to more conventional business workflows, the actual scientific workflow poses a quite different set of challenges due to the special needs for large-scale distributed data collection and evaluation. We tried to specify Confious through dynamics of a workflow management system, to identify the PC Chair's responsibilities and to facilitate their qualitative accomplishment during the coordination process. In order to address portability, reliability and scalability issues, a modular architecture approach has been adopted keeping the functionality independent of the repository used. We are confident that the rational and algorithmic ground on which Confious has been designed and developed will catch the attention of the interested reader and will exert a pull on conference organizers and scientific committees to consider Confious for their future conferences.

References

1. Malone T. and Crowstone K.: The Interdisciplinary Study of Coordination. ACM Computer Surveys, 26(1):87-119, 1994.
2. Rethinking the Conference Reviewing Process. SIGMOD 2004 Panel

3. Ciancarini P., Rossi D., and Vitali F.: A case study in designing a document-centric coordination application over the Internet. In D. Clarke an A. Dix and F. Dix, editors, Proc. Workshop on the Active Web, pages 41–56, Jan 1999.
4. Mathews G. and Jacobs B.: Electronic Management of the Peer Review Process. Computer Networks and ISDN Systems, 28(7-11):1523, Nov. 1996.
5. Nierstrasz O.: Identify the Champion, Pattern Languages of Program Design. N. Harrison, B. Foote, H. Rohnert (Ed.), Addison-Wesley, vol. 4, 2000
6. Snodgrass R.: Summary of Conference Management Software.
   http://www.acm.org/sigs/sgb/summary.html
7. http://www.informatik.uni-trier.de/~ley/db/
8. http://www.confious.com

Tool Support for Model-Driven Development of Web Applications[1]

Jaime Gómez, Alejandro Bia, and Antonio Parraga

Web Engineering Research Group,
Departamento de Lenguajes y Sistemas Informáticos,
University of Alicante,
03690 - Alicante
{gomez, abia, aparraga}dlsi.ua.es

Abstract. This paper describes the engineering foundations of VisualWADE, a CASE tool to automate the production of Web applications. VisualWADE follows a model-driven approach focusing on requirements analysis, high level design, and rapid prototyping. In this way, an application evolves smoothly from the first prototype to the final product, and its maintenance is a natural consequence of development. The paper also discusses the lessons learned in the development of the tool and its application to several case studies in the industrial context.

1 Introduction

The rapid evolution of Internet in general and of the WWW in particular has promoted in recent years intensive research in the field of conceptual modeling of Web applications. This fact has induced a new research trend within Software Engineering known as Web Engineering. In this context, different methods, languages, tools and design patterns for web modeling have been proposed. Some of the most relevant studied so far are HDM [4], WebML[2], OOHDM [7], UWE [10], ADM [1], and OO-H [6]. These methods are centered mainly in the definition of navigational and presentational aspects relative to the semantic of models to capture relevant properties of web environments. However, few are the proposals that have tried to apply their methods to solve complex real cases to verify the effectiveness of their modeling approach. Much lesser have been the attempts (successful or not) of building specific purpose tools for Web Engineering. We can mention WebRatio [9] developed at the Politecnico di Milano (Italy) under the technical direction of Prof. Piero Fraternali, or ArgoUWE [11] developed at the Luwdig Maximilians University of Munich (Germany) under the technical direction of Dr. Nora Koch.

This paper describes the engineering foundations of VisualWADE, a CASE tool for the design and automatic production of Web applications based on the OO-H method developed at the University of Alicante. The underlying idea behind VisualWADE consists of an appropriate combination of simple concepts (modeling

---

[1] This article has been supported by the MEC through the METASIGN project, reference number: TIN2004-00779.

M. Kitsuregawa et al. (Eds.): WISE 2005, LNCS 3806, pp. 721–730, 2005.

elements), that allow the designer to model and automatically generate any type of web-based system, from a web-portal or company intranet to a secure web site for electronic commerce. VisualWADE exploits a group of very well-known concepts to capture the complexity of real web applications. The underlying method, OO-H (object oriented hypermedia), provides specific modeling elements to represent navigation maps based on a notation compatible with UML. The captured specification is compiled making use of model-based code generation techniques, and as a result, it produces a web application with a default user interface. This user interface can be refined within the environment to obtain the final appearance of the web application with the consequent increment of development productivity. The paper is organized as follows: section 2 provides a brief introduction to the OO-H method to familiarize the reader with the modeling notation. Section 3 describes the basic aspects of modeling organized according to three different perspectives through which a web application is modeled with VisualWADE (structure, navigation and presentation). A running example (web-based mail system) is used to describe the tool support. Section 4 describes the lessons learned in the application of VisualWADE in the development of real web engineering projects on various application domains (tax management, Internet banking, digital signatures). Finally, the paper ends with some conclusions, based on our experience, about the evolution and the future of web engineering methods, techniques and tools.

2   A Brief Introduction to the OO-H Method

The OO-H method (object oriented hypermedia) is a generic method based on the object oriented paradigm that provides a specific notation and semantics for the development of web based applications. OO-H defines a set of diagrams, techniques and tools that altogether comprise a complete approach for the modeling of web application. The method includes: a design process, a navigational access diagram (NAD), an abstract presentation diagram (APD) and finally, a CASE tool that supports and automates the development process. With OO-H, a traditional business application can be "converted" to a web-compliant application by adding two new views (diagrams) that complement the structure (class diagram) and behavior views (interaction and state transition diagrams). The first of them, the NAD, is used to specify a navigation view. The second, the APD, captures concepts related to the final-interface presentation details. The NAD enriches a domain model with navigation and interaction characteristics. It also defines constraints about navigation and information which should be showed to the web user. For this purpose, OO-H uses the object constraint language OCL [8]). In this way, a precise navigation diagram can be obtained. On the other hand, the APD contains the definition of abstract pages (pages that are not attached to any specific web language) based on a set of XML templates that capture the relevant presentational properties of the web interface under construction. OO-H is a well-recognized Web design method in the field of Web Engineering an several publications [5,6] provide detailed information about it. Due to fact that the focus of this paper is to describe the OO-H tool (called VisualWADE), interested readers are redirected to the references commented above. In the next section, we describe the basic aspects to model a web application with

VisualWADE. A running example focused on a web-based mail system is used to introduce the relevant concepts about the method.

3   VisualWADE: Basic Aspects

Domain Modeling

The starting point to approach the design of a web application is the domain model represented with a class diagram (see Figure 1).

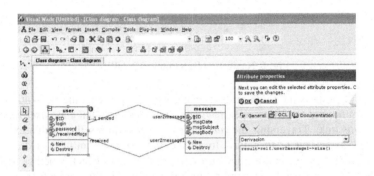

Fig. 1. A class diagram in VisualWADE

The notation of this diagram is based on UML which makes it quite intuitive for a designer familiarized with object oriented analysis and design. The application helps the designer throughout the whole edition process by means of a simple, but yet powerful and intuitive graphical interface. The creation of classes, attributes and relationships is carried out with simple mouse actions. The availability within the environment of zoom buttons and global views help the organization and management of complex diagrams comprised of several classes. In Figure 1, a class diagram corresponding to the web-based mail system can be observed. In this case, the *user* class and the *message* class are specified and between them two associations to capture the information corresponding to the messages *sent* and *received* by the user. Derived attributes can also be specified within the class diagram. Attributes stereotyped as *"derived"* has an associated OCL formula that specifies how the value of the attribute is obtained. This is the case of the attribute *receivedMsgs* of the *user* class, whose value is obtained by navigating through the *user2message1* role and calculating the number of instances of the *message* class (*size()* function). Obviously, we have implemented within the environment an OCL compiler that allows the syntactic and semantic validation of the OCL formulas.

Navigation Modeling

A navigation view shows the way in which attributes and services provided by the classes defined in the domain model are accessed. In Figure 2 a partial view of the NAD diagram for a web user is shown.

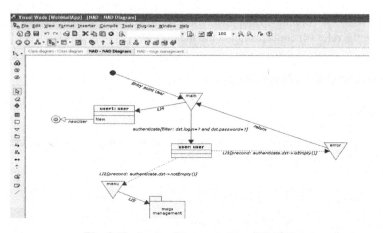

Fig. 2. Navigation Diagram in VisualWADE

The entry point is the *main* abstract page, which represents the navigation starting node. From *main* the web user can navigate to the navigational class *user* through the *authenticate* link. Traversing the *authenticate* link requires the evaluation of filter (expressed as an OCL formula). In this case, the user must provide the *login* information (*dst.login*) and a *password* (*dst.password*) to check whether he/she is a valid user for the system. Depending on the success of this validation process the preconditions associated to links *LI2* and *LI3* will determine which of these links will be activated and therefore the destination abstract page (*menu* or *error*) to continue the navigation process. The *notEmpty()* and *isEmpty()* OCL functions provide the necessary information to know if a user is or not registered in the system. Continuing with the description of this navigation diagram, from the *main* abstract page and through the *LI4* link the *newUser* service of the navigational class *user* is accessed. This modeling situation allow a web user to activate the service *newUser* to register new users into the system.. Finally, from the *menu* abstract page the navigation continues to the navigational target *message management* while with the *error* abstract page it returns to the *main* starting page. In Figure 2, the toolbar on the left contains the modeling elements that can be inserted in a NAD. By mouse selections, the internal properties of each element can be edited. For example, a link connects an origin element with a destination element. Link properties allow to specify whether the information of the origin element must be shown in the same page that the information of the destination element or not. The visual environment also includes very useful functions such as copy/paste, do/undo, zoom-in/zoom-out, quick element search and finally rules to check the model's consistency (model checking) and the corresponding warning messages. This last feature will be discussed later on.

Presentation Modeling

Once the designer has specified the navigation diagram (completed or partially completed), this diagram can be compiled. As a result a set of XML [3] pages that fulfills the navigation specifications are generated. The XML pages constitute the web application and contain a preliminary web user interface. This preliminary web user interface can be refined within the environment to render the final look and feel.

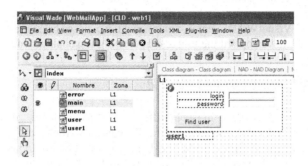

Fig. 3. Presentation Diagram in VisualWADE

The aspects that can be refined are those corresponding to the properties of styles, location, colors, just as it could be done with any authoring tool like Frontpage or Dreamweaver.. Figure 3 shows the abstract presentation diagram, result of compiling the NAD of Figure 2. Several zones can be observed: on the left side the page viewer can be observed. It contains the abstract pages that have been generated, alphabetically ordered (*error*, *messages*, *menu*, *main*, *user*, *user1*). On the right side can be seen the editing area where the content of the abstract pages is visualized. The information of the *main* page is showed in this case. As a result of the compilation process from NAD to APD, a form has been generated with the fields *login* and *password* and the corresponding button to execute the action (*OK*). Also shown is the link *user1* which enables the navigation to register a *new user* into the system. This preliminary web user interface can be animated by means of the animation tool ☝.

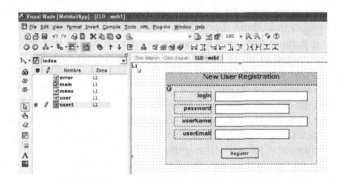

Fig. 4. Refinement and animation in the APD

When the animation tool is active the links and buttons of the interface become sensitive to mouse selections allowing the corresponding navigation jumps. While a model is being animated it is still possible to select the edition tool to modify any property of the elements of the interface. Figure 4 is the result of having activated the animation tool, having selected with the mouse the link *user1* of Figure 3, and finally having used the edition tool to modify the look of the page. It can be observed that within these refinements a help text has been included and the position, size and color of the users' creation form have been changed. Once we have introduced the basic features of the VisualWADE environment, next we describe some of the relevant projects were we have applied the tool and interesting lessons learned.

4   VisualWADE: Lessons Learned

VisualWADE has been used in such different environments as: the Autonomous Organization of Tax Administration of the Province of Alicante (SUMA) [12], the Mediterranean Savings Bank (CAM) [13], the Association of Industrial Technical Engineers of the Province of Alicante (COITI) [14], as well as to create VisualWADE's own website [15]. In this section we will present some of the characteristics of the systems that have been designed with VisualWADE within these companies. In SUMA Tax Administration, several Web applications have been developed, most of which are data-oriented. Among them, we highlight in chronological order: an inventory management system, SUMA's intranet and its Internet portal. The inventory management system is an application to manage the computer material inventory which is distributed along its 250 offices in the province of Alicante. Actually, inventory management can be seen as a traditional desktop application with a Web user interface. This was the first application that we completely designed using VisualWADE and also the one where more design errors were made. The reason was that we were strongly influenced by the type of user interfaces that the company was accustomed to use, and we were forced to carry out an "unnatural" design for a Web environment. Few Web visualization patterns were used so that the navigation was not intuitive and it was directed by the set of services offered from the interface (the same as in their traditional applications). Inventory management had more than 150 available services in the application. The experience of this development made both the SUMA team and the VisualWADE team to mature very much in a parallel way, and to realize that doing design like this prevented us from taking advantage of all the benefits of Web environments. The second project carried out at SUMA was its intranet. Basically, the intranet provides the necessary functionality to manage the group of news, events, tools and internal documents of the company through an intuitive and user-friendly Web interface. It is the first application that was designed for several user profiles, among them the administrator whose fundamental role is to supervise the information entered to the system from the different departments. Currently, the intranet of SUMA provides services to more than 400 users, and by the third month of operation it had increased its visits by more than 300% compared to the same period of the previous year. The last project carried out was the portal of SUMA. With a navigation design similar to that of the intranet, this application offers new and interesting services to citizens and city councils. In its design, some of the advanced characteristics provided by VisualWADE have been used, like multi-language support and template-based interface generation. In fact, the graphic design was developed by a subcontracted external company. Later, this graphic design was adapted to the generated navigation model. Regarding the

Mediterranean Savings Bank (CAM), the use of VisualWADE was more limited there, mainly for reasons of security which are described in the next section. Coordinated with the team of the CAM-directo service, whose responsibility is to maintain the group of applications to provide bank service through Internet, we used VisualWADE only to design the user interface navigation of the CAM-directo system itself. In this case, none of the capabilities of VisualWADE to generate predefined services was used, since the functionality already existed and had to be simply invoked from the navigation environment. To do so, we used the VisualWADE Web services integration modules (not described in this paper) that "encapsulated" the calls to the different necessary operations through a WSDL specification. The most difficult part was to adapt the return of parameters from the services to the navigation engine for later presentation on the Web interface. Regrettably, this task of integration with Web services still has to be made by hand. The experience was very positive, but we also realized that much of the potential use of VisualWADE is lost, since only a few of the characteristics of the environment like the interface generator were used. The need for privacy and security demanded by bank environments forced us to modify the Web design environments so that these security requirements are treated as first level elements. In this sense, we have created a workgroup with the CAM-directo team to identify and propose a set of modeling primitives that should be incorporated to a security model of Web applications. The PROVE (proyecto visados electronicos) project developed in the COITI (industrial engineer association of the province of Alicante) has been another system where VisualWADE has been applied successfully. The aim of this project is to provide a web-based application to manage electronic documents following the digital signature standards. PROVE makes an intensive use of Web services to offer digital signature services provided by the public key infrastructure (PKI) of the Generalitat Valenciana [16]. PROVE, is the first system developed with VisualWADE that connects three different information systems; the PKI Web server, the CAM-directo system and the COITI system. Conceptually, an industrial engineer can send through the PROVE system a digitally signed electronic document (pdf file that contains the description of a project), pay the corresponding administrative rates through the CAM-directo system, and submit it automatically to the department of COITI for registration. Just like the case of SUMA, the integration with Web services had to be carried out by hand. This is therefore a pending area for improvement in future versions of the tool. PROVE currently serves more than 1350 members, processing more than 15.000 projects per year. Finally, the conceptual design and generation of the VisualWADE website itself has been carried out using the tool. The VisualWADE portal is also based on templates and provides a set of very interesting navigation functionalities. All these functionalities have been fully generated using the properties of VisualWADE. For instance, the possibility to register at the website to access the free download of the tool, or to participate in discussion forums, or even to execute a project's task-management application example. Contrary to the systems that have been presented previously, in the VisualWADE portal there is no use of any functionality from third-party developers. In this sense, we could have used any free software for forum management available in Internet, but we preferred to build it from scratch to demonstrate the power and ease of use of the environment. The VisualWADE portal is open since November 2004. Currently it manages a transfer rate of more than 15

Gb por month, and more than 600 downloads of the tool from all over the world have already taken place. Although all these systems that have been briefly presented here constitute a real fact about the usability of advanced web development environments, our current purpose is to make VisualWADE available to the highest number of possible interested users with the objective of exploring new uses and development experiences. We are sure that this new phase will highlight interesting experiences yet to discover.

Next we present some of our experiences acquired during the development of the Web information systems described. We intend to provide some of the experiences of the VisualWADE team in the application of the tool for the resolution of real cases. As common denominator, all these cases required Web based solutions for their information systems. Most of these solutions (85 percent approximately) did not require new developments, but adaptations of existent information systems to the new Web environment, while only the remaining (15 percent approximately) could be considered as new developments, although in fact they were small extensions of functionalities not available until then. As mentioned before, VisualWADE provides, on one hand, predefined operations to support the design of date-intensive Web applications. This type of operations has demonstrated to be enough to provide basic business logic in applications like the inventory management or the intranet of SUMA. In fact, a great number of the Web applications demanded by companies are data-oriented. Therefore, it is particularly important to provide CRUD services for the great majority of Web environments that companies require, particularly companies that possess organizational information systems. On the other hand, the ability to specify and to use Web services in VisualWADE has facilitated the integration of functions that, in the form of legacy software, were needed in the new environment. For reasons dealing with security, privacy and complexity among others, these inherited functions could not be rewritten again but rather they had to be integrated into the new solutions. Consider that many of these companies have invested heavily in the past so that their information systems could reach the maturity and reliability desired. Therefore, what these companies need are not tools for the construction of Web software from scratch, but tools that facilitate the migration of their systems to the new environment, preserving the highly-reliable existent functionality. Regarding the primitives and navigation patterns, our experience shows the necessity of an intensive use of structures like index, show-all and guided-tours in the designed and generated applications. Also, the great volume of information managed by them often requires information to be presented by pieces. Therefore, it became indispensable to offer constructors to paginate the results. In VisualWADE such constructors are an implicit part of the navigation primitives, allowing the designer to enable or disable the pagination property as well as the number of objects per page. We have also identified some lacks related to navigation primitives of particular usefulness that unfortunately VisualWADE does not support at this time, among them, the nested indexes and the multiple attribute selection. It has been detected that with these two navigation primitives some pending modeling situations, which were not possible to specify or had to be specified in another less efficient way, could have been covered in a satisfactory way. The animation capabilities provided within the presentation diagram proves to be highly productive in several senses. On one hand, it helps to reduce the learning curve of the tool by a 25% approximately, especially on navigation diagram concepts since from the animation environment the effect of a modeling specification on the end-user interface can be seen at a glance. On the other hand, the development speed is increased by a factor of 10 by providing specific model compilers that faithfully reproduce the appearance and the behavior of the animated interface. In all the companies where VisualWADE has been applied we had to carry out periods of computer personnel's training. Our experience in this sense shows that an important update is required by most of the personnel, especially regarding object oriented analysis and design techniques, which we found quite surprising. The computer personnel of these companies possess an adequate knowledge of data modeling, and therefore to understand or to specify a class diagram was not a problem for them. However, we had to struggle to explain the navigation diagram and particularly its most advanced concepts such as the use of OCL to specify filters and preconditions on links and services. In the case of the CAM project, this situation did not happen and the transfer of knowledge was much more agile due to the personnel's high training. Another thing that we have learned is that it is very important that the navigation models take into account temporal data about the navigated information. Unfortunately, the great majority of the existent Web design methods and tools, do not keep in mind this dimension when specifying a navigation space. When modeling the SUMA intranet project, we needed to support navigational requirements to maintain the expiration period of news and events that were generated within the intranet itself and we realized that we needed some means to deal with time in the navigation model of VisualWADE. In this case, we opted for a solution based on extending the OCL language of VisualWADE by adding time primitives. This allowed us to consider operations between dates, etc., within the environment. The experience of working with VisualWADE in the CAM-directo team has been very productive. Especially, to learn both restrictions of the environment and situations that would have been impossible to realize without this experience. For example, the CAM team did not like that VisualWADE's model compilers produce a fixed generation skeleton (architecture). They said that anyone who knew how the different artifacts generated communicate to each other, had a very valuable information to attempt against the security of the generated code. For this reason, our efforts to improve model compilers are directed to provide mechanisms based on MDD/MDA to produce different generation skeletons based on a set of architecture templates.

5   Conclusions

Web developers should improve the productivity and quality to satisfy market needs and reduce delivery times and costs. Regrettably, the methods and standard techniques that are used for Web development still present several deficiencies: models and tools for analysis and design lack appropriate concepts to capture the development properties in this type of environments. As a consequence most of the application code is written by hand and difficult to reuse; documentation is scarce and of low quality, especially for user interfaces; costs and development time are difficult to predict and quickly get out of control during the maintenance and evolution phases of the application. VisualWADE, in its current state, solves some of these demands, and at present, is being used for the resolution of complex real cases in institutions like SUMA Tax Administration (Alicante), Mediterranean Savings Bank (CAM), and the Association of Industrial Technical Engineers of the Province of Alicante. VisualWADE and OO-H are under permanent development. Our next challenge is to integrate the new development paradigm based on MDD/MDA into the environment. We invite the interested reader to download the latest version of the tool and to experience the benefits of advanced web development environments.

References

1. P. Atzeni, G. Mecca, and P. Merialdo. Design and Maintenance of Data-Intensive Web Sites. In Advances in Database Technology - EDBT'98, pages 436–449, 03 1998.
2. S. Ceri, P. Fraternali, and A. Bongio. Web Modeling Language (WebML): a modeling language for designing Web sites. In Position Paper, Web Engineering Workshop, WWW9, 05 2000.
3. eXtensible Markup Language (XML). http://www.w3.org/XML/.
4. F. Garzotto and P. Paolini. HDM A Model-Based Approach to Hypertext Application Design. ACM Transactions on Information Systems (TOIS), 11(1):1–26, 01 1993.
5. J. Gómez, C. Cachero and O. Pastor. Extending a Conceptual Modelling Approach to Web Application Design. CAiSE 2000: 79-93. LNCS 1789. 2000.
6. J. Gómez, C. Cachero, and O. Pastor. Conceptual Modeling of Device-Independent Web Applications. IEEE Multimedia 8(2): 20-32. 2001.
7. D. Schwabe, G. Rossi, and D. J. Barbosa. Systematic Hypermedia Application Design with OOHDM. In Proceedings of the seventh ACM conference on HYPERTEXT '96, page 166, 1996.
8. Jos Warmer and Anneke Kleppe. The Object Constraint Language. Precise Modeling with UML. Addison-Wesley, 1998.
9. WebRatio Web Site http://www.webratio.com.
10. N. Koch, A. Kraus: The Expressive Power of UML-based Web Engineering, In Proc. of the 2nd. IWWOST, CYTED, Málaga, Spain, June 2002, 105-119.
11. A. Knapp, N. Koch, F. Moser, G. Zhang. ArgoUWE: A CASE Tool for Web Applications. EMSISE03, 14 pages, online publication at http://www.pst.informatik.uni-muenchen.de/~kochn
12. SUMA Gestion Tributaria. http://www.suma.es
13. Mediterranean Savings Bank. http://www.cam.es
14. PROVE. http://www.copitial.org
15. VisualWADE. http://www.visualwade.com
16. PKI Generalitat Valenciana http://pki.gva.es

Web Personalization: My Own Web Based on Open Content Platform

Seiyoung Lee[1,2] and Hwan-Seung Yong[2]

[1] Yahoo! Korea
Glass Tower, 946-1, Daechi-dong, Gangnam-gu, Seoul, Korea
imp230@kr.yahoo-inc.com
[2] Department of Computer Science, Ewha Womans University
Daehyun-dong, Seodaemun-gu, Seoul, Korea
hsyong@ewha.ac.kr

Abstract. The key word in the 2nd round of portal competition will be Personalization. This study reviewed recent core research related to Web Personalization and thus showed the ideal next generation model based on recent personalization strategies of major portals. The model is mainly composed of the following: Open Content strategy based on RSS; Personalized Search based on a user's preferences, Desktop Search, My Web storage, etc; Social Network, the concept that a user can share information with others depending on his interests; and Ubiquitous Computing that can merge people, computers and materials with the help of various multimedia technologies.

1 Introduction

As the Web continues to grow in size and use, the problem of excessive information being shown whenever browsing and searching has become more severe. To alleviate this problem, we need Personalization on the Web. This will be achieved by customizing the Web environment towards the user's preferences. This Personalization means the timely presentation of the preferred information to the user at the right moment. Also, Personalization will be embodied in such a way as to customize the interactions on a website based upon the user's explicit and/or implicit interests and desires. In order to learn about a specific user, the system has to collect and analyze related information and store the results in the users' profile.

In spite of its importance, Web Personalization faces several tough challenges that distinguish it from other main stream issues of Data Mining such as: Scalability [6], Accuracy [7], Evolving User Interests [6,8], Data Collection and Preprocessing [9], Integrating Multiple Sources of Data [10,11], Conceptual Modeling for Web usage Mining [12], and Privacy Concerns [13]. As a result, many users feel that Web Personalization is still far from reality. In addition, there are those who feel that Personalization is not useful or cost-effective [5]. With all these challenges, portals and their search engines are still trying hard to implement it. These systems have been launched by major portals such as Yahoo! and Google.

Through reviews on related theories and resultant studies, this paper proposes an ideal model of the next generation system. The model is based on present strategies

M. Kitsuregawa et al. (Eds.): WISE 2005, LNCS 3806, pp. 731–739, 2005.

for Web Personalization adopted from major portals. The technical background of Web Personalization is reviewed in Section 2. The current trend of major portals is reviewed in Section 3. Finally, an ideal model for Web Personalization based on the above analysis is proposed in Section 4.

2   Overview on Web Personalization

Web Personalization can be defined as the process of customizing the contents and structure of a Web site to the specific and individual needs of each user based upon the user's behavior. The steps for Web Personalization are composed of: (a) the Collection of web data, (b) the Preprocessing of web data, (c) the Analysis of the collected data, and (d) the Decision Making/Final Recommendation [15,19]. Details are shown in the following paragraphs. [2,3,4]

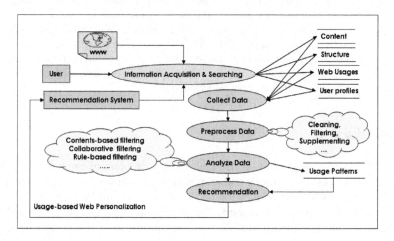

Fig. 1. Overview of the Usage-based Web Personalization process

Regarding (a) the "Collection of Web data", implicit and explicit information, will be collected. Implicit data is generally composed of a user's past activities and the click streams of the activities recorded in Web server logs. At the same time, explicit data are collected from registration forms and rating questionnaires. In (b) the "Preprocessing of Web data", a structured format will be prepared for the input data prior to (c) the "Analysis of the collected data". That is, data displaying inconsistent data will be cleaned, and data irrelevant to the goal of the analysis will be filtered out. Finally, links that are missed due to caching will be completed through incomplete clickthrough paths. Step (c) the "Analysis of the collected data", known as Web Usage Mining, is meant to discover interesting usage patterns and statistical correlations between Web pages and user groups with the help of technologies such as Machine Learning and Data Mining [16,17,18]. This step frequently results in automatic user profiling, and is typically applied offline, so that it does not burden the Web server. The final step of Personalization, (d) the "Decision Making/Final Recommendation", recommendations deduced from the preceding steps will be delivered to the specific user. The generation process of dynamic web contents is typically delivered with it.

The tools used for analyzing collected data include Content-based filtering, Collaborative filtering and Rule-based filtering. Content-based filtering is based on individual users' preferences. It tracks each user's behavior and recommends similar items that the user preferred in the past. This approach has worked well for Amazon™ [14]. Collaborative filtering is based on the assumption that users present habits that are consistent with their past behavior in areas such as rating, browsing or purchasing. Of course, the system may recommend items that are preferred by other users with similar interests [15]. This approach relies on historical records of all user interests that can be inferred from their ratings of the items such as products and web pages on a website. Rule-based filtering is generally used to customize products at e-commerce sites such as Dell on Line™. The user answers several questions and then receives customized results such as a list of products. This approach is mostly based on heavy planning, manual concoctions of a judicious set of questions, possible answer combinations, and customization by an expert. However, it suffers from a lack of intelligence due to non-automatic learning, and tends to be static. All three of these are currently being combined to deduce more exact results. Regardless, this Web Usage Mining yields more fruitful sets of patterns on which the users' navigational behavior are well reflected. The system adequately adopts this kind of knowledge and uses it to personalize the website according to each user's behavior and profile. Figure 1 shows an overview of the Usage-based Web Personalization process.

3   The Present Trend of Major Portals

3.1   Open Content Platform

RSS (Really Simple Syndication) is an XML-based format for easily distributing and aggregating Web content such as news headlines. Users determine their favorite websites and a properly configured RSS aggregator will syndicate selected lists of hyperlinks and headlines, along with other information about the websites, and then display the contents on the user's desktop at regular intervals. The user decides to follow the link or not.

RSS-based contents have given rise to the trend of sharing in the online world. The recently redesigned MY Yahoo! incorporates a prototype of RSS-aware program that has been successful [21,22]. Once any kind of RSS-format sources are referred to in "My Page", any format of the new updated data can be displayed. Furthermore, users can choose various contents inside and outside of Yahoo! via special modules, to overcome the simplicity of information given in RSS-format. Open content platform based on RSS is very significant, in that it lowers barriers to entry for competitors.

RSS is going mainstream. Companies continue to experiment with ways to use and distribute RSS feeds. Changes in the future of content are likely to be driven by RSS and many possible devices are used to capture RSS feeds. RSS is not limited to web pages. RSS feeds have been popping up in many services. The lightweight nature of its code makes it ideally suited for new devices. Figure 2 shows a basic concept of Open Content Platform. By adding value to the content providers, third-party service providers, and the end users, RSS can provide a very simple way of creating thousands of different forms, customized to the device and to the user.

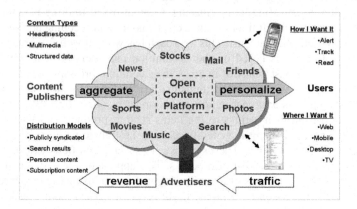

Fig. 2. Open Content Platform based on RSS

3.2 Social Network

Network searching has the potential to be a more dynamic force than Personalization. Networking includes both physical and social network technologies. The recent search engine, Eureckster [29], has been designed to return more personalized results based on Social Network. Users can easily make a Social Network through Eureckster and share the same interests with others on the Network. Considering that it uses keywords and searches websites relevant to the given queries, it seems very similar to the existent search engines. However, it is distinguished from the other engines, in that it can reorder search results, depending on the interests of people related to the specific group. Cyworld [30], in Korea, which was greeted enthusiastically by the public, is a good example of the power of Social Network. Of course, services using the network may not only be related to a certain group of people, but may also be accompanied by physical network technologies such as Online storage and Web publishing. Flickr and Yahoo 360°, that recently have both been launched, are also good examples. Sooner or later, services could be provided in any environment; irrespective of whether they are located on a PC or on the Web.

3.3 Personalized Search

The Web Search engines, unlike any other applications, have the luxury of a huge user base. The existing search engines rely on automated algorithms and static link structure: The search engines' potential is far from being fulfilled, as they cannot return useful results for over 50% of queries. This is usually caused by many factors, for example, short and ambiguous queries, lack of structured information and lack of knowledge of users' preferences. In order to reduce unsatisfactory results and improve search capability, Personalized Search is a must. It will enable search results to be more focused on the user's interests. Various studies on Personalized Search are ongoing, such as: Methods for returning more valuable documents based on the under-standing of the Context of the search requests [23], Effective personalization based on Association Rule Discovery from Web usage data [24], Ontology based Personalized search [25], and Establishment of the Term Vector Database [26].

The Personalized Search beta that Google has recently launched can deliver custom search results based on a profile describing a user's area of interest. The adapted algo-rithms can dynamically reorder results by weighting the user's interests. It is now considered a successful prototype, one that can deliver relevant search results [27]. Also, Yahoo! has enhanced its search service with My Web recently. It has similar functions to Bookmark, in which search results can be saved and shared, specific URLs can be blocked, and research is possible within the existent search results [28]. Furthermore, search results that are saved on My Web can be added to the RSS con-tents of My Yahoo! through categorization. This model is well-fitted with Personal-ization Policy, which is based on open contents. If search engines based on users' preferences and Desktop-Based Search are added to this model, it will become much more powerful.

4   Future Outlook on Web Personalization

4.1   Social Search

After years of development, and especially since the introduction of link counting and anchor text, web search has gotten amazingly powerful in its ability to surface nearly any kind of information within the billions of pages that comprise the Web. However, as powerful and large as today's web search engines are, they are still limited in their ability to deliver key services to their user.

For example, a person's definition of "the best plasma TV review site" depends on the user's tastes as well the opinions and recommendations of friends and authorities they trust. Web Search engines do not have the ability to deliver the right answer because they do not always capture the most trusted and valued sources for that user. Today's search engines can deliver great results, especially with very specific queries, but typically do a poor job of connecting us with new items that might be interesting, timely, and personally relevant. Our friends and people who share common interests are better sources for this information.

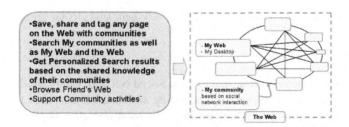

Fig. 3. The Next Main Features of Personalized Search, based on Social Network

To address these kinds of limits to today's search experience, Yahoo! is releasing an early beta version of My Web 2.0 for a limited number of users. It is a new kind of search engine - a social search engine- that complements Web Search by enabling users to search the knowledge and expertise of their friends and community in addition to the Web. Figure 3 shows the next main features of Personalized Search based on Social Network.

4.2 Personalization Platform

A Unified Personalization Platform is a must to encourage more users to engage more deeply with more services. It will make users' experience more personally relevant and consistent. Figure 4 shows actionable attributes for targeting through Use Profile Services extension on the Personalization Platform. Raw data sources such as User profiles, Web logs and other sources from the Web or PC could be processed into Unified User Model through the Profiling Engine. The Profiling Engine extracts raw data, maps them into categories, holds the categorized data, and then populates attributes into appropriate services.

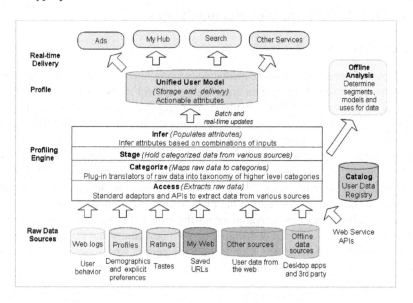

Fig. 4. User Profile service extension: actionable attributes for targeting

4.3 My Own Web

Open Content Strategy, Personalization and Social Network can be used to define the current behavior in major portals in attracting and maintaining "User Loyalty". According to Eric Schmidt, CEO of Google, "The most important factor for search engines is shifting from the return of the exact search results to Personalization". Thus, Desktop Search could be the trigger which stimulates this shift. It is possible to estimate the patterns of Personal Search based on various information stored on the user's PC. Also, the huge disks that are provided by email are capable of storing data sufficiently for personal profile application. Furthermore, Blogs and Instant Messenger Applications are obviously useful tools in the implementation of Personalized services.

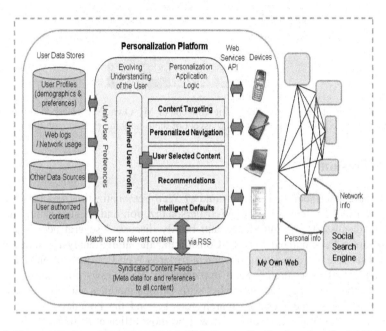

Fig. 5. Concept Design of "My Own Web": Web Personalization based on Social Networks

RSS technology is also valuable. RSS feeds can be used in place of frequent, inefficient browsing or search engines. Things like Email, Instant Messaging, maybe VoiP and Video conferencing, music and search will play an important role, too. A rich media RSS standard(RM RSS) would allow publishers to make such content available online in the same way news articles are today. This could be the true Personalized Web and the basis of a Ubiquitous Computing environment. Figure 5 shows a conceptual design of "My Own Web" based on Personalization Platform and Social Network. Personalization Platform seamlessly integrates users' preferences, information and media across the Web.

It should be mentioned that the area of Web Personalization should not simply be restricted to the customized "MY" service provided by a specific website, but should be extended to "My Own Web". The concept of My Own Web refers to the user's new ability to exercise more control over every aspect of their daily interaction with the Web. (refer to Figure 6) If My Own Web is connected to various multimedia and information technologies, it will soon be the heart of the Ubiquitous Computing environment in our lives.

Fig. 6. The Zen of "My Own Web". The concept of My Own Web refers to the user's new ability to exercise more control over every aspect of their daily interaction with the Web.

5   Conclusion

In this paper, the theoretical background of Web Personalization was reviewed. The application of RSS technology to Web Personalization and its successful adaptation was also discussed. We introduced and briefly discussed several access points for implementing Personalized Search. Considering the above analysis, it can be concluded that there is a consistent movement towards Web Personalization. The following technologies have already been implemented: RSS draws information from any website to the users; My Web furnishes with various modules and utilities, as per the users' preferences; and Desktop Search goes beyond the boundary of the personal computer and the Web. In addition, it will be most efficient to integrate Social Network concept and Ubiquitous Computing technology in conjunction with the most recent developments in Web Personalization for utmost utility and user satisfaction.

Acknowledgement

This work was supported by Korea Science and Engineering Foundation (KOSEF) grants 20044014.

References

1. The Personalization Consortium, http://www.personalization.org/personalization.html
2. Eirinaki, M., Vazirgiannis, M.: Web mining for web personalization. ACM Transactions On Internet Technology (TOIT), 3(1) (2003) 1-27.
3. Nasraoui, O.: World Wide Web Personalization. Invited chapter in "Encyclopedia of Data Mining and Data Warehousing", J. Wang, Ed, Idea Group (2005)
4. Shahabi, C., Chen Y.: Web Information Personalization-Challenges and Approaches. Datbases in Networked Information Systems, Japan (DNIS) (2003)
5. McGovern G.: Thinking-Why personalization hasn't worked. New Thinking Newsletter (2003)

6. Nasraoui O., Cardona C., Rojas C., Gonzalez F.: Mining Evolving User Profiles in Noisy Web Clickstream Data with a Scalable Immune System Clustering Algorithm. KDD Workshop (2003) 71-81.
7. Nasraoui O. and Pavuluri M.: Complete this Puzzle: A Connectionist Approach to Accurate Web Recommendations based on a Committee of Predictors. WebKDD workshop (2004).
8. Desikan P. and Srivastava J.: Mining Temporally Evolving Graphs. WebKDD workshop (2004)
9. Berendt B., Bamshad M, Spiliopoulou M., Wiltshire J.: Measuring the accuracy of session-izers for web usage analysis, In Workshop on Web Mining, the First SIAM International Conference on Data Mining (2001) 7-14.
10. Li J. and Zaiane O.: Using Distinctive Information Channels for a Mission-based Web Recommender System. WebKDD workshop (2004)
11. Berendt B., Hotho A., and Stumme G.: Towards semantic web mining. In Proc. International Semantic Web Conference (ISWC02) (2002)
12. Meo R., Lanzi P., Matera M., Esposito R.: Integrating Web Conceptual Modeling and Web Usage Mining. WebKDD workshop (2004)
13. Agrawal R. and Srikant R.: Privacy-preserving data mining, In Proc. of the ACM SIGMOD Conference on Management of Data, Dallas, Texas (2000) 439-450.
14. Linden G., Smith B., and York J.: Amazon.com Recommendations Item-to-item collaborative filtering, IEEE Internet Computing, 7(1), (2003) 76-80
15. Schafer J.B., Konstan J., and Reidel J.: Recommender Systems in E-Commerce, In Proc. ACM Conf. E-commerce (1999) 158-166
16. Spiliopoulou M. and Faulstich L. C.: WUM: A Web utilization Miner, in Proc. of EDBT workshop WebDB98, Valencia, Spain (1999)
17. Srivastava, J., Cooley, R.: Deshpande, M., And Tan, P-N. Web usage mining: Discovery and applications of usage patterns from web data, SIGKDD Explorations, 1(2) (2000) 12-23.
18. Nasraoui O., Krishnapuram R., and Joshi A.: Mining Web Access Logs Using a Relational Clustering Algorithm Based on a Robust Estimator, 8th International World Wide Web Conference, Toronto (1999) 40-41.
19. Mobasher B., Dai H., Luo T., Nakagawa M.: Effective personalization based on association rule discovery from Web usage data, ACM Workshop (2001)
20. RSS at Harvard Law, http://blogs.law.harvard.edu/tech/rss
21. My Yahoo! RSS FAQ, http://my.Yahoo.com/s/rss-faq.html
22. My Yahoo!, http://my.Yahoo.com
23. Lawrenc, S.: Context in Web Search, Data Engineering Bulletin, Vol 23, Number 3 (2000)
24. Mobasher, B., Dai, H., Luo, T., Nakagawa M.: Effective Personalization Based on Association Rule Discovery from Web Usage Data. ACM Workshop (WIDM) (2001) 103-112.
25. Gauch, S., Chaffee, J., Pretschner, A.: Ontology-Based Personalized Search and Browsing. Web Intelligence and Agent System archive Vol 1, Issue 3-4 (2003) 219-234
26. Stata, R., Bharat, K., Maghou, F.: The Term Vector Database: fast access to indexing terms for Web pages. Computer Networks: The International Journal of Computer and Telecommunications Networking archive, Vol 33, Issue 1-6 (2000) 247-255
27. Google Personalized Search Beta site, http://labs.Google.com/personalized/
28. My! Yahoo! Search Beta site, http://mysearch.Yahoo.com/
29. Eurekster, http://www.eurekster.com/
30. Cyworld, http://cyworld.nate.com/main2/index.htm
31. Google Desktop Search Beta site, http://desktop.Google.com/

An Effective Approach for Content Delivery in an Evolving Intranet Environment - A Case Study of the Largest Telecom Company in Taiwan

Chih-Chin Liang [1,2], Ping-Yu Hsu [2], Jun-Der Leu [2], and Hsing Luh [3]

[1] Customer Service Information Tech. Lab,
Telecommunication Laboratories, ChungHwa Telecom Co.,
Ltd No.21-3, Sec. 1, Sinyi Rd., Jhongjheng District,
Taipei City, Taiwan 100, R.O.C.
[2] Department of Management, National Central University,
No. 300, Jung-da Rd., Jung-li City, Taoyuan,
Taiwan 320, R.O.C.
{pyhsu, leujunder}@mgt.ncu.edu.tw
lgcwow@gmail.com
http://www.chttl.com.tw/chttlwww/eindex.htm
[3] Department of Mathematical Sciences, National Chengchi University,
No.64, Sec. 2, Jhihnan Rd., Wen-Shan District,
Taipei City, Taiwan 116, R.O.C.
slu@nccu.edu.tw

Abstract. Being the dominant telecommunication company in Taiwan, ChungHwa Telecom Co., Ltd., CHT is her symbol listed on the New York Stock Exchange, provides major communication services to more than 23 million people living in Taiwan. CHT has vast number of software developed on client-server or web-based architectures with client software installed in more than ten thousand client computers spreading over the entire nation. Since telecommunication industry evolved in fast pace, the software functions are constantly changing. The changes have to be reflected in all client software before new services can be launched. Thus, the cost and time in distributing contents to client computers has become a major concern in CHT. To improve the efficiency of contents distribution, this research helps CHT develop new software to automatically distribute contents to client computers. To minimize the chance of system locks and balance contents distribution loading, in the new system, each dispatching server sends update contents to no more than three other servers. The contents are delivered with hybrid routing strategy that combines both fixed and adaptive routing strategies. With its low error rate and speedy distribution, the new system reduces the man-minutes per year required to manage the contents distribution of a client server system from 14,227.2 minutes to 1,144 minutes, namely reduces 92% of the time. The user satisfaction of the system was also found to be above 80% among six factors of the measurement designed by Bailey, et al. [1].

Keywords: intranet systems, system integration, routing algorithms.

M. Kitsuregawa et al. (Eds.): WISE 2005, LNCS 3806, pp. 740–749, 2005.
© Springer-Verlag Berlin Heidelberg 2005

1 Introduction

Improving customer services is listed as one of the most important operational strategies by many companies, and it is especially critical for those in the service industry
[2]. ChungHwa Telecom, listed on the New York Stock Exchanges with the symbol of
CHT since July, 2003, is such a service oriented company. ChungHwa Telecom is the
dominant integrated telecom service provider in Taiwan. Its services include city calls,
Internet services, broadband networking, satellite communication, intelligent network,
mobile data, and multimedia broadband. The services are delivered to more than 23
million people living in Taiwan and offshore isles. In March 2005, the company had a
capital of $2.84 billion.

   CHT has over 10,000 personal computers used by clerks spread over operation
centers in Taiwan for processing business transactions. In average, each personal
computer hosts seven different types of client software, each of which links to a system
in the back offices. The systems are designed in either client-server or web-based architecture. Even though the latter architecture is the trend, there are still many systems
designed with the former architecture in big enterprises [3][4]. With the client-server
architecture, applications and some data such as promotion codes, area codes, and
customer codes are stored on the personal computers. With the coexistence of both
architectures, web based systems may also write data to the personal computers for the
references of client software of other client-server systems.

   With the fierce competition faced by CHT and the high variety of services offered by
CHT, the data and applications on the personal computers are changed constantly for
the introduction of new services or promotion plans. The changes can be as frequently
as four times a week. The changes may include both data and enhancement of applications. All the changes have to be successfully delivered to related clerks personal
computers before corresponding promotions and new services can be launched [5].
Therefore the contents delivery issue of data and applications of personal computers
becomes a serious business issue in CHT [6][7][8].

   Software, such as Interwoven TeamSite Content Server and Microsoft System
Management Server [9] are designed to help delivery contents in organizations [10].
However, these systems are not adapted by CHT due to either technology or management problems. For example, one system requires all computers be managed by
Microsoft Active Directory [11], which only operates on the latest versions of Microsoft operating systems. However, CHT owns many computers installed with
non-Microsoft platforms or older versions of Windows Operating Systems. Another
product charges US$100 per computer per year; the cost of delivering contents with
such software would have cost CHT US$1M per year.

   With these technology and managerial problems, the team decided to develop its own
content delivery system. The system had to delivery the contents along the organizational hierarchy to get supports from all business units. The system also had to be robust
so that the failure of any servers on the distribution routes did not bring the distribution
to a halt. The system also had to work efficiently so that contents could be distributed to
all personal computers before the scheduled service or promotion launched. With the
requirements, the research strived to develop a contents distribution system that employed hybrid routing strategy to deliver contents along physical organizational hier-

archy, protect system robustness, and work efficiently at the same time. Although originally designed for CHT, the system developed in this research can be applied to enterprises which require information being effectively and reliably distributed along organization hierarchies with low operation cost. The contribution of the research is potentially significant, even though networks enable peer to peer communications among servers, most communications in organizations still function along management hierarchy [12].

CHT originally developed a contents distribution system that was plagued by the problems of content lock and traffic bursting problems. The paper reports a new system, named as FnFDS (Fire and Forget Distribution System), which overcomes the two problems and is applied to distribute update contents of an ordering management system. The engineers needed to trigger and supervise the distributions are reduced from two experienced engineers to one trained staff member. The average distribution time is reduced from 14,227.2 minutes per year to 1,144 minutes per year. The pay of the engineers operating the original system and the FnFDS is US$4,400 and US$857.14 per month, respectively. Furthermore, with its success, the system is now being applied to deliver the update contents to more than fifteen vital softwares such as ordering system and billing system, which support the daily operations of the enterprise.

To measure the satisfaction of the front end clerks toward the FNFDS, a survey based on Bailey's measurements was also conducted. The result showed that users are satisfied with the service of the system in the factors of feeling of control, reliability, security of data, flexibility, documentation, and expectation.

The rest of the paper is organized as following. In Section 2, issues and problems faced by CHT in contents delivery are illustrated. In Section 3, the hybrid routing algorithm employed by FnFDS is presented. In Section 4, the complexity, cost saved, and user satisfaction of FnFDS are discussed. The conclusion of the paper is shown in Section 5.

2   Contents Delivery in CHT

The client-server architecture is popular in modern organizations since it leverages existing technology and organization resources to perform business processing [13]. However, the architecture requires organizations to devote considerable resources to maintain client software [14].

However, the resources required of contents delivery can be potentially huge in organizations like CHT, since the installation base of client software is large and the programs run on the clients and servers are consistently updated with the incessant launching of new services in the organization. For example, the billing client software needs to load new billing types and billing rules whenever a new service is provided. In general, in one intranet application, client updates are performed four times in one week. With each update, all 10,000 computers needed to be successfully updated in the specified time window; otherwise, the company will not be able to launch consistent new services to all of its customers in time.

To better manage the updates of client contents in such complex environment, CHT has decided to develop an information system to distribute the update contents and to monitor the progress since 2001[15]. To design a system to efficiently distribute update contents, three issues must be addressed. The contents must be delivered along the organizational hierarchy. The delivery must be done with the minimum human intervention in order to save cost and speed up the distribution. The last but not the least issue is that no server can be shut down when delivery fails since these servers may host other important applications. The distribution system had to make reasonable retries until contents arrive at the destination safely.

Fig. 1 shows the organizational hierarchy of CHT, which has three business groups, each of which has its own regional administrative center to manage the group computers and networks. Each business group has numerous regional centers such as the Service Center, the Line Center, the Construction Unit, etc. Each regional center also has staff managing its computers and networks. The client computers reside in regional centers.

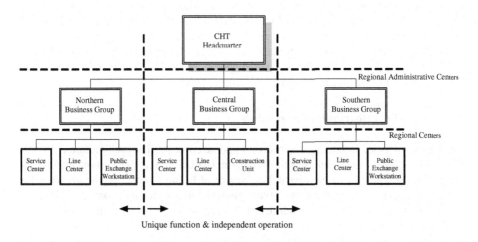

Fig. 1. The organization chart of CHT

Before the Internet became popular, CHT updated its systems with deliveryman carrying diskettes or magnetic tapes holding update contents to regional administrative centers and regional centers. After receiving the updating media, the business groups dispatched agents to regional center to distribute the contents and revised the clients.

With the arrival of the Internet, CHT replaced deliverymen with programs running on dispatching servers. In the scheme, HQ and every regional administrative center and regional center assign some computers as dispatching servers. The update contents are stored in the dispatching server in the headquarters and all dispatching servers in the regional administrative centers and regional centers connect to the HQ server to download contents. The seemingly easy solution has three major drawbacks: traffic jams, content lock and lacking of quality control. The first problem arises from the simultaneous contents transfer requests coming from all dispatching servers in regional administrative centers and regional centers. The requests put serious burden on the network and the server host the contents. The second problem is the content lock problem, which is caused by failed transmission. When a content which is stored in a file is transmitted, the file is locked by the operating system. When the transmission aborted, the lock may not be released properly and hence prevent the content from being fetched by other dispatching servers. The third problem comes from incomplete transmission of contents. The computers may not detect the contents downloaded are incomplete and apply the contents to the client software which may cause serious errors in the client software. To monitor the progress of contents distributions and handle crisis in the processes, CHT used to dedicate two engineers.

3   Distributed Contents by FnF Delivering System

To relieve the pain from contents distribution managers and increase the efficiency of contents distribution, a new generation of contents distribution algorithm is designed. The new system is designed to reduce the network traffic, to automate transmission process, namely, minimizing the chances of content lock and to guarantee that the contents transmitted are correct. Since the goal is to eliminate human interventions in the distribution process, the new system is named as FnFDS, which is an acronym of Fire and Forget Distribution System.

3.1   The FnFDS Distribution Algorithm

FnFDS uses a 4-tier architecture to transmit update contents. The architecture coincides with the business hierarchy originally. When FnFDS starts, the system checks the availability of contents in the dispatching server of headquarters, and then notifies the dispatching servers in the administrative regional centers to fetch the data from it. After data soundly arriving regional administrative centers, the system then notifies the leaders of dispatching servers in the regional centers to fetch the contents from their corresponding dispatching servers in the administrative regional centers. Dispatching servers in regional centers are organized into groups to perform load balance and failover. Each group elects a leader in the run time to fetch contents from the corresponding dispatching server in the administrative regional center. After the leader soundly fetching the contents, FnFDS then notifies all dispatching servers in the group to fetch data from the leader. After each group has the update contents distributed and notified the FnFDS the availability of dispatching servers, the system then notifies client computers to get update contents from the nearest available dispatching servers in the same regional centers. If a client is disconnected from the network when contents are distributed, it can contact to the dispatching server in the corresponding regional administrative center after reconnecting to the network. Fig. 2 shows the transmission schema. Node *HQ* in the first layer is the dispatching servers located at headquarters of organization. *RAC1, RAC2* and *RAC3* in the second layer are dispatching servers in the three regional administrative centers locate at corresponding Business Group. Third layer consists of groups of dispatching servers in the regional center. In Fig. 2, the first group is composed by four servers marked with *RAC1-Group1-Server1* to *RAC1-Group1-Server4*. The fourth layer is composed by client computers which are the final destinations of the update contents.

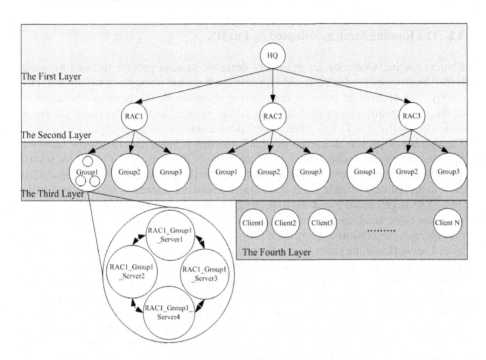

Fig. 2. The 4-tier Architecture of FnFDS

The algorithm FnFDS contains four components, namely, FnFDS_HQ, FnFDS_RAC, FnFDS_AC, and FnFDS_Client. FnFDS_HQ launchs the distribution process and triggers FnFS_RAC operates in regional administrative center to fetch the update data. After being triggered by FnFDS_HQ, the algorithms of FnFDS_RACs fetch update contents from FnFDS_HQ and store them in the corresponding servers. The algorithm of FnFDS_RC operates in regional center and keeps polling corresponding FnFDS_RAC servers to check the availability of update contents. When update contents are available in FnFDS_RAC server, FnFDS_RCs work with the same FnFDS_RAC will elect one as leader to fetch the update contents. Other FnFDS_RC servers in the same group then fetch the file from the leader. FnFDS_Clients are triggered by FnFDS_HQ when update contents are available at the functioning FnFDS_RC.

The program of FnFDS_Client is activated by a client computer when the computer receives signals from the FnFDS_HQ or when the client computer is reconnected to network and found that there are update contents waiting for it from checking the entries stored in the severs in regional administrative centers or headquarters. The entries are stored in more than one dispatching servers so that even if one of them goes down, the client computers still get the latest update contents. With the approach, FnF_HQ can terminate the distribution process even if some client computers are disconnected from the network and the disconnected client computers can fetch the latest updates at the moment connecting to the server.

3.2 The Routing Strategy Adopted by FnFDS

Content routing strategies are originally designed to send packets through networks [16]. The strategy is adapted in algorithm to route update contents in the intranet efficiently. The differences between these two applications lie on the sizes of data delivered and the frequencies of such delivery taking places. The size of network packets is typically smaller than 1k bits whereas the update contents can be as large as 10M bytes. The number of packets delivered in a packet switch network can be several hundreds per min whereas the average times of update contents delivered with FnFDS are several a day. The differences forces FnFDS to detect the network conditions only immediately prior to the delivery of updating contents to save network resources, whereas traditional routing strategies require systems to probe network conditions constantly.

On the other hand, since several research claims that multi-path routing mechanism may increase the network performance [17], FnF routing strategy (FnFRS) employees a hybrid network routing strategy which combines traditional fixed and adaptive routing strategies to fit business infrastructure [18]. Based on the infrastructure of Fig. 2, contents distribution between the headquarters and the administrative regional centers follows fixed routing strategy, namely, contents always follow the same route to the same destinations. On the other hand, the contents distribution between administrative regional centers and regional centers employ the adaptive routing strategy. Adjusting itself to the network traffic periodically, an adaptive routing decides an optimized route for each delivery. In FnFDS, the routing between each regional administrative center and its groups is adaptive in the sense that the leader elected in each distribution may be different and the speed of the connection between the elected leader and the dispatching server in the corresponding regional administrative center is potentially the best among the servers in the same group since the leader's petition is the first one reaching the dispatching server in the regional administrative center. Deploying contents among servers in the same group follows fixed routing strategy; since the contents are broadcasted to all servers from the leader directly.

4 Complexity and Implementation Results

The complexity and system performance of FnFDS are discussed in the section. Also included in the section are the financial contribution of the system and the measure of user satisfactions toward the system.

4.1 System Performance

Given M clients and N servers with each server connected to k other servers, the level of the network hierarchy is $\log_k N$. The complexity of the system is $O(\log_k N + M/(k*\log_k N))$. N is thirty six and k is three in this case.

An experiment was also performed to compare the complexity of FnFDS and the original approach employed by CHT. One content with the size of 10,000K was sent over the net for 12 times without maintenance issue occurred. The average time required to distribute the content from the dispatching server in HQ to the dispatching servers in regional centers was 300.08 seconds (around five minutes) and 680.50 seconds (around eleven minutes) through FnFDS and the original system, respectively.

Besides, the error rate of contents distribution was dramatically reduced from 80% to 10%. The errors included content lock, dispatching servers malfunction or disconnected from the networks. In the original system, content lock was the most serious problem, whereas in FnFDS, content lock was reduced to almost none. The content lock situation needed two engineers to spend 40 minutes to fix them in the original system and the maintenance issue took only 10 minutes of one trained staff member in FnFDS.

4.2 Cost Saved

In average, this company needs to distribute update contents at least four times a week for each application. Hence, the yearly average numbers of distribution with error handling for the original and FnFDS systems are 166.4 times and 20.8 times, respectively. In other words, the average numbers of successful distributions for the original and FnFDS systems are 41.6 times and 187.2 times. The man-minutes spending in each year in fixing the problems in the original system and FnFDS is 13,312 minutes and 208 minutes respectively. The man-minutes spending in each year in general situation in the original system and FnFDS is 915.2 minutes and 936 minutes, respectively. The total man-minutes needed to operate and correct the errors of the content distributions are 14,227.2 minutes and 1,144 minutes in the original system and FnFDS, respectively.

Since the procedure of trouble shooting is a lot easier in the FnFDS than unlocking the locked contents in the original system, the FnFDS is now operated by trained staff member whose hourly pay is lower than that of the engineers operate the original system. In this case, the pay of the two senior engineers operating the original system and one trained staff member operating the FnFDS system is US$4,400 and US$857.14 per month, respectively. We can reduce the salary cost by change the person in charge easily.

Table 1 shows the summaries of costs and time saved by FnFDS to update one/client server system. In CHT, there are more than forty intranet applications that needed to be maintained.

Table 1. The Time and Cost saved by FnFDS applying to 40 applications

Organization	Original System	FnFDS
Error Rate (%)	80%	10%
The Averaged Distribution Time per Year	569,088 minutes (14,227.2 minutes * 40 applications)	45,760 minutes (1,144 minutes * 40 applications)
	92% Time Saved	
The Salary Cost per Year	$2,112,000 ($4,400 * 12 months * 40 applications)	$411,427.2 ($857.14 * 12 months * 40 applications)
	80.5% Cost Saved	

4.3 Clerks' Satisfaction

A study was conducted to collect samples from CHT's three major business regions, namely, northern, central and southern Taiwan. Survey questionnaires were sent to five groups of CHT employees: staff members, customer service personnel, researchers, managers and others. All participants in the target groups have used the FnFDS or been engaged in work related to the FnFDS for at least 12 months. The measurement vehicle was adopted from the 13 factors proposed by Bailey, et al., namely, flexibility, accuracy, reliability, system integration, response/turn-around time, convenience of access, documentation, degree of training, job effects, feeling of control, format and output, security of data, and expectation [1]. With a pretest performed with 107 surveys, we found that the significant factors were feeling of control, reliability, security of data, flexibility, documentation, and expectation.

600 questionnaires were randomly distributed to the target groups and 339 valid questionnaires were collected. The response rate was 56.5%. This survey showed that user satisfaction was 87.7% for feeling of control, 87.4% for reliability, 93% for security of data, 83% for flexibility, 85.6% for documentation, and 90.3% for expectation.

5   Conclusion

Client contents distribution is a serious issue that needs to be addressed for companies that have fast evolving intranet environment with huge number of client installation bases. Furthermore, contents distribution is very important for web-based systems that still have client application and data files. In other words, the same version of update contents must arrive all on-line personal computers before a required deadline so that companies can upgrade corresponding client software and business processes.

CHT is the largest telecom company with layers of organizational hierarchy in Taiwan which offers both data and voice services. The company deploys more than ten thousand personal computers for clerks facing customers directly and in average, has to distribute update contents four times a week to support service upgrades and promotions. The original contents distribution system is plagued with the problems of network congestions, content locks, and incomplete contents transmission. With the original contents distribution system, CHT used to dedicate two engineers to monitor and control the progress of update contents distribution in one intranet application. The man-minutes per year spent is around 14,227.2 minutes and CHT must employ 2 engineers in the salary of US$4,400 per month. With around forty systems operating in CHT, the resource saved can be potentially huge.

To overcome the technical issues entangled in the contents distribution system and save the cost of managing the distribution process, an improved system, termed as FnF Delivery System (FnFDS) is designed. The FnFDS reduces traffic burst and increases system robustness with hybrid routing. With the check of content size in each delivery, FnFDS also greatly reduces the chance of incomplete contents distribution. With the technical merits, FnFDS significantly reduces the chance of content lock and therefore decreases the need of human interventions during contents distribution. With FnFDS, the company now only needs to assign a trained staff member to oversee the process. The man-minutes per year spent to monitor the distribution is reduced by 92%, and salary cost is reduced by 80.5%. A survey was conducted to evaluate user satisfaction of the system and showed that user attitude were affirmative in six significant factors, include feeling of control, reliability, security of data, flexibility, documentation, and expectation, with at least 80% of satisfaction, among which the security of data even reached 93%.

Acknowledgement

This study is supported by National Science Council, Taiwan, Republic of China, through the Project No. 94-2416-H-008-013.

References

1. Bailey, J. E., Orlikowski W. J.: A Short-form Measure of User Information Satisfaction: A Psychometric Evaluation and Notes on Use. J Mana Inform Syst, 4(1988) 44-59.
2. Gokhale, A. A.: Enterprise-wide networking for manufacturing. Comput & Ind Eng, 35(1998) 259-262.
3. Mills, R. J., Paper, D., Lawless, K. A., Kulikowich, J. M.: Hypertext navigation- an intrinsic component of the corporate intranet. J Comput Inform Syst, 43(2002) 44-50.
4. Conti, M., Gregori, E., Lapenna, W.: Client-side content delivery policies in replicated web services: parallel access versus single server approach. Perform Eva, 59 (2005) 137-157.
5. Ranganathan, C., Ganpathy, S.: Key dimensions of business-to-customer web sites. Inform & Mana, 39(2002) 457-465.
6. Stuckenschmidt, H., van Harmelen, F.: Generating and managing metadata for web-based information systems. Knowledge-Based Syst, 17(2004) 201-206.
7. Taylor, M. J., Mcwilliam, J., England D., Akomode, J.: Skills required in developing electronic commerce for small and medium enterprises: case based generalization approach. Elec Commerce Res & Appl, 3(2004) 253-265.
8. Fry, M., MacLarty, G.: Policy-based content delivery: an active network approach. Comput Commun, 24(2001) 241-248.
9. Rosenblatt, B.: Enterprise content integration: a progress report. Seybold Report: Analyzing Publish Technologies, 3(2003) 9-14.
10. Frank, C, Gardoni M.: Information content management with shared ontologies- at corporate research centre of EADS. Int J Inform Mana. 25(2005) 55-70.
11. Kaminski, J, Olivo Jr., O. A.: Up close with SMS 2003. Netw Comput, 15(2004) 84-86.
12. Demange, G: On group stability in hierarchies and networks. J. Polit Econ. 112(2005) 754-778.
13. Ruffer, S.M., Yen, D., Lee, S.: Client-server computing technology: a framework for feasibility analysis and implementation. Int J Inform Mana 15(1995) 135-150.
14. de Vries, W. A., Fieck, R. A.: Client-server infrastructure: a case study in planning and conversion. Ind Mana & Data Syst, 97(1997), 222-236.
15. Wang, W. M., Liang, C. C., Lu, H. Z., Chow, W. S., Chang, K. Y.: Research of Testing Process: The Case of TOPS-System Delivery Process. TL Tech J, 34(2004) 7-34.
16. Beaubrun, R., Pierre, S.: A routing algorithm for distributed communication networks. IEEE Conference on Computer Networks, LCN 97 (1997) 99-105.
17. Pham, P. P., Perreau, S.: Increasing the network performance using multi-path routing mechanism with load balance. Ad Hoc Netw, 2(2004) 433-459.
18. Bertsekas, D., Gallager, R.: Data Netwwork, Prentice Hall, Englewood Cliffs, New Jersey (1987).

Achieving Decision Consistency Across the SOA-Based Enterprise Using Business Rules Management Systems

James Taylor

Fair Isaac Corporation, Vice President of Product Marketing, 181 Metro Dr., Suite 600,
San Jose, CA 95110, United States,
JamesTaylor@FairIsaac.com

Abstract. The adoption of a **service-oriented architecture (SOA)** provides businesses with the ability to rapidly deploy new applications and easily integrate with other component applications both inside and outside the organization. This decentralized application environment provides a great deal of flexibility for business units and IT departments, but it also creates difficulty in managing the consistency of business decisions delivered through various applications. **Business rules management systems (BRMS)** provide a mechanism for managing decision logic and act as a conductor in order to align application decision behavior.

The key to BRMS is the use of a centralized rules repository, within which resides the decision logic applications use to interact with their customers. Applications communicate with a rules engine in order to process those business rules specific to the decision required for the particular application and situational context.

This paper will show how business rules management systems fit within a service-oriented architecture, how BRMS can act as intermediary between service-based applications and legacy applications, and how companies are using BRMS to manage decision processes across the enterprise.

1 Introduction

The widespread implementation of service-oriented architectures within large-scale enterprise systems has shown that we have moved past the early adoption phase. The era of monolithic all-encompassing enterprise applications is over, and the vendors of such applications (such as the major ERP and CRM systems vendors) have moved towards componentization, while simultaneously redesigning their products for standards-based integration. Both IT customers and vendors have come to realize that the name of the game is to create a set modular software applications which can work together and allow each component of the system to focus on what it does best. Using a SOA approach, new applications can be created and implemented more quickly than through previous development approaches, and these new service-based applications can easily be designed to interact with other "services" both inside and outside of the organization.

While the decentralized SOA application environment provides a great deal of flexibility for business units and IT departments, it also creates a new set of

M. Kitsuregawa et al. (Eds.): WISE 2005, LNCS 3806, pp. 750–761, 2005.

challenges: how can organizations effectively manage the consistency of business decisions delivered through various applications; and how can organizations reliably implement changes to business decision logic across all their services. Business rules management systems provide a highly effective and efficient mechanism for managing decision logic and acting as a conductor in order to align decision behavior. The key to BRMS is the use of a centralized rules repository, within which resides the decision logic that applications use in their process interactions. This paper will show how business rules management systems fit within a service-oriented architecture, and how BRMS act both as an intermediary between applications and as the decision management component for application behavior.

2   BRMS Description

The primary goal of business rules management is the separation of business decision processes from the mechanics of application I/O and control code. A BRMS allows for the storage and management of business rules, as well as the ability to execute decision processes through a rules engine.

There are four main benefits to using a business rules management approach within any enterprise architecture:

- The ability to have disparate operational systems act consistently in their outputs without having to maintain duplicate decision logic in each system.
- The ability to change decision logic without having to make any changes within the code of operational systems, thereby significantly reducing QA testing when new decision logic is implemented.
- The ability to define decision logic using sophisticated methods not possible through standard coding, such as decision tables, decision trees, scorecards and the use decision inferencing among chains of inter-related rules.
- The ability to automate many operational decisions that have previously been made manually.

2.1   BRMS Applicability

The types of applications using BRMS to handle decision logic cover many different industries and types of functionality. The following list provides a sample of ways that organizations are using BRMS:

- benefits eligibility determination
- claims handling
- credit approval and limit determination
- credit collection strategies
- data validation
- diagnostic advice
- insurance underwriting and policy pricing
- problem resolution procedures
- product assembly configuration validation
- product recommendations
- regulatory compliance management

3 BRMS Rule Definition and Architecture

Business rules management systems define business decision logic as rules, and these rules are stored in a rule repository. Using the BRMS rule development environment, individual rules are then combined into **rulesets**, functional blocks defining decision logic for a subtask. Rulesets can be combined in a procedural decision flow (**rule-flow**) to conditionally use the assigned rulesets in a sequence which achieves a desired business decision. This combination of ruleflows, rulesets and individual rules are utilized within rule-based services (**rule service**) which are used to guide the decision logic for a specific business process. Rule services can be combined and are made executable within a **decision management service**. Decision management services use the BRMS rule engine to process the inputs from operational system applications through rule services, as well as processing data (from separate data sources) and analytic models (embedded within rule services) as required in order to return the optimal decision output back to the client application.

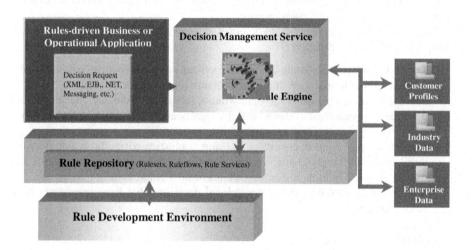

Fig. 1. BRMS components integrate external applications and data with rules management functions

The differentiation between individual rules, rulesets, ruleflows and rule services provides the highest level of flexibility in the re-use and sharing of decision logic across multiple applications. As the functionality across each application is different, so to is each application's use of rules. Several applications may require a common rule, but each may have its own unique set of related rules or decision processes that need to be associated with that specific rule.

3.1 BRMS Evolution

Business rules management systems started to become available in the late 1990's as the next generation of Expert Systems. While Expert Systems were designed to help solve specific types of problems, BRMS were designed as middleware applications which could be easily integrated with enterprise applications, information systems and databases. The initial group of BRMS vendors developed their products using Java technology; now, some have .NET and even COBOL-based versions to allow the rules engine to manage decision logic more effectively across a heterogeneous application environment. As middleware, robust connectivity is an important aspect of BRMS functionality. In a SOA environment, the primary means of communication between services and BRMS is through the use of XML/SOAP, but other methods of communication include HTTP, EJB, COM+/.NET and messaging protocols (MQ Series and JMS). In many cases, decision management services are implemented within application servers, such as those from IBM, BEA, Oracle, Sun and Microsoft. Application servers provide built-in security protocols, which resolves one of the primary concerns that enterprise architects have when moving their systems to a service-oriented architecture.

4   Transitioning to a SOA-Based Environment Using a BRMS

Implementation of a BRMS is a good first step in moving to a SOA-based environment. In fact, the transition to SOA is not an all-or-none proposition; many organizations start by implementing new applications as services, but it is also possible to tie new service-based applications and existing applications together using a BRMS as the common decisioning mechanism. This is especially useful in legacy modernization efforts. In many cases, organizations rely on older mainframe systems to handle many crucial business functions, and it just not feasible to completely replace these systems. Instead, a more practical approach is to slowly transition portions of functionality off of legacy systems while allowing them to continue to perform their primary processing responsibilities. Removing decision logic from operational application code is a good initial step in legacy modernization efforts. By doing this, legacy systems are actually stabilized, since fewer changes need to be made to the core code over time. Decision logic code is replaced with a simple invocation call to a decision management service, along with a mechanism for receiving the output from the BRMS. When decision logic (rules) is changed, the legacy system code is unaffected since the changes are made within the BRMS. Core processing functions within legacy systems can then be transitioned to new service-based applications incrementally, and legacy systems can be decommissioned as their functionality is fully replaced by newer systems.

The use of BRMS also allows for faster creation and deployment of new services within a service-oriented architecture. The decoupling of application functionality and decision logic allows developers to focus on core application functionality while having a separate group of business analysts create the rule services that will manage the outputs of the new application. Once both the application and the corresponding rule services are ready for testing, the developers need to create a decision management service to handle the interaction between the application and the rules engine (the major BRMS vendors provide wizard-driven facilities for setting up a decision management services using the standard SOA methods as described previously in the paper). The ability to work in parallel on both application development and decision management definition, along with having developers focus their attention on core application functionality, greatly reduces the time required to bring new services into production.

5 BRMS Case Study – California Department of Motor Vehicles

The California Department of Motor Vehicles (DMV) is responsible for collecting approximately \$4.1 billion annually in vehicle registration fees. Centralized computer systems in Sacramento communicate with local systems across 167 field offices throughout the state to handle the complex task of calculating registration fees for the nation's largest population of new and used autos, trucks, motorcycles, vessels and other vehicle types. In 2000, the DMV realized that they needed to update and unite the two separate vehicle fee systems, and move to a modern system that would meet the state's strategic realignment towards eGovernment with future public access via the internet.

The DMV began the Vehicle Registration Fee Computation (VR Fee Comp) project to consolidate and streamline the fee generation processes that were implemented across two different computing platforms, two computing languages and two distinct systems:

- The DMV Automated fee system (DMVA) is deployed on servers at each of the DMV's 167 field offices and its headquarters. It processes customer initiated vehicle registration transactions in real time in IBM's proprietary Event Driven Language (EDL).
- The DMV Batch fee (DMVB) systems are deployed on mainframe computers at the Teale Data Center, where the renewal notices are generated and the Remittance Processing system handles most of the "DMV by mail" processing in Common Business Oriented Language (COBOL).

5.1 Information Systems Challenges at the California DMV

Because of the two different computing platforms, changes and updates required two separate development efforts, two different analyst teams, and two different databases. This made it difficult to coordinate changes and ensure consistency between the two systems. "Most of the computer programs composing the DMV legacy fee systems have been used for more than three decades with constant updates and work-arounds grafted into the code by multiple people over the years," says Jerrianne Seitz, Data Processing Manager at the California DMV. "Making changes to the system was no easy task as one change could introduce numerous side effects."

Due to the complexity of the programs and duplication of effort required to make changes to two separate systems, the DMV was challenged to meet legislatively mandated deadlines for fee changes. Even minor changes required extensive analysis and programming efforts by the legacy system's development staff. There also was a real and practical need to update the systems as they had met their physical limitation; the DMV reached a point where they couldn't add more statements to the system.

5.2 Systems Reengineering Process at the California DMV

After discovering all of the places where Vehicle Fee calculation rules had been programmed, the VR Fee Comp team's analysis uncovered that instead of simply recoding the existing systems, they needed to look at newer technologies and methodologies for managing their business processes. The team recognized that a business rules management system would enable the separation of business logic, policies and processes from the actual application programming. The ability to give the power of business policies and business changes to analysts instead of programmers was a monumental change to the current application development process for the DMV, as often a limited amount of programming resources resulted in long delays to system updates. In addition to faster system changes, a BRMS could enforce the greatest levels of compliance with the legislative mandates.

With a keen sense for developing a solution that would easily integrate with future technology and assure the solution's life-cycle longevity, the VR Fee Comp team was at the forefront of evaluating newer technologies, such as Java, and Java applications servers that would allow for an open and internet-ready system to facilitate future goals of web enabling components of the vehicle registration process. Any BRMS would have to be understandable and usable by non-technical analysts responsible for overseeing legislative compliance. It would also require an intuitive user interface that would allow comprehensive control and testing of rules without obscure programming syntax. From a technical standpoint, it must run quickly and scale to handle massive numbers of transactions on a variety of computer systems, from the largest mainframes to office servers. And it would have to do all this without requiring replacement or rewriting of the vast majority of the legacy applications and systems in place throughout the DMV infrastructure. According to Seitz, "Many people within the organization felt our rules were so complex that a third-party software package wouldn't be able to handle the task. We needed to evaluate and demonstrate functionality and performance in any solution we planned to bring in."

The DMV was committed to seeking innovative technology to create a new solution. Upon delving into the project, however, the DMV realized the necessity existed to also conduct a best practice review of their business policies and practice methodologies. The resulting clearer understanding of their decision infrastructure proved to be an invaluable process. They examined a business rules methodology, created a blueprint of their business processes, and looked at normalizing and understanding the terms and policies that were already in place. It was necessary to look at the existing business policies, the legislation that affects them, and how a consolidation of lookups and interrelations could be architected to simplify future updates.

The DMV's Vehicle Registration team reengineered a vehicle registration fee system that could work in conjunction with both systems in a manner that would be transparent to the end user. The revised solution used Fair Isaac's Blaze Advisor BRMS, IBM WebSphere application server, and a Java 2 Enterprise Edition (J2EE) solution operating on a mainframe computer.

Leveraging the power of a centralized decision management service built by the DMV technical development team, using the Blaze Advisor development environment and its associated web-based rule maintenance services, the DMV successfully gives the non-technical analysts who are responsible for overseeing legislative compliance the ability to ensure proper implementation of the policy rules across the DMV vehicle registration fee systems without having to become programmers. They also defined "templates" for certain types of rules that business analysts should be able to create on their own. These maintenance facilities are available through automatically generated web pages that eliminate formal rule syntax and custom editing environments.

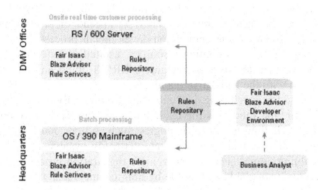

Fig. 2. California DMV Rules Processing and Development Workflow

5.3 Reengineering Results at the California DMV

The first phase of the project implemented the new technical environment and fee business rules for vessels (i.e. boats and other watercraft). Vessels were selected for the first implementation because it represented a lower volume transaction count and therefore a lower impact to DMV field office operations. This phase was completed and successfully released to production in March 2003. The second phase of the project implemented the new fee business rules supporting expedited legislation for the Vehicle Registration Penalty (Reg penalty) fees which could not be implemented in the legacy fee system due to its limitations. This phase went live across the DMVA system in April 2003. The Reg penalty fees system processes 60,000 to 75,000 business transactions per day. The third phase of the VR Fee Comp project went into production in February 2005. Phase three implemented the rules and fees for autos, commercial vehicles, trailers, motorcycles and off-highway vehicles. It required over 2,000 rules and numerous rulesets, ruleflows, tables and processes for several hundred thousand business transactions per day. While many projects boast tens of thousands of rules, the DMV team's methodology resulted in an effective rule-set of 2,100.

With the deployment of the fourth phase of the project to production, the team will move on to the consolidation of the DMVA and DMVB systems. Coupled with the IBM's WebSphere Applications Server, Blaze Advisor positions the DMV to make future system enhancements more easily and to add centralized and consistent rules to new external-facing services such as a self-service web site and telephone response systems. "The upcoming implementation of the VR Fee Calculator on the internet will further support our strategic business and IT goals by improving the integrity and quality of its products and services to customers," adds Seitz. "The new rules-powered system and resulting business practices should continue to lower our operating costs by decreasing the number of telephone calls and transactions in the California DMV Field Offices and Telephone Service Centers."

6 BRMS Case Study – First American Field Services

First American Field Services (FAFS) is one of the largest default mortgage field services company in the United States, providing inspection, maintenance, and service repairs on more than 150,000 properties per month. When a property goes into delinquency, foreclosure, or bankruptcy, financial institutions retain FAFS to help protect their investment. Many of the properties are covered by government-backed loans and are regulated by U.S. government agencies such as the Department of Housing and Urban Development (HUD), the Federal Housing Administration (FHA), and the Department of Veterans Affairs (VA). Any work performed on homes backed by FHA and VA loans must be carried out in accordance with voluminous federal regulations, including tight timetables, which must be met in order to receive payment.

6.1 Information Systems Challenges at First American Field Services

Using its network of more than 1,000 field representatives, FAFS has built an excellent reputation within the U.S. mortgage industry. But the company's IT infrastructure needed updating. Too many processes were paper-based. Work orders from banks would be electronically transmitted to First American Field Services' aging IBM AS/400 system. From the AS/400, work orders would be printed and then sent by fax or express carrier to contractors and First American employees in the field. Paper-based processing continued as handwritten reports from the field were sent back to First American, where they would be re-keyed into the AS/400 system for record-keeping and invoicing.

"Our contractors in the field would do the work and fill in forms with pencils or pens, and then they'd send by express carrier or fax the job information back to us," says Mark Davis, Development Manager, Management Information Services at First American Field Services. "We had whole groups of people who were dedicated to opening express carrier packages, keeping paper in the fax machines, and processing all the paperwork to get it into our legacy system."

Although the company was able to deliver excellent service to its customers, the process was time-consuming and didn't scale well. "Because we couldn't automate the handling of the paper flow, we wound up requiring more and more people," Davis says. "This is a thin-margin business, so these inefficiencies were impacting our bottom line. Of course with people having to decipher handwriting sent across a fax, and with all the re-keying, there was also the chance for errors. Ensuring errors didn't enter our system created even more overhead. It was a messy and time-consuming situation."

In addition to the inefficiencies and delays inherent to a paper-based workflow, FAFS needed a better way of ensuring that HUD regulations were followed. HUD regulations fill hundreds of pages of paper that fill many three-ring binders, which must be updated frequently and sent out to the field, making it difficult to ensure that all regulations were being adhered to consistently. The company also needed a more efficient and less expensive way to customize its services to meet the needs of each of its banking customers. "Every bank has its own preferences," says Davis. "For example, when we mail a notification to a home owner, some banks want their name included, some do not. Some want their phone number included, some do not. The list of customizations goes on to cover almost every facet of our business relationship as we provide service to the banks. Because our legacy systems were so hard to change, we wound up doing all of that customization manually."

6.2 Systems Reengineering Process at First American Field Services

As FAFS looked toward updating its infrastructure it identified key needs, including:

- Eliminating paper-based workflow to enhance project time efficiency and accuracy.
- Embedding HUD regulations and other requirements into the system to ensure compliance.
- Making it easier to customize services for customers.
- Ensuring interoperability with legacy systems that were essential for other roles.

First American Field Services created a new application called the Property Inspection and Maintenance System (PIMS) to automate workflow that had been done manually. Complex regulations that used to be stored in 3-ring binders are automatically integrated with work orders, and documents from the field are filed electronically, doing away with the constant need for express carriers, faxing, and re-keying data. The solution was created using Microsoft® Visual Studio® .NET development system and the Microsoft .NET Framework. The .NET Framework is an integral component of the Microsoft Windows Server™ operating system that provides a programming model and runtime for Web services, Web applications, and smart-client applications. FAFS chose Fair Isaac Blaze Advisor as the BRMS to provide an application for automating implementation of rules, a function that serves as the heart of the PIMS solution. FAFS uses Blaze Advisor for .NET as a rules engine to automatically embed relevant HUD regulations, other requirements, and bank-specific customizations into work orders.

Blaze Advisor for .NET handles a spectrum of functions that were previously done manually, including:

- Automation of instructions to contractors according to HUD regulations
- Management of order distribution to the field
- Client pricing and vendor payment
- Queue management and escalations for exception processing
- Automatic generation of new orders based on results of other orders
- Maximums and caps for each line item on each order

The .NET-connected PIMS application has a three-tier architecture that includes:

- Presentation Tier – Users access the PIMS system through a Web-based interface created by First American developers using Visual Studio .NET 2003 and the .NET Framework. The application is supported by Microsoft Internet Information Services version 6.0 running on the Standard Edition of Microsoft

Windows Server™ 2003, the foundation of the Microsoft Windows Server System™ integrated server software, and Windows 2000 Server. The presentation tier for internal users is hosted on three load-balanced Hewlett Packard (HP) ProLiant DL380G2 servers, dual processor computers with 4GB of RAM, running Windows 2000 Server with Service Pack 4. The presentation tier for external users is hosted on three HP ProLiant BL20 blade computers with dual processors and 3 GB of RAM running Windows Server 2003 Standard Edition. The presentation tier servers are located in Dallas, Texas, and are accessed by the other tiers, located in Sterling, Virginia, using .NET Remoting.

- Business Tier – The business tier includes .NET-connected applications and the Blaze Advisor for .NET rules engine. The .NET-connected applications, and a .NET data bus, control workflow in and out of the rules engine, and coordinates communication with the database tier. The .NET-connected applications run on Windows 2000 Server, and are hosted on three load-balanced HP ProLiant DL380G2 dual processor computers with 4GB of RAM running Windows 2000 Server with Service Pack 4. Blaze Advisor for .NET runs on Windows Server 2003 Standard Edition and is hosted on two HP ProLiant DL380G2 servers, dual processor computers with 4 GB of memory and running Windows 2000 Server with Service Pack 4.

- Data Tier – PIMS-related data for reporting is stored on SQL Server 2000™ Enterprise Edition running on Windows Server 2003 Standard Edition and hosted on three HP ProLiant DL380G2 servers, dual processor computers with 4GB of RAM running Windows 2000 Server with Service Pack 4. SQL Server 2000 is part of Microsoft Windows Server System integrated server software. SQL Server 2000 Reporting Services is hosted on a separate server. The data tier also includes an IBM DB2 database running on the AS/400. The SQL Server database communicates with the AS/400 using OLE DB components and the ADO.NET feature of the .NET Framework.

6.3   Reengineering Results at First American Field Services

First American Field Services has enjoyed a number of benefits since deploying its .NET-connected PIMS application, including consistent application of complex regulations, faster and more accurate project completion, rapid return on investment, enhanced developer productivity, and faster time to market for new products.

The Blaze Advisor for .NET rules engine helps FAFS ensure that HUD regulations, customer preferences, and other business rules are consistently applied across the organization. Using Blaze Advisor, First American creates a set of Standard Operating Procedures (SOP) for each banking client and contractor. "Blaze Advisor has been a huge benefit in helping us consistently apply the vast number of regulations that guide our work," says Davis. "For example, when a house is vacant, FHA may want the lawn cut, but the frequency for which it will pay for this varies from state to state, according to the climate. Or if a window is broken in a vacant house in Florida, we can board it up with one thickness plywood, unless it is hurricane season, when a different thickness of plywood is required, except in designated high risk hurricane areas where another thickness of plywood may be required all year round. So there are exceptions on top of exceptions that go on and on." Prior to the PIMS system with Blaze Advisor, HUD, FHA, and other regulations filled hundreds of pages stored in multiple three-ring binders. "It is tough to carry all of that information in your head," Davis says. "People would tape lists to the wall, and develop other methods of keeping track of what needed to be done for each instance, but we are gaining huge value from having these rules automatically applied to all of our work orders. Everything you need to know from a regulatory standpoint is right there on the work order. Our people no longer have to worry about consulting a shelf of 3-ring binders."

FAFS is enjoying the value of faster project completion since deployment of its PIMS .NET-connected solution. Timeliness is especially important because government regulations prohibit payment for some services unless completed and invoiced within a specified period. In the past, First American sometimes had to go uncompensated for services it performed. "The Microsoft .NET technology tightly integrates with Blaze Advisor to create a unified solution. Our increased timeliness is thanks to the Microsoft .NET part of the application, and accuracy is thanks to the Blaze Advisor part of the application," says Davis. "Our Microsoft .NET-connected applications on the business tier have freed us from the burden of paperwork because everything is electronic, from distributing work orders to collecting field reports and invoicing." The old paperwork ate up time. "A contractor in the field might finish a job in just one hour, but with our old paper system it could take us three weeks to process the work order and invoice it," says Davis. "Now we turn this around within 48 hours."

Enhanced accuracy provides another huge help. "With Blaze Advisor implementing business rules, we just aren't seeing the mistakes that we used to," Davis says. "We are automatically giving our people everything they need to know to properly complete a project. This has been a huge help."

PIMS has helped FAFS decrease its expenses in a number of areas, and enjoy a rapid return on investment. For example the company used to spend $90,000 a month on express carrier-handling paperwork to and from the field. It has also brought operational savings. "We can now respond to regulatory changes from a federal agency, or customization requests from our customers 75 percent faster than we could before PIMS because we no longer have to deal directly with our legacy systems," says Davis. "We have also been able to reduce the size of our IT staff by more than half for the same reasons." Other savings are coming from redeploying resources in departments that used to manage the flow of paper-based work, and the ability to handle increased customers without adding more people. "First American headcount is shrinking while the business is able to grow, thanks to our .NET-connected PIMS application," says Davis. "Between the Blaze Advisor rules engine and our .NET-connected PIMS application, it is very easy for us to bring on new clients or to customize the services we provide for existing clients. We're able to give the clients what they want, when they want it, without bringing on more people."

Removing the need to deal directly with the legacy system, or to create manual work-arounds, has greatly decreased the time it takes to bring new product offerings to market. "It used to be a big chore to create a new product," says Davis. "It used to take us six months to introduce a new product working with the legacy system. Working with Blaze Advisor and our .NET-connected application environment we can do that in a month. And only two weeks of that is coding, the other two weeks are for analysis, and testing. Our new ability to bring new service-based products to market more quickly provides us with a competitive advantage."

7 Conclusion

The powerful advantages of a componentized, service-based application architecture have been shown to help organizations become more productive and nimble in their ability to build new applications. The use of a business rules management system within a service-oriented architecture provides clear benefits through the separation of decision logic from application functionality. Using a BRMS ensures that disparate applications behave consistently, are able to automate complex decisions and quickly adapt to changing business requirements. Business rules management systems also offer organizations the ability to incrementally transition from legacy systems to a service-oriented architecture.

Service Design, Implementation and Description (Tutorial)

Marlon Dumas[1] and Andreas Wombacher[2]

[1] Queensland University of Technology, Brisbane, Australia
m.dumas@qut.edu.au
[2] University of Twente, The Netherlands
a.wombacher@utwente.nl

Summary

There is an increasingly widespread acceptance of service-oriented architectures as a paradigm for integrating heterogeneous software applications. In this paradigm, independently developed and operated applications are exposed as (Web) services that are then interconnected using a set of standard protocols and languages. While the technology for developing basic services and interconnecting them on a point-to-point basis has attained a certain degree of maturity, there remain open challenges when it comes to building and managing services that participate in interactions that do not follow simple request-response patterns.

This tutorial will present a critical overview of current, emerging, and prospective practices in the area of service development, with a focus on design, implementation and description. High-level approaches, including multi-viewpoint design techniques, will be stressed. These high-level concepts will then be linked to lower-level ones, for example by showing implementations (e.g. in BPEL) of higher-level service designs (e.g. in UML).

The tutorial will consider service discovery as an essential aspect of service development. Since service discovery is the comparison of the description of a service request with a description of a service offering, the tutorial will review different dimensions of service description as well as corresponding comparison operations. The tutorial will then discuss process-based service description as a basis for enabling the comparison of services from a behavioral perspective.

From this tutorial, the attendees can expect to gain an appreciation of the concepts and principles underpinning service development practices, as well as an understanding of the limitations of these practices and how they are being addressed by ongoing research efforts.

Outline

1. General principles of service-oriented architectures
2. Service-oriented design
3. Implementation of Web services
4. Service description and comparison
5. Open issues in service-oriented development

M. Kitsuregawa et al. (Eds.): WISE 2005, LNCS 3806, p. 762, 2005.
© Springer-Verlag Berlin Heidelberg 2005

WISE-2005 Tutorial: Web Content Mining

Bing Liu

Department of Computer Science, University of Illinois at Chicago,
851 S. Morgan Street, Chicago, IL 60607
liub@cs.uic.edu

Abstract. Web mining aims to develop a new generation of techniques to effectively mine useful information or knowledge from the Web. It consists of Web usage mining, Web structure mining, and Web content mining. Web usage mining refers to the discovery of user access patterns from Web usage logs. Web structure mining tries to discover useful knowledge from the structure of Web hyperlinks. Web content mining aims to extract and mine useful information or knowledge from Web page contents. This tutorial focuses on Web Content Mining. In the past few years, there was a rapid expansion of activities in this area. In this tutorial, I will introduce the main web content mining tasks and problems and state-of-the-art techniques for dealing with them. All parts of the tutorial have a mix of research and industry flavor, addressing seminal research concepts and looking at the technology from an industry angle.

Main Topics

1. Data/information extraction: The focus is on extraction of structured data from Web pages, such as products and search results. Extracting such data allows one to provide value-added services, e.g., comparative shopping, and meta-search. Two main types of techniques, machine learning and automatic extraction, are covered.
2. Web information integration and schema matching: Although the Web contains a huge amount of data, different web sites (or even pages) represent similar information differently. How to identify or match semantically similar data is a very important problem with many practical applications. Several existing techniques and problems will be examined.
3. Mining online opinion sources: There are many online opinion sources, e.g., customer reviews of products, forums, blogs and chat rooms. Mining opinions (especially consumer opinions) is of great importance for marketing intelligence and product benchmarking. We will introduce some interesting tasks and techniques to mine such sources.
4. Mining the Web to build concept hierarchies or ontology: Concept hierarchies or ontology are useful in many applications. However, generating them manually is very time consuming. Some existing methods that explore the information redundancy on the Web to perform the task will be presented.
5. Segmenting Web pages and detecting noise: In many Web applications, one only wants the main content of the Web page without advertisements, navigation links, copyright notices. Automatically segmenting Web pages to extract the main content of the pages is interesting problem. A number of techniques have been proposed in the past few years.

M. Kitsuregawa et al. (Eds.): WISE 2005, LNCS 3806, pp. 763, 2005.
© Springer-Verlag Berlin Heidelberg 2005

An Introduction to Data Grid Management Systems

Arun Jagatheesan

San Diego Supercomputer Center (SDSC),
University of California, San Diego,
9500 Gilman Drive, MC0505, La Jolla, CA 92093
arun@sdsc.edu

Abstract. We describe a "grid" as a coordinated infrastructure, formed by combining resources that might be owned by distributed and autonomous administrative domains. A data grid infrastructure facilitates a logical view of distributed resources that are shared between autonomous administrative domains. An emerging data storage problem is the management of unstructured data storage resources for inter/intra/multi-enterprise collaborative efforts. A new paradigm in data management systems, apart from traditional file systems and database systems is required. Data grids are being built around the world for coordinated sharing and management of unstructured data storage resources that are distributed at collaborating teams from the same or different enterprises. Data Grid Management System (DGMS) middleware will soon become part of the software infrastructure in many enterprises.

A Data Grid is a logical unified view of a grid's data storage infrastructure. Data storage middleware (DGMS) create a federated, location independent, logical infrastructure namespace that dynamically spreads across the grid's administrative domains. Datagrids support sharing data collections and storage resources between autonomous administrative domains. A *shared collection* is a logical aggregation of digital entities, (e.g.) files, data streams, etc., which are physically distributed in multiple physical storage resources. The digital entities or the storage resources used in a shared collection could be owned by multiple administrative domains. A *shared resource* allows users from multiple administrative domains to share the storage space in a resource. The success for data grids could be attributed to "data virtualization".

Data Virtualization is the concept of bringing together different heterogeneous data and storage resources into one or more logical views, so that the distributed and replicated data appear as a single logical data source managed by a single data management system. The underlying concept behind datagrids and data virtualization is similar to relational databases: to isolate physical organization of data from logical schema (view). In data virtualization, instead of completely hiding the physical organization of the storage resources where the data resides, another logical namespace of storage resources is provided to the applications. The SDSC Storage Resource Broker (SRB) is a DGMS that currently manages around a Petabyte of data in multiple data grid environments. We observe many open research problems for these new data management environments.

M. Kitsuregawa et al. (Eds.): WISE 2005, LNCS 3806, pp. 764, 2005.

Are We Ready for the Service Oriented Architecture?

Stephane Gagnon

New Jersey Institute of Technology,Newark, NJ 07102, USA
gagnon@njit.edu

Abstract. This Industry Track Panel poses a strategic question, "Are We Ready for the Service Oriented Architecture (SOA)?" We discuss this issue from both vendor and adopter perspectives in the company of 5 IT Executives. In particular, we go beyond the discussion of SOA standards as such, and try to assess the importance of this approach from the point of view of related technologies, such as Business Process Management, Enterprise Architecture, Configuration Management, Business Rules Systems, and Open Source Solutions.

Panelists

- Greg Carter, CTO, Metastorm Inc.
- James McGovern, Enterprise Architect, Hartford Financial Services Group Inc.
- Swapnil Shah, CEO, mValent Inc.
- James Taylor, VP Marketing, Fair Isaac Corp.
- Bob Zurek, Dir. Advanced Technology, IBM Software Group

This Industry Track Panel is focused on one of today's most strategic question: "Are We Ready for the Service Oriented Architecture (SOA)?" The emergence of Web Services standards has led to a revival of this long established architectural approach, which was until recently supported mainly by messaging, distributed object, and connector technologies. The potential for interoperability and seamless integration has never been as strong as today. Yet it is not clear to what extent vendors are moving fast enough in bringing the latest SOA and especially WS technologies as core product features. In addition, the diversity and integration of WS-enabled and pre-WS solutions presents a major challenge for IT projects operating on increasingly small budgets. Finally, as adopting firms continue to maintain traditional architectures while experimenting with an SOA, they encounter major development productivity issues.

We discuss this issue from both vendor and adopter perspectives in the company of 5 IT Executives. The Panel question will lead us to reflect on further issues, such as: Are existing approaches to enterprise IT ready for the SOA? Can the SOA be applied using existing vendor tools and methodologies? Or do we need radical changes in how we conceive applications, and what vendors we use to do so?

In particular, this discussion will go beyond existing SOA standards and try to assess the importance of this architecture from the point of view of related technologies, such as Business Process Management, Enterprise Architecture, Configuration Management, Business Rules Systems, and Open Source Solutions.

M. Kitsuregawa et al. (Eds.): WISE 2005, LNCS 3806, pp. 765, 2005.

Data Engineering Approach to Design of Web Services

George Feuerlicht

Department of Software Engineering, Faculty of Information Technology,
University of Technology, Sydney, P.O. Box 123, Broadway, NSW 2007, Australia
jiri@it.uts.edu.au

Abstract. With the wide acceptance of Web Services as the preferred implementation platform for service-oriented applications there is increased interest
in how such applications should be designed. While there are similarities between software components and services there is now a general agreement that
mapping existing components directly to Web Services leads to suboptimal design and results in poor performance and scalability. Most practitioners recommend the use of *coarse-grained,* message-oriented Web Service that minimize
the number of messages and avoid the need to maintain state information between invocations. We argue that the design of message structures used as Web
Services payloads directly impacts on application interoperability, and that excessive use of coarse-grained, document-centric message structures results in
poor reuse and undesirable interdependencies between services. Our approach
provides a framework for the design message structures using data engineering
principles. We consider the impact of increasing message granularity on cohesion and coupling of service-oriented applications and analyze associated design trade-offs.

1 Introduction

Web services are being increasingly used to implement e-business applications in
various industry sectors. Examples range from relatively simple Web services APIs
(Application Programming Interfaces) designed to provide programmatic access to
popular websites such as Google (google.com) and Amazon (amazon.com), to comprehensive Web services solutions provided by travel industry companies such as
Sabre (www.sabre-holdings.com/). There is some evidence that practitioners involved
in implementing Web Services solutions are paying only limited attention to how
such applications should be designed. Web Services design is an active area of research, but at present there are no comprehensive design methodologies. Most existing
approaches focus on designing Web Services from existing components and use object-
oriented methods or component-based techniques [1], [2], [3]. Although there are similarities between software components and services, mapping components directly to
Web Services leads to suboptimal design and results in poor performance and scalability. Most practitioners recommend the use of coarse-grained, message-oriented
Web Service that produce fewer messages and therefore have lower communication
overheads [4]. The principal limitation of this (message-oriented) approach is its use

M. Kitsuregawa et al. (Eds.): WISE 2005, LNCS 3806, pp. 766–767, 2005.
© Springer-Verlag Berlin Heidelberg 2005

of composite document structures that implicitly represent complex business processes and contain embedded business rules. From a software engineering perspective, service operations need to be designed to maximize cohesion and minimize coupling [5]. Applying these principles to service interface design leads to reduction in undesirable side effects, and improved flexibility of applications [6], but at the same time produces finer-granularity operations, and therefore conflicts with performance considerations. Balancing performance and software engineering design objectives requires understanding of the impact of granularity service operations on cohesion and coupling of service operations.

2   Conclusions

Our design methodology for Web Services applies data engineering principles to design of Web Services applications [7], [8]. The design approach relies on the principles of orthogonality, maximizing method cohesion, and minimizing method coupling, and uses data normalization techniques to avoid externalization of redundant data elements. The proposed design framework facilitates design decisions about service granularity based on the theory of normalization applied to service interfaces.

References

1. Ambler, S.W. (2002) Deriving Web Services from UML models, Part :1Establishing the process .Available on: http://www-.106ibm.com/developerworks/webservices/library/ws uml/1
2. Levi, K. and A. Arsanjani (2002) A goal-driven approach to enterprise component identification and specification. Communications of the ACM. Vol. 45:(10). (2002) 45 - 52
3. Oberleitner, J., Dustdar, S. 2003, 'Constructing Web Services out of Generic Component Compositions', in International Conference ICWS-Europe 2003, eds M. Jeckle & L.-j. Zhang, Springer, Erfurt, Germany, pp. 37-48.
4. Huhns, Michael N. and Munindar P. Singh, "Service-Oriented Computing: Key Concepts and Principles," IEEE Internet Computing, vol. 9, no. 1, 2005, pp. 75-81.
5. Feuerlicht, G, Designing Service-Oriented e-Business Applications using Data Engineering Techniques, The Third Workshop on e-Business, in conjunction with ICIS 2004, December 11, 2004, Washington D.C., USA, ISBN:957-01-9161-9
6. Venners, B. (1998) Introduction to Design Techniques . Available on: http://www.javaworld.com/javaworld/jw-/1998-02jw--02techniques.html, February, .1998
7. Feuerlicht, G., Design of Service Interfaces for e-Business Applications using Data Normalization Techniques, Journal of Information Systems and e-Business Management, Springer-Verlag GmbH, 26 July 2005, pages 1-14, ISS:1617-98
8. Feuerlicht, G., Meesathit, S., Software Development Methodology for Web Services, accepted for publication in the Proceedings of the 4th International Conference on New Software Methodologies, Tools and Techniques, SoMet 05, Tokyo, Japan, September 28-30, 2005

Author Index

Lecture Notes in Computer Science

For information about Vols. 1–3684

please contact your bookseller or Springer

Vol. 3731: F. Wang (Ed.), Formal Techniques for Networked and Distributed Systems - FORTE 2005. XII, 558 pages. 2005.

Vol. 3729: Y. Gil, E. Motta, R.V. Benjamins, M.A. Musen (Eds.), The Semantic Web – ISWC 2005. XXIII, 1073 pages. 2005.

Vol. 3728: V. Paliouras, J. Vounckx, D. Verkest (Eds.), Integrated Circuit and System Design. XV, 753 pages. 2005.

Vol. 3726: L.T. Yang, O.F. Rana, B. Di Martino, J.J. Dongarra (Eds.), High Performance Computing and Communcations. XXVI, 1116 pages. 2005.

Vol. 3725: D. Borrione, W. Paul (Eds.), Correct Hardware Design and Verification Methods. XII, 412 pages. 2005.

Vol. 3724: P. Fraigniaud (Ed.), Distributed Computing. XIV, 520 pages. 2005.

Vol. 3723: W. Zhao, S. Gong, X. Tang (Eds.), Analysis and Modelling of Faces and Gestures. XI, 4234 pages. 2005.

Vol. 3722: D. Van Hung, M. Wirsing (Eds.), Theoretical Aspects of Computing – ICTAC 2005. XIV, 614 pages. 2005.

Vol. 3721: A. Jorge, L. Torgo, P.B. Brazdil, R. Camacho, J. Gama (Eds.), Knowledge Discovery in Databases: PKDD 2005. XXIII, 719 pages. 2005. (Subseries LNAI).

Vol. 3720: J. Gama, R. Camacho, P.B. Brazdil, A. Jorge, L. Torgo (Eds.), Machine Learning: ECML 2005. XXIII, 769 pages. 2005. (Subseries LNAI).

Vol. 3719: M. Hobbs, A.M. Goscinski, W. Zhou (Eds.), Distributed and Parallel Computing. XI, 448 pages. 2005.

Vol. 3718: V.G. Ganzha, E.W. Mayr, E.V. Vorozhtsov (Eds.), Computer Algebra in Scientific Computing. XII, 502 pages. 2005.

Vol. 3717: B. Gramlich (Ed.), Frontiers of Combining Systems. X, 321 pages. 2005. (Subseries LNAI).

Vol. 3716: L. Delcambre, C. Kop, H.C. Mayr, J. Mylopoulos, Ó. Pastor (Eds.), Conceptual Modeling – ER 2005. XVI, 498 pages. 2005.

Vol. 3715: E. Dawson, S. Vaudenay (Eds.), Progress in Cryptology – Mycrypt 2005. XI, 329 pages. 2005.

Vol. 3714: J. H. Obbink, K. Pohl (Eds.), Software Product Lines. XIII, 235 pages. 2005.

Vol. 3713: L.C. Briand, C. Williams (Eds.), Model Driven Engineering Languages and Systems. XV, 722 pages. 2005.

Vol. 3712: R. Reussner, J. Mayer, J.A. Stafford, S. Overhage, S. Becker, P.J. Schroeder (Eds.), Quality of Software Architectures and Software Quality. XIII, 289 pages. 2005.

Vol. 3711: F. Kishino, Y. Kitamura, H. Kato, N. Nagata (Eds.), Entertainment Computing - ICEC 2005. XXIV, 540 pages. 2005.

Vol. 3710: M. Barni, I. Cox, T. Kalker, H.J. Kim (Eds.), Digital Watermarking. XII, 485 pages. 2005.

Vol. 3709: P. van Beek (Ed.), Principles and Practice of Constraint Programming - CP 2005. XX, 887 pages. 2005.

Vol. 3708: J. Blanc-Talon, W. Philips, D.C. Popescu, P. Scheunders (Eds.), Advanced Concepts for Intelligent Vision Systems. XXII, 725 pages. 2005.

Vol. 3707: D.A. Peled, Y.-K. Tsay (Eds.), Automated Technology for Verification and Analysis. XII, 506 pages. 2005.

Vol. 3706: H. Fuks, S. Lukosch, A.C. Salgado (Eds.), Groupware: Design, Implementation, and Use. XII, 378 pages. 2005.

Vol. 3704: M. De Gregorio, V. Di Maio, M. Frucci, C. Musio (Eds.), Brain, Vision, and Artificial Intelligence. XV, 556 pages. 2005.

Vol. 3703: F. Fages, S. Soliman (Eds.), Principles and Practice of Semantic Web Reasoning. VIII, 163 pages. 2005.

Vol. 3702: B. Beckert (Ed.), Automated Reasoning with Analytic Tableaux and Related Methods. XIII, 343 pages. 2005. (Subseries LNAI).

Vol. 3701: M. Coppo, E. Lodi, G. M. Pinna (Eds.), Theoretical Computer Science. XI, 411 pages. 2005.

Vol. 3700: J.F. Peters, A. Skowron (Eds.), Transactions on Rough Sets IV. X, 375 pages. 2005.

Vol. 3699: C.S. Calude, M.J. Dinneen, G. Păun, M. J. Pérez-Jiménez, G. Rozenberg (Eds.), Unconventional Computation. XI, 267 pages. 2005.

Vol. 3698: U. Furbach (Ed.), KI 2005: Advances in Artificial Intelligence. XIII, 409 pages. 2005. (Subseries LNAI).

Vol. 3697: W. Duch, J. Kacprzyk, E. Oja, S. Zadrożny (Eds.), Artificial Neural Networks: Formal Models and Their Applications – ICANN 2005, Part II. XXXII, 1045 pages. 2005.

Vol. 3696: W. Duch, J. Kacprzyk, E. Oja, S. Zadrożny (Eds.), Artificial Neural Networks: Biological Inspirations – ICANN 2005, Part I. XXXI, 703 pages. 2005.

Vol. 3695: M.R. Berthold, R.C. Glen, K. Diederichs, O. Kohlbacher, I. Fischer (Eds.), Computational Life Sciences. XI, 277 pages. 2005. (Subseries LNBI).

Vol. 3694: M. Malek, E. Nett, N. Suri (Eds.), Service Availability. VIII, 213 pages. 2005.

Vol. 3693: A.G. Cohn, D.M. Mark (Eds.), Spatial Information Theory. XII, 493 pages. 2005.

Vol. 3692: R. Casadio, G. Myers (Eds.), Algorithms in Bioinformatics. X, 436 pages. 2005. (Subseries LNBI).

Vol. 3691: A. Gagalowicz, W. Philips (Eds.), Computer Analysis of Images and Patterns. XIX, 865 pages. 2005.

Vol. 3690: M. Pĕchouček, P. Petta, L.Z. Varga (Eds.), Multi-Agent Systems and Applications IV. XVII, 667 pages. 2005. (Subseries LNAI).

Vol. 3689: G.G. Lee, A. Yamada, H. Meng, S.H. Myaeng (Eds.), Information Retrieval Technology. XVII, 735 pages. 2005.

Vol. 3688: R. Winther, B.A. Gran, G. Dahll (Eds.), Computer Safety, Reliability, and Security. XI, 405 pages. 2005.

Vol. 3687: S. Singh, M. Singh, C. Apte, P. Perner (Eds.), Pattern Recognition and Image Analysis, Part II. XXV, 809 pages. 2005.

Vol. 3686: S. Singh, M. Singh, C. Apte, P. Perner (Eds.), Pattern Recognition and Data Mining, Part I. XXVI, 689 pages. 2005.

Vol. 3685: V. Gorodetsky, I. Kotenko, V.A. Skormin (Eds.), Computer Network Security. XIV, 480 pages. 2005.